9^e

INTRODUCTION TO
Marketing

INTRODUCTION TO

Marketing

9^e

Carl McDaniel
Chair, Department of Marketing
University of Texas at Arlington

Charles W. Lamb
M.J. Neeley School of Business
Texas Christian University

Joseph F. Hair, Jr.
Department of Marketing
Kennesaw State University

THOMSON
™
SOUTH-WESTERN

Australia · Brazil · Canada · Mexico · Singapore · Spain · United Kingdom · United States

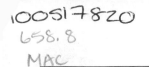

THOMSON

SOUTH-WESTERN

Introduction to Marketing, 9e

Carl McDaniel, Charles W. Lamb, and Joseph F. Hair, Jr.

VP/Editorial Director:
Jack W. Calhoun

Publisher:
Neil Marquardt

Acquisitions Editor:
Neil Marquardt

Developmental Editor:
Jamie Gleich Bryant, B-Books

Marketing Manager:
Nicole Moore

Content Project Manager:
Tamborah Moore

Manager, Editorial Media:
John Barans

Technology Project Manager:
Pam Wallace

Marketing Communications Manager:
Sarah Greber

Manufacturing Coordinator:
Diane Gibbons

Production House:
Lachina Publishing Services

Printer:
China Translation and
Printing Services

Art Director:
Stacy Jenkins Shirley

Internal Designer:
Beckmeyer Design

Cover Images:
© Getty Images

Photography Manager:
John Hill

Photo Researcher:
Rose Alcorn

Library of Congress Control Number:
2006937490

For more information about our products,
contact us at:

Thomson Learning Academic Resource
Center
1-800-423-0563

Thomson Higher Education
5191 Natorp Boulevard
Mason, OH 45040
USA

80/01/81

Brief Contents

Contents

PART 1
The World of Marketing 2

**PART 2
Analyzing Marketing Opportunities 142**

PART 5
Promotion 436

PART 6
Pricing Decisions 534

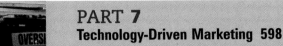

ABOUT THIS EDITION

Your students are going places—not only in the future, but right now—and *Introduction to Marketing, 9e* can take them wherever they need to go. Its lively presentation of concepts will pique student interest in a marketing major and provide a memorable reference point for majors in other business disciplines. Our book is strong enough to support a student looking ahead to an MBA or jumping right into the workplace. Wherever your students want to go, McDaniel, Lamb, and Hair's *Introduction to Marketing 9e* can take them there.

SO WHAT'S NEW?

If you are already familiar with *Introduction to Marketing,* you may be asking, "So what's new?" The answer is quite a bit.

New Content

In addition to the dozens of new examples in each chapter, we have added new topical content and revised and updated existing material throughout the book.

PART 1 We have retained the proven format of Chapter 1 (An Overview of Marketing) and the Career Appendix that introduces students to various aspects of a career in marketing, like types of marketing jobs, pay scales, preparation for interviewing, and what to expect the first year on the job. Chapter 2 (Strategic Planning for Competitive Advantage) reintegreates the BCG portfolio matrix and culminates with a brand new Marketing Plan Appendix on E-motion software, a real company based in Massachusetts. The thorough—and real—marketing plan helps students better understand the level of detail needed in plotting out a marketing strategy. A thoroughly revised Chapter 3 (Social Responsibility, Ethics, and the Marketing Environment) includes new content on ethical values and norms for marketers, tackles the issue of sustainability, and offers new content on demo-

graphics, including new material on time-pressed consumers and women as principal economic decision makers. We added a section on Tweens to complement our fully revised sections on Generation Y, Generation X, baby boomers, Hispanic Americans, African Americans, and Asian Americans. The chapter also contains new information on consumer privacy and related legislation. Chapter 4 (Developing a Global Vision) has been greatly revised to reflect constant changes in the global marketplace. There is new material on the Doha Round of WTO talks and on the Central American Free Trade Agreement. Information about the U.S. Commercial Service has been updated, as has the content related to the effects of purchasing power across nations, global distribution of wealth, the World Bank, the International Monetary Fund, and the effects of exchange rates.

PART 2 Chapter 5 (Consumer Decision Making) has a new section on how blogging is changing the concept of opinion leadership. Chapter 6 (Business Marketing) has a completely revised section on business marketing on the Internet and a reworked section on strategic alliances and trust in business relationships. In Chapter 7 (Segmenting and Targeting Markets) we've condensed the section on one-to-one marketing to give your students what they need to know and have updated all the sections on age, gender, and ethnic segmentation. Chapter 8 (Decision Support Systems and Marketing Research) has new sections on the uses of blogging for marketing research, marketing research aggregators, ethnographic research, and online focus groups.

PART 3 Chapter 9 (Product Concepts) has new statistics on top brands, and Chapter 10 (Developing and Managing Products) adds new content on the roles of innovation and the Internet in product development.

PART 4 Companies everywhere are working to squeeze inefficiencies out of their supply chains, so in Chapter 12 (Supply Chain Management) we discuss how technology is affecting multiple aspects of the distribution channel. Chapter 13 (Retailing) contains an enhanced section on Internet retailing, a better explanation of interactivity, and the most current retailing statistics.

PART 5 Chapter 14 (Integrated Marketing Communications) explores the role and responsibility of marketing for public health and how blogging is changing the basic marketing communication model. Chapter 15 (Advertising and Public Relations) stays abreast of a wide variety of alternative media. The impact of digital video recorders (DVRs) like TiVo are debated, and there is new information on product placement. We've also reorganized the discussion of sponsorships to make it more intuitive for the student.

PART 6 Chapter 17 (Pricing Concepts) includes a revised section on the role of the Internet in pricing structures and the related impact on demand. New content on psychological pricing (which digits in the price matter most to consumers) is included in Chapter 18 (Setting the Right Price), where we also cover the lastest cases in price fixing.

PART 7 You may be wondering what we've done with the Internet chapter. Because the Internet touches every aspect of marketing, we have moved the content from that chapter into relevant chapters throughout the book. You'll read integrated Internet content in every chapter. Customer Relationship Management is now covered in Chapter 19.

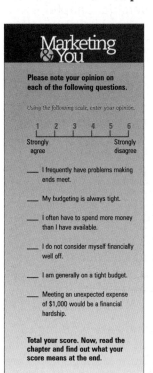

New Marketing and You Surveys

Today's students demand their courses be relevant, and to help you make that connection, we have added a short survey to each chapter opener. Adapted from material in the *Marketing*

Scales Handbook, these short polls are an engaging way to introduce students to a new concept. Even though this is their first marketing course, Marketing & You polls show them that they already have experience with marketing. Scoring instructions are given, and general results provided. Marketing & You is *not* meant to be used in a scientific context; it is just an interesting and fun way to introduce the chapter material.

New Videos on Modern Companies

For the Ninth Edition of *Introduction to Marketing,* we have created a set of entirely new videos on companies your students and you will recognize. Company Clips segments average 8 minutes in length, which is enough time to cover

core marketing issues facing Method, ReadyMade Magazine, Sephora, Vans, Kodak, and Acid+All. Segments are rich enough to allow you to teach through the video, integrating lecture and video to create a richer learning experience. Tips on how to do this are included in the Instructor Manual with Video Guide.

New Integrated Coverage of the Internet

The Internet touches all aspects of marketing. For this reason, the Ninth Edition contains Internet coverage in almost every chapter. For example, different aspects and applications of blogging are covered in 5 chapters! That's because blogging is a critical part of the external environment, changing who is considered an opinion leader; opening new avenues for marketing research; altering the basic marketing communications model; and becoming a hot advertising medium. Integrated coverage of the Internet allows students to encounter this revolutionary aspect of marketing multiple times over the course of the semester, rather than just once at the end.

New Design

A new feature worth mentioning is the clean design of the Ninth Edition. Research has told us that students were having trouble focusing on the main material because of the number of distractions on each page. This edition maintains visual interest without overwhelming the students.

CLASSIC FEATURES HAVE BEEN UPDATED AND ENHANCED

Looking Forward

Each chapter begins with a new, current, real-world story about a marketing decision or situation facing a company. These vignettes have been carefully prepared to stimulate student interest in topics to come in the chapter and can be used to begin class discussion. In the Ninth Edition, you'll read about companies like Kiehl's, Beacon Street Girls, General Electric, Wal-Mart, Procter & Gamble, GAP, Porsche, Starbucks, Virgin Mobile, XM Satellite Radio, and others.

Visual Learning Outcome Summaries

Through our years of teaching, we know that not all students learn the material the same way. Some can read books and understand the concepts just from their verbal presentation. Other students need to rewrite the material in their own words in order to understand it completely. Still others learn best from diagrams and exhibits. Student focus groups have confirmed this experience in a more quantitative way.

For this reason, we have retained our visual **Review Learning Outcomes,** which are designed to give students a picture of the content, to help them recall the material. For example, Learning Outcome 4 in Chapter 4 discusses the various ways of entering the global marketing place. The detailed discussion, of everything from exporting to direct investment, ends with the following review:

These reviews are not meant to repeat every nuance of the chapter content. Rather, they are meant to provide visual cues that prompt the student to recall the salient points in the chapter.

Global Perspectives Boxes

Today most businesses compete not only locally and nationally, but globally as well. Companies that may have never given a thought to exporting now face competition abroad. Thinking globally should be a part of every manager's tactical and strategic planning. Accordingly, we address this topic in detail early in Chapter 4. Global marketing is fully integrated throughout the book, cases, and videos, as well.

Our **Global Perspectives** boxes provide expanded global examples of the marketing issues facing companies on several continents. Each box concludes with thought-provoking questions carefully prepared to stimulate class discussion. You'll read about consumer behavior in Poland, how to do business in India, how Carrefour approaches discounting, pricing for South American airlines, and more.

GLOBAL Perspectives

Persuading Italians to Drink Water on the Go

Nestlé's bottled water is among the top five international brands of bottled water in volume of sales and is sold in 35 countries. More than 90 percent of Nestlé's water sales occur in North America and Europe.

Italians have the highest average annual consumption of bottled water in the world. Although the tap water in Italy is drinkable, Italians prefer bottled water, and about 265 different brands of bottled water are available there. Nevertheless, Italians do not drink their bottled water on the go. Instead, they buy large bottles of water to serve at meals. Italian mothers tell their children that eating and drinking while walking can cause indigestion and that it's bad manners to eat or drink anywhere but at the table. Even if Italians wanted to drink bottled water on the street, they would have difficulty finding it. Although bottled water can be purchased in bars or at kiosks near tourist attractions such as the Colosseum in Rome, it isn't widely available on the street. Strict licensing laws restrict sales of food or drinks at places like newsstands.

Now Nestlé is trying to grow its market in Italy by changing these long-standing traditions. It has developed a marketing strategy designed to get Italian consumers to drink water on the go.

The company started its campaign with Acqua Panna, a brand aimed at women. Television ads featured a fashionable cartoon character named Lulu who carries a purse containing Acqua Panna in a squeezable hourglass-shaped bottle, called Panna 75. The bottle has a newly designed membrane top created by Nestlé to prevent water from leaking into a leather handbag. The ads show the bottle tipped over to demonstrate that it doesn't leak. Nestlé also hired apparel designer Roberto Cavalli to create a limited edition label for the water, and a small plastic purse that he designed to hold Panna 75 was given out at one of his fashion shows in Milan. Finally, to encourage Italians to drink water outdoors, Nestlé managers organize pickup soccer games and aerobic sessions on Italian beaches. Of course, Nestlé bottled water is passed around at all these events.

With these efforts, Nestlé increased its share of the $3 billion Italian water market to 29 percent in 2004, up from 25.8 percent in 2003. Almost all of the increase was due to sales of water in smaller, more portable bottles.[10]

Do you think that Nestlé should try to change deep-seated Italian habits in order to sell more drinking water? Explain your answer.

Ethics in Marketing Boxes

In this edition we continue our emphasis on ethics. The **Ethics in Marketing** boxes, complete with questions focusing on ethical decision making, have all been revised. This feature offers provocative examples of how ethics comes into play in many marketing decisions. Are packaged-food companies responsible for childhood obesity levels? Should Nestlé charge for bottled water in developing nations? What should companies do to ensure that consumers' personal data is protected? Is tweaking someone else's invention an ethical way to develop new products?

Students will consider these and many other hotly debated, ethical questions.

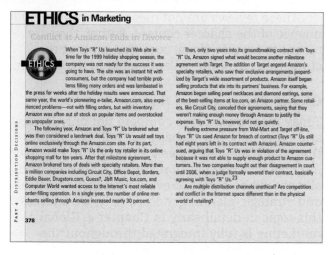
Some examples are researching the complete supply chain for a specified product; creating an advertising campaign for a product, using the rules from the Hasbro game Taboo; role playing a televised interview after a marketing crisis; and much more.

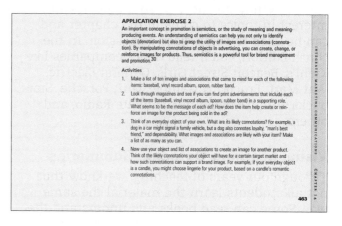

APPLICATION EXERCISE 2

An important concept in promotion is semiotics, or the study of meaning and meaning-producing events. An understanding of semiotics can help you not only to identify objects (denotation) but also to grasp the utility of images and associations (connotation). By manipulating connotations of objects in advertising, you can create, change, or reinforce images for products. Thus, semiotics is a powerful tool for brand management and promotion.[30]

Activities

1. Make a list of ten images and associations that come to mind for each of the following items: baseball, vinyl album, spoon, rubber band.

2. Look through magazines and see if you can find print advertisements that include each of the items (baseball, vinyl record album, spoon, rubber band) in a supporting role. What seems to be the message of each ad? How does the item help create or reinforce an image for the product being sold in the ad?

3. Think of an everyday object of your own. What are its likely connotations? For example, a dog in a car might signal a family vehicle, but a dog also connotes loyalty, "man's best friend," and dependability. What images and associations are likely with your item? Make a list of as many as you can.

4. Now use your object and list of associations to create an image for another product. Think of the likely connotations your object will have for a certain target market and how such connotations can support a brand image. For example, if your everyday object is a candle, you might choose lingerie for your product, based on a candle's romantic connotations.

INTEGRATED MARKETING COMMUNICATIONS CHAPTER 14

463

Review and Applications

To help students focus their study time, we continue to group end-of-chapter discussions and writing questions with their related learning outcome summary. Questions are numbered according to the learning outcome to which they correspond. For example, the summary point for Chapter 10, Learning Outcome 5 has three related questions. They are numbered 5.1, 5.2, and 5.3. This organization helps students identify questions pertinent to the learning outcome they are studying, allowing each chapter to function as a series of content blocks that can be read over multiple study sessions.

LO5 Explain the diffusion process through which new products are adopted. The diffusion process is the spread of a new product from its producer to ultimate adopters. Adopters in the diffusion process belong to five categories: innovators, early adopters, the early majority, the late majority, and laggards. Product characteristics that affect the rate of adoption include product complexity, compatibility with existing social values, relative advantage over existing substitutes, observability, and "trialability." The diffusion process is facilitated by word-of-mouth communication from marketers to consumers.

5.1 Describe some products whose adoption rates have been affected by complexity, compatibility, relative advantage, observability, and/or "trialability."

5.2 What type of adopter behavior do you typically follow? Explain.

5.3 Review Exhibit 10.3. Analyze each product on the graph according to the characteristics that influence the rate of adoption. For example, what can you conclude from the data about the relative advantage of DVD audio? Write one to two pages explaining your analysis.

Application Exercises

Application exercises at the end of each chapter give students the opportunity to work with marketing concepts in various real-world contexts. We incorporate activities (rather than questions) to help students appreciate the width and depth of the marketing industry. These exercises come from instructors around the country who have contributed their teaching ideas to our unique supplement, **Great Ideas in Teaching Marketing,** since the First Edition. Each exercise selected was a winner in the "Best of the Great Ideas in Teaching Marketing," as voted by a panel of 35 faculty judges. You can be sure that these applications will be successful whether used as classroom activities or team projects assignments.

Entrepreneurship Case

Entrepreneurship, whether in the newest dot com or in America's largest corporations, is what fueled the greatest period of expansion in American history. Ten chapters have new entrepreneurship cases, highlighting the challenges facing entrepreneurs in the 21st century. These cases focus on a wide variety of companies, like Ethel's Chocolate Boutiques, CamelBak (maker of personal hydration systems for outdoor enthusiasts and the military), *Wicked* (the fantastically successful Broadway production), NetFlix, and American icon Ron Popeil, among others.

But we also recognize that entrepreneurial activities take place across the *Fortune* 500, so we profile industry giants like Apple and its new Garage Band software, Best Buy, and Cirque du Soleil. All have used a highly entrepreneurial approach in various parts of their business. Your students will find these cases an exciting and challenging aspect of each chapter.

Entrepreneurship Case

NETFLIX READY FOR PRIMETIME

Shocked at the $40 fee he incurred for a late return of *Apollo 13*, Netflix founder Reed Hastings decided that in the age of the Internet, there had to be a better way to rent videos for home viewing. Thus, in 1997, he started an Internet-based, DVD rental service that offered direct-to-home deliveries with no late fees. A mere decade and 4 million subscribers later, Netflix has taken on established video rental companies such as Blockbuster, Hollywood Video, and Wal-Mart and emerged as the leader in innovation and customer service.

In addition to betting that the Internet would be the future of the video rental market, Hastings made a few other key predictions that helped him develop a company with almost $700 million in revenue in under ten years. He watched as moviegoers fled public theaters for the comfort of home theater systems, and he observed those same consumers embracing the features, capacity, and high-quality format of the DVD. Realizing that the Internet could allow those same convenience seekers 24-hour browsing and selection access to an unprecedented volume of movie titles in a single digital

©PAUL SAKUMA/ASSOCIATED PRESS

AN OVERVIEW OF MARKETING CHAPTER

Biz Flix

Biz Flix gives you a captivating modality to launch your lecture. These 2- to 3-minute clips  from feature films provide an entertaining and metaphoric look at marketing. Some depict concrete marketing concepts, like the clip on pricing from the cult classic *Fast Times at Ridgemont High,* and the clip from *The Jerk,* showing Steven Martin embodying the marketing concept with his portrayal of Navin Johnson. Other clips provide a quick, engaging way to start the class: a brand montage from *Josie and the Pussycats;* and a money-handling scene from *Casino* narrated by Robert De Niro, whose description sounds a lot like a marketing channel. Other clips are from *Family Man, The Bourne Identity, The Money Pit, Jaws, Man's Favorite Sport,* and more.

Marketing Miscues

Mistakes can have tough consequences, but they also offer a great lesson. This is especially true in  marketing. At the end of each part, you will find new cases that describe good and bad ideas that couldn't make it in the rough-and-tumble marketplace. Often amusing and always interesting, these cases about iPod's troubles with the Nano, Burger King's troubles with Coq Roq, and *Grand Theft Auto*'s trouble with ratings, will help your students avoid the same mistakes made by these well-known companies. After all, making smart decisions is at the heart of successful marketing.

Critical Thinking Cases

In today's dynamic business environment, managers must constantly make decisions. For that reason, marketers must be able to quickly evaluate data and craft appropriate response strategies. In the hope of better preparing the next generation of business leaders, *Introduction to Marketing,* Ninth Edition, helps students develop critical thinking skills with a more challenging comprehensive case at the end of each of the seven major parts—all of them new for this edition. Critical Thinking Cases feature issues confronting well-known brands like Whole Foods Market, NASCAR, Yahoo, and HGTV, and ask students to evaluate the situation, identify key issues, and make decisions.

OUR PEDAGOGY IS DESIGNED WITH YOUR STUDENTS IN MIND

All of our new and exciting content is anchored by the cornerstone of our text, our fully **Integrated Learning System (ILS).** The text and all major supplements are organized around the learning outcomes that appear at the beginning of each chapter, so *Introduction to Marketing* is both easy to teach from and to learn.

A numbered icon like the one shown here identifies each objective in each chapter and appears next to its related material throughout the text, Instructor's Manual, Test Bank, PowerPoint, and Study Guide.

LO ¹ In addition, we consider multiple learning styles in the organization of our text pedagogy.

Our Text Pedagogy Excites and Reinforces Learning

Pedagogical features are meant to reinforce learning, but that doesn't mean that they have to be boring. We have created teaching tools within the text itself that will excite student interest as well as teach. Not one of our features is casually included: each has been designed and written to meet a specific learning need, level, or style.

- **Cross-Functional Connections:** No marketer is an island. Marketing professionals work with every functional area of the company. The Cross-Functional Connections that open every part explore the give-and-take between marketing and all other business functions. Solutions to the topical questions are provided in the instructor manual.
- **Online:** Activities with URLs appear in the  margins throughout each chapter and are tied either to organizations mentioned in the text or to the concepts being discussed. Because each activity calls for student effort and feedback, you can use these

mini-exercises as additional assignments or quizzing opportunities.

- **Quick Check:** This quick checklist helps students take inventory of their retention. Quick Check lets students evaluate how confident they are by scoring themselves on how well they think they understand the chapter concepts: How well can they describe the concept of exchange; explain the marketing concept; outline the creative decisions in advertising? Based on their scores, students are directed to move on to the applications, reread the chapter, or visit their instructor during office hours.

- **Terms:** Key terms appear in boldface in the text, with definitions in the margins, making it easy for students to check their understanding of key definitions. A complete alphabetical list of key terms appears at the end of each chapter as a study checklist, with page citations for easy reference.

- **Review and Applications:** The end of each chapter contains a section titled Review and Applications, a summary that distills the main points of the chapter. Chapter summaries are organized around the learning outcomes so that students can quickly check their understanding of chapter concepts. Discussion questions and activities are under the learning outcome to which they pertain.

- **Writing Questions:** To help students improve their writing skills, we have included writing exercises in the review section at the end of each chapter. These exercises are marked with the icon shown here. The writing questions are designed to be brief, so that students can accomplish writing assignments in a short time and instructors' grading time is minimized.

- **Team Activities:** The ability to work collaboratively is a key to success in today's business world. End-of-chapter team activities, identified by the icon shown here, give students opportunities to learn to work together by engaging in consensus building and problem solving.

- **Application Exercise:** These activities are based on winning teaching ideas from the "Best of the Great Ideas in Teaching Marketing" contest held in conjunction with the publication of the Eighth Edition. Developed by professors across the country, these exercises allow students to explore the principles of marketing in greater detail through engaging and enjoyable activities.

- **Entrepreneurship Case:** All chapters contain an entrepreneurship case with questions that help students work through problems facing real small businesses today.

All components of our comprehensive support package have been developed to help you prepare lectures and tests as quickly and easily as possible. We provide a wealth of information and activities beyond the text to supplement your lectures, as well as teaching aids in a variety of formats to fit your own teaching style.

Who Wants to Be a Marketer?

When we debuted **Who Wants to Be a Marketer?** with the Sixth Edition, we did not anticipate how popular it would become. Developed by John Drea of Western Illinois University, this exciting supplement to the Ninth Edition of *Introduction to Marketing* by McDaniel, Lamb, and Hair is an in-class, computer-based game. Who Wants to Be a Marketer? is a fun and exciting way to review terminology and concepts with students.

Those teaching in a traditional classroom can use the version of the game formatted for Microsoft PowerPoint. The game has two rounds of fifty original questions per chapter, for a total of 1,500 questions! The game Who Wants to Be a Marketer? is available only for adopters of *Introduction to Marketing* by McDaniel, Lamb, and Hair.

INNOVATIVE AND VALUABLE INSTRUCTOR SUPPLEMENTS

Managing your classroom resources is now easier than ever. The Instructor's Manual, Certified Test Bank, and PowerPoint, Who Wants to Be a Marketer?, and ExamView testing software are available at www.thomsonedu.com/aise.

New Video Package

The video package to accompany *Introduction to Marketing, 9e,* contiues to provide you multiple options for your class. Each chapter has both a movie clip and a longer segment showcasing the nuts and bolts of marketing at modern companies. The rich Company Clip videos will help reinforce what you've learned by showing people who are doing marketing every day—and not according to thematic units.

A Value-Added Instructor Manual Like No Other

Our Instructor's Manual is the core of our **Integrated Learning System**. For the Ninth Edition of *Introduction to Marketing,* we have made our popular Instructor's Manual even more valuable for new and experienced instructors alike. Here is a list of the features that will reduce class preparation time:

- Suggested syllabi for 12- and 16-week terms.
- A pedagogy grid for each chapter briefly laying out 1) all the options the professor has in the chapter, and 2) the key points addressed by the features in each chapter. The features included on the grid are Looking Forward, the boxed features, Application Exercise, Ethics Exercise, Entrepreneurship Case, and each video option.
- Three suggested lesson plans for each chapter: a lecture lesson plan, a small-group work lesson plan, and a video lesson plan.

We have retained the proven features like the chapter outline, lists of support material, additional class activities, and solutions for all Review and Applications, Entrepreneurship, Marketing Miscues, and Critical Thinking Cases in the book. There are also teaching tips for setting up each of the Application Exercises. Our manual is truly "one-stop shopping" for instructors teaching any size marketing course.

Certified Test Bank and Windows Testing Software

The Test Bank of the Ninth Edition has been reviewed by a panel of marketing faculty across the country who helped identify questions that may cause problems in their implementation. Faculty reviewers have helped us cull any troublesome questions. You can be sure that, no matter which questions you select for quizzes, tests, and exams, they are of the best quality. The Test Bank is organized around the learning outcomes to help you prepare on a class-by-class basis; and all questions are tagged with relevant AACSB standards to help you monitor trends in student performance necessary for accreditation. The Test Bank is available in print and new Windows software formats (ExamView testing software).

With ExamView, you can choose to prepare tests that cover all learning outcomes or that emphasize only those you feel are most important. This updated Test Bank is one of the most comprehensive on the market, with over 3,500 true/false, multiple-choice, scenario, and essay questions. Our testing database, combined with the ease of ExamView, takes the pain out of exam preparation.

Other Outstanding Supplements

- **Handbook for New Instructors: Getting Started with Great Ideas:** This helpful supplement was specifically designed for instructors preparing to teach their first course in principles of marketing. We have bolstered our helpful hints on everything from developing a course outline to grading, with winning general teachings from our "Best of the Great Ideas in Teaching Marketing" contest. To give you a complete resource for teaching ideas, we have included all of the winning entries, nearly one hundred in all, at the end of the Handbook. You'll find great teaching ideas for every chapter, plus a wealth of general tips. If you're new, let professors from around the country help you get started teaching principles of marketing!

- *Wall Street Journal* **Edition:** South-Western and WSJ have teamed up to offer you the option of a WSJ package. If you are interested in ordering *Introduction to Marketing,* 9e with WSJ, please contact your local representative. This package includes a card entitling learners to receive a subscription to *The Wall Street Journal* and WSJ.com, giving them access to many articles used as examples in this textbook. This *Wall Street Journal* edition makes it easy to relate marketing concepts to daily news stories. Instructors with 10 or more students who redeem their subscription offers will receive their own free subscription.

MEET THE AUTHORS

Carl McDaniel

Carl McDaniel is a professor of marketing at the University of Texas–Arlington, where he has been chairman of the marketing department since 1976. He has been an instructor for more than 20 years and is the recipient of several awards for outstanding teaching. McDaniel has also been a district sales manager for Southwestern Bell Telephone Company. Currently, he serves as a board member of the North Texas Higher Education Authority, a billion-dollar financial institution.

In addition to *Introduction to Marketing*, McDaniel has co-authored numerous textbooks in marketing and business. McDaniel's research has appeared in such publications as the *Journal of Marketing, Journal of Business Research, Journal of the Academy of Marketing Science,* and *California Management Review.*

McDaniel is a member of the American Marketing Association, the Academy of Marketing Science, and the Society for Marketing Advances. In addition to his academic experience, McDaniel has business experience as the co-owner of a marketing research firm. Recently, McDaniel served as senior consultant to the International Trade Centre (ITC), Geneva, Switzerland. The ITC's mission is to help developing nations increase their exports. He has a bachelor's degree from the University of Arkansas and his master's degree and doctorate from Arizona State University.

Charles W. Lamb

Charles W. Lamb is the M.J. Neeley Professor of Marketing, M.J. Neeley School of Business, Texas Christian University. He served as chair of the department of marketing from 1982 to 1988 and again from 1997 to 2003. He is currently chair of the Department of Information Systems and Supply Chain Management and president of the Academy of Marketing Science.

Lamb has authored and co-authored more than a dozen books and anthologies on marketing topics and over 150 articles that have appeared in academic journals and conference proceedings.

In 1997, he was awarded the prestigious Chancellor's Award for Distinguished Research and Creative Activity at TCU. This is the highest honor that the university bestows on its faculty. Other key honors he has received include the M.J. Neeley School of Business Research Award and selection as a Distinguished Fellow of the Academy of Marketing Science and a Fellow of the Southwestern Marketing Association.

Lamb earned an associate degree from Sinclair Community College, a bachelor's degree from Miami University, an MBA from Wright State University, and a doctorate from Kent State University. He previously served as assistant and associate professor of marketing at Texas A&M University.

Joseph F. Hair, Jr.

Joseph Hair is Professor of Marketing at Kennesaw State University. Before that, he was the Alvin C. Copeland Endowed Chair of Franchising and Director, Entrepreneurship Institute, Louisiana State University. Before that, Hair held the Phil B. Hardin Chair of Marketing at the University of Mississippi. He has taught graduate and undergraduate marketing and marketing research courses.

Hair has authored 30 books, monographs, and cases, and over 60 articles in scholarly journals. He has also participated on many university committees and has chaired numerous departmental task forces. He serves on the editorial review boards of several journals.

He is a member of the American Marketing Association, Academy of Marketing Science, Southern Marketing Association, and Southwestern Marketing Association. He was the 2004 recipient of the Academy of Marketing Science Excellence in Teaching Award.

Hair holds a bachelor's degree in economics, a master's degree in marketing, and a doctorate in marketing, all from the University of Florida. He also serves as a marketing consultant to businesses in a variety of industries, ranging from food and retail, to financial services, health care, electronics, and the U.S. Departments of Agriculture and Interior.

Acknowledgments

This book could not have been written and published without the generous expert assistance of many people. First we wish to thank Julie Baker, Texas Christian University, for her contributions to several chapters. We would also like to recognize and thank Vicky Crittenden, Boston College, and Bill Crittenden, Northeastern University, for contributing the Cross-Functional Connections that open each part. Vicky also did an excellent job on the Critical Thinking cases and Marketing Miscues. Thank you to Robin and Randy Stuart of Kennesaw State University, who provided valuable insights into revisions and new directions for the Ninth Edition. We must also thank Jeffrey Gleich for contributing all of the new Entrepreneurship cases.

We also wish to thank each of the following persons for their work on the best supplement package that is available today. Our gratitude goes out to: Thomas and Betty Pritchett of Kennesaw State University for revising our comprehensive Test Bank and for writing the quizzes that appear in other parts of the package; Eric Brengle of Indiana University for designing the fantastic PowerPoint templates, and Deborah Baker of Texas Christian University for executing the revision beautifully.

Administrative assistant Fran Eller at TCU typed the manuscript, provided important quality control, and helped keep the project (and us) on schedule. Jeannette Hood, UTA administrative assistant, played a major role in managing the marketing office so that Carl could write. Their dedication, hard work, and support were exemplary.

Our deepest gratitude goes to the team at Thomson Learning that has made this text a market leader. Jamie Bryant, our developmental editor at B-books, is world-class in her abilities and dedication. Tamborah Moore, our production editor, helped make this text a reality. A special thanks goes to Neil Marquardt, our publisher, for his suggestions and support.

Finally, we are particularly indebted to our reviewers and to faculty who have contributed to this edition and throughout the years:

Keith Absher
University of North Alabama

Roshan (Bob) D. Ahuja
Xavier University

Wayne Alexander
Moorhead State University

Jackie Anderson
Davenport University School of Business

Joseph Anderson
Northern Arizona University

Linda Anglin
Mankato State University

Christopher Anicich
California State University, Fullerton

Barry Ashmen
Bucks County Community College

Stephen Baglione
Saint Leo University

Kathleen M. Bailey
Loyola University of New Orleans

Gregory J. Baleja
Alma College

Andrew Banasiewicz
Louisiana State University

Barry L. Bayus
University of North Carolina–Chapel Hill

Fred Beasley
Northern Kentucky University

John L. Beisel
Pittsburgh State University

Christine A. Bell
Albright College

Ken Bell
Ellsworth Community College

Thomas S. Bennett
Gaston Community College

Marcel L. Berard
Community College of Rhode Island

Deirdre Bird
Providence College

Robert J. Blake
Concordia University

David M. Blanchette
Rhode Island College

L. Michelle Bobbitt
Bradley University

James C. Boespflug
Arapahoe Community College

Larry Borgen
Normandale Community College

William H. Brannen
Creighton University

David Brennan
Webster University

Rich Brown
Freed-Hardeman University

William G. Browne
Oregon State University

Pat LeMay Burr
University of Incarnate Word

Richard M. Burr
Trinity University

Victoria Bush
University of Mississippi

Deborah Chiviges Calhoun
College of Notre Dame of Maryland

Joseph E. Cantrell
DeAnza College

Shery Carder
Lake City Community College

G. L. Carr
University of Alaska, Anchorage

Stephen B. Castleberry
University of Minnesota, Duluth

Ed Cerny
University of South Carolina

Meg Clark
Cincinnati State Technical and Community College

Irvine Clarke III
James Madison University

Barbara Coleman
Augusta College

Robert A. Compton
Valley Forge Military College

Brian I. Connett
California State University, Northridge

John Alan Davis
Mohave Community College

Debra Decelles
State University of New York College–Brockport

Ronald Decker
University of Wisconsin, Eau Claire

William M. Diamond
SUNY – Albany

Gary M. Donnelly
Casper College

John T. Drea
Western Illinois University

Debbie Easterling
University of Maryland–Eastern Shore

Jacqueline K. Eastman
Valdosta State University

Kevin M. Elliott
Mankato State University

G. Scott Erickson
Ithaca College

Karen A. Evans
Herkimer County Community College

Theresa B. Flaherty
Old Dominion University

P. J. Forrest
Mississippi College

Raymond Frost
Central Connecticut State University

John Gardner
State University of New York College–Brockport

S. J. Garner
Eastern Kentucky University

Leonard R. Geiser
Goshen College

Cornelia J. Glenn
Owensboro Community College

James H. Glenn
Owensboro Community College

Lynn R. Godwin
University of St. Thomas

Daniel J. Goebel
University of Southern Mississippi

Jana G. Goodrich
Pennsylvania State University

Darrell Goudge
University of Central Oklahoma

Reginald A. Graham
Eastern Montana College

Gordon T. Gray
Oklahoma City University

Donna H. Green
Wayne State University

Mark Green
Simpson College

Dwayne D. Gremler
University of Idaho

Alice Griswold
Clarke College

Barbara Gross
California State University at Northridge

Richard A. Halberg
Houghton College

Randall S. Hansen
Stetson University

David M. Hardesty
University of Miami

Martha Hardesty
College of St. Catherine

Dorothy R. Harpool
Wichita State University

Hari S. Hariharan
University of Wisconsin, Madison

L. Jean Harrison-Walker
University of Houston–Clear Lake

Michael Hartford
Morehead State University

James W. Harvey
George Mason University

Timothy S. Hatten
Black Hills State University

Paula J. Haynes
University of Tennessee at Chattanooga

James E. Hazeltine
Northeastern Illinois University

Charlane Bomrad Held
Onondaga Community College

Tom Hickey
Oswego State University of New York

Patricia M. Hopkins
California State Polytechnic

Mark B. Houston
University of Missouri

Kristen B. Hovsepian
Ashland University

Amy R. Hubbert
University of Nebraska at Omaha

R. Vish Iyer
University of Northern Colorado

Anita Jackson
Central Connecticut State University

Anupam Jaju
George Mason University

Bruce H. Johnson
Gustavus Adolphus College

Russell W. Jones
University of Central Oklahoma

Mathew Joseph
University of South Alabama

Vaughn Judd
Auburn University–Montgomery

Jacqueline J. Kacen
University Illinois

Ira S. Kalb
University of Southern California

William J. Kehoe
University of Virginia

J. Steven Kelly
DePaul University

Philip R. Kemp
De Paul University

Raymond F. Keyes
Boston College

Sylvia Keyes
Bridgewater State College

G. Dean Kortge
Central Michigan University

John R. Kuzma
Minnesota State University, Mankato

Bernard P. Lake
Kirkwood Community College

Thomas J. Lang
University of Miami

J. Ford Laumer, Jr.
Auburn University

Kenneth R. Lawrence
New Jersey Institute of Technology

Richard M. Lei
Northern Arizona University

Ron Lennon
Barry University

Judith J. Leonard
Eastern Kentucky University

J. Gordon Long
Georgia College

Sandra L. Lueder
Sacred Heart University

Michael Luthy
Bellarmine College

James L. Macke
Cincinnati State Technical and Community College

Charles S. Madden
Baylor University

Deanna R. D. Mader
Marshall University

Fred H. Mader
Marshall University

Larry Maes
Davenport University

Shirine Mafi
Otterbein College

Jack K. Mandel
Nassau Community College

Karl Mann
Tennessee Tech University

Phylis M. Mansfield
Pennsylvania State University—Erie/Behrend

Cathy L. Martin
Northeast Louisiana University

Gregory S. Martin
University of West Florida

Irving Mason
Herkimer County Community College

Lee H. McCain
Seminole Community College

Michael McCall
Ithaca College

Nancy Ryan McClure
University of Central Oklahoma

Kim McKeage
University of Maine

Bronna McNeely
Midwestern State University

Sanjay S. Mehta
Sam Houston State University

Taylor W. Meloan
University of Southern California

Ronald E. Michaels
University of Central Florida

Charles E. Michaels, Jr.
University of South Florida

Mark A. Mitchell
Coastal Carolina University

William C. Moncrief
Texas Christian University

Michael C. Murphy
Langston University

Elwin Myers
Texas A&M University

Suzanne Altobello Nasco
Southern Illinois University

Murugappan Natesan
University of Alberta

N. Chinna Natesan
Southwest Texas State University

Roy E. Nicely
Valdosta State College

Carolyn Y. Nicholson
Stetson University

Chuck Nielson
Louisiana State University

Robert O'Keefe
DePaul University

Patrick A. Okonkwo
Central Michigan University

Brian Olson
Johnson County Community College

Anil M. Pandya
Northeastern Illinois University

Michael M. Pearson
Loyola University, New Orleans

John Perrachione
Truman State University

Monica Perry
California State University, Fullerton

Constantine G. Petrides
Borough of Manhattan Community College

Julie M. Pharr
Tennessee Technological University

Chris Pullig
University of Virginia

William Rech
Bucks County Community College

Allan C. Reddy
Valdosta State University

Joseph Reihing
State University of New York, Nassau

Jamie M. Ressler
Palm Beach Atlantic University

Sandra Robertson
Thomas Nelson Community College

John Ronchetto
University of San Diego

Dick Rose
University of Phoenix (deceased)

Al Rosenbloom
Dominican University

Barbara-Jean Ross
Louisiana State University

Lawrence Ross
Florida Southern College

Anthony Rossi
State University of New York College–Brockport

Carl Saxby
University of Southern Indiana

Jan Napoleon Saykiewicz
Duquesne University

Deborah Reed Scarfino
William Jewel College

Jeffrey Schmidt
University of Illinois

Peter A. Schneider
Seton Hall University

James A. Seaman
Nyack College

Trina Sego
Boise State University

Donald R. Self
Auburn University – Montgomery

Matthew D. Shank
Northern Kentucky University

John Shapiro
Northeastern State University

David L. Sherrell
University of Memphis

Peggy O. Shields
University of Southern Indiana

Mandeep Singh
Western Illinois University

Lois J. Smith
University of Wisconsin–Whitewater

Mark T. Spence
Southern Connecticut State College

James V. Spiers
Arizona State University

Thomas Stevenson
University of North Carolina–Charlotte

Karen L. Stewart
Richard Stockton College

James E. Stoddard
University of New Hampshire

Judy Strauss
University of Nevada, Reno

Susan Sunderline
State University of New York College–Brockport

Albert J. Taylor
Austin Peay State University

Janice E. Taylor
Miami University of Ohio

Ronald D. Taylor
Mississippi State University

James L. Thomas
Jacksonville State University

Kay Blythe Tracy
Gettysburg College

Gregory P. Turner
College of Charleston

Richard Turshen
Pace University

Sandra T. Vernon
Fayetteville Technical Community College

Franck Vingeron
California State University at Northridge

Charles R. Vitaska
Metro State College, Denver

James Ward
Arizona State University

Beth A. Walker
Arizona State University

Jim Wenthe
Georgia College and State University

Stacia Wert-Gray
University of Central Oklahoma

Janice K. Williams
University of Central Oklahoma

Laura A. Williams
San Diego State University

Elizabeth J. Wilson
Boston College

Robert D. Winsor
Loyola Marymount University

Leon Winer
Pace University

Arch G. Woodside
Boston College

Barbara Ross-Wooldridge
University of Tampa

Linda Berns Wright
Mississippi State University

William R. Wynd
Eastern Washington University

Merv H. Yeagle
University of Maryland

The World
of Marketing

CROSS-FUNCTIONAL
CONNECTIONS

As a major business function, marketing cannot be accomplished in isolation. The concept of a customer orientation has encompassed the business community, which has made marketing both a strategic thrust and a functional process. Though ownership of the marketing function remains with the marketers, the concept of marketing must permeate the entire organization.

Companies are managed vertically but are run horizontally. The vertical management of companies has led to the creation of functional silos in corporations. Traditionally, the need for functional expertise has resulted in workers who are experts in specialized portions of the organization's tasks. For example, a functional-level marketing strategist resolves questions concerning what products deliver customer satisfaction and value, what price to charge, how to distribute the products, and what type of marketing communication activities will have the desired impact. The functional-level manufacturing strategist decides what products manufacturing can make, at what rate to produce, and how to make the products. Since such functional activities require expertise in only one functional area, managers have traditionally been trained to manage "vertically." Furthermore, an employee working in a functional silo generally does not acknowledge the importance of other functional processes in providing the final product or service to the customer.

Companies are increasingly finding that the rigidity of such functional groupings is unable to meet the demands of today's dynamic, market-oriented marketplace. Consequently, a significant trend in modern organizations is an effort to increase collaboration and integration across functional areas of the business. Successful interactions between marketing and other functional areas do not occur

Though ownership of the marketing function remains with the marketers, the concept of marketing must permeate the entire organization.

easily, however, and often result in conflict. Reasons for cross-functional conflict include divergent personalities, physical separation, data differences, and suboptimal reward systems.

Marketing people tend to be extroverted and interact easily with others, whereas research and development and manufacturing people are frequently introverted and feel most comfortable working with individual work processes and output. In addition to having distinct personalities, marketers and their product management colleagues in R&D and manufacturing are often housed in different locations, which is surprising considering the overlapping effects that all three groups have on a company's product.

The marketing department is typically located in the company's headquarters, which may be in the heart of a major business district, with sales located strategically close to customers. The manufacturing group is often located in low-wage areas or low-rent districts, possibly close to suppliers. The manufacturing group may even be located in a different country. Given this physical sepa-

ration, it is easy for each department to "do its own thing," particularly if the groups are separated by language differences as well as time zones.

Another major source of conflict between marketing and its R&D and manufacturing counterparts is the type of data collected and used in decision making. Technical specialists in R&D and manufacturing have a difficult time understanding how marketers can work without "hard" data. It is difficult to mesh marketing's attitudinal data with data on cycle times or tensile strength. For example, while marketing's forecasts are rarely 100 percent accurate, manufacturing can determine the precise costs associated with production processes.

Not surprisingly, marketing's reward system, based on increased sales, is often in direct conflict with manufacturing and R&D's reward systems that are driven by cost reduction. Marketing may be able to increase sales by offering consumers more depth in the product line. Unfortunately, that increased depth leads to more changeover in production lines, which, in turn, drives up the cost of production.

A major challenge for marketers has been to develop mechanisms for reducing conflict between the marketing department and other business functions. In addition to cross-functional teams and job rotations, marketers have begun using the vast information technology infrastructure to facilitate interactions across functions. For example, retailers are now able to transmit orders directly to a supplier's computer via the electronic highway. The supplier's computer automatically sends the order to the shop floor, while simultaneously reconciling the order with the retail store's credit history. This reduction in the need for human intervention not only speeds up the transaction process but also lessens the chance for error and conflict across functional groups.

Recognition of the customer's role in the organization and the empowerment of employees are both necessary for success in today's business environment. Successful cross-functional coordination is critical to having a satisfied, loyal customer, which in turn is necessary for success in today's marketplace.

Questions

1. Why is cross-functional coordination necessary to have a customer-oriented firm?

2. What roles do teamwork and technology play in cross-functional coordination?

An Overview
of Marketing

Learning Outcomes

LO¹   Define the term *marketing*

LO²   Describe four marketing management philosophies

LO³   Discuss the differences between sales and market orientations

LO⁴   Describe several reasons for studying marketing

building customer
relationships at **Kiehl's**

Luxury makeup-counter employees are the used-car salesmen of the department-store world. Stop by for a simple tube of lipstick, and a plastic-looking clerk guilts you into buying ointments that promise to cure every wrinkle, spot, or dark circle you never had.

Contrast that with Kiehl's, where there are no mirrors to magnify your flaws. The Spartan packaging of its products—dishwashing soap is sexier than this—seduces rather than screams. And when one of the 154-year-old brand's white-coat-clad sales reps approaches you, you're urged to take a free sample and see if it works before you buy.

Any sales techniques taught are more a lesson on what not to do: "Don't send customers away without free samples. And don't use words like fabulous."

The sample program, under which Kiehl's gives away more than 12 million packets and tubes a year, is the "cornerstone of Kiehl's customer-service philosophy," taking the pressure off both reps and customers, says Cammie Cannella, assistant VP of global education development. "It's very important that

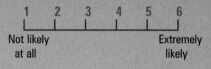

our customers believe in the quality," she says. "There is no other way to do that than have reps who educate customers about what's in our products and then let them try them out firsthand."

When L'Oreal acquired the brand in 2000 and expanded it to 16 stores and 150 department-store counters nationwide, it kept Kiehl's sample program—a winning, if investment-heavy, formula for building trusting customer relationships. Such gentle, generous tactics have proven a potent prescription.

Complementing the free samples is a highly knowledgeable staff, which Kiehl's invests in heavily to train. The company uses nearly 10 percent of its compensation budget to send new hires to an up to four-week residency in New York, Miami, or San Francisco. Any sales techniques taught are more a lesson on what not to do: "Don't send customers away without free samples. And don't use words like *fabulous.*"

That sort of high-touch, low-pressure service is the beauty of Kiehl's, says customer Sean Cambern. He'd never had any interest in skin care until he followed his wife into a Kiehl's store one afternoon. "Now I'm always stopping by," he says. "You'll never feel like you're being sold to." Now there's a formula for sales success.[1]

Explain Kiehl's philosophy of business. Describe and evaluate its formula for building trusting customer relationships.

What Is Marketing?

What does the term *marketing* **mean to you?** Many people think it means the same as personal selling. Others think marketing is the same as personal selling and advertising. Still others believe marketing has something to do with making products available in stores, arranging displays, and maintaining inventories of products for future sales. Actually, marketing includes all of these activities and more.

Marketing has two facets. First, it is a philosophy, an attitude, a perspective, or a management orientation that stresses customer satisfaction. Second, marketing is an organization function and a set of processes used to implement this philosophy. This is the marketing process.

The American Marketing Association's definition encompasses both perspectives: "**Marketing** is an organizational function and a set of processes for creating, communicating, and delivering value to customers and for managing customer relationships in ways that benefit the organization and its stakeholders."[2]

Marketing involves more than just activities performed by a group of people in a defined area or department. In the often-quoted words of David Packard, cofounder of Hewlett-Packard, "marketing is too important to be left only to the marketing department." Marketing is a process that focuses on delivering value and benefits to customers, not just selling goods, services, and/or ideas. It uses communication, distribution, and pricing strategies to provide customers and other stakeholders with the goods, services, ideas, values, and benefits they desire when and where they want them. It involves building long-term, mutually rewarding relationships when these benefit all parties concerned. Marketing also entails an understanding that organizations have many connected stakeholder "partners," including employees, suppliers, stockholders, distributors, and others.

When an organization creates a high level of employee satisfaction, this leads to greater effort, which leads to higher-quality goods and services, which lead to more repeat business, which leads to higher growth and profits, which lead to higher stockholder satisfaction, which leads to more investment, and so on.[3] The motto of Wegmans Food Markets, the Rochester-based grocery chain ranked by *Fortune* magazine as the best company to work for in America, states, "Employees first, customers second." The rationale is that if employees are happy, customers will be too.[4]

One desired outcome of marketing is an **exchange**; people giving up something to receive something they would rather have. Normally, we think of money as the medium of exchange. We "give up" money to "get" the goods and services we want. Exchange does not require money, however. Two persons may barter or trade such items as baseball cards or oil paintings.

An exchange can take place only if the following five conditions exist:

1. There must be at least two parties.

2. Each party has something that might be of value to the other party.

3. Each party is capable of communication and delivery.

4. Each party is free to accept or reject the exchange offer.

5. Each party believes it is appropriate or desirable to deal with the other party.[5]

Exchange will not necessarily take place even if all these conditions exist. They are, however, necessary for exchange to be possible. For example, you may place an advertisement in your local newspaper stating that your used automobile is for sale at a certain price. Several people may call you to ask about the car, some may test-drive it, and one or more may even make you an offer. All five conditions are necessary for an exchange to exist. But unless you reach an agreement with a buyer and actually sell the car, an exchange will not take place. Notice that marketing can occur even if an exchange does not occur. In the example just discussed, you would have engaged in marketing even if no one bought your used automobile.

marketing
An organizational function and a set of processes for creating, communicating, and delivering value to customers and for managing customer relationships in ways that benefit the organization and its stakeholders.

exchange
People giving up something to receive something they would rather have.

LO¹ Define the term *marketing*

Customer value and beneficial relationships

Creating value

Product | Place

Exchange
A ↔ B

Price | Promotion

Delivering value

Communicating value

LO²
Marketing Management Philosophies

Four competing philosophies strongly influence an organization's marketing processes. These philosophies are commonly referred to as production, sales, market, and societal marketing orientations.

PRODUCTION ORIENTATION

A **production orientation** is a philosophy that focuses on the internal capabilities of the firm rather than on the desires and needs of the marketplace. A production orientation means that management assesses its resources and asks these questions: "What can we do best?" "What can our engineers design?" "What is easy to produce, given our equipment?" In the case of a service organization, managers ask, "What services are most convenient for the firm to offer?" and "Where do our talents lie?" Some have referred to this orientation as a *Field of Dreams* orientation, from the movie's well-known line, "If we build it, they will come." The furniture industry is infamous for its disregard of customers and for its slow cycle times. This has always been a production-oriented industry.

There is nothing wrong with assessing a firm's capabilities; in fact, such assessments are major considerations in strategic marketing planning (see Chapter 2). A production orientation falls short because it does not consider whether the goods and services that the firm produces most efficiently also meet the needs of the marketplace. Sometimes what a firm can best produce is exactly what the market wants. For example, the research and development department of 3M's commercial tape division developed and patented the adhesive component of Post-It Notes a year before a commercial application was identified. In other situations, as when competition is weak or demand exceeds supply, a production-oriented firm can survive and even prosper. More often, however, firms that succeed in competitive markets have a clear understanding that they must first determine what customers want and then produce it, rather than focusing on what company management thinks should be produced.

© R. ALCORN/THOMSON

SALES ORIENTATION

A **sales orientation** is based on the ideas that people will buy more goods and services if aggressive sales techniques are used and that high sales result in high profits. Not only are sales to the final buyer emphasized but intermediaries are also encouraged to push manufacturers' products more aggressively. To sales-oriented firms, marketing means selling things and collecting money.

The fundamental problem with a sales orientation, as with a production orientation, is a lack of understanding of the needs and wants of the marketplace. Sales-oriented companies often find that, despite the quality of their sales force, they cannot convince people to buy goods or services that are neither wanted nor needed.

Some sales-oriented firms simply fail to understand what is important to their customers. Many so-called dot-com businesses that came into existence in the late 1990s are no longer around because they focused on the technology rather than the customer.

Kimberly Knickle couldn't have been happier when she signed up with online grocer Streamline.com. Streamline installed a refrigerator in her garage to make deliveries when

production orientation
A philosophy that focuses on the internal capabilities of the firm rather than on the desires and needs of the marketplace.

sales orientation
The idea that people will buy more goods and services if aggressive sales techniques are used and that high sales result in high profits

she wasn't home, picked up the dry cleaning, delivered stamps, and dropped off parcel shipments. The best part was the customer service. When something went wrong, Streamline instantly credited her account. She could always get someone on the phone. As the company expanded its customer base, however, the deliveries became inconsistent, telephone customer service put her on hold more often, and the company overcharged her several times. The big blow came when it revamped its Web site: in the past, she could place an order for 30 items quickly, but the company switched to a new system that checked inventory in real time, slowing down the interface tremendously. "The grocery store is two minutes away," Knickle says. "In 25 minutes, I could get two-thirds of my shopping done at the store. This was supposed to make my life easier."[6]

Satisfying customer needs and wants is the cornerstone of the marketing concept. Hamid Hashmi understands this marketing fundamental. He is CEO of the Muvico Theater in Boca Raton, Florida, which boasts 20 theaters ranging from 100 to 450 seats, a full-service bar, a 230+ seat restaurant, and a day-care center available to customers as well as the company's 350 employees.

MARKET ORIENTATION

The **marketing concept** is a simple and intuitively appealing philosophy that articulates a market orientation. It states that the social and economic justification for an organization's existence is the satisfaction of customer wants and needs while meeting organizational objectives. It is based on an understanding that a sale does not depend on an aggressive sales force, but rather on a customer's decision to purchase a product. What a business thinks it produces is not of primary importance to its success. Instead, what customers think they are buying—the perceived value—defines a business. The marketing concept includes the following:

- Focusing on customer wants and needs so that the organization can distinguish its product(s) from competitors' offerings

- Integrating all the organization's activities, including production, to satisfy these wants

- Achieving long-term goals for the organization by satisfying customer wants and needs legally and responsibly

Firms that adopt and implement the marketing concept are said to be market oriented. Achieving a **market orientation** involves obtaining information about customers, competitors, and markets; examining the information from a total business perspective; determining how to deliver superior customer value; and implementing actions to provide value to customers.

For example, Coach interviews at least 10,000 customers every year to keep track of perceptions of the brand. It also tests each product in a limited number of stores six months before the product actually comes out. This helps the company assess the final design and forecast demand.[7] Coach also works to establish and maintain rewarding relationships with its customers. You can bring in your Coach bag any time and have it repaired free for the natural life of the bag. The company fixes 100,000 bags each year.[8]

Understanding your competitive arena and competitors' strengths and weaknesses is a critical component of a market orientation. This includes assessing what existing or potential competitors might be intending to do tomorrow as well as what they are doing today. Western Union failed to define its competitive arena as telecommunications, concentrating instead on telegraph services, and was eventually outflanked by fax technology. Had Western Union been a market-oriented company, its management might have better understood the changes taking place, seen the competitive threat, and developed strategies to counter the threat. (See the Online exercise at the top of the page to find out more about Western Union's situation.)

marketing concept
The idea that the social and economic justification for an organization's existence is the satisfaction of customer wants and needs while meeting organizational objectives.

market orientation
A philosophy that assumes that a sale does not depend on an aggressive sales force but rather on a customer's decision to purchase a product. It is synonymous with the marketing concept.

© GENERAL MILLS INC.

Even the lid is good for you.

Save Lids to Save Lives.

For every pink lid you mail back by December 31, 2003, Yoplait will make a 10-cent donation to the Susan G. Komen Breast Cancer Foundation, up to $1.2 million. Combined with Yoplait's guaranteed donation of $830,000, we can raise $2 million. Yoplait and you — partners in the fight against breast cancer. This September and October, look for Yoplait pink lids at a store near you. www.YoplaitUSA.com.

Although Yoplait is not founded on a societal marketing orientation in the same way as, say, the Sierra Club, the company still communicates to its customers its concern about women's health. For each pink lid redeemed by a Yoplait customer, the company donates 10 cents to the Susan G. Komen Breast Cancer Foundation.

Western Union
Has Western Union rebounded from its failure to define its competitive arena as telecommunications? Evaluate the company's Web site to find out. Describe, if you can, the company's value proposition, the market it serves, and whom it seems to be competing against in the twenty-first century.

http://www.westernunion.com

Online

SOCIETAL MARKETING ORIENTATION

One reason a market-oriented organization may choose not to deliver the benefits sought by customers is that these benefits may not be good for individuals or society. This philosophy, called a **societal marketing orientation**, states that an organization exists not only to satisfy customer wants and needs and to meet organizational objectives but also to preserve or enhance individuals' and society's long-term best interests. Marketing products and containers that are less toxic than normal, are more durable, contain reusable materials, or are made of recyclable materials is consistent with a societal marketing orientation. Duracell and Eveready battery companies have reduced the levels of mercury in their batteries and will eventually market mercury-free products. Turtle Wax car wash products and detergents are biodegradable and can be "digested" by waste treatment plants. The company's plastic containers are made of recyclable plastic, and its spray products do not use propellants that damage the ozone layer in the earth's upper atmosphere.

LO³
Differences between Sales and Market Orientations

The differences between sales and market orientations are substantial. The two orientations can be compared in terms of five characteristics: the organization's focus, the firm's business, those to whom the product is directed, the firm's primary goal, and the tools used to achieve those goals.

THE ORGANIZATION'S FOCUS

Personnel in sales-oriented firms tend to be "inward looking," focusing on selling what the organization

REVIEW LEARNING OUTCOME

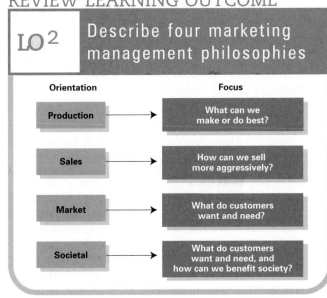

LO² Describe four marketing management philosophies

Orientation	Focus
Production	What can we make or do best?
Sales	How can we sell more aggressively?
Market	What do customers want and need?
Societal	What do customers want and need, and how can we benefit society?

societal marketing orientation
The idea that an organization exists not only to satisfy customer wants and needs and to meet organizational objectives but also to preserve or enhance individuals' and society's long-term best interests.

makes rather than making what the market wants. Many of the historic sources of competitive advantage—technology, innovation, economies of scale—allowed companies to focus their efforts internally and prosper. Today, many successful firms derive their competitive advantage from an external, market-oriented focus. A market orientation has helped companies such as Dell, Inc., the Royal Bank of Canada, and Southwest Airlines outperform their competitors. These companies put customers at the center of their business in ways most companies do poorly or not at all.

A sales orientation has led to the demise of many firms including Streamline.com, the Digital Entertainment Network, and Urban Box Office. As one technology industry analyst put it, "no one has ever gone to a Web site because they heard there was great Java running."9

Customer Value

Customer value is the relationship between benefits and the sacrifice necessary to obtain those benefits. Customer value is not simply a matter of high quality. A high-quality product that is available only at a high price will not be perceived as a good value, nor will bare-bones service or low-quality goods selling for a low price. Instead, customers value goods and services that are of the quality they expect and that are sold at prices they are willing to pay. Value can be used to sell a Mercedes-Benz as well as a $3 Tyson frozen chicken dinner.

The automobile industry illustrates the importance of creating customer value. To penetrate the fiercely competitive luxury automobile market, Lexus adopted a customer-driven approach, with particular emphasis on service. Lexus stresses product quality with a standard of zero defects in manufacturing. The service quality goal is to treat each customer as one would treat a guest in one's home, to pursue the perfect person-to-person relationship, and to strive to improve continually. This pursuit has enabled Lexus to establish a clear quality image and capture a significant share of the luxury car market. Marketers interested in customer value

- *Offer products that perform*: This is the bare minimum requirement. Consumers have lost patience with shoddy merchandise.

- *Earn trust.* Diane Hessan, CEO of Communispace in Watertown, Massachusetts, says that "selling is all about the right to do business with someone. Put yourself in their shoes, and understand what the issues are. In today's business environment, the most critical element of any sale is trust. Ultimately, when someone says yes to you, they are saying, 'I'm betting on what this person is telling me.'"10

- *Avoid unrealistic pricing*: E-marketers are leveraging Internet technology to redefine how prices are set and negotiated. With lower costs, e-marketers can often offer lower prices than their brick-and-mortar counterparts. The enormous popularity of auction sites such as eBay and Amazon.com and the customer-bid model used by Priceline illustrates that online customers are interested in bargain prices. Many are not willing to pay a premium for the convenience of examining the merchandise and taking it home with them.

- *Give the buyer facts*: Today's sophisticated consumer wants informative advertising and knowledgeable salespeople. Web sites that don't provide enough information are among the top ten things that "irk" Internet shoppers most.

- *Offer organization-wide commitment in service and after-sales support*: People fly Southwest Airlines because the airline offers superior value. Although passengers do not get assigned seats or meals (just peanuts or crackers) when they use the airline, its service is reliable and friendly and costs less than most major airlines. All Southwest employees are involved in the effort to satisfy customers. Pilots tend to the boarding gate when their help is needed, and ticket agents help move luggage. One reservation agent flew from Dallas to Tulsa with a frail, elderly woman whose son was afraid she couldn't handle the change of planes by herself on her way to St. Louis.

Customer Satisfaction

Customer satisfaction is the customer's evaluation of a good or service in terms of whether that good or service has met the customer's needs and expectations. Failure to meet needs and expectations results in dissatisfaction with the good or service.11 Keeping current customers satisfied is just as important as attracting new ones and a lot less expensive. One study showed that reducing customer attrition by just 5 to 10 percent could increase annual profits by as much as 75 percent.12 Firms that have a reputation for delivering high levels of customer satisfaction do things differently from their competitors.

customer value
The relationship between benefits and the sacrifice necessary to obtain those benefits.

customer satisfaction
Customers' evaluation of a good or service in terms of whether it has met their needs and expectations.

Top management is obsessed with customer satisfaction, and employees throughout the organization understand the link between their job and satisfied customers. The culture of the organization is to focus on delighting customers rather than on selling products.

Nordstrom's impeccable reputation for customer service comes not from its executives or its marketing team, but from the customers themselves. The retail giant is willing to take risks, do unusual and often expensive favors for shoppers, and reportedly even accept returns on items not purchased there. But big risks often yield big gains. People tell their friends that a company is doing crazy things for its customers, and the word spreads. Pretty soon this word of mouth, or viral marketing, lures new people to the store—even people who have no idea what's inside want to experience what it's like to shop there.[13]

Building Relationships

Attracting new customers to a business is only the beginning. The best companies view new-customer attraction as the launching point for developing and enhancing a long-term relationship. Companies can expand market share in three ways: attracting new customers, increasing business with existing customers, and retaining current customers. Building relationships with existing customers directly addresses two of the three possibilities and indirectly addresses the other.

Relationship marketing is a strategy that focuses on keeping and improving relationships with current customers. It assumes that many consumers and business customers prefer to have an ongoing relationship with one organization than to switch continually among providers in their search for value.[14] USAA is a good example of a company focused on building long-term relationships with customers. Customer retention was a core value of the company long before customer loyalty became a popular business concept. USAA believes so strongly in the importance of customer retention that managers and executives' bonuses are based, in part, on this dimension.[15]

Most successful relationship marketing strategies depend on customer-oriented personnel, effective training programs, employees with authority to make decisions and solve problems, and teamwork.

Customer-Oriented Personnel   For an organization to be focused on building relationships with customers, employees' attitudes and actions must be customer oriented. An employee may be the only contact a particular customer has with the firm. In that customer's eyes, the employee is the firm. Any person, department, or division that is not customer oriented weakens the positive image of the entire organization. For example, a potential customer who is greeted discourteously may well assume that the employee's attitude represents the whole firm.

Some companies, such as Coca-Cola, Delta Air Lines, Hershey Company, Kellogg, Nautilus, and Sears, have appointed chief customer officers (CCOs). These customer advocates provide an executive voice for customers and report directly to the CEO.[16] Their responsibilities include assuring that the company maintains a customer-centric culture and that all company employees remain focused on delivering customer value.[17]

The Role of Training   Leading marketers recognize the role of employee training in customer service and relationship building. Edward Jones Company, ranked number one among *Fortune*'s "100 Best Companies to Work For," for two straight years, spends 3.8 percent of its payroll on training, with an average of 146 hours for every employee. New brokers get more than four times that much.[18] It is no coincidence that the public companies on this list such as Southwest Airlines and Cisco Systems perform much better than other firms in their respective industries. All new employees at Disneyland and Walt Disney World must attend Disney University, a special training program for Disney employees. They must first pass Traditions 1, a daylong course focusing on the Disney philosophy and operational procedures. Then they go on to specialized training. Similarly, McDonald's has Hamburger University. At American Express's Quality University, line employees and managers learn how to treat customers. There is an extra payoff for companies such as Disney and McDonald's that train their employees to be customer oriented. When employees make their customers happy, the employees are more likely to derive satisfaction from their jobs. Having contented workers who are committed to their jobs leads to better customer service and greater employee retention.

relationship marketing
A strategy that focuses on keeping and improving relationships with current customers.

Empowerment In addition to training, many market-oriented firms are giving employees more authority to solve customer problems on the spot. The term used to describe this delegation of authority is **empowerment**. Employees develop ownership attitudes when they are treated like part-owners of the business and are expected to act the part. These employees manage themselves, are more likely to work hard, account for their own performance and the company's, and take prudent risks to build a stronger business and sustain the company's success. FedEx customer service representatives are trained and empowered to resolve customer problems. Although the average FedEx transaction costs only $16, the customer service representatives are empowered to spend up to $100 to resolve a customer problem.

At Wegmans Food Markets, employees are encouraged to do just about anything on the spot, without consulting a higher-up, to satisfy a customer. That could entail cooking a family's Thanksgiving turkey at the store because the one purchased was too big to fit in the family's oven or going to a customer's home to rescue a meal. Empowering employees goes beyond having them make house calls, though. It means creating an environment where employees can do the right things, unburdened by hierarchies. According to Heather Pawlowski, a Wegmans vice president, "We're taking customers to a place they've not been before. And once they arrive, shoppers don't want to leave."[19]
Empowerment gives customers the feeling that their concerns are being addressed and gives employees the feeling that their expertise matters. The result is greater satisfaction for both customers and employees.

Teamwork Many organizations, such as Southwest Airlines and Walt Disney World, that are frequently noted for delivering superior customer value and providing high levels of customer satisfaction assign employees to teams and teach them team-building skills. **Teamwork** entails collaborative efforts of people to accomplish common objectives. Job performance, company performance, product value, and customer satisfaction all improve when people in the same department or work group begin supporting and assisting each other and emphasize cooperation instead of competition. Performance is also enhanced when cross-functional teams align their jobs with customer needs. For example, if a team of telecommunications service representatives is working to improve interaction with customers, back-office people such as computer technicians or training personnel can become part of the team with the ultimate goal of delivering superior customer value and satisfaction.

THE FIRM'S BUSINESS

A sales-oriented firm defines its business (or mission) in terms of goods and services. A market-oriented firm defines its business in terms of the benefits its customers seek. People who spend their money, time, and energy expect to receive benefits, not just goods and services. This distinction has enormous implications.

Because of the limited way it defines its business, a sales-oriented firm often misses opportunities to serve customers whose wants can be met through a wide range of product offerings instead of specific products. For example, in 1989, 220-year-old Britannica had estimated revenues of $650 million and a worldwide sales force of 7,500. Just five years later, after three consecutive years of losses, the sales force had collapsed to as few as 280 representatives. How did this respected company sink so low? Britannica managers saw that competitors were beginning to use CD-ROMs to store huge masses of information but chose to ignore the new computer technology, as well as an offer to team up with Microsoft.

It's not hard to see why parents would rather give their children an encyclopedia on a compact disc instead of a printed one. The CD-ROM versions were either given away or sold by other publishers for under $400. A full 32-volume set of *Encyclopaedia Britannica* weighs about 120 pounds, costs a minimum of $1,500, and takes up four and one-half feet of shelf space. If Britannica had defined its business as providing information instead of publishing books, it might not have suffered such a precipitous fall.

empowerment
Delegation of authority to solve customers' problems quickly—usually by the first person that the customer notifies regarding a problem.

teamwork
Collaborative efforts of people to accomplish common objectives.

Britannica

Go to Britannica's Web site. What evidence do you see that Britannica has redefined its core business? What do you think its business definition currently is? How has the company met the challenges of CD-ROM technology and online content distribution?

http://www.britannica.com

Online

Adopting a "better late than never" philosophy, Britannica has made its complete 32-volume set available free on the Internet. The company no longer sells door-to-door and hopes to return to profitability by selling advertising on its Web site.

Answering the question "What is this firm's business?" in terms of the benefits customers seek, instead of goods and services, offers at least three important advantages:

- It ensures that the firm keeps focusing on customers and avoids becoming preoccupied with goods, services, or the organization's internal needs.

- It encourages innovation and creativity by reminding people that there are many ways to satisfy customer wants.

- It stimulates an awareness of changes in customer desires and preferences so that product offerings are more likely to remain relevant.

Having a market orientation and focusing on customer wants do not mean that customers will always receive everything they want. It is not possible, for example, to profitably manufacture and market automobile tires that will last for 100,000 miles for $25. Furthermore, customers' preferences must be mediated by sound professional judgment as to how to deliver the benefits they seek. As one adage suggests, "People don't know what they want—they only want what they know." Consumers have a limited set of experiences. They are unlikely to request anything beyond those experiences because they are not aware of benefits they may gain from other potential offerings. For example, before the Internet, many people thought that shopping for some products was boring and time consuming, but could not express their need for electronic shopping.

THOSE TO WHOM THE PRODUCT IS DIRECTED

A sales-oriented organization targets its products at "everybody" or "the average customer." A market-oriented organization aims at specific groups of people. The fallacy of developing products directed at the average user is that relatively few average users actually exist. Typically, populations are characterized by diversity. An average is simply a midpoint in some set of characteristics. Because most potential customers are not "average," they are not likely to be attracted to an average product marketed to the average customer. Consider the market for shampoo as one simple example. There are shampoos for oily hair, dry hair, and dandruff. Some shampoos remove the gray or color hair. Special shampoos are marketed for infants and elderly

We make bathtime tangle free.

With JOHNSON'S® BUDDIES™ Easy-comb Shampoo, tangles don't stand a chance. And it's just one in a line of bath products designed specially for toddlers. You'll love the fun shapes, because they're simple for little hands to hold, and kids love the bright colors. So bathtime's easier for both of you.

Johnson's Buddies™

Johnson's markets its Easy-Comb Shampoo towards the parents of young children.

people. There is even shampoo for people with average or normal hair (whatever that is), but this is a fairly small portion of the total market for shampoo.

A market-oriented organization recognizes that different customer groups want different features or benefits. It may therefore need to develop different goods, services, and promotional appeals. A market-oriented organization carefully analyzes the market and divides it into groups of people who are fairly similar in terms of selected characteristics. Then the organization develops marketing programs that will bring about mutually satisfying exchanges with one or more of those groups.

Paying attention to the customer isn't exactly a new concept. Back in the 1920s, General Motors began designing cars for every lifestyle and pocketbook. This was a breakthrough for an industry that had been largely driven by production needs ever since Henry Ford promised any color as long as it was black. Chapter 7 thoroughly explores the topic of analyzing markets and selecting those that appear to be most promising to the firm.

This chapter's "Global Perspectives" box illustrates the challenges facing companies that think that all customers are the same. Clearly, what works in the United States will not always work in developing countries such as India.

THE FIRM'S PRIMARY GOAL

A sales-oriented organization seeks to achieve profitability through sales volume and tries to convince potential customers to buy, even if the seller knows that the customer and product are mismatched. Sales-oriented organizations place a higher premium on making a sale than on developing a long-term relationship with a customer. In contrast, the ultimate goal of most market-oriented organizations is to make a profit by creating customer value, providing customer satisfaction, and building long-term relationships with customers. The exception is so-called nonprofit organizations that exist to achieve goals other than profits. Nonprofit organizations can and should adopt a market orientation. Nonprofit organization marketing is explored further in Chapter 11.

TOOLS THE ORGANIZATION USES TO ACHIEVE ITS GOALS

Sales-oriented organizations seek to generate sales volume through intensive promotional activities, mainly personal selling and advertising. In contrast, market-oriented organizations recognize that promotion decisions are only one of four basic marketing mix decisions that have to be made: product decisions, place (or distribution) decisions, promotion decisions, and pricing decisions. A market-oriented organization recognizes that each of these four components is important. Furthermore, market-oriented organizations recognize that marketing is not just a responsibility of the marketing department. Interfunctional coordination means that skills and resources throughout the organization are needed to create, communicate, and deliver superior customer service and value.

A market-oriented organization uses many tools to promote its products. Sherwin-Williams uses a variety of promotional activities, including advertising and offering free samples, to market its paints.

A Beginner's Guide to Indian Marketing

Cultural barriers, poor infrastructure, and government restrictions make marketing in India a challenge even though it is one of the world's fastest-growing economies. Here are some of the lessons learned by foreign pioneers who have positioned their companies to cash in on India's remarkable progress.

- *Scale down:* Americans snap up supersize containers at Costco, but Indians save cash by buying smaller quantities. Revlon reduced the size of its nail polish bottles and saw sales volume increase.

- *Price for mass appeal:* The average income for a middle-class Indian worker is just $1,200 a year. Phone equipment maker UTStarcom found that spending constraints trickle down: it had to design cheaper network switches to sell to local phone companies.

- *Tailor products to Indian tastes:* In most countries, Subway carries only one or two menu items based on the local cuisine, but in India, the franchise offers separate vegetarian counters and a specialized "Indian Delights" menu.

- *Localize your message:* In the 1990s, Pepsi ran the same commercials in India that it aired elsewhere. But the brand didn't take off until it tapped local talent like Sharukh Khan, India's biggest box-office star, and Schin Tendulkar, a hugely popular cricket batsman.

- *Find a good partner:* India's fragmented distribution channels present a challenge to foreign companies. Tap into booming local chains like Foodworld, Pantaloon, and Shopper's Stop, which offer access to India's middle class.[20]

How might a bicycle manufacturer such as Schwinn adapt its marketing program to appeal to the Indian market? Review Schwinn's Web site (**http://www.schwinnbike.com**) for ideas.

A WORD OF CAUTION

This comparison of sales and market orientations is not meant to belittle the role of promotion, especially personal selling, in the marketing mix. Promotion is the means by which organizations communicate with present and prospective customers about the merits and characteristics of their organization and products. Effective promotion is an essential part of effective marketing. Salespeople who work for market-oriented organizations are generally perceived by their customers to be problem solvers and important links to supply sources and new products. Chapter 16 examines the nature of personal selling in more detail.

REVIEW LEARNING OUTCOME

LO3 Discuss the differences between sales and market orientations

	What is the organization's focus?	What business are you in?	To whom is the product directed?	What is your primary goal?	How do you seek to achieve your goal?
Sales Orientation	Inward, on the organization's needs	Selling goods and services	Everybody	Profit through maximum sales volume	Primarily through intensive promotion
Market Orientation	Outward, on the wants and preferences of customers	Satisfying customer wants and needs and delivering superior value	Specific groups of people	Profit through customer satisfaction	Through coordinated marketing and interfunctional activities

LO4
Why Study Marketing

Now that you understand the meaning of the term *marketing*, why it is important to adopt a marketing orientation, how organizations implement this philosophy, and how one-to-one marketing is evolving, you may be asking, "What's in it for me?" or "Why should I study marketing?" These are important questions, whether you are majoring in a business field other than marketing (such as accounting, finance, or management information systems) or a nonbusiness field (such as journalism, economics, or agriculture). There are several important reasons to study marketing: Marketing plays an important role in society, marketing is important to businesses, marketing offers outstanding career opportunities, and marketing affects your life every day.

MARKETING PLAYS AN IMPORTANT ROLE IN SOCIETY

The total population of the United States exceeds 295 million people.[21] Think about how many transactions are needed each day to feed, clothe, and shelter a population of this size. The number is huge. And yet it all works quite well, partly because the well-developed U.S. economic system efficiently distributes the output of farms and factories. A typical U.S. family, for example, consumes 2.5 tons of food a year. Marketing makes food available when we want it, in desired quantities, at accessible locations, and in sanitary and convenient packages and forms (such as instant and frozen foods).

MARKETING IS IMPORTANT TO BUSINESS

The fundamental objectives of most businesses are survival, profits, and growth. Marketing contributes directly to achieving these objectives. Marketing includes the following activities, which are vital to business organizations: assessing the wants and satisfactions of present and potential customers, designing and managing product offerings, determining prices and pricing policies, developing distribution strategies, and communicating with present and potential customers.

All businesspeople, regardless of specialization or area of responsibility, need to be familiar with the terminology and fundamentals of accounting, finance, management, and marketing. People in all business areas need to be able to communicate with specialists in other areas. Furthermore, marketing is not just a job done by people in a marketing department. Marketing is a part of the job of everyone in the organization. Therefore, a basic understanding of marketing is important to all businesspeople.

MARKETING OFFERS OUTSTANDING CAREER OPPORTUNITIES

Between a fourth and a third of the entire civilian workforce in the United States performs marketing activities. Marketing offers great career opportunities in such areas as professional selling, marketing research, advertising, retail buying, distribution management, product management, product development, and wholesaling. Marketing career opportunities also exist in a variety of nonbusiness organizations, including hospitals, museums, universities, the armed forces, and various government and social service agencies. (See Chapter 11.)

As the global marketplace becomes more challenging, companies all over the world and of all sizes are going to have to become better marketers. For a comprehensive look at career opportunities in marketing and a variety of other useful information about careers, read the Career Appendix at the end of this chapter.

MARKETING AFFECTS YOUR LIFE EVERY DAY

Marketing plays a major role in your everyday life. You participate in the marketing process as a consumer of goods and services. About half of every

REVIEW LEARNING OUTCOME

LO4 Describe several reasons for studying marketing

Why Study Marketing?

- Important to society
- Important to business
- Good career opportunities

+

Marketing affects you every day!

dollar you spend pays for marketing costs, such as marketing research, product development, packaging, transportation, storage, advertising, and sales expenses. By developing a better understanding of marketing, you will become a better-informed consumer. You will better understand the buying process and be able to negotiate more effectively with sellers. Moreover, you will be better prepared to demand satisfaction when the goods and services you buy do not meet the standards promised by the manufacturer or the marketer.

Quick Check

Now that you've read the chapter, do you get it? Take a moment for a quick check using this scale:

1 *Not at all*; 2 *Not very well*; 3 *Ok*; 4 *Well*; 5 *Very Well*

Can you . . .

____ recite the definition of marketing?

____ describe the concept of exchange?

____ explain the marketing concept?

____ name the four marketing management orientations?

____ distinguish between the sales and marketing orientations?

____ list the reasons why studying marketing is a good idea?

____ explain the difference between customer satisfaction and customer value?

____ identify the elements companies use to develop long-term relationships with customers?

____ TOTAL

Score: 35–40, you're ready to move on to the applications below; 30–34, skim the chapter one more time before moving on to the applications; 20–29, reread the sections giving you the most trouble and go to ThomsonNOW for guided tutorials; under 20, you better reread the chapter to get a grasp of the fundamentals. If you've reread the chapter and still have a low score, visit your professor or TA during office hours.

Review and Applications

LO 1 Define the term *marketing*. Marketing is an organizational function and a set of processes for creating, communicating, and delivering value to customers and for managing customer relationships in ways that benefit the organization and its stakeholders.

 1.1 What is the AMA? What does it do? How do its services benefit marketers? **http://www.marketingpower.com**

LO 2 Describe four marketing management philosophies. The role of marketing and the character of marketing activities within an organization are strongly influenced by its philosophy and orientation. A production-oriented organization focuses on the internal capabilities of the firm rather than on the desires and needs of the marketplace. A sales orientation is based on the beliefs that people will buy more products if aggressive sales techniques are used and that high sales volumes produce high profits. A market-oriented organization focuses on satisfying customer wants and needs while meeting organizational objectives. A societal marketing orientation goes beyond a market orientation to include the preservation or enhancement of individuals' and society's long-term best interests.

 2.1 Your company president has decided to restructure the firm to make it more market oriented. She is going to announce the changes at an upcoming meeting. She has asked you to prepare a short speech outlining the general reasons for the new company orientation.

2.2 Donald E. Petersen, former chairman of the board of Ford Motor Company, remarked, "If we aren't customer driven, our cars won't be either." Explain how this statement reflects the marketing concept.

2.3 Give an example of a company that might be successfully following a production orientation. Why might a firm in this industry be successful following such an orientation?

LO3 Discuss the differences between sales and market orientations. First, sales-oriented firms focus on their own needs; market-oriented firms focus on customers' needs and preferences. Second, sales-oriented companies consider themselves to be deliverers of goods and services, whereas market-oriented companies view themselves as satisfiers of customers. Third, sales-oriented firms direct their products to everyone; market-oriented firms aim at specific segments of the population. Fourth, although the primary goal of both types of firms is profit, sales-oriented businesses pursue maximum sales volume through intensive promotion, whereas market-oriented businesses pursue customer satisfaction through coordinated activities.

3.1 A friend of yours agrees with the adage "People don't know what they want—they only want what they know." Write your friend a letter expressing the extent to which you think marketers shape consumer wants.

3.2 Your local supermarket's slogan is "It's your store." However, when you asked one of the stock people to help you find a bag of chips, he told you it was not his job and that you should look a littler harder. On your way out, you noticed a sign with an address for complaints. Draft a letter explaining why the supermarket's slogan will never be credible unless the employees carry it out.

3.3 How does Philip Morris handle the sensitive issues associated with marketing tobacco? What kind of information does its Web site at **http://www.philipmorris .com/** provide about smoking and its negative effects on health? How do you think Philip Morris is able to justify such marketing tactics? After checking around the site, do you think that approach makes the company more or less trustworthy?

LO4 Describe several reasons for studying marketing. First, marketing affects the allocation of goods and services that influence a nation's economy and standard of living. Second, an understanding of marketing is crucial to understanding most businesses. Third, career opportunities in marketing are diverse, profitable, and expected to increase significantly during the coming decade. Fourth, understanding marketing makes consumers more informed.

4.1 Write a letter to a friend or family member explaining why you think that a course in marketing will help you in your career in some field other than marketing.

Key Terms

customer satisfaction	10	market orientation	8	relationship marketing	11
customer value	10	marketing	6	sales orientation	7
empowerment	12	marketing concept	8	societal marketing orientation	9
exchange	6	production orientation	7	teamwork	12

Exercises

APPLICATION EXERCISE

Understanding the differences among the various marketing management philosophies is the starting point for understanding the fundamentals of marketing.[22] From reading the chapter, you may be convinced that the market orientation is the most appealing philosophy and the one best suited to creating a competitive advantage. Not all companies, however, use the market orientation. And even companies that follow it may not execute well in all areas.

Activities

1. Visit your local grocery store and go through the cereal, snack-food, and dental hygiene aisles. Go up and down each aisle slowly, noticing how many different products are available and how they are organized on the shelves.

2. Count the varieties of product in each product category. For example, how many different kinds of cereal are on the shelves? How many different sizes? Do the same for snack food and toothpaste.

3. Now try to find a type of product in the grocery store that does not exhibit such variety. There may not be many. Why do you think there are enough kinds of cereals to fill an entire aisle (and then some), but only a few different types of, say, peanut butter? Can this difference be explained in terms of marketing management philosophy (peanut butter manufacturers do not follow the marketing concept) or by something else entirely?

4. Have you ever wanted to see a particular kind of cereal or snack food on the shelf? Think of product varietals (like grapefruit-flavored toothpaste or peanut butter-covered popcorn) that you have never seen on the shelf but would be interested in trying if someone would make it. Write a letter or send an e-mail to an appropriate company, suggesting that it add your concept to its current product line.

Entrepreneurship Case

NETFLIX READY FOR PRIMETIME

Shocked at the $40 fee he incurred for a late return of *Apollo 13*, Netflix founder Reed Hastings decided that in the age of the Internet, there had to be a better way to rent videos for home viewing. Thus, in 1997, he started an Internet-based, DVD rental service that offered direct-to-home deliveries with no late fees. A mere decade and 4 million subscribers later, Netflix has taken on established video rental companies such as Blockbuster, Hollywood Video, and Wal-Mart and emerged as the leader in innovation and customer service.

In addition to betting that the Internet would be the future of the video rental market, Hastings made a few other key predictions that helped him develop a company with almost $700 million in revenue in under ten years. He watched as moviegoers fled public theaters for the comfort of home theater systems, and he observed those same consumers embracing the features, capacity, and high-quality format of the DVD. Realizing that the Internet could allow those same convenience seekers 24-hour browsing and selection access to an unprecedented volume of movie titles in a single digital catalog, Hastings shrewdly designed a service that outperforms traditional, store-based video rentals.

Netflix allows consumers to choose from a variety of subscription plans. The most popular plan offers three DVDs for $17.99 per month. Once a subscriber builds a list of favorite movies and TV shows from a selection of over 60,000 titles, Netflix mails out the three titles at the top of the list, along with return-addressed prestamped envelopes. After viewing the DVDs, the customer simply mails them back to Netflix in the supplied packaging. When the titles are scanned in at one of the distribution warehouses, the customer is simultaneously sent the next selections on the favorites list.

With 34 strategically placed distribution centers, Netflix can deliver 92 percent of its movies within one day of being ordered. That outstanding delivery service is just the tip of the iceberg. Netflix's Web site takes personalization to new levels through its high-powered recommendation software, called Cinematch. Cinematch uses over a million lines of code and over half a billion customer-supplied ratings to suggest rental choices upon request.

Amazingly, over 60 percent of the titles added to users' favorites lists come from Cinematch recommendations, and over a million ratings are sent to Netflix every day. Just how effective is Cinematch? Netflix uses fewer than 50 customer service reps to support its entire customer base! Of those, 10 are authorized to make direct callbacks to customers with complaints to find out how the problem could have been prevented in the first place. It's that kind of attention to customers that forced retail giant Wal-Mart to give up and turn over its entire customer list to Netflix.

Netflix even added two key features to its service in response to customer requests. The first is the ability to generate multiple favorites lists for a single account, allowing families to build multiple wish lists that can differ as much as *Steel Magnolias* and *Old School*. The second is the addition of a community feature called "Friends." Friends enables users to share the titles, ratings, and preferences for recently viewed shows with those they invite to be part of their network.

Always looking to the future, Hastings wants to diversify Netflix by adding high-definition DVD rentals to its current service, selling previously rented DVDs in the rapidly growing used-DVD market, and developing an on-demand video download service. Though it's impossible to tell exactly what blockbuster service Netflix will deliver next, it's a safe bet its customers will applaud.[23]

Questions

1. Describe the elements of the exchange process as they occur between Netflix and its customers.

2. How does Netflix's approach to relationship marketing increase customer satisfaction?

3. Which marketing management philosophy does Netflix subscribe to?

COMPANY CLIPS

Method – Live Clean

Method, the innovative branding concept in household cleaning, was conceived by roommates Eric Ryan and Adam Lowry during their drive to a ski lodge. Eric had been thinking of ways to introduce design to the home care industry (i.e., cleaning products) and began talking about his vision to Adam. A chemical engineer from Stanford University with a degree in environmental science, Adam was the perfect sounding board. He soon realized that he could use his expertise to create naturally-derived, biodegradable formulas for the beautiful products Eric had in mind.

Questions

1. Is method best described as having a market orientation or a societal-marketing orientation?

2. How does method implement the marketing concept?

BIZ FLIX

The Jerk

As an encore to reviewing and studying the overview of marketing presented in this chapter, watch the scene from *The Jerk*. It features Steve Martin in his first starring role as Navin Johnson, an insecure fellow trying to get a successful start at a St. Louis gas station. The scene is an edited sequence from The New Phone Book segment that appears in the first twenty-six minutes of the film. Does Navin quickly identify Stan Fox's (Bill Macy) customer needs and desires about his falling eyeglasses? How does Navin get customer information so he can design a product solution? Does he exceed those needs with his innovative solution? Does the product appear to offer superior customer value? Why or why not?

Marketing & You Results

The higher your score, the more likely you are to do business with the company you thought of and recommend it to others. That is you have a commitment to the organization and are likely a loyal customer. As you read in Chapter 1, building relationships is a central part of the market orientation!

CAREERS

One of the most important decisions in your life is choosing a career. Not only will your career choice affect your income and lifestyle, but it also will have a major impact on your happiness and self-fulfillment.

You can use many of the basic concepts of marketing introduced in this book to get the career you want by marketing yourself. The purpose of marketing is to create exchanges that satisfy individual as well as organizational objectives, and a career is certainly an exchange situation for both you and an organization. The purpose of this appendix is to help you market yourself to prospective employers by providing some helpful tools and information.

AVAILABLE CAREERS

Marketing careers have a bright outlook into the next decade. The U.S. Bureau of Labor Statistics estimates that employment in marketing fields will grow between 21 and 35 percent through 2012. Many of these increases will be in the areas of sales, public relations, retailing, advertising, marketing research, product management, and marketing management.

- *Sales:* There are more opportunities in sales than in any other area of marketing. Sales positions vary greatly among companies. Some selling positions focus more on providing information; others emphasize locating potential customers, making presentations to committees, and closing the sale. Because compensation is often in the form of salary plus commission, there are few limits on the amount of money a person can make and therefore great potential. Sales positions can be found in many organizations, including manufacturing, wholesaling, retailing, insurance, real estate, financial services, and many other service businesses.

- *Public relations:* Public relations firms help create an image or a message for an individual or organization and communicate it effectively to a desired audience. All types of firms, profit and nonprofit organizations, individuals, and even countries employ public relations specialists. Communication skills, both written and oral, are critical for success in public relations.

- *Retailing:* Retail careers require many skills. Retail personnel may manage a sales force or other personnel, select and order merchandise, and be responsible for promotional activities, inventory control, store security, and accounting. Large retail stores have a variety of positions, including store or department manager, buyer, display designer, and catalog manager.

- *Advertising:* Many organizations employ advertising specialists. Advertising agencies are the largest employers; however, manufacturers, retailers, banks, radio and television stations, hospitals, and insurance agencies all have advertising departments. Creativity, artistic talent, and communication skills are a few of the attributes needed for a successful career in advertising. Account executives serve as a liaison between the advertising agency and the client. Account executives must have a good knowledge of business practices and possess excellent sales skills.

- *Marketing management:* Marketing managers develop the firm's detailed marketing strategy. With the help of subordinates, including market research managers and product development managers, they determine the demand for products and services offered by the firm and its competitors. In addition, they identify potential markets—for example, business firms, wholesalers, retailers, government, or the general public. Marketing managers develop pricing straegy with an eye toward maximizing the firm's share of the market and its profits while ensuring that the firm's customers are satisfied. In collaboration with sales, product development, and other managers, they monitor trends that indicate the need for new products and services and oversee product development. Marketing managers work with advertising and promotion managers to promote the firm's products and services and to attract potential users.

- *Marketing research:* The most rapid growth in marketing careers is in marketing research. Marketing research firms, advertising agencies, universities, private firms, nonprofit organizations, and governments provide growing opportunities in marketing research. Researchers conduct industry research, advertising research, pricing and packaging research, new-product testing, and test marketing. Researchers are involved in one or more stages of the research process, depending on the size of the organization conducting the research. Marketing research requires knowledge of statistics, data processing and analysis, psychology, and communication.

- *Product management:* Product managers coordinate all or most of the activities required to market a product. Thus, they need a general knowledge of all aspects of marketing. Product managers are responsible for the successes and failures of a product and are compensated well for this responsibility. Most product managers have previous sales experience and skills in communication. The position of product manager is a major step in the career path of top-level marketing executives.

Starting in a marketing job is also one of the *best routes to the top* of any organization. More CEOs come from sales and marketing backgrounds than from any other field. As examples, Lee Iacocca (Chrysler), Phil Lippincott (Scott Paper), John Akers (IBM), John Sparks (Whirlpool), and Bruno Bich (Bic Pen) came up through sales and marketing. Typically, a college graduate enters the marketing field in a sales position, then moves to sales supervisor, and next sales manager at the district, regional, and national levels. Individuals who prefer to advance through the ranks of marketing management can usually make a career move into product or brand management or another marketing headquarters job after serving for a couple of years in the initial sales position.

Probably the most difficult part of job hunting is deciding exactly what type of work you would like. Many students have had no working experience other than summer jobs, so they are not sure what career to pursue. Too often, college students and their parents rush toward occupational fields that seem to offer the highest monetary payoff or are currently "hot," instead of looking at the long run over a 40- to 50-year working life. One straightforward approach to deciding what type of job to undertake is to do a "self-analysis." This involves honestly asking yourself what your skills, abilities, and interests really are and then identifying occupational fields that match up well with your personality profile. Some students prefer to take various vocational aptitude tests to help identify their interests and abilities. Your college's placement office or psychology department can inform you about the availability of these tests. You may find it useful to develop a FAB (feature–advantage–benefit) matrix that shows what your skills are, why they offer an advantage, and how they would benefit an employer. Exhibit 1 shows an example.

Exhibit 1

The FAB Matrix

Need of Employer This job requires . . .	Feature of Job Applicant I have . . .	Advantage of Feature This feature means that . . .	Benefit to Employer You will . . .
• Frequent sales presentations to individuals and groups.	• Taken 10 classes that required presentations.	• I require limited or no training in making presentations.	• Save on the cost of training and have an employee with the ability and confidence to be productive early.
• Knowledge of personal computers, software, and applications.	• Taken a personal computer course and used Lotus in most upper-level classes.	• I can already use Word, Excel, dBase, SAS, SPSS, and other software.	• Save time and money on training.
• A person with management potential.	• Been president of a student marketing group and social fraternity president for two years.	• I have experience leading people.	• Save time because I am capable of stepping into a leadership position as needed.

YOUR FIRST MARKETING ASSIGNMENT

Marketing yourself to a prospective employer will usually be your first big marketing assignment. With your services (as represented by your qualifications, education, training, and personal characteristics) as the product, you must convince prospective employers that they should buy your services over those of many other candidates for the job. All the steps of the marketing and sales process apply: identifying opportunities, developing yourself as a product, prospecting for potential employers, planning your approach to them, approaching with a résumé and cover letter, making your sales presentation and demonstrating your qualifications in a personal interview, dealing with objections or giving reasons why the employer should hire you over other candidates, attempting to close the sale by enthusiastically asking for the job and employing appropriate closing techniques, and following up by thanking the prospective employer for the interview and reinforcing a positive impression.

Prospecting for a Potential Employer

After you have determined what you're selling (your skills, abilities, interests, and so forth) and identified the type of job you think you would like, you might begin your personal selling process by looking at the *College Placement Annual* at your college placement office. The *College Placement Annual* provides a variety of information about prospective employers and lists the organizations according to the types of jobs they have available—for example, advertising, banking, marketing research, and sales. Another very important source is an online search on the Internet. Other sources of information about prospective employers include directories such as those published by Dun and Bradstreet, Standard & Poor's, and trade associations; the annual American Marketing Association membership directory (company listings); the Yellow Pages of telephone books in cities where you would like to live and work; and classified sections of the *Wall Street Journal* or city newspapers. Before contacting a particular company, look up its annual report and stock evaluation (from *Value Line* or various other sources) in your college library to learn as much as possible about the company and its prospects for the future. You might also obtain a list of articles on the company from the *Business Periodicals Index (BPI)*.

College Placement Office

Use your college placement office to find out which companies are going to be interviewing on campus on what dates; then sign up for interviews with those companies that seem to best match your job skills and requirements. Usually, the college placement office has books, pamphlets, or files that will give you leads on other prospective employers that may not be interviewing on campus that term.

Job-Hunting Expenses

Although campus interviews are convenient, students seldom get a job without follow-up interviews with more senior managers—usually at company headquarters. These additional interviews generally take a full day and may involve long-distance trips. You should be forewarned that job hunting can be expensive. Printing your résumé, typing cover letters, buying envelopes and stamps, making long-distance telephone calls, incurring travel expenses, and buying new clothing will require a sizable outlay of money. Even though most companies eventually reimburse you for expenses incurred on a company visit, they seldom pay in advance. Reimbursement can take several weeks, so you may encounter some cash-flow problems over the short run.

Exhibit 2

Helpful Internet Addresses for Job Searches/Résumé Writing

The Monster board	http://www.monster.com
JobWeb	http://www.jobweb.org
Career Mosaic	http://www.careermosaic.com
Proven Resumes.com	http://www.provenresumes.com/
WSJ Career Journal	http://www.careerjournal.com

The Internet

The Internet is the fastest-growing medium for job searching today. Many companies are using the Internet to assist them in their recruiting efforts. Some companies are even conducting initial interviews online via videoconferencing. Just as some companies post jobs on a bulletin board, companies can list job opportunities on job posting Web sites. Some of the more popular job search Web sites are listed in Exhibit 2. These sites also contain information about résumé writing and interviewing, as well as tips that you can use to secure the job that you want.

Employment Agencies

Although many employment agencies receive fees from employers for providing good job candidates, others charge job seekers huge fees (sometimes thousands of dollars) for helping them find jobs. Therefore, make sure you fully understand the fee arrangement before signing up with an employment agency. Some employment agencies may not be worth your time and/or money because they use a programmed approach to helping you write your résumé and cover letter and prospect for potential employers. Potential employers have seen these "canned" formats and approaches so many times that your personal advertisement (your résumé and cover letter) will be almost indistinguishable from others.

The Hidden Job Market

It has been estimated that nearly 90 percent of available jobs are never advertised and never reach employment agency files, so creative resourcefulness often pays off in finding the best jobs. Consider every reasonable source for leads. Sometimes your professors, deans, or college administrators can give you names and contact persons at companies that have hired recent graduates.

Do not be bashful about letting other people know that you are looking for work. Classmates, friends, and business associates of your family may be of help not only directly but also indirectly, acting as extra pairs of eyes and ears alert to job opportunities for you.

Planning Your Approach (the Preapproach)

After conducting your self-analysis and identifying potential employers looking for people with your abilities and interests, you need to prepare your *résumé* (or personal advertisement). Your résumé should focus on your achievements to date, your educational background, your work experience, and your special abilities and interests. Some students make the mistake of merely listing their assigned responsibilities on different jobs without indicating what they accomplished on the job. If you achieved something on the job, say it—for example, "Helped computerize office files," "Increased sales in my territory by 10 percent," "Received a 15 percent raise after three months on the job," or "Promoted to assistant store manager after four months." When looking for a job, remember that employers are looking for a *track record of achievement*, so you must distinguish yourself from those who may have had the same assigned job responsibilities as you did but performed poorly. If your work experience is minimal, consider a "skills" résumé, in which you emphasize your particular abilities, such as organizing, programming, or leadership skills, and give supporting evidence whenever you can. Examples of various types of résumés can be found in the *College Placement Annual* and in various other job-hunting publications (ask your college business reference librarian to direct you). Exhibit 2 lists some Web sites where you can learn about résumé formats.

Remember that there is no one correct format for your résumé. A little tasteful creativity can help differentiate your résumé from countless look-alike résumés. If you are a young college graduate, your résumé will usually be only one page long, but do not worry about going to a second page if you have something important to present. One student so blindly followed the one-page résumé rule that he left out having served in the military—service that is usually viewed very positively by prospective employers, especially if it involved significant leadership responsibilities or work experience.

If you know what job you want, you may want to put your *job objective* near the top of your résumé. If you are not sure what job you want or want to send out the same résumé for several different jobs, then you can describe your job objective in your *cover letter*. A key element in the cover letter is convincing the prospective employer to grant you an interview. Thus, you must talk in terms of the employer's interests, not just your own. You are answering the question: "Why should we hire you?" You may need to send a letter with your résumé enclosed to a hundred or more companies to obtain five to ten interviews, so do not be discouraged if you get replies from only a few companies or are told by many companies that they have no job opportunities at present. You will probably need only a few interviews and just one job offer to get your career started.

Review some of the publications and sources mentioned in the previous section on prospecting (e.g., *College Placement Annual*, Dun and Bradstreet directories, and annual reports) to learn as much as you can about your prospective employer so that you can tailor your cover letter. Remember, the employer is thinking in terms of the company's needs, not yours. For one example of a résumé, see Exhibit 3. A cover letter is illustrated in Exhibit 4.

Exhibit 3
Sample Résumé

Making Your Approach

RACHEL E. SANFORD
2935 Mountain View Road
Ellington, PA 19401
(216) 567-0000

JOB OBJECTIVE	Sales representative for a consumer-products company
EDUCATION	Graduated *cum laude* with BS in Marketing Management (June 2006), University of Southern Pennsylvania. Career-related courses included Selling and Sales Management, Public Speaking, Business Writing, Public Relations, Marketing Research, Computer Programming, and Multivariate Data Analysis.
ACTIVITIES AND HONORS	President, Student Marketing Association; Vice president, Chi Omega Sorority; Captain, women's varsity tennis team; sportswriter for the *Campus View* student newspaper. Named to Who's Who among American College Students, 2004–2005. On Dean's List all four years. Overall grade point average = 3.65.

WORK EXPERIENCE

Summer 2005	*Sales representative,* Peabody Manufacturing Company. Sold women's blouses to boutiques and small department stores in southeastern Pennsylvania. Exceeded assigned sales quota by 20%; named "outstanding" summer employee for 2005.
Summer 2004	*Buyer,* Hamm's Department Stores, Inc., Midway, Pa. Developed purchase plan, initiated purchase orders, monitored and controlled expenditures for nearly $2 million worth of women's clothing. Made monthly progress reports (written and oral) to Hamm's Executive Committee. Received 15% bonus as #2 buyer in the six stores of the Hamm's chain in special "Back to School" purchasing competition.
Summer 2003	*Retail clerk,* Hamm's Department Stores, Inc., Midway, Pa. After 3 months, received 10% pay raise and promotion to evening salesclerk supervisor over seven part-time salesclerks. Devised new inventory control system for handbags and accessories that cut costs over $50,000 annually.
Summer 2002	*Cosmetics salesperson,* Heavenly Charm, Inc., Midway, Pa. Sold $63,000 worth of Heavenly Charm cosmetics door to door. Named #1 salesperson in the sales region. Offered full-time job as sales supervisor.
INTERESTS	Tennis, golf, public speaking, short story writing, and reading biographies.

Prospective employers can be approached by mail, telephone, the Internet, or personal contact. Personal contact is best, but this usually requires that you know someone with influence who can arrange an interview for you. Of course, a few enterprising students have devised elaborate and sometimes successful schemes to get job interviews. For example, we know of one young man who simply went to the headquarters of the company he wanted to work for and asked to see the president. Told that the president of the company could not see him, the student said that he was willing to wait until the president had time. This audacious individual went back three different days until the president finally agreed to see him, perhaps mainly out of curiosity about what sort of young man would be so outrageous in his job search.

Fortunately for this young man, he had a lot to offer and was able to communicate this to the president, so he was hired. This unorthodox approach shows how far people have gone to impress potential employers, and if you feel comfortable doing it, then go ahead. A personal contact within the company certainly can win you some special attention and enable you to avoid competing head-on with the large number of other candidates looking for a job. Most students, however, start their approach in the traditional way by mailing their résumé and cover letter to the recruiting department of the company. More recently, students have begun to e-mail their résumés, and some companies are requiring this as a means of screening out applicants who are not computer literate. Unless your résumé matches a particular need at that time, it will probably be filed away for possible future reference or merely discarded. To try to get around the system, some students send their letter by express mail or mailgram or address it to a key executive, with "Personal" written on the envelope. These students believe that bypassing the company's personnel office will increase the likelihood that their cover letter and résumé will be read by someone with authority to hire. Other students send their résumé on a CD or DVD, and one student in Louisiana sent a King Cake to the recipient of the résumé, while another sent a packet of Louisiana spices. Using gimmicks, no matter how creative, to get a job interview will offend some executives and thus cause you to be rejected from consideration for a job. But you can probably also be sure that a few executives will admire your efforts and grant you an interview.

Only you know how comfortable you feel with different approaches to obtaining a job interview. We advise you not to use an approach that is out of character for you and thus will make you feel awkward and embarrassed.

Exhibit 4
Sample Cover Letter

Rachel E. Sanford
2935 Mountain View Road
Ellington, PA 19401

Mr. Samuel Abramson
District Sales Manager
Hixson Appliance Company
Philadelphia, PA 19103

Dear Mr. Abramson:

Hixson has been a familiar name to me ever since I was barely able to see over my mother's kitchen counter. Virtually every appliance we had was a Hixson, so I know firsthand what fine quality products you sell. My career interest is in sales, and there is no company that I would rather work with than Hixson Appliance.

I will be graduating this June from Southern Pennsylvania University with a BS in marketing management, and I would like you to consider me for a job as a sales representative with your company. As you can see in my enclosed résumé, I have successfully worked in sales jobs during three of the last four summers. My college course electives (e.g., public speaking, business writing, and public relations) have been carefully selected with my career objective in mind. Even my extracurricular activities in sports and campus organizations have helped prepare me for working with a variety of people and competitive challenges.

Will you please grant me an interview so that I can convince you that I'm someone you should hire for your sales team? I'll call you next Thursday afternoon to arrange an appointment at your convenience.

Look forward to meeting you soon.

Sincerely,

Rachel E. Sanford

Enclosure

Exhibit 5
Before the Interview

- **Practice**
  - ✓ Questions you may be asked
  - ✓ Questions you want to ask about the position and organization
  - ✓ Role-playing an interview
- **Self-assessment**
  - ✓ Goals
  - ✓ Skills, abilities, accomplishments
  - ✓ Work values (important factors you look for in a job)
  - ✓ Experiences
  - ✓ Personality
- **Research**
  - ✓ Obtain company literature
  - ✓ Write or visit the organization
  - ✓ Talk to people familiar with the organization
- **Obtain references**
- **Plan ahead**
  - ✓ Attire to be worn to the interview
  - ✓ Directions to the interview site
  - ✓ Time of arrival (get there with at least 5–10 minutes to spare)

Making Your Sales Presentation

Your personal sales presentation will come during the interview with the prospective employer's recruiters or interviewers. Like any presentation, it requires thorough preparation and an effective follow-up, as well as a solid performance during the interview itself.

Pre-Interview Considerations

Preparing for the interview is crucial. You will already have gathered information on the company, as suggested in the preceding sections; you should review it now. Exhibit 5 shows a pre-interview checklist that can help you prepare. In addition, the self-assessment test in Exhibit 6 can help you determine if you're ready for the interview.

Keep the following in mind in preparing for your interview:

- Find out the exact place and time of the interview.
- Be certain you know the interviewer's name and how to pronounce it if it looks difficult.
- Do some research on the company with which you are interviewing—talk to people and read the company literature to know what its products or services are, where its offices are located, what its growth has been, and how its prospects look for the future.
- Think of two or three good questions that you would like to ask during your interview.
- Plan to arrive at the designated place for your interview a little early so that you will not feel rushed and worried about being on time.
- Plan to dress in a manner appropriate to the job for which you are interviewing.

A guide for the interview conversation itself is to prepare nine positive thoughts before you go in for the interview:

- Three reasons why you selected the employer to interview
- Three reasons you particularly like the employer
- Three assets you have that should interest the employer

Try to make a positive impression on everyone you encounter in the company, even while waiting in the lobby for your interview. Sometimes managers will ask their receptionists and secretaries for an opinion of you, and your friendliness, courtesy, professional

Exhibit 6

Self-Assessment Test

How assertive are you (or will you be) as you interview for a position? Listed below are questions that will help you to evaluate yourself: answer yes or no to the questions, being honest with yourself. If you have five or fewer yes answers, you still have some work to do. A good score is seven or more yes answers.

Yes	No	
――	――	Have you made an effort to research the company before the interview?
――	――	Have you prepared several questions that you want to ask?
――	――	If an interviewer asks a personal question unrelated to the job, will you be able to tactfully call this to his attention?
――	――	If an interviewer gives you a hypothetical job-related problem, do you have confidence in your ability to respond in a timely and succinct manner?
――	――	If the interviewer seems distracted or uninterested during your interview, will you be able to steer the interview back on track and gain her attention?
――	――	When you meet the interviewer, will you be the first to introduce yourself and begin the conversation?
――	――	If the interviewer continually interrupts when you are responding to questions or giving information about yourself, can you politely handle this?
――	――	If the interviewer never gives you the opportunity to talk about yourself and you have only five minutes remaining in the interview, have you thought about phrases or ways to redirect the interview and regain control of the process?
――	――	When the interviewer is beginning to close the interview, are you prepared to ask questions about how you stand, what the determining factors are for candidate selection, and by what date you will have an answer?

demeanor, personal habits, and the like will all be used to judge you. Even the magazines you choose to read while waiting can be a positive or negative factor. For instance, it will probably be less impressive if you leaf through a popular magazine like *People* or *Sports Illustrated* than if you read something more professional such as *Business Week* or the *Wall Street Journal*.

During the Interview

During the interview, do not be merely a passive respondent to the interviewer's questions. Being graciously assertive by asking reasonable questions of your own will indicate to the interviewer that you are alert, energetic, and sincerely interested in the job. The personal interview is your opportunity to persuade the prospective employer that you should be hired. To use a show business analogy, you will be onstage for only a short time (during the personal interview), so try to present an honest but positive image of yourself. Perhaps it will help you to be alert and enthusiastic if you imagine that you are being interviewed on television. Exhibit 7 lists a number of questions that are frequently asked during interviews.

Sometimes prospective employers will ask you to *demonstrate* certain abilities by having you write a timed essay about some part of your life, sell something (such as a desk calculator) to the interviewer, or respond to hostile questions. Be calm and confident during any such unorthodox interviewing approaches and you will make a good impression. Remember, most employers want you to perform well because they are looking for the best people they can find in a given time frame for the money they have to offer.

If you are given intelligence, aptitude, or psychological tests, you should try to be honest so that you do not create unrealistic expectations that you will not be able to fulfill. It is just as important that you do not create a false impression and begin with a company that is not right for you as it is to secure employment in the first place. Many experts say that it is not very difficult to "cheat" on aptitude or psychological tests if you are able to "play the role" and provide the answers that you know the company wants to read. Usually, the so-called safe approach in most personality and preference (interest) tests is to not take extreme positions on anything that is not clearly associated with the job you are applying for. For sales jobs, it is probably safe to come across as highly extroverted and interested in group activities, but it may not be safe to appear to be overly interested in literature, music, art, or any solitary activity. In addition, the "right" answers tend to indicate a conservative, goal-oriented, money-motivated, and gregarious personality.

Dealing with Objections. Sometimes interviewers will bluntly ask, "Why should we hire you?" This requires that you think in terms of the employer's needs and present in concise form all your major "selling points." Also, sometimes the interviewer may bring up reasons why

Exhibit 7

Some Questions Frequently Asked during a Job Interview

- Of the jobs you've had to date, which one did you like best? Why?
- Why do you want to work for our company?
- Tell me what you know about our company.
- Do any of your relatives or friends work for our company? If so, in what jobs?
- Tell me about yourself, your strengths, weaknesses, career goals, and so forth.
- Is any member of your family a professional marketer? If so, what area of marketing?
- Why do you want to start your career in marketing?
- Persuade me that we should hire you.
- What extracurricular activities did you participate in at college? What leadership positions did you have in any of these activities?
- What benefits have you derived from participation in extracurricular activities that will help you in your career?
- Where do you see yourself within our company in five years? In ten years? Twenty years?
- What is your ultimate career goal?
- What do you consider your greatest achievement to date?
- What is your biggest failure to date?
- What is (was) your favorite subject in school? Why?
- Are you willing to travel and possibly relocate?
- How would the people who know you describe you?
- How would you describe yourself?
- What do you like most about marketing?
- What do you like least about marketing?
- If we hire you, how soon could you start work?
- What is the minimum we would have to offer you to come with us?
- What goals have you set for yourself? How are you planning to achieve them?
- Who or what has had the greatest influence on the development of your career interests?
- What factors did you consider in choosing your major?
- Why are you interested in our organization?
- What can you tell me about yourself?
- What two or three things are most important to you in a position?
- What kind of work do you want to do?
- What can you tell me about a project you initiated?
- What are your expectations of your future employer?
- What is your GPA? How do you feel about it? Does it reflect your ability?
- How do you resolve conflicts?
- What do you feel are your strengths? Your weaknesses? How do you evaluate yourself?
- What work experience has been the most valuable to you and why?
- What was the most useful criticism you ever received, and who was it from?
- Can you give an example of a problem you have solved and the process you used?
- Can you describe the project or situation that best demonstrates your analytical skills?
- What has been your greatest challenge?
- Can you describe a situation where you had a conflict with another individual and explain how you dealt with it?
- What are the biggest problems you encountered in college? How did you handle them? What did you learn from them?
- What are your team-player qualities? Give examples.
- Can you describe your leadership style?
- What interests or concerns you about the position or the company?
- In a particular leadership role you had, what was the greatest challenge?
- What idea have you developed and implemented that was particularly creative or innovative?

Exhibit 7

Some Questions Frequently Asked during a Job Interview (continued)

- What characteristics do you think are important for this position?
- How have your educational and work experiences prepared you for this position?
- Can you take me through a project where you demonstrated skills?
- How do you think you have changed personally since you started college?
- Can you tell me about a team project that you are particularly proud of and discuss your contribution?
- How do you motivate people?
- Why did you choose the extracurricular activities you did? What did you gain? What did you contribute?
- What types of situations put you under pressure, and how do you deal with the pressure?
- Can you tell me about a difficult decision you have made?
- Can you give an example of a situation in which you failed and explain how you handled it?
- Can you tell me about a situation when you had to persuade another person of your point of view?
- What frustrates you the most?
- Knowing what you know now about your college experience, would you make the same decisions?
- What can you contribute to this company?
- How would you react to having your credibility questioned?
- What characteristics are important in a good manager? How have you displayed one of these characteristics?
- What challenges are you looking for in a position?
- What two or three accomplishments have given you the most satisfaction?
- Can you describe a leadership role of yours and tell why you committed your time to it?
- How are you conducting your job search, and how will you make your decision?
- What is the most important lesson you have learned in or out of school?
- Can you describe a situation where you had to work with someone who was difficult? How was the person difficult, and how did you handle it?
- We are looking at a lot of great candidates; why are you the best person for this position?
- How would your friends describe you? Your professors?
- What else should I know about you?

you are not the ideal candidate. For example, he or she may say: (1) "We're really looking for someone with a little more experience"; (2) "We'd like to get someone with a more technical educational background"; or (3) "We need someone to start work within two weeks." These kinds of statements are similar to objections or requests for additional information. In other words, the interviewer is saying, "Convince me that I shouldn't rule you out for this reason." To overcome such objections, you might respond to each, respectively, along the following lines:

(1) "I've had over a year's experience working with two different companies during my summer vacations, and I've worked part-time with a third company all during college. I'm a fast learner, and I've adapted well to each of the three companies, so I feel that my working experience is equivalent to that of someone who has had three or four years' experience with the same company."

(2) "Although I didn't choose to earn a technical undergraduate degree, I've taken several technical courses in college, including basic engineering courses, chemistry, physics, and two years of math. I'm very confident that I can quickly learn whatever is necessary technically to do the job, and my real strength is that my education has been a blend of technical and managerial courses."

(3) "Well, I do have one more term of school, so I couldn't start full-time work in two weeks, but perhaps we could work out an arrangement in which I could work part-time—maybe Friday, Saturday, and Sunday or on weekends until I graduate."

Good "salespeople" do not allow an objection to block a sale. Providing reasonable solutions or alternative perspectives can often overcome objections or, at least, allow room for further negotiation toward a compromise solution.

How to Act during the Interview. The following can help you behave appropriately during the interview:

- *Think positive.* Be enthusiastic, interested, knowledgeable, and confident.
- *Take few notes.* It is acceptable to take notes during the interview, but limit them to things that are essential to remember. You want to focus more on listening and observing rather than writing.
- *Relate to the interviewer.* Build positive rapport with the interviewer. Listen and observe; relate yourself to the employer or position.
- *Watch your body language.* Be aware of nervousness (fidgeting, shaking leg, tapping, etc.). Project confidence (eye contact, firm handshake, upright posture).
- *Be aware of the questions the employer asks.* Answer with information relevant to the position. Provide a direct answer; avoid being long-winded.
- *Think about the questions you ask.* They should indicate that you know something about the job. Avoid questions that could easily be answered elsewhere (through research). Obtain information you need to know to be satisfied with the job (interviewing is a two-way process). Salary and benefit questions should be asked after the job is offered.
- *Achieve effective closure.* Ask when the employer expects to make a decision. Restate your interest and ability to perform the job. Show confidence and enthusiasm (smile, end with a firm handshake). Obtain the employer's business card, if possible (it may be useful when writing a thank-you letter).

Interview Questions. Too many employment applicants spend all their time preparing for the questions employers will ask them. Too often, they fail to ask vital questions that would help them learn if a job is right for them. Failing to ask important questions during the interview often leads to jobs that offer neither interest nor challenge. Too often, uninformed applicants accept positions hoping that they will develop into something more meaningful and rewarding later. Exhibit 8 suggests questions that you may want to ask.

Closing the Sale

Although it is not likely that a prospective employer will offer you a job immediately after the job interview, you should nevertheless let the interviewer know that you definitely want the job and are confident that you will do an excellent job for the employer. You will need to use your best judgment on how to best do this.

In each stage of the personal selling process, you should be looking for feedback from the interviewer's body language and voice inflections or tone.

Following Up the Interview

Within a few days after any job interview, whether you want the job or not, it is business courtesy to write thank-you letters to interviewers. In these letters you can reinforce the positive impression you made in the interview and again express your keen interest in working for the company. If you do not hear from the company within a few weeks, it may be appropriate to write another letter expressing your continuing interest in the job and asking for a decision so that you can consider other options if necessary. As a possible reason for this follow-up letter, you might mention an additional personal achievement since the interview, give a more detailed answer to one of the interviewer's questions, or perhaps send a newspaper or magazine article of interest. A neat, well-written, courteous follow-up letter gives you a chance not only to make a stronger impression on the interviewer but also to exhibit positive qualities such as initiative, energy, sensitivity to others' feelings, and awareness of business protocol.

Many applicants fail to write a thank-you letter after an interview, yet many employers say that the deciding factor between several similar job candidates is often the thank-you note. The thank-you letter should be typewritten. If the interviewer is a very technology-driven person, a thank-you e-mail may also be appropriate. However, the personal touch of a typewritten and hand-signed letter leaves a better impression.

Be sure to write a follow-up letter in all of the following situations:

- *After two or three weeks of no reply.*
- *When a job has been refused.* Express your regret that no job is available and ask if you might be considered in the future. Also, ask how you could improve yourself to better fit what the company is looking for.
- *After an interview.* Express your thanks for the interviewer's time and courtesy. Answer any unanswered questions and clarify any misconceptions.

Exhibit 8

Sample Interview Questions to Be Asked by Job Candidates

- Where is the organization going? What plans or projects are being developed to maintain or increase its market share? Have many new product lines been decided upon recently? Is the sales growth in the new product line sustainable?
- Who are the people with whom I will be working? May I speak with some of them?
- May I have a copy of the job description?
- What might be a typical first assignment?
- Do you have a performance appraisal system? How is it structured? How frequently will I be evaluated?
- What is the potential for promotion in the organization? In promotions, are employees ever transferred between functional fields? What is the average time to get to _____ level in the career path? Is your policy to promote from within, or are many senior jobs filled by experienced people from outside? Do you have a job posting system?
- What type of training will I receive? When does the training program begin? Is it possible to move through your program faster? About how many individuals go through your internship program?
- What is the normal routine of a (an) _____ like? Can I progress at my own pace, or is it structured? Do employees normally work overtime?
- How much travel is normally expected? Is a car provided to traveling personnel?
- How much freedom is given to new people? How much discipline is required? How much input does the new person have? How much decision-making authority is given to new personnel?
- How frequently do you relocate employees? Is it possible to transfer from one division to another?
- What is the housing market for a single person in _____ (city)? Is public transportation adequate?
- How much contact with and exposure to management is there?
- How soon should I expect to report to work?

- *To accept a job (even if previously done in person or on the phone).* State your acceptance. Reiterate the agreement, the time for beginning work, and the like. Do not start asking for favors.
- *To refuse a job offer.* Graciously decline the offer. Be warm and interested and indicate that you appreciate the offer.

Follow-up letters are also appropriate after you have received replies to both solicited and unsolicited letters of inquiry. Always make certain that your letters possess the attitude, quality, and skill of a professional.

ON THE JOB

Working Conditions

Advertising, marketing, promotions, public relations, and sales managers work in offices close to those of top managers. Long hours, including evenings and weekends, are common. About 44 percent of advertising, marketing, and public relations managers work more than 40 hours per week. Substantial travel may also be involved. For example, attendance at meetings sponsored by associations or industries is often mandatory. Sales managers travel to local, regional, and national offices and to various dealers and distributors. Advertising and promotions managers may travel to meet with clients or representatives of communications media. At times, public relations managers travel to meet with special interest groups or government officials. Job transfers between headquarters and regional offices are common, particularly among sales managers.

Moving Up the Ladder

Most advertising, marketing, promotions, public relations, and sales management positions are filled by promoting experienced staff or related professional personnel. For example, many managers are former sales representatives, purchasing agents, buyers, or product, advertising, promotions, or public relations specialists. In small firms, where the number of positions is limited, advancement to a management position usually comes slowly. In large firms, promotion may occur more quickly.

Although experience, ability, and leadership are emphasized for promotion, advancement can be accelerated by participation in management training programs conducted by many large firms. Many firms also provide their employees with continuing education opportunities, either in-house or at local colleges and universities, and encourage employee participation in seminars and conferences, often provided by professional societies. In collaboration with colleges and universities, numerous marketing and related associations sponsor national or local management training programs. Staying abreast of what is happening in your industry and getting involved in related industry associations can be important for your career advancement.

YOUR EARLY WORKING CAREER

Even though you want to choose a company that you will stay with throughout your working life, it is realistic to recognize that you will probably work for three, four, or more companies during your career. If you are not fully satisfied with your job or company during the first few years of your full-time working life, remember that you are building experience and knowledge that will increase your marketability for future job opportunities. Keep a positive outlook and do the best you can in all job assignments—and your chance for new opportunities will come. Do not be too discouraged by mistakes that you may make in your career; nearly every successful person has made and continues to make many mistakes. View these mistakes largely as learning experiences, and they will not be too traumatic or damaging to your confidence.

Good luck in your marketing career!

Strategic Planning
for Competitive Advantage

Learning Outcomes

LO 1 Understand the importance of strategic marketing and know a basic outline for a marketing plan

LO 2 Develop an appropriate business mission statement

LO 3 Describe the criteria for stating good marketing objectives

LO 4 Explain the components of a situation analysis

LO 5 Identify sources of competitive advantage

LO 6 Identify strategic alternatives

LO 7 Discuss target market strategies

LO 8 Describe the elements of the marketing mix

LO 9 Explain why implementation, evaluation, and control of the marketing plan are necessary

LO 10 Identify several techniques that help make strategic planning effective

a marketing strategy for
Beacon Street Girls

Concerned about the provocative images and scantily clad girls in books and other media aimed at pre-teenagers, Addie Schwartz decided to develop an alternative. She founded B*tween Productions, which publishes Beacon Street Girls, a line of books and accessories aimed at the "tween" market—the more than 10 million girls who are between toys and boys. These 9- to 13-year-olds represent a market estimated to be worth more than $40 billion annually.

Schwartz's goal was to create characters that girls could identify with and learn from. "I wanted to use the media to empower girls in a positive way," she

"I wanted to use the media to empower girls in a positive way,"

explains. In 2002, Schwartz and her team created composites of the characters and decided that the books would be set in the real-life town of Brookline, Massachusetts. Schwartz then conducted 30 focus groups with girls from the target age group. The characters who emerged reflected the diverse interests and backgrounds of the focus group participants. Among the characters are Avery, a soccer player who was adopted from Korea; Katani, an African American who designs her own clothes; and Maeve, who is dyslexic and loves boys and old movies.

Beacon Street Girls is modeled after the American Girl brand—a very suc-cessful line of dolls, books, and accessories aimed at girls age 7 and older. Schwartz says her brand is the next step for American Girl fans who no longer play with dolls. Like American Girl, Beacon Street Girls has an extensive product line that includes accessories; an interactive Web site with games, quizzes, and guidelines for healthy living; and a book club. Schwartz is planning to add clothing and tech gadgets as well. Beacon Street's products are priced lower than American Girl's, however. An American Girl doll costs $84, whereas Beacon Street accessories range from a $2.99 spiral notebook to a $54 duffel bag.

The books are distributed through retail bookstores. Although the big chains such as Barnes & Noble and Border's offered only standard shelf space, about 70 independent bookstores nationwide feature Beacon Street merchandising displays that call attention to the series.

Although Beacon Street Girls' advertising budget is small, it has gained free publicity via partnerships with organizations such as Girls, Inc., a nonprofit organization dedicated to inspiring girls to be strong, smart, and bold. The partnership is planning a nationwide program to help girls use literature to explore contemporary issues that can affect their self-esteem and development. The character Maeve, who is dyslexic, recently appeared on the Web site of the Charles and Helen Schwab Foundation for children with learning disabilities.[1]

What are the elements of Beacon Street Girls' marketing strategy? How would you describe its competitive advantage? Why do you think the product is so successful?

LO¹
The Nature of Strategic Planning

Strategic planning is the managerial process of creating and maintaining a fit between the organization's objectives and resources and the evolving market opportunities. The goal of strategic planning is long-run profitability and growth. Thus, strategic decisions require long-term commitments of resources.

A strategic error can threaten a firm's survival. On the other hand, a good strategic plan can help protect and grow the firm's resources. For instance, if the March of Dimes had decided to focus on fighting polio, the organization would no longer exist. Most of us view polio as a conquered disease. The March of Dimes survived by making the strategic decision to switch to fighting birth defects.

Strategic marketing management addresses two questions: What is the organization's main activity at a particular time? How will it reach its goals? Here are some examples of strategic decisions:

- The decision of Sears to buy Lands' End, a successful clothing catalog and online retail business. The move could upgrade Sears' image and increase its presence in the catalog business and on the Internet. Lands' End clothing will enjoy greater retail distribution in Sears stores.

- Reebok's decision to stop competing with Nike in the hard-core sports market. Instead, it plans to become the top shoe brand for hip-hoppers, hipsters, and other fashion-forward consumers.[2]

- McDonald's decision to offer more healthful foods by focusing on fresh fruits and vegetables with its new line of premium salads.[3]

- S. C. Johnson's introduction of Shout Color Catchers, a laundry sheet for the washer that collects loose dyes and prevents clothes from bleeding color onto other laundry items.

New Doublemint Twins are different. They're mints.

Mints with a blend of two flavors. *Enjoy yourself.*

© WM. WRIGLEY JR. COMPANY

Strategic planning is critical to business success. Doublemint has adapted to its changing market by deciding to sell mints in addition to chewing gum.

strategic planning
The managerial process of creating and maintaining a fit between the organization's objectives and resources and evolving market opportunities.

planning
The process of anticipating future events and determining strategies to achieve organizational objectives in the future.

marketing planning
Designing activities relating to marketing objectives and the changing marketing environment.

marketing plan
A written document that acts as a guidebook of marketing activities for the marketing manager.

All these decisions have affected or will affect each organization's long-run course, its allocation of resources, and ultimately its financial success. In contrast, an operating decision, such as changing the package design for Post's cornflakes or altering the sweetness of a Kraft salad dressing, probably won't have a big impact on the long-run profitability of the company.

How do companies go about strategic marketing planning? How do employees know how to implement the long-term goals of the firm? The answer is a marketing plan.

WHAT IS A MARKETING PLAN?

Planning is the process of anticipating future events and determining strategies to achieve organizational objectives in the future. **Marketing planning** involves designing activities relating to marketing objectives and the changing marketing environment. Marketing planning is the basis for all marketing strategies and decisions. Issues such as product lines, distribution channels, marketing communications, and pricing are all delineated in the **marketing plan**. The marketing plan is a written document that acts as a guidebook of marketing activities for the marketing manager. In this chapter, you will learn the importance of writing a marketing plan and the types of information contained in a marketing plan.

Why Write a Marketing Plan?

By specifying objectives and defining the actions required to attain them, a marketing plan provides the basis by which actual and expected performance can be compared. Marketing can be one of the most expensive and complicated business activities, but it is also one of the most important. The written marketing plan provides clearly stated activities that help employees and managers understand and work toward common goals.

Writing a marketing plan allows you to examine the marketing environment in conjunction with the inner workings of the business. Once the marketing plan is written, it serves as a reference point for the success of future activities. Finally, the marketing plan allows the marketing manager to enter the marketplace with an awareness of possibilities and problems.

Marketing Plan Elements

Marketing plans can be presented in many different ways. Most businesses need a written marketing plan because a marketing plan is large and can be complex. Details about tasks and activity assignments may be lost if communicated orally. Regardless of the way a marketing plan is presented, some elements are common to all marketing plans. These include defining the business mission and objectives, performing a situation analysis, delineating a target market, and establishing components of the marketing mix. Exhibit 2.1 shows these elements, which are also described further below. Other elements that may be included in a plan are budgets, implementation timetables, required marketing research efforts, or elements of advanced strategic planning. An example of a marketing plan appears in the appendix to this chapter (pp. 58–64).

Selecting which alternative to pursue depends on the overall company philosophy and culture. The choice also depends on the tool used to make the decision. Companies generally have one of two philosophies about when they expect profits. They either pursue profits right away or first seek to increase market share and then pursue profits. In the long run, market share and profitability are compatible goals. Many companies have long followed this credo: Build market share, and profits will surely follow. Michelin, the tire producer, consistently sacrifices short-term profits to achieve market share. On the other hand, IBM stresses profitability and stock valuation over market share, quality, and customer service. As you can see, the same strategic alternative may be viewed entirely differently by different firms.

A number of tools exist to help managers select a strategic alternative. The most common of these tools are in matrix form. The portfolio matrix is described here in more detail.

WRITING THE MARKETING PLAN

The creation and implementation of a complete marketing plan will allow the organization to achieve marketing objectives and succeed. However, the marketing plan is only as good as the information it contains and the effort, creativity, and thought that went into its creation. Having a good marketing information system and a wealth of competitive intelligence (covered in Chapter 8) is critical to a thorough and accurate situation analysis. The role of managerial intuition is also important in the creation

DMusic
Use Exhibit 2.1 to create a sample summary marketing plan for Dmusic.com, an Internet start-up created by a teenage entrepreneur.
http://www.dmusic.com

Online

Exhibit 2.1

Elements of a Marketing Plan

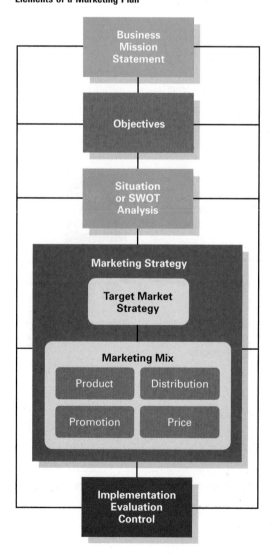

and selection of marketing strategies. Managers must weigh any information against its accuracy and their own judgment when making a marketing decision.

Note that the overall structure of the marketing plan (Exhibit 2.1) should not be viewed as a series of sequential planning steps. Many of the marketing plan elements are decided on simultaneously and in conjunction with one another. Further, every marketing plan has a different content, depending on the organization, its mission, objectives, targets, and marketing mix components. The example of a marketing plan in the chapter appendix should not be regarded as the only correct format for a marketing plan. Many organizations have their own distinctive format or terminology for creating a marketing plan. Every marketing plan should be unique to the firm for which it was created. Remember, however, that although the format and order of presentation should be flexible, the same types of questions and topic areas should be covered in any marketing plan. As you can see by the extent of the marketing plan in the appendix, creating a complete marketing plan is not a simple or quick effort.

REVIEW LEARNING OUTCOME

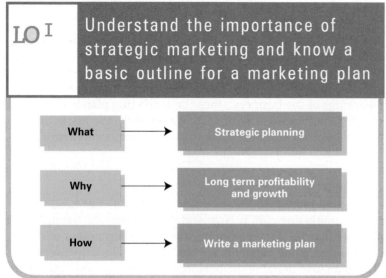

LO 1 Understand the importance of strategic marketing and know a basic outline for a marketing plan

What	→	Strategic planning
Why	→	Long term profitability and growth
How	→	Write a marketing plan

LO 2
Defining the Business Mission

The foundation of any marketing plan is the firm's **mission statement,** which answers the question, "What business are we in?" The way a firm defines its business mission profoundly affects the firm's long-run resource allocation, profitability, and survival. The mission statement is based on a careful analysis of benefits sought by present and potential customers and an analysis of existing and anticipated environmental conditions. The firm's mission statement establishes boundaries for all subsequent decisions, objectives, and strategies. The American Marketing Association's mission statement is shown in Exhibit 2.2.

A mission statement should focus on the market or markets the organization is attempting to serve rather than on the good or service offered. Otherwise, a new technology may quickly make the good or service obsolete and the mission statement irrelevant to company functions. Business mission statements that are stated too narrowly suffer from **marketing myopia**—defining a business in terms of goods

mission statement
A statement of the firm's business based on a careful analysis of benefits sought by present and potential customers and an analysis of existing and anticipated environmental conditions.

marketing myopia
Defining a business in terms of goods and services rather than in terms of the benefits that customers seek.

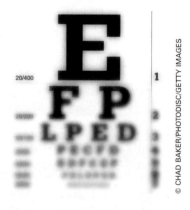

© CHAD BAKER/PHOTODISC/GETTY IMAGES

Exhibit 2.2

American Marketing Association's Mission Statement

The American Marketing Association is an international professional organization for people involved in the practice, study, and teaching of marketing. Our principal roles are:

- To always understand and satisfy the needs of marketers so as to provide them with products and services that will help them be better marketers.
- To empower marketers through information, education, relationships, and resources that will enrich their professional development and careers.
- To advance the thought, application, and ethical practice of marketing.

SOURCE: http://www.marketingpower.com/about/ama/mission/, November 1, 2006.

and services rather than in terms of the benefits that customers seek. In this context, *myopia* means narrow, short-term thinking. For example, Frito-Lay defines its mission as being in the snack-food business rather than in the corn chip business. The mission of sports teams is not just to play games but to serve the interests of the fans.

Alternatively, business missions may be stated too broadly. "To provide products of superior quality and value that improve the lives of the world's consumers" is probably too broad a mission statement for any firm except Procter & Gamble. Care must be taken when stating what business a firm is in. For example, the mission of Ben & Jerry's centers on three important aspects of its ice cream business: (1) Product: "To make, distribute and sell the finest quality all natural ice cream and related products in a wide variety of innovative flavors made from Vermont Dairy products;" (2) Economic: "To operate the company on a sound financial basis of profitable growth, increasing value for our shareholders, and creating career opportunities and financial rewards for our employees;" and (3) Social: "To operate the company in a way that actively recognizes the central role that business plays in the structure of society by initiating innovative ways to improve the quality of life of a broad community—local, national, and international."[4] By correctly stating the business mission in terms of the benefits that customers seek, the foundation for the marketing plan is set. Many companies are focusing on designing more appropriate mission statements because these statements are frequently displayed on the company's Web sites.

The organization may need to define a mission statement and objectives for a **strategic business unit (SBU)**, which is a subgroup of a single business or a collection of related businesses within the larger organization. A properly defined SBU should have a distinct mission and specific target market, control over its resources, its own competitors, and plans independent of the other SBUs in the organization. Thus, a large firm such as Kraft Foods may have marketing plans for each of its SBUs, which include breakfast foods, desserts, pet foods, and beverages.

LO 3
Setting Marketing Plan Objectives

Before the details of a marketing plan can be developed, objectives for the plan must be stated. Without objectives, there is no basis for measuring the success of marketing plan activities.

A **marketing objective** is a statement of what is to be accomplished through marketing activities. To be useful, stated objectives should meet several criteria. First, objectives should be realistic, measurable, and time specific. It is tempting to state that the objective is "to be the best marketer of cat food." However, what is "best" for one firm might be sales of one million pounds of cat food per year, whereas to another firm, "best" might mean dominant market share. It may also be unrealistic for start-up firms or new products to command dominant market share, given other competitors in the marketplace. Finally, by what time should the objective be met? A more realistic objective would be "To achieve 10 percent dollar market share in the cat food market within 12 months of product introduction."

Second, objectives must also be consistent with and indicate the priorities of the organization. Specifically, objectives flow from the business mission statement to the rest of the marketing plan. Exhibit 2.3 shows some well-stated and some poorly stated objectives. Notice how well they do or do not meet the aforementioned criteria.

strategic business unit (SBU)
A subgroup of a single business or a collection of related businesses within the larger organization.

marketing objective
A statement of what is to be accomplished through marketing activities.

Exhibit 2.3

Examples of Marketing Objectives

Poorly Stated Objectives	Well-Stated Objectives
Our objective is to be a leader in the industry in terms of new-product development.	Our objective is to spend 12 percent of sales revenue between 2007 and 2008 on research and development in an effort to introduce at least five new products in 2008.
Our objective is to maximize profits.	Our objective is to achieve a 10 percent return on investment during 2007, with a payback on new investments of no longer than four years.
Our objective is to better serve customers.	Our objective is to obtain customer satisfaction ratings of at least 90 percent on the 2007 annual customer satisfaction survey, and to retain at least 85 percent of our 2007 customers as repeat purchasers in 2008.
Our objective is to be the best that we can be.	Our objective is to increase market share from 30 percent to 40 percent in 2007 by increasing promotional expenditures by 14 percent.

REVIEW LEARNING OUTCOME

LO3 Describe the criteria for stating good marketing objectives

Realistic, measurable, and time-specific objectives consistent with the firm's objectives:

1. Communicate marketing management philosophy

2. Provide management direction

3. Motivate employees

4. Force executives to think clearly

5. Allow for better evaluation of results

Carefully specified objectives serve several functions. First, they communicate marketing management philosophies and provide direction for lower-level marketing managers so that marketing efforts are integrated and pointed in a consistent direction. Objectives also serve as motivators by creating something for employees to strive for. When objectives are attainable and challenging, they motivate those charged with achieving the objectives. Additionally, the process of writing specific objectives forces executives to clarify their thinking. Finally, objectives form a basis for control; the effectiveness of a plan can be gauged in light of the stated objectives.

LO4 Conducting a Situation Analysis

Before specific marketing activities can be defined, marketers must understand the current and potential environment that the product or service will be marketed in. A situation analysis is sometimes referred to as a **SWOT analysis**; that is, the firm should identify its internal strengths (S) and weaknesses (W) and also examine external opportunities (O) and threats (T).

When examining internal strengths and weaknesses, the marketing manager should focus on organizational resources such as production costs, marketing skills, financial resources, company or brand image, employee capabilities, and available technology. For example, a potential weakness for AirTran Airways (formerly ValuJet) is the age of its airplane fleet, which could project an image of danger or low quality. Other weaknesses include high labor turnover rates and limited flights. A potential strength is the airline's low operating costs, which translate into lower prices for consumers. Another issue to consider in this section of the marketing plan is the historical background of the firm—its sales and profit history.

When examining external opportunities and threats, marketing managers must analyze aspects of the marketing environment. This process is called **environmental** scanning—the collection and interpretation of information about forces, events, and relationships in the external environment that may affect the future of the organization or the implementation of the marketing plan. Environmental scanning helps identify market opportunities and threats and provides guidelines for the design of marketing strategy. The six most often studied macroenvironmental forces are social, demographic, economic, technological, political and legal, and competitive. These forces are examined in detail in Chapter 3. For example, H&R Block, a tax preparation service, benefits from complex changes in the tax codes that motivate citizens to have their tax returns prepared by a professional. Alternatively, tax-simplification or flat-tax plans would allow people to easily prepare their own returns.

LO 5
Competitive Advantage

Performing a SWOT analysis allows firms to identify their competitive advantage. A competitive advantage is a set of unique features of a company and its products that are perceived by the target market as significant and superior to the competition. It is the factor or factors that cause customers to patronize a firm and not the competition. There are three types of competitive advantages: cost, product/service differentiation, and niche strategies.

COST COMPETITIVE ADVANTAGE

Cost leadership can result from obtaining inexpensive raw materials, creating an efficient scale of plant operations, designing products for ease of manufacture, controlling overhead costs, and avoiding marginal customers. DuPont, for example, has an exceptional cost competitive advantage in the production of titanium dioxide. Technicians created a production process using low-cost feedstock, giving DuPont a 20 percent cost advantage over its competitors. The cheaper feedstock technology is complex and can be duplicated only by investing about $100 million and several years of testing time. Having a **cost competitive advantage** means being the low-cost competitor in an industry while maintaining satisfactory profit margins.

A cost competitive advantage enables a firm to deliver superior customer value. Wal-Mart, the world's leading low-cost general merchandise store, offers good value to customers because it focuses on providing a large selection of merchandise at low prices and good customer service. Wal-Mart is able to keep its prices down because it has strong buying power in its relationships with suppliers.

Costs can be reduced in a variety of ways.

- *Experience curves:* **Experience curves** tell us that costs decline at a predictable rate as experience with a product increases. The experience curve effect encompasses a broad range of manufacturing, marketing, and administrative costs. Experience curves reflect learning by doing, technological advances, and economies of scale. Firms like Boeing use historical experience curves as a basis for predicting and setting prices. Experience curves allow management to forecast costs and set prices based on anticipated costs as opposed to current costs.

- *Efficient labor:* Labor costs can be an important component of total costs in low-skill, labor-intensive industries such as product assembly and apparel manufacturing.

SWOT analysis
Identifying internal strengths (S) and weaknesses (W) and also examining external opportunities (O) and threats (T).

environmental scanning
Collection and interpretation of information about forces, events, and relationships in the external environment that may affect the future of the organization or the implementation of the marketing plan.

competitive advantage
The set of unique features of a company and its products that are perceived by the target market as significant and superior to the competition.

cost competitive advantage
Being the low-cost competitor in an industry while maintaining satisfactory profit margins.

experience curves
Curves that show costs declining at a predictable rate as experience with a product increases.

One way companies can create competetive advantage through cost leadership is by reducing labor costs. In the bicycle industry, this labor reduction comes from outsourcing manufacturing operations. The Giant Bicycle company used to manufacture products in Taiwan but now manufactures in neighboring China because of lower wages, plentiful land, and lax environmental regulations.

Many U.S. manufacturers such as Nike, Levi Strauss, and Liz Claiborne have gone offshore to achieve cheaper manufacturing costs. Many American companies are also outsourcing activities such as data entry and other labor-intensive jobs.

- *No-frills goods and services:* Marketers can lower costs by removing frills and options from a product or service. Southwest Airlines, for example, offers low fares but no seat assignments or meals. Low prices give Southwest a higher load factor and greater economies of scale, which, in turn, mean even lower prices such as Southwest's "Friends Fly Free" promotions.

- *Government subsidies:* Governments may provide grants and interest-free loans to target industries. Such government assistance enabled Japanese semiconductor manufacturers to become global leaders.

- *Product design:* Cutting-edge design technology can help offset high labor costs. BMW is a world leader in designing cars for ease of manufacture and assembly. Reverse engineering—the process of disassembling a product piece by piece to learn its components and obtain clues as to the manufacturing process—can also mean savings. Reverse engineering a low-cost competitor's product can save research and design costs. Japanese engineers have reversed many products, such as computer chips coming out of Silicon Valley.

- *Reengineering:* Reengineering entails fundamental rethinking and redesign of business processes to achieve dramatic improvements in critical measures of performance. It often involves reorganizing from functional departments such as sales, engineering, and production to cross-disciplinary teams.

- *Production innovations:* Production innovations such as new technology and simplified production techniques help lower the average cost of production. Technologies such as computer-aided design and computer-aided manufacturing (CAD/CAM) and increasingly sophisticated robots help companies like Boeing, Ford, and General Electric reduce their manufacturing costs.

- *New methods of service delivery:* Medical expenses have been substantially lowered by the use of outpatient surgery and walk-in clinics. Airlines, such as Delta, are lowering reservation and ticketing costs by encouraging passengers to use the Internet to book flights and by providing self-check-in kiosks at the airport.

PRODUCT/SERVICE DIFFERENTIATION COMPETITIVE ADVANTAGE

product/service differentiation competitive advantage
The provision of something that is unique and valuable to buyers beyond simply offering a lower price than the competition's

Because cost competitive advantages are subject to continual erosion, product/service differentiation tends to provide a longer lasting competitive advantage. The durability of this strategy tends to make it more attractive to many top managers. A **product/service differentiation competitive advantage** exists when a firm provides something unique that is valuable to buyers beyond simply offering a low price. Examples include brand names (Lexus), a strong dealer network (Caterpillar Tractor for construction work), product reliability (Maytag appliances), image (Neiman Marcus in retailing), or service (FedEx). A great example of a company that has a strong product/service competitive

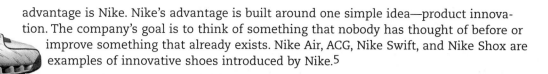

advantage is Nike. Nike's advantage is built around one simple idea—product innovation. The company's goal is to think of something that nobody has thought of before or improve something that already exists. Nike Air, ACG, Nike Swift, and Nike Shox are examples of innovative shoes introduced by Nike.[5]

NICHE COMPETITIVE ADVANTAGE

A **niche competitive advantage** seeks to target and effectively serve a single segment of the market (see Chapter 7). For small companies with limited resources that potentially face giant competitors, niching may be the only viable option. A market segment that has good growth potential but is not crucial to the success of major competitors is a good candidate for developing a niche strategy.

Many companies using a niche strategy serve only a limited geographic market. Buddy Freddy's is a very successful restaurant chain but is found only in Florida. Migros is the dominant grocery chain in Switzerland. It has no stores outside that small country.

Block Drug Company uses niching by focusing its product line on tooth products. It markets Polident to clean false teeth, Poligrip to hold false teeth, and Sensodyne toothpaste for persons with sensitive teeth. The Orvis Company manufactures and sells everything that anyone might ever need for fly fishing. Orvis is a very successful nicher.

BUILDING SUSTAINABLE COMPETITIVE ADVANTAGE

The key to having a competitive advantage is the ability to sustain that advantage. A **sustainable competitive advantage** is one that cannot be copied by the competition. Nike, discussed earlier, is a good example of a company that has a sustainable competitive advantage. Others include Rolex (high-quality watches), Nordstrom department stores (service), and Southwest Airlines (low price). In contrast, when Datril was introduced into the pain-reliever market, it was touted as being exactly like Tylenol, only cheaper. Tylenol responded by lowering its price, thus destroying Datril's competitive advantage and ability to remain on the market. In this case, low price was not a sustainable competitive advantage. Without a competitive advantage, target customers don't perceive any reason to patronize an organization instead of its competitors.

The notion of competitive advantage means that a successful firm will stake out a position unique in some manner from its rivals. Imitation of competitors indicates a lack of competitive advantage and almost ensures mediocre performance. Moreover, competitors rarely stand still, so it is not surprising that imitation causes managers to feel trapped in a seemingly endless game of catch-up. They are regularly surprised by the new accomplishments of their rivals.

Companies need to build their own competitive advantages rather than copy a competitor. The sources of tomorrow's competitive advantages are the skills and assets of the organization. Assets include patents, copyrights, locations, and equipment and technology that are superior to those of the competition. Skills are functions such as customer service and promotion that the firm performs better than its competitors. Travelocity, for example, is known for the ease of its online travel reservation system. Marketing managers should continually focus the firm's skills and assets on sustaining and creating competitive advantages.

Remember, a sustainable competitive advantage is a function of the speed with which competitors can imitate a leading company's strategy and plans. Imitation requires a competitor to identify the leader's competitive advantage, determine how it is achieved, and then learn how to duplicate it.

niche competitive advantage
The advantage achieved when a firm seeks to target and effectively serve a small segment of the market.

sustainable competitive advantage
An advantage that can not be copied by the competition.

REVIEW LEARNING OUTCOME

LO5 Identify sources of competitive advantage

To create sustainable competitive advantage, don't copy someone else, build your own:

Sources of Competitive Advantage

- Cost $
- Product/ Service Differentiation A vs. B vs. C
- Niche Strategies

LO⁶
Strategic Directions

The end result of the SWOT analysis and identification of a competitive advantage is to evaluate the strategic direction of the firm. Selecting a strategic alternative is the next step in marketing planning.

STRATEGIC ALTERNATIVES

To discover a marketing opportunity, management must know how to identify the alternatives. One method for developing alternatives is Ansoff's strategic opportunity matrix (see Exhibit 2.4), which matches products with markets. Firms can explore these four options:

- *Market penetration*: A firm using the **market penetration** alternative would try to increase market share among existing customers. If Kraft Foods started a major campaign for Maxwell House coffee, with aggressive advertising and cents-off coupons to existing customers, it would be following a penetration strategy. McDonald's sold the most Happy Meals in history with a promotion that included Ty's Teeny Beanie Babies. Customer databases, discussed in Chapters 8 and 19, helped managers implement this strategy.

- *Market development*: **Market development** means attracting new customers to existing products. Ideally, new uses for old products stimulate additional sales among existing customers while also bringing in new buyers. McDonald's, for example, has opened restaurants in Russia, China, and Italy and is eagerly expanding into Eastern European countries. Coca-Cola and Pepsi have faster growth in their new foreign markets than at home. In the nonprofit area, the growing emphasis on continuing education and executive development by colleges and universities is a market development strategy.

- *Product development*: A **product development** strategy entails the creation of new products for present markets. Several makers of men's suits have introduced new suits designed to be worn in hot weather. For example, Brooks Brothers has introduced a line of poplin suits with polyester fibers that move moisture away from the body. Joseph A. Bank Clothiers has created suits that contain the same fibers NASA developed for spacesuits to prevent astronauts from getting overheated.[6]

  Managers following the product development strategy can rely on their extensive knowledge of the target audience. They usually have a good feel for what customers like and dislike about current products and what existing needs are not being met. In addition, managers can rely on established distribution channels.

- *Diversification*: **Diversification** is a strategy of increasing sales by introducing new products into new markets. For example, LTV Corporation, a steel producer, diversified into the monorail business. Sony practiced a diversification strategy when it acquired Columbia Pictures; although motion pictures are not a new product in the marketplace, they were a new product for Sony. Coca-Cola manufactures and markets water-treatment and water-conditioning equipment, which has

market penetration
A marketing strategy that tries to increase market share among existing customers.

market development
A marketing strategy that entails attracting new customers to existing products.

product development
A marketing strategy that entails the creation of new products for current customers.

diversification
A strategy of increasing sales by introducing new products into new markets.

Exhibit 2.4

Ansoff's Strategic Opportunity Matrix

	Present Product	New Product
Present Market	**Market penetration:** McDonald's sells more Happy Meals with Disney movie promotions.	**Product development:** McDonald's introduces premium salads and McWater.
New Market	**Market development:** McDonald's opens restaurants in China.	**Diversification:** McDonald's introduces line of children's clothing.

PART I   THE WORLD OF MARKETING

been a very challenging task for the traditional soft drink company. A diversification strategy can be risky when a firm is entering unfamiliar markets. On the other hand, it can be very profitable when a firm is entering markets with little or no competition.

SELECTING A STRATEGIC ALTERNATIVE

Portfolio Matrix

Recall that large organizations engaged in strategic planning may create strategic business units. Each SBU has its own rate of return on investment, growth potential, and associated risk. Management must find a balance among the SBUs that yields the overall organization's desired growth and profits with an acceptable level of risk. Some SBUs generate large amounts of cash, and others need cash to foster growth. The challenge is to balance the organization's "portfolio" of SBUs for the best long-term performance.

To determine the future cash contributions and cash requirements expected for each SBU, managers can use the Boston Consulting Group's portfolio matrix. The **portfolio matrix** classifies each SBU by its present or forecast growth and market share. The underlying assumption is that market share and profitability are strongly linked. The measure of market share used in the portfolio approach is *relative market share*, the ratio between the company's share and the share of the largest competitor. For example, if firm A has a 50 percent share and the competitor has 5 percent, the ratio is 10 to 1. If firm A has a 10 percent market share and the largest competitor has 20 percent, the ratio is 0.5 to 1.

If you had wanted a pair of **yellow pants,** you wouldn't have paid **$46 for these.**

TIDE WITH BLEACH ALTERNATIVE KEEPS WHITES WHITER, LONGER. SO THE LOOK YOU LOVE WILL LAST.

Tide knows fabrics best

Companies often try to profit by expanding the lines of their most profitable brands (cash cows). Tide, for instance, has been expanded to include the Tide With Bleach Alternative featured in this advertisement.

Exhibit 2.5 is a hypothetical portfolio matrix for a large computer manufacturer. The size of the circle in each cell of the matrix represents dollar sales of the SBU relative to dollar sales of the company's other SBUs. The following categories are used in the matrix:

portfolio matrix
A tool for allocating resources among products or strategic business units on the basis of relative market share and market growth rate.

star
In the portfolio matrix, a business unit that is a fast-growing market leader.

cash cow
In the portfolio matrix, a business unit that usually generates more cash than it needs to maintain its market share.

- *Stars:* A **star** is a market leader and growing fast. For example, computer manufacturers have identified subnotebook and handheld models as stars. Star SBUs usually have large profits but need a lot of cash to finance rapid growth. The best marketing tactic is to protect existing market share by reinvesting earnings in product improvement, better distribution, more promotion, and production efficiency. Management must strive to capture most of the new users as they enter the market.

- *Cash cows:* A **cash cow** is an SBU that usually generates more cash than it needs to maintain its market share. It is in a low-growth market, but the product has a dominant market share. Personal computers and laptops are categorized as cash cows in Exhibit 2.5. The basic strategy for a cash cow is to maintain market dominance by being the price leader and making technological improvements in the product. Managers should resist pressure to extend the basic line unless they can

Exhibit 2.5

Portfolio Matrix for a Large Computer Manufacturer

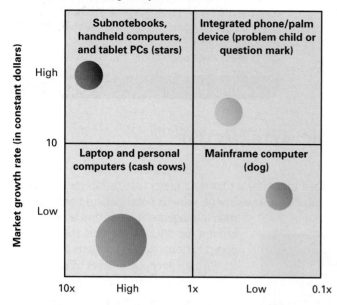

NOTE: The size of the circle represents the dollar sales relative to sales of other SBUs on the matrix—for example, 10x means sales are ten times greater than those of the next largest competitor.

problem child (question mark)
In the portfolio matrix, a business unit that shows rapid growth but poor profit margins.

dog
In the portfolio matrix, a business unit that has low growth potential and a small market share

marketing strategy
The activities of selecting and describing one or more target markets and developing and maintaining a marketing mix that will produce mutually satisfying exchanges with target markets.

market opportunity analysis (MOA)
The description and estimation of the size and sales potential of market segments that are of interest to the firm and the assessment of key competitors in these market segments.

---

dramatically increase demand. Instead, they should allocate excess cash to the product categories where growth prospects are the greatest. For instance, the Clorox Company owns Kingsford charcoal, the Glad brand of products, Fresh Step, Scoop Away and other pet litters, Black Flag pest control products, Brita water filtration systems, and K. C. Masterpiece barbeque sauce, among others. Traditionally, the company's cash cow has been Clorox bleach, which owns the lion's share of a low-growth market. The Clorox Company has been highly successful in stretching the Clorox line to include scented chlorine bleach as well as Clorox 2, a chlorine-free bleach for colored clothing. Another example is Heinz, which has two cash cows: ketchup and Weight Watchers frozen dinners.

- *Problem children:* A **problem child,** also called a **question mark,** shows rapid growth but poor profit margins. It has a low market share in a high-growth industry. Problem children need a great deal of cash. Without cash support, they eventually become dogs. The strategy options are to invest heavily to gain better market share, acquire competitors to get the necessary market share, or drop the SBU. Sometimes a firm can reposition the products of the SBU to move them into the star category.

- *Dogs:* A **dog** has low growth potential and a small market share. Most dogs eventually leave the marketplace. In the computer manufacturer example, the mainframe computer has become a dog. Other examples include Jack-in-the-Box shrimp dinners. Warner-Lambert's Reef mouthwash, and Campbell's Red Kettle soups. Frito-Lay has produced several dogs, including Stuffers cheese-filled snacks, Rumbles granola nuggets, and Toppels cheese-topped crackers—a trio irreverently known as Stumbles, Tumbles, and Twofers. The strategy options for dogs are to harvest or divest.

After classifying the company's SBUs in the matrix, the next step is to allocate future resources for each. The four basic strategies are to

- *Build:* If an organization has an SBU that it believes has the potential to be a star (probably a problem child at present), building would be an appropriate goal. The organization may decide to give up short-term profits and use its financial resources to achieve this goal. Procter & Gamble built Pringles from a money loser into a record profit maker.

- *Hold:* If an SBU is a very successful cash cow, a key goal would surely be to hold or preserve market share so that the organization can take advantage of the very positive cash flow. Bisquick has been a prosperous cash cow for General Mills for over two decades.

- *Harvest:* This strategy is appropriate for all SBUs except those classified as stars. The basic goal is to increase the short-term cash return without too much concern for the long-run impact. It is especially worthwhile when more cash is needed from a cash cow with long-run prospects that are unfavorable because of low market growth rate. For instance, Lever Brothers has been harvesting Lifebuoy soap for a number of years with little promotional backing.

Market development = ↑ customers

Market penetration = ↑ share

Product development = ↑ products

Diversification = ↑ new products + ↑ new markets

- *Divest*: Getting rid of SBUs with low share markets is often appropriate. Problem childr are most suitable for this strategy. Procter & Ga dropped Cincaprin, a coated aspirin, because of it growth potential.

LO7
Describing the Target Market

Marketing strategy involves the activities of selecting and describing one or more target markets and developing and maintaining a marketing mix that will produce mutually satisfying exchanges with target markets.

TARGET MARKET STRATEGY

A market segment is a group of individuals or organizations that share one or more characteristics. They therefore may have relatively similar product needs. For example, parents of newborn babies need products such as formula, diapers, and special foods. The target market strategy identifies the market segment or segments on which to focus. This process begins with a **market opportunity analysis (MOA)**—the description and estimation of the size and sales potential of market segments that are of interest to the firm and the assessment of key competitors in these market segments. After the firm describes the market segments, it may target one or more of them. There are three general strategies for selecting target markets. Target market(s) can be selected by appealing to the entire market with one marketing mix, concentrating on one segment, or appealing to multiple market segments using multiple marketing mixes. The characteristics, advantages, and disadvantages of each strategic option are examined in Chapter 7. Target markets could be smokers who are concerned about white teeth (the target of Topol toothpaste), people concerned about sugar and calories in their soft drinks (Diet Pepsi), or college students needing inexpensive about-town transportation (Yamaha Razz scooter).

Any market segment that is targeted must be fully described. Demographics, psychographics, and buyer behavior should be assessed. Buyer behavior is covered in Chapters 5 and 6. If segments are differentiated by ethnicity, multicultural aspects of the marketing mix should be examined. If the

We Can Dream, Can't We?

mountaindew.com   DO THE DEW

Companies often use a mix of positioning bases to reach their target audience. Mountain Dew is one of these products. This ad combines the element of youth, outdoor fun, and even irreverence.

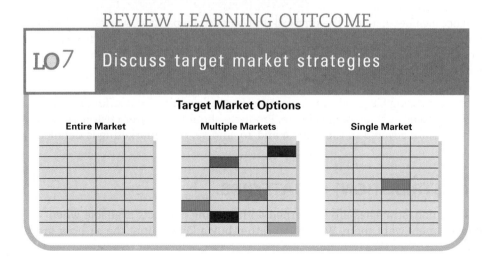

Target Market Options

Entire Market	Multiple Markets	Single Market

target market is international, it is especially important to describe differences in culture, economic and technological development, and political structure that may affect the marketing plan. Global marketing is covered in more detail in Chapter 4.

LO⁸

The Marketing Mix

The term **marketing mix** refers to a unique blend of product, place (distribution), promotion, and pricing strategies (often referred to as the **four Ps**) designed to produce mutually satisfying exchanges with a target market. The marketing manager can control each component of the marketing mix, but the strategies for all four components must be blended to achieve optimal results. Any marketing mix is only as good as its weakest component. For example, the first pump toothpastes were distributed over cosmetic counters and failed. Not until pump toothpastes were distributed the same way as tube toothpastes did the products succeed. The best promotion and the lowest price cannot save a poor product. Similarly, excellent products with poor placing, pricing, or promotion will likely fail.

Successful marketing mixes have been carefully designed to satisfy target markets. At first glance, McDonald's and Wendy's may appear to have roughly identical marketing mixes because they are both in the fast-food hamburger business. However, McDonald's has been most successful at targeting parents with young children for lunchtime meals, whereas Wendy's targets the adult crowd for lunches and dinner. McDonald's has playgrounds, Ronald McDonald the clown, and children's Happy Meals. Wendy's has salad bars, carpeted restaurants, and no playgrounds.

Variations in marketing mixes do not occur by chance. Astute marketing managers devise marketing strategies to gain advantages over competitors and best serve the needs and wants of a particular target market segment. By manipulating elements of the marketing mix, marketing managers can fine-tune the customer offering and achieve competitive success.

PRODUCT STRATEGIES

Typically, the marketing mix starts with the product "P." The heart of the marketing mix, the starting point, is the product offering and product strategy. It is hard to design a place strategy, decide on a promotion campaign, or set a price without knowing the product to be marketed.

The product includes not only the physical unit but also its package, warranty, after-sale service, brand name, company image, value, and many other factors. A Godiva chocolate has many product elements: the chocolate itself, a fancy gold wrapper, a customer satisfaction guarantee, and the prestige of the Godiva brand name. We buy things not only for what they do (benefits) but also for what they mean to us (status, quality, or reputation).

Products can be tangible goods such as computers, ideas like those offered by a consultant, or services such as medical care. Products should also offer customer value. Product decisions are covered in Chapters 9 and 10, and services marketing is detailed in Chapter 11.

PLACE (DISTRIBUTION) STRATEGIES

Place, or distribution, strategies are concerned with making products available when and where customers want them. Would you rather buy a kiwi fruit at the 24-hour gro-

marketing mix
A unique blend of product, place, promotion, and pricing strategies designed to produce mutually satisfying exchanges with a target market.

four Ps
Product, place, promotion, and price, which together make up the marketing mix.

The role of promotion is to inform, persuade, and remind. Chik-Fil-A's popular "Eat Mor Chikin" cows have been the subject of outdoor advertising, television advertising, and even a yearly calendar that contains over $20 worth of coupons for free food.

REVIEW LEARNING OUTCOME

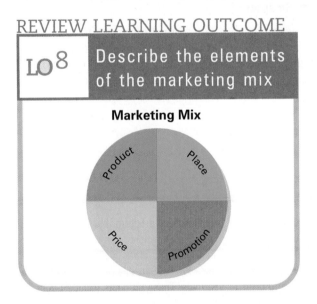

LO8 Describe the elements of the marketing mix

Marketing Mix

Product
Place
Price
Promotion

cery store within walking distance or fly to Australia to pick your own? A part of this place "P" is physical distribution, which involves all the business activities concerned with storing and transporting raw materials or finished products. The goal is to make sure products arrive in usable condition at designated places when needed. Place strategies are covered in Chapters 12 and 13.

PROMOTION STRATEGIES

Promotion includes advertising, public relations, sales promotion, and personal selling. Promotion's role in the marketing mix is to bring about mutually satisfying exchanges with target markets by informing, educating, persuading, and reminding them of the benefits of an organization or a product. A good promotion strategy, like using the Dilbert character in a national promotion strategy for Office Depot, can dramatically increase sales. Good promotion strategies do not guarantee success, however. Despite massive promotional campaigns, the movies *The Alamo* and *The Ladykillers* had disappointing box-office returns. Each element of the promotion "P" is coordinated and managed with the others to create a promotional blend or mix. These integrated marketing communications activities are described in Chapters 14, 15, and 16. Technology-driven aspects of promotional marketing are covered in Chapter 19. The "Ethics in Marketing" box highlights several issues regarding advertising to children.

PRICING STRATEGIES

Price is what a buyer must give up to obtain a product. It is often the most flexible of the four marketing mix elements—the quickest element to change. Marketers can raise or lower prices more frequently and easily than they can change other marketing mix variables. Price is an important competitive weapon and is very important to the organization because price multiplied by the number of units sold equals total revenue for the firm. Pricing decisions are covered in Chapters 17 and 18.

LO9
Following Up on the Marketing Plan

implementation
The process that turns a marketing plan into action assignments and ensures that these assignments are executed in a way that accomplishes the plan's objectives.

IMPLEMENTATION

Implementation is the process that turns a marketing plan into action assignments and ensures that these assignments are executed in a way that accomplishes the plan's objectives. Implementation activities may involve detailed job assignments, activity descriptions, timelines, budgets, and lots of communication. Although implementation is essentially "doing what you said you were going to do," many organizations repeatedly experience failures in strategy implementation. Brilliant marketing plans are doomed to fail if they are not properly implemented. These detailed communications may or may not be part of the written marketing plan. If they are not part of the plan, they should be specified elsewhere as soon as the plan has been communicated.

EVALUATION AND CONTROL

After a marketing plan is implemented, it should be evaluated. **Evaluation** entails gauging the extent to which marketing objectives have been achieved during the specified time period. Four common reasons for failing to achieve a marketing objective are unrealistic marketing objectives, inappropriate marketing strategies in the plan, poor implementation, and changes in the environment after the objective was specified and the strategy was implemented.

Once a plan is chosen and implemented, its effectiveness must be monitored. **Control** provides the mechanisms for evaluating marketing results in light of the plan's objectives and for correcting actions that do not help the organization reach those objectives within budget guidelines. Firms need to establish formal and informal control programs to make the entire operation more efficient.

Perhaps the broadest control device available to marketing managers is the **marketing audit**—a thorough, systematic, periodic evaluation of the objectives, strategies, structure, and performance of the marketing organization. A marketing audit helps management allocate marketing resources efficiently. It has four characteristics:

- *Comprehensive:* The marketing audit covers all the major marketing issues facing an organization and not just trouble spots.

- *Systematic:* The marketing audit takes place in an orderly sequence and covers the organization's marketing environment, internal marketing system, and specific marketing activities. The diagnosis is followed by an action plan with both short-run and long-run proposals for improving overall marketing effectiveness.

evaluation
Gauging the extent to which the marketing objectives have been achieved during the specified time period.

control
Provides the mechanisms for evaluating marketing results in light of the plan's objectives and for correcting actions that do not help the organization reach those objectives within budget guidelines.

marketing audit
A thorough, systematic, periodic evaluation of the objectives, strategies, structure, and performance of the marketing organization.

ETHICS in Marketing

Does Advertising "Junk" Food to Children Contribute to Obesity?

During the decades from 1960 until 1980 about 6 percent of children in the United States were overweight, according to government data. Since 1980, however, the rate of obesity in children aged 6 to 11 has more than doubled, and the rate in adolescents has tripled.

A 2004 study commissioned by the U.S. government found that advertising contributes to childhood obesity. Kraft Foods, the nation's biggest food company, spends about $90 million annually advertising directly to children. In January 2005, Kraft announced it would stop advertising certain products to kids under 12. This move put Kraft at odds with competitors and came with the risk that Kraft might lose market share and millions in sales. On the other hand, Kraft was the only food manufacturer named to California's "Honor Roll" for its efforts to fight obesity.

By early 2006, Kraft had stopped advertising products such as Oreo and Chips Ahoy cookies and Kool-Aid in television, radio, and print media viewed primarily by children between the ages of 6 and 11. The company already had a policy of not advertising to children under the age of 6. In conjunction with its advertising

ban, Kraft also developed a labeling program that features a Sensible Solution flag, based on nutritional criteria derived from the 2005 U.S. Dietary Guidelines and other public health authorities. Kraft foods that qualify for the Sensible Solution flag are marketed to 6- to 11-year-olds. These products include Sugar-Free Kool-Aid, Lunchables Fun Pack Chicken Dunks, and Sugar-Free Fruity Pebbles cereal.

Kraft took these steps because it feared that failure to act could result in the government imposing restrictions on children's advertising and might also lead to bad publicity and lawsuits. The company also acknowledged that it was aware of the public's growing concern over the role of food marketing in childhood obesity.

Critics claim, however, that Kraft has too much discretion in deciding what is healthy and what is not. They argue that the company still reaches young children through cartoon characters on its packaging. In addition, Kraft continues to market all of its products to children 12 and older.[7]

Do you think that food companies should be held responsible for the growing rate of childhood obesity? Do you think government regulations are needed?

LO 9 Explain why implementation, evaluation, and control of the marketing plan are necessary

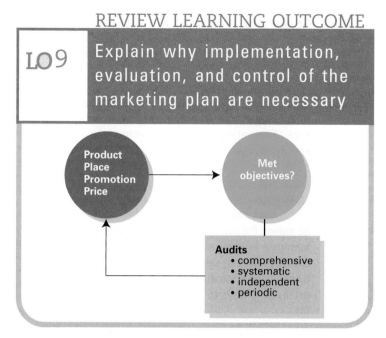

- *Independent*: The marketing audit is normally conducted by an inside or outside party who is independent enough to have top management's confidence and to be objective.

- *Periodic*: The marketing audit should be carried out on a regular schedule instead of only in a crisis. Whether it seems successful or is in deep trouble, any organization can benefit greatly from such an audit.

Although the main purpose of the marketing audit is to develop a full profile of the organization's marketing effort and to provide a basis for developing and revising the marketing plan, it is also an excellent way to improve communication and raise the level of marketing consciousness within the organization. It is a useful vehicle for selling the philosophy and techniques of strategic marketing to other members of the organization.

LO 10
Effective Strategic Planning

Effective strategic planning requires continual attention, creativity, and management commitment. Strategic planning should not be an annual exercise, in which managers go through the motions and forget about strategic planning until the next year. It should be an ongoing process because the environment is continually changing and the firm's resources and capabilities are continually evolving.

Sound strategic planning is based on creativity. Managers should challenge assumptions about the firm and the environment and establish new strategies. For example, major oil companies developed the concept of the gasoline service station in an age when cars needed frequent and rather elaborate servicing. They held on to the full-service approach, but independents were quick to respond to new realities and moved to lower-cost self-service and convenience-store operations. The majors took several decades to catch up.

Perhaps the most critical element in successful strategic planning is top management's support and participation. For example, Michael Anthony, CEO of Brookstone, Inc., and the Brookstone buying team earn hundreds of thousands of frequent flyer miles searching the world for manufacturers and inventors of unique products that can be carried in its retail stores, catalogs, and Internet site. Anthony has codeveloped some of these products and has also been active in remodeling efforts for Brookstone's 250 permanent and seasonal stores.

LO 10 Identify several techniques that help make strategic planning effective

Quick Check ✔

Now that you've read the chapter, do you get it?
Take a moment for a quick check using this scale:

1 Not at all; 2 Not very well; 3 Ok; 4 Well; 5 Very Well

Can you . . .

____ outline the elements of a marketing plan?

____ identify an appropriate business mission?

____ explain the components of a situational analysis?

____ describe several sources of competitive advantage?

____ label the BCG matrix?

____ describe target market strategies?

____ list the elements in the marketing mix?

____ identify the strategic alternatives companies can use?

____ explain why a marketing plan is important for companies?

____ distinguish between the different kinds of marketing audits?

____ TOTAL

Score: 41–50, you're ready to move on to the applications below; 31–40, skim the chapter one more time before moving on to the applications; 21–30, reread the sections giving you the most trouble and go to ThomsonNOW for guided tutorials; under 20, you better reread the chapter to get a grasp of the fundamentals. If you've reread the chapter and still have a low score, visit your professor or TA during office hours.

Review and Applications

LO 1 Understand the importance of strategic marketing and know a basic outline for a marketing plan. Strategic marketing planning is the basis for all marketing strategies and decisions. The marketing plan is a written document that acts as a guidebook of marketing activities for the marketing manager. By specifying objectives and defining the actions required to attain them, a marketing plan provides the basis by which actual and expected performance can be compared.

Although there is no set formula or a single correct outline, a marketing plan should include basic elements such as stating the business mission, setting objectives, performing a situation analysis of internal and external environmental forces, selecting target market(s), delineating a marketing mix (product, place, promotion, and price), and establishing ways to implement, evaluate, and control the plan.

1.1 Your cousin wants to start his own business, and he is in a hurry. He has decided not to write a marketing plan because he thinks that preparing one would take too long. He says he doesn't need a formal proposal because he has already received funding from your uncle. Explain why it is important for him to write a plan anyway.

1.2 After graduation, you decide to take a position as the marketing manager for a small snack-food manufacturer. The company, Shur Snak, is growing, and this is the first time that the company has ever employed a marketing manager. Consequently, there is no marketing plan in place for you to follow. Outline a basic marketing plan for your boss to give her an idea of the direction you want to take the company.

1.3 How are Coke and Pepsi using their Web sites, **http://www.coke.com** and **http://www.pepsi.com**, to promote their newest product offerings? Do you see hints of any future strategies the companies might implement? Where?

LO 2 Develop an appropriate business mission statement. The mission statement is based on a careful analysis of benefits sought by present and potential customers and an analysis of existing and anticipated environmental conditions. The firm's mission statement establishes boundaries for all subsequent decisions, objectives, and strategies. A mission statement should focus on the market or markets the organization is attempting to serve rather than on the good or service offered.

2.1 How can a new company best define its business mission statement? Can you find examples of good and bad mission statements on the Internet? How might you improve the bad ones?

2.2 Thinking back to question 1.2, write a business mission statement for Shur Snak. What elements should you include? Evaluate the mission statement you wrote against some of those you found online in question 2.1.

LO 3   Describe the criteria for stating good marketing objectives. **Objectives should be realistic, measurable, and time specific. Objectives must also be consistent and indicate the priorities of the organization.**

3.1   Building on the Shur Snak example, imagine that your boss has stated that the marketing objective of the company is to do the best job of satisfying the needs and wants of the customer. Explain that although this objective is admirable, it does not meet the criteria for good objectives. What are these criteria? What is a specific example of a better objective for Shur Snak?

LO 4   Explain the components of a situation analysis. **In the situation (or SWOT) analysis, the firm should identify its internal strengths (S) and weaknesses (W) and also examine external opportunities (O) and threats (T). When examining external opportunities and threats, marketing managers must analyze aspects of the marketing environment in a process called environmental scanning. The six most often studied macroenvironmental forces are social, demographic, economic, technological, political and legal, and competitive.**

4.1   Competition in the private courier sector is fierce. UPS and FedEx dominate, but other companies, such as DHL and even the United States Postal Service (USPS), still have a decent chunk of the express package delivery market. Perform a mini-situation analysis on one of the companies listed below by stating one strength, one weakness, one opportunity, and one threat. You may want to consult the following Web sites as you build your grid:

UPS   **http://www.ups.com**
FedEx   **http://www.fedex.com**
DHL   **http://www.dhl-usa.com**
USPS   **http://www.usps.gov**

LO 5   Identify sources of competitive advantage. **A competitive advantage is a set of unique features of a company and its products that are perceived by the target market as significant and superior to the competition. There are three types of competitive advantages: cost, product/service differentiation, and niche strategies. Sources of cost competitive advantages include experience curves, efficient labor, no-frills goods and services, government subsidies, product design, reengineering, product innovations, and new methods of service delivery. A product/ service differentiation competitive advantage exists when a firm provides something unique that is valuable to buyers beyond just low price. Niche competitive advantages come from targeting unique segments with specific needs and wants. The goal of all these sources of competitive advantage is to be sustainable.**

5.1   Break into small groups and discuss examples (at least two per person) of the last few products you have purchased. What specific strategies were used to achieve competitive advantage? Is that competitive advantage sustainable against the competitors?

LO 6   Identify strategic alternatives. **The strategic opportunity matrix can be used to help management develop strategic alternatives. The four options are market penetration, product development, market development, and diversification. In selecting a strategic alternative, managers may use a portfolio matrix, which classifies strategic business units as stars, cash cows, problem children, or dogs, depending on their present or projected growth and market share.**

6.1   Based on your SWOT analysis, decide what the strategic growth options are for the company you chose in question 4.1.

LO 7 Discuss target market strategies. The target market strategy identifies which market segment or segments to focus on. This process begins with a market opportunity analysis (MOA), which describes and estimates the size and sales potential of market segments that are of interest to the firm. In addition, an assessment of key competitors in these market segments is performed. After the market segments are described, one or more may be targeted by the firm. The three strategies for selecting target markets are appealing to the entire market with one marketing mix, concentrating on one segment, or appealing to multiple market segments using multiple marketing mixes.

7.1 You are given the task of deciding the marketing strategy for a transportation company. How do the marketing mix elements change when the target market is (a) low-income workers without personal transportation, (b) corporate international business travelers, or (c) companies with urgent documents or perishable materials to be delivered to customers?

LO 8 Describe the elements of the marketing mix. The marketing mix (or four Ps) is a blend of product, place, promotion, and pricing strategies designed to produce mutually satisfying exchanges with a target market. The starting point of the marketing mix is the product offering. Products can be tangible goods, ideas, or services. Place (distribution) strategies are concerned with making products available when and where customers want them. Promotion includes advertising, public relations, sales promotion, and personal selling. Price is what a buyer must give up to obtain a product and is often the easiest to change of the four marketing mix elements.

8.1 Choose three or four other students and make up a team. Create a marketing plan to increase enrollment in your school. Describe the four marketing mix elements that make up the plan.

LO 9 Explain why implementation, evaluation, and control of the marketing plan are necessary. Before a marketing plan can work, it must be implemented; that is, people must perform the actions in the plan. The plan should also be evaluated to see if it has achieved its objectives. Poor implementation can be a major factor in a plan's failure. Control provides the mechanisms for evaluating marketing results in light of the plan's objectives and for correcting actions that do not help the organization reach those objectives within budget guidelines.

9.1 Have your school enrollment marketing plan team (from question 8.1) develop a plan to implement, evaluate, and control the marketing strategy.

9.2 Using the *Wall Street Journal's* archive at **http://wsj.com**, trace the history of Kimberly-Clark's marketing plan and strategy for Cottonelle Fresh Rollwipes (premoistened toilet paper). Once you have a basic understanding of the product development and launch history, evaluate the plan set in motion by Kimberly-Clark. Does the company consider the product (and hence the plan) a success? Has the product been well received in the market? Are competitors moving in to take away market share with their own versions? Write a brief report giving a two-sentence synopsis of the product history and then describing what went right with the plan and what went wrong (if anything). If you identify flaws in the plan, say what the company could have done to avoid those problems.

LO 10 Identify several techniques that help make strategic planning effective. First, management must realize that strategic planning is an ongoing process and not a once-a-year exercise. Second, good strategic planning involves a high level of creativity. The last requirement is top management's support and cooperation.

10.1 What techniques can make your school enrollment marketing plan more effective?

Key Terms

Exercises

APPLICATION EXERCISE

As you now know from reading the chapter, an important part of the strategy-making process involves scanning the environment for changes that affect your marketing efforts. This exercise is designed to introduce you to the business press and to help you make the connection between the concepts you learn in the classroom and real-world marketing activities.[8]

Activities

1. Find a current article of substance in the business press (the *Wall Street Journal*, the *Financial Times, Fortune, BusinessWeek, Inc.*, etc.) that discusses topics you have covered in this course. Although this is only Chapter 2, you will be surprised by the amount of terminology you have already learned. If you are having trouble finding an article, read through the table of contents at the beginning of the book to familiarize yourself with the names of concepts that will be presented later in the course. Read your article carefully, making notes about relevant content.

2. Write a one-paragraph summary of the key points in your article; then write a list of the terms or concepts critical to understanding the article. Provide definitions of those terms. If you are unfamiliar with a term or concept that is central to the article, do some research in your textbook or see your professor during office hours. Relate these key points to the concepts in your text by citing page numbers.

3. How are the strategic elements of target market and marketing mix relevant to the article?

4. Explain the environments that are relevant to the situation presented in the article. (Chapter 3 contains a full list of environmental factors.)

(You may find this exercise useful throughout the term, as reading material from outside the text will reinforce the concepts you are learning in your course. The business press is also the place to find fully contextual examples that can aid in understanding difficult material.)

Entrepreneurship Case

CIRQUE DU SOLEIL: THE FIRE WITHIN

A 27-foot-long bronze clown shoe is the only indication that there is something other-worldly within the concrete walls of the large, rather nondescript building. Located in Montreal, the building is home to what many feel is the most successful entertainment company in the world—Cirque du Soleil.

The company's massive headquarters houses practice rooms the size of airplane hangars where cast members work on their routines. More than 300 seamstresses, engineers, and makeup artists sew, design, and build custom materials for exotic shows with stage lives of 10 to 12 years. In fact, the production staff often invents materials, such as the special waterproof makeup required for the production of *O*, a show performed mostly in a 1.5 million-gallon pool of water that was also specially designed and engineered by Cirque employees. Another key in-house resource is Cirque's team of 32 talent scouts and casting staff that recruits and cultivates performers from all over the world. The department maintains a database of 20,000 names, any of whom could be called at any time to join the members of Cirque's cast, who number 2,700 and speak 27 languages.

Shows with exotic names like *Mystère, La Nouba, O, Dralion, Varekai*, and *Zumanity* communicate through style and tone that they are intended to do more than just amuse. Cirque designs productions with distinct personalities that are meant to evoke awe, wonder, inspiration, and reflection. As one cast member put it, "The goal of a Cirque performer is not just to perform a quadruple somersault, but to treat it as some manifestation of a spiritual, inner life. Like in dance, the goal is . . . to have a language, a conversation, with the audience."

Incredibly, every one of the 15 shows that Cirque has produced over its 20-year history has returned a profit. In contrast, 90 percent of the high-budget Broadway shows that strive to reach the same target market fail to break even. Cirque's statistics, however, are eye-popping. *Mystère*, which opened at the Treasure Island hotel and casino in Las Vegas in 1993 and still runs today, cost $45 million to produce and has returned over $430 million; *O*, which opened at the Bellagio hotel and casino in 1998, cost $92 million to produce and has already returned over $480 million. Though the company splits about half of its profits with its hotel and casino partners, those same partners sometimes absorb up to 75 percent of Cirque's production costs.

At the helm of this incredible business machine is the dynamic duo of Franco Dragone and Daniel Lamarre. Dragone, a Belgian, is the creative force behind most of the company's ten current productions, and Lamarre, a former television executive, presides over show and new venture development. Together, they have transformed a one-tour, one-residence circus company into an entertainment powerhouse with five simultaneous world tours; four permanent facilities in Las Vegas—Treasure Island, the Bellagio, New York–New York, and the MGM Grand—all of which are part of the Mirage family of casinos; another permanent theater at Disney World; and a series of shows on the cable television channel Bravo that has already won an Emmy.

Lamarre claims that his business is successful because he and his staff "let the creative people run it." He guides the company with an invisible hand, making sure that business policies do not interfere with the creative process; it is Dragone and his team of creative and production personnel, not a predetermined budget, that defines the content, style, and material requirements for each project. Because of their sound planning, Cirque du Soleil can claim that it is one of the world's elite businesses, as well as one of the world's elite entertainment companies.[9]

Questions

1. Based on what you have read in the case, outline a rudimentary SWOT analysis for Cirque du Soleil.

2. Explain how Cirque du Soleil implements, evaluates, and controls the elements of its marketing plan.

3. List and describe at least three keys to Cirque du Soleil's competitive advantage.

COMPANY CLIPS

Method – Healthy Home

Cash-strapped startup companies generally do not spend a great deal of time and money on planning. Founders are so busy with the rudiments of business—finding customers and creating, manufacturing, and delivering the product—that they may even forget important things, like invoicing. Eric Lowry reinforces this notion in the opening of the second method video segment. Nonetheless, strategic planning is an important part of successful marketing. Listen closely to the segment, which introduces method's CEO, Alastair Dorward, and gauge for yourself how much planning you think this innovative startup did before launching its brand.

Questions

1. Based on what you heard in the video, does method have a marketing plan?

2. Explain the elements that make up method's competitive advantage. Is it sustainable?

3. What are the elements in method's marketing mix?

4. What are method's target market strategies and how does it use them in its operations?

BIZ FLIX

U-571

Now that you have worked through the chapter, you may be ready to "think outside the box" about strategy. As an encore to your work, watch the film clip from *U-571*, starring Harvey Keitel and Matthew McConaughey. This action-packed World War II thriller shows a U.S. submarine crew's efforts to retrieve an Enigma encryption device from a disabled German submarine. After the crew gets the device, a German vessel torpedoes and sinks their submarine. The survivors must now use the disabled German submarine to escape from the enemy with their prize.

How are the concepts of competitive advantage, situation analysis, and strategic objective illustrated in the clip?

Marketing & You Results

The higher your score the greater importance you place on planning. You also develop plans more often and devote more energy to the planning process. High scores also indicate a motivation to work "smart" and efficiently. If your score was low, you are less inclined to spend energy planning and, as a result, may have lower performance.

Marketing Plan
Appendix

e-motionsoftware
we keep the business of business moving

I Company Description

Scott Keohane and a partner founded e-motion software in 2003 and established its worldwide headquarters in Austin, Texas. They envisioned software solutions that conformed to a particular business, not the other way around, with products designed to (1) improve operating efficiency, (2) empower users, (3) enhance security, (4) improve return on investment (ROI), and (5) streamline business processes. Ultimately, however, Keohane's partner decided to leave the company. Keohane converted the partner's shares into a note, according to the partnership agreement the two had in place.

The origins of the company were based in Keohane's ten years of entrepreneurial endeavors, four years of which were spent as an independent consultant in the Oracle applications marketplace. Oracle is the world's largest enterprise software company. According to Oracle's Web site, the company's business is information—how to manage it, use it, share it, and protect it. Commercial enterprise information management software systems, such as those offered by Oracle, promise seamless integration of all information flowing through a company.

In a global marketplace in which external company collaborations are driving business efforts and internal cross-functional integration is critical for timely decision making, enterprise systems can help position companies in this highly competitive environment. Enterprise systems, such as the Oracle E-Business Suite, provide a simplified, unifying corporate technology platform. This type of platform enables companies to utilize high-quality internal and external information both strategically and tactically. The E-Business Suite includes numerous product families (e.g., advanced procurement, contracts, performance management, customer data/relationship management, financial, human resource management, logistics, manufacturing, marketing, order management, projects, sales, service, and supply chain management).

As an independent consultant, Keohane was continually asked to customize existing Oracle technology or create one-off applications to meet common requirements. When he identified the need for third-party products that would withstand upgrades to the underlying Oracle architecture, he formed e-motion software, LP. The overall business concept was to utilize the Oracle E-Business Suite as the underlying framework for customization to fit a particular customer's needs. Soon after its founding, e-motion software became a member of the Oracle Partner Network. By joining the Oracle Partner Network, e-motion software gained access to Oracle Software Licenses, technical training, marketing funds, and comarketing opportunities.

II Business Mission

E-motion software is committed to the Oracle E-Business Suite of Applications and will provide a level of support that is unmatched in the industry. The company's goals are to make Oracle Applications more reliable, to enhance the Applications' functionality, and to make the Suite's use more efficient. The company's products offer an attractive alternative to in-house development and support. E-motion software's customers will be utilizing functional products that are self-funding. That is, the savings achieved through a more efficient workforce and enhanced security will far exceed the cost of the company's products. The company's commitment extends from the methods used to build e-motion software products to the company's simple installation procedures to the postinstallation service. E-motion software products run on multiple server platforms, require no customization, and are fully compatible with existing hardware and software warranties.

III Marketing Objective

The marketing objective is to establish the company as an expert in the third-party marketplace. The third-party product market for functions that are specifically designed for integration with Oracle Applications is still in its infancy. E-motion software has to establish itself as a leader in this new marketplace. To accomplish this objective, customers must see that e-motion software products are safe and secure and that they do not affect existing Oracle functionality or their Oracle warranty.

Objective Metric: **Three major Oracle clients by the end of 2005**

To accomplish this marketing objective, e-motion software must obtain three major Oracle clients by the end of 2005. These clients will serve as reference sites for the company. These clients will enable e-motion software to demonstrate the gains achieved by using its products. As such, the clients need to be vocal and create viral marketing within the industry.

Objective Metric: **One client in each region of the United States by the end of 2006**

Given the close-knit nature of Oracle clients through organizations such as the Oracle Application User's Group (OAUG), e-motion software needs to obtain clients within each of the major geographic areas in the United States: Northeast, Mid-Atlantic, Southeast, Midwest, Northwest, and West Coast.

IV Situation Analysis

Industry Analysis

Trends

The Enterprise Resource Planning (ERP) community has undergone a radical change since the turn of the century. Historically, applications were designed for the professional user or technology expert. Today's marketplace, however, has shifted from the professional user to employee users. That is, employees in all functional areas have access to and utilize information from ERP applications. Thus, ERP providers are now developing applications intended for individual employee use instead of bigger applications designed for the professional user. These self-service, employee-based applications have fundamentally changed the way ERP applications are sold, implemented, and administered. Professional users are no longer the keepers of the data, manually entering and updating data from forms and memos. They have now become administrators in charge of ensuring data integrity. The promise of transforming departments, such as human resources and benefits, from manual-intensive data entry shops into proactive reporting shops has shifted the marketplace to self-service suite applications. This emerging trend has prompted the development of self-service applications that enable employees to utilize systems that are within their individual realms of expertise, yet are integrated across the firm.

Competitors

E-motion software represents a new voice within the Oracle community. The company is creating a new niche in the marketplace and therefore faces competition from a variety of sources. There are currently no head-to-head competitors. The existing competition can be split into three very distinct groups: Oracle, consulting firms, and in-house development centers.

Apart from creating the ERP industry, Oracle has resources that dwarf every other company in the ERP marketplace. With its available capital and the size of its development group, Oracle could simply reallocate a small development team to work on competing products. Oracle has, however, repeatedly released products that were little more than advanced betas, resulting in weeks of downtime for companies implementing the new products. By building applications that require no customization to Oracle code, e-motion software can confidently assure its customers that its products will work.

Consulting firms could advise the client to include the cost of custom application development into the total cost of the consulting engagement. This is standard protocol for competing consultancies and would effectively stop e-motion software from entering into a client site. Most consultancies, however, do not have a support and development center to handle ongoing system management. E-motion software will compete directly with consultancies by providing superior service at an affordable price.

In-house development centers (IHDCs) pose a tricky problem for e-motion software. If a company has an IHDC, it is usually a trusted source that knows the company, its standards, and its software.

Additionally, the IHDC is usually considered a "no-cost" center because salaries are already included in the company's budget. Thus, program development and implementation are considered just another project with no additional cost. On the positive side, information technology (IT) budgets have been slashed and IT departments scaled down over the past few years. Though IT spending has begun to trend upward again, the creation of IHDC units has lagged this spending trend. E-motion software plans to capitalize on this lag in IHDC unit development and upward spending trend.

Customer Profile

The marketplace has moved from professional users to employee users. Basically, professional users are now babysitters, ensuring that employees do not enter incorrect information into the system. This creates quite a quandary, however. Professional users must maintain the integrity of the system, while releasing control of it at the same time. This often forces the professional user to become a reactive unit, rushing to fix things when they break down. Employee users generally do not know the many idiosyncrasies of the ERP system. Thus, to maintain system integrity and ensure data reliability, professional users must often spend time double-checking employees' data entry and answering help desk calls about how to use the system. This is not what a self-service ERP solution is designed to deliver, however. E-motion software proposes to enter the self-service arena with a broad range of products designed to regain the efficiencies promised by self-service applications.

Technology

The costs of developing and maintaining an ERP solution require that the underlying technology be relevant for several years after the product is purchased and installed. The rapid emergence of Internet-based transactions (e.g., banking, loan applications) brought self-service applications to the forefront of business opportunity. Initially, Oracle attempted to use a mix of PL/SQL and DHTML code in the self-service offerings, but the applications resulting from this mix were not very good looking, had little functionality, and were difficult to implement. Oracle then switched to using Java Server Pages (JSP) as its self-service foundation, with PL/SQL and HTML as the accessory languages. Products with the JSP foundation were well received in the marketplace. E-motion software plans to adhere to Oracle's decision to use JSP, especially since JSP offers e-motion software some key benefits: (1) JSP is robust and flexible, allowing all applications to use the same coding techniques; (2) JSP is recyclable, which means that e-motion software can leverage existing code across new applications; (3) JSP is accessible because Java is one of the best-known programming languages; (4) JSP is portable, allowing e-motion software to easily enter other ERP markets; and (5) the use of JSP means that e-motion software will always comply with Oracle-approved practices.

SWOT Analysis

The strengths, weaknesses, opportunities, and threats (SWOT) analysis provides a snapshot of e-motion software's internal strengths and weaknesses and external opportunities and threats.

Strengths
- Founder—Scott Keohane is extremely knowledgeable about the third-party marketplace, and he is also personally and financially dedicated to making the business a success.
- Active and committed advisory council.
- Reliable products and product support.
- Member of Oracle Partner Network.

Weaknesses
- A one-person company that has to supplement the company with independent consulting services.
- Not enough time dedicated to company development.
- Though it has considerable anecdotal information, the company is lacking in marketing research.
- Financial resources.

Opportunities
- Changing marketplace that coincides with e-motion software's product development.
- The move toward employee users instead of professional users.
- Growth market.
- Technological changes.
- Refocus on IT applications.
- Persistent threat of security breaches.
- Growing focus on cross-functional interactions in the business press.
- New entries into the workforce (e.g., recent college graduates) are trained to use computers in decision making and thus expect companies to have data programs in place.

Threats
- Competitors—all three groups of competitors are likely to have deeper pockets than e-motion software.
- Offerings can be duplicated by knowledgeable experts.
- Limited market access across the United States.
- Economies of scale in larger companies such as Oracle.
- IT departments do not have unlimited budgets.

V Marketing Strategy

Target Market Strategy

E-motion software's sales plan is based on the company's understanding of the marketplace and on how it will resolve inefficiencies with the use of the

Oracle E-Business Suite of Applications. From his consulting experience in helping potential clients install and maintain their individualized suite of applications, Keohane has considerable understanding of users' needs. To obtain clients, e-motion software will rely on continuing existing relationships with prospective clients, maintaining ongoing relationships with other consulting firms, and reaching new clients via marketing and sales initiatives.

Geographically, e-motion software will direct its marketing and sales efforts within the contiguous United States. Though global operations are potential clients, the current size of e-motion software suggests that the U.S. marketplace is more viable at this time. Within this marketplace, e-motion software will focus on companies that have between 500 and 10,000 employees. These are the small-to-midsize companies that utilize the Oracle E-Business Suite of Applications. Companies of this size are unlikely to have their own development staffs in place or have the desire to develop and/or support home-grown applications. Within these small-to-midsize companies, the individual target customer varies by the product offering. For example, a database administrator will be targeted for the company's system administrator products, and the IT director will be targeted for the functional line of product offerings.

Marketing Mix

Product

E-motion software develops applications specifically for the Oracle E-Business Suite. For clients of Oracle Applications who desire greater efficiency and an increase in ROI on their installed ERP systems, e-motion software will offer a line of products designed specifically to improve performance of the existing Oracle Application installation. Clients that have in-house development staff will be able to lower the total cost of ownership of a product by having e-motion software upgrade their Oracle installation. Clients without in-house staffs, however, are more likely to benefit from e-motion software installations because they will now be able to perform a greater number of tasks that are not offered by Oracle.

As a product-based company, e-motion software cannot ignore the importance of product marketing. The three product attributes that will drive the business are level of service, usability, and clear return on purchase price. The reluctance of some customers to install relatively new third-party products in their ERP systems is an obstacle to overcome via product marketing. The company has to deliver on its promise that "e-motion software products make the business process of our customers more efficient, while easily understanding the upgrades to the underlying Oracle Application." E-motion must remain focused on this promise during both the product development and the product delivery process.

E-motion software's product line consists of functions that respond to inefficiencies identified from years of experience with Oracle ERP systems. Since the product portfolio is built expressly for the Oracle Applications E-Business Suite, the products are updated continually to maintain compatibility as well as to take advantage of new technologies and capabilities released by Oracle. All products enjoy the following characteristics: tight integration with Oracle, intuitive design, compatible architecture, and streamlined interfaces. Product offerings are iPraise, Responsibility Management, Password Reset, and Global Directory.

iPraise: The employee appraisal system developed by e-motion software is the most dynamic appraisal system available to Oracle customers. Combining e-motion software's commitment to streamlined application interfaces with the vast functionality available to Oracle E-Business Suite customers, iPraise represents the next generation of appraisal systems. The system is flexible, allowing it to be configured to meet the specific needs of the organization. Using the appraisal configuration engine, the customer can choose to include or omit several aspects of the appraisal process and even determine in which order they are to be constructed. Thus, iPraise is a complete solution for Oracle customers. Customers can opt to integrate other modules of Oracle that have been configured previously with the E-Business Suite. Installing iPraise is fast and easy.

Responsibility Management: Responsibility Management solves one of the most important questions faced by all Oracle system administrators: "Who has access to which data?" Using Responsibility Management, a system administrator or database administrator can quickly, easily, and accurately identify who has access to which data in real time. Responsibility Management can inform the administrator of the following:

- Employees with particular responsibility
- Employees without a single responsibility
- User names that are not attached to any employee
- User names that are attached to more than one employee
- User accounts that are expiring in x number of days
- User accounts created in x days prior
- All users that have been given y responsibilities in x days prior

Results are displayed in a simple table that can be arranged and sorted. The table can also be exported to Excel for further investigation.

In addition to the query capabilities, Responsibility Management enables the system administrator to make changes to the user account, such as:

- End date a responsibility
- User account expiration update for a particular responsibility

- Bulk assignment of responsibilities (by organization, job, location, etc.)
- Bulk end-dating of responsibilities (by organization, job, location, etc.)

Overall, Responsibility Management enables system administrators to enforce security policies by providing a simple, easy-to-use function to identify who has what responsibility. Each day that a person has access not identified with his or her position is unnecessary and insecure.

Password Reset: Forgotten passwords are the single largest end-user issue. Every day, help desks are bombarded with calls from end-users who have forgotten their passwords. The standard Oracle log-in link does not provide a solution for this problem, so end users are forced to call the help desk to reset the password. E-motion software's Password Reset function is the solution.

Password Reset is modeled after the standard password reset functionality available on most Web sites. Even if the user is using Password Reset for the first time, all the components will seem familiar, and the user will know where to go next without receiving complex instructions or training. Password Reset functions as part of the Oracle Applications. There are no outside Web sites to access or other applications to open. The user simply clicks on a link from the log-in page, enters the required information, and the password is reset. The user can then log in immediately with the new password. Password Reset validates a user's identity by going directly to the Oracle database and running queries against it. This tight integration ensures reliability.

Global Directory: Most companies utilize a separate system for their corporate directory. This requires entering and maintaining all employee information in Oracle and then re-entering that information into a separate system. Worse yet, they print the company directory from a separate system. Not only is this extremely inefficient, but there is a great chance for error. In today's fast-changing world, employee information can change on a weekly basis. As a result, the "other" system is often neglected, and its data are unreliable. Global Directory solves this issue by "going to source" and gathering data directly from the Oracle database; thus Global Directory has up-to-the-minute validity. Global Directory allows users to query the database for a wide variety of information. The results can be customized to give employees the depth of knowledge they require.

Global Directory functions as part of the Oracle Applications. There are no outside Web sites to access or other applications to open. Using the export function, users can transfer results into Excel, XML, or CSV, making it possible to utilize the information for such items as contact lists, distribution forms, and mailing labels.

Place/Distribution

E-motion software is now headquartered in Bedford, Massachusetts. However, home office location has little to do with the actual distribution of e-motion software's products since the products are installed and implemented at the client company. E-motion software will perform its own marketing channel functions (e.g., transactional, logistical, and facilitating) and does not foresee the need for any intermediaries in this process. However, e-motion software is a strong supporter of industry groups, such as the Oracle Applications User Group, and related industry events. Such support allows the company to become recognized as a vendor among Oracle Applications clients.

E-motion software does offer a partner program for companies that wish to resell or refer e-motion software products to Oracle ERP clients. The program is segmented into two separate categories. The Alliance Partner Referral Program is tailored for businesses that have customer relationships with companies in specific industries or with businesses or IT needs that e-motion software programs can uniquely address. An Alliance Partner will identify e-motion software customers and refer them to e-motion software for a share of the revenue from the referred account. As part of the program, Alliance Partner members receive all the training and materials needed to promote e-motion software solutions to their client base. The Alliance Solution Provider Program is designed for qualified Oracle-focused consultancies with a strong track record for providing top-notch service to their clients. Partner program members are trained and certified by e-motion software. Once certified, implementation partners can then configure and implement e-motion software products with unparalleled service and support.

Promotion

As a third-party purveyor of products for Oracle, it is important for e-motion software to convey, clearly and succinctly, its "reason for being." Company material will have the heading: "e-motion software: we keep the business of business moving." It will emphasize the Oracle connection with the following statement on documents, as appropriate: "Oracle clients around the country are realizing true gains in productivity and efficiency by taking every day tasks and putting them in motion."

E-motion software will adhere to mainstream thinking regarding the promotion of third-party products for ERP solutions.

- A cohesive, easy-to-maneuver, and user-friendly Web site (**http://www.e-motionsoftware.com**)
- Recorded demos on the company Web site (requires users to register for a demo user account)
- Press releases as a member of the Certified Oracle Partner Network

- Demonstrations presented at trade shows and events
- Word-of-mouth and reference sites
- The Internet via Google AdWords campaigns to drive potential clients to the company Web site
- Product datasheets that provide pertinent product data, features, and benefits of installation (available on the company Web site or via hard copy)

Importantly, e-motion software is a company that relies heavily on direct selling to reach potential customers. This promotional method requires a large amount of cold calling. E-motion software purchases the names of potential customers from marketing services that collect such information from customers of Oracle ERP products.

Price

E-motion software prices its products to sufficiently cover the costs associated with development, sales, and support and to provide cash flow for future growth and development. The following table provides the company's standard price list. These list prices can vary, however, as there is a trickle-down effect in the industry. Essentially, pricing starts with Oracle, trickles through the consulting firm, and then down to e-motion products.

Prices are based on industry standards for classification. For example, Password Reset, as an enterprise system product, has a total purchase price of $15,000, with a $2,700 software update and support fee. Responsibility Management, iPraise, and Global Directory are priced on a per employee (user) basis with a minimum purchase of 2,000 employees. For example, Global Directory is $2 per employee with a minimum purchase of 2,000 employees. Thus, the least amount a company could purchase this product for is $4,000. The 18 percent annual maintenance fee is the industry standard.

VI Implementation, Evaluation, and Control

Marketing Research

The company needs to keep abreast of two distinct segments in the marketplace: its clients' needs and Oracle's direction. E-motion software needs to understand its clients and their ongoing needs. This includes meeting current needs and forecasting future needs as the Oracle Application Suite continues to evolve. E-motion software must also maintain up-to-date and accurate intelligence on both current Oracle offerings and planned initiatives. By doing this, it will be able to introduce products that complement new Oracle functions and will be less likely to offer products that compete for functions included at no charge in an Oracle license.

Organizational Structure and Plan

As a start-up company, e-motion software currently has only one member on its staff, Scott Keohane. As e-motion software matures into a stable, profitable organization, the need for employees will grow. The first foreseeable employee need is in the area of sales. The plan is to hire a salesperson in early 2006 to allow Mr. Keohane to continue his consulting on a regular basis, while at the same time ensuring a steady supply of funds for continued development efforts. To obtain the financial flexibility needed to manage its cash flow successfully, the company has made contractors a significant component of its workforce. Contractors are used in the following areas: application development, database administration, and marketing. Current contractors have been associated with e-motion software almost since the company's inception and are largely credited with its early successes.

To provide a management resource from which Keohane can receive regular advice and guidance, e-motion software has assembled a nonvoting, nonbinding advisory council to assist in decision making, overall strategy, and execution. The advisory council is composed of four outside members who have made a commitment to provide their expertise and experience, free of charge, to e-motion software. Advisory members interact quarterly via teleconference.

PRODUCT PRICING SHEET

	License Price	Software Update & Support	Licensing Metric	Minimum
Application Infrastructure				
Password Reset	$15,000	$2,700/year	Enterprise	N/A
Responsibility Management	$6	18%/year	User	2,000
User Application				
iPraise	$10	18%/year	User	2,000
Corporate Information				
Global Directory	$2	18%/year	User	2,000

Financial Projections

The financial objective is to be financially solvent within the first two years of operation.

Objective Metric: Sales of $250,000 by the end of 2005
Sales of $2 million by the end of 2007
Gross margin higher than 80 percent
Positive cash flow yearly

The five-year financial projection plan (in U.S. dollars) for e-motion software is:

Keohane's current consultancies, a dedicated salesperson could more readily identify potential e-motion software clients. Of major concern is that the current financial strategy of supporting the new business by personal funds from consulting may prove to be too onerous for Keohane.

Ultimately, the goal is to "make it big." The hope is that, over the next five years, the small products that e-motion software has developed will generate cash sufficient to build a larger module that one of the larger ERP companies (e.g., Oracle) will want to acquire.[10]

FIVE YEARS FINANACIAL PROJECTION PLAN	2006	2007	2008	2009	2010
Revenues:					
iPraise	$50,000	$100,000	$600,000	$2,225,000	$5,500,000
Responsibility Mgt	60,000	80,000	160,000	420,000	700,000
Password Reset	225,000	180,000	180,000	150,000	75,000
Global Directory	45,000	75,000	180,000	300,000	465,000
Cost of Goods Sold	0	0	0	0	0
General & Administrative	$350,000	$765,000	$1,600,000	$2,165,000	$2,600,000

Implementation Timetable

2005

- The company plans to have three major Oracle clients by the end of 2005.

2006

- The company plans to have secured at least one client in each region of the United States by the end of 2006. This would mean at least one customer in the Northeast, the Mid-Atlantic, the Southeast, the Midwest, the Northwest, and the West Coast.
- Keohane plans to hire one full-time salesperson.

Summary

E-motion software continually monitors activities with current and potential clients. As a consultant in the industry, Keohane is always on the lookout for potential clients. He has set quarterly and yearly sales targets, and actual sales will be compared to these quarterly plans. Additionally, Keohane will continue his efforts to enlist at least one client in each of the major geographic regions of the United States. However, it may take a qualified salesperson to devote the time necessary to acquire new customers. Additionally, by not being restricted to

Social Responsibility,

CHAPTER

3

Ethics, and the Marketing Environment

Learning Outcomes

LO¹ Discuss corporate social responsibility

LO² Describe the role of ethics and ethical decisions in business

LO³ Discuss the external environment of marketing, and explain how it affects a firm

LO⁴ Describe the social factors that affect marketing

LO⁵ Explain the importance to marketing managers of current demographic trends

LO⁶ Explain the importance to marketing managers of multiculturalism and growing ethnic markets

LO⁷ Identify consumer and marketer reactions to the state of the economy

LO⁸ Identify the impact of technology on a firm

LO⁹ Discuss the political and legal environment of marketing

LO¹⁰ Explain the basics of foreign and domestic competition

© MICHAEL OKONIEWSKI/ASSOCIATED PRESS
© HENRI KROEGER/ISTOCKPHOTO INTERNATIONAL, INC.

corporate citizenship
at **General Electric**

Recently, Jeffrey R. Immelt, the chairman and chief executive officer of General Electric, one of the world's most valuable and most admired companies, stood before 200 of GE's corporate officers and said it would take four things to keep the company on top. Three of those were predictable: execution, growth, and great people. The fourth was not: virtue. And it was at the top of his list.

Virtue is not the first thing that comes to mind when people think about GE, an industrial and financial-services giant that is on track to generate over $150 billion in revenues in 2007. Under

To be a great company today, he likes to say, you also have to be a good company.

Jack Welch, the CEO before Immelt, GE was known for hard-driving management and for delivering market-beating shareholder returns. But Immelt doesn't want to stop there. To be a great company today, he likes to say, you also have to be a good company. Immelt takes it as a given that companies have an obligation to help solve the world's problems, and not just to make money and obey the law. "Good leaders give back," he says. "The era we live in belongs to people who believe in themselves but are focused on the needs of others."

"The world's changed," Immelt says. "Businesses today aren't admired. Size is

not respected. There's a bigger gulf today between haves and have-nots than ever before. It's up to us to use our platform to be a good citizen. Because not only is it a nice thing to do, it's a business imperative." Today, GE audits its suppliers in the developing world to make sure they comply with labor, environmental, health, and safety standards. It has performed 3,100 audits since the program began in 2002.

When people in GE's African American Forum asked whether the company could do more in Africa, Immelt responded. He couldn't see a way to locate a business there, so he looked for other ways to help. GE formed a broad partnership with Ghana's public health service, committing $20 million over five years. The company donated ultrasound equipment, X-rays, patient monitors, incubators, refrigerators, and freezers to the hospital.

The knowledge and goodwill generated in Ghana could eventually pay off monetarily for GE. "If you look over the long term, there is a decent chance that the continent of Africa becomes a market that we want to understand," Immelt says.

The more you listen to Immelt and his people, the more it becomes clear that GE's practice of corporate citizenship is guided by this kind of business calculus. Immelt says as much: "If this wasn't good for business, we probably wouldn't do it."[1]

Why is a company like GE placing so much emphasis on social responsibility? Is GE acting in the stockholders' best interest by giving away $20 million in equipment? How do uncontrollable factors in the environment affect these and other companies? We will examine these issues and more in Chapter 3.

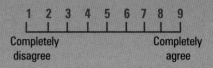

Using the following scale, enter the numbers that reflect your opinions.

```
1  2  3  4  5  6  7  8  9
└──┴──┴──┴──┴──┴──┴──┴──┘
Completely              Completely
disagree                    agree
```

_____ The ethics and social responsibility of a firm are essential to its long-term profitability.

_____ Business ethics and social responsibility are critical to the survival of a business enterprise.

_____ The overall effectiveness of a business can be determined to a great extent by the degree to which it is ethical and socially responsible.

_____ Good ethics is often good business.

_____ Business has a social responsibility beyond making a profit.

_____ Corporate planning and goal-setting sessions should include discussions of ethics and social responsibility.

_____ Social responsibility and profitability can be compatible.

Now, total your score. Find out what it means after you read the chapter.

LO¹
Corporate Social Responsibility

Corporate social responsibility is a business's concern for society's welfare. This concern is demonstrated by managers who consider both the long-range best interests of the company and the company's relationship to the society within which it operates. The newest theory in social responsibility is called **sustainability**. This refers to the idea that socially responsible companies will outperform their peers by focusing on the world's social problems and viewing them as opportunities to build profits and help the world at the same time. It is also the notion that companies cannot thrive for long (i.e., lack sustainability) in a world where billions of people are suffering and are desperately poor. Thus, it is in business's interest to find ways to attack society's ills. Only business organizations have the talent, creativity, and executive ability to do the job.

Skeptics say business should focus on making a profit and leave social and environmental problems to nonprofit organizations (like the World Wildlife Federation or the Sierra Club) and government. Economist Milton Friedman believes that the free market, not companies, should decide what is best for the world. He asks, "If businesspeople do have a social responsibility other than making maximum profits for stockholders, how are they to know what it is?"[2] Friedman argues that when business executives spend more money than they need to—to purchase delivery vehicles with hybrid engines, or to pay higher wages in developing countries, or even to donate company funds to charity—they are spending shareholders' money to further their own agendas. Better to pay dividends and let the shareholders give the money away, if they choose.

Proponents of corporate social responsibility say that's a false dichotomy. Smart companies, they say, can prosper and build shareholder value by tackling global problems. For General Electric, selling more wind power and energy-efficient locomotives is a no-brainer. When it comes to philanthropy, or supply chain audits designed to keep GE from being linked to sweatshops, or decisions about granting domestic-partner benefits, the business case usually comes down to GE's reputation and its desire to attract and engage great people. Some years back, for example, GE decided not to sell low-end ultrasound machines in China (and to put warning labels on the high-end machines it did sell), because it did not want the machines to be used for gender screening that could lead to abortions. The potential harm to GE's image was too great to take the risk.

But applying that kind of cost-benefit analysis to decisions with moral dimensions is a tricky business. Although GE operates in more than 100 countries, it has decided not to do business in Myanmar because the government there is a notorious violator of human rights and has been spotlighted by human-rights groups—and because the business upside is limited. GE has judged that it has more to lose than gain by being there.[3]

One theorist suggests that total corporate social responsibility has four components: economic, legal, ethical, and philanthropic.[4] The **pyramid of corporate social responsibility** portrays economic performance as the foundation for the other three responsibilities. At the same time that it pursues profits (economic responsibility), however, a business is expected to obey the law (legal responsibility); to do what is right, just, and fair (ethical responsibilities); and to be a good corporate citizen (philanthropic responsibility). These four compo-

Furniture | Kitchen Cabinetry | Closets | Doors | Home Theatre | Shoji | Architectural Woodwork

Eco *logical*
Smart kitchens. Natural materials. Custom-crafted.
For a free brochure on our *Sereno* bamboo kitchen, visit berkeleymills.com or give us a call.

Berkeley Mills
east-west furniture design®
2830 7th Street, Berkeley, California | 877-426-4557 | berkeleymills.com

© BERKELEY MILLS

Many companies hope to profit by demonstrating concern for the environment. This Berkeley Mills ad suggests that the company's products are natural and ecologically friendly.

LO 1 Discuss corporate social responsibility

Philanthropic responsibilities
Be a good corporate citizen.
Contribute resources to the
community; improve the
quality of life.

Ethical responsibilities
Be ethical.
Do what is right, just, and
fair. Avoid harm.

Legal responsibilities
Obey the law.
Law is society's codification
of right and wrong. Play by
the rules of the game.

Economic responsibilities
Be profitable.
Profit is the foundation
on which all other
responsibilities rest.

nents are distinct but together constitute the whole. Still, if the company doesn't make a profit, then the other three responsibilities are moot.

Though being "most admired" and social responsibility are not the same thing, it is difficult to imagine that a company lacking in social responsibility would be highly admired. According to a recent survey, Dell, General Electric, Starbucks, Wal-Mart, Southwest Airlines, FedEx, Berkshire Hathaway, Microsoft, Johnson & Johnson, and Procter & Gamble are America's most admired companies, all of which engage in socially responsible activities.[5] Yet, does being socially responsible create additional demand for the company's goods and services? The answer is quite complex. In some cases, it is "yes," and in others, "no." For example, one factor is the issue on which the company focuses, such as health, education, or charitable giving and how this is perceived by the target market. Other factors are product/service quality and how the target market perceives the importance of social responsibility.[6]

In summary, the evidence that corporate social responsibility drives profit and growth is inconclusive. There's also the difficulty of defining social responsibility. Socially responsible investment funds have generally tracked the broader stock market. Since its inception in 1991, the Domini Social Equity fund, the oldest and largest such fund, has gained an average of 8.66 percent annually, while the Standard & Poor's 500 has gained 9 percent. On the other hand, a recent study by Governance Metrics International, which rates companies on their governance policies, labor practices, environmental activities, and litigation history, found that stocks of the top-ranked firms significantly outperformed the market, while low-rated companies trailed the indexes.[7] For now, about the most one can say is that there doesn't seem to be a financial penalty for embracing socially responsible programs.

Paul Tebo, a chemical engineer at DuPont, sees the question differently. Tebo argues that both the world and the company are better off because of the progress DuPont has made. It has dramatically reduced greenhouse gas emissions and hazardous waste, even after accounting for the sale of Conoco, and its waste-treatment costs are down. Looking ahead, DuPont wants to generate 25 percent of revenues from renewable resources by 2010.[8]

LO 2
Ethical Behavior in Business

Social responsibility and ethics go hand in hand. Ethics refers to the moral principles or values that generally govern the conduct of an individual or a group. Ethics can also be viewed as the standard of behavior by which conduct is judged. Standards that are legal may not always be ethical, and vice versa. Laws are the values and standards enforceable by the courts. Ethics consists of personal moral principles and values rather than societal prescriptions.

Defining the boundaries of ethicality and legality can be difficult. Often, judgment is needed to determine whether an action that may be legal is an ethical or unethical act. Also, judgment is required to determine if an unethical act is legal or illegal. For example, a jury recently found Richard Scrushy, charged with a $1.4 billion fraud at Health-South Corporation, innocent on all counts. On the other hand, Bernard Ebbers, former

ethics
The moral principles or values that generally govern the conduct of an individual.

CEO of WorldCom, was found guilty of securities fraud and filing false documents and was sentenced to 25 years in prison.

Morals are the rules people develop as a result of cultural values and norms. Culture is a socializing force that dictates what is right and wrong. Moral standards may also reflect the laws and regulations that affect social and economic behavior. Thus, morals can be considered a foundation of ethical behavior.

Morals are usually characterized as good or bad. "Good" and "bad" have different connotations, including "effective" and "ineffective." A good salesperson makes or exceeds the assigned quota. If the salesperson sells a new stereo or television set to a disadvantaged consumer—knowing full well that the person can't keep up the monthly payments—is the salesperson still a good one? What if the sale enables the salesperson to exceed his or her quota?

"Good" and "bad" can also refer to "conforming" and "deviant" behaviors. A doctor who runs large ads offering discounts on open-heart surgery would be considered bad, or unprofessional, in the sense of not conforming to the norms of the medical profession. "Bad" and "good" are also used to express the distinction between criminal and law-abiding behavior. And finally, different religions define "good" and "bad" in markedly different ways. A Muslim who eats pork would be considered bad, as would a fundamentalist Christian who drinks whiskey.

MORALITY AND BUSINESS ETHICS

Today's business ethics actually consist of a subset of major life values learned since birth. The values businesspeople use to make decisions have been acquired through family, educational, and religious institutions.

Ethical values are situation specific and time oriented. Nevertheless, everyone must have an ethical base that applies to conduct in the business world and in personal life. One approach to developing a personal set of ethics is to examine the consequences of a particular act. Who is helped or hurt? How long lasting are the consequences? What actions produce the greatest good for the greatest number of people? A second approach stresses the importance of rules. Rules come in the form of customs, laws, professional standards, and common sense. Consider these examples of rules:

- Always treat others as you would like to be treated.

- Copying copyrighted computer software is against the law.

- It is wrong to lie, bribe, or exploit.

Another approach emphasizes the development of moral character within individuals. Ethical development can be thought of as having three levels:9

- *Preconventional morality*, the most basic level, is childlike. It is calculating, self-centered, and even selfish, based on what will be immediately punished or rewarded. Fortunately, most businesspeople have progressed beyond the self-centered and manipulative actions of preconventional morality.

- *Conventional morality* moves from an egocentric viewpoint toward the expectations of society. Loyalty and obedience to the organization (or society) become paramount. At the level of conventional morality, a marketing decision maker would be concerned only with whether the proposed action is legal and how it will be viewed by others. This type of morality could be likened to the adage "When in Rome, do as the Romans do."

- *Postconventional morality* represents the morality of the mature adult. At this level, people are less concerned about how others might see them and more concerned about how they see and judge themselves over the long run. A marketing decision maker who has attained a postconventional level of morality might ask, "Even though it is legal and will increase company profits, is it right in the long run? Might it do more harm than good in the end?"

ETHICAL DECISION MAKING

How do businesspeople make ethical decisions? There is no cut-and-dried answer. Some of the ethical issues managers face are shown in Exhibit 3.1. Studies show that the following factors tend to influence ethical decision making and judgments:[10]

Exhibit 3.1

Unethical Practices Marketing Managers May Have to Deal With

- Entertainment and gift giving
- False or misleading advertising
- Misrepresentation of goods, services, or company capabilities
- Lying to customers in order to get the sale
- Manipulation of data (falsifying or misusing statistics or information)
- Misleading product or service warranties
- Unfair manipulation of customers
- Exploitation of children or disadvantaged groups
- Stereotypical portrayals of women, minority groups, or senior citizens
- Invasion of customer privacy
- Sexually oriented advertising appeals
- Product or service deception
- Unsafe products or services
- Price deception
- Price discrimination
- Unfair or inaccurate statements about competitors
- Smaller amounts of product in the same-size packages

- *Extent of ethical problems within the organization*: Marketing professionals who perceive fewer ethical problems in their organizations tend to disapprove more strongly of "unethical" or questionable practices than those who perceive more ethical problems. Apparently, the healthier the ethical environment, the more likely that marketers will take a strong stand against questionable practices.

- *Top-management actions on ethics*: Top managers can influence the behavior of marketing professionals by encouraging ethical behavior and discouraging unethical behavior.

- *Potential magnitude of the consequences*: The greater the harm done to victims, the more likely that marketing professionals will recognize a problem as unethical.

- *Social consensus*: The greater the degree of agreement among managerial peers that an action is harmful, the more likely that marketers will recognize a problem as unethical.

- *Probability of a harmful outcome*: The greater the likelihood that an action will result in a harmful outcome, the more likely that marketers will recognize a problem as unethical.

- *Length of time between the decision and the onset of consequences*: The shorter the length of time between the action and the onset of negative consequences, the more likely that marketers will perceive a problem as unethical.

- *Number of people to be affected*: The greater the number of persons affected by a negative outcome, the more likely that marketers will recognize a problem as unethical.

ETHICAL GUIDELINES

Many organizations have become more interested in ethical issues. One sign of this interest is the increase in the number of large companies that appoint ethics officers—from virtually none seven years ago to almost 33 percent of large corporations now. More and more companies are providing ethics resources for their employees. Today over 70 percent of employees in the United States can seek advice on ethics questions via telephone, e-mail, Web, or in-person. (See http://www.ethics.org for more information.) In addition, many companies of various sizes have developed a **code of ethics** as a guideline to help marketing managers and other employees make better decisions. In fact, a national study found that 60 percent of companies surveyed had a code of ethics, 33 percent offered ethics training, and 33 percent employed an ethics officer.[11] Some of the most highly praised codes of ethics are those of Boeing, Hewlett-Packard, Johnson & Johnson, and Costco.

Creating ethics guidelines has several advantages:

code of ethics
A guideline to help marketing managers and other employees make better decisions.

- The guidelines help employees identify what their firm recognizes as acceptable business practices.

- A code of ethics can be an effective internal control on behavior, which is more desirable than external controls like government regulation.

Exhibit 3.2

Ethics Checklist

- Does the decision benefit one person or group but hurt or not benefit other individuals or groups? In other words, is my decision fair to all concerned?

- Would individuals or groups, particularly customers, be upset if they knew about my decision?

- Has important information been overlooked because my decision was made without input from other knowledgeable individuals or groups?

- Does my decision presume that my company is an exception to a common practice in this industry and that I therefore have the authority to break a rule?

- Would my decision offend or upset qualified job applicants?

- Will my decision create conflict between individuals or groups within the company?

- Will I have to pull rank or use coercion to implement my decision?

- Would I prefer to avoid the consequences of my decision?

- Did I avoid truthfully answering any of the above questions by telling myself that the risks of getting caught are low or that I could get away with the potentially unethical behavior?

- A written code helps employees avoid confusion when determining whether their decisions are ethical.

- The process of formulating the code of ethics facilitates discussion among employees about what is right and wrong and ultimately leads to better decisions.

Businesses, however, must be careful not to make their code of ethics too vague or too detailed. Codes that are too vague give little or no guidance to employees in their day-to-day activities. Codes that are too detailed encourage employees to substitute rules for judgment. For instance, if employees are involved in questionable behavior, they may use the absence of a written rule as a reason to continue behaving that way, even though their conscience may be saying no. The checklist in Exhibit 3.2 is an example of a simple but helpful set of ethical guidelines. Following the checklist will not guarantee the "rightness" of a decision, but it will improve the chances that the decision will be ethical. Although many companies have issued policies on ethical behavior, marketing managers must still put the policies into effect. They must address the classic "matter of degree" issue. For example, marketing researchers must often resort to deception to obtain unbiased answers to their research questions. Asking for a few minutes of a respondent's time is dishonest if the researcher knows the interview will last 45 minutes. Not only must management post a code of ethics, but it must also give examples of what is ethical and unethical for each item in the code. Moreover, top management must stress to all employees the importance of adhering to the company's code of ethics. Without a detailed code of ethics and top management's support, creating ethical guidelines becomes an empty exercise.

Ethics training is an excellent way to help employees put good ethics into practice. Raytheon, one of the world's largest defense contractors, requires all its employees to attend formal classroom ethics awareness training each year. In addition, all employees must complete online scenario-based ethics and business conduct training annually. At Niagara

REVIEW LEARNING OUTCOME

LO 2 Describe the role of ethics and ethical decisions in business

MORALITY		
Preconventional	Conventional	Post-conventional
What's in it for me?	Everyone else is doing it!	Is this good in the long run?
Will I get caught?	When in Rome . . .	

ETHICAL CLIMATE
TOP-MANAGEMENT'S ETHICS
MAGNITUDE OF CONSEQUENCES
SOCIAL CONSENSUS
PROBABILITY OF HARM
LENGTH OF TIME BETWEEN DECISION AND IMPACT
NUMBER OF PEOPLE AFFECTED
ETHICAL TRAINING

Exhibit 3.3

Ethical Norms and Values for Marketers

Norms

- Marketers must first do no harm.
- Marketers must foster trust in the marketing system.
- Marketers should embrace, communicate, and practice the fundamental ethical values that will improve consumer confidence in the integrity of the marketing exchange system.

Ethical Values

- Honesty—This means being truthful and forthright in our dealings with customers and stakeholders.
- Responsibility—This involves accepting the consequences of our marketing decisions and strategies.
- Fairness—This has to do with justly trying to balance the needs of the buyer with the interests of the seller.
- Respect—This addresses the basic human dignity of all stakeholders.
- Openness—This focuses on creating transparency in our marketing operations.
- Citizenship—This involves a strategic focus on fulfilling the economic, legal, philanthropic and societal responsibilities that serve stakeholders.

SOURCE: American Marketing Association.

Mohawk, an electric and natural gas utility, an Ethics and Compliance Office manages a company-wide ethics program that includes a code of conduct detailing employee responsibilities to avoid conflicts of interest. Niagara Mohawk recently won the Better Business Bureau's International Torch Award for business ethics.

The American Marketing Association's code of ethics highlights three general norms and six ethical values. These are shown in Exhibit 3.3.

LO³ The External Marketing Environment

All managerial decision making should be grounded in a good ethical base. In other words, proper ethics should permeate every managerial action. Perhaps the most important decisions a marketing manager must make relate to the creation of the marketing mix.

Recall from Chapters 1 and 2 that a marketing mix is the unique combination of product, place (distribution), promotion, and price strategies. The marketing mix is, of course, under the firm's control and is designed to appeal to a specific group of potential buyers. A **target market** is a defined group that managers feel is most likely to buy a firm's product.

Over time, managers must alter the marketing mix because of changes in the environment in which consumers live, work, and make purchasing decisions. Also, as markets mature, some new consumers become part of the target market; others drop out. Those who remain may have different tastes, needs, incomes, lifestyles, and buying habits than the original target consumers.

Although managers can control the marketing mix, they cannot control elements in the external environment that continually mold and reshape the target market. Review Learning Outcome 3 shows the controllable and uncontrollable variables that affect the target market, whether it consists of consumers or business purchasers. The uncontrollable elements in the center of the diagram continually evolve and create changes in the target market. In contrast, managers can shape and reshape the marketing mix, depicted on the left side of the diagram, to influence the target market. That is, managers react to changes in the external environment and attempt to create a more effective marketing mix.

UNDERSTANDING THE EXTERNAL ENVIRONMENT

Unless marketing managers understand the external environment, the firm cannot intelligently plan for the future. Thus, many organizations assemble a team of specialists to continually collect and evaluate environmental information, a process called *environmental scanning*. The goal in gathering the environmental data is to identify future market opportunities and threats.

For example, as technology continues to blur the line between personal computers, television, and movies, a company like Dell may find itself competing against a company like Sony. Research shows that children would like to find more games bundled with computer software, while adults are more likely to desire various word-processing and business-related software. Is this information an opportunity or a threat to Dell marketing managers?

target market
A defined group most likely to buy a firm's product.

ENVIRONMENTAL MANAGEMENT

No one business is large or powerful enough to create major change in the external environment. Thus, marketing managers are basically adapters rather than agents of change. For example, despite the huge size of General Motors and Ford, these companies are continually challenged to meet the competitive push by the Japanese for an ever-growing share of the U.S. automobile market. Competition is basically an uncontrollable element in the external environment.

A firm is not always completely at the mercy of the external environment, however. Sometimes a firm can influence external events. For example, extensive lobbying by FedEx has enabled it to acquire virtually all of the Japanese routes that it has sought. Japan had originally opposed new cargo routes for FedEx. The favorable decision was based on months of lobbying by FedEx at the White House, at several agencies, and in Congress for help in overcoming Japanese resistance. When a company implements strategies that attempt to shape the external environment within which it operates, it is engaging in **environmental management**.

The factors within the external environment that are important to marketing managers can be classified as social, demographic, economic, technological, political and legal, and competitive.

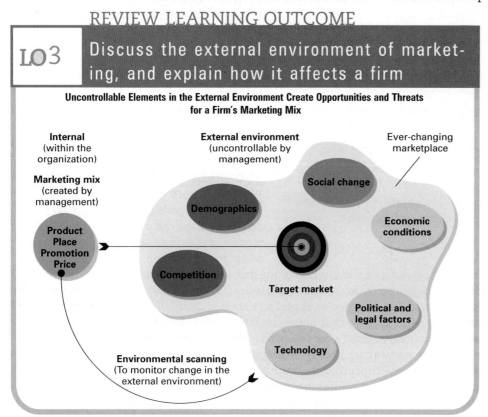

REVIEW LEARNING OUTCOME

LO3 Discuss the external environment of marketing, and explain how it affects a firm

Uncontrollable Elements in the External Environment Create Opportunities and Threats for a Firm's Marketing Mix

Internal (within the organization)

Marketing mix (created by management)

Product Place Promotion Price

External environment (uncontrollable by management)

Ever-changing marketplace

Social change

Demographics

Economic conditions

Competition

Target market

Political and legal factors

Technology

Environmental scanning (To monitor change in the external environment)

LO4
Social Factors

Social change is perhaps the most difficult external variable for marketing managers to forecast, influence, or integrate into marketing plans. Social factors include our attitudes, values, and lifestyles. Social factors influence the products people buy, the prices paid for products, the effectiveness of specific promotions, and how, where, and when people expect to purchase products.

AMERICAN VALUES

A *value* is a strongly held and enduring belief. During the United States' first 200 years, four basic values strongly influenced attitudes and lifestyles:

- *Self-sufficiency*: Every person should stand on his or her own two feet.

- *Upward mobility*: Success would come to anyone who got an education, worked hard, and played by the rules.

- *Work ethic*: Hard work, dedication to family, and frugality were moral and right.

- *Conformity*: No one should expect to be treated differently from everybody else.

environmental management
When a company implements strategies that attempt to shape the external environment within which it operates.

One social factor that has recently had an important impact on the marketing of food products is the popularity of the South Beach diet. Since the diet restricts intake of carbohydrates, manufacturers of breads, cereals, and snack foods, like Frito-Lay, have retooled product offerings and promotional messages to appeal to this growing market segment and to maintain demand for their products.

These core values still hold for a majority of Americans today. A person's values are key determinants of what is important and not important, what actions to take or not to take, and how one behaves in social situations.

People typically form values through interaction with family, friends, and other influencers such as teachers, religious leaders, and politicians. The changing environment can also play a key role in shaping one's values. For example, people born during the 1980s and 1990s tend to be more comfortable with technology and its importance in the home than persons born in the 1960s.

Values influence our buying habits. Today's consumers are demanding, inquisitive, and discriminating. No longer willing to tolerate products that break down, they are insisting on high-quality goods that save time, energy, and often calories. U.S. consumers rank the characteristics of product quality as (1) reliability, (2) durability, (3) easy maintenance, (4) ease of use, (5) a trusted brand name, and (6) a low price. Shoppers are also concerned about nutrition and want to know what's in their food, and many have environmental concerns.

THE GROWTH OF COMPONENT LIFESTYLES

People in the United States today are piecing together **component lifestyles.** A lifestyle is a mode of living; it is the way people decide to live their lives. In other words, they are choosing products and services that meet diverse needs and interests rather than conforming to traditional stereotypes.

In the past, a person's profession—for instance, banker—defined his or her lifestyle. Today, a person can be a banker and also a gourmet, fitness enthusiast, dedicated single parent, and Internet guru. Each of these lifestyles is associated with different goods and services and represents a target audience. For example, for the gourmet, marketers offer cooking utensils, wines, and exotic foods through magazines like *Bon Appetit* and *Gourmet.* The fitness enthusiast buys adidas equipment and special jogging outfits and reads *Runner* magazine. Component lifestyles increase the complexity of consumers' buying habits. The banker may own a BMW but change the oil himself or herself. He or she may buy fast food for lunch but French wine for dinner, own sophisticated photographic equipment and a low-priced home stereo, and shop for socks at Kmart or Wal-Mart and suits or dresses at Brooks Brothers. The unique lifestyles of every consumer can require a different marketing mix.

THE CHANGING ROLE OF FAMILIES AND WORKING WOMEN

component lifestyles
The practice of choosing goods and services that meet one's diverse needs and interests rather than conforming to a single, traditional lifestyle.

Component lifestyles have evolved because consumers can choose from a growing number of goods and services, and most have the money to exercise more options. The growth of dual-income families has resulted in increased purchasing power. Approximately 63 percent of all females between 16 and 65 years old are now in the workforce. Today, more than 9 million women-owned businesses in the United States generate $3.6 trillion in revenues.[12] The phenomenon of working women has probably had a greater effect on marketing than any other social change.

As women's earnings grow, so do their levels of expertise, experience, and authority. Working-age women are not the same group businesses targeted 30 years ago. They expect different things in life—from their jobs, from their spouses, and from the products and services they buy. Not all companies understand this notion. Even though women spend about $55 billion of the total $95 billion spent on consumer electronics, experts say companies continue to assume women aren't very interested in high-tech products or respond only to "technology-made-simple" themes.[13]

Not only do women purchase the bulk of technology products, but they also still do most of the grocery shopping. In one study by Baltimore-based Vertis, 85 percent of the women surveyed said that they personally do 60 percent or more of the household grocery shopping. Of the women surveyed, about 71 percent of those who read grocery advertising inserts make lists and plan their grocery shopping trips around the items they see advertised. About 48 percent of Generation X women (those born between 1965 and 1978) who read advertising inserts said they regularly use coupons from the inserts or circulars.[14]

Nearly 30 percent of the women reported that the Internet was very important for their retail-related decisions compared to 14 percent who said the same about newspapers, 4 percent about magazines, 3 percent about radio, and just 6 percent who said the same thing about TV.[15]

Mothers, in particular, are finding the Internet to be a useful tool for shopping decisions. A study by America Online found that 80 percent of mothers in the United States who are online save time every week by using the Internet to do chores and other activities. About 75 percent use the Internet for planning and researching trips, 67 percent do research on products to buy, 66 percent get health information, and 55 percent search for discounts and coupons. Overall, mothers who use the Internet spend an average of seven hours per week online, not including at-work usage.[16]

Marriage is a declining institution in America. In the 1950s, the likelihood that someone would be married during his or her lifetime was 95 percent. Today, it's only 85 percent.[17]

Whereas 80 percent of all households in the 1950s included a married couple, just above 50 percent do today. The traditional American family of two adults with kids at home accounted for 40 percent of U.S. households in 1970. Today, that percentage has fallen below 25 percent for the first time ever, and it's projected to be only 20 percent by 2010.[18]

The shift has been to single households, which now outnumber married households with kids. In 1970, the reverse was true by a margin of more than two to one. Single people made up 17 percent of U.S. households in 1970. Today, they account for more than 25 percent, and that percentage is projected to grow to 30 percent by 2010. Already, single people account for 42 percent of the workforce, 40 percent of home buyers, and 35 percent of voters. Single-parent households have also grown from 11 to 16 percent. One-third of children born today have single parents.[19]

Single working women are now the second largest group of home buyers after couples. Both Home Depot and Lowe's estimate that about half of all purchases in their stores are made by women. In addition, married women often influence buying decisions made as a couple or when the husband shops alone. Currently, all Home Depot stores offer classes and

Single women are now the second largest group of homebuyers after couples. Reflecting this trend are the changing demographics of customers at Home Depot and Lowe's, which both indicate that about half of the purchases made in their stores are by women. As a result, both companies have made adjustments to how they market to women.

clinics that are open to both men and women. Several years ago the company began offering women-only classes in some stores as an alternative to *Monday Night Football*.

THERE IS NEVER ENOUGH TIME

Research shows that the large percentage of people who say they never have enough time to do all that they need to do keeps inching up. In 2001, it was 73 percent; in 2002, 75 percent; in 2003, 76 percent; in 2004, 77 percent. Year to year, these shifts are unremarkable, but over several years clearly ever more people are worried about having too little time.[20]

Over 31 percent of college-educated male workers are regularly working 50 or more hours a week, up from 22 percent in 1980. About 40 percent of American adults get less than seven hours of sleep on weekdays, up from 34 percent in 2001. Almost 60 percent of meals are rushed, and 34 percent of lunches are eaten on the run.[21] To manage their scarce time, about 74 percent of working adults engage in multitasking—doing more than one thing at a time.[22] They're talking on their cell phones while rushing to work or school, answering e-mails during conference calls, waking up at 4 A.M., and generally multitasking day and night.

Not only is there not enough time available, but BlackBerrys, cell phones, e-mail, and other high-tech gear are eroding traditional boundaries between the office, school, and home. As a result, most Americans feel that they don't have enough time for their families. But many busy families are learning to turn technology to their advantage, using it to stay in touch and, at the same time, increase family time. Forty-eight percent of working women have increased their use of the Internet in the past 12 months. The Internet saves shopping time and enables working women to stay in touch with their families.

REVIEW LEARNING OUTCOME

LO4 Describe the social factors that affect marketing

Time pressure

Component lifestyles

Values

Changing role of women

Social Factors

LO5
Demographic Factors

Another uncontrollable variable in the external environment—also extremely important to marketing managers—is **demography**, the study of people's vital statistics, such as their age, race and ethnicity, and location. Demographics are significant because the basis for any market is people. Demographic characteristics are strongly related to consumer buyer behavior in the marketplace.

We turn our attention now to a closer look at age groups, their impact, and the opportunities they present for marketers. The cohorts have been given the names of tweens, Generation Y, Generation X, and baby boomers. You will find that each cohort group has its own needs, values, and consumption patterns.

TWEENS

They watch cable channels designed just for them, they cruise the Net with ease, they know what they want—and often get it. They are America's tweens (today's pre- and early adolescents, ages 8 to 14), a population 29 million strong. With attitudes, access to information, and sophistication well beyond their years and purchasing power to match, each of these young consumers will spend an average of $1,500 in 2007, for an aggregate total of $39 billion. Add to this the nearly $126 billion parents will spend on their tweens by year-end, a number expected to balloon to $150 billion by 2008, and one grasps the importance and potential of this market.

Tweens overwhelmingly (92 percent) recognize television commercials for what they are—"just advertising." About three-quarters regard billboards and radio spots as paid

demography
The study of people's vital statistics, such as their age, race and ethnicity, and location.

advertising, and about half recognize promotional mediums such as product placements on television shows.[23]

Just because tweens get the business motive behind ads, however, doesn't mean they are averse to them. Of the tweens surveyed, 43 percent think advertising is "funny," 39 percent find it "informative," and around 35 percent consider it "entertaining" or "interesting." Yet tweens are discerning. A majority of the tweens surveyed (52 percent) said they tune out during television commercials, mainly because the commercials are repeats or are "boring."[24]

Tweens around the world are emerging as "the richest generation" and "the most influential generation in history" as the "Global Perspectives" box describes.

GENERATION Y

Those designated by demographics as **Generation Y** were born between 1979 and 1994. They are about 60 million strong, more than three times as large as Generation X. And though Generation Y is much smaller than the baby boom, which lasted nearly 20 years and produced 78 million children, its members are plentiful enough to put their own footprints on society. Most Gen Yers are the children of baby boomers and hence are also referred to as "echo boomers."

Gen Yers range from college graduates to kids still in their tween years. They already spend nearly $200 billion annually and over their lifetimes will likely spend about $10 trillion.[26] Some have already started their careers and are making major purchasing decisions such as cars and homes; at the very least, they are buying lots of computers, MP3 players, cell phones, DVDs, and sneakers.

Researchers have found Gen Yers to be:

- *Impatient:* Gen Y has grown up in a world that's always been automated, and they've had access to computers, CD-ROMs, the Internet, DVD players, chat rooms, instant messaging, and the like, for as long as they can remember, so it's no surprise that they expect things to be done *now.*

- *Family-oriented:* Unlike Gen X before them, overall Gen Yers had relatively stable childhoods. They also grew up in a very family-focused time when even big companies strived to become more family- and kid-friendly. It's the generation that inspired spin-off stores like babyGap and the makeover of Las Vegas into a family vacation destination.

- *Inquisitive:* Knowing more than their parents about computers and technology has always been a source of pride for the echo boomers. It's led to a natural inquisitiveness that many still possess. They want to know why things happen, how things work, and what they can do next.

- *Opinionated:* From the time they were children, Gen Yers have been encouraged to share their opinions by their parents, teachers, and other authority figures. That's translated to a group who feel that their opinions are always needed and welcomed.

- *Diverse:* This is the most ethnically diverse generation the nation has ever seen, and many don't identify themselves as being only one race. Consequently, they're much more accepting overall of people who are different from themselves.

- *Time managers:* Their entire lives have been scheduled—from playgroups to soccer camp to Little League. So, it's no surprise that they've picked up a knack for planning along the way.

- *"Street Smart":* The term isn't used in the literal sense, but simply means that these young people have seen a lot. With the Internet and 24-hour cable TV news exposing them to recounts of violence, war, and sexuality at a young age, they're

Generation Y
People born between 1979 and 1994.

Tweens around the World

Across the globe, an endless variety of disposable goods and leisure products are being designed specifically for tweens. By the time they reach their tween years, young people today are already experienced consumers and savvy about advertising. Consider that an average child in the United States, Australia, and the United Kingdom sees between 20,000 and 40,000 commercials a year. Children spend 60 percent more time watching television each year than they spend in school. Children's financial spending has roughly doubled every ten years over the past three decades. Today, tweens are estimated to control and influence an astounding $1.18 trillion per year around the globe via their pocket money and their general influence on their parents' purchasing decisions. And this is exactly where this generation differs from previous generations—their ability to influence their parents to a degree never seen before.

Three aspects of this generation make them extremely interesting. First, in addition to being a very rich generation with considerable financial potential, they have a remarkable ability to persuade their parents. Studying tweens across 11 countries, researchers learned that in most countries including the United States, the United Kingdom, Australia, Germany, and other northern European countries, tweens have developed highly persuasive skills. They can muster well-planned arguments to help ensure that family purchases go their way.

Secondly, tweens affect their parents' brand choices—even when the brand is aimed at the parents. New research from more than 70 cities in the United States and 14 other countries throughout Europe, Asia, and South America, reveals that in up to 80 percent of all brand choices, tweens control the final decision. Even when it comes to the choice of a car, more than 60 percent of all tweens have a substantial influence on the final decision.

Finally, tweens put a premium on straight talk and are drawn to brands that project utter confidence and offer full-on accountability. Procter & Gamble has launched several campaigns based precisely on this straight-talk philosophy. Its Old Spice High Endurance deodorant put its reputation on the line with a money-back guarantee and an invitation to phone 1-800-PROVEIT. The tweens love it—and they've embraced the brand and the product.

Tweens hate brands that take themselves too seriously, but embrace those that are able to laugh at themselves. The Yoo-hoo Chocolate Beverage Corporation is not afraid to make fun of itself by sending a garbage truck painted in the brand's signature yellow and blue to hand out samples of its chocolate milk. The man behind the drink, the top flavor guru, is Dr. Yoo-hoo, who's introduced as "The Tsar of Tastiness! The Sultan of Scrumptiousness! The Maharaja of Mmmmm."[25]

Why do you think that tweens have so much influence on brand choice within the family? Do you think that this varies from country to country? How would companies like Dell and Ford effectively promote brands to tweens?

---

not easily shocked. They're much more aware of the world around them than earlier generations were.[27]

Gen Yers are the most sophisticated generation ever when it comes to media. They create their own Web sites, make their own CDs and DVDs, and take a cynical view of packaged messages. Instead, they take their cues from each other. A well-placed product on one of their pop idols, like Paris Hilton and Ashton Kutcher, can launch a brand of $40 T-shirts and trucker hats. But they also shop at vintage clothing shops.

One of the things that can reach this generation is word of mouth. In marketing to them, buzz is more important than ever before. Toyota is already betting hundreds of millions of dollars that it can create that buzz by launching an entire new car division aimed exclusively at echo boomers. "They've affected clothing. They've affected beverages. And now, they're just about to affect the car business," says Jim Farley, head of Toyota's Scion division.[28] Toyota is quietly promoting its new $15,000 cars, with air conditioning and power windows, by sponsoring events like street basketball/break dance festivals, where it always has cars on hand for people to look at and sometimes even test-drive. "People kind of just stumble on our products, and it's cool that way," says Farley. "That's what the company wants. This is like regular car companies are on TV. This is our regular activity. This is how we expose our cars to young people."[29]

Gen Yers tend to prefer word of mouth promotion to traditional advertising. Toyota has taken advantage of this preference by using its promotion budget to sponsor street events and create an informal buzz around its Scion division.

Seventy percent of Scion's promotion budget is spent on such events. Only 30 percent is spent on traditional advertising, and much of that is on the Internet, where Gen Yers can fill out a Scion order form, customize their car with 40 different options, and drop off the form at the dealership without ever hearing a sales pitch.

GENERATION X

Generation X—people born between 1965 and 1978—consists of 40 million consumers. It was the first generation of latchkey children—products of dual-career households or, in roughly half of the cases, of divorced or separated parents. Gen Xers have been bombarded by multiple media since their cradle days; thus, they are savvy and cynical consumers.

With careers launched and families started, Gen Xers are at the stage in life when suddenly a host of demands are competing for their time—and their budgets. As a result, Gen X spending is quite diffuse: food, housing, transportation. Time is at a premium for harried Gen Xers, so they're outsourcing the tasks of daily life, which include everything from domestic help to babysitting. Xers spend 78 percent more than average on personal services, more than any other age group, and therefore spend 15 percent less than average on housekeeping supplies.[30]

Over the next 10 years, most Gen Xers will enter into their 40s, historically individuals' money-making years. Over the past 30 years, people aged 45 to 54 earned 60 percent more on average than any other age group.

Although Gen Xers are buying homes and spending money to decorate and renovate them, most companies still ignore them, focusing instead on the larger demographic groups—baby boomers and Gen Y. However, some furniture retailers, such as Williams-Sonoma's Pottery Barn and Crate & Barrel, target Gen Xers who want to mix and match different styles. Ethan Allen is now attracting Gen Xers with its new TV ads. Williams-Sonoma also appeals to more Gen Xers with West Elm, its newer furniture concept, which offers edgier designs and lower prices than those found at Pottery Barn.

Gen Xers are careful shoppers when it comes to home furnishings. Some 31 percent of Gen Xers polled said they checked at least four stores before buying, and 65 percent held no loyalty to any retail brand (only 13 percent did) while 41 percent said they'd shop at any store "that had a good deal." Asked what furniture brands come immediately to mind, the largest bloc of respondents (35 percent) said "none," and 70 percent cited brand as the least important factor in buying.[31]

Gen Xers are a highly desired target for travel providers such as Holiday Inn Select. Gen Xers have no qualms about taking a midweek trip for fun as many work at home and have more flexibility than baby boomers who tend to take weekend or week-long vacations. "The influence of Gen X is going to drive affinity for midweek business, and brands that respond well to their preferences are the ones that will get the lion's share of the Gen X business," said Mark Snyder, senior vice president for brand management at Holiday Inn Hotels and Resorts in the Americas.[32]

Researchers have found that a male Gen X traveler is more likely than a boomer to pick a hotel with a sports bar. But the pub must be genuine and the workout room cutting edge. So Holiday Inn Select is adding *Sporting News* Grill restaurants and Fitness by Nautilus workout centers to its offerings. In-room amenities will include Wolfgang Puck coffee, Moen showerheads, and Garden Botanika bath products.

Why does tailoring the merchandise to particular age groups matter? One reason is that each generation enters a life stage with its own tastes and biases, and tailoring products to what customers value is key to sales.

BABY BOOMERS—AMERICA'S MASS MARKET

When Vespa motor scooters came puttering back into the U.S. market in 2000 after a 15-year absence, managers at the Italian company figured their biggest customers would be twentysomethings looking for a cheap way to get around. But executives at Piaggio, Vespa's parent company, noticed something odd as they scootered back and forth to their Manhattan offices: the most enthusiastic sidewalk gawkers were often aging baby boomers who remembered the candy-colored bikes from their youth. It turns out that boomers have lost none of their affection for Vespa. Better yet, now they can afford to buy top-of-the-line models with all the trimmings. Much to the company's surprise, consumers age 50 and older now buy a quarter of the scooters Vespa sells in the United States.

There are 77 million **baby boomers** (persons born between 1946 and 1964), making them the largest demographic segment in the population today. The oldest have already turned 60 years old. With average life expectancy at an all-time high of 77.4 years, more and more Americans over 50 consider middle age a new start on life. Fewer than 20 percent say they expect to stop work altogether as they age. Of those who plan to keep working at least part-time, 67 percent said they'll do so to stay mentally active, and 57 percent said to stay physically active. People now in their 50s may well work longer than any previous generation; more than 60 percent of men aged 60 to 64 are expected to be in the workforce in 2012, up from about 54 percent in 1992, according to the Bureau of Labor Statistics.[33]

Boomers' incomes will continue to grow as they keep working. As a group, people aged 50 to 60 have more than $1 trillion of spending power a year, about double the spending power of today's 60- to 70-year-olds. They're likely to be vigorous consumers as they empty the nest, take on new jobs, relocate, support the children they had in their 40s, go back to school, start a second or third career, remarry, inherit money from their savings-minded parents, pursue new hobbies, and tackle the health issues of aging.

Many marketers believe that consumers' brand preferences are locked in by age 40. That might have been true for previous generations. But today's over-50 crowd is just as likely, and in some cases more likely, as everyone else to try different brands within a product category. According to Yankelovich, Inc., 33 percent of consumers older than 50 agree that it's "risky" to buy an unfamiliar brand. That's less than the 36 percent of respondents aged 16 to 34 and only a little more than the 30 percent of people aged 35 to 49 who agree with that notion.[34] In some categories such as cosmetics and electronics, older consumers are even more willing to brand-hop than younger ones.

Procter & Gamble's Cover Girl brand, which depends on women older than 55 for about 20 percent of its sales, has just launched its first line of makeup aimed at older women. The name of the product, Advanced Radiance Age-Defying makeup, hints that advancing age can be pretty. And while ads still show a stunningly gorgeous face, that face belongs to an older woman—51-year-old former supermodel Christie Brinkley.

Baby boomers are not a monolithic group. A recent lifestyle study divided this huge market into four segments:

- *"Looking for balance"* boomers: About one-quarter of boomers (27 percent) fall into this very active and busy segment. They represent an excellent market for companies that can offer them time-saving products and services. Though money is important, saving time is equally important to this segment. Companies engaged in travel-related businesses and food-service businesses will find key opportunities here.

- *"Confident and living well"* boomers: Confident and living well boomers represent 23 percent of all boomers. They have the highest incomes of all the segments and relish the chance to be the first to purchase a new product or service. They are technologically oriented and care about what is stylish and trendy. They are the most active boomers, and travel is one of their favorite interests. Marketers offering luxury goods and services will find prime boomer prospects here.

- *"At ease"* boomers: At ease boomers represent 31 percent of all boomers. They are at peace with themselves and do not worry about the future, job security, or financial security. They express the least interest in luxury goods and services and don't travel much. They are the most home-centric and family-oriented segment of the boomers. Marketers of traditional household products and services will find this group of boomers most receptive to their offerings. New products and innovations are least likely to appeal to this group. Established and trusted brand names will resonate most strongly with this boomer segment.

baby boomers
People born between 1946 and 1964.

A generation as unique as this needs a new generation of personal financial planning.

Because your generation is about to reinvent what retirement means.

And we're reinventing the personal financial planning to help get you there.

With more CERTIFIED FINANCIAL PLANNER™ professionals than any other company.

Over a century of financial services experience.

And more than 10,000 personal financial advisors ready to work with you one-to-one, face-to-face, from day one.

Call 1-800-Ameriprise now to get started with a Free-for-Life IRA, or visit us at ameriprise.com.

The Personal Advisors of
Ameriprise
Financial

What's next. Financial Planning ▶ Retirement ▶ Investments ▶ Insurance

*Ameriprise Financial will waive your annual IRA custodial fee for life when you invest $10,000 or more in new assets into a new Traditional, Roth or SEP IRA by April 30, 2006. The annual custodial fee waiver does not include product fees or sales charges. Financial advisory services and investments available through Ameriprise Financial Services, Inc., Member NASD and SIPC. CERTIFIED FINANCIAL PLANNER is a trademark owned by CFP Board. © 2006 Ameriprise Financial, Inc. All rights reserved.

Baby boomers are eager to maintain their active lifestyle, so marketers, like Ameriprise, are finding new ways to reach them as they approach retirement.

- *"Overwhelmed" boomers:* As the smallest segment of the boomer population, overwhelmed boomers represent less than 20 percent of boomers. This group has the lowest income of all the segments. They worry about the future and their financial security. This segment is also the least active, and health is a big concern for them. They are also the least social boomers, spending little time with family and friends. These boomers are also far less accepting of technology and are well below average on using electronic, digital, and tech products.35

AMERICANS ON THE MOVE

The average U.S. citizen moves every six years—a trend that has implications for marketing. A large influx of people into an area creates many new opportunities for all types of businesses. Conversely, significant out-migration from a city or town may force many of its businesses to move or close down and markets to dry up. Most people who move don't go far, however. Sixty percent stay in their home county, and another 20 percent move to another county in the same state.36 The remaining 20 percent are part of a new migration trend from the North to the South and West. A belt stretching from North Carolina south to Florida and then west to California is America's region of net in-migration. Over time cities that lose population like Boston, Cleveland, Detroit, Milwaukee, Minneapolis, Philadelphia, and Toledo, Ohio, could have problems paying for things like health-care services due to a lower tax base. Over the next 20 years, an exodus of 30 million middle-class and affluent households to the South and West will drastically change markets.37

In addition to migration within its borders, the United States experiences immigration from other countries. The six states with the highest levels of immigration from abroad are California, New York, New Jersey, Illinois, Texas, and Massachusetts. The presence of large numbers of immigrants in an area creates a need for markets that cater to their unique needs and desires.

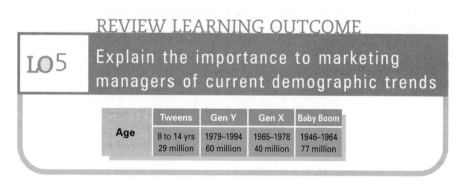

REVIEW LEARNING OUTCOME

LO 5 Explain the importance to marketing managers of current demographic trends

Age	Tweens	Gen Y	Gen X	Baby Boom
	8 to 14 yrs	1979–1994	1965–1978	1946–1964
	29 million	60 million	40 million	77 million

LO 6
Growing Ethnic Markets

By 2008, Hispanics will wield more than $1 trillion in spending power, an increase of 340 percent since 1990. By that same year, African Americans' spending will top $921 billion, and Asian Americans' spending power will have soared over 400 percent since 1990, to $526 billion—far outpacing total U.S. growth in buying power.38

Hispanics are America's largest minority group with 12.5 percent of the population followed by African Americans with 12.3 percent and Asian Americans with 3.6 percent.39 In both Texas and California, minorities now account for over half of the population. The same is also true for Hawaii and New Mexico, but this has been the case for many years. The projected U.S. population by race in 2050 is shown in Exhibit 3.4.

Exhibit 3.4

U.S. Population by Race

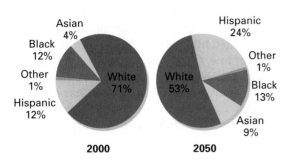

2000   2050

SOURCE: U.S. Census Bureau.

Companies across the United States have recognized that diversity can result in bottom-line benefits. More than ever, diversity is emerging as a priority goal for visionary leaders who embrace the incontestable fact that the United States is becoming a truly multicultural society. Smart marketers increasingly are reaching out and tapping these growing markets. Recently, Pepsi attributed one percentage point of its 7.4 percent revenue growth, or about $250 million, to new products inspired by diversity efforts. Those products included guacamole-flavored Doritos chips and Gatorade Xtremo, aimed at Hispanics, and Mountain Dew Code Red, which tends to appeal to African Americans.[40]

MARKETING TO HISPANIC AMERICANS

The term *Hispanic* encompasses people of many different backgrounds. Nearly 60 percent of Hispanic Americans are of Mexican descent. The next largest group, Puerto Ricans, make up just under 10 percent of Hispanics. Other groups, including Central Americans, Dominicans, South Americans, and Cubans, each account for less than 5 percent of all Hispanics.[41]

The diversity of the Hispanic population and the language differences create many challenges for those trying to target this market. Hispanics, especially recent immigrants, often prefer products from their native country. Therefore, many retailers along the southern U.S. border import goods from Mexico. In New York City, more than 6,000 *bodegas* (grocery stores) sell such items as plantains, chorizo (pork sausage), and religious candles to Puerto Rican Americans. The *bodegas* also serve as neighborhood social centers. Fresh produce is usually very important to Hispanics because of the tradition of shopping every day at open-air produce markets in their native country.

In general, Hispanics tend to be very brand loyal, but they often are not aware of many mainstream U.S. brands. Instead, many Hispanics are loyal to the brands found in their homeland. If these are not available, Hispanics will choose brands that reflect their native values and culture. This preference for brands from home has helped Mexico's Jarritos become one of the fastest-growing soft drinks in the United States. Yet until recently it was *una marca desapareciendo*—a dying brand. Despite having name recognition in its homeland that rivaled that of Coca-Cola, the 55-year-old soda was losing ground to imported U.S. rivals. So parent company Novamex boldly crossed the border. In the past few years, it has moved onto the competition's turf with marketing that speaks to Mexican Americans' thirst for the good old days. Today, Jarritos's 11 flavors are sold in more than 50,000 U.S. outlets. Sales at privately held Novamex, which now distributes 11 Mexican brands, are set to grow 23 percent this year to an estimated $225 million, thanks mostly to Jarritos.[42]

Wal-Mart has been the largest retailer in Mexico since 2000. But until recently, it has taken a low key approach to targeting Hispanics in the United States. Now the world's largest retailer is stepping up efforts to attract America's fastest-growing immigrant group. In 2004, Wal-Mart began printing its monthly ad circulars in English and Spanish. It also launched its own Hispanic magazine, called *Viviendo* (Living), which it distributes free at 1,300 stores heavily shopped by Hispanics. The glossy quarterly magazine features profiles of Latino leaders and celebrities next to ads highlighting Wal-Mart's expanding line of products and services geared toward Hispanics.

In another move, Wal-Mart recently teamed up with Sprint to offer a new prepaid wireless service expressly targeted to Hispanics. Wal-Mart is also stocking a line of bathroom and tabletop accessories from New York restaurateur and cookbook author Zarela Martinez, whose designs are inspired by Mexican folk art and culture. And Wal-Mart's three-year-old financial-services department offers cut-rate fees on money wire transfers, a big lure for immigrants who support family back home.[43]

About 12 million U.S. Hispanics—nearly half of all adult U.S. Hispanics—have home Internet access. Hispanics who use the Internet are, on average, much younger than the general online population. Sixty-three percent of Hispanics who have Internet access use the Web to look for information, rather than to play games or hang out in chat rooms, versus 52 percent of the general population.[44] Kraft Foods has realized that the Net is a good way to connect with Hispanics. The company launched **http://www.comidakraft.com**, where Hispanics can share or post their recipes online, through what's called the Recipe Connection. The Recipe Connection page encourages Hispanic consumers to submit a favorite recipe containing at least one Kraft food product, "perhaps one that has been passed down in your family or an original creation from your own kitchen." Many of the recipes later appear in the magazine, *comida y familia,* a Spanish-language recipe index published by Kraft.

MARKETING TO AFRICAN AMERICANS

Many firms are creating new and different products for the African American market. Often entrepreneurial African Americans are the first to realize unique product opportunities. For example, when Yla Eason couldn't find an African American superhero doll to buy for her son, she founded Olmec Corporation. Now this New York–based toy manufacturer is a $2 million company, marketing more than 60 kinds of African American and Hispanic dolls. Eason has a distribution partnership with Hasbro.

Several companies owned by African Americans—such as Soft Sheen, M&M, Johnson, and ProLine—target the African American market for health and beauty aids. Huge corporations like Revlon, Gillette, and Alberto-Culver have either divisions or major product lines for this market as well. Alberto-Culver's hair-care line for this segment includes 75 products. In fact, hair-care items are the largest single category in the African American health and beauty aid industry. Maybelline with its Shades of You product line has the largest share (28 percent) of the African American health and beauty aid market.

Allstate has been targeting black consumers for several decades. Each year it spends more of its advertising budget to reach the African American market. Allstate offers *The Black Enterprise African American Travel Guide* and gives away Allstate-branded hand fans, extolling Allstate's aid to black families, at churches with predominantly black congregations. The African American twist Allstate adds to its "You're in good hands . . ." tagline is the connotation, "Only Allstate respects you enough to give you the insurance experience you truly deserve."[45]

The promotional dollars spent on African Americans continue to rise, as does the number of black media choices. BET, the black cable TV network, has 62 million viewers.[46] The 36-year-old *Essence* magazine reaches one-third of all black females ages 18 to 49. But radio holds a special appeal. African Americans spend considerable time with radio (an astounding 4 hours a day versus 2.8 hours for other groups), and urban audiences have an intensely personal relationship with the medium. ABC Radio Network's Tom Joyner reaches an audience of 7 million in 100 markets, and Doug Banks is heard by 1.5 million listeners in 36 markets. Pepsi used radio to raise the level of Mountain Dew awareness and its market share in urban markets. Artists like Busta Rhymes personify the image of Mountain Dew and create the lyrics and the vibe that sells the product.

During Black History Month, Pepsi asked African American students to "Write Your Own History." Pepsi created a Web site featuring black history and art where "Write Your Own History" entry forms were readily available. Retail tie-ins with major chain stores also provided entry points for the contest, which awarded 10 college tuition scholarships of $10,000 as first prizes, Dell computers as second prizes, as well as software and 12-packs of Pepsi.

MARKETING TO ASIAN AMERICANS

Asian Americans, who represent only 4.2 percent of the U.S. population, have the highest average family income of all groups. At $66,500, it exceeds the average U.S. household income by more than $10,000. Sixty percent of all Asian Americans have at least a bachelor's degree.[47]

Because Asian Americans are younger and better educated and have higher incomes than average, they are sometimes called a "marketer's dream." Not only is their purchasing power expected to grow, but as a group, Asian Americans are more comfortable with technology than the general population is. They are far more likely to use automated teller machines, and many more of them own DVD players, compact disc players, microwave ovens, home computers, and telephone answering machines.

Multicultural Marketing Resources
As a marketer, what does MMR have to help you with multicultural marketing? Consider attending events posted to the MMR calendar that will take place in your area.
http://www.multiculturalmarketingresources.com

Online

A number of products have been developed specifically for the Asian American market. For example, Kayla Beverly Hills salon draws Asian American consumers because the firm offers cosmetics formulated for them. Anheuser-Busch's agricultural products division targets the Asian American market with eight varieties of California-grown rice, each with a different label, to cover a range of nationalities and tastes.

Cultural diversity within the Asian American market complicates promotional efforts. "There really isn't one Asian American market," says Nancy Shimamoto of San Francisco–based Hispanic & Asian Marketing Research, Inc., a division of Cheskin.[48] Instead, she says, marketers must recognize the cultural and linguistic differences that exist among the Chinese American, Filipino, Japanese, Vietnamese, Korean, Indian, and Pakistani markets. "There is absolutely no common language or culture, and to find the ties that bind is extraordinarily difficult," she says.[49]

Although Asian Americans embrace the values of the larger U.S. population, they also hold on to the cultural values of their particular subgroup. Consider language. Many Asian Americans, particularly Koreans and Chinese, speak their native tongue at home. Filipinos are far less likely to do so. Or consider big-ticket purchases. In Japanese American homes, the husband alone makes the decision on such purchases nearly half the time; the wife decides only about 6 percent of the time. In Filipino families, however, wives make these decisions a little more often than their husbands do, although by far the most decisions are made by husbands and wives jointly or with the input of other family members.[50]

Asian Americans like to shop at stores owned and managed by other Asian Americans. Small businesses such as flower shops, grocery stores, and appliance stores are often best equipped to offer the products that Asian Americans want. For example, at first glance the Ha Nam supermarket in Los Angeles's Koreatown might be any other grocery store. But next to the Kraft American singles and the State Fair corn dogs are jars of whole cabbage kimchi. A snack bar in another part of the store cooks up aromatic mung cakes, and an entire aisle is devoted to dried seafood.

Some entrepreneurs are building large enclosed malls that cater to Asian consumers. At the Aberdeen Centre near Vancouver, British Columbia, nearly 80 percent of the merchants are Chinese Canadians, as are 80 percent of the customers. The mall offers fashions made in Hong Kong, a shop for traditional Chinese medicines, and a theater showing Chinese movies. Kung fu martial-arts demonstrations and Chinese folk dances are held in the mall on weekends.

ETHNIC AND CULTURAL DIVERSITY

Multiculturalism occurs when all major ethnic groups in an area—such as a city, county, or census tract—are roughly equally represented. Because of its current demographic transition, the trend in the United States is toward greater multiculturalism.

San Francisco County is the most diverse county in the nation. The proportions of major ethnic groups are closer to being equal there than anywhere else. People of many ancestries have long been attracted to the area. Elsewhere, however, a careful examination of the statistics from the latest U.S. Census Bureau reveals that the nation's minority groups, especially Hispanics and Asians, are heavily clustered in selected regions and markets. Rather than witnessing the formation of a homogeneous national melting pot, we are seeing the creation of numerous mini-melting pots, while the rest of America remains much less diverse.

multiculturalism
When all major ethnic groups in an area—such as a city, county, or census tract—are roughly equally represented.

In a broad swath of the country, the minority presence is still quite limited. America's racial and ethnic patterns have taken on distinctly regional dimensions. Hispanics dominate large portions of counties in a span of states stretching from California to Texas. Blacks are strongly represented in counties of the South as well as selected urban areas in the Northeast and Midwest. The Asian presence is relatively small and highly concentrated in a few scattered counties, largely in the West. And Native Americans are concentrated in select pockets in Oklahoma, the Southeast, the upper Midwest, and the West. Multiethnic counties are most prominent in California and the Southwest, with mixes of Asians and Hispanics, or Hispanics and Native Americans.

REVIEW LEARNING OUTCOME

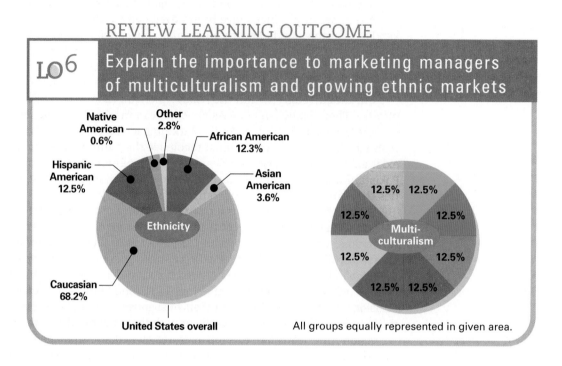

LO6 Explain the importance to marketing managers of multiculturalism and growing ethnic markets

Native American 0.6%
Other 2.8%
African American 12.3%
Hispanic American 12.5%
Asian American 3.6%
Ethnicity
Caucasian 68.2%
United States overall

Multi-culturalism
12.5% 12.5%
12.5% 12.5%
12.5% 12.5%
12.5% 12.5%
All groups equally represented in given area.

LO7
Economic Factors

In addition to social and demographic factors, marketing managers must understand and react to the economic environment. The three economic areas of greatest concern to most marketers are consumers' incomes, inflation, and recession.

CONSUMERS' INCOMES

As disposable (or after-tax) incomes rise, more families and individuals can afford the "good life." In recent years, however, U.S. incomes have risen at a rather slow pace. After adjustment for inflation, the median household income in the United States in 2007 was projected to be approximately $45,000. This means half of all U.S. households earned less and the other half earned more.[51]

Education is the primary determinant of a person's earning potential. For example, only 1 percent of those with only a high school education earn over $100,000 annually. By comparison, 13 percent of college-educated workers earn six figures or more.[52] Along with "willingness to buy," or "ability to buy," income is a key determinant of target markets. A marketer who knows where the money is knows where the markets are. If you are seeking a new store location for Dollar General, a retail chain that caters to lower-income consumers, you would probably concentrate on the South and Midwest because most households with annual incomes of less than $45,000 are concentrated in these areas.

The slow pace of income growth has contributed to another trend: consumers are strapped for cash. Twenty-eight percent of Americans say that once they have paid for their essential living expenses, they have no spare cash; by comparison, only 19 percent of Canadian consumers say the same.[53] So millions of Americans have turned to credit to buy the things they want. Credit gives middle- and lower-income consumers the financial flexibility that only the rich used to enjoy. Since 1990, income for the median American household has risen only 11 percent after adjusting for inflation, but median household spending has jumped by 30 percent. How can the typical family afford to spend so much? Over the same period, median household debt outstanding leaped by 80 percent.[54] Debt, of course, means that consumers must eventually use their income to make interest payments instead of buying more goods and services. Too much debt can ultimately lead to financial ruin.

The Financial Power of Women

Another trend in consumers' income is the growing financial power of women in the United States. Women bring in half or more of the income in the majority of U.S. households and women control 51.3 percent of the private wealth in the United States. Women also control most of the spending in U.S. households—about 80 percent.[55] And, women have become the primary buyers of many types of products including those that are historically male-dominated products. For example, women purchase:

- 68 percent of new cars
- 66 percent of computers
- 60 percent of home improvements
- 53 percent of investments
- 51 percent of consumer electronics[56]

Women are important to marketers because they control the majority of household purchases and bring in the majority of household income. This advertisement for *To the Contrary* explores issues that are important to working mothers.

PURCHASING POWER

Rising incomes don't necessarily mean a higher standard of living. Increased standards of living are a function of purchasing power. **Purchasing power** is measured by comparing income to the relative cost of a set standard of goods and services in different geographic areas, usually referred to as the cost of living. Another way to think of purchasing power is income minus the cost of living (i.e., expenses). In general, a cost of living index takes into account housing, food and groceries, transportation, utilities, health care, and miscellaneous expenses such as clothing, services, and entertainment. Homefair's salary calculator uses these metrics when it figures that the cost of living in New York City is almost three times the cost of living in Youngstown, Ohio. This means that a worker living in New York must earn nearly $279,500 to have the same standard of living as someone making $100,000 in Youngstown.

When income is high relative to the cost of living, people have more discretionary income. That means they have more money to spend on nonessential items (in other words, on wants rather than needs). This information is important to marketers for obvious reasons. Consumers with high purchasing power can afford to spend more money without jeopardizing their budget for necessities, like food, housing, and utilities. They also have the ability to purchase higher-priced necessities, for example, a more expensive car, a home in a more expensive neighborhood, or a designer handbag versus a purse from a discount store.

purchasing power
A comparison of income versus the relative cost of a set standard of goods and services in different geographic areas.

INFLATION

Inflation is a measure of the decrease in the value of money, generally expressed as the percentage reduction in value since the previous year, which is the rate of inflation. Thus, in simple terms an inflation rate of 5 percent means you will need 5 percent more units of money than you would have needed last year to buy the same basket of products. If inflation is 5 percent, you can expect that, on average, prices have risen by about 5 percent since the previous year. Of course, if pay raises are matching the rate of inflation, then employees will be no worse off in terms of the immediate purchasing power of their salaries.

In times of low inflation, businesses seeking to increase their profit margins can do so only by increasing their efficiency. If they significantly increase prices, no one will purchase their goods or services.

In more inflationary times, marketers use a number of pricing strategies to cope. (See Chapter 18 for more on these strategies.) But in general, marketers must be aware that inflation causes consumers to either build up or diminish their brand loyalty. In one research session, a consumer panelist noted, "I used to use just Betty Crocker mixes, but now I think of either Betty Crocker or Duncan Hines, depending on which is on sale." Another participant said, "Pennies count now, and so I look at the whole shelf, and I read the ingredients. I don't really understand, but I can tell if it's exactly the same. So now I use this cheaper brand, and honestly, it works just as well." Inflation pressures consumers to make more economical purchases. Nevertheless, most consumers try hard to maintain their standard of living.

In creating marketing strategies to cope with inflation, managers must realize that, regardless of what happens to the seller's cost, the buyer is not going to pay more for a product than the subjective value he or she places on it. No matter how compelling the justification might be for a 10 percent price increase, marketers must always examine its impact on demand. Many marketers try to hold prices level as long as is practical.

inflation
A measure of the decrease in the value of money, expressed as the percentage reduction in value since the previous year.

recession
A period of economic activity characterized by negative growth, which reduces demand for goods and services.

RECESSION

A **recession** is a period of economic activity characterized by negative growth, which reduces demand for goods and services. During a recession, the growth rates of income, production, and employment all fall below zero percent. For example, in a true recession, you wouldn't just receive a smaller raise than in previous years; your pay would actually be cut. In 2001, the slowdown in the high-tech sector, overextended consumer credit, and the terrorist attacks on America resulted in the economy slipping into a recession that lasted

REVIEW LEARNING OUTCOME

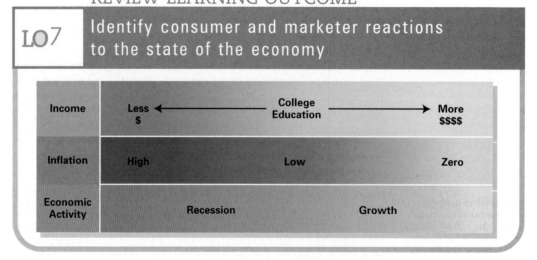

| LO7 | Identify consumer and marketer reactions to the state of the economy |

Income	Less $ ←———— College Education ————→ More $$$$
Inflation	High	Low	Zero
Economic Activity	Recession	Growth

until early 2003. The problems of inflation and recession go hand in hand, yet recession requires different marketing strategies:

- *Improve existing products and introduce new ones:* The goal is to reduce production hours, waste, and the cost of materials. Recessions increase the demand for goods and services that are economical and efficient, offer value, help organizations streamline practices and procedures, and improve customer service.

- *Maintain and expand customer services:* In a recession, many organizations postpone the purchase of new equipment and materials. Sales of replacement parts and other services may become an important source of income.

- *Emphasize top-of-the-line products and promote product value:* Customers with less to spend will seek demonstrated quality, durability, satisfaction, and capacity to save time and money. High-priced, high-value items consistently fare well during recessions.

LO⁸ Technological Factors

Sometimes new technology is an effective weapon against inflation and recession. New machines that reduce production costs can be one of a firm's most valuable assets. The power of a personal-computer microchip doubles about every 18 months. Our ability, as a nation, to maintain and build wealth depends in large part on the speed and effectiveness with which we invent and adopt machines that lift productivity. For example, coal mining is typically thought of as unskilled, backbreaking labor. But visit Cyprus Amax Mineral Company's Twenty-mile Mine near Oak Creek, Colorado, and you will find workers with push-button controls who walk along massive machines that shear 30-inch slices from an 850-foot coal wall. Laptop computers help miners track equipment breakdowns and water quality.

RESEARCH

The United States excels at both basic and applied research. **Basic research** (or *pure research*) attempts to expand the frontiers of knowledge but is not aimed at a specific, pragmatic problem. Basic research aims to confirm an existing theory or to learn more about a concept or phenomenon. For example, basic research might focus on high-energy physics. **Applied research,** in contrast, attempts to develop new or improved products. The United States has dramatically improved its track record in applied research. For example, the United States leads the world in applying basic research to aircraft design and propulsion systems.

Rather than invention for the sake of invention, many firms are turning to the marketing concept to guide their research. To give its scientists guidance, Dow first interviews customers to find out their wants and needs. A wish list of products and/or technical characteristics helps the scientists create inventions with market value. Dow recently created a fiber called XLA after learning that apparel makers wanted a "soft stretch" fiber with a natural feel. Dow thinks that the product might deliver sales of $300 million within ten years.

Although developing new technology internally is a key to creating and maintaining a long-term competitive advantage, external technology is also important to managers for two reasons. First, by acquiring the technology, the firm may be able to operate more efficiently or create a better product. Second, a new technology may render your existing products obsolete. The debut of George Eastman's Kodak camera in 1888 marked the birth of film-based photography. In 2003, for the first time digital cameras outsold traditional cameras that use film. You can imagine the profound impact this shift has had on Kodak. The firm has been struggling ever since.

basic research
Pure research that aims to confirm an existing theory or to learn more about a concept or phenomenon.

applied research
An attempt to develop new or improved products.

mVibe presents:

The evolution of breaking news.

Newsboy, c. 1950s   Mobile phone, c. 2005

Daily text alerts from mVIBE.
Just text **JOIN** to mVIBE (68423) to sign up!

Get the low down straight from the street.

*Get bling for your mobile phone with
ringtones, wallpapers, and more from mVIBE!
Visit mobile.vibe.com and get your download on!

DG
MVIBE

New technologies are creating opportunities for marketers who want to observe emerging consumer opinions. This advertisement for MVibe emphasizes immediate delivery.

GLOBAL INNOVATION

Microsoft spent $80 million to open an Advanced Technology Center outside Beijing, China. With nearly 500 engineers, Ph.D. students, and visiting professors, it is one of Microsoft's most important facilities for developing graphics, handwriting-recognition, and voice-synthesizing technologies. The technology center illustrates how innovation is increasingly becoming a global process conducted at worldwide research and development operations. Like Microsoft, IBM has facilities around the world including major labs in China, Israel, Switzerland, Japan, and India.

General Electric has become a leader in wind energy technology by tapping into a global network. The technology for GE's new wind turbines comes from the following countries:

- *United States.:* The main research center in Niskayuna, New York, handles basic research, while other centers in New York, Pennsylvania, South Carolina, California, and Virginia tackle other design and engineering aspects.

- *Canada:* Engineers at GE Consumer & Industrial in Peterborough, Ontario, provided the manufacturing technology for the generator.

- *India:* Researchers at Bangalore have crafted a series of analytical models and turbine system design tools that affect the entire turbine.

- *China:* Researchers in Shanghai are in charge of the turbine simulator to test new products and conduct high-end tests for variable-speed power electronics.

- *Germany:* The lead experts on the gearbox work at GE Wind operations in Salzbergen. Researchers in Munich design sensors and monitor advanced controls.[57]

RSS AND BLOGGING

New technologies may also create new opportunities. The recent explosion in the popularity of blogs has presented several intriguing opportunities for marketers. RSS (Really Simple Syndication) enables automated, seamless delivery of updated news content or marketing messages to blog sites or mobile phones. For example, if you are interested in extreme sports, opera, and exotic fish (or whatever), you can set up an RSS feed that will pull down articles on those topics every day. Advancing technology also allows today's marketers to use natural language search technolo gies to scan blogs and learn about consumer opinion as its being generated. Instead of looking for formulas or keywords alone, marketers can use these search tools to scan for speech that reflects how people actually talk and to determine what certain speech patterns and word combinations mean to the speaker. That, in turn, allows marketers to discover what people are saying about their products and how they are saying it. And by expanding their searches to include publicly posted blog content such as photos, user profiles, and hyperlinks, marketers are able to segment markets and profile individuals with newfound speed and accuracy.

REVIEW LEARNING OUTCOME

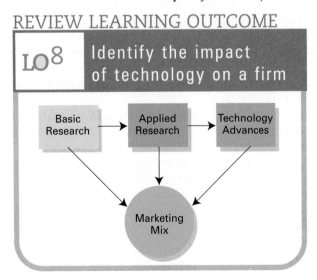

LO8 Identify the impact of technology on a firm

Basic Research → Applied Research → Technology Advances → Marketing Mix

Political and Legal Factors

Business needs government regulation to protect innovators of new technology, the interests of society in general, one business from another, and consumers. In turn, government needs business because the marketplace generates taxes that support public efforts to educate our youth, pave our roads, protect our shores, and so on. The private sector also serves as a counterweight to government. The decentralization of power inherent in a private-enterprise system supplies the limitation on government essential for the survival of a democracy.

Every aspect of the marketing mix is subject to laws and restrictions. It is the duty of marketing managers or their legal assistants to understand these laws and conform to them, because failure to comply with regulations can have major consequences for a firm. Sometimes just sensing trends and taking corrective action before a government agency acts can help avoid regulation. The tobacco industry failed to do this. As a result, Joe Camel and the Marlboro Man are fading into the sunset along with other strategies used to promote tobacco products.

The challenge is not simply to keep the marketing department out of trouble, however, but to help it implement creative new programs to accomplish marketing objectives. It is all too easy for a marketing manager or sometimes a lawyer to say "no" to a marketing innovation that actually entails little risk. For example, an overly cautious lawyer could hold up sales of a desirable new product by warning that the package design could prompt a copyright infringement suit. Thus, it is important to have a thorough understanding of the laws established by the federal government, state governments, and regulatory agencies to govern marketing-related issues.

FEDERAL LEGISLATION

Federal laws that affect marketing fall into several categories. First, the Sherman Act, the Clayton Act, the Federal Trade Commission Act, the Celler-Kefauver Antimerger Act, and the Hart-Scott-Rodino Act were passed to regulate the competitive environment. Second, the Robinson-Patman Act was designed to regulate pricing practices. Third, the Wheeler-Lea Act was created to control false advertising. These key pieces of legislation are summarized in Exhibit 3.5. The primary federal laws that protect consumers are shown in Exhibit 3.6.

Exhibit 3.5

Primary U.S. Laws That Affect Marketing

LEGISLATION	IMPACT ON MARKETING
Sherman Act of 1890	Makes trusts and conspiracies in restraint of trade illegal; makes monopolies and attempts to monopolize a misdemeanor.
Clayton Act of 1914	Outlaws discrimination in prices to different buyers; prohibits tying contracts (which require the buyer of one product to also buy another item in the line); makes illegal the combining of two or more competing corporations by pooling ownership of stock.
Federal Trade Commission Act of 1914	Created the Federal Trade Commission to deal with antitrust matters; outlaws unfair methods of competition.
Robinson-Patman Act of 1936	Prohibits charging different prices to different buyers of merchandise of like grade and quantity; requires sellers to make any supplementary services or allowances available to all purchasers on a proportionately equal basis.
Wheeler-Lea Amendments to the FTC Act of 1938	Broadens the Federal Trade Commission's power to prohibit practices that might injure the public without affecting competition; outlaws false and deceptive advertising.
Lanham Act of 1946	Establishes protection for trademarks.
Celler-Kefauver Antimerger Act of 1950	Strengthens the Clayton Act to prevent corporate acquisitions that reduce competition.
Hart-Scott-Rodino Act of 1976	Requires large companies to notify the government of their intent to merge.

Exhibit 3.6

Primary U.S. Laws Protecting Consumers

Federal Food and Drug Act of 1906	Prohibits adulteration and misbranding of foods and drugs involved in interstate commerce; strengthened by the Food, Drug, and Cosmetic Act (1938) and the Kefauver-Harris Drug Amendment (1962).
Federal Hazardous Substances Act of 1960	Requires warning labels on hazardous household chemicals.
Kefauver-Harris Drug Amendment of 1962	Requires that manufacturers conduct tests to prove drug effectiveness and safety.
Consumer Credit Protection Act of 1968	Requires that lenders fully disclose true interest rates and all other charges to credit customers for loans and installment purchases.
Child Protection and Toy Safety Act of 1969	Prevents marketing of products so dangerous that adequate safety warnings cannot be given.
Public Health Smoking Act of 1970	Prohibits cigarette advertising on TV and radio and revises the health hazard warning on cigarette packages.
Poison Prevention Labeling Act of 1970	Requires safety packaging for products that may be harmful to children.
National Environmental Policy Act of 1970	Established the Environmental Protection Agency to deal with various types of pollution and organizations that create pollution.
Public Health Cigarette Smoking Act of 1971	Prohibits tobacco advertising on radio and television.
Consumer Product Safety Act of 1972	Created the Consumer Product Safety Commission, which has authority to specify safety standards for most products.
Child Protection Act of 1990	Regulates the number of minutes of advertising on children's television.
Children's Online Privacy Protection Act of 1998	Empowers the FTC to set rules regarding how and when marketers must obtain parental permission before asking children marketing research questions.
Aviation Security Act of 2001	Requires airlines to take extra security measures to protect passengers, including the installation of stronger cockpit doors, improved baggage screening, and increased security training for airport personnel.
Homeland Security Act of 2002	Protects consumers against terrorist acts. Created the Department of Homeland Security.
Do Not Call Law of 2003	Protects consumers against unwanted telemarketing calls.
CAN-SPAM Act of 2003	Protects consumers against unwanted e-mail, or spam.

STATE LAWS

Legislation that affects marketing varies state by state. Oregon, for example, limits utility advertising to 0.5 percent of the company's net income. California has forced industry to improve consumer products and has enacted legislation to lower the energy consumption of refrigerators, freezers, and air conditioners. Several states, including New Mexico and Kansas, are considering levying a tax on all in-state commercial advertising.

REGULATORY AGENCIES

Although some state regulatory bodies actively pursue violators of their marketing statutes, federal regulators generally have the greatest clout. The Consumer Product Safety Commission, the Federal Trade Commission, and the Food and Drug Administration are the three federal agencies most directly and actively involved in marketing affairs. These agencies, plus others, are discussed throughout the book, but a brief introduction is in order at this point.

The sole purpose of the **Consumer Product Safety Commission (CPSC)** is to protect the health and safety of consumers in and around their homes. The CPSC has the power to set mandatory safety standards for almost all products that consumers use (about 15,000 items). The CPSC consists of a five-member committee and about 1,100 staff members, including technicians, lawyers, and administrative help. The commission can fine offending firms up to $500,000 and sentence their officers to up to a year in prison. It can also ban dangerous products from the marketplace. Recently, Graco Children's Products agreed to pay $4 million to settle charges that it failed to inform the CPSC in a timely manner that more than 12 million of its products were hazardous to young children.[58]

Consumer Product Safety Commission (CPSC)
A federal agency established to protect the health and safety of consumers in and around their homes.

The **Federal Trade Commission (FTC)** also consists of five members, each holding office for seven years. The FTC is empowered to prevent persons or corporations from using unfair methods of competition in commerce. It is authorized to investigate the practices of business combinations and to conduct hearings on antitrust matters and deceptive advertising. The FTC has a vast array of regulatory powers (see Exhibit 3.7). Nevertheless, it is not invincible. For example, the FTC had proposed to ban all advertising to children under age 8, to ban all advertising of the sugared products that are most likely to cause tooth decay to children under age 12, and to require the food industry to pay for dental health and nutritional advertisements. Business reacted by lobbying to reduce the FTC's power. The two-year lobbying effort resulted in passage of the FTC Improvement Act of 1980. The major provisions of the act are as follows:

> It bans the use of unfairness as a standard for industrywide rules against advertising. All the proposals concerning children's advertising were therefore suspended, because they were based almost entirely on the unfairness standard. It requires oversight hearings on the FTC every six months. This congressional review is designed to keep the commission accountable. Moreover, it keeps Congress aware of one of the many regulatory agencies it has created and is responsible for monitoring.

Businesses rarely band together to create change in the legal environment as they did to pass the FTC Improvement Act. Generally, marketing managers react only to legislation, regulation, and edicts. It is usually less costly to stay attuned to the regulatory environment than to fight the government. If marketers had toned down their hard-hitting advertisements to children, they might have avoided an FTC inquiry altogether. The FTC also regulates advertising on the Internet as well as Internet abuses of consumer privacy (discussed in Chapter 8). The **Food and Drug Administration (FDA)**, another powerful agency, is charged with enforcing regulations against selling and distributing adulterated, misbranded, or hazardous food and drug products. In the last decade it took a very aggressive stance against tobacco products and is now paying attention to the fast-food industry.

THE BATTLE OVER CONSUMER PRIVACY

The popularity of the Internet for direct marketing, for collecting consumer data, and as a repository for sensitive consumer data has alarmed privacy-minded consumers. So many online users have complained about "spam," the Internet's equivalent of junk mail, that the U.S. Congress passed the CAN-SPAM Act in an attempt to regulate it. The act, which took effect on January 1, 2004, does not ban spam, but it does prohibit commercial e-mailers from using a false address and presenting false or misleading information. It

Federal Trade Commission
As a marketing manager, how would you use the FTC Web site in designing a new marketing campaign?
http://www.ftc.gov

Online

Federal Trade Commission (FTC)
A federal agency empowered to prevent persons or corporations from using unfair methods of competition in commerce.

Food and Drug Administration (FDA)
A federal agency charged with enforcing regulations against selling and distributing adulterated, misbranded, or hazardous food and drug products.

Exhibit 3.7

Powers of the Federal Trade Commission

REMEDY	PROCEDURE
Cease-and-Desist Order	A final order is issued to cease an illegal practice—and is often challenged in the courts.
Consent Decree	A business consents to stop the questionable practice without admitting its illegality.
Affirmative Disclosure	An advertiser is required to provide additional information about products in advertisements.
Corrective Advertising	An advertiser is required to correct the past effects of misleading advertising. (For example, 25 percent of a firm's media budget must be spent on FTC-approved advertisements or FTC-specified advertising.)
Restitution	Refunds are required to be given to consumers misled by deceptive advertising. According to a 1975 court-of-appeals decision, this remedy cannot be used except for practices carried out after the issuance of a cease-and-desist order.
Counteradvertising	The FTC proposed that the Federal Communications Commission permit advertisements in broadcast media to counteract advertising claims (also that free time be provided under certain conditions).

also requires commercial e-mailers to provide a way for recipients to "opt out" of receiving further e-mail from the sender.

Another problem is that Web surfers, including children who are using the Internet, are routinely asked to divulge personal information in order to access certain screens or purchase goods or services online. Internet users who once felt fairly anonymous when using the Web are now disturbed by the amount of information marketers collect on them and their children as they visit various sites in cyberspace.

Most consumers are unaware of how technology is used to collect personal data or how the personal information is used and distributed after it is collected. The government actively sells huge amounts of personal information to list compilers. State motor vehicle bureaus sell names and addresses of individuals who get driver's licenses. Hospitals sell the names of women who just gave birth on their premises. Consumer credit databases, developed and maintained by large providers such as Equifax Marketing Services and TransUnion, are often used by credit-card marketers to prescreen targets for solicitations.

While privacy policies for companies in the United States are largely voluntary and there are almost no regulations on the collection and use of personal data, collecting consumer data outside the United States is a different matter. Database marketers venturing into new data territories must carefully navigate foreign privacy laws. The European Union's *European Data Protection Directive,* for instance, states that any business that trades with a European organization must comply with the EU's rules for handling information about individuals or risk prosecution. This directive prohibits the export of personal data to countries not doing enough to protect privacy, in particular, the United States.

More than 50 nations have, or are developing, privacy legislation. Europe has the strictest legislation regarding the collection and use of consumer data, and other countries look to that legislation when formulating their policies. Australia, for instance, recently introduced legislation that would require private companies to follow a set of guidelines regarding the collection, storage, use, and transfer of personal information about individuals. Common privacy rules include obtaining data fairly and lawfully, using the information only for the original purpose specified, making sure it is accurate and up-to-date, and destroying data after the purpose for collection is completed. The EU requires that consumers be presented with an opt-out provision at the point of data collection.

Identity Theft

People are right to be concerned about their personal information. Identity theft cost $53 billion in 2005.[59] One company that has come under fire is ChoicePoint. Since spinning off from the credit bureau Equifax in 1997, it has been buying up databases and data-mining operations. Businesses, individuals, and even the FBI now rely on its storehouse. But its customers have also included Nigerian scammers who apparently used the data to steal people's identities.

To ensure that only certain businesses had access to its data, ChoicePoint set up requirements for potential customers, but those safeguards proved unreliable. A man named Olatunji Oluwatosin—and possibly others—used fake names and the fax machine at a Hollywood copy shop to create fictitious small businesses requesting ChoicePoint service. Before Oluwatosin was caught—after someone at ChoicePoint became suspicious about one of his applications—he accessed at least 145,000 names. (Oluwatosin pleaded no contest to felony identity theft in California in February 2005; he is serving a 16-month sentence.)[60] ChoicePoint announced in March 2005 that it will no longer sell consumer data that includes driver's license numbers and Social Security numbers.[61]

Later in 2005, Citi Financial notified 3.9 million customers that computer tapes containing their personal information were missing. Data on the tapes included account information, payment histories, and Social Security numbers.[62] Were the data simply lost? We did not have an answer as the book went to press.

LO9 Discuss the political and legal environment of marketing

Protect Consumers

Protect Consumers Marketers Innovators

Legislation

Consumer	Marketers
Federal – Clayton Act – Robinson-Patman Act – Wheeler-Lea Amendments – All laws in Exhibit 3.6 and all items in Exhibit 3.7	Federal – Sherman Act – Lanham Act – Celler-Kefauver Act – Hart-Scott Rodino Act – Federal Trade Commission Act
State Municipal	State Municipal

Marketing Mix

Agencies

CPSC FDA FTC	FDA FTC

Governmental Actions

Three key laws (one a state law) have been passed to protect consumers from identity theft. The federal laws are:

- *Gramm-Leach-Bliley Act (Financial Services Modernization Act):* This act is aimed at financial companies. It requires those corporations to tell their customers how they use their personal information and to have policies that prevent fraudulent access to it. Partial compliance has been required since 2001.

- *Health Insurance Portability and Accountability Act:* This law is aimed at the health-care industry. It limits disclosure of individuals' medical information and imposes penalties on organizations that violate privacy rules. Compliance has been required for large companies since 2003.

The state law is:

- *California's Notice of Security Breach Law:* If any company or agency that has collected personal information about a California resident discovers that nonencrypted information has been taken by an unauthorized person, the company or agency must tell the resident. Compliance has been required since 2003. (Some 30 other states are considering similar laws.)

LO10
Competitive Factors

The competitive environment encompasses the number of competitors a firm must face, the relative size of the competitors, and the degree of interdependence within the industry. Management has little control over the competitive environment confronting a firm.

COMPETITION FOR MARKET SHARE AND PROFITS

As U.S. population growth slows, costs rise, and available resources tighten, firms find that they must work harder to maintain their profits and market share regardless of the form of the competitive market. Take, for example, the competition among airlines. In the aftermath of September 11, 2001, the airline industry imploded. Proud competitors, including United Airlines, Delta Air Lines, and Northwest Airlines, declared bankruptcy as rising fuel prices added to their woes. American Airlines, the world's largest airline, teetered on the brink of going under. Survival in such a horrific environment meant drastically cutting costs and squeezing out revenue wherever possible. Yet one competitor not only survived, but managed to earn a profit. Southwest Airlines made money and avoided layoffs with its efficient strategy based on one type of plane and lower labor costs.

The airlines' problems have made the competitive environment more challenging for firms in the commercial aircraft industry. American aircraft manufacturer Boeing still faces competition from European company Airbus, even though Airbus recently lost its edge in that $50 billion market. In 2006, Airbus was beset with problems, while Boeing's new 787 Dreamliner gave the company a much needed lift. Marketers tout the Dreamliner's features, which include large windows, mood lighting, electronic shades, wider seats and aisles, and a state-of-the-art climate control system, as providing a unique flying experience.

Boeing's idea is to include an outreach to passengers, along with spreadsheets and fuel consumption data, in its sales pitch to airline executives. Just as Intel created a desire for personal computers containing its microchips and Nokia used its unique cell phone features to drive demand among Verizon and Cingular customers, Boeing intends to create demand for the 787s by including postsale service that highlights to passengers the benefits the planes provide and that are consistent with the carrier's brand. "The more people fly, the more they develop a preference for the type of aircraft they fly in," asserts Robert Pollack, Boeing's vice president for brand and marketing positioning. "A lot more can be done to suggest to consumers that the airline they fly in the future can make a difference in their air travel."[63]

Boeing is betting that creating a bond with consumers by cobranding with partner airlines can give the company an edge against Airbus. The first cobranding effort could come from Continental Airlines, which ordered ten 787s to be delivered in 2009. Already, China Airlines, Air Berlin, and Ryanair have executed campaigns with assistance from Boeing's advertising agency.

The cola wars are another area where competition is brutal. Recently, PepsiCo made Diet Pepsi the star of the company's U.S. marketing efforts—and trimmed advertising spending on sugar-sweetened Pepsi-Cola. Pepsi says it plans to double its marketing spending on Diet Pepsi, while the budget for Pepsi-Cola will fall slightly. The move reflects the continued loss of fizz by Pepsi-Cola, which was invented in 1898 and is the second-biggest brand in the soft-drink aisle.

As part of the reordered priorities, Diet Pepsi will be marketed as a hip, cool brand for everyone, including teenagers and baby boomers. The new campaign will allow Diet Pepsi to escape the advertising shadow of Pepsi-Cola and have its own new tagline, "Light. Crisp. Refreshing."[64] Meanwhile, Pepsi is narrowing its sales pitch for regular Pepsi-Cola to soda drinkers younger than 25, Latinos, African Americans, and sports fans.

Both PepsiCo and Coca-Cola have been reluctant to turn away from having the sugary brand be the leader despite five years of deteriorating sales for regular sodas. As a result, diet sodas—the industry's real growth engine—often have suffered from neglect and inconsistent marketing. Yet, even with their recent struggles, regular sugary soft drinks still account for more than 70 percent of industry sales in the United States and maintain a big presence on store shelves. Overseas, sugared sodas are even more dominant, particularly in developing countries.

REVIEW LEARNING OUTCOME

LO 10 Explain the basics of foreign and domestic competition

Highly Competitive Marketplace

Mature Industries

Slow growth/
No growth

Can only increase market share by taking it from a competitor.

GLOBAL COMPETITION

Boeing, PepsiCo, and Coca-Cola are savvy international competitors conducting business throughout the world. Many foreign competitors also consider the United States to be a ripe target market. Thus, a U.S. marketing manager can no longer focus only on domestic competitors. In automobiles, textiles, watches, televisions, steel, and many other areas, foreign competition has been strong. In the past, foreign firms penetrated U.S. markets by concentrating on price, but today the emphasis has switched to product quality. Nestlé, Sony, Rolls-Royce, and Sandoz Pharmaceuticals are noted for quality, not cheap prices.

© DYSON/PRNEWSFOTO (AP TOPIC GALLERY)

For a century, vacuuming has been synonymous with one brand, whose iconic status is such that the British and French still refer to "hoovering the carpet." But two years after launching his bagless cleaners in the United States, English inventor James Dyson's company now makes America's best-selling vacuum. Dyson has captured 21 percent of the U.S. market, leaving Canton, Ohio–based Hoover with 16 percent. Dyson's clean sweep is all the more surprising given that his product goes for $399 to $550 while an average vacuum costs $150.[65]

Global competition is discussed in much more detail in Chapter 4.

Quick Check ✔

Now that you've read the chapter, do you get it? Take a moment for a quick check using this scale:

1 Not at all; 2 Not very well; 3 Ok; 4 Well; 5 Very Well

Can you . . .

____ define sustainability?

____ outline the levels of corporate social responsibility?

____ describe the levels of ethical development?

____ recite the elements in the external marketing environment?

____ differentiate the generations in terms of their marketing behavior?

____ explain how economic factors influence consumers and marketers?

____ recite the primary U.S. laws that affect marketing?

____ identify how the ethnic composition of the population determines marketing strategy?

____ identify the main U.S. regulatory agencies and explain what they are responsible for?

____ write a paragraph about changing social factors?

____ explain which competitive factors have the greatest impact on marketing?

____ TOTAL

Score: 46–55, you're ready to move on to the applications; 36–45, skim the chapter one more time before moving on to the applications; 26–35, reread the sections giving you the most trouble and go to ThomsonNow for guided tutorials; 25 and under, you better reread the chapter to get a grasp of the fundamentals. If you've reread the chapter and still have a low score, visit your professor or TA during office hours.

Review and Applications

LO 1 Discuss corporate social responsibility. Responsibility in business refers to a firm's concern for the way its decisions affect society. Social responsibility has four components: economic, legal, ethical, and philanthropic. These are intertwined, yet the most fundamental is earning a profit. If a firm does not earn a profit, the other three responsibilities are moot. Most businesspeople believe they should do more than pursue profits. Although a company must consider its economic needs first, it must also operate within the law, do what is ethical and fair, and be a good corporate citizen. The concept of sustainability is that socially responsible companies will outperform their peers by focusing on the world's social problems and viewing them as an opportunity to earn profits and help the world at the same time.

1.2 Describe at least three situations in which you would not purchase the products of a firm even though it is very socially responsible.

1.2 A firm's only responsibility to society is to earn a fair profit. Comment.

1.3 Is sustainability a viable concept for America's businesses?

LO 2 Describe the role of ethics and ethical decisions in business. Business ethics may be viewed as a subset of the values of society as a whole. The ethical conduct of businesspeople is shaped by societal elements, including family, education, religion, and social movements. As members of society, businesspeople are morally obligated to consider the ethical implications of their decisions.

Ethical decision making is approached in three basic ways. The first approach examines the consequences of decisions. The second approach relies on rules and laws to guide decision making. The third approach is based on a theory of moral development that places individuals or groups in one of three developmental stages: preconventional morality, conventional morality, or postconventional morality.

Many companies develop a code of ethics to help their employees make ethical decisions. A code of ethics can help employees identify acceptable business practices, be an effective internal control on behavior, help employees avoid confusion when determining whether decisions are ethical, and facilitate discussion about what is right and wrong.

2.2 Write a paragraph discussing the ethical dilemma in the following situation and identfying possible solutions: An insurance agent forgets to get the required signature from one of her clients who is buying an automobile insurance policy. The client acknowledges the purchase by giving the agent a signed personal check for the full amount. To avoid embarrassment and inconvenience, the agent forges the client's signature on the insurance application and sends it to the insurance company for processing.

2.3 Discuss the relationship between ethics and social responsibility.

2.4 Do you think that a code of ethics will actually influence an employee's behavior? Why or why not?

LO3 Discuss the external environment of marketing, and explain how it affects a firm. The external marketing environment consists of social, demographic, economic, technological, political and legal, and competitive variables. Marketers generally cannot control the elements of the external environment. Instead, they must understand how the external environment is changing and the impact of that change on the target market. Then marketing managers can create a marketing mix to effectively meet the needs of target customers.

3.1 What is the purpose of environmental scanning? Give an example.

3.2 Form six teams and make each one responsible for one of the uncontrollable elements in the marketing environment. Your boss, the company president, has asked each team to provide one-year and five-year forecasts of the major trends the firm will face. The firm is in the telecommunications equipment industry. It has no plans to become a telecommunications service provider like, for example, Verizon and AT&T. Each team should use the library, the Internet, and other data sources to make its forecasts. Each team member should examine a minimum of one data source. The team members should then pool their data and prepare a recommendation. A spokesperson for each team should present the findings to the class.

LO4 Describe the social factors that affect marketing. Within the external environment, social factors are perhaps the most difficult for marketers to anticipate. Several major social trends are currently shaping marketing strategies. First, people of all ages have a broader range of interests, defying traditional consumer profiles. Second, changing gender roles are bringing more women into the workforce and increasing the number of men who shop. Third, an increase in the number of dual-career families has created demand for time-saving goods and services.

4.1 Every country has a set of core values and beliefs. These values may vary somewhat from region to region of the nation. Identify five core values for your area of the country. Clip magazine advertisements that reflect these values and bring them to class.

4.2 Give an example of component lifestyles based on someone you know.

LO5 Explain the importance to marketing managers of current demographic trends. Today, several basic demographic patterns are influencing marketing mixes. Because the U.S. population is growing at a slower rate, marketers can no longer rely on profits from generally expanding markets. Marketers are also faced with increasingly experienced consumers among the younger generations such as tweens and Gen Y. And because the population is also growing older, marketers are offering more products that appeal to middle-aged and older consumers.

5.1 Baby boomers in America are aging. Describe how this might affect the marketing mix for the following:

    a. Bally's Health Clubs
    b. McDonald's
    c. Whirlpool Corporation
    d. The state of Florida
    e. Target Stores

5.2 You have been asked to address a local Chamber of Commerce on the subject of "Generation Y." Prepare an outline for your talk.

5.3 How should Ford Motor Company market differently to Generation Y, Generation X, and baby boomers?

LO6 Explain the importance to marketing managers of multiculturalism and growing ethnic markets. Multiculturalism occurs when all major ethnic groups in an area are roughly equally represented. Growing multiculturalism makes the marketer's task more challenging. America is not a melting pot but numerous mini-melting pots. Hispanics are the fastest-growing segment of the population followed by African Americans. Many companies are now creating departments and product lines to effectively target multicultural market segments. Companies have quickly found that ethnic markets are not homogeneous.

6.1 Go to the library and look up a minority market such as the Hispanic market. Write a memo to your boss that details the many submarkets within this segment.

6.2 Using the library and the Internet, find examples of large companies directing marketing mixes to each major ethnic group.

LO7 Identify consumer and marketer reactions to the state of the economy. In recent years, many households have gone into debt as the rise in consumer spending has outpaced the growth in income. At the same time, the financial power of women has increased, and they are making the purchasing decisions for many products in traditionally male-dominated areas. During a time of inflation, marketers generally attempt to maintain level pricing to avoid losing customer brand loyalty. During times of recession, many marketers maintain or reduce prices to counter the effects of decreased demand; they also concentrate on increasing production efficiency and improving customer service.

7.1 Explain how consumers' buying habits may change during a recessionary period.

7.2 Periods of inflation require firms to alter their marketing mix. Suppose a recent economic forecast predicts that inflation will be almost 10 percent during the next 18 months. Your company manufactures hand tools for the home gardener. Write a memo to the company president explaining how the firm may have to alter its marketing mix.

LO8 Identify the impact of technology on a firm. Monitoring new technology is essential to keeping up with competitors in today's marketing environment. The United States excels in basic research and, in recent years, has dramatically improved its track record in applied research. Without innovation, U.S. companies can't compete in global markets. Innovation is increasingly becoming a global process.

8.1 Give three examples of how technology has benefited marketers. Also, give several examples of firms that have been hurt because they did not keep up with technological changes.

LO 9 Discuss the political and legal environment of marketing. All marketing activities are subject to state and federal laws and the rulings of regulatory agencies. Marketers are responsible for remaining aware of and abiding by such regulations. Some key federal laws that affect marketing are the Sherman Act, Clayton Act, Federal Trade Commission Act, Robinson-Patman Act, Wheeler-Lea Amendments to the FTC Act, Lanham Act, Celler-Kefauver Antimerger Act, and Hart-Scott-Rodino Act. Many laws, including privacy laws, have been passed to protect the consumer as well. The Consumer Product Safety Commission, the Federal Trade Commission, and the Food and Drug Administration are the three federal agencies most involved in regulating marketing activities.

9.1 The Federal Trade Commission and other governmental agencies have been both praised and criticized for their regulation of marketing activities. To what degree do you think the government should regulate marketing? Explain your position.

9.2 Can you think of any other areas where consumer protection laws are needed?

9.3 What topics are currently receiving attention in FDA News (**http://www.fdanews.com**)? What effect has the attention had on market share?

LO 10 Explain the basics of foreign and domestic competition. The competitive environment encompasses the number of competitors a firm must face, the relative size of the competitors, and the degree of interdependence within the industry. Declining population growth, rising costs, and shortages of resources have heightened domestic competition.

10.1 Explain how the nature of competition is changing in America.

10.2 Might there be times when a company becomes too competitive? If so, what could be the consequences?

Key Terms

applied research	89	demography	77	morals	70
baby boomers	81	environmental management	74	multiculturalism	85
basic research	89	ethics	69	purchasing power	87
code of ethics	71	Federal Trade Commission (FTC)	93	pyramid of corporate social	
component lifestyles	75	Food and Drug Administration (FDA)	93	responsibility	68
Consumer Product Safety		Generation X	80	recession	88
Commission (CPSC)	92	Generation Y	78	sustainability	68
corporate social responsibility	68	inflation	88	target market	73

Exercises

APPLICATION EXERCISE

Demographic factors play a large role in shaping the external marketing environment. One of those demographic factors is culture. The importance of cultural understanding cannot be overstated, especially in today's global marketplace and our own multicultural country. In general, Americans tend to be ethnocentric; that is, they are quick to prejudge other cultural norms as wrong (or of less significance) because they differ from American practices.

One way to be exposed to another culture is by examining the foods typical of that culture. In this exercise, you will need to work in a team to create a guide to ethnic dining in your city or area. The finished guide will be descriptive in nature; it is not meant to be a rating guide.[66]

Activities

1. Identify ethnic dining categories for inclusion in your guide. Once you have identified categories for your area, make a list of restaurants for each category.

2. You will need to create a data collection form so that the same information is collected from each restaurant. For example, you will want to include the name, address, and phone number for each restaurant. Think of other information that would be helpful.

3. Divide up the restaurant list your team generated in activity 1 so that each team member is responsible for collecting information from a certain number of restaurants. Consider dividing the list geographically so that each team member can visit an assortment of ethnic restaurants. If your budget allows, eat at a few of the restaurants in addition to collecting the information. After you have all the information, meet to review and compare your findings.

4. Was there a meal or type of food that you particularly liked? Disliked? Which type of ethnic restaurant seemed most foreign to you? Why do you think that was?

Entrepreneurship Case

ROCKSTAR GAMES: CAUGHT IN THEIR OWN VICE?

In Oakland, California, police arrest a gang of teens who now face charges for five homicides, several carjackings, and a slew of armed robberies. Roughly 2,000 miles away in Tennessee, stepbrothers Joshua and William Buckner, ages 14 and 16, are arrested and plead guilty to reckless homicide, aggravated assault, and reckless endangerment for fatally shooting one motorist and critically wounding a second.

The tie that binds these seemingly unrelated crimes is a video game—Rockstar Games' *Grand Theft Auto: Vice City*. When questioned about their crimes, both sets of perpetrators cited boredom and a desire to emulate the action of the main character in *Vice City* as the cause of their violent behavior.

In *Vice City*, players assume the role of Tommy Vercetti, an ex-con who loses cocaine and money in a botched drug deal. To recoup his losses, he must accomplish various missions in an attempt to ascend the hierarchy of *Vice City*'s underworld. The game awards points to players for mass shootings, graphic rapes, liaisons with prostitutes, car thefts, and drug sales. The violence is extreme and often grotesque. In one mission, players controlling Vercetti can earn points for raping a woman in the back of a stolen car and then deciding whether to kick her to death, cut her to pieces with a machete, or fatally shoot her.

Its graphic violence and sexually explicit material have earned *Vice City* an M rating from the Entertainment Software Rating Board, which indicates to consumers that the game is intended only for gamers aged 17 or older. Younger gamers, however, are playing the game in large numbers, and critics, parents, and politicians are horrified to find that children are being exposed to a game that glorifies such behavior. Racism rears its head in the game too, as Vercetti at one point is instructed by a narrator to "shoot the Haitians."

The backlash against Rockstar Games has been significant. Haitian and Cuban groups have filed suit against the company in Florida, where state legislators have proposed a bill that would increase the fines levied against retailers who rent or sell M-rated video games to minors. The lawmakers note that several small towns and cities have already passed such legislation.

In New York, Rockstar's racial insensitivity aroused the ire of the state attorney general, New York City Mayor Michael Bloomberg, and the Anti-Defamation League. Their pressure persuaded Rockstar to remove the racially offensive line from all future copies of the game. Other than that, Rockstar has officially declined to comment on any other inquiries. The Interactive Entertainment Merchants Association, an industry group including giant retailers such as Wal-Mart and Blockbuster, Inc., has reacted by adopting procedures intended to stop the sale of mature and adult video games to minors.

Despite the negative reactions, the game has gained mass-market acceptance. *Vice City* alone accounted for nearly half of Rockstar's $1.04 billion in revenue in 2003—a year when revenue for all M-rated video games actually declined from $910 million to $833 million. Rockstar currently dominates the adult segment of the market with the ten M-rated games it produces. Players of the game say its plot lines are pure fantasy, and the chief operating officer of Rockstar Games, Terry Donovan, defends his company by claiming that if the popular HBO television series *The Sopranos* was a video game, it would be *Grand Theft Auto*.

His customers, he asserts, are young male professionals who are willing to spend serious money on intense simulation-type games that provide primal stress release. Donovan and many others believe that the M rating is enough to alert parents to the games' adult content and that legislation from the government infringes on freedom of speech. At the moment, the popular counterargument is that like drugs, alcohol, and pornography, the games represent a threat to the psychological development of young people and should be controlled as such.[67]

Questions

1. Do you think Rockstar Games' chief operating officer, Terry Donovan, displays adequate concern for corporate social responsibility? Explain.

2. Describe the technological, social, and political forces acting on the video game industry.

3. How is Rockstar responding to its environmental conditions? Do you agree with Rockstar's approach? Why or why not?

COMPANY CLIPS

Method – People against Dirty

Method's first "lab" was the kitchen of founders Eric Ryan and Adam Lowry, two friends whose goal was to evolve the household cleaner from a toxic object that hid under the sink to an all-natural, biodegradable, and stylish counter-top accessory. This video segment shows method through yet another lens, that of corporate social responsibility (CSR) and sustainability. Chemical engineer Adam Lowry outlines the chemical aspects of traditional cleaning products and describes how method's products are healthier. As you watch the video, keep in mind the various marketing orientations you learned in Chapter 1.

Questions

1. Does method have a societal marketing orientation, or is it just a market-oriented company that integrates a number of environmental practices into its operations? Explain.

2. How is method practicing sustainability?

3. Discuss the changing social factors that have made it possible for method to be so successful.

BIZ FLIX

Jaws

Now that you have finished studying Chapter 3, you may be ready to think metaphorically about marketing ethics and external environments. As an encore to your work, watch the film clip from Jaws, starring Roy Scheider, Richard Dreyfuss, and Robert Shaw. You are probably familiar with the movie's plot: A giant great white shark terrorizes an east coast community's beaches. In this scene, the community's police chief, mayor, and others disagree on how to handle the situation. Special effects add much shock value to an early Steven Spielberg directorial effort—his sixth feature film.

Which ethical decision-making concepts are illustrated in this clip? Can you see how it relates to marketing?

Marketing & You Results

The higher your score, the more important you think ethics and socially responsible behavior are to achieving corporate objectives. A high score also suggests that you are an ethical idealist, or someone who sees right and wrong as absolute, rather than an ethical relativist, or someone who sees right and wrong as situation dependent.

Developing a

CHAPTER
4
Global Vision

Learning Outcomes

LO¹ Discuss the importance of global marketing

LO² Discuss the impact of multinational firms on the world economy

LO³ Describe the external environment facing global marketers

LO⁴ Identify the various ways of entering the global marketplace

LO⁵ List the basic elements involved in developing a global marketing mix

LO⁶ Discover how the Internet is affecting global marketing

a global vision at **Philips Electronics**

f you live in Shanghai and want a new cell phone, plasma TV, CD player, or electric razor, then go to Yolo—a brightly lit, wide-aisled hypermarket that looks like a Chinese clone of Best Buy. Grand new stores like this are where Dutch giant Royal Philips Electronics ($38 billion in sales) sold 80 percent of its electronics wares in China last year. It's where the few with lots of money go to shop.

It's a different story in India, where big chain outlets account for less than 15 percent of Philips's $570 million in sales. In urban areas, most Philips products are sold from 35,000 small, family-owned stores. To reach customers in rural areas, where 72 percent of the population lives,

China and India are two of the fastest-growing and most exciting markets in the world.

 Philips has 300 distributors whose yellow vans trundle over bumpy dirt roads selling hand-cranked radios for $3.25 and 14-inch "starter" TVs for $125. In other words, go after the many with very little to spend.

In China, Philips has 35 factories and offices with 20,000 employees and another 30,000 Chinese workers employed by contract manufacturers and minority-owned joint ventures. By contrast, the company's Indian investment is largely in white-collar workers—software engineers who make a quarter of what they'd earn in Silicon Valley. Philips has 1,500 engineers in Bangalore—a quarter of all its engineers worldwide—to write the software for all of Philips's DVD players, most of its digital TVs, and some of its X-ray and magnetic resonance imaging machines. Another 250 accountants and financial analysts work out of offices in Chennai and Kolkata doing back-office support for worldwide operations.

In deploying very different strategies for these two huge Asian markets, Philips CEO Gerard Kleisterlee is betting that the company can capture "the couple of hundred million" middle-income people who will be "the consumers of tomorrow."

Certainly, others have learned that a one-size-fits-all strategy for Asia doesn't necessarily work. Unilever, for instance, had great success in the 1990s selling single-use foil packages of shampoo for pennies each in tens of thousands of India's small retail outlets. But when it tried to import the same packaging and far-reaching distribution system to China, it flopped: the Chinese preferred to buy bottles of shampoo at department stores and hypermarkets.[1]

China and India are two of the fastest-growing and most exciting markets in the world. To successfully penetrate these markets, a firm, such as Philips, must have a global vision. What is a global vision? What environmental factors should a company consider when it enters the global marketplace? What are several alternative methods of "going global"?

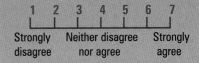

How would you describe your interest in other cultures? Enter your answers on the lines provided.

1	2	3	4	5	6	7

Strongly disagree   Neither disagree nor agree   Strongly agree

_____ I would like to have opportunities to meet people from other countries.

_____ I am very interested in trying food from different countries.

_____ We should have a respect for traditions, cultures, and ways of life of other nations.

_____ I would like to learn more about other countries.

_____ I have a strong desire for overseas travel.

_____ I would like to know more about foreign cultures and customs.

_____ I have a strong desire to meet and interact with people from foreign countries.

Now, total your score. Read the chapter, and find out what your score means at the end.

Rewards of Global Marketing

Today, global revolutions are under way in many areas of our lives: management, politics, communications, technology. The word *global* has assumed a new meaning, referring to a boundless mobility and competition in social, business, and intellectual arenas. No longer just an option, **global marketing**—marketing that targets markets throughout the world—has become imperative for business.

U.S. managers must develop a global vision not only to recognize and react to international marketing opportunities but also to remain competitive at home. Often a U.S. firm's toughest domestic competition comes from foreign companies. Moreover, a global vision enables a manager to understand that customer and distribution networks operate worldwide, blurring geographic and political barriers and making them increasingly irrelevant to business decisions. In summary, having a **global vision** means recognizing and reacting to international marketing opportunities, using effective global marketing strategies, and being aware of threats from foreign competitors in all markets.

Over the past two decades, global trade has climbed from $200 billion a year to over $7 trillion. Countries and companies that were never considered major players in global marketing are now important, and some of them show great skill.

Today, marketers face many challenges to their customary practices. Product development costs are rising, the life of products is getting shorter, and new technology is spreading around the world faster than ever. But marketing winners relish the pace of change instead of fearing it.

An example of a young company with a global vision that has capitalized on new technology is Ashtech in Sunnyvale, California. Ashtech makes equipment to capture and convert satellite signals from the U.S. government's Global Positioning System. Ashtech's chief engineer and his team of ten torture and test everything built by Ashtech—expensive black boxes of chips and circuits that use satellite signals to tell surveyors, farmers, mining machine operators, and others where they are with great accuracy. Over half of Ashtech's output is exported. Its biggest customer is Japan.

Adopting a global vision can be very lucrative for a company. Gillette, for example, gets about two-thirds of its revenue from its international division. H. J. Heinz, the ketchup company, gets over half of its revenue from international sales. Although Cheetos and Ruffles haven't done very well in Japan, the potato chip has been quite successful. PepsiCo's (owner of Frito-Lay) overseas snack business brings in more than $3.25 billion annually.

Another company with a global vision is Pillsbury. The Pillsbury Doughboy is used in India to sell a product that the company had just about abandoned in America: flour. Pillsbury (owned by General Mills) has many higher-margin products such as microwave pizzas in other parts of the world, but it discovered that in this tradition-bound market, it needed to push the basics.

Even so, selling packaged flour in India has been almost revolutionary, because most Indian housewives still buy raw wheat in bulk, clean it by hand, store it in huge metal hampers, and, every week, carry some to a neighborhood mill, or *chakki*, where it is ground between two stones.

To help reach those housewives, the Doughboy himself has gotten a makeover. In TV advertising, he presses his palms together and bows in the traditional Indian greeting. He speaks six regional languages.

Global marketing is not a one-way street, whereby only U.S. companies sell their wares and services throughout the world. Foreign competition in the domestic market used to be relatively rare but now is found in almost every industry. In fact, in many industries U.S. businesses have lost significant market share to imported products. In electronics, cameras, automobiles, fine china, tractors, leather goods, and a host of other consumer and industrial products, U.S. companies have struggled at home to maintain their market shares against foreign competitors. In 2005, General Motors laid off more than 30,000 workers because of intense foreign competition in the American market.

global marketing
Marketing that targets markets throughout the world.

global vision
Recognizing and reacting to international marketing opportunities, using effective global marketing strategies, and being aware of threats from foreign competitors in all markets.

IMPORTANCE OF GLOBAL MARKETING TO THE UNITED STATES

Many countries depend more on international commerce than the United States does. For example, France, Britain, and Germany all derive more than 19 percent of their gross domestic product (GDP) from world trade, compared to about 12 percent for the United States. Nevertheless, the impact of international business on the U.S. economy is still impressive:

- The United States exports about a fifth of its industrial production.

- One in every ten jobs in the United States is directly or indirectly supported by exports.[2]

- U.S. businesses export over $800 billion in goods to foreign countries every year, and almost a third of U.S. corporate profits comes from international trade and foreign investment.

- Exports account for 25 percent of U.S. economic growth.

- The United States is the world's leading exporter of farm products, selling more than $60 billion in agricultural exports to foreign countries each year.

- Chemicals, office machinery and computers, automobiles, aircraft, and electrical and industrial machinery make up almost half of all nonagricultural exports.

These statistics might seem to imply that practically every business in the United States is selling its wares throughout the world, but nothing could be further from the truth. About 85 percent of all U.S. exports of manufactured goods are shipped by 250 companies; less than 10 percent of all manufacturing businesses, or around 25,000 companies, export their goods on a regular basis. Most small- and medium-sized firms are essentially nonparticipants in global trade and marketing. Only the very large multinational companies have seriously attempted to compete worldwide. Fortunately, more of the smaller companies are now aggressively pursuing international markets.

Estela Pacheco sews pajamas for Wal-Mart at a textile factory located 15 miles from San Salvador, El Salvador. Frustrated by stalled international free trade talks, El Salvador is leading negotiations to create a giant trade bloc across the Americas in an effort to bring more industrial jobs to the country.

THE FEAR OF TRADE AND GLOBALIZATION

The protests during meetings of the World Trade Organization, the World Bank, and the International Monetary Fund (the three organizations are discussed later in the chapter) show that many people fear world trade and globalization. What do they fear? The negatives of global trade are as follows:

- Millions of Americans have lost jobs due to imports, production shifts abroad, or outsourcing of tech jobs. Most find new jobs—that often pay less.

- Millions of others fear losing their jobs, especially at those companies operating under competitive pressure.

- Employers often threaten to outsource jobs if workers do not accept pay cuts.

- Service and white-collar jobs are increasingly vulnerable to operations moving offshore.

LO 1   Discuss the importance of global marketing

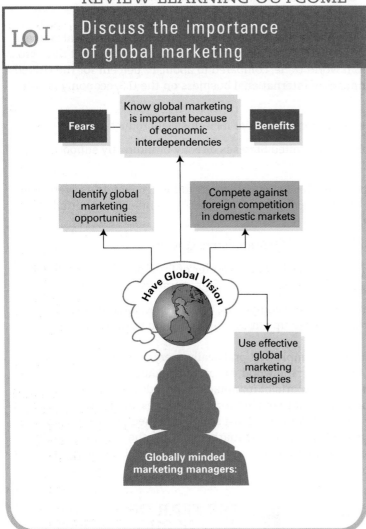

BENEFITS OF GLOBALIZATION

Traditional economic theory says that globalization relies on competition to drive down prices and increase product and service quality. Business goes to the countries that operate most efficiently and/or have the technology to produce what is needed. Many companies move their factories to countries where labor is cheap because the bulk of the work is labor-intensive, requiring few skills, and thus can be done more efficiently in countries that have an abundance of less educated workers. In return, these countries buy more higher-valued goods made by skilled workers in developed countries.

In summary, globalization expands economic freedom, spurs competition, and raises the productivity and living standards of people in countries that open themselves to the global marketplace. For less developed countries, globalization also offers access to foreign capital, global export markets, and advanced technology while breaking the monopoly of inefficient and protected domestic producers. Faster growth, in turn, reduces poverty, encourages democratization, and promotes higher labor and environmental standards. Though government officials may face more difficult choices as a result of globalization, their citizens enjoy greater individual freedom. In this sense, globalization acts as a check on governmental power by making it more difficult for governments to abuse the freedom and property of their citizens.

LO 2
Multinational Firms

The United States has a number of large companies that are global marketers. Many of them have been very successful. A company that is heavily engaged in international trade, beyond exporting and importing, is called a **multinational corporation.** Multinational corporations move resources, goods, services, and skills across national boundaries without regard to the country in which the headquarters is located. The world's leading multinational firms are listed in Exhibit 4.1. In 2006, to be ranked as one of the 500 largest multinationals, a firm needed revenue of $12.4 billion. That is more than the GDP of Jordan or Jamaica.[3] These organizations are as big as small countries! Indeed, Wal-Mart's annual sales are larger than the GDP of all but 30 nations in the world.

Multinationals often develop their global business in stages. In the first stage, companies operate in one country and sell into others. Second-stage multinationals set up foreign subsidiaries to handle sales in one country. In the third stage, they operate an entire line of business in another country. The fourth stage has evolved primarily due to the Internet and involves mostly high-tech companies. For these firms, the executive suite is virtual. Their top executives and core corporate functions are in different countries, wherever the firms can gain a competitive edge through the availability of talent or

multinational corporation
A company that is heavily engaged in international trade, beyond exporting and importing.

Exhibit 4.1

The World's Largest Multinational Corporations

Rank	Company	Country	Revenues ($ millions)
1	Wal-Mart Stores	U.S.	287,989.0
2	BP	Britain	285,059.0
3	ExxonMobil	U.S.	270,772.0
4	Royal Dutch/Shell Group	Britain/Netherlands	268,690.0
5	General Motors	U.S.	193,517.0
6	DaimlerChrysler	Germany	176,687.5
7	Toyota Motor	Japan	172,616.3
8	Ford Motor	U.S.	172,233.0
9	General Electric	U.S.	152,866.0
10	Total	France	152,609.5
11	Chevron	U.S.	147,967.0
12	ConocoPhillips	U.S.	121,663.0
13	AXA	France	121,606.3
14	Allianz	Germany	118,937.2
15	Volkswagen	Germany	110,648.7
16	Citigroup	U.S.	108,276.0
17	ING Group	Netherlands	105,886.4
18	Nippon Telegraph & Telephone	Japan	100,545.3
19	American International Group	U.S.	97,987.0
20	International Business Machines	U.S.	96,293.0
21	Siemens	Germany	91,493.2
22	Carrefour	France	90,381.7
23	Hitachi	Japan	83,993.9
24	Assicurazioni Generali	Italy	83,267.6
25	Matsushita Electric Industrial	Japan	81,077.7

SOURCE: "World's Largest Corporations," *Fortune*, July 25, 2005, 119.

capital, low costs, or proximity to their most important customers.

A good example of a fourth-stage company is Trend Micro, an Internet antivirus software company.[4] Its top executives, engineers, and support staff are spread around the world so that they can respond quickly to new virus threats—which can start anywhere and spread like wildfire. The main virus response center is in the Philippines, where 250 ever-vigilant engineers work evening and midnight shifts as needed. Six other labs are scattered from Munich to Tokyo.

Trend Micro's financial headquarters is in Tokyo, where it went public; product development is in Ph.D.-rich Taiwan; and most of its sales are in Silicon Valley—inside the giant American market. When companies fragment this way, they are no longer limited to the strengths, or hobbled by the weaknesses, of their native lands.

Such fourth-stage multinationals are being created around the world. They include business-intelligence-software maker Business Objects, with headquarters in France and San Jose, California; Wipro, a tech-services supplier with headquarters in India and Santa Clara, California; and computer-peripherals maker Logitech International, with headquarters in Switzerland and Fremont, California.

A multinational company may have several worldwide headquarters, depending on where certain markets or technologies are. Britain's APV, a maker of food-processing equipment, has a different headquarters for each of its worldwide businesses. ABB Asea Brown Boveri, the European electrical engineering giant based in Zurich, Switzerland, groups its thousands of products and services into 50 or so business areas. Each is run by a leadership team that crafts global business strategy, sets product development priorities, and decides where to make its products. None of the teams work out of the Zurich headquarters; instead, they are scattered around the world. Leadership for power transformers is based in Germany, electric drives in Finland, and process automation in the United States.

The role of multinational corporations in developing nations is a subject of controversy. Multinationals' ability to tap financial, physical, and human resources from all over the world and combine them economically and profitably can be of benefit to any country. They also often possess and can transfer the most up-to-date technology. Critics, however, claim that often the wrong kind of technology is transferred to developing nations. Usually, it is **capital-intensive** (requiring a greater expenditure for equipment than for labor) and thus does not substantially increase employment. A "modern sector" then emerges in the nation, employing a small proportion of the labor force at relatively high productivity and income levels and with increasingly capital-intensive technologies. In addition, multinationals sometimes support reactionary and oppressive

capital-intensive
Using more capital than labor in the production process.

regimes if it is in their best interests to do so. Other critics say that the firms take more wealth out of developing nations than they bring in, thus widening the gap between rich and poor nations. The petroleum industry in particular has been heavily criticized in the past for its actions in some developing countries.

To counter such criticism, more and more multinationals are taking a proactive role in being good global citizens. Sometimes companies are spurred to action by government regulation, and in other cases multinationals are attempting to protect their good brand name. The "Ethics in Marketing" box explains in more detail.

GLOBAL MARKETING STANDARDIZATION

Traditionally, marketing-oriented multinational corporations have operated somewhat differently in each country. They use a strategy of providing different product features, packaging, advertising, and so on. However, Ted Levitt, a Harvard professor, described a trend toward what he referred to as "global marketing," with a slightly different meaning.[6] He contended that communication and technology have made the world smaller so that almost all consumers everywhere want all the things they have heard about, seen, or experienced. Thus, he saw the emergence of global markets for standardized consumer products on a huge scale, as opposed to segmented foreign markets with different products. In this book, global marketing is defined as individuals and organizations using a global vision to effectively market goods and services across national boundaries. To make the distinction, we can refer to Levitt's notion as **global marketing standardization.**

global marketing standardization
Production of uniform products that can be sold the same way all over the world.

Global marketing standardization presumes that the markets throughout the world are becoming more alike. Firms practicing global marketing standardization produce "globally standardized products" to be sold the same way all over the world. Uniform production should enable companies to lower production and marketing costs and increase profits.

ETHICS in Marketing

Globalization: A Race to the Bottom or to the Top?

One of the most common perceptions of globalization is that it involves poor people in developing nations working in unsafe conditions to produce goods for consumers in the West. It's part of what corporate critics invariably call a "race to the bottom." Multinational companies, they say, seek out places where labor is cheap and safety, health, and environmental laws are weak.

But a closer look at globalization shows that the idea of a race to the bottom obscures more than it explains. Yes, U.S. companies roam the globe in search of low-cost labor—but some of them export health and safety standards when they open factories in the developing world, while others keep an eye on suppliers to avoid having a sweatshop label attached to their brand.

There's more: U.S.-based companies that sell globally are scrambling to comply with an array of European environmental laws that are much stricter than those they face at home. Regulations enacted in Brussels now govern how computers, cell phones, and aircraft engines are designed. In Europe, companies are responsible for recycling. As a result, Dell will now pick up its equipment from anyone and recycle it at no extra charge—in Europe or the United States. Dell is also rethinking the design of its computers. The company uses fewer screws and no glue, so its machines are easier to disassemble. Plastic parts are labeled

to aid recycling, and an internal chassis is made of steel that can be reused or melted down.

China is also having an impact as it begins to grapple with energy and pollution problems so severe that they demand innovative solutions. For example, more than 170 Chinese cities have banned brick in new housing because making bricks in vast quantities requires too much soil and energy. So big chemical companies are developing energy-efficient building materials that will be used worldwide. You could call these unexpected consequences of globalization a "race to the top."

The drive to meet rising global standards of one kind or another is affecting just about every multinational company. Spurred by regulation in Europe and the prospect of sales to China, General Electric is investing $1.5 billion over the next five years in research into energy-efficient and environmentally friendly products like wind turbines, clean coal technology, and appliances that save water or electricity. Intel, Xerox, Motorola, and Dell are revamping their supply chains to get lead out of microprocessors, copiers, cell phones, and computers. And at considerable expense, Nike and Gap are dispatching inspectors who monitor hundreds of their suppliers in the developing world.[5]

Do you think that most of the positive actions taken by multinationals are a result of high ethical standards? Do you think that workers in poor countries are better off because of multinationals?

Levitt cited Coca-Cola, Colgate-Palmolive, and McDonald's as successful global marketers. His critics point out, however, that the success of these three companies is really based on variation, not on offering the same product everywhere. McDonald's, for example, changes its salad dressings and provides self-serve espresso for French tastes. It sells bulgogi burgers in South Korea and falafel burgers in Egypt. It also offers different products to suit tastes in Germany (where it offers beer) and Japan (where it offers sake). Further, the fact that Coca-Cola and Colgate-Palmolive sell some of their products in more than 160 countries does not signify that they have adopted a high degree of standardization for all their products globally. Only three Coca-Cola brands are standardized, and one of them, Sprite, has a different formulation in Japan. Some Colgate-Palmolive products are marketed in just a few countries. Axion paste dishwashing detergent, for example, was formulated for developing countries, and La Croix Plus detergent was custom made for the French market. Colgate toothpaste is marketed the same way globally, although its advanced Gum Protection Formula is used in only 27 nations.

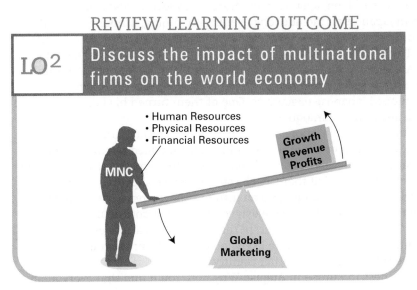

REVIEW LEARNING OUTCOME

LO² Discuss the impact of multinational firms on the world economy

- Human Resources
- Physical Resources
- Financial Resources

MNC

Growth
Revenue
Profits

Global
Marketing

Nevertheless, some multinational corporations are moving toward a degree of global marketing standardization. 3M markets some of its industrial tapes the same way around the globe. Procter & Gamble calls its new philosophy "global planning." The idea is to determine which product modifications are necessary from country to country while trying to minimize those modifications. P&G has at least four products that are marketed similarly in most parts of the world: Camay soap, Crest toothpaste, Head and Shoulders shampoo, and Pampers diapers. However, the smell of Camay, the flavor of Crest, and the formula of Head and Shoulders, as well as the advertising, vary from country to country.

LO³
External Environment Facing Global Marketers

A global marketer or a firm considering global marketing must consider the external environment. Many of the same environmental factors that operate in the domestic market also exist internationally. These factors include culture, economic and technological development, political structure and actions, demographic makeup, and natural resources.

CULTURE

Central to any society is the common set of values shared by its citizens that determines what is socially acceptable. Culture underlies the family, the educational system, religion, and the social class system. The network of social organizations generates overlapping roles and status positions. These values and roles have a tremendous effect on people's preferences and thus on marketers' options. A company that does not understand a country's culture is doomed to failure in that country. Cultural blunders lead to misunderstandings and often perceptions of rudeness or even incompetence. For example, when people in India shake hands, they sometimes do so rather limply. This isn't a sign of weakness or disinterest; instead, a soft handshake conveys respect. Avoiding eye contact is also a sign of deference in India.[7]

A U.S. luggage manufacturer found out that culture also affects thinking and perception. The company designed a new Middle East advertising campaign around the image of its luggage being carried on a magic flying carpet. Many of the participants in a group in a marketing research study thought they were seeing advertising for Samsonite *carpets*. Green Giant learned that it could not use its Jolly Green Giant in parts of Asia where wearing a green hat signifies that a man has an unfaithful wife.

Language is another important aspect of culture. Marketers must take care in translating product names, slogans, instructions, and promotional messages so as not to convey the wrong meaning. For example, Mitsubishi Motors had to rename its Pajero model in Spanish-speaking countries because the term describes a sexual activity. Toyota Motors' MR2 model dropped the number 2 in France because the combination sounds like a French swearword. The literal translation of Coca-Cola in Chinese characters means "bite the wax tadpole."

Each country has its own customs and traditions that determine business practices and influence negotiations with foreign customers. In many countries, personal relationships are more important than financial considerations. For instance, skipping social engagements in Mexico may lead to lost sales. Negotiations in Japan often include long evenings of dining, drinking, and entertaining, and only after a close personal relationship has been formed do business negotiations begin. The Japanese go through a very elaborate ritual when exchanging business cards. An American businesswoman was unaware of this important cultural tradition. She came into a meeting and tossed some of her business cards across the table at a group of stunned Japanese executives. One of them turned his back on her and walked out. The deal never went through.

Making successful sales presentations abroad requires a thorough understanding of the country's culture. Germans, for example, don't like risk and need strong reassurance. A successful presentation to a German client will emphasize three points: the bottom-line benefits of the product or service, that there will be strong service support, and that the product is guaranteed. In southern Europe, it is an insult to show a price list. Without negotiating, you will not close the sale. The English want plenty of documentation for product claims and are less likely to simply accept the word of the sales representative. Scandinavian and Dutch companies are more likely to approach business transactions as Americans do than are companies in any other country.

Never try to do business in Europe in August. Why not? You'll find that everyone has gone on vacation. Today, all European countries have laws requiring companies to provide employees with vacations of at least four weeks (the standard in Belgium, Britain, Germany, and Italy, among others) to five weeks (as in Austria, Denmark, France, and Sweden). But most workers get more vacation time because of collective agreements negotiated by unions or other compensation arrangements.

When actual vacation time is calculated, workers average 7.9 weeks in Italy, 7.8 weeks in Germany, and 7 weeks in France. In the United States, workers average 3.9 weeks of vacation and holiday time, but 23 percent of U.S. private-sector workers, including part-time workers, get no paid vacation time at all.[8]

ECONOMIC AND TECHNOLOGICAL DEVELOPMENT

A second major factor in the external environment facing the global marketer is the level of economic development in the countries where it operates. In general, complex and sophisticated industries are found in developed countries, and more basic industries are found in less developed nations. Average family incomes are higher in more developed countries than in the less developed countries. Larger incomes mean greater purchasing power and demand not only for consumer goods and services but also for the machinery and workers required to produce consumer goods.

According to the World Bank, the combined gross national income (GNI) of the 234 nations for which data are available is approximately $34 trillion. Divide that up among the world's 6.5 billion inhabitants, and you get just $5,230 for every man, woman, and child on Earth. The United States accounts for almost a third of the income earned worldwide, or $12.3 trillion—more than any other single country. If America's GNI were divided equally among its 297 million residents, each American would receive $41,400—6.6 times the

Exhibit 4.2

Where the Global Money Is and Is Not

Country	Gross National Income per Capita*
Luxembourg	$56,230
Norway	52,030
Switzerland	48,230
United States	41,400
Denmark	40,650
Iceland	38,620
Japan	37,180
Sweden	35,770
Ireland	34,280
United Kingdom	33,940
Finland	32,790
Austria	32,300
Italy	26,120
Hungary	8,270
Mexico	6,770
Turkey	3,750
Russia	3,410
Samoa	1,860
Bolivia	960
India	620
Haiti	390
Congo	120
Burundi	90

*GNI per capita refers to a country's gross national income divided by the total population of the country.
SOURCE: World Bank Development Indicators 2005.

world average. Even so, Americans are still not the richest people on the planet. That title goes to the residents of Luxembourg, where the per capita GNI is $56,230 (see Exhibit 4.2).[9]

In low-income countries where the annual GNI per capita is $745 or less, the average life expectancy is only 58.9 years, compared with 77.5 years in the United States. Eighty out of every 1,000 newborns die in low-income countries each year, versus only seven in the United States. Just 59.8 percent of children are immunized against measles in those nations, compared with 91 percent of children stateside. And there are only 6 computers per 1,000 residents; in America there are 625.[10]

Just because a country has a low GNI per capita doesn't mean that everyone is poor. In fact, some of these countries have large and growing pockets of wealth. The average Bentley automobile costs around $600,000. Bentley opened showrooms in China in May 2002 and sold 50 cars in its first eight months, compared with 80 in Japan for all 2002. Chinese consumers also buy about 30 Ferraris and 70 Maseratis per year—an indication of the speed at which China's young entrepreneurs are garnering wealth. Chinese buyers of superluxury cars tend to be younger than in other markets—typically, they are 35 to 50 years old and have made their money in real estate or with their own companies.

POLITICAL STRUCTURE AND ACTIONS

Political structure is the third important variable facing global marketers. Government policies run the gamut from no private ownership and minimal individual freedom to little central government and maximum personal freedom. As rights of private property increase, government-owned industries and centralized planning tend to decrease. But a political environment is rarely at one extreme or the other. India, for instance, is a republic with elements of socialism, monopoly capitalism, and competitive capitalism in its political ideology.

A recent World Bank study found that the least amount of business regulation fosters the strongest economies.[11] The least regulated and most efficient economies are concentrated among countries with well-established common-law traditions, including Australia, Canada, New Zealand, the United Kingdom, and the United States. On a par with the best performers are Singapore and Hong Kong. Not far behind are Denmark, Norway, and Sweden, social democracies that recently streamlined their business regulation.

The countries with the least efficient across-the-board regulations and political structures are Bolivia, Burkina Faso, Chad, Costa Rica, Guatemala, Mali, Mozambique, Paraguay, the Philippines, and Venezuela.

In extreme cases, governments have been known to expropriate the assets of multinational corporations. In a recent example, President Hugo Chávez of Venezuela ordered oil companies to set up joint ventures controlled by Petrólos de Venezuela (PDVSA), the state oil company; he also hiked royalties from 16.7 to 30 percent. Chávez now has targeted more than 700 plants, particularly in the food industry, that are idle or not operating at capacity for possible expropriation.[12]

Legal Considerations

Closely related to and often intertwined with the political environment are legal considerations. In France, nationalistic sentiments led to a law that requires pop music stations to play at least 40 percent of their songs in French (even though French teenagers love American and English rock and roll).

Many legal structures are designed to either encourage or limit trade. Here are some examples:

- *Tariff: a tax levied on the goods entering a country.* The United States maintains tariffs as high as 27 percent on Canadian softwood lumber. U.S. lumber producers and environmentalists have alleged that Canada's provincial governments subsidize the softwood industry by charging below-market rates to cut trees and not enforcing environmental laws.

- *Quota: a limit on the amount of a specific product that can enter a country.* The United States has strict quotas for imported textiles, sugar, and many dairy products. Several U.S. companies have sought quotas as a means of protection from foreign competition. For example, Harley-Davidson convinced the U.S. government to place quotas on large motorcycles imported to the United States. These quotas gave the company the opportunity to improve its quality and compete with Japanese motorcycles.

- *Boycott: the exclusion of all products from certain countries or companies.* Governments use boycotts to exclude companies from countries with which they have a political dispute. Several Arab nations boycotted Coca-Cola because it maintained distributors in Israel.

- *Exchange control: a law compelling a company earning foreign exchange from its exports to sell it to a control agency, usually a central bank.* A company wishing to buy goods abroad must first obtain foreign currency exchange from the control agency. Generally, exchange controls limit the importation of luxuries. For instance, Avon Products drastically cut back new production lines and products in the Philippines because exchange controls prevented the company from converting pesos to dollars to ship back to the home office. The pesos had to be used in the Philippines. China restricts the amount of foreign currency each Chinese company is allowed to keep from its exports. Therefore, Chinese companies must usually get the government's approval to release funds before they can buy products from foreign companies.

- *Market grouping (also known as a common trade alliance): occurs when several countries agree to work together to form a common trade area that enhances trade opportunities.* The best-known market grouping is the European Union (EU), which will be discussed in more detail later. The EU, which was known as the European Community before 1994, has been evolving for more than four decades, yet until recently, many trade barriers existed among its member nations.

- *Trade agreement: an agreement to stimulate international trade.* Not all government efforts are meant to stifle imports or investment by foreign corporations. The Uruguay Round of trade negotiations is an example of an effort to encourage trade, as was the grant of most favored nation (MFN) status to China. The largest Latin American trade agreement is **Mercosur**, which includes Argentina, Bolivia, Brazil, Chile, Colombia, Ecuador, Paraguay, Peru, and Uruguay. The elimination of most tariffs among the trading partners has resulted in trade revenues of over $16 billion annually. The economic boom created by Mercosur will undoubtedly cause other nations to seek trade agreements on their own or to enter Mercosur. The European Union hopes to have a free trade pact with Mercosur in the future.

Uruguay Round and Doha Round

The **Uruguay Round** is an agreement that has dramatically lowered trade barriers worldwide. Adopted in 1994, the agreement has been signed by 148 nations. It is the most ambitious global trade agreement ever negotiated. The agreement has reduced tar-

Mercosur
The largest Latin American trade agreement; includes Argentina, Bolivia, Brazil, Chile, Colombia, Ecuador, Paraguay, Peru, and Uruguay.

Uruguay Round
An agreement to dramatically lower trade barriers worldwide; created the World Trade Organization.

iffs by one-third worldwide—a move that is
expected to raise global income by $235 bil-
lion annually. Perhaps most notable is the
recognition of new global realities. For the
first time an agreement covers services,
intellectual property rights, and trade-
related investment measures such as
exchange controls.

The Uruguay Round made several major changes in world trading practices:

- *Entertainment, pharmaceuticals, integrated circuits, and software*: The rules protect
  patents, copyrights, and trademarks for 20 years. Computer programs receive 50
  years of protection and semiconductor chips receive 10 years'. But many developing nations were given a decade to phase in patent protection for drugs. France,
  which limits the number of U.S. movies and TV shows that can be shown, refused
  to liberalize market access for the U.S. entertainment industry.

- *Financial, legal, and accounting services*: Services came under international trading
  rules for the first time, creating a vast opportunity for these competitive U.S.
  industries. Now it is easier for managers and key personnel to be admitted to a
  country. Licensing standards for professionals, such as doctors, cannot discriminate against foreign applicants. That is, foreign applicants cannot be held to
  higher standards than domestic practitioners.

- *Agriculture*: Europe is gradually reducing farm subsidies, opening new opportunities for such U.S. farm exports as wheat and corn. Japan and Korea are beginning
  to import rice. But U.S. growers of sugar and citrus fruit have had their subsidies
  trimmed.

- *Textiles and apparel*: Strict quotas limiting imports from developing countries are
  being phased out, causing further job losses in the U.S. clothing trade. But retailers and consumers are the big winners, because past quotas have added $15 bil-
  lion a year to clothing prices.

- *A new trade organization*: The **World Trade Organization (WTO)** replaced the old
  General Agreement on Tariffs and Trade (GATT), which was created in 1948.
  The old GATT contained extensive loopholes that enabled countries to avoid the
  trade-barrier reduction agreements—a situation similar to obeying the law only if
  you want to! Today, all WTO members must fully comply with all agreements
  under the Uruguay Round. The WTO also has an effective dispute settlement procedure with strict time limits to resolve disputes.

The latest round of WTO trade talks began in Doha, Qatar, in 2001. For the most part,
the periodic meetings of WTO members under the Doha Round have been very con-
tentious. Typically, the discussions find developing countries on one side of the argument and the rich developed countries on the other. A major goal of the Doha Round is
to bolster the developing economies of Africa, Asia, and Latin America where up to two-
thirds of the population work in agriculture. To this end, efforts have been made to persuade the developed countries to lower their barriers on food imports and reduce the
subsidies they provide to their own farmers. At the same time, the United States hopes
to end the rampant piracy of patents and copyrights in developing countries, to increase
opportunities abroad for U.S. service companies, and to obtain lower tariffs for U.S.
exports to other countries.

To date there has been little agreement between the developed and developing
nations. Negotiations in Cancún, Mexico, collapsed when the developing nations, led by
Brazil, India, and China, demanded that the United States and the European Union drop
agricultural tariffs and slash domestic agricultural subsidies faster and deeper than either
was willing to do. The $300 billion a year in domestic subsidies to farmers encourages

**World Trade
Organization (WTO)**
A trade organization that
replaced the old General
Agreement on Tariffs and
Trade (GATT).

**General Agreement
on Tariffs and Trade
(GATT)**
A trade agreement that
contained loopholes that
enabled countries to avoid
trade-barrier reduction
agreements.

DEVELOPING A GLOBAL VISION

CHAPTER 4

115

huge amounts of excess production. This, in turn, depresses global agricultural prices and makes it difficult, or impossible, for developing countries to compete. France, in particular, has balked at trimming subsidies to its inefficient farmers and has threatened to capsize a modest EU subsidy-trimming plan. For their part, developing nations, led by Brazil and India, have threatened to retain import barriers and keep on making knockoff pharmaceuticals and software.

The WTO Ministerial Conference of all 148 members met in December 2005 in Hong Kong to try to get the stalled Doha Round moving forward. Clearly, neither the EU nor the United States is ready to confront politically powerful farm interests. But most of the WTO's 148 members believe in free trade—that's why they are members. Their citizens, though, are less comfortable with the wrenching changes brought by rapid globalization.

The trend toward globalization has resulted in the creation of additional agreements and organizations: the North American Free Trade Agreement, the Central America Free Trade Agreement, the European Union, the World Bank, and the International Monetary Fund.

North American Free Trade Agreement

At the time it was instituted, the **North American Free Trade Agreement (NAFTA)** created the world's largest free trade zone. Ratified by the U.S. Congress in 1993, the agreement includes Canada, the United States, and Mexico, with a combined population of 360 million and economy of $6 trillion.

Canada, the largest U.S. trading partner, entered a free trade agreement with the United States in 1988. Thus, many of the new long-run opportunities for U.S. business under NAFTA have been in Mexico, America's second largest trading partner. Tariffs on Mexican exports to the United States averaged just 4 percent before the treaty was signed, and most goods entered the United States duty-free. Therefore, the main impact of NAFTA was to open the Mexican market to U.S. companies. When the treaty went into effect, tariffs on about half the items traded across the Rio Grande disappeared. The pact removed a web of Mexican licensing requirements, quotas, and tariffs that limited transactions in U.S. goods and services. For instance, the pact allowed U.S. and Canadian financial-services companies to own subsidiaries in Mexico for the first time in 50 years.

The real question is whether NAFTA can continue to deliver rising prosperity in all three countries. America has certainly benefited from cheaper imports and more investment opportunities abroad. Over the years, Mexico has also made huge economic gains due to NAFTA. The U.S.-Mexico cross border trade now averages over $750 million a day.[13] Over $1 billion in trade flows daily between the United States and Canada. During the 1990s, many Canadian manufacturers switched from producing a broad cross section of products to higher-value niche-products that were less prone to competitive pressures such as wood products, clothing, and transportation equipment.

Although Mexico has thrived under NAFTA, its prospects are not as bright as in the past. It is losing its advantage as a low-cost producer to countries such as India and China. American businesses complain that Mexico has a dysfunctional judicial system, unreliable power supplies, poor roads, high corporate tax rates, and unfriendly labor relations. This has given companies pause when considering investing in Mexico. Mexico still has a lot to offer, but it must improve its infrastructure.

Central America Free Trade Agreement

The newest free trade agreement is the **Central America Free Trade Agreement (CAFTA)** instituted in 2005. Besides the United States, the agreement includes Costa Rica, the Dominican Republic, El Salvador, Guatemala, Honduras, and Nicaragua. The United States is already the principal exporter to these nations, so economists think that it will not result in a major increase in U.S. exports. It will, however, reduce tariffs on exports to CAFTA countries. Already, some 80 percent of the goods imported into the United States from CAFTA nations are tariff-free. CAFTA countries may benefit from the new permanent trade deal if U.S. multinational firms deepen their investment in the region.

North American Free Trade Agreement (NAFTA)
An agreement between Canada, the United States, and Mexico that created the world's largest free trade zone.

Central America Free Trade Agreement (CAFTA)
A trade agreement, instituted in 2005, that includes Costa Rica, the Dominican Republic, El Salvador, Guatemala, Honduras, Nicaragua, and the United States.

Exhibit 4.3

The European Union

Europe's New Look			
	GDP (€ billions)*	Population (millions)	GDP per capita(€)*
Current EU	9,097.8	377.6	24,094
2004 entrants	429.5	74.7	5,750

SOURCE: http://www.eurounion.org/profile.

© SHARON MEREDITH/ISTOCKPHOTO INTERNATIONAL, INC.

European Union
A free trade zone encompassing 25 European countries.

European Union

One of the world's most important free trade zones is the **European Union**, which now encompasses most of Europe. In 2004, the EU expanded from 15 members (Austria, Belgium, Denmark, Finland, France, Germany, Greece, Iceland, Italy, Luxembourg, the Netherlands, Portugal, Spain, Sweden, and the United Kingdom) to 25 members with a combined population of 450 million (see Exhibit 4.3). The new members are Cyprus, the Czech Republic, Estonia, Hungary, Latvia, Lithuania, Malta, Poland, Slovakia, and Slovenia. The new entrants differ in several ways from the older members. Eight of the new members are former Soviet satellites and remain saddled with inefficient government offices, state-controlled enterprises, and large, protected farm sectors. Most economists predict that it will take 50 years or longer before the productivity and living standards of the new entrants catch up to those of western Europe.[14]

Nonetheless, the primary goal of the EU is to create a unified European market. Common foreign, security, and defense policies are also goals, as well as European citizenship—whereby any EU citizen can live, work, vote, and run for office anywhere in the member countries. The EU is creating standardized trade rules and coordinated health and safety standards. Duties, customs procedures, and taxes have also been standardized. A driver hauling cargo from Amsterdam to Lisbon can now clear four border crossings by showing a single piece of paper. Before the formation of the EU, the same driver would have carried two pounds of paper to cross the same borders. The standardized rules and procedures have helped to create an estimated 2.5 million jobs since.

Nevertheless, many regulations still are not standardized. Since 1997, Kellogg has faced obstacle after obstacle as it tries to persuade regulators in different EU countries to allow it to put the same vitamins in all of its corn flakes. Denmark doesn't want any vitamins added, fearing that cereal eaters who already take multivitamins might exceed recommended daily doses, which some experts say can damage internal organs. Dutch officials don't believe that either Vitamin D or folic acid is beneficial, so they don't want them added. Finland likes more Vitamin D than other countries to help Finns make up for sun deprivation.[15] Caterpillar, Inc., has encountered similar problems. It sells tractors throughout Europe, but in Germany, it must install a louder backup horn and locate the lights in different places. Requirements for yield signs and license-plate holders on the backs of vehicles also differ, sometimes just by centimeters, from country to country.

Some economists have called the EU the "United States of Europe." It is an attractive market, with purchasing power almost equal to that of the United States. But the EU will probably never be a United States of Europe. For one thing, even if a united Europe achieves standardized regulations, marketers will not be able to produce a single Europroduct for a generic Euroconsumer. With more than 15 different languages and individual national customs, Europe will always be far more diverse than the United States. Thus, product differences will continue to be necessary. It will be a long time, for instance, before the French begin drinking the instant coffee that Britons enjoy. Preferences for washing machines also differ: British homemakers want front-loaders, and the French want top-loaders; Germans like lots of settings and high spin speeds;

Italians like lower speeds. Even European companies that think they understand Euroconsumers often have difficulties producing "the right product." Atag Holdings NV, a diversified Dutch company whose main business is kitchen appliances, was confident it could cater to both the "potato" and "spaghetti" belts—marketers' terms for consumer preferences in northern and southern Europe. But Atag quickly discovered that preferences vary much more than that. For example, on its ovens, burner shape and size, knob and clock placement, temperature range, and colors vary greatly from country to country. Although Atag's kitchenware unit has lifted foreign sales to 25 percent of its total from 4 percent in the mid-1990s, it now believes that its range of designs and speed in delivering them, rather than the magic bullet of a Europroduct, will keep it competitive.

An entirely different type of problem facing global marketers is the possibility of a protectionist movement by the EU against outsiders. For example, European automakers have proposed holding Japanese imports at roughly their current 10 percent market share. The Irish, Danes, and Dutch don't make cars and have unrestricted home markets; they would be unhappy about limited imports of Toyotas and Datsuns. But France has a strict quota on Japanese cars to protect Renault and Peugeot. These local carmakers could be hurt if the quota is raised at all.

The EU is a very tough antitrust enforcer—tougher than the United States, some would say. The EU, for example, blocked a merger between General Electric and Honeywell (both American companies) even after U.S. regulators had approved the deal! Unlike U.S. law, EU laws allow officials to seal corporate offices for unspecified periods to prevent destruction of evidence and enter the homes, cars, yachts, and other personal property of executives suspected of abusing their companies' market power or conspiring to fix prices. In 2005, the European offices of Intel were raided by EU antitrust officials looking for evidence of abuse of monopoly power. Advanced Micro Devices (AMD) claimed that Intel had achieved its 90 percent share of the global market through threats and kickbacks.[16]

Microsoft has been fighting the European Court since 2002, with no quick end in sight. The court fined Microsoft for monopolizing Internet access by offering Internet Explorer with its Windows software. The company is also appealing a court decision requiring it to share code with "open-source" companies. Another big American company, Coca-Cola, settled a six-year antitrust dispute with the European Court by agreeing to strict limits on its sales tactics. Coke can't sign exclusive agreements with retailers that would ban competing soft drinks. It can't give retailers rebates based on sales volume; and it must give rivals, like Pepsi, 20 percent of the space in Coke coolers so that they can stock their own brands. If Coke violates the terms of the agreement, it will be fined 10 percent of its worldwide revenue (over $2 billion).[17]

The World Bank and International Monetary Fund

Two international financial organizations are instrumental in fostering global trade. The **World Bank** offers low-interest loans to developing nations. Originally, the purpose of the loans was to help these nations build infrastructure such as roads, power plants, schools, drainage projects, and hospitals. Now the World Bank offers loans to help developing nations relieve their debt burdens. To receive the loans, countries must pledge to lower trade barriers and aid private enterprise. In addition to making loans, the World Bank is a major source of advice and information for developing nations. The United States has granted the organization $60 million to create knowledge databases on nutrition, birth control, software engineering, creating quality products, and basic accounting systems.

The **International Monetary Fund (IMF)** was founded in 1945, one year after the creation of the World Bank, to promote trade through financial cooperation and eliminate trade barriers in the process. The IMF makes short-term loans to member nations that are unable to meet their budgetary expenses. It operates as a lender of last resort for troubled nations. In exchange for these emergency loans, IMF lenders frequently extract significant commitments from the borrowing nations to address the problems

World Bank
An international bank that offers low-interest loans, advice, and information to developing nations.

International Monetary Fund (IMF)
An international organization that acts as a lender of last resort, providing loans to troubled nations, and also works to promote trade through financial cooperation.

that led to the crises. These steps may include curtailing imports or even devaluing the currency.

DEMOGRAPHIC MAKEUP

The three most densely populated nations in the world are China, India, and Indonesia. But that fact alone is not particularly useful to marketers. They also need to know whether the population is mostly urban or rural, because marketers may not have easy access to rural consumers. In Belgium about 90 percent of the population lives in an urban setting, whereas in Kenya almost 80 percent of the population lives in a rural setting. Belgium is thus the more attractive market. Just as important as population is personal income within a country. Exhibit 4.2 showed gross national income per capita in selected countries.

Another key demographic consideration is age. There is a wide gap between the older populations of the industrialized countries and the vast working-age populations of developing countries. This gap has enormous implications for economies, businesses, and the competitiveness of individual countries. It means that while Europe and Japan struggle with pension schemes and the rising cost of health care, countries like China, Brazil, and Mexico can reap the fruits of what's known as a demographic dividend: falling labor costs, a healthier and more educated population, and the entry of millions of women into the workforce.

The demographic dividend is a gift of falling birthrates, and it causes a temporary bulge in the number of working-age people. Population experts have estimated that one-third of East Asia's economic miracle can be attributed to a beneficial age structure. But the miracle occurred only because the governments had policies in place to educate their people, create jobs, and improve health.

NATURAL RESOURCES

A final factor in the external environment that has become more evident in the past decade is the shortage of natural resources. For example, petroleum shortages have created huge amounts of wealth for oil-producing countries such as Norway, Saudi Arabia, and the United Arab Emirates. Both consumer and industrial markets have blossomed in these countries. Other countries—such as Indonesia, Mexico, and Venezuela—were able to borrow heavily against oil reserves in order to develop more rapidly. On the other hand, industrial countries like Japan, the United States, and much of western Europe experienced an enormous transfer of wealth to the petroleum-rich nations. The high price of oil in 2005 and 2006 created inflationary pressures in petroleum-importing nations. It also created major problems for airlines and other petroleum-dependent industries.

Petroleum is not the only natural resource that affects international marketing. Warm climate and lack of water mean that many of Africa's countries will remain importers of foodstuffs. The United States, on the other hand, must rely on Africa for many precious metals. Japan depends heavily on the United States for timber and logs. A Minnesota company manufactures and sells a million pairs of disposable chop-sticks to Japan each year. The list could go on, but the point is clear. Vast differences in natural resources create international dependencies, huge shifts of wealth, inflation and recession, export opportunities for countries with abundant resources, and even a stimulus for military intervention.

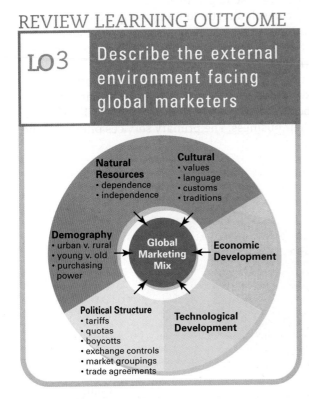

REVIEW LEARNING OUTCOME

LO3 Describe the external environment facing global marketers

Cultural
• values
• language
• customs
• traditions

Natural Resources
• dependence
• independence

Demography
• urban v. rural
• young v. old
• purchasing power

Global Marketing Mix

Economic Development

Political Structure
• tariffs
• quotas
• boycotts
• exchange controls
• market groupings
• trade agreements

Technological Development

Global Marketing by the Individual Firm

A company should consider entering the global marketplace only after its management has a solid grasp of the global environment. Some relevant questions are "What are our options in selling abroad?" "How difficult is global marketing?" and "What are the potential risks and returns?" Concrete answers to these questions would probably encourage the many U.S. firms not selling overseas to venture into the international arena. Foreign sales can be an important source of profits.

Companies decide to "go global" for a number of reasons. Perhaps the most important is to earn additional profits. Managers may feel that international sales will result in higher profit margins or more added-on profits. A second stimulus is that a firm may have a unique product or technological advantage not available to other international competitors. Such advantages should result in major business successes abroad. In other situations, management may have exclusive market information about foreign customers, marketplaces, or market situations. While exclusivity can provide an initial motivation for international marketing, managers must realize that competitors can be expected to catch up with the firm's information advantage. Finally, saturated domestic markets, excess capacity, and potential for economies of scale can also be motivators to "go global." Economies of scale mean that average per-unit production costs fall as output is increased.

Many firms form multinational partnerships—called strategic alliances—to assist them in penetrating global markets; strategic alliances are examined in Chapter 6. Five other methods of entering the global marketplace are, in order of risk, exporting, licensing and franchising, contract manufacturing, the joint venture, and direct investment (see Exhibit 4.4).

EXPORTING

When a company decides to enter the global market, exporting is usually the least complicated and least risky alternative. Exporting is selling domestically produced products to buyers in another country. A company can sell directly to foreign importers or buyers. Exporting is not limited to huge corporations such as General Motors or 3M. Indeed, small companies account for 96 percent of all U.S. exporters, but only 30 percent of the export volume.[18] The United States is the world's largest exporter.

The U.S. Commercial Service within the Department of Commerce promotes itself as "Your Global Business Partner." It offers trade specialists in more than a hundred U.S. cities and 150 overseas offices to help beginning exporters, and helps those already engaged in global marketing increase their business. The primary services offered by the

exporting
Selling domestically produced products to buyers in another country.

Exhibit 4.4

Risk Levels for Five Methods of Entering the Global Marketplace

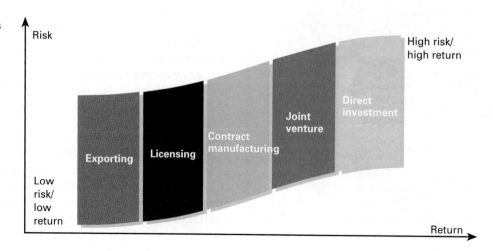

U.S. Commercial Service are marketing research, locating qualified buyers and partners, trade events, and global business consulting. These services are explained in more detail in Exhibit 4.5.

Recently, the U.S. Commercial Service launched BuyUSA.com. This Internet service offers one-on-one export counseling provided by the U.S. Commercial Service. In addition, the site provides Web-based sales leads to exporters. A U.S. exporter fills out a questionnaire on its product offerings and receives access to qualified foreign buyers. We suggest that you go to the Web site and take the BuyUSA tour and demo to learn more about how the U.S. Commercial Service aids American firms wanting to "go global." For those interested in international business, a nongovernmental Web site that offers links to hundreds of useful sites is available from the International Federation of International Trade Associations (**http://fita.org**).

Instead of selling directly to foreign buyers, a company may decide to sell to intermediaries located in its domestic market. The most common intermediary is the export merchant, also known as a **buyer for export**, which is usually treated like a domestic customer by the domestic manufacturer. The buyer for export assumes all risks and sells internationally for its own account. The domestic firm is involved only to the extent that its products are bought in foreign markets.

A second type of intermediary is the **export broker**, who plays the traditional broker's role by bringing buyer and seller together. The manufacturer still retains title and assumes all the risks. Export brokers operate primarily in agricultural products and raw materials.

Export agents, a third type of intermediary, are foreign sales agents-distributors who live in the foreign country and perform the same functions as domestic manufacturers' agents, helping with international financing, shipping, and so on. The U.S. Department of Commerce has an agent-distributor service that helps about 5,000 U.S. companies a year find an agent or distributor in virtually any country of the world. A second category of agents resides in the manufacturer's country but represents foreign buyers. This type of agent acts as a hired purchasing agent for foreign customers operating in the exporter's home market.

LICENSING AND FRANCHISING

Another effective way for a firm to move into the global arena with relatively little risk is to sell a license to manufacture its product to someone in a foreign country. **Licensing** is the legal process whereby a licensor allows another firm to use its manufacturing process, trademarks, patents, trade secrets, or other proprietary knowledge. The licensee, in turn, pays the licensor a royalty or fee agreed on by both parties.

Because licensing has many advantages, U.S. companies have eagerly embraced the concept, sometimes in unusual ways. Caterpillar, the producer of heavy machinery, has licensed Wolverine World Wide to make "CAT" brand shoes and boots. Europeans have latched onto CAT gear as the new symbol of American outdoor culture. CAT is one of Europe's hottest brands, which translates into almost $1 billion in licensing revenues. CAT also granted Overland Appean Limited a global license to produce CAT apparel.

A licensor must make sure it can exercise sufficient control over the licensee's activities to ensure proper quality, pricing, distribution, and so on. Licensing may also create a new competitor in the long run, if the licensee decides to void the license agreement. International law is often ineffective in stopping such actions. Two common ways of maintaining effective control over licensees are shipping one or more critical components from the United States or locally registering patents and trademarks to the U.S. firm, not to the licensee. Garment companies maintain control by delivering only so many labels per day; they also supply their own fabric, collect the scraps, and do accurate unit counts.

Caterpillar Heavy Equipment

Is it obvious from Caterpillar's home page that it is in the apparel business? Visit the Caterpillar Web site to find out. Does CAT handle the manufacturing and distribution of any of its apparel in any markets? Does that surprise you? Why or why not?

http://www.cat.com

Online

buyer for export
An intermediary in the global market that assumes all ownership risks and sells globally for its own account.

export broker
An intermediary who plays the traditional broker's role by bringing buyer and seller together.

export agent
An intermediary who acts like a manufacturer's agent for the exporter. The export agent lives in the foreign market.

licensing
The legal process whereby a licensor agrees to let another firm use its manufacturing process, trademarks, patents, trade secrets, or other proprietary knowledge.

Counseling and Advocacy

- **Advocacy:** Get a competitive edge with U.S. Commercial Service advocacy. U.S. diplomats and other officials help your company when unanticipated problems arise—resolve payment issues, settle disputes, win contracts, and overcome regulatory hurdles. Support can include government-to-government meetings by U.S. Commercial Service officers and ambassadors with high-level foreign government officials, in addition to direct intervention with international companies.

- **Counseling:** Increase your export sales and enter new international markets with U.S. Commercial Service export counseling. Trade specialists in more than 100 U.S. cities and 80 countries provide in-depth export consulting and customized business solutions. Our trade specialists near you work with our team of experts overseas in getting you the information and advice that you need to succeed.

- **Platinum Key Service:** Get long-term, comprehensive, customized support to achieve your business goals. The Platinum Key Service is solution oriented and custom-tailored to your needs. Identify markets, launch products, develop major project opportunities, resolve market entry questions, and receive assistance on regulatory matters. Our in-country trade specialists will work closely with you to identify needs, provide progress reports, and ensure timely resolution.

Market Research

- **Market Research Library:** Accurate, up-to-date information lets you target the best international markets. Our comprehensive market research includes overviews on doing business in more than 120 countries and profiles of 110 industry sectors. You can also get updates on new regulations, currency fluctuations, business trends, and government-financed projects. Much of this research is available at no charge.

- **Customized Market Research:** Receive specific intelligence on the export prospects for your product or service in a potential market.

- **Business Facilitation Service:** Get low-cost logistical and administrative support when you're on international business travel. Our Business Facilitation Service offers flexible solutions to let you do business when you're away from home.

Finding International Partners

- **International Partner Search:** Find qualified international buyers, partners, or agents without traveling overseas. U.S. Commercial Service specialists will deliver detailed company information on up to five prescreened international companies that have expressed an interest in your company's products and services.

- **Gold Key Matching Service:** Save time and money by letting the U.S. Commercial Service help you find a buyer, partner,

agent, or distributor. The Gold Key Service provides you with one-on-one appointments with prescreened potential agents, distributors, sales representatives, association and government contracts, licensing or joint venture partners, and other strategic business partners in your targeted export market.

- **Commercial News USA:** Promote your products and services to more than 400,000 international buyers in 145 countries. Commercial News USA is a product catalog distributed by U.S. embassies and consulates worldwide and has a proven track record of high response rates and solid sales results.

- **Trade Leads:** View announcements from qualified international companies looking to source U.S. products and services and advertise government tender projects through our trade leads database. All of our trade leads are prescreened by our U.S. embassy or consulate staff overseas and are provided as a free service for U.S. exporters.

- **International Company Profile:** Prevent costly mistakes with quick, low-cost credit checks or due-diligence reports on international companies. Before you do business with a prospective agent, distributor, or partner, the International Company Profile will give you the background information you need to evaluate the company.

Trade Events and Related Services

- **U.S. Pavilions at Certified Trade Fairs:** Exhibit at U.S. Pavilions certified by the U.S. Commercial Service and increase your chances of finding new business. Certified U.S. Pavilions offer one-on-one business matching, business counseling from trade specialists, and special exhibit services designed to help U.S. exporters maximize returns from trade shows and make more international sales.

- **Trade Fair Certification:** Exhibiting at a trade show abroad can lead to tremendous export opportunities for U.S. companies. This is why the Trade Fair Certification Program was created: to help companies like yours make important exhibiting decisions and free you of many of the concerns you may have about exhibiting outside the United States.

- **International Buyer Program:** Find new international business partners at U.S. trade shows with the International Buyer Program. The IBP recruits more than 125,000 foreign buyers and distributors to 32 top U.S. trade shows per year. U.S. Commercial Service trade specialists arrange meetings for U.S. exporters and international delegates and provide export counseling at the show's International Business Center.

- **Trade Missions:** Meet face-to-face with prescreened international business contacts in promising markets with U.S. Commercial Service trade missions. Trade missions save you time and money by allowing you to maximize contact with qualified distributors, sales representatives, or partners in one to four countries.

Entertainment characters and properties, such as Celine Dion, Antonio Banderas, and SpongeBob SquarePants, account for 24 percent of worldwide retail sales of licensed goods. Total license sales now run over $110 billion annually. Corporate trademark/brand properties and fashion labels each account for 21 percent of the total. The United States and Canada account for 65 percent of all global licensing sales.[19]

Franchising is a form of licensing that has grown rapidly in recent years. More than 400 U.S. franchisors operate more than 40,000 outlets in foreign countries, bringing in sales of over $9 billion.[20] Over half of the international franchises are for fast-food restaurants and business services. Relationships with franchisees are not always harmonious, however. Coca-Cola Femsa, Coke's biggest bottler in Latin America and the second largest worldwide, was upset to learn from Coke USA that prices in Mexico would gradually increase starting in 2007 for beverage concentrate, the main ingredient in soft drinks and Coke's primary source of income. Femsa officials said the price rise would cost the company an additional $20 million in 2007 and an extra $60 million annually by 2009. They plan to cut their marketing dollars on Coke's sodas "to offset the impact to our profitability that such concentrate prices represent." Coke's second largest bottler in Mexico, Embotelladoras Arca, said it was considering a similar cutback in marketing.[21]

CONTRACT MANUFACTURING

Firms that do not want to become involved in licensing or to become heavily involved in global marketing may engage in **contract manufacturing**, which is private-label manufacturing by a foreign company. The foreign company produces a certain volume of products to specification, with the domestic firm's brand name on the goods. The domestic company usually handles the marketing. Thus, the domestic firm can broaden its global marketing base without investing in overseas plants and equipment. After establishing a solid base, the domestic firm may switch to a joint venture or direct investment.

Recently, particularly in China, contract manufacturers have been making overruns and selling the excess production directly to either consumers or retailers. New Balance, for example, found that a contract manufacturer was producing extra running shoes and selling them to unauthorized retailers. The retailers were selling the knockoff New Balance shoes for $20, while authorized retailers were trying to sell the same shoe for $60. Recently, New Balance changed its relationship with its suppliers. It cut the number of factories it uses in China to six and monitors them more closely. It has also begun using high-tech shoe labels to better spot counterfeits and keep control of its own production.

Other companies have experienced similar problems. Unilever discovered that one of its suppliers in Shanghai had been making excess cases of soap and selling them directly to retailers. Procter & Gamble says one of its Chinese suppliers sold empty P&G shampoo bottles to another company, which filled them with counterfeit shampoo. P&G fired the supplier.[22]

contract manufacturing
Private-label manufacturing by a foreign company.

JOINT VENTURE

Joint ventures are somewhat similar to licensing agreements. In an international **joint venture**, the domestic firm buys part of a foreign company or joins with a foreign company to create a new entity. A joint venture is a quick and relatively inexpensive way to go global and to gain needed expertise.[23] For example, Robert Mondavi Wineries entered into a joint venture with Baron Philippe de Rothschild, owner of Bordeaux's First Growth chateau, Mouton-Rothschild. They created a wine in California called Opus One. It was immediately established as the American vanguard of quality and price. Mondavi has entered other joint ventures with the Frescobaldi family in Tuscany and with Errazuriz in Chile.

Joint ventures can be very risky. Many fail; others fall victim to a takeover, in which one partner buys out the other. Sometimes joint venture partners simply can't agree on management strategies and policies. Though joint ventures are very popular in the auto industry, many have not worked out. Joint venture factories—General Motors/Toyota, Suzuki/GM, Mazda/Ford, DaimlerChrysler/Mitsubishi—have not been particular successes. DaimlerChrysler and BMW built an engine plant in Brazil that failed to meet expectations.[24] Nevertheless, automakers continue to form joint ventures. DaimlerChrysler and Volkswagen are working together on a minivan for VW. GM, DaimlerChrysler, and BMW are jointly developing hybrid vehicles. There's a DaimlerChrysler/Hyundai JV engine plant in Michigan, and VW and Porsche combined to create the Porsche Cayenne and the VW Touareg. Mazda and Ford recently announced plans to build an engine plant in China. Ford says that the project is key to its expansion plans in China.[25]

joint venture
When a domestic firm buys part of a foreign company or joins with a foreign company to create a new entity.

direct foreign investment
Active ownership of a foreign company or of overseas manufacturing or marketing facilities.

Many U.S. companies practice direct investment by building manufacturing or marketing facilities in foreign countries, like the Chinese Wal-Mart Supercenter pictured here.

© CLARO CORTES IV/REUTERS/CORBIS

DIRECT INVESTMENT

Active ownership of a foreign company or of overseas manufacturing or marketing facilities is **direct foreign investment**. Direct foreign investment by U.S. firms is currently about $2,100 billion. Direct investors have either a controlling interest or a large minority interest in the firm. Thus, they have the greatest potential reward and the greatest potential risk.

For example, Mexico has attracted top U.S. candy manufacturers looking for cheap labor, cheap sugar, and a youthful Mexican market with a sweet tooth. American confectioners are also using Mexico as a platform to export back into the U.S. market, more than tripling Mexican candy sales in the United States to around $150 million a year from less than $50 million in 1993, the year before NAFTA went into effect. That sales surge is behind the shrinking candy workforce north of the border. All of the Big Three U.S. candy makers—Mars, Inc., Tootsie Roll Industries, and the Hershey Company—operate plants in Mexico.[26]

Wal-Mart now has over 2,000 stores located outside the United States. In 2005, international sales were over $60 billion. About one-third of all new Wal-Mart stores are opened in global markets. Wal-Mart already has 151 stores in Brazil, for example, and is opening about two more there each month. Today, the company reaches about half of Brazil's 180 million consumers. Wal-Mart's total sales of $300 billion are almost equal to half of Brazil's GDP.[27] Wal-Mart occasionally stumbles in its quest for international growth. To American eyes, the Wal-Mart ethics code is standard stuff. But when the company distributed the newly translated code to German employees, it caused a furor. They read a caution against supervisor-employee relationships as a puritanical ban on interoffice romance, while a call to report improper behavior was taken as an invitation to spy on coworkers. Competitors continue to chuckle about the reaction customers had when Wal-Mart tried to offer services such as grocery bagging. It turned out that Germans didn't want strangers handling their groceries. And when female clerks followed orders to smile at shoppers, male customers took it as a come-on.[28]

Direct investment by American companies in China's rapidly expanding economy has mushroomed. General Motors, for example, offers a range of vehicles for various market segments. For China's newly rich, there are $75,000-plus Cadillac SRX sport-utility vehicles and $55,000 CTS sedans. A bit lower down, the $30,000 Buick Regal is positioned as the vehicle for cost-conscious entrepreneurs who want a prestigious car. For mid-level managers, there are various models of the $15,000-to-$20,000 Buick Excelle. And for younger urbanites buying their first cars, GM's Chevrolet division offers the $19,000 Epica sedan, the $10,000-to-$12,000 Aveo hatchback, and the $5,700 Spark minicar. Meanwhile, in the countryside GM offers the Wuling, which goes for $4,000 to $6,500. This boxy minivan can carry seven passengers, a couple of hogs, or a dozen sacks of potatoes.

GM isn't alone in discovering that China is not a monolithic market. The country, with 1.3 billion citizens speaking more than 100 dialects, is wildly diverse. What people eat, wear, and drive differs greatly from north to south, east to west, rich to poor, young to old, city to countryside. Appliance and electronics maker Samsung discovered that customers living in steamy Guangdong Province need larger refrigerators than those in the more temperate north, so it started shipping bigger fridges south. Procter & Gamble has won over consumers in China's hinterlands with a budget detergent called Tide Clean White, while holding onto city customers with the more expensive Tide Triple Action. P&G reaches China's urban strivers by sponsoring a popular reality TV show called *Absolute Challenge*, in which contestants vie to win jobs as product representatives for Crest or Cover Girl. At the same time, it blankets village kiosks and mom-and-pop stores with advertising emphasizing the value offered by Tide Clean White and low-end versions of Crest and Oil of Olay skin cream.[29]

Sometimes firms make direct investments because they can find no suitable local partners. Direct investments also avoid the communication problems and conflicts of interest that can arise with joint ventures. Other firms simply don't want to share their technology, which they fear may be stolen or ultimately used against them by creating a new competitor. Texas Instruments has historically been one of the latter companies.

A firm may make a direct foreign investment by acquiring an interest in an existing company or by building new facilities. It might do so because it has trouble transferring some resource to a foreign operation or getting that resource locally. One important resource is personnel, especially managers. If the local labor market is tight, the firm may buy an entire foreign firm and retain all its employees instead of paying higher salaries than competitors.

The United States is a popular place for direct investment by foreign companies. In 2007, the value of foreign-owned businesses in the United States was more than $600 billion.

REVIEW LEARNING OUTCOME

LO4 Identify the various ways of entering the global marketplace

International Trade

Exporting
Licensing and franchising
Contract manufacturing
Joint venture
Direct investment

Lower Risk

Higher Risk

LO5
The Global Marketing Mix

To succeed, firms seeking to enter into foreign trade must still adhere to the principles of the marketing mix. Information gathered on foreign markets through research is the basis for the four Ps of global marketing strategy: product, place (distribution), promotion, and price. Marketing managers who understand the advantages and disadvantages of different ways of entering the global market and the effect of the external environment on the firm's marketing mix have a better chance of reaching their goals.

The first step in creating a marketing mix is developing a thorough understanding of the global target market. Often this knowledge can be obtained through the same types of marketing research used in the domestic market (see Chapter 8). However, global marketing research is conducted in vastly different environments. Conducting a survey can be difficult in developing countries, where telephone ownership is growing but is not always common and mail delivery is slow or sporadic. Drawing samples based on known population parameters is often difficult because of the lack of data. In some cities in South America, Mexico, Africa, and Asia, street maps are unavailable, streets are unidentified, and houses are unnumbered. Moreover, the questions a marketer can ask may differ in other cultures. In some cultures, people tend to be more private than in the United States and will not respond to personal questions on surveys. For instance, in France, questions about one's age and income are considered especially rude.

PRODUCT AND PROMOTION

With the proper information, a good marketing mix can be developed. One important decision is whether to alter the product and the promotion for the global marketplace. Other options are to radically change the product or to moderately adjust either the promotional message or the product to suit local conditions.

One Product, One Message

The strategy of global marketing standardization, which was discussed earlier, means developing a single product for all markets and promoting it the same way all over the world. For instance, Procter & Gamble uses the same product and promotional themes for Head and Shoulders in China as it does in the United States. The advertising draws attention to a person's dandruff problem, which stands out in a nation of black-haired people. Head and Shoulders is now the best-selling shampoo in China despite costing over 300 percent more than local brands. Buoyed by its success with Head and Shoulders, P&G is using the same product and same promotion strategy with Tide detergent in China. It also used another common promotion tactic that has been successful in the United States. The company spent half a million dollars to reach agreements with local washing machine manufacturers, which now include a free box of Tide with every new washer.

Other multinational firms are also applying uniform branding around the world on products such as Dove, Perrier, L'Oréal, and Hellmann's. Nestlé has been transitioning from Carnation to Nestlé on nutritional products such as infant formula and instant breakfast in the United States to achieve global harmonization. Unilever recently began a transition from its Lipton side dish line in the United States to the more globally prominent Knorr brand.

Opened in 1982, Honda's Marysville, Ohio, plant was the first built by a Japanese manufacturer in the United States. Now, several Asian and European automakers have plants here—even BMW.

Global media—especially satellite and cable TV networks like CNN International, MTV Networks, and British Sky Broadcasting—make it possible to beam advertising to audiences unreachable a few years ago. Eighteen-year-olds in Paris often have more in common with 18-year-olds in New York than with their own parents. Almost all of MTV's advertisers run

Disneyland Resort Paris
How does Disney vary its park information to suit specific cultural tastes? Compare the presentation of theme park information for the U.S., Tokyo, and Paris resorts. What similarities and differences do you notice?
http://disney.go.com

Online

unified, English-language campaigns in the nations the firm reaches. The audiences buy the same products, go to the same movies, listen to the same music, and sip the same colas. Global advertising works on that simple premise. Although teens throughout the world prefer movies above all other forms of television programming, they are closely followed by music videos, stand-up comedy, and then sports.

Global marketing standardization can sometimes backfire. Unchanged products may fail simply because of cultural factors. The game *Trivial Pursuit* failed in Japan. It seems that getting the answers wrong can be seen as a loss of face. Any type of war game tends to do very poorly in Germany, even though Germany is by far the world's biggest game-playing nation. A successful game in Germany has plenty of details and thick rulebooks.

Sometimes the desire for absolute standardization must give way to practical considerations and local market dynamics. For example, because of the feminine connotations of the word *diet,* the European version of Diet Coke is Coca-Cola Light. In France, its country of origin, the leading brand of yogurt is called Danone, whereas in the United States, it goes by its anglicized name, Dannon. Even if the brand name differs by market—as with Lay's potato chips, which are Sabritas in Mexico—a strong visual relationship may be created by uniform application of the brandmark and graphic elements on packaging.[30]

Product Invention

In the context of global marketing, product invention can be taken to mean either creating a new product for a market or drastically changing an existing product. For the Japanese market, Nabisco had to remove the cream filling from its Oreo cookies because Japanese children thought they were too sweet. Campbell Soup invented a watercress and duck gizzard soup that is now selling well in China. It is also considering a cream of snake soup. Frito-Lay's most popular potato chip in Thailand is shrimp flavored. Popular ice cream flavors in Japan include pickled orchid, eel, fish, sea slug, whale meat, soft-shelled turtle, and cedar chips.

Whirlpool has launched what it bills as the world's cheapest automatic washer, with an eye on low-income consumers who thought they could never afford one. Whirlpool invested $30 million over 18 months to develop the washing machine in Brazil. But the Ideale (the machine's brand name) is a global project because it is also being manufactured in China and India. The washer was launched first in Brazil and China (where its Chinese name means Super Hand-Washing Washer). It followed in India a few months later. Soon it will be marketed in other developing countries. The target retail price: $150 to $200. Just about a quarter of Brazilian households have an automatic washing machine, and penetration is only about 8 percent in China and 4.5 percent in India.[31]

Consumers in different countries use products differently. For example, in many countries, clothing is worn much longer between washings than in the United States, so a more durable fabric must be produced and marketed. For Peru, Goodyear developed a tire that contains a higher percentage of natural rubber and has better treads than tires manufactured elsewhere in order to handle the tough Peruvian driving conditions. Rubbermaid has sold millions of open-top wastebaskets in America; Europeans, picky about garbage peeking out of bins, want bins with tight lids that snap into place.

Product Adaptation

Another alternative for global marketers is to slightly alter a basic product to meet local conditions. Sometimes it is as simple as changing the package size. In India, Unilever

Successful global marketers have discovered that the path to profitability is through tailoring products to various tastes and desires. A Japanese salesclerk displays a package of flounder and spinach stew, a jar of white bait porridge, and a wild duck cream stew, all produced by America's leading baby-food maker, Gerber. The Japanese baby-food market has tripled in the past 15 years, and more than four hundred infant entries jostle for spots on Japan's jam-packed supermarket shelves.

sells single-use sachets of Sunsilk shampoo for 2 to 4 cents. Unilever's Rexona brand deodorant sticks sell for 16 cents and up. They are big hits in India, the Philippines, Bolivia, and Peru—where Unilever has grabbed 60 percent of the deodorant market. A nickel-size Vaseline package and a tube containing enough Close Up toothpaste for 20 brushings sell for about 8 cents each. In Nigeria, Unilever sells 3-inch-square packets of margarine that don't need refrigeration.[32]

Sometimes power sources and/or voltage must be changed on electronic products. It may be necessary, for example, to change the size and shape of the electrical plug. In other cases, the change may be a bit more radical. In India, people often lack reliable access to electricity or can't afford batteries. So, Freeplay Energy Group of London created a radio that is charged by cranking a handle.

Starbucks coffee has invaded England, upsetting the tea cart in a country famous for its afternoon tea. London already has some 200 Starbucks outlets, surpassing New York City, which has 190. All told, there are 466 Starbucks in the United Kingdom. Meanwhile, British tea sales have declined 12 percent in the past five years. That is a momentous shift. After all, tea has been a British staple since the 1600s, and the British Empire's expansion was, at least in part, a search for land to grow tea plants.

For years, coffee in Britain was almost always made from instant powder, a pale imitation of the fresh-brewed drink that Americans have long enjoyed. But in 1998, the first Starbucks shops opened in affluent London neighborhoods. At first, the chain struggled with high real estate costs and management problems. But after a change in leadership, it started to spread to smaller towns throughout Britain. Starbucks in Britain does come with some twists. Its menu includes cheese and marmite sandwiches. (Marmite is a black yeast spread that only the British—and the citizens of some of their former colonies—seem able to stomach.) Its local product-development team has also come up with a cold creamy drink called Strawberries and Cream Frappuccino. Otherwise, it is like any Starbucks in America.[33]

When IKEA, the Sweden-based furniture retailer, entered the U.S. market, it kept the same items but dropped the smaller-sized beds, linens, and other furniture. American houses are twice as big as the average European home, and thus the furniture is larger.

Message Adaptation

Another global marketing strategy is to maintain the same basic product but alter the promotional strategy. Bicycles are mainly pleasure vehicles in the United States. In many parts of the world, however, they are a family's main mode of transportation. Thus, promotion in these countries should stress durability and efficiency. In contrast, U.S. advertising may emphasize escaping and having fun.

Harley-Davidson decided that its American promotion theme, "One steady constant in an increasingly screwed-up world," wouldn't appeal to the Japanese market. The Japanese ads combine American images with traditional Japanese ones: American riders passing a geisha in a rickshaw, Japanese ponies nibbling at a Harley motorcycle. Waiting lists for Harleys in Japan are now six months long.

Kit Kat bars are a hit the world over, but Nestlé didn't have much luck selling them in Japan until it figured out how to crack the teen market. In Japan, the product's name is pronounced "kitto katsu," which roughly translates to "I hope you win." Fueling a rumor that Kit Kats bring success at crucial school exams, Nestlé rolled out packages combining the candy with other good-luck charms. Now 90 percent of Japanese schoolkids say they've heard of Kit Kat bars, and Kit Kat sales have soared 28 percent.[34]

Some cultures view a product as having less value if it has to be advertised. In other nations, claims that seem commonplace by U.S. standards may be viewed negatively or even not allowed. Germany does not permit advertisers to state that their products are "the best" or "better" than those of competitors, descriptions commonly used in U.S. advertising. The hard-sell tactics and sexual themes so common in U.S. advertising are taboo in many countries. Procter & Gamble's advertisements for Cheer detergents were voted least popular in Japan because they used hard-sell testimonials. The negative reaction forced P&G to withdraw Cheer from the Japanese market. In the Middle East, pictures of women in print advertisements have been covered with censors' ink.

Language barriers, translation problems, and cultural differences have generated numerous headaches for international marketing managers. Consider these examples:

- A toothpaste claiming to give users white teeth was especially inappropriate in many areas of Southeast Asia, where the well-to-do chew betel nuts and black teeth are a sign of higher social status.

- Procter & Gamble's Japanese advertising for Camay soap nearly devastated the product. In one commercial, a man meeting a woman for the first time immediately compared her skin to that of a fine porcelain doll. Although the ad had worked in other Asian countries, the man came across as rude and disrespectful in Japan.

- A teenager careening down a store aisle on a grocery cart in a Coca-Cola ad was perceived as too rebellious in Singapore.

- In China, Toyota had to pull and formally apologize for 30 magazine and newspaper advertisements depicting stone lions—a traditional sign of Chinese power—saluting and bowing to a Prado Land Cruiser sport-utility vehicle. "You cannot but respect the Prado," the ad said. But Chinese words often have multiple meanings. *Prado* translates into Chinese as *badao,* which also means "rule by force" or "overbearing." Consumer critics who called Toyota and posted scathing—occasionally profane—messages in Internet discussion groups said the lions resembled those flanking the Marco Polo Bridge, the site near Beijing of the opening battle in Japan's 1937 invasion of China.[35]

PLACE (DISTRIBUTION)

Solving promotional and product problems does not guarantee global marketing success. The product still has to get adequate distribution. For example, Europeans don't play sports as much as Americans do, so they don't visit sporting-goods stores as often. Realizing this, Reebok started selling its shoes in about 800 traditional shoe stores in France. In one year, the company doubled its French sales. Harley-Davidson had to open two company-owned stores in Japan to get distribution for its Harley clothing and clothing accessories.

The Japanese distribution system is considered the most complicated in the world. Imported goods wind their way through layers of agents, wholesalers, and retailers. For example, a bottle of 96 aspirins costs about $20 because the bottle passes through at least six wholesalers, each of whom increases the selling price. As a result, the Japanese consumer pays the world's most exorbitant prices. These distribution channels seem to be based on historical and traditional patterns of socially arranged trade-offs, which Japanese officials claim are very hard for the government to change. Today, however, the system seems to be changing because of pressure from Japanese consumers, who are putting more emphasis on low prices in their purchasing decisions. The retailer who can cut distribution costs and therefore the retail price gets the sale. For example, Kojima, a Japanese electronics superstore chain like the U.S. chains Circuit City and Best Buy, had to bypass General Electric's Japanese distribution partner Toshiba to import its merchandise at a good price. Toshiba's distribution system required refrigerators to pass through too many hands before they reached the retailer. Kojima went directly to GE headquarters in the United States and persuaded the company to sell it refrigerators, which were then shipped directly to Kojima. It is now selling GE refrigerators for about $800—half the price of a typical Japanese model.

Innovative distribution systems can create a competitive advantage for savvy companies. Every day, dozens of flights touch down at Kenya's Nairobi Airport, unloading tourists. But when some of those same KLM and Kenya Airlines aircraft take off for the late-night trip home, they're carrying far more than weary travelers returning from African safaris. Their planes are crammed with an average 25 tons apiece of fresh beans, bok choy, okra, and other produce that was harvested and packaged just the day before. It's all bound for eager—and growing—markets in Brussels, London, Paris, and other European cities.

Those flights are integral parts of an innovative supply chain that might make Michael Dell envious. Vegpro Kenya, one of the nation's top produce exporters, operates seven farms within a two-hour drive of the airport. Every morning, trucks full of just-picked vegetables—30 varieties in all—dash to the airport. There, inside Vegpro's 27,000-square-foot air-conditioned cargo bay, more than 1,000 workers wash and sort the vegetables before they are rushed onto planes, ensuring that there's no break in the "cool chain" before the produce arrives in European stores the next day.

To combat distribution problems, companies are using creative strategies. Colgate-Palmolive has introduced villagers in India to the concept of brushing teeth by rolling into villages with video vans that show half-hour infomercials on the benefits of toothpaste. The company received more than half of its revenue in that nation from rural areas in 2006. Until recently, the rural market was virtually invisible, due to a lack of distribution. Unilever's Indian subsidiary, Hindustan Lever, sells its cosmetics, toothpastes, and detergents door-to-door. It plans to have over a million direct-sales consultants by 2008. In many developing nations, channels of distribution and the physical infrastructure are inadequate. In China, only 1 percent of the roads are Western-standard expressways, and airfreight accounts for less than 1 percent of all freight volume.[36] Therefore, the main modes of transport are truck and train. But in a fragmented trucking industry with few major companies, multinationals have difficulty determining which companies are reliable. In the rail system, theft is a major problem.

If China is bad, India is worse. The nation's highway network stretches just 124,000 miles, compared with 870,000 miles in China. Most Indian roads are simple two-lane affairs, maintained badly if at all. Shipping goods by rail costs twice as much on average as in developed countries and three times as much as in China. At India's ports, shipments often languish for days waiting for customs clearance and loading berths; goods typically take 6 to 12 weeks to reach the United States, compared with 2 to 3 weeks for goods from China.[37]

The lack of distribution infrastructure and cultural differences are creating problems for Dell in China. While Dell has focused on large business and government customers in the country's major cities, demand is emerging elsewhere—in hundreds of smaller cities, where Dell doesn't sell as effectively as its rivals and where even some business customers want to see products before they buy. That's where competitors Lenovo, Hewlett-Packard, and Founder have been selling briskly through retail shops. In not pursuing consumers, Dell has neglected an area that is growing much faster than the business sector. If it does start marketing to consumers, Dell's direct-sales strategy might falter because relatively few Chinese customers use credit cards, and those who do aren't accustomed to buying over the phone or the Internet. "The reality is, Dell needs to establish more of a presence on the street," either through sales kiosks or retailers, says Roger L. Kay, president of consulting firm Endpoint Technologies Associates, Inc., in Wayland, Massachusetts.[38]

American companies importing goods to the United States are facing other problems. Logistics has been a growing challenge for U.S. companies seeking to cut costs by shifting more production to countries where manufacturing is cheaper. Now, however, the rising costs for shipping goods are adding to their profit pressures. The surge in global trade in recent years has added to strains and charges for all forms of transport. As a result, some manufacturers are developing costly buffer stocks—which can mean setting up days' or weeks' worth of extra components—to avoid shutting down production lines and failing to make timely deliveries. Others are shifting to more expensive but more-reliable modes of transport, like airfreight, which is faster and less prone to delays than ocean shipping. Some companies are turning to new information technology to keep supply chains flowing and hiring experts to help determine the best U.S. ports to use each week.

PRICING

Once marketing managers have determined a global product and promotion strategy, they can select the remainder of the marketing mix. Pricing presents some unique problems in the global sphere.[39] Exporters must not only cover their production costs but also consider transportation costs, insurance, taxes, and tariffs. When deciding on a final price, marketers must also determine what customers are willing to spend on a particular product. Marketers also need to ensure that their foreign buyers will pay the price. Because developing nations lack mass purchasing power, selling to them often poses special pricing problems. Sometimes a product can be simplified in order to lower the price. The firm must not assume that low-income countries are willing to accept lower quality, however. Although the nomads of the Sahara are very poor, they still buy expensive fabrics to make their clothing. Their survival in harsh conditions and extreme temperatures requires this expense. Additionally, certain expensive luxury items can be sold almost anywhere.

Exchange Rates

The exchange rate is the price of one country's currency in terms of another country's currency. If a country's currency *appreciates*, less of that currency is needed to buy another country's currency. If a country's currency *depreciates*, more of that currency will be needed to buy another country's currency.

How do appreciation and depreciation affect the prices of a country's goods? If, say, the U.S. dollar depreciates relative to the Japanese yen, U.S. residents have to pay more dollars to buy Japanese goods. To illustrate, suppose the dollar price of a yen is $0.012 and that a Toyota is priced at 2 million yen. At this exchange rate, a U.S. resident pays $24,000 for a Toyota ($0.012 × 2 million yen = $24,000). If the dollar depreciates to $0.018 to one yen, then the U.S. resident will have to pay $36,000 for a Toyota.

As the dollar depreciates, the prices of Japanese goods rise for U.S. residents, so they buy fewer Japanese goods—thus, U.S. imports may decline. At the same time, as the dollar depreciates relative to the yen, the yen appreciates relative to the dollar. This means prices of U.S. goods fall for the Japanese, so they buy more U.S. goods—and U.S. exports rise.

Currency markets operate under a system of **floating exchange rates**. Prices of different currencies "float" up and down based on the demand for and the supply of each currency. Global currency traders create the supply of and demand for a particular country's currency based on that country's investment, trade potential, and economic strength.

Dumping

Dumping is the sale of an exported product at a price lower than that charged for the same or a like product in the "home" market of the exporter. This practice is regarded as a form of price discrimination that can potentially harm the importing nation's competing industries. Dumping may occur as a result of exporter business strategies that

floating exchange rates
Prices of different currencies move up and down based on the demand for and the supply of each currency.

dumping
The sale of an exported product at a price lower than that charged for the same or a like product in the "home" market of the exporter.

include (1) trying to increase an overseas market share, (2) temporarily distributing products in overseas markets to offset slack demand in the home market, (3) lowering unit costs by exploiting large-scale production, and (4) attempting to maintain stable prices during periods of exchange rate fluctuations.

Historically, the dumping of goods has presented serious problems in international trade. As a result, dumping has led to significant disagreements among countries and diverse views about its harmfulness. Some trade economists view dumping as harmful only when it involves the use of "predatory" practices that intentionally try to eliminate competition and gain monopoly power in a market. They believe that predatory dumping rarely occurs and that antidumping rules are a protectionist tool whose cost to consumers and import-using industries exceeds the benefits to the industries receiving protection.

Recently, the United States imposed antidumping duties (taxes) on shrimp from eight countries that the government determined were dumping shrimp on the U.S. market. China was hit worst, with maximum duties of 112.81 percent. The maximums for Brazil and Vietnam were 67.8 percent and 25.76 percent, respectively, but Ecuador, India, and Thailand got off relatively lightly.[40]

Countertrade

Global trade does not always involve cash. Countertrade is a fast-growing way to conduct global business. In **countertrade,** all or part of the payment for goods or services is in the form of other goods or services. Countertrade is thus a form of barter (swapping goods for goods), an age-old practice whose origins have been traced back to cave dwellers. The U.S. Department of Commerce says that roughly 30 percent of all global trade is countertrade. In fact, both India and China have made billion-dollar government purchasing lists, with most of the goods to be paid for by countertrade. Recently, the Malaysian government bought 20 diesel-powered locomotives and paid for them with palm oil.

One common type of countertrade is straight barter. For example, PepsiCo sends Pepsi syrup to Russian bottling plants and in payment gets Stolichnaya vodka, which is then marketed in the West. Another form of countertrade is the compensation agreement. Typically, a company provides technology and equipment for a plant in a developing nation and agrees to take full or partial payment in goods produced by that plant. For example, General Tire Company supplied equipment and know-how for a Romanian truck tire plant. In turn, General Tire sold the tires it received from the plant in the United States under the Victoria brand name. Pierre Cardin gives technical advice to China in exchange for silk and cashmere. In these cases, both sides benefit even though they don't use cash.

countertrade
A form of trade in which all or part of the payment for goods or services is in the form of other goods or services.

REVIEW LEARNING OUTCOME

LO5 List the basic elements involved in developing a global marketing mix

Global Marketing Mix

PRODUCT + PROMOTION	PLACE (Distribution)	PRICE
One Product, One Message	Channel Choice	Dumping
Product Invention	Channel Structure	Countertrade
Product Adaptation	Country Infrastructure	Exchange Rates
Message Adaptation		Purchasing Power

LO6
The Impact of the Internet

In many respects "going global" is easier than it has ever been before. Opening an e-commerce site on the Internet immediately puts a company in the international marketplace. Sophisticated language translation software can make any site accessible to persons around the world. Global shippers such as UPS, FedEx, and DHL help solve international e-commerce distribution complexities. E4X, Inc., offers software to ease currency

Worshipers at Zeniarai Benten shrine south of Tokyo wash their money in the trickling spring water of a tiny cave. Cleanse your money here, the saying goes, and it will multiply. The practice exemplifies the culture's firm belief in cash and abhorrence of credit, which explains the reluctance of Japanese consumers to make Internet purchases using credit.

© SHIZUO KAMBAY ASHI/ASSOCIATED PRESS

conversions. Sites that use E4X's software can post prices in U.S. dollars, then ask their customers what currency they wish to use for payment. If the answer is a currency other than dollars, E4X takes over the transaction and translates the price into any of 22 currencies, collects the payment from the customer, and pays the site in dollars, just as though it were any other transaction. Customers never realize they're dealing with a third party.

Nevertheless, the promise of "borderless commerce" and the global "Internet economy" are still being restrained by the old brick-and-mortar rules, regulations, and habits. For example, Lands' End is not allowed to mention its unconditional refund policy on its e-commerce site in Germany because German retailers, which normally do not allow returns after 14 days, sued and won a court ruling blocking mention of it. Credit cards may be the currency of the Internet, but not everyone uses them. Whereas Americans spend an average of $6,500 per year by credit card, Japanese spend less than $2,000. Many Japanese don't even have a credit card. So how do they pay for e-commerce purchases? 7-Eleven Japan, with over 8,000 convenience stores, has come to the rescue. eS-Books, the Japanese Web site partner of Yahoo! Japan, lets shoppers buy books and videos on the Internet, then specify to which 7-Eleven the merchandise is to be shipped. The buyer goes to that specific store and pays cash for the e-purchase.

Like the Japanese, Scandinavians are reluctant to use credit cards, and the French have an *horreur* of revealing the private information that Net retailers often request. French Web sites tend to be decidedly French. For example, FNAC, the largest French video, book, and music retailer, offers a daily "cultural newspaper" at its site. A trendy Web site in France will have a black background, while bright colors and a geometrical layout give a site a German feel. Dutch surfers are keen on video downloads, and Scandinavians seem to have a soft spot for images of nature.

REVIEW LEARNING OUTCOME

LO⁶ Discover how the Internet is affecting global marketing

Global Marketing →

E-commerce

Brick & Mortar
Rules
Regulations
Habits

Review and Applications

LO¹ Discuss the importance of global marketing. Businesspeople who adopt a global vision are better able to identify global marketing opportunities,

Quick Check ✔

Now that you've read the chapter, do you get it?
Take a moment for a quick check using this scale:

1 Not at all; 2 Not very well; 3 Ok; 4 Well; 5 Very Well

Can you . . .

____ explain why global marketing is important?

____ outline the stages of multinational corporations?

____ list the main regional trading agreements that govern global business?

____ differentiate between tariffs, quotas, boycotts, and exchange controls?

____ rank the different methods of going global according to the risk involved?

____ explain global marketing mix strategies?

____ write a paragraph comparing dumping and countertrade?

____ explain how the Internet has affected global marketing?

____ TOTAL

Score: 32–40, you're ready to move on to the applications below; 25–31, skim the chapter one more time before moving on to the applications; 16–24, reread the sections giving you the most trouble and go to ThomsonNow for guided tutorials; 15 and under, you better reread the chapter to get a grasp of the fundamentals. If you've reread the chapter and still have a low score, visit your professor or TA during office hours.

understand the nature of global networks, create effective global marketing strategies, and compete against foreign competition in domestic markets.

1.2 What is meant by "having a global vision"? Why is it important?

1.2 Isolationists have suggested that America would be much better off economically and politically if we just "built a wall" around the country and didn't deal with outsiders. Do you agree? Why or why not?

LO2 Discuss the impact of multinational firms on the world economy. Multinational corporations are international traders that regularly operate across national borders. Because of their vast size and financial, technological, and material resources, multinational corporations have a great influence on the world economy. They have the ability to overcome trade problems, save on labor costs, and tap new technology.

2.1 Rubbermaid, the U.S. manufacturer of kitchen products and other household items, is considering moving to global marketing standardization. What are the pros and cons of this strategy?

2.2 Do you believe that multinationals are beneficial or harmful to developing nations? Why? What could foreign governments do to make them more beneficial?

LO3 Describe the external environment facing global marketers. Global marketers face the same environmental factors as they do domestically: culture, economic and technological development, political structure and actions, demography, and natural resources. Cultural considerations include societal values, attitudes and beliefs, language, and customary business practices. A country's economic and technological status depends on its stage of industrial development, which, in turn, affects average family incomes. The political structure is shaped by political ideology and such policies as tariffs, quotas, boycotts, exchange controls, trade agreements, and market groupings. Demographic variables include the size of a population and its age and geographic distribution.

3.1 Many marketers now believe that teenagers in the developed countries are becoming "global consumers." That is, they all want and buy the same goods and services. Do you think this is true? If so, what has caused the phenomenon?

3.2 Renault and Peugeot dominate the French market but have no presence in the U.S. market. Why do you think that this is true?

3.3 Suppose that your state senator has asked you to contribute a brief article to her constituents' newsletter that answers the question, "Will there ever be a United States of Europe?" Write a draft of your article, and include reasons why or why not.

3.4 Divide into six teams. Each team will be responsible for one of the following industries: entertainment; pharmaceuticals; computers and software; financial, legal, or accounting services; agriculture; and textiles and apparel. Interview one or more executives in each of these industries to determine how the WTO, NAFTA, and CAFTA have affected and will affect their organizations. If a local firm cannot be contacted in your industry, use the library and the Internet to prepare your report.

3.5 What are the major barriers to international trade? Explain how government policies may be used to either restrict or stimulate global marketing.

LO4 Identify the various ways of entering the global marketplace. Firms use the following strategies to enter global markets, in descending order of risk and profit: direct investment, joint venture, contract manufacturing, licensing and franchising, and exporting.

4.1 Candartel, an upscale manufacturer of lamps and lampshades in America, has decided to "go global." Top management is having trouble deciding how to develop the market. What are some market entry options for the firm?

4.2 Explain how the U.S. Commercial Service can help companies wanting to enter the international market.

4.3 What are some of the advantages and potential disadvantages of entering a joint venture?

4.4 Why is direct investment considered risky?

LO5 List the basic elements involved in developing a global marketing mix. A firm's major consideration is how much it will adjust the four Ps—product, promotion, place (distribution), and price—within each country. One strategy is to use one product and one promotion message worldwide. A second strategy is to create new products for global markets. A third strategy is to keep the product basically the same but alter the promotional message. A fourth strategy is to slightly alter the product to meet local conditions.

5.1 The sale of cigarettes in many developed countries either has peaked or is declining. However, the developing markets represent major growth markets. Should U.S. tobacco companies capitalize on this opportunity?

5.2 Describe at least three situations where an American company might want to keep the product the same but alter the promotion. Also, give three examples where the product must be altered.

5.3 Explain how exchange rates can affect a firm's global sales.

LO6 Discover how the Internet is affecting global marketing. Simply opening a Web site can open the door for international sales. International carriers, like UPS, can help solve logistics problems. Language translation software can help an e-commerce business become multilingual. Yet cultural differences and old-line rules, regulations, and taxes hinder rapid development of e-commerce in many countries.

6.1 Describe how "going global" via the Internet presents opportunities and challenges.

6.2 Give several examples of how culture may hinder "going global" via the Internet.

Key Terms

Exercises

APPLICATION EXERCISE

To be effective as a marketer, it is important to know geography. How will you be able to decide whether to expand into a new territory (domestic or foreign) if you don't know where it is and something about its culture, currency, and economy? If you can't place the European countries on a blank map, or if you can't label the lower 48 states without a list to help you, you're not alone. In one study, students incorrectly located over 50 percent of European countries and over 25 percent of the states in the Unites States. To help you brush up on your geography, we've compiled some tools that you may find useful.[41]

Activities

1. To review domestic geography, go to **http://www.50states.com/tools/usamap.htm** and print the blank map of the United States. Label the map. For a challenge, add the state capitals to the map.

2. To be a global marketer, it is not enough to know where countries are located. You will need to know about the culture, the main exports, the currency, and even the main imports. Select a half-dozen or so countries with which you are unfamiliar, and research basic geographic information about them.

3. Once you have successfully labeled the U.S. map, you may be ready to try labeling a world map. If so, go to **http://www.clickandlearn.com** and view the free, printable, blackline maps. Under the category of world maps, choose the blackline detail map. This shows country outlines, whereas the basic blackline outline map shows only the continents. You will notice that there are also blackline maps for each continent, so if taking on the entire world is too daunting, start with more manageable blocks.

Entrepreneurship Case

MTV: ROCKING THE WORLD ONE NATION AT A TIME

To most people, MTV is as American as apple pie, baseball, and freedom of speech. It is a cultural icon to every American who grew up in the 1980s or 1990s, and it is easily one of the most palpable influence on the behavior of the demographic it targets with its programming. A closer look at MTV's business, however, reveals that its true significance is its ability to translate its formula for success into the many languages of the world. The network now owns 33 distinct channels that broadcast shows in 18 languages to 1.8 billion viewers in over 160 countries.

MTV Networks International, a subsidiary of MTV that actually dwarfs its parent, took its first steps on foreign soil with MTV Europe in 1987 and soon thereafter became Europe's largest television network. With a blueprint for success in hand, the large subsidiary turned its attention to the global youth market, which today includes over 2.5 billion people between the ages of 10 and 34. As it watched demand for television sets and paid programming services explode in rapidly developing markets, such as China, Latin America, and India, MTV was poised to capitalize.

Large and diverse markets, however, are difficult to understand and expensive to penetrate. Initially, MTV simply tried to export a standardized version of its American programming, but it quickly discovered that teens from around the world—while they do enjoy American music—are mostly interested in what's happening in their own regions. MTV responded by undertaking the costly and complex task of producing localized content for specific markets. Now, veejay selection, programming, and service offerings are all unique in any given market.

Digital television and interactive services are very popular in Europe, so MTV UK developed a service that allows viewers to obtain information on CDs, check concert dates, and vote for their favorite performers during the MTV European Music Awards directly from their TV sets. In Asia, a virtual animated veejay named LiLi can interact with viewers in five different languages. Controlled by an actor behind the image, LiLi can also interview guests and provide popular culture tips. Brazilian viewers, who also tend to be huge soccer fans, enjoy *Rockgol*, an MTV-produced soccer championship that has been opposed by Brazilian record industry executives and musicians.

MTV Japan, a joint venture between MTV Networks and local investment firm H&Q Asia Pacific, operates in the world's second largest music market and one of the world's most advanced mobile telecommunications markets. Identifying those two trends, MTV Japan developed a service that lets subscribers use their mobile phones to download entertainment news and new music or vote for their favorite veejay.

The development cycle is long for such detailed international projects, but MTV Networks International president Bill Roedy is a patient man. He spent ten years working with Chinese officials for the right to air MTV programming for just six hours a day. The payoff? Forty cable providers now carry MTV Mandarin into 60 million Chinese homes. Roedy is also sensitive to foreign leaders' fears that their culture will be "Americanized" by MTV. Before his networks enter markets with extreme cultural differences, such as Israel, Singapore, Cuba, or China, Roedy meets with key political figures to allay their fears. "We've had very little resistance once we explain that we're not in the business of exporting American culture," he notes.[42]

Questions

1. Discuss MTV's global product strategy.

2. Identity the key environmental challenges MTV has faced in its effort to expand globally, and discuss how MTV has overcome them.

3. What is MTV's global market entry strategy? Discuss whether you agree with MTV's approach, and identify its advantages and disadvantages.

COMPANY CLIPS

Method—Global Beginnings

In the twenty-first century, startups can become global businesses much faster than in anytime in history. So, while new companies are forging their way domestically, they may also experience an added layer of challenges from trying to enter global markets at the same time. In this final video segment on method, founder Eric Ryan and CEO Alastair Dorward describe their company's perspective on global expansion and which foreign markets represent good opportunities for method.

Questions

1. Is method a multinational company? Explain.

2. Which environmental factors facing all global marketers is method confronting as it begins to expand into foreign markets?

3. Outline method's global marketing mix.

4. What is innovative about how method envisions moving into foreign markets? Would method's strategy for global expansion work for other companies or industries? Which ones? Explain.

BIZ FLIX

Lost in Translation

Now that you have a sense about the issues marketers must consider before entering foreign markets, you may be better able to appreciate how drastic cultural differences can be. The film *Lost in Translation*, starring Scarlett Johansson and Bill Murray, illustrates these differences expertly. Based on director Sophia Coppola's Academy Award winning screenplay, this film was shot entirely on location in Japan. It offers extraordinary views of various parts of Japanese culture that are not available to you without a visit.

Marketing & You Results

This questionnaire measures cultural openness. The higher your score, the more interested you are in learning about other cultures and interacting with people from other countries. People with high cultural openness tend to be less ethnocentric and more open to buying imported products than people with low cultural openness. As you read Chapter 4, cultural openness is an important aspect of developing a global vision.

Marketing Miscue

Mental Health Advocates Not Crazy about Valentine's Day Offering

Valentine's Day 2005 was memorable for many people in Vermont and, in particular, for those at Vermont Teddy Bear Company. The company's "Crazy for You" teddy bear garnered more attention than the company had anticipated. Though the teddy bear did spark a same-period sales increase from the previous year, the company may have wondered whether the controversy set off by the bear's strait jacket was worth the additional sales.

Providing handcrafted, American-made teddy bears, Vermont Teddy Bear Company is a pioneer of direct marketing. The company sells direct to consumers via its 1-800-829-BEAR phone number or online at **http://www.vermontteddybear.com**. The company is pursuing an aggressive growth strategy in a competitive battle with the floral delivery providers. Every year its Bear-Gram service delivers over 450,000 Vermont Teddy Bears. Additionally, more than 150,000 tourists each year visit the company's two factory retail stores in Shelburne and Waterbury, Vermont, and many purchase a bear.

The company offers over 100 bears, with special-occasion bears for special events and holidays. With 92 percent of Americans celebrating Valentine's Day, the holiday ranks fourth in holiday sales transactions and third in dollar volume. Thus, it is not surprising that Vermont Teddy Bear offers a wide variety of Bear-Grams for this Valentine's Day. Customers can choose from specialty teddy bears, such as "Fool for Love," "Heart Throb," "Country Lovin'," "All Star Lover," "Playbear Playmate," "Playboy," "Love Match," "Romantic at Heart," "Love Me Tender," "Jailhouse Rock," "Redhot Lover," and "Purple Passion," that range in price from around $60 to $100 each. In 2005, customers could also order the "Crazy for You" bear.

With a direct to consumer price of $69.95, the "Crazy for You" bear came with its own straitjacket to restrain its paws and a commitment report. The accessories upset mental health advocates across the United States. In a letter to the company, the executive director of the Vermont chapter of the National Alliance for the Mentally Ill said that these accessories were completely inappropriate. He explained that straitjackets are used as a method of involuntary restraint to prevent persons in severe psychological crisis from injuring themselves or others and that commitment reports are used to involuntarily commit individuals to psychiatric treatment when they are temporarily incapable of making informed decisions on their own behalf. Using these symbols of serious mental illness to sell teddy bears was tasteless. Vermont's governor described the "Crazy for You" bear as very insensitive and said that it stigmatized those suffering from mental health problems. Meanwhile, the executive director of the Vermont Human Rights Commission suggested that the company divert a portion of the bear's profits to assist those struggling with mental illnesses.

In response to these criticisms, Vermont Teddy Bears' CEO Elisabeth Robert (pronounced "ro-BEAR") announced that the company would not withdraw the bear from the market. She pointed out that not only had the concept received a positive response in pretesting but that, once on the market, the bear was being enthusiastically purchased by customers. Therefore, she said, the company would continuing selling the bear, which was intended for a one-time Valentine's Day offering, until it was sold out.

The furor began on January 12, 2005, with national media attention, and the "Crazy for You" bear sold out on February 3, 2005. Though the total number of "Crazy for You" bears sold was not reported publicly, the company did receive Valentine's Day orders well in advance of its normal holiday selling season and reported an increase of 29 percent over the 2004 same-period sales.

Though Vermont Teddy Bear fared well, in the short term, from sales of the "Crazy for You" bear, CEO Robert was asked to give up her seat on the board of Vermont's largest hospital, Fletcher Allen Health Care. Her perceived disparagement of the mentally ill was thought to be contrary to the mission of the hospital. Meanwhile, critics wondered if the company would suffer longer-term damage. Would the way Vermont Teddy Bear handled the controversy cause it to lose sales and/or investors? As one public relations expert noted, society would have forgiven a mistake (the introduction of the bear), but it might not forgive arrogance (the company's refusal to withdraw the bear after it was criticized as insensitive).[1]

Questions:

1. Did Vermont Teddy Bear Company violate the requirements of corporate social responsibility? Why or why not?

2. Was the controversy a positive or a negative for the company? For Robert?

Critical Thinking Case

Pharmaceutical Marketing—Direct to Consumers or Not?

There is growing controversy over the estimated $4 billion the pharmaceutical industry spends annually on direct-to-consumer (DTC) advertising. Prior to 1997, pharmaceutical advertising and promotion focused on physicians. Companies advertised their products in professional medical journals and sent sales personnel to visit doctors (referred to as "detailing") and provide them with free samples, which were then passed on to their patients. Since 1997, however, when the Food and Drug Administration (FDA) relaxed pharmaceutical advertising rules, companies have been shifting advertising dollars toward DTC advertising. The marketing issue boils down to whether pharmaceutical companies should influence prescription choices via the physician or the patient.

According to estimates pharmaceutical companies spend close to $25 billion a year promoting new drugs in the United States. With an estimated 80,000 drug company representatives visiting physicians every day, detailing accounts for around $5 billion of this amount, and free drug samples account for slightly over $16 billion. An estimated 80–95 percent of medical doctors see drug company representatives on a regular basis. Nevertheless, research has shown that such marketing tactics have little impact on the prescribing behavior of physicians.

The question, however, is whether DTC advertising affects physician prescribing behavior. Critics say that it does and that consumer ads prompt patients to seek medications they do not need. Additionally, they argue, advertising benefits the market leader because that company can afford to spend the most on advertising and then gains sales from new patients seeking treatment. Some research indicates that doctors comply with patient requests for drugs 85 percent of the time—drugs the patients learned about via DTC ads. At the same time, critics say, creating brand awareness for a particular product makes it more difficult for physicians to prescribe equivalent drugs and plays on consumers' lack of knowledge instead of the physician's level of expertise. In addition, critics claim, ads may encourage overconsumption of some drugs by creating a false impression of a drug's capabilities and exaggerating its effect on the disease or illness. Opponents also argue that DTC advertising is driving up prescription costs and leads to higher individual drug prices as companies seek to cover expensive advertising costs.

Proponents of DTC pharmaceutical advertising contend that it offers several benefits. First, they say, the changing role of information in the health-care system has created a need for DTC advertising. Patients have much greater access to health-care information (via the Internet) and are entering into a patient-doctor relationship empowered by this information. Thus, advertising, as a major means of mass communication, is a primary form of information dissemination. In particular, sufferers of certain diseases and medical conditions benefit from the advertising. For example, disease awareness ads help patients recognize symptoms at an early stage when the disease can still be treated. Ads can help remove the stigma of some illnesses, particularly mental illness. Thus, ads can serve to educate the public. Another benefit of drug advertising is that it encourages compliance. Many conditions (e.g., high cholesterol) do not exhibit outward signs of improvement when the patient takes the medication. These conditions require medical monitoring to determine if the drug is working. Ads can help remind patients to take their medication and to have prescriptions refilled. Furthermore, proponents point out that there does not appear to be a direct correlation between advertising expenditures and product price, and the annual growth in marketing expenditures has remained relatively constant—although there has been a shift of funds from doctor-focused to patient-focused ads.

Pharmaceutical advertising is regulated by the FDA's Division of Drug Marketing, Advertising, and Communications. Division employees review between 30,000 and 40,000 ads a year. Although the annual number of complaints received by the FDA has remained about the same since DTC advertising began in 1997, the number of citations issued to drug manufacturers has dropped about 80 percent during this same time period.

Prescription drug spending is projected to be one of the fastest-growing segments of health-care costs. It is estimated that, by 2012, prescription drugs will account for 14.5 percent of the $3.1 trillion that the United States spends on health care (compared to 10 percent in 2001). Is marketing the reason behind the increased expenditures? Or are knowledgeable consumers taking more drugs and thereby avoiding other health-care costs?[2]

Questions:

1. Who are the customers in the pharmaceutical drug market?

2. Is there a difference between the marketing of pharmaceuticals and the marketing of other consumer products (e.g., computers)? Why or why not?

PART 2

Analyzing Marketing Opportunities

CROSS-FUNCTIONAL CONNECTIONS

W hether a company is trying to determine individual buying behavior, sharpen its target marketing skills, or understand competitive actions, information is the key to success. Traditionally, information gathering has been regarded as the "job" of the marketing department. Companies must realize, however, that the marketplace belongs to the entire company, making it everyone's responsibility to gather and maintain marketplace information.

Clearly, MTV Networks understands the need for information integration. The network thrives on being a trendy, hip entertainment provider. It uses cultural anthropologists to acquire information about the target audience and to disseminate this market research information within the network's organizational structure. These cultural anthropologists gather information from target viewers by visiting their homes, talking with them on the street, and observing them as they go about their daily lives. Internally, the programming, marketing, and scheduling departments share this marketplace information. The ultimate goal is to bring the thoughts and feelings of MTV's target audience into the organization's mainstream functional processes.

Unfortunately, nonmarketing functional areas often

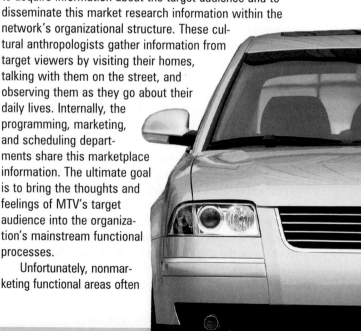

perceive anthropological information such as that used by MTV as too abstract for decision making. The debate often centers on the qualitative-versus-quantitative format of data used by various functional areas. For example, it is often difficult to get engineers, accountants, financial analysts, and production specialists to recognize the reliability of qualitative marketing data. Additionally, though marketing researchers are experts at statistical methods, other functional areas may be suspicious of the source of marketing data because it is often perceptual. For functional experts who are used to dealing with facts, the abstraction found in perceptual data can be difficult to trust.

Employees must realize, however, that the marketplace belongs to the entire company, making it everyone's responsibility to gather and maintain marketplace information.

Not only must the information-gathering process engage all functional areas, but the warehousing or storing of these data also requires considerable cross-functional interactions. Studies examining the maintenance of databases have found that cross-functional misalignments are a critical problem in the successful implementation and use of data warehouses. Companies must assemble and manage cross-functional teams that will make sure market intelligence combines information from both internal and external sources.

Aside from the need for a general cross-functional sharing of data, there are three major areas in which the information-gathering and dissemination processes need to be formally integrated across functions:

1. Benchmarking studies

2. Customer satisfaction studies

3. Forecasting

Benchmarking is the process of comparing a firm's performance in various activities against the performance of other companies that have completed similar activities. A benchmarking study could focus on cross-company comparisons of purchasing processes, inventory management, product development cycles, hiring practices, payroll processes, order fulfillment,

and overall performance of various marketing activities. Gathering information on a firm's competitors during a benchmarking study requires an extensive amount of secondary research. Recently, cross-functional "shadow teams" have been formed to improve the benchmarking of competitive activities. These shadow teams integrate internal information with all externally available information on specific competitors.

Customer satisfaction is driven by issues related to all functions within the firm. Companies such as Enterprise Rent-A-Car link results from customer satisfaction studies with employee promotions. For employees at a particular Enterprise branch to be eligible for promotion, customer satisfaction must be at or above the corporate average. This direct link between customer satisfaction and employee achievement requires that Enterprise have customer metrics that allow for accurate accountability on customer satisfaction.

Forecasting crosses the boundaries of multiple business functions. For example, marketing may offer a discount on a particular product. Key functional partners in a price discount are manufacturing and finance. From a production perspective, the price discount might indicate the need for increased production of the discounted item, assuming the discount is not solely an attempt to sell off excess merchandise. Financially, a price discount connects clearly with gross margins. A drop in price means a decrease in the gross margin, assuming costs remain constant. Unfortunately, marketing's ability to make price changes quickly has been the cause of much conflict between marketing and manufacturing and between marketing and finance.

Marketplace information is a key driver in all decisions made by a company. Therefore, it is imperative that all functional areas participate in gathering and disseminating information. Success in today's global environment depends on all functional areas understanding the firm's customers and competitors.

Questions:

1. What data differences exist across functional areas?

2. What roles do the various functions play in collecting and maintaining marketplace knowledge?

Consumer

Decision Making

Learning Outcomes

LO¹ Explain why marketing managers should understand consumer behavior

LO² Analyze the components of the consumer decision-making process

LO³ Explain the consumer's postpurchase evaluation process

LO⁴ Identify the types of consumer buying decisions and discuss the significance of consumer involvement

LO⁵ Identify and understand the cultural factors that affect consumer buying decisions

LO⁶ Identify and understand the social factors that affect consumer buying decisions

LO⁷ Identify and understand the individual factors that affect consumer buying decisions

LO⁸ Identify and understand the psychological factors that affect consumer buying decisions

Virgin Mobile USA **courts Gen Y**

dentifying changes in consumer behavior often requires picking up a small blip on a marketer's radar that over time becomes more and more obvious. Virgin Mobile USA took advantage of Gen Yers' discontent with the current product and service offerings in the wireless phone market by creating marketing campaigns and calling plans aimed directly at this group of consumers, including lots of ring tones, no contracts, and phones that play music and video.

Many Gen Yers associated existing brands, like Nextel, with their parents, so Virgin Mobile repositioned its line of phones with a new slogan: "Live with-

Virgin Mobile USA's Gen Y campaigns have been a big success.

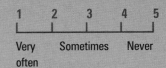

out a plan. The phone of choice for hipsters, slackers, and many people in between." Virgin Mobile's pay-as-you-go plan appeals to Gen Yers because many of them do not have the credit card required to activate a phone. The pay-as-you-go plan also gives users more control over their minutes by offering them three options designed for individuals with different usage patterns—Month2Month, Day2Day, and Minute2Minute. To further entice Gen Yers, some Virgin handsets are cobranded with MTV; all of them bear hip names such as the Party Animal, Slider, Vox, Rave, and most recently Snapper, which is Java- and 3G-enabled and features a 1.8-inch, 65K color display.

Virgin Mobile offers other value-added benefits such as rings from popular artists like Mystikal, Linkin Park, and JayZ; movie theme rings; and the "res-

cue ring," which is a preprogrammed incoming call to help you "escape from a bad date." Over 40 percent of subscribers use *MTV, which allows users to access music news and gossip, play games, vote for videos, and text message the popular MTV show *Total Request Live*.

Over 60 percent of Virgin Mobile subscribers send more than 25 text messages per month—more than twice the activity of the average consumer. Howard Handler, chief marketing officer of Virgin Mobile USA, says, "IM is a huge part of our customers' lives. It's an everyday form of communication for them." For that reason, Virgin Mobile recently partnered with OZ to bring the AOL Instant Messenger service to the youth market.

Virgin Mobile USA's Gen Y campaigns have been a big success. The company now has over three million subscribers—a remarkable achievement considering the product was launched just a little over three years ago—and continues to sign up thousands of young adults every day. Not only is Virgin Mobile attracting customers, but it is focusing on their needs and desires in terms of postpurchase services. In a study by Market Strategies, Inc., Virgin Mobile rated 95 percent in customer satisfaction. Another independent study rated Virgin Mobile USA number one in customer satisfaction among all prepaid wireless services.[1]

If you get your phone from a carrier other than Virgin Mobile, what makes your current plan more appealing, and what might motivate you to switch? What factors are likely to affect mobile phone service purchasing decisions of Gen Yers in the future?

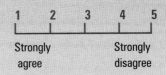

What is your buying behavior?

Using the scales below, enter your answers.

1	2	3	4	5
Very often		Sometimes		Never

_____ I have felt others would be horrified if they knew of my spending habits.

_____ I've bought things even though I couldn't afford them.

_____ I've written a check when I knew I didn't have enough money in the bank to cover it.

_____ I've bought myself something in order to make myself feel better.

_____ I've felt anxious or nervous on days I didn't go shopping.

_____ I've made only the minimum payments on my credit cards.

1	2	3	4	5
Strongly agree				Strongly disagree

_____ If I have any money left at the end of the pay period, I just have to spend it.

_____ Having more money would solve my problems.

_____ I have bought something, arrived home, and didn't know why I had bought it.

Now, total your score. Read the chapter and find out what your score means at the end.

LO¹
The Importance of Understanding Consumer Behavior

Consumers' product and service preferences are constantly changing. In order to address this constant state of flux and to create a proper marketing mix for a well-defined market, marketing managers must have a thorough knowledge of consumer behavior. **Consumer behavior** describes how consumers make purchase decisions and how they use and dispose of the purchased goods or services. The study of consumer behavior also includes an analysis of factors that influence purchase decisions and product use.

Understanding how consumers make purchase decisions can help marketing managers in several ways. For example, if a manager knows through research that gas mileage is the most important attribute for a certain target market, the manufacturer can redesign the product to meet that criterion. If the firm cannot change the design in the short run, it can use promotion in an effort to change consumers' decision-making criteria. In the opening vignette, you learned that Virgin Mobile USA understood that Gen Yers wanted freedom and control over their calling plan and value-added services such as ring tones, instant messaging, and music. The company successfully appealed to this market segment by developing a marketing strategy that met its targeted consumers' needs, wants, and desires.

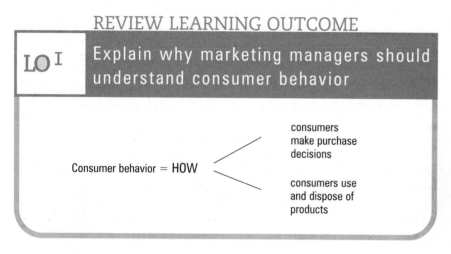

REVIEW LEARNING OUTCOME

LO¹ Explain why marketing managers should understand consumer behavior

Consumer behavior = HOW
— consumers make purchase decisions
— consumers use and dispose of products

LO²
The Consumer Decision-Making Process

When buying products, consumers generally follow the **consumer decision-making process** shown in Exhibit 5.1: (1) need recognition, (2) information search, (3) evaluation of alternatives, (4) purchase, and (5) postpurchase behavior. These five steps represent a general process that can be used as a guide for studying how consumers make decisions. It is important to note, though, that consumers' decisions do not always proceed in order through all of these steps. In fact, the consumer may end the process at any time or may not even make a purchase. The section on the types of consumer buying decisions later in the chapter discusses why a consumer's progression through these steps may vary. Before addressing this issue, however, we will describe each step in the process in greater detail.

NEED RECOGNITION

The first stage in the consumer decision-making process is need recognition. **Need recognition** occurs when consumers are faced with an imbalance between actual and desired states. For example, have you ever gotten blisters from an old running shoe? Or maybe you have seen a TV commercial for a new sports car and wanted to buy it. Need recognition is triggered when a consumer is exposed to either an internal or an external **stimulus**. *Internal stimuli* are occurrences you experience, such as hunger or thirst. For example, you may hear your stomach growl and then realize that you are hungry. *External stimuli* are influences from an outside source such as someone's recommenda-

---

consumer behavior
Processes a consumer uses to make purchase decisions, as well as to use and dispose of purchased goods or services; also includes factors that influence purchase decisions and product use.

consumer decision-making process
A five-step process used by consumers when buying goods or services.

need recognition
Result of an imbalance between actual and desired states.

stimulus
Any unit of input affecting one or more of the five senses: sight, smell, taste, touch, hearing.

tion of a new restaurant, the color of an automobile, the design of a package, a brand name mentioned by a friend, or an advertisement on television or radio.

A marketing manager's objective is to get consumers to recognize an imbalance between their present status and their preferred state. Advertising and sales promotion often provide this stimulus. Surveying buyer preferences provides marketers with information about consumer wants and needs that can be used to tailor products and services. For example, Procter & Gamble frequently surveys consumers regarding their wants and needs. P&G used the Internet to test market its Crest Whitestrips home-bleaching kit, as well as its extensions of the initial product such as Whitestrips Premium/Whitestrips Premium Plus and Night Effects/Night Effects Premium. The test revealed that 80 percent of potential buyers were women between the ages of 35 and 54, thus identifying the best target market for the product. The company was then able to fine-tune its marketing plan before launching the product nationwide.[2] In another example of how far P&G will go to learn about market trends, the company videotapes consumers at home in its own version of reality TV to learn things about them that surveys do not reveal.[3]

Marketing managers can create wants on the part of the consumer. A **want** exists when someone has an unfulfilled need and has determined that a particular good or service will satisfy it. When college students move in to their own apartment or dorm room, they often need to furnish it and want new furniture rather than hand-me-downs from their parents. A want can be for a specific product, or it can be for a certain attribute or feature of a product. In this example, the college students not only need home furnishings, but also want items that reflect their personal sense of style. Similarly, consumers may want ready-to-eat meals, drive-through dry-cleaning service, and Internet shopping to fill their need for convenience.

Another way marketers create new products and services is by observing trends in the marketplace. IKEA, the home furnishing giant, watches the home decor trends and then creates affordable, trendy furniture. For example, marketers at IKEA realized that Generation Y consumers prefer furniture that is stylish, easy to clean, multifunctional, and portable. As a result, IKEA uses "bold orange, pink and green colors." The wood boasts a lacquered finish that can be wiped clean and doesn't need polish. IKEA also

want
Recognition of an unfulfilled need and a product that will satisfy it.

Exhibit 5.1

Consumer Decision-Making Process

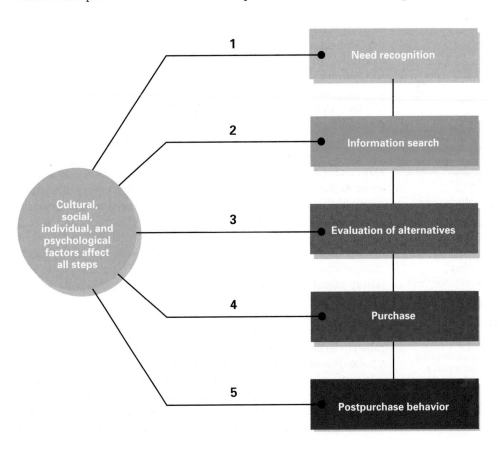

1 Need recognition

2 Information search

3 Evaluation of alternatives

4 Purchase

5 Postpurchase behavior

Cultural, social, individual, and psychological factors affect all steps

offers a space-saving, multifunction desk that can be converted into a dining table; it has wheels so that it can be easily moved.[4]

Consumers recognize unfulfilled wants in various ways. The two most common occur when a current product isn't performing properly and when the consumer is about to run out of something that is generally kept on hand. Consumers may also recognize unfulfilled wants if they become aware of a product that seems superior to the one currently used. Such wants are usually created by advertising and other promotional activities. For example, aware of the popularity of MP3s and consumers' desire to take their music with them, car stereo manufacturers such as Sonicblue and Kenwood have added MP3 interfaces. Other companies, including Apple, Microsoft, RCA, and Creative Technology, are hoping to fulfill consumer desires for smaller audio and video players, referred to as portable media centers. The newest devices have wireless Internet connection capabilities providing access to downloadable movies and TV as well as music and video games. But Apple continues to lead the field with its iPod Shuffle and Nano and extensive downloadable music and TV programs.[5]

Marketers selling their products in global markets must carefully observe the needs and wants of consumers in various regions. Unilever hit on an unrecognized need of European consumers when it introduced Persil Tablets, premeasured laundry detergent in tablet form. Though the tablets are more expensive than regular detergents, Unilever found that European consumers considered laundry a chore and wanted the process to be as simple and uncomplicated as possible. Unilever launched the tablets as a less messy and more convenient alternative. The laundry tablets were an immediate success in the United Kingdom and enabled Unilever's Persil brand to beat out rival Procter & Gamble's best-selling Ariel powder detergent.[6]

INFORMATION SEARCH

After recognizing a need or want, consumers search for information about the various alternatives available to satisfy it. For example, as gasoline prices increase, many people are searching for information on vehicles that use alternatives to gasoline, such as Honda's hybrid models. An information search can occur internally, externally, or both. In an **internal information search,** the person recalls information stored in the memory. This stored information stems largely from previous experience with a product. For example, while traveling with your family, you encounter a hotel where you stayed during spring break earlier that year. By searching your memory, you can probably remember whether the hotel had clean rooms and friendly service.

In contrast, an **external information search** seeks information in the outside environment. There are two basic types of external information sources: nonmarketing-controlled and marketing-controlled. A **nonmarketing-controlled information source** is not associated with marketers promoting a product. These information sources include personal experiences (trying or observing a new product); personal sources (family, friends, acquaintances, and coworkers who may recommend a product or service); and public sources, such as Underwriters Laboratories, *Consumer Reports*, and other rating organizations that comment on products and services. For example, if you are in the mood to go to the movies, you may search your memory for past experiences at various cinemas when determining which one to go to (personal experience). To choose which movie you will see, you may rely on the recommendation of a friend or family member (personal sources). Alternatively, you may read the critical reviews in the newspaper or online (public sources). Marketers gather information on how these information sources work and use it to attract customers. For example, car manufacturers know that younger customers are likely to get information from friends and family, so they try to develop enthusiasm for their products via word of mouth.

On the other hand, a **marketing-controlled information source** is biased toward a specific product, because it originates with marketers promoting that product. Marketing-controlled information sources include mass-media advertising (radio, newspaper, television, and magazine advertising), sales promotion (contests, displays, premiums, and so forth), salespeople, product labels and packaging, and the Internet. Many

internal information search
The process of recalling past information stored in the memory.

external information search
The process of seeking information in the outside environment.

nonmarketing-controlled information source
A product information source that is not associated with advertising or promotion.

marketing-controlled information source
A product information source that originates with marketers promoting the product.

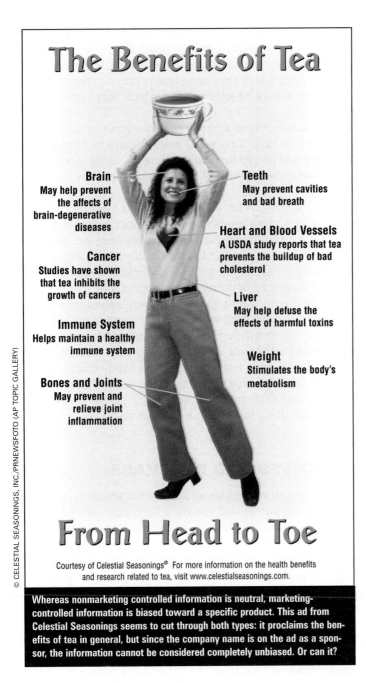

The Benefits of Tea

Brain
May help prevent the affects of brain-degenerative diseases

Teeth
May prevent cavities and bad breath

Heart and Blood Vessels
A USDA study reports that tea prevents the buildup of bad cholesterol

Cancer
Studies have shown that tea inhibits the growth of cancers

Liver
May help defuse the effects of harmful toxins

Immune System
Helps maintain a healthy immune system

Weight
Stimulates the body's metabolism

Bones and Joints
May prevent and relieve joint inflammation

From Head to Toe

Courtesy of Celestial Seasonings® For more information on the health benefits and research related to tea, visit www.celestialseasonings.com.

Whereas nonmarketing controlled information is neutral, marketing-controlled information is biased toward a specific product. This ad from Celestial Seasonings seems to cut through both types: it proclaims the benefits of tea in general, but since the company name is on the ad as a sponsor, the information cannot be considered completely unbiased. Or can it?

consumers, however, are wary of the information they receive from marketing-controlled sources, believing that most marketing campaigns stress the product's attributes and ignore its faults. These sentiments tend to be stronger among better educated and higher-income consumers. For instance, in spite of extensive advertising highlighting its philanthropic activities, Philip Morris continues to have a poor reputation among consumers. In fact, after a survey revealed that an extensive image campaign had not changed consumer opinion about the company, Philip Morris decided to change its corporate name to Altria to shift the focus away from the Philip Morris brand and onto the company's other brands like Kraft Foods, Maxwell House, Nabisco, Oscar Meyer, Post, and Tang. In another example, surveys showed that consumers were skeptical about quality assurance advertisements made by Bridgestone's Firestone Tires in the wake of the company's massive tire recall.[7]

The extent to which an individual conducts an external search depends on his or her perceived risk, knowledge, prior experience, and level of interest in the good or service. Generally, as the perceived risk of the purchase increases, the consumer enlarges the search and considers more alternative brands. For example, suppose that you want to purchase a surround sound system for your home stereo. The decision is relatively risky because of the expense and technical nature of the stereo system, so you are motivated to search for information about models, prices, options, compatibility with existing entertainment products, and capabilities. You may decide to compare attributes of many speaker systems because the value of the time expended finding the "right" stereo will be less than the cost of buying the wrong system. In contrast, more than 60 percent of bar patrons don't know what they will drink until seconds before they place their order, challenging the marketers of alcoholic beverages to find ways of "educating" potential customers on the spot.[8]

A consumer's knowledge about the product or service will also affect the extent of an external information search. A consumer who is knowledgeable and well informed about a potential purchase is less likely to search for additional information. In addition, the more knowledgeable consumers are, the more efficiently they will conduct the search process, thereby requiring less time to search. For example, many consumers know that AirTran and other discount airlines have much lower fares, so they generally use the discounters and do not even check fares at other airlines.

The extent of a consumer's external search is also affected by confidence in one's decision-making ability. A confident consumer not only has sufficient stored information about the product but also feels self-assured about making the right decision. People lacking this confidence will continue an information search even when they know a great deal about the product. Consumers with prior experience in buying a certain product will have less perceived risk than inexperienced consumers. Therefore, they will spend less time searching and limit the number of products that they consider.

A third factor influencing the external information search is product experience. Consumers who have had a positive prior experience with a product are more likely to limit their search to items related to the positive experience. For example, when flying, consumers are likely to choose airlines with which they have had positive experiences, such as consistent on-time arrivals. They will avoid airlines with which they had a negative experience, such as lost luggage.

Product experience can also play a major role in a consumer's decision to make a high-risk purchase. For example, TiVo, the maker of personal video recorders, found that due to the expensive and complex nature of its product, advertising was only moderately effective in generating sales. Instead, personal experience is the most important factor in the decision to purchase a PVR.[9]

Finally, the extent of the search is positively related to the amount of interest a consumer has in a product. A consumer who is more interested in a product will spend more time searching for information and alternatives. For example, suppose you are a dedicated runner who reads jogging and fitness magazines and catalogs. In searching for a new pair of running shoes, you may enjoy reading about the new brands available and spend more time and effort than other buyers in deciding on the right shoe.

The consumer's information search should yield a group of brands, sometimes called the buyer's **evoked set** (or **consideration set**), which are the consumer's most preferred alternatives. From this set, the buyer will further evaluate the alternatives and make a choice. Consumers do not consider all brands available in a product category, but they do seriously consider a much smaller set. For example, from the many brands of pizza available, consumers are likely to consider only the alternatives that fit their price range, location, take-out/delivery needs, and taste preferences. Having too many choices can, in fact, confuse consumers and cause them to delay the decision to buy or, in some instances, cause them to not buy at all.

EVALUATION OF ALTERNATIVES AND PURCHASE

After getting information and constructing an evoked set of alternative products, the consumer is ready to make a decision. A consumer will use the information stored in memory and obtained from outside sources to develop a set of criteria. These standards help the consumer evaluate and compare alternatives. One way to begin narrowing the number of choices in the evoked set is to pick a product attribute and then exclude all products in the set that don't have that attribute. For example, assume Jane and Jill, both college sophomores, are looking for their first apartment. They need a two-bedroom apartment, reasonably priced, and located near campus. They want the apartment to have a swimming pool, washer and dryer, and covered parking. Jane and Jill begin their search with all apartments in the area and then systematically eliminate possibilities that lack the features they need. Hence, if there are 50 alternatives in the area, they may reduce their list to just 10 apartments that possess all of the desired attributes.

Another way to narrow the number of choices is to use cutoffs. Cutoffs are either minimum or maximum levels of an attribute that an alternative must pass to be considered. Suppose Jane and Jill set a maximum of $1,000 to spend on combined rent. Then all apartments with rent higher than $1,000 will be eliminated, further reducing the list of apartments from ten to eight. A final way to narrow the choices is to rank the attributes under consideration in order of importance and evaluate the products based on how well each performs on the most important attributes. To reach a final decision on one of the remaining eight apartments, Jane and Jill may decide proximity to campus is the most important attribute. As a result, they will choose to rent the apartment closest to campus.

If new brands are added to an evoked set, the consumer's evaluation of the existing brands in that set changes. As a result, certain brands in the original set may become more desirable. Suppose Jane and Jill find two apartments located equal distance from campus, one priced at $800 and the other at $750. Faced with this choice, they may decide that the $800 apartment is too expensive given that a comparable apartment is cheaper. If they add a $900 apartment to the list, however, then they may perceive the $800 apartment as more reasonable and decide to rent it.

evoked set (consideration set)
A group of brands, resulting from an information search, from which a buyer can choose.

The goal of the marketing manager is to determine which attributes have the most influence on a consumer's choice. Several attributes may collectively affect a consumer's evaluation of products. A single attribute, such as price, may not adequately explain how consumers form their evoked set. Moreover, attributes the marketer thinks are important may not be very important to the consumer. For example, if you are buying a laptop computer or iBook, you will first have to determine which computers are in your price range. But, in making a final decision, you may also consider weight, screen size, software included, processor speeds, CD and DVD drives, service packages, and reputation.

A brand name can also have a significant impact on a consumer's ultimate choice. One online survey found that Johnson & Johnson has the best corporate reputation among American companies, benefiting from its heritage as the premier maker of baby powder and shampoo. Respondents uniformly cited the familiarity and comfort they feel in using J&J products on their children. When faced with dozens of products on the drugstore shelf, consumers naturally gravitate toward J&J products. By providing consumers with a certain set of promises, brands in essence simplify the consumer decision-making process so consumers do not have to rethink their options every time they need something.[10]

Following the evaluation of alternatives, the consumer decides which product to buy or decides not to buy a product at all. If he or she decides to make a purchase, the next step in the process is an evaluation of the product after the purchase.

REVIEW LEARNING OUTCOME

LO 2 Analyze the components of the consumer decision-making process

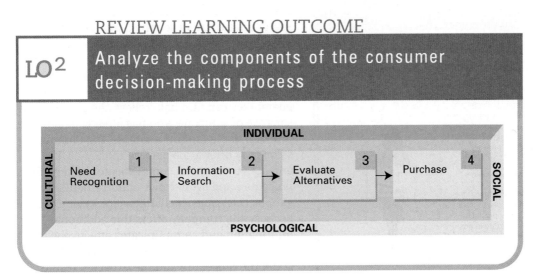

LO 3
Postpurchase Behavior

When buying products, consumers expect certain outcomes from the purchase. How well these expectations are met determines whether the consumer is satisfied or dissatisfied with the purchase. For example, if a person bids on a used car stereo from eBay and wins, he may have fairly low expectations regarding performance. If the stereo's performance turns out to be of superior quality, then the person's satisfaction will be high because his expectations were exceeded. Conversely, if the person bid on a new car stereo expecting superior quality and performance, but the stereo broke within one month, he would be very dissatisfied because his expectations were not met. Price often influences the level of expectations for a product or service.

For the marketer, an important element of any postpurchase evaluation is reducing any lingering doubts that the decision was sound. This is particularly important because 75 percent of all consumers say they had a bad experience in the last year with a product or service they purchased.[11] When people recognize inconsistency between their values or opinions and their behavior, they tend to feel an inner tension called **cognitive dissonance**. For example, suppose a person who normally tans in a tanning bed decides to try a new "airbrush" tanning method, called a "Hollywood" or "mystic" tanning. Mystic tanning costs $30 to $50, significantly more than "fake tanner" or a tanning bed. Prior to spending more on the tan, the person may feel inner tension or anxiety, which is a feeling of dissonance. This feeling occurs because she knows the product has

cognitive dissonance
Inner tension that a consumer experiences after recognizing an inconsistency between behavior and values or opinions.

some disadvantages, such as being expensive, and some advantages, such as being free of harmful ultraviolet rays. In this case, the disadvantage of higher cost battles the advantage of no harmful UV rays.[12]

Consumers try to reduce dissonance by justifying their decision. They may seek new information that reinforces positive ideas about the purchase, avoid information that contradicts their decision, or revoke the original decision by returning the product. To ensure satisfaction, thereby reducing dissonance, consumers using the "mystic tanning" mentioned above may ask several friends about their experiences, do online research, and talk with the tanning booth representative to obtain additional information about the procedure. In some instances, people deliberately seek contrary information in order to refute it and reduce dissonance. Dissatisfied customers sometimes rely on word of mouth to reduce cognitive dissonance, by letting friends and family know they are displeased.

Marketing managers can help reduce dissonance through effective communication with purchasers. For example, a customer service manager may slip a note inside the package congratulating the buyer on making a wise decision. Postpurchase letters sent by manufacturers and dissonance-reducing statements in instruction booklets may help customers feel at ease with their purchase. Advertising that displays the product's superiority over competing brands or guarantees can also help relieve the possible dissonance of someone who has already bought the product. In the tanning example, the tanning salon may offer a 100 percent money-back guarantee. The mystictan.com Web site explains the procedure and even shows endorsements from various celebrities, including actor Kevin Dillon. Because the company offers this additional information and communicates effectively with its customers, they are more likely to understand the procedure and the expected results; hence, it is likely that the outcome will meet or exceed their expectations rather than being disappointing.[13]

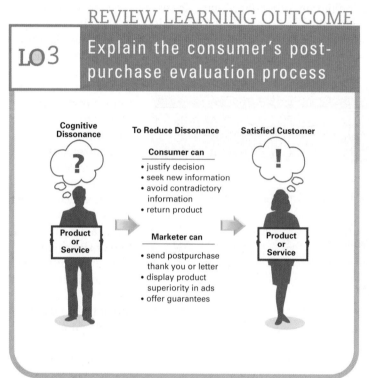

REVIEW LEARNING OUTCOME

LO3 Explain the consumer's post-purchase evaluation process

LO4
Types of Consumer Buying Decisions and Consumer Involvement

All consumer buying decisions generally fall along a continuum of three broad categories: routine response behavior, limited decision making, and extensive decision making (see Exhibit 5.2). Goods and services in these three categories can best be described in terms of five factors: level of consumer involvement, length of time to make a decision, cost of the good or service, degree of information search, and the number of alternatives considered. The level of consumer involvement is perhaps the most significant determinant in classifying buying decisions. **Involvement** is the amount of time and effort a buyer invests in the search, evaluation, and decision processes of consumer behavior.

Frequently purchased, low-cost goods and services are generally associated with **routine response behavior**. These goods and services can also be called low-involvement products because consumers spend little time on search and decision before making the purchase. Usually, buyers are familiar with several different brands in the product category but stick with one brand. Consumers engaged in routine response behavior normally don't experience need recognition until they are exposed to advertising or see the product displayed on a store shelf. Consumers buy first and evaluate later, whereas the reverse is true

involvement
The amount of time and effort a buyer invests in the search, evaluation, and decision processes of consumer behavior.

routine response behavior
The type of decision making exhibited by consumers buying frequently purchased, low-cost goods and services; requires little search and decision time.

152

Exhibit 5.2
Continuum of Consumer Buying Decisions

	Routine	Limited	Extensive
Involvement	low	low to moderate	high
Time	short	short to moderate	long
Cost	low	low to moderate	high
Information Search	internal only	mostly internal	internal and external
Number of Alternatives	one	few	many

for extensive decision making. A consumer who has previously purchased a whitening toothpaste and was satisfied with it will probably walk to the toothpaste aisle and select that same brand without spending 20 minutes examining all other alternatives.

Limited decision making typically occurs when a consumer has previous product experience but is unfamiliar with the current brands available. Limited decision making is also associated with lower levels of involvement (although higher than routine decisions) because consumers do expend moderate effort in searching for information or in considering various alternatives. But what happens if the consumer's usual brand of whitening toothpaste is sold out? Assuming that toothpaste is needed, the consumer will be forced to choose another brand. Before making a final decision, the consumer will likely evaluate several other brands based on their active ingredients, their promotional claims, and the consumer's prior experiences.

Consumers practice **extensive decision making** when buying an unfamiliar, expensive product or an infrequently bought item. This process is the most complex type of consumer buying decision and is associated with high involvement on the part of the consumer. This process resembles the model outlined in Exhibit 5.1. These consumers want to make the right decision, so they want to know as much as they can about the product category and available brands. People usually experience cognitive dissonance only when buying high-involvement products. Buyers use several criteria for evaluating their options and spend much time seeking information. Buying a home or a car, for example, requires extensive decision making.

The type of decision making that consumers use to purchase a product does not necessarily remain constant. For instance, if a routinely purchased product no longer satisfies, consumers may practice limited or extensive decision making to switch to another brand. And people who first use extensive decision making may then use limited or routine decision making for future purchases. For example, when a family gets a new puppy, they will spend a lot of time and energy trying out different toys to determine which one the dog prefers. Once the new owners learn that the dog prefers a bone to a ball, however, the purchase no longer requires extensive evaluation and will become routine.

FACTORS DETERMINING THE LEVEL OF CONSUMER INVOLVEMENT

limited decision making
The type of decision making that requires a moderate amount of time for gathering information and deliberating about an unfamiliar brand in a familiar product category.

extensive decision making
The most complex type of consumer decision making, used when buying an unfamiliar, expensive product or an infrequently bought item; requires use of several criteria for evaluating options and much time for seeking information.

The level of involvement in the purchase depends on the following five factors:

- *Previous experience:* When consumers have had previous experience with a good or service, the level of involvement typically decreases. After repeated product trials, consumers learn to make quick choices. Because consumers are familiar with the product and know whether it will satisfy their needs, they become less involved in the purchase. For example, a consumer purchasing cereal has many brands to choose from—just think of any grocery store cereal aisle. If the consumer always buys the same brand because it satisfies his hunger, then he has a low level of involvement. When a consumer purchases cereal for the first time, however, it likely will be a much more involved purchase.

- *Interest:* Involvement is directly related to consumer interests, as in cars, music, movies, bicycling, or electronics. Naturally, these areas of interest vary from one individual to another. A person highly involved in bike racing will be very interested in the type of bike she owns and will spend quite a bit of time evaluating different bikes. If a person wants a bike only for recreation, however, he

PHILIPS

Let's make things better

The Philips High-Definition Flat TV as seen from two points of view. His. And Hers.
Now there's a TV for both you and your better half. One that offers a larger-than-life image without taking up your whole living room. Philips Flat TVs are available in a wide range of screen sizes ranging from 15" to 50" in standard and widescreen formats. With a depth of less than 4.5 inches, Flat TVs not only save space, the incredible high-definition picture is flat-out amazing. And the design is enough to enhance any room. So any way you look at it, a Philips Flat TV will give you maximum impact with minimal disruption of your home. And, quite possibly, your marriage.

See More with Less TV. Experience More with Philips HD Flat TV.'

Learn more about Philips Flat TV at www.flattv.philips.com.

As the level of purchasing involvement increases, so does the marketing manager's responsibility to provide extensive and informative promotional materials to potential customers. This ad for Philips's high-definition flat TV appeals to both men and women with detailed copy that is also a tool for reducing cognitive dissonance.

may be fairly uninvolved in the purchase and just look for a bike from the most convenient location.

- *Perceived risk of negative consequences:* As the perceived risk in purchasing a product increases, so does a consumer's level of involvement. The types of risks that concern consumers include financial risk, social risk, and psychological risk. First, financial risk is exposure to loss of wealth or purchasing power. Because high risk is associated with high-priced purchases, consumers tend to become extremely involved. Therefore, price and involvement are usually directly related: As price increases, so does the level of involvement. For example, someone who is purchasing a new car for the first time (higher perceived risk) will spend much more time and effort making this purchase than someone who has purchased several new cars (lower perceived risk). Second, consumers take social risks when they buy products that can affect people's social opinions of them (for example, driving an old, beat-up car or wearing unstylish clothes). Third, buyers undergo psychological risk if they feel that making the wrong decision might cause some concern or anxiety. For example, some consumers feel guilty about eating foods that are not healthy, such as regular ice cream rather than fat-free frozen yogurt.

- *Situation:* The circumstances of a purchase may temporarily transform a low-involvement decision into a high-involvement one. High involvement comes into play when the consumer perceives risk in a specific situation. For example, an individual might routinely buy low-priced brands of liquor and wine. When the boss visits, however, the consumer might make a high-involvement decision and buy more prestigious brands.

- *Social visibility:* Involvement also increases as the social visibility of a product increases. Products often on social display include clothing (especially designer labels), jewelry, cars, and furniture. All these items make a statement about the purchaser and, therefore, carry a social risk.

MARKETING IMPLICATIONS OF INVOLVEMENT

Marketing strategy varies according to the level of involvement associated with the product. For high-involvement product purchases, marketing managers have several responsibilities. First, promotion to the target market should be extensive and informative. A good ad gives consumers the information they need for making the purchase decision, as well as specifying the benefits and unique advantages of owning the product. For example, Philips Magnavox, the leading manufacturer of high-definition, flat-screen televisions, features a print ad that not only provides extensive product information, such as size parameters and screen alternatives (wide or standard), but also appeals to consumers' sense of style and their need to save space. Most importantly, the ad's tagline is aimed at both men and women as a couple: "The Philips High-Definition Flat TV as seen from two points of view. His. And Hers."[14]

Purchasing online involves added risk for many consumers, even in limited decision-making situations. To overcome the challenges of getting shoppers to complete purchases online, Landsend.com created a virtual three-dimensional model that customers can use to try on clothes. It also offers an online "personal shopper" to help customers identify items they might like. Purchase rates have been 26 percent higher among online shoppers who use the model and 80 percent higher among customers who use the personal shopper.[15]

For low-involvement product purchases, consumers may not recognize their wants until they are in the store. Therefore, in-store promotion is an important tool when promoting low-involvement products. Marketing managers focus on package design so the product will be eye-catching and easily recognized on the shelf. Examples of products that take this approach are Campbell's soups, Tide detergent, Velveeta cheese, and Heinz ketchup. In-store displays also stimulate sales of low-involvement products. A good display can explain the product's purpose and prompt recognition of a want. Displays of health and beauty aid items in supermarkets have been known to increase sales many times above normal. Coupons, cents-off deals, and two-for-one offers also effectively promote low-involvement items.

Linking a product to a higher-involvement issue is another tactic that marketing managers can use to increase the sales of a low-involvement product. For example, many food products are no longer just nutritious but also low in carbohydrate, fat, or cholesterol. Although packaged food may normally be a low-involvement product, reference to health issues raises the involvement level. To take advantage of aging baby boomers' interest in healthier foods, producers of Silk soy milk and Gardenburger meatless burgers, both of which contain soy protein, tout soy's health benefits, such as reducing the risk of coronary heart disease, preventing certain cancers, and reducing the symptoms of menopause. Sales of soy-based products, long shunned in the United States for their taste, have skyrocketed as a result of these health claims.[16]

REVIEW LEARNING OUTCOME

LO4 Identify the types of comsumer buying decisions and discuss the significance of consumer involvement

Previous experience
Interest
Perceived risk of negative consequences
Situation
Social visibility

Extensive

Limited

Routine

Factors Influencing Consumer Buying Decisions

The consumer decision-making process does not occur in a vacuum. On the contrary, underlying cultural, social, individual, and psychological factors strongly influence the decision process. These factors have an effect from the time a consumer perceives a stimulus through postpurchase behavior. Cultural factors, which include culture and values, subculture, and social class, exert the broadest influence over consumer decision making. Social factors sum up the social interactions between a consumer and influential groups of people, such as reference groups, opinion leaders, and family members. Individual factors, which include gender, age, family life-cycle stage, personality, self-concept, and lifestyle, are unique to each individual and play a major role in the type of products and services consumers want. Psychological factors determine how consumers perceive and interact with their environments and influence the ultimate decisions consumers make. They include perception, motivation, learning, beliefs, and attitudes. Exhibit 5.3 summarizes these influences.

Exhibit 5.3
Factors That Affect the Consumer Decision-Making Process

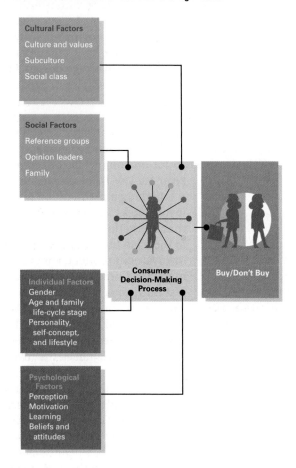

Cultural Factors
Culture and values
Subculture
Social class

Social Factors
Reference groups
Opinion leaders
Family

Individual Factors
Gender
Age and family
life-cycle stage
Personality,
self-concept,
and lifestyle

Psychological
Factors
Perception
Motivation
Learning
Beliefs and
attitudes

Consumer
Decision-Making
Process

Buy/Don't Buy

LO5
Cultural Influences on Consumer Buying Decisions

Of all the factors that affect consumer decision making, cultural factors exert the broadest and deepest influence. Marketers must understand the way people's culture and its accompanying values, as well as their subculture and social class, influence their buying behavior.

CULTURE AND VALUES

Culture is the essential character of a society that distinguishes it from other societal groups. The underlying elements of every culture are the values, language, myths, customs, rituals, and laws that shape the behavior of the people, as well as the material artifacts, or products, of that behavior as they are transmitted from one generation to the next. Exhibit 5.4 lists some defining components of American culture.

Culture is pervasive. Cultural values and influences are the ocean in which individuals swim, and yet most are completely unaware that it is there. What people eat, how they dress, what they think and feel, and what language they speak are all dimensions of culture. It encompasses all the things consumers do without conscious choice because their culture's values, customs, and rituals are ingrained in their daily habits.

Culture is functional. Human interaction creates values and prescribes acceptable behavior for each culture. By establishing common expectations, culture gives order to society. Sometimes these expectations are enacted into laws. For example, drivers in our culture must stop at a red light. Other times these expectations are taken for granted. For example, grocery stores and hospitals are open 24 hours whereas banks are open only during bankers' hours.

Culture is learned. Consumers are not born knowing the values and norms of their

Exhibit 5.4
Components of American Culture

COMPONENT	EXAMPLES
Values	Success through hard work
	Emphasis on personal freedom
Language	English as the dominant language
Myths	George Washington never told a lie.
	Abraham Lincoln walked a mile to return a penny.
Customs	Bathing daily
	Shaking hands when greeting new people
	Standard gratuity of 15 to 20 percent at restaurants
Rituals	Thanksgiving Day dinner
	Singing the "Star Spangled Banner" before baseball games
	Going to religious services on the appropriate day
Laws	Child labor laws
	Sherman Anti-Trust Act guarantees competition
Material artifacts	Diamond engagement rings
	Cell phones

SOURCE: Adapted from *Consumer Behavior* by William D. Wells and David Prensky. Copyright © 1996 by John Wiley & Sons, Inc. Reprinted by permission of John Wiley & Sons, Inc. All Rights Reserved.

Constant **cell-phone** chatter.

Hair-trigger **tempers.**

Faster-than-**fast-paced**
lifestyles.

Where's the politeness,
the compassion,
the **civility?**

*No one knows good manners
like* Town & Country.

With humorous and eloquent
insights from Andy Rooney, Jamie
Lee Curtis, Frank McCourt and
many more, this sparkling
collection of essays is worth
reading—and following.

1-58816-454-3
Only $17.95 (Canada $25.95) in hardcover.
Available wherever books are sold
or call 1-866-338-3778 to order.

Also Available:

Town&Country
MODERN MANNERS
THE THINKING PERSON'S
GUIDE TO SOCIAL GRACES

EDITED BY THOMAS P. FARLEY

HEARST BOOKS

***Modern Manners* explores the ways in which new technologies,
like cell-phones, have changed American culture.**

culture
The set of values, norms,
attitudes, and other meaningful symbols that shape
human behavior and the
artifacts, or products, of
that behavior as they are
transmitted from one gen-
eration to the next.

value
The enduring belief that a
specific mode of conduct
is personally or socially
preferable to another
mode of conduct.

society. Instead, they must learn what is acceptable from family and friends. Children learn the values that will govern their behavior from parents, teachers, and peers. As members of our society, they learn to shake hands when they greet someone, to drive on the right-hand side of the road, and to eat pizza and drink Coca-Cola.

Culture is dynamic. It adapts to changing needs and an evolving environment. The rapid growth of technology in today's world has accelerated the rate of cultural change. Television has changed entertainment patterns and family communication and has heightened public awareness of political and other news events. Automation has increased the amount of leisure time we have and, in some ways, has changed the traditional work ethic. Cultural norms will continue to evolve because of our need for social patterns that solve problems.

In the United States, rapidly increasing diversity is causing major shifts in culture. For example, the growth of the Hispanic community is influencing American food, music, clothing, and entertainment. Additionally, African American culture has been embraced by the mainstream. Indeed, African American women make up one of the fastest-growing segments of the American population. The projected growth rate of this segment is 8 percent compared to 4 percent for the total U.S. population. Additionally, "one in two married black women is the primary decision maker in buying a house, versus one in four married white women." Traditionally, marketers have not taken advantage of the opportunity to market to African American women. Now, however, many companies are taking note of this rapidly growing segment of the population. For example, Kraft's Honey Bunches of Oats cereal developed an advertising campaign that focused on black women. Research showed that African American women do not like to eat cereal when others are around, so the print ad shows a black woman eating a bowl of cereal alone with the caption "Take a breather. This moment is yours. Just you and your bowl of Honey Bunches of Oats."[17] Avon has hired Venus and Serena Williams, sisters and tennis stars, to be spokespersons for its color cosmetics and a new jewelry line. But they are doing more than just promoting Avon products. They are also recruiting African American sales representatives. In addition to featuring the famous tennis stars, Avon has used a multicultural beauty advisory board to develop new products for African American women. In fact, Avon is revamping all its promotional materials to reflect the demographics of the United States.[18]

The most defining element of a culture is its **values**—the enduring beliefs shared by a society that a specific mode of conduct is personally or socially preferable to another mode of conduct. People's value systems have a great effect on their consumer behavior. Consumers with similar value systems tend to react alike to prices and other marketing-related inducements. Values also correspond to consumption patterns. For example, Americans place a high value on convenience. This value has created lucrative markets for products such as breakfast bars, energy bars, and nutrition bars that allow consumers to eat on the go.[19] Values can also influence consumers' TV viewing habits or the magazines they read. For instance, people who strongly object to violence avoid crime shows, and those who oppose pornography do not buy *Hustler*. Core American values—those considered central to the American way of life—are presented in Exhibit 5.5.

The personal values of target consumers have important implications for marketing managers. When marketers understand the core values that underlie the attitudes that

Exhibit 5.5
Core American Values

Success	Americans admire hard work, entrepreneurship, achievement, and success. Those achieving success in American society are rewarded with money, status, and prestige. For example, Bill Gates, once a nerdy computer buff, built Microsoft Corporation into an internationally known giant. Gates is now one of the richest people in the world.
Materialism	Americans value owning tangible goods. American society encourages consumption, ownership, and possession. Americans judge others based on their material possessions; for example, the type of car they own, where they live, and what type of clothes they wear.
Freedom	The American culture was founded on the principle of religious and political freedom. The U.S. Constitution and the Bill of Rights assure American citizens the right to life, liberty, and the pursuit of happiness. These freedoms are fundamental to the legal system and the moral fiber of American culture. The Internet, for example, is built on the principle of the right to free speech. Lawmakers who have attempted to limit the material available on the Internet have met with tough opposition from proponents of free speech. Spam has become such a major problem in recent years, however, that individuals are becoming more receptive to laws restricting spam even if they limit spammers' free speech.
Progress	Technological advances, as well as advances in medicine, science, health, and the quality of products and services, are important to Americans. Each year, for example, more than 20,000 new or improved consumer products are introduced on America's supermarket shelves.*
Youth	Americans are obsessed with youth and spend a good deal of time on products and procedures that make them feel and look younger. Americans spend millions each year on health and beauty aids, health clubs, and healthy foods. Media and advertising encourage the quest for youth by using young, attractive, slim models, such as those in ads from fashion designer Calvin Klein.
Capitalism	Americans believe in a free enterprise system characterized by competition and the chance for monetary success. Capitalism creates choices, quality, and value for Americans. Laws prohibit monopolistic control of a market and regulate free trade. Americans encourage small business success, such as that found by Apple Computer, Wal-Mart, and McDonald's, all of which started as small enterprises with a better idea that toppled the competition.

*Data obtained from the Food Marketing Institute Web site at **http://www.fmi.org**, 2004.
SOURCE: From *Consumer Behavior* by William D. Wells and David Prensky. Copyright © 1996 John Wiley & Sons, Inc. Reprinted by permission of John Wiley & Sons, Inc. All Rights Reserved.

shape the buying patterns of America's consumers and how these values were molded by experiences, they can target their message more effectively. For example, the personal value systems of older consumers, baby boomers, Generation Xers, and Generation Yers are quite different. The key to understanding older consumers, or everyone born before 1945, is recognizing the impact of the Great Depression and World War II on their lives. Facing these two immense challenges shaped a generation characterized by discipline, self-denial, financial and social conservatism, and a sense of obligation. Boomers, those individuals nurtured in the bountiful postwar period between 1945 and 1964, believe they are entitled to the wealth and opportunity that seemed endless in their youth. Generation Xers are very accepting of diversity and individuality. They are also a very entrepreneurial-driven generation, ready to tackle life's challenges for themselves rather than as part of a crowd.[20] Gen Yers are more serious and socially conscious than Gen Xers. Some of the defining events of their lives include Columbine, the O. J. Simpson trial, the Clinton impeachment, the 2000 presidential election, and the terrorist attacks of September 11, 2001. They grew up with cable television, computers, debit cards, and cell phones, making them the most well connected generation to date—a fact that has important implications for word-of-mouth influence.

Gen Yers are notorious for being one of the most difficult market segments to reach. They are the "most unpredictable, advertising-saturated and marketing-skeptical group of adults America has ever seen,"[21] and they also have a tendency to ignore media. When Toyota launched its new Scion, the marketing department put the car on display outside coffee shops and raves to encourage word-of-mouth marketing. From its approximately $13,000 price to its design, the vehicle is focused on Gen Yers' lifestyle. The seats fully recline for a nap between classes; a 15-volt outlet allows students to connect their computer, and the audio system reads MP3 files. The importance of these features to Gen Yers is underscored by a study conducted by MTV. It asked Gen Yers how many hours a day they spent Web surfing, chatting with friends, and downloading music. Surprisingly, the survey revealed that these consumers are spending more than 24 hours a day on these activities—a result that can be explained by Gen Yers' ability to multitask. They can download music, watch TV, and talk to friends via instant messaging all at the same time.

Values represent what is most important in people's lives. Therefore, marketers watch carefully for shifts in consumers' values over time. For example, millions of Americans have an interest in spirituality, as evidenced by the soaring sales of books with religious or spiritual themes and the popularity of television shows with similar themes. Similarly, after the September 11 terrorist attacks, when many people were fearful and concerned about self-protection, gun sales soared as did the sale of drugs to cure anthrax.

The Source
What culture does the material at The Source Web site appeal to? How would you define it? Consider that culture in terms of its components, and explain why you think The Source transcends the typical racial segmentation of culture.
http://www.thesource.com

Online

UNDERSTANDING CULTURE DIFFERENCES

Underlying core values can vary across cultures. Most Americans are more concerned about their health than their weight. But for many Brazilian women, being thin is more important than being healthy. In fact, one survey found that 75 percent of Brazilian women over the age of 20 who wanted to lose weight had taken prescription diet drugs for obesity even though less than one-third of the women were obese and the drugs presented the risk of side effects such as heart and lung damage. In contrast, most Chinese women do not place a high value on thinness and show little concern about being overweight.[22]

As more companies expand their operations globally, the need to understand the cultures of foreign countries becomes more important. A firm has little chance of selling products in a culture it does not understand. Like people, products have cultural values and rules that influence their perception and use. Culture, therefore, must be understood before the behavior of individuals within the cultural context can be understood. Colors, for example, may have different meanings in global markets than they do at home. In China, white is the color of mourning and brides wear red. In the United States, black is for mourning and brides wear white. American designers at Universal Studios had to learn about Japanese culture when planning a new theme park for Japan. Surveys showed that many of their original ideas for Japanese attractions would not appeal to Japanese consumers who were hoping for an authentic American theme park that catered to their cultural differences. After extensive surveys and product testing, the result was a Universal Studios theme park with an orderly clockwise layout, Japanese-style American food, and a Jurassic Park water slide designed to prevent riders from getting wet.[23]

Language is another important aspect of culture that global marketers must deal with. When translating product names, slogans, and promotional messages into foreign languages, they must be careful not to convey the wrong message. General Motors discovered too late that Nova (the name of an economical car) literally means "doesn't go" in Spanish; Coors encouraged its English-speaking customers to "Turn it loose," but the phrase in Spanish means "Suffer from diarrhea."

Though marketers expanding into global markets generally adapt their products and business formats to the local culture, some fear that increasing globalization, as well as the proliferation of the Internet, will result in a homogeneous world culture in the future. U.S. companies in particular, they fear, are Americanizing the world by exporting bastions of American culture, such as McDonald's fast-food restaurants, Starbucks coffeehouses, Microsoft software, and American movies and entertainment.

subculture
A homogeneous group of people who share elements of the overall culture as well as unique elements of their own group.

SUBCULTURE

A culture can be divided into subcultures on the basis of demographic characteristics, geographic regions, national and ethnic background, political beliefs, and religious beliefs. A **subculture** is a homogeneous group of people who share elements of the overall culture as well as cultural elements unique to their own group. Within subcultures, people's

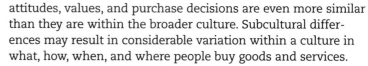

Grateful Dead
What kind of marketing program could you design to attract the subculture of Grateful Dead followers? Visit the GD Online Store to see how marketers are currently doing this. What other elements of the site could help you design a successful program?

http://www.dead.net

Online

attitudes, values, and purchase decisions are even more similar than they are within the broader culture. Subcultural differences may result in considerable variation within a culture in what, how, when, and where people buy goods and services.

In the United States alone, countless subcultures can be identified. Many are concentrated geographically. People belonging to the Mormon religion, for example, are clustered mainly in Utah; Cajuns are located in the bayou regions of southern Louisiana. Many Hispanics live in states bordering Mexico, whereas the majority of Chinese, Japanese, and Korean Americans are found on the West Coast.

Other subcultures are geographically dispersed. Computer hackers, people who are hearing or visually impaired, Harley-Davidson bikers, military families, university professors, and gays may be found throughout the country. Yet they have identifiable attitudes, values, and needs that distinguish them from the larger culture. For example, Nokia Corporation sells phones that flash or vibrate for people with hearing problems while other companies, such as Nike and Pfizer, have aired commercials featuring people with various disabilities.[24] Similarly, Burger King has had good results in Chicago targeting people who work at night and crave dinner-type food in the morning by advertising and offering burgers in the morning instead of waiting until 10:30 A.M. like most of its competitors.[25]

Once marketers identify subcultures, they can design special marketing programs to serve their needs. According to the U.S. Census Bureau, the Hispanic population is the largest and fastest-growing subculture, increasing four times as fast as the general population. To tap into this large and growing segment, marketers have been spending a larger percentage of their marketing budgets advertising to Hispanics. Companies like Procter & Gamble, Anheuser-Busch, Hershey, and Chuck E. Cheese all have Hispanic marketing campaigns, as do major league sports teams like the Texas Rangers and the Dallas Mavericks. The campaigns often feature both English and Spanish advertising and appeal to cultural pride.[26]

Other companies have been successful in targeting much smaller subcultures that are often overlooked. For example, Shaklee Corporation, a multilevel marketing company, has targeted subcultures such as the Amish, Mennonites, and Hasidic Jews. To recruit salespeople in these subcultures, Shaklee caters to their special needs. For example, Amish and Mennonite salespeople can earn a "bonus buggy" instead of the more traditional new car. To accommodate Hasidic customers, Shaklee toughened standards on its kosher products.[27]

SOCIAL CLASS

The United States, like other societies, has a social class system. A **social class** is a group of people who are considered nearly equal in status or community esteem, who regularly socialize among themselves both formally and informally, and who share behavioral norms.

A number of techniques have been used to measure social class, and a number of criteria have been used to define it. One view of contemporary U.S. status structure is shown in Exhibit 5.6.

As you can see from Exhibit 5.6, the upper and upper middle classes comprise the small segment of affluent and wealthy Americans. The upper social classes are more likely than other classes to contribute something to society—for example, by volunteer work or active participation in civic affairs. In terms of consumer buying patterns, the affluent are more likely to own their own home and purchase new cars and trucks and are less likely to smoke. The very rich flex their financial muscles by spending more on vacation homes, vacations and cruises, and housekeeping and gardening services. The most affluent consumers are more likely to attend art auctions and galleries, dance performances, operas, the theater, museums, concerts, and sporting events. Marketers often pay attention to the superwealthy. For example, the Mercedes-Benz Maybach 62, touted as the "world's most

Exhibit 5.6
U.S. Social Classes

Upper Classes		
Capitalist class	1%	People whose investment decisions shape the national economy; income mostly from assets, earned or inherited; university connections
Upper middle class	14%	Upper-level managers, professionals, owners of medium-sized businesses; well-to-do, stay-at-home homemakers who decline occupational work by choice; college-educated; family income well above national average
Middle Classes		
Middle class	33%	Middle-level white-collar, top-level blue-collar; education past high school typical; income somewhat above national average; loss of manufacturing jobs has reduced the population of this class
Working class	32%	Middle-level blue-collar, lower-level white-collar; income below national average; largely working in skilled or semi-skilled service jobs
Lower Classes		
Working poor	11–12%	Low-paid service workers and operatives; some high school education; below mainstream in living standard; crime and hunger are daily threats
Underclass	8–9%	People who are not regularly employed and who depend primarily on the welfare system for sustenance; little schooling; living standard below poverty line

SOURCE: Adapted from Richard P. Coleman, "The Continuing Significance of Social Class to Marketing," Journal of Consumer Research, December 1983, 267; Dennis Gilbert and Joseph A. Kahl, *The American Class Structure: A Synthesis* (Homewood, IL: Dorsey Press, 1982), ch. 11, **http://en.wikipedia.org/wiki/social_structure_of_the_united_states**, May 2006.

luxurious car," is aimed at this group. Priced at $375,000, the car features electronic doors, reclining seats with footrests, a workstation with media capability, a champagne cooler, and lots more. Similarly, New York–based designer Calvin Stewart sells A.P.O. jeans featuring fully customized denim embellished with diamond, gold, and platinum details—starting at $1,000 a pair.[28]

The majority of Americans today define themselves as middle class, regardless of their actual income or educational attainment. This phenomenon most likely occurs because working-class Americans tend to aspire to the middle-class lifestyle while some of those who do achieve affluence may downwardly aspire to respectable middle-class status as a matter of principle. Attaining goals and achieving status and prestige are important to middle-class consumers. People falling into the middle class live in the gap between the haves and the have-nots. They aspire to the lifestyle of the more affluent but are constrained by the economic realities and cautious attitudes they share with the working class.

The working class is a distinct subset of the middle class. Interest in organized labor is one of the most common attributes among the working class. This group often rates job security as the most important reason for taking a job. The working-class person depends heavily on relatives and the community for economic and emotional support. The emphasis on family ties is one sign of the group's intensely local view of the world. They like the local news far more than do middle-class audiences who favor national and world coverage. They are also more likely to vacation closer to home.

Lifestyle distinctions between the social classes are greater than the distinctions within a given class. The most significant difference between the classes occurs between the middle and lower classes, where there is a major shift in lifestyles. Members of the lower class typically have incomes at or below the poverty level. This social class has the highest unemployment rate, and many individuals or families are subsidized through the welfare system. Many are illiterate, with little formal education. Compared to more affluent consumers, lower-class consumers have poorer diets and typically purchase very different types of foods when they shop.

Social class is typically measured as a combination of occupation, income, education, wealth, and other variables. For instance, affluent upper-class consumers are more likely to be salaried executives or self-employed professionals with at least an undergraduate degree. Working-class or middle-class consumers are more likely to be hourly service workers or blue-collar employees with only a high school education. Educational attainment, however, seems to be the most reliable indicator of a person's social and

social class
A group of people in a society who are considered nearly equal in status or community esteem, who regularly socialize among themselves both formally and informally, and who share behavioral norms.

Exhibit 5.7
Social Class and Education

Educational Profile	Median Household Income
Those with less than a 9th grade education	$ 17,261
Those with a 9th–12th grade education (no diploma)	$ 21,737
High school graduates	$ 35,744
College graduates, B.A.	$ 64,406
College graduates, M.A.	$ 74,476
Professional degree holders	$ 100,000

SOURCE: U.S. Census Bureau, 1999, accessed at **http://www.pbs.org/peoplelikeus/resources/stats.html**, May 2006

REVIEW LEARNING OUTCOME

LO5 Identify and understand the cultural factors that affect consumer buying decisions.

economic status (see Exhibit 5.7). Those with college degrees or graduate degrees are more likely to fall into the upper classes, while those people with some college experience fall closest to traditional concepts of the middle class.

Marketers are interested in social class for two main reasons. First, social class often indicates which medium to use for advertising. Suppose an insurance company seeks to sell its policies to middle-class families. It might advertise during the local evening news because middle-class families tend to watch more television than other classes do. If the company wants to sell more policies to upscale individuals, it might place a print ad in a business publication like the *Wall Street Journal*. The Internet, long the domain of more educated and affluent families, is becoming an important advertising outlet for advertisers hoping to reach blue-collar workers and homemakers. As the middle class rapidly adopts the medium, marketers are having to do more research to find out which Web sites will reach their audience.

Second, knowing what products appeal to which social classes can help marketers determine where to best distribute their products. For example, a survey of consumer spending in the Washington, D.C. area reveals a stark contrast between Brie-eaters and Velveeta-eaters. The buyers of Brie, the soft and savory French cheese, are concentrated in the upscale neighborhoods of Northwest D.C. and the western suburbs of Montgomery County, Maryland, and Fairfax County, Virginia, where most residents are executives, white-collar professionals, or politicians. Brie fans tend to be college-educated professionals with six-figure incomes and an activist spirit. In contrast, aficionados of Velveeta, a processed cheese marketed by Kraft, are concentrated in the middle-class, family-filled suburbs of Prince George's County and the predominantly black D.C. neighborhoods. Velveeta buyers tend to be married with children, high school educated, and employed at modestly paying service and blue-collar jobs.[29]

LO6
Social Influences on Consumer Buying Decisions

Most consumers are likely to seek out the opinions of others to reduce their search and evaluation effort or uncertainty, especially as the perceived risk of the decision increases. Consumers may also seek out others' opinions for guidance on new products or services, products with image-related attributes, or products where attribute information is lacking or uninformative. Specifically, consumers interact socially with reference groups, opinion leaders, and family members to obtain product information and decision approval.

Japanese teenage girls have long provided the marketing litmus test companies need before launching new products. Perhaps their success in this area is due to the fact that they are caught in a pivotal clash between a tradition of collectivism and a growing sense of individualism.

reference group
A group in society that influences an individual's purchasing behavior.

primary membership group
A reference group with which people interact regularly in an informal, face-to-face manner, such as family, friends, or fellow employees.

secondary membership group
A reference group with which people associate less consistently and more formally than a primary membership group, such as a club, professional group, or religious group.

aspirational reference group
A group that someone would like to join.

norm
A value or attitude deemed acceptable by a group.

REFERENCE GROUPS

All the formal and informal groups that influence the buying behavior of an individual are that person's **reference groups.** Consumers may use products or brands to identify with or become a member of a group. They learn from observing how members of their reference groups consume, and they use the same criteria to make their own consumer decisions.

Reference groups can be categorized very broadly as either direct or indirect (see Exhibit 5.8). Direct reference groups are face-to-face membership groups that touch people's lives directly. They can be either primary or secondary. **Primary membership groups** include all groups with which people interact regularly in an informal, face-to-face manner, such as family, friends, and coworkers. In contrast, people associate with **secondary membership groups** less consistently and more formally. These groups might include clubs, professional groups, and religious groups.

Consumers also are influenced by many indirect, non-membership reference groups they do not belong to. **Aspirational reference groups** are those a person would like to join. To join an aspirational group, a person must at least conform to the norms of that group. (**Norms** are the values and attitudes deemed acceptable by the group.) Thus, a person who wants to be elected to public office may begin to dress more conservatively, as other politicians do. He or she may go to many of the restaurants and social engagements that city and business leaders attend and try to play a role that is acceptable to voters and other influential people. Similarly, teenagers today may dye their hair and experiment with body piercing and tattoos. Athletes are an aspirational group for several market segments. To appeal to the younger market, Coca-Cola signed basketball star LeBron James to be the spokesperson for its Sprite and POWERade brands, and Nike signed a sneaker deal with him reportedly worth $90 million. Coca-Cola and Nike assumed James would encourage

Exhibit 5.8
Types of Reference Groups

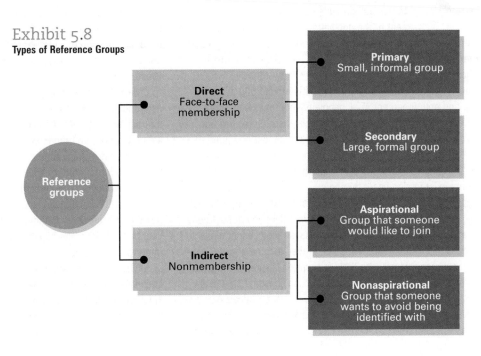

consumers to drink Coke brands and buy Nike shoes because they would like to identify with him.[30] Read the "Global Perspectives" box for an example of how aspirational brands and social class have created a unique market in Poland.

Nonaspirational reference groups, or dissociative groups, influence our behavior when we try to maintain distance from them. A consumer may avoid buying some types of clothing or car, going to certain restaurants or stores, or even buying a home in a certain neighborhood in order to avoid being associated with a particular group.

The activities, values, and goals of reference groups directly influence consumer behavior. For marketers, reference groups have three important implications: (1) they serve as information sources and influence perceptions; (2) they affect an individual's aspiration levels; and (3) their norms either constrain or stimulate consumer behavior. For example, Teenage Research Unlimited, an Illinois research firm devoted to uncovering what's cool in the teen market, recently identified four loose groups among today's teens based on their interests in clothes, music, and activities. Tracking these groups reveals how products become cool and how groups influence the adoption of cool products by other groups. According to Teenage Research Unlimited, a trend or fad often starts with "Edge" teens who have the most innovative tastes. These teens are on the cutting edge of fashion and music, and they wear their attitude all over their bodies in the form of tattoos, body piercing, studded jewelry, or colored tresses. Certain fads embraced by Edgers will spark an interest in the small group of teens called "Influencers," who project the look other teens covet. Influencers also create their own trends like rap music, baggy jeans, and pro sports clothes. Once a fad is embraced and adopted by Influencers, the look becomes cool and desirable. "Conformers" and "Passives" comprise the majority of the teen population, but they will not embrace a fad until it gets its seal of approval from the Influencers.[32]

nonaspirational reference group
A group with which an individual does not want to associate.

GLOBAL Perspectives

The Polish Profile

During its 11 years of preparation for full membership in the European Union, Poland became a nation of contradictions. Modern buildings are going up in the cities, while villages and small towns remain underdeveloped. Forty-two percent of the population have mobile phones, 26 percent have lap tops or personal computers, and 20 percent have Internet access, yet 42 percent say they cannot afford to meet their basic needs.

The average monthly salary in Poland is around 500 euros ($600), and only 6 percent of all people paying taxes earn more than 7,400 euros ($8,100) a year. Thus, class structures are not clearly defined. In financial terms, Poland has almost no upper class (only a few hundred millionaires) and a very small middle class. Nevertheless, in terms of education and family ties, both segments exist in significant numbers.

Typically, Polish consumers spend most of their money on food, energy, and telecommunications. More than a third do not buy meat, fruits, and vegetables, however, either because they cannot afford to or because they grow their own. Some of their income goes for clothes, but proportionally very little is spent on leisure, education, or holidays. With such limited incomes, Polish consumers generally have little opportunity to broaden their horizons or try novelties.

Given this overall financial picture, marketers must adjust their offerings to match the buying behavior of Polish consumers, for whom price is the key purchase criterion. For marketers, this often means selling older technology or slightly poorer quality and less functional equipment, lowering profit margins, or changing a brand's positioning. For example, Western Europe's mainstram brands, like Lipton tea, are considered premium brands in Poland. Lipton competes with Saga, the local brand, and even though Saga is gaining on Lipton, Lipton has a higher market share because its unit price is not a barrier for people with aspirations to the Western European lifestyle.

Marketers must also pay attention to the psychographic and aspirational aspects of the market. The availability of reputable international brands in Poland has aroused desire, and people now aspire to premium brands and buy more expensive brands that they can afford. Aspirations toward foreign brands, promising better quality and a modern lifestyle, allow global brands to find their market positions. A good example is the popularity of Mercedes-Benz automobiles. Poland is second to Germany in terms of the number of Mercedes on the road, but in Poland, they are often 15 years old or older. The aspirational image of the brand plays a very important role, albeit at a secondhand price.[31]

What kind of strategies could a global marketer use to succeed in Poland? What opportunities do you see for global marketers in Poland? For domestic marketers?

Understanding the effect of reference groups on a product is important for marketers as they track the life cycle of their products. Retailer Abercrombie & Fitch noticed it was beginning to lose its target audience of college students when its stores began attracting large numbers of high school students trying to be more like college students. To solve the problem, A&F created its Hollister store chain specifically for high school students.[33]

In Japan, companies have long relied on the nation's high school girls to give them advice during product testing. Fads that catch on among teenage girls often become big trends throughout the country and among Japanese consumers in general. Food manufacturers frequently recruit Tokyo schoolgirls to sample potato chip recipes or chocolate bars. Television networks survey high school girls to fine-tune story lines for higher ratings on prime-time shows. Other companies pay girls to keep diaries of what they buy. Warner-Lambert hired high school girls to help choose a new gum flavor. After extensive chewing and comparing, the girls settled on a flavor that became Trickle, now Japan's best-selling bubble gum.[34]

OPINION LEADERS

Reference groups frequently include individuals known as group leaders, or **opinion leaders**—those who influence others. Obviously, it is important for marketing managers to persuade such people to purchase their goods or services. Many products and services that are integral parts of Americans' lives today got their initial boost from opinion leaders. For example, DVDs and SUVs (sport-utility vehicles) were purchased by opinion leaders well ahead of the general public.

Opinion leaders are often the first to try new products and services out of pure curiosity. They are typically self-indulgent, making them more likely to explore unproven but intriguing products and services. Technology companies have found that teenagers, because of their willingness to experiment, are key opinion leaders for the success of new technologies. For example, text messaging became popular with teenagers before it gained widespread appeal. As a result, many technology companies include it in their marketing programs targeted to teens. Similarly, Jet Blue Airways, Redken, FreshLook Color Contacts, and Bombay Sapphire gin advertise on *Fashion Week TV*. The show reaches 20,000 viewers described as "fashion insiders and media and socialite attendees." In addition to their commercials, these advertisers are featured in *Fashion Week* programs and VIP lounges. One VIP lounge showcased airline seats and flight attendants both outfitted in Jet Blue regalia. The flight attendants wore FreshLook Contacts and served Bombay Sapphire martinis. By reaching opinion leaders, these companies hope to start a trend that will carry into the mass market.[35]

Opinion leadership is a casual, face-to-face phenomenon and usually inconspicuous, so locating opinion leaders can be a challenge. Thus, marketers often try to create opinion leaders. They may use high school cheerleaders to model new fall fashions or civic leaders to promote insurance, new cars, and other merchandise. Revatex, the maker of JNCO jeans, sponsors extreme-sports athletes who appeal to the teen market. It also gives free clothes to trendsetters among teens in the hopes they will influence others to purchase the brand. JNCO outfits big-name DJs in the rave scene, as well as members of hip, alternative bands favored by the teen crowd. Similarly, the Web site of New York retailer Alloy Online (http://www.alloyonline.com) offers style tips, quizzes on topics like "Are you a teenage drama queen?" and "What is your ideal guy type?" as well as gossip about teen idols such as hip-hop star Mary J. Blige.[36]

On a national level, companies sometimes use movie stars, sports figures, and other celebrities to promote products, hoping they are appropriate opinion leaders. The effectiveness of celebrity endorsements varies, though, depending largely on how credible and attractive the spokesperson is and how familiar people are with him or her. Endorsements are most likely to succeed if a reasonable association between the spokesperson and the product can be established. Respected organizations such as the American Heart Association or the American Cancer Society may also serve as opinion leaders. Marketers may seek endorsements from them as well as from schools, churches, cities, the military, and fraternal organizations as a form of group opinion leadership.

opinion leader
An individual who influences the opinions of others.

Salespeople often ask to use opinion leaders' names as a means of achieving greater personal influence in a sales presentation.

How Blogs Are Defining Today's Opinion Leaders

Increasingly, marketers are looking to Web logs, or blogs, as they're commonly called, to find opinion leaders.[37] In 2005, 10 percent of consumers read blogs—twice as many as in the previous year. The problem, though, is that with over 25 million unique blogs and 70,000 new ones coming online every day, it's getting harder to separate the true opinion leaders from intermediate Web users who are just looking to share random thoughts or vacation photos with family and friends. One way marketers are doing this is by looking to teen blogs to identify the social trends that are shaping consumer behavior.

During the research phase of development for its teen-targeted RED Blogs service, AOL discovered that over 50 percent of teens do not mind sharing their feelings in public forums. This is especially evident at social networking sites like Myspace, FaceBook, and Xanga, where teens and twenty-somethings post extensive personal profiles, photo collections, links to user groups they belong to, and detailed descriptions of their social events.

Raised with MTV, 500-channel cable services, a rapidly maturing Internet, and ever-expanding cell phone capabilities, teens have unprecedented access to the world around them. Furthermore, they are no longer passive observers of the culture their parents have created. They can follow their favorite bands, actors, or athletes via their Web sites and blogs and expect to interact with them instead of just admiring them from afar. With their unprecedented ability to network and communicate with each other, young people rely on each others' opinions more than marketing messages when making purchase decisions. And blogs are becoming a key way that teens communicate their opinions. Consequently, today's marketers are reading teen blogs, developing products that meet the very specific needs that teens express there, and learning unique and creative ways to put key influencers in charge of marketing their brands for them.

FAMILY

The family is the most important social institution for many consumers, strongly influencing values, attitudes, self-concept—and buying behavior. For example, a family that strongly values good health will have a grocery list distinctly different from that of a family that views every dinner as a gourmet event. Moreover, the family is responsible for the **socialization process**, the passing down of cultural values and norms to children. Children learn by observing their parents' consumption patterns, and so they will tend to shop in a similar pattern.

Decision-making roles among family members tend to vary significantly, depending on the type of item purchased. Family members assume a variety of roles in the purchase process. *Initiators* suggest, initiate, or plant the seed for the purchase process. The initiator can be any member of the family. For example, Sister might initiate the product search by asking for a new bicycle as a birthday present. *Influencers* are those members of the family whose opinions are valued. In our example, Mom might function as a price-range watchdog, an influencer whose main role is to veto or approve price ranges. Brother may give his opinion on certain makes of bicycles. The *decision maker* is the family member who actually makes the decision to buy or not to buy. For example, Dad or Mom is likely to choose the final brand and model of bicycle to buy after seeking further information from Sister about cosmetic features such as color and imposing additional criteria of his or her own, such as durability and safety. The *purchaser* (probably Dad or Mom) is the one who actually exchanges money for the product. Finally, the *consumer* is the actual user—Sister, in the case of the bicycle.

Marketers should consider family purchase situations along with the distribution of consumer and decision-maker roles among family members. Ordinary marketing views the individual as both decision maker and consumer. Family marketing adds several other possibilities: Sometimes more than one family member or all family members are involved in the decision; sometimes only children are involved in the decision; sometimes more than one consumer is involved; and sometimes the decision maker and the

socialization process
How cultural values and norms are passed down to children.

Exhibit 5.9

Relationships among Purchasers and Consumers in the Family

	Purchase Decision Maker		
Consumer	**Parent(s) Only**	**Child/Children Only**	**Some or All Family Members**
Parent(s)	golf clubs cosmetics wine	Mother's Day card	Christmas gifts minivan
Child/Children	diapers breakfast cereal	candy small toys	bicycle
Some Family Members	videos long-distance phone service	children's movies	computers sports events
All Family Members	clothing life insurance	fast-food restaurant	swim club membership vacations

SOURCE: From "Pulling the Family's Strings" by Robert Boutillier, *American Demographics*, August 1993. © 1993 PRIMEDIA Intertec, Stamford, CT. Reprinted with permission.

REVIEW LEARNING OUTCOME

LO6
Identify and understand the social factors that affect consumer buying decisions

Reference Groups	Direct		Indirect	
	Primary	Secondary	Aspirational	Nonaspirational

Opinion Leaders	People you know	Celebrities

Family	Socialization Process		
	Initiators	Decision Makers	Consumers
	Influencers		Purchasers

consumer are different people. Exhibit 5.9 represents the patterns of family purchasing relationships that are possible.

Children can have great influence over the purchase decisions of their parents. In many families, with both parents working and short on time, children are encouraged to participate. In addition, children in single-parent households become more involved in family decisions at an earlier age. Children are especially influential in decisions about food and eating out, so food companies listen closely to what children want. Children also are more interested in entertainment than food. Therefore, McDonald's and Burger King spend about $4 billion annually on toys for their kid meals; Quaker Oatmeal features hidden treasures. Ketchup, margarine, jelly, and even peanut butter now come in squeezable bottles designed to allow small hands to create pictures. Promotions for food products aimed at children include a Web site that illustrates how to build a fort with french fries and books that teach children to count using Cheerios, M&Ms, and Oreos.[38] Children influence purchase decisions for many more products and services than food. Even though they are usually not the actual purchasers of such items, children often participate in decisions about toys, clothes, vacations, recreation, automobiles, and many other products.

LO7
Individual Influences on Consumer Buying Decisions

A person's buying decisions are also influenced by personal characteristics that are unique to each individual, such as gender; age and life-cycle stage; and personality, self-concept, and lifestyle. Individual characteristics are generally stable over the course of one's life. For instance, most people do not change their gender, and the act of changing personality or lifestyle requires a complete reorientation of one's life. In the case of age and life-cycle stage, these changes occur gradually over time.

GENDER

Physiological differences between men and women result in different needs, such as health and beauty products. Just as important are the distinct cultural, social, and economic roles played by men and women and the effects that these have on their decision-making processes. For example, many networks have programming targeted to women, while Spike TV calls itself the "first network for men." Two magazines are geared to men who like to shop: *Cargo* is modeled after *Lucky*, a women's shopping magazine; and *Vitals*, a free magazine, is positioned as a "luxury shopping magazine" for men.[39]

Indeed, men and women do shop differently. Studies show that men and women share similar motivations in terms of where to shop—that is, seeking reasonable prices, merchandise quality, and a friendly, low-pressure environment—but they don't necessarily feel the same about shopping in general. Most women enjoy shopping. Their male counterparts claim to dislike the experience and shop only out of necessity. Further, men desire simple shopping experiences, stores with less variety, and convenience. Men are more interested than women in stores that are easy to shop in, are near home or office, or have knowledgeable personnel.[40] The Internet appeals to men who find it an easy way to shop for clothing and gifts. Many Internet retailers are designing their sites to attract male gift buyers. Banana Republic's Web site prompts customers purchasing gifts to choose a price range and then returns many suggestions for gifts in that range. To help its male shoppers, intimate apparel retailer Victoria's Secret lets women create password-protected wish lists and then zap them to their significant others to ensure there's no mistaking colors or sizes.

Trends in gender marketing are influenced by the changing roles of men and women in society. For instance, as women around the world are working and earning more, many industries are attracting new customers by marketing to women. The video game industry, which has traditionally targeted 18- to 22-year-old men with games featuring guns and explosions, is developing games based on popular female characters, like Barbie and Nancy Drew, aimed at capturing female customers. In South Korea, major credit-card companies target working women by offering benefits attractive to women such as discounts at department and bridal stores and disfigurement insurance for plastic surgery.[41]

The changing roles of women are also forcing companies that have traditionally targeted women to develop new strategies. One reason is because women's decision making tends to be multi-minded and integrative, meaning that they consider and move back and forth among many criteria, as opposed to being single-minded and focused. They tend to view shopping as a learning process, educating themselves on the available options and typically adding criteria as they learn more. It is not unusual for a woman to shift back to an earlier stage of the decision process as she learns something that may cause her even to change categories. For example, a woman may have decided to buy an SUV because her friends all love theirs and she likes the looks of the new models. Once on the showroom floor, however, she may see a new minivan that offers great storage and fuel mileage. Suddenly, she's including minivans in her consideration set and has added two new criteria to the qualifying list.[42]

AGE AND FAMILY LIFE-CYCLE STAGE

The age and family life-cycle stage of a consumer can have a significant impact on consumer behavior. How old a consumer is generally indicates what products he or she may be interested in purchasing. Consumer tastes in food, clothing, cars, furniture, and recreation are often age related. For example, researchers from *American Demographics* magazine and the research firm Encino examined the correlation between television shows and the age of viewers. As expected, the target audience of many TV shows directly coincided with the viewers. *American Juniors* on Fox was most popular with the 13–16 age range, *8 Simple Rules for Dating My Teenage Daughter* on ABC was most popular with the 17–20 age range, and *Big Brother* on CBS was most popular with the 21–25 age range. For more mature audiences, the most popular shows were *Desperate Housewives*, *Sex and the City*, *Lost*, *The Sopranos*, and crime shows like *CSI* and its various spinoffs.[43]

Related to a person's age is his or her place in the family life cycle. As Chapter 7 explains in more detail, the *family life cycle* is an orderly series of stages through which consumers' attitudes and behavioral tendencies evolve through maturity, experience, and changing income and status. Marketers often define their target markets in terms of family life cycle, such as "young singles," "young married with children," and "middle-aged married without children." For instance, young singles spend more than average on alcoholic beverages, education, and entertainment. New parents typically increase their spending on health care, clothing, housing, and food and decrease their spending on alcohol, education, and transportation. Households with older children spend more on food, entertainment, personal care products, and education, as well as cars and gasoline. After their children leave home, spending by older couples on vehicles, women's clothing, health care, and long-distance calls typically increases. For instance, the presence of children in the home is the most significant determinant of the type of vehicle that's driven off the new-car lot. Parents are the ultimate need-driven car consumers, requiring larger cars and trucks to haul their children and all their belongings. It comes as no surprise then that for all households with children, SUVs rank either first or second among new-vehicle purchases followed by minivans.

Marketers should also be aware of the many nontraditional life-cycle paths that are common today and provide insights into the needs and wants of such consumers as divorced parents, lifelong singles, and childless couples. Three decades ago, married couples with children under 18 accounted for about half of U.S. households. Today, such families make up only 23 percent of all households, while people living alone or with nonfamily members represent more than 30 percent. Furthermore, according to the U.S. Census Bureau, the number of single-mother households grew by 25 percent over the last decade. The shift toward more single-parent households is part of a broader societal change that has put more women on the career track. Although many marketers continue to be wary of targeting nontraditional families, Charles Schwab targeted single mothers in an advertising campaign featuring Sarah Ferguson, the Duchess of York and a divorced mom. The idea was to appeal to single mothers' heightened awareness of the need for financial self-sufficiency.[44]

PERSONALITY, SELF-CONCEPT, AND LIFESTYLE

Each consumer has a unique personality. **Personality** is a broad concept that can be thought of as a way of organizing and grouping how an individual typically reacts to situations. Thus, personality combines psychological makeup and environmental forces. It includes people's underlying dispositions, especially their most dominant characteristics. Although personality is one of the least useful concepts in the study of consumer behavior, some marketers believe that personality influences the types and brands of products purchased. For instance, the type of car, clothes, or jewelry a consumer buys may reflect one or more personality traits.

Self-concept, or self-perception, is how consumers perceive themselves. Self-concept includes attitudes, perceptions, beliefs, and self-evaluations. Although self-concept may change, the change is often gradual. Through self-concept, people define their identity, which in turn provides for consistent and coherent behavior.

Self-concept combines the **ideal self-image** (the way an individual would like to be) and the **real self-image** (how an individual actually perceives himself or herself). Generally, we try to raise our real self-image toward our ideal (or at least narrow the gap). Consumers seldom buy products that jeopardize their self-image. For example, someone who sees herself as a trendsetter wouldn't buy clothing that doesn't project a contemporary image.

personality
A way of organizing and grouping the consistencies of an individual's reactions to situations.

self-concept
How consumers perceive themselves in terms of attitudes, perceptions, beliefs, and self-evaluations.

ideal self-image
The way an individual would like to be.

real self-image
The way an individual actually perceives himself or herself.

Dove's most recent marketing campaign aims to recast women's self-concept in a positive way. Women of all ages, races, and sizes have become models for the successful series of television and print advertisements, called "Campaign for Real Beauty."

Human behavior depends largely on self-concept. Because consumers want to protect their identity as individuals, the products they buy, the stores they patronize, and the credit cards they carry support their self-image. No other product quite reflects a person's self-image as much as the car he or she drives. For example, many young consumers do not like family sedans like the Honda Accord or Toyota Camry and say they would buy one for their mom, but not for themselves. Likewise, younger car buyers may avoid minivans because they do not want to sacrifice the youthful image they have of themselves just because they have new responsibilities. To combat decreasing sales, marketers of the Nissan Quest minivan decided to reposition it as something other than a "mom mobile" or "soccer mom car." They chose the ad copy "Passion built it. Passion will fill it up," followed by "What if we made a minivan that changed the way people think of minivans?"[45]

By influencing the degree to which consumers perceive a good or service to be self-relevant, marketers can affect consumers' motivation to learn about, shop for, and buy a certain brand. Marketers also consider self-concept important because it helps explain the relationship between individuals' perceptions of themselves and their consumer behavior.

An important component of self-concept is *body image*, the perception of the attractiveness of one's own physical features. For example, individuals who have cosmetic surgery often experience significant improvement in their overall body image and self-concept. Moreover, a person's perception of body image can be a stronger reason for trying to lose weight than either good health or other social factors.[46] With the median age of Americans rising, many companies are introducing products and services aimed at aging baby boomers who are concerned about their age and physical appearance. Bank of America has featured Harley-riding seniors in its advertisements for its private-bank marketing campaign, and high-end anti-aging creams are flying off department store shelves. Finally marketers are also seeing boomers respond to products aimed at younger audiences. For instance, new Starwood "W" Hotels, designed and advertised to attract a young, hip crowd, are attracting large numbers of boomers.[47]

Personality and self-concept are reflected in lifestyle. A **lifestyle** is a mode of living, as identified by a person's activities, interests, and opinions. *Psychographics* is the analytical technique used to examine consumer lifestyles and to categorize consumers. Unlike personality characteristics, which are hard to describe and measure, lifestyle characteristics are useful in segmenting and targeting consumers. Lifestyle and psychographic analysis explicitly addresses the way consumers outwardly express their inner selves in their social and cultural environment.

Many companies now use psychographics to better understand their market segments. For many years, marketers selling products to mothers conveniently assumed that all moms were fairly homogeneous and concerned about the same things—the health and well-being of their children—and that they could all be reached with a similar message. But recent lifestyle research has shown that there are traditional, blended, and nontraditional moms, and companies like Procter & Gamble and Pillsbury are using strategies to reach these different types of mothers. Psychographics is also effective with other segments. Gap, one of the leading proponents of "lifestyle" advertising, consistently uses celebrities to market each season's line. In an attempt to bring back baby boomers and their children, Gap used stars such as Madonna, Missy Elliot, Sarah Jessica Parker, and Josh Duhamel in its advertising campaigns. Cord jeans for women and other products were featured in 30- and 60-second TV spots. To further entice consumers, a limited edition CD remix was offered in stores and online.[48] Psychographics and lifestyle segmentation are discussed in more detail in Chapter 7.

lifestyle
A mode of living as identified by a person's activities, interests, and opinions.

REVIEW LEARNING OUTCOME

LO7 Identify and understand the cultural factors that affect consumer buying decisions

Individual Influences

Gender

Age and Family Life Cycle

Personality, Self-Concept Lifestyle

LO⁸
Psychological Influences on Consumer Buying Decisions

An individual's buying decisions are further influenced by psychological factors: perception, motivation, learning, and beliefs and attitudes. These factors are what consumers use to interact with their world. They are the tools consumers use to recognize their feelings, gather and analyze information, formulate thoughts and opinions, and take action. Unlike the other three influences on consumer behavior, psychological influences can be affected by a person's environment because they are applied on specific occasions. For example, you will perceive different stimuli and process these stimuli in different ways depending on whether you are sitting in class concentrating on the instructor, sitting outside of class talking to friends, or sitting in your dorm room watching television.

PERCEPTION

The world is full of stimuli. A stimulus is any unit of input affecting one or more of the five senses: sight, smell, taste, touch, hearing. The process by which we select, organize, and interpret these stimuli into a meaningful and coherent picture is called **perception**. In essence, perception is how we see the world around us and how we recognize that we need some help in making a purchasing decision.

People cannot perceive every stimulus in their environment. Therefore, they use **selective exposure** to decide which stimuli to notice and which to ignore. A typical consumer is exposed to more than 2,500 advertising messages a day but notices only between 11 and 20.

The familiarity of an object, contrast, movement, intensity (such as increased volume), and smell are cues that influence perception. Consumers use these cues to identify and define products and brands. The shape of a product's packaging, such as Coca-Cola's signature contour bottle, for instance, can influence perception. Color is another cue, and it plays a key role in consumers' perceptions. Packaged foods manufacturers use color to trigger unconscious associations for grocery shoppers who typically make their shopping decisions in the blink of an eye. Red, for instance, used on packages of Campbell's soups and SunMaid raisins, is associated with prolonged and increased eating. Green is associated with environmental well-being and healthy, low-fat foods. Healthy Choice entrées and SnackWells cookies use green. Premium products, like Sheba cat food, Ben & Jerry's ice cream, and Godiva chocolate use black, brown, and gold on their packaging to convey their use of superior ingredients.[49] The shape and look of a product's packaging can also influence perception. Ivory Soap created special packaging based on the original late nineteenth-century design to take advantage of a consumer trend toward simplifying life by emphasizing the brand's heritage and image of purity.[50]

What is perceived by consumers may also depend on the stimuli's vividness or shock value. Graphic warnings of the hazards associated with a product's use are perceived more readily and remembered more accurately than less vivid warnings or warnings that are written in text. "Sexier" ads excel at attracting the attention of younger consumers. Companies like Calvin Klein and Guess use sensuous ads to "cut through the clutter" of competing ads and other stimuli to capture the attention of the target audience.

Two other concepts closely related to selective exposure are selective distortion and selective retention. **Selective distortion** occurs when consumers change or distort information that conflicts with their feelings or beliefs. For example, suppose a college student buys a Sonicblue Rio MP3 player. After the purchase, if the student gets new information about an alternative brand, such as an Apple iPod, he or she may distort the information to make it more consistent with the prior view that the Sonicblue Rio is just as good as the iPod, if not better. Business travelers who fly often may distort or discount information about airline crashes because they must use air travel constantly in their jobs.

perception
The process by which people select, organize, and interpret stimuli into a meaningful and coherent picture.

selective exposure
The process whereby a consumer notices certain stimuli and ignores others.

selective distortion
A process whereby a consumer changes or distorts information that conflicts with his or her feelings or beliefs.

Selective retention is remembering only information that supports personal feelings or beliefs. The consumer forgets all information that may be inconsistent. After reading a pamphlet that contradicts one's political beliefs, for instance, a person may forget many of the points outlined in it. Similarly, consumers may see a news report on suspected illegal practices by their favorite retail store, but soon forget the reason the store was featured on the news.

Which stimuli will be perceived often depends on the individual. People can be exposed to the same stimuli under identical conditions but perceive them very differently. For example, two people viewing a TV commercial may have different interpretations of the advertising message. One person may be thoroughly engrossed by the message and become highly motivated to buy the product. Thirty seconds after the ad ends, the second person may not be able to recall the content of the message or even the product advertised.

Marketing Implications of Perception

Marketers must recognize the importance of cues, or signals, in consumers' perception of products. Marketing managers first identify the important attributes, such as price or quality, that the targeted consumers want in a product and then design signals to communicate these attributes. For example, consumers will pay more for candy in expensive-looking foil packages. But shiny labels on wine bottles signify less expensive wines; dull labels indicate more expensive wines. Marketers also often use price as a signal to consumers that the product is of higher quality than competing products. Gibson Guitar Corporation briefly cut prices on many of its guitars to compete with Japanese rivals Yamaha and Ibanez but found that it sold more guitars when it charged more for them. Consumers perceived that the higher price indicated a better quality instrument.[51]

Of course, brand names send signals to consumers. The brand names of Close-Up toothpaste, DieHard batteries, and Caress moisturizing soap, for example, identify important product qualities. Names chosen for search engines and sites on the Internet, such as Yahoo!, Amazon.com, and Excite, are intended to convey excitement, intensity, and vastness. Companies may even change their names to send a message to consumers. As today's utility companies increasingly enter unregulated markets, many are shaking their stodgy "Power & Light & Electric" names in favor of those that let consumers know they are not just about electricity anymore, such as Reliant Resources, Entergy, and Cinergy.

Consumers also associate quality and reliability with certain brand names. Companies watch their brand identity closely, in large part because a strong link has been established between perceived brand value and customer loyalty. Brand names that consistently enjoy high perceived value from consumers include Kodak, Disney, National Geographic, Mercedes-Benz, and Fisher-Price. Naming a product after a place can also add perceived value by association. Brand names using the words Santa Fe, Dakota, or Texas convey a sense of openness, freedom, and youth, but products named after other locations might conjure up images of pollution and crime.

Marketing managers are also interested in the *threshold level of perception*: the minimum difference in a stimulus that the consumer will notice. This concept is sometimes referred to as the "just-noticeable difference." For example, how much would Apple have to drop the price of its iPod Shuffle before consumers recognized it as a bargain—$25? $50? or more? One study found that the just-noticeable difference in a stimulus is about a 20 percent change. For example, consumers will likely notice a 20 percent price decrease more quickly than a 15 percent decrease. This marketing principle can be applied to other marketing variables as well, such as package size or loudness of a broadcast advertisement.[52]

Another study showed that the bargain-price threshold for a name brand is lower than that for a store brand. In other words, consumers perceive a bargain more readily when stores offer a small discount on a name-brand item than when they offer the same discount on a store brand; a larger discount is needed to achieve a similar effect for a store brand.[53] Researchers also found that for low-cost grocery items, consumers typically do not see past the second digit in the price. For instance, consumers do not

selective retention
A process whereby a consumer remembers only that information that supports his or her personal beliefs.

perceive any real difference between two comparable cans of tuna, one priced at $1.52 and the other at $1.59, because they ignore the last digit.[54]

Besides changing such stimuli as price, package size, and volume, marketers can change the product or attempt to reposition its image. Realtors, for example, have changed a property's address to enhance its image. In fact, one San Francisco real estate company almost lost a major deal when one of its potential clients refused to move into an office whose address was 444 Market Street because of the association of the number four with death in the Chinese community. The company saved the deal by renovating the lobby to include a new entrance and changing the building's address to One Front Street.[55] But marketers must be careful when adding features. How many new services will discounter Target Stores need to add before consumers perceive it as a full-service department store? How many sporty features will General Motors have to add to a basic two-door sedan before consumers start perceiving it as a sports car?

Marketing managers who intend to do business in global markets should be aware of how foreign consumers perceive their products. For instance, in Japan, product labels are often written in English or French, even though they may not translate into anything meaningful. Many Japanese associate foreign words on product labels with the exotic, the expensive, and high quality.

Marketers have often been suspected of sending advertising messages subconsciously to consumers in what is known as *subliminal perception*. The controversy began when a researcher claimed to have increased popcorn and Coca-Cola sales at a movie theater after flashing "Eat popcorn" and "Drink Coca-Cola" on the screen every five seconds for 1/300th of a second, although the audience did not consciously recognize the messages. Almost immediately consumer protection groups became concerned that advertisers were brainwashing consumers, and this practice was pronounced illegal in California and Canada. Although the researcher later admitted to making up the data and scientists have been unable to replicate the study since, consumers are still wary of hidden messages that advertisers may be sending.

MOTIVATION

By studying motivation, marketers can analyze the major forces influencing consumers to buy or not buy products. When you buy a product, you usually do so to fulfill some kind of need. These needs become motives when aroused sufficiently. For instance, suppose this morning you were so hungry before class that you needed to eat something. In response to that need, you stopped at McDonald's for an Egg McMuffin. In other words, you were motivated by hunger to stop at McDonald's. **Motives** are the driving forces that cause a person to take action to satisfy specific needs.

Why are people driven by particular needs at particular times? One popular theory is **Maslow's hierarchy of needs,** shown in Exhibit 5.10, which arranges needs in ascending order of importance: physiological, safety, social, esteem, and self-actualization. As a person fulfills one need, a higher level need becomes more important.

The most basic human needs are *physiological*—that is the needs for food, water, and shelter. Because they are essential to survival, these needs must be satisfied first. Ads showing a juicy hamburger or a runner gulping down Gatorade after a marathon are examples of appeals to satisfy the physiological needs of hunger and thirst.

Safety needs include security and freedom from pain and discomfort. Marketers sometimes appeal to consumers' fears and anxieties about safety to sell their products. For example, aware of the aging population's health fears, the retail medical imaging centers Heart Check America and HealthScreen America advertise that they offer consumers a full body scan for early detection of health problems such as coronary disease and cancer. On the other hand, some companies or industries advertise to allay consumer fears. For example, in the wake of the September 11 terrorist attacks, the airline industry found itself having to conduct an image campaign to reassure consumers about the safety of air travel.[56]

After physiological and safety needs have been fulfilled, *social needs*—especially love and a sense of belonging—become the focus. Love includes acceptance by one's peers, as

motive
A driving force that causes a person to take action to satisfy specific needs.

Maslow's hierarchy of needs
A method of classifying human needs and motivations into five categories in ascending order of importance: physiological, safety, social, esteem, and self-actualization.

Exhibit 5.10

**Maslow's Hierarchy
of Needs**

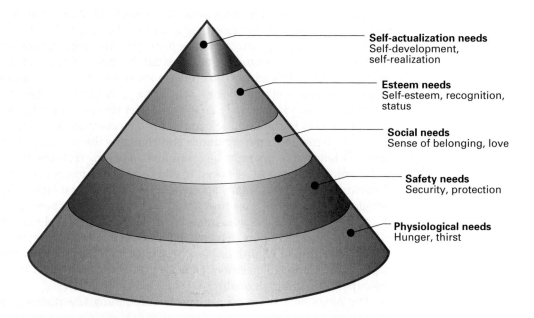

Self-actualization needs
Self-development,
self-realization

Esteem needs
Self-esteem, recognition,
status

Social needs
Sense of belonging, love

Safety needs
Security, protection

Physiological needs
Hunger, thirst

well as sex and romantic love. Marketing managers probably appeal more to this need than to any other. Ads for clothes, cosmetics, and vacation packages suggest that buying the product can bring love. The need to belong is also a favorite of marketers, especially those marketing products to teens. Shoes and clothing brands such as Nike, adidas, Tommy Hilfiger, Gap, JNCO, and Abercrombie & Fitch score high with teenagers as "cool" brands. Teens who wear these labels feel and look like they belong to the in-crowd.

Love is acceptance without regard to one's contribution. Esteem is acceptance based on one's contribution to the group. *Self-esteem needs* include self-respect and a sense of accomplishment. Esteem needs also include prestige, fame, and recognition of one's accomplishments. Mont Blanc pens, Mercedes-Benz automobiles, and Neiman Marcus stores all appeal to esteem needs. Most high-end spas and health clubs appeal to consumers' self-esteem needs. Like exclusive country clubs, clubs such as Chicago's East Bank Club are designed to make members feel proud of their commitment to fitness while also giving them a sense of social accomplishment. In fact, the clubs can be so effective that even during an economic recession, patrons will not give up their membership because to do so would be a public admission of financial problems.[57]

Asian consumers, in particular, are strongly motivated by status and appearance. Asians tend to be conscious of their place in a group, institution, or society as a whole. The importance of gaining social recognition turns Asians into some of the most image-conscious consumers in the world. Status-conscious Asians will not hesitate to spend freely on premium brands, such as BMW, Mercedes-Benz, and the best Scotch whiskey and French cognac. Indeed, marketers of luxury products such as Gucci, Louis Vuitton, and Prada find that demand for their products is so strong among image-conscious consumers that their sales are generally unaffected by economic downturns. In some cases, companies have been able to make up for sluggish European and U.S. sales by raising prices and volume in Asia.

The highest human need is *self-actualization*. It refers to finding self-fulfillment and self-expression, reaching the point in life at which "people are what they feel they should be."

More than one motive may drive a consumer's purchase. This Asics advertisement encourages consumers to buy sneakers by highlighting an unconventional benefit of running instead of a more traditional one, like exercise.

Maslow felt that very few people ever attain this level. Even so, advertisements may focus on this type of need. For example, American Express ads convey the message that acquiring its card is one of the highest attainments in life. Microsoft appealed to consumers' needs for self-actualization when it chose "Your Potential Our Passion" as the Windows XP slogan; similarly, the U.S. Army changed its slogan from "Be all that you can be" to "Army of One," and the U.S. Navy adopted a slogan urging young people to "Accelerate Your Life."

LEARNING

Almost all consumer behavior results from **learning**, which is the process that creates changes in behavior through experience and practice. It is not possible to observe learning directly, but we can infer when it has occurred by a person's actions. For example, suppose you see an advertisement for a new and improved cold medicine. If you go to the store that day and buy that remedy, we infer that you have learned something about the cold medicine.

There are two types of learning: experiential and conceptual. *Experiential learning* occurs when an experience changes your behavior. For example, if the new cold medicine does not relieve your symptoms, you may not buy that brand again. *Conceptual learning*, which is not acquired through direct experience, is the second type of learning. Assume, for example, that you are standing at a soft drink machine and notice a new diet flavor with an artificial sweetener. Because someone has told you that diet beverages leave an aftertaste, you choose a different drink. You have learned that you would not like this new diet drink without ever trying it.

Reinforcement and repetition boost learning. Reinforcement can be positive or negative. If you see a vendor selling frozen yogurt (stimulus), buy it (response), and find the yogurt to be quite refreshing (reward), your behavior has been positively reinforced. On the other hand, if you buy a new flavor of yogurt and it does not taste good (negative reinforcement), you will not buy that flavor of yogurt again (response). Without positive or negative reinforcement, a person will not be motivated to repeat the behavior pattern or to avoid it. Thus, if a new brand evokes neutral feelings, some marketing activity, such as a price change or an increase in promotion, may be required to induce further consumption. Learning theory is helpful in reminding marketers that concrete and timely actions are what reinforce desired consumer behavior.

Repetition is a key strategy in promotional campaigns because it can lead to increased learning. Most marketers use repetitious advertising so that consumers will learn what their unique advantage is over the competition. Generally, to heighten learning, advertising messages should be spread over time rather than clustered together.

A related learning concept useful to marketing managers is stimulus generalization. In theory, **stimulus generalization** occurs when one response is extended to a second stimulus similar to the first. Marketers often use a successful, well-known brand name for a family of products because it gives consumers familiarity with and knowledge about each product in the family. Such brand-name families spur the introduction of new products and facilitate the sale of existing items. Jell-O frozen pudding pops rely on the familiarity of Jell-O gelatin; Clorox bathroom cleaner relies on familiarity with Clorox bleach; and Dove shampoo relies on familiarity with Dove soap. Microsoft entered the video game industry, hoping that the Microsoft brand would guarantee sales for the Xbox. Initial response to the Xbox was strong based on Microsoft's reputation. Since then Microsoft has worked hard to be successful in an industry dominated by other brand giants Sony and Nintendo. The latest generation Xbox 360, introduced in December 2005, has jaw-dropping high-definition graphics, unmatched online play, and compelling digital entertainment; it plays music and movies stored in an array of devices including MP3 players and displays photos from digital cameras. Branding is examined in more detail in Chapter 9.

Another form of stimulus generalization occurs when retailers or wholesalers design their packages to resemble well-known manufacturers' brands. Such imitation often confuses consumers, who buy the imitation thinking it's the original. U.S. manufacturers

learning
A process that creates changes in behavior, immediate or expected, through experience and practice.

stimulus generalization
A form of learning that occurs when one response is extended to a second stimulus similar to the first.

in foreign markets have sometimes found little, if any, brand protection. In South Korea, Procter & Gamble's Ivory soap competes head-on with the Korean brand Bory, which has an almost identical logo on the package. Consumers dissatisfied with Bory may attribute their dissatisfaction to Ivory, never realizing that Bory is an imitator. Counterfeit products are also produced to look exactly like the original. For example, counterfeit Levi's jeans made in China are hot items in Europe, where Levi Strauss has had trouble keeping up with demand. The knockoffs look so much like the real thing that unsuspecting consumers don't know the difference—until after a few washes, when the belt loops fall off and the rivets begin to rust.

The opposite of stimulus generalization is **stimulus discrimination,** which means learning to differentiate among similar products. Consumers may perceive one product as more rewarding or stimulating. For example, some consumers prefer Coca-Cola and others prefer Pepsi. Many insist they can taste a difference between the two brands.

With some types of products—such as aspirin, gasoline, bleach, paper towels—marketers rely on promotion to point out brand differences that consumers would otherwise not recognize. This process, called *product differentiation*, is discussed in more detail in Chapter 7. Usually, product differentiation is based on superficial differences. For example, Bayer tells consumers that it's the aspirin "doctors recommend most."

BELIEFS AND ATTITUDES

stimulus discrimination
A learned ability to differentiate among similar products.

belief
An organized pattern of knowledge that an individual holds as true about his or her world.

attitude
A learned tendency to respond consistently toward a given object.

Beliefs and attitudes are closely linked to values. A **belief** is an organized pattern of knowledge that an individual holds as true about his or her world. A consumer may believe that Sony's camcorder makes the best home videos, tolerates hard use, and is reasonably priced. These beliefs may be based on knowledge, faith, or hearsay. Consumers tend to develop a set of beliefs about a product's attributes and then, through these beliefs, form a *brand image*—a set of beliefs about a particular brand. In turn, the brand image shapes consumers' attitudes toward the product.

An **attitude** is a learned tendency to respond consistently toward a given object, such as a brand. Attitudes rest on an individual's value system, which represents personal standards of good and bad, right and wrong, and so forth; therefore, attitudes tend to be more enduring and complex than beliefs.

For an example of the nature of attitudes, consider the differing attitudes of consumers around the world toward the practice of purchasing on credit. Americans have long been enthusiastic about charging goods and services and are willing to pay high interest rates for the privilege of postponing payment. To many European consumers, doing what amounts to taking out a loan—even a small one—to pay for anything seems absurd. Germans especially are reluctant to buy on credit. Italy has a sophisticated credit and banking system well suited to handling credit cards, but Italians prefer to carry cash, often huge wads of it. Although most Japanese consumers have credit cards, card purchases amount to less than 1 percent of all consumer transactions. The Japanese have long looked down on credit purchases but acquire cards to use while traveling abroad.

If a good or service is meeting its profit goals, positive attitudes toward the product merely need to be reinforced. If the brand is not succeeding, however, the marketing manager must strive to

In our FlexFuel Vehicles, Yellow means Go.

livegreen **goyellow**

Struggling brands must work to change consumers' negative beliefs about them. General Motors is running advertisements stressing its efforts to reduce greenhouse gas emissions. GM hopes to improve its brand image by convincing consumers that it is concerned about the environment.

COPYRIGHT © 2006 GENERAL MOTORS CORPORATION

change target consumers' attitudes toward it. Changes in attitude tend to grow out of an individual's attempt to reconcile long-held values with a constant stream of new information. This change can be accomplished in three ways: changing beliefs about the brand's attributes, changing the relative importance of these beliefs, and adding new beliefs.

Changing Beliefs about Attributes

The first technique is to turn neutral or negative beliefs about product attributes into positive ones. For example, many consumers believe that it is easier and cheaper to take traditional film to be developed than it is to print their own digital photos. To change this belief, Kodak has begun setting up kiosks in retail outlets that let consumers print their digital photos. The kiosks eliminate the need for consumers to purchase their own high-quality printer. Similarly, companies like It's Never 2 Late are trying to change senior citizens' belief that computers are too complicated for them to learn by providing software and hardware with larger type, fewer options, and more graphics to make it easier for seniors to use a PC.

Changing beliefs about a service can be more difficult because service attributes are intangible. Convincing consumers to switch hairstylists or lawyers or go to a mall dental clinic can be much more difficult than getting them to change brands of razor blades. Image, which is also largely intangible, significantly determines service patronage. For example, Tomra, a Norwegian recycling giant, hopes to increase the number of Americans who recycle by changing their perception that recycling is an unsavory chore. By building new rePlanet recycling kiosks in communities as an alternative to neighborhood recycling centers, Tomra is offering Americans a clean, convenient, service-oriented way to be responsible citizens.[58] Service marketing is explored in detail in Chapter 11.

Changing the Importance of Beliefs

The second approach to modifying attitudes is to change the relative importance of beliefs about an attribute. Cole Haan, originally a men's shoe outfitter, used boats and cars in its ads for years to associate the brand with active lifestyles, an important attribute for men. Now that it is selling women's products, such as handbags and shoes, some of its ads use models and emphasize how the products look, an important attribute for women. The company hopes the ads will change customers' perceptions and beliefs that it only sells men's products.[59]

Marketers can also emphasize the importance of some beliefs over others. For example, DaimlerChrysler's Jeep unit positions itself as being rugged but promotes its luxury features. The newest Grand Cherokees have even more off-road capability, but very few owners ever take them off-road. Luxury features include a climate-control system with infrared beams that track drivers' and passengers' skin temperature to automatically adjust air conditioning and heat, his and her key rings

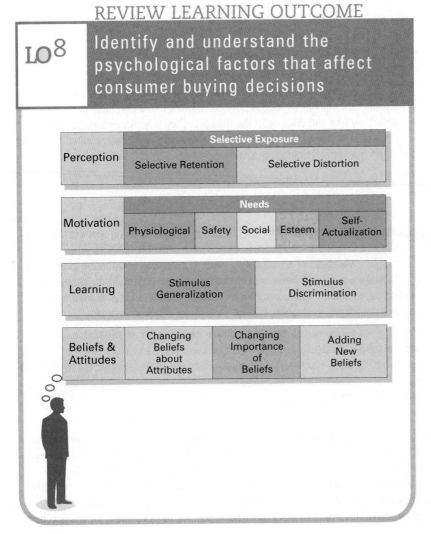

REVIEW LEARNING OUTCOME

LO 8 — Identify and understand the psychological factors that affect consumer buying decisions

Perception	Selective Exposure	
	Selective Retention	Selective Distortion

Motivation	Needs				
	Physiological	Safety	Social	Esteem	Self-Actualization

Learning	Stimulus Generalization	Stimulus Discrimination

Beliefs & Attitudes	Changing Beliefs about Attributes	Changing Importance of Beliefs	Adding New Beliefs

that remember settings for power seats and mirrors, a system to reprogram radio stations for different drivers, and many other comforts.

Adding New Beliefs

The third approach to transforming attitudes is to add new beliefs. Although changes in consumption patterns often come slowly, cereal marketers are betting that consumers will eventually warm up to the idea of cereal as a snack. A print ad for General Mills's Cookie-Crisp cereal features a boy popping the sugary nuggets into his mouth while he does his homework. Koch Industries, the manufacturer of Dixie paper products, is also attempting to add new beliefs about the uses of its paper plates and cups with an advertising campaign aimed at positioning its product as a "home cleanup replacement." Commercials pitch Dixie paper plates as an alternative to washing dishes after everyday meals.

U.S. companies attempting to market their goods overseas may need to help consumers add new beliefs about a product in general. Coca-Cola and PepsiCo have both found it challenging to sell their diet cola brands to consumers in India partly because diet foods of any kind are a new concept in that country where malnutrition was widespread not too many years ago. Indians also have deep-rooted attitudes that anything labeled "diet" is meant for a sick person, such as a diabetic. As a general rule, most Indians are not diet-conscious, preferring food prepared in the traditional manner that tastes good. Indians are also suspicious of the artificial sweeteners used in diet colas. India's Health Ministry has required warning labels on cans and bottles of Diet Coke and Diet Pepsi saying "Not Recommended for Children."[60]

Review and Applications

LO 1 Explain why marketing managers should understand consumer behavior. Consumer behavior describes how consumers make purchase decisions and how they use and dispose of the products they buy. An understanding of consumer behavior reduces marketing managers' uncertainty when they are defining a target market and designing a marketing mix.

1.1 The type of decision making a consumer uses for a product does not necessarily remain constant. Why? Support your answer with an example from your own experience.

LO 2 Analyze the components of the consumer decision-making process. The consumer decision-making process begins with need recognition, when stimuli trigger awareness of an unfulfilled want. If additional information is required to make a purchase decision, the consumer may engage in an internal or external information search. The consumer then evaluates the additional information and establishes purchase guidelines. Finally, a purchase decision is made.

2.1 Visit Carpoint's Web site at **http://autos.msn.com/home/carresearch.aspx?src=msnhp**. How does the site assist consumers in the evaluation stage of choosing a new car? Develop your own hypothetical evoked set of three or four car models and present your comparisons. Which vehicle attributes would be most important in your purchase decision?

LO 3 Explain the consumer's postpurchase evaluation process. Consumer postpurchase evaluation is influenced by prepurchase expectations, the prepurchase information search, and the consumer's general level of self-confidence. Cognitive dissonance is the inner tension that a consumer experiences after recognizing a purchased product's disadvantages. When a purchase creates cognitive dissonance, consumers tend to react by seeking positive reinforcement for the purchase

Quick Check ✔

Now that you've read the chapter, do you get it? Take a moment for a quick check using this scale:

1 Not at all; 2 Not very well; 3 Ok; 4 Well; 5 Very Well

Can you . . .

____ explain what consumer behavior is?

____ outline the steps of the consumer decision-making process?

____ describe the kinds of information searches and information sources and explain how they differ?

____ teach a friend not in the class about cognitive dissonance?

____ explain how social class is measured in the United States?

____ draw a diagram showing the relationship between different reference groups?

____ describe how personality and self-concept influence what someone buys?

____ write a paragraph about selective exposure, selective retention, and selective distortion?

____ label Maslow's hierarchy of needs with information marketers would find useful at each level?

____ explain how marketers can change consumers' attitudes toward a product?

____ TOTAL

Score: 41–50, you're ready to move on to the applications; 31–40, skim the chapter one more time before moving on to the applications; 21–30, reread the sections giving you the most trouble and go to Thomson NOW for guided tutorials; 20 and under, you better reread the chapter to get a grasp of the fundamentals. If you've reread the chapter and still have a low score, visit your professor or TA during office hours.

---

decision, avoiding negative information about the purchase decision, or revoking the purchase decision by returning the product.

3.1 Recall an occasion when you experienced cognitive dissonance about a purchase. In a letter to a friend, describe the event and explain what you did about it.

LO4 Identify the types of consumer buying decisions and discuss the significance of consumer involvement. Consumer decision making falls into three broad categories. First, consumers exhibit routine response behavior for frequently purchased, low-cost items that require very little decision effort; routine response behavior is typically characterized by brand loyalty. Second, consumers engage in limited decision making for occasional purchases or for unfamiliar brands in familiar product categories. Third, consumers practice extensive decision making when making unfamiliar, expensive, or infrequent purchases. High-involvement decisions usually include an extensive information search and a thorough evaluation of alternatives. In contrast, low-involvement decisions are characterized by brand loyalty and a lack of personal identification with the product. The main factors affecting the level of consumer involvement are previous experience, interest, perceived risk of negative consequences (financial, social, and psychological), situation, and social visibility.

4.1 Describe the three categories of consumer decision-making behavior. Name typical products for which each type of consumer behavior is used.

4.2 Describe the level of involvement and the involvement factors likely to be associated with buying a new computer. Do you think Apple's Web site at **http://www.apple.com** simplifies or complicates the process for the average consumer? Explain.

LO5 Identify and understand the cultural factors that affect consumer buying decisions. Cultural influences on consumer buying decisions include culture and values, subculture, and social class. Culture is the essential character of a society that distinguishes it from other cultural groups. The underlying elements of every culture are the values, language, myths, customs, rituals, laws, and artifacts, or products, that are transmitted from one generation to the next. The most defining element of a culture is its values—the enduring beliefs shared by a society that a specific mode of conduct is personally or socially preferable to another mode of conduct. A culture can be divided into subcultures on the basis of demographic characteristics, geographic regions, national and ethnic background, political beliefs, and religious beliefs.

Subcultures share elements of the overall culture as well as cultural elements unique to their own group. A social class is a group of people who are considered nearly equal in status or community esteem, who regularly socialize among themselves both formally and informally, and who share behavioral norms.

5.1 You are a new marketing manager for a firm that produces a line of athletic shoes to be targeted to the college student subculture. In a memo to your boss, list some product attributes that might appeal to this subculture and the steps in your customers' purchase processes, and recommend some marketing strategies that can influence their decision.

LO6 Identify and understand the social factors that affect consumer buying decisions. Social factors include such external influences as reference groups, opinion leaders, and family. Consumers seek out others' opinions for guidance on new products or services and products with image-related attributes or because attribute information is lacking or uninformative. Consumers may use products or brands to identify with or become a member of a reference group. Opinion leaders are members of reference groups who influence others' purchase decisions. Family members also influence purchase decisions; children tend to shop in similar patterns as their parents.

6.1 Family members play many different roles in the buying process: initiator, influencer, decision maker, purchaser, and consumer. Identify the person in your family who might play each of these roles in the purchase of a dinner at Pizza Hut, a summer vacation, Froot Loops breakfast cereal, an Abercrombie & Fitch sweater, golf clubs, an Internet service provider, and a new car.

LO7 Identify and understand the individual factors that affect consumer buying decisions. Individual factors that affect consumer buying decisions include gender; age and family life-cycle stage; and personality, self-concept, and lifestyle. Beyond obvious physiological differences, men and women differ in their social and economic roles and that affects consumer buying decisions. How old a consumer is generally indicates what products he or she may be interested in purchasing. Marketers often define their target markets in terms of consumers' life-cycle stage, following changes in consumers' attitudes and behavioral tendencies as they mature. Finally, certain products and brands reflect consumers' personality, self-concept, and lifestyle.

7.1 Assume you are involved in the following consumer decision situations: (a) renting a DVD to watch with your roommates, (b) choosing a fast-food restaurant to go to with a new friend, (c) buying a popular music compact disc, (d) buying jeans to wear to class. List the individual factors that would influence your decision in each situation and explain your responses.

LO8 Identify and understand the psychological factors that affect consumer buying decisions. Psychological factors include perception, motivation, learning, values, beliefs, and attitudes. These factors allow consumers to interact with the world around them, recognize their feelings, gather and analyze information, formulate thoughts and opinions, and take action. Perception allows consumers to recognize their consumption problems. Motivation is what drives consumers to take action to satisfy specific consumption needs. Almost all consumer behavior results from learning, which is the process that creates changes in behavior through experience. Consumers with similar beliefs and attitudes tend to react alike to marketing-related inducements.

8.1 How do beliefs and attitudes influence consumer behavior? How can negative attitudes toward a product be changed? How can marketers alter beliefs about a product? Give some examples of how marketers have changed negative attitudes about a product or added or altered beliefs about a product.

Key Terms

Exercises

APPLICATION EXERCISE

Principles of consumer behavior are evident in many areas of marketing. Perhaps the easiest place to see this critical foundation of marketing activity is in print ads.[61]

Activities

1. Because pictures can help reinforce understanding, consider doing this exercise for each chapter in the book. At the end of the semester, you will have a portfolio of ads that illustrate the concepts in the entire book, which can help you study. Simply look through your portfolio and try to recall the concepts at work in each advertisement. This exercise can be a prelude to a longer study session for comprehensive exams.

2. Review the main concepts in this chapter and create a checklist that itemizes them. Then, comb through your favorite magazines and newspapers for advertisements that illustrate each concept. To get a wide variety of ads, you will need to look through several magazines. If you don't have many magazines at your disposal, go to the campus library periodical room. Photocopy the ads you select to support this chapter.

© JEFF ROBERSON/ASSOCIATED PRESS

Entrepreneurship Case

BACK TO THE FUTURE? CHOCOLATE LOUNGES TASTE SWEET SUCCESS

The chocolate house dates back to seventeenth-century London, when members of society's elite would gather in luxurious surroundings to relax and sip hot chocolate. Later, Europeans expanded on that idea and developed solid chocolate treats that sold in upscale boutiques. Lacking the resources and economy of established continentals, bootstrapping American settlers pioneered the development of cheaper chocolate bars for the masses.

Centuries have passed, however, and the American palate has tired of the taste of mass-produced chocolate. The U.S. chocolate industry has experienced growth of less than 3 percent since the turn of the millennium, and the lack of industry innovation has left a bad taste in chocolate purveyors' mouths, too. Enter Ethel's Chocolate Lounges, named in honor of the matriarch of the Mars family, who founded the candy company with her husband Frank in 1911.

Now Ethel Mars's name adorns the signs at the company's latest attempt to breathe fresh life into chocolate. Aware that chocolate sales at upscale retail outlets, like Godiva and Starbucks grew by nearly 20 percent from 2002 to 2004, Mars opened Ethel's Chocolate Lounge in the Lincoln Park neighborhood of Chicago in April 2005. More Ethel's have opened since then, and the chic chocolate houses are Mars's bet that well-heeled and sweet-toothed consumers will take to premium chocolate the same way that well-to-do coffee lovers flock to Starbucks for high-priced java. Ethel's Lounges are designed to coddle patrons in the lap of luxury, but Mars president John Haugh maintains that what makes Ethel's special is that it offers "approachable gourmet chocolate." In other words, you don't have to be a millionaire to enjoy the sweet taste of the good life.

Prices are not for everyone's wallet, however. Truffles and Tea for Two, which features all 11 of Ethel's truffles served on a silver platter, sells for $15. Chocolates and Cocoa for Two includes two cocoas and 10 pieces of chocolate for $18, and a box of 48 chocolates is $42. Five "Collections" offer over 50 individual chocolates that sell for between $.90 and $1.50.

Supporting Haugh's claim of approachability, though, the menus at Ethel's feature icons and descriptions of the chocolates' contents so that customers won't experience an unwanted surprise. A multitude of hot and cold beverages give visitors more reasons to extend their stays.

But it's not just the chocolate that makes Ethel's such a desirable destination. Advertising describes Ethel's as "a place for chocolate and chitchat." Generously stuffed pink couches with brown accents combine upscale modern and traditional looks to give the stores a hip and classy feel. For those who don't immediately get it, a sign behind the counter reads, "Chocolate is the new black." The stores' appeal is their relaxing ambience and neighborhood vibe—like a modern American coffeehouse, these shops encourage socializing and extending lounging. The effect is carefully planned. Mars's research revealed that even calorie-conscious consumers will splurge for the good stuff as long as a broader social experience comes with it.

Parallels to the Starbucks-led American coffee revival are obvious and inescapable. Confectionary industry insiders note that chocolate cafés are taking hold, and research confirms their belief. Datamonitor, a research firm specializing in trend identification, described chocolate as "the new coffee" on its list of the top ten trends to watch in 2006. The popularity of the Chocolate Bar in New York, billed as a "candy store for grown-ups," and South Bend Chocolate's ten chocolate cafés shows that the trend is for real. Even some Hershey's stores now offer seating for patrons.

Joan Steuer, president of Chocolate Marketing, claims that, for women, enjoying chocolate in a luxurious lounge is like taking a candle-lit bubble bath. She notes, too, that much of the appeal is that the experience is testimony to the person's upward mobility. It's a perfect way to cater to the American desire to have the best that money can buy.[62]

Questions

1. List the factors that might influence a consumer to spend money and time at Ethel's. Which factor do you think will motivate a consumer the most? Why?

2. Review the core American values in Exhibit 5.5. Which value does the Ethel's experience appeal to most? Explain.

3. What type of consumer buying decision best describes the choice to indulge at Ethel's?

COMPANY CLIPS

ReadyMade—Do-it-Yourself

In 2001 when Grace Hawthorne, CEO, and Shoshana Berger, Editor-in-Chief, came up with their idea for ReadyMade there were no other publications with their unique do-it-yourself (DIY) theme. ReadyMade was to be a magazine about fun and creative projects for the home. Since its development, the bimonthly magazine has enjoyed a loyal subscriber base and continues to gain readership across the country. All issues include numerous do-it-yourself (DIY) projects, each rated by their level of difficulty, as well as several feature articles exploring the latest in innovation and design. In this video, pay attention to ReadyMade's methods as they launched their magazine. Note also how ReadyMade uses its knowledge of its consumer base to tailor the product.

Questions

1. While the ReadyMade magazine was still in the design stages, very little research was done to determine whether an interested market existed. Did this adversely affect the magazine as it moved forward to publication? Explain.

2. How does the cover of ReadyMade magazine reflect the principles of packaging design as influenced by the known behaviors of its consumers?

3. To what extent does ReadyMade rely on opinion leaders to promote the magazine? Is this a successful tactic?

BIZ FLIX

The Family Man (I)

See the theories in Chapter 5 at work in this clip from *The Family Man*, starring Nicolas Cage (Jack) and Tea Leoni (Kate). In the selected scene, Jack is still trying to adapt to his new life as husband, father, and tire salesman. He walks into the men's department of a mall department store and begins to admire the suits. How does this scene relate to the many factors that affect the consumer decision-making process shown in Exhibit 5.1? Can you describe Jack's decision using terms and concepts from the chapter?

Marketing & You Results

High scores suggest that you tend to shop for value, whereas lower scores indicate compulsive buying, or excessive shopping relative to your disposable income. Lower scores also suggest that you may use excessive shopping to deal with undesirable moods or negative feelings. Even though your mood might improve afterward, beware: the change is temporary, compulsive shopping behavior is very difficult to stop, and you can experience harmful consequences as a result.

Business

Marketing

Learning Outcomes

LO¹   Describe business marketing

LO²   Describe the role of the Internet in business marketing

LO³   Discuss the role of relationship marketing and strategic alliances in business marketing

LO⁴   Identify the four major categories of business market customers

LO⁵   Explain the North American Industry Classification System

LO⁶   Explain the major differences between business and consumer markets

LO⁷   Describe the seven types of business goods and services

LO⁸   Discuss the unique aspects of business buying behavior

Goodyear **tries to regain dealers' trust**

oodyear Tire & Rubber Company, the world's largest tire company, once boasted the premier tire reseller network in the United States. In the 1970s and 1980s, it earned dealer loyalty through aggressive pricing, on-time deliveries, and marketing fueled by the famous Goodyear name. So how did one of the most recognized brands in American corporate history turn off the very people who handle the bulk of its sales? Easy.

After assuring its dealers that it would not sell through discount merchandisers, Goodyear announced a distribution deal with Sears. Similar pacts with

"We lost sight of the fact that it's in our interest that our dealers succeed"

Wal-Mart and Sam's Club pitted dealers against the nation's most powerful retailers. Many other tire manufacturers now do the same thing, but dealers say Goodyear has gone about it the wrong way. For one thing, they complain that Goodyear's "fill rate"—the number of tires dealers receive divided by the number they ordered—has been as low as 50

percent, making it difficult for dealers to compete. (Ninety percent is considered standard.) In addition, to sell more tires, the company until recently offered bulk discounts to its biggest retailers and wholesalers. The result was pricing insanity: Some smaller dealers were paying more for tires than the price Sears charged at retail. Yet dealers were expected to honor warranties and recalls. "Goodyear opened a Pandora's box," says Larry Hauck, owner of Wells Tire of Alton, Illinois, an exclusive Goodyear dealer until the late 1990s.

Under CEO Robert Keegan—who since taking his post in 2003 has brought Goodyear back to a semblance of financial health—the company is finally owning up to its dealer problems. "We lost sight of the fact that it's in our interest that our dealers succeed," says Jack Winterton, Goodyear's vice president for replacement tire sales.

Keegan is also attempting to mend fences. Dealer sales are now organized through a handful of wholesalers to unify pricing, and fill rates have improved. "We still have a long way to go on this," Winterton admits.[1]

How did Goodyear lose the trust and commitment of its dealers? What needs to change for it to regain dealer support?

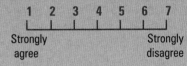

Marketing & You

Think about the last time you dealt with a salesperson when making a major purchase. Then, using the following scales, indicate your opinions of that salesperson.

Using the scales below, enter your answers.

```
1    2    3    4    5    6    7
└────┴────┴────┴────┴────┴────┘
Strongly                  Strongly
agree                     disagree
```

_____ This salesperson was frank in dealing with me.

_____ This salesperson did not make false claims.

_____ I do not think this salesperson was completely open in dealing with me.*

_____ This salesperson was only concerned about himself/herself.*

_____ This salesperson did not seem to be concerned with my needs.*

_____ I did not trust this salesperson.*

_____ This salesperson was not trustworthy.*

Now, total your score, reversing your answers for the items followed by an asterisk. That is, if you put a 2, change it to a 6; if you put a 3, change it to a 5, and so forth. Read the chapter and find out what your score means at the end.

LO¹
What Is Business Marketing?

Business marketing is the marketing of goods and services to individuals and organizations for purposes other than personal consumption. The sale of a personal computer to your college or university is an example of business marketing. Business products include those that are used to manufacture other products, become part of another product, or aid the normal operations of an organization. The key characteristic distinguishing business products from consumer products is intended use, not physical characteristics. A product that is purchased for personal or family consumption or as a gift is a consumer good. If that same product, such as a personal computer or a cell phone, is bought for use in a business, it is a business product.

The size of the business market in the United States and most other countries substantially exceeds that of the consumer market. In the business market, a single customer can account for a huge volume of purchases. For example, General Motors' purchasing department spends more than $85 billion per year on goods and services. General Electric, DuPont, and IBM spend over $60 million per day on business purchases.[2]

REVIEW LEARNING OUTCOME

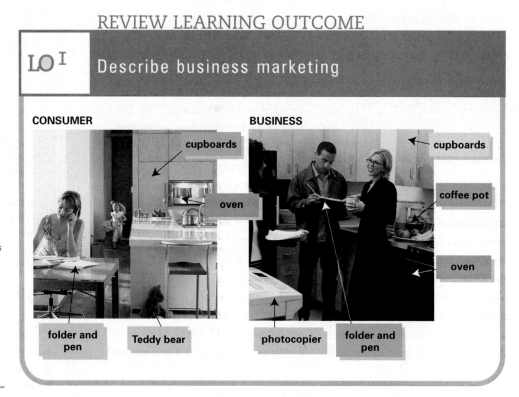

LO²
Business Marketing on the Internet

It is hard to imagine that commercial use of the Internet began as recently as the mid-1990s. In 1995, the commercial Web sites that did exist were static. Only a few had data-retrieval capabilities. Frames, tables, and styles were not available. Security of any sort was rare, and streaming video did not exist. In 2005, there were over one billion Internet users worldwide.

The use of the Internet to facilitate activities between organizations is called **business-to-business electronic commerce** (B-to-B or B2B e-commerce). This method of conducting business has evolved and grown rapidly throughout its short history. In 2006, the United States alone was expected to account for over $800 billion of

business marketing
The marketing of goods and services to individuals and organizations for purposes other than personal consumption.

business-to-business electronic commerce
The use of the Internet to facilitate the exchange of goods, services, and information between organizations.

Exhibit 6.1

Internet Sites Specifically for Small Businesses

http://www.allbusiness.com AllBusiness provides entrepreneurs with the knowledge and tools to start, manage, and grow their business. The site links to hundreds of how-to articles and provides expert answers to questions.

http://www.bcentral.com Microsoft bCentral offers small-business solutions such as assistance in establishing an online business presence, enhancing sales or services, or managing business operations. The site also contains practical tips, advice, and links to how-to articles.

http://office.com Office.com offers practical information on how to start or run a business and how to transform an existing company into an e-business. Users access over 500 databases for news that affects their companies or industries. Office.com is one of the ten most visited business Web sites on the Internet.

http://www.quicken.com/small_business/ This site offers information on starting, running, and growing a small business. It also provides links to a variety of other Quicken sites that are useful to small-business owners and managers.

B2B e-commerce.[3] Online B2B transactions in the European Union were expected to reach 2.2 trillion euros (about $1.8 trillion) in 2006, representing 22 percent of all B2B transactions.[4] This phenomenal growth is not restricted to large companies. Exhibit 6.1 identifies some popular Internet sites that cater to small businesses.

MEASURING ONLINE SUCCESS

To understand what works and what doesn't work online, marketers must be able to comprehend the vast amount of data stored in the log files generated by their Web servers. Not all of these data are relevant for planning an online strategy, but by combining certain log file results with sales information, a marketer can fine-tune the marketing effort to maximize online success.

In the mid-1990s, many Web sites displayed hit counters on their pages. This software device counted the number of file requests made of the server to create the pages seen by visitors. Unfortunately, the hit counters didn't record who visited, how many times they visited, or even what interested the visitors. The counters didn't provide much useful information, and that's why they're rarely seen now.

For marketers today, three of the most important measurements are recency, frequency, and monetary value. *Recency* relates to the fact that customers who have made a purchase recently are more likely to purchase again in the near future than customers who haven't purchased for a while. *Frequency* data help marketers identify frequent purchasers who are definitely more likely to repeat their purchasing behavior in the future. The *monetary value* of sales is important because big spenders can be the most profitable customers for your business.

NetGenesis, a company that has been purchased by SPSS, has devised a number of equations that can help online marketers better understand their data. For example, combining frequency data with the length of time a visitor spent on the Web site (duration) and the number of site pages viewed during each visit (total site reach) can provide an analytical measure of a site's **stickiness** factor:

$$\text{Stickiness} = \text{Frequency} \times \text{Duration} \times \text{Site Reach}$$

By measuring the stickiness factor of a Web site before and after a design or function change, the marketer can quickly determine whether visitors embraced the change. By adding purchase information to determine the level of stickiness needed to provide a desired purchase volume, the marketer gains an even more precise understanding of how a site change affected business. An almost endless number of factor combinations can be created to provide a quantitative method for determining buyer behavior online. First, though, the marketer must determine what measures are required and which factors can be combined to arrive at those measurements.[5]

TRENDS IN B2B INTERNET MARKETING

Over the last decade marketers have become more and more sophisticated in their use of the Internet. Exhibit 6.2 compares three prominent Internet business marketing strategy initiatives from the late 1990s to five that are currently being pursued. In previous

stickiness
A measure of a Web site's effectiveness; calculated by multiplying the frequency of visits times the duration of a visit times the number of pages viewed during each visit (site reach).

Exhibit 6.2

Evolution of E-Business Initiatives

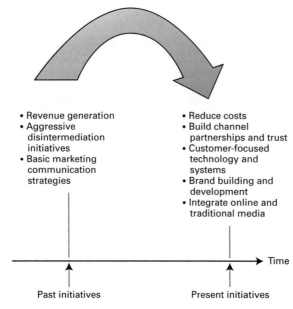

- Revenue generation
- Aggressive disintermediation initiatives
- Basic marketing communication strategies

- Reduce costs
- Build channel partnerships and trust
- Customer-focused technology and systems
- Brand building and development
- Integrate online and traditional media

Time

Past initiatives

Present initiatives

SOURCE: Andrew J. Rohm and Fareena Sultan, "The Evolution of E-Business," *Marketing Management*, January/February, 2004, p. 35. Used by permission.

years, online marketing objectives focused on attracting new prospects and promoting brands. Today, savvy business marketers use the Internet to achieve a wide range of objectives.[6] The best online strategy often integrates conventional and Internet marketing strategies. New applications that provide additional information about present and potential customers, increase efficiency, lower costs, increase supply chain efficiency, or enhance customer retention, loyalty, and trust are being developed each year. Chapter 19 on customer relationship management, describes several of these applications.

One term in Exhibit 6.2 that may be unfamiliar is **disintermediation**, which means eliminating intermediaries such as wholesalers or distributors from a marketing channel. A prime example of disintermediation is Dell, Inc., which sells directly to business buyers and consumers. Large retailers such as Wal-Mart use a disintermediation strategy to help reduce costs and prices.[7]

A few years ago, many people thought that the Internet would eliminate the need for distributors. Why would customers pay for distributor markups when they could buy directly from the manufacturers with a few mouse clicks? Yet Internet disintermediation has occurred less frequently than many expected. The reason is that distributors often perform important functions such as providing credit, aggregation of supplies from multiple sources, delivery, and processing returns. Many business customers, especially small firms, depend on knowledgeable distributors for information and advice that are not available to them online. You will notice in Exhibit 6.2 that building channel partnerships and trust has replaced aggressive disintermediation initiatives as a priority for most firms.

disintermediation
The elimination of intermediaries such as wholesalers or distributors from a marketing channel.

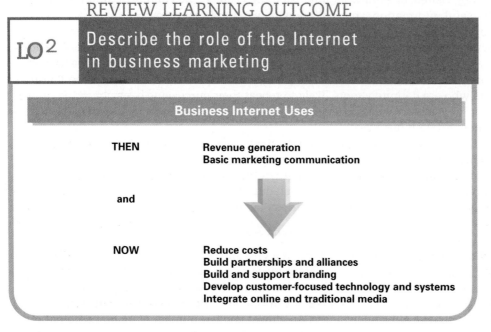

REVIEW LEARNING OUTCOME

LO 2 Describe the role of the Internet in business marketing

Business Internet Uses

THEN
Revenue generation
Basic marketing communication

and

NOW
Reduce costs
Build partnerships and alliances
Build and support branding
Develop customer-focused technology and systems
Integrate online and traditional media

LO 3
Relationship Marketing and Strategic Alliances

As Chapter 1 explained, relationship marketing is a strategy that entails seeking and establishing ongoing partnerships with customers. Relationship marketing has become an important business marketing strategy as customers have become more demanding and competition has become more intense. Loyal customers are also more profitable than those who are price-sensitive and perceive little or no difference among brands or suppliers. Building long-term relationships with customers offers companies a way to build competitive advantage that is hard for competitors to copy. For example, the FedEx Powership program includes a series of automated shipping, tracking, and invoicing systems that save customers time and money while solidifying their loyalty to FedEx. This produces a win-win situation. FedEx has a satisfied loyal customer, and the customer saves time and money shipping products to its customers. Similarly, Dell, Inc., provides a customized Web page for each of its premier customers that individual employees in the customer organization can access for information and technical support.

Although relationships are expected to produce win-win outcomes, it doesn't always work out this way. Just a few years ago Kodak was the exclusive provider of photo-developing services for Walgreen Company. This relationship rapidly deteriorated as Kodak shifted its focus from film to digital technologies and began competing directly with its film-processing partners. As a result, Walgreen has shifted much of its film-processing business to Kodak's archrival Fuji Photo Film.[8] The tension between Goodyear Tire & Rubber and its distributors, described at the beginning of this chapter, is another example of a relationship that developed problems when the environment and one company's strategy changed.

STRATEGIC ALLIANCES

A **strategic alliance**, sometimes called a *strategic partnership*, is a cooperative agreement between business firms. Strategic alliances can take the form of licensing or distribution agreements, joint ventures, research and development consortia, and partnerships. They may be between different manufacturers, manufacturers and customers, manufacturers and suppliers, and manufacturers and channel intermediaries.

Business marketers form strategic alliances to leverage what they have (technology, financial resources, access to markets) by combining these assets with those of other firms. Rival retail supply chain exchanges Agentrics LLC and WorldWide Retail Exchange LLC have formed a combined online marketplace aimed at reducing the cost of buying goods and making it easier for stores and suppliers to compete more effectively with retail giant Wal-Mart.[9] Sometimes alliance partners' assets are complementary. For example, Microsoft and SAP AG will jointly develop and sell software that combines their leading lines of business programs. The new product integrates Microsoft's Office suite of desktop applications with SAP's mySAP suite of enterprise resource planning tools. The goal is to enable workers to use familiar desktop software from Microsoft to display and manipulate back-office systems from SAP.[10]

Some alliances are formed with competitors to achieve increased productivity and lower costs for all participants. For example, Boeing and Lockheed Martin have agreed to form a joint venture to launch military, spy, and civilian research rockets and satellites for the U.S. government. The joint venture will presumably end years of bitter rivalry and litigation between the two companies.[11]

Other alliances are formed between companies that operate in completely different industries. Choice Hotels and 1-800-Flowers share call-center employees because doing so is a cheaper alternative than outsourcing. When one company experiences increased demand for its products and services, it can call on its partner's employees rather than add staff or use a temporary agency. At a given time, as many as 100 call-center agents may be taking orders for the other company. Both companies report higher employee retention and better recruitment.[12]

For an alliance to succeed in the long term, it must be built on commitment and trust. **Relationship commitment** means that a firm believes that an ongoing relationship with some other firm is so important that it warrants maximum efforts at maintaining it indefinitely.[13] A perceived reduction in commitment by one of the parties often leads to a breakdown in the relationship, as illustrated by the Kodak/Walgreen and Goodyear examples.

strategic alliance (strategic partnership)
A cooperative agreement between business firms.

relationship commitment
A firm's belief that an ongoing relationship with another firm is so important that the relationship warrants maximum efforts at maintaining it indefinitely.

Trust exists when one party has confidence in an exchange partner's reliability and integrity.[14] Some alliances fail when participants lack trust in their trading partners. General Motors, Ford, DaimlerChrysler, Nissan Motor Company, and Renault SA created an Internet automobile parts exchange, called Covisint, that was expected to account for $300 billion in sales per year. The auto manufacturers assumed that if they built a Web site, trading volume would follow. But the industry is characterized by mistrust between buyers and sellers. After a decade of being forced to accept price concessions, suppliers were in no hurry to participate. The manufacturers didn't help by boasting that Covisint would squeeze an additional 30 percent in savings out of vendors.

Another example of a failed alliance was a partnership between pharmaceutical giant Eli Lilly and a small biotechnology company, Amylin Pharmaceuticals, Inc. The plan was to jointly develop and market a new diabetes drug. The relationship reached a low point when the marketing chiefs from Lilly and Amylin engaged in a shouting match in a hallway following a joint presentation to senior management at Lilly. The main problem: mutual distrust.[15]

RELATIONSHIPS IN OTHER CULTURES

Although the terms *relationship marketing* and *strategic alliances* are fairly new, and popularized mostly by American business executives and educators, the concepts have long been familiar in other cultures. Businesses in Mexico, China, Japan, Korea, and much of Europe rely heavily on personal relationships. Chapter 19 explores customer relationship management in detail.

In Japan, for example, exchange between firms is based on personal relationships that are developed through what is called *amae*, or indulgent dependency. *Amae* is the feeling of nurturing concern for, and dependence on, another. Reciprocity and personal relationships contribute to *amae*. Relationships between companies can develop into a keiretsu—a network of interlocking corporate affiliates. Within a keiretsu, executives may sit on the boards of their customers or their suppliers. Members of a keiretsu trade with each other whenever possible and often engage in joint product development, finance, and marketing activity. For example, the Toyota Group keiretsu includes 14 core companies and another 170 that receive preferential treatment. Toyota holds an equity position in many of these 170 member firms and is represented on many of their boards of directors.

Many American firms have found that the best way to compete in Asian coun-

trust
The condition that exists when one party has confidence in an exchange partner's reliability and integrity.

keiretsu
A network of interlocking corporate affiliates.

REVIEW LEARNING OUTCOME

LO3 Discuss the role of relationship marketing and strategic alliances in business marketing

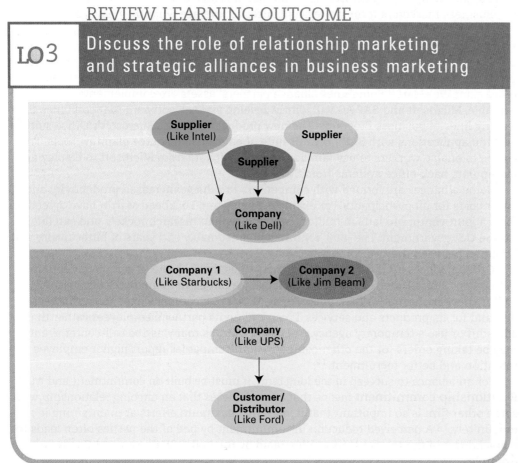

tries is to form relationships with Asian firms. For example, Fuji-Xerox markets copiers in Japan and other Asian countries. Whirlpool has spent over $200 million buying controlling interests in competing firms in China and in India. Both General Motors and Volkswagen have formed partnerships with giant Chinese car producer Shanghai Automotive Industry Corporation (SAIC). GM and VW already produce more than 600,000 autos per year in Shanghai factories. GM plans to begin building Cadillacs in Shanghai soon. SAIC's goal is to become one of the world's six largest automakers by 2020.[16]

LO4
Major Categories of Business Customers

The business market consists of four major categories of customers: producers, resellers, governments, and institutions.

PRODUCERS

The producer segment of the business market includes profit-oriented individuals and organizations that use purchased goods and services to produce other products, to incorporate into other products, or to facilitate the daily operations of the organization. Examples of producers include construction, manufacturing, transportation, finance, real estate, and food service firms. In the United States there are over 13 million firms in the producer segment of the business market. Some of these firms are small, and others are among the world's largest businesses.

Producers are often called **original equipment manufacturers** or **OEMs**. This term includes all individuals and organizations that buy business goods and incorporate them into the products that they produce for eventual sale to other producers or to consumers. Companies such as General Motors that buy steel, paint, tires, and batteries are said to be OEMs.

maharam

maharam.com

THE STORY OF MY LIFE BY MAIRA KALMAN

800.645.3943

The producer segment of the business market includes manufacturing, like Maharam's textile production, as well as construction, finance, transportation, real estate, and others. In addition to being a producer, Maharam sells only to business marketers (called "to the trade" in the textile industry).

original equipment manufacturers (OEMs) Individuals and organizations that buy business goods and incorporate them into the products that they produce for eventual sale to other producers or to consumers.

RESELLERS

The reseller market includes retail and wholesale businesses that buy finished goods and resell them for a profit. A retailer sells mainly to final consumers; wholesalers sell mostly to retailers and other organizational customers. There are approximately 1.5 million retailers and 500,000 wholesalers operating in the United States. Consumer-product firms like Procter & Gamble, Kraft Foods, and Coca-Cola sell directly to large retailers and retail chains and through wholesalers to smaller retail units. Retailing is explored in detail in Chapter 13.

Business product distributors are wholesalers that buy business products and resell them to business customers. They often carry thousands of items in stock and employ sales forces to call on business customers. Businesses that wish to buy a gross of pencils or a hundred pounds of fertilizer typically purchase these items from local distributors rather than directly from manufacturers such as Empire Pencil or Dow Chemical.

GOVERNMENTS

A third major segment of the business market is government. Government organizations include thousands of federal, state, and local buying units. They make up what may be the largest single market for goods and services in the world.

Contracts for government purchases are often put out for bid. Interested vendors submit bids (usually sealed) to provide specified products during a particular time. Sometimes the lowest bidder is awarded the contract. When the lowest bidder is not awarded the contract, strong evidence must be presented to justify the decision. Grounds for rejecting the lowest bid include lack of experience, inadequate financing, or poor past performance. Bidding allows all potential suppliers a fair chance at winning government contracts and helps ensure that public funds are spent wisely.

Federal Government

Name just about any good or service and chances are that someone in the federal government uses it. The U.S. federal government buys goods and services valued at over $590 billion per year, making it the world's largest customer.

Although much of the federal government's buying is centralized, no single federal agency contracts for all the government's requirements, and no single buyer in any agency purchases all that the agency needs. We can view the federal government as a combination of several large companies with overlapping responsibilities and thousands of small independent units.

One popular source of information about government procurement is *Commerce Business Daily*. Until recently, businesses hoping to sell to the federal government found the document unorganized, and it often arrived too late to be useful. The online version (**http://www.cbd-net.com**) is more timely and lets contractors find leads using keyword searches. *Doing Business with the General Services Administration, Selling to the Military*, and *Selling to the U.S. Air Force* are other examples of publications designed to explain how to do business with the federal government.

North American Industry Classification System (NAICS)
A detailed numbering system developed by the United States, Canada, and Mexico to classify North American business establishments by their main production processes.

State, County, and City Government

Selling to states, counties, and cities can be less frustrating for both small and large vendors than selling to the federal government. Paperwork is typically simpler and more manageable than it is at the federal level. On the other hand, vendors must decide which of the over 82,000 government units are likely to buy their wares. State and local buying agencies include school districts, highway departments, government-operated hospitals, and housing agencies.

REVIEW LEARNING OUTCOME

LO4 Identify the four major categories of business market customers

Business Marketing

- **Producers**
  - OEMs
- **Resellers**
  - Wholesalers
  - Retailers
- **Governments**
  - Federal
  - State
  - Municipal
  - County
- **Institutions**
  - Unions
  - Civic Clubs
  - Other
  - Churches
  - Foundations
  - Nonprofits

INSTITUTIONS

The fourth major segment of the business market consists of institutions that seek to achieve goals other than the standard business goals of profit, market share, and return on investment. This segment includes schools, hospitals, colleges and universities, churches, labor unions, fraternal organizations, civic clubs, foundations, and other so-called nonbusiness organizations. Xerox offers educational and medical institutions the same prices as government agencies (the lowest that Xerox offers) and has a separate sales force that calls on these customers.

LO⁵

The North American Industry Classification System

The **North American Industry Classification System (NAICS)** is an **industry classification system** introduced in 1997 to replace the standard industrial classification system (SIC). NAICS (pronounced *nakes*) is a system for classifying North American business establishments. The system, developed jointly by the United States, Canada, and Mexico, provides a common industry classification system for the North American Free Trade Agreement (NAFTA) partners. Goods- or service-producing firms that use identical or similar production processes are grouped together.

NAICS is an extremely valuable tool for business marketers engaged in analyzing, segmenting, and targeting markets. Each classification group is relatively homogeneous in terms of raw materials required, components used, manufacturing processes employed, and problems faced. The more digits in a code, the more homogeneous the group is. Therefore, if a supplier understands the needs and requirements of a few firms within a classification, requirements can be projected for all firms in that category. The number, size, and geographic dispersion of firms can also be identified. This information can be converted to market potential estimates, market share estimates, and sales forecasts. It can also be used for identifying potential new customers. NAICS codes can help identify firms that may be prospective users of a supplier's goods and services.

Exhibit 6.3 provides an overview of NAICS. Exhibit 6.4 illustrates the six-digit classification system for two of the 20 NAICS economic sectors: manufacturing and information. The hierarchical structure of NAICS allows industry data to be summarized at several levels of detail. To illustrate:

- The first two digits designate a major economic sector such as agriculture (11) or manufacturing (31–33).

Exhibit 6.3

NAICS Two-Digit Codes and Corresponding Economic Sectors

NAICS Code	Economic Sector
11	Agriculture, forestry, and fishing
21	Mining
22	Utilities
23	Construction
31–33	Manufacturing
43	Wholesale trade
44–45	Retail trade
47–48	Transportation
51	Information
52	Finance and insurance
53	Real estate and rental and leasing
56	Professional and technical services
57	Management and support services
61	Education services
62	Health and social assistance
71	Arts, entertainment, and recreation
72	Food services, drinking places, and accommodations
81	Other services, except public administration
93	Public administration
98	Estates and trusts
99	Nonclassifiable

Exhibit 6.4

Examples of NAICS Hierarchy

NAICS Level	Example 1 NAICS Code	Example 1 Description	Example 2 NAICS Code	Example 2 Description
Sector	31–33	Manufacturing	51	Information
Subsector	334	Computer and electronic product manufacturing	513	Broadcasting and telecommunications
Industry group	3346	Manufacturing and reproduction of magnetic and optical media	5133	Telecommunications
Industry	33461	Manufacturing and reproduction of magnetic and optical media	51332	Wireless telecommunications carriers, except satellite
U.S. industry	334611	Reproduction of software	513321	Paging

SOURCE: U.S. Census Bureau, "New Code System in NAICS," **http://www.census.gov/epcd/www/naics.html**.

- The third digit designates an economic subsector such as crop production or apparel manufacturing.

- The fourth digit designates an industry group, such as grain and oil seed farming or fiber, yarn, and thread mills.

- The fifth digit designates the NAICS industry, such as wheat farming or broad-woven fabric mills.

- The sixth digit, when used, identifies subdivisions of NAICS industries that accommodate user needs in individual countries.[17]

For a complete listing of all NAICS codes, see **http://www.censusgov/epcd/www/ naics.html.**

REVIEW LEARNING OUTCOME

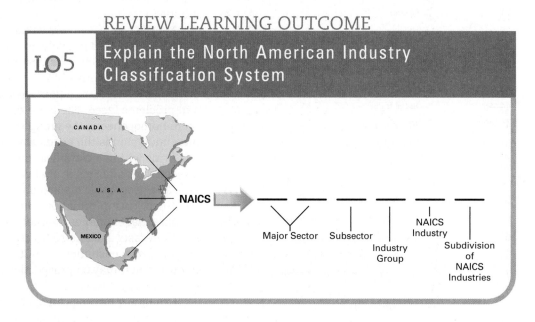

LO5 Explain the North American Industry Classification System

LO6
Business versus Consumer Markets

The basic philosophy and practice of marketing are the same whether the customer is a business organization or a consumer. Business markets do, however, have characteristics different from consumer markets.

DEMAND

Consumer demand for products is quite different from demand in the business market. Unlike consumer demand, business demand is derived, inelastic, joint, and fluctuating.

Derived Demand

The demand for business products is called **derived demand** because organizations buy products to be used in producing their customers' products. For example, the market for CPUs, hard drives, and CD-ROMs is derived from the demand for personal computers. These items are only valuable as components of computers. Demand for these items rises and falls with the demand for PCs.

Because demand is derived, business marketers must carefully monitor demand patterns and changing preferences in final consumer markets, even though their customers are not in those markets. Moreover, business marketers must carefully monitor their customers' forecasts, because derived demand is based on expectations of future demand for those customers' products.

derived demand
The demand for business products.

Some business marketers not only monitor final consumer demand and customer forecasts but also try to influence final consumer demand. Aluminum producers use television and magazine advertisements to point out the convenience and recycling opportunities that aluminum offers to consumers who can choose to purchase soft drinks in either aluminum or plastic containers.

Inelastic Demand

The demand for many business products is inelastic with regard to price. *Inelastic demand* means that an increase or decrease in the price of the product will not significantly affect demand for the product. This will be discussed further in Chapter 17.

The price of a product used in the production of, or as part of, a final product is often a minor portion of the final product's total price. Therefore, demand for the final consumer product is not affected. If the price of automobile paint or spark plugs rises significantly, say, 200 percent in one year, do you think the number of new automobiles sold that year will be affected? Probably not.

Joint Demand

Joint demand occurs when two or more items are used together in a final product. For example, a decline in the availability of memory chips will slow production of microcomputers, which will in turn reduce the demand for disk drives. Likewise, the demand for Apple operating systems exists as long as there is demand for Apple computers. Sales of the two products are directly linked.

Fluctuating Demand

The demand for business products—particularly new plants and equipment—tends to be less stable than the demand for consumer products. A small increase or decrease in consumer demand can produce a much larger change in demand for the facilities and equipment needed to make the consumer product. Economists refer to this phenomenon as the **multiplier effect** (or **accelerator principle**).

Cummins Engine Company, a producer of heavy-duty diesel engines, uses sophisticated surface grinders to make parts. Suppose Cummins is using 20 surface grinders. Each machine lasts about ten years. Purchases have been timed so two machines will wear out and be replaced annually. If the demand for engine parts does not change, two grinders will be bought this year. If the demand for parts declines slightly, only 18 grinders may be needed and Cummins won't replace the worn ones. However, suppose that next year demand returns to previous levels plus a little more. To meet the new level of demand, Cummins will need to replace the two machines that wore out in the first year, the two that wore out in the second year, plus one or more additional machines. The multiplier effect works this way in many industries, producing highly fluctuating demand for business products.

PURCHASE VOLUME

Business customers buy in much larger quantities than consumers. Just think how large an order Kellogg typically places for the wheat bran and raisins used to manufacture Raisin Bran. Imagine the number of tires that DaimlerChrysler buys at one time.

joint demand
The demand for two or more items used together in a final product.

multiplier effect (accelerator principle)
Phenomenon in which a small increase or decrease in consumer demand can produce a much larger change in demand for the facilities and equipment needed to make the consumer product.

NUMBER OF CUSTOMERS

Business marketers usually have far fewer customers than consumer marketers. The advantage is that it is a lot easier to identify prospective buyers, monitor current customers' needs and levels of satisfaction, and personally attend to existing customers. The main disadvantage is that each customer becomes crucial—especially for those manufacturers that have only one customer. In many cases, this customer is the U.S. government. The success or failure of one bid can make the difference between prosperity and bankruptcy. After five years of development, testing, and politicking,

One difference between consumer and business markets is that business customers are more likely to be located in certain states, like Ohio. This advertisement lists reasons for Ohio's large population of business buyers.

the Pentagon awarded Lockheed Martin a multidecade contract to build 3,000 jet fighter airplanes. Boeing Aircraft Company, the only other bidder on the $200 billion contract, immediately announced plans for substantial layoffs.

LOCATION OF BUYERS

Business customers tend to be much more geographically concentrated than consumers. For instance, more than half the nation's business buyers are located in New York, California, Pennsylvania, Illinois, Ohio, Michigan, and New Jersey. The aircraft and microelectronics industries are concentrated on the West Coast, and many of the firms that supply the automobile manufacturing industry are located in and around Detroit.

DISTRIBUTION STRUCTURE

Many consumer products pass through a distribution system that includes the producer, one or more wholesalers, and a retailer. In business marketing, however, because of many of the characteristics already mentioned, channels of distribution are typically shorter. Direct channels, where manufacturers market directly to users, are much more common. The use of direct channels has increased dramatically in the past decade with the introduction of various Internet buying and selling schemes. One such technique is a **business-to-business online exchange**, which is an electronic trading floor that provides companies with integrated links to their customers and suppliers. The goal of a B2B online exchange is to simplify business purchasing and make it more efficient. For example, Exostar, the aerospace industry's online exchange, has over 12,000 participating suppliers and conducts more than 20,000 transactions each week.[18] Exchanges such as Exostar facilitate direct channel relationships between producers and their customers.

NATURE OF BUYING

Unlike consumers, business buyers usually approach purchasing rather formally. Businesses use professionally trained purchasing agents or buyers who spend their entire career purchasing a limited number of items. They get to know the items and the sellers well. Some professional purchasers earn the designation of Certified Purchasing Manager (CPM) after participating in a rigorous certification program.

NATURE OF BUYING INFLUENCE

Typically, more people are involved in a single business purchase decision than in a consumer purchase. Experts from fields as varied as quality control, marketing, and finance, as well as professional buyers and users, may be grouped in a buying center (discussed later in this chapter).

TYPE OF NEGOTIATIONS

Consumers are used to negotiating price on automobiles and real estate. In most cases, however, American consumers expect sellers to set the price and other conditions of sale, such as time of delivery and credit terms. In contrast, negotiating is com-

business-to-business online exchange
An electronic trading floor that provides companies with integrated links to their customers and suppliers.

mon in business marketing. Buyers and sellers negotiate product specifications, delivery dates, payment terms, and other pricing matters. Sometimes these negotiations occur during many meetings over several months. Final contracts are often very long and detailed.

USE OF RECIPROCITY

Business purchasers often choose to buy from their own customers, a practice known as **reciprocity**. For example, General Motors buys engines for use in its automobiles and trucks from Borg Warner, which in turn buys many of the automobiles and trucks it needs from GM. This practice is neither unethical nor illegal unless one party coerces the other and the result is unfair competition. Reciprocity is generally considered a reasonable business practice. If all possible suppliers sell a similar product for about the same price, doesn't it make sense to buy from those firms that buy from you?

reciprocity
The practice of business purchasers choosing to buy from their own customers.

major equipment (installations)
Capital goods such as large or expensive machines, mainframe computers, blast furnaces, generators, airplanes, and buildings.

USE OF LEASING

Consumers normally buy products rather than lease them. But businesses commonly lease expensive equipment such as computers, construction equipment and vehicles, and automobiles. Leasing allows firms to reduce capital outflow, acquire a seller's latest products, receive better services, and gain tax advantages.

The lessor, the firm providing the product, may be either the manufacturer or an independent firm. The benefits to the lessor include greater total revenue from leasing compared to selling and an opportunity to do business with customers who cannot afford to buy.

REVIEW LEARNING OUTCOME

LO6 Explain the major differences between business and consumer markets

Characteristic	Business Market	Consumer Market
Demand	Organizational	Individual
Purchase volume	Larger	Smaller
Number of customers	Fewer	Many
Location of buyers	Geographically concentrated	Dispersed
Distribution structure	More direct	More indirect
Nature of buying	More professional	More personal
Nature of buying influence	Multiple	Single
Type of negotiations	More complex	Simpler
Use of reciprocity	Yes	No
Use of leasing	Greater	Lesser
Primary promotional method	Personal selling	Advertising

PRIMARY PROMOTIONAL METHOD

Business marketers tend to emphasize personal selling in their promotion efforts, especially for expensive items, custom-designed products, large-volume purchases, and situations requiring negotiations. The sale of many business products requires a great deal of personal contact. Personal selling is discussed in more detail in Chapter 16.

LO7
Types of Business Products

Business products generally fall into one of the following seven categories, depending on their use: major equipment, accessory equipment, raw materials, component parts, processed materials, supplies, and business services.

MAJOR EQUIPMENT

Major equipment includes such capital goods as large or expensive machines, mainframe computers, blast furnaces, generators, airplanes, and buildings. (These items are also commonly called **installations**.) Major equipment is depreciated over time rather than charged as an expense in the year it is purchased. In addition, major equipment is often custom-designed for each customer. Personal selling is an important part of the marketing strategy for major equipment because distribution channels are almost always direct from the producer to the business user.

ACCESSORY EQUIPMENT

Accessory equipment is generally less expensive and shorter-lived than major equipment. Examples include portable drills, power tools, microcomputers, and fax machines. Accessory equipment is often charged as an expense in the year it is bought rather than depreciated over its useful life. In contrast to major equipment, accessories are more often standardized and are usually bought by more customers. These customers tend to be widely dispersed. For example, all types of businesses buy microcomputers.

Local industrial distributors (wholesalers) play an important role in the marketing of accessory equipment because business buyers often purchase accessories from them. Regardless of where accessories are bought, advertising is a more vital promotional tool for accessory equipment than for major equipment.

RAW MATERIALS

© BOISE PAPER SOLUTIONS/PRNEWSFOTO (AP TOPIC GALLERY)

Even though the Internet has greatly affected the consumption of many supplies, like envelopes, paper is still in high demand. In fact, computer technology has increased the demand for paper rather than squelched it.

Raw materials are unprocessed extractive or agricultural products—for example, mineral ore, timber, wheat, corn, fruits, vegetables, and fish. Raw materials become part of finished products. Extensive users, such as steel or lumber mills and food canners, generally buy huge quantities of raw materials. Because there is often a large number of relatively small sellers of raw materials, none can greatly influence price or supply. Thus, the market tends to set the price of raw materials, and individual producers have little pricing flexibility. Promotion is almost always via personal selling, and distribution channels are usually direct from producer to business user.

COMPONENT PARTS

accessory equipment
Goods, such as portable tools and office equipment, that are less expensive and shorter-lived than major equipment.

raw materials
Unprocessed extractive or agricultural products, such as mineral ore, timber, wheat, corn, fruits, vegetables, and fish.

component parts
Either finished items ready for assembly or products that need very little processing before becoming part of some other product.

Component parts are either finished items ready for assembly or products that need very little processing before becoming part of some other product. Caterpillar diesel engines are component parts used in heavy-duty trucks. Other examples include spark plugs, tires, and electric motors for automobiles. A special feature of component parts is that they can retain their identity after becoming part of the final product. For example, automobile tires are clearly recognizable as part of a car. Moreover, because component parts often wear out, they may need to be replaced several times during the life of the final product. Thus, there are two important markets for many component parts: the original equipment manufacturer (OEM) market and the replacement market.

Many of the business features listed on page 197 in the review for Learning Outcome 6 characterize the OEM market. The difference between unit costs and selling prices in the OEM market is often small, but profits can be substantial because of volume buying.

The replacement market is composed of organizations and individuals buying component parts to replace worn-out parts. Because components often retain their identity in final products, users may choose to replace a component part with the same brand used by the manufacturer—for example, the same brand of automobile tires or battery. The replacement market operates differently from the OEM market, however. Whether replacement buyers are organizations or individuals, they tend to demonstrate the characteristics of consumer markets that were shown in the review for Learning Outcome 6. Consider, for example, an automobile replacement part. Purchase volume is usually small and there are many customers, geographically dispersed, who typically buy from car dealers or parts stores. Negotiations do not occur, and neither reciprocity nor leasing is usually an issue.

Manufacturers of component parts often direct their advertising toward replacement buyers. Cooper Tire & Rubber, for example, makes and markets component parts—automobile and truck tires—for the replacement market only. General Motors and other car makers compete with independent firms in the market for replacement automobile parts.

PROCESSED MATERIALS

Processed materials are products used directly in manufacturing other products. Unlike raw materials, they have had some processing. Examples include sheet metal, chemicals, specialty steel, lumber, corn syrup, and plastics. Unlike component parts, processed materials do not retain their identity in final products.

Most processed materials are marketed to OEMs or to distributors servicing the OEM market. Processed materials are generally bought according to customer specifications or to some industry standard, as is the case with steel and plywood. Price and service are important factors in choosing a vendor.

SUPPLIES

Supplies are consumable items that do not become part of the final product—for example, lubricants, detergents, paper towels, pencils, and paper. Supplies are normally standardized items that purchasing agents routinely buy. Supplies typically have relatively short lives and are inexpensive compared to other business goods. Because supplies generally fall into one of three categories—maintenance, repair, or operating supplies—this category is often referred to as MRO items.

Competition in the MRO market is intense. Bic and Paper Mate, for example, battle for business purchases of inexpensive ballpoint pens.

BUSINESS SERVICES

Business services are expense items that do not become part of a final product. Businesses often retain outside providers to perform janitorial, advertising, legal, management consulting, marketing research, maintenance, and other services. Hiring an outside provider makes sense when it costs less than hiring or assigning an employee to perform the task and when an outside provider is needed for particular expertise.

processed materials
Products used directly in manufacturing other products.

supplies
Consumable items that do not become part of the final product.

business services
Expense items that do not become part of a final product.

REVIEW LEARNING OUTCOME

LO7 Describe the seven types of business goods and services

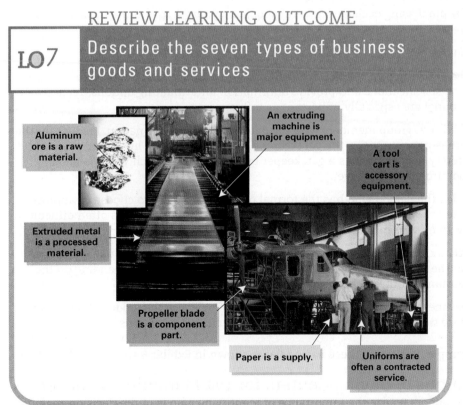

Aluminum ore is a raw material.

An extruding machine is major equipment.

A tool cart is accessory equipment.

Extruded metal is a processed material.

Propeller blade is a component part.

Paper is a supply.

Uniforms are often a contracted service.

LO⁸
Business Buying Behavior

As you probably have already concluded, business buyers behave differently from consumers. Understanding how purchase decisions are made in organizations is a first step in developing a business selling strategy. Business buying behavior has five important aspects: buying centers, evaluative criteria, buying situations, business ethics, and customer service.

BUYING CENTERS

A **buying center** includes all those persons in an organization who become involved in the purchase decision. Membership and influence vary from company to company. For instance, in engineering-dominated firms like Bell Helicopter, the buying center may consist almost entirely of engineers. In marketing-oriented firms like Toyota and IBM, marketing and engineering have almost equal authority. In consumer goods firms like Procter & Gamble, product managers and other marketing decision makers may dominate the buying center. In a small manufacturing company, almost everyone may be a member.

The number of people involved in a buying center varies with the complexity and importance of a purchase decision. The composition of the buying group will usually change from one purchase to another and sometimes even during various stages of the buying process. To make matters more complicated, buying centers do not appear on formal organizational charts.

For example, even though a formal committee may have been set up to choose a new plant site, it is only part of the buying center. Other people, like the company president, often play informal yet powerful roles. In a lengthy decision-making process, such as finding a new plant location, some members may drop out of the buying center when they can no longer play a useful role. Others whose talents are needed then become part of the center. No formal announcement of "who is in" and "who is out" is ever made.

Roles in the Buying Center

As in family purchasing decisions, several people may play a role in the business purchase process:

- *Initiator:* the person who first suggests making a purchase.

- *Influencers/evaluators:* people who influence the buying decision. They often help define specifications and provide information for evaluating options. Technical personnel are especially important as influencers.

- *Gatekeepers:* group members who regulate the flow of information. Frequently, the purchasing agent views the gatekeeping role as a source of his or her power. A secretary may also act as a gatekeeper by determining which vendors get an appointment with a buyer.

- *Decider:* the person who has the formal or informal power to choose or approve the selection of the supplier or brand. In complex situations, it is often difficult to determine who makes the final decision.

- *Purchaser:* the person who actually negotiates the purchase. It could be anyone from the president of the company to the purchasing agent, depending on the importance of the decision.

- *Users:* members of the organization who will actually use the product. Users often initiate the buying process and help define product specifications.

An example illustrating these basic roles is shown in Exhibit 6.5.

Implications of Buying Centers for the Marketing Manager

Successful vendors realize the importance of identifying who is in the decision-making unit, each member's relative influence in the buying decision, and each member's evalu-

buying center
All those persons in an organization who become involved in the purchase decision.

ative criteria. Successful selling strategies often focus on determining the most important buying influences and tailoring sales presentations to the evaluative criteria most important to these buying-center members.

Loctite Corporation
What evidence do you see on Loctite's Web site that its marketing efforts focus on engineers? Read some of its online literature.
http://www.loctite.com/

Online

For example, Loctite Corporation, the manufacturer of Super Glue and industrial adhesives and sealants, found that engineers were the most important influencers and deciders in adhesive and sealant purchase decisions. As a result, Loctite focused its marketing efforts on production and maintenance engineers.

Exhibit 6.5

Buying-Center Roles for Computer Purchases

Role	Illustration
Initiator	Division general manager proposes to replace company's computer network.
Influencers/ evaluators	Corporate controller's office and vice president of data processing have an important say about which system and vendor the company will deal with.
Gatekeepers	Corporate departments for purchasing and data processing analyze company's needs and recommend likely matches with potential vendors.
Decider	Vice president of administration, with advice from others, selects vendor the company will deal with and system it will buy.
Purchaser	Purchasing agent negotiates terms of sale.
Users	All division employees use the computers.

EVALUATIVE CRITERIA

Business buyers evaluate products and suppliers against three important criteria: quality, service, and price—in that order.

Quality

In this case, quality refers to technical suitability. A superior tool can do a better job in the production process, and superior packaging can increase dealer and consumer acceptance of a brand. Evaluation of quality also applies to the salesperson and the salesperson's firm. Business buyers want to deal with reputable salespeople and companies that are financially responsible. Quality improvement should be part of every organization's marketing strategy.

Service

Almost as much as they want satisfactory products, business buyers want satisfactory service. A purchase offers several opportunities for service. Suppose a vendor is selling heavy equipment. Prepurchase service could include a survey of the buyer's needs. After thorough analysis of the survey findings, the vendor could prepare a report and recommendations in the form of a purchasing proposal. If a purchase results, postpurchase service might consist of installing the equipment and training those who will be using it. Postsale services may also include maintenance and repairs. Another service that business buyers seek is dependability of supply. They must be able to count on delivery of what was ordered when it is scheduled to be delivered. Buyers also welcome services that help them sell their finished products. Services of this sort are especially appropriate when the seller's product is an identifiable part of the buyer's end product.

Price

Business buyers want to buy at low prices—at the lowest prices, under most circumstances. However, a buyer who pressures a supplier to cut prices to a point where the supplier loses money on the sale almost forces shortcuts on quality. The buyer also may, in effect, force the supplier to quit selling to him or her. Then a new source of supply will have to be found.

BUYING SITUATIONS

Often business firms, especially manufacturers, must decide whether to make something or buy it from an outside supplier. The decision is essentially one of economics. Can an item of similar quality be bought at a lower price elsewhere? If not, is manufacturing it in-house the best use of limited company resources? For example, Briggs & Stratton Corporation, a major manufacturer of four-cycle engines, might be able to save

$150,000 annually on outside purchases by spending $500,000 on the equipment needed to produce gas throttles internally. Yet Briggs & Stratton could also use that $500,000 to upgrade its carburetor assembly line, which would save $225,000 annually. If a firm does decide to buy a product instead of making it, the purchase will be a new buy, a modified rebuy, or a straight rebuy.

New Buy

A **new buy** is a situation requiring the purchase of a product for the first time. For example, suppose a manufacturing company needs a better way to page managers while they are working on the shop floor. Currently, each of the several managers has a distinct ring, for example, two short and one long, that sounds over the plant intercom whenever he or she is being paged by anyone in the factory. The company decides to replace its buzzer system of paging with handheld wireless radio technology that will allow managers to communicate immediately with the department initiating the page. This situation represents the greatest opportunity for new vendors. No long-term relationship has been established for this product, specifications may be somewhat fluid, and buyers are generally more open to new vendors.

If the new item is a raw material or a critical component part, the buyer cannot afford to run out of supply. The seller must be able to convince the buyer that the seller's firm can consistently deliver a high-quality product on time.

Modified Rebuy

A **modified rebuy** is normally less critical and less time-consuming than a new buy. In a modified-rebuy situation, the purchaser wants some change in the original good or service. It may be a new color, greater tensile strength in a component part, more respondents in a marketing research study, or additional services in a janitorial contract.

Because the two parties are familiar with each other and credibility has been established, buyer and seller can concentrate on the specifics of the modification. But in some cases, modified rebuys are open to outside bidders. The purchaser uses this strategy to ensure that the new terms are competitive. An example would be the manufacturing company buying radios with a vibrating feature for managers who have trouble hearing the ring over the factory noise. The firm may open the bidding to examine the price/quality offerings of several suppliers.

Straight Rebuy

A **straight rebuy** is a situation vendors prefer. The purchaser is not looking for new information or other suppliers. An order is placed and the product is provided as in previous orders. Usually, a straight rebuy is routine because the terms of the purchase have been agreed to in earlier negotiations. An example would be the previously cited manufacturing company purchasing additional radios for new managers from the same supplier on a regular basis.

One common instrument used in straight-rebuy situations is the purchasing contract. Purchasing contracts are used with products that are bought often and in high volume. In essence, the purchasing contract makes the buyer's decision making routine and promises the salesperson a sure sale. The advantage to the buyer is a quick, confident decision an to the salesperson, reduced or eliminated competition.

Suppliers must remember not to take straight-rebuy relationships for granted. Retaining existing customers is much easier than attracting new ones.

BUSINESS ETHICS

As we noted in Chapter 3, ethics refers to the moral principles or values that generally govern the conduct of an individual or a group. Ethics can also be viewed as the standard of behavior by which conduct is judged.

Although we have heard a lot about corporate misbehavior in recent years, most people, and most companies, follow ethical practices. To help achieve this, over half of all major corporations offer ethics training to employees. Many companies also have

new buy
A situation requiring the purchase of a product for the first time.

modified rebuy
A situation where the purchaser wants some change in the original good or service.

straight rebuy
A situation in which the purchaser reorders the same goods or services without looking for new information or investigating other suppliers.

codes of ethics that help guide buyers and sellers. See the "Ethics in Marketing" box for an example of a corporate code of ethics,

CUSTOMER SERVICE

Business marketers are increasingly recognizing the benefits of developing a formal system to monitor customer opinions and perceptions of the quality of customer service. Companies like McDonald's, L.L. Bean, and Lexus build their strategies not only around products but also around a few highly developed service skills. These companies understand that keeping current customers satisfied is just as important as attracting new ones, if not more so. These leading-edge firms are obsessed not only with delivering high-quality customer service, but also with measuring satisfaction, loyalty, relationship quality, and other indicators of nonfinancial performance.

Most firms find it necessary to develop measures unique to their own strategy, value propositions, and target market. For example, Anderson Corporation assesses the loyalty of its trade customers by their willingness to continue carrying its windows and doors, recommend its products to colleagues and customers, increase their volume with the company, and put its products in their own homes. Basically, each firm's measures should not only ask "what are your expectations?" and "how are we doing?" but should also reflect what the firm wants its customers to do.

Some customers are more valuable than others. They may have greater value because they spend more, buy higher-margin products, have a well-known name, or have the

Institute for Supply Management
Familiarize yourself with the Institute for Supply Management (ISM) by reading about the organization on its Web site. Based on what you read, do you think a purchasing manager can be effective without being certified by the ISM? How does the ISM help its members with ethical dilemmas?

http://www.ism.ws

Online

ETHICS in Marketing

Code of Ethics at Lockheed Martin

Lockheed Martin's board of directors has adopted the booklet *Setting the Standard* (updated in January 2005) as the company's Code of Ethics and Business Conduct. It summarizes the principles that guide the company's actions in the global marketplace. The Code applies to all Lockheed Martin employees, members of the board of directors, agents, consultants, contract labor, and others, when they are representing or acting for the corporation. Contractors and suppliers are expected to follow these standards as well. The Code promotes "doing the right things," as well as "doing things right" to maintain personal and institutional integrity.

The personal integrity of each employee and the commitment of all employees to the highest standards of personal and professional conduct underlie the ethical culture of Lockheed Martin. The Code requires more than simply complying with the laws, rules, and regulations. The company values teamwork, sets team goals, assumes collective accountability for actions, embraces diversity, and shares leadership. It is committed to excellence and pursues superior performance in every activity.

While maintaining sensitivity to the diverse social and cultural settings in which the company conducts business, Lockheed Martin aims to *set the standard* for ethical conduct at all of its locations throughout the world. The company strives to achieve this through behavior in accordance with six principles: honesty, integrity, respect, trust, responsibility, and citizenship.

THE CODE

- *Honesty:* to be truthful in all our endeavors; to be honest and forthright with one another and with our customers, communities, suppliers, and shareholders.
- *Integrity:* to say what we mean, to deliver what we promise, to fulfill our commitments, and to stand for what is right.
- *Respect:* to treat one another with dignity and fairness, appreciating the diversity of our workforce and the uniqueness of each employee.
- *Trust:* to build confidence through teamwork and open, candid communication.
- *Responsibility:* to take responsibility for our actions, and to speak up—without fear of retribution—and report concerns in the workplace, including violations of laws, regulations, and company policies, and seek clarification and guidance whenever there is doubt.
- *Citizenship:* to obey all the laws of the United States and other countries in which we do business, and to do our part to make the communities in which we live and work better.[19]

Discuss the similarities and differences in Lockheed Martin's Code and the American Marketing Association's Ethical Values, which are part of its "Ethical Norms and Values for Marketers" at **http://www.marketingpower.com**.

BUSINESS MARKETING

CHAPTER 6

203

Rackspace – Managed Hosting Backed by Fanatical Support™

Fast servers, secure data centers and maximum bandwidth are all well and good. In fact, we invest a lot of money in them every year. But we believe hosting enterprise class web sites and web applications takes more than technology. It takes Fanatical Support.

Fanatical Support isn't a clever slogan, but the day to day reality our customers experience working with us. It's how we have reimagined customer service to bring unprecedented responsiveness and value to everything we do for our customers. It starts the first time you talk with us. And it never ends.

Contact us to see how Fanatical Support works for you.

1.888.571.8961 or visit www.rackspace.com

rackspace MANAGED HOSTING

© RACKSPACE LTD.

Because satisfying current customers can be just as essential as attracting new ones, customer service plays an important role in maintaining productive business relationships. This Rackspace advertisement emphasizes the company's customer support instead of its product.

potential of becoming a bigger customer in the future. Some companies selectively provide different levels of service to customers based on their value to the business. By giving the most valuable customers superior service, a firm is more likely to keep them happy, hopefully increasing retention of these high-value customers and maximizing the total business value they generate over time.

To achieve this goal, the firm must be able to divide customers into two or more groups based on their value. It must also create and apply policies that govern how service will be allocated among groups. Policies might establish which customers' phone calls get "fast tracked" and which customers are directed to use the Web and/or voice self-service, how specific e-mail questions are routed, and who is given access to online chat and who isn't.[20]

Providing different customers with different levels of service is a very sensitive matter. It must be handled very carefully and very discreetly to avoid offending lesser value, but still important customers.

REVIEW LEARNING OUTCOME

LO8 Discuss the unique aspects of business buying behavior

Review and Applications

LO1 Describe business marketing. Business marketing provides goods and services that are bought for use in business rather than for personal consumption. Intended use, not physical characteristics, distinguishes a business product from a consumer product.

1.1 As the marketing manager for Huggies diapers made by Kimberly-Clark, you are constantly going head-to-head with Pampers, produced by rival Procter & Gamble. You are considering unlocking the potential of the business market to increase your share of the disposable diaper market, but how? Write an outline of several ways you could transform this quintessentially consumer product into a successful business product as well.

LO2 Describe the role of the Internet in business marketing. The rapid expansion and adoption of the Internet have made business markets more competitive than ever before. The number of business buyers and sellers using the Internet is rapidly increasing. Firms are seeking new and better ways to expand markets and sources of supply, increase sales and decrease costs, and better

Quick Check ✔

Now that you've read the chapter, do you get it?
Take a moment for a quick check using this scale:

1 Not at all; 2 Not very well; 3 Ok; 4 Well; 5 Very Well

Can you . . .

____ differentiate between business and consumer marketing?

____ describe the ways companies build strategic alliances?

____ list the four types of business customers?

____ explain how a NAICS code works?

____ construct a table showing the differences between consumer and business markets?

____ identify the seven types of business goods and services?

____ write a paragraph describing the roles in the buying center?

____ compare the three buying situations?

____ explain how the Internet has influenced business marketing practices?

____ **TOTAL**

Score: 41–50, you're ready to move on to the applications; 31–40, skim the chapter one more time before moving on to the applications; 21–30, reread the sections giving you the most trouble and go to Thomson NOW for guided tutorials; 20 and under, you better reread the chapter to get a grasp of the fundamentals. If you've reread the chapter and still have a low score, visit your professor or TA during office hours.

serve customers. Marketers are becoming more sophisticated in their use of the Internet and are developing quantitative methods that can be used to better measure online success.

2.1 How could you use the Web site **http://www.BtoBonline.com** to help define a target market and develop a marketing plan?

2.2 Reconsider question 1.1. How could you use the Internet in your business marketing of Huggies diapers?

LO3 Discuss the role of relationship marketing and strategic alliances in business marketing. Relationship marketing entails seeking and establishing long-term alliances or partnerships with customers. A strategic alliance is a cooperative agreement between business firms. Firms form alliances to leverage what they do well by partnering with others that have complementary skills.

3.1 Why is relationship or personal selling the best way to promote in business marketing?

LO4 Identify the four major categories of business market customers. Producer markets consist of for-profit organizations and individuals that buy products to use in producing other products, as components of other products, or in facilitating business operations. Reseller markets consist of wholesalers and retailers that buy finished products to resell for profit. Government markets include federal, state, county, and city governments that buy goods and services to support their own operations and serve the needs of citizens. Institutional markets consist of very diverse nonbusiness institutions whose main goals do not include profit.

4.1 Understanding businesses is key to business marketing. Publications like *Manufacturing Automation, Computer Weekly, Power Generation Technology & Markets*, and *Biotech Equipment Update* can give you insights into many business marketing concepts. Research the industrial publications to find an article on a business marketer that interests you. Write a description of the company using as many concepts from the chapter as possible. What major category or categories of business market customers does this firm serve?

4.2 What do you have to do to get a government contract? Check out the Web sites **http://www.fedbizopps.gov** and **http://www.governmentbids.com** to find out. Does it seem worth the effort?

LO5 Explain the North American Industry Classification System. The NAICS provides a way to identify, analyze, segment, and target business and government markets. Organizations can be identified and compared by a numeric code indicating business sector, subsector, industry group, industry, and country industry. NAICS is a valuable tool for analyzing, segmenting, and targeting business markets.

5.1 Explain how a marketer can use the Web site **http://www.census.gov/epcd/www/naics.html** to convert SIC data to the NAICS.

5.2 Pick a product and determine its NAICS code. How easy was it to trace the groups and sectors?

LO 6 Explain the major differences between business and consumer markets. In business markets, demand is derived, price-inelastic, joint, and fluctuating. Purchase volume is much larger than in consumer markets, customers are fewer in number and more geographically concentrated, and distribution channels are more direct. Buying is approached more formally using professional purchasing agents, more people are involved in the buying process, negotiation is more complex, and reciprocity and leasing are more common. And, finally, selling strategy in business markets normally focuses on personal contact rather than on advertising.

6.1 How might derived demand affect the manufacturing of an automobile?

6.2 Your boss has just asked you, the company purchasing manager, to buy new computers for an entire department. Since you have just recently purchased a new home computer, you are well-educated about the various products available. How will your buying process for the company differ from your recent purchase for yourself?

LO 7 Describe the seven types of business goods and services. Major equipment includes capital goods, such as heavy machinery. Accessory equipment is typically less expensive and shorter-lived than major equipment. Raw materials are extractive or agricultural products that have not been processed. Component parts are finished or near-finished items to be used as parts of other products. Processed materials are used to manufacture other products. Supplies are consumable and not used as part of a final product. Business services are intangible products that many companies use in their operations.

7.1 In small groups, brainstorm examples of companies that feature the products in different business categories. (Avoid examples already listed in the chapter.) Compile a list of ten specific business products including at least one in each category. Then match up with another group. Have each group take turns naming a product and have the other group identify its appropriate category. Try to resolve all discrepancies by discussion. Some identified products may appropriately fit into more than one category.

LO 8 Discuss the unique aspects of business buying behavior. Business buying behavior is distinguished by five fundamental characteristics. First, buying is normally undertaken by a buying center consisting of many people who range widely in authority level. Second, business buyers typically evaluate alternative products and suppliers based on quality, service, and price—in that order. Third, business buying falls into three general categories: new buys, modified rebuys, and straight rebuys. Fourth, the ethics of business buyers and sellers are often scrutinized. Fifth, customer service before, during, and after the sale plays a big role in business purchase decisions.

8.1 A colleague of yours has sent you an e-mail seeking your advice as he attempts to sell a new voice-mail system to a local business. Send him a return e-mail describing the various people who might influence the customer's buying decision. Be sure to include suggestions for dealing with the needs of each of these individuals.

8.2 Intel Corporation supplies microprocessors to Hewlett-Packard for use in its computers. Describe the buying situation in this relationship, keeping in mind the rapid advance of technology in this industry.

Key Terms

Exercises

APPLICATION EXERCISE

Purchasing agents are often offered gifts and gratuities. Increasingly, though, companies are restricting the amount and value of gifts that their purchasing managers can accept from vendors. The idea is that purchasing managers should consider all qualified vendors during a buying decision instead of only those who pass out great event tickets. This exercise asks you to consider whether accepting various types of gifts is ethical.[21]

Activities

1. Review the following list of common types of gifts and favors. Put a checkmark next to the items that you think it would be acceptable for a purchasing manager to receive from a vendor.

    —Advertising souvenirs   —Automobiles
    —Clothing   —Dinners
    —Discounts on personal purchases   —Food and liquor
    —Golf outings   —Holiday gifts
    —Large appliances   —Loans of money
    —Lunches   —Small-value appliances
    —Tickets (sports, theater, amusement parks, etc.)   —Trips to vendor plants
    —Vacation trips

2. Now look at your list of acceptable gifts through various lenses. Would your list change if the purchasing manager's buying decision involved a low-cost item (say, pens)? Why or why not? What if the decision involved a very expensive purchase (like a major installation)?

3. Form a team and compare your lists. Discuss (or debate) any discrepancies.

Entrepreneurship Case

THEY'VE GOT YOUR 'BAK

In 1989, Michael Eidson probably never imagined that his homemade, do-it-yourself fix for dehydration during long cycling races would evolve into the world's premier hydration device for outdoor enthusiasts, soldiers, and law enforcement personnel. That is exactly what happened to the CamelBak backpack, however.

The first version, which used medical tubing to flow water from an intravenous drip bag that was insulated by a sock and strapped to the back of his shirt, was born as most inventions are—out of necessity. The special pack made it possible for Eidson to take in fluids while sitting upright without having to sacrifice speed by reaching down for a water bottle during a race. The packs gained fame during the 1991 Gulf War as extreme sports enthusiasts in the U.S. Special Forces carried their personal CamelBaks into combat during Desert Storm. Thereafter, the CamelBak name would be forever associated with extreme performance and the U.S. Armed Forces.

By 1995, Eidsen sold the company for $4 million. Its buyer, Kransco, introduced the first camouflaged models, and the packs continued to gain acclaim. In 1999, two years after buying his first CamelBak pack, cyclist Chuck Hunter left Lockheed Martin to join the upstart company in hopes of growing its military business. He promptly moved the company to the Sonoma Valley, built a research and development center, and leveraged his experience in the defense industry to launch a military-specific line of packs.

Hunter partnered with DuPont to help CamelBak develop the Low Infrared Reflective (LIRR) system. LIRR applies specially developed materials to a pack's compartments, buckles, and straps to shield soldiers from enemy detection systems. As advanced identification and kill technologies are increasingly being deployed on the battlefield, individual protection applications like the LIRR will be the camouflage of tomorrow.

Other CamelBak innovations include the WaterBeast reservoir, a fluid storage system that boasts 30 percent more rigidity than other packs on the market. The WaterBeast has the ability to withstand lengthy field engagements, aided by its silver-ion reservoir and tube linings that eliminate 99.99 percent of all fungus and bacteria in the water delivery system. The WaterBeast reservoir is now a standard feature on all CamelBak packs, as is the company's proprietary drinking nozzle, or bite valve, which must withstand 10,000 compressions to guarantee it will last through three years of combat use.

Another CamelBak first is its CBR 4.0 pack system, which is specially designed to perform under chemical or biological weapons attack. The CBR 4.0 took five years to develop, and like all CamelBak military and law enforcement products, it was created to meet the specific requests and requirements of the target market. Since its introduction in 2005, the U.S. Special Forces, New York Police Department, U.S. Secret Service, Department of Health and Human Services, and a myriad of HAZMAT, law enforcement, and government agencies from around the world have adopted and deployed the CBR 4.0.

Though CamelBak specializes in offering extreme performance packs for the military, industrial, and professional markets, it also sells a variety of products for hunting, extreme sports, recreational, and "light" law enforcement applications. Having claimed more than 90 percent of the military market for hydration packs, product manager Shawn Cullen likens CamelBak to Kleenex: "Everyone calls a hydration system a CamelBak," he says. Ironically, the company's biggest customer is its biggest competitor. While it continues to use CamelBaks, the U.S. Army is working with a former supplier to develop its own version, most likely in an attempt to reduce costs.

At prices up to $200 for combat-ready systems, one thing CamelBaks aren't is cheap. But then again, neither is CamelBak itself. Its strong product lines, history of innovation, secure strategic relationships, and dominance in government and institutional markets drove its value to over $200 million when investment bank Bear Stearns Company bought the outfit from Kransco in 2003—not bad for a product that started life as an intravenous fluid bag wrapped in a sock.[22]

Questions

1. What type of business product is a CamelBak backpack?

2. Discuss how business relationships and strategic partnerships have helped to increase the value of CamelBak's products and the business itself.

3. What type(s) of business market customers does CamelBak sell to?

4. Review the types of demand that most influence business markets. Which ones do you think are most important for CamelBak to consider in its marketing strategy? Why?

© NKP MEDIA, INC./THOMSON

COMPANY CLIPS

ReadyMade—Making Business Relationships

Like most periodicals, ReadyMade relies on advertisers for much of its revenue. Finding companies interested in advertising in the magazine and cultivating those relationships is an important component of making the company successful. ReadyMade must constantly market its product to potential investors through personal contact and solicitation. ReadyMade also must develop relationships with distributors and other businesses that will directly or indirectly promote the magazine and help make it successful. As you watch this video, notice the strategies that Darci Andresen describes as she explains the process she goes through as head of Advertising Sales & Special Promotions when seeking new advertisers.

Questions

1. When marketing to potential advertisers, what strategies could ReadyMade use to promote itself without having to rely on hard statistics about its readers?

2. What sort of strategic alliances does ReadyMade maintain? In what ways are these partnerships beneficial to the magazine?

3. Go to ReadyMade's website, www.readymademag.com. What evidence do you see of its business partnerships? How does it use its Web site to market itself to businesses?

BOWFINGER/CORBIS

BIZ FLIX

Bowfinger

Think more metaphorically about business marketing by watching a clip from *Bowfinger*, starring Steve Martin (Bowfinger), Eddie Murphy (Kit Ramsey), and Robert Downey, Jr. (Jerry Renfro). In this funny look at Hollywood filmmaking, Bobby Bowfinger wants to make a movie featuring action star Kit Ramsey, but the film budget is paltry at best. The selected scene shows you how Bowfinger works to get a deal with a producer.

As you watch the scene, think of it as a buying situation. What kind of buy is it? For what kind of product? What kind of business relationship do you think Bowfinger wants? What about Renfro, the producer? If you haven't already seen the movie, you might want to rent it to see how the product and the business relationship change over the course of the film.

Marketing & You Results

A high score indicates that you found the salesperson to be credible and concerned about your needs. Because you found the salesperson to be open and concerned, you had a higher level of trust in the salesperson than did someone with a lower score. As you read in Chapter 6, trust is an important element in building strategic alliances and in cultivating business clients.

Segmenting and Targeting Markets

CHAPTER

7

Learning Outcomes

LO¹   Describe the characteristics of markets and market segments

LO²   Explain the importance of market segmentation

LO³   Discuss criteria for successful market segmentation

LO⁴   Describe the bases commonly used to segment consumer markets

LO⁵   Describe the bases for segmenting business markets

LO⁶   List the steps involved in segmenting markets

LO⁷   Discuss alternative strategies for selecting target markets

LO⁸   Explain one-to-one marketing

LO⁹   Explain how and why firms implement positioning strategies and how product differentiation plays a role

Changing directions at **Wal-Mart**

Wal-Mart Stores, Inc., has begun a fundamental rethinking of the formula that made it the world's largest retailer. The company grew enormous by cramming its shelves with merchandise at the lowest prices possible. Now, responding to big shifts it sees in the American economy, Wal-Mart is changing the way it does business to reach out to more upscale shoppers. Wal-Mart's predicament reflects broader changes in the United States. The country's uneven economic recovery has benefited high-income Americans more than the traditional Wal-Mart customer, who

Wal-Mart needs to appeal to the shopper who loves a great deal on socks but also can splurge on merchandise with fatter profit margins.

values price over image. Executives now say that Wal-Mart needs to appeal to the shopper who loves a great deal on socks but also can splurge on merchandise with fatter profit margins, such as 400-thread-count sheets or a stereo.

After surveying its customers and concluding they were "starved for fashion," Wal-Mart has started to bring in more stylish merchandise. The company still does all its apparel buying out of Bentonville, Arkansas. But two years ago, it opened a New York office, located on Fifth Avenue near the Empire State Building, to spot hot styles. Last year, the office persuaded headquarters to take a chance on long, patterned skirts embellished with sequins. They sold out in all stores within weeks.

Wal-Mart has also created a new store prototype with wider aisles, lower shelves, and more elegant displays of pricey products. The retailer once prided itself on selling the first DVD player under $100. Now it also offers 42-inch flat-panel plasma TVs for $1,648 to $1,998. It's a significant gamble, because Wal-Mart must be careful not to alienate its traditional base while it pursues more affluent shoppers. Lower-income rural shoppers have always been the core customers of this nearly $300 billion-a-year company. Other retailers have flopped when they tried to pursue growth outside their areas of expertise. A decade ago, JCPenney, the mid-market department store chain, failed to woo new customers and alienated old ones when it tried to go upscale.[1]

Three of the major concepts addressed in this chapter are market segmentation, targeting, and positioning. Explain Wal-Mart's old and new strategies using these terms. What major barriers must Wal-Mart overcome to achieve success? Why do you think the new strategy will (or will not) be successful?

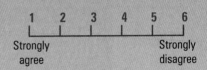

Marketing & You

Please note your opinion on each of the following questions.

Using the following scale, enter your opinion.

1	2	3	4	5	6

Strongly agree   Strongly disagree

____ I frequently have problems making ends meet.

____ My budgeting is always tight.

____ I often have to spend more money than I have available.

____ I do not consider myself financially well off.

____ I am generally on a tight budget.

____ Meeting an unexpected expense of $1,000 would be a financial hardship.

Total your score. Now, read the chapter and find out what your score means at the end.

LO¹
Market Segmentation

The term _market_ means different things to different people. We are all familiar with the supermarket, stock market, labor market, fish market, and flea market. All these types of markets share several characteristics. First, they are composed of people (consumer markets) or organizations (business markets). Second, these people or organizations have wants and needs that can be satisfied by particular product categories. Third, they have the ability to buy the products they seek. Fourth, they are willing to exchange their resources, usually money or credit, for desired products. In sum, a **market** is (1) people or organizations with (2) needs or wants and with (3) the ability and (4) the willingness to buy. A group of people or an organization that lacks any one of these characteristics is not a market.

Within a market, a **market segment** is a subgroup of people or organizations sharing one or more characteristics that cause them to have similar product needs. At one extreme, we can define every person and every organization in the world as a market segment because each is unique. At the other extreme, we can define the entire consumer market as one large market segment and the business market as another large segment. All people have some similar characteristics and needs, as do all organizations.

From a marketing perspective, market segments can be described as somewhere between the two extremes. The process of dividing a market into meaningful, relatively similar, and identifiable segments or groups is called **market segmentation**. The purpose of market segmentation is to enable the marketer to tailor marketing mixes to meet the needs of one or more specific segments.

Exhibit 7.1 illustrates the concept of market segmentation. Each box represents a market consisting of seven persons. This market might vary as follows: one homogeneous market of seven people, a market consisting of seven individual segments, a market composed of two segments based on gender, a market composed of three age segments, or a market composed of five age and gender market segments. Age and gender and many other bases for segmenting markets are examined later in this chapter.

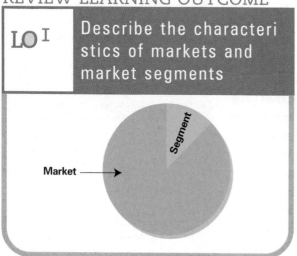
Exhibit 7.1

Concept of Market Segmentation

No market segmentation

Fully segmented market

Market segmentation by gender: M, F

Market segmentation by age group: 1, 2, 3

Market segmentation by gender and age group

LO²
The Importance of Market Segmentation

Until the 1960s, few firms practiced market segmentation. When they did, it was more likely a haphazard effort than a formal marketing strategy. Before 1960, for example, the Coca-Cola Company produced only one beverage and aimed it at the entire soft drink market. Today, Coca-Cola offers over a dozen different products to market segments based on diverse consumer preferences for flavors and calorie and caffeine content.

Coca-Cola offers traditional soft drinks, energy drinks (such as POWERade), flavored teas, fruit drinks (Fruitopia), and water (Dasani).

Market segmentation plays a key role in the marketing strategy of almost all successful organizations and is a powerful marketing tool for several reasons. Most importantly, nearly all markets include groups of people or organizations with different product needs and preferences. Market segmentation helps marketers define customer needs and wants more precisely. Because market segments differ in size and potential, segmentation helps decision makers more accurately define marketing objectives and better allocate resources. In turn, performance can be better evaluated when objectives are more precise.

Chico's, a successful women's fashion retailer, thrives by marketing to women aged 35 to 55 who like to wear comfortable, yet stylish clothing. It sells private-label clothing that comes in just a few nonjudgmental sizes: zero (regular sizes 4–6), one (8–10), two (10–12), and three (14–16).

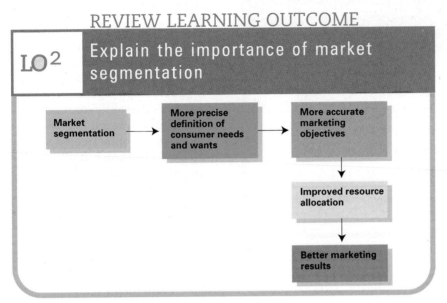
LO³
Criteria for Successful Segmentation

Marketers segment markets for three important reasons. First, segmentation enables marketers to identify groups of customers with similar needs and to analyze the characteristics and buying behavior of these groups. Second, segmentation provides marketers with information to help them design marketing mixes specifically matched with the characteristics and desires of one or more segments. Third, segmentation is consistent with the marketing concept of satisfying customer wants and needs while meeting the organization's objectives.

To be useful, a segmentation scheme must produce segments that meet four basic criteria:

- *Substantiality:* A segment must be large enough to warrant developing and maintaining a special marketing mix. This criterion does not necessarily mean that a segment must have many potential customers. Marketers of custom-designed homes and business buildings, commercial airplanes, and large computer systems typically develop marketing programs tailored to each potential customer's needs. In most cases, however, a market segment needs many potential customers to make commercial sense. In the 1980s, home banking failed because not enough people owned personal computers. Today, a larger number of people own computers, and home banking is a growing industry.

- *Identifiability and measurability:* Segments must be identifiable and their size measurable. Data about the population within geographic boundaries, the number of people in various age categories, and other social and demographic characteristics are often easy to get, and they provide fairly concrete measures of segment size. Suppose that a social service agency wants to identify segments by their readiness to participate in a drug and alcohol program or in prenatal care. Unless the agency can measure how many people are willing, indifferent, or unwilling to participate, it will have trouble gauging whether there are enough people to justify setting up the service.

market
People or organizations with needs or wants and the ability and willingness to buy.

market segment
A subgroup of people or organizations sharing one or more characteristics that cause them to have similar product needs.

market segmentation
The process of dividing a market into meaningful, relatively similar, and identifiable segments or groups.

- *Accessibility:* The firm must be able to reach members of targeted segments with customized marketing mixes. Some market segments are hard to reach—for example, senior citizens (especially those with reading or hearing disabilities), individuals who don't speak English, and the illiterate.

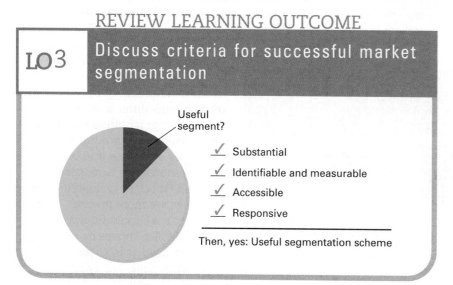

Useful segment?

✓ Substantial

✓ Identifiable and measurable

✓ Accessible

✓ Responsive

Then, yes: Useful segmentation scheme

- *Responsiveness:* As Exhibit 7.1 illustrates, markets can be segmented using any criteria that seem logical. Unless one market segment responds to a marketing mix differently from other segments, however, that segment need not be treated separately. For instance, if all customers are equally price-conscious about a product, there is no need to offer high-, medium-, and low-priced versions to different segments.

LO 4
Bases for Segmenting Consumer Markets

Marketers use **segmentation bases**, or **variables**, which are characteristics of individuals, groups, or organizations, to divide a total market into segments. The choice of segmentation bases is crucial because an inappropriate segmentation strategy may lead to lost sales and missed profit opportunities. The key is to identify bases that will produce substantial, measurable, and accessible segments that exhibit different response patterns to marketing mixes.

Markets can be segmented using a single variable, such as age group, or several variables, such as age group, gender, and education. Although it is less precise, single-variable segmentation has the advantage of being simpler and easier to use than multiple-variable segmentation. The disadvantages of multiple-variable segmentation are that it is often harder to use than single-variable segmentation; usable secondary data are less likely to be available; and as the number of segmentation bases increases, the size of individual segments decreases. Nevertheless, the current trend is toward using more rather than fewer variables to segment most markets. Multiple-variable segmentation is clearly more precise than single-variable segmentation.

Consumer goods marketers commonly use one or more of the following characteristics to segment markets: geography, demographics, psychographics, benefits sought, and usage rate.

GEOGRAPHIC SEGMENTATION

Geographic segmentation refers to segmenting markets by region of a country or the world, market size, market density, or climate. Market density means the number of people within a unit of land, such as a census tract. Climate is commonly used for geographic segmentation because of its dramatic impact on residents' needs and purchasing behavior. Snowblowers, water and snow skis, clothing, and air-conditioning and heating systems are products with varying appeal, depending on climate.

Consumer goods companies take a regional approach to marketing for four reasons. First, many firms need to find new ways to generate sales because of sluggish and intensely competitive markets. Second, computerized checkout stations with scanners give retailers an accurate assessment of which brands sell best in their region. Third,

segmentation bases (variables)
Characteristics of individuals, groups, or organizations.

many packaged-goods manufacturers are introducing new regional brands intended to appeal to local preferences. Fourth, a more regional approach allows consumer goods companies to react more quickly to competition. For example, Cracker Barrel, a restaurant known in the South for home-style cooking, is altering its menu outside its core southern market to reflect local tastes. Customers in upstate New York can order Reuben sandwiches, and those in Texas can get eggs with salsa. Miller Lite developed the "Miller Lite True to Texas" marketing program, a state-wide campaign targeting Texas beer drinkers.

DEMOGRAPHIC SEGMENTATION

Marketers often segment markets on the basis of demographic information because it is widely available and often related to consumers' buying and consuming behavior. Some common bases of **demographic segmentation** are age, gender, income, ethnic background, and family life cycle.

Avon, a brand associated with older generations, is attempting to break into a more youthful market with its Mark brand of beauty products. Carleigh Krubiner, a sophomore at the University of Pennsylvania and sales representative for Mark, holds a sample of the new products. She sells the brightly colored makeup in funky packaging from her dorm room.

Age Segmentation

Marketers use a variety of terms to refer to different age groups. Examples include newborns, infants, young children, tweens, teens, young adults, baby boomers, Generation X, Generation Y, and seniors. Age segmentation can be an important tool, as a brief exploration of the market potential of several age segments illustrates.

Through allowances, earnings, and gifts, children account for, and influence, a great deal of consumption. For example, there are about 20 million so-called tweens (ages 9–12) in the United States. This group spends over $20 billion per year and influences how another $200 billion is spent.[2] Tweens desire to be kids, but also want some of the fun of being a teenager. Many retailers such as Limited Too and Abercrombie serve this market with clothing that is similar in style to that worn by teenagers and young adults.

The teenage market includes about 22 million individuals[3] and accounts for over $100 billion in purchasing power.[4] Teens spend most of their money on clothing, entertainment, and food. Boost Mobile and Virgin Mobile USA market cell phone services to teens. The handsets come in funky colors or are cobranded with edgy companies such as women's surf-gear maker Roxy. Both Boost and Virgin avoid traditional distribution channels, selling instead at surf shops, record stores, and other places where teens hang out. Customers don't have to worry about credit checks or binding contracts—the company relies on pay-as-you-go plans. Rather than receive a monthly bill, customers can purchase prepaid chunks of airtime, in increments ranging from $20 to $50, at places like 7-Eleven and Target. Communicating to this group is also different from communicating to their parents. Teens spend an average of 17 hours per week online and 14 hours watching television.[5] They don't visit the same Web sites, watch the same TV programs, or read the same magazines as their parents. Magazines specifically designed to appeal to teenage girls include *Teen Vogue, Teen People, CosmoGIRL!, Elle Girl, and Seventeen.*[6] Clothing marketers such as Ralph Lauren, Guess, DKNY, Dior, Giorgio Armani, and Dooney & Bourke advertise heavily in these magazines.[7]

People born between 1946 and 1964 are often called "baby boomers." Together, baby boomers and the older generation—seniors—form a large and very lucrative market. Every 7.5 seconds one or more of the 77 million baby boomers in the United States turns 50. Individuals 50 years old and older own 80 percent of the financial assets in the United States and account for 50 percent of discretionary income.[8] As a group, they represent more than $2 trillion in spending power per year, or almost half of total consumer

geographic segmentation
Segmenting markets by region of a country or the world, market size, market density, or climate.

demographic segmentation
Segmenting markets by age, gender, income, ethnic background, and family life cycle.

spending in the United States.[9] Like the other age groups we have discussed, baby boomers represent tremendous market potential for a wide range of products including retirement properties, health and wellness products, automobiles with features designed for them, and other goods and services you might not expect. For example, customers 50 years old and older account for one-fourth of all Vespa motor scooters sold in the United States. Not only are baby boomers often nostalgic and eager to continue their active lives, but they now can afford to buy top-of-the-line models of these products from their youth.[10] For those looking for a retirement home, Pulte Homes Inc. and Del Webb's retirement community divisions focus on communities for senior citizens.[11] As the "Global Perspectives" box in this chapter illustrates, Japanese automaker Toyota is introducing a variety of new products to appeal to older consumers in Japan and elsewhere. Nissan is also developing new features and products for older consumers such as wheelchair ramps for big vans, swivel seats, and motorized cranes to lift walkers and wheelchairs into car trunks.[12] The challenges facing marketers who target boomers are great. Unlike yesterday's generation of 60-year-olds, today's boomers refuse to believe they're aging, so marketers who want to appeal to this segment cannot use any kind of messaging that refers to aging. Rather, they must appeal to boomers' interests, lifestyles, and values—anything but age. Companies as diverse as Whirlpool, Gap, Moen, Fila, and OXO are doing this with great success.

The president of OXO, the company that makes Good Grips cooking utensils with the thick black handles, says, "The last thing they want is the kind of patronizing, help-me-do-something kind of tools. We have almost a cult-like following among older consumers. At the same time, we have just as strong a following from people in the 20-to-40 age range because the products look cool."[13]

OXO is not the only company to find the 20-to-40 age group appealing. The approximately 58 million people classified as young adults, between 20 and 34 years of age, are frequently targeted by beer, wine, and spirits companies. For example, Bacardi, Ltd., hired a young marketing team to develop ads for Dewars Scotch. The team dropped the "mixa-

GLOBAL Perspectives

Adapting to an Aging Population

For a hint at what Toyota Motor Corporation sees when it peers into the future, have a look at the TAO-Light II, a sleek new addition to its lineup with a top speed of four miles per hour. That may be slow, but the TAO-Light II isn't a car. It is a wheelchair made from car parts, developed by Aisin Seiki Company, a member of the Toyota family of businesses that supplies transmissions and drive trains. The TAO is among a slew of new products from Toyota and its hundreds of affiliated suppliers that tap the market of elderly Japanese and the families who care for them. Though executives won't say how much Toyota has invested in products for the graying market, the company is clearly intent on turning Japan's stark demographic trends into a growth opportunity.

Toyota's efforts amount to a case study on maneuvering around a tricky marketing challenge: How does a company grow sales as the population begins to age rapidly? According to government projections, a quarter of Japan's population will be 65 years or older by 2015. By the year 2050, 35 percent will be over 65. Japanese families are having fewer children, so the number of youths is shrinking, and the overall population peaked in 2006 at 128 million. Japan's average life expectancy of 82 years is one of the highest in the world. And while Japan is aging faster than other countries, the trend is global: the United Nations forecasts that the world population of people 65 and over, currently at 472 million, will reach 598 million by 2015 and 823 million by 2025.

Few doubt the potential of the burgeoning elderly market. Expenditures for medical care and welfare services are expected to reach $650 billion by 2010, more than a 25 percent increase over 2002, according to Japanese government figures. What's more, since 2000, Japan has offered financial incentives for products like wheelchairs and reclining beds in an effort to encourage more families to take care of the elderly at home and reduce national health-care costs.

Toyota engineers continue to hone their lineup of products targeting the elderly. These include an upgraded version of the TAO-Light II wheelchair. Aisin, working with electronics company Fujitsu, Ltd., has developed the TAO Aicle, a new electric wheelchair that can be programmed to carry the driver to destinations on autopilot mode.[14]

Define the target market for Toyota's TAO-Light II. Why has Toyota selected this target market? Is this a good idea? What do you think about an automobile company marketing wheelchairs?

bility" angle stressed in previous ads and revived the famous Dewars profiles campaign, showing adventure-seeking 25- to 34-year olds. In the United States and the United Kingdom, the average Bordeaux wine drinker is between 35 and 45 years of age. This region's wine association would like to target drinkers as young as 25, says the president of Sopexa, the trade association for French food and wine. The group is backing fashion shows in Los Angeles, London, and Paris and organizing wine tasting courses, called "Wine Uncorked," for law and business school students at Ivy League universities. It has also launched an ad campaign featuring attractive young guests at a cocktail party with the slogan "Be Seduced" that is running in women's magazines such as *Harper's Bazaar*.[15]

Gender Segmentation

In the United States, women handle 75 percent of family finances, make or influence 80 percent of consumer purchases, and buy 51 percent of the new electronics sold, 75 percent of over-the-counter drugs, and 65 percent of new cars. That means that women are making decisions when it comes to the purchase of a huge variety of goods and services, not just the packaged goods that have traditionally been marketed to them.[16]

Historically, women took two-thirds of the home photographs and ordered most of the prints. Digital technology changed that. As men assumed the lead role in taking pictures, sales of film and printing fell dramatically. To reverse this trend, Kodak developed more female-friendly cameras, stand-alone photo printers, retail kiosks, and online development services. The result has been a slow but steady turnaround as women have become more involved in digital photography.[17]

Other marketers that traditionally focused most of their attention on males are also recognizing the potential of the female market segment. For example, Ameritrade recently launched its first print and online campaign directed to women.[18] The number of women shopping at hardware stores such as Home Depot and Lowe's Home Improvement Warehouse has been rising in recent years. A survey by Ace Hardware revealed that 42 percent of its customers are women and that they spend 30 to 40 percent more than men per visit. Home improvement stores are reaching out to women by creating a grocery store–type experience with wider, well-lit aisles, clear signage, and instructions on product use.[19]

Similarly, other brands that have been targeted to men, such as Gillette razors and Rogaine baldness remedy, are increasing their efforts to attract women. For example, athletic apparel manufacturers like Nike and Reebok have typically targeted men, and when they did target women, just copied the hard-edged, sports-marketing strategies that made them so popular with men. Mindy Grossman, vice president of global apparel for Reebok, says, "We were taking the men's formula—big athlete, big marketing—and trying to apply it to women. But that's not how she [sic] reponds." Reebok is developing apparel for the variety of activities women do, which more often than not, include fitness dance and yoga instead of traditional, competitive sports.[20]

At the same time that marketers of traditionally male products are reaching out to women, marketers that traditionally focused almost exclusively on women have now recognized the importance and potential of the male segment. For example, males are increasingly involved in wedding planning, deciding on everything from the site, seating plans, and table decorations to the wedding cake and keepsakes for guests. As males get more involved with their weddings, businesses such as engagement consultants, resorts, and spas are beginning to create special packages designed to attract men.[21] To illustrate, the Fairmont

Many companies have profited from redesigning traditionally feminine products and marketing them towards men. Here, L'Oréal advertises an anti-wrinkle cream that has been packaged to appeal to men.

Princess Resort in Scottsdale, Arizona, wanted to target men in addition to its female clientele and hired a cultural anthropologist who uncovered intrinsic differences in the way men and women approached a spa. Research led the resort to:

- Use darker woods and colors to create a club-like ambiance so men wouldn't feel they were entering female territory

- Install televisions in locker rooms (to reduce awkwardness felt by males in spa wear)

- Develop customized packages, including "Keep Your Shorts On" and "Golf Performance Treatment"

- Reposition the "European Facial," as translated for men into "Barber Facial"[22]

Marketers of products such as clothing, cosmetics, personal-care items, magazines, jewelry, and footwear still commonly segment markets by gender. Sports Clips is a hair salon designed to appeal to men and boys. The waiting room features a TV with a 52-inch screen, and customers can buy sports memorabilia, pro team caps, and college charcoal grills as well as hair-care products. Men aged 18 to 49 are the segment most likely to purchase goods online. Many Internet companies advertise to this group to build their brands and get exposure for their sites. For example, Blue Nile, one of the most successful online jewelry retailers, targets men who dislike jewelry stores, even though most of the jewelry it sells is for women.

Income Segmentation

Income is a popular demographic variable for segmenting markets because income level influences consumers' wants and determines their buying power. Many markets are segmented by income, including the markets for housing, clothing, automobiles, and food. For example, wholesale clubs Costco and Sam's Club appeal to different income segments. Costco attracts more upscale customers with warehouse prices for gourmet foods and upscale brands like Waterford crystal, Raymond Weil watches, and Ralph Lauren clothing. Sam's Club, on the other hand, originally focused more on members' business needs, offering bulk packages of the kinds of items sold in Wal-Mart's discount stores and supercenters. Sam's Club is trying to win more upscale customers by adding items like jewelry and gourmet food.

Ethnic Segmentation

In the past, ethnic groups in the United States were expected to conform to a homogenized, Anglo-centric ideal. This was evident both in the marketing of mass-marketed products and in the selective way that films, television, advertisements, and popular music portrayed America's diverse population. Until the 1970s, ethnic foods were rarely sold except in specialty stores. The racial barrier in entertainment lasted nearly as long, except for supporting movie and TV roles—often based on stereotypes dating back to the nineteenth century.[23] Increasing numbers of ethnic minorities in the U.S. along with increased buying power have changed this. Hispanic Americans, African Americans, and Asian Americans are the three largest ethnic groups in the United States. According to projections, these three groups collectively will make up one-third of the country's population by 2010 and have a combined buying power of more than $1 trillion annually. Today, companies such as Procter & Gamble, Allstate Insurance, Bank of America, and Reebok have developed multicultural marketing initiatives designed to better understand and serve the wants and preferences of U.S. minority groups. Many consumer goods companies spend 5 to 10 percent of their marketing budgets specifically targeting multicultural consumers. This proportion will likely increase in the future as ethnic groups represent larger and larger percentages of the U.S. population.

Experts say that regardless of the segment being targeted, marketers need to stay educated about the consumer they are pursuing, convey a message that is relevant to each particular market, use the Internet as a vehicle to educate ethnic markets about brands and products, and use integrated marketing techniques to reinforce the message in various ways.[24] As Catherine Linder, Walgreens divisional vice president and general merchandise manager for beauty and fashion, noted, "Our customers are as diverse as the communities we serve."[25]

Keeping a finger on the pulse of ethnic communities is one of the most challenging, and most important, tasks of a multicultural marketer. AT&T stays abreast of the African American, Asian American, and Hispanic communities through its involvement with national organizations, including the National Council of La Raza (NCLR), a private, non-profit Hispanic organization based in Washington; Organization of Chinese Americans (OCA), also in Washington; Chicago-based Rainbow/PUSH Coalition, a multiracial, multi-issue, international membership organization founded by Rev. Jesse L. Jackson Sr.; National Association for the Advancement of Colored People (NAACP), based in Baltimore; and Chicago-based U.S. Hispanic Leadership Institute. AT&T's involvement with such national and political groups is an extension of its long-standing grassroots efforts within ethnic communities.[26] The company supports these organizations financially both to show its commitment to diversity and to learn about the unique needs, preferences, and lifestyles of each group.

Some companies have found that segmenting by ethnicity is not precise enough. In many instances, the Hispanic market segment is not one segment but several. There are roughly 42 million Hispanics in the United States. Latinos of Mexican, Puerto Rican, and Cuban ancestry comprise roughly three-quarters of this group. Latinos from different ancestry respond to marketing messages differently. Marketers should ask the following questions:

- What are the general characteristics of your total target Latino population (size, growth rate, and spending power)?

- Who exactly are they (demographics, psychographics, attitudes, values, beliefs, and motivations)?

- What are their behaviors, in terms of products, services, media, language, and so on?

- How are they different from the general market and each other, based on country of origin?[27]

This applies to all ethnic groups that are generally segmented on the basis of ancestry.

Alternatively, some companies have abandoned the notion that ethnic group youths require separate marketing mixes. Instead, they are focusing on "urban youth," regardless of race or ethnicity, in cities such as New York and Los Angeles, because these are the places where trends typically start.[28]

Family Life-Cycle Segmentation

The demographic factors of gender, age, and income often do not sufficiently explain why consumer buying behavior varies. Frequently, consumption patterns among people of the same age and gender differ because they are in different stages of the family life cycle. The **family life cycle (FLC)** is a series of stages determined by a combination of age, marital status, and the presence or absence of children.

The life-cycle stage consisting of the married-couple household, used to be considered the traditional family in the United States. Today, however, married couples make up just 50.7 percent of households, down from nearly 80 percent in the 1950s. This means that the 86 million single adults in the United States could soon define the new majority. Already, unmarried Americans make up 42 percent of the workforce, 40 percent of home buyers, and one of the most potent consumer groups on record.[29]

Exhibit 7.2 illustrates numerous FLC patterns and shows how families' needs, incomes, resources, and expenditures differ at each stage. The horizontal flow shows the traditional family life cycle. The lower part of the exhibit gives some of the characteristics and purchase patterns of families in each stage of the traditional life cycle. The exhibit also acknowledges that about half of all first marriages end in divorce. When young marrieds move into the young divorced stage, their consumption patterns often revert back to those of the young single stage of the cycle. About four out of five divorced

family life cycle (FLC)
A series of stages determined by a combination of age, marital status, and the presence or absence of children.

persons remarry by middle age and reenter the traditional life cycle, as indicated by the "recycled flow" in the exhibit.

Consumers are especially receptive to marketing efforts at certain points in the life cycle. Soon-to-be-married couples are typically considered to be most receptive because they are making brand decisions about products that could last longer than their marriages. To illustrate, research shows that 67 percent of women wear the same fragrance they wore when they got married, 96 percent shop at the same stores they used when engaged, and 81 percent are using the same brands.[30] Furthermore, U.S. newlyweds spend a total of $70 billion in the first year after marriage.

Exhibit 7.2

Family Life Cycle

- ●—— Usual flow
- ●—— Recycled flow
- ▪ Traditional flow

[Flow diagram of family life cycle stages: Young single → Young married without children → Young married with children → Middle-aged married with children → Middle-aged married without dependent children → Older married → Older unmarried; with branches: Young divorced without children, Middle-aged divorced without children, Middle-aged married without children, Young divorced with children, Middle-aged divorced with children, Middle-aged divorced without dependent children]

Young single	Young married or divorced without children	Young married or divorced with children	Middle-aged married or divorced with or without children	Middle-aged married or divorced without children	Older married	Older unmarried
Few financial burdens	Better off financially than they will be in near future	Home purchasing at peak	Financial position still better	Home ownership at peak	Drastic cut in income	Drastic cut in income
Fashion opinion leaders	Highest purchase rate and highest average purchase of durables	Liquid assets low	More wives work	Most satisfied with financial position and money saved	Keep home	Special need for attention, affection, and security
Recreation-oriented	Buy: cars, refrigerators, stoves, sensible and durable furniture, vacations	Dissatisfied with financial position and amount of money saved	Some children get jobs	Interested in travel, recreation, self-education	Buy: medical appliances, medical care, products that aid health, sleep, and digestion	Buy: same medical and product needs as other retired group
Buy: basic kitchen equipment, basic furniture, cars, equipment for mating game, vacations		Interested in new products	Hard to influence with advertising	Make gifts and contributions		
		Like advertised products	High average purchase of durables	Not interested in new products		
		Buy: washers, dryers, televisions, baby food, chest rubs, cough medicine, vitamins, dolls, wagons, sleds, skates	Buy: new and more tasteful furniture, auto travel, unnecessary appliances, boats, dental	Buy: vacations, luxuries, home improvements		

PSYCHOGRAPHIC SEGMENTATION

Age, gender, income, ethnicity, family life-cycle stage, and other demographic variables are usually helpful in developing segmentation strategies, but often they don't paint the entire picture. Demographics provides the skeleton, but psychographics adds meat to the bones. **Psychographic segmentation** is market segmentation on the basis of the following variables:

- *Personality:* Personality reflects a person's traits, attitudes, and habits. According to a national survey by Roper, almost half of Americans believe their cars match their personalities. For example, SUVs deliver the heady feeling of being independent and above it all. Convertibles epitomize wind-in-the-hair freedom, and off-roaders convey outdoor adventure. About 25 percent of people surveyed say that their cars make them feel powerful.[31]

- *Motives:* Marketers of baby products and life insurance appeal to consumers' emotional motives—namely, to care for their loved ones. Using appeals to economy, reliability, and dependability, carmakers like Subaru and Suzuki target customers with rational motives. Carmakers like Mercedes-Benz, Jaguar, and Cadillac appeal to customers with status-related motives.

- *Lifestyles:* Lifestyle segmentation divides people into groups according to the way they spend their time, the importance of the things around them, their beliefs, and socioeconomic characteristics such as income and education. For example, a recent study of the women's market places women into four categories based on lifestyle distinctions that drive their behavior. *Explorers* are comfortable with themselves and are not obsessed with physical appearance. They also express strong or old-fashioned values such as admiring classical art, literature, and history. *Achievers* care about balance in their lives as much as they do about achieving their goals. They care much more about their own individual view of what success means than about society's expectations. *Builders* struggle between their need for material possessions to support their lives and the desire for simplicity and balance. They also take more time for themselves, even with families to care for. *Masters* are living simplified lives but are not internally settled. They have an active interest in health and beauty, but don't want to be told how they can stay young; they want support in being beautiful and living life to the fullest.[32]

- *Geodemographics:* **Geodemographic segmentation** clusters potential customers into neighborhood lifestyle categories. It combines geographic, demographic, and lifestyle segmentations. Geodemographic segmentation helps marketers develop marketing programs tailored to prospective buyers who live in small geographic regions, such as neighborhoods, or who have very specific lifestyle and demographic characteristics. H-E-B Grocery Company, a 304-store, Texas-based supermarket chain, specializes in developing its own branded products designed to meet the needs and tastes of specific communities. In the Rio Grande Valley, where summers are hot and many residents don't have air conditioning, H-E-B markets its own brand of rubbing oil that helps cool the skin while adding moisturizers. Along the southern border, the grocer stocks *discos,* large metal disks that Mexican Americans use to cook their

psychographic segmentation
Market segmentation on the basis of personality, motives, lifestyles, and geodemographics.

geodemographic segmentation
Segmenting potential customers into neighborhood lifestyle categories.

Marketers need to tailor their products and advertising to the lifestyle and demographic characteristics of the group they are trying to sell to. For example, this ad for Tractor Supply Co. targets consumers who live in the country and maintain rural lifestyles.

© TRACTOR SUPPLY COMPANY

brisket. Further north it sells gas grills that appeal to Anglo Americans.33 Stores in predominant Asian, Latino, or African American neighborhoods carry merchandise specifically selected for each geodemographic target market.

Psychographic variables can be used individually to segment markets or be combined with other variables to provide more detailed descriptions of market segments. One combination approach is the Claritas PRIZM Lifestyle software program that divides Americans into 66 "clusters," or consumer types, all with catchy names. The clusters combine basic demographic data such as age, ethnicity, and income with lifestyle information, such as magazine and sports preferences, taken from consumer surveys. For example, the "Kids and Cul-de-Sacs" group consists of upscale, married couples with children who live in recently built subdivisions. These families have a median household income of $70, 233, tend to own a Honda Odyssey, and are likely to spend large sums of money for child-centered products and services such as video games and Chuck E. Cheese. The "Bohemian Mix" cluster is made up of urbanites under age 35. These young singles and couples, students, and professionals has a median income of $51,100, is an early adopter in many product categories, tends to shop at Banana Republic, and is likely to read *Vanity Fair* magazine.34 The program also predicts to which neighborhoods across the country the clusters are likely to gravitate.

BENEFIT SEGMENTATION

benefit segmentation
The process of grouping customers into market segments according to the benefits they seek from the product.

Benefit segmentation is the process of grouping customers into market segments according to the benefits they seek from the product. Most types of market segmentation are based on the assumption that this variable and customers' needs are related. Benefit segmentation is different because it groups potential customers on the basis of their needs or wants rather than some other characteristic, such as age or gender. The snack-food market, for example, can be divided into six benefit segments, as shown in Exhibit 7.3.

Customer profiles can be developed by examining demographic information associated with people seeking certain benefits. This information can be used to match marketing strategies with selected target markets. Procter & Gamble introduced Pampers Rash Guard, a diaper designed to combat diaper rash. The many different types of performance energy bars with various combinations of nutrients are aimed at consumers

Exhibit 7.3

Lifestyle Segmentation of the Snack-Food Market

	Nutritional Snackers	Weight Watchers	Guilty Snackers	Party Snackers	Indiscriminate Snackers	Economical Snackers
% of Snackers	22%	14%	9%	15%	15%	18%
Lifestyle Characteristics	Self-assured, controlled	Outdoorsy, influential, venturesome	Highly anxious, isolated	Sociable	Hedonistic	Self-assured, price-oriented
Benefits Sought	Nutritious, without artificial ingredients, natural	Low in calories, quick energy	Low in calories, good tasting	Good to serve guests, served with pride, goes well with beverages	Good tasting, satisfies hunger	Low in price, best value
Consumption Level of Snacks	Light	Light	Heavy	Average	Heavy	Average
Type of Snacks Usually Eaten	Fruits, vegetables, cheese	Yogurt, vegetables	Yogurt, cookies, crackers, candy	Nuts, potato chips, crackers, pretzels	Candy, ice cream, cookies, potato chips, pretzels, popcorn	No specific products
Demographics	Better educated, have younger children	Younger, single	Younger or older, female, lower socio-economic status	Middle-aged, nonurban	Teenager	Have large family, better educated

looking for different benefits. For example, PowerBar is designed for athletes looking for long-lasting fuel, while PowerBar Protein Plus is aimed at those who want extra protein for replenishing muscles after strength training. Carb Solutions High Protein Bars are for those on low-carb diets; Luna Bars are targeted to women who want a bar with fewer calories, soy protein, and calcium; and Clif Bars are for people who want a natural bar with ingredients like rolled oats, soybeans, and organic soy flour.[35]

USAGE-RATE SEGMENTATION

Usage-rate segmentation divides a market by the amount of product bought or consumed. Categories vary with the product, but they are likely to include some combination of the following: former users, potential users, first-time users, light or irregular users, medium users, and heavy users. Segmenting by usage rate enables marketers to focus their efforts on heavy users or to develop multiple marketing mixes aimed at different segments. Because heavy users often account for a sizable portion of all product sales, some marketers focus on the heavy-user segment.

The **80/20 principle** holds that 20 percent of all customers generate 80 percent of the demand. Although the percentages usually are not exact, the general idea often holds true. For example, in the fast-food industry, the heavy user accounts for only one of five fast-food patrons, but makes about 60 percent of all visits to fast-food restaurants. Fewer than 10 percent of the subscribers to Time Warner's cable unit consume more than 75 percent of its bandwidth.[36]

Developing customers into heavy users is the goal behind many frequency/loyalty programs like the airlines' frequent flyer programs. Many supermarkets and other retailers have also designed loyalty programs that reward the heavy-user segment with deals available only to them, such as in-store coupon dispensing systems, loyalty card programs, and special price deals on selected merchandise.

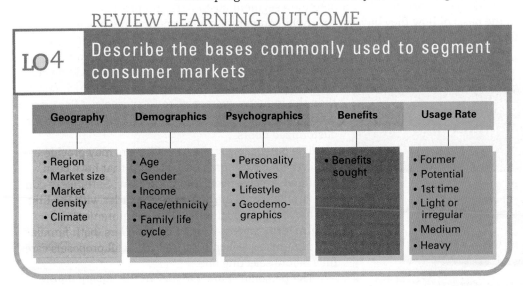

REVIEW LEARNING OUTCOME

LO4 Describe the bases commonly used to segment consumer markets

Geography	Demographics	Psychographics	Benefits	Usage Rate
• Region • Market size • Market density • Climate	• Age • Gender • Income • Race/ethnicity • Family life cycle	• Personality • Motives • Lifestyle • Geodemographics	• Benefits sought	• Former • Potential • 1st time • Light or irregular • Medium • Heavy

LO5
Bases for Segmenting Business Markets

The business market consists of four broad segments: producers, resellers, government, and institutions (for a detailed discussion of the characteristics of these segments, see Chapter 6). Whether marketers focus on only one or on all four of these segments, they are likely to find diversity among potential customers. Thus, further market segmentation offers just as many benefits to business marketers as it does to consumer-product marketers.

usage-rate segmentation
Dividing a market by the amount of product bought or consumed.

80/20 principle
A principle holding that 20 percent of all customers generate 80 percent of the demand.

COMPANY CHARACTERISTICS

Company characteristics, such as geographic location, type of company, company size, and product use, can be important segmentation variables. Some markets tend to be regional because buyers prefer to purchase from local suppliers, and distant suppliers may have difficulty competing in terms of price and service. Therefore, firms that sell to geographically concentrated industries benefit by locating close to their markets.

Segmenting by customer type allows business marketers to tailor their marketing mixes to the unique needs of particular types of organizations or industries. Many companies are finding this form of segmentation to be quite effective. For example, Home Depot, one of the largest do-it-yourself retail businesses in the United States, has targeted professional repair and remodeling contractors in addition to consumers.

Volume of purchase (heavy, moderate, light) is a commonly used basis for business segmentation. Another is the buying organization's size, which may affect its purchasing procedures, the types and quantities of products it needs, and its responses to different marketing mixes. Banks frequently offer different services, lines of credit, and overall attention to commercial customers based on their size.

Many products, especially raw materials like steel, wood, and petroleum, have diverse applications. How customers use a product may influence the amount they buy, their buying criteria, and their selection of vendors. For example, a producer of springs may have customers that use the product in applications as diverse as making machine tools, bicycles, surgical devices, office equipment, telephones, and missile systems.

BUYING PROCESSES

Many business marketers find it helpful to segment customers and prospective customers on the basis of how they buy. For example, companies can segment some business markets by ranking key purchasing criteria, such as price, quality, technical support, and service. Atlas Corporation has developed a commanding position in the industrial door market by providing customized products in just 4 weeks, which is much faster than the industry average of 12 to 15 weeks. Atlas's primary market is companies with an immediate need for customized doors.

The purchasing strategies of buyers may provide useful segments. Two purchasing profiles that have been identified are satisficers and optimizers. **Satisficers** contact familiar suppliers and place the order with the first one to satisfy product and delivery requirements. **Optimizers** consider numerous suppliers (both familiar and unfamiliar), solicit bids, and study all proposals carefully before selecting one.

The personal characteristics of the buyers themselves (their demographic characteristics, decision style, tolerance for risk, confidence level, job responsibilities, etc.) influence their buying behavior and thus offer a viable basis for segmenting some business markets. IBM computer buyers, for example, are sometimes characterized as being more risk averse than buyers of less expensive computers that perform essentially the same functions. In advertising, therefore, IBM stressed its reputation for high quality and reliability.

satisficers
Business customers who place an order with the first familiar supplier to satisfy product and delivery requirements.

optimizers
Business customers who consider numerous suppliers, both familiar and unfamiliar, solicit bids, and study all proposals carefully before selecting one.

REVIEW LEARNING OUTCOME

LO5 Describe the bases for segmenting business markets

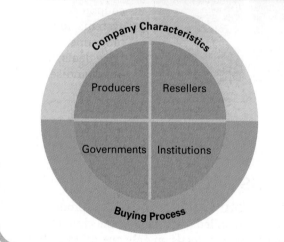

Company Characteristics

Producers | Resellers
Governments | Institutions

Buying Process

LO6
Steps in Segmenting a Market

The purpose of market segmentation, in both consumer and business markets, is to identify marketing opportunities.

1. *Select a market or product category for study*: Define the overall market or product category to be studied. It may be a market in which the firm already competes, a new but related market or product category, or a totally new one. For instance, Anheuser-Busch closely examined the beer market before introducing Michelob Light and Bud Light. Anheuser-Busch also carefully studied the market for salty snacks before introducing the Eagle brand.

2. *Choose a basis or bases for segmenting the market*: This step requires managerial insight, creativity, and market knowledge. There are no scientific procedures for selecting segmentation variables. However, a successful segmentation scheme must produce segments that meet the four basic criteria discussed earlier in this chapter.

3. *Select segmentation descriptors*: After choosing one or more bases, the marketer must select the segmentation descriptors. Descriptors identify the specific segmentation variables to use. For example, if a company selects demographics as a basis of segmentation, it may use age, occupation, and income as descriptors. A company that selects usage segmentation needs to decide whether to go after heavy users, nonusers, or light users.

4. *Profile and analyze segments*: The profile should include the segments' size, expected growth, purchase frequency, current brand usage, brand loyalty, and long-term sales and profit potential. This information can then be used to rank potential market segments by profit opportunity, risk, consistency with organizational mission and objectives, and other factors important to the firm.

5. *Select target markets*: Selecting target markets is not a part of but a natural outcome of the segmentation process. It is a major decision that influences and often directly determines the firm's marketing mix. This topic is examined in greater detail later in this chapter.

6. *Design, implement, and maintain appropriate marketing mixes*: The marketing mix has been described as product, place (distribution), promotion, and pricing strategies intended to bring about mutually satisfying exchange relationships with target markets. Chapters 9 through 18 explore these topics in detail.

Markets are dynamic, so it is important that companies proactively monitor their segmentation strategies over time. Often, once customers or prospects have been assigned to a segment, marketers think their task is done. Once customers are assigned to an age segment, for example, they stay there until they reach the next age bracket or category, which could be ten years in the future. Thus, the segmentation classifications are static, but the customers and prospects are changing. Dynamic segmentation approaches adjust to fit the changes that occur in customers' lives. Tesco, a British

REVIEW LEARNING OUTCOME

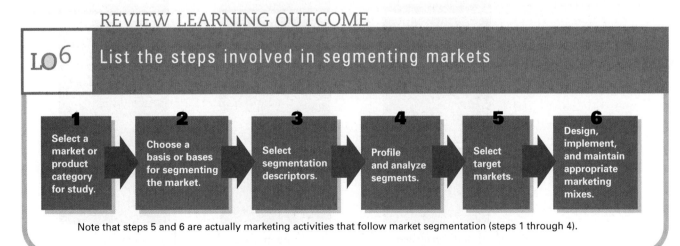

LO 6   List the steps involved in segmenting markets

1	2	3	4	5	6
Select a market or product category for study.	Choose a basis or bases for segmenting the market.	Select segmentation descriptors.	Profile and analyze segments.	Select target markets.	Design, implement, and maintain appropriate marketing mixes.

Note that steps 5 and 6 are actually marketing activities that follow market segmentation (steps 1 through 4).

supermarket company, has a frequent shopper card that gathers data and tracks the purchases of 7 million customers on every shopping occasion. Using these data, Tesco can reclassify every customer every week. Some customers move to different segments, and some don't, but all are evaluated, allowing the company to understand changes in customer behavior on a real-time, ongoing basis. Based on these changes, Tesco can continuously update its marketing programs to accommodate customers' behaviors. Tesco has become number one in food store sales in the United Kingdom primarily by knowing more about its customers than its competitors do.[37]

LO7
Strategies for Selecting Target Markets

So far this chapter has focused on the market segmentation process, which is only the first step in deciding whom to approach about buying a product. The next task is to choose one or more target markets. A **target market** is a group of people or organizations for which an organization designs, implements, and maintains a marketing mix intended to meet the needs of that group, resulting in mutually satisfying exchanges. Because most markets will include customers with different characteristics, lifestyles, backgrounds, and income levels, it is unlikely that a single marketing mix will attract all segments of the market. Thus, if a marketer wishes to appeal to more than one segment of the market, it must develop different marketing mixes. For example, Sunlight Saunas makes saunas that retail at various prices between $1,695 and $5,595. The company segments its customer base into luxury and health markets based on data it gathers from visits to its Web site and conversations with potential customers. The same saunas appeal to both market segments, but the different groups require different marketing messages.[38] The three general strategies for selecting target markets— undifferentiated, concentrated, and multisegment targeting—are illustrated in Exhibit 7.4. Exhibit 7.5 illustrates the advantages and disadvantages of each targeting strategy.

UNDIFFERENTIATED TARGETING

A firm using an **undifferentiated targeting strategy** essentially adopts a mass-market philosophy, viewing the market as one big market with no individual segments. The firm uses one marketing mix for the entire market. A firm that adopts an undifferentiated targeting strategy assumes that individual customers have similar needs that can be met with a common marketing mix.

target market
A group of people or organizations for which an organization designs, implements, and maintains a marketing mix intended to meet the needs of that group, resulting in mutually satisfying exchanges.

undifferentiated targeting strategy
A marketing approach that views the market as one big market with no individual segments and thus uses a single marketing mix.

Exhibit 7.4

Three Strategies for Selecting Target Markets

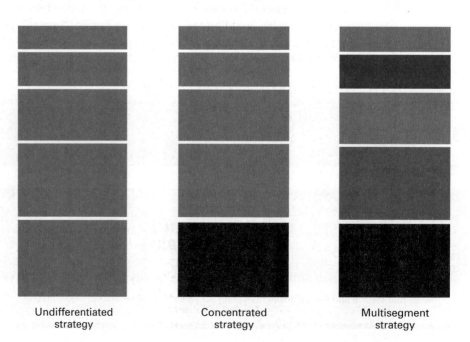

| Undifferentiated strategy | Concentrated strategy | Multisegment strategy |

Exhibit 7.5

Advantages and
Disadvantages of Target
Marketing Strategies

Targeting Strategy	Advantages	Disadvantages
Undifferentiated Targeting	• Potential savings on production/marketing costs • Company more susceptible to competition	• Unimaginative product offerings
Concentrated Targeting	• Concentration of resources • Can better meet the needs of a narrowly defined segment • Allows some small firms to better compete with larger firms • Strong positioning	• Segments too small, or changing • Large competitors may more effectively market to niche segment
Multisegment Targeting	• Greater financial success • Economies of scale in producing/marketing	• High costs • Cannibalization

The first firm in an industry sometimes uses an undifferentiated targeting strategy. With no competition, the firm may not need to tailor marketing mixes to the preferences of market segments. Henry Ford's famous comment about the Model T is a classic example of an undifferentiated targeting strategy: "They can have their car in any color they want, as long as it's black." At one time, Coca-Cola used this strategy with a single product and a single size of its familiar green bottle. Marketers of commodity products, such as flour and sugar, are also likely to use an undifferentiated targeting strategy.

One advantage of undifferentiated marketing is the potential for saving on production and marketing. Because only one item is produced, the firm should be able to achieve economies of mass production. Also, marketing costs may be lower when there is only one product to promote and a single channel of distribution. Too often, however, an undifferentiated strategy emerges by default rather than by design, reflecting a failure to consider the advantages of a segmented approach. The result is often sterile, unimaginative product offerings that have little appeal to anyone.

Another problem associated with undifferentiated targeting is that it makes the company more susceptible to competitive inroads. Hershey lost a big share of the candy market to Mars and other candy companies before it changed to a multisegment targeting strategy. Coca-Cola forfeited its position as the leading seller of cola drinks in supermarkets to Pepsi-Cola in the late 1950s, when Pepsi began offering several sizes of containers.

You might think a firm producing a standard product like toilet tissue would adopt an undifferentiated strategy. However, this market has industrial segments and consumer segments. Industrial buyers want an economical, single-ply product sold in boxes of a hundred rolls. The consumer market demands a more versatile product in smaller quantities. Within the consumer market, the product is differentiated with designer print or no print, cushioned or noncushioned, and economy priced or luxury priced. Fort Howard Corporation, the market share leader in industrial toilet paper, does not even sell to the consumer market.

Undifferentiated marketing can succeed in certain situations, though. A small grocery store in a small, isolated town may define all of the people that live in the town as its target market. It may offer one marketing mix and generally satisfy everyone in town. This strategy is not likely to be as effective if there are three or four grocery stores in the town.

concentrated targeting strategy
A strategy used to select one segment of a market for targeting marketing efforts.

niche
One segment of a market.

CONCENTRATED TARGETING

With a **concentrated targeting strategy**, a firm selects a market niche (one segment of a market) for targeting its marketing efforts. Because the firm is appealing to a single segment, it can concentrate on understanding the needs, motives, and satisfactions of that segment's members and on developing and maintaining a highly specialized marketing mix. Some firms find that concentrating resources and meeting the needs of a narrowly defined market segment is more profitable than spreading resources over several different segments.

For example, Starbucks became successful by focusing on consumers who want gourmet coffee products. America Online (AOL) became one of the worlds' leading Internet providers by targeting Internet newcomers. By making the Internet interface easy to use, AOL was able to attract millions of people who otherwise might not have subscribed to an online service. Watch makers Patek Philippe, Rolex, and Breguet selling watches priced at $200,000 or more are definitely pursuing a concentrated targeting strategy. AARP pursues a concentrated strategy if you consider people over 50 years old to be a single market segment of the overall population.

Small firms often adopt a concentrated targeting strategy to compete effectively with much larger firms. For example, Enterprise Rent-A-Car rose to number one in the car rental industry by catering to people with cars in the shop. It has now expanded into the airport rental market. Majestic Athletic is able to compete with apparel makers several times its size by focusing its attention on one market segment—professional baseball. It recently beat out adidas, Nike, and Reebok to become the sole supplier to Major League Baseball and its exclusive licensee.39

Some firms, on the other hand, use a concentrated strategy to establish a strong position in a desirable market segment. Porsche, for instance, targets an upscale automobile market through "class appeal, not mass appeal."

Concentrated targeting violates the old adage "Don't put all your eggs in one basket." If the chosen segment is too small or if it shrinks because of environmental changes, the firm may suffer negative consequences. For instance, OshKosh B'Gosh, Inc., was highly successful selling children's wear in the 1980s. It was so successful, however, that the children's line came to define OshKosh's image to the extent that the company could not sell clothes to anyone else. Attempts at marketing older children's clothing, women's casual clothes, and maternity wear were all abandoned. Recognizing it was in the children's wear business, the company expanded into products such as kids' shoes, children's eyewear, and plush toys.

"This is Paul Frank too."

paul frank says:
"the whole reason for naming it paul frank industries was because i wanted to be able to make anything!"

some people have been having a hard time locking down exactly what paul frank is. maybe because the wide range of quality products designed by paul frank industries don't easily pigeonhole us into a certain demographic or marketing scheme. so i'll just keep making unique things i am proud of. and let you decide where to put it. thanks.

paul frank is your friend.

small paul
by paul frank
www.paulfrank.com

Brands with a multisegment targeting approach develop marketing mixes for more than one distinct market segment. In this advertisement, Paul Frank displays the versatility of its brand by pointing out that it makes clothing for children as well as for teenagers and young adults.

A concentrated strategy can also be disastrous for a firm that is not successful in its narrowly defined target market. Before Procter & Gamble introduced Head and Shoulders shampoo, several small firms were already selling antidandruff shampoos. Head and Shoulders was introduced with a large promotional campaign, and the new brand captured over half the market immediately. Within a year, several of the firms that had been concentrating on this market segment went out of business.

MULTISEGMENT TARGETING

A firm that chooses to serve two or more well-defined market segments and develops a distinct marketing mix for each has a **multisegment targeting strategy**. Many universities offer full-time (day) MBA programs, professional (evening) programs, and executive (weekend) programs, each targeted at a distinctly different market segment. Many programs are targeting mothers returning to the workplace. Cosmetics companies seek to increase sales and market share by targeting multiple age and ethnic groups. Maybelline and Cover Girl, for example, market different lines to teenage women, young adult women, older women, and African American women. CitiCard offers its Upromise Card to those who want to earn money to save for college, its Platinum Select Card to those who want no annual fee and a competitive interest rate, its Diamond Preferred Rewards Card to customers who want to earn free rewards like travel and brand-name merchandise, and its Citi AAdvantage Card to those who want to earn

American Airlines Advantage frequent flyer miles to redeem for travel. Many credit-card companies even have programs specifically designed for tweens, teens, and college students.[40] Wal-Mart has historically followed a concentrated strategy that targeted lower income segments. Recently, however, the company has made a bold effort to target upscale shoppers in Plano, Texas, by opening a pilot store that stocks plasma televisions, fine jewelry, hundreds of types of wine (including some priced at $500 a bottle), and even boasts a sushi bar, an espresso bar, and free wireless Internet access—but no layaways. Wal-Mart's core middle-class customer base is slipping, so the company must expand its strategy to attract upper-end consumers, who define value differently than shoppers of moderate income.[41]

Sometimes organizations use different promotional appeals, rather than completely different marketing mixes, as the basis for a multisegment strategy. Beer marketers such as Adolph Coors and Anheuser-Busch advertise and promote special events targeted toward African American, Hispanic American, and Asian American market segments. The beverages and containers, however, do not differ by ethnic market segment.

Multisegment targeting is used for stores and shopping formats, not just brands. In the past, Best Buy treated all its customers as if they were the same, according to CEO Bradbury Anderson. But its customers aren't the same.[42] The company has identified five types of customers and has given each type a name: "Jill," a busy suburban mom; "Buzz," a focused, active younger male; "Ray," a family man who likes his technology practical; "BB4B" (short for Best Buy for Business), a small employer; and "Barry," an affluent professional male who's likely to drop tens of thousands of dollars on a home theater system.

Over the next few years, each of Best Buy's 608 stores will focus on one or two of the five segments.[43] Gap, Inc., takes a different approach. It uses family and individual branding for its alternative format outlets that target different market segments. Stores operating under the family brand include Gap, Gapkids, babyGap, GapBody, and Gap Outlet. Individual brands other than Gap include Banana Republic, Old Navy, and Forth & Towne. The newest addition, Forth & Towne, caters to women over 35 with clothes for all occasions. The nearly 40 million American female baby boomers are a demographic group that hasn't had many apparel stores created solely for them.[44] This group represents a $41 billion business with $27 billion of that spent on themselves.[45]

Multisegment targeting offers many potential benefits to firms, including greater sales volume, higher profits, larger market share, and economies of scale in manufacturing and marketing. Yet it may also involve greater product design, production, promotion, inventory, marketing research, and management costs. Before deciding to use this strategy, firms should compare the benefits and costs of multisegment targeting to those of undifferentiated and concentrated targeting.

cannibalization
A situation that occurs when sales of a new product cut into sales of a firm's existing products.

Another potential cost of multisegment targeting is **cannibalization,** which occurs when sales of a new product cut into sales of a firm's existing products. In many cases, however, companies prefer to steal sales from their own brands rather than lose sales to a competitor. Also, in today's fast-paced world of Internet business, some companies are willing to cannibalize existing business to build new business. Code Red, part of PepsiCo's multisegmentation approach, gets a quarter of its volume from existing Mountain Dew drinkers.[46]

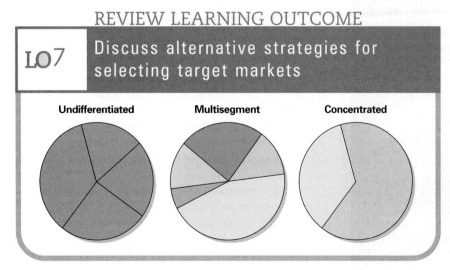

REVIEW LEARNING OUTCOME

LO7 Discuss alternative strategies for selecting target markets

Undifferentiated   Multisegment   Concentrated

SEGMENTING AND TARGETING MARKETS

CHAPTER 7

LO⁸
One-to-One Marketing

Most businesses today use a mass-marketing approach designed to increase *market share* by selling their products to the greatest number of people. For many businesses, however, it is more efficient and profitable to use one-to-one marketing to increase *share of customer*—in other words, to sell more products to each customer. **One-to-one marketing** is an individualized marketing method that utilizes customer information to build long-term, personalized, and profitable relationships with each customer. The goal is to reduce costs through customer retention and increase revenue through customer loyalty. For example, Tesco, the British supermarket chain, sends out a mailing each quarter to 11 million households—but it produces 4 million different versions, tailored to the interests of its diverse customer base.[47]

The difference between one-to-one marketing and the traditional mass-marketing approach can be compared to shooting a rifle and a shotgun. If you have good aim, a rifle is the more efficient weapon to use. A shotgun, on the other hand, increases your odds of hitting the target when it is more difficult to focus. Instead of scattering messages far and wide across the spectrum of mass media (the shotgun approach), one-to-one marketers look for opportunities to communicate with each individual customer (the rifle approach).

Anya Hndmarch, one of Britain's leading handbag and accessory designers, invites her customers to participate in the creation of their handbags by providing a personal photograph that she expertly transposes onto one of her beautifully designed bags. Customers may also participate in the design process in other ways to create a unique, one-of-a-kind, customer-designed handbag.[48]

Lands' End also engages in one-to-one marketing by custom designing clothing. On Lands' End's Web site, customers provide information by answering a series of questions that takes about 20 minutes. Customer sizing information is saved, and reordering is simple. Customers who customize have been found to be more loyal. Reorder rates for Lands' End custom-clothing buyers are 34 percent higher than for buyers of its standard-sized clothing.[49]

Is one-to-one marketing just the latest fad, or will it continue to grow and spread? Several factors suggest that personalized communications and product customization will continue to expand as more and more companies understand why and how their customers make and execute purchase decisions. At least four trends will lead to the continuing growth of one-to-one marketing.

one-to-one marketing
An individualized marketing method that utilizes customer information to build long-term, personalized, and profitable relationships with each customer.

First, the one-size-fits-all marketing of yesteryear no longer fits. Consumers do not want to be treated like the masses. Instead, they want to be treated as the individuals they are, with their own unique sets of needs and wants. By its personalized nature, one-to-one marketing can fulfill this desire.

Second, more direct and personal marketing efforts will continue to grow to meet the needs of consumers who no longer have the time to spend shopping and making purchase decisions. With the personal and targeted nature of one-to-one marketing, consumers can spend less time making purchase decisions and more time doing the things that are important.

Third, consumers will be loyal only to those companies and brands that have earned their loyalty and reinforced it at every purchase occasion. One-to-one marketing techniques focus on finding a firm's best customers, rewarding them for their loyalty, and thanking them for their business.

How serious are companies about giving customers individualized attention? Levi Strauss has a shrink tub in its San Francisco megastore so that customers can shrink their jeans to fit. After the shrink tub, they pass through the human dryer before leaving the store.

© REUTERS NEWMEDIA INC./CORBIS

Fourth, mass-media approaches will decline in importance as advances in market research and database technology allow marketers to collect detailed information on their customers, not just the approximation offered by demographics but the specific names and addresses. New technology offers one-to-one marketers a more cost-effective way to reach customers and enables businesses to personalize their messages. For example, MyYahoo.com greets each user by name and offers information in which the user has expressed interest. Similarly, RedEnvelope.com helps customers keep track of special occasions and offers personalized gift recommendations. Dell, Inc., and Starbucks are well-known examples of one-to-one product customization, but more and more companies are making it possible for customers to customize their purchases. With the help of database technology, one-to-one marketers can track their customers as individuals, even if they number in the millions.

One-to-one marketing is a huge commitment and often requires a 180-degree turnaround for marketers who spent the last half of the twentieth century developing and implementing mass-marketing efforts. Although mass marketing will probably continue to be used, especially to create brand awareness or to remind consumers of a product, the advantages of one-to-one marketing cannot be ignored.

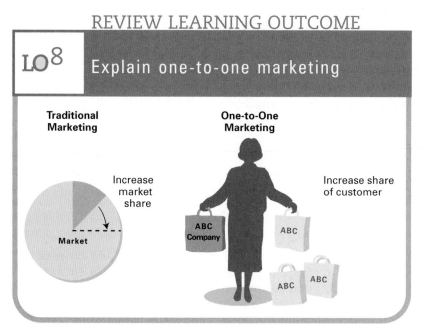

LO8 Explain one-to-one marketing

Traditional Marketing

One-to-One Marketing

Increase market share

Market

Increase share of customer

ABC Company

ABC

ABC   ABC

LO9
Positioning

The development of any marketing mix depends on **positioning**, a process that influences potential customers' overall perception of a brand, product line, or organization in general. **Position** is the place a product, brand, or group of products occupies in consumers' minds relative to competing offerings. Consumer goods marketers are particularly concerned with positioning. Procter & Gamble, for example, markets 11 different laundry detergents, each with a unique position, as illustrated in Exhibit 7.6.

Positioning assumes that consumers compare products on the basis of important features. Marketing efforts that emphasize irrelevant features are therefore likely to misfire. For example, Crystal Pepsi and a clear version of Coca-Cola's Tab failed because consumers perceived the "clear" positioning as more of a marketing gimmick than a benefit.

Effective positioning requires assessing the positions occupied by competing products, determining the important dimensions underlying these positions, and choosing a position in the market where the organization's marketing efforts will have the greatest impact. For example, Campbell's "Select" brand targets what the company calls "Food Explorers." This line of products is positioned as a brand for upscale adults who adventurously seek new taste experiences.[50] ProFlowers' business model is to ship flowers directly from growers to consumers, which allows bouquets to stay fresh longer. The company's position statement is, "The art of fresher flowers."[51]

As the previous examples illustrate, **product differentiation** is a positioning strategy that many firms use to distinguish their products from those of competitors. The distinctions can be either real or perceived. Tandem Computer designed machines with two central processing units and two memories for computer systems that can never afford to be down or lose their databases (for example, an airline reservation system). In

positioning
Developing a specific marketing mix to influence potential customers' overall perception of a brand, product line, or organization in general.

position
The place a product, brand, or group of products occupies in consumers' minds relative to competing offerings.

product differentiation
A positioning strategy that some firms use to distinguish their products from those of competitors.

Exhibit 7.6

Positioning of Procter & Gamble Detergents

Brand	Positioning	Market Share
Tide	Tough, powerful cleaning	31.1%
Cheer	Tough cleaning and color protection	8.2%
Bold	Detergent plus fabric softener	2.9%
Gain	Sunshine scent and odor-removing formula	2.6%
Era	Stain treatment and stain removal	2.2%
Dash	Value brand	1.8%
Oxydol	Bleach-boosted formula, whitening	1.4%
Solo	Detergent and fabric softener in liquid form	1.2%
Dreft	Outstanding cleaning for baby clothes, safe for tender skin	1.0%
Ivory Snow	Fabric and skin safety on baby clothes and fine washables	0.7%
Ariel	Tough cleaner, aimed at Hispanic market	0.1%

this case, Tandem used product differentiation to create a product with very real advantages for the target market. However, many everyday products, such as bleaches, aspirin, unleaded regular gasoline, and some soaps, are differentiated by such trivial means as brand names, packaging, color, smell, or "secret" additives. The marketer attempts to convince consumers that a particular brand is distinctive and that they should demand it over competing brands.

Some firms, instead of using product differentiation, position their products as being similar to competing products or brands. Artificial sweeteners advertised as tasting like sugar or margarine tasting like butter are two examples.

PERCEPTUAL MAPPING

perceptual mapping
A means of displaying or graphing, in two or more dimensions, the location of products, brands, or groups of products in customers' minds.

Perceptual mapping is a means of displaying or graphing, in two or more dimensions, the location of products, brands, or groups of products in customers' minds. For example, after several years of decreasing market share and the perception of teenagers that Levi's were not "cool," Levi Strauss developed a number of youth-oriented fashions, as well as apparel appealing to adults by extending the Dockers and Slates casual-pants brands. To target high-end customers, Levi offers styles such as its Vintage line. These jeans sell for $85 to $220 in stores like Neiman Marcus. The perceptual map in Exhibit 7.7 shows Levi's dozens of brands and subbrands, from cheap basics to high-priced fashion.

Exhibit 7.7

Perceptual Map and Positioning Strategy for Levi Strauss Products

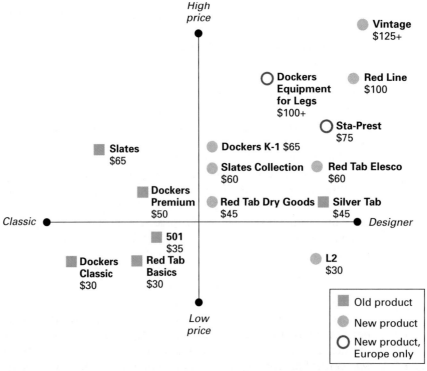

SOURCE: Nina Munk, "How Levi's Trashed a Great American Brand," *Fortune*, April 12, 1999, p. 84.

POSITIONING BASES

Firms use a variety of bases for positioning, including the following:

- *Attribute:* A product is associated with an attribute, product feature, or customer benefit. Rockport shoes are positioned as an always comfortable brand that is available in a range of styles from working shoes to dress shoes.

- *Price and quality:* This positioning base may stress high price as a signal of quality or emphasize low price as an indication of value. Neiman Marcus uses the high-price strategy; Wal-Mart has successfully followed the low-price and value strategy. The mass merchandiser Target has developed an interesting position based on price and quality. It is an "upscale discounter," sticking to low prices but offering higher quality and design than most discount chains.

- *Use or application:* Stressing uses or applications can be an effective means of positioning a product with buyers. Kahlúa liqueur used advertising to point out 228 ways to consume the product. Snapple introduced a new drink called "Snapple a Day" that is intended for use as a meal replacement.

- *Product user:* This positioning base focuses on a personality or type of user. Zale Corporation has several jewelry store concepts, each positioned to a different user. The Zale stores cater to middle-of-the-road consumers with traditional styles. Its Gordon's stores appeal to a slightly older clientele with a contemporary look. Guild is positioned for the more affluent 50-plus consumer.

- *Product class:* The objective here is to position the product as being associated with a particular category of products; for example, positioning a margarine brand with butter. Alternatively, products can be disassociated with a category; for example, the "We're not your father's Oldsmobile" ad campaign.

- *Competitor:* Positioning against competitors is part of any positioning strategy. The Avis rental car positioning as number two exemplifies positioning against specific competitors.

- *Emotion:* Positioning using emotion focuses on how the product makes customers feel. A number of companies use this approach. For example, Nike's "Just Do It" campaign didn't tell consumers what "it" was, but most got the emotional message of achievement and courage. Budweiser's advertising featuring talking frogs and lizards emphasized fun. Kodak has long used emotional positioning revolving around family and memories when advertising its cameras and film.

It is not unusual for a marketer to use more than one of these bases. A print ad in the "Got Milk?" campaign featuring Joan Lunden sporting a milk mustache read as follows:

> Most people think I must drink at least 10 cups of coffee to be so perky in the morning. But the truth is, I like skim milk first thing. It has all the same nutrients as whole milk without all the fat. And, besides, my husband got the coffee maker.

This ad reflects the following positioning bases:

- *Product attribute/benefit:* The "same nutrients as whole milk without all the fat" describes a product attribute, and that skim milk makes her "perky" is a benefit.

Repositioning can help companies attract new customers. This Wal-Mart ad is part of the company's effort to reposition into the upscale discounting segment dominated by Target. Wal-Mart's change in strategy reflects the company's need to sell to higher income customers, like those that can afford a plasma TV.

- *Use or application*: Lunden drinks milk first thing in the morning.

- *Product user*: The use of Lunden, a successful, independent woman, shows that milk is not just for kids.

- *Product class (disassociation)*: The ad differentiates skim milk from whole milk, showing that skim milk is healthier.

- *Competitor (indirect)*: She drinks milk instead of coffee.

- *Emotion*: The ad conveys an upbeat, contemporary attitude.[52]

REPOSITIONING

Sometimes products or companies are repositioned in order to sustain growth in slow markets or to correct positioning mistakes. **Repositioning** is changing consumers' perceptions of a brand in relation to competing brands. For example, Gap, Inc., is trying to reposition Banana Republic as a more fashion-oriented retailer. Management hopes that this repositioning will help distinguish Banana Republic from its sister store Gap, which is known for khakis and other basics. The four-pronged strategy entails emphasizing trendier styles and colors over basics and neutrals, making stores feel more upscale, persuading fashion editors to use the chain's clothes in their editorial pages, and depicting ordinary, real-world settings in ads so that clothes appear accessible and wearable.[53]

An entire industry of firms that need to think about repositioning is the supermarket industry. For over a decade, Wal-Mart has been expanding in both rural and metro areas. The result has generally been devastating to competitors, especially independent grocers. Consulting firm Retail Forward predicts that two supermarkets will go out of business for every Wal-Mart supercenter that opens in the United States. The Strategic Resource Group adds that 27 leading national and regional supermarket operators have either gone bankrupt or have liquidated since Wal-Mart went national with supercenters.[54] So what are competitors to do? Wal-Mart owns the low price position. Successful competitors will have to establish viable alternative positions.

Safeway is trying to avoid Wal-Mart by repositioning itself as upscale with more produce, organics, prepared food, and wine. H-E-B stores in Hispanic areas in Texas are tailoring their product mix to appeal to this market segment. H-E-B has also opened Asian wet markets in some stores. Its Central Market format is definitely upscale with unique products and very high-quality perishables. Research shows that over half of all families with incomes between $50,000 and $100,000 are willing to pay more for high-quality items in a more pleasant shopping environment.[55] Other chains are also experimenting with new positioning strategies. Publix is testing new Hispanic-oriented stores called Publix Sabor and GreenWise, an organic/natural foods format. Stop & Shop is also focusing more on organics.[56]

It is too early to tell which, if any, of these repositioning strategies will be successful. Clearly, though, competing head-on with Wal-Mart is not a good idea.

repositioning
Changing consumers' perceptions of a brand in relation to competing brands.

REVIEW LEARNING OUTCOME

LO9 Explain how and why firms implement positioning strategies and how product differentiation plays a role

Each car occupies a position in consumers' minds.
Cars can be positioned according to attribute (sporty, conservative, etc.),
to price/quality (affordable, classy, etc.) or other bases.
Cadillac has repositioned itself as a car for younger drivers with edgier ads.

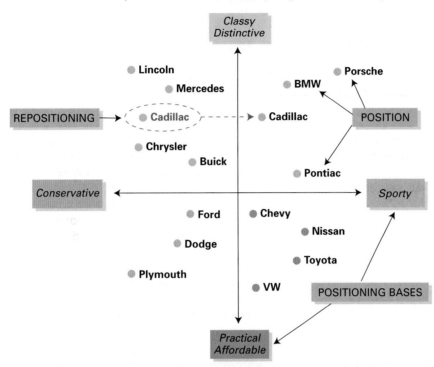

Review and Applications

LO1 Describe the characteristics of markets and market segments. **A market is composed of individuals or organizations with the ability and willingness to make purchases to fulfill their needs or wants. A market segment is a group of individuals or organizations with similar product needs as a result of one or more common characteristics.**

1.1 Mercedes-Benz is thinking about advertising its cars to college students. Do you think that college students are a viable potential market for Mercedes? Why or why not?

1.2 Go to the Web site **http://www.careermag.com**. How are visitors to the site segmented when seeking relevant job openings? Report your results:

LO2 Explain the importance of market segmentation. **Before the 1960s, few businesses targeted specific market segments. Today, segmentation is a crucial marketing strategy for nearly all successful organizations. Market segmentation enables marketers to tailor marketing mixes to meet the needs of particular population segments. Segmentation helps marketers identify consumer needs and preferences, areas of declining demand, and new marketing opportunities.**

2.1 Describe market segmentation in terms of the historical evolution of marketing.

235

Quick Check ✔

Now that you've read the chapter, do you get it? Take a moment for a quick check using this scale:

1 Not at all; 2 Not very well; 3 Ok; 4 Well; 5 Very Well

Can you . . .

____ differentiate a market, a market segment, and a target market?

____ explain how companies determine if a market segment is viable?

____ draw a diagram illustrating the different bases marketers use to segment consumer markets?

____ compare benefit and usage-rate segmentation?

____ list the steps in segmenting a market?

____ write a paragraph on the advantages and disadvantages of the three target market strategies?

____ account for the rise of one-to-one marketing?

____ draw a perceptual map for a market of your choosing?

____ explain to a friend not in the class what position, positioning, and repositioning are?

____ identify several positioning bases?

____ **TOTAL**

Score: 41–50, you're ready to move on to the applications; 31–40, skim the chapter one more time before moving on to the applications; 21–30, reread the sections giving you the most trouble and go to Thomson NOW for guided tutorials; 20 and under, you better reread the chapter to get a grasp of the fundamentals. If you've reread the chapter and still have a low score, visit your professor or TA during office hours.

LO3 Discuss criteria for successful market segmentation. Successful market segmentation depends on four basic criteria: (1) a market segment must be substantial and have enough potential customers to be viable; (2) a market segment must be identifiable and measurable; (3) members of a market segment must be accessible to marketing efforts; and (4) a market segment must respond to particular marketing efforts in a way that distinguishes it from other segments.

3.1 As a marketing consultant for a chain of hair salons, you have been asked to evaluate the kids' market as a potential segment for the chain to target. Write a memo to your client discussing your evaluation of the kids' segment in terms of the four criteria for successful market segmentation.

LO4 Describe the bases commonly used to segment consumer markets. Five bases are commonly used for segmenting consumer markets. Geographic segmentation is based on region, size, density, and climate characteristics. Demographic segmentation is based on age, gender, income level, ethnicity, and family life-cycle characteristics. Psychographic segmentation includes personality, motives, and lifestyle characteristics. Benefits sought is a type of segmentation that identifies customers according to the benefits they seek in a product. Finally, usage segmentation divides a market by the amount of product purchased or consumed.

4.1 Choose magazine ads for five different consumer products. For each ad, write a description of what you think the demographic characteristics of the targeted market are.

4.2 Investigate how Delta Air Lines (**http://www.delta.com**) uses its Web site to cater to its market segments.

4.3 Is it possible to identify a single market for two distinctly different products? For example, how substantial is the market comprised of consumers who use Apple *and* who drive Volkswagens? Can you think of other product combinations that would interest a single market? (Do not use products that are complementary, like a bike and a bike helmet. Think of products, like the iPod and the car, that are very different.) Complete the following sentences and describe sentences and describe the market for each set of products you pair together.

Consumers of:

Propel fitness water could also be a target market for _____.

Proactiv Solution skin care products could also be a target market for _____.

Alienware computers could also be a target market for _____.

Specialty luggage tags could also be a target market for _____.

LO5 Describe the bases for segmenting business markets. Business markets can be segmented on two general bases. First, businesses segment markets based on company characteristics, such as customers' geographic location, type of company, company size, and product use. Second, companies may segment customers based on the buying processes those customers use.

5.1 Choose five ads from business publications such as the *Wall Street Journal*, *Fortune*, and *BusinessWeek*. For each ad, write a description of how you think the company has segmented its business market.

LO6 List the steps involved in segmenting markets. Six steps are involved when segmenting markets: (1) selecting a market or product category for study; (2) choosing a basis or bases for segmenting the market; (3) selecting segmentation descriptors; (4) profiling and evaluating segments; (5) selecting target markets; and (6) designing, implementing, and maintaining appropriate marketing mixes.

6.1 Write a letter to the president of your bank suggesting ideas for increasing profits and enhancing customer service by improving segmentation and targeting strategies.

LO7 Discuss alternative strategies for selecting target markets. Marketers select target markets using three different strategies: undifferentiated targeting, concentrated targeting, and multisegment targeting. An undifferentiated targeting strategy assumes that all members of a market have similar needs that can be met with a single marketing mix. A concentrated targeting strategy focuses all marketing efforts on a single market segment. Multisegment targeting is a strategy that uses two or more marketing mixes to target two or more market segments.

7.1 Form a team with two or three other students. Create an idea for a new product. Describe the segment (or segments) you are going to target with the product, and explain why you chose the targeting strategy you did.

7.2 Go to the Web sites of JCPenney, **http://www.jcpenney.com**, and Target, **http://www.target.com**. Compare the presentation of women's fashions at the Web sites. What are the major differences? Which site is more designer focused, and which is more brand focused? Which company's approach do you think will appeal more to the "Holy Grail" target market of 25- to 35-year-old women?

LO8 Explain one-to-one marketing. One-to-one marketing is an individualized marketing method that utilizes customer information to build long-term, personalized, and profitable relationships with each customer. Successful one-to-one marketing comes from understanding customers and collaborating with them, rather than using them as targets for generic messages. Database technology makes it possible for companies to interact with customers on a personal, one-to-one basis.

8.1 You are the marketing manager for a specialty retailer that sells customized handbags. Write a memo to your boss describing how the company could benefit from one-to-one marketing.

LO9 Explain how and why firms implement positioning strategies and how product differentiation plays a role. Positioning is used to influence consumer perceptions of a particular brand, product line, or organization in relation to competitors. The term *position* refers to the place that the offering occupies in consumers' minds. To establish a unique position, many firms use product differentiation, emphasizing the real or perceived differences between competing offerings. Products may be differentiated on the basis of attribute, price and quality, use or application, product user, product class, or competitor.

9.1 Choose a product category (e.g., pick-up trucks), and identify at least three different brands and their respective positioning strategies. How is each position communicated to the target audience?

Key Terms

Exercises

APPLICATION EXERCISE

How tightly do you fit into a particular market segment? Do you think you can be neatly classified? If you think your purchasing habits make you an enigma to marketers, you may need to think again.[57]

Activities

1. Go to the Claritas Web site (**http://www.claritas.com**) and follow its "You Are Where You Live" link to find out what your ZIP code says about you. The database will generate many cluster descriptions based on your ZIP code. Depending on the functionality of the Web site at the time you access the database, you may need to reenter your ZIP code multiple times if you want to read all the cluster descriptions.

2. Now pick a product category, like automobiles, athletic shoes, beverages, or health and beauty products. Then think about which products in that category would appeal to each of the clusters generated by your ZIP code search. For example, a car that appeals to a cluster titled "Young Bohemians" may not be the car of choice for the cluster "Pools and Patios." If your search generated only one cluster type, you may wish to enter other ZIP codes for your area of town or for your region.

3. Create a perceptual map for the product you chose. Write a short statement that describes the overall position of each product with an explanation of why you located it where you did on the perceptual map.

© ROYALTY-FREE/CORBIS

Entrepreneurship Case

VIVA LAS VEGAS

In 2003, more than 35.5 million travelers made Las Vegas their destination of choice. It was the second largest volume of visitors the city has ever entertained, lagging just slightly behind the 35.8 million recorded for the year 2000. Those numbers are remarkable given the recent slump in the travel industry, and the city has the Las Vegas Convention and Visitors Authority to thank. For almost 50 years, the LVCVA has been promoting Las Vegas in an effort to maximize occupancy for the city's hoteliers who suffer from the cyclical demand in the travel industry. The authority's marketing of the city's convention, lodging, and entertainment facilities to convention organizers, meeting planners, and leisure travelers plays an integral role in keeping hotel rooms and convention facilities occupied during off-peak times of the year.

Many types of visitors go to Las Vegas for a variety of reasons, and the LVCVA uses a multilevel promotions strategy to reach them all. The organization's promotional mix includes national television advertising, grassroots marketing, and relationship building with a variety of organizations. Each element is specifically designed to address issues within particular segments of its growing target market, such as changes in the composition of the visitor pool, shifts in visitors' travel preferences, the emergence of potentially lucrative metropolitan markets, and trends in foreign visitors.

An LVCVA study of the area's visitors for 2001, for example, found that African Americans, Hispanics, and Asian Americans accounted for 9, 5, and 4 percent, respectively, of the total visitor pool. The same study also revealed that the number of visitors from each of those groups had been steadily rising and that all U.S. visitors were beginning to prefer two- or three-day stays to weeklong vacations. With those data in hand, the LVCVA produced its award-winning "Vegas Stories" series of TV commercials. These irreverent ads poke fun at the sticky situations travelers may find themselves in as a result of too much revelry in the desert.

Using the tagline, "What happens here, stays here," the spots from the "Vegas Stories" campaign include an older Asian woman trying to alter an after-the-trip love letter while Roy Orbison's "Only the Lonely" plays in the background and a bachelorette party of African American women riding quietly in a limousine until the group is slowly overcome with sheepish laughter. Other commercials depict elderly couples, businesswomen, and young professional males. The LVCVA also produced its first-ever commercial recorded entirely in Spanish, which was written specifically to appeal to Hispanics' historical preference for family or group activities for vacations. Additionally, the authority's director of diversity began promoting Las Vegas to ethnic chambers of commerce and organizations like the International Association of Hispanic Meeting Planners and the National Coalition of Black Meeting Planners.

Other research performed by the LVCVA identified Portland, Oregon, and Atlanta as emerging regional markets based on their median household incomes, their available flights to Las Vegas, the cost of advertising in those markets, and the propensity of their citizens to gamble. The LVCVA then bought billboards in each city, cruised the towns in a specially prepared van featuring an Elvis impersonator and a traditional Vegas showgirl, and offered special travel deals to promote the entertainment options that Las Vegas offers in addition to gambling.

The authority's message carries beyond the borders of the United States, too. When it noticed significant drops in the visitor volume from Canada—Las Vegas's leading source of international travelers—the LVCVA sent an official delegation to Toronto. The group canvassed Toronto's Canadian Meeting & Incentive Travel Symposium & Trade Show to persuade convention operators to host their future productions in the desert. Representatives also met with private convention and leisure travel planners and attended events in Montreal and Vancouver to promote their cause.

Las Vegas is clearly on the rise again thanks to the tireless work of the LVCVA, and the authority has the hard data to prove it. As long as the LVCVA continues to understand its many diverse customers and communicate with them appropriately, the city of lights should continue to shine brightly for many years to come.[58]

Questions

1. What bases does the LVCVA use for segmenting its target market?

2. Does the LVCVA use an undifferentiated, a concentrated, or a multisegment targeting strategy? Why? Should the LVCVA be concerned with cannibalization?

3. Think of the many reasons a person might want to travel to Las Vegas. Given a target market of all U.S. citizens aged 18 to 75, speculate how you might segment that market by lifestyle.

4. What do you think makes the LVCVA so successful?

COMPANY CLIPS

ReadyMade—Focus and Segmentation

ReadyMade markets itself as a magazine catering to GenNest, the group of consumers ages 25 to 35 who are just settling down after college. This group of young couples is buying its first houses and taking on domestic and decorating roles for the first time. They are interested in being stylish, while at the same time maintaining their own unique personalities. But ReadyMade appeals to a wide variety of readers than just GenNest. The magazine has subscribers in all age groups, from teens looking to spruce up their rooms to retirees looking for projects to enliven their homes. This diversity offers a unique challenge to ReadyMade as it tries to promote itself to advertisers who need to know what sort of people will be reached through advertisements appearing in the publication.

Questions

1. How does ReadyMade communicate the demographics of its reader base to advertisers who want to see specific statistics that do not easily represent ReadyMade's target market?

2. What sort of segmentation does ReadyMade use when it markets to businesses and investors?

3. What ideas do you have that would help ReadyMade reach out to new subscribers without alienating its loyal base?

BIZ FLIX

The Breakfast Club

Carefully review this chapter's discussion of segmenting and targeting markets, especially noting Exhibit 7.1, "Concept of Market Segmentation." The scene is an edited version of the "Lunchtime" sequence that appears in the first third of the film. John Hughes's careful look at teenage culture in a suburban Chicago High School focuses on a group of teenagers from the school's different subcultures. View this film scene as a metaphor for market segmentation. What market segments can you identify in the scene? What are your criteria or bases for those segments or divisions? Why would market segmentation be important if you were marketing products or services to the people shown in the scene?

Marketing & You Results

A high score indicates that you operate within budget constraints. Living on a budget doesn't necessarily mean that you change your shopping behavior or your price comparison behavior, however. Low scores relate to financial health and a tendency to be brand loyal. After reading Chapter 7, you can see why income and financial situation can be an important segmentation variable!

Decision Support

CHAPTER 8

Systems and Marketing Research

Learning Outcomes

LO¹ Explain the concept and purpose of a marketing decision support system

LO² Define marketing research and explain its importance to marketing decision making

LO³ Describe the steps involved in conducting a marketing research project

LO⁴ Discuss the profound impact of the Internet on marketing research

LO⁵ Discuss the growing importance of scanner-based research

LO⁶ Explain the concept of competitive intelligence

finding out what **Students want**

How can advertisers reach college students who spend $175 billion annually? The over 16 million students enrolled in American colleges and universities represent a tempting target market with high long-term earnings potential. To help marketers better understand how to reach this target market, Harris Interactive queried more than 1,600 18- to 30-year-old U.S. students working toward a degree at two- and four-year colleges. Among other things, the study examined student preferences for products and the marketing media used to deliver them.

Though TV advertising continues to have an impact, its influence is fading—

Though TV advertising continues to have an impact, its influence is fading—at least in consumers' opinions.

at least in consumers' opinions. Of those who watch TV, 83 percent say they do something else while watching (87 percent of females versus 77 percent of males). Multitasking is on the rise: 45 percent of students access the Internet (versus 33 percent in 2002) while the tube's on, 37 percent do homework (versus 28 percent), and 36 percent talk on the phone. Since they aren't exactly sitting front and center while commercials are airing, it's little surprise that only 38 percent consider TV ads the most influential form of marketing. On the other hand, 91 percent said they pay attention to nontraditional marketing methods, such as word of mouth, and 70 percent of those who did said these messages influence their buying decisions. Nearly half (48 percent) consider product sampling the method most likely to drive them to purchase.

Another traditional ad strategy—hiring an influential celebrity as brand endorser—seems to be losing steam among students. Only 5 percent said they prefer brands used by a favorite celebrity. Instead, they would rather see a reflection of themselves or "everyday people" in advertising (36 percent).

College students, like many consumers, tend to switch between mass brands and class (elite) brands. Here is what they said about brands:

- I try to buy brands that are on sale: 80 percent
- I prefer brands that are environmentally safe: 31 percent
- I like to try new brands before other people: 28 percent.
- I am willing to pay more for a brand with a great image: 26 percent
- I prefer brands that give back to the community: 26 percent.
- I prefer brands that are totally new and different: 24 percent.
- It is important that I use certain brands: 20 percent.
- I prefer brands that are connected to a cause: 20 percent.
- I prefer the same brands as my friends: 19 percent.
- I am willing to pay more for a brand not everyone has access to: 18 percent.
- I prefer brands that make me feel like part of the "in" crowd: 12 percent.
- I prefer brands that my favorite celebrity is using: 5 percent.[1]

What are some of the reasons that managers do marketing research? What are the techniques for conducting marketing research? Should managers always conduct marketing research before making a decision? How does marketing research relate to decision support systems? We will explore all these topics and others in Chapter 8.

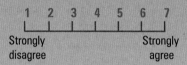

Marketing & You

Please note your opinion on each of the following questions.

Using the following scale, enter your opinion.

1	2	3	4	5	6	7

Strongly disagree   Strongly agree

During a marketing project, a marketing manager should have formal or informal processes

____ For continuously collecting information from customers.

____ For continuously collecting information about competitors' activities.

____ For continuously collecting information about relevant publics other than customers and competitors.

____ For continuously reexamining the value of information collected in previous studies.

____ For continuously collecting information from external experts, such as consultants.

Total your score. Now, read the chapter and find out what your score means at the end.

LO¹
Marketing Decision Support Systems

Accurate and timely information is the lifeblood of marketing decision making. Good information can help an organization maximize sales and efficiently use scarce company resources. To prepare and adjust marketing plans, managers need a system for gathering everyday information about developments in the marketing environment—that is, for gathering **marketing information**. The system most commonly used these days for gathering marketing information is called a *marketing decision support system.*

A marketing **decision support system (DSS)** is an interactive, flexible computerized information system that enables managers to obtain and manipulate information as they are making decisions. A DSS bypasses the information-processing specialist and gives managers access to useful data from their own desks.

These are the characteristics of a true DSS:

- *Interactive:* Managers give simple instructions and see immediate results. The process is under their direct control; no computer programmer is needed. Managers don't have to wait for scheduled reports.

- *Flexible:* A DSS can sort, regroup, total, average, and manipulate the data in various ways. It will shift gears as the user changes topics, matching information to the problem at hand. For example, the CEO can see highly aggregated figures, and the marketing analyst can view very detailed breakouts.

- *Discovery-oriented:* Managers can probe for trends, isolate problems, and ask "what if" questions.

- *Accessible:* Managers who aren't skilled with computers can easily learn how to use a DSS. Novice users should be able to choose a standard, or default, method of using the system. They can bypass optional features so they can work with the basic system right away while gradually learning to apply its advanced features.

marketing information
Everyday information about developments in the marketing environment that managers use to prepare and adjust marketing plans.

decision support system (DSS)
An interactive, flexible computerized information system that enables managers to obtain and manipulate information as they are making decisions.

As a hypothetical example of how a DSS can be used, consider Renee Smith, vice president and manager of new products for Central Corporation. To evaluate sales of a recently introduced product, Renee can "call up" sales by the week, then by the month, breaking them out at her option by, say, customer segments. As she works at her desktop computer, her inquiries can go in several directions, depending on the decision at hand. If her train of thought raises questions about monthly sales last quarter compared to forecasts, she can use her DSS to analyze problems immediately. Renee might see that her new product's sales were significantly below forecasts. Were her forecasts too optimistic? She compares other products' sales to her forecasts and finds that the targets were very accurate. Was something wrong with the product? Is her sales department getting insufficient leads, or is it not putting leads to good use? Thinking a minute about how to examine that question, she checks ratios of leads converted to sales, product by product. The results disturb her. Only 5 percent of the new product's leads generated orders, compared to the company's 12 percent all-product average. Why? Renee guesses

REVIEW LEARNING OUTCOME

LO¹ Explain the concept and purpose of a marketing decision support system

- Interactive
- Flexible
- Discovery-oriented
- Accessible

DSS

Internal and External Marketing Information

that the sales force is not supporting the new product vigorously enough. Quantitative information from the DSS could perhaps provide more evidence to back that suspicion. But already having enough quantitative knowledge to satisfy herself, the VP acts on her intuition and experience and decides to have a chat with her sales manager.

Perhaps the fastest-growing use of DSSs is for **database marketing**, which is the creation of a large computerized file of customers' and potential customers' profiles and purchase patterns. It is usually the key tool for successful one-to-one marketing, which relies on very specific information about a market. Huge databases can raise a number of concerns about the safety and use of personal data as the "Ethics in Marketing" box explains.

LO²
The Role of Marketing Research

database marketing
The creation of a large computerized file of customers' and potential customers' profiles and purchase patterns.

marketing research
The process of planning, collecting, and analyzing data relevant to a marketing decision.

Marketing research is the process of planning, collecting, and analyzing data relevant to a marketing decision. The results of this analysis are then communicated to management. Marketing research plays a key role in the marketing system. It provides decision makers with data on the effectiveness of the current marketing mix and also with insights for necessary changes. Furthermore, marketing research is a main data source for both management information systems and DSS. In other words, the findings of a marketing research project become data in a DSS.

Each year about $7 billion is spent on marketing research in the United States. That money is used to study products, advertising, prices, packages, names, logos, services, buying habits, taglines, colors, uses, awareness, familiarity, new concepts, traffic patterns, wants, needs, and politics.

ETHICS in Marketing

The Downside of Databases

ChoicePoint, Inc., has 19 billion data files, full of personal information about nearly every American adult. In minutes, it can produce a report listing someone's former addresses, old roommates, family members, and neighbors. The company's computers can tell its clients if an insurance applicant has ever filed a claim and whether a job candidate has ever been sued or faced a tax lien.

But in October 2004, after its databases were accessed by a man bent on identity theft, there was one thing ChoicePoint struggled to do: Figure out just what records had been stolen. "They said it was a huge task, and they didn't have to staff to do it," said Robert Costa, head of the Los Angeles County sheriff's department identity-theft squad. "Apparently, their technology wasn't built so you were able to find the electronic footsteps these guys left."

Months passed before ChoicePoint was able to estimate the number of people whose personal data had been compromised, which it pegged at 145,000. It couldn't say whether any of the data had been used to steal from the victims or get fraudulent loans. The sheriff's department, meanwhile, came to more alarming conclusions. It estimated that data had been downloaded on millions of people and used to run up millions of dollars in fraudulent credit-card charges.

The vulnerability of the company's data and its difficulty in tracking the breach point to a paradox. ChoicePoint and similar data sellers pitch their troves of private information as a way to restore personal security in a society fraught with anxiety over terrorism and crime. For a time, one could even buy ChoicePoint background-check kits at Sam's Club for $39.99, though ChoicePoint says it required buyers to prove a valid business purpose for using them. The company pulled the product after a few months, saying it had been just a test. The chief executive of ChoicePoint, Derek Smith, still maintains that society is better off if everyone can check the background of anyone else. Yet the very existence of these vast information stockpiles—vulnerable to both error and stealing—has spawned new sources of worry and risk.[2]

Marketers use databases to save countless dollars by getting the right product and message to the right consumer. American Express uses its database to tell how and where individual cardholders transact business. Allstate uses its new database to determine which of its 1,500 rates it will charge a specific customer for auto insurance. The company examines not only the person's driving history but also things like record of late payments and credit-card balances. 7-Eleven has found databases indispensable in deciding what merchandise to stock in which store.

Do databases store too much personal data on consumers? Should companies have the right to acquire personal information if doing so will help lower marketing costs and better target the right customers? Should government impose more or less regulation on databases? Why?

Marketing research has three roles: descriptive, diagnostic, and predictive. Its *descriptive* role includes gathering and presenting factual statements. For example, what is the historic sales trend in the industry? What are consumers' attitudes toward a product and its advertising? Its *diagnostic* role includes explaining data. For instance, what was the impact on sales of a change in the design of the package? Its *predictive* function is to address "what if" questions. For example, how can the researcher use the descriptive and diagnostic research to predict the results of a planned marketing decision?

MANAGEMENT USES OF MARKETING RESEARCH

Marketing research can help managers in several ways. It improves the quality of decision making and helps managers trace problems. Most important, sound marketing research helps managers focus on the paramount importance of keeping existing customers, aids them in better understanding the marketplace, and alerts them to marketplace trends.

Marketing research also helps managers gauge the perceived value of their goods and services as well as the level of customer satisfaction. For example, research revealed which brands of plumbing fixtures were traditional to New York City. This helped the Brooklyn Home Depot's store manager Rich Kantor to arrange his small pilot store so that it was designed to meet the needs of urban communities.

Improving the Quality of Decision Making

Managers can sharpen their decision making by using marketing research to explore the desirability of various marketing alternatives. For example, on the heels of the successful launch of its Young & Tender line of bagged spinach, NewStar, a Salinas, California–based produce firm, was wondering what to do for an encore. A line of salad kits featuring spinach in combination with a dressing and/or other ingredients seemed like a natural idea. But rather than introducing a me-too product to the already-crowded salad kit market, the company wanted to add a gourmet twist.

The process began with an idea generation phase, says Christie Hoyer, vice president of product development and evaluation at the National Food Laboratory (NFL). Sessions were conducted with NFL chefs, food technologists, and other culinary arts workers. "We did a number of brainstorming sessions, game-playing, and other, more coordinated exercises. From that we came up with numerous flavor concepts for the salads and the sauté mixes."

Next came the first round of consumer testing. At this stage, Hoyer says, NFL wanted to validate the product concepts and also gauge reactions to them. A four-phase process was conducted with male and female consumers ages 21 to 64 who were their family's primary grocery shopper and were positive toward spinach salad and cooked fresh spinach.

The first phase gathered reactions to the concept of a line of gourmet salad and sauté kits and determined purchase intent for each flavor (based on descriptions of the flavors, not actual tasting). Next the respondents tried the product prototypes, which were rotated so that half of the group tried the sautés first and half tried the salads first.

The third phase was a test of packaging. Respondents were taken to a separate area featuring a mock store display of three packaging concepts and asked to rank their preferences for the different graphics. In the fourth phase, the consumers viewed a large copy of the nutritional information for a salad kit and a sauté kit. "Without specifically asking about it, we were interested in their reaction to things such as fat content," Hoyer says.

Since the salad and sauté mixes were introduced, they have been a hit with retailers and with consumers. Marketing research paved the way![3]

Tracing Problems

Another way managers use marketing research is to find out why a plan backfired. Was the initial decision incorrect? Did an unforeseen change in the external environment cause the plan to fail? How can the same mistake be avoided in the future?

Keebler introduced Sweet Spots, a shortbread cookie with a huge chocolate drop on it. It has had acceptable sales and is still on the market, but only after the company used marketing research to overcome several problems. Soon after the cookie's introduction, Keebler increased the box size from 10 ounces at $2.29 to 15 ounces at $3.19. Demand immediately fell. Market research showed that Sweet Spots were now considered more of a luxury than an everyday item. Keebler lowered the price and went back to the 10-ounce box. Even though Sweet Spots originally was aimed at upscale adult females, the company also tried to appeal to kids. In subsequent research, Keebler found that the package graphics appealed to mothers but not to children.

Focusing on the Paramount Importance of Keeping Existing Customers

An inextricable link exists between customer satisfaction and customer loyalty. Long-term relationships don't just happen but are grounded in the delivery of service and value by the firm. Customer retention pays big dividends for organizations. Powered by repeat sales and referrals, revenues and market share grow. Costs fall because firms spend less money and energy attempting to replace defectors. Steady customers are easy to serve because they understand the modus operandi and make fewer demands on employees' time. Increased customer retention also drives job satisfaction and pride, which lead to higher employee retention. In turn, the knowledge employees acquire as they stay longer increases productivity. A Bain & Co. study estimated that a 5 percent decrease in the customer defection rate can boost profits by 25 to 95 percent.[4] Another study found that the customer retention rate has a major impact on the value of the firm.[5]

The ability to retain customers is based on an intimate understanding of their needs. Sometimes companies think that they are meeting customer needs when they are not. UPS, Inc., for example, had always assumed that on-time delivery was the paramount concern of its customers. Consequently, UPS's definition of quality centered almost exclusively on the results of time-and-motion studies. Knowing the average time elevator doors took to open on a certain city block and figuring how long people took to answer their doorbells were critical parts of the customer satisfaction equation. So was pushing drivers to meet exacting schedules. The problem was that UPS's marketing research survey was asking the wrong questions. It asked customers if they were pleased with delivery times and whether they thought delivery could be even faster.

When UPS began asking broader questions about how it could improve service, it discovered that its customers weren't as obsessed with on-time delivery as the company had thought. The biggest surprise was that customers wanted more interaction with drivers, who provided the only face-to-face contact customers had with the company. Less harried drivers who were more willing to chat could offer customers some practical advice on shipping.

In a sharp departure from tradition, the company now encourages its 62,000 delivery drivers to get out of their trucks and go along with salespeople to visit customers. It also allows drivers an additional 30 minutes a week to spend at their discretion to strengthen ties with customers and perhaps bring in new sales. Drivers use the Internet to report customer needs to the sales team. If a salesperson makes a sale based on that lead, the driver is given points on a debit card that can be used as cash. This has increased sales and encourages drivers to become more aware of customer needs. Using marketing research to understand its customers has enabled UPS to achieve consistently high customer satisfaction scores on the University of Michigan's 200-company Customer Satisfaction Index.[6]

Understanding the Ever-Changing Marketplace

Marketing research also helps managers understand what is going on in the marketplace and take advantage of opportunities. Historically, marketing research has been practiced for as long as marketing has existed. The early Phoenicians carried out market demand studies as they traded in the various ports of the Mediterranean Sea. Marco Polo's diary indicates he was performing marketing research as he traveled to China. There is even evidence that the Spanish systematically conducted "market surveys" as they explored the New World, and there are examples of marketing research conducted during the Renaissance.

Today, Internet marketing research can help companies quickly and efficiently understand what is happening in the marketplace. Internet research told AvantGo Mobile, Inc., a mobile Internet service, that 40 percent of its users were also American Airlines frequent flyers. Armed with that information, AvantGo pitched advertising on its PDA service to the airline. Now, AvantGo offers an American Airlines channel, including flight lookup, weekly Netsaver fares, promotions, special offers, contact numbers, and the locations of airport lounges.

California-based computer accessory maker Iogear uses a sample from its opt-in panel created on its Web site (**http://www.Iogear.com**) to find out what its customers want. The company surveyed users to find out whether they would prefer to buy a mouse for a notebook computer rather than use a touchpad. Of 9,400 users, 500 responded, and 72 percent said they preferred a mouse. That information was included in a press release, introducing three new mini-mice, that was sent to members of the technical media.[7]

LO 3
Steps in a Marketing Research Project

Virtually all firms that have adopted the marketing concept engage in some marketing research because it offers decision makers many benefits. Some companies spend millions on marketing research; others, particularly smaller firms, conduct informal, limited-scale research studies. For example, when Eurasia restaurant, serving Eurasian cuisine, first opened along Chicago's ritzy Michigan Avenue, it drew novelty seekers. But it turned off the important business lunch crowd, and sales began to decline. The owner surveyed several hundred businesspeople working within a mile of the restaurant. He found that they were confused by Eurasia's concept and wanted more traditional Asian fare at lower prices. In response, the restaurant altered its concept; it hired a Thai chef, revamped the menu, and cut prices. The dining room was soon full again.

Whether a research project costs $200 or $2 million, the same general process should be followed. The marketing research process is a scientific approach to decision making that maximizes the chance of getting accurate and meaningful results. Exhibit 8.1 traces the steps: (1) identifying and formulating the problem/opportunity, (2) planning the research design and gathering primary data, (3) specifying the sampling procedures, (4) collecting the data, (5) analyzing the data, (6) preparing and presenting the report, and (7) following up.

The research process begins with the recognition of a marketing problem or opportunity. As changes occur in the firm's external environment, marketing managers are faced with the questions, "Should we change the existing marketing mix?" and, if so, "How?" Marketing research may be used to evaluate product, promotion, distribution, or pricing alternatives.

During a recent summer, Starbucks wanted to answer this question: Do the company's out-of-home media (such as billboards, kiosk ads, vehicle wraps, vinyl signs that can be placed on cars and trucks) reach and affect people as efficiently as its television, radio, and print advertising? Previously, the Starbucks name had not been closely associated with summertime drinks. One of the objectives of the summer advertising was to change that.

To determine the effects of its advertising, Starbucks hired Bruzzone Research, which conducted the study online. By doing this, the research company was able to show each respondent almost every piece of advertising that Starbucks used over the

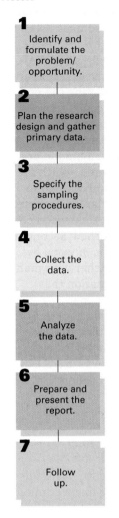

Exhibit 8.1

The Marketing Research Process

1
Identify and formulate the problem/ opportunity.

2
Plan the research design and gather primary data.

3
Specify the sampling procedures.

4
Collect the data.

5
Analyze the data.

6
Prepare and present the report.

7
Follow up.

marketing research problem
Determining what information is needed and how that information can be obtained efficiently and effectively.

marketing research objective
The specific information needed to solve a marketing research problem; the objective should be to provide insightful decision-making information.

management decision problem
A broad-based problem that uses marketing research in order for managers to take proper actions.

secondary data
Data previously collected for any purpose other than the one at hand

summer. The research found that virtually all of Starbucks advertising worked. When people noticed any of it, they ended up buying more of the summer drinks being advertised than people who didn't notice the advertising. The study also found that some of the ads worked a lot better than others.

Among the survey's other results were the following:

- Reminding people of the appropriateness of Starbucks' cold drinks during the summer worked well.

- Simply announcing what products were now available, and where, did not work as well.

- Simple illustrations of the drinks with palm trees, beaches, and blue sky worked well.

- More complex "what is this?" graphics did not work as well.

- The depiction of gratification was critical. The results showed specifically what conveyed gratification and what didn't.

- Starbucks' green straws, featured in some advertising, produced mixed results.

- Limits needed to be set on the amount spent on a single execution, and the results helped show where to set the limits. Starbucks found a number of cases where spending more did not produce more buyers.[8]

The Starbucks story illustrates an important point about problem/opportunity definition. The **marketing research problem** is information oriented. It involves determining what information is needed and how that information can be obtained efficiently and effectively. The **marketing research objective**, then, is to provide insightful decision-making information. This requires specific pieces of information needed to answer the marketing research problem. Managers must combine this information with their own experience and other information to make a proper decision. Starbucks' marketing research problem was to gather information online to determine recall and impact of out-of-home media. The marketing research objective was to measure recall and purchase of specific products featured in the promotions via billboards, kiosk ads, and vehicle wraps.

Whereas the marketing research problem is information oriented, the **management decision problem** is action oriented. Management problems tend to be much broader in scope and far more general than marketing research problems, which must be narrowly defined and specific if the research effort is to be successful. Sometimes several research studies must be conducted to solve a broad management problem. The management decision problem for Starbucks was: "Do the company's out-of-home media reach and affect people as efficiently as its television, radio, and print advertising?" Or, as the Starbucks vice-president for promotion might simply ask, "How do I get the most bang for my bucks (sales) from my advertising budget?"

SECONDARY DATA

A valuable tool throughout the research process, but particularly in the problem/opportunity identification stage is **secondary data**—data previously collected for any purpose, other than the one at hand. Secondary information originating within the company includes documents such as annual reports, reports to stockholders, product testing results perhaps made available to the news media, and house periodicals composed by the company's personnel for communication to employees, customers, or others. Often this information is incorporated into a company's internal database.

Innumerable outside sources of secondary information also exist, principally coming from government (federal, state, and local) departments and agencies that compile and publish summaries of business data. Trade and industry associations also publish secondary data. Still more data are available in business periodicals and other news media that regularly publish studies and articles on the economy, specific industries, and even individual companies. The unpublished summarized secondary information from these sources corresponds to internal reports, memos, or special-purpose analyses with limited circulation. Economic considerations or priorities in the organization may preclude publication of these summaries. Most of the sources listed above can be found on the Internet.

Secondary data save time and money if they help solve the researcher's problem. Even if the problem is not solved, secondary data have other advantages. They can aid in formulating the problem statement and suggest research methods and other types of data needed for solving the problem. In addition, secondary data can pinpoint the kinds of people to approach and their locations and serve as a basis of comparison for other data. The disadvantages of secondary data stem mainly from a mismatch between the researcher's unique problem and the purpose for which the secondary data were originally gathered, which are typically different. For example, a major consumer-products manufacturer wanted to determine the market potential for a fireplace log made of coal rather than compressed wood by-products. The researcher found plenty of secondary data about total wood consumed as fuel, quantities consumed in each state, and types of wood burned. Secondary data were also available about consumer attitudes and purchase patterns of wood by-product fireplace logs. The wealth of secondary data provided the researcher with many insights into the artificial log market. Yet, nowhere was there any information that would tell the firm whether consumers would buy artificial logs made of coal.

The quality of secondary data may also pose a problem. Often secondary data sources do not give detailed information that would enable a researcher to assess their quality or relevance. Whenever possible, a researcher needs to address these important questions: Who gathered the data? Why were the data obtained? What methodology was used? How were classifications (such as heavy users versus light users) developed and defined? When was the information gathered?

THE NEW AGE OF SECONDARY INFORMATION: THE INTERNET

Gathering secondary data, though necessary in almost any research project, has traditionally been a tedious and boring job. The researcher often had to write to government agencies, trade associations, or other secondary data providers and then wait days or weeks for a reply that might never come. Often, one or more trips to the library were required and the researcher might find that needed reports were checked out or missing. Now, however, the rapid development of the Internet has eliminated much of the drudgery associated with the collection of secondary data.

Finding Secondary Data on the Internet

Although there is probably no single best way to search the Web, we can recommend a five-step strategy:

- *Step One:* Analyze your topic to decide where to begin. A suggested worksheet is shown in Exhibit 8.2.

- *Step Two:* Test run a word or phrase in a search engine such as Google. Consider synonyms or equivalent terms.

- *Step Three:* Learn as you go and vary your approach with what you learn. Don't assume that you know what you want to find. Look at the search results and see what else you might use in addition to what you tried.

- *Step Four:* Don't get bogged down in strategy that doesn't work. Consider using a subject directory. A few of the best are the Librarian's Index, **http://lii.org**; Infomine, **http://infomine.ucr.edu**; Academic Info, **http://www.academicinfo.net**; Google Directory, **http://directory.google.com**; About.com, **http://www.about.com**;

Exhibit 8.2
Internet Search Topic Worksheet

Jot down a topic or subject you'd like to explore on the Web, and begin the presearch analysis:

1. **What UNIQUE WORDS, DISTINCTIVE NAMES, ABBREVIATIONS, or ACRONYMS are associated with your topic?** These may be the places to begin because their specificity will help you zero in on relevant pages.

2. **Can you think of societies, organizations, or groups that might have information on your subject via their pages?** Search these as a "phrase in quotes," looking for a home page that might contain links to other pages, journals, discussion groups, or databases on your subject. You may require the "phrase in quotes" to be in the document's title by preceding it by **title:[no space]**

3. **What other words are likely to be in ANY Web documents on your topic?** You may want to require these by joining them with **AND** or preceding each by **+[no space]**

4. **Do any of the words in 1, 2, or 3 belong in phrase or strings—together in a certain order, like a cliché?** Search these as a "phrase in quotes" (e.g., "observation research" or "marketing research aggregator").

5. **For any of the terms in 4, can you think of synonyms, variant spellings, or equivalent terms you would also accept in relevant documents?** You may want to allow these terms by joining them by **OR** and including each set of equivalent terms in **( )** (e.g., surveys or interviews).

6. **Can you think of any extraneous or irrelevant documents these words might pick up?** You may want to exclude terms or phrases with **– [no space]** before each term or use **AND NOT** (e.g., surveys or interviews –job).

7. **What BROADER terms could your topic be covered by?** When browsing subject categories or searching sites of webliographies or databases on your topic, try broader categories (e.g., marketing research).

SOURCE: Copyright 2004 by the Regents of the University of California. All Rights Reserved. Created by Joe Barker, Teaching Library, UC Berkeley.

and Yahoo Directory, **http://dir.yahoo.com**. Many researchers switch back and forth between directories and search engines.

- *Step Five:* If you haven't found what you want, go back to the earlier steps better informed. 9

Effective searching on the Internet is part art, part science, and part luck.

Marketing Research Aggregators

The **marketing research aggregator** industry is a $100 million business that is growing by about 6 percent a year. Companies in this field acquire, catalog, reformat, segment, and resell reports already published by large and small marketing research firms. Even Amazon.com has added a marketing research aggregation area to its high-profile e-commerce site.

The role of aggregator firms is growing because their databases of research reports are getting bigger and more comprehensive—and more useful—as marketing research firms get more comfortable using resellers as a sales channel. Meanwhile, advances in Web technology are making the databases easier to search and deliveries speedier. Research aggregators are also indirectly tapping new markets for traditional research firms. By slicing and repackaging research reports into narrower, more specialized sections for resale to small- and medium-sized clients that often cannot afford to commission their own studies or buy full reports, the aggregators are nurturing a new target market for the information.

Prior to the emergence of research aggregators, a lot of marketing research was available only as premium-priced subscription services. For example, a 17-chapter $2,800 report from Wintergreen Research (based in Lexington, Massachusetts) was recently broken up and sold (on AllNetResearch.com) for $350 per chapter, significantly boosting the overall revenue generated by the report.

In addition to AllNetResearch.com, other major aggregators are Profound.com, Bitpipe.com, USADATA.com, and MarketResearch.com.

PLANNING THE RESEARCH DESIGN AND GATHERING PRIMARY DATA

Good secondary data can help researchers conduct a thorough situation analysis. With that information, researchers can list their unanswered questions and rank them.

marketing research aggregator
A company that acquires, catalogs, reformats, segments, and resells reports already published by marketing research firms.

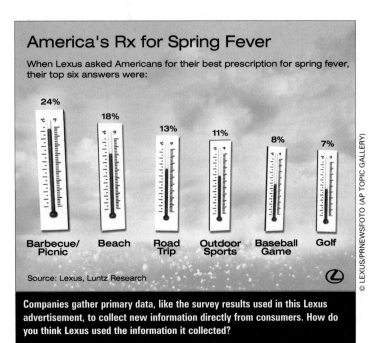

America's Rx for Spring Fever

When Lexus asked Americans for their best prescription for spring fever, their top six answers were:

24% Barbecue/Picnic
18% Beach
13% Road Trip
11% Outdoor Sports
8% Baseball Game
7% Golf

Source: Lexus, Luntz Research

© LEXUS/PRNEWSFOTO (AP TOPIC GALLERY)

Companies gather primary data, like the survey results used in this Lexus advertisement, to collect new information directly from consumers. How do you think Lexus used the information it collected?

Researchers must then decide the exact information required to answer the questions. The **research design** specifies which research questions must be answered, how and when the data will be gathered, and how the data will be analyzed. Typically, the project budget is finalized after the research design has been approved.

Sometimes research questions can be answered by gathering more secondary data; otherwise, primary data may be needed. **Primary data,** or information collected for the first time, is used for solving the particular problem under investigation. The main advantage of primary data is that they will answer a specific research question that secondary data cannot answer. For example, suppose Pillsbury has two new recipes for refrigerated dough for sugar cookies. Which one will consumers like better? Secondary data will not help answer this question. Instead, targeted consumers must try each recipe and evaluate the taste, texture, and appearance of each cookie. Moreover, primary data are current, and researchers know the source. Sometimes researchers gather the data themselves rather than assign projects to outside companies. Researchers also specify the methodology of the research. Secrecy can be maintained because the information is proprietary. In contrast, much secondary data is available to all interested parties for relatively small fees or for free.

Gathering primary data is expensive; costs can range from a few thousand dollars for a limited survey to several million for a nationwide study. For instance, a nationwide, 15-minute telephone interview with 1,000 adult males can cost $50,000 for everything, including a data analysis and report. Because primary data gathering is so expensive, firms may cut back on the number of in-person interviews to save money and use an Internet study instead. Larger companies that conduct many research projects use another cost-saving technique. They *piggyback studies,* or gather data on two different projects using one questionnaire. The drawback is that answering questions about, say, dog food and gourmet coffee may be confusing to respondents. Piggybacking also requires a longer interview (sometimes a half hour or longer), which tires respondents. The quality of the answers typically declines, with people giving curt replies and thinking, "When will this end!" A lengthy interview also makes people less likely to participate in other research surveys.

Nevertheless, the disadvantages of primary data gathering are usually offset by the advantages. It is often the only way of solving a research problem. And with a variety of techniques available for research—including surveys, observations, and experiments—primary research can address almost any marketing question.

Survey Research

The most popular technique for gathering primary data is **survey research**, in which a researcher interacts with people to obtain facts, opinions, and attitudes. Exhibit 8.3 summarizes the characteristics of traditional forms of survey research.

In-Home Personal Interviews Although in-home personal interviews often provide high-quality information, they tend to be very expensive because of the interviewers' travel time and mileage costs. Therefore, they are rapidly disappearing from the American and European marketing researcher's survey toolbox. They are, however, still popular in many countries around the globe.

Mall Intercept Interviews The **mall intercept interview** is conducted in the common area of a shopping mall or in a market research office within the mall. It is the economy version of the door-to-door interview with personal contact between interviewer and respon-

research design
Specifies which research questions must be answered, how and when the data will be gathered, and how the data will be analyzed.

primary data
Information that is collected for the first time; used for solving the particular problem under investigation.

survey research
The most popular technique for gathering primary data, in which a researcher interacts with people to obtain facts, opinions, and attitudes.

mall intercept interview
A survey research method that involves interviewing people in the common areas of shopping malls.

Exhibit 8.3
Characteristics of Traditional Forms of Survey Research

Characteristic	In-Home Personal Interviews	Mall Intercept Interviews	Central-Location Telephone Interviews	Self-Administered and One-Time Mail Surveys	Mail Panel Surveys	Executive Interviews	Focus Groups
Cost	High	Moderate	Moderate	Low	Moderate	High	Low
Time span	Moderate	Moderate	Fast	Slow	Relatively slow	Moderate	Fast
Use of interviewer probes	Yes	Yes	Yes	No	Yes	Yes	Yes
Ability to show concepts to respondent	Yes (also taste tests)	Yes (also taste tests)	No	Yes	Yes	Yes	Yes
Management control over interviewer	Low	Moderate	High	n/a	n/a	Moderate	High
General data quality	High	Moderate	High to moderate	Moderate to low	Moderate	High	Moderate
Ability to collect large amounts of data	High	Moderate	Moderate to low	Low to moderate	Moderate	Moderate	Moderate
Ability to handle complex questionnaires	High	Moderate	High, if computer-aided	Low	Low	High	N/A

dent, because the interviewer saves on travel time and mileage costs. To conduct this type of interview, the research firm rents office space in the mall or pays a significant daily fee. One drawback is that it is hard to get a representative sample of the population this way.

However, an interviewer can also probe when necessary—a technique used to clarify a person's response. For example, an interviewer might ask, "What did you like best about the salad dressing you just tried?" The respondent might reply, "Taste." This answer doesn't provide a lot of information, so the interviewer could probe by saying, "Can you tell me a little bit more about taste?" The respondent then elaborates: "Yes, it's not too sweet, it has the right amount of pepper, and I love that hint of garlic."

Mall intercept interviews must be brief. Only the shortest ones are conducted while respondents are standing. Usually, researchers invite respondents to their office for interviews, which are still generally less than 15 minutes long. The researchers often show respondents concepts for new products or a test commercial or have them taste a new food product. The overall quality of mall intercept interviews is about the same as telephone interviews.

Marketing researchers are applying computer technology in mall interviewing. The first technique is **computer-assisted personal interviewing**. The researcher conducts in-person interviews, reads questions to the respondent off a computer screen, and directly keys the respondent's answers into the computer. A second approach is **computer-assisted self-interviewing**. A mall interviewer intercepts and directs willing respondents to nearby computers. Each respondent reads questions off a computer screen and directly keys his or her answers into a computer. The third use of technology is fully automated self-interviewing. Respondents are guided by interviewers or independently approach a centrally located computer station or kiosk, read questions off a screen, and directly key their answers into the station's computer.

Telephone Interviews Compared to the personal interview, the telephone interview costs less, but cost is rapidly increasing due to respondent refusals to participate. Most telephone interviewing is conducted from a specially designed phone room called a **central-location telephone (CLT) facility**. A phone room has many phone lines, individual interviewing stations, sometimes monitoring equipment, and headsets. The research firm typically will interview people nationwide from a single location. The federal "Do Not Call" law does not apply to survey research.

Most CLT facilities offer computer-assisted interviewing. The interviewer reads the questions from a computer screen and enters the respondent's data directly into the computer. The researcher can stop the survey at any point and immediately print out the

computer-assisted personal interviewing
An interviewing method in which the interviewer reads the questions from a computer screen and enters the respondent's data directly into the computer.

computer-assisted self-interviewing
An interviewing method in which a mall interviewer intercepts and directs willing respondents to nearby computers where the respondent reads questions off a computer screen and directly keys his or her answers into a computer.

central-location telephone (CLT) facility
A specially designed phone room used to conduct telephone interviewing.

survey results. Thus, a researcher can get a sense of the project as it unfolds and fine-tune the research design as necessary. An online interviewing system can also save time and money because data entry occurs as the response is recorded rather than as a separate process after the interview. Hallmark Cards found that an interviewer administered a printed questionnaire for its Shoebox Greeting cards in 28 minutes. The same questionnaire administered with computer assistance took only 18 minutes.

Mail Surveys Mail surveys have several benefits: relatively low cost, elimination of interviewers and field supervisors, centralized control, and actual or promised anonymity for respondents (which may draw more candid responses). Some researchers feel that mail questionnaires give the respondent a chance to reply more thoughtfully and to check records, talk to family members, and so forth. A disadvantage is that mail questionnaires usually produce low response rates.

Low response rates pose a problem because certain elements of the population tend to respond more than others. The resulting sample may therefore not represent the surveyed population. For example, the sample may have too many retired people and too few working people. In this instance, answers to a question about attitudes toward Social Security might indicate a much more favorable overall view of the system than is actually the case. Another serious problem with mail surveys is that no one probes respondents to clarify or elaborate on their answers.

Mail panels like those operated by Market Facts, National Family Opinion Research, and NPD Research offer an alternative to the one-shot mail survey. A mail panel consists of a sample of households recruited to participate by mail for a given period. Panel members often receive gifts in return for their participation. Essentially, the panel is a sample used several times. In contrast to one-time mail surveys, the response rates from mail panels are high. Rates of 70 percent (of those who agree to participate) are not uncommon.

Executive Interviews Marketing researchers use **executive interviews** to conduct the industrial equivalent of door-to-door interviewing. This type of survey involves interviewing businesspeople, at their offices, concerning industrial products or services. For example, if Dell wanted information regarding user preferences for different features that might be offered in a new line of computer printers, it would need to interview prospective user-purchasers of the printers. It is appropriate to locate and interview these people at their offices.

This type of interviewing is very expensive. First, individuals involved in the purchase decision for the product in question must be identified and located. Sometimes lists can be obtained from various sources, but more frequently screening must be conducted over the telephone. A particular company is likely to have individuals of the type being sought, but locating those people within a large organization can be expensive and time-consuming. Once a qualified person is located, the next step is to get that person to agree to be interviewed and to set a time for the interview. This is not as hard as it might seem because most professionals seem to enjoy talking about topics related to their work.

Finally, an interviewer must go to the particular place at the appointed time. Long waits are frequently encountered, and cancellations are not uncommon. This type of survey requires the very best interviewers because they are frequently interviewing on topics that they know very little about. Executive interviewing has essentially the same advantages and disadvantages as in-home interviewing.

Focus Groups A **focus group** is a type of personal interviewing. Often recruited by random telephone screening, seven to ten people with certain desired characteristics form a focus group. These qualified consumers are usually offered an incentive (typically $30 to $50) to participate in a group discussion. The meeting place (sometimes resembling a living room, sometimes featuring a conference table) has audiotaping and perhaps videotaping equipment. It also likely has a viewing room with a one-way mirror so that clients (manufacturers or retailers) may watch the session. During the session, a moderator, hired by the research company, leads the group discussion.

executive interviews
A type of survey that involves interviewing businesspeople at their offices concerning industrial products or services.

focus group
Seven to ten people who participate in a group discussion led by a moderator.

Focus groups are much more than question-and-answer interviews. Market researchers draw a distinction between "group dynamics" and "group interviewing." The interaction provided in **group dynamics** is essential to the success of focus-group research; this interaction is the reason for conducting group rather than individual research. One of the essential postulates of group-session usage is the idea that a response from one person may become a stimulus for another, thereby generating an interplay of responses that may yield more information than if the same number of people had contributed independently.

Focus groups are occasionally used to brainstorm new product ideas or to screen concepts for new products. Ford Motor Company, for example, asked consumers to drive several automobile prototypes. These "test drivers" were then brought together in focus groups. During the discussions, consumers complained that they were scuffing their shoes because the rear seats lacked foot room. In response, Ford sloped the floor underneath the front seats, widened the space between the seat adjustment tracks, and made the tracks in the Taurus and Sable models out of smooth plastic instead of metal.

A system created by Focus Vision Network allows client companies and advertising agencies to view live focus groups in over 300 cities worldwide. For example, the private satellite network lets a General Motors researcher observing a San Diego focus group control two cameras in the viewing room. The researcher can get a full-group view or a close-up, zoom, or pan the participants. The researcher can also communicate directly with the moderator using an ear receiver. Ogilvy & Mather (a large New York advertising agency whose clients include StarKist Sea Foods, Seagram's, MasterCard, and Burger King) has installed the system.

Increasingly, focus groups are being conducted online. Online focus groups are examined in detail later in the chapter.

CreateSurvey.com
Design a marketing questionnaire to post on your class Web site using the tools offered by CreateSurvey. Visit the demo polls on the site for ideas and tips.

http://www.createsurvey.com/

Online

Questionnaire Design

All forms of survey research require a questionnaire. Questionnaires ensure that all respondents will be asked the same series of questions. Questionnaires include three basic types of questions: open-ended, closed-ended, and scaled-response (see Exhibit 8.4). An **open-ended question** encourages an answer phrased in the respondent's own words. Researchers get a rich array of information based on the respondent's frame of reference. In contrast, a **closed-ended question** asks the respondent to make a selection from a limited list of responses. Traditionally, marketing researchers separate the two-choice question (called *dichotomous*) from the many-item type (often called *multiple choice*). A **scaled-response question** is a closed-ended question designed to measure the intensity of a respondent's answer.

Closed-ended and scaled-response questions are easier to tabulate than open-ended questions because response choices are fixed. On the other hand, unless the researcher designs the closed-ended question very carefully, an important choice may be omitted.

For example, suppose a food study asked this question: "Besides meat, which of the following items do you normally add to a taco that you prepare at home?"

Avocado	1	Olives (black/green)	6	
Cheese (Monterey Jack/cheddar)	2	Onions (red/white)	7	
Guacamole	3	Peppers (red/green)	8	
Lettuce	4	Pimento	9	
Mexican hot sauce	5	Sour cream	0	

The list seems complete, doesn't it? However, consider the following responses: "I usually add a green, avocado-tasting hot sauce"; "I cut up a mixture of lettuce and spinach"; "I'm a vegetarian; I don't use meat at all. My taco is filled only with guacamole." How would you code these replies? As you can see, the question needs an "other" category.

group dynamics
Group interaction essential to the success of focus-group research.

open-ended question
An interview question that encourages an answer phrased in the respondent's own words.

closed-ended question
An interview question that asks the respondent to make a selection from a limited list of responses.

scaled-response question
A closed-ended question designed to measure the intensity of a respondent's answer.

© CATHLEEN CLAPPER/ISTOCKPHOTO INTERNATIONAL INC.

Exhibit 8.4
Types of Questions Found on Questionnaires for National Market Research

Open-Ended Questions	Closed-Ended Questions	Scaled-Response Question

Open-Ended Questions

1. What advantages, if any, do you think ordering from a mail-order catalog offers compared to shopping at a local retail outlet?
   (*Probe:* What else?)

2. Why do you have one or more of your rugs or carpets professionally cleaned rather than cleaning them yourself or having someone else in the household clean them?

3. What is there about the color of the eye shadow that makes you like it the best?

Closed-Ended Questions

Dichotomous

1. Did you heat the Danish product before serving it?
   Yes 1
   No 2

2. The federal government doesn't care what people like me think.
   Agree 1
   Disagree 2

Multiple choice

1. I'd like you to think back to the last footwear of any kind that you bought. I'll read you a list of descriptions and would like for you to tell me which category they fall into. *(Read list and circle proper category.)*
   Dress and/or formal 1
   Casual 2
   Canvas/trainer/gym shoes 3
   Specialized athletic shoes 4
   Boots 5

2. In the last three months, have you used Noxzema skin cream . . .
   (Circle all that apply.)
   As a facial wash .1
   For moisturizing the skin 2
   For treating blemishes 3
   For cleansing the skin 4
   For treating dry skin 5
   For softening skin 6
   For sunburn 7
   For making the facial skin smooth 8

Scaled-Response Question

Now that you have used the rug cleaner, would you say that you . . . *(Circle one.)*
Would definitely buy it 1
Would probably buy it 2
Might or might not buy it 3
Probably would not buy it 4
Definitely would not buy it 5

A good question must also be clear and concise, and ambiguous language must be avoided. Take, for example, the question "Do you live within ten minutes of here?" The answer depends on the mode of transportation (maybe the person walks), driving speed, perceived time, and other factors. Instead, respondents should see a map with certain areas highlighted and be asked whether they live in one of those areas.

Clarity also implies using reasonable terminology. A questionnaire is not a vocabulary test. Jargon should be avoided, and language should be geared to the target audience. A question such as "What is the level of efficacy of your preponderant dishwasher powder?" would probably be greeted by a lot of blank stares. It would be much simpler to say "Are you (1) very satisfied, (2) somewhat satisfied, or (3) not satisfied with your current brand of dishwasher powder?"

Stating the survey's purpose at the beginning of the interview also improves clarity. The respondents should understand the study's intentions and the interviewer's expectations. Sometimes, of course, to get an unbiased response, the interviewer must disguise the true purpose of the study. If an interviewer says, "We're conducting an image study for American National Bank" and then proceeds to ask a series of questions about the bank, chances are the responses will be biased. Many times respondents will try to provide answers that they believe are "correct" or that the interviewer wants to hear.

Finally, to ensure clarity, the interviewer should avoid asking two questions in one; for example, "How did you like the taste and texture of the Pepperidge Farm coffee cake?" This should be divided into two questions, one concerning taste and the other texture.

A question should also be unbiased. A question such as "Have you purchased any quality Black & Decker tools in the past six months?" biases respondents to think of the topic in a certain way (in this case, to link quality and Black & Decker tools). Questions

One interesting observation situation is toy-testing day camp. Pictured here, Fama Ana tries on a pair of "spy glasses" at Duracell Toy Testing Camp. In one week, over a thousand children in 15 cities test 25 different toys while marketers look on.

can also be leading: "Weren't you pleased with the good service you received last night at the Holiday Inn?" (The respondent is all but instructed to say yes.) These examples are quite obvious; unfortunately, bias is usually more subtle. Even an interviewer's clothing or gestures can create bias.

Observation Research

In contrast to survey research, **observation research** depends on watching what people do. Specifically, it can be defined as the systematic process of recording the behavioral patterns of people, objects, and occurrences without questioning them. A market researcher using the observation technique witnesses and records information as events occur or compiles evidence from records of past events. Carried a step further, observation may involve watching people or phenomena and may be conducted by human observers or machines. Examples of these various observational situations are shown in Exhibit 8.5.

Two common forms of people-watching-people research are mystery shoppers and one-way mirror observations. **Mystery shoppers** are researchers posing as customers who gather observational data about a store (i.e., are the shelves neatly stocked?) and collect data about customer/employee interactions. In the latter case, of course, there is communication between the mystery shopper and the employee. The mystery shopper may ask, "How much is this item?" "Do you have this in blue?" or "Can you deliver this by Friday?" The interaction is not an interview, and communication occurs only so that the mystery shopper can observe the actions and comments of the employee. Mystery shopping is, therefore, classified as an observational marketing research method even though communication is often involved. Conducted on a continuous basis, mystery shopping can motivate and recognize service performance. Used as a benchmark, mystery shopping can pinpoint strengths and weaknesses for training operations and policy refinements.

At the Fisher-Price Play Laboratory, children are invited to spend 12 sessions playing with toys. Toy designers watch through one-way mirrors to see how children react to Fisher-Price's and other makers' toys. Fisher-Price, for example, had difficulty designing a toy lawn mower that children would play with. A designer, observing behind the mirror, noticed the children's fascination with soap bubbles. He then created a lawn mower that spewed soap bubbles. It sold over a million units in the first year.

observation research
A research method that relies on four types of observation: people watching people, people watching an activity, machines watching people, and machines watching an activity.

mystery shoppers
Researchers posing as customers who gather observational data about a store.

ethnographic research
The study of human behavior in its natural context; involves observation of behavior and physical setting.

Ethnographic Research

Ethnographic research comes to marketing from the field of anthropology. The technique is becoming increasingly popular in commercial marketing research. **Ethnographic research,** or the study of human behavior in its natural context, involves observation of behavior and physical setting. Ethnographers directly observe the population they are

Exhibit 8.5

Observational Situations

Situation	Example
People watching people	Observers stationed in supermarkets watch consumers select frozen Mexican dinners; the purpose is to see how much comparison shopping people do at the point of purchase.
People watching phenomena	Observer stationed at an intersection counts traffic moving in various directions.
Machines watching people	Movie or videotape cameras record behavior as in the people-watching-people example above.
Machines watching phenomena	Traffic-counting machines monitor traffic flow.

studying. As "participant observers," ethnographers can use their intimacy with the people they are studying to gain richer, deeper insights into culture and behavior—in short, what makes people do what they do.

For managers at Cambridge SoundWorks, it was a perplexing problem: in retail outlets across the country, men stood wide-eyed as sales reps showed off the company's hi-fi, "blow-your-hair-back" stereo speakers. So why didn't such unabashed enthusiasm for the product translate into larger—and bigger ticket—sales?

To find out, the Andover, Massachusetts–based manufacturer and retailer of stereo equipment hired research firm Design Continuum, in West Newton, Massachusetts, to follow a dozen prospective customers over the course of two weeks. The researchers' conclusion: the high-end speaker market suffered from "the spouse acceptance factor." While men adored the big black boxes, women hated their unsightly appearance. Concerned about the way the speakers would look in the living room, women would talk their husbands out of buying a cool but hideous and expensive piece of stereo equipment. Even those who had purchased the product had trouble showing it off: men would attempt to display the loudspeakers as trophies in living rooms, while women would hide them behind plants, vases, and chairs. "Women would come into the store, look at the speakers and say, 'that thing is ugly,'" says Ellen Di Resta, a principal at Design Continuum. "The men would lose the argument and leave the store without a stereo. The solution was to give the target market what men and women *both* wanted: a great sound system that looks like furniture so you don't have to hide it."

Armed with this knowledge, Cambridge SoundWorks unveiled a new line. The furniture-like Newton Series of speakers and home theater systems comes in an array of colors and finishes. The result: the Newton Series is the fastest-growing and best-selling product line in the firm's history.[10]

Experiments

An **experiment** is a method a researcher can use to gather primary data. The researcher alters one or more variables—price, package design, shelf space, advertising theme, advertising expenditures—while observing the effects of those alterations on another variable (usually sales). The best experiments are those in which all factors are held constant except the ones being manipulated. The researcher can then observe that changes in sales, for example, result from changes in the amount of money spent on advertising.

Holding all other factors constant in the external environment is a monumental and costly, if not impossible, task. Such factors as competitors' actions, weather, and economic conditions are beyond the researcher's control. Yet market researchers have ways to account for the ever-changing external environment. Mars, the candy company, was losing sales to other candy companies. Traditional surveys showed that the shrinking candy bar was not perceived as a good value. Mars wondered whether a bigger bar sold at the same price would increase sales enough to offset the higher ingredient costs. The company designed an experiment in which the marketing mix stayed the same in different markets but the size of the candy bar varied. The substantial increase in sales of the bigger bar quickly proved that the additional costs would be more than covered by the additional revenue. Mars increased the bar size—and its market share and profits.

SPECIFYING THE SAMPLING PROCEDURES

Once the researchers decide how they will collect primary data, their next step is to select the sampling procedures they will use. A firm can seldom take a census of all possible users of a new product, nor can they all be interviewed. Therefore, a firm must select a sample of the group to be interviewed. A **sample** is a subset from a larger population.

Several questions must be answered before a sampling plan is chosen. First, the population, or **universe**, of interest must be defined. This is the group from which the sample will be drawn. It should include all the people whose opinions, behavior, preferences,

experiment
A method a researcher uses to gather primary data.

sample
A subset from a larger population.

universe
The population from which a sample will be drawn.

attitudes, and so on are of interest to the marketer. For example, in a study whose purpose is to determine the market for a new canned dog food, the universe might be defined to include all current buyers of canned dog food.

After the universe has been defined, the next question is whether the sample must be representative of the population. If the answer is yes, a probability sample is needed. Otherwise, a nonprobability sample might be considered.

Probability Samples

A **probability sample** is a sample in which every element in the population has a known statistical likelihood of being selected. Its most desirable feature is that scientific rules can be used to ensure that the sample represents the population.

One type of probability sample is a **random sample**—a sample arranged in such a way that every element of the population has an equal chance of being selected as part of the sample. For example, suppose a university is interested in getting a cross section of student opinions on a proposed sports complex to be built using student activity fees. If the university can acquire an up-to-date list of all the enrolled students, it can draw a random sample by using random numbers from a table (found in most statistics books) to select students from the list. Common forms of probability and nonprobability samples are shown in Exhibit 8.6.

Nonprobability Samples

Any sample in which little or no attempt is made to get a representative cross-section of the population can be considered a **nonprobability sample.** Therefore the probability of selection of each sampling unit is not known. A common form of a nonprobability sample is the **convenience sample,** which uses respondents who are convenient or readily accessible to the researcher—for instance, employees, friends, or relatives.

Nonprobability samples are acceptable as long as the researcher understands their nonrepresentative nature. Because of their lower cost, nonprobability samples are the basis of much marketing research.

Types of Errors

Whenever a sample is used in marketing research, two major types of error may occur: measurement error and sampling error. **Measurement error** occurs when there is a

probability sample
A sample in which every element in the population has a known statistical likelihood of being selected.

random sample
A sample arranged in such a way that every element of the population has an equal chance of being selected as part of the sample.

nonprobability sample
Any sample in which little or no attempt is made to get a representative cross section of the population.

convenience sample
A form of nonprobability sample using respondents who are convenient or readily accessible to the researcher—for example, employees, friends, or relatives.

measurement error
An error that occurs when there is a difference between the information desired by the researcher and the information provided by the measurement process.

Exhibit 8.6

Types of Samples

Probability Samples	
Simple Random Sample	Every member of the population has a known and equal chance of selection.
Stratified Sample	The population is divided into mutually exclusive groups (such as gender or age); then random samples are drawn from each group.
Cluster Sample	The population is divided into mutually exclusive groups (such as geographic areas); then a random sample of clusters is selected. The researcher then collects data from all the elements in the selected clusters or from a probability sample of elements within each selected cluster.
Systematic Sample	A list of the population is obtained—i.e., all persons with a checking account at XYZ Bank—and a *skip interval* is obtained by dividing the sample size by the population size. If the sample size is 100 and the bank has 1,000 customers, then the skip interval is 10. The beginning number is randomly chosen within the skip interval. If the beginning number is 8, then the skip pattern would be 8, 18, 28, ...
Nonprobability Samples	
Convenience Sample	The researcher selects the easiest population members from which to obtain information.
Judgment Sample	The researcher's selection criteria are based on personal judgment that the elements (persons) chosen will likely give accurate information.
Quota Sample	The researcher finds a prescribed number of people in several categories—i.e., owners of large dogs versus owners of small dogs. Respondents are not selected on probability sampling criteria.
Snowball Sample	Additional respondents are selected on the basis of referrals from the initial respondents. This method is used when a desired type of respondent is hard to find—i.e., persons who have taken round-the-world cruises in the last three years. This technique employs the old adage "Birds of a feather flock together."

difference between the information desired by the researcher and the information provided by the measurement process. For example, people may tell an interviewer that they purchase Coors beer when they do not. Measurement error generally tends to be larger than sampling error.

Sampling error occurs when a sample somehow does not represent the target population. Sampling error can be one of several types. Nonresponse error occurs when the sample actually interviewed differs from the sample drawn. This error happens because the original people selected to be interviewed either refused to cooperate or were inaccessible. For example, people who feel embarrassed about their drinking habits may refuse to talk about them.

Frame error, another type of sampling error, arises if the sample drawn from a population differs from the target population. For instance, suppose a telephone survey is conducted to find out Chicago beer drinkers' attitudes toward Coors. If a Chicago telephone directory is used as the *frame* (the device or list from which the respondents are selected), the survey will contain a frame error. Not all Chicago beer drinkers have a phone, and many phone numbers are unlisted. An ideal sample (for example, a sample with no frame error) matches all important characteristics of the target population to be surveyed. Could you find a perfect frame for Chicago beer drinkers?

Random error occurs when the selected sample is an imperfect representation of the overall population. Random error represents how accurately the chosen sample's true average (mean) value reflects the population's true average (mean) value. For example, we might take a random sample of beer drinkers in Chicago and find that 16 percent regularly drink Coors beer. The next day we might repeat the same sampling procedure and discover that 14 percent regularly drink Coors beer. The difference is due to random error.

Error is common to all surveys, yet it is often not reported or is underreported. Typically, the only error mentioned in a written report is sampling error. When errors are ignored, misleading results can result in poor information and, perhaps, bad decisions.

COLLECTING THE DATA

Marketing research field service firms collect most primary data. A **field service firm** specializes in interviewing respondents on a subcontracted basis. Many have offices, often in malls, throughout the country. A typical marketing research study involves data collection in several cities, requiring the marketer to work with a comparable number of field service firms. Besides conducting interviews, field service firms provide focus-group facilities, mall intercept locations, test product storage, and kitchen facilities to prepare test food products.

ANALYZING THE DATA

After collecting the data, the marketing researcher proceeds to the next step in the research process: data analysis. The purpose of this analysis is to interpret and draw conclusions from the mass of collected data. The marketing researcher tries to organize and analyze those data by using one or more techniques common to marketing research: one-way frequency counts, cross-tabulations, and more sophisticated statistical analysis. Of these three techniques, one-way frequency counts are the simplest. One-way frequency tables record the responses to a question. For example, the answers to the question "What brand of microwave popcorn do you buy most often?" would provide a one-way frequency distribution. One-way frequency tables are always done in data analysis, at least as a first step, because they provide the researcher with a general picture of the study's results.

A **cross-tabulation,** or "cross-tab," lets the analyst look at the responses to one question in relation to the responses to one or

---

sampling error
An error that occurs when a sample somehow does not represent the target population.

frame error
An error that occurs when a sample drawn from a population differs from the target population.

random error
An error that occurs when the selected sample is an imperfect representation of the overall population.

field service firm
A firm that specializes in interviewing respondents on a subcontracted basis.

cross-tabulation
A method of analyzing data that lets the analyst look at the responses to one question in relation to the responses to one or more other questions.

Exhibit 8.7

Hypothetical Cross-Tabulation between Gender and Brand of Microwave Popcorn Purchased Most Frequently

| Brand | Purchase by Gender | |
	Male	Female
Orville Reddenbacher	31%	48%
T.V. Time	12	6
Pop Rite	38	4
Act Two	7	23
Weight Watchers	4	18
Other	8	0

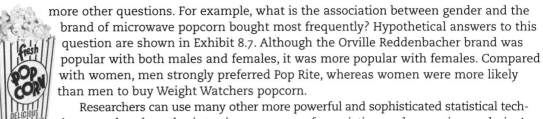

more other questions. For example, what is the association between gender and the brand of microwave popcorn bought most frequently? Hypothetical answers to this question are shown in Exhibit 8.7. Although the Orville Reddenbacher brand was popular with both males and females, it was more popular with females. Compared with women, men strongly preferred Pop Rite, whereas women were more likely than men to buy Weight Watchers popcorn.

Researchers can use many other more powerful and sophisticated statistical techniques, such as hypothesis testing, measures of association, and regression analysis. A description of these techniques goes beyond the scope of this book but can be found in any good marketing research textbook. The use of sophisticated statistical techniques depends on the researchers' objectives and the nature of the data gathered.

REVIEW LEARNING OUTCOME

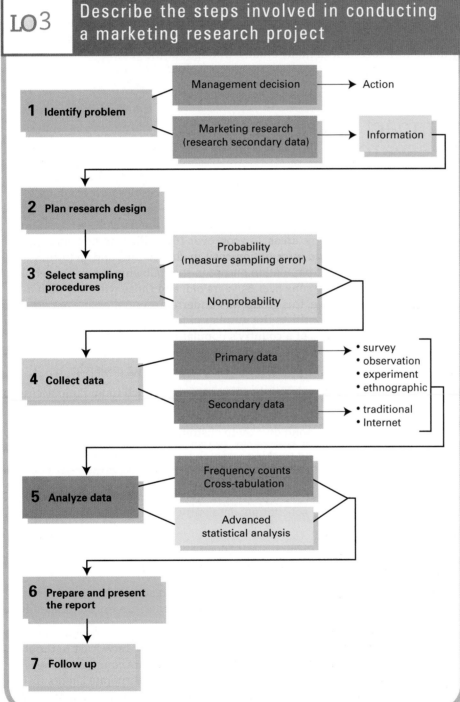

LO3 Describe the steps involved in conducting a marketing research project

1 Identify problem
- Management decision → Action
- Marketing research (research secondary data) → Information

2 Plan research design

3 Select sampling procedures
- Probability (measure sampling error)
- Nonprobability

4 Collect data
- Primary data
  - survey
  - observation
  - experiment
  - ethnographic
- Secondary data
  - traditional
  - Internet

5 Analyze data
- Frequency counts Cross-tabulation
- Advanced statistical analysis

6 Prepare and present the report

7 Follow up

PREPARING AND PRESENTING THE REPORT

After data analysis has been completed, the researcher must prepare the report and communicate the conclusions and recommendations to management. This is a key step in the process. If the marketing researcher wants managers to carry out the recommendations, he or she must convince them that the results are credible and justified by the data collected.

Researchers are usually required to present both written and oral reports on the project. Today, the written report is no more than a copy of the PowerPoint slides used in the oral presentation. Both reports should be tailored to the audience. They should begin with a clear, concise statement of the research objectives, followed by a complete, but brief and simple, explanation of the research design or methodology employed. A summary of major findings should come next. The conclusion of the report should also present recommendations to management.

Most people who enter marketing will become research users rather than research suppliers. Thus, they must know what to notice in a report. As with many other items we purchase, quality is not always readily apparent. Nor does a high price guarantee superior quality. The basis for measuring the quality of a marketing research report is the research proposal. Did the report meet the objectives established in the proposal? Was the methodology outlined in the proposal followed? Are the conclusions based on logical deductions from the data analysis? Do the recommendations seem prudent, given the conclusions?

FOLLOWING UP

The final step in the marketing research process is to follow up. The researcher should determine why management did or did not carry out the recommendations in the report. Was sufficient decision-making information included? What could have been done to make the report more useful to management? A good rapport between the product manager, or whoever authorized the project, and the market researcher is essential. Often they must work together on many studies throughout the year.

LO⁴
The Profound Impact of the Internet on Marketing Research

The way survey research is conducted has changed forever because of the Internet. The vast majority (88 percent) of U.S. research firms are now conducting marketing research online.[11]

In the United States, the online population is now closely tracking the United States population in most key demographic areas. In 2005, over 164 million Americans logged on each month to shop, e-mail, find information, visit in chat rooms, and so forth.[12] These Web users mirrored the U.S. population except in the following areas: households earning over $200,000 annually, persons over 65 years old, and those with less than a high school education. In each case, this group was underrepresented online as compared with the total U.S. population.[13] As the number of Internet users continues to grow worldwide, the characteristics of a country's population and of Internet users tend to meld.

There are several reasons for the success of Internet marketing research:

- It allows for better and faster decision making through much more rapid access to business intelligence.

- It improves the ability to respond quickly to customer needs and market shifts.

- It makes follow-up studies and tracking research much easier to conduct and more fruitful.

- It slashes labor- and time-intensive research activities (and associated costs), including mailing, telephone solicitation, data entry, data tabulation, and reporting.

ADVANTAGES OF INTERNET SURVEYS

The huge growth in the popularity of Internet surveys is the result of the many advantages offered by the Internet. The specific advantages of Internet surveys are related to many factors:

- *Rapid development, real-time reporting:* Internet surveys can be broadcast to thousands of potential respondents simultaneously. Respondents complete surveys simultaneously; then results are tabulated and posted for corporate clients to view as the returns arrive. The result: survey results can be in a client's hands in significantly less time than would be required for traditional surveys.

- *Dramatically reduced costs:* The Internet can cut costs by 25 to 40 percent and provide results in half the time it takes to do traditional telephone surveys. Data collection costs account for a large proportion of any traditional market research budget. Telephone surveys are labor-intensive efforts incurring training, telecommunications, and management costs. Electronic methods eliminate these completely. While costs for traditional survey techniques rise proportionally with the number of interviews desired, electronic solicitations can grow in volume with little increase in project costs.

- *Personalized questions and data:* Internet surveys can be highly personalized for greater relevance to each respondent's own situation, thus speeding the response process. Respondents enjoy a personalized survey because they are asked to answer only pertinent questions, can pause and resume the survey as needed, and can see previous responses and correct inconsistencies.

- *Improved respondent participation:* Busy respondents may be growing increasingly intolerant of "snail mail" or telephone-based surveys. Internet surveys take half as much time to complete as phone interviews, can be accomplished at the respondent's convenience (after work hours), and are much more stimulating and engaging. Graphics, interactivity, links to incentive sites and real-time summary reports make the interview enjoyable. The result? Much higher response rates.

- *Contact with the hard-to-reach:* Certain groups—doctors, high-income professionals, top management in Global 2000 firms—are among the most surveyed on the planet and the most difficult to reach. Many of these groups are well represented online. Internet surveys provide convenient anytime/anywhere access that makes it easy for busy professionals to participate.

USES OF THE INTERNET BY MARKETING RESEARCHERS

Marketing researchers are using the Internet to administer surveys, conduct focus groups, and perform a variety of other types of marketing research.

Internet Samples

Internet samples may be classified as unrestricted, screened, or recruited. In an **unrestricted Internet sample,** anyone who desires can complete the questionnaire. It is fully self-selecting and probably representative of nothing except Web surfers. The problem is exacerbated if the same Internet user can access the questionnaire repeatedly. For example, *InfoWorld*, a computer user magazine, decided to conduct its Readers Choice survey for the first time on the Internet. The results were so skewed by repeat voting for one product that the entire survey was publicly abandoned and the editor asked for readers' help to avoid the problem again. A simple solution to repeat respondents is to lock respondents out of the site after they have filled out the questionnaire.

Screened Internet samples adjust for the unrepresentativeness of the self-selected respondents by imposing quotas based on some desired sample characteristics. These are often demographic characteristics such as gender, income, and geographic region, or product-related criteria such as past purchase behavior, job responsibilities, or current product use. The applications for screened samples are generally similar to those for unrestricted samples.

Screened sample questionnaires typically use a branching or skip pattern for asking screening questions to determine whether the full questionnaire should be presented to a respondent. Some Web survey systems can make immediate market segment calculations that first assign a respondent to a particular segment based on screening questions and then select the appropriate questionnaire to match the respondent's segment.

Recruited Internet Samples **Recruited Internet samples** are used in surveys that require more control over the makeup of the sample. Recruited samples are ideal for applications in which there is already a database from which to recruit the sample. For

unrestricted Internet sample
A survey in which anyone with a computer and Internet access can fill out the questionnaire.

screened Internet sample
An Internet sample with quotas based on desired sample characteristics.

recruited Internet sample
A sample in which respondents are prerecruited and must qualify to participate. They are then e-mailed a questionnaire or directed to a secure Web site.

example, a good application would be a survey that used a customer database to recruit respondents for a purchaser satisfaction study.

Respondents are recruited by telephone, mail, or e-mail, or in person. After qualification, they are sent the questionnaire by e-mail or are directed to a Web site that contains a link to the questionnaire. At Web sites, passwords are normally used to restrict access to the questionnaire to recruited sample members. Since the makeup of the sample is known, completions can be monitored; to improve the participation rate, follow-up messages can be sent to those who have not completed the questionnaire.

Recruited Panels By far, the most popular form of Internet sampling is the recruited panel. In the early days of Internet recruiting, panels were created by means of Web-based advertising, or posting, that offered compensation for participation in online studies. This method allowed research firms to build large pools of individuals who were available to respond quickly to the demands of online marketing research. Internet panels have grown rapidly and now account for over 40 percent of all custom research sampling in the United States.[14]

Renting Internet Panels Very few marketing research companies build their own Internet panels because of the huge expense involved. Instead, they rent a sample from an established panel provider. The largest and oldest sample provider in the nation is Survey Sampling, Inc. Today, it offers the marketing research industry a huge Internet panel called Survey Spot that has over 5 million members. As with its other (non-Internet) panels, Survey Sampling offers subsets of its main panel, which is balanced demographically. In other words, its panel looks exactly like the U.S. population in terms of demographics, based on the U.S. Census.

Online Focus Groups

A recent development in qualitative research is the online focus group. A number of organizations are currently offering this new means of conducting focus groups. The process is fairly simple.

- The research firm builds a database of respondents via a screening questionnaire on its Web site.

- When a client comes to a firm with a need for a particular focus group, the firm goes to its database and identifies individuals who appear to qualify. It sends an e-mail message to these individuals, asking them to log on to a particular site at a particular time scheduled for the group. The firm pays them an incentive for their participation.

- The firm develops a discussion guide similar to the one used for a conventional focus group.

- A moderator runs the group by typing in questions online for all to see. The group operates in an environment similar to that of a chat room so that all participants see all questions and all responses.

- The firm captures the complete text of the focus group and makes it available for review after the group has finished.

The Moderator's Role The basic way the moderator communicates with respondents in an online focus group is "freestyle" or "on the fly." That is, the moderator types in all questions, instructions, and probes into the text-entry area of the chat room in real-time (live, on-the-spot). In a variation on this method, the moderator copies and pastes questions from an electronic version of the guide into the text-entry area. Here, the moderator will toggle back and forth between the document and the chat room. An advantage of the freestyle method is that it forces the moderator to adapt to the group rather than use a series of canned questions. A disadvantage is that typing everything freestyle (or even copying and pasting from a separate document) takes time.

One way respondents can see stimuli (e.g., a concept statement, a mockup of a print ad, or a short product demonstration on video) is for the moderator to give the respondents a URL. Respondents then copy the URL from the chat stream, open another browser window, paste in the URL, and view it. An advantage of this approach is its simplicity. However, there are several disadvantages. First, if the respondents do not copy the URL correctly, they will not see it. Another disadvantage is that once respondents open another browser, they have "left the room" and the moderator has lost their attention; researchers must hope that respondents will return within the specified amount of time.

More advanced virtual focus group software reserves a frame (section) of the screen for stimuli to be shown. Here, the moderator has control over what is shown in the stimulus area. The advantage of this approach is that the respondent does not have to do any work to see the stimuli.

Types of Online Focus Groups Decision Analyst, one of America's most progressive firms in applying Internet technology to marketing research, offers two types of online focus groups:

1. *Real-time online focus groups:* These are live, interactive sessions with four to six participants and a moderator in a chat room format. The typical session does not last longer than 45 to 50 minutes. This technique is best for simple, straightforward issues that can be covered in limited time. The results tend to be superficial compared to in-person focus groups—but this is acceptable for certain types of projects. Typically, three to four groups are recommended as a minimum. Clients can view the chat room as the session unfolds and communicate with the moderator.

2. *Time-extended online focus groups:* These sessions follow a message board format and usually last five to ten days. The 15 to 20 participants must comment at least two or three times per day and spend 15 minutes a day logged in to the discussion. The moderator reviews respondents' comments several times per day (and night) and probes or redirects the discussion as needed. This technique provides three to four times as much content as the average in-person focus group. Time-extended online focus groups give participants time to reflect, talk to others, visit a store, or check the pantry. This extra time translates into richer content and deeper insights. Clients can view the online content as it is posted and may communicate with the moderator at any time.[15]

Using Channel M2 to Conduct Online Focus Groups Channel M2 provides market researchers with user-friendly virtual interview rooms, recruiting, and technical support for conducting virtual qualitative research, efficiently and effectively. By using Channel M2, the moderator and client can see and hear every respondent. You can see a demo at **http://www.channelM2.com.**

To recruit focus groups (from a global panel with access to over 15 million online consumers), Channel M2 uses a blend of e-mail and telephone verification and confirmation. Specifically, e-mails elicit involvement and direct participants to an online qualification questionnaire to ensure that each meets screening criteria. Telephone follow-up confirms that respondents qualify. Participants are sent a Web camera so that both verbal and nonverbal reactions can be recorded. Channel M2 tech support helps participants install the Webcam one to two days prior to the interview. Before participating, respondents must show a photo ID (their driver's license) to their Webcam so that their identity can be verified.

Participants are then provided instructions via e-mail including a link to the Channel M2 interviewing room and a toll-free teleconference number to call. Upon clicking on the link, participants sign on and see the Channel M2 interview room, complete with live video of the other participants, text chat, screen or slide sharing, and whiteboard (see Exhibit 8.8).

Exhibit 8.8
An M2 Online Focus Group Under Way

© 2005 CHANNEL M2, LLC.

SOURCE: Channel M2.

Thus, in a Channel M2 focus group, all the participants can see and hear each other and communicate in a group setting. Once the focus group is under way, questions and answers occur in "real time" in a lively setting. Participants comment spontaneously, both verbally and via text messaging, yet the moderator can provide direction exactly as would be done in a traditional setting.[16]

Advantages of Online Focus Groups Many advantages are claimed for cyber groups. Cyber Dialogue, a marketing research company specializing in cyber groups, lists the following benefits of online focus groups on its Web site:

- *Speed:* Typically, focus groups can be recruited and conducted, with delivery of results, within five days of client approval.

- *Cost-effectiveness:* Off-line focus groups incur costs for facility rental, airfare, hotel, and food. None of these costs is incurred with online focus groups.

- *Broad geographic scope:* In a given focus group, you can speak to people in Boise, Idaho, and Miami, Florida, at the same time.

- *Accessibility:* Online focus groups give you access to individuals who otherwise might be difficult to recruit (e.g., business travelers, doctors, mothers with infants).

- *Honesty:* From behind their screen names, respondents are anonymous to other respondents and tend to talk more freely about issues that might create inhibitions in a face-to-face group.

Cyber Dialogue charges $3,000 for its focus groups. This compares very favorably to a cost in the range of $7,000 (without travel costs) for conventional focus groups.

The Role of Blogs in Marketing Research

Cutting-edge, technology-driven, marketing research companies, like Nielsen BuzzMetrics (formerly Intelliseek), are now using more refined Internet search technologies to monitor, interpret, and report on comments, opinions, and feedback generated on blogs.[17] Their automated and sophisticated technologies combine machine learning and natural language processing to mine volumes of unstructured data, such as billions of lines of plain text, and identify the intelligence buried within. It is a rich source of information that allows researchers and marketers to identify and respond to key trends almost instantaneously. BuzzMetrics even dispatches experts to meet with clients, interpret the data, and suggest strategic responses.

Its most revolutionary product, BlogPulse, monitors keywords and phrases, detects authors' sentiments, classifies data in terms of relevance, and unearths specific facts and data points about the brands, products, or companies that are the subject of bloggers' attention. Major clients like Sony, AOL, Porsche, Yahoo, and VH1 use BlogPulse to monitor consumers' opinions about their products or services on a daily, or even hourly, basis. BlogPulse can also identify the Internet's most influential bloggers, which is something marketers dearly love to know. A higher level of development of a consumer's sphere of influence indicates a greater potential to empower word-of-mouth marketing by leveraging the volume, frequency, and quality of the communications. "Influence matters, and BlogPulse's new features offer one-click access to meaningful analysis that helps [clients] understand the impact of blogs," notes chief marketing officer, Pete Blackshaw.

Though blog monitoring can be far more revealing than standard focus groups and surveys, some marketing research projects combine modern technology with direct human input. 3iYing is a budding design and marketing firm that is leveraging the power of the blogosphere and direct involvement from opinion leaders to help its clients establish relevance with a very specific target market—teenage females. The company recruits panel members from the New York High School of Art & Design and LaGuardia High School of Music & Performing Arts because they tend to have advanced senses of design and are generally well-networked opinion leaders.

After determining which of their clients' products and ad campaigns are ill-conceived or out of touch, 3iYing's team of young girls survey their networks of friends via e-mail, instant messaging, or blog postings at Internet community sites. They generate lists of what girls really want and of the key product features or marketing messages that girls find appealing. The design team then configures products and marketing campaigns that resonate with the target audience. 3iYing's work for Virgin Mobile allowed the company to more effectively encourage girls to put pressure on their parents to help them with their higher-than-average cell phone fees. Girls talk on cell phones more than male teenagers and need either a parent's help with the bills or cheaper service. Instead of lowering fees, Virgin used what it learned from 3iYing to create a magazine ad with a perforated cell phone that ran in *CosmoGIRL!* Readers could pull out the gimmick and "talk" on their fake phones to shame parents into providing money for a real phone or more minutes. According to 3iYing's CEO, Heidi Dangelmaier, "Such group creativity and content sharing make a product far superior to anything that you will ever find."

Other Uses of the Internet by Marketing Researchers

The Internet revolution in marketing research has had an impact on more than just the way surveys and focus groups are conducted. The management of the research process and the dissemination of information have also been greatly enhanced by the Internet. Several key areas have been affected by the Internet:

- *The distribution of requests for proposals (RFPs) and proposals:* Companies can now quickly and efficiently send RFPs to a select e-mail list of research suppliers. In turn, research suppliers can develop proposals and e-mail them back to clients. A process that used to take days using snail mail now occurs in a matter of hours.

- *Collaboration between the client and the research supplier in the management of a research project:* Now a researcher and client may both be looking at a proposal, RFP, report, or some type of statistical analysis at the same time on their respective computer screens while discussing it over the telephone. This is very powerful and efficient. Changes in the sample size, quotas, and other aspects of the research plan can be discussed and made immediately.

- *Data management and online analysis:* Clients can access their survey via the research supplier's secure Web site and monitor the data gathering in real time. The client can use sophisticated tools to actually do data analysis as the survey develops.

REVIEW LEARNING OUTCOME

LO4 Discuss the profound impact of the Internet on marketing research

By driving down time and cost of collecting data, the Internet has increased in popularity, has become easier to use, and therefore is used in a growing number of research applications.

scanner-based research
A system for gathering information from a single group of respondents by continuously monitoring the advertising, promotion, and pricing they are exposed to and the things they buy.

BehaviorScan
A scanner-based research program that tracks the purchases of 3,000 households through store scanners in each research market.

This real-time analysis may result in changes in the questionnaire, sample size, or the types of respondents being interviewed. The research supplier and the client become partners in "just-in-time" marketing research.

- *Publication and distribution of reports:* Reports can be published to the Web directly from programs such as PowerPoint and all the latest versions of leading word-processing, spreadsheet, and presentation software packages. This means that results are available to appropriate managers worldwide on an almost instantaneous basis. Reports can be searched for the content of interest using the same Web browser used to view the report.

- *Viewing of oral presentations of marketing research surveys by widely scattered audiences:* By placing oral presentations on password-protected Web sites, managers throughout the world can see and hear the actual client presentation. This saves time and money by avoiding the need for the managers to travel to a central meeting site.[18]

LO5
Scanner-Based Research

Scanner-based research is a system for gathering information from a single group of respondents by continuously monitoring the advertising, promotion, and pricing they are exposed to and the things they buy. The variables measured are advertising campaigns, coupons, displays, and product prices. The result is a huge database of marketing efforts and consumer behavior. Scanner-based research is bringing ever closer the Holy Grail of marketing research: an accurate, objective picture of the direct causal relationship between different kinds of marketing efforts and actual sales.

InfoScan
A scanner-based sales-tracking service for the consumer packaged-goods industry.

The two major scanner-based suppliers are Information Resources, Inc. (IRI), and the A. C. Nielsen Company. Each has about half the market. However, IRI is the founder of scanner-based research.

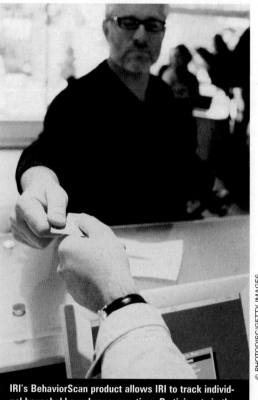

IRI's BehaviorScan product allows IRI to track individual household purchases over time. Participants in the household panel present an ID card at the checkout of a scanner-equipped grocery store.

© PHOTODISC/GETTY IMAGES

IRI's first product is called **BehaviorScan.** A household panel (a group of 3,000 long-term participants in the research project) has been recruited and maintained in each BehaviorScan town. Panel members shop with an ID card, which is presented at the checkout in scanner-equipped grocery stores and drugstores, allowing IRI to track electronically each household's purchases, item by item, over time. It uses microcomputers to measure TV viewing in each panel household and can send special commercials to panel member television sets. With such a measure of household purchasing, it is possible to manipulate marketing variables, such as TV advertising or consumer promotions, or to introduce a new product and analyze real changes in consumer buying behavior.

IRI's most successful product is InfoScan—a scanner-based sales-tracking service for the consumer packaged-goods industry. Retail sales, detailed consumer purchasing information (including measurement of store loyalty and total grocery basket expenditures), and promotional activity by manufacturers and retailers are monitored and evaluated for all bar-coded products. Data are collected weekly from more than 32,000 supermarkets, drugstores, and mass merchandisers.

When Should Marketing Research Be Conducted?

When managers have several possible solutions to a problem, they should not instinctively call for marketing research. In fact, the first decision to make is whether to conduct marketing research at all.

Some companies have been conducting research in certain markets for many years. Such firms understand the characteristics of target customers and their likes and dislikes about existing products. Under these circumstances, further research would be repetitive and waste money. Procter & Gamble, for example, has extensive knowledge of the coffee market. After it conducted initial taste tests with Folgers Instant Coffee, P&G went into national distribution without further research. Consolidated Foods Kitchen of Sara Lee followed the same strategy with its frozen croissants, as did Quaker Oats with Chewy Granola Bars. This tactic, however, does not always work. P&G marketers thought they understood the pain reliever market thoroughly, so they bypassed market research for Encaprin aspirin in capsules. Because it lacked a distinct competitive advantage over existing products, however, the product failed and was withdrawn from the market.

Managers rarely have such great trust in their judgment that they would refuse more information if it were available and free. But they might have enough confidence that they would be unwilling to pay very much for the information or to wait a long time to receive it. The willingness to acquire additional decision-making information depends on managers' perceptions of its quality, price, and timing. Of course, if perfect information were available—that is, the data conclusively showed which alternative to choose—decision makers would be willing to pay more for it than for information that still left uncertainty. In summary, research should be undertaken only when the expected value of the information is greater than the cost of obtaining it.

LO5 — Discuss the growing importance of scanner-based research

BehaviorScan

Panel information from specific groups of people, enables researchers to manipulate variables and see real results

InfoScan

Aggregate consumer information on all bar-coded products

LO6 — Competitive Intelligence

Derived from military intelligence, competitive intelligence is an important tool for helping a firm overcome a competitor's advantage. Specifically, competitive intelligence can help identify the advantage and play a major role in determining how it was achieved.

Competitive intelligence (CI) helps managers assess their competitors and their vendors in order to become a more efficient and effective competitor. Intelligence is analyzed information. It becomes decision-making intelligence when it has implications for the organization. For example, one of your firm's primary competitors may have plans to introduce a product with performance standards equal to your own but with a 15 percent cost advantage. The new product will reach the market in eight months. This intelligence has important decision-making and policy consequences for management. Competitive intelligence and environmental scanning (where management gathers data about the external environment—see Chapter 2) combine to create marketing intelligence. Marketing intelligence is then used as input into a marketing decision support system. Nine out of ten large companies have employees dedicated to the CI function. Many firms spend several million dollars a year on the function.

The top corporate CI officer at a multibillion-dollar global technology company claims that competitive intelligence helped his company recover after it began losing market share to a competitor. The rival, after competing directly with the company for years, had figured out its bidding strategy. Instead of competing on price with an off-the-shelf offering, the rival was beginning to offer prospects a customized solution—and it was winning. When the CI officer's company changed to a customized approach, it won hundreds of millions of dollars in new business the following year. At Pergo, Inc., a maker of laminate flooring, CI helped win a major contract. When Pergo told a national

competitive intelligence (CI)
An intelligence system that helps managers assess their competition and vendors in order to become more efficient and effective competitors.

retailer what it had learned from a mutual supplier—that the rival would not be able to launch a new product when it said it would— the retailer signed with Pergo instead.

Cognos, which sells planning and budgeting programs to clients such as Dow Chemical, recently turned CI into a company-wide event. Any of the firm's 3,000 workers can submit information about Cognos competitors through an internal Web site called Street Fighter. The site has drawn more than 200 entries per month. R&D and sales executives pore over it daily, and bona fide tips are rewarded with prizes like DVD players.[19]

SOURCES OF COMPETITIVE INTELLIGENCE

The Internet and its databases are a great source of CI. CI researchers can use Internet databases to answer these and other questions:

- What articles were written about this market?
- What companies are associated with this product group?
- What patents have been filed for this technology?
- What are the major magazines or texts in this industry?
- What are the chances that I will find something in print on the target company?
- How many companies are in the same industry as the target company?
- Who are the reporters studying this industry?
- How can I be updated on industry and company events without having to constantly request the information?
- How can I compile a list of the leading experts in the industry and the key institutions they are associated with?

Non-computer-based sources of CI can be found in a variety of areas:

- A company's salespeople, who can directly observe and ask questions about the competition.
- Experts with in-depth knowledge of a subject or activity.
- CI consultants, who can use their knowledge and experience to gather needed information quickly and efficiently.
- Government agencies, a valuable source of all types of data.
- Uniform Commercial Code (UCC) filings, a system that identifies goods that are leased or pledged as collateral. This is an excellent source for learning about a company's latest additions to plant assets.
- Suppliers, a group that may offer information on products shipped to a competitor.
- Periodicals, a good source for timely articles on successes, failures, opportunities, and threats.
- The Yellow Pages, which often provide data on a number of competitors, trading areas, and special offerings.
- Trade shows, official gatherings where competitors display their latest offerings.

This list is not exhaustive, but it does provide an idea of how CI can be gathered.

REVIEW LEARNING OUTCOME

LO 6 Explain the concept of competitive intelligence

CI

- Part of a sound marketing strategy
- Helps companies respond to competitive threats
- Helps reduce unnecessary costs

Quick Check ✔

Now that you've read the chapter, do you get it?
Take a moment for a quick check using this scale:

1 Not at all; 2 Not very well; 3 Ok; 4 Well; 5 Very Well

Can you . . .

___ list the roles of marketing research?

___ outline the steps of the marketing research process?

___ explain the benefits of secondary and primary data?

___ describe the multiple ways the Internet is used as a marketing research tool?

___ identify several types of survey research?

___ write examples of open-ended, close-ended, dichotomous, and scaled-response questions?

___ compare BehaviorScan and InfoScan?

___ draw a table organizing and describing the types of samples market researchers can use?

___ differentiate between the various types of errors?

___ describe how blogging is becoming a tool for marketing research?

___ TOTAL

Score: 41–50, you're ready to move on to the applications; 31–40, skim the chapter one more time before moving on to the applications; 21–30, reread the sections giving you the most trouble and go to Thomson NOW for guided tutorials; 20 and under, you better reread the chapter to get a grasp of the fundamentals. If you've reread the chapter and still have a low score, visit your professor or TA during office hours.

Review and Applications

LO¹ Explain the concept and purpose of a marketing decision support system. A decision support system (DSS) makes data instantly available to marketing managers and allows them to manipulate the data themselves to make marketing decisions. Four characteristics make DSSs especially useful to marketing managers: They are interactive, flexible, discovery oriented, and accessible. Decision support systems give managers access to information immediately and without outside assistance. They allow users to manipulate data in a variety of ways and to answer "what if" questions. And, finally, they are accessible to novice computer users.

1.1 In the absence of company problems, is there any reason to develop a marketing DSS?

1.2 Explain the difference between marketing research and a DSS.

LO² Define marketing research and explain its importance to marketing decision making. Marketing research is a process of collecting and analyzing data for the purpose of solving specific marketing problems. Marketers use marketing research to explore the profitability of marketing strategies. They can examine why particular strategies failed and analyze characteristics of specific market segments. Managers can use research findings to help keep current customers. Moreover, marketing research allows management to behave proactively, rather than reactively, by identifying newly emerging patterns in society and the economy.

2.1 The task of marketing is to create exchanges. What role might marketing research play in the facilitation of the exchange process?

2.1 Marketing research has traditionally been associated with manufacturers of consumer goods. Today, however, an increasing number of organizations, both profit and nonprofit, are using marketing research. Why do you think this trend exists? Give some examples of specific reasons why organizations might use marketing research.

2.3 Write a reply to the following statement: "I own a restaurant in the downtown area. I see customers every day whom I know on a first-name basis. I understand their likes and dislikes. If I put something on the menu and it doesn't sell, I know that they didn't like it. I also read the magazine *Modern Restaurants*, so I know what the trends are in the industry. This is all of the marketing research I need to do."

2.4 Give an example of (a) the descriptive role of marketing research, (b) the diagnostic role, and (c) the predictive function of marketing research.

LO3 Describe the steps involved in conducting a marketing research project. The marketing research process involves several basic steps. First, the researcher and the decision maker must agree on a problem statement or set of research objectives. The researcher then creates an overall research design to specify how primary data will be gathered and analyzed. Before collecting data, the researcher decides whether the group to be interviewed will be a probability or nonprobability sample. Field service firms are often hired to carry out data collection. Once data have been collected, the researcher analyzes them using statistical analysis. The researcher then prepares and presents oral and written reports, with conclusions and recommendations, to management. As a final step, the researcher determines whether the recommendations were implemented and what could have been done to make the project more successful.

3.1 Critique the following methodologies and suggest more appropriate alternatives:

  a. A supermarket was interested in determining its image. It dropped a short questionnaire into the grocery bag of each customer before putting in the groceries.

  b. To assess the extent of its trade area, a shopping mall stationed interviewers in the parking lot every Monday and Friday evening. Interviewers walked up to people after they had parked their cars and asked them for their ZIP codes.

  c. To assess the popularity of a new movie, a major studio invited people to call a 900 number and vote yes, they would see it again, or no, they would not. Each caller was billed a $2 charge.

3.2 You have been charged with determining how to attract more business majors to your school. Write an outline of the steps you would take, including the sampling procedures, to accomplish the task.

3.3 Why are secondary data sometimes preferable to primary data?

3.4 What is a marketing research aggregator? What role do these aggregators play in marketing research?

3.5 Discuss when focus groups should and should not be used.

3.6 Divide the class into teams of eight persons. Each group will conduct a focus group on the quality and number of services that your college is providing to its students. One person from each group should be chosen to act as moderator. Remember, it is the moderator's job to facilitate discussion, not to lead the discussion. These groups should last approximately 45 minutes. If possible, the groups should be videotaped or recorded. Upon completion, each group should write a brief report of its results. Consider offering to meet with the dean of students to share the results of your research.

3.7 Ethnographic research is a new (and expensive) trend in marketing research. Find an article on ethnographic research. Read and summarize the article. What is your opinion of ethnographic research? Do you think it will be the wave of the future? Explain your reasoning.

LO4 Discuss the profound impact of the Internet on marketing research. The Internet has vastly simplified the secondary data search process, placing more sources of information in front of researchers than ever before. Internet survey research is surging in popularity. Internet surveys can be created rapidly and reported in real time. They are also relatively inexpensive and can easily be personalized. Often researchers can use the Internet to contact respondents who are difficult to reach by other means. The Internet can also be used to conduct focus groups, to distribute research proposals and reports, and to facilitate collaboration between the client and the research supplier. Clients can access real-time data and analyze the information as the collection process continues.

4.1 Go to **http://www.SRIC-bi.com** and take the VALS Survey. Report on how marketing researchers are using this information.

4.2 Divide the class into teams. Each team should go to a different opt-in survey site on the Web and participate in an online survey. A spokesperson for each team should report the results to the class.

4.3 What are various ways to obtain respondents for online surveys?

4.4 Describe the advantages and disadvantages of online surveys.

LO5 Discuss the growing importance of scanner-based research. **A scanner-based research system enables marketers to monitor a market panel's exposure and reaction to such variables as advertising, coupons, store displays, packaging, and price. By analyzing these variables in relation to the panel's subsequent buying behavior, marketers gain useful insight into sales and marketing strategies.**

5.1 Why has scanner-based research been seen as "the ultimate answer" for marketing researchers? Do you see any disadvantages of this methodology?

5.2 Detractors claim that scanner-based research is like "driving a car down the road looking only in the rearview mirror." What does this mean? Do you agree?

LO6 Explain the concept of competitive intelligence. **Competitive intelligence (CI) helps managers assess their competition and their vendors in order to become more efficient and effective competitors. Intelligence is analyzed information, and it becomes decision-making intelligence when it has implications for the organization.**

By helping managers assess their competition and vendors, CI leads to fewer surprises. CI allows managers to predict changes in business relationships, guard against threats, forecast a competitor's strategy, and develop a successful marketing plan.

The Internet and databases accessed via the Internet offer excellent sources of CI. Company personnel, particularly sales and service representatives, are usually good sources of CI. Many companies require their salespersons to routinely fill out CI reports. Other external sources of CI include experts, CI consultants, government agencies, UCC filings, suppliers, newspapers and other publications, Yellow Pages, and trade shows.

6.1 Why do you think that CI is so hot in today's environment?

6.2 Prepare a memo to your boss at JetBlue Airlines and outline why the organization needs a CI unit.

6.3 Form a team with three other students. Each team must choose a firm in the PC manufacturing industry and then go to the Web site of the firm and acquire as much CI as possible. Each team will then prepare a five-minute oral presentation on its findings.

Key Terms

Exercises

APPLICATION EXERCISE

For its *Teens and Healthy Eating: Oxymoron or Trend?* study, New York–based BuzzBack Market Research focused on snacking. Among its findings: Teens eat an average of three snacks per day; breakfast is the meal they skip most often. Though scads of snacks are stacked on store shelves, when it comes to healthier treats targeting adolescents, it's a bit of a teenage wasteland. BuzzBack asked 532 teen respondents to conjure up new foods they'd gobble up. The following are some of their ideas:

- "Travel fruit. Why can't fruit be in travel bags like chips or cookies? Canned fruit is too messy. Maybe have a dip or something sold with it, too."—Female, age 17.

- "A drink that contains five servings of fruits and vegetables."—Male, age 16, Caucasian.

- "I would invent all natural and fat-free, vitamin-enhanced cookies and chips that had great flavor."—Female, age 16.

- "I would make fruit-based cookies."—Male, age 16, Caucasian.

- "Low-carb trail mix, because trail mix is easy to eat but it has a lot of fat/carbs."— Female, age 15, Caucasian.

- "I would create some sort of microwavable spaghetti."—Male, age 16, Caucasian.

- "Something quick and easy to make that's also cheap. I'll be in college next year, and I'm trying to find things that are affordable, healthier than cafeteria food and easy to make."—Female, age 17.

- "*Good* vegan mac n'cheese."—Female, age 18, Caucasian.

- "A smoothie where you could get all the nutrients you need, that tastes good, helps you stay in shape, and is good for you. Has vitamins A, B_3, B_{12}, C, ginkgo. Packaging would be bright."—Female, age 16, African American.

- "A breakfast shake for teens. Something easy that tastes good, not necessarily for dieters like Slim Fast, etc. Something to balance you off in the morning."—Male, age 18.[20]

Activities

1. You are a new-product development specialist at Kraft. What guidance can you get from the BuzzBack study?

2. Choose one of the suggestions from the above list of healthy snack concepts. Imagine that your company is interested in turning the idea into a new product but wants to conduct market research before investing in product development. Design a marketing research plan that will give company managers the information they need before engaging in new-product development of the idea. (Hint: Use steps 1–3 in Exhibit 8.1 as a guide.)

3. Once you have finished your plan, collect the data. Depending on the data-collection methods you have outlined in your plan, you may need to make adjustments so that you can collect actual data to analyze.

4. Analyze the data you collected and create a report for your company either recommending that the company pursue the idea you chose or investigate another.

Entrepreneurship Case

LOOK-LOOK

You can't always believe what you hear, particularly in the fast-moving world of youth trends. That is, unless you listen to Sharon Lee and DeeDee Gordon, founders of Look-Look, the most accurate information resource on the global youth culture. The pair founded the company in 1999, determined to find whatever makes the cultural spider-sense tingle—music, shoes, clothes, games, makeup, food, and technology. Lee and Gordon took Look-Look online in 2000, and the company has since risen to be the paragon of trend forecasting in the youth market. How?

When Sharon Lee needs to know what's cool, she taps into a network of experts the CIA would envy. It's a Web-linked weave of over 35,000 volunteers and part-timers, aged 14 to 35, recruited over several years at clubs and hangouts around the country, from New York to Los Angeles and points in between, to report on their world.

Look-Look's human database brims with youthful hipsters from all over the planet who log in to the company's Web site to answer surveys and polls, register opinions, and communicate ideas. Some of the recruits communicate through Look-Look–supplied digital or video cameras, from which they upload pictures, document reports, and post content to the firm's intranet message boards.

Some, such as Portland, Oregon's Emily Galash, receive small monthly sums—Emily's is $125 per month—for capturing and sharing the moments of their personal lives. Gordon and Lee welcome images from anything as private as underground parties to simple adornments like posters on bedroom walls.

Look-Look relies on "early adopters" and "influencers" to provide depth to information that traditional research practices only skim. For Look-Look, focus groups are strictly passé; such conventional tactics would not have raised its clients' awareness of incoming trends such as under-a-dollar stores, fold-up scooters, or over-the-shoulder bags. Strangely enough, however, Gordon and Lee and counterparts, such as Jane Buckingham's Intelligence Group, Irma Zandl's Zandl Group, and Faith Popcorn's BrainReserve, now run the risk of being out of date themselves.

Once known as "cool seekers or "cool hunters," they now prefer to refer to themselves as "futurists" and "planners." The Web-connected reality of instant digital feedback and content generation through blogs, text messages, and music, photo, and video hosting sites such as MySpace.com causes trends to flash before us and dissipate before most know they existed in the first place.

"Cool" isn't even cool anymore, and marketers to this age group must spot what's going to be "in" before or as it develops. Look-Look's success is well documented, however, and that's the reason companies like Telemundo, Procter & Gamble, Nike, Kellogg's, and Coca-Cola rely on its help to stay in the running for the $175 billion wielded by teen consumers.

Recently, Look-Look began working with Microsoft to tap into the culture of the twenty-first-century teenager. On a project designed to help the software giant's PC-gaming unit connect with the growing female presence in the video gaming market, Look-Look selected 30 teens from its database and asked them to keep blogs about their experiences with Microsoft PC games. Lisa Sikora, group product manager for Windows gaming, acknowledged Look-Look's relevance, noting that companies like hers need to "start talking to this audience in their way, not our way."

But Look-Look doesn't stop there. In addition to finding the future, Look-Look is defining it, too. Working with Virgin Mobile, an extremely youth-oriented marketer, Look-Look came up with two unique ideas. The first was to hold an art contest among members of its human database to devise cell phone covers. The top five designs, from artists aged 17 to 20 years old, are now officially sold in stores as covers for the Kyocera K10 Royale.

Remember Emily Galash? The money she earns is for the 30 to 40 pictures she sends to Look-Look every month. Instead of attempting to interpret her pictures for the sake of reporting on trends, Look-Look bolts select shots directly to the pages of Virgin

Mobile's internationally viewable Web site because they *are* trends. Amateur work like Emily's and that of the artists who designed the Kyocera face plates is valued because it maintains its authenticity, individuality, and credibility with its target audience.

Clients also ask Look-Look to identify which products are the hottest in a given market. After a small army is canvassed through online polls and surveys, the results are arranged into categories. "The turnaround," says Lee, "can be as little as 48 hours." Look-Look categorizes information into ten channels: fashion, entertainment, technology, activities, eating and drinking, health and beauty, mood of culture (how kids feel about life), spirituality, city guide, and Look Out (a "best of" findings in a snapshot). The information is put through rigorous paces. "Methodology is crucial, especially with the quantity and quality of the sample," says Lee. "We can take a sample of 300 or thousands. That's up to Gallup standards."

Still, cool is as hard to pin down as a weather forecast for next week. But the real arbiters of cool are those who can afford to lead. "Ultimately," says Que Gaskins, chief marketing officer of the avant-garde, multicultural marketing Ad*itive, "the future of cool belongs to whoever has the most buying power."[21]

Questions

1. Describe the role of the Internet in youth trend spotting. Do you think a research firm can accurately forecast youth trends without an online component to its research plan?

2. What is Look-Look offering businesses that traditional market research firms cannot offer?

3. Make a list of products or companies that you think could benefit from Look-Look's form of predictive market research. Next to each item, write a brief explanation of why and how you think cool seeking would benefit the company or product.

4. Go to Look-Look's Web site at **http://www.look-look.com** and check out some of the free information in each category. How accurate do you find the information? Have you seen any of these trends in your city or region, or among your friends and classmates?

COMPANY CLIPS

ReadyMade—Ready Research

Having been in business for five years, ReadyMade now has a lot of research on the various characteristics of its readers. Its knowledge of GenNesters has made the magazine a leader in identifying and describing that segment. As a new business, ReadyMade found that businesses had little interest in marketing to this group. Now that businesses have become more aware of GenNester influence, however, ReadyMade is able to fill the need for information. ReadyMade has statistics on the ages at which people are marrying and the interests of couples that have just married. Because the magazine is ahead of the curve on gathering information on this segment, ReadyMade can help other businesses figure out how to tailor their marketing efforts to fit the needs of GenNesters.

Questions

1. How has ReadyMade been able to help Toyota promote its new line of cars? What benefit has ReadyMade seen from the partnership?

2. How does ReadyMade use new technology to gain information about its consumers?

3. What sorts of long-term decisions is ReadyMade making that could be aided by research? What would you recommend?

BIZ FLIX

Apollo 13

Now that you have read about how critical information is to good marketing decision making, watch this clip from *Apollo 13*. This scene shows a crisis in space that the astronauts and mission control need to work out in order to avoid catastrophe. What evidence of a decision support system do you see in the clip? What kind of information do the astronauts use to assess their situation (akin to identifying the research problem)? Can you draw parallels between what you see in the clip and the job of a market researcher?

Higher scores indicates that you place greater importance on collecting primary and secondary information when developing marketing campaigns or projects. A lower score means you would be less aggressive in collecting information and might plow ahead regardless of how much information you do (or don't) have. After reading Chapter 8, you can see how involved gathering and analyzing market information can be, but also how critical it is to success.

Marketing Miscue

Has eBay Forgotten Its Faithful Followers?

By the time it celebrated its tenth anniversary in 2005, eBay had become a cultural phenomenon with a community of customers devoted to buying and selling online. Unfortunately for eBay however, this cultural phenomenon is no longer unique to the company, as online auction competitors have entered the marketplace.

eBay began as a weekend project for Pierre Omidyar and has evolved into one of the largest Internet companies. Based in San Jose, California, the company has approximately 61 million *active* users (almost 150 million *registered* users worldwide), with quarterly revenue topping $1 billion in the first quarter of 2005. Collectively, merchandise sold on eBay during 2004 amounted to around $34 billion.

In 2005, however, discontent erupted among eBay's sellers when the company announced rather steep fee increases. The changes affected all types of sellers. The monthly cost for store owners (the larger sellers) increased

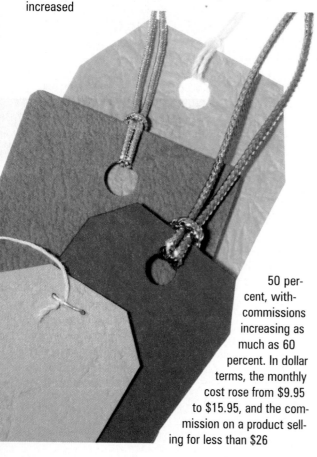

50 percent, with commissions increasing as much as 60 percent. In dollar terms, the monthly cost rose from $9.95 to $15.95, and the commission on a product selling for less than $26

increased from 5.25 percent to 8 percent. Under the new fee plan, individuals (the smaller sellers) would pay $0.35 for posting a thumbnail picture of a product, up from $0.25, and listing an item for a ten-day auction would cost $0.40, up from $0.20. Though these individual increases seemed relatively minor, the cost over hundreds or thousands of transactions for the sellers was considerable.

More interesting, however, is that the anger over the fee hike uncovered a growing discontent among sellers. Entrepreneurs expressed concern that the company was catering to the professional sellers (e.g., big-ticket electronics vendors and industrial manufacturers) and ignoring smaller home-based sellers who might also be enthusiasts or collectors. Yet it was these faithful enthusiasts who had helped eBay grow during its early years. In addition, sellers began grumbling about issues such as the receipt of automated messages when contacting the company, the lack of shopping carts to enable multiple purchases at the same time, the slowing growth in a market reaching maturity, and the company's hands-off approach to fraud. They complained that eBay was raising prices without attempting to increase traffic or provide better service.

Regardless of whether the fee hikes were warranted, the buzz instigated by the increases was an advantage to eBay's fledging competitors. Combined, Overstock, Yahoo, and Bidville have only 3.5 million items listed for sale at any given time. By comparison, eBay's listings amount to around 50 million items. Thus, even a small piece of eBay's business would be big business for the newcomers. Though not expecting users to defect from eBay entirely, these competitors are hoping that sellers will begin listing merchandise on multiple Web-based auction sites.

Company leaders at eBay were uncertain how many of its users were unhappy. Since the company was still growing, they knew that satisfied users outnumbered dissatisfied ones. Nevertheless, the company's earnings growth missed Wall Street expectations in the fourth quarter of 2004. Though the shortfall was only one penny, this was the first time in recent memory that eBay had fallen short. The company's stock, which had soared in 2003 and 2004, lost 19 percent of its value on the earnings news.[1] Had eBay only added salt to the wound by increasing fees and thereby generating more negative publicity for the firm?

Questions

1. How can eBay segment its market?

2. What type of market research does an online auction company need?

Critical Thinking Case

The Marketing Challenge at Lyon College

Lyon College (**http://www.lyon.edu**) is an independent, residential, coeducational, four-year undergraduate liberal arts college affiliated with the Presbyterian Church. Founded in 1872, it is the oldest independent college in Arkansas operating under its original charter. Situated on 136 acres in the scenic foothills of the Ozark Mountains, the college is located in Batesville, Arkansas. Batesville, which has 9,445 residents, is approximately 90 miles northeast of Little Rock (the state capital) and about 110 miles northwest of Memphis, Tennessee. A 2005 economic impact study conducted by EconImpact showed that Lyon College contributes $41 million annually to the economy of north central Arkansas. This includes $6.4 million in direct spending, $3.9 million in secondary spending, $19.2 million in increased alumni earnings, $10.5 million in social benefits, and $1.2 million in local government benefits.

Conferring the bachelor of arts and bachelor of science degrees, Lyon College offers majors in accounting, art, biology, business administration, chemistry, computer science, early childhood/elementary education, economics, English, environmental studies, history, mathematics, music, political science, psychology, religion and philosophy, Spanish, and theater. The college enrolls around 500 students from 20 states and 17 countries. The middle 50 percent of entering freshmen score between 21 and 28 on the American College Test (ACT), and 60 percent rank in the top quartile of their high school graduating class. Faculty members at the college are talented teachers and scholars. Over 90 percent of the full-time faculty hold a Ph.D. or other terminal degree appropriate to their field. In 2005, a Lyon College faculty member was named as Arkansas Professor of the Year. This was the twelfth time in 17 years that a Lyon College professor had received this honor from the Council for Advancement and Support of Education (CASE). This record is unmatched by any other liberal arts college in the country; no other Arkansas institution of higher learning has won more than four times.

Lyon regularly ranks among the nation's best liberal arts colleges in *U.S. News & World Report*'s annual list of "America's Best Colleges" (the list includes more than 200 liberal arts colleges that focus almost exclusively on offering bachelor degrees and award at least 50 percent of these degrees in the liberal arts). Heading the *U.S. News* list are institutions such as Williams College and Amherst College in Massachusetts and Swarthmore College in Pennsylvania. Joining Lyon in the third tier are institutions such as Eckerd College in Florida, Ogelthorpe University and Morehouse College in Georgia, Cornell College in Iowa, and Guilford College in North Carolina. Based on surveys of over 110,000 students at 360 colleges, Lyon was one of 140 schools receiving the "Best in the Southeast" designation from the *Princeton Review*.

The college has developed a long-term strategic plan, "The Strategic Plan for Lyon College: 2005–2010," that reaffirms its mission to offer a liberal arts education of superior quality in a personalized setting and envisions a time when the school will be recognized as one of the finest liberal arts colleges in the South. For the fall of 2006, the college's objective was to enroll 160 well-qualified freshman students. The college's recruiting has traditionally focused on the state of Arkansas and the adjoining six states (Louisiana, Mississippi, Missouri, Oklahoma, Tennessee, and Texas). These seven states were expected to have 485,000 high school graduates in 2006, with 30,000 of them in Arkansas. Of these 30,000 Arkansans, 18,000 were expected to attend college, and approximately one-half of them were likely to score over 21 on the ACT.

Typically, applicants to Lyon College apply to at least four other colleges or universities. Lyon's in-state public competitors include the University of Arkansas (Fayetteville), the University of Central Arkansas (Conway), and Arkansas State University (Jonesboro). Major private college competitors include Hendrix College (in Conway, Arkansas) and Rhodes College (in Memphis); both are considerably more expensive than Lyon. At $19,990 (tuition, room and board), Lyon is the fourth most expensive college in Arkansas, where the per capita income is $22,000. In choosing a college, high school graduates consider many factors including the college's size, location, and curriculum, and their own ability or willingness to pay the tuition. One issue the college faces in recruiting students is the interactive aspect of the college choice process. That is, the college knows that it has to target its prospects (future college students), but a multitude of influencers will affect a prospect's choice (parents, teachers, counselors, friends). Thus, for Lyon to meet its short-term recruitment goal as well as fulfill its longer-term vision, the college must distinguish itself from its competitors while developing lasting relationships with these multiple constituencies.[2]

Questions

1. Describe the consumer decision-making process employed in the college selection process.

2. How could Lyon College segment and reach its potential market(s)?

PART 3

Product Decisions

CROSSING FUNCTIONAL
LINES IN SPEEDING
PRODUCTS TO MARKET

Today's consumers have come to expect continual upgrades and improvements in products. This is especially true in the consumer electronics industry, where products such as the cell phone, MP3 player, and laptop computer must incorporate the latest technological innovations. This speed-to-market phenomenon is possible because companies are becoming more and more adept at integrating functions. This functional integration allows marketing, research and development, manufacturing, and finance/accounting to work simultaneously to develop and commercialize new and improved products.

The mantra of "move fast or lose out" is evident in companies such as Dell (which has cut the development time for notebook computers in half over the last decade) and Apple Computer (which has reduced the development time for its iPod from two years to eight months). In another example of simultaneous product development, Motorola moved from an engineering-focused company to a consumer-oriented company when it developed and introduced its Razr cell phone. The company listened to customers' desires for style and built a cool, trendy phone using its core foundation in engineering.

The Razr not only exemplified the possibilities created when functions work together in the product development phase, but it also helped Motorola usurp Nokia's position as the leading marketer of cell phones worldwide.

Historically, marketers focused on the company's products or services from a *demand-side* perspective. Through marketing research, marketers determined consumers' current and future wants and needs. Marketing then expected R&D to develop a device that would satisfy these wants and needs. The expectation then was that manufacturing would produce the device. The device became a true product with the development of a marketing program that added value in customers' minds.

The key to providing new and improved products quickly is a multidisciplinary approach to business.

On the flip side, the manufacturing and R&D departments have traditionally viewed products from a *supply-side* perspective. In this framework, new-product conception was the job of the R&D group for design, with the device then produced by the manufacturing group. The supply-side role of marketing was to entice the marketplace to want the product. From this perspective, marketing was the functional group that told the marketplace about the product's performance, but it had no input as to what actually went into the product or service.

R&D and manufacturing functional groups have become quite efficient at working together, using processes such as "design-factory fit," "concurrent engineering," "design for manufacturability and assembly," and "early manufacturing involvement." Basically, all of these concepts refer to advance linkage between a product's design and its manufacturing needs so that the manufacturing group will be ready to make the product once it has been designed. Companies have also focused on meeting "mass customization" and speed-to-market demands through "modularization."

A consumer-products company that has been extremely successful

with modularity is Build-A-Bear Workshops. Using modular components, the company (with simultaneous input from the customer) can construct a stuffed toy exactly to the customer's specifications and deliver it immediately to the customer. Though modularity might not seem at first to apply to stuffed animals, it enables the company to sell individually customized stuffed toys. In technical terms, modularity reduces the number of individual parts, allowing Build-A-Bear Workshop to quickly customize a product beyond the core architecture of a stuffed toy.

In today's fast-paced speed-to-market world, companies recognize the need to include all functions simultaneously in the process of developing new and improved products. These cross-functional integrative attempts have now spread even more widely in large corporations through cross-pollination. Cross-pollination brings together various units within a company to develop a new product by utilizing expertise across the company. For example, Gillette's new M3Power is the result of collaboration among the company's razor unit, its Duracell battery unit, and its Braun small-appliance division.

The key to providing new and improved products quickly is a multidisciplinary approach to business. Marketplace demands of immediacy and customization have focused attention on marketing, R&D, and manufacturing. Traditionally, products were conceptualized by one function, given to another function to produce, and then handed over to another function to sell. In a speed-to-market world, however, time-based competition in providing new products has done away with such a linear product development process. Now, the expectation is that the final product is of high quality and has moved through the company's functional processes in half the time required for the traditional linear process. Today's marketplace is increasingly demanding that companies compete on both time and customization.

Questions

1. What are some of the popular business terms used to describe cross-functional integration?

2. How is cross-functional integration different from cross-pollination?

Product Concepts

© BEN MARGOT/ASSOCIATED PRESS
© BART SADOWSKI/ISTOCKPHOTO INTERNATIONAL INC.

CHAPTER

9

Learning Outcomes

LO¹ Define the term *product*

LO² Classify consumer products

LO³ Define the terms *product item, product line,* and *product mix*

LO⁴ Describe marketing uses of branding

LO⁵ Describe marketing uses of packaging and labeling

LO⁶ Discuss global issues in branding and packaging

LO⁷ Describe how and why product warranties are important marketing tools

how could **eBay** extend its brand?

Once a brand is successfully established, the company may consider extending the brand to other products. Vivaldi Partners, a New York marketing consulting firm, surveyed more than 4,500 consumers about their perceptions of brand extension opportunities for 20 growth brands. The survey asked consumers whether they thought a particular brand could move into many different categories, as well as which specific products might be appropriate extensions. At the head of the list was eBay, which 66 percent of the study participants felt had many different expansion opportunities. In second place was Amazon.com.

The table shows the top 10 brands mentioned and the product categories that consumers thought would be a good fit for extending the brand.[1]

Once a brand is successfully established, the company may consider extending the brand to other products.

Rank	Brand	Expansion Opportunities
1	eBay	Dating network, loans, skills swapping
2	Amazon.com	Airline tickets, groceries, financial products, concert tickets
3	Samsung	Electric cars, alarm systems, gaming consoles, cell phone service
4	Whole Foods	High-end restaurants, cookware, culinary college, organic apparel
5	Google	Dating network, children's toys, video games, instant messenger
6	Yahoo!	Banking, cell phone service, coffeehouses, Yahoo! brand clothing
7	Apple Computer	Cell phones, car stereos, televisions
8	Nike	Sports drinks, trips/tours, jeans
9	Coach	Home decor, children's apparel, jackets
10	Victoria's Secret	Bags, beauty service, bath towels

SOURCE: Vivaldi Partners.

Do you think the products consumers chose represent good brand expansion opportunities? Why or why not?

What Is a Product?

The product offering, the heart of an organization's marketing program, is usually the starting point in creating a marketing mix. A marketing manager cannot determine a price, design a promotion strategy, or create a distribution channel until the firm has a product to sell. Moreover, an excellent distribution channel, a persuasive promotion campaign, and a fair price have no value when the product offering is poor or inadequate.

A **product** may be defined as everything, both favorable and unfavorable, that a person receives in an exchange. A product may be a tangible good like a pair of shoes, a service like a haircut, an idea like "don't litter," or any combination of these three. Packaging, style, color, options, and size are some typical product features. Just as important are intangibles such as service, the seller's image, the manufacturer's reputation, and the way consumers believe others will view the product.

To most people, the term *product* means a tangible good. However, services and ideas are also products. (Chapter 11 focuses specifically on the unique aspects of marketing services.) The marketing process identified in Chapter 1 is the same whether the product marketed is a good, a service, an idea, or some combination of these.

REVIEW LEARNING OUTCOME

LO¹ Define the term *product*

Product

Good
Service
Idea

LO²

Types of Consumer Products

Products can be classified as either business (industrial) or consumer products, depending on the buyer's intentions. The key distinction between the two types of products is their intended use. If the intended use is a business purpose, the product is classified as a business or industrial product. As explained in Chapter 6, a **business product** is used to manufacture other goods or services, to facilitate an organization's operations, or to resell to other customers. A **consumer product** is bought to satisfy an individual's personal wants. Sometimes the same item can be classified as either a business or a consumer product, depending on its intended use. Examples include lightbulbs, pencils and paper, and computers.

We need to know about product classifications because business and consumer products are marketed differently. They are marketed to different target markets and tend to use different distribution, promotion, and pricing strategies.

Chapter 6 examined seven categories of business products: major equipment, accessory equipment, component parts, processed materials, raw materials, supplies, and services. The current chapter examines an effective way of categorizing consumer products. Although there are several ways to classify them, the most popular approach includes these four types: convenience products, shopping products, specialty products, and unsought products (see Exhibit 9.1). This approach classifies products according to how much effort is normally used to shop for them.

CONVENIENCE PRODUCTS

A **convenience product** is a relatively inexpensive item that merits little shopping effort—that is, a consumer is unwilling to shop extensively for such an item. Candy, soft drinks, combs, aspirin, small hardware items, dry cleaning, and car washes fall into the convenience product category.

product
Everything, both favorable and unfavorable, that a person receives in an exchange.

business product (industrial product)
A product used to manufacture other goods or services, to facilitate an organization's operations, or to resell to other customers.

consumer product
A product bought to satisfy an individual's personal wants.

convenience product
A relatively inexpensive item that merits little shopping effort.

Exhibit 9.1

Classification of Consumer Products

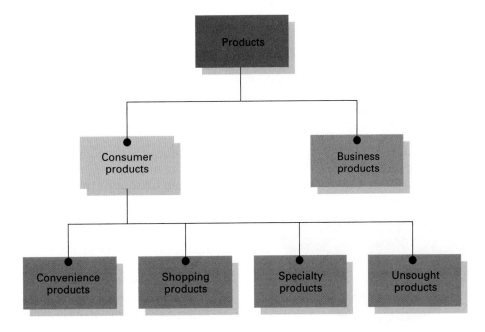

```
                           Products
                              |
              +---------------+----------------+
              |                                |
         Consumer                          Business
         products                          products
              |
     +--------+--------+--------+--------+
     |        |        |        |
Convenience  Shopping  Specialty  Unsought
 products    products  products   products
```

Consumers buy convenience products regularly, usually without much planning. Nevertheless, consumers do know the brand names of popular convenience products, such as Coca-Cola, Bayer aspirin, and Right Guard deodorant. Convenience products normally require wide distribution in order to sell sufficient quantities to meet profit goals. For example, the gum Dentyne Ice is available everywhere, including Wal-Mart, Walgreens, Shell gas stations, newsstands, and vending machines.

SHOPPING PRODUCTS

A **shopping product** is usually more expensive than a convenience product and is found in fewer stores. Consumers usually buy a shopping product only after comparing several brands or stores on style, practicality, price, and lifestyle compatibility. They are willing to invest some effort into this process to get the desired benefits.

There are two types of shopping products: homogeneous and heterogeneous. Consumers perceive *homogeneous* shopping products as basically similar—for example, washers, dryers, refrigerators, and televisions. With homogeneous shopping products, consumers typically look for the lowest-priced brand that has the desired features. For example, they might compare Kenmore, Whirlpool, and General Electric refrigerators.

In contrast, consumers perceive *heterogeneous* shopping products as essentially different—for example, furniture, clothing, housing, and universities. Consumers often have trouble comparing heterogeneous shopping products because the prices, quality, and features vary so much. The benefit of comparing heterogeneous shopping products is "finding the best product or brand for me"; this decision is often highly individual. For example, it would be difficult to compare a small, private university with a large, public university.

SPECIALTY PRODUCTS

When consumers search extensively for a particular item and are very reluctant to accept substitutes, that item is a **specialty product**. Rolex watches, Rolls Royce automobiles, Bose speakers, Ruth's Chris Steak House, and highly specialized forms of medical care are generally considered specialty products.

shopping product
A product that requires comparison shopping because it is usually more expensive than a convenience product and is found in fewer stores.

specialty product
A particular item that consumers search extensively for and are very reluctant to accept substitutes.

© MARK STOKES/ISTOCKPHOTO INTERNATIONAL INC.

PRODUCT CONCEPTS

CHAPTER 9

285

LO 2 Classify consumer products

Marketers of specialty products often use selective, status-conscious advertising to maintain their product's exclusive image. Distribution is often limited to one or a very few outlets in a geographic area. Brand names and quality of service are often very important.

UNSOUGHT PRODUCTS

A product unknown to the potential buyer or a known product that the buyer does not actively seek is referred to as an **unsought product**. New products fall into this category until advertising and distribution increase consumer awareness of them.

Some goods are always marketed as unsought items, especially needed products we do not like to think about or care to spend money on. Insurance, burial plots, encyclopedias, and similar items require aggressive personal selling and highly persuasive advertising. Salespeople actively seek leads to potential buyers. Because consumers usually do not seek out this type of product, the company must go directly to them through a salesperson, direct mail, or direct-response advertising.

LO 3
Product Items, Lines, and Mixes

Rarely does a company sell a single product. More often, it sells a variety of things. A **product item** is a specific version of a product that can be designated as a distinct offering among an organization's products. Campbell's Cream of Chicken soup is an example of a product item (see Exhibit 9.2).

A group of closely related product items is a **product line**. For example, the column in Exhibit 9.2 titled "Soups" represents one of Campbell's product lines. Different container sizes and shapes also distinguish items in a product line. Diet Coke, for example, is available in cans and various plastic containers. Each size and each container are separate product items.

An organization's **product mix** includes all the products it sells. Together, all of Campbell's products—soups, sauces, frozen entrées, beverages, and biscuits—constitute its product mix. Each product item in the product mix may require a separate marketing strategy. In some cases, however, product lines and even entire product mixes share some marketing strategy components. Nike promoted all of its product items and lines with the theme "Just Do It."

Organizations derive several benefits from organizing related items into product lines, including the following:

- *Advertising economies:* Product lines provide economies of scale in advertising. Several products can be advertised under the umbrella of the line. Campbell's can talk about its soup being "m-m-good" and promote the entire line.

- *Package uniformity:* A product line can benefit from package uniformity. All packages in the line may have a common look and still keep their individual identities. Again, Campbell's soup is a good example.

- *Standardized components:* Product lines allow firms to standardize components, thus reducing manufacturing and inventory costs. For example, many of the components Samsonite uses in its folding tables and chairs are also used in its patio furniture. General Motors uses the same parts on many automobile makes and models.

unsought product
A product unknown to the potential buyer or a known product that the buyer does not actively seek.

product item
A specific version of a product that can be designated as a distinct offering among an organization's products.

product line
A group of closely related product items.

product mix
All products that an organization sells.

- *Efficient sales and distribution:* A product line enables sales personnel for companies like Procter & Gamble to provide a full range of choices to customers. Distributors and retailers are often more inclined to stock the company's products if it offers a full line. Transportation and warehousing costs are likely to be lower for a product line than for a collection of individual items.

- *Equivalent quality:* Purchasers usually expect and believe that all products in a line are about equal in quality. Consumers expect that all Campbell's soups and all Mary Kay cosmetics will be of similar quality.

Product mix width (or breadth) refers to the number of product lines an organization offers. In Exhibit 9.2, for example, the width of Campbell's product mix is five product lines. **Product line depth** is the number of product items in a product line. As shown in Exhibit 9.2, the sauces product line consists of four product items; the frozen entrée product line includes three product items.

Firms increase the *width* of their product mix to diversify risk. To generate sales and boost profits, firms spread risk across many product lines rather than depend on only one or two. Firms also widen their product mix to capitalize on established reputations. The Oreo Cookie brand has been extended to include items such as breakfast cereal, ice cream, Jell-O pudding, and cake mix.

Firms increase the *depth* of their product lines to attract buyers with different preferences, to increase sales and profits by further segmenting the market, to capitalize on economies of scale in production and marketing, and to even out seasonal sales patterns. Procter & Gamble is adding some lower-priced versions of its namesake brands, including Bounty Basic and Charmin Basic. These brands are targeted to more price-sensitive customers, a segment that P&G had not been serving with its more premium brands.[2] As another example, Oreo Cookies now come in a variety of flavors, including Double Delight Mint Creme, Chocolate Creme, Uh-Oh Oreos (vanilla cookie, chocolate filling), and Double Delight Peanut Butter and Chocolate.

Exhibit 9.2
Campbells Product Lines and Product Mix

	Width of the Product Mix				
	Soups	Sauces	Frozen Entrées	Beverages	Biscuits
Depth of the Product Lines	Cream of Chicken	Mild Cheese	Chicken á la King	Tomato Juice	Arnott's:
	Cream of Mushroom	Alfredo	Beef Stew	V-8 Juice	Water Cracker
	Vegetable Beef	Italian Tomato	Chicken Lasagna	V-8 Splash	Butternut Snap
	Chicken Noodle	Marinara			Chocolate Chip
	Tomato				Fruit Oat
	Bean with Bacon				White Fudge
	Minestrone				
	Clam Chowder				
	French Onion				
	more . . .				

ADJUSTMENTS TO PRODUCT ITEMS, LINES, AND MIXES

Over time, firms change product items, lines, and mixes to take advantage of new technical or product developments or to respond to changes in the environment. They may adjust by modifying products, repositioning products, or extending or contracting product lines.

Product Modification

Marketing managers must decide if and when to modify existing products. **Product modification** changes one or more of a product's characteristics:

- *Quality modification:* change in a product's dependability or durability. Reducing a product's quality may let the manufacturer lower the price and appeal to target markets unable to afford the original product. Conversely, increasing quality can help the firm compete with rival firms. Increasing quality can also result in

product mix width
The number of product lines an organization offers.

product line depth
The number of product items in a product line.

product modification
Changing one or more of a product's characteristics.

EVERY KID GOES THROUGH STAGES. FORTUNATELY, SO DO OUR NEW BRUSHES.

INTRODUCING NEW
Oral-B
Stages

Oral-B's Stages toothbrushes represent a functional modification to adult toothbrushes. Numerous colors and designs of a single-stage toothbrush would be a style modification.

increased brand loyalty, greater ability to raise prices, or new opportunities for market segmentation. Inexpensive ink-jet printers have improved in quality to the point that they produce photo-quality images. These printers are now competing with camera film. To appeal to a more upscale market, Robert Mondavi Winery introduced a high-end wine called Twin Oaks to prestigious restaurants and hotels. This wine is positioned as a higher-quality wine than the one Mondavi sells in supermarkets.

- *Functional modification:* change in a product's versatility, effectiveness, convenience, or safety. Tide with Downy combines the functions of cleaning power and fabric softening into one product. Lea & Perrins offers its steak sauce in a value-priced squeeze bottle with a "no mess, stay clean" cap.

- *Style modification:* aesthetic product change, rather than a quality or functional change. Procter & Gamble has added Febreze scents to its Tide liquid laundry detergent, Downy liquid fabric softener, and Bounce dryer sheets. These products all promise their usual function, with a touch of scent to improve the aesthetics of each brand.[3] Clothing and auto manufacturers also commonly use style modifications to motivate customers to replace products before they are worn out. **Planned obsolescence** is a term commonly used to describe the practice of modifying products so that those that have already been sold become obsolete before they actually need replacement. Some argue that planned obsolescence is wasteful; some claim it is unethical. Marketers respond that consumers favor style modifications because they like changes in the appearance of goods like clothing and cars. Marketers also contend that consumers, not manufacturers and marketers, decide when styles are obsolete.

Repositioning

Repositioning, as Chapter 7 explained, involves changing consumers' perceptions of a brand. A promotion by the Diamond Trading Company, a division of De Beers, encouraged women to buy their own "right-hand" diamonds. The company wanted to reposition its diamond rings as an expression of a woman's individuality and style, rather than a symbol of love and commitment.[4]

Changing demographics, declining sales, or changes in the social environment often motivate firms to reposition established brands. The clothing retailer Banana Republic started out selling safari-style clothing, but the concept soon became outdated. Gap acquired the chain and repositioned it as a more upscale retailer offering business casual clothing. Research told Hormel that consumers ages 18 to 35 were familiar with the Spam brand, but were put off by the inconvenience and negative image of the can it had traditionally come in. In response, Hormel changed Spam's packaging to a high-tech foil pouch that contains single slices in an effort to appeal to these younger consumers with active lifestyles.[5]

Product Line Extensions

A **product line extension** occurs when a company's management decides to add products to an existing product line in order to compete more broadly in the industry. Coca-Cola has developed a brand extension for Diet Coke that is designed to appeal to men ages 18 to 34 who want a lower-calorie drink, but see Diet Coke as a woman's drink.[6] Kraft has extended a number of its popular Nabisco brands by adding small-portioned packages. Targeted to people with active lifestyles, the packages each offer a portion providing 100 calories, zero to three grams of fat, and zero grams of trans fat.[7] Johnson & Johnson expanded its Viactiv

planned obsolescence
The practice of modifying products so those that have already been sold become obsolete before they actually need replacement.

product line extension
Adding additional products to an existing product line in order to compete more broadly in the industry.

line of soft calcium chews by adding a multivitamin product targeted to women.[8]

Product Line Contraction

Does the world really need 31 varieties of Head and Shoulders shampoo? Or 52 versions of Crest? Or poultry and seafood from Heinz? Heinz has decided the answer is no. The company is deleting a number of product lines, such as vegetables, poultry, frozen foods, and seafood, so that it can concentrate on the products it sells best: ketchup, sauces, frozen snacks, and baby food.[9] Symptoms of product line overextension include the following:

- Some products in the line do not contribute to profits because of low sales or because they cannibalize sales of other items in the line.

- Manufacturing or marketing resources are disproportionately allocated to slow-moving products.

- Some items in the line are obsolete because of new product entries in the line or new products offered by competitors.

Three major benefits are likely when a firm contracts overextended product lines. First, resources become concentrated on the most important products. Second, managers no longer waste resources trying to improve the sales and profits of poorly performing products. Third, new product items have a greater chance of being successful because more financial and human resources are available to manage them.

kate spade
NEW YORK

NEW YORK   HONG KONG   TOKYO   SAN FRANCISCO   CHICAGO
SHOP KATESPADE.COM

Adding new products to an existing line helps companies create variety and compete more broadly in their industries. This Kate Spade advertisement depicts a diverse collection of shoes and purses.

REVIEW LEARNING OUTCOME

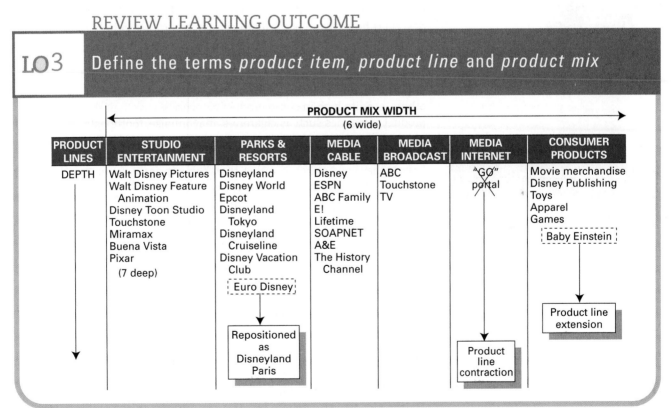

LO3   Define the terms *product item*, *product line* and *product mix*

PRODUCT LINES	STUDIO ENTERTAINMENT	PARKS & RESORTS	MEDIA CABLE	MEDIA BROADCAST	MEDIA INTERNET	CONSUMER PRODUCTS
DEPTH	Walt Disney Pictures Walt Disney Feature Animation Disney Toon Studio Touchstone Miramax Buena Vista Pixar (7 deep)	Disneyland Disney World Epcot Disneyland Tokyo Disneyland Cruiseline Disney Vacation Club Euro Disney Repositioned as Disneyland Paris	Disney ESPN ABC Family E! Lifetime SOAPNET A&E The History Channel	ABC Touchstone TV	"GO" portal Product line contraction	Movie merchandise Disney Publishing Toys Apparel Games Baby Einstein Product line extension

PRODUCT MIX WIDTH (6 wide)

LO⁴ Branding

The success of any business or consumer product depends in part on the target market's ability to distinguish one product from another. Branding is the main tool marketers use to distinguish their products from the competition's.

A **brand** is a name, term, symbol, design, or combination thereof that identifies a seller's products and differentiates them from competitors' products. A **brand name** is that part of a brand that can be spoken, including letters (GM, YMCA), words (Chevrolet), and numbers (WD-40, 7-Eleven). The elements of a brand that cannot be spoken are called the **brand mark**—for example, the well-known Mercedes-Benz and Delta Air Lines symbols.

BENEFITS OF BRANDING

Branding has three main purposes: product identification, repeat sales, and new-product sales. The most important purpose is *product identification*. Branding allows marketers to distinguish their products from all others. Many brand names are familiar to consumers and indicate quality.

The term **brand equity** refers to the value of company and brand names. A brand that has high awareness, perceived quality, and brand loyalty among customers has high brand equity. Starbucks, Volvo, and Dell are companies with high brand equity. A brand with strong brand equity is a valuable asset.

The term **global brand** has been used to refer to brands where at least 20 percent of the product is sold outside the home country or region. Exhibit 9.3 lists the top five global brands, and the top five North American brands. Yum! Brands, which owns Pizza Hut, KFC, and Taco Bell, is a good example of a company that has developed strong global brands. Yum believes that it has to adapt its restaurants to local tastes and different cultural and political climates. In Japan, for instance, KFC sells tempura crispy strips. In northern England, KFC focuses on gravy and potatoes, and in Thailand it offers rice with soy or sweet chili sauce. Sometimes a company attempts to change consumers' attitudes as well as adapting its product. This chapter's "Global Perspectives" box describes how Nestlé is trying to change traditions in Italy in order to sell more bottled water.

The best generator of *repeat sales* is satisfied customers. Branding helps consumers identify products they wish to buy again and avoid those they do not. **Brand loyalty,** a consistent preference for one brand over all others, is quite high in some product categories. Over half the users in product categories such as cigarettes, mayonnaise, toothpaste, coffee, headache remedies, photographic film, bath soap, and ketchup are loyal to one brand. Many students come to college and purchase the same brands they used at home, rather than being "price" buyers. Brand identity is essential to developing brand loyalty.

The third main purpose of branding is to *facilitate new-product sales.* Company and brand names like those listed in Exhibit 9.3 are extremely useful when introducing new products.

The Internet provides firms a new alternative for generating brand awareness, promoting a desired brand image, stimulating new and repeat brand sales, and enhancing brand loyalty and building brand equity. Nearly all packaged-goods firms have a presence online. Tide.com offers a useful feature called Stain Detective, a digital tip sheet on how to remove almost any substance from almost any fabric.

BRANDING STRATEGIES

Firms face complex branding decisions. As Exhibit 9.4 illustrates, the first decision is whether to brand at all. Some firms actually use the lack of a brand name as a selling

modern furnishings for loft, apartment, home.

©B2

a new destination from Crate and Barrel. in chicago: 800 w. north ave [312.787.8329] and 3757 n. lincoln ave [773.755.3900]. cb2.com. tripod lamp 169. zoom chair 499. dolcor table 149. accessories 2.95 to 39.95.

© CB2

Crate and Barrel has established CB2 in order to appeal to urban consumers. This advertisement identifies the new brand as a supplier of modern furniture and accessories.

brand
A name, term, symbol, design, or combination thereof that identifies a seller's products and differentiates them from competitors' products.

brand name
That part of a brand that can be spoken, including letters, words, and numbers.

brand mark
The elements of a brand that cannot be spoken.

brand equity
The value of company and brand names.

global brand
A brand where at least 20 percent of the product is sold outside its home country or region.

brand loyalty
A consistent preference for one brand over all others.

Persuading Italians to Drink Water on the Go

Nestlé's bottled water is among the top five international brands of bottled water in volume of sales and is sold in 35 countries. More than 90 percent of Nestlé's water sales occur in North America and Europe.

Italians have the highest average annual consumption of bottled water in the world. Although the tap water in Italy is drinkable, Italians prefer bottled water, and about 265 different brands of bottled water are available there. Nevertheless, Italians do not drink their bottled water on the go. Instead, they buy large bottles of water to serve at meals. Italian mothers tell their children that eating and drinking while walking can cause indigestion and that it's bad manners to eat or drink anywhere but at the table. Even if Italians wanted to drink bottled water on the street, they would have difficulty finding it. Although bottled water can be purchased in bars or at kiosks near tourist attractions such as the Colosseum in Rome, it isn't widely available on the street. Strict licensing laws restrict sales of food or drinks at places like newsstands.

Now Nestlé is trying to grow its market in Italy by changing these long-standing traditions. It has developed a marketing strategy designed to get Italian consumers to drink water on the go.

The company started its campaign with Acqua Panna, a brand aimed at women. Television ads featured a fashionable cartoon character named Lulu who carries a purse containing Acqua Panna in a squeezable hourglass-shaped bottle, called Panna 75. The bottle has a newly designed membrane top created by Nestlé to prevent water from leaking into a leather handbag. The ads show the bottle tipped over to demonstrate that it doesn't leak. Nestlé also hired apparel designer Roberto Cavalli to create a limited edition label for the water, and a small plastic purse that he designed to hold Panna 75 was given out at one of his fashion shows in Milan. Finally, to encourage Italians to drink water outdoors, Nestlé managers organize pickup soccer games and aerobic sessions on Italian beaches. Of course, Nestlé bottled water is passed around at all these events.

With these efforts, Nestlé increased its share of the $3 billion Italian water market to 29 percent in 2004, up from 25.8 percent in 2003. Almost all of the increase was due to sales of water in smaller, more portable bottles.[10]

Do you think that Nestlé should try to change deep-seated Italian habits in order to sell more drinking water? Explain your answer.

---

point. These unbranded products are called generic products. Firms that decide to brand their products may choose to follow a policy of using manufacturers' brands, private (distributor) brands, or both. In either case, they must then decide among a policy of individual branding (different brands for different products), family branding (common names for different products), or a combination of individual branding and family branding.

Generic Products versus Branded Products

generic product
A no-frills, no-brand-name, low-cost product that is simply identified by its product category.

A **generic product** is typically a no-frills, no-brand-name, low-cost product that is simply identified by its product category. (Note that a generic product and a brand name that becomes generic, such as cellophane, are not the same thing.)

Exhibit 9.3

The Top Five Global and North American Brands

Global	North American
1. Apple	1. Apple
2. Google	2. Google
3. IKEA	3. Target
4. Starbucks	4. Starbucks
5. Al Jazeera	5. Pixar

SOURCE: Deborah L. Vence, "*Not Taking Care of Business,*" *Marketing News,* March 15, 2005, p. 19.

Exhibit 9.4

Major Branding Decisions

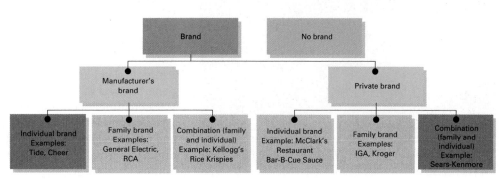

The main appeal of generics is their low price. Generic grocery products are usually 30 to 40 percent less expensive than manufacturers' brands in the same product category and 20 to 25 percent less expensive than retailer-owned brands.

Pharmaceuticals are an example of a product category where generics have made large inroads. When patents on successful pharmaceutical products expire, low-cost generics rapidly appear on the market. For example, when the patent on Merck's popular antiarthritis drug Clinoril expired, sales declined by 50 percent almost immediately.

Manufacturers' Brands versus Private Brands

The brand name of a manufacturer—such as Kodak, La-Z-Boy, and Fruit of the Loom—is called a **manufacturer's brand**. Sometimes "national brand" is used as a synonym for "manufacturer's brand." This term is not always accurate, however, because many manufacturers serve only regional markets. Using "manufacturer's brand" more precisely defines the brand's owner.

A **private brand**, also known as a private label or store brand, is a brand name owned by a wholesaler or a retailer. Private brands include Wal-Mart's Ol' Roy dog food, which has surpassed Nestlé's Purina as the world's top-selling dog food, and the George line of apparel, which has knocked Liz Claiborne's clothing out of Wal-Mart. Private labels and products made exclusively by retailers account for one of every five items sold in the United States, representing more than $50 billion in annual sales.[11] An A. C. Nielsen 2005 online survey found that more than two-thirds of global customers think private-label products are a good alternative to other brands, that they are an extremely good value, and that they offer quality at least as good as that of major manufacturers' brands.[12] At JCPenney, 40 percent of sales come from private-label brands.[13] Staples is adding several hundred private-branded products every year; in 2004, they accounted for 15 percent of the company's sales. Staples is unusual in that it is developing its own products rather than just putting its name on existing ones.[14]

Retailers love consumers' greater acceptance of private brands. Because overhead is low and there are no marketing costs, private-label products bring 10 percent higher margins, on average, than manufacturers' brands. More than that, a trusted store brand can differentiate a chain from its competitors. For example, many shoppers will drive the extra mile to Costco, a wholesale club, to buy the store's Kirkland brands and will also buy other goods while they are there.[15] Exhibit 9.5 illustrates key issues that wholesalers and retailers should consider in deciding whether to sell manufacturers' brands or private brands. Many firms offer a combination of both. Competition from private brands is causing some manufacturers' brands to more aggressively protect their trademarks and brand equity. In the first quarter of 2006, Procter & Gamble filed four lawsuits against various private-label companies, accusing them of trademark infringement, false advertising, and unfair competition. P&G claims the companies have been knocking off the packaging of popular P&G brands, like Pantene, Head and Shoulders, and Crest, which each generate over $1 billion in annual sales for P&G. With U.S. consumer spending on private-label personal care products growing faster than sales of private-label food and beverage, it's no wonder that P&G is responding vigorously to private brands that knockoff its successful brands.[16]

striped rugby shirt $24.99
cherry-print pleated skirt $29.99
yellow canvas bag $34.99

leather bomber jacket $149.99
neck tie shirt $19.99
patched denim miniskirt $24.99

short-sleeve polo $16.99
strapless dress $39.99

style selection varies by store.

wear is luella?

London-based Luella Bartley brings her cool Brit fashions to Target...
and at prices that are sure to please all you thieving fashionistas.

© TARGET CORPORATION

EXPECT MORE. PAY LESS.

Branding products from cutting-edge designers, like Luella Bartley, has contributed to Target's success as an upscale discount retailer. Here, Target advertises an exclusive line of designer clothing that it has established as a private brand.

Exhibit 9.5
Comparing Manufacturers' and Private Brands from the Reseller's Perspective

Key Advantages of Carrying Manufacturers' Brands	Key Advantages of Carrying Private Brands
• Heavy advertising to the consumer by manufacturers like Procter & Gamble helps develop strong consumer loyalties.	• A wholesaler or retailer can usually earn higher profits on its own brand. In addition, because the private brand is exclusive, there is less pressure to mark the price down to meet competition.
• Well-known manufacturers' brands, such as Kodak and Fisher-Price, can attract new customers and enhance the dealer's (wholesaler's or retailer's) prestige.	• A manufacturer can decide to drop a brand or a reseller at any time or even to become a direct competitor to its dealers.
• Many manufacturers offer rapid delivery, enabling the dealer to carry less inventory.	• A private brand ties the customer to the wholesaler or retailer. A person who wants a Die-Hard battery must go to Sears.
• If a dealer happens to sell a manufacturer's brand of poor quality, the customer may simply switch brands and remain loyal to the dealer.	• Wholesalers and retailers have no control over the intensity of distribution of manufacturers' brands. Wal-Mart store managers don't have to worry about competing with other sellers of Sam's American Choice products or Ol' Roy dog food. They know that these brands are sold only in Wal-Mart and Sam's Wholesale Club stores.

Individual Brands versus Family Brands

individual branding
Using different brand names for different products.

family brand
Marketing several different products under the same brand name.

cobranding
Placing two or more brand names on a product or its package.

Many companies use different brand names for different products, a practice referred to as **individual branding**. Companies use individual brands when their products vary greatly in use or performance. For instance, it would not make sense to use the same brand name for a pair of dress socks and a baseball bat. Procter & Gamble targets different segments of the laundry detergent market with Bold, Cheer, Dash, Dreft, Era, Gain, Ivory Snow, Oxydol, Solo, and Tide. Marriott International also targets different market segments with Courtyard by Marriott, Residence Inn, and Fairfield Inn.

In contrast, a company that markets several different products under the same brand name is using a **family brand**. Sony's family brand includes radios, television sets, stereos, and other electronic products. A brand name can only be stretched so far, however. Do you know the differences among Holiday Inn, Holiday Inn Express, Holiday Inn Select, Holiday Inn Sunspree Resort, Holiday Inn Garden Court, and Holiday Inn Hotel & Suites? Neither do most travelers.

Cobranding

Cobranding entails placing two or more brand names on a product or its package. Three common types of cobranding are ingredient branding, cooperative branding, and complementary branding. *Ingredient branding* identifies the brand of a part that makes up the product. Examples of ingredient branding are Intel (a microprocessor) in a personal computer, such as Dell, or a satellite radio (XM) in an automobile (Cadillac). *Cooperative branding* occurs when two brands receiving equal treatment (in the context of an advertisement) borrow from each other's brand equity. A promotional contest jointly sponsored by Ramada Inns, American Express, and Continental Airlines is an example of cooperative branding. Guests at Ramada who paid with an American Express card were automatically entered in the contest and were eligible to win more than a hundred getaways for two at any Ramada in the continental United States and round-trip airfare from Continental. Finally, with *complementary branding*, products are advertised or marketed together to suggest usage, such as a spirits brand (Seagram's) and a compatible mixer (7-Up).

Cobranding is a useful strategy when a combination of brand names enhances the prestige or perceived value of a product or when it benefits brand owners and users. When Intel launched its Centrino wireless processor, it established cobranding relationships with T-Mobile and hotel chains Marriott International and Westin Hotels & Resorts because there was mutual value in establishing these relationships. T-Mobile was able to set up global "hot spots" to

The cobranded shoes in this advertisement feature both Bathing Ape and Marvel Comics brand names. This arrangement helps Marvel Comics to branch out and establish a market share in the shoe industry and Bathing Ape to increase the number of shoe designs it offers.

PRODUCT CONCEPTS

CHAPTER 9

reach Intel's target market of mobile professionals, while the hotel chains enabled Intel to target business professionals.[17] Yum! Brands leads in volume for retail franchise cobranding concepts. This company has a mix of KFCs and Taco Bells, KFCs and A&Ws, Taco Bells and Long John Silver's, and Pizza Huts and WingStreets.[18]

Cobranding may be used to increase a company's presence in markets where it has little or no market share. For example, Coach was able to build a presence in a whole new category when its leather upholstery with logo was used in Lexus automobiles.[19]

European firms have been slower to adopt cobranding than U.S. firms have. One reason is that European customers seem to be more skeptical than U.S. customers about trying new brands. European retailers also typically have less shelf space than their U.S. counterparts and are less willing to give new brands a try.

TRADEMARKS

A **trademark** is the exclusive right to use a brand or part of a brand. Others are prohibited from using the brand without permission. A **service mark** performs the same function for services, such as H&R Block and Weight Watchers. Parts of a brand or other product identification may qualify for trademark protection. Some examples are

- Shapes, such as the Jeep front grille and the Coca-Cola bottle

- Ornamental color or design, such as the decoration on Nike tennis shoes, the black-and-copper color combination of a Duracell battery, Levi's small tag on the left side of the rear pocket of its jeans, or the cutoff black cone on the top of Cross pens

- Catchy phrases, such as Prudential's "Own a piece of the rock," Merrill Lynch's "We're bullish on America," and Budweiser's "This Bud's for you"

- Abbreviations, such as Bud, Coke, or The Met

- Sounds, such as General Electric Broadcasting Company's ship's bell clock sound and the MGM lion's roar.

It is important to understand that trademark rights come from use rather than registration. A company must have a genuine intention to use a trademark when it files an intent-to-use application with the U.S. Patent and Trademark Office and must actually use the mark within three years of the application being granted. Trademark protection typically lasts for ten years.[20] To renew the trademark, the company must prove it is using the mark. Rights to a trademark last as long as the mark is used. Normally, if the firm does not use it for two years, the trademark is considered abandoned, and a new user can claim exclusive ownership of it.

In November 1999, legislation went into effect that explicitly applies trademark law to the online world. This law includes financial penalties for those who violate trademarked products or register an otherwise trademarked term as a domain name.

Companies that fail to protect their trademarks face the possibility that their product names will become generic. A **generic product name** identifies a product by class or type and cannot be trademarked. Former brand names that were not sufficiently protected by their owners and were subsequently declared to be generic product names by U.S. courts include aspirin, cellophane, linoleum, thermos, kerosene, monopoly, cola, and shredded wheat.

Companies like Rolls Royce, Cross, Xerox, Levi Strauss, Frigidaire, and McDonald's aggressively enforce their trademarks. Rolls Royce, Coca-Cola, and Xerox even run newspaper and magazine ads stating that their names are trademarks and should not be used as descriptive or generic terms. Some ads threaten lawsuits against competitors that violate trademarks.

trademark
The exclusive right to use a brand or part of a brand.

service mark
A trademark for a service.

generic product name
Identifies a product by class or type and cannot be trademarked.

LO4 Describe marketing uses of branding

Brand name: MGM

Brand mark:

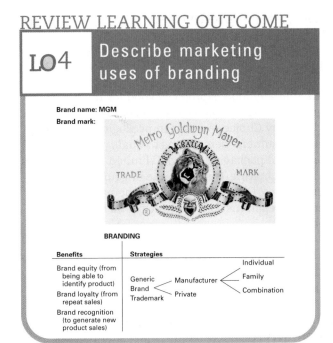

BRANDING

Benefits	Strategies	
Brand equity (from being able to identify product)	Generic Brand Trademark ‹ Manufacturer ‹ Private	Individual Family Combination
Brand loyalty (from repeat sales)		
Brand recognition (to generate new product sales)		

Despite severe penalties for trademark violations, trademark infringement lawsuits are not uncommon. One of the major battles is over brand names that closely resemble another brand name. Donna Karan filed a lawsuit against Donnkenny, Inc., whose Nasdaq trading symbol—DNKY—was too close to Karan's DKNY trademark.

Companies must also contend with fake or unauthorized brands, such as fake Levi's jeans, Microsoft software, Rolex watches, Reebok and Nike footwear, and Louis Vuitton handbags. Knockoffs of Burberry's trademarked tan, black, white, and red plaid are easy to find in cheap shops all over the world, and loose imitations are found in some reputable department stores as well. One Web site sells a line of plaid bags, hats, and shoes that it says are "inspired by Burberry." Burberry says it spends a couple million pounds a year running ads in trade publications and sending letters to trade groups, textile manufacturers, and retailers reminding them about its trademark rights. It also works with customs officials and local law enforcement to seize fakes, sues infringers, and scans the Internet to pick up online chatter about counterfeits.[21]

In Europe, you can sue counterfeiters only if your brand, logo, or trademark is formally registered. Until recently, formal registration was required in each country in which a company sought protection. A company can now register its trademark in all European Union (EU) member countries with one application.

LO5
Packaging

Packages have always served a practical function—that is, they hold contents together and protect goods as they move through the distribution channel. Today, however, packaging is also a container for promoting the product and making it easier and safer to use.

PACKAGING FUNCTIONS

The three most important functions of packaging are to contain and protect products, promote products, and facilitate the storage, use, and convenience of products. A fourth function of packaging that is becoming increasingly important is to facilitate recycling and reduce environmental damage.

Containing and Protecting Products

The most obvious function of packaging is to contain products that are liquid, granular, or otherwise divisible. Packaging also enables manufacturers, wholesalers, and retailers to market products in specific quantities, such as ounces.

Physical protection is another obvious function of packaging. Most products are handled several times between the time they are manufactured, harvested, or otherwise produced and the time they are consumed or used. Many products are shipped, stored, and inspected several times between production and consumption. Some, like milk, need to be refrigerated. Others, like beer, are sensitive to light. Still others, like medicines and bandages, need to be kept sterile. Packages protect products from breakage, evaporation, spillage, spoilage, light, heat, cold, infestation, and many other conditions.

Promoting Products

Packaging does more than identify the brand, list the ingredients, specify features, and give directions. A package differentiates a product from competing products and may associate a new product with a family of other products from the same manufacturer.

Welch's repackaged its line of grape juice–based jams, jellies, and juices to unify the line and get more impact on the shelf.

Packages use designs, colors, shapes, and materials to try to influence consumers' perceptions and buying behavior. For example, marketing research shows that health-conscious consumers are likely to think that any food is probably good for them as long as it comes in green packaging. Two top brands of low-fat foods—SnackWell's and Healthy Choice—use green packaging. Packaging can also influence consumers' perceptions of quality and/or prestige. Nestlé is using gold packaging to signal limited-edition flavors for some items in its Signature Treasures line of gourmet candy.[22]

Packaging has a measurable effect on sales. Quaker Oats revised the package for Rice-a-Roni without making any other changes in marketing strategy and experienced a 44 percent increase in sales in one year.

Facilitating Storage, Use, and Convenience

Wholesalers and retailers prefer packages that are easy to ship, store, and stock on shelves. They also like packages that protect products, prevent spoilage or breakage, and extend the product's shelf life.

Consumers' requirements for storage, use, and convenience cover many dimensions. Consumers are constantly seeking items that are easy to handle, open, and reclose, although some consumers want packages that are tamperproof or childproof. Research indicates that hard-to-open packages are among consumers' top complaints.[23] Surveys conducted by *Sales & Marketing Management* magazine revealed that consumers dislike—and avoid buying—leaky ice cream boxes, overly heavy or fat vinegar bottles, immovable pry-up lids on glass bottles, key-opener sardine cans, and hard-to-pour cereal boxes. Such packaging innovations as zipper tear strips, hinged lids, tab slots, screw-on tops, and pour spouts were introduced to solve these and other problems. Nestlé is making an effort to improve all its packaging to make it easier for people to rip open its pouches, twist off its caps, and reseal its tubs. Easy openings are especially important for kids and aging baby boomers. The company's package designers spent nine months developing a plastic lid for ice cream that is easier to pull off when the ice cream is frozen and ribbed corners for ice cream cartons that are easier to grip when scooping.[24]

Some firms use packaging to segment markets. For example, a C&H sugar carton with an easy-to-pour, reclosable top is targeted to consumers who don't do a lot of baking and are willing to pay at least 20 cents more for the package. Different-size packages appeal to heavy, moderate, and light users. Salt is sold in package sizes ranging from single serving to picnic size to giant economy size. Campbell's soup is packaged in single-serving cans aimed at the elderly and singles market segments. Beer and soft drinks are similarly marketed in various package sizes and types. Packaging convenience can increase a product's utility and, therefore, its market share and profits. To appeal to women, Dutch Boy designed a square plastic paint container with a side handle and a spout to replace the traditional wire-handled round metal paint can. Women make up a large part of the interior paint customer base, thanks to popular do-it-yourself television programs, such as *Decorating Cents* and *Trading Spaces*.[25]

The Internet will soon give consumers more packaging options. Indeed, the Internet may significantly change the purpose and appearance of packaging. Packaging for products sold on the Internet will be more under the customer's control and will be customized by consumers to fit their needs. Some designers are already offering to personalize, for a fee, packages such as wine bottle labels.

Facilitating Recycling and Reducing Environmental Damage

One of the most important packaging issues today is compatibility with the environment. Some firms use their packaging to target environmentally concerned market segments. Brocato International markets shampoo and hair conditioner in bottles that are biodegradable in landfills. Procter & Gamble markets Sure Pro and Old Spice in "eco-friendly" pump-spray packages that do not rely on aerosol propellants. Other firms that

persuasive labeling
A type of package labeling that focuses on a promotional theme or logo with consumer information being secondary.

informational labeling
A type of package labeling designed to help consumers make proper product selections and lower their cognitive dissonance after the purchase.

universal product codes (UPCs)
A series of thick and thin vertical lines (bar codes), readable by computerized optical scanners, that represent numbers used to track products.

Now lunch at work can make you feel right at home.

Introducing Progresso® Microwavable Bowls, in six delicious flavors.

Wherever you are, a taste of the good life. **PROGRESSO**

The soup featured in this advertisement is packaged in both persuasive and informational labeling. The familiar Progresso logo and the word "new!" persuade consumers to try the product, while the nutrition facts and heating instructions on the other side of the can provide basic information.

have introduced pump sprays include S.C. Johnson (Pledge furniture polish) and Reckitt Benckiser Household Products (Woolite rug cleaner).

Food and Drug Administration
Just what does the label on your snack foods have to say? What about your makeup? Go to the Food and Drug Administration's Web site to read the exact requirements for labeling various products. Pick a product and report back to the class.

http://www.fda.gov

Online

LABELING

An integral part of any package is its label. Labeling generally takes one of two forms: persuasive or informational. **Persuasive labeling** focuses on a promotional theme or logo, and consumer information is secondary. Price Pfister developed a new, persuasive label—featuring a picture of a faucet, the brand name, and the logo—with the goal of strengthening brand identity and becoming known as a brand instead of as a manufacturer. Note that the standard promotional claims—such as "new," "improved," and "super"—are no longer very persuasive. Consumers have been saturated with "newness" and thus discount these claims.

Informational labeling, in contrast, is designed to help consumers make proper product selections and lower their cognitive dissonance after the purchase. Sears attaches a "label of confidence" to all its floor coverings. This label gives such product information as durability, color, features, cleanability, care instructions, and construction standards. Most major furniture manufacturers affix labels to their wares that explain the products' construction features, such as type of frame, number of coils, and fabric characteristics. The Nutritional Labeling and Education Act of 1990 mandated detailed nutritional information on most food packages and standards for health claims on food packaging. An important outcome of this legislation has been guidelines from the Food and Drug Administration for using terms like *low fat, light, reduced cholesterol, low sodium, low calorie,* and *fresh.*

UNIVERSAL PRODUCT CODES

The **universal product codes (UPCs)** that appear on most items in supermarkets and other high-volume outlets were first introduced in 1974. Because the numerical codes appear as a series of thick and thin vertical lines, they are often called *bar codes.* The lines are read by computerized optical scanners that match codes with brand names, package sizes, and prices. They also print information on cash register tapes and help retailers rapidly and accurately prepare records of customer purchases, control inventories, and track sales. The UPC system and scanners are also used in single-source research (see Chapter 8).

REVIEW LEARNING OUTCOME

LO5 Describe marketing uses of packaging and labeling

PACKAGING FUNCTIONS:
containing and protecting products
promoting products
facilitating storage, use, and convenience
facilitating recycling and disposal

PERSUASIVE LABELING

NOW Even More **RICE CRUNCH** with **marshmallow balls**

Nutrition Info
%
%
%
Sugar 10g
Fiber 2g
Carb 3g
Protein 9g
Ingredients

INFORMATIONAL LABELING

UPC

24 oz. 1 gram ©Distribution

LO⁶
Global Issues in Branding and Packaging

International marketers must address several concerns regarding branding and packaging.

BRANDING

When planning to enter a foreign market with an existing product, a firm has three options for handling the brand name:

Hugo enjoys fame in more than 40 countries and is one of the strongest global brands in children's entertainment. Orion has the exclusive license to distribute Hugo in the U.S.

- *One brand name everywhere:* This strategy is useful when the company markets mainly one product and the brand name does not have negative connotations in any local market. The Coca-Cola Company uses a one-brand-name strategy in 195 countries around the world. The advantages of a one-brand-name strategy are greater identification of the product from market to market and ease of coordinating promotion from market to market.

- *Adaptations and modifications:* A one-brand-name strategy is not possible when the name cannot be pronounced in the local language, when the brand name is owned by someone else, or when the brand name has a negative or vulgar connotation in the local language. The Iranian detergent "Barf," for example, might encounter some problems in the U.S. market.

- *Different brand names in different markets:* Local brand names are often used when translation or pronunciation problems occur, when the marketer wants the brand to appear to be a local brand, or when regulations require localization. Gillette's Silkience hair conditioner is called Soyance in France and Sientel in Italy. The adaptations were deemed to be more appealing in the local markets. Coca-Cola's Sprite brand had to be renamed Kin in Korea to satisfy a government prohibition on the unnecessary use of foreign words. Because of the feminine connotations of the word *diet*, the European version of Diet Coke is Coca Cola Light.²⁶

PACKAGING

Three aspects of packaging that are especially important in international marketing are labeling, aesthetics, and climate considerations. The major *labeling* concern is properly translating ingredient, promotional, and instructional information on labels. In Eastern Europe, packages of Ariel detergent are printed in 14 languages, from Latvian to Lithuanian. Care must also be employed in meeting all local labeling requirements. Several years ago, an Italian judge ordered that all bottles of Coca-Cola be removed from retail shelves because the ingredients were not properly labeled. Labeling is also harder in countries like Belgium and Finland, which require it to be bilingual.

Package *aesthetics* may also require some attention. The key is to stay attuned to cultural traits in host countries. For example, colors may have different connotations. Red is associated with witchcraft in some countries, green may be a sign of danger, and white may be symbolic of death. Aesthetics also influence package size. Soft drinks are not sold in six-packs in countries that lack refrigeration. In some countries, products like detergent may be bought only in small quantities because of a lack of storage space. Other products, like cigarettes, may be bought in small quantities, and even single units, because of the low purchasing power of buyers.

On the other hand, simple visual elements of the brand, such as a symbol or logo, can be a standardizing element across products and countries. For example, in Mexico,

LO 6 — Discuss global issues in branding and packaging

Branding choices:	Packaging considerations:
1 name	Labeling
Modify or adapt 1 name	Aesthetics
Different names in different markets	Climate

Lay's potato chips are known as Sabritas, but the packaging carries the same brand mark and graphic elements as in the United States.[27]

Extreme *climates* and long-distance shipping necessitate sturdier and more durable packages for goods sold overseas. Spillage, spoilage, and breakage are all more important concerns when products are shipped long distances or frequently handled during shipping and storage. Packages may also have to ensure a longer product life if the time between production and consumption lengthens significantly.

LO 7 — Product Warranties

warranty
A confirmation of the quality or performance of a good or service.

express warranty
A written guarantee.

implied warranty
An unwritten guarantee that the good or service is fit for the purpose for which it was sold.

Just as a package is designed to protect the product, a **warranty** protects the buyer and gives essential information about the product. A warranty confirms the quality or performance of a good or service. An **express warranty** is a written guarantee. Express warranties range from simple statements—such as "100 percent cotton" (a guarantee of quality) and "complete satisfaction guaranteed" (a statement of performance)—to extensive documents written in technical language. In contrast, an **implied warranty** is an unwritten guarantee that the good or service is fit for the purpose for which it was sold. All sales have an implied warranty under the Uniform Commercial Code.

Congress passed the Magnuson-Moss Warranty–Federal Trade Commission Improvement Act in 1975 to help consumers understand warranties and get action from manufacturers and dealers. A manufacturer that promises a full warranty must meet certain minimum standards, including repair "within a reasonable time and without charge" of any defects and replacement of the merchandise or a full refund if the product does not work "after a reasonable number of attempts" at repair. Any warranty that does not live up to this tough prescription must be "conspicuously" promoted as a limited warranty.

LO 7 — Describe how and why product warranties are important marketing tools

Express warranty	=	written guarantee
Implied warranty	=	unwritten guarantee

Review and Applications

LO 1 Define the term *product*. A product is anything, desired or not, that a person or organization receives in an exchange. The basic goal of purchasing decisions is to receive the tangible and intangible benefits associated with a product. Tangible aspects include packaging, style, color, size, and features. Intangible qualities include service, the retailer's image, the manufacturer's reputation, and the social status associated with a product. An organization's product offering is the crucial element in any marketing mix.

1.1 Form a team of four or five members. Have the team determine what the tangible and intangible benefits are for a computer, a tube of toothpaste, a beauty salon, and a dentist.

Quick Check

Now that you've read the chapter, do you get it? Take a moment for a quick check using this scale:

1 Not at all; 2 Not very well; 3 Ok; 4 Well; 5 Very Well

Can you...

___ explain the relationship between product items, product lines, and product mixes?

___ give the rationale behind organizing products into product lines?

___ explain how companies adjust product items, lines, and mixes?

___ draw a diagram depicting the product line depth and the product mix width for your favorite company or brand?

___ identify multiple branding strategies and explain why a marketer would choose each?

___ explain the difference between a brand and a trademark?

___ identify the various ways to cobrand products?

___ list the functions of product packaging?

___ write a paragraph comparing persuasive and informational labeling—and give examples of each?

___ tell a friend the difference between an implied and an express warranty?

___ **TOTAL**

Score: 41–50, you're ready to move on to the applications; 31–40, skim the chapter one more time before moving on to the applications; 21–30, reread the sections giving you the most trouble and go to Thomson NOW for guided tutorials; 20 and under, you better reread the chapter to get a grasp of the fundamentals. If you've reread the chapter and still have a low score, visit your professor or TA during office hours.

LO² Classify consumer products. Consumer products are classified into four categories: convenience products, shopping products, specialty products, and unsought products. Convenience products are relatively inexpensive and require limited shopping effort. Shopping products are of two types: homogeneous and heterogeneous. Because of the similarity of homogeneous products, they are differentiated mainly by price and features. In contrast, heterogeneous products appeal to consumers because of their distinct characteristics. Specialty products possess unique benefits that are highly desirable to certain customers. Finally, unsought products are either new products or products that require aggressive selling because they are generally avoided or overlooked by consumers.

2.1 Break into groups of four or five. Have the members of the group classify each of the following products into the category (convenience, shopping, specialty, unsought) that they think fits best from their perspective as consumers (i.e., if they were buying the product): Coca-Cola (brand), car stereo, winter coat, pair of shoes, life insurance, blue jeans, fast-food hamburgers, shampoo, canned vegetables, curtains.

2.2 Although major appliances, like washers and dryers, are usually considered homogeneous shopping products, the high-efficiency, front-loaders that boast many more features than standard machines are gaining in popularity. Do you think high-efficiency technology is enough to make washers and dryers heterogeneous shopping products? Explain.

LO³ Define the terms *product item, product line,* and *product mix.* A product item is a specific version of a product that can be designated as a distinct offering among an organization's products. A product line is a group of closely related products offered by an organization. An organization's product mix includes all the products it sells. Product mix width refers to the number of product lines an organization offers. Product line depth is the number of product items in a product line. Firms modify existing products by changing their quality, functional characteristics, or style. Product line extension occurs when a firm adds new products to existing product lines.

3.1 A local civic organization has asked you to give a luncheon presentation about planned obsolescence. Rather than pursuing a negative approach by talking about how businesses exploit customers through planned obsolescence, you have decided to talk about the benefits of producing products that do not last forever. Prepare a one-page outline of your presentation.

3.2 Go to Unilever's Web site at **http://www.unilever.com.** Can Unilever delete anything from its product lines? Visit the company's product category pages on its "Brands" Web page to see the number of existing products and new products planned. Write a proposal for contracting one of Unilever's product lines.

LO4 Describe marketing uses of branding. A brand is a name, term, or symbol that identifies and differentiates a firm's products. Established brands encourage customer loyalty and help new products succeed. Branding strategies require decisions about individual, family, manufacturers', and private brands.

4.1 A local supermarket would like to introduce its own brand of paper goods (i.e., paper towels, facial tissue, etc.) to sell alongside its current inventory. The company has hired you to generate a report outlining the advantages and disadvantages of doing so. Write the report.

4.2 How does Hormel use its Web site (**http://www.hormel.com**) to promote its store brands? Is the site designed more to promote the company or its brands? Check out the Spam Web site at **http://www.spam.com**. How do you think Hormel is able to successfully sustain this brand that is often the punch line to a joke?

LO5 Describe marketing uses of packaging and labeling. Packaging has four functions: containing and protecting products; promoting products; facilitating product storage, use, and convenience; and facilitating recycling and reducing environmental damage. As a tool for promotion, packaging identifies the brand and its features. It also serves the critical function of differentiating a product from competing products and linking it with related products from the same manufacturer. The label is an integral part of the package, with persuasive and informational functions. In essence, the package is the marketer's last chance to influence buyers before they make a purchase decision.

5.1 Find a product at home that has a distinctive package. Write a paragraph evaluating that package based on the four functions of packaging discussed in the chapter.

LO6 Discuss global issues in branding and packaging. In addition to brand piracy, international marketers must address a variety of concerns regarding branding and packaging, including choosing a brand-name policy, translating labels and meeting host-country labeling requirements, making packages aesthetically compatible with host-country cultures, and offering the sizes of packages preferred in host countries.

6.1 List the countries to which Levi Strauss & Co. markets through the Web site **http://www.levi.com**. How do the product offerings differ between the U.S. and European selections?

LO7 Describe how and why product warranties are important marketing tools. Product warranties are important tools because they offer consumers protection and help them gauge product quality.

7.1 Lands' End and L.L. Bean are renowned for their product guarantees. Find and read the exact wording of their guarantees on their Web sites (**http://www.landsend.com** and **http://www.llbean.com**). Do you think a company could successfully compete against either without offering the same guarantee?

Key Terms

Exercises

APPLICATION EXERCISE

What is your favorite brand of sandwich cookie? If you're like most Americans, chances are it's Oreo. In fact, Oreos are so popular that many people think Oreo was the original sandwich cookie. But they're wrong. Sunshine first marketed its Hydrox sandwich cookie in 1908. Hydrox thrived until 1912, when Nabisco (now part of Kraft) launched Oreo. With Nabisco's superior distribution and advertising, Hydrox was soon out-matched. By 1998, Hydrox sales totaled $16 million, while Oreo's revenues were at $374 million. Hydrox has been purchased by Keebler (subsequently purchased by Kellogg), whose elves are trying to give the cookie a major facelift. You are part of the Keebler team deciding what to do with the Hydrox brand.[28]

Activities

1. Can you re-create Hydrox through a name change? What kind of brand name could go head-to-head with Oreo? (Most people unfamiliar with Hydrox think it is a cleaning product.) Make a list of three to five possibilities.

2. How can you package your renewed sandwich cookie to make it more attractive on the shelf than Oreo? What about package size? Draft a brief packaging plan for the new Hydrox (or whatever name you chose).

3. Can you modify the original formula to make something new and more competitive? Will a brand extension work here? Why or why not?

Entrepreneurship Case

FINALLY, A GARAGE BAND THAT REALLY ROCKS

Steve Jobs's keynote address at the 2004 MacWorld conference was roundly criticized for being blasé and void of any exciting new developments. It did, however, have one major and perhaps easily overlooked bright spot—the unveiling of the latest version of Apple's iLife software. The standard suite of iLife products includes the popular and much heralded iTunes music management software, as well as a digital photograph manipulator and organizer called iPhoto, a digital video-editing program named iMovie, and a DVD mastering program called iDVD. The big news at MacWorld was that Apple has added a new program to iLife '04 called GarageBand. Complete with GarageBand, iLife '04 comes free on all new Apple computers and is available as an upgrade to own-ers of older systems for a mere $49.

That $49 buys more than a thousand prerecorded Apple loops (or riffs), over 50 vir-tual instruments, and a virtual recording engineer (which performs over 200 effects). Put simply, GarageBand helps any aspiring musician or hobbyist compose music, and all of those features turn any owner's computer into a pretty substantial home recording studio. Whether the musician needs a drumbeat to back up an external electric guitar for a jam session or a full range of orchestral instruments to provide the background to a keyboard solo, GarageBand makes sure that all selected loops come together on time and in key. The user can even manipulate loops to create an entire song without using any instruments at all. The loops are royalty-free, so new songwriters don't have to worry about paying licensing fees to loop creators if they happen to make the next Hip Hop chart topper.

The software provides a synthesizer-like keyboard that displays on the screen for those who wish to play the plethora of virtual instruments via their computer keyboards, but plugging in an external keyboard allows the aspiring or accomplished musician to seriously expand his or her range. Whether the user selects a Stratocaster guitar, a Steinway piano, a pop organ, or a big-band bass from the library of virtual instruments, the keyboard assumes its identity. Any notes or chords played on it will produce the exact sounds that would emulate from the original version of the virtual instrument. To the delight of guitar players, GarageBand also offers virtual amplifiers that allow them to extract the sounds of the British invasion, arena rock, or cool jazz from their axes.

GarageBand comes with a vast array of effects that composers can apply to their arrangements, too. Loops and any recorded pieces can be faded, reverberated, brightened, echoed, compressed, or tweaked in any number of ways to obtain just the right sound. When masterpieces are finished, GarageBand automatically exports them to iTunes where they are filed in a play list under the composer's name. The program also integrates new compositions with the rest of the iLife programs so that users can match soundtracks to their slide shows and movies. In fact, the programs are so well integrated that Apple is advertising them as "just like Microsoft Office, for the rest of your life."

GarageBand is the latest push by Jobs and Apple to make its computers the hubs of digital home entertainment centers. Unlike iTunes, GarageBand is compatible only with Apple computers. Jobs is betting that with an active musician in one of every two U.S. households, GarageBand will draw a virtually untapped market of more than a hundred million amateur musicians to Apple computers. Considering that iTunes' music store owns 70 percent of the legal music download market and that the iPod is the best-selling digital music playback device, that bet looks like a sound one.[29]

Questions

1. Is GarageBand a new product or a modification of an existing product? If it is a modification, what type of modification is it? Explain.

2. What type of product is GarageBand?

3. To which of Apple's product lines does GarageBand belong?

COMPANY CLIPS

Kodak—Reinventing the Brand

Unquestionably, Kodak is one of most recognized brands in the United States and the world. For over a century, Kodak was known as the company that brought the technology of photography into the everyday, aptly summed up in the tag line, "Celebrate the Moments of Your Life." Grocery stores, convenient stores, and camera stores contained aisles full of little yellow boxes of Kodak film in every possible speed. But after Kodak invented the digital camera, the company was faced with the challenge of leveraging the equity of its brand in new competitive market—one that didn't include film.

Questions

1. Using Exhibit 9.1 as a guide, create a diagram that organizes the Kodak products mentioned in the video. How are changes in the company's product mix necessitating changes to the way managers market Kodak's offerings?

2. List the attributes of the Kodak brand. What benefits of branding has the company experienced over time? Have there been pitfalls to having a brand with such strong associations?

3. Describe the functions of packaging of a disposable camera.

BIZ FLIX

Josie and the Pussycats

JOSIE AND THE PUSSYCATS/CORBIS

Now that you understand product concepts, watch the clip from *Josie and the Pussycats*, a film based on the cartoon show and comic book. A little-known, teen rock and roll trio, "The Pussycats," gets an unexpected career boost from a record executive who embeds subliminal advertising into the group's recordings. The fiendish executive plans to use the altered recordings to control the minds, product choices, and spending habits of the nation's teenagers.

The edited scene is a montage of many different product placements throughout the film. As you watch the clip the first time, try to remember all the brands you see. Do some appear more than once? Even if you can't see what's in the shopping bags, can you make assumptions about the types of products they contain (i.e., convenience, shopping, specialty, unsought)? How well do the brands in the clip match what you perceive to be the wants and needs of teenagers?

Marketing &You Results

A higher score on this scale indicates that you are very brand conscious when you shop. You prefer to buy brands that are nationally known rather than private brands or generic brands. Conversely, a lower score suggests that you are not so brand conscious and tend to choose lower-priced, lesser-known brands.

Developing and

Managing Products

Learning Outcomes

LO¹ Explain the importance of developing new products and describe the six categories of new products

LO² Explain the steps in the new-product development process

LO³ Explain why some products succeed and others fail

LO⁴ Discuss global issues in new-product development

LO⁵ Explain the diffusion process through which new products are adopted

LO⁶ Explain the concept of product life cycles

© R. ALCORN/THOMSON

Procter & Gamble *extends a brand by sweeping up*

When Robert Godfroid, a senior scientist for Procter & Gamble's Swiffer brand, started visiting consumers' homes in 2003, he was looking for anything disagreeable or inconvenient. "We wanted to know what tasks they found unpleasant," he says. He watched carefully as consumers cleaned the floor, dusted their furniture, and vacuumed the carpet. He scattered dirt around their living room rugs to see how they would deal with it.

Godfroid was hoping to find a way to

The new product is the seventh major Swiffer brand extension since the initial mop was introduced.

push the popular Swiffer mop, which comes in four varieties, onto carpets. According to P&G, roughly 75 percent of America's floors are covered with carpet, but Swiffer, which was introduced as a dry mop in 1999, worked on hard floors only. So just as early Swiffer efforts centered on replacing a traditional mop and bucket, Godfroid's job was to find a way to sideline the traditional vacuum.

After 22 months of research on what irritates consumers about vacuuming, P&G introduced a cordless carpet sweeper. The Swiffer CarpetFlick is designed to clean up small patches of dirt on carpets so that consumers won't have to drag out their traditional vacuum cleaners for small jobs. P&G hopes its new contraption can extend the run of the Swiffer brand.

The new CarpetFlick resembles an old-fashioned manual sweeper but operates on a different principle. The plastic on the base of the CarpetFlick pushes down on dirt and then flicks the particles up through an opening in the sweeper into a cavity containing a sticky adhesive sheet that captures the debris. P&G says the mechanism is similar to the one used in the game Tiddlywinks. Like other Swiffer products, the adhesive is disposable and replaceable. The suggested retail price is $12.99, with replacement adhesives priced at $4.29 for a pack of six.

The new Swiffer has a window that allows people to see how much dirt is stuck to the adhesive sheet, but the window is tinted orange so the refuse won't be too visible. "They don't like that nasty bagful of dirt," that comes with a traditional vacuum cleaner, says Godfroid. "But at the same time they want to see the dirt because it is a signal that they are getting the floor clean."

The new product is the seventh major Swiffer brand extension since the initial mop was introduced. P&G will have to guard against knockoffs from competitors, which have already been adept at mimicking Swiffer products. Clorox's ReadyMop and S.C. Johnson's Pledge Grab-it quickly followed Swiffer's original market launch.[1]

Do you think the Swiffer CarpetFlick is a new product? Why or why not? What do you think about the way P&G came up with the idea for the Swiffer CarpetFlick? What are the strengths and weaknesses of this approach?

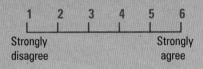

Marketing & You

Using the following scale, indicate your opinion on the line before each item.

1	2	3	4	5	6

Strongly disagree — Strongly agree

____ I like introducing new brands and products to my friends.

____ I like helping people by providing them with information about many kinds of products.

____ People ask me for information about products, places to shop, or sales.

____ If someone asked where to get the best buy on several types of products, I could tell him or her where to shop.

____ My friends think of me as a good source of information when it comes to new products or sales.

____ I know a lot of different products, stores, and sales, and I like sharing this information.

Total your score. Read the chapter and find out what your score means at the end.

The Importance of New Products

New products are important to sustain growth, increase revenues and profits, and replace obsolete items. "There is tremendous pressure on industry to innovate more, and do it more quickly," notes the director of IBM's 200-engineer Zurich Research Laboratory.[2] According to a Boston Consulting Group survey of senior executives, more than two-thirds cite innovation as a priority, but 57 percent are dissatisfied with the returns they get on their innovation investments.[3] No wonder! According to Doblin Group innovation consultants, the overall innovation initiative success rate is a dismal 4.5 percent.[4] Companies that do a particularly good job at product innovation include Apple, 3M, Microsoft, General Electric, and Sony.[5] The average fast-moving consumer goods company introduces 70 to 80 new products per year.[6] PepsiCo introduced over 200 new products in one recent year. Kellogg introduced over 100 in the first half of 2004. For both PepsiCo and Kellogg, the percentage of sales from new products far exceeds their respective industry average.[7]

© LYSOL/PRNEWSFOTO (AP TOPIC GALLERY)

New product lines are a type of new product that allows a company to enter an established market. With its Ready Brush toilet cleaning system, Lysol is entering the market for cleaning tools (toilet brushes, sponges, mops, etc.), which is dominated by companies like Ocello and Quickie.

CATEGORIES OF NEW PRODUCTS

The term **new product** is somewhat confusing because its meaning varies widely. Actually, the term has several "correct" definitions. A product can be new to the world, to the market, to the producer or seller, or to some combination of these. There are six categories of new products:

- *New-to-the-world products* (also called *discontinuous innovations*): These products create an entirely new market. Ten of the most important new-to-the-world products introduced in the past 100 years are:[8]

  1. Penicillin
  2. Transistor radio
  3. Polio vaccine
  4. Mosaic (the first graphic Web browser)
  5. Microprocessor
  6. Black-and-white television
  7. Plain paper copier
  8. Alto personal computer (prototype of today's PCs)
  9. Microwave oven
  10. Arpanet network (the groundwork for the Internet)

  New-to-the-world products represent the smallest category of new products.

- *New product lines:* These products, which the firm has not previously offered, allow it to enter an established market. After Procter & Gamble purchased Iams pet food brand, worldwide sales doubled and profits tripled. The brand moved from the fifth best-selling pet food brand in the United States to the top spot in less than five years.[9]

- *Additions to existing product lines:* This category includes new products that supplement a firm's established line. Examples of product line additions include Huggies Pull-Ups and Pampers Easy-Ups brands of disposable training pants and Pampers Kandoo wipes and other personal-care products for kids.

new product
A product new to the world, the market, the producer, the seller, or some combination of these.

- *Improvements or revisions of existing products*: The "new and improved" product may be significantly or slightly changed. Gillette's Fusion and Fusion Power razors are examples of product improvements. New formulations of Tide such as Tide With Bleach, Tide Free (which has no fragrance), Tide Wear Care (that purports to keep fabrics vibrant longer), and Tide With Bleach Powder are also examples of improvements or revisions of existing products. Another type of revision is package improvement. The Heinz EZ Squirt Ketchup bottle is short and made from easy-to-squeeze plastic; its needle-shaped nozzle lets small hands use it to decorate food. Tide Kick's package includes a nozzle so that detergent can be rubbed directly into a stain. Most new products fit into the revision or improvement category.

- *Repositioned products*: These are existing products targeted at new markets or market segments. General Motors has done the seemingly impossible with Cadillac, taking a tired, defeated luxury brand two decades past its peak and repositioning it as a direct competitor to European brands such as BMW and Lexus.[10] Cadillac Escalade sport-utility vehicles and CTS sedans are showing up in Miami's trendy South Beach district and similar locations. The average age of Cadillac buyers has dropped from 64 to 59. The new XLR, SRX, and STS models are all aimed at a younger, "hipper" target market.[11]

- *Lower-priced products*: This category refers to products that provide performance similar to competing brands at a lower price. Hewlett-Packard Laser Jet 3100 is a scanner, copier, printer, and fax machine combined. This new product is priced lower than many conventional color copiers and much lower than the combined price of the four items purchased separately. Wal-Mart is making headway penetrating the low-price fashion market dominated by Target.

REVIEW LEARNING OUTCOME

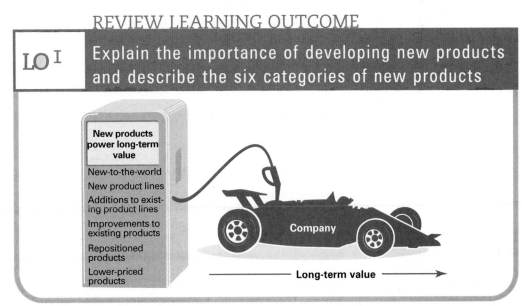

LO¹ Explain the importance of developing new products and describe the six categories of new products

New products power long-term value
- New-to-the-world
- New product lines
- Additions to existing product lines
- Improvements to existing products
- Repositioned products
- Lower-priced products

Company

Long-term value →

LO²
The New-Product Development Process

The management consulting firm Booz, Allen, & Hamilton has studied the new-product development process for over 30 years. After analyzing five major studies undertaken during this period, the firm concluded that the companies most likely to succeed in developing and introducing new products are those that take the following actions:

- Make the long-term commitment needed to support innovation and new-product development.

- Use a company-specific approach, driven by corporate objectives and strategies, with a well-defined new-product strategy at its core.

Exhibit 10.1

**New-Product Development
Process**

1 New-product strategy

2 Idea generation

3 Idea screening

4 Business analysis

5 Development

6 Test marketing

7 Commercialization

New product

- Capitalize on experience to achieve and maintain competitive advantage.

- Establish an environment—a management style, organizational structure, and degree of top-management support—conducive to achieving company-specific new-product and corporate objectives.

Most companies follow a formal new-product development process, usually starting with a new-product strategy. Exhibit 10.1 traces the seven-step process, which is discussed in detail in this section. The exhibit is funnel-shaped to highlight the fact that each stage acts as a screen. The purpose is to filter out unworkable ideas.

NEW-PRODUCT STRATEGY

A **new-product strategy** links the new-product development process with the objectives of the marketing department, the business unit, and the corporation. A new-product strategy must be compatible with these objectives, and in turn, all three objectives must be consistent with one another. A new-product strategy is part of the organization's overall marketing strategy. It sharpens the focus and provides general guidelines for generating, screening, and evaluating new-product ideas. The new-product strategy specifies the roles that new products must play in the organization's overall plan and describes the characteristics of products the organization wants to offer and the markets it wants to serve.

The importance of having a well-thought-out new-product strategy is illustrated by a Dun & Bradstreet finding that for each successful new product introduced, a company needs between 50 and 60 other new-product ideas somewhere in the new-product development process.[12] Gillette aims for 40 percent of annual sales to be generated from products less than five years old.[13]

IDEA GENERATION

New-product ideas come from many sources, including customers, employees, distributors, competitors, vendors, research and development (R&D), and consultants.

- *Customers:* The marketing concept suggests that customers' wants and needs should be the springboard for developing new products. Many of today's most innovative and successful marketers are introducing fewer new products, but they are taking steps to ensure that these "chosen few" are truly unique and better and, above all, really do address unmet consumer needs. How do they do that? They begin and end development with the customer.[14] The most common techniques for gathering new-product ideas from consumers are surveys and focus groups. These research tools were discussed extensively in Chapter 8. Other useful techniques include observation and mining blogs.

    The Swiffer brand duster and carpet sweeper discussed at the beginning of this chapter are examples of successful new-product ideas generated by watching people perform routine tasks in their homes. Mining blogs is another way to gather new-product ideas and learn about consumers' assessment of the company's and competitor's brands. Umbria Communications scours 13 million blogs to determine what consumers are saying about new products and trends. Electronic Arts uses Umbria to determine what bloggers are saying about upcoming games so it can predict demand.[15]

- *Employees:* Marketing personnel—advertising and marketing research employees, as well as salespeople—often create new-product ideas because they analyze and are involved in the marketplace. The very successful introduction of Post-It Notes started with an employee's idea. In 1974, the R&D department of 3M's commercial tape division developed and patented the adhesive component of Post-It Notes. However, it was a year before an employee of the commercial tape division, who

new-product strategy
A plan that links the new-product development process with the objectives of the marketing department, the business unit, and the corporation.

sang in a church choir, identified a use for the adhesive. He had been using paper clips and slips of paper to mark places in hymn books. But the paper clips damaged his books, and the slips of paper fell out. The solution, as we now all know, was to

IDEO
What are some recent innovations to come out of IDEO? Who are its clients? Which innovation do you like best?
http://www.ideo.com

Online

apply the adhesive to small pieces of paper and sell them in packages.

Encouraging employees from different divisions to exchange ideas is also a useful strategy. The developers of Mr. Clean AutoDry turned to scientists who worked on PUR water purification and Cascade dishwashing detergent to learn how to dry dishes without spotting.[16]

Some firms reward employees for coming up with creative new ideas. Procter & Gamble gives stock options. At W. L. Gore, if any employee can convince his or her peers that an idea has merit and they are willing to spend time helping with it, it suddenly becomes an official project.[17] At Google, employees can spend up to 20 percent of their time working on individual projects called "Googlettes."[18]

- *Distributors*: A well-trained sales force routinely asks distributors about needs that are not being met. Because they are closer to end users, distributors are often more aware of customer needs than are manufacturers. The inspiration for Rubbermaid's litter-free lunch box, named Sidekick, came from a distributor. The distributor suggested that Rubbermaid place some of its plastic containers inside a lunch box and sell the box as an alternative to plastic wrap and paper bags.

- *Competitors*: No firms rely solely on internally generated ideas for new products. A big part of any organization's marketing intelligence system should be monitoring the performance of competitors' products. One purpose of competitive monitoring is to determine which, if any, of the competitors' products should be copied.

  There is plenty of information about competitors on the World Wide Web. For example, AltaVista (**http://www.altavista.digital.com**) is a powerful index tool that can be used to locate information about products and companies. Fuld & Co.'s competitive intelligence guide provides links to a variety of market intelligence sites.

  As we noted in Chapter 6, many companies form alliances with competitors to market new and existing products. Procter & Gamble and Clorox teamed up to use P&G's patented adhesive-film technology to develop Glad Press 'n Seal food storage bags.[19]

- *Vendors*: 7-Eleven regularly forges partnerships with vendors to create proprietary products such as Candy Gulp (a plastic cup filled with gummies) and Blue Vanilla Laffy Taffy Rope candy developed by Nestlé's Wonka division exclusively for 7-Eleven.

- *Research and development*: R&D is carried out in four distinct ways. Basic research is scientific research aimed at discovering new technologies. Applied research takes these new technologies and tries to find useful applications for them. **Product development** goes one step further by converting applications into marketable products. *Product modification* makes cosmetic or functional changes in existing products. Many new-product breakthroughs come from R&D activities. Ynjö Neuvo, head of R&D at Nokia, offers five tips for successful new-product development:[20]

  - Don't locate your R&D in a single place, especially not near the smothering influence of headquarters. Disperse R&D around the globe.

  - Keep teams small—no larger than 50 if possible—and give individual engineers and their managers a lot of power and authority.

  - Flatten hierarchy and stay as close as possible to your engineers. Hierarchy dissipates energy.

  - Encourage engineers to generate crazy new ideas outside their official work assignments by celebrating secret tinkering and side projects—and get innovations into production with rocket speed.

  - Welcome mistakes. If you're not making them, you're not pushing the envelope hard enough.

product development
A marketing strategy that entails the creation of marketable new products; the process of converting applications for new technologies into marketable products.

Every year, companies in the Standard & Poor's 500 index spend over $100 billion on R&D.[21] Still, 40 percent of American managers surveyed by International Survey Research Corporation thought their companies were not doing enough to develop new products.[22] Balancing the need to develop new products with demands to lower costs creates a difficult dilemma for many managers. Two examples of companies that have made major commitments to building competitive advantage through R&D are Procter & Gamble, with 7,500 researchers located in 20 technical facilities in nine countries,[23] and Toyota Motor Corporation, which spends $14 billion per year on research and product development—twice as much as either General Motors or Ford spends.[24]

Some companies are establishing innovation laboratories to complement or even replace R&D programs, where scientists spend years coming up with new-product ideas and then pass these ideas along to product developers, then to designers, and finally to marketers.[25] Ideas labs focus on substantially increasing the speed of innovation. Motorola's Razr telephone was developed in an innovation lab called Moto City, located about 50 miles from company headquarters. Most of the development work was done by a team of engineers, designers, and marketers who worked in open spaces and waist-high cubicles. Many normal practices, such as soliciting input from regional managers around the world, were omitted to foster teamwork and speed development.[26] Innovation labs are used by a wide range of organizations including Boeing, Wrigley, Procter & Gamble, and the Mayo Clinic.

- *Consultants:* Outside consultants are always available to examine a business and recommend product ideas. Examples include the Weston Group; Booz, Allen, & Hamilton; and Management Decisions. Traditionally, consultants determine whether a company has a balanced portfolio of products and, if not, what new-product ideas are needed to offset the imbalance. For instance, an outside consultant conceived Airwick's highly successful Carpet Fresh carpet cleaner.

Creativity is the wellspring of new-product ideas, regardless of who comes up with them. A variety of approaches and techniques have been developed to stimulate creative thinking. The two considered most useful for generating new-product ideas are brainstorming and focus-group exercises. The goal of **brainstorming** is to get a group to think of unlimited ways to vary a product or solve a problem. Group members avoid criticism of an idea, no matter how ridiculous it may seem. Objective evaluation is postponed. The sheer quantity of ideas is what matters. As noted in Chapter 8, an objective of focus-group interviews is to stimulate insightful comments through group interaction. Focus groups usually consist of seven to ten people. Sometimes consumer focus groups generate excellent new-product ideas—for example, Cycle dog food, Stick-Up room deodorizers, and Dustbuster vacuum cleaners. In the industrial market, machine tools, keyboard designs, aircraft interiors, and backhoe accessories have evolved from focus groups.

IDEA SCREENING

After new ideas have been generated, they pass through the first filter in the product development process. This stage, called **screening**, eliminates ideas that are inconsistent with the organization's new-product strategy or are obviously inappropriate for some other reason. The new-product committee, the new-product department, or some other formally appointed group performs the screening review. General Motors' Advanced Portfolio Exploration Group (APEx) knows that only one out of every 20 new car concepts developed by the group will ever become a reality. That's not a bad percentage. In the pharmaceutical business, one new product out of 5,000 ideas is not uncommon.[27] Most new-product ideas are rejected at the screening stage.

Concept tests are often used at the screening stage to rate concept (or product) alternatives. A **concept test** evaluates a new-product idea, usually before any prototype has been created. Typically, researchers get consumer reactions to descriptions and visual representations of a proposed product.

brainstorming
The process of getting a group to think of unlimited ways to vary a product or solve a problem.

screening
The first filter in the product development process, which eliminates ideas that are inconsistent with the organization's new-product strategy or are obviously inappropriate for some other reason.

concept test
A test to evaluate a new-product idea, usually before any prototype has been created.

Concept tests are considered fairly good predictors of success for line extensions. They have also been relatively precise predictors of success for new products that are not copycat items, are not easily classified into existing product categories, and do not require major changes in consumer behavior—such as Betty Crocker Tuna Helper, Cycle dog food, and Libby Fruit Float. However, concept tests are usually inaccurate in predicting the success of new products that create new consumption patterns and require major changes in consumer behavior—such as microwave ovens, videocassette recorders, computers, and word processors.

BUSINESS ANALYSIS

New-product ideas that survive the initial screening process move to the **business analysis** stage, where preliminary figures for demand, cost, sales, and profitability are calculated. For the first time, costs and revenues are estimated and compared. Depending on the nature of the product and the company, this process may be simple or complex.

The newness of the product, the size of the market, and the nature of the competition all affect the accuracy of revenue projections. In an established market like soft drinks, industry estimates of total market size are available. Forecasting market share for a new entry is a bigger challenge.

Analyzing overall economic trends and their impact on estimated sales is especially important in product categories that are sensitive to fluctuations in the business cycle. If consumers view the economy as uncertain and risky, they will put off buying durable goods like major home appliances, automobiles, and homes. Likewise, business buyers postpone major equipment purchases if they expect a recession.

These questions are commonly asked during the business analysis stage:

business analysis
The second stage of the screening process where preliminary figures for demand, cost, sales, and profitability are calculated.

development
The stage in the product development process in which a prototype is developed and a marketing strategy is outlined.

- What is the likely demand for the product?

- What impact would the new product probably have on total sales, profits, market share, and return on investment?

- How would the introduction of the product affect existing products? Would the new product cannibalize existing products?

- Would current customers benefit from the product?

- Would the product enhance the image of the company's overall product mix?

- Would the new product affect current employees in any way? Would it lead to hiring more people or reducing the size of the workforce?

- What new facilities, if any, would be needed?

- How might competitors respond?

- What is the risk of failure? Is the company willing to take the risk?

Answering these questions may require studies of markets, competition, costs, and technical capabilities. But at the end of this stage, management should have a good understanding of the product's market potential. This understanding is important as costs increase dramatically once a product idea enters the development stage.

DEVELOPMENT

In the early stage of **development**, the R&D or engineering department may develop a prototype of the product. During this stage, the firm should start sketching a marketing strategy. The marketing department should decide on the product's packaging, branding, labeling, and so forth. In addition, it should map out preliminary promotion, price, and

New-product development is the lifeblood of many companies. IBM is working on a flexible panel/e-newspaper device that will allow users to download news services through wireless access.

distribution strategies. The feasibility of manufacturing the product at an acceptable cost should be thoroughly examined.

The development stage can last a long time and thus be very expensive. Crest toothpaste was in the development stage for 10 years. It took 18 years to develop Minute Rice, 15 years to develop the Polaroid Colorpack camera, 15 years to develop the Xerox copy machine, and 51 years to develop television. Gillette developed three shaving systems over a 27-year period (TracII, Atra, and Sensor) before introducing the Mach3 in 1998 and Fusion in 2006.[28] Gillette expects the Fusion to account for $1 billion in sales within three years.[29]

The development process works best when all the involved areas (R&D, marketing, engineering, production, and even suppliers) work together rather than sequentially, a process called **simultaneous product development**. This approach allows firms to shorten the development process and reduce costs. With simultaneous product development, all relevant functional areas and outside suppliers participate in all stages of the development process. Rather than proceeding through highly structured stages, the cross-functional team operates in unison. Involving key suppliers early in the process capitalizes on their knowledge and enables them to develop critical component parts. In 1996, it took General Motors more than 48 months to develop a new vehicle. Simultaneous product development has helped GM reduce that time to about 18 months.[30]

The Internet is a useful tool for implementing simultaneous product development. On the Net, multiple partners from a variety of locations can meet regularly to assess new-product ideas, analyze markets and demographics, and review cost information. Ideas judged to be feasible can quickly be converted into new products. Without the Internet it would be impossible to conduct simultaneous product development from different parts of the world. Global R&D is important for two reasons. First, large companies have become global and are no longer focused only on one market. Global R&D is necessary to connect with customers in different parts of the world. Second, companies want to tap into the world's best talent—which isn't always found in the United States.[31]

Some firms use online brain trusts to solve technical problems. InnoCentive, Inc., is a network of 80,000 self-selected science problem solvers in 173 countries. Its clients include Boeing, DuPont, and Procter & Gamble. More than one-third of the two dozen requests submitted to InnoCentive's network by P&G have been solved. Problem solvers are paid $5,000 or more for their solutions. As a result of working with InnoCentive and other initiatives, P&G has increased the proportion of new products derived from outside sources from 20 to 35 percent in a three-year period.[32]

Innovative firms are also gathering a variety of R&D input from customers online. Google polls millions of Web page creators to determine the most relevant search results. LEGO Group uses the Internet to identify its most enthusiastic customers and to help design and market products. Dow Chemical, Eli Lilly & Co., and Hewlett-Packard are among the firms that conduct online R&D activities.[33]

Laboratory tests are often conducted on prototype models during the development stage. User safety is an important aspect of laboratory testing, which actually subjects products to much more severe treatment than is expected by end users. The Consumer Product Safety Act of 1972 requires manufacturers to conduct a "reasonable testing program" to ensure that their products conform to established safety standards.

Many products that test well in the laboratory are also tried out in homes or businesses. Examples of product categories well suited for such use tests include human and pet food products, household cleaning products, and industrial chemicals and supplies. These products are all relatively inexpensive, and their performance characteristics are apparent to users. For example, Procter & Gamble tests a variety of personal and home-care products in the community around its Cincinnati, Ohio headquarters.

TEST MARKETING

After products and marketing programs have been developed, they are usually tested in the marketplace. **Test marketing** is the limited introduction of a product and a marketing program to determine the reactions of potential customers in a market situation. Test marketing allows management to evaluate alternative strategies and to assess how

simultaneous product development
A team-oriented approach to new-product development.

test marketing
The limited introduction of a product and a marketing program to determine the reactions of potential customers in a market situation.

PART 3   PRODUCT DECISIONS

314

well the various aspects of the marketing mix fit together. Quaker Oats test marketed the Take Heart line of food products including ready-to-eat cereals, snack bars, and fruit juice beverages in selected markets in the New York State area before introducing the line nationwide.[34] Even established products are test marketed to assess new marketing strategies. One-dollar bottles of chocolate, strawberry, and coffee-flavored milk, distributed through vending machines, were offered in schools in Texas, California, Massachusetts, Nebraska, and Florida to assess this alternative distribution strategy. Initial weekly sales ran about 200 bottles per machine.[35]

The cities chosen as test sites should reflect market conditions in the new product's projected market area. Yet no "magic city" exists that can universally represent market conditions, and a product's success in one city doesn't guarantee that it will be a nationwide hit. When selecting test market cities, researchers should therefore find locations where the demographics and purchasing habits mirror the overall market. The company should also have good distribution in test cities. Moreover, test locations should be isolated from the media. If the TV stations in a particular market reach a very large area outside that market, the advertising used for the test product may pull in many consumers from outside the market. The product may then appear more successful than it really is. Exhibit 10.2 provides a useful checklist of criteria for selecting test markets.

The High Costs of Test Marketing

Test marketing frequently takes one year or longer, and costs can exceed $1 million. Some products remain in test markets even longer. McDonald's spent 12 years developing and testing salads before introducing them. Despite the cost, many firms believe it is a lot better to fail in a test market than in a national introduction.

Because test marketing is so expensive, some companies do not test line extensions of well-known brands. For example, because the Folgers brand is well known, Procter & Gamble faced little risk in distributing its instant decaffeinated version nationally. Consolidated Foods Kitchen of Sara Lee followed the same approach with its frozen croissants. Other products introduced without being test marketed include General Foods' International Coffees, Quaker Oats' Chewy Granola Bars and Granola Dipps, and Pillsbury's Milk Break Bars.

The high cost of test marketing is not just financial. One unavoidable problem is that test marketing exposes the new product and its marketing mix to competitors before its introduction. Thus, the element of surprise is lost. Hamilton Beach sued both Honeywell and Holmes Products for copying its TrueAir odor eliminator. The device in question, about the size of a hardcover book, claimed to eliminate odors within a six-foot radius by pulling air through a filter.[36] Another strategy for piggybacking on someone else's R&D efforts is called "design-around." This chapter's "Ethics in Marketing" box explains how the practice works. Competitors can also sabotage or "jam" a testing program by introducing their own sales promotion, pricing, or advertising campaign. The purpose is to hide or distort the normal conditions that the testing firm might expect in the market.

Alternatives to Test Marketing

Many firms are looking for cheaper, faster, safer alternatives to traditional test marketing. In the

Merwyn

Do you think test marketing can be simulated successfully? Go to Merwyn.com and read how the company uses algorithms to create test market results. If you have an idea, try it out. Do you think this is a suitable and effective substitute for real test marketing?

http://www.merwyn.com

Online

Exhibit 10.2

Checklist for Selecting Test Markets

In choosing a test market, many criteria need to be considered, especially the following:

- Similarity to planned distribution outlets
- Relative isolation from other cities
- Availability of advertising media that will cooperate
- Diversified cross section of ages, religions, cultural-societal preferences, etc.
- No atypical purchasing habits
- Representative population size
- Typical per capital income
- Good record as a test city, but not overly used
- Not easily "jammed" by competitors
- Stability of year-round sales
- No dominant television station; multiple newspapers, magazines, and radio stations
- Availability of research and audit services
- Availability of retailers that will cooperate
- Freedom from unusual influences, such as one industry's dominance or heavy tourism

Finding a Way around Patents

Nebraska rancher Gerald Gohl had a bright idea: create a remote-controlled spotlight, so he wouldn't have to roll down the window of his pickup truck and stick out a handheld beacon to look for his cattle on cold nights. By 1997, Gohl held a patent on the RadioRay, a wireless version of his spotlight that could rotate 360 degrees and was mounted using suction cups or brackets. Retail price: more than $200. RadioRay started to catch on with ranchers, boaters, hunters, and even police.

Wal-Mart Stores, Inc., liked it, too, and called Gohl to discuss carrying the RadioRay as a "wow" item, an unusual product that might attract lots of attention and sales. Gohl said no, worrying that selling to Sam's Club could drive the spotlight's price lower and poison his relationships with distributors.

Soon after, Sam's Club was selling its own wireless, remote-controlled searchlight—for about $60. It looked nearly identical to the RadioRay except for a small plastic part restricting the light's rotation to slightly less than 360 degrees. Golight, Inc., Gohl's company, sued Wal-Mart alleging patent infringement. The retailer countered that Gohl's invention was obvious and that its light wasn't an exact copy of the RadioRay's design.

The legal battle between Gohl and the world's largest retailer—which Wal-Mart lost in a federal district court and on appeal and is now considering taking to the Supreme Court—reflects a growing trend in the high-stakes, persnickety world of patents and product design. Patent attorneys say that companies increasingly are imitat-ing rivals' inventions while trying to make their own versions just different enough to avoid infringing on a patent. The near-copycat procedure, which among other things helps companies avoid paying royalties to patent holders, is called a "design-around."

Design-arounds underscore the pressure that companies feel to keep pace with the innovations of competitors. And U.S. courts have repeatedly concluded that designing around—and even copying products left unprotected—can be good for consumers by lowering prices and encouraging innovation.

"We design around competitor patents on a regular basis," says James O'Shaughnessy, vice president and chief intellectual property counsel at Rockwell Automation, Inc., in Milwaukee, a maker of industrial automation equipment. "Anybody who is really paying attention to the patent system, who respects it, will still nevertheless try to find ways—either offshore production or a design-around—to produce an equivalent product that doesn't infringe."

Design-arounds are particularly common in auto parts, semiconductors, and other industries with enormous markets that are attractive to newcomers looking for a way to break in. The practice also happens in mature industries, where there are few big breakthroughs and competitors rely on relatively small changes to gain a competitive advantage. Patented products are attractive targets for an attempted end run because they command premium prices, making them irresistible amid razor-thin profit margins and expanding global competition.[37]

Do you think that design-arounds are ethical? What effects do they have on R&D costs? What about their effects on prices?

---

early 1980s, Information Resources, Inc., pioneered one alternative: single-source research using supermarket scanner data (discussed in Chapter 8). A typical supermarket scanner test costs about $300,000. Another alternative to traditional test marketing is **simulated (laboratory) market testing**. Advertising and other promotional materials for several products, including the test product, are shown to members of the product's target market. These people are then taken to shop at a mock or real store, where their purchases are recorded. Shopper behavior, including repeat purchasing, is monitored to assess the product's likely performance under true market conditions. Research firms offer simulated market tests for $25,000 to $100,000, compared to $1 million or more for full-scale test marketing.

Online Test Marketing

Despite these alternatives, most firms still consider test marketing essential for most new products. The high price of failure simply prohibits the widespread introduction of most new products without testing. Many firms are finding that the Internet offers a fast, cost-effective way to conduct test marketing.

Procter & Gamble is an avid proponent of using the Internet as a means of gauging customer demand for potential new products. The company reportedly conducts 40 percent of its product tests and other studies online and hopes to cut its $140 million annual research budget in half by shifting efforts to the Internet.[38]

Many products that are not available in grocery stores or drugstores can be sampled or purchased from P&G's corporate Web site **http://pg.com**. The company's home tooth-

simulated (laboratory) market testing
The presentation of advertising and other promotion materials for several products, including a test product, to members of the product's target market.

© RIC FELD/ASSOCIATED PRESS

bleaching kit Crest Whitestrips provides an illustration. When the company was ready to launch Crest Whitestrips, management wasn't sure that consumers would be willing to pay the proposed $44 retail price. P&G then began an eight-month campaign offering the strips exclusively on http://whitestrips.com. TV spots and magazine ads were run to promote the online sale. In eight months, 144,000 whitening kits were sold online. The product was then introduced in retail outlets, and $50 million worth of kits were sold in the first three months at the initial $44 per kit price.39

Other consumer goods firms that have recently begun online test marketing include General Mills and Quaker Oats. Other sites have appeared that offer consumers prototype products developed by all sizes of firms.

New Product Works

Not all new products are well received in the marketplace. Go to New Product Works' Web site and read the polls for an overview of products the company expects to "hit" and some it expects to "miss." What is your opinion of the products listed?

http://www.newproductworks.com

Online

COMMERCIALIZATION

The final stage in the new-product development process is **commercialization**, the decision to market a product. The decision to commercialize the product sets several tasks in motion: ordering production materials and equipment, starting production, building inventories, shipping the product to field distribution points, training the sales force, announcing the new product to the trade, and advertising to potential customers.

The time from the initial commercialization decision to the product's actual introduction varies. It can range from a few weeks for simple products that use existing equipment to several years for technical products that require custom manufacturing equipment.

The total cost of development and initial introduction can be staggering. Gillette spent $750 million developing the Mach3, and the first-year marketing budget for the new three-bladed razor was $300 million.

For some products, a well-planned Internet campaign can provide new-product information for people who are looking for the solutions that a particular new product offers. Attempting to reach customers at the point in time when they need a product is much more cost-effective and efficient than communicating with a target market that may eventually have a need for the product.

commercialization
The decision to market a product.

REVIEW LEARNING OUTCOME

LO² Explain the steps in the new-product development process

Number of new product ideas / Time

- Idea generation
- Idea screening
- Business analysis
- Development
- Test marketing
- Commercialization

LO³
Why Some Products Succeed and Others Fail

Despite the amount spent on developing and testing new products, a large proportion of new-product introductions fail. In the consumer goods industry, 70 to 90 percent of all new products fail within the first year.40 Products fail for a number of reasons. One common reason is that they simply do not offer any discernible benefit compared to existing products. Another commonly cited factor in new-product failures is a poor match between product features and customer desires. For example, there are telephone systems on the market with over 700 different functions, although the average user is happy with just 10 functions.

Other reasons for failure include overestimation of market size, incorrect positioning, a price too high or too low, inadequate distribution, poor promotion, or simply an inferior product compared to those of competitors.

Failure can be a matter of degree. Absolute failure occurs when a company cannot recoup its development, marketing, and production costs. The product actually loses money for the company. A relative product failure results when the product returns a profit but fails to achieve sales, profit, or market share goals.

High costs and other risks of developing and testing new products do not stop many companies, such as Rubbermaid, Colgate-Palmolive, Campbell's Soup, 3M, and Procter & Gamble, from aggressively developing and introducing new products.

The most important factor in successful new-product introduction is a good match between the product and market needs—as the marketing concept would predict. Successful new products deliver a meaningful and perceivable benefit to a sizable number of people or organizations and are different in some meaningful way from their intended substitutes. Firms that routinely experience success in new-product introductions tend to share the following characteristics:

- A history of carefully listening to customers

- An obsession with producing the best product possible

- A vision of what the market will be like in the future

- Strong leadership

- A commitment to new-product development

- A project-based team approach to new-product development

- Getting every aspect of the product development process right

REVIEW LEARNING OUTCOME

LO3 Explain why some products succeed and others fail

New Product — Market Needs

Good match leads to success

New Product — Market Needs

Mismatch can mean failure

LO4
Global Issues in New-Product Development

Increasing globalization of markets and of competition provides a reason for multinational firms to consider new-product development from a worldwide perspective. That perspective includes developing countries as well as more established markets. Procter & Gamble, Unilever, and Colgate-Palmolive generate 20, 35, and 45 percent, respectively, of their revenues in developing countries.[41] A firm that starts with a global strategy is better able to develop products that are marketable worldwide. In many multinational corporations, every product is developed for potential worldwide distribution, and unique market requirements are built in whenever possible. Procter & Gamble introduced Pampers Phases into global markets within one month of introducing the product in the United States. P&G's goal was to have the product on the shelf in 90 countries within one year. The objective was to establish brand loyalty among dealers and consumers before foreign competitors could react.

Some global marketers design their products to meet regulations in their major markets and then, if necessary, meet smaller markets' requirements country by country. Nissan develops lead-country car models that, with minor changes, can be sold in most markets. With this approach, Nissan has been able to reduce the number of its basic models from 48 to 18.

Kids dressed as Colonel Harland Sanders (Kentucky Fried Chicken's founder) promote egg tarts in a KFC restaurant in Shanghai, China. KFC sells food that appeals to local tastes, like egg tarts, Peking duck rolls, and Dragon Twists, and promotes them in unique and memorable ways.

Some products, however, have little potential for global market penetration without modification. Russia and China represent two huge automobile markets but not at prevailing international prices. General Motors, Ford Motor Company, Fiat, Renault, and others are working with Russian partners to produce cars that can retail for $15,000 or less. GM, Toyota, and Volkswagen AG are focusing on China. In an unusual turn of events, the Chinese carmaker Chery Automotive Company has announced plans to introduce Chery vehicles into the U.S. market in 2007.[42]

Some companies could not sell their products at affordable prices and still make an adequate profit in many countries. To counter this problem, Procter & Gamble uses subcontractors to combine proprietary ingredients with standard chemicals and package the products.[43] The result is lower cost to P&G.

We often hear about how popular American products are in foreign countries. Recently, U.S. companies such as Levi Strauss, Coca-Cola, RJR Nabisco, and Nike have been finding that products popular in foreign markets can become hits in the United States. Häagen-Dazs' ice cream flavor *dulce de leche*, named after a caramelized milk drink that is popular in Argentina, was originally introduced in Buenos Aires. Enova, a cooking oil that helps cut body weight and fat, was the top-selling brand in Japan before it was introduced in the United States.

Other companies are applying a new twist on the popular international business aphorism, "think global, act local." At Coca-Cola, this means giving country managers more autonomy in new-product development. The idea has resulted in several new brands of energy drinks, waters, and teas being introduced in various Asian countries. More beverages are planned to diversify beyond colas. Results have been impressive.

REVIEW LEARNING OUTCOME

LO4 Discuss global issues in new-product development

- Single product worldwide
- Modification of products
- Multiple products in multiple countries

LO5
The Spread of New Products

Managers have a better chance of successfully marketing products if they understand how consumers learn about and adopt products. A person who buys a new product never before tried may ultimately become an **adopter**, a consumer who was happy enough with his or her trial experience with a product to use it again.

DIFFUSION OF INNOVATION

adopter
A consumer who was happy enough with his or her trial experience with a product to use it again.

innovation
A product perceived as new by a potential adopter.

diffusion
The process by which the adoption of an innovation spreads.

An **innovation** is a product perceived as new by a potential adopter. It really doesn't matter whether the product is "new to the world" or some other category of new product. If it is new to a potential adopter, it is an innovation in this context. **Diffusion** is the process by which the adoption of an innovation spreads.

Five categories of adopters participate in the diffusion process:

- *Innovators*: the first 2.5 percent of all those who adopt the product. Innovators are eager to try new ideas and products, almost as an obsession. In addition to having higher incomes, they are more worldly and more active outside their community than noninnovators. They rely less on group norms and are more self-confident. Because they are well educated, they are more likely to get their information from scientific sources and experts. Innovators are characterized as being venturesome.

The original
Seatbeltbag
BUILT IN THE USA by harveys

* for stores, go to **seatbeltbag.com** *

Early adopters are opinion leaders who encourage others to buy a new product; they are often essential to successful product innovation. Harveys hopes to attract early adopters by presenting its Seatbeltbag as a trendy and versatile product.

- *Early adopters*: the next 13.5 percent to adopt the product. Although early adopters are not the very first, they do adopt early in the product's life cycle. Compared to innovators, they rely much more on group norms and values. They are also more oriented to the local community, in contrast to the innovators' worldly outlook. Early adopters are more likely than innovators to be opinion leaders because of their closer affiliation with groups. The respect of others is a dominant characteristic of early adopters.

- *Early majority*: the next 34 percent to adopt. The early majority weighs the pros and cons before adopting a new product. They are likely to collect more information and evaluate more brands than early adopters, therefore extending the adoption process. They rely on the group for information but are unlikely to be opinion leaders themselves. Instead, they tend to be opinion leaders' friends and neighbors. The early majority is an important link in the process of diffusing new ideas because they are positioned between earlier and later adopters. A dominant characteristic of the early majority is deliberateness. Most of the first residential broadband users were classic early adopters—white males, well educated and wealthy, with a great deal of Internet experience.

- *Late majority*: the next 34 percent to adopt. The late majority adopts a new product because most of their friends have already adopted it. Because they also rely on group norms, their adoption stems from pressure to conform. This group tends to be older and below average in income and education. They depend mainly on word-of-mouth communication rather than on the mass media. The dominant characteristic of the late majority is skepticism.

- *Laggards*: the final 16 percent to adopt. Like innovators, laggards do not rely on group norms, but their independence is rooted in their ties to tradition. Thus, the past heavily influences their decisions. By the time laggards adopt an innovation, it has probably become outmoded and been replaced by something else. For example, they may have bought their first black-and-white TV set after color television was already widely diffused. Laggards have the longest adoption time and the lowest socioeconomic status. They tend to be suspicious of new products and alienated from a rapidly advancing society. The dominant value of laggards is tradition. Marketers typically ignore laggards, who do not seem to be motivated by advertising or personal selling.

Note that some product categories, such as monochrome televisions, may never be adopted by 100 percent of the population. The adopter categories refer to all of those who will eventually adopt a product, not the entire population.

PRODUCT CHARACTERISTICS AND THE RATE OF ADOPTION

Five product characteristics can be used to predict and explain the rate of acceptance and diffusion of a new product:

- *Complexity*: the degree of difficulty involved in understanding and using a new product. The more complex the product, the slower is its diffusion. For instance, DVD recorders have been around for a few years, but they have been bought mostly by early adopters willing to go to the trouble of linking the gadgets to their PCs or to pay high prices for the first stand-alone machines that connect to a TV.

LO5 Explain the diffusion process through which new products are adopted

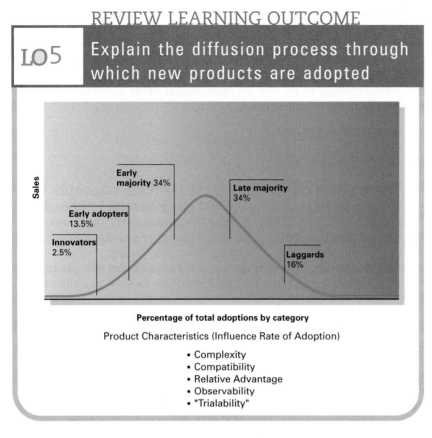

Sales

Innovators 2.5%

Early adopters 13.5%

Early majority 34%

Late majority 34%

Laggards 16%

Percentage of total adoptions by category

Product Characteristics (Influence Rate of Adoption)

- Complexity
- Compatibility
- Relative Advantage
- Observability
- "Trialability"

- *Compatibility*: the degree to which the new product is consistent with existing values and product knowledge, past experiences, and current needs. Incompatible products diffuse more slowly than compatible products. For example, the introduction of contraceptives is incompatible in countries where religious beliefs discourage the use of birth control techniques.

- *Relative advantage*: the degree to which a product is perceived as superior to existing substitutes. For example, because it reduces cooking time, the microwave oven has a clear relative advantage over a conventional oven.

- *Observability*: the degree to which the benefits or other results of using the product can be observed by others and communicated to target customers. For instance, fashion items and automobiles are highly visible and more observable than personal-care items.

- *"Trialability"*: the degree to which a product can be tried on a limited basis. It is much easier to try a new toothpaste or breakfast cereal than a new automobile or microcomputer. Demonstrations in showrooms and test-drives are different from in-home trial use. To stimulate trials, marketers use free-sampling programs, tasting displays, and small package sizes.

Exhibit 10.3 shows the rate of adoption of five audio products introduced in the last 25 years. Satellite radio has been adopted more quickly than any other innovative audio product.

Exhibit 10.3
Sales of New Audio Products

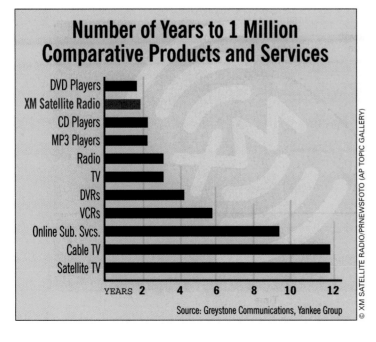

Number of Years to 1 Million Comparative Products and Services

DVD Players
XM Satellite Radio
CD Players
MP3 Players
Radio
TV
DVRs
VCRs
Online Sub. Svcs.
Cable TV
Satellite TV

YEARS 2 4 6 8 10 12

Source: Greystone Communications, Yankee Group

© XM SATELLITE RADIO/PRNEWSFOTO (AP TOPIC GALLERY)

MARKETING IMPLICATIONS OF THE ADOPTION PROCESS

Two types of communication aid the diffusion process: *word-of-mouth communication* among consumers and communication from marketers to consumers. Word-of-mouth communication within and across groups speeds diffusion. Opinion leaders discuss new products with their followers and with other opinion leaders. Marketers must therefore ensure that opinion leaders have the types of information desired in the media that they use. Suppliers of some products, such as professional and health-care services, rely almost solely on word-of-mouth communication for new business.

The second type of communication aiding the diffusion process is *communication directly from the marketer to potential adopters*. Messages directed toward early adopters should normally use different appeals than messages directed toward the early majority, the late majority, or the laggards. Early adopters are more important than innovators because they make up a larger group, are more socially active, and are usually opinion leaders.

As the focus of a promotional campaign shifts from early adopters to the early majority and the late majority, marketers should study the dominant characteristics, buying behavior, and media characteristics of these target markets. Then they should revise messages and media strategy to fit. The diffusion model helps guide marketers in developing and implementing promotion strategy.

LO⁶
Product Life Cycles

The product life cycle (PLC) one of the most familiar concepts in marketing. Few other general concepts have been so widely discussed. Although some researchers and consultants have challenged the theoretical basis and managerial value of the PLC,[44] many believe it is a useful marketing management diagnostic tool and a general guide for marketing planning in various "life-cycle" stages.

The product life cycle is a biological metaphor that traces the stages of a product's acceptance, from its introduction (birth) to its decline (death). As Exhibit 10.4 shows, a product progresses through four major stages: introduction, growth, maturity, and decline.

The PLC concept can be used to analyze a brand, a product form, or a product category. The PLC for a product form is usually longer than the PLC for any one brand. The exception would be a brand that was the first and last competitor in a product form market. In that situation, the brand and product form life cycles would be equal in length. Product categories have the longest life cycles. A **product category** includes all brands that satisfy a particular type of need such as shaving products, passenger automobiles, or soft drinks.

The time a product spends in any one stage of the life cycle may vary dramatically. Some products, such as fad items, move through the entire cycle in weeks. Others, such as electric clothes washers and dryers, stay in the maturity stage for decades. Exhibit 10.4 illustrates the typical life cycle for a consumer durable good, such as a washer or dryer. In contrast, Exhibit 10.5 illustrates typical life cycles for styles (such as formal, business, or casual clothing), fashions (such as miniskirts or baggy jeans), and fads (such as leopard-print clothing). Changes in a product, its uses, its image, or its positioning can extend that product's life cycle.

The PLC concept does not tell managers the length of a product's life cycle or its duration in any stage. It does not dictate marketing strategy. It is simply a tool to help marketers forecast future events and suggest appropriate strategies. Look at Exhibit 10.6 on page 323. What conclusions can you draw about the PLC of nondigital TVs, digital TVs, and flat panel TVs based on four and a half years of sales data?

product life cycle (PLC)
A biological metaphor that traces the stages of a product's acceptance, from its introduction (birth) to its decline (death).

product category
All brands that satisfy a particular type of need.

Exhibit 10.4

Four Stages of the Product Life Cycle

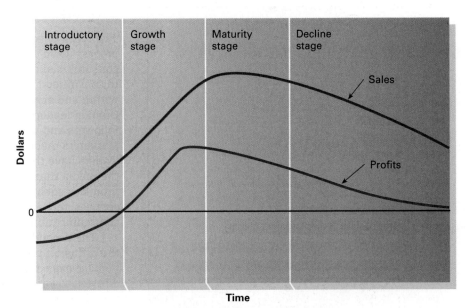

Introductory stage | Growth stage | Maturity stage | Decline stage; Dollars; 0; Sales; Profits; Time

INTRODUCTORY STAGE

introductory stage
The first stage of the product life cycle in which the full-scale launch of a new product into the marketplace occurs.

The **introductory stage** of the product life cycle represents the full-scale launch of a new product into the marketplace. Computer databases for personal use, room-deodorizing air-conditioning filters, and wind-powered home electric generators are all product categories that have recently entered the PLC. A high failure rate, little competition, frequent product modification, and limited distribution typify the introductory stage of the PLC.

Marketing costs in the introductory stage are normally high for several reasons. High dealer margins are often needed to obtain adequate distribution, and incentives are needed to get consumers to try the new product. Advertising expenses are high because of the need to educate consumers about the new product's benefits. Production costs are also often high in this stage, as product and manufacturing flaws are identified and corrected and efforts are undertaken to develop mass-production economies.

As Exhibit 10.4 illustrates, sales normally increase slowly during the introductory stage. Moreover, profits are usually negative because of R&D costs, factory tooling, and high introduction costs. The length of the introductory phase is largely determined by product characteristics, such as the product's advantages over substitute products, the educational effort required to make the product known, and management's commitment of resources to the new item. A short introductory period is usually preferred to help reduce the impact of negative earnings and cash flows. As soon as the product gets off the ground, the financial burden should begin to diminish. Also, a short introduction helps dispel some of the uncertainty as to whether the new product will be successful.

Promotion strategy in the introductory stage focuses on developing product awareness and informing consumers about the product category's potential benefits. At this stage, the communication challenge is to stimulate primary demand—demand for the product in general rather than for a specific brand. Intensive personal selling is often required to gain acceptance for the product among wholesalers and retailers. Promotion of convenience products often requires heavy consumer sampling and couponing. Shopping and specialty products demand educational advertising and personal selling to the final consumer.

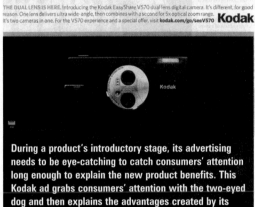

During a product's introductory stage, its advertising needs to be eye-catching to catch consumers' attention long enough to explain the new product benefits. This Kodak ad grabs consumers' attention with the two-eyed dog and then explains the advantages created by its dual-lens digital camera.

Exhibit 10.5
Product Life Cycles for Styles, Fashions, and Fads

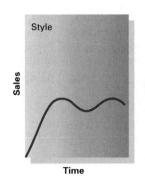

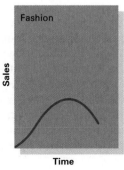

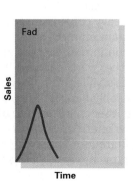

Exhibit 10.6
U.S. Sales of Televisions, in Billions of Dollars

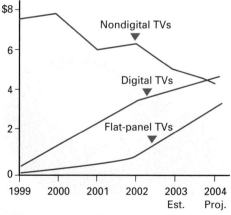

SOURCE: Consumer Electronics Association as seen in Evan Ramstad, "Flat-Panel, Plasma TV Sets Bring a Flood of New Brands," *Wall Street Journal*, January 13, 2004, B1.

Interestingly, the introductory stage of the PLC seems to vary among European countries. As Exhibit 10.7 shows, the average introductory stage ranges from just under 4 years in Denmark to about 9 years in Greece. Cultural factors seem to be largely responsible for these differences. Scandinavians are often more open to new ideas than people in other European countries.[45]

Exhibit 10.7

The European Divide

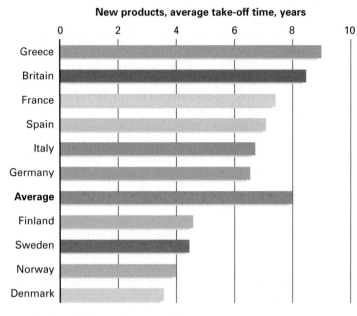

New products, average take-off time, years

Greece	
Britain	
France	
Spain	
Italy	
Germany	
Average	
Finland	
Sweden	
Norway	
Denmark	

SOURCE: Gerard J. Tellis, Stefan Stremersch, and Eden Yin. Reprinted from "When will It Fly?" *The Economist*, August 9, 2003, 332.

growth stage
The second stage of the product life cycle when sales typically grow at an increasing rate, many competitors enter the market, large companies may start acquiring small pioneering firms, and profits are healthy.

maturity stage
The third stage of the product life cycle during which sales increase at a decreasing rate.

GROWTH STAGE

If a product category survives the introductory stage, it advances to the **growth stage** of the life cycle. In this stage, sales typically grow at an increasing rate, many competitors enter the market, and large companies may start to acquire small pioneering firms. Profits rise rapidly in the growth stage, reach their peak, and begin declining as competition intensifies. Emphasis switches from primary demand promotion (for example, promoting personal digital assistants, or PDAs) to aggressive brand advertising and communication of the differences between brands (for example, promoting Casio versus Palm and Visor).

Distribution becomes a major key to success during the growth stage, as well as in later stages. Manufacturers scramble to sign up dealers and distributors and to build long-term relationships. Without adequate distribution, it is impossible to establish a strong market position.

MATURITY STAGE

A period during which sales increase at a decreasing rate signals the beginning of the **maturity stage** of the life cycle. New users cannot be added indefinitely, and sooner or later the market approaches saturation. Normally, this is the longest stage of the product life cycle. Many major household appliances are in the maturity stage of their life cycles.

For shopping products and many specialty products, annual models begin to appear during the maturity stage. Product lines are lengthened to appeal to additional market segments. Service and repair assume more important roles as manufacturers strive to distinguish their products from others. Product design changes tend to become stylistic (How can the product be made different?) rather than functional (How can the product be made better?).

As prices and profits continue to fall, marginal competitors start dropping out of the market. Dealer margins also shrink, resulting in less shelf space for mature items, lower dealer inventories, and a general reluctance to promote the product. Thus, promotion to dealers often intensifies during this stage in order to retain loyalty.

Heavy consumer promotion by the manufacturer is also required to maintain market share. Consider these well-known examples of competition in the maturity stage: the "cola war" featuring Coke and Pepsi, the "beer war" featuring Anheuser-Busch's Budweiser brands and Philip Morris's Miller brands, and the "burger wars" pitting leader McDonald's against challengers Burger King and Wendy's.

Another characteristic of the maturity stage is the emergence of "niche marketers" that target narrow, well-defined, underserved segments of a market. Starbucks Coffee targets its gourmet line at the only segment of the coffee market that is growing: new, younger, more affluent coffee drinkers.

DECLINE STAGE

A long-run drop in sales signals the beginning of the **decline stage**. The rate of decline is governed by how rapidly consumer tastes change or substitute products are adopted. Many convenience products and fad items lose their market overnight, leaving large inventories of unsold items, such as designer jeans. Others die more slowly.

U.S. sales of traditional 35mm cameras have been on a steady decline since 2000. In one recent year, film camera sales dropped 15 percent. The worldwide shift to digital photography has led Eastman Kodak to stop selling reloadable film-based consumer cameras in the United States, Canada, and Europe. Kodak hasn't made a profit selling film cameras for several years. It continued selling the cameras only to aid the sale of film. Kodak's first consumer camera was introduced in 1888.[46]

Some firms have developed successful strategies for marketing products in the decline stage of the product life cycle. They eliminate all nonessential marketing expenses and let sales decline as more and more customers discontinue purchasing the products. Eventually, the product is withdrawn from the market.

Management sage Peter Drucker says that all companies should practice "organized abandonment," which entails reviewing every product, service, and policy every two or three years and asking the critical question, "If we didn't do this already, would we launch it now?" Would we introduce the product, service, or policy now? If the answer is no, it's time to begin the abandonment process.[47]

IMPLICATIONS FOR MARKETING MANAGEMENT

The product life cycle concept encourages marketing managers to plan so that they can take the initiative instead of reacting to past events. The PLC is especially useful as a predicting or forecasting tool. Because products pass through distinctive stages, it is often possible to estimate a product's location on the curve using historical data. Profits, like sales, tend to follow a predictable path over a product's life cycle.

Exhibit 10.8 shows the relationship between the adopter categories and stages of the PLC. Note that the various categories of adopters first buy products in different stages of the life cycle. Almost all sales in the maturity and decline stages represent repeat purchasing.

decline stage
The fourth stage of the product life cycle, characterized by a long-run drop in sales.

Exhibit 10.8

Relationship between the Diffusion Process and the Product Life Cycle

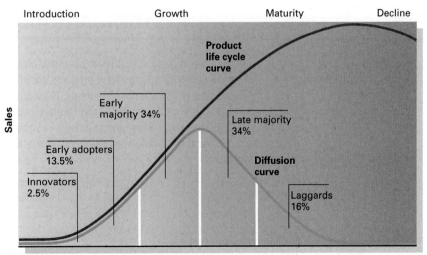

LO6 Explain the concept of product life cycles

Marketing Mix Strategy	Product Life Cycle Stage			
	Introductory	Growth	Maturity	Decline
Product Strategy	Limited number of models; frequent product modifications	Expanded number of models; frequent product modifications	Large number of models	Elimination of unprofitable models and brands
Distribution Strategy	Distribution usually limited, depending on product; intensive efforts and high margins often needed to attract wholesalers and retailers	Expanded number of dealers; intensive efforts to establish long-term relationships with wholesalers and retailers	Extensive number of dealers; margins declining; intensive efforts to retain distributors and shelf space	Unprofitable outlets phased out
Promotion Strategy	Develop product awareness; stimulate primary demand; use intensive personal selling to distributors; use sampling and couponing for consumers	Stimulate selective demand; advertise brand aggressively	Stimulate selective demand; advertise brand aggressively; promote heavily to retain dealers and customers	Phase out all promotion
Pricing Strategy	Prices are usually high to recover development costs (see Chapter 17)	Prices begin to fall toward end of growth stage as result of competitive pressure	Prices continue to fall	Prices stabilize at relatively low level; small price rises are possible if competition is negligible

Sales (vertical axis)

Time (horizontal axis)

Review and Applications

LO1
Explain the importance of developing new products and describe the six categories of new products. New products are important to sustain growth and profits and to replace obsolete items. New products can be classified as new-to-the-world products (discontinuous innovations), new product lines, additions to existing product lines, improvements or revisions of existing products, repositioned products, or lower-priced products. To sustain or increase profits, a firm must innovate.

1.1 How many new products can you identify? Visit the supermarket and make a list of at least 15 items with the word "New" on the label. Include on your list anything that looks like a new product. Next to each item on your list, write the category of new product that best describes the item. Share your results with the class.

1.2 New entertainment products aren't necessarily media products. Form a team of three or four students and brainstorm new nonmedia entertainment products. Try to identify one item for each of the categories of new products discussed in the chapter.

Quick Check ✔

Now that you've read the chapter, do you get it?
Take a moment for a quick check using this scale:

1 Not at all; 2 Not very well; 3 Ok; 4 Well; 5 Very Well

Can you . . .

____ identify the categories of new products?

____ give the rationale behind new-product development?

____ outline the steps in the new-product development process?

____ explain the pros and cons of test marketing?

____ account for why new products fail?

____ draw a diagram illustrating the diffusion of innovation?

____ identify the product characteristics that influence the rate of adoption?

____ describe the product life cycle?

____ construct a table explaining how the marketing mix strategy changes at each stage of the product life cycle?

____ TOTAL

Score: 37–45, you're ready to move on to the applications; 28–36, skim the chapter one more time before moving on to the applications; 19–27, reread the sections giving you the most trouble and go to Thomson NOW for guided tutorials; 18 and under, you better reread the chapter to get a grasp of the fundamentals. If you've reread the chapter and still have a low score, visit your professor

LO 2 Explain the steps in the new-product development process. First, a firm forms a new-product strategy by outlining the characteristics and roles of future products. Then new-product ideas are generated by customers, employees, distributors, competitors, vendors, and internal R&D personnel. Once a product idea has survived initial screening by an appointed screening group, it undergoes business analysis to determine its potential profitability. If a product concept seems viable, it progresses into the development phase, in which the technical and economic feasibility of the manufacturing process is evaluated. The development phase also includes laboratory and use testing of a product for performance and safety. Following initial testing and refinement, most products are introduced in a test market to evaluate consumer response and marketing strategies. Finally, test market successes are propelled into full commercialization. The commercialization process involves starting up production, building inventories, shipping to distributors, training a sales force, announcing the product to the trade, and advertising to consumers.

2.1 List the advantages of simultaneous product development.

 2.2 You are a marketing manager for Nike. Your department has come up with the idea of manufacturing a baseball bat for use in colleges around the nation. Assuming you are in the business analysis stage, write a brief analysis based on the questions in the "Business Analysis" section of the chapter.

2.3 What are the major disadvantages to test marketing, and how might they be avoided?

 2.4 How could information from customer orders at **http://www.pizzahut.com** help the company's marketers plan new-product developments?

LO 3 Explain why some products succeed and others fail. The most important factor in determining the success of a new product is the extent to which the product matches the needs of the market. Good matches are frequently successful. Poor matches are not.

 3.1 In small groups, brainstorm ideas for a new wet-weather clothing line. What type of product would potential customers want and need? Prepare and deliver a brief presentation to your class.

LO 4 Discuss global issues in new-product development. A marketer with global vision seeks to develop products that can easily be adapted to suit local needs. The goal is not simply to develop a standard product that can be sold worldwide. Smart global marketers also look for good product ideas worldwide.

 4.1 Visit **http://pg.com** and look at the brands it offers around the world. What conclusions can you draw about Procter & Gamble's global new-product development strategy?

LO5 Explain the diffusion process through which new products are adopted. The diffusion process is the spread of a new product from its producer to ultimate adopters. Adopters in the diffusion process belong to five categories: innovators, early adopters, the early majority, the late majority, and laggards. Product characteristics that affect the rate of adoption include product complexity, compatibility with existing social values, relative advantage over existing substitutes, observability, and "trialability." The diffusion process is facilitated by word-of-mouth communication and communication from marketers to consumers.

5.1 Describe some products whose adoption rates have been affected by complexity, compatibility, relative advantage, observability, and/or "trialability."

5.2 What type of adopter behavior do you typically follow? Explain.

5.3 Review Exhibit 10.3. Analyze each product on the graph according to the characteristics that influence the rate of adoption. For example, what can you conclude from the data about the relative advantage of DVD audio? Write one to two pages explaining your analysis.

LO6 Explain the concept of product life cycles. All brands and product categories undergo a life cycle with four stages: introduction, growth, maturity, and decline. The rate at which products move through these stages varies dramatically. Marketing managers use the product life cycle concept as an analytical tool to forecast a product's future and devise effective marketing strategies.

6.1 What is Cheerios doing to compete successfully in the maturity stage? Go to its Web site **http://www.cheerios.com** to find out.

Key Terms

Exercises

APPLICATION EXERCISE

A simple statistical analysis will help you better understand the types of new products. As in the Application Exercise in Chapter 5, you will be using print advertisements, but you will also be adding information from other sources (TV ads, trips to the store, and the like).[48]

Activities

1. Compile a list of 100 new products. If you are building a portfolio of ads (see the Application Exercise in Chapter 5), you can generate part of this list as you collect print advertisements for the topics in this chapter. Consider tabulating television ads for new products that are aired during programs you normally watch. A trip to the grocery could probably yield your entire list, but then your list would be limited to consumer products.

2. Make a table with six columns labeled as follows: new-to-the-world products, new product line, addition to existing product line, improvement/revision of existing product line, repositioned product, and lower-priced product.

3. Place each of your 100 new products into one of the six categories. Tabulate your results at the bottom of each column. What conclusions can you draw from the distribution of your products? Consider adding your results together with the rest of the class to get a larger and more random sample.

Entrepreneurship Case

WELCOME TO THE KANDY KASTLE, BUT BEWARE—THINGS ARE NOT WHAT THEY SEEM

Meet Larry Jones, a former toy designer for the likes of Hasbro, Mattel and Playmates Toys. Displaced when the industry turned to electronic toys, the irrepressible Jones is hard at play designing captivating candy concepts for niche manufacturer Kandy Kastle. He is not a confectioner, nor does he aspire to be one. Instead, Jones tinkers with candy delivery mechanisms and silly, sometimes grotesque names sure to capture the eyes, imaginations, and tummies of youngsters.

His products belong to the $250 million, nonchocolate segment of the U.S. novelty candy market. It's the third largest segment of the sweets market, behind chocolate and chewy treats such as gummy candies, licorice, and taffy. The market has been flat in recent years, but several former toy designers and a slew of hobbyist designers are beginning to breathe new life into the industry.

Their creations range from the simply fun to the outright goofy, and candy makers pay handsomely in hopes of landing the next big hit. Two of Jones's latest hits include the Big Barf and the Big Burp. Repulsive though they sound, both are just mouth-shaped, sound-generating dispensers for harmless gumballs. Though items like the Big Barf reek of a style unique to Larry Jones, he is just one of a new breed of novelty candy container designers who are hoping to create the next confection legend that might someday be mentioned in the same breath as the almighty Pez.

As action figures, toy trains, and other traditional toys are increasingly overshadowed by their digital counterparts, inventors and their employers are betting that products that combine toys with candy curiosities are positioned to capture the dollars left behind by that fading market. Deirdre Gonzalez, vice president of marketing for Cap Candy, says the reinvigorated novelty candy market is "a hybrid business between the two industries." Often priced from $.99 to $1.29, candy items sold with toy novelties are now attracting dollars that used to be reserved for low-end toy purchases.

And the competition is as fierce as children's tastes are fickle. In addition to Kandy Kastle, companies like Cap Candy and Candy Planet race each other to develop new products, while the likes of Willy Wonka and Jelly Belly battle to promote their lines with tie-ins to blockbuster children's movies. Even independent entrepreneurs are getting in on the act. Two married couples quit their postal service jobs to form BAAT Enterprises (from their names: Bill, Ann, Ann, and Tom) and introduced the Spin Pop, a rotating motorized sucker. A modern take on the Ring Pop, the Spin Pop sold almost 6 million units in under two years.

What's cool with kids is fleeting, though. New products must be developed every month to keep up. Larry Jones, for example, did not rest on the laurels of his gastrointestinal gumball designs. He is also the wiz behind Ear Wax, Big Toe Goo, Tar Pits, Hose Nose, Brain Drain, and glow-in-the-dark Lightning Bugs. "What I'm after is to have the kid have a little bit of magic or a little giggle while eating his candy," Jones says. Kandy Kastle is relying on him to come up with a host of interesting fare based on the hugely popular Hello Kitty brand, too. Originality is key. The children in this market space, aged 4 to 12 years, are increasingly savvy consumers and they are gaining in influence and even buying power.

Influence with parents is crucial, of course, but sway with other kids in the peer group is more critical. Rose Downey, marketing manager at Au'Some Candy Company, puts extra emphasis on word-of-mouth endorsements for her company's novelty products. "We feel that the right way to grasp the kids' attention is word-of-mouth advertising," she says. "Kids trust other kids' judgment," she continues. "If Child A buys the product and it tastes great and looks cool and is fun, Child B is going to want the product and so on. Trust the kids. They know best when it comes to candy."[49]

Questions

1. To what category of new products does the Spin Pop belong?

2. Visit **http://www.KandyKastle.com** and review the product descriptions. Discuss the characteristics that influence their rate of adoption, and predict and explain their rates of acceptance and diffusion.

3. Based on what you read in the case, what do you think Kandy Kastle's new-product development strategy is? Why do you think the development of the Hello Kitty product line is important?

4. In what part of the product life cycle are the candy and toy categories? What kind of future do you predict for the novelty candy category?

COMPANY CLIPS

Kodak—Reinventing Photography

Designing usable and intriguing products is an integral part of Kodak's marketing process. Paul Porter, director of corporate design and usability, focuses on creating interesting, functional, and intuitive equipment. (Recall the striking ad on page 323 for the dual-lens camera.) To make sure the company is on the right track with product development, Kodak marketers interview customers and visit them in their own homes, observing how families use digital photography. The understanding gained from these interactions helps the company create a wide range of products targeted at different market segments.

Questions

1. EasyShare 1 didn't sell very well, but Paul Porter claimed this wasn't the purpose of that particular product. What was the purpose of the product?

2. What kind of new product was EasyShare 1?

3. Discuss the product development process at Kodak.

4. Place Kodak's digital cameras in the product life cycle.

BIZ FLIX

October Sky

Watch the *October Sky* film scenes after you have studied the discussion of developing and managing products in Chapter 10. The film tells the true story of Homer Hickam's (Jake Gylenhaal) rise from a West Virginia coal-mining town to become a NASA engineer. The scenes are an edited composite of parts of the "Rocket Roulette" and "Splitting the Sky" sequences that appear a third of the way into the film. Although Homer and his friends are not developing a new product for sale, the process they use to develop their rocket has many characteristics of the new-product development process described in this chapter. Which process characteristics do you see in these scenes? Are there examples of idea generation and idea screening in the scenes? What are they? Companies develop new products to sustain their profits and growth. What motivates Homer and his friends to solve their rocket functioning problem? Which new product category discussed at the beginning of this chapter best fits the result of their efforts?

Marketing & You Results

If your score is high, you are most likely a "market maven." You are aware of new products earlier and talk about a variety of products to your friends. High scores also indicate a greater interest in and attentiveness to the market. Conversely, the lower your score, the less interested you are in the market and new products.

Services and
CHAPTER 11 Nonprofit Organization Marketing

Learning Outcomes

LO¹ Discuss the importance of services to the economy

LO² Discuss the differences between services and goods

LO³ Describe the components of service quality and the gap model of service quality

LO⁴ Develop marketing mixes for services

LO⁵ Discuss relationship marketing in services

LO⁶ Explain internal marketing in services

LO⁷ Discuss global issues in services marketing

LO⁸ Describe nonprofit organization marketing

Humane Society *upgrades and increases adoptions*

A growing number of animal shelters across the country are fixing up their facilities, adding innovative architecture, retail space, and even Starbucks coffee, in order to improve the conditions of—and to show off—the homeless occupants. For example, at the Humane Society/Society for the Prevention of Cruelty to Animals in San

Animals live in homelike settings complete with televisions, couches, natural lighting, and art on the walls.

Antonio, Texas, cats and dogs play in specially designed "cottages" and "palaces" behind glass walls that face the street. Soft music plays to help keep the animals calm. The facility's executive director notes that potential adopters coming in are willing to stay longer because they smell fresh air, not animals.

In addition to improving its physical facility, the San Antonio shelter moved its location from a run-down neighborhood to a busy retail district. Positioned near a Target store, a mall, and a medical center, the new shelter experienced increased foot traffic and adoptions right away.

The movement to spruce up animal shelters started in California, where shelters in San Francisco and Oakland changed the way homeless animals were housed. One of the first organizations to create new pet adoption facilities was the San Francisco SPCA. In 1998, it built a $7 million, 27,000-square-foot addition with more than 80 "condos" and "apartments," where animals live in homelike settings complete with televisions, couches, natural lighting, and art on the walls. The shelter's former director estimates that up to 100 shelters nationwide have made similar changes.[1]

How does providing a service, like an animal shelter, differ from providing goods, such as soft drinks, automobiles, or blue jeans? What components of the marketing mix were changed in the animal shelters described here?

LO¹
The Importance of Services

service
The result of applying human or mechanical efforts to people or objects.

A **service** is the result of applying human or mechanical efforts to people or objects. Services involve a deed, a performance, or an effort that cannot be physically possessed. Today, the service sector substantially influences the U.S. economy, accounting for 81 percent of both U.S. gross domestic product and U.S. employment.[2] The demand for services is expected to continue. According to the Bureau of Labor Statistics, service occupations will be responsible for nearly all net job growth through the year 2012. Much of this demand results from demographics. An aging population will need nurses, home health care, physical therapists, and social workers. Two-earner families need child-care, housecleaning, and lawn-care services. Also increasing will be the demand for information managers, such as computer engineers and systems analysts. There is also a growing market for service companies worldwide.

The marketing process described in Chapter 1 is the same for all types of products, whether they are goods or services. Many ideas and strategies discussed throughout this book have been illustrated with service examples. In many ways, marketing is marketing, regardless of the product's characteristics. In addition, although a comparison of goods and services marketing can be beneficial, in reality it is hard to distinguish clearly between manufacturing and service firms. Indeed, many manufacturing firms can point to service as a major factor in their success. For example, maintenance and repair services offered by the manufacturer are important to buyers of copy machines. General Electric makes most of its revenues from finance operations rather than from products. Nevertheless, services have some unique characteristics that distinguish them from goods, and marketing strategies need to be adjusted for these characteristics.

REVIEW LEARNING OUTCOME

LO¹ Discuss the importance of services to the economy

Services ⟶ Deed / Performance / Effort

Services as a percentage of GDP

10% 20% 30% 40% 50% 60% 70% 80% 90% 100%

81%

Services as a percentage of employment

10% 20% 30% 40% 50% 60% 70% 80% 90% 100%

81%

LO²
How Services Differ from Goods

intangibility
The inability of services to be touched, seen, tasted, heard, or felt in the same manner that goods can be sensed.

search quality
A characteristic that can be easily assessed before purchase.

experience quality
A characteristic that can be assessed only after use.

credence quality
A characteristic that consumers may have difficulty assessing even after purchase because they do not have the necessary knowledge or experience.

Services have four unique characteristics that distinguish them from goods. Services are intangible, inseparable, heterogeneous, and perishable.

INTANGIBILITY

The basic difference between services and goods is that services are intangible performances. Because of their **intangibility**, they cannot be touched, seen, tasted, heard, or felt in the same manner that goods can be sensed. Services cannot be stored and are often easy to duplicate.

Evaluating the quality of services before or even after making a purchase is harder than evaluating the quality of goods because, compared to goods, services tend to exhibit fewer search qualities. A **search quality** is a characteristic that can be easily assessed before purchase—for instance, the color of an appliance or automobile. At the same time, services tend to exhibit more experience and credence qualities. An **experience quality** is a characteristic that can be assessed only after use, such as the quality of a meal in a restaurant or the actual experience of a vacation. A **credence quality** is a characteristic that

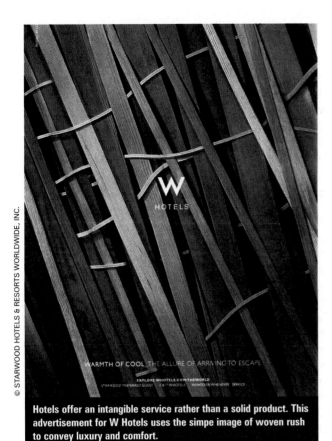

Hotels offer an intangible service rather than a solid product. This advertisement for W Hotels uses the simpe image of woven rush to convey luxury and comfort.

consumers may have difficulty assessing even after purchase because they do not have the necessary knowledge or experience. Medical and consulting services are examples of services that exhibit credence qualities.

These characteristics also make it harder for marketers to communicate the benefits of an intangible service than to communicate the benefits of tangible goods. Thus, marketers often rely on tangible cues to communicate a service's nature and quality. For example, Travelers' Insurance Company's use of the umbrella symbol helped make tangible the benefit of protection that insurance provides.

The facilities that customers visit, or from which services are delivered, are a critical tangible part of the total service offering. Messages about the organization are communicated to customers through such elements as the decor, the clutter or neatness of service areas, and the staff's manners and dress. The 167 land ports of entry along U.S. borders are undergoing a design overhaul to enhance and rebuild their facilities. The chief architect of the General Services Administration noted that the border stations should "speak positively to what lies beyond."[3] The design and development team at Bass Pro Shops believes that in-store displays are not just fixtures, but marketing tools that will attract customers if designed to reflect local culture. So, for example, the Destin, Florida store incorporates indigenous seagulls and swordfish in the chandeliers.[4]

INSEPARABILITY

Goods are produced, sold, and then consumed. In contrast, services are often sold, produced, and consumed at the same time. In other words, their production and consumption are inseparable activities. This **inseparability** means that, because consumers must be present during the production of services like haircuts or surgery, they are actually involved in the production of the services they buy. That type of consumer involvement is rare in goods manufacturing.

Simultaneous production and consumption also means that services normally cannot be produced in a centralized location and consumed in decentralized locations, as goods typically are. Services are also inseparable from the perspective of the service provider. Thus, the quality of service that firms are able to deliver depends on the quality of their employees.

inseparability
The inability of the production and consumption of a service to be separated. Consumers must be present during the production.

heterogeneity
The variability of the inputs and outputs of services, which cause services to tend to be less standardized and uniform than goods.

HETEROGENEITY

One great strength of McDonald's is consistency. Whether customers order a Big Mac and french fries in Fort Worth, Tokyo, or Moscow, they know exactly what they are going to get. This is not the case with many service providers. Because services have greater **heterogeneity** or variability of inputs and outputs, they tend to be less standardized and uniform than goods. For example, physicians in a group practice or barbers in a barber shop differ within each group in their technical and interpersonal skills. A given physician's or barber's performance may even vary depending on time of day, physical health, or some other factor. Because services tend to be labor-intensive and production and consumption are inseparable, consistency and quality control can be hard to achieve.

Standardization and training help increase consistency and reliability. Limited-menu restaurants like Pizza Hut and KFC offer customers high consistency from one visit to the next because of standardized preparation procedures. Another way to increase consistency is to mechanize the process. Banks have reduced the inconsistency of teller services by providing automated teller machines (ATMs). Automatic coin receptacles and electronic toll collection systems such as E-Z Pass have replaced human collectors on toll roads.

PERISHABILITY

The fourth characteristic of services is their **perishability**, which means that they cannot be stored, warehoused, or inventoried. An empty hotel room or airplane seat produces no revenue that day. The revenue is lost. Yet service organizations are often forced to turn away full-price customers during peak periods.

One of the most important challenges in many service industries is finding ways to synchronize supply and demand. The philosophy that some revenue is better than none has prompted many hotels to offer deep discounts on weekends and during the off-season and has prompted airlines to adopt similar pricing strategies during off-peak hours. Car rental agencies, movie theaters, and restaurants also use discounts to encourage demand during nonpeak periods.

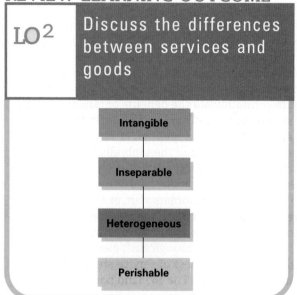

REVIEW LEARNING OUTCOME

LO2 Discuss the differences between services and goods

Intangible

Inseparable

Heterogeneous

Perishable

LO3
Service Quality

Because of the four unique characteristics of services, service quality is more difficult to define and measure than is the quality of tangible goods. Business executives rank the improvement of service quality as one of the most critical challenges facing them today.

Research has shown that customers evaluate service quality by the following five components:[5]

- *Reliability*: the ability to perform the service dependably, accurately, and consistently. Reliability is performing the service right the first time. This component has been found to be the one most important to consumers.

- *Responsiveness*: the ability to provide prompt service. Examples of responsiveness include calling the customer back quickly, serving lunch fast to someone who is in a hurry, or mailing a transaction slip immediately. The ultimate in responsiveness is offering service 24 hours a day, seven days a week. For example, Zappos.com, a successful online shoe company, keeps its warehouse open 24/7 so that customers can order shoes at 11 P.M. and still get next-day delivery.[6]

- *Assurance*: the knowledge and courtesy of employees and their ability to convey trust. Skilled employees who treat customers with respect and make customers feel that they can trust the firm exemplify assurance.

- *Empathy*: caring, individualized attention to customers. Firms whose employees recognize customers, call them by name, and learn their customers' specific requirements are providing empathy. Ritz-Carlton, the only service company that has twice won the prestigious Malcolm Baldrige National Quality Award, has a rig-

perishability
The inability of services to be stored, warehoused, or inventoried.

reliability
The ability to perform a service dependably, accurately, and consistently.

responsiveness
The ability to provide prompt service.

assurance
The knowledge and courtesy of employees and their ability to convey trust.

empathy
Caring, individualized attention to customers.

© LIBBY CHAPMAN/ISTOCKPHOTO INTERNATIONAL INC.

orous training program for its employees. For example, bellhops have to learn 28 steps to greeting a guest that includes offering a warm, sincere greeting and using the guest's name when possible.[7]

- *Tangibles:* the physical evidence of the service. The tangible parts of a service include the physical facilities, tools, and equipment used to provide the service, such as a doctor's office or an ATM, and the appearance of personnel. For example, Enterprise Rent-A-Car has strict dress codes for its employees. Female employees have 30 guidelines including that pants must be creased, skirts must not be shorter than two inches above the knee, and legs must be in stockings. Male employees have to follow 26 dress rules, including dress shirts with coordinated ties and no beards. In fact, "distinctive professional dress" is mentioned in Enterprise's written founding values. Hospitals have found that improving their layouts and looks can translate into better health for their patients. After the Barbara Ann Karmanos Cancer Institute in Detroit was renovated, using soft colors, warm indirect lighting, wider hallways and doors, and pullout sofas for visitors, hospital administrators found that patients dealt more effectively with their pain than they had before the remodeling.[8]

tangibles
The physical evidence of a service, including the physical facilities, tools, and equipment used to provide the service.

gap model
A model identifying five gaps that can cause problems in service delivery and influence customer evaluations of service quality.

Overall service quality is measured by combining customers' evaluations for all five components.

THE GAP MODEL OF SERVICE QUALITY

A model of service quality called the **gap model** identifies five gaps that can cause problems in service delivery and influence customer evaluations of service quality.[9] These gaps are illustrated in Exhibit 11.1:

- *Gap 1:* the gap between what customers want and what management thinks customers want. This gap results from a lack of understanding or a misinterpretation of the customers' needs, wants, or desires. A firm that does little or no customer satisfaction research is likely to experience this gap. An important step in closing gap 1 is to keep in touch with what customers want by doing research on customer needs and customer satisfaction. Ritz-Carlton has an in-house database called the Customer Loyalty Anticipation Satisfaction System that stores guest preferences, such as whether an individual likes Seagram's ginger ale or Canada Dry.[10]

- *Gap 2:* the gap between what management thinks customers want and the quality specifications that management develops to provide the service. Essentially, this gap is the result of management's inability to translate customers' needs into delivery systems within the firm. For example, Kentucky Fried Chicken once rated its managers' success according to "chicken efficiency," or how much chicken they threw away at the end of the night. Customers who came in late at night would either have to wait for chicken to be cooked or settle for chicken several hours old. The "chicken efficiency" measurement did not take customers into account.

Exhibit 11.1
Gap Model of Service Quality

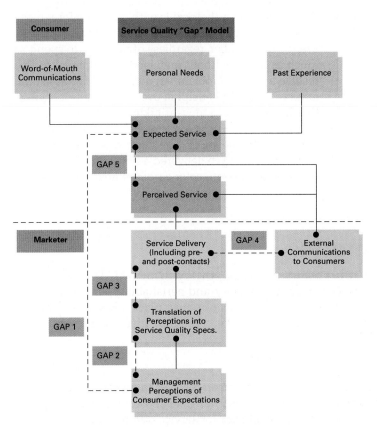

SOURCE: Valerie A. Zeithaml, Mary Jo Bitner, and Dwayne Gremler, *Services Marketing* (New York: McGraw-Hill, 2006).

- *Gap 3*: the gap between the service quality specifications and the service that is actually provided. If both gaps 1 and 2 have been closed, then gap 3 is due to the inability of management and employees to do what should be done. Poorly trained or poorly motivated workers can cause this gap. Management needs to ensure that employees have the skills and the proper tools to perform their jobs. Other techniques that help to close gap 3 are training employees so they know what management expects and encouraging teamwork. For example, Ritz-Carlton's employee training includes a 2-day introduction to the company, followed by a 21-day course on job responsibilities. In addition, every day at all the company's hotels, employees participate in a 15-minute session where they talk about Ritz-Carlton's core values.[11]

- *Gap 4*: the gap between what the company provides and what the customer is told it provides. This is clearly a communication gap. It may include misleading or deceptive advertising campaigns promising more than the firm can deliver or doing "whatever it takes" to get the business. To close this gap, companies need to create realistic customer expectations through honest, accurate communication about what the firms can provide.

- *Gap 5*: the gap between the service that customers receive and the service they want. This gap can be positive or negative. For example, if a patient expects to wait 20 minutes in the physician's office before seeing the physician but waits only 10 minutes, the patient's evaluation of service quality will be high. However, a 40-minute wait would result in a lower evaluation.

REVIEW LEARNING OUTCOME

LO3 Describe the components of service quality and the gap model of service quality

SERVICE

Reliability · Responsiveness · Assurance · Empathy · Tangibles

When one or more of these gaps are large, service quality is perceived as low. As the gaps shrink, service quality improves. For instance, Ritz-Carlton has excelled in closing gap 3. Not only does this hotel firm give its employees thorough training, as described above, but even before they are hired, it puts potential employees through a comprehensive screening process to match their skills with positions for which they are naturally inclined. The company also allows every staff member, regardless of position, to spend as much as $2,000 without management approval to resolve a guest's problem. An administrative assistant at Ritz-Carlton Philadelphia overheard a guest saying that he would have to wear hiking boots to an important meeting the next morning because he had forgotten his formal shoes. The guest was awestruck when the employee delivered a new pair of shoes in his size and favorite color early the next morning.[12]

LO4
Marketing Mixes for Services

Services' unique characteristics—intangibility, inseparability of production and consumption, heterogeneity, and perishability—make marketing more challenging. Elements of the marketing mix (product, place, promotion, and pricing) need to be adjusted to meet the special needs created by these characteristics.

PRODUCT (SERVICE) STRATEGY

A product, as defined in Chapter 9, is everything a person receives in an exchange. In the case of a service organization, the product offering is intangible and consists in large part of a process or a series of processes. Product strategies for service offerings include deci-

Dry cleaning is an example of a possession-processing service. These types of services require less focus on attractive physical environments and customer service training than people-processing services like hairdressers and airlines.

sions on the type of process involved, core and supplementary services, standardization or customization of the service product, and the service mix.

Service as a Process

Two broad categories of things get processed in service organizations: people and objects. In some cases, the process is physical, or tangible, while in others the process is intangible. Based on these characteristics, service processes can be placed into one of four categories:[13]

- *People processing* takes place when the service is directed at a customer. Examples are transportation services, hairstyling, health clubs, and dental and health care.

- *Possession processing* occurs when the service is directed at customers' physical possessions. Examples are lawn care, car repair, dry cleaning, and veterinary services.

- *Mental stimulus processing* refers to services directed at people's minds. Examples are entertainment, spectator sports events, theater performances, and education.

- *Information processing* describes services that use technology or brainpower directed at a customer's assets. Examples are insurance, banking, and consulting.

Because customers' experiences and involvement differ for each of these types of services, marketing strategies may also differ. For example, people-processing services require customers to enter the *service factory*, which is a physical location, such as an aircraft, a physician's office, or a hair salon. In contrast, possession-processing services typically do not require the presence of the customer in the service factory; the customer may simply leave the car at the garage for repairs, for example. Marketing strategies for the former would therefore focus more on an attractive, comfortable physical environment and employee training on employee-customer interaction issues than would strategies for the latter.

core service
The most basic benefit the consumer is buying.

supplementary services
A group of services that support or enhance the core service.

Core and Supplementary Service Products

The service offering can be viewed as a bundle of activities that includes the **core service**, which is the most basic benefit the customer is buying, and a group of **supplementary services** that support or enhance the core service. Exhibit 11.2 illustrates these concepts for FedEx. The core service is overnight transportation and delivery of packages, which involves possession processing. The supplementary services, some of which involve information processing, include problem solving, advice and information, billing statements, and order taking. Starbucks has added a wireless Internet service called "T-Mobile HotSpot" that enhances its core offering—the Starbucks' experience of high-quality coffee served in a coffeehouse atmosphere. Starbucks is not trying to become an Internet coffeehouse, but to become the "other place" where people want to be connected to the Internet.[14]

In many service industries, the core service becomes a commodity as competition increases. Thus, firms usually emphasize supplementary services to create a competitive advantage. First-class passengers on Virgin Atlantic's flight from Miami to London enjoy seats that convert into flat beds, a bar and bartender, and a chance for a massage. When

Exhibit 11.2

Core and Supplementary Services for FedEx

SOURCE: From *Services Marketing* 5th ed., by Christopher H. Lovelock and Jochen Wirtz © 2004. Reprinted by permission of Prentice Hall, Inc., Upper Saddle River, NJ.

Making services more personalized is the goal of mass customization. For example, airlines are rolling out personal interactive entertainment systems on airplanes so that passengers can watch movies when they want, rather than only at a set time during the flight.

© AP/WIDE WORLD PHOTOS

passengers land, they may shower in a special lounge and then be taken by limousine to their destinations.[15] On the other hand, some firms are positioning themselves in the marketplace by greatly reducing supplementary services. For example, Microtel Inn is an amenity-free hotel concept known as "fast lodging." These low-cost hotels have one- and two-bedroom accommodations and a swimming pool, but no meeting rooms or other services.

Customization/Standardization

An important issue in developing the service offering is whether to customize or standardize it. Customized services are more flexible and respond to individual customers' needs. They also usually command a higher price. The traditional law firm, which treats each case differently according to the client's situation, offers customized services. Standardized services are more efficient and cost less. Unlike the traditional law firm, for example, Hyatt Legal Services offers low-cost, standardized service "packages" for those with uncomplicated legal needs, such as drawing up a will or mediating an uncontested divorce.

Instead of choosing to either standardize or customize a service, a firm may incorporate elements of both by adopting an emerging strategy called **mass customization**. Mass customization uses technology to deliver customized services on a mass basis, which results in giving each customer whatever she or he asks for.

For example, a feature on Lands' End Web site allows women to define their figures online, receive advice on what swimsuits will flatter their shapes, and mix and match more than 216 combinations of colors and styles. Several airlines are designing services to cater to travelers' individual needs and preferences. Some will serve dinner to passengers when they want to eat it, rather than when the airline wants to serve it. More airlines are offering video-on-demand systems, which let passengers start or stop their movie anytime they want.

The Service Mix

Most service organizations market more than one service. For example, ChemLawn offers lawn care, shrub care, carpet cleaning, and industrial lawn services. Each organization's service mix represents a set of opportunities, risks, and challenges. Each part of the service mix should make a different contribution to achieving the firm's goals. To succeed, each service may also need a different level of financial support.

Designing a service strategy therefore means deciding what new services to introduce to which target market, what existing services to maintain, and what services to eliminate. For example, to increase membership, AAA added financial services, credit cards, and travel perks. Hilton has seven hotel brands that are targeted to different customer segments. For example, the Conrad, in the tower of Hilton's Waldorf Astoria, is one of the fanciest, and most expensive, Hilton hotels. The Hampton Inn is a basic, inexpensive hotel, and Embassy Suites are upscale inns that offer a homelike experience, including kitchen facilities.[16]

mass customization
A strategy that uses technology to deliver customized services on a mass basis.

PLACE (DISTRIBUTION) STRATEGY

Distribution strategies for service organizations must focus on such issues as convenience, number of outlets, direct versus indirect distribution, location, and scheduling. A key factor influencing the selection of a service provider is *convenience*. Therefore, service firms must offer convenience. Many banks have opened small branches in supermarkets and discount stores like Wal-Mart to make it more convenient for customers to use their services. Restaurants such as Chili's and Macaroni Grill deliver take-out food to customers waiting in their cars. Some doctors are even starting to make house calls to elderly and infirm patients.

An important distribution objective for many service firms is the *number of outlets* to use or the number of outlets to open during a certain time. Generally, the intensity of distribution should meet, but not exceed, the target market's needs and preferences. Having too few outlets may inconvenience customers; having too many outlets may boost costs unnecessarily. Intensity of distribution may also depend on the image desired. Having only a few outlets may make the service seem more exclusive or selective.

The next service distribution decision is whether to distribute services to end users *directly* or *indirectly* through other firms. Because of the intangible nature of services, many service firms have to use direct distribution or franchising. Examples include legal, medical, accounting, and personal-care services. The newest form of direct distribution is the Internet. Most of the major airlines are now using online services to sell tickets directly to consumers, which results in lower distribution costs for the airline companies. Merrill Lynch offers Merrill Lynch Online, an Internet-based service that connects clients with company representatives. Other firms with standardized service packages have developed indirect channels using independent intermediaries. For example, Bank of America is offering teller services and loan services to customers in small satellite facilities located in Albertson's grocery stores in Texas.

The *location* of a service most clearly reveals the relationship between its target market strategy and its distribution strategy. Reportedly, Conrad Hilton claimed that the three most important factors in determining a hotel's success are "location, location, and location." An interesting location trend has started in the banking industry. In the past few years, banks aggressively directed customers away from branches and toward ATMs and the Internet. In a recent about-face, banks are trying to entice customers back into the branches. For example, Washington Mutual, Inc., based in Seattle, is designing new branches and remodeling old ones to resemble Gap stores.

For time-dependent service providers like airlines, physicians, and dentists, scheduling is often a more important factor. Scheduling is sometimes the most important factor in a customer's choice of airline. MinuteClinic has opened no-appointment-necessary clinics in eight CVS pharmacies in the Atlanta, Georgia area. The goal is to diagnose patients in 15 minutes, start to finish. The drugstore chain rents space to the company under the assumption that patients will pick up their medicines at CVS stores. The advantage for patients is that MinuteClinic is fast and convenient.[17]

PROMOTION STRATEGY

Consumers and business users have more trouble evaluating services than goods because services are less tangible. In turn, marketers have more trouble promoting intangible services than tangible goods. Here are four promotion strategies they can try:

- *Stressing tangible cues:* A tangible cue is a concrete symbol of the service offering. To make their intangible services more tangible, hotels turn down the bedcovers and put mints on the pillows. Insurance companies use symbols like rocks, blankets, umbrellas, and hands to help make their intangible services appear tangible. Merrill Lynch uses a bull to help give its services substance.

- *Using personal information sources:* A personal information source is someone consumers are familiar with (such as a celebrity) or someone they know or can relate to personally. Celebrity endorsements are sometimes used to reduce customers' perceived risk in choosing a service. Service firms may also seek to simulate positive word-of-mouth communication among present and prospective customers by using real customers in their ads.

- *Creating a strong organizational image:* One way to create an image is to manage the evidence, including the physical environment of the service facility, the appearance

The owner of 112 McDonald's restaurants in Switzerland leveraged the company's strong organizational image (quality, service, cleanliness, and hygiene) and created a hotel. The four-star Golden Arch Hotel has an ultramodern design, offers wireless Internet connections through the television, and is priced as if it were a two-star hotel, at only around $90 per night.

of the service employees, and the tangible items associated with a service (like stationery, bills, and business cards). For example, McDonald's has created a strong organizational image with its Golden Arches, relatively standardized interiors, and employee uniforms. Another way to create an image is through branding. Disney brands include Disneyland, Disney World, the Disney Channel, and Disney Stores.

- *Engaging in post-purchase communication:* Postpurchase communication refers to the follow-up activities that a service firm might engage in after a customer transaction. Postcard surveys, telephone calls, brochures, and various other types of follow-up show customers that their feedback matters and their patronage is appreciated.

PRICE STRATEGY

Considerations in pricing a service are similar to the pricing considerations to be discussed in Chapters 17 and 18. However, the unique characteristics of services present two special pricing challenges.

First, in order to price a service, it is important to define the unit of service consumption. For example, should pricing be based on completing a specific service task (cutting a customer's hair), or should it be time based (how long it takes to cut a customer's hair)? Some services include the consumption of goods, such as food and beverages. Restaurants charge customers for food and drink rather than the use of a table and chairs. Some transportation firms charge by distance; others charge a flat rate.

Second, for services that are composed of multiple elements, the issue is whether pricing should be based on a "bundle" of elements or whether each element should be priced separately. A bundled price may be preferable when consumers dislike having to pay "extra" for every part of the service (for example, paying extra for baggage or food on an airplane), and it is simpler for the firm to administer. For instance, MCI offered a basic communications package that included 30 minutes of telephone time, five hours of Internet access, a personal number that could route calls to several locations, and a calling card all

REVIEW LEARNING OUTCOME

LO4 Develop marketing mixes for services

PRODUCT = SERVICE	PLACE	PROMOTION	PRICE
Process	Number of outlets	Tangible cues	Revenue oriented
Core and supplementary	Direct	Personal information services	Operations oriented
Mass customization	Indirect	Strong organizational image	Patronage oriented
Standardization	Location	Post–purchase communication	

for one price. Alternatively, customers may not want to pay for service elements they do not use. Many furniture stores now have "unbundled" delivery charges from the price of the furniture. Customers who wish to can pick up the furniture at the store, saving on the delivery fee.

Marketers should set performance objectives when pricing each service. Three categories of pricing objectives have been suggested:[18]

- *Revenue-oriented pricing* focuses on maximizing the surplus of income over costs. A limitation of this approach is that determining costs can be difficult for many services.

- *Operations-oriented pricing* seeks to match supply and demand by varying prices. For example, matching hotel demand to the number of available rooms can be achieved by raising prices at peak times and decreasing them during slow times.

- *Patronage-oriented pricing* tries to maximize the number of customers using the service. Thus, prices vary with different market segments' ability to pay, and methods of payment (such as credit) are offered that increase the likelihood of a purchase.

A firm may need to use more than one type of pricing objective. In fact, all three objectives probably need to be included to some degree in a pricing strategy, although the importance of each type may vary depending on the type of service provided, the prices that competitors are charging, the differing ability of various customer segments to pay, or the opportunity to negotiate price. For customized services (for example, legal services and construction services), customers may also have the ability to negotiate a price. This chapter's "Global Perspectives" box describes how discount pricing in the airline industry is changing the way people travel in Latin America.

GLOBAL Perspectives

Discount Airlines Offer an Alternative to Taking the Bus in Latin America

Until recently, people who traveled long distances in Latin American countries like Mexico and Brazil had to take expensive full-fare flights, often on small charter airlines, or endure a long uncomfortable ride on a bus. Now, a fast-growing group of discount airlines is offering an alternative. Modeled on discounters like Southwest Airlines, these carriers are offering fares as low as $20 between São Paulo and Rio de Janeiro. In some cases, one-way promotional fares have been less than a dollar.

The growth of budget airlines in Latin America has been facilitated by aviation officials who are making it easier to offer cross-border flights. For example, regulators in Peru and Brazil agreed to allow 28 flights a week between the two countries—more than triple the previous quota of 8 flights a week.

The new airlines are primarily targeting the millions of middle- and lower-middle-class Latin Americans who are tired of bumpy, cramped, ten-hour-plus bus rides between cities. Besides, the bus fares, which can run as high as $75 to $100 on some routes, are nearly as costly as a discount plane ticket—or even higher than the special promotional fares.

Foreign tourists are another potential market for the budget airlines. Tourism to Latin America is on the rise, with many people coming from the United States. U.S.-based travelers can purchase tickets on the airlines' Web sites, many of which have English options and allow bookings with major credit cards. Some of the airlines also offer hotel and rental car packages targeted to tourists. Tikal Jets, which flies from Guatemala City to Belize City, offers discounts at the Radisson and Grand Tikal Futura hotels in Guatemala City when tickets are bought through its Web site. Click, a budget airline in Mexico, will offer domestic routes from Mexico City to popular but hard-to-reach beach towns like Ixtapa and Puerto Escondito. So far, however, none of the discount carriers is listed on the sites of the big travel agencies like Travelocity and Orbitz.[19]

Do you think the new discount airlines will be successful in Latin America? Why or why not? Will culture be a factor?

Relationship Marketing in Services

Many services involve ongoing interaction between the service organization and the customer. Thus, they can benefit from relationship marketing, the strategy described in Chapter 1, as a means of attracting, developing, and retaining customer relationships. The idea is to develop strong loyalty by creating satisfied customers who will buy additional services from the firm and are unlikely to switch to a competitor. Satisfied customers are also likely to engage in positive word-of-mouth communication, thereby helping to bring in new customers.

Many businesses have found that it is more cost-effective to hang on to the customers they have than to focus only on attracting new ones. A bank executive, for example, found that increasing customer retention by 2 percent can have the same effect on profits as reducing costs by 10 percent.

Services that purchasers receive on a continuing basis (for example, cable TV, banking, insurance) can be considered membership services. This type of service naturally lends itself to relationship marketing. When services involve discrete transactions (for example, a movie theater, a restaurant, public transportation), it may be more difficult to build membership-type relationships with customers. Nevertheless, services involving discrete transactions may be transformed into membership relationships using marketing tools. For example, the service could be sold in bulk (for example, a theater series subscription or a commuter pass on public transportation). Or a service firm could offer special benefits to customers who choose to register with the firm (for example, loyalty programs for hotels, airlines, and car rental firms). The service firm that has a more formalized relationship with its customers has an advantage because it knows who its customers are and how and when they use the services offered.[20]

It has been suggested that relationship marketing can be practiced at three levels:[21]

This E*Trade advertisement encourages consumers to sign up for the company's membership service by offering a free portfolio review to new users. The ad also provides a message to existing users about the benefits of the company's services.

- *Level 1:* The firm uses pricing incentives to encourage customers to continue doing business with it. Examples include the frequent flyer programs offered by many airlines and the free or discounted travel services given to frequent hotel guests. This level of relationship marketing is the least effective in the long term because its price-based advantage is easily imitated by other firms.

- *Level 2:* This level of relationship marketing also uses pricing incentives but seeks to build social bonds with customers. The firm stays in touch with customers, learns about their needs, and designs services to meet those needs. 1-800-FLOWERS, for example, developed an online Gift Reminder Program. Customers who reach the company via its Web site can register unlimited birthdays, anniversaries, or other special occasions. Five days before each occasion and at their request, 1-800-FLOWERS sends them an e-mail reminder. Level 2 relationship marketing has a higher potential for keeping the firm ahead of the competition than does level 1 relationship marketing.

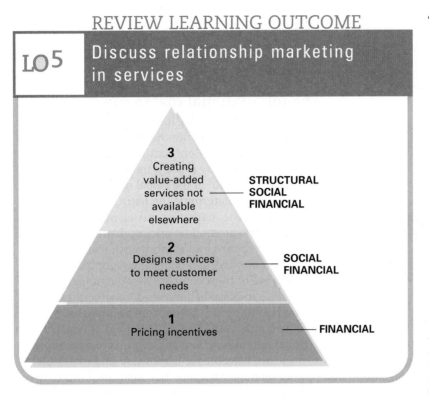

LO 5 Discuss relationship marketing in services

3
Creating value-added services not available elsewhere — STRUCTURAL SOCIAL FINANCIAL

2
Designs services to meet customer needs — SOCIAL FINANCIAL

1
Pricing incentives — FINANCIAL

- *Level 3:* At this level, the firm again uses financial and social bonds but adds structural bonds to the formula. Structural bonds are developed by offering value-added services that are not readily available from other firms. Hertz's #1 Club Gold program allows members to call and reserve a car, board a courtesy bus at the airport, tell the driver their name, and get dropped off in front of their car. Hertz also starts up the car and turns on the air conditioning or heat, depending on the temperature. Marketing programs like this one have the strongest potential for sustaining long-term relationships with customers.

LO 6
Internal Marketing in Service Firms

internal marketing
Treating employees as customers and developing systems and benefits that satisfy their needs.

Services are performances, so the quality of a firm's employees is an important part of building long-term relationships with customers. Employees who like their jobs and are satisfied with the firm they work for are more likely to deliver superior service to customers. In other words, a firm that makes its employees happy has a better chance of keeping its customers coming back. Studies show that replacing an employee costs roughly 1.5 times a year's pay. Also, companies with highly committed employees have been found to post sharply higher shareholder returns. Thus, it is critical that service firms practice **internal marketing**, which means treating employees as customers and developing systems and benefits that satisfy their needs.

Companies have instituted a wide variety of programs designed to satisfy employees. Zappos .com, the online shoe company, pays 100 percent of the health insurance premiums for its employees, and every employee gets a free lunch every day.[22] Chipotle Mexican Grill provides its Spanish-speaking employees with English-language instruction, which builds the workers' self-confidence and results in lower employee turnover. [23] The Container Store's turnover rate is less than 10 percent for full-time employees and 30 to 35 percent for part-timers in an industry with an average turnover rate of more than 70 percent. Applicants who get a callback are put in group interviews with as many as ten other job candidates, which gives managers an opportunity to see how people might perform as part of a team. New hires go through a 241-hour training program that stretches out over a year and are paired with training "buddies" who help them with everything from sales techniques to learning the features of the modular storage system that is the company's best-seller.[24] These examples illustrate how service firms can invest in their most important resource—their employees.

LO 6 Explain internal marketing in services

Management   Employees   Customers

Good service flows from management to customers through employees.

LO7 Discuss global issues in services marketing

U. S. A.

United States is world's largest exporter of services.

LO7
Global Issues in Services Marketing

The international marketing of services is a major part of global business, and the United States has become the world's largest exporter of services. Competition in international services is increasing rapidly, however.

To be successful in the global marketplace, service firms must first determine the nature of their core product. Then the marketing mix elements (additional services, place, promotion, pricing, distribution) should be designed to take into account each country's cultural, technological, and political environment.

Because of their competitive advantages, many U.S. service industries have been able to enter the global marketplace. U.S. banks, for example, have advantages in customer service and collections management. The field of construction and engineering services offers great global potential; U.S. companies have vast experience in this industry, so economies of scale are possible for machinery and materials, human resource management, and project management. The U.S. insurance industry has substantial knowledge about underwriting, risk evaluation, and insurance operations that it can export to other countries.

LO8
Nonprofit Organization Marketing

A nonprofit organization is an organization that exists to achieve some goal other than the usual business goals of profit, market share, or return on investment. Nonprofit organizations share important characteristics with private-sector service firms. Both market intangible products. Both often require the customer to be present during the production process. Both for-profit and nonprofit services vary greatly from producer to producer and from day to day, even from the same producer. Neither for-profit nor nonprofit services can be stored in the way that tangible goods can be produced, saved, and sold at a later date.

Few people realize that nonprofit organizations account for over 20 percent of the economic activity in the United States. The cost of government (i.e., taxes), the predominant form of nonprofit organization, has become the biggest single item in the American family budget—more than housing, food, or health care. Together, federal, state, and local governments collect tax revenues that amount to more than a third of the U.S. gross domestic product. Moreover, they employ nearly one of every five nonagricultural civilian workers. In addition to government entities, nonprofit organizations include hundreds of thousands of private museums, theaters, schools, and churches.

nonprofit organization
An organization that exists to achieve some goal other than the usual business goals of profit, market share, or return on investment.

nonprofit organization marketing
The effort by nonprofit organizations to bring about mutually satisfying exchanges with target markets.

WHAT IS NONPROFIT ORGANIZATION MARKETING?

Nonprofit organization marketing is the effort by nonprofit organizations to bring about mutually satisfying exchanges with target markets. Although these organizations vary substantially in size and purpose and operate in different environments, most perform the following marketing activities:

- Identify the customers they wish to serve or attract (although they usually use another term, such as *clients, patients, members,* or *sponsors*)

- Explicitly or implicitly specify objectives

- Develop, manage, and eliminate programs and services

- Decide on prices to charge (although they use other terms, such as *fees, donations, tuition, fares, fines,* or *rates*)

- Schedule events or programs, and determine where they will be held or where services will be offered

- Communicate their availability through brochures, signs, public service announcements, or advertisements

Often, the nonprofit organizations that carry out these functions do not realize they are engaged in marketing.

UNIQUE ASPECTS OF NONPROFIT ORGANIZATION MARKETING STRATEGIES

Like their counterparts in business organizations, nonprofit managers develop marketing strategies to bring about mutually satisfying exchanges with target markets. However, marketing in nonprofit organizations is unique in many ways—including the setting of marketing objectives, the selection of target markets, and the development of appropriate marketing mixes.

Objectives

In the private sector, the profit motive is both an objective for guiding decisions and a criterion for evaluating results. Nonprofit organizations do not seek to make a profit for redistribution to owners or shareholders. Rather, their focus is often on generating enough funds to cover expenses. The Methodist Church does not gauge its success by the amount of money left in offering plates. The Museum of Science and Industry does not base its performance evaluations on the dollar value of tokens put into the turnstile.

Most nonprofit organizations are expected to provide equitable, effective, and efficient services that respond to the wants and preferences of multiple constituencies. These include users, payers, donors, politicians, appointed officials, the media, and the general public. Nonprofit organizations cannot measure their success or failure in strictly financial terms.

The lack of a financial "bottom line" and the existence of multiple, diverse, intangible, and sometimes vague or conflicting objectives make prioritizing objectives, making decisions, and evaluating performance hard for nonprofit managers. They must often use approaches different from the ones commonly used in the private sector. For example, Planned Parenthood has devised a system for basing salary increases on how employees perform in relation to the objectives they set each year.

Target Markets

Three issues relating to target markets are unique to nonprofit organizations:

- *Apathetic or strongly opposed targets:* Private-sector organizations usually give priority to developing those market segments that are most likely to respond to particular offerings. In contrast, nonprofit organizations must often target those who are apathetic about or strongly opposed to receiving their services, such as vaccinations, family-planning guidance, help for problems of drug or alcohol abuse, and psychological counseling.

- *Pressure to adopt undifferentiated segmentation strategies:* Nonprofit organizations often adopt undifferentiated strategies (see Chapter 7) by default. Sometimes they fail to recognize the advantages of targeting, or an undifferentiated approach may appear to offer economies of scale and low per capita costs. In other instances, nonprofit organizations are pressured or required to serve the maximum number of people by targeting the average user. The problem with developing services targeted at the average user is that there are few "average" users. Therefore, such strategies typically fail to fully satisfy any market segment.

- *Complementary positioning:* The main role of many nonprofit organizations is to provide services, with available resources, to those who are not adequately served by private-sector organizations. As a result, the nonprofit organization must often complement, rather than compete with, the efforts of others. The positioning task is to identify underserved market segments and to develop marketing programs that match their needs rather than to target the niches that may be most profitable. For example, a university library may see itself as complementing the services of the public library, rather than competing with it.

Product Decisions

There are three product-related distinctions between business and nonprofit organizations:

- *Benefit complexity:* Rather than simple product concepts, like "Fly the friendly skies" or "We make money the old-fashioned way," nonprofit organizations often market complex behaviors or ideas. Examples include the need to exercise or eat right, not to drink and drive, and not to smoke tobacco. The benefits that a person receives are complex, long term, and intangible and therefore are more difficult to communicate to consumers.

- *Benefit strength:* The benefit strength of many nonprofit offerings is quite weak or indirect. What are the direct, personal benefits to you of driving 55 miles per hour, donating blood, or asking your neighbors to contribute money to a charity? In contrast, most private-sector service organizations can offer customers direct, personal benefits in an exchange relationship.

- *Involvement:* Many nonprofit organizations market products that elicit either very low involvement ("Prevent forest fires" or "Don't litter") or very high involvement ("Join the military" or "Stop smoking"). The typical range for private-sector goods is much narrower. Traditional promotional tools may be inadequate to motivate adoption of either low- or high-involvement products.

Place (Distribution) Decisions

A nonprofit organization's capacity for distributing its service offerings to potential customer groups when and where they want them is typically a key variable in determining the success of those service offerings. For example, most state land-grant universities offer extension programs throughout their state to reach the general public. Many large universities have one or more satellite campus locations to provide easier access for students in other areas. Some educational institutions also offer classes to students at off-campus locations via interactive video technology.

The extent to which a service depends on fixed facilities has important implications for distribution decisions. Obviously, services like rail transit and lake fishing can be delivered only at specific points. Many nonprofit services, however, do not depend on special facilities. Counseling, for example, need not take place in agency offices; it may occur wherever counselors and clients can meet. Probation services, outreach youth programs, and educational courses taught on commuter trains are other examples of deliverable services.

Promotion Decisions

Many nonprofit organizations are explicitly or implicitly prohibited from advertising, thus limiting their promotion

Recycling that's easy to wrap around.

Wrapping yourself around a plan that recycles your used rechargeable batteries is easy. Just check the rechargeable batteries in your cordless phones, laptop computers, camcorders, cell phones, two-way radios and power tools. If they no longer hold a charge, recycle them by visiting www.call2recycle.org, calling 877-2-RECYCLE, or by dropping them off at one of the listed national retailers.

Recycle your rechargeable batteries.

call 2 recycle
A Rechargeable Battery Recycling Corporation program

Recycle at one of these national retailers: BatteriesPlus +   Office DEPOT   RadioShack   Sears   STAPLES   TARGET

© 2006 Rechargeable Battery Recycling Corporation. Founded in 1994, RBRC is a non-profit organization dedicated to recycling rechargeable batteries and cellular phones. For more information: www.rbrc.org or 1-800-8-BATTERY.

© RECHARGEABLE BATTERY RECYCLING CORPORATION

Nonprofits that request action on the part of consumers must make sure their locations are convenient and accessible. This call2recycle advertisement lists a number of national retailers where consumers can drop off their old batteries for recycling. Consumers will most likely already be visiting these locations to purchase new batteries, making them convenient recycling locations.

options. Most federal agencies fall into this category. Other nonprofit organizations simply do not have the resources to retain advertising agencies, promotion consultants, or marketing staff. However, nonprofit organizations have a few special promotion resources to call on:

Advertising Council
What are the most compelling PSAs on the Ad Council site at the moment?
http://www.adcouncil.org

Online

- *Professional volunteers:* Nonprofit organizations often seek out marketing, sales, and advertising professionals to help them develop and implement promotion strategies. In some instances, an advertising agency donates its services in exchange for potential long-term benefits. One advertising agency donated its services to a major symphony because the symphony had a blue-ribbon board of directors. Donated services create goodwill, personal contacts, and general awareness of the donor's organization, reputation, and competency.

- *Sales promotion activities:* Sales promotion activities that make use of existing services or other resources are increasingly being used to draw attention to the offerings of nonprofit organizations. Sometimes nonprofit charities even team up with other companies for promotional activities.

- *Public service advertising:* A **public service advertisement (PSA)** is an announcement that promotes a program of a federal, state, or local government or of a nonprofit organization. Unlike a commercial advertiser, the sponsor of the PSA does not pay for the time or space. Instead, it is donated by the medium. The Advertising Council has developed PSAs that are some of the most memorable advertisements of all time. For example, Smokey the Bear reminded everyone to be careful not to start forest fires.

Communication with your teens can be a form of prevention. In fact, teens whose parents lay out rules and expectations for them are far less likely to try pot and other drugs. Be clear. Be firm. Be a parent. For information, call 1-800-788-2800 or visit www.theantidrug.com.

if
you're
not
telling
them
NO
you're telling them
YES

PARENTS.
THE ANTI-DRUG.

Nonprofits often rely on public service advertisements to spread their messages because space and time are donated by the advertising medium rather than paid for by the sponsor. Pictured here is one print advertisement in the multimedia campaign titled "Parents: The Anti Drug", which encourages parents to discuss the negative effects of drug use with their children.

Pricing Decisions

Five key characteristics distinguish the pricing decisions of nonprofit organizations from those of the profit sector:

- *Pricing objectives:* The main pricing objective in the profit sector is revenue or, more specifically, profit maximization, sales maximization, or target return on sales or investment. Many nonprofit organizations must also be concerned about revenue. Often, however, nonprofit organizations seek to either partially or fully defray costs rather than to achieve a profit for distribution to stockholders. Nonprofit organizations also seek to redistribute income—for instance, through taxation and sliding-scale fees. Moreover, they strive to allocate resources fairly among individuals or households or across geographic or political boundaries.

- *Nonfinancial prices:* In many nonprofit situations, consumers are not charged a monetary price but instead must absorb nonmonetary costs. The importance of those costs is illustrated by the large number of eligible citizens who do not take advantage of so-called free services for the poor. In many public assistance programs, about half the people who are eligible don't participate. Nonmonetary costs consist of the opportunity cost of time, embarrassment costs, and effort costs.

public service advertisement (PSA)
An announcement that promotes a program of a federal, state, or local government or of a nonprofit organization.

- *Indirect payment:* Indirect payment through taxes is common to marketers of "free" services, such as libraries, fire protection, and police protection. Indirect payment is not a common practice in the profit sector.

- *Separation between payers and users:* By design, the services of many charitable organizations are provided for those who are relatively poor and largely paid for by those who are better off financially. Although examples of separation between payers and users can be found in the profit sector (such as insurance claims), the practice is much less prevalent.

- *Below-cost pricing:* An example of below-cost pricing is university tuition. Virtually all private and public colleges and universities price their services below full cost.

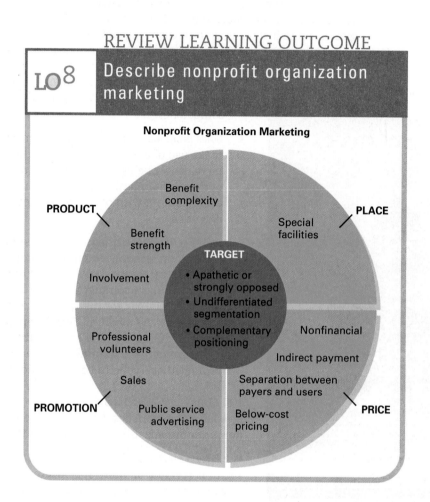

REVIEW LEARNING OUTCOME

LO 8 Describe nonprofit organization marketing

Nonprofit Organization Marketing

PRODUCT
- Benefit complexity
- Benefit strength
- Involvement

PLACE
- Special facilities

TARGET
- Apathetic or strongly opposed
- Undifferentiated segmentation
- Complementary positioning

PRICE
- Nonfinancial
- Indirect payment
- Separation between payers and users
- Below-cost pricing

PROMOTION
- Professional volunteers
- Sales
- Public service advertising

Review and Applications

LO 1 Discuss the importance of services to the economy. The service sector plays a crucial role in the U.S. economy, employing more than 80 percent of the workforce and accounting for a similar percentage of the gross domestic product.

1.1 To keep track of how service employment is affecting the U.S. economy, go to **http://www.bls.gov/bdm/home.html**. Look at the right sidebar which gives the latest numbers for Business Employment Dynamics. What trends to you see? Do the numbers support the information from the chapter?

LO 2 Discuss the differences between services and goods. Services are distinguished by four characteristics. Services are intangible performances in that they lack clearly identifiable physical characteristics, making it difficult for

Quick Check ✔

Now that you've read the chapter, do you get it? Take a moment for a quick check using this scale:

1 Not at all; 2 Not very well; 3 Ok; 4 Well; 5 Very Well

Can you . . .

___ explain why services are important?

___ describe the unique characteristics of services?

___ identify the five metrics against which consumers measure service quality?

___ explain what happens at each stage of the gap model of service delivery?

___ identify the core and supplementary services at your favorite service provider?

___ draw a diagram showing how service providers use a marketing mix?

___ define internal marketing and explain why it is important?

___ describe the unique aspects of the target markets of nonprofit organizations?

___ explain how the marketing mix differs for nonprofit organizations and for-profit organizations?

___ TOTAL

Score: 37–45, you're ready to move on to the applications; 28–36, skim the chapter one more time before moving on to the applications; 19–27, reread the sections giving you the most trouble and go to Thomson NOW for guided tutorials; 18 and under, you better reread the chapter to get a grasp of the fundamentals. If you've reread the chapter and still have a low score, visit your professor or TA during office hours.

marketers to communicate their specific benefits to potential customers. The production and consumption of services occur simultaneously. Services are heterogeneous because their quality depends on such elements as the service provider, individual consumer, location, and so on. Finally, services are perishable in the sense that they cannot be stored or saved. As a result, synchronizing supply with demand is particularly challenging in the service industry.

2.1 Assume that you are a manager of a bank branch. Write a list of the implications of intangibility for your firm.

2.2 Over 25 years ago, Tim and Nina Zagat began publishing leisure guides containing reviews of restaurants. Today, the renowned *Zagat* guides still contain reviews of restaurants, but they also rate hotels, entertainment, nightlife, movies, shopping, and even music. Go to **http://www.zagat.com**. In your opinion, are *Zagat* survey guides goods or services? Explain your reasoning.

LO3 Describe the components of service quality and the gap model of service quality.

Service quality has five components: reliability (ability to perform the service dependably, accurately, and consistently), responsiveness (providing prompt service), assurance (knowledge and courtesy of employees and their ability to convey trust), empathy (caring, individualized attention), and tangibles (physical evidence of the service).

The gap model identifies five key discrepancies that can influence customer evaluations of service quality. When the gaps are large, service quality is low. As the gaps shrink, service quality improves. Gap 1 is found between customers' expectations and management's perceptions of those expectations. Gap 2 is found between management's perception of what the customer wants and specifications for service quality. Gap 3 is found between service quality specifications and delivery of the service. Gap 4 is found between service delivery and what the company promises to the customer through external communication. Gap 5 is found between customers' service expectations and their perceptions of service performance.

3.1 Analyze a recent experience that you have had with a service business (for example, hairdresser, movie theater, dentist, restaurant, car repair) in terms of your expectations and perceptions about each of the five components of service quality.

LO4 Develop marketing mixes for services. "Product" (service) strategy issues include what is being processed (people, possessions, mental stimulus, information), core and supplementary services, customization versus standardization, and the service mix. Distribution decisions involve convenience, number of outlets, direct versus indirect distribution, and scheduling. Stressing tangible cues, using personal sources of information, creating strong organizational images, and engaging in postpurchase communication are effective promotion strategies. Pricing objectives for services can be revenue oriented, operations oriented, patronage oriented, or any combination of the three.

4.1 Form a team with at least two other classmates, and come up with an idea for a new service. Develop a marketing mix strategy for the new service.

LO5 Discuss relationship marketing in services. Relationship marketing in services involves attracting, developing, and retaining customer relationships. There are three levels of relationship marketing: level 1 focuses on pricing incentives; level 2 uses pricing incentives and social bonds with customers; and level 3 uses pricing, social bonds, and structural bonds to build long-term relationships.

5.1 For the new service developed for question 4.1, have the members of the team discuss how they would implement a relationship marketing strategy.

LO6 Explain internal marketing in services. Internal marketing means treating employees as customers and developing systems and benefits that satisfy their needs. Employees who like their jobs and are happy with the firm they work for are more likely to deliver good service.

6.1 Choose a service firm with which you do a lot of business. Write a memo to the manager explaining the importance of internal marketing and outlining the factors internal marketing includes.

6.2 Return to **http://www.zagat.com** and investigate what the site offers. How does *Zagat* propose to help companies with internal services marketing?

LO7 Discuss global issues in services marketing. The United States has become the world's largest exporter of services. Although competition is keen, the United States has a competitive advantage because of its vast experience in many service industries. To be successful globally, service firms must adjust their marketing mix for the environment of each target country.

7.1 What issues would you have to think about in going global with the new service that you developed in the questions above? How would you change your marketing mix to address those issues?

LO8 Describe nonprofit organization marketing. Nonprofit organizations pursue goals other than profit, market share, and return on investment. Nonprofit organization marketing facilitates mutually satisfying exchanges between nonprofit organizations and their target markets. Several unique characteristics distinguish nonbusiness marketing strategy, including a concern with services and social behaviors rather than manufactured goods and profit; a difficult, undifferentiated, and in some ways marginal target market; a complex product that may have only indirect benefits and elicit very low involvement; distribution that may or may not require special facilities depending on the service provided; a relative lack of resources for promotion; and prices only indirectly related to the exchange between the producer and the consumer of services.

8.1 Form a team with two or three classmates. Using the promotion strategies discussed in the nonprofit section of this chapter, develop a promotion strategy for your college or university.

Key Terms

Exercises

APPLICATION EXERCISE

All people know quality when they see it—or do they? Let's take a look at some goods and services and then think about assessing their quality. For this exercise, work in teams of two to three and discuss each item before determining its final placement.[25]

Activities

1. Using the abbreviations in parentheses, place each of the following products and services along the continuum below: a new car (C), designer jeans (J), car oil change (O), dress dry cleaning (D), haircut (H), tax preparation software (T), college education (E).

   100% physical good _____ 100% service

2. Once you have placed the items along the continuum, consider how easy it is to assess the quality of each item.

   Easy to assess quality _____ Difficult to assess quality

3. What assumptions can you make about the ability to assess the quality of goods compared to services? Is it easier to assess the quality of some goods than others? What about for services?

Entrepreneurship Case

CAST IN THE LEADING ROLE, PLAYBILL SHINES

© ADAM WOOLFITT/CORBIS

Anyone who has ever attended live theater has probably, at some point, flipped through a copy of *Playbill*. Established in New York City in 1884 as the program of choice for Broadway and off-Broadway theaters, Playbill the company publishes and distributes the near-ubiquitous black and white program with the familiar yellow and black cover to theaters in almost every major and medium-sized city in the United States. Over 3 million theatergoers read the programs every month.

Complete with cast rosters and biographies, show synopsis, lists of prominent theater sponsors, insider gossip columns, and various feature articles on nationally known actors and theater personalities, *Playbill* provides its readers with a panoramic view of the performing arts. Playbill distributes its programs free to theaters, which, in turn, give them to show attendees as a complimentary item included with the price of their tickets. Like most magazine publishers, Playbill earns revenue simply by selling the advertising space—a lot of it—within its pages. Thanks to its broad distribution network and its wealth of proprietary and nationally oriented editorial content, Playbill is able to extend its revenue base with a mix of local, regional, and national advertisers.

Although the audiences at the many performing arts centers represent a highly coveted and affluent consumer demographic, Playbill's competition has been limited to one national and several regional program publishers. To establish itself as the lone national brand, Playbill purchased its primary rival, Stagebill, which publishes *Performing Arts* magazine, in 2002. Though Playbill's purchase of Stagebill could be interpreted as a move to exert its dominance, closer inspection of the deal and the state of the industry reveals that Playbill was motivated simply by survival. Program publishers suffer from exceptionally low profit margins, and continual pressure to cut costs left Playbill with the ability to supply programs to only a select few of Stagebill's most lucrative former customers.

Though Playbill has eliminated its most serious rival, fallout from the takeover emboldened the theater owners who were left behind. Consequently, demand for locally published programs has increased. Sizable theater consortiums in major markets such as San Francisco, Chicago, Seattle, and Los Angeles now work with local publishers who afford them more editorial control over their programs' content. To venue owners in those markets, providing locally focused news, information, and personal profiles is the key to building audience support for live theater in their particular market. To help offset their publishing costs, some even assume responsibility for selling advertising space in their programs in exchange for a share of the ad revenue they generate.

Despite the new gains by regional consortiums, Playbill still retains an effective monopoly on the national market for printed programs. The company has further extended its appeal to advertisers by forming the necessary business partnerships to take its product to the airwaves and into cyberspace. Recently, Playbill and Sirius Satellite Radio formed a strategic alliance to provide daily news features, live programming, music, special programming, and information from the world of Broadway for Sirius Radio's Broadway's Best channel. In return for the increased brand exposure, Playbill promotes Sirius in printed editions of Playbill and through Playbill Online, at Playbill.com.

Playbill.com uses a mix of exclusive content, feature articles pulled from the printed *Playbill*, show schedules, and seating charts for all of Playbill's partner theaters around the world to generate 20 million hits each month. Playbill has used the Web site to coordinate partnerships with ticket agencies, restaurants, and hotels that offer discounts to the hundreds of thousands of subscribers to Playbill Online's Playbill Club. Consumers can join the club for free, and it offers tremendous exposure for Playbill's business partners who are able to place their products or services directly in front of individuals with an average yearly income of $80,000.

Clearly, Playbill is on solid ground. Nevertheless, it still faces the challenge of finding innovative ways to earn a profit from a product that doesn't cost its end customers a single cent.[26]

Questions

1. What role does the alliance with Sirius play in Playbill's marketing mix? Do you think the alliance will enhance demand for Playbill's services? Explain.

2. Using the material in Learning Outcome 4 as a template, outline Playbill's marketing mix. Discuss its product, core and supplementary services, mass customization, service mix, distribution, promotion, and pricing.

3. Is *Playbill* a good, a service, or both? Explain.

COMPANY CLIPS

Kodak—Reinventing the Mix

You probably think of Kodak as selling only products. In fact, the company has an entire division, the Graphic Communications Group, dedicated to delivering service solutions to business customers. Mark Webber is vice president of worldwide sales partnerships for Kodak's digital printing solutions group, which provides services to the b-to-b (business-to-business) market. In this video, he explains how Kodak creates both digital and analog printing solutions for a wide variety of clients and how the company is taking advantage of new technology to meet evolving customer demands.

Questions

1. Would you describe Kodak's services as customized or standardized? Why?

2. Describe Kodak's services mix.

3. Outline Kodak's pricing strategy for its services.

BIZ FLIX

Intolerable Cruelty

Now that you have worked through this chapter, you will be able to see the concepts in a more nuanced situation. As an encore to your study, watch the film clip from *Intolerable Cruelty*, starring George Clooney (Miles Massey), Stacey Travis (Mrs. Donaly), and Catherine Zeta-Jones (Marylin Rexroth). The selected scene shows the introductory interview between Mr. Massey and Mrs. Donaly. Mrs. Donaly is hiring Mr. Massey as her divorce attorney. As you watch the clip, think about what Massey is communicating about his service. How is his service customized? How is it standardized? What is your assessment of how Mrs. Donaly is evaluating the service she is buying (i.e., does she seem satisfied, dissatisfied, or ambivalent by the end of the clip)? What other service concepts from the chapter can you relate to the film clip?

A high score means you have a positive attitude about charitable operations and most likely think that nonprofit organizations fulfill an important role in society. A high score does not necessarily mean you give more to charity, however.

Marketing Miscue

Manufacturing Defect Results in Quite a Stir for iPod Nano

Innovation has been key in Apple Computer's transition from just a computer company into a consumer electronics company as well. One of Apple's most prominent consumer electronics product introductions has been the iPod. Though companies such as Dell countered with competing products (e.g., the Dell DJ), the iPod quickly became synonymous with MP3 players. Without a doubt, the iPod has been a runaway success for Apple. With estimated quarterly shipments of almost 7 million iPods, Apple continues to crush competitors.

The company recognized that, as with any cool product offering, it had to keep the spotlight on the iPod. To do so, Apple introduced the iPod Nano in the fall of 2005. Considered by some to be the coolest iPod yet, the iPod Nano was a hybrid of the iPod Shuffle, the iPod Mini, and full-sized color iPods. Combining key features from all three products, plus some new features, the iPod Nano brought new meaning to the phrase "thin is in." With dimensions of 3.5 by 1.6 inches and a back-to-front depth of 0.27 inches, the iPod Nano could fit into a business card wallet.

Two models of this pencil-thin player, available in black or white, were introduced. Starting at $199, the 2GB model could hold 500 songs. The 4GB model could hold 1,000 songs and had an expected retail price starting at $249. Accessories for the Nano included lanyard headphones, an armband, tubes in five colors that looked cool and also served as safety protection, in-ear earphones, a dock, a USB power adapter, and a USB cable. Apple expected the accessories to contribute significantly to its profits from the Nano.

The new iPod was introduced with much fanfare, with Steve Jobs literally pulling the iPod Nano out of his pocket. This demonstration of where to carry the iPod Nano may linger in the minds of many purchasers, particularly those who retrieved their new iPod Nanos from their pockets only to find the color display screen scratched so badly that images were distorted. One Nano owner, Matthew Peterson, did something about the problem. Apparently, Peterson had the iPod Nano in his pocket while he was walking only to have the screen shatter when he sat down—and no, he didn't sit on it. Peterson took his Nano to the nearest Apple Store for repair or replacement, but the staff at the store declined to replace the broken unit or to admit any responsibility on the part of the company. According to Apple, the damage was not covered under the product warranty.

At that point, Peterson felt that his only recourse was to see if there were any other disenchanted iPod Nano customers. So, he created a Web site, **http://www.flawedmusicplayer.com**, where he posted an autopsy photo of the Nano that showed the damage sustained after only four days of what should have been normal use (at least according to the way Jobs presented the product). The Web site quickly became an online gathering place for dissatisfied iPod Nano customers. Soon, close to 300 threads were posted on the Web site's discussion board relating stories of damage ranging from severe scratches to shattered LCD screens. Ultimately, the Web site got Apple's attention (which was Peterson's mission), and the company began investigating the problem. In the interim, however, customers became even more irate when at least one iPod repair company, overwhelmed by the demand for its services, temporarily raised the price of repairing Nano LCD screens because of limited screen availability.

Three weeks after introducing the iPod Nano, Apple took responsibility for the flawed product and offered to replace screens that cracked too easily. The company attempted to downplay what it referred to as a "minor issue" by saying that the defective screens were due to a vendor quality problem that affected less than one-tenth of 1 percent of all the iPod Nanos that had been sold. The company insisted that the defects were not a design problem attributable to the size of the iPod Nano.[1]

Questions

1. Why did it take an international Web site to get Apple's attention to this matter?

2. Do you think sales of the iPod Nano will be affected by the reports about defective screens?

Critical Thinking Case

Dallas Mavericks—The Total Entertainment Experience

Mark Cuban, ranked as number 327 on *Forbes* magazine's list of the world's richest people, paid $280 million for a losing product when he bought the Dallas Mavericks in January 2000. At the time, he described the sports franchise as a beaten organization, but one that had a culture of survival. As the new owner, Cuban began immediately to revitalize the product by changing the face of the organization. His objective was to transform Mavericks games into a total entertainment experience that would offer much more than just a basketball game.

Internal changes paved the way for enhancing the customer's experience. Cuban immediately tripled the size of the sales staff. Every sales representative was required to make 100 cold calls per day until games began to sell out. The new mantra was, "Every minute of every day, it's selling time." More important, however, was what these sales reps were selling. Cuban told them that they no longer sold basketball—they were selling fun, throats sore from yelling, and hands sore from clapping.

Within three years, Mavericks fans had a sense of pride in their team, which had developed into a winning basketball franchise. Once a perpetual loser, the team was winning games, making the playoffs, and boasting franchise-best records. Though the team's winning record was capturing fans, Cuban knew that he would have to offer a wide array of related products and enhancements if he was to continue to beat out his entertainment competitors in Northeast Texas.

The Dallas Mavericks reside in a city with all of the "big four" professional sports teams. In addition to the Mavericks, Dallas is home to the Dallas Cowboys (football), the Dallas Stars (hockey), and the Texas Rangers (baseball). The Mavericks' entertainment competitors also include the Texas Motor Speedway, Lone Star Park, Dallas Desperados Dancers, and Dallas Burn and Sidekicks soccer teams, as well as countless restaurants, bars, movie theaters, and music venues. Local collegiate sports teams (e.g., Southern Methodist University, the University of North Texas, and the University of Texas at Arlington) also compete for entertainment time and dollars.

As a competitor in this vast entertainment marketplace, the Mavericks offered not just a winning team, but a great in-arena experience. The Mavs ManiAAC's (men between the ages of 21 and 50) made their dancing debut at the first playoff game in 2001, and fans were entertained regularly by the Mavs Man mascot and the Mavs Dancers. The entertainment experience also included the merchandise sold, the music and videos played, the free entry of painted fans, and the team's own version of Duke's Cameron Crazies (allegedly some of the rowdiest, wittiest, and best-organized college basketball fans).

The team's attendance figures testify to Cuban's ability to create a successful product. Since December 2001, the team has sold out every home game at the American Airlines Center. With this goal accomplished, team management had a new objective: to increase the team's fan base in the Fort Worth area. Although the Mavericks consider themselves a Metroplex (Dallas–Fort Worth) team, they had not made a concentrated effort to market the team outside the city of Dallas.

Demographically, Dallas and Fort Worth are very comparable. Fort Worth is located approximately 30 miles west of Dallas, with two major highways connecting the two cities. Like the Minnesota Timberwolves (Minneapolis and St. Paul) and the Golden State Warriors (Oakland and San Francisco), the Mavericks have easy access to markets in two large cities. The combined population of Dallas and Fort Worth is slightly over 1.7 million (compared to a market of almost 660,000 for the Timberwolves and around 1.2 million for the Warriors).

Though Fort Worth does not boast a hometown professional team, the Texas Rangers claim Fort Worth, Dallas, and Arlington as their hometowns. Additionally, Fort Worth has minor league teams such as the Fort Worth Cats baseball team and the Fort Worth Brahmas hockey team. On the collegiate scene, the Horned Frogs of Texas Christian University have become a national phenomenon and draw considerable support. Other entertainment offerings in Fort Worth include Six Flags over Texas, Six Flags Hurricane Harbor, the Fort Worth Stock Show and Rodeo, the Bass Performance Hall, and the Will Rogers Coliseum and Museum district. Despite this competition, Cuban's goal was to make the Mavericks a hometown brand in Fort Worth by 2005, while continuing to fill their arena to capacity.[2]

Questions:

1. What is the product?

2. What does the term *brand equity* mean in relation to the attempt by team management to expand the fan base without necessarily selling more game tickets?

PART 4

Distribution Decisions

CROSS-FUNCTIONAL CONNECTIONS

To achieve customer satisfaction, a company must have the right product at the right place at the right time. Accomplishing this requires considerable interaction among marketing and its internal and external partners. Manufacturing has been a key marketing partner in making the distribution process successful. Advanced manufacturing systems have been developed that not only reduce costs (ultimately affecting the price charged to the customer) but also allow faster product delivery. Two popular advanced manufacturing systems are just-in-time (JIT) and electronic data interchange (EDI).

With a JIT manufacturing system, the product is produced as needed instead of being produced for stock. Ultimately, such a manufacturing system can change the structure of the distribution channel. Customers may be able to receive products directly from the manufacturer rather than via a longer distribution channel. Not only are products available faster, but costs are lowered with fewer channel members. Marketing must make certain, however, that the new channel structure is more effective as well as more efficient. If the eliminated channel intermediary provided a service that will not be available when the product is shipped directly to the customer from the manufacturer, the longer channel may be necessary.

The use of EDI can significantly increase the efficiency of operations between the shop floor and distribution of the product. EDI permits the exchange of information electronically. Data collected at the point of sale are transmitted automatically to the manufacturing department. Thus, manufacturing knows the exact number of desired units at any point in time, allowing the manufacturing group to time its production and delivery to meet the customer's specific needs. In some instances, retail sales data transmitted electronically to the manufacturing group start the machines on the shop floor. Such quick response to channel needs can dramatically reduce the time from order entry to delivery.

Lowering costs, while maintaining high quality, is critical to successful manufacturing operations. MfgQuote.com is an online collaborative service that utilizes process innovation to bring together engineers and

> *More and more companies are combining cross-functional skills with information technology infrastructures to better serve customers.*

purchasing managers so that the bidding and buying process is streamlined. In doing this, MfgQuote.com helps manufacturers lower costs, reduce retail prices, purchase higher-quality raw materials, and have them delivered on time. One user credits the cross-functional online service with a 30 to 50 percent savings on raw materials. Such savings are ultimately reflected in the interactions that marketers have with the company's end users.

One important aspect of the channel of distribution is the actual delivery of the company's products. The equipment used to make deliveries is an important decision that the company faces. Decisions regarding the type of transportation equipment (from aircraft to railcars) receive considerable input from both the marketing and the finance/accounting groups. For example, marketing might prefer that its perishable product be delivered by air to avoid any spoilage. From a cost-effectiveness viewpoint, however, the financial group might determine that the product should be shipped via truck because the savings would offset the costs associated with any spoiled product. The two functional groups have to balance customer demands with the relative costs of shipment. The manufacturing group must be involved as well to ensure that appropriate and cost-effective packaging is used for the transportation method ultimately selected.

The role of the delivery provider is particularly prominent in the release of much-

hyped products such as the Xbox 360 and new Harry Potter books. While the interactions between the manufacturer/publisher and the retailer with respect to release dates tend to receive the most attention, the planning that must take place with the home delivery carrier (e.g., FedEx) cannot be overlooked. Customers who have pre-ordered an Xbox 360 or a new Harry Potter book are promised delivery on the date of release. Such guaranteed delivery affects internal scheduling at the chosen carrier. In addition to working intimately with the manufacturer/publisher, the carrier must plan its delivery schedule so that recipients of other products are not delayed because of the expectations of one client.

Coordination between marketing and other business functions is necessary to get a high-quality, competitively priced product or service to the end user in a timely manner. Operational efficiencies in linking production and distribution are the result of well-thought-out cross-functional plans. Technology is a powerful force behind improvements in distribution, and more and more companies are combining cross-functional skills with information technology infrastructures to better serve customers.

Questions

1. What are the popular advanced manufacturing systems, and how do they interact with marketing?

2. What functional areas were involved in the timely release of the Xbox 360?

Marketing Channels

and Supply Chain Management

Learning Outcomes

LO 1   Explain what a marketing channel is and why intermediaries are needed

LO 2   Define the types of channel intermediaries and describe their functions and activities

LO 3   Describe the channel structures for consumer and business products and discuss alternative channel arrangements

LO 4   Define supply chain management and discuss its benefits

LO 5   Discuss the issues that influence channel strategy

LO 6   Explain channel leadership, conflict, and partnering

LO 7   Describe the logistical components of the supply chain

LO 8   Discuss new technology and emerging trends in supply chain management

LO 9   Discuss channels and distribution decisions in global markets

LO 10   Identify the special problems and opportunities associated with distribution in service organizations

multichannel distribution works
at **Starbucks**

Since going public in 1992, Starbucks has grown to become the number one coffee retailer in the world and a *Fortune* 500 company. Annual revenues topped $8 billion in 2005. Starbucks reaches customers at over 11,000 locations in more than 36 countries on six continents.

One way Starbucks fuels such growth is through multichannel distribution. In addition to selling coffee through its retail outlets, Starbucks developed a suite of products specifically for wholesale distribution: a bottled iced coffee called Frappuccino, DoubleShot espresso, and a line of superpremium ice creams.

Starbucks reaches customers at over 11,000 locations in more than 36 countries on six continents.

Starbucks carries these products in its stores, but wholesale distributors like Pepsi, Kraft, and Dreyer's are responsible for making these products available at over 10,000 grocery, drug, and convenience stores. Licensed vendors (grocery stores, offices and educational institutions, airlines, and health-care facilities) provide a third channel through which consumers can purchase Starbucks products.

Starbucks' core business is purchasing and roasting high-quality coffee beans that are used to create brewed coffee, espresso, ice cream, and ready-to-drink beverages. To reach consumers who do not drink coffee, Starbucks launched Tazo teas and Tiazzi, a blended juice and tea drink. Starbucks also owns the Seattle's Best Coffee and Torrefazione Italia coffee brands, which offer an alternative variety of coffee flavors that appeal to a broader consumer base.

More than 80 percent of the Starbucks stores in the United States are company owned and operated. When expanding into new overseas markets, however, the company always seeks a local business partner. In Japan, Starbucks has partnered with Sazaby, Inc., and in Korea with Shinsegae Company. Each partner has special capabilities in food distribution.

In the early 2000s, Starbucks pushed its brand into a new space with the Duetto Visa card, which functions as a dual Visa credit card and reloadable Starbucks drink card. Cardholders are rewarded based on usage with Duetto dollars, coffee beans, and gift certificates. Starbucks is also expanding its Hear Music Coffeehouses as another strategy for building loyalty. These new coffeehouses offer the traditional Starbucks experience and allow music lovers—who might not otherwise be reached through traditional channels—to discover and buy new music over a cup of coffee. The coffeehouses carry an extensive inventory of CDs that has been handpicked by the Starbucks Hear Music content team to appeal to local and regional tastes in each market. The loyalty programs, supported by marketing alliances with XM Satellite Radio, T-Mobile, and United Airlines, have all contributed to enhancing the Starbucks experience.[1]

What are the advantages to pursuing a multichannel strategy, as Starbucks has? Can you think of any disadvantages? What new channels could Starbucks enter without much difficulty?

Marketing & You

Using the following scale, indicate your opinions on the lines before the items.

1	2	3	4	5	6

Strongly disagree   Strongly agree

____ I would prefer to be a leader.

____ I see myself as a good leader.

____ I will be a success.

____ People always seem to recognize my authority.

____ I have a natural talent for influencing people.

____ I am assertive.

____ I like to have authority over other people.

____ I am a born leader.

Now, total your score. Read the chapter and find out what your score means at the end.

Marketing Channels

The term *channel* is derived from the Latin word *canalis,* which means canal. A marketing channel can be viewed as a large canal or pipeline through which products, their ownership, communication, financing and payment, and accompanying risk flow to the consumer. Formally, a **marketing channel** (also called a **channel of distribution**) is a business structure of interdependent organizations that reach from the point of product origin to the consumer with the purpose of moving products to their final consumption destination. Marketing channels facilitate the physical movement of goods through the supply chain, representing "place" or "distribution" in the marketing mix (product, price, promotion, and place) and encompassing the processes involved in getting the right product to the right place at the right time.

Many different types of organizations participate in marketing channels. **Channel members** (also called *intermediaries, resellers,* and *middlemen*) negotiate with one another, buy and sell products, and facilitate the change of ownership between buyer and seller in the course of moving the product from the manufacturer into the hands of the final consumer. An important aspect of marketing channels is the joint effort of all channel members to create a continuous and seamless supply chain. The **supply chain** is the connected chain of all of the business entities, both internal and external to the company, that perform or support the marketing channel functions. As products move through the supply chain, channel members facilitate the distribution process by providing specialization and division of labor, overcoming discrepancies, and providing contact efficiency.

A local supermarket has no stockroom. But always has lime soda. Can you see it?

IBM
ibm.com/ondemand

Marketing channels aid in overcoming discrepancies of quantity, like the one suggested by this ad for IBM supply chain management software.

marketing channel (channel of distribution)
A set of interdependent organizations that ease the transfer of ownership as products move from producer to business user or consumer.

channel members
All parties in the marketing channel that negotiate with one another, buy and sell products, and facilitate the change of ownership between buyer and seller in the course of moving the product from the manufacturer into the hands of the final consumer.

supply chain
The connected chain of all of the business entities, both internal and external to the company, that perform or support the logistics function.

PROVIDING SPECIALIZATION AND DIVISION OF LABOR

According to the concept of *specialization and division of labor,* breaking down a complex task into smaller, simpler ones and allocating them to specialists will create greater efficiency and lower average production costs. Manufacturers achieve economies of scale through the use of efficient equipment capable of producing large quantities of a single product.

Marketing channels can also attain economies of scale through specialization and division of labor by aiding producers who lack the motivation, financing, or expertise to market directly to end users or consumers. In some cases, as with most consumer convenience goods, such as soft drinks, the cost of marketing directly to millions of consumers—taking and shipping individual orders—is prohibitive. For this reason, producers hire channel members, such as wholesalers and retailers, to do what the producers are not equipped to do or what channel members are better prepared to do. Channel members can do some things more efficiently than producers because they have built good relationships with their customers. Therefore, their specialized expertise enhances the overall performance of the channel.

OVERCOMING DISCREPANCIES

Marketing channels also aid in overcoming discrepancies of quantity, assortment, time, and space created by economies of scale in production. For example, assume that Pillsbury can efficiently produce its Hungry Jack instant pancake mix only at a rate of 5,000 units in a typical day. Not even the most ardent pancake fan could consume that amount in a year, much less in a day. The quantity produced to achieve low unit costs has created a **discrepancy of quantity,** which is the difference between the amount of product produced and the amount an end user wants to buy. By storing the product and distributing it in the appropriate amounts, marketing channels overcome quantity discrepancies by making products available in the quantities that consumers desire.

Mass production creates not only discrepancies of quantity but also discrepancies of assortment. A **discrepancy of assortment** occurs when a consumer does not have all of the items needed to receive full satisfaction from a product. For pancakes to provide maximum satisfaction, several other products are required to complete the assortment. At the very least, most people want a knife, fork, plate, butter, and syrup. Others might add orange juice, coffee, cream, sugar, eggs, and bacon or sausage. Even though Pillsbury is a large consumer-products company, it does not come close to providing the optimal assortment to go with its Hungry Jack pancakes. To overcome discrepancies of assortment, marketing channels assemble in one place many of the products necessary to complete a consumer's needed assortment.

A **temporal discrepancy** is created when a product is produced but a consumer is not ready to buy it. Marketing channels overcome temporal discrepancies by maintaining inventories in anticipation of demand. For example, manufacturers of seasonal merchandise, such as Christmas or Halloween decorations, are in operation all year even though consumer demand is concentrated during certain months of the year.

Furthermore, because mass production requires many potential buyers, markets are usually scattered over large geographic regions, creating a **spatial discrepancy.** Often global, or at least nationwide, markets are needed to absorb the outputs of mass producers. Marketing channels overcome spatial discrepancies by making products available in locations convenient to consumers. For example, if all the Hungry Jack pancake mix is produced in Boise, Idaho, then Pillsbury must use an intermediary to distribute the product to other regions of the United States. Consumers elsewhere would be unwilling to drive to Boise to purchase pancake mix.

PROVIDING CONTACT EFFICIENCY

The third need fulfilled by marketing channels is that they provide contact efficiency. Marketing channels provide contact efficiencies by reducing the number of stores customers must shop in to complete their purchases. Think about how much time you would spend shopping if supermarkets, department stores, and shopping malls did not exist. For example, suppose you had to buy your milk at a dairy and your meat at a stockyard. Imagine buying your eggs and chicken at a hatchery and your fruits and vegetables at various farms. You would spend a great deal of time, money, and energy just shopping for a few groceries. Supply chains simplify distribution by cutting the number of transactions required to get products from manufacturers to consumers and making an assortment of goods available in one location.

Consider the example illustrated in Exhibit 12.1. Four consumers each want to buy a television set. Without a retail intermediary like Circuit City, television manufacturers JVC, Zenith, Sony, Toshiba, and RCA would each have to make four contacts to reach the four buyers who are in the target market, for a total of 20 transactions. However, when Circuit City acts as an intermediary between the producer and consumers, each producer has to make only one contact, reducing the number of transactions to 9. Each producer sells to one retailer rather than to four consumers. In turn, consumers buy from one retailer instead of from five producers.

Contact efficiency is being enhanced even more by information technology. Better information on product availability and pricing increasingly is reducing the need for

discrepancy of quantity
The difference between the amount of product produced and the amount an end user wants to buy.

discrepancy of assortment
The lack of all the items a customer needs to receive full satisfaction from a product or products.

temporal discrepancy
A situation that occurs when a product is produced but a customer is not ready to buy it.

spatial discrepancy
The difference between the location of a producer and the location of widely scattered markets.

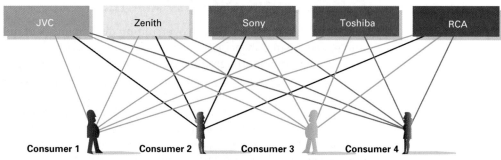

Without an intermediary: 5 producers x 4 consumers = 20 transactions

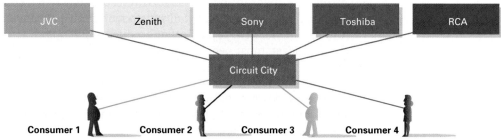

With an intermediary: 5 producers + 4 consumers = 9 transactions

REVIEW LEARNING OUTCOME

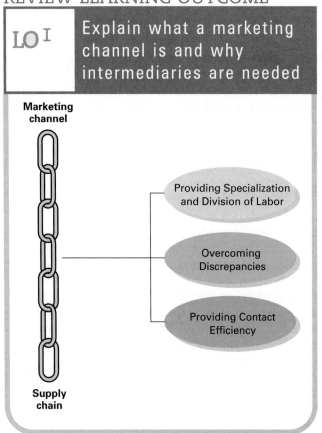

LO 1 Explain what a marketing channel is and why intermediaries are needed

Marketing channel

Providing Specialization and Division of Labor

Overcoming Discrepancies

Providing Contact Efficiency

Supply chain

consumers to actually shop for bargains or view ads in a traditional manner. By making information on products and services easily accessible over the Internet, Google, Yahoo, and similar information assemblers are becoming the starting point for finding and buying products and services. As they cull and organize huge digital warehouses of news, images, traffic and weather reports, and information on automobiles, real estate, and other consumer products, inefficiencies will be reduced, as will prices. These developments are revolutionizing marketing channels and benefiting consumers because shoppers can find out where the best bargains are without having to search for them.[2]

LO 2
Channel Intermediaries and Their Functions

Intermediaries in a channel negotiate with one another, facilitate the change of ownership between buyers and sellers, and physically move products from the manufacturer to the final consumer. The most prominent difference separating intermediaries is whether they take title to the product. *Taking title* means they own the merchandise and control the terms of the sale—for example, price and delivery date. Retailers and merchant wholesalers are examples of intermediaries that take title to products in the marketing channel and resell them. **Retailers** are firms that sell mainly to consumers. Retailers will be discussed in more detail in Chapter 13.

Merchant wholesalers are organizations that facilitate the movement of products and services from the manufacturer to producers, resellers, governments, institutions, and retailers. All merchant wholesalers take title to the goods they sell, and most of them operate one or more warehouses where they receive goods, store them, and later reship them. Customers are mostly small- or moderate-sized retailers, but merchant wholesalers also market to manufacturers and institutional clients.

Other intermediaries do not take title to goods and services they market but do facilitate the exchange of ownership between sellers and buyers. **Agents and brokers** simply facilitate the sale of a product from producer to end user by representing retailers, wholesalers, or manufacturers. Title reflects ownership, and ownership usually implies control. Unlike wholesalers, agents or brokers only facilitate sales and generally have little input into the terms of the sale. They do, however, get a fee or commission based on sales volume. For example, when selling a home, the owner usually hires a real estate agent who then brings potential buyers to see the house. The agent facilitates the sale by bringing the buyer and owner together, but never actually takes ownership of the home.

Variations in channel structures are due in large part to variations in the numbers and types of wholesaling intermediaries. Generally, product characteristics, buyer considerations, and market conditions determine the type of intermediary the manufacturer should use.

- *Product characteristics* that may require a certain type of wholesaling intermediary include whether the product is standardized or customized, the complexity of the product, and the gross margin of the product. For example, a customized product such as insurance is sold through an insurance agent or broker who may represent one or multiple companies. In contrast, a standardized product such as gum is sold through a merchant wholesaler that takes possession of the gum and reships it to the appropriate retailers.

- *Buyer considerations* affecting the wholesaler choice include how often the product is purchased and how long the buyer is willing to wait to receive the product. For example, at the beginning of the school term, a student may be willing to wait a few days for a textbook to get a lower price by ordering online. Thus, this type of product can be distributed directly. But, if the student waits to buy the book until right before an exam and needs the book immediately, it will have to be purchased at the school bookstore.

- *Market characteristics* determining the wholesaler type include how many buyers are in the market and whether they are concentrated in a general location or are widely dispersed. Gum and textbooks, for example, are produced in one location and consumed in many other locations. Therefore, a merchant wholesaler is needed to distribute the products. In contrast, in a home sale, the buyer and seller are localized in one area, which facilitates the use of an agent/broker relationship.

Exhibit 12.2 shows the factors determining the type of wholesaling intermediary.

CHANNEL FUNCTIONS PERFORMED BY INTERMEDIARIES

Retailing and wholesaling intermediaries in marketing channels perform several essential functions that make the flow of goods between producer and buyer possible. The three basic functions that intermediaries perform are summarized in Exhibit 12.3.

Transactional functions involve contacting and communicating with prospective buyers to make them aware of existing products and explain their features, advantages, and benefits. Intermediaries in the supply chain also provide *logistical* functions.

retailer
A channel intermediary that sells mainly to consumers.

merchant wholesaler
An institution that buys goods from manufacturers and resells them to businesses, government agencies, and other wholesalers or retailers and that receives and takes title to goods, stores them in its own warehouses, and later ships them.

agents and brokers
Wholesaling intermediaries who do not take title to a product but facilitate its sale from producer to end user by representing retailers, wholesalers, or manufacturers.

Exhibit 12.2

Factors Suggesting Type of Wholesaling Intermediary to Use

Factor	Merchant Wholesalers	Agents or Brokers
Nature of Product	Standard	Nonstandard, custom
Technicality of Product	Complex	Simple
Product's Gross Margin	High	Low
Frequency of Ordering	Frequent	Infrequent
Time between Order and Receipt of Shipment	Buyer desires shorter lead time	Buyer satisfied with long lead time
Number of Customers	Many	Few
Concentration of Customers	Dispersed	Concentrated

SOURCE: Reprinted by permission of the publisher. From Donald M. Jackson and Michael F. D'Amico, "Products and Markets Served by Distributors and Agents," 27–33 in *Industrial Marketing Management.* Copyright 1989 by Elsevier Science Inc.

Logistics is the process of strategically managing the efficient flow and storage of raw materials, in-process inventory, and finished goods from point of origin to point of consumption. Logistical functions include transporting, storing, sorting out, accumulating, allocating, and assorting products into either homogeneous or heterogeneous collections. For example, grading agricultural products typifies the sorting-out process while consolidation of many lots of grade A eggs from different sources into one lot illustrates the accumulation process. Supermarkets or other retailers perform the assorting function by assembling thousands of different items that match their customers' desires. Similarly, while large companies typically have direct channels, many small companies depend on wholesalers to promote and distribute their products. For example, small beverage manufacturers like Jones Soda, Honest Tea, and Energy Brands depend on wholesalers to distribute their products in a marketplace dominated by large competitors like Coca-Cola and Pepsi.

The third basic channel function, *facilitating*, includes research and financing. Research provides information about channel members and consumers by getting answers to key questions: Who are the buyers? Where are they located? Why do they buy? Financing ensures that channel members have the money to keep products moving through the channel to the ultimate consumer.

A single company may provide one, two, or all three functions. Consider Kramer Beverage Company, a Coors beer distributor. As a beer distributor, Kramer provides transactional, logistical, and facilitating channel functions. Sales representatives contact local bars and restaurants to negotiate the terms of the sale, possibly giving the customer a discount for large purchases, and arrange for delivery of the beer. At the same time, Kramer also provides a facilitating function by extending credit to the customer. Kramer merchandising representatives, meanwhile, assist in promoting the beer on a local level by hanging Coors beer signs and posters. Kramer also provides logistical functions by accumulating the many types of Coors beer from the Coors manufacturing plant in Golden, Colorado, and storing them in its refrigerated warehouse. When an order needs to be filled, Kramer then sorts the beer into heterogeneous collections for each particular customer. For example, the local Chili's Grill & Bar may need two kegs of Coors, three kegs of Coors Light, and two cases of Killian's Red in bottles. The beer will then be loaded

logistics
The process of strategically managing the efficient flow and storage of raw materials, in-process inventory, and finished goods from point of origin to point of consumption.

Exhibit 12.3

Marketing Channel Functions Performed by Intermediaries

Type of Function	Description
Transactional functions	**Contacting and promoting:** Contacting potential customers, promoting products, and soliciting orders
	Negotiating: Determining how many goods or services to buy and sell, type of transportation to use, when to deliver, and method and timing of payment
	Risk taking: Assuming the risk of owning inventory
Logistical Functions	**Physically distributing:** Transporting and sorting goods to overcome temporal and spatial discrepancies
	Storing: Maintaining inventories and protecting goods
	Sorting: Overcoming discrepancies of quantity and assortment by
	Sorting out: Breaking down a heterogeneous supply into separate homogeneous stocks
	Accumulating: Combining similar stocks into a larger homogeneous supply
	Allocating: Breaking a homogeneous supply into smaller and smaller lots ("breaking bulk")
	Assorting: Combining products into collections or assortments that buyers want available at one place
Facilitating Functions	**Researching:** Gathering information about other channel members and consumers
	Financing: Extending credit and other financial services to facilitate the flow of goods through the channel to the final consumer

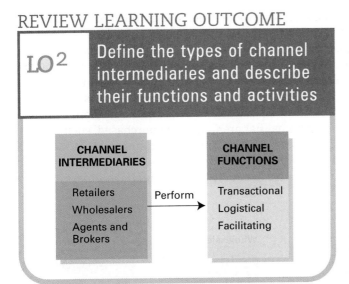

onto a refrigerated truck and transported to the restaurant. Upon arrival, the Kramer delivery person will transport the kegs and cases of beer into the restaurant's refrigerator and may also restock the coolers behind the bar.

Although individual members can be added to or deleted from a channel, someone must still perform these essential functions. They can be performed by producers, end users or consumers, channel intermediaries such as wholesalers and retailers, and sometimes nonmember channel participants. For example, if a manufacturer decides to eliminate its private fleet of trucks, it must still have a way to move the goods to the wholesaler. This task may be accomplished by the wholesaler, which may have its own fleet of trucks, or by a nonmember channel participant, such as an independent trucking firm. Nonmembers also provide many other essential functions that may at one time have been provided by a channel member. For example, research firms may perform the research function; advertising agencies may provide the promotion function; transportation and storage firms, the physical distribution function; and banks, the financing function.

LO³
Channel Structures

A product can take many routes to reach its final consumer.

Marketers search for the most efficient channel from the many alternatives available. Marketing a consumer convenience good like gum or candy differs from marketing a specialty good like a Mercedes-Benz. The two products require very different distribution channels. Likewise, the appropriate channel for a major equipment supplier like Boeing Aircraft would be unsuitable for an accessory equipment producer like Black & Decker. The next sections discuss the structures of typical marketing channels for consumer and business-to-business products. Alternative channel structures are also discussed.

CHANNELS FOR CONSUMER PRODUCTS

Exhibit 12.4 illustrates the four ways manufacturers can route products to consumers. Producers use the **direct channel** to sell directly to consumers. Direct marketing activities—including telemarketing, mail-order and catalog shopping, and forms of electronic retailing like online shopping and shop-at-home television networks—are a good example of this type of channel structure. For example, home computer users can purchase Dell computers directly over the telephone or from Dell's Internet Web site. There are no intermediaries. Producer-owned stores and factory outlet stores—like Sherwin-Williams, Polo Ralph Lauren, Oneida, and West Point Pepperel—are other examples of direct channels. Farmers' markets are also direct channels. Direct marketing and factory outlets are discussed in more detail in Chapter 13.

At the other end of the spectrum, an *agent/broker channel* involves a fairly complicated process. Agent/broker channels are typically used in markets with many small manufacturers and many retailers that lack the resources to find each other. Agents or brokers bring manufacturers and wholesalers together for negotiations, but they do not take title to merchandise. Ownership passes directly to one or more wholesalers and then to retailers. Finally, retailers sell to the ultimate consumer of the product. For example, a food broker represents buyers and sellers of grocery products. The broker acts on behalf of many different producers and negotiates the sale of their products to wholesalers that specialize in foodstuffs. These wholesalers in turn sell to grocers and convenience stores.

direct channel
A distribution channel in which producers sell directly to consumers.

Most consumer products are sold through distribution channels similar to the other two alternatives: the retailer channel and the wholesaler channel. A *retailer channel* is most common when the retailer is large and can buy in large quantities directly from the manufacturer. Wal-Mart, Target, JCPenney, and car dealers are examples of retailers that often bypass a wholesaler. A *wholesaler channel* is commonly used for low-cost items that are frequently purchased, such as candy, cigarettes, and magazines. For example, M&M/Mars sells candies and chocolates to wholesalers in large quantities. The wholesalers then break these quantities into smaller quantities to satisfy individual retailer orders.

Exhibit 12.4

Marketing Channels for Consumer Products

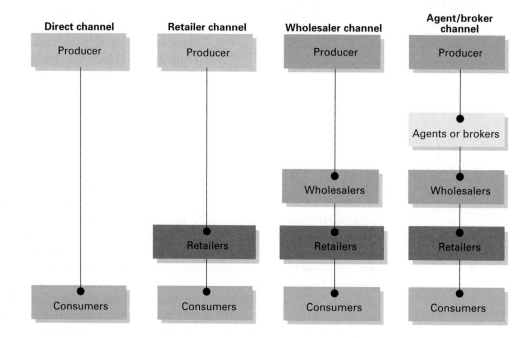

CHANNELS FOR BUSINESS AND INDUSTRIAL PRODUCTS

As Exhibit 12.5 on the next page illustrates, five channel structures are common in business and industrial markets. First, direct channels are typical in business and industrial markets. For example, manufacturers buy large quantities of raw materials, major equipment, processed materials, and supplies directly from other manufacturers. Manufacturers that require suppliers to meet detailed technical specifications often prefer direct channels. The direct communication required between DaimlerChrysler and its suppliers, for example, along with the tremendous size of the orders, makes anything but a direct channel impractical. The channel from producer to government buyers is also a direct channel. Since much government buying is done through bidding, a direct channel is attractive. Dell, for example, the top seller of desktop computers to federal, state, and local government agencies in the United States, sells the computers through direct channels.

Companies selling standardized items of moderate or low value often rely on *industrial distributors*. In many ways, an industrial distributor is like a supermarket for organizations. Industrial distributors are wholesalers and channel members that buy and take title to products. Moreover, they usually keep inventories of their products and sell and service them. Often small manufacturers cannot afford to employ their own sales force. Instead, they rely on manufacturers' representatives or selling agents to sell to either industrial distributors or users.

Today, though, the traditional industrial distributor is facing many challenges. Manufacturers are getting bigger due to growth, mergers, and consolidation. Through

Exhibit 12.5

Channels for Business and Industrial Products

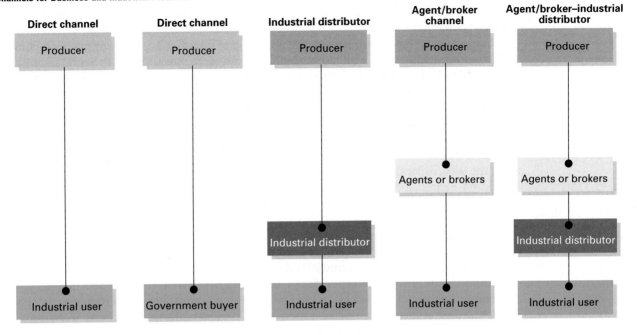

technology, manufacturers and customers have access to information that in the past only the distributor had. Consequently, many manufacturers and customers are bypassing distributors and going direct, often via the Internet. The Internet has enabled virtual distributors to emerge and forced traditional industrial distributors to expand their business model. An example of how the Internet has revolutionized industrial distribution is **http://www.Pumpbiz.com**, which sells pumps for chemicals, wastewater, sumps, water, coolants, and all other industrial process fluids. Pump types available include centrifugal, diaphragm, vertical, magnetic drive, and metering pumps. The site offers 24/7 purchasing and provides access to information on major manufacturers of pumps, including side-by-side comparisons and reviews; copies of manuals, diagrams, and other installation and repair documentation; warranted installers in the customer's local area; and instant access to past purchasing and related information on a customer's account.[3]

The Internet has also led to the emergence of three other new forms of industrial distribution. Some companies serve as agents that link buyers and sellers and charge a fee. For example, Expedia.com links business travelers to airlines, hotels, and car rental companies. A second form of marketplace has been developed by existing companies looking for a way to drop the intermediary from the supply chain. For example, the Worldwide Retail Exchange is a marketplace created by 17 major retailers including Target, JCPenney, and Walgreens. Retailers use the exchange to make purchases that in the past would have required telephone, fax, or face-to-face sales calls. Retailers using the exchange estimate they have saved approximately 15 percent in their purchasing costs. Finally, a third type of Internet marketplace is a "private exchange." Private exchanges allow companies to automate their supply chains while sharing information only with select suppliers. Ace Hardware and Hewlett-Packard, for example, use private exchanges to manage their inventory supplies.[4] Another example is I-textile, which enables companies in the textile business to communicate over a secure online platform to place orders, update information, and standardize transactions.[5]

ALTERNATIVE CHANNEL ARRANGEMENTS

Rarely does a producer use just one type of channel to move its product. It usually employs several different or alternative channels, which include multiple channels, nontraditional channels, and strategic channel alliances.

Multiple Channels

When a producer selects two (or more) channels to distribute the same product to target markets, this arrangement is called **dual distribution** (or **multiple distribution**). As more people have access to the Internet and embrace online shopping, an increasing number of retailers are using multiple channels of distribution. For example, companies such as Limited Brands, which includes The Limited, Express, Victoria's Secret, and Bath and Body Works, sell in-store, online, and through catalogs. Other examples are Sears and Avon. Since Sears purchased Lands' End, a traditional direct business-to-consumer clothing manufacturer, Lands' End products are available in Sears stores, and Sears credit cards are accepted on the Lands' End Web site. Avon, a direct supplier of health and beauty products for women, offers consumers four alternatives for purchasing products. They can contact a representative in person (the original business model), purchase on the Web, order direct from the company, or pick up products at an Avon Salon & Spa. Limited, Sears/Lands' End, and Avon, are each distributing identical products to existing markets using more than one channel of distribution.[6]

Nontraditional Channels

Often nontraditional channel arrangements help differentiate a firm's product from the competition. For example, manufacturers may decide to use nontraditional channels such as the Internet, mail-order channels, or infomercials, to sell products instead of going through traditional retailer channels. Although nontraditional channels may limit a brand's coverage, they can give a producer serving a niche market a way to gain market access and customer attention without having to establish channel intermediaries. Nontraditional channels can also provide another avenue of sales for larger firms. For example, a London publisher sells short stories through vending machines in the London Underground. Instead of the traditional book format, the stories are printed like folded maps making them an easy-to-read alternative for commuters.

Kiosks, long a popular method for ordering and registering for wedding gifts, dispersing cash through ATMs, and facilitating airline check-in, are finding new uses. Ethan Allen furniture stores use kiosks as a product locator tool for consumers and salespeople. Kiosks on the campuses of Cheney University allow students to register for classes, see their class schedule and grades, check account balances, and even print transcripts. The general public, when it has access to the kiosks, can use them to gather information about the university.[7]

Strategic Channel Alliances

Companies often form **strategic channel alliances**. Such an alliance enables a company to use another manufacturer's already established channel. Alliances are used most often when the creation of marketing channel relationships may be too expensive and time-consuming. Recall from the opening example that Starbucks, the world's premier coffee marketer, uses strategic alliances both domestically and around the world. When Starbucks wanted to develop ready-to-drink (RTD) coffee beverages for supermarkets and other outlets, it decided not to develop a new channel from scratch. Rather, Starbucks signed an agreement with Pepsi to develop and bottle a Starbucks brand of RTD coffee, a category that had been extremely difficult to develop. The resulting Frappuccino and DoubleShot were so successful when they were launched that they were constantly

dual distribution (multiple distribution)
The use of two (or more) channels to distribute the same product to target markets.

strategic channel alliance
A cooperative agreement between business firms to use the other's already established distribution channel.

CONSUMER CHANNELS	BUSINESS CHANNELS	ALTERNATIVE CHANNELS
• Direct	• Direct	• Multiple
• Retail	• Industrial	• Nontraditional
• Wholesaler	• Agent/broker	• Strategic alliances
• Agent/broker	• Agent/broker–industrial	

sold out. Today, nearly 15 years since the Pepsi/Starbucks alliance first was forged, Pepsi is still the sole distributor for Starbucks RTD beverages like Frappuccino and DoubleShot, and Starbucks has continued access to the thousands of outlets where Pepsi is sold.[8] Similarly, Accenture and Cisco Systems have formed an alliance to work together in the joint development, marketing, and deployment of global network solutions. The combination of Accenture's network consulting services and Cisco's advanced technology will result in cost savings in asset acquisition and service delivery for their customers.[9] Strategic channel alliances are proving to be more successful for growing businesses than mergers and acquisitions. This is especially true in global markets where cultural differences, distance, and other barriers can prove challenging. For example, Heinz has a strategic alliance with Kagome, one of Japan's largest food companies. The companies are working together to find ways to reduce operating costs while expanding both brands' market presence globally.[10]

LO4
Supply Chain Management

In today's sophisticated marketplace, many companies are turning to supply chain management for competitive advantage. The goal of **supply chain management** is to coordinate and integrate all of the activities performed by supply chain members into a seamless process from the source to the point of consumption, ultimately giving supply chain managers "total visibility" of the supply chain both inside and outside the firm. The philosophy behind supply chain management is that by visualizing the entire supply chain, supply chain managers can maximize strengths and efficiencies at each level of the process to create a highly competitive, customer-driven supply system that is able to respond immediately to changes in supply and demand.

An important element of supply chain management is that it is completely customer driven. In the mass-production era, manufacturers produced standardized products that were "pushed" down through the supply channel to the consumer. In contrast, in today's marketplace, products are being driven by customers, who expect to receive product configurations and services matched to their unique needs. For example, Dell only builds computers according to its customers' precise specifications, such as the amount of RAM memory; type of monitor, modem, or CD drive; and amount of hard disk space. Similarly, car companies offer customers the option to customize even economy-priced cars. For about $20,000, customers can order a Ford Mustang with a V-6 engine, a six-disc CD changer, MP3 player, and eight speakers. The focus is on pulling products into the marketplace and partnering with members of the supply chain to enhance customer value. Customizing an automobile is now possible because of new supply chain relationships between the automobile manufacturers and the after-market auto-parts industry.[11]

This reversal of the flow of demand from a "push" to a "pull" has resulted in a radical reformulation of both market expectations and traditional marketing, production, and distribution functions. Through the channel partnership of suppliers, manufacturers, wholesalers, and retailers along the entire supply chain who work together toward the common goal of creating customer value, supply chain management allows companies to respond with the unique product configuration and mix of services demanded by the customer. Today, supply chain management plays a dual role: first, as a *communicator* of customer demand that extends from the point of sale all the way back to the supplier, and second, as a *physical flow process* that engineers the timely and cost-effective movement of goods through the entire supply pipeline.

Accordingly, supply chain managers are responsible for making channel strategy decisions, coordinating the sourcing and procurement of raw materials, scheduling production, processing orders, managing inventory, transporting and storing supplies and finished goods, and coordinating customer service activities. Supply chain managers are also responsible for the management of information that flows through the supply chain. Coordinating the relationships between the company and its external partners, such as vendors, carriers, and third-party companies, is also a critical function of supply

supply chain management
A management system that coordinates and integrates all of the activities performed by supply chain members into a seamless process, from the source to the point of consumption, resulting in enhanced customer and economic value.

chain management. Because supply chain managers play such a major role in both cost control and customer satisfaction, they are more valuable than ever. In fact, demand for supply chain managers has increased substantially in recent years.

In summary, supply chain managers are responsible for directing raw materials and parts to the production department and the finished or semifinished product through warehouses and eventually to the intermediary or end user. Above all, supply chain management begins and ends with the customer. Instead of forcing into the market a product that may or may not sell quickly, supply chain managers react to actual customer demand. By doing so, they minimize the flow of raw materials, finished product, and packaging materials at every point in the supply chain, resulting in lower costs and increased customer value. Exhibit 12.6 depicts the supply chain process.

Exhibit 12.6
The Supply Chain Process

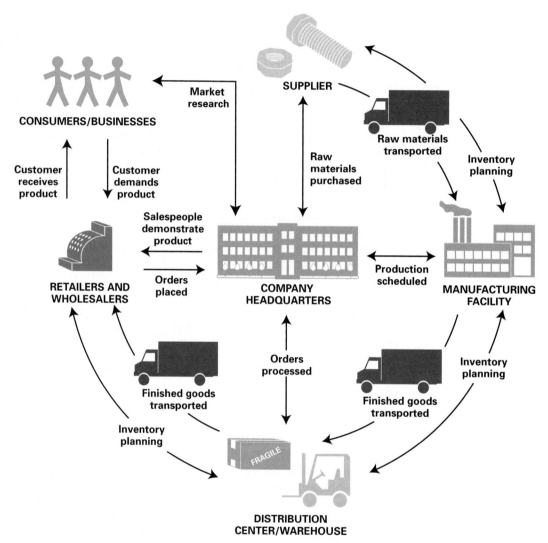

BENEFITS OF SUPPLY CHAIN MANAGEMENT

Supply chain management is a key means of differentiation for a firm and a critical component in marketing and corporate strategy. Companies that focus on supply chain management commonly report lower inventory, transportation, warehousing, and packaging costs; greater supply chain flexibility; improved customer service; and higher revenues. Research has shown a clear relationship between supply chain performance and profitability. Specific benefits from effective implementation of supply chain procedures include an almost 20 percent increase in cash flow, a more than 50 percent increase in flexibility of supply chain activities, and a reduction of 5 to 10 percent in supply chain costs.[12]

Dreyer's Ice Cream's successful logistics systems starts with its state-of-the-art manufacturing facility. The return on investment the company experienced subsequent to its supply chain upgrades was extremely impressive.

Dreyer's, the largest ice cream manufacturer in the United States, manufactures products for such well-known brands as Nestlé Drumstick and Crunch, Butterfinger, Toll House, Carnation, and Starbucks. The company owes much of its success to its logistics system. It has invested several hundred million dollars in new trucks, manufacturing centers, and a computerized supply chain system that enables dispatchers to design delivery routes around sales volume, mileage, traffic patterns, road tolls, and stores' hours of operation. Dreyer's has seen a substantial return on its investment: the number of sales accounts has increased by more than 30 percent, over 40,000 unnecessary stops have been eliminated, and it has saved millions of dollars in fuel and labor costs, resulting in higher profits. In fact, the system provides such strong customer service capability and cost savings that nearly one-third of Dreyer's revenue comes from deals to distribute its competitors' brands such as Häagen-Dazs and Ben & Jerry's.[13] On a more individual level, one materials analyst for a company that produces seat belts reported that when her company began focusing on supply chain management, it shortened her workweek by 15 to 20 hours and reduced her inventory costs by 75 percent.[14]

REVIEW LEARNING OUTCOME

LO4 Define supply chain management and discuss its benefits

Well-managed supply chains . . .

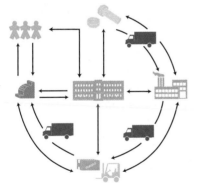

lead to . . .

✓ reduced costs
✓ increased flexibility
✓ improved customer service
✓ greater revenue

LO5
Making Channel Strategy Decisions

Devising a marketing channel strategy requires several critical decisions. Supply chain managers must decide what role distribution will play in the overall marketing strategy. In addition, they must be sure that the channel strategy chosen is consistent with product, promotion, and pricing strategies. In making these decisions, marketing managers must determine what factors will influence the choice of channel and what level of distribution intensity will be appropriate.

FACTORS AFFECTING CHANNEL CHOICE

Supply chain managers must answer many questions before choosing a marketing channel. The final choice depends on the analysis of several factors, which often interact. These factors can be grouped as market factors, product factors, and producer factors.

Market Factors

Among the most important market factors affecting the choice of distribution channel are target customer considerations. Specifically, supply chain managers should answer the following questions: Who are the potential customers? What do they buy? Where do they buy? When do they buy? How do they buy? Additionally, the choice of channel depends on whether the producer is selling to consumers or to industrial customers. Industrial customers' buying habits are very different from those of consumers. Industrial customers tend to buy in larger quantities and require more customer service. For example, Toyota Industrial Equipment manufactures the leading lift truck used to move materials in and out of warehouses and other industrial facilities. Its business customers buy large numbers of trucks at one time and require additional services such as data tracking on how the lift truck is used.[15] In contrast, consumers usually buy in very small quantities and sometimes do not mind if they get little or no service, such as in a discount store like Wal-Mart or Target.

The geographic location and size of the market are also important to channel selection. As a rule, if the target market is concentrated in one or more specific areas, then direct selling through a sales force is appropriate. When markets are more widely dispersed, intermediaries would be less expensive. The size of the market also influences channel choice. Generally, larger markets require more intermediaries. For instance, Procter & Gamble has to reach millions of consumers with its many brands of household goods. It needs many intermediaries, including wholesalers and retailers.

Product Factors

Products that are more complex, customized, and expensive tend to benefit from shorter and more direct marketing channels. These types of products sell better through a direct sales force. Examples include pharmaceuticals, scientific instruments, airplanes, and mainframe computer systems. On the other hand, the more standardized a product is, the longer its distribution channel can be and the greater the number of intermediaries that can be involved. For example, with the exception of flavor and shape, the formula for chewing gum is about the same from producer to producer. Chewing gum is also very inexpensive. As a result, the distribution channel for gum tends to involve many wholesalers and retailers.

The product's life cycle is also an important factor in choosing a marketing channel. In fact, the choice of channel may change over the life of the product. For example, when photocopiers were first available, they were typically sold by a direct sales force. Now, however, photocopiers can be found in several places, including warehouse clubs, electronics superstores, and mail-order catalogs. As products become more common and less intimidating to potential users, producers tend to look for alternative channels. Gatorade was originally sold to sports teams, gyms, and fitness clubs. As the drink became more popular, mainstream supermarket channels were added, followed by convenience stores and drugstores. Now Gatorade can be found in vending machines and even in some fast-food restaurants.

Another factor is the delicacy of the product. Perishable products like vegetables and milk have a relatively short life span. Fragile products like china and crystal require a minimum amount of handling. Therefore, both require fairly short marketing channels. Online retailers such as eBay facilitate the sale of unusual or difficult-to-find products that benefit from a direct channel.

Producer Factors

Several factors pertaining to the producer itself are important to the selection of a marketing channel. In general, producers with large financial, managerial, and marketing resources are better able to use more direct channels. These producers have the ability to hire and train their own sales force, warehouse their own goods, and extend credit to their customers. For example, variety store Dollar Tree distributes products through retail locations at low prices. To increase cost-efficiency, Dollar Tree has a coast-to-coast logistics network of nine distribution centers to service its almost 3,000 stores.[16] Smaller or weaker firms, on the other hand, must rely on intermediaries to provide these services for them. Compared to producers with only one or two product lines, producers that sell several products in a related area are able to choose channels that are more direct. Sales expenses then can be spread over more products.

A producer's desire to control pricing, positioning, brand image, and customer support also tends to influence channel selection. For instance, firms that sell products with exclusive brand images, such as designer perfumes and clothing, usually avoid channels in which discount retailers are present. Manufacturers of upscale products, such as Gucci (handbags) and Godiva (chocolates), may sell their wares only in expensive stores in order to maintain an image of exclusivity. Many producers have opted to risk their image, however, and test sales in discount channels. Levi Strauss expanded its distribution to include JCPenney, Sears, and Wal-Mart. Wal-Mart is now Levi Strauss's biggest customer.

LEVELS OF DISTRIBUTION INTENSITY

Organizations have three options for intensity of distribution: intensive distribution, selective distribution, or exclusive distribution (see Exhibit 12.7).

Intensive Distribution

Intensive distribution is a form of distribution aimed at maximum market coverage. The manufacturer tries to have the product available in every outlet where potential customers might want to buy it. If buyers are unwilling to search for a product (as is true of convenience goods and operating supplies), the product must be very accessible to buyers. A low-value product that is purchased frequently may require a lengthy channel. For example, candy, chips, and other snack foods are found in almost every type of retail store imaginable. These foods typically are sold to retailers in small quantities by food or candy wholesalers. The Wrigley Company could not afford to sell its gum directly to every service station, drugstore, supermarket, and discount store. The cost would be too high. Sysco delivers food and related products to restaurants and other food service companies that prepare meals for customers dining out. It is not economically feasible for restaurants to go to individual vendors for each product. Therefore, Sysco serves as an intermediary by delivering all products necessary to fulfill restaurants' needs.[17]

Most manufacturers pursuing an intensive distribution strategy sell to a large percentage of the wholesalers willing to stock their products. Retailers' willingness (or unwillingness) to handle items tends to control the manufacturer's ability to achieve intensive distribution. For example, a retailer already carrying ten brands of gum may show little enthusiasm for one more brand.

Selective Distribution

Selective distribution is achieved by screening dealers and retailers to eliminate all but a few in any single area. Because only a few are chosen, the consumer must seek out the product. For example, when Heeling Sports Ltd. launched Heelys, thick-soled sneakers with a wheel embedded in each heel, the company hired a group of 40 teens to perform Heelys exhibitions in targeted malls, skate parks, and college campuses across the country to create demand. Then the company made the decision to avoid large stores like Target and to distribute the shoes only through selected mall retailers and skate and surf shops in order to position the product as "cool and kind of irreverent."[18]

intensive distribution
A form of distribution aimed at having a product available in every outlet where target customers might want to buy it.

selective distribution
A form of distribution achieved by screening dealers to eliminate all but a few in any single area.

Exhibit 12.7
Intensity of Distribution Levels

Intensity Level	Distribution Intensity Objective	Number of Intermediaries in Each Market	Examples
Intensive	Achieve mass-market selling; popular with health and beauty aids and convenience goods that must be available everywhere	Many	Pepsi-Cola, Frito-Lay potato chips, Huggies diapers, Alpo dog food, Crayola crayons
Selective	Work closely with selected intermediaries who meet certain criteria; typically used for shopping goods and some specialty goods	Several	Donna Karan clothing, Hewlett-Packard printers, Burton snowboards, Aveda aromatherapy products
Exclusive	Work with a single intermediary for products that require special resources or positioning; typically used for specialty goods and major industrial equipment	One	BMW cars, Rolex watches

Selective distribution strategies often hinge on a manufacturer's desire to maintain a superior product image so as to be able to charge a premium price. DKNY clothing, for instance, is sold only in select retail outlets, mainly full-price department stores. Likewise, premium pet food brands such as Hill's Pet Nutrition and Ralston-Purina's ProPlan are distributed chiefly through specialty pet food stores and veterinarians, rather than mass retailers like Wal-Mart, so that a premium price can be charged. Manufacturers sometimes expand selective distribution strategies, believing that doing so will enhance revenues without diminishing their product's image. For example, when Procter & Gamble purchased premium pet food brand Iams, it expanded the brand's selective distribution strategy and began selling Iams food in mass retailer Target. Even though the new strategy created channel conflict with breeders and veterinarians who had supported the product, sales increased.[19]

exclusive distribution
A form of distribution that establishes one or a few dealers within a given area.

EXCLUSIVE DISTRIBUTION

The most restrictive form of market coverage is **exclusive distribution,** which entails only one or a few dealers within a given area. Because buyers may have to search or travel extensively to buy the product, exclusive distribution is usually confined to consumer specialty goods, a few shopping goods, and major industrial equipment. Products such as Rolls-Royce automobiles, Chris-Craft power boats, and Pettibone tower cranes are distributed under exclusive arrangements. Sometimes exclusive territories are granted by new companies (such as franchisors) to obtain market coverage in a particular area. Limited distribution may also serve to project an exclusive image for the product.

Retailers and wholesalers may be unwilling to commit the time and money necessary to promote and service a product unless the manufacturer guarantees them an exclusive territory. This arrangement shields the dealer from direct competition and enables it to be the main beneficiary of the manufacturer's promotion efforts in that geographic area. With exclusive distribution, channels of communication are usually well established because the manufacturer works with a limited number of dealers rather than many accounts.

Exclusive distribution also takes place within a retailer's store rather than a geographic area—for example, when a retailer agrees not to sell a manufacturer's competing brands. Mossimo, traditionally an apparel wholesaler, developed an agreement with Target to design clothing and related items sold exclusively at Target stores. Other exclusive distributors involved in this successful model include Thomas O'Brien domestics, Sonia Kashuk makeup, Isaac Mizrahi domestics and apparel, and Todd Oldham home furnishings for the college student.[20]

REVIEW LEARNING OUTCOME

LO5 Discuss the issues that influence channel strategy

Factors	Distribution
Market	Intensive
Product	Selective
Producer	Exclusive

Channel Strategy

LO6
Managing Channel Relationships

A marketing channel is more than a set of institutions linked by economic ties. Social relationships play an important role in building unity among channel members. A critical aspect of supply chain management, therefore, is managing the social relationships among channel members to achieve synergy. The basic social dimensions of channels are power, control, leadership, conflict, and partnering.

CHANNEL POWER, CONTROL, AND LEADERSHIP

Channel power is a channel member's capacity to control or influence the behavior of other channel members. **Channel control** occurs when one channel member affects another member's behavior. To achieve control, a channel member assumes channel leadership and exercises authority and power. This member is termed the **channel leader,** or **channel captain.** In one marketing channel, a manufacturer may be the leader because it controls new-product designs and product availability. In another, a retailer may be the channel leader because it wields power and control over the retail price, inventory levels, and postsale service.

The exercise of channel power is a routine element of many business activities in which the outcome is often greater control over a company's brands. Apple started its line of retail stores because management was dissatisfied with how distributors were selling the company's computers (i.e., with its lack of control). Macintosh displays were often buried inside other major retail stores, surrounded by personal computers running the more popular Windows operating systems by Microsoft. To regain a position of power in the marketing channel, Apple hired a retail executive to develop a retail strategy, which relied heavily on company-owned stores that reflected Apple's design sensibilities. The new strategy has paid off tremendously: in the first three months of 2006 alone, sales at Apple stores topped $1 billion.[21]

CHANNEL CONFLICT

Inequitable channel relationships often lead to **channel conflict,** which is a clash of goals and methods among the members of a distribution channel. In a broad context, conflict may not be bad. Often it arises because staid, traditional channel members refuse to keep pace with the times. Removing an outdated intermediary may result in reduced costs for the entire supply chain. The Internet has forced many intermediaries to offer services such as merchandise tracking and inventory availability online.

Conflicts among channel members can be due to many different situations and factors. Oftentimes, conflict arises because channel members have conflicting goals. For instance, athletic footwear retailers want to sell as many shoes as possible in order to maximize profits, regardless of whether the shoe is manufactured by Nike, adidas, or Saucony. But the Nike manufacturer wants a certain sales volume and market share in each market.

Conflict can also arise when channel members fail to fulfill expectations of other channel members—for example, when a franchisee does not follow the rules set down by the franchisor, or when communications channels break down between channel members. As another example, if a manufacturer shortens the period of warranty coverage and fails to inform dealers of this change, conflict may occur when dealers make repairs expecting that they will be reimbursed by the manufacturer. Further, ideological differences and different perceptions of reality can also cause conflict among channel members. For instance, retailers may believe "the customer is always right" and offer a very liberal return policy. Wholesalers and manufacturers may feel that people "try to get something for nothing" or don't follow product instructions carefully. Their differing views of allowable returns will undoubtably conflict with those of retailers.

Conflict within a channel can be either horizontal or vertical. **Horizontal conflict** occurs among channel members on the same level, such as two or more different wholesalers or two or more different retailers, that handle the same manufacturer's brands. This type of channel conflict is found most often when manufacturers practice dual or multiple distribution strategies. When Apple changed its distribution strategy and began opening its own stores, it angered Apple's traditional retail partners, some of whom ultimately filed lawsuits against the company. The primary allegation was that Apple stores were competing unfairly with them and that Apple favored its own stores when allocating desirable inventory (like iPods). Horizontal conflict can also occur when some channel members feel that other members on the same level are being treated differently by the manufacturer. For example, the American Booksellers Association, a group representing

channel power
The capacity of a particular marketing channel member to control or influence the behavior of other channel members.

channel control
A situation that occurs when one marketing channel member intentionally affects another member's behavior.

channel leader (channel captain)
A member of a marketing channel that exercises authority and power over the activities of other channel members.

channel conflict
A clash of goals and methods between distribution channel members.

horizontal conflict
A channel conflict that occurs among channel members on the same level.

small independent booksellers, filed a lawsuit against bookstore giants Barnes & Noble and Borders, claiming they had violated antitrust laws by using their buying power to demand "illegal and secret" discounts from publishers. These deals, the association contended, put independent booksellers at a serious competitive disadvantage.

Many regard horizontal conflict as healthy competition. Much more serious is **vertical conflict,** which occurs between different levels in a marketing channel, most typically between the manufacturer and wholesaler or the manufacturer and retailer. Producer-versus-wholesaler conflict occurs when the producer chooses to bypass the wholesaler and deal directly with the consumer or retailer.

Dual distribution strategies can also cause vertical conflict in the channel. For example, high-end fashion designers traditionally sold their products through luxury retailers such as Neiman Marcus and Saks Fifth Avenue. Interested in increasing sales and gaining additional control over presentation, many designers such as Giorgio Armani, Donna Karan, and Louis Vuitton opened their own boutiques in the same shopping centers anchored by the luxury retailers. As a result, the retailers lost substantial revenues on the designers' items. Similarly, manufacturers experimenting with selling to customers directly over the Internet create conflict with their traditional retailing intermediaries. For example, Walgreens sells about 2 billion photo prints a year, all of which once were printed on Kodak paper using Kodak chemicals. When Kodak launched Ofoto.com, a site where customers could upload digital prints to the Internet, view them, and order prints directly from Kodak, Walgreens took exception. It installed 2,300 traditional and digital photo kiosks made by Fuji, Kodak's main competitor. The channel conflict will cost Kodak $500 million a year in sales.[22] This chapter's "Ethics in Marketing" box describes a channel conflict involving Amazon.com.

Producers and retailers may also disagree over the terms of the sale or other aspects of the business relationship. When Procter & Gamble introduced "everyday low pricing" to its retail channel members, a strategy designed to standardize wholesale prices and eliminate

vertical conflict
A channel conflict that occurs between different levels in a marketing channel, most typically between the manufacturer and wholesaler or between the manufacturer and retailer.

channel partnering (channel cooperation)
The joint effort of all channel members to create a supply chain that serves customers and creates a competitive advantage.

ETHICS in Marketing

Conflict at Amazon Ends in Divorce

When Toys "R" Us launched its Web site in time for the 1999 holiday shopping season, the company was not ready for the success it was going to have. The site was an instant hit with consumers, but the company had terrible problems filling many orders and was lambasted in the press for weeks after the holiday results were announced. That same year, the world's pioneering e-tailer, Amazon.com, also experienced problems—not with filling orders, but with inventory. Amazon was often out of stock on popular items and overstocked on unpopular ones.

The following year, Amazon and Toys "R" Us brokered what was then considered a landmark deal. Toys "R" Us would sell toys online exclusively through the Amazon.com site. For its part, Amazon would make Toys "R" Us the only toy retailer in its online shopping mall for ten years. After that milestone agreement, Amazon brokered tons of deals with specialty retailers. More than a million companies including Circuit City, Office Depot, Borders, Eddie Bauer, Drugstore.com, Guess?, J&R Music, Ice.com, and Computer World wanted access to the Internet's most reliable order-filling operation. In a single year, the number of online merchants selling through Amazon increased nearly 30 percent.

Then, only two years into its groundbreaking contract with Toys "R" Us, Amazon signed what would become another milestone agreement with Target. The addition of Target angered Amazon's specialty retailers, who saw their exclusive arrangements jeopardized by Target's wide assortment of products. Amazon itself began selling products that ate into its partners' business. For example, Amazon began selling pearl necklaces and diamond earrings, some of the best-selling items at Ice.com, an Amazon partner. Some retailers, like Circuit City, canceled their agreements, saying that they weren't making enough money through Amazon to justify the expense. Toys "R" Us, however, did not go quietly.

Feeling extreme pressure from Wal-Mart and Target off-line, Toys "R" Us sued Amazon for breach of contract (Toys "R" Us still had eight years left in its contract with Amazon). Amazon countersued, arguing that Toys "R" Us was in violation of the agreement because it was not able to supply enough product to Amazon customers. The two companies fought out their disagreement in court until 2006, when a judge formally severed their contract, basically agreeing with Toys "R" Us.[23]

Are multiple distribution channels unethical? Are competition and conflict in the Internet space different than in the physical world of retailing?

Exhibit 12.8
Transaction- versus Partnership-Based Firms

	Transaction-Based	Partnership-Based
Relationships between Manufacturer and Supplier	• Short-term • Adversarial • Independent • Price more important	• Long-term • Cooperative • Dependent • Value-added services more important
Number of Suppliers	Many	Few
Level of Information Sharing	Minimal	High
Investment Required	Minimal	High

SOURCE: David Frederick Ross, *Competing Through Supply Chain Management: Creating Market-Winning Strategies Through Supply Chain Partnerships* (New York: Chapman & Hall, 1998), 61.

REVIEW LEARNING OUTCOME

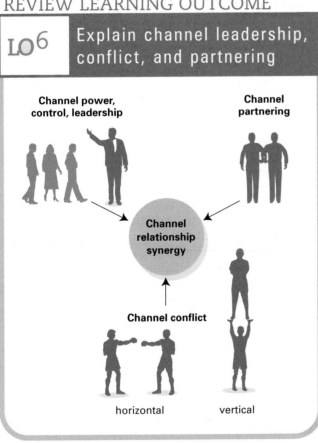

LO6 Explain channel leadership, conflict, and partnering

Channel power, control, leadership

Channel partnering

Channel relationship synergy

Channel conflict

horizontal   vertical

most trade promotions, many retailers retaliated. Some cut the variety of P&G sizes they carried or eliminated marginal brands. Others moved P&G brands from prime shelf space to less visible shelves.

CHANNEL PARTNERING

Regardless of the locus of power, channel members rely heavily on one another. Even the most powerful manufacturers depend on dealers to sell their products; even the most powerful retailers require the products provided by suppliers. In sharp contrast to the adversarial relationships of the past between buyers and sellers, contemporary management thought emphasizes the development of close working partnerships among channel members. **Channel partnering,** or **channel cooperation,** is the joint effort of all channel members to create a supply chain that serves customers and creates a competitive advantage. Channel partnering is vital if each member is to gain something from other members. By cooperating, retailers, wholesalers, manufacturers, and suppliers can speed up inventory replenishment, improve customer service, and reduce the total costs of the marketing channel.

Channel alliances and partnerships help supply chain managers create the parallel flow of materials and information required to leverage the supply chain's intellectual, material, and marketing resources. The rapid growth in channel partnering is due to new enabling technology and the need to lower costs. A comparison between companies that approach the marketplace unilaterally and those that engage in channel cooperation and form partnerships is detailed in Exhibit 12.8.

Collaborating channel partners meet the needs of consumers more effectively by ensuring that the right products are available at the right time and for a lower cost, thus boosting sales and profits. Forced to become more efficient, many companies are turning formerly adversarial relationships into partnerships. For example, Kraft is the largest coffee purchaser in the world. Rather than clash with coffee bean growers, Kraft partners with them to help build customer demand and develop "sustainable" coffee production (growing coffee in a way that reduces the impact on the environment, provides quality ingredients for manufacturers to meet consumer needs, and is more valuable to the farmer).[24]

LO7
Managing the Logistical Components of the Supply Chain

Now that you are familiar with the structure and strategy of marketing channels and the role of supply chain management, it is important to also understand the physical means through which products move through the supply chain.

As mentioned earlier, supply chain management coordinates and integrates all of the activities performed by supply chain members into a seamless process. The supply chain consists of several interrelated and integrated logistical components: (1) sourcing and procurement of raw materials and supplies, (2) production scheduling, (3) order processing, (4) inventory control, (5) warehousing and materials-handling, and (6) transportation.

The **logistics information system** is the link connecting all of the logistics components of the supply chain. The components of the system include, for example, software for materials acquisition and handling, warehouse-management and enterprise-wide solutions, data storage and integration in data warehouses, mobile communications, electronic data interchange, RFID chips, and the Internet. Working together, the components of the logistics information system are the fundamental enablers of successful supply chain management.

The **supply chain team,** in concert with the logistics information system, orchestrates the movement of goods, services, and information from the source to the consumer. Supply chain teams typically cut across organizational boundaries, embracing all parties who participate in moving the product to market. The best supply chain teams also move beyond the organization to include the external participants in the chain, such as suppliers, transportation carriers, and third-party logistics suppliers. Members of the supply chain communicate, coordinate, and cooperate extensively.

Today's corporate supply chain logisticians have become so efficient that the U.S. Marine Corps is now consulting with companies like Wal-Mart, UPS, and Unilever to improve its own supply chain efficiency. The Marine Corps's goal is to reduce the time it takes to deliver supplies to the front lines from one week to 24 hours and lower costs by cutting inventories in half.

SOURCING AND PROCUREMENT

One of the most important links in the supply chain is the one between the manufacturer and the supplier. Purchasing professionals are on the front lines of supply chain management. Purchasing departments plan purchasing strategies, develop specifications, select suppliers, and negotiate price and service levels.

The goal of most sourcing and procurement activities is to reduce the costs of raw materials and supplies. Purchasing professionals have traditionally relied on tough negotiations to get the lowest price possible from suppliers of raw materials, supplies, and components. Perhaps the biggest contribution purchasing can make to supply chain management, however, is in the area of vendor relations. Companies can use the purchasing function to strategically manage suppliers in order to reduce the total cost of materials and services. Through enhanced vendor relations, buyers and sellers can develop cooperative relationships that reduce costs and improve efficiency with the aim of lowering prices and enhancing profits. By integrating suppliers into their companies' businesses, purchasing managers have become better able to streamline purchasing processes, manage inventory levels, and reduce overall costs of the sourcing and procurement operations.

logistics information system
The link that connects all of the logistics components of the supply chain.

supply chain team
An entire group of individuals who orchestrate the movement of goods, services, and information from the source to the consumer.

PRODUCTION SCHEDULING

In traditional mass-market manufacturing, production begins when forecasts call for additional products to be made or inventory control systems signal low inventory levels. The firm then makes a product and transports the finished goods to its own warehouses or those of intermediaries, where the goods wait to be ordered by retailers or customers. Many types of convenience goods, such as toothpaste, deodorant, and detergent, are manufactured based on past sales and demand and then sent to retailers to resell. Production scheduling based on pushing a product down to the consumer obviously has its disadvantages, the most notable being that companies risk making products that may become obsolete or that consumers don't want in the first place.

In a customer "pull" manufacturing environment, which is growing in popularity, production of goods or services is not scheduled until an order is placed by the customer specifying the desired configuration. As you read in Chapter 11, this process, known as **mass customization,** or **build-to-order,** uniquely tailors mass-market goods and services to the needs of the individuals who buy them. Companies as diverse as BMW, Dell, Levi Strauss, Mattel, and a slew of Web-based businesses are adopting mass customization to maintain or obtain a competitive edge.

As more companies move toward mass customization—and away from mass marketing—of goods, the need to stay on top of consumer demand is forcing manufacturers to make their supply chains more flexible. Flexibility is critical to a manufacturer's success when dramatic swings in demand occur. To meet consumers' demand for customized products, companies are forced to adapt their manufacturing approach or even create a completely new process. For years, Nike sold its shoes through specialty retailers to hard-core runners who cared little what the shoes looked like. Over time, however, runners began to demand more stylish designs and technologically advanced footwear. To keep pace with rapidly changing fashions and trends, Nike launched NikeID, a set of specialty stores and a Web site through which you can design and order athletic shoes. You can even personalize them with an eight-character brand statement.[25]

Just-in-Time Manufacturing

An important manufacturing process common today among manufacturers is just-in-time manufacturing. Borrowed from the Japanese, **just-in-time production (JIT),** sometimes called *lean production,* requires manufacturers to work closely with suppliers and transportation providers to get necessary items to the assembly line or factory floor at the precise time they are needed for production. For the manufacturer, JIT means that raw materials arrive at the assembly line in guaranteed working order "just in time" to be installed, and finished products are generally shipped to the customer immediately after completion. For the supplier, JIT means supplying customers with products in just a few days, or even a few hours, rather than weeks. For the ultimate consumer, JIT means lower costs, shorter lead times, and products that more closely meet the consumer's needs. For example, Zara, a European clothing manufacturer and retailer with over 600 stores in 48 countries, uses the JIT process to ensure that its stores are stocked with the latest fashion trends. Using its salespeople to track which fashions are selling fastest, the company can increase production of hot items and ship them to its stores in 15 days. Because Zara stores do not maintain large inventories, they can respond quickly to fashion trends and offer their products for less, giving Zara a distinct advantage over more traditional retailers like Gap that place orders months in advance.[26]

JIT benefits manufacturers most by reducing their raw materials inventories. For example, at Dell's Texas plant, computer components often are delivered just minutes before they are needed. Chips, boards, and drives are kept in trucks backed into bays located 50 feet from the beginning of the production line. On average, Dell takes only about a week from buying parts to selling them as a finished product. Similarly, Customized Transportation, Inc., works with General Motors to coordinate delivery of interior door panels at the moment they are needed for production. CTI also helps GM manage its supply chain by issuing purchase orders, buying the raw materials from vendors, assembling the components, and packaging them for delivery.

JIT also shortens lead times—the time it takes to get parts from a supplier after an order has been placed. Manufacturers enjoy better relationships with suppliers and can decrease their production and storeroom costs. Because there is little safety stock, and therefore no margin for error, the manufacturer cannot afford to make a mistake. As a result, a manufacturer using JIT must be sure it receives high-quality parts from all vendors, be confident that the supplier will meet all delivery commitments, and have a crisis management plan to handle any disruptions. Finally, JIT tends to reduce the amount of paperwork.

mass customization (build-to-order)
A production method whereby products are not made until an order is placed by the customer; products are made according to customer specifications.

just-in-time production (JIT)
A process that redefines and simplifies manufacturing by reducing inventory levels and delivering raw materials just when they are needed on the production line.

ORDER PROCESSING

The order is often the catalyst that sets the supply chain in motion, especially in the build-to-order environments of leading computer manufacturers such as Dell. The **order processing system** processes the requirements of the customer and sends the information into the supply chain via the logistics information system. The order goes to the manufacturer's warehouse. If the product is in stock, the order is filled and arrangements are made to ship it. If the product is not in stock, it triggers a replenishment request that finds its way to the factory floor.

The role of proper order processing in providing good service cannot be overemphasized. As an order enters the system, management must monitor two flows: the flow of goods and the flow of information. Often marketers' best-laid plans get entangled in the order processing system. Obviously, good communication among sales representatives, office personnel, and warehouse and shipping personnel is essential to correct order processing. Shipping incorrect merchandise or partially filled orders can create just as much dissatisfaction as stockouts or slow deliveries. The flow of goods and information must be continually monitored so that mistakes can be corrected before an invoice is prepared and the merchandise shipped.

Order processing is becoming more automated through the use of computer technology known as **electronic data interchange (EDI)**. The basic idea of EDI is to replace the paper documents that usually accompany business transactions, such as purchase orders and invoices, with electronic transmission of the needed information. A typical EDI message includes all the information that would traditionally be included on a paper invoice such as product code, quantity, and transportation details. The information is usually sent via private networks, which are more secure and reliable than the networks used for standard e-mail messages. Most importantly, the information can be read and processed by computers, significantly reducing costs and increasing efficiency. Companies that use EDI can reduce inventory levels, improve cash flow, streamline operations, and increase the speed and accuracy of information transmission. EDI also creates a closer relationship between buyers and sellers.

It should not be surprising that retailers have become major users of EDI. For Wal-Mart, Target, and the like, logistics speed and accuracy are crucial competitive tools in an overcrowded retail environment. Many big retailers are helping their suppliers acquire EDI technology so that they can be linked into the system. EDI works hand in hand with retailers' *efficient consumer response* programs, which are designed to have the right products on the shelf, in the right styles and colors, at the right time, through improved inventory, ordering, and distribution techniques. (See Chapter 13 for more discussion of retailers' use of EDI techniques.)

INVENTORY CONTROL

Closely interrelated with the procurement, manufacturing, and ordering processes is the **inventory control system**—a method that develops and maintains an adequate assortment of materials or products to meet a manufacturer's or a customer's demands.

Inventory decisions, for both raw materials and finished goods, have a big impact on supply chain costs and the level of service provided. If too many products are kept in inventory, costs increase—as do risks of obsolescence, theft, and damage. If too few products are kept on hand, then the company risks product shortages and angry customers, and ultimately lost sales. For example, negative sales forecasts for the Christmas buying season in the past few years caused many retailers to cut back on orders because they were afraid of having to discount large end-of-the-year inventories. As a result, many com-

order processing system
A system whereby orders are entered into the supply chain and filled.

electronic data interchange (EDI)
Information technology that replaces the paper documents that usually accompany business transactions, such as purchase orders and invoices, with electronic transmission of the needed information to reduce inventory levels, improve cash flow, streamline operations, and increase the speed and accuracy of information transmission.

inventory control system
A method of developing and maintaining an adequate assortment of materials or products to meet a manufacturer's or a customer's demand.

7-Eleven Japan turns its inventory in less than a week using the "sense and respond" method. Managers pour over sales and demographic data daily (sense) and make changes to the items they stock, in what amounts, and where in each of the company's 10,000 stores (respond).

© NG HAN GUAN/ASSOCIATED PRESS

panies including Panasonic and Lands' End lost sales due to inventory shortages on popular items. The goal of inventory management, therefore, is to keep inventory levels as low as possible while maintaining an adequate supply of goods to meet customer demand.

Managing inventory from the supplier to the manufacturer is called **materials requirement planning (MRP)**, or **materials management**. This system also encompasses the sourcing and procurement operations, signaling purchasing when raw materials, supplies, or components will need to be replenished for the production of more goods. The system that manages the finished goods inventory from manufacturer to end user is commonly referred to as **distribution resource planning (DRP)**. Both inventory systems use various inputs, such as sales forecasts, available inventory, outstanding orders, lead times, and mode of transportation to be used, to determine what actions must be taken to replenish goods at all points in the supply chain. Demand in the system is collected at each level in the supply chain, from the retailer back up the chain to the manufacturer. With the use of electronic data interchange, the information can be transmitted much faster to meet the quick-response needs of today's competitive marketplace. Exhibit 12.9 provides an example of inventory replenishment using DRP from the retailer to the manufacturer.

Just-in-time manufacturing processes have had a significant impact on reducing inventory levels. Since JIT requires supplies to be delivered at the time they are needed on the factory floor, little inventory is needed. With JIT the purchasing firm can reduce the amount of raw materials and parts it keeps on hand by ordering more often and in smaller amounts. And lower inventory levels due to JIT can give firms a competitive edge through the flexibility to halt production of struggling products in favor of those gaining popularity with consumers. Savings also come from having less capital tied up in inventory and from the reduced need for storage facilities.

WAREHOUSING AND MATERIALS-HANDLING

Supply chain logisticians oversee the constant flow of raw materials from suppliers to manufacturer and finished goods from the manufacturer to the ultimate consumer.

materials requirement planning (MRP) (materials management)
An inventory control system that manages the replenishment of raw materials, supplies, and components from the supplier to the manufacturer.

distribution resource planning (DRP)
An inventory control system that manages the replenishment of goods from the manufacturer to the final consumer.

Exhibit 12.9
Inventory Replenishment Example

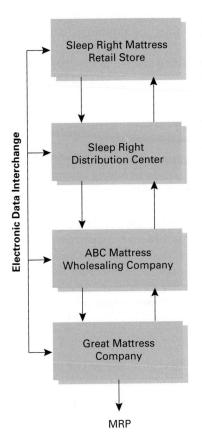

Sleep Right is planning a promotion on the Great Mattress Company's Gentle Rest mattress. Sales forecast is for 50 units to be sold. Sleep Right has 10 open Gentle Rest orders with its distribution center. New mattresses must be delivered in two weeks in time for the promotion.

Sleep Right's Distribution Center is electronically notified of the order of 50 new Gentle Rest mattresses. It currently has 20 Gentle Rest mattresses in inventory and begins putting together the transportation plans to deliver these to the Sleep Right Store. Delivery takes one day. It orders 40 new mattresses from its mattress wholesaler to make up the difference.

ABC Mattress Wholesaling Company is electronically notified of Sleep Right DC's order of 40 new Gentle Rest mattresses. It currently does not have any of these in stock but electronically orders 40 from the Great Mattress Company's factory. Once it receives the new mattresses, it can have them delivered to the Sleep Right DC in two days.

The Great Mattress Company electronically receives ABC's order and forwards it to the factory floor. Production of a new mattress takes 20 minutes. The total order of 40 mattresses can be ready to be shipped to ABC in two days. Delivery takes one day. Raw material supplies for this order are electronically requested from Great Mattress's supply partners, who deliver the needed materials just-in-time to its stitching machines.

Although JIT manufacturing processes may eliminate the need to warehouse many raw materials, manufacturers may often keep some safety stock on hand in the event of an emergency, such as a strike at a supplier's plant or a catastrophic event that temporarily stops the flow of raw materials to the production line. Likewise, the final user may not need or want the goods at the same time the manufacturer produces and wants to sell them. Products like grain and corn are produced seasonally, but consumers demand them year-round. Other products, such as Christmas ornaments and turkeys, are produced year-round, but consumers do not want them until autumn or winter. Therefore, management must have a storage system to hold these products until they are shipped.

Storage is what helps manufacturers manage supply and demand, or production and consumption. It provides time utility to buyers and sellers, which means that the seller stores the product until the buyer wants or needs it. Even when products are used regularly, not seasonally, many manufacturers store excess products in case the demand surpasses the amount produced at a given time. Storing additional product does have disadvantages, however, including the costs of insurance on the stored product, taxes, obsolescence or spoilage, theft, and warehouse operating costs. Another drawback is opportunity costs—that is, the opportunities lost because money is tied up in stored product instead of being used for something else.

Because businesses are focusing on cutting supply chain costs, the warehousing industry is also changing to better serve its customers. For example, many warehouses are putting greater emphasis on more efficient unloading and reloading layouts and customized services that move merchandise through the warehouse faster, often in the same day. They also are investing in services using sophisticated tracking technology such as materials-handling systems.

A **materials-handling system** moves inventory into, within, and out of the warehouse. Materials-handling includes these functions:

- Receiving goods into the warehouse or distribution center

- Identifying, sorting, and labeling the goods

- Dispatching the goods to a temporary storage area

- Recalling, selecting, or picking the goods for shipment (may include packaging the product in a protective container for shipping)

The goal of the materials-handling system is to move items quickly with minimal handling. With a manual, nonautomated materials-handling system, a product may be handled more than a dozen times. Each time it is handled, the cost and risk of damage increase; each lifting of a product stresses its package. Consequently, most manufacturers today have moved to automated systems. Scanners quickly identify goods entering and leaving a warehouse through bar-coded labels affixed to the packaging. Electronic storage and retrieval systems automatically store and pick goods in the warehouse or distribution center. Automated materials-handling systems decrease product handling, ensure accurate placement of product, and improve the accuracy of order picking and the rates of on-time shipment.

At Dell, the OptiPlex system runs the factory. The computer software receives orders, sends requests for parts to suppliers, orders components, organizes assembly of the product, and even arranges for it to be shipped. Thus, instead of hundreds of workers, often fewer than six are working at one time. An order for a few hundred computers can be filled in less than eight hours using the automated system. With the OptiPlex system, productivity has increased 160 percent per person per hour.[27]

TRANSPORTATION

Transportation typically accounts for 5 to 10 percent of the price of goods. Supply chain logisticians must decide which mode of transportation to use to move products from supplier to producer and from producer to buyer. These decisions are, of course, related to all other logistics decisions. The five major modes of transportation are railroads,

materials-handling system
A method of moving inventory into, within, and out of the warehouse.

Exhibit 12.10

Criteria for Ranking Modes of Transportation

	Highest				Lowest
Relative Cost	Air	Truck	Rail	Pipe	Water
Transit Time	Water	Rail	Pipe	Truck	Air
Reliability	Pipe	Truck	Rail	Air	Water
Capability	Water	Rail	Truck	Air	Pipe
Accessibility	Truck	Rail	Air	Water	Pipe
Traceability	Air	Truck	Rail	Water	Pipe

motor carriers, pipelines, water transportation, and airways. Supply chain managers generally choose a mode of transportation on the basis of several criteria:

- *Cost:* The total amount a specific carrier charges to move the product from the point of origin to the destination

- *Transit time:* The total time a carrier has possession of goods, including the time required for pickup and delivery, handling, and movement between the point of origin and the destination

- *Reliability:* The consistency with which the carrier delivers goods on time and in acceptable condition

- *Capability:* The ability of the carrier to provide the appropriate equipment and conditions for moving specific kinds of goods, such as those that must be transported in a controlled environment (for example, under refrigeration)

- *Accessibility:* A carrier's ability to move goods over a specific route or network

- *Traceability:* The relative ease with which a shipment can be located and transferred

The mode of transportation used depends on the needs of the shipper, as they relate to these six criteria. Exhibit 12.10 compares the basic modes of transportation on these criteria.

REVIEW LEARNING OUTCOME

LO7 Describe the logistical components of the supply chain

Supply Chain Team

Logistics Information System

- Sourcing and procurement of raw materials and supplies
- Production scheduling
- Order processing and customer service
- Inventory control
- Warehousing and materials-handling
- Transportation

In many cases, especially in a JIT manufacturing environment, the transportation network replaces the warehouse or eliminates the expense of storing inventories as goods are timed to arrive the moment they're needed on the assembly line or for shipment to customers. In fact, Toyota is so committed to JIT that it has no parts warehouses in the United States. Instead, it works closely with its suppliers to make sure that parts will be delivered on time even during a crisis. For example, Continental Teves, Inc., supplies Toyota with German-made steering sensors for its Sequoia SUV. Traditionally, the parts were flown from Germany and delivered to Toyota when they were needed for installation. Recently, however, because terrorist attacks can shut down airspace, Continental has been shipping the parts via ship to ensure that they will arrive on time even if U.S. airspace is shut down.

LO⁸
Trends in Supply Chain Management

Several technological advances and business trends are affecting the job of the supply chain manager today. Three of the most important trends are advanced computer technology, outsourcing of logistics functions, and electronic distribution.

ADVANCED COMPUTER TECHNOLOGY

Advanced computer technology has boosted the efficiency of logistics dramatically with tools such as automatic identification systems (auto ID) using bar coding and radio-frequency technology, communications technology, and supply chain software systems that help synchronize the flow of goods and information with customer demand. Amazon.com's state-of-the-art distribution centers, for instance, use sophisticated order picking systems that utilize computer terminals to guide workers through the picking and packing process. Radio-frequency technology, which uses radio signals that work with scanned bar codes to identify products, directs Amazon's workers to the exact locations in the warehouse where the product is stored. Warehouse management software examines pick rates, location, and picking and storage patterns, and builds combinations of customer orders for shipping. After installing these supply chain technology tools, Amazon saw a 70 percent improvement in operational efficiency.[28]

Procter & Gamble and many other companies use radio-frequency identification (RFID) tags in shipments to Wal-Mart stores. RFID tags are chips attached to a pallet of goods that allow the goods to be tracked from the time they are packed at the manufacturing plant until the consumer purchases them. Benefits include increased revenue for Wal-Mart because the shelves are always full and reduced inventory management costs because overstocking and time spent counting items and are minimized. Wal-Mart requires all vendors to use RFID technology.[29]

One of the major goals of technology is to bring up-to-date information to the supply chain manager's desk. The transportation system has long been referred to as a "black hole," where products and materials fall out of sight until they reappear some time later in a plant, store, or warehouse. Now carriers have systems that track freight, monitor the speed and location of carriers, and make routing decisions on the spur of the moment. Roadway Express, named one of the "Top 100 U.S. Motor Carriers" by Inbound Logistics, handles more than 70,000 shipments a day, many for large retailers like Wal-Mart, Target, and Home Depot. Information technology systems enable each package to be tracked from the minute it is received at one of Roadway's terminals until it is delivered. Customers can check on the progress of their shipment anytime by logging on to Roadway's Web site and entering the tracking number. Companies needing trucking services can go to the Inbound Logistics Web site and use their Trucking Decision Support Tool to identify motor carriers that can meet their service needs.[30] Swedish-based communications giant Ericsson, whose operations span the globe, uses specialized supply chain software to gain visibility over the 50,000 outbound shipments it makes a year. As products leave its manufacturing facilities, transportation providers transmit status information at specified intervals to Ericsson's information system, which is accessible to management using a standard Web browser. The company has benefited greatly from the increased visibility of shipments the system has provided. Ericsson's management is now in a position to identify bottlenecks and respond before a crisis occurs, as well as measure the performance of its supply chain at different checkpoints.[31]

OUTSOURCING LOGISTICS FUNCTIONS

outsourcing (contract logistics) A manufacturer's or supplier's use of an independent third party to manage an entire function of the logistics system, such as transportation, warehousing, or order processing.

External partners are becoming increasingly important in the efficient deployment of supply chain management. **Outsourcing, or contract logistics,** is a rapidly growing segment of the distribution industry in which a manufacturer or supplier turns over an

UPS offers more services than its hallmark package delivery. In fact, UPS helps companies open new global supply chains, manage raw material, and add distribution channels. To find out more, visit www.ups.com/supplychain.

entire function of the logistics system, such as buying and managing transportation or warehousing, to an independent third party. Many manufacturers are turning to outside partners for their logistics expertise in an effort to focus on the core competencies that they do best. Partners create and manage entire solutions for getting products where they need to be, when they need to be there. Logistics partners offer staff, an infrastructure, and services that reach consumers virtually anywhere in the world. Because a logistics provider is focused, clients receive service in a timely, efficient manner, thereby increasing customers' level of satisfaction and boosting their perception of added value to a company's offerings.

Third-party contract logistics allow companies to cut inventories, locate stock at fewer plants and distribution centers, and still provide the same service level or even better. The companies then can refocus investment on their core business. Ford Motor Company uses third-party logistics provider UPS Worldwide Logistics Group to manage the delivery of Ford, Lincoln, and Mercury cars and trucks in the United States, Canada, and Mexico. The alliance between Ford and UPS has substantially reduced the time it takes to move vehicles from Ford's assembly plants to dealers and customers. Moreover, the Web-based system enables Ford and its dealers to track an individual vehicle's location from production through delivery to the final destination. Similarly, in the hospitality industry, procurement services company Avendra enables Fairmont Hotels & Resorts, Hyatt Hotels, Intercontinental Hotels Group, Marriott International, and others to enjoy significant savings and value-added supply chain services.[32] Avendra negotiates with suppliers to obtain virtually everything a hotel might need, from food and beverages to golf course maintenance. By relying on Avendra to manage many aspects of the supply chain, the hotels are able to concentrate on their core function—providing hospitality.

electronic distribution
A distribution technique that includes any kind of product or service that can be distributed electronically, whether over traditional forms such as fiber-optic cable or through satellite transmission of electronic signals.

Many firms are taking outsourcing one step further by allowing business partners to take over the final assembly of their product or its packaging in an effort to reduce inventory costs, speed up delivery, or meet customer requirements better. Ryder Truck Lines assembles and packages 22 different combinations of shrink-wrapped boxes that contain the ice trays, drawers, shelves, doors, and other accessories for the various refrigerator models Whirlpool sells. Similarly, outsourcing firm StarTek, Inc., packages and ships products for Microsoft, provides technical support to customers of America Online, and maintains AT&T communication systems.[33]

ELECTRONIC DISTRIBUTION

Electronic distribution is the most recent development in the logistics arena. Broadly defined, **electronic distribution** includes any kind of product or service that can be distributed electronically, whether over traditional forms such as fiber-optic cable or through satellite transmission of electronic signals. For instance, instead of buying and installing software from stores, computer users purchase software over the Internet and download it electronically to their personal computers or rent the same software

movie tickets.com ™
YOUR OWN PERSONAL BOX OFFICE™

Electronic distribution has become a viable channel for many products, including tax preparation software, postage stamps, and even movie tickets, which can be purchased over the Internet prior to a show.

from Internet services that have the program available for use on their servers. For example, Intuit, Inc., allows people to fill out their tax returns on its Web site rather than buying its TurboTax software. Consumers can purchase tickets to sporting events, concerts, and movies over the Internet and print the tickets at home. And music, television shows, and movies have long been delivered to consumers through electronic pipelines. (Apple sold over 20 million songs and TV shows through iTunes in 2005 alone.)[34]

One of the most innovative electronic distribution ventures of late has come from ESPN. The sports broadcaster has leased high-speed network capacity from Sprint to create Mobile ESPN. Through a special cell phone, Mobile ESPN broadcasts a rich multimedia package of news, scores, statistics, and videos unlike anything else. Its sports service includes news, scores, videos, alerts, fantasy teams, ESPN columnists, and more. There's a special section where users can select to receive news and stats about their favorite players and teams.[35]

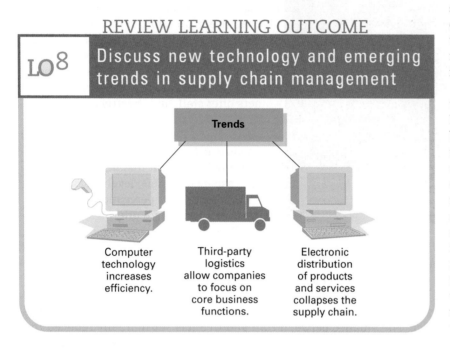

REVIEW LEARNING OUTCOME

LO8 Discuss new technology and emerging trends in supply chain management

Trends

Computer technology increases efficiency.

Third-party logistics allow companies to focus on core business functions.

Electronic distribution of products and services collapses the supply chain.

LO9
Channels and Distribution Decisions for Global Markets

With the spread of free-trade agreements and treaties, such as the European Union and the North American Free Trade Agreement (NAFTA) in recent decades, global marketing channels and management of the supply chain have become increasingly important to U.S. corporations that export their products or manufacture abroad.

DEVELOPING GLOBAL MARKETING CHANNELS

Executives should recognize the unique cultural, economic, institutional, and legal aspects of each market before trying to design marketing channels in foreign countries. Manufacturers introducing products in global markets face a tough decision: what type of channel structure to use. Specifically, should the product be marketed directly, mostly by company salespeople, or through independent foreign intermediaries, such as agents and distributors? Using company salespeople generally provides more control and is less risky than using foreign intermediaries. However, setting up a sales force in a foreign country also entails a greater commitment, both financially and organizationally.

Marketers should be aware that channel structures and types abroad may differ from those in the United States. For instance, the more highly developed a nation is economically, the more specialized its channel types. Therefore, a marketer wishing to sell in Germany or Japan will have several channel types to choose from. Conversely, developing countries like India, Ethiopia, and Venezuela have limited channel types available; there are typically few mail-order channels, vending machines, or specialized retailers and wholesalers. Some countries also regulate channel choices. Until 2004, Chinese regulations required foreign retailers to have a local partner. So, when IKEA, the Swedish home furnishings retailer, opened its first two stores in China, it used joint ventures.

When the regulations were lifted, however, IKEA opened its first wholly owned store in Guangzhou and then a Beijing store that is almost as big as eight football fields, second in size only to the company's flagship store in Stockholm.[36]

Marketers must also be aware that many countries have "gray" marketing channels in which products are distributed through unauthorized channel intermediaries. It is estimated that sales of counterfeit luxury items like Prada handbags and Big Bertha golf clubs have reached almost $2 billion a year. The new fakes are harder to detect and hit the market almost instantly. For instance, a fake Christian Dior saddlebag was available just weeks after the original arrived on retailers' shelves. Similarly, Chinese companies are producing so many knockoffs of Yamaha, Honda, and Suzuki motorcycles that the Japanese companies are seeing a drop in sales. What's more, many companies are getting so good at design piracy that they are beginning to launch their own new products.[37]

The Internet has also proved to be a way for pirates to circumvent authorized distribution channels, especially in the case of popular prescription drugs. In recent years, the U.S. Customs Service has seized millions of dollars worth of prescription drugs, most of which were purchased from foreign Internet sites. Some were seized because they had not been approved for use in the United States, others because they did not comply with U.S. labeling laws. Most sites offer just a handful of the most popular drugs, such as Viagra; consumers can get the drugs after obtaining the approval of a doctor who is affiliated with the site and who never sees the patient.

GLOBAL LOGISTICS AND SUPPLY CHAIN MANAGEMENT

As global trade becomes a more decisive factor in success or failure for firms of all sizes, a well-thought-out global logistics strategy becomes more important.

One of the most critical global logistical issues for importers of any size is coping with the legalities of trade in other countries. Shippers and distributors must be aware of the permits, licenses, and registrations they may need to acquire and, depending on the type of product they are importing, the tariffs, quotas, and other regulations that apply in each country. This multitude of different rules is why multinational companies like Eastman Kodak are so committed to working through the World Trade Organization to develop a global set of rules and to encourage countries to participate. Other goals for these companies include reducing trade barriers such as tariffs. As these barriers fall, the flow of merchandise across borders is increasing due to more companies sourcing from multiple countries. For instance, a Kodak camera sold in France may have been assembled there, but the camera mechanism probably came from China and the film from the United States.

The presence of different rules hasn't slowed the spread of supply chain globalization, however. In spite of the added costs associated with importing and exporting goods, many companies are looking to other countries for their sourcing and procurement needs. For example, Applica, Inc., a U.S. maker of small appliances, is committed to using technology to improve its relationships with suppliers in Mexico. The company has linked its suppliers directly to sales data from Wal-Mart stores to help manage production and inventory costs.[38]

Transportation can also be a major issue for companies dealing with global supply chains. Uncertainty regarding shipping usually tops the list of reasons why companies, especially smaller ones, resist international markets. Even companies that have scored overseas successes often are vulnerable to logistical problems. Large companies have the capital to create global logistics systems, but smaller companies often must rely on the services of carriers and freight forwarders to get their products to overseas markets.

In some instances, poor infrastructure makes transportation dangerous and unreliable. And the process of moving goods across the borders of even the most industrialized nations can still be complicated by government regulations. For example, NAFTA was supposed to improve the flow of goods across the continent, but moving goods across the border still requires approvals from dozens of government agencies, broker intervention, and hours spent at border checks. Shipping companies like Ryder are working to make the process easier. Currently, Ryder operates a cross-border facility in San Antonio to help

REVIEW LEARNING OUTCOME

LO9

Discuss channels and distribution decisions in global markets

Distribute directly or through foreign partners

Different channel structures than in domestic markets

Illegitimate "gray" marketing channels

Legal and infrastructure differences

clients like General Motors and Xerox with customs and logistics costs. The company also is part of a pilot project to automate border crossings with technology similar to that of an E-Z pass. The new system sends and receives short-range radio signals containing information on the load to tollbooths, weigh stations, and border crossings. If the cargo meets requirements, the truck or train receives a green light to go ahead. Questionable cargo is set aside for further inspection. Transportation industry experts say the system can reduce delivery times by more than three hours.[39]

LO¹⁰

Channels and Distribution Decisions for Services

The fastest-growing part of our economy is the service sector. Although distribution in the service sector is difficult to visualize, the same skills, techniques, and strategies used to manage inventory can also be used to manage service inventory—for instance, hospital beds, bank accounts, or airline seats. The quality of the planning and execution of distribution can have a major impact on costs and customer satisfaction.

One thing that sets service distribution apart from traditional manufacturing distribution is that, in a service environment, production and consumption are simultaneous. In manufacturing, a production setback can often be remedied by using safety stock or a faster mode of transportation. Such substitution is not possible with a service. The benefits of a service are also relatively intangible—that is, you normally can't see the benefits of a service, such as a doctor's physical exam. But a consumer can normally see the benefits provided by a product—for example, cold medicine relieving a stuffy nose.

Because service industries are so customer oriented, customer service is a priority. To manage customer relationships, many service providers, such as insurance carriers, physicians, hair salons, and financial services, use technology to schedule appointments, manage accounts, and disburse information. Service distribution focuses on three main areas:

- *Minimizing wait times:* Minimizing the amount of time customers wait in line to deposit a check, wait for their food at a restaurant, or wait in a doctor's office for an appointment is a key factor in maintaining the quality of service. People tend to overestimate the amount of time they spend waiting in line, researchers report, and unexplained waiting seems longer than explained waits. To reduce anxiety among waiting customers, some restaurants give patrons pagers that allow them to roam around or go to the bar. Banks sometimes install electronic boards displaying stock quotes or sports scores. Car rental companies reward repeat customers by eliminating their waits altogether. Airports have designed comfortable sitting areas with televisions and children's play areas for those waiting to board planes. Some service companies are using sophisticated technology to further ease their customers' waiting time. Similarly, many hotels and airlines are using electronic check-in kiosks. Travelers can insert their credit cards to check in upon arrival, receive their room key, get directions, print maps to area restaurants and attractions, and print out their hotel bills.

- *Managing service capacity:* For product manufacturers, inventory acts as a buffer, enabling them to provide the product during periods of peak demand without extraordinary efforts. Service firms don't have this luxury. If they don't have the capacity to meet demand, they must either turn down some prospective customers, let service levels slip, or expand capacity. For instance, at tax time a tax preparation firm may have so many customers desiring its services that it has to either turn business away or add temporary offices or preparers. Popular restaurants risk losing business when seating is unavailable or the wait is too long. To manage their capacity, travel Web sites allow users to find last-minute deals to fill up empty airline seats and hotel rooms.

Does your bank deliver any of its services online? Visit its Web site to find out. Which online services would you be inclined to use? Are there any that you would definitely *not* use? Why not?

Online

© SHOWCASE OF HOMES/PRNEWSFOTO (AP TOPIC GALLERY)

Keller Williams Realty has changed the distribution channel for its real estate services by opening a storefront in a shopping mall. The Showcase of Homes store includes a kiosk where potential customers can browse the multiple listing service database for homes of interest.

- *Improving service delivery:* Like manufacturers, service firms are now experimenting with different distribution channels for their services. Choosing the right distribution channel can increase the times that services are available (such as using the Internet to disseminate information and services 24/7) or add to customer convenience (like pizza delivery, walk-in medical clinics, or a dry cleaner located in a supermarket). The airline industry has found that using the Internet for ticket sales both reduces distribution costs and raises the level of customer service by making it easier for customers to plan their own travel. Cruise lines, on the other hand, have found that travel agents add value by helping customers sort through the abundance of information and complicated options available when booking a cruise. In the real estate industry, realtors are placing kiosks in local malls that enable consumers to directly access listings.

The Internet is fast becoming an alternative channel for delivering services. Consumers can now purchase plane tickets, plan a vacation cruise, reserve a hotel room, pay bills, purchase mutual funds, and receive electronic newspapers in cyberspace. Insurance giant Allstate, for instance, now sells auto and home insurance directly to consumers in some states through the Internet in addition to its traditional network of agents. The effort reduces costs so that Allstate can stay competitive with rival insurance companies Progressive and Geico that already target customers directly. Similarly, several real estate Web sites are making it easier for customers to shop for a new home on the Web.

REVIEW LEARNING OUTCOME

LO 10 Identify the special problems and opportunities associated with distribution in service organizations

Minimizing wait times is a key factor in maintaining service quality.

Managing service capability is critical to successful service distribution.

Improving service delivery makes it easier and more convenient for consumers to use the service.

Traditionally, the only way for customers to gain access to realtors' listings was to work through a real estate agent who would search the listings and then show customers homes that met their requirements. The new companies offer direct access to the listings, enabling customers to review properties for sale on their own, and choose which ones they would like to visit.

Review and Applications

LO 1 Explain what a marketing channel is and why intermediaries are needed. A marketing channel is a business structure of interdependent organizations that reach from the point of product origin to the consumer with the purpose of physically moving products to their final consumption destination, representing "place" or "distribution" in the marketing mix and encompassing the processes involved in getting the right product to the right place at the right time. Members of a marketing channel create a continuous and seamless supply chain that performs or supports the marketing channel functions. Channel members provide economies to the distribution process in the form of specialization and division of labor; overcoming discrepancies in quantity, assortment, time, and space; and providing contact efficiency.

1.1 Your family runs a specialty ice cream parlor, Graeter's, that manufactures its own ice cream in small batches and sells it only in pint-sized containers. After someone not affiliated with the company sent six pints of its ice cream to Oprah Winfrey, she proclaimed on her national TV show that it was the best ice cream she had ever eaten. Immediately after the broadcast, orders came flooding in, overwhelming your small-batch production schedule and your rudimentary distribution system. The company's shipping manager thinks she can handle it, but you disagree. List the reasons why you need to restructure your supply chain.[40]

LO 2 Define the types of channel intermediaries and describe their functions and activities. The most prominent difference separating intermediaries is whether they take title to the product. Retailers and merchant wholesalers take title, but agents and brokers do not. Retailers are firms that sell mainly to consumers. Merchant wholesalers are organizations that facilitate the movement of products and services from the manufacturer to producers, resellers, governments, institutions, and retailers. Agents and brokers do not take title to the goods and services they market, but they do facilitate the exchange of ownership between sellers and buyers. Channel intermediaries perform three basic types of functions. Transactional functions include contacting and promoting, negotiating, and risk taking. Logistical functions performed by channel members include physical distribution, storing, and sorting functions. Finally, channel members may perform facilitating functions, such as researching and financing.

2.1 What kind of marketing channel functions can be performed over the Internet? Why do you think so?

LO3 Describe the channel structures for consumer and business products and discuss alternative channel arrangements. Marketing channels for consumer and business products vary in degree of complexity. The simplest consumer-product channel involves direct selling from producers to consumers. Businesses may sell directly to business or government buyers. Marketing channels grow more complex as intermediaries become involved. Consumer-product channel intermediaries include agents, brokers, wholesalers, and retailers. Business-product channel intermediaries include agents, brokers, and industrial distributors. Marketers often use alternative channel arrangements to move their products to the consumer. With dual distribution or multiple distribution, they choose two or more different channels to distribute the same product. Nontraditional channels help differentiate a firm's product from the competitor's or provide a manufacturer with another avenue for sales. Finally, strategic channel alliances are arrangements that use another manufacturer's already established channel.

3.1 Describe the most likely marketing channel structure for each of these consumer products: candy bars, Tupperware products, nonfiction books, new automobiles, farmers' market produce, and stereo equipment. Now, construct alternative channels for these same products.

3.2 You have been hired to design an alternative marketing channel for a firm specializing in the manufacturing and marketing of novelties for college student organizations. In a memo to the president of the firm, describe how the channel operates.

3.3 Building on question 1.1, determine a new channel structure for Graeter's. Write a proposal to present to your key managers.

LO4 Define supply chain management and discuss its benefits. Supply chain management coordinates and integrates all of the activities performed by supply chain members into a seamless process from the source to the point of consumption. The responsibilities of a supply chain manager include developing channel design strategies, managing the relationships of supply chain members, sourcing and procurement of raw materials, scheduling production, processing orders, managing inventory and storing product, and selecting transportation modes. The supply chain manager is also responsible for managing customer service and the information that flows through the supply chain. The benefits of supply chain management include reduced costs in inventory management, transportation, warehousing, and packaging; improved service through techniques like time-based delivery and make-to-order; and enhanced revenues, which result from such supply chain–related achievements as higher product availability and more customized products.

4.1 Discuss the benefits of supply chain management. How does the implementation of supply chain management result in enhanced customer value?

LO5 Discuss the issues that influence channel strategy. When determining marketing channel strategy, the supply chain manager must determine what market, product, and producer factors will influence the choice of channel. The manager must also determine the appropriate level of distribution intensity. Intensive distribution is distribution aimed at maximum market coverage. Selective distribution is achieved by screening dealers to eliminate all but a few in any single area. The most restrictive form of market coverage is exclusive distribution, which entails only one or a few dealers within a given area.

5.1 Decide which distribution intensity level—intensive, selective, or exclusive—is used for each of the following products, and explain why: Piaget watches, Land Rover sport-utility vehicles, M&Ms, special edition Barbie dolls, Crest toothpaste.

5.2 Now that you have a basic channel structure for Graeter's (from question 3.3), form a team of three to four students and list the market, product, and producer factors that will affect your final channel structure.

LO6 Explain channel leadership, conflict, and partnering. Power, control, leadership, conflict, and partnering are the main social dimensions of marketing channel relationships. Channel power refers to the capacity of one channel member to control or influence other channel members. Channel control occurs when one channel member intentionally affects another member's behavior. Channel leadership is the exercise of authority and power. Channel conflict occurs when there is a clash of goals and methods among the members of a distribution channel. Channel conflict can be either horizontal, between channel members at the same level, or vertical, between channel members at different levels of the channel. Channel partnering is the joint effort of all channel members to create a supply chain that serves customers and creates a competitive advantage. Collaborating channel partners meet the needs of consumers more effectively by ensuring that the right products reach shelves at the right time and at a lower cost, boosting sales and profits.

6.1 Procter & Gamble and Wal-Mart are key partners in a shared supply chain. P&G is one of Wal-Mart's biggest suppliers, and Wal-Mart provides extremely detailed scanner data about customer purchases of P&G products. Wal-Mart has begun selling its own brand of Sam's Choice laundry detergent in bright orange bottles alongside P&G's Tide, but for a greatly reduced price. What do you think will be the impact of this new product on what has been a stable channel relationship?

LO7 Describe the logistical components of the supply chain. The logistics supply chain consists of several interrelated and integrated logistical components: (1) sourcing and procurement of raw materials and supplies, (2) production scheduling, (3) order processing, (4) inventory control, (5) warehousing and materials-handling, and (6) transportation. The logistics information system is the link connecting all of the logistics components of the supply chain. Information technology connects the various components and partners of the supply chain into an integrated whole. The supply chain team, in concert with the logistics information system, orchestrates the movement of goods, services, and information from the source to the consumer. Supply chain teams typically cut across organizational boundaries, embracing all parties who participate in moving product to market. Procurement deals with the purchase of raw materials, supplies, and components according to production scheduling. Order processing monitors the flow of goods and information (order entry and order handling). Inventory control systems regulate when and how much to buy (order timing and order quantity). Warehousing provides storage of goods until needed by the customer while the materials-handling system moves inventory into, within, and out of the warehouse. Finally, the major modes of transportation are railroads, motor carriers, pipelines, waterways, and airways.

7.1 Discuss the impact of just-in-time production on the entire supply chain. Specifically, how does JIT affect suppliers, procurement planning, inventory levels, mode of transportation selected, and warehousing? What are the benefits of JIT to the end consumer?

7.2 Assume that you are the supply chain manager for a producer of expensive, high-tech computer components. Identify the most suitable method(s) of transporting your product in terms of cost, transit time, reliability, capability, accessibility, and traceability. Now, assume you are the supply chain manager for a producer of milk. How does this change your choice of transportation?

LO8 Discuss new technology and emerging trends in supply chain management. Several emerging trends are changing the job of today's supply chain manager. Technology and automation are bringing up-to-date distribution information to the decision maker's desk. Technology is also linking suppliers, buyers, and carriers for joint decision making, and it has created a new electronic distribution channel. Many companies are saving money and time by outsourcing third-party carriers to handle some or all aspects of the distribution process.

8.1 Visit the Web site of Menlo Logistics at **http://www.menlolog.com**. What logistics functions can this third-party logistics supplier provide? How does its mission fit in with the supply chain management philosophy?

LO9 Discuss channels and distribution decisions in global markets. Global marketing channels are becoming more important to U.S. companies seeking growth abroad. Manufacturers introducing products in foreign countries must decide what type of channel structure to use—in particular, whether the product should be marketed through direct channels or through foreign intermediaries. Marketers should be aware that channel structures in foreign markets may be very different from those they are accustomed to in the United States. Global distribution expertise is also emerging as an important skill for supply chain managers as many countries are removing trade barriers.

9.1 Go to the World Trade Organization's Web site at **http://www.wto.org**. What can you learn at the site about how globalization affects supply chain management and other aspects of business?

LO10 Identify the special problems and opportunities associated with distribution in service organizations. Managers in service industries use the same skills, techniques, and strategies to manage logistics functions as managers in goods-producing industries. The distribution of services focuses on three main areas: minimizing wait times, managing service capacity, and improving service delivery.

10.1 Assume that you are the marketing manager of a hospital. Write a report indicating the distribution functions that concern you. Discuss the similarities and dissimilarities of distribution for services and for goods.

Key Terms

Exercises

APPLICATION EXERCISE

It may be easy to understand how supply chain management works just from reading, but you may still not appreciate the scope of distribution channels. This exercise will help you see for yourself how deep and complex a single distribution channel is. Then, when you think of the number of products and services available on the market at any one time, you will understand how tremendous the national (and international) distribution network actually is.[41]

Activities

1. Pick a product with which you are familiar or that you anticipate being able to research easily. You may want to consult family members, relatives, or even a former or current employer who can give you details of the business.

2. Trace the distribution network of your product as far back as is feasible. A simple example is a diamond sold by a local jewelry store, purchased direct from diamond wholesalers in the Netherlands, bought by wholesalers from diamond centers in South Africa, brought out of mines owned by a company in South Africa. Identify participants in the channel by company name and location as much as possible.

3. Identify the mode of transportation used between each stage in the channel.

4. Identify by name and location the component parts of the product, if any. For example, let's expand the diamond example from a single diamond to a diamond necklace. You would need to trace the distribution history of the chain until the point at which the diamond and chain are combined to form the diamond necklace.

Entrepreneurship Case

CURRENT TV PLUGS INTO THE 'NET GENERATION

Ten years ago, the Internet began a revolution that has forever changed the way consumers shop for goods, send and receive mail, find and read news, and acquire and listen to music. A relatively new electronic distribution channel, the Web enables billions of near-instantaneous commercial, consumer, and information exchanges each day. And with the widespread dispersion of increasingly powerful and portable digital technologies, marketers are witnessing a new phenomenon—consumers devoting considerable time to archiving and sharing the personal events of their lives.

Tech-savvy members of Generations X and Y are photographing, recording, cataloging, uploading, blogging, hyperlinking, downloading, and sharing peer-to-peer files at an accelerating pace. Moreover, the independent Web sites where those opinions, files, and reports are located are becoming an increasingly valid means of staying connected with the world. Quite simply, this phenomenon is turning traditional media channels on their collective ear.

Few companies really comprehend that the digital technologies driving homemade reporting and entertainment productions are simultaneously increasing demand for them. One company that understands, and even anticipated, this trend is start-up cable channel Current TV. Cofounded, chaired, and shaped by the vision of former vice president Al Gore, Current predicted the relevance of do-it-yourself (DIY) media some time ago. Gore's objective, as stated on Current TV's Web site, is to democratize the production, distribution, and consumption of television.

Years ago Gore recognized that the proliferation of affordable digital technology would make it possible to create "a powerful new brand of television that doesn't treat audiences as merely viewers, but as collaborators." And those collaborations, fueled by viewer-created content (VCC), are powering the DIY media boom. Shari Anne Brill, vice president and director of programming at the Carat Group, an independent media agency, predicts that "Current will appeal to a much younger-skewing and very unique audience. It opens up tremendous avenues between Internet and television, and it's a very interesting way to reach out to viewers who want to participate in the viewing experience."

Current TV's Web site already hosts a menu of more than 50 "pods" containing program lists chosen for their appeal to independent spirits who have grown disenchanted with the staid format of mainstream television. Recent feature programs on Current TV have included a piece on a man who spends his free time jumping from cliffs and bridges, a first-person perspective on the rescue efforts in the aftermath of Hurricane Katrina, and an in-depth report on a San Francisco rock band produced by a local college student.

Most programs relate to current affairs, but other topics routinely covered include lifestyle themes such as art, fashion, culture, the environment, music, language, relationships, careers, travel, movies, and more. Regardless of subject, all Current TV programming has an intimate and unpretentious feel. Ever mindful of past pitfalls, Current is adamant that it will not devolve into a twenty-first century version of the public access fiascoes that gave VCC a bad name many years ago.

To protect program quality, only one-third of Current's programming is viewer created, but the company doesn't think that will dissuade viewers as long as its professionally produced work has credibility, relevance, and appeal. The viewer-submitted content that is aired is also paid for, though it is repeated quite a bit, and watchers have the ability to vote for shows at Current TV's Web site.

What would enable Current to run more VCC? The answer, in a word, is access. At this time, Current distributes its programming to only 20 million residences in select metropolitan areas via Comcast, DirecTV, and Time Warner. It lacks support from the major cable and satellite companies that, together, feed popular stations to around 80 million homes. Current needs access to viewers in order to appeal to their creative alter egos and fuel the DIY cycle.

In an age when countless business models have seen explosive growth followed by a dramatic collapse, Current's approach and situation look promising. Its concept has recently been validated by MTV's purchase of independent, Web-based VCC site iFilm.com. MTV Networks Music Group president, Brian Graden, says that VCC "is obviously the next wave, and the purchase by Viacom of iFilm is probably the strongest statement that we're very much on to that. The more control you put of everything into the viewers' hands in this sort of multiplatform, on-demand age, that's the only way you're going to win."[42]

Questions

1. Explain Current TV's channel strategy. What factors influence it the most? Why?

2. Who are Current's channel partners? What do you think will be needed to sustain those relationships?

3. Describe Current TV's channel arrangement. What role do the intermediaries play? What potential conflicts would you predict for Current?

COMPANY CLIPS

Sephora—Business is Beautiful

The beauty-retail store, Sephora, was founded in 1969 in France and since then has become a leader in sales of heath and beauty-aid products. It opened its first store in the United States in 1998 on 5th Avenue in New York City and prides itself on being ahead of the market in skin care trends. Its luxurious environment is the selling point for over 250 brands. On its shelves, Sephora maintains a balance of big brand names with lesser known, up-and-coming brands. Sephora also carries its own private brand that it promotes independently in the store. Each sales representative in a Sephora store is trained to best help customers find the products that best fit their skin types and lifestyles. Watch the video to learn what techniques Sephora uses to keep its shelves stocked and customers happy.

Questions

1. Why is important to customers that Sephora keep detail information about their inventory? What does Sephora do to insure their numbers are accurate?

2. How does Sephora manage its supply chain? What information goes into decide which suppliers become incorporated?

BIZ FLIX

Casino

Now that you have learned the concrete fundamentals of marketing supply chains, you can expand your thinking of channels. As an encore to your study, watch the first film clip from Martin Scorsese's *Casino,* starring Robert De Niro, Joe Pesci, and Sharon Stone. The selected scene comes from the film's opening sequence, which gives important background about casino operations. Although the sequence does not depict a marketing channel in the sense of the chapter's definition, we can still think metaphorically about the scene. That is, we can think of the activities shown in the scene as being *like* a marketing channel in many ways. For example, how is the flow of money like a channel? Who are the "channel" members? Can you see examples of specialization of "channel" members? How efficient is the casino's "channel"? Why do you think that is? Remember, to be relevant and insightful, the clip doesn't have to be literal. As you watch the clip, just think, "This is *like* a channel because . . ."

Marketing & You Results

A higher score indicates that you like to be a leader and use authority. Studies have linked authority to vanity, so a high score also suggests a high level of vanity. In particular, "achievement view vanity," which means you have very high opinions of your accomplishments and think that others consider you successful as well, is strongly linked to authority.

Retailing

Learning Outcomes

LO 1   Discuss the importance of retailing in the U.S. economy

LO 2   Explain the dimensions by which retailers can be classified

LO 3   Describe the major types of retail operations

LO 4   Discuss nonstore retailing techniques

LO 5   Define franchising and describe its two basic forms

LO 6   List the major tasks involved in developing a retail marketing strategy

LO 7   Describe new developments in retailing

With its family of brands, Gap, Inc., is a leading global specialty retailer offering clothing, accessories, and personal-care products for men, women, children, and babies. Its brand names include Gap, Banana Republic, Old Navy, and most recently Forth & Towne, as well as GapKids,

Bringing back the luster may be a struggle for a company that was once the leader in its category.

babyGap, GapBody, and GapMaternity. The company has more than 3,000 stores worldwide in various countries, including the United States, Canada, the United Kingdom, France, and Japan.

Gap was founded in 1969 and expanded to include new target markets by establishing stores with a similar look but different price points and quality, such as Old Navy and Banana Republic. For years, Gap was a trendsetter. In recent years, however, Gap stores have paid less attention to their "bread and butter" market—maturing, loyal customers looking for clothing and accessories to enhance their personal style at a great value. The Old Navy and Banana Republic stores have also lost their fashion leadership image among younger customers.

In 2005, Gap's overall sales were down almost 10 percent. Yet, sales for specialty apparel retailers as a group were up 3 percent, a clear indication that Gap has lost market share to the competition.

One problem is that Gap has lost the baby boomers to competitors such as upscale discounter Target and mall-based specialty chains such as Chico FAS, which have their own particular looks. To win back the boomers, Gap recently opened Forth & Towne, its first new store concept in more than a decade, targeted toward career women ages 35 to 44. This segment accounts for almost 40 percent of women's apparel expenditures and thus represents a major opportunity for Gap. To distinguish itself from the competition, Forth & Towne will offer the high level of service of a boutique, the broad offerings of a department store, attractive fitting rooms—and a forgiving fit.

But Gap must do more than reach out to boomers. The company must also develop strategies to attract younger customers to Banana Republic and Old Navy. Gap has hired new leadership to design and introduce more attractive merchandise for its brands, but bringing back the luster may be a struggle for a company that was once the leader in its category.[1]

What will be Gap's major challenges in making the new concept for boomers work? Should Gap be opening a new store concept targeted at boomers, or should it focus on its Old Navy and Banana Republic stores, which account for almost 60 percent of company sales? Are you shopping at Old Navy and Banana Republic as often as you used to? If not, where are you shopping and why?

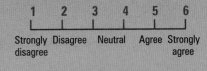

Marketing & You

How much do you enjoy shopping? Enter your answers on the lines provided.

1	2	3	4	5	6
Strongly disagree	Disagree	Neutral		Agree	Strongly agree

____ I shop because buying things makes me happy.

____ Shopping is fun.

____ I get a real "high" from shopping.

____ I enjoy talking with salespeople and other shoppers who are interested in the same things I am.

____ I like having a salesperson bring merchandise out for me to choose from.

____ I enjoy seeing mall exhibits while shopping.

Total your score, and find out what it means after you read the chapter.

The Role of Retailing

retailing
All the activities directly related to the sale of goods and services to the ultimate consumer for personal, nonbusiness use.

Retailing—all the activities directly related to the sale of goods and services to the ultimate consumer for personal, nonbusiness use—has enhanced the quality of our daily lives. When we shop for groceries, hair styling, clothes, books, and many other products and services, we are involved in retailing. The millions of goods and services provided by retailers mirror the needs and styles of U.S. society.

Exhibit 13.1

Ten Largest U.S. Retailers

2000 Rank	Company	Retailing Formats	2005 Revenues (in billions)	2005 Number of Stores
1	**Wal-Mart** Bentonville, Arkansas	Discount stores, supercenters, and warehouse clubs	$312.4	6,131
2	**The Home Depot** Atlanta, Georgia	Home centers	$81.5	2,042
3	**Kroger** Cincinnati, Ohio	Supermarkets and convenience stores	$60.6	3,726
4	**Sears Holdings*** Hoffman Estates, Illinois	Department stores, catalogs, home centers, and specialty	$53.9	3,770
5	**Costco** Issaquah, Washington	Warehouse clubs	$52.9	461
6	**Target Corporation** Minneapolis, Minnesota	Discount stores	$52.6	1,397
7	**Lowe's** Mooresville, North Carolina	Home centers	$43.2	1,225
8	**Walgreens** Deerfield, Ill.	Drugstores	$42.2	4,953
9	**Albertson's** Boise, Idaho	Supermarkets	$40.4	2,500
10	**Safeway** Pleasanton, California	Supermarkets	$38.4	1,775

* Renamed Sears Holdings after merger with Kmart; formerly was Sears Roebuck.
SOURCE: STORES, July 2006, **http://www.stores.org.** Sales figures include international sales.

Retailing affects all of us directly or indirectly. The retailing industry is one of the largest employers; over 1 million U.S. retailers employ more than 15 million people. Retail trade accounts for 11.6 percent of all U.S. employment, and almost 13 percent of all businesses are considered retail under NAICS. At the store level, retailing is still largely a mom-and-pop business. Almost nine out of ten retail companies employ fewer than 20 employees, and, according to the National Retail Federation, over 90 percent of all retailers operate just one store.[2]

The U.S. economy is heavily dependent on retailing. Retailers ring up almost $4 trillion in sales annually, about 40 percent of the gross domestic product (GDP).[3] Although most retailers are quite small, a few giant organizations dominate the industry, most notably Wal-Mart, whose annual U.S. sales alone account for about 5 percent of all retail sales. Who are these giants? Exhibit 13.1 lists the ten largest U.S. retailers.

REVIEW LEARNING OUTCOME

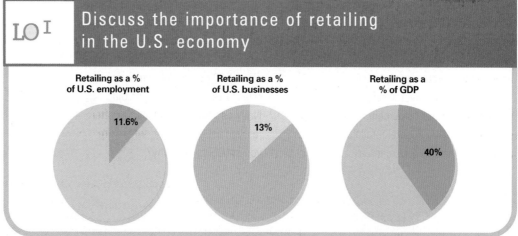

LO¹ Discuss the importance of retailing in the U.S. economy

Retailing as a % of U.S. employment — 11.6%

Retailing as a % of U.S. businesses — 13%

Retailing as a % of GDP — 40%

LO²
Classification of Retail Operations

A retail establishment can be classified according to its ownership, level of service, product assortment, and price. Specifically, retailers use the latter three variables to position themselves in the competitive marketplace. (As noted in Chapter 7, positioning is the strategy used to influence how consumers perceive one product in relation to all competing products.) These three variables can be combined in several ways to create distinctly different retail operations. Exhibit 13.2 lists the major types of retail stores discussed in this chapter and classifies them by level of service, product assortment, price, and gross margin.

Exhibit 13.2

Types of Stores and Their Characteristics

Type of Retailer	Level of Service	Product Assortment	Price	Gross Margin
Department store	Moderately high to high	Broad	Moderate to high	Moderately high
Specialty store	High	Narrow	Moderate to high	High
Supermarket	Low	Broad	Moderate	Low
Convenience store	Low	Medium to narrow	Moderately high	Moderately high
Drugstore	Low to moderate	Medium	Moderate	Low
Full-line discount store	Moderate to low	Medium to broad	Moderately low	Moderately low
Discount specialty store	Moderate to low	Medium to broad	Moderately low to low	Moderately low
Warehouse clubs	Low	Broad	Low to very low	Low
Off-price retailer	Low	Medium to narrow	Low	Low
Restaurant	Low to high	Narrow	Low to high	Low to high

OWNERSHIP

Retailers can be broadly classified by form of ownership: independent, part of a chain, or franchise outlet. Retailers owned by a single person or partnership and not operated as part of a larger retail institution are **independent retailers.** Around the world, most retailers are independent, operating one or a few stores in their community. Local florists, shoe stores, and ethnic food markets typically fit this classification.

Chain stores are owned and operated as a group by a single organization. Under this form of ownership, many administrative tasks are handled by the home office for the entire chain. The home office also buys most of the merchandise sold in the stores. Gap and Starbucks are examples of chains.

Franchises are owned and operated by individuals but are licensed by a larger supporting organization, such as Subway or Quiznos. The franchising approach combines the advantages of independent ownership with those of the chain store organization. Franchising is discussed in more detail later in the chapter.

LEVEL OF SERVICE

The level of service that retailers provide can be classified along a continuum, from full service to self-service. Some retailers, such as exclusive clothing stores, offer high levels of service. They provide alterations, credit, delivery, consulting, liberal return policies, layaway, gift wrapping, and personal shopping. Discount stores usually offer fewer services. Retailers like factory outlets and warehouse clubs offer virtually no services.

PRODUCT ASSORTMENT

The third basis for positioning or classifying stores is by the breadth and depth of their product line. Specialty stores—for example, Hallmark card stores, Lady Foot Locker, and TCBY yogurt shops—have the most concentrated product assortments, usually carrying single or narrow product lines but in considerable depth. On the other end of the spectrum,

independent retailers
Retailers owned by a single person or partnership and not operated as part of a larger retail institution.

chain stores
Stores owned and operated as a group by a single organization.

franchise
The right to operate a business or to sell a product.

full-line discounters typically carry broad assortments of merchandise with limited depth. For example, Target carries automotive supplies, household cleaning products, and pet food. Typically, though, it carries only four or five brands of dog food. In contrast, a specialty pet store, such as Petsmart, may carry as many as 20 brands in a large variety of flavors, shapes, and sizes.

Other retailers, such as factory outlet stores, may carry only part of a single line. Nike stores sell only certain items of its own brand. Discount specialty stores like Home Depot and Rack Room Shoes carry a broad assortment in concentrated product lines, such as building and home supplies or shoes.

PRICE

Price is a fourth way to position retail stores. Traditional department stores and specialty stores typically charge the full "suggested retail price." In contrast, discounters, factory outlets, and off-price retailers use low prices as a major lure for shoppers.

The last column in Exhibit 13.2 shows the typical **gross margin**—how much the retailer makes as a percentage of sales after the cost of goods sold is subtracted. The level of gross margin and the price level generally match. For example, a traditional jewelry store has high prices and high gross margins. A factory outlet has low prices and low gross margins. Markdowns on merchandise during sale periods and price wars among competitors, in which stores lower prices on certain items in an effort to win customers, cause gross margins to decline. When Wal-Mart entered the grocery business in a small Arkansas community, a fierce price war ensued. By the time the price war was in full swing, the price of a quart of milk had plummeted by more than 50 percent (below the price of a pint) and a loaf of bread sold for only 9 cents—prices at which no retailer could make a profit.

REVIEW LEARNING OUTCOME

LO 2 Explain the dimensions by which retailers can be classified

STORE
- Ownership
- Level of service
- Product assortment
- Price

LO 3
Major Types of Retail Operations

Traditionally, there have been several distinct types of retail stores, each offering a different product assortment, type of service, and price level, according to its customers' shopping preferences.

In a recent trend, however, retailers are experimenting with alternative formats that make it harder to classify them. For instance, supermarkets are expanding their nonfood items and services; discounters are adding groceries; drugstores are becoming more like convenience stores; and department stores are experimenting with smaller stores. Nevertheless, many stores still fall into the basic types.

DEPARTMENT STORES

A **department store** carries a wide variety of shopping and specialty goods, including apparel, cosmetics, housewares, electronics, and sometimes furniture. Purchases are generally made within each department rather than at one central checkout area. Each department is treated as a separate buying center to achieve economies in promotion, buying, service, and control. Each department is usually headed by a **buyer,** a department head who not only selects the merchandise for his or her department but may also be responsible for promotion and personnel. For a consistent, uniform store image, central management sets broad policies about the types of merchandise carried and price

gross margin
The amount of money the retailer makes as a percentage of sales after the cost of goods sold is subtracted.

department store
A store housing several departments under one roof.

buyer
A department head who selects the merchandise for his or her department and may also be responsible for promotion and personnel.

ranges. Central management is also responsible for the overall advertising program, credit policies, store expansion, customer service, and so on.

Large independent department stores are rare today. Most are owned by national chains. Among the largest U.S. department store chains are Federated Department Stores, JCPenney, Sears, Dillard's, and Nordstrom. Federated Department Stores owns the Bloomingdale's and Macy's brands. Dillard's is known for its distribution expertise. Nordstrom offers innovative customer service.

In recent years, consumers have become more cost conscious and value oriented. Specialty retailers, discounters, catalog outlets, and even online Internet shopping alternatives are offering superior merchandise selection and presentation, sharper pricing, and greater convenience to take sales away from department stores. They have also been quicker to adopt new technology and invest in labor-saving strategies. In addition, their leaner cost structure translates into lower prices for the customer. Meanwhile, manufacturers like Bass, Calvin Klein, Guess, and Polo Ralph Lauren have opened outlet stores of their own, and discount stores such as Wal-Mart and Target have upgraded their apparel assortments, taking more sales away from department stores.

SPECIALTY STORES

Specialty store formats allow retailers to refine their segmentation strategies and tailor their merchandise to specific target markets. A **specialty store** is not only a type of store but also a method of retail operations—namely, specializing in a given type of merchandise. Examples include children's clothing, men's clothing, candy, baked goods, gourmet coffee, sporting goods, and pet supplies. A typical specialty store carries a deeper but narrower assortment of specialty merchandise than does a department store. Generally, specialty stores' knowledgeable sales clerks offer more attentive customer service. The format has become very powerful in the apparel market and other areas. In fact, consumers buy more clothing from specialty stores than from any other type of retailer. The Children's Place, Gadzooks, Williams-Sonoma, Foot Locker, and Tower Records are examples of successful chain specialty retailers.

Consumers usually consider price to be secondary in specialty outlets. Instead, the distinctive merchandise, the store's physical appearance, and the caliber of the staff determine its popularity. For example, Sharper Image, a national retail chain, has grown quickly by offering high-tech gadgets for consumers. Gadgets are created either by the in-house design department or by independent innovators who sell ideas to Sharper Image. The retailer avoids price wars by packing products with distinguishing features, creating all-in-one product combinations, and keeping pace with demand for innovative gizmos.[4] Because of their attention to the customer and limited product line, manufacturers often favor introducing new products in small specialty stores before moving on to larger retail and department stores.

Small specialty stores also provide a low-risk testing ground for many new products. Nike, for instance, often uses athletic footwear retailer Foot Locker as its venue for new shoe introductions. As an example, Nike introduced its $130 Tuned Air running shoe exclusively at Foot Locker shoe outlets. While the arrangement protected Foot Locker from price competition from other retailers, allowing it to charge full retail price, it also created an image of exclusivity for Nike.

SUPERMARKETS

U.S. consumers spend about a tenth of their disposable income in **supermarkets.** Supermarkets are large, departmentalized, self-service retailers that specialize in food and some nonfood items. Supermarkets have experienced declining sales in recent years. Some of this decline has been the result of increased competition from discounter Wal-Mart and Sam's Clubs. But demographic and lifestyle changes have also affected the supermarket industry.

One major change has been the increase in dual-income and single-parent families that eat out more or are just too busy to prepare meals at home. According to the U.S. Department of Agriculture, Americans spend about 60 percent of their food money in retail

specialty store
A retail store specializing in a given type of merchandise.

supermarket
A large, departmentalized, self-service retailer that specializes in food and some nonfood items.

grocery stores, and 40 percent on food away from home. In comparison, Americans spent over three-fourths of their food money in grocery stores in 1950.

As stores seek to meet consumer demand for one-stop shopping, conventional supermarkets are being replaced by bigger *superstores*, which are usually twice the size of supermarkets. Superstores meet the needs of today's customers for convenience, variety, and service. Superstores offer one-stop shopping for many food and nonfood needs, as well as many services—including pharmacies, flower shops, salad bars, in-store bakeries, takeout food sections, sit-down restaurants, health food sections, video rentals, dry-cleaning services, shoe repair, photo processing, and banking. Some even offer family dentistry or optical shops. This tendency to offer a wide variety of nontraditional goods and services under one roof is called **scrambled merchandising.** Safeway supermarkets are a good example of scrambled merchandising. In addition to including a liquor store, floral department, and pharmacy, they also lease space to Starbucks and local banks. Another trend in supermarket diversification is the addition of store-owned gas stations. The gas stations are not only a revenue source for the supermarkets and a convenience for customers, but they also attract customers to the location by offering lower prices than can usually be found at a traditional gas station. Store-owned stations are expected to account for as much as 20 percent of overall gasoline sales in the near future.

Another demographic trend affecting supermarkets is expanding ethnicity. If current trends in shopping patterns among ethnic groups continue, demographic changes promise to have a vast impact on supermarket retailers. For example, both African American and Hispanic households now outspend white American households on weekly grocery shopping. In terms of shopping habits, African Americans and Hispanics tend to be conservative, looking for products and brands they know and trust and shopping at stores that reliably meet their needs. It will also be increasingly important for supermarkets to tailor their stores' product mix to reflect the demographics of the population they serve. For example, thousands of retailers now carry Hispanic-owned Goya Foods.[5]

To stand out in an increasingly competitive marketplace, many supermarket chains are tailoring marketing strategies to appeal to specific consumer segments. Most notable is the shift toward *loyalty marketing programs* that reward loyal customers carrying frequent shopper cards with discounts or gifts. Once scanned at the checkout, frequent shopper cards help supermarket retailers electronically track shoppers' buying habits. More than half of the customers who shop at the over 600 Piggly Wiggly stores carry the Pig's Favorite loyalty card. Customers use their card each time they shop to get special discounts on items. Piggly Wiggly also uses consumer purchase data stored in its database to determine customer preferences. If management sees that a customer buys flowers regularly, then it sends that customer a coupon redeemable in its floral department.[6]

DRUGSTORES

Drugstores stock pharmacy-related products and services as their main draw. Consumers are most often attracted to a drugstore by its pharmacy or pharmacist, its convenience, or because it honors their third-party prescription drug plan. Drugstores also carry an extensive selection of over-the-counter (OTC) medications, cosmetics, health and beauty aids, seasonal merchandise, specialty items such as greeting cards and a limited selection of toys, and some nonrefrigerated convenience foods. As competition has increased from mass merchandisers and supermarkets with their own pharmacies, as well as from direct-mail prescription services, drugstores have added value-added services such as 24-hour operations, drive-through pharmacies, and low-cost health clinics staffed by nurse practitioners.

Demographic trends in the United States look favorable for the drugstore industry. As the baby boom population continues to age, they will spend an increasing percentage of their disposable income on health care and wellness. In fact, the average 60-year-old pur-

© KENNETH C. ZIRKEL/ISTOCKPHOTO INTERNATIONAL INC.

scrambled merchandising
The tendency to offer a wide variety of nontraditional goods and services under one roof.

drugstore
A retail store that stocks pharmacy-related products and services as its main draw.

chases 15 prescriptions per year, nearly twice as many as the average 30-year-old. Because baby boomers are attentive to their health and keenly sensitive about their looks, the increased traffic at the pharmacy counter in the future should also spur sales in other traditionally strong drugstore merchandise categories, most notably OTC drugs, vitamins, and health and beauty aids.

CONVENIENCE STORES

A **convenience store** can be defined as a miniature supermarket, carrying only a limited line of high-turnover convenience goods. These self-service stores are typically located near residential areas and are open 24 hours, seven days a week. Convenience stores offer exactly what their name implies: convenient location, long hours, and fast service. However, prices are almost always higher at a convenience store than at a supermarket. Thus, the customer pays for the convenience.

When the original convenience stores added self-service gas pumps, full-service gas stations fought back by closing service bays and opening miniature stores of their own, selling convenience items like cigarettes, sodas, and snacks. Supermarkets and discount stores also wooed customers with one-stop shopping and quick checkout. To combat the gas stations' and supermarkets' competition, convenience store operators have changed their strategy. They have expanded their offerings of nonfood items with video rentals and health and beauty aids and added upscale sandwich and salad lines and more fresh produce. Some convenience stores are even selling Pizza Hut, Subway, and Taco Bell products prepared in the store. For example, Exxon On the Run features Mountain Coffee Roasters, BLIMPIE subs and salads, and an On the Run Café that offers everything from fresh sandwiches and fresh fruits to a grilled hamburger and french fries.[7]

DISCOUNT STORES

A **discount store** is a retailer that competes on the basis of low prices, high turnover, and high volume. Discounters can be classified into four major categories: full-line discount stores, specialty discount stores, warehouse clubs, and off-price discount retailers.

Full-Line Discount Stores

Compared to traditional department stores, **full-line discount stores** offer consumers very limited service and carry a much broader assortment of well-known, nationally branded "hard goods," including housewares, toys, automotive parts, hardware, sporting goods, and garden items, as well as clothing, bedding, and linens. Some even carry limited nonperishable food items, such as soft drinks, canned goods, and potato chips. As with department stores, national chains dominate the discounters. Full-line discounters are often called mass merchandisers. **Mass merchandising** is the retailing strategy whereby retailers use moderate to low prices on large quantities of merchandise and lower service to stimulate high turnover of products.

Wal-Mart is the largest full-line discount store in terms of sales. Wal-Mart initially expanded rapidly by locating on the outskirts of small towns and absorbing business for miles around. In recent years, most of its growth has come in larger cites. Today, it has over 5,000 stores. Much of Wal-Mart's success has been attributed to its merchandising foresight, cost consciousness, efficient communication and distribution systems, and involved, motivated employees. Wal-Mart is credited with pioneering the retail strategy of "everyday low pricing," a strategy now widely copied by retailers the world over. Besides expanding throughout all 50 states and Puerto Rico, Wal-Mart has expanded globally into Mexico, Canada, Brazil, Argentina, China, Germany, Korea, and the United Kingdom. Wal-Mart has also become a formidable retailing giant in online shopping, concentrating on toys and electronics. With tie-ins to its stores across the country, Wal-Mart offers online shopping with in-store kiosks linking to the site and the ability to handle returns and exchanges from Internet sales at its physical stores.[8]

Supercenters combine a full line of groceries and general merchandise with a wide range of services, including pharmacy, dry cleaning, portrait studios, photo finishing, hair

convenience store
A miniature supermarket, carrying only a limited line of high-turnover convenience goods.

discount store
A retailer that competes on the basis of low prices, high turnover, and high volume.

full-line discount stores
A retailer that offers consumers very limited service and carries a broad assortment of well-known, nationally branded "hard goods."

mass merchandising
A retailing strategy using moderate to low prices on large quantities of merchandise and lower service to stimulate high turnover of products.

supercenter
A retail store that combines groceries and general merchandise goods with a wide range of services.

salons, optical shops, and restaurants—all in one location. For supercenter operators like Wal-Mart, food is a customer magnet that sharply increases the store's overall volume, while taking customers away from traditional supermarkets. Wal-Mart now operates over 1,000 supercenters and plans to keep opening them at a rate of more than 150 a year for the near future. Although Target was the last major discounter to embrace the supercenter concept, it recently doubled the number of Super Target stores and is investing in the development of private-label grocery products.[9]

Supercenters are also threatening to push Europe's traditional small and medium-sized food stores into extinction. Old-fashioned corner stores and family businesses are giving way to larger chains that offer food, drugs, services, and general merchandise all in one place. Today, the largest British food retailer is Tesco, a chain operator that is expanding rapidly and now has over 1,800 stores in the United Kingdom and almost 2,500 stores globally, including a joint venture with Safeway in the United States.

Many European countries, however, are passing legislation to make it more difficult for supercenters to open. In France, for example, laws ban authorizations for new supercenters over 1,000 square meters (10,800 square feet). Belgium and Portugal have passed similar bans. In Britain and the Netherlands, areas outside towns and cities are off limits to superstores. By imposing planning and building restrictions for large stores, these countries are trying to accommodate environmental concerns, movements to revive city centers, and the worries of small shopkeepers.

An increasingly popular variation of full-line discount stores is *extreme-value retailing,* the most notable examples being Dollar General and Family Dollar. Extreme-value retailers have grown in popularity as major discounters continue to shift toward the supercenter format, broadening their customer base and increasing their offerings of higher-priced goods aimed at higher-income consumers. This has created an opening for extreme-value retailers to entice shoppers from the low-income segment. Low- and fixed-income customers are drawn to extreme-value retailers, whose stores are located within their communities. Extreme-value retailers also build smaller stores (a typical store is about the size of one department in a Wal-Mart superstore) with a narrower selection of merchandise emphasizing day-to-day necessities. Rock-bottom prices are also key to their success. With the average transaction under $10, extreme-value retailers have found low price to be far more critical to building traffic and loyalty than any other retailing format.[10]

Specialty Discount Stores

Another discount niche includes the single-line **specialty discount stores**—for example, stores selling sporting goods, electronics, auto parts, office supplies, housewares, or toys. These stores offer a nearly complete selection of single-line merchandise and use self-service, discount prices, high volume, and high turnover to their advantage. Specialty discount stores are often termed **category killers** because they so heavily dominate their narrow merchandise segment. Examples include Toys "R" Us in toys, Circuit City and Best Buy in electronics, Staples and Office Depot in office supplies, Home Depot and Lowe's in home improvement supplies, IKEA in home furnishings, Bed Bath & Beyond in kitchen and bath accessories, and Dick's in sporting goods.

Toys "R" Us was the first category killer, offering a giant selection of toys, usually over 15,000 different items per store, at prices usually 10 to 15 percent less than competitors'. When Toys "R" Us came on the retail scene, department stores were generally limiting their toy assortments to the Christmas season. Toys "R" Us offered a broad assortment of inventory all year long. Additionally, the playing field was scattered with many small toy chains or mom-and-pop stores. With its bright warehouse-style stores, Toys "R" Us gobbled up market share, causing many small toy stores to fail and department stores to eliminate their toy departments. At its peak, Toys "R" Us had over 1,500 stores, about half of them outside the United States. Its Babies "R" Us division became the largest baby product specialty store chain in the world and a leader in the juvenile industry. The Babies "R" Us stores have continued to do well, but in recent years, sales at Toys "R" Us stores have declined as the stores have faced increasing competition from Wal-Mart and Target. In an effort to revive the company, it was sold to a group of investors in July 2005.[11]

specialty discount store
A retail store that offers a nearly complete selection of single-line merchandise and uses self-service, discount prices, high volume, and high turnover.

category killers
Specialty discount stores that heavily dominate their narrow merchandise segment.

Category killers have emerged in other specialty segments as well, creating retailing empires in highly fragmented mom-and-pop markets. For instance, the home improvement industry, which for years was served by professional builders and small hardware stores, is now dominated by Home Depot and Lowe's. Similarly, prior to the creation of Petsmart and Petco pet supplies chains, the pet industry was dominated by thousands of independent neighborhood pet stores. Another industry that was very fragmented was the office products industry. As more people began to work from home, replacing their typewriters with personal computers and purchasing fax machines, the local stationery store, with its limited selection of paper and writing materials, quickly became obsolete. The industry is now dominated by Office Depot, Staples, and OfficeMax, which each stock 5,000 to 7,000 different types of products. Category-dominant retailers like these serve their customers by offering a large selection of merchandise, stores that make shopping easy, and low prices every day, which eliminates the need for time-consuming comparison shopping.

Warehouse Membership Clubs

Warehouse membership clubs sell a limited selection of brand-name appliances, household items, and groceries. These are usually sold in bulk from warehouse outlets on a cash-and-carry basis to members only. Individual members of warehouse clubs are charged low or no membership fees. Currently, the leading stores in this category are Wal-Mart's Sam's Club, Costco, and BJ's Wholesale Club.

Warehouse clubs have had a major impact on supermarkets. With 90,000 square feet or more, warehouse clubs offer 60 to 70 percent general merchandise and health- and beauty-care products, with grocery-related items making up the difference. Warehouse club members tend to be more educated and more affluent and have a larger household than regular supermarket shoppers. These core customers use warehouse clubs to stock up on staples; then they go to specialty outlets or food stores for perishables.

Off-Price Retailers

An **off-price retailer** sells at prices 25 percent or more below traditional department store prices because it pays cash for its stock and usually doesn't ask for return privileges. Off-price retailers buy manufacturers' overruns at cost or even less. They also absorb goods from bankrupt stores, irregular merchandise, and unsold end-of-season output. Nevertheless, much off-price retailer merchandise is first-quality, current goods. Because buyers for off-price retailers purchase only what is available or what they can get a good deal on, merchandise styles and brands often change monthly. Today, there are hundreds of off-price retailers, including T. J. Maxx, Ross Stores, Marshall's, HomeGoods, and Tuesday Morning.

Factory outlets are an interesting variation on the off-price concept. A **factory outlet** is an off-price retailer that is owned and operated by a manufacturer. Thus, it carries one line of merchandise—its own. Each season, from 5 to 10 percent of a manufacturer's output does not sell through regular distribution channels because it consists of closeouts (merchandise being discontinued), factory seconds, and canceled orders. With factory outlets, manufacturers can regulate where their surplus is sold, and they can realize higher profit margins than they would by disposing of the goods through independent wholesalers and retailers. Factory outlet malls typically locate in out-of-the-way rural areas or near vacation destinations. Most are situated 10 to 15 miles from urban or suburban shopping areas so that manufacturers don't alienate their department store accounts by selling the same goods virtually next door at a discount.

Manufacturers reaping the benefits of outlet mall popularity include Gap, J. Crew, and Calvin Klein clothiers; West Point Pepperel textiles; Pottery Barn and Crate & Barrel

warehouse member-ship clubs
Limited-service merchant wholesalers that sell a limited selection of brand-name appliances, household items, and groceries on a cash-and-carry basis to members, usually small businesses and groups.

off-price retailer
A retailer that sells at prices 25 percent or more below traditional department store prices because it pays cash for its stock and usually doesn't ask for return privileges.

factory outlet
An off-price retailer that is owned and operated by a manufacturer.

home products; Oneida silversmiths; and Dansk kitchenwares. Top-drawer department stores have also opened outlet stores to sell hard-to-move merchandise. Dillard's has opened a series of clearance centers to make final attempts to move merchandise that failed to sell in the department store. To move their clearance items, Nordstrom operates Nordstrom Rack, Saks Fifth Avenue has Off Fifth, and Neiman Marcus has Last Call.

RESTAURANTS

Restaurants straddle the line between retailing establishments and service establishments. Restaurants do sell tangible products—food and drink—but they also provide a valuable service for consumers in the form of food preparation and food service. Most restaurants could even fall into the definition of a specialty retailer given that most concentrate their menu offerings on a distinctive type of cuisine—for example, Olive Garden Italian restaurants, Starbucks coffeehouses, Popeye's Fried Chicken, and Pizza Hut pizza restaurants.

As a retailing institution, restaurants must deal with many of the same issues as a more traditional retailer, such as personnel, distribution, inventory management, promotion, pricing, and location. Restaurants and food-service retailers run the spectrum from those offering limited service and inexpensive food, such as fast-food chains or the local snack bar or coffeehouse, to those that offer sit-down service and moderate to high prices, such as the Outback Steakhouse & Saloon chain or a local trendy Italian bistro.

Eating out is an important part of Americans' daily activities and is growing in strength. According to the National Restaurant Association, more than 70 billion meals are eaten in restaurants or cafeterias annually. This means that Americans consume an average of 4.8 commercially prepared meals per week. Food away from home accounts for about 25 percent of the household food budget for lower-income families and as much as 50 percent for those with higher incomes. The trend toward eating out has been fueled by the increase in working mothers and dual-income families who have more money to eat out and less time to prepare meals at home. By 2010 almost 55 percent of household food budgets is expected to be spent on food eaten away from home.[12]

The restaurant industry is one of the most entrepreneurial of businesses and one of the most competitive. Because barriers to entering the restaurant industry are low, the opportunity appeals to many people. The risks, however, are great. About 50 percent of all new restaurants fail within the first year of operation. Restaurants face competition not only from other restaurants but also from the consumer who can easily choose to cook at home. Competition has fostered innovation and ever-changing menus in most segments of the restaurant industry. Another way restaurants are competing is by targeting underserved distribution niches. For example, fast-food operators are locating in hospitals, airports, and highway rest stops. Companies like Subway, Dunkin' Donuts, and Church's Fried Chicken also are partnering with branded service stations to offer customers one-stop shopping. These partnerships save money on leases, lure more customers, and stimulate innovation. Many restaurants are now competing directly with supermarkets by offering takeout and delivery in an effort to capture more of the home meal replacement market.

REVIEW LEARNING OUTCOME

LO3 Describe the major types of retail operations

The retailing methods discussed so far have been in-store methods, in which customers must physically shop at stores. In contrast, **nonstore retailing** is shopping without visiting a store. Because consumers demand convenience, nonstore retailing is currently growing faster than in-store retailing. The major forms of nonstore retailing are automatic vending, direct retailing, direct marketing, and electronic retailing.

© STONYFIELD FARM/PR NEWSWIRE PHOTO SERVICE (NEWS COM)

AUTOMATIC VENDING

A low-profile yet important form of retailing is **automatic vending,** the use of machines to offer goods for sale—for example, the soft drink, candy, or snack vending machines found in college cafeterias and office buildings. Vending is the most pervasive retail business in the United States, with about six million vending machines selling $40 billion annually. Food and beverages account for about 85 percent of all sales from vending machines. Due to the convenience, consumers are willing to pay higher prices for products from a vending machine than for the same products in traditional retail settings.

Retailers are constantly seeking new opportunities to sell via vending. For example, United Artists Theaters offer moviegoers the option of purchasing hot popcorn, Tombstone pizza, Kraft macaroni-and-cheese, and chicken fingers from a vending machine instead of waiting in line at the concession stand. Many vending machines today also sell nontraditional kinds of merchandise, such as videos, toys, stickers, sports cards, office-type supplies, film, and disposable cameras. In a sign of the times, Macy's shoppers can purchase iPod music players and accessories from specially designed Zoom Store vending machines located in select stores.

Of course, vending machines are also an important tool in the ongoing cola wars between Coca-Cola and Pepsi. Both companies are constantly looking for new ways to improve vending machine sales. For example, Coca-Cola is implementing Intelligent Vending, a "cashless" payment system. Vending machines with this system accept credit cards, RFID devices, and hotel room keys and can be accessed via cell phone (mobile e-commerce, or m-commerce, as discussed later in this chapter).[13]

DIRECT RETAILING

In **direct retailing,** representatives sell products door-to-door, office-to-office, or at home sales parties. Companies like Avon, Mary Kay Cosmetics, The Pampered Chef, Usbourne Books, and World Book Encyclopedia have used this approach for years. But recently direct retailers' sales have suffered as women have entered the workforce. Working women are not home during the day and have little time to attend selling parties. Although most direct sellers like Avon and Silpada still advocate the party plan method, the realities of the marketplace have forced them to be more creative in reaching their target customer. Direct sales representatives now hold parties in offices, parks, and even parking lots. Others hold informal gatherings where shoppers can drop in at their convenience or offer self-improvement classes. Many direct retailers are also turning to direct mail, telephone, or more traditional retailing venues to find new avenues to their customers and increase sales. Avon, for instance, has begun opening cosmetic

nonstore retailing
Shopping without visiting a store.

automatic vending
The use of machines to offer goods for sale.

direct retailing
The selling of products by representatives who work door-to-door, office-to-office, or at home parties.

Avon

What advantages do you think the Avon site has over a visit from an Avon representative? Can you get the same amount of product information from each? Does Avon offer any products that you would prefer to order from a representative?

http://www.avon.com

Online

kiosk counters, called Avon Beauty Centers, in malls and strip centers. Avon has also launched a new brand—Mark, a beauty "experience" for young women. Most Mark representatives are students who typically sell the product as an afterschool part-time job. Prospective representatives and consumers can buy products or register to be a representative in person, online, or over the phone.[14]

Direct retailers are also using the Internet as a channel to reach more customers and increase sales. Amway launched Quixtar.com, an online channel for its products that generated over $1 billion in revenues in its first year. Customers access the site using a unique referral number for each Amway rep, a system that ensures that the reps earn their commissions. Best known for its health and beauty offerings, Quixtar features hundreds of products from leading brand-name companies in many categories, including apparel, athletic gear, photography, electronics, appliances, and furniture. Avon, Tupperware, and Mary Kay also have Internet retail sites. At Avon's site, individual reps have their own home pages that link from Avon's home page so that sales are credited to them.

In response to the decline in U.S. sales, many direct retailers are exploring opportunities in other countries. For example, Mary Kay, Avon, and Amway have started successful operations in China by adapting their business models to China's laws. Mary Kay agents in China do not purchase and resell the products but are paid a sales commission instead. The company also changed its slogan from "God First, Family Second, Career Third," to "Faith First, Family Second, Career Third."[15]

DIRECT MARKETING

Direct marketing, sometimes called **direct-response marketing,** refers to the techniques used to get consumers to make a purchase from their home, office, or other non-retail setting. These techniques include direct mail, catalogs and mail order, telemarketing, and electronic retailing. Shoppers using these methods are less bound by traditional shopping situations. Time-strapped consumers and those who live in rural or suburban areas are most likely to be direct-response shoppers because they value the convenience and flexibility that direct marketing provides.

Direct Mail

Direct mail can be the most efficient or the least efficient retailing method, depending on the quality of the mailing list and the effectiveness of the mailing piece. According to the Direct Marketing Association, companies spent more than $160 billion on direct marketing in the United States in 2005 and generated about $1.85 trillion in sales. With direct mail, marketers can precisely target their customers according to demographics, geographics, and even psychographics. Good mailing lists come from an internal database or from list brokers for about $35 to $150 per thousand names.

Direct mailers are becoming more sophisticated in targeting the "right" customers. Using statistical methods to analyze census data, lifestyle and financial information, and past-purchase and credit history, direct mailers can pick out those most likely to buy their products. For example, Range Rover recently launched a direct-mail campaign that invited 150,000 potential customers to one of six test-drive events. Approximately 1,000 people attended each event, and of those approximately 12 people bought the new sport-utility vehicle at each event. Overall, a total of 775 new SUVs were sold to those who received the mailer. To compile the list, Range Rover used current customers, subscribers of selected Condé Nast magazines, and American Express platinum cardholders. By targeting the solicitation to only the best prospects, the company saved millions in postage while still generating new sales. For more expensive products, direct mailers are using videocassettes in place of letters and brochures to deliver their sales messages.[16]

direct marketing (direct-response marketing)
Techniques used to get consumers to make a purchase from their home, office, or another nonretail setting.

Catalogs and Mail Order

Consumers can now buy just about anything through the mail, from the mundane, like books, music, and polo shirts, to the outlandish, such as the $5 million diamond-and-ruby-studded bra available through the Victoria's Secret catalog. Although women make up the bulk of catalog shoppers, the percentage of male catalog shoppers has recently soared. As changing demographics have shifted more of the shopping responsibility to men, they are viewing shopping via catalog, mail order, and the Internet as more sensible than a trip to the mall.

Successful catalogs usually are created and designed for highly segmented markets. For example, Schwan Food Company recently launched Impromptu Gourmet, which offers convenient gourmet and fine dining frozen foods. Certain types of retailers are using mail order successfully. For example, computer manufacturers have discovered that mail order is a lucrative way to sell personal computers to home and small-business users, evidenced by Dell's tremendous success. Dell has used its direct business model to become a $55 billion company and the number one PC seller worldwide. With a global market share of almost 20 percent, it sells about $50 million in computers and equipment online every day.[17]

Improved customer service and quick delivery policies have boosted consumer confidence in mail order. L.L. Bean and Lands' End are two catalog companies known for their excellent customer service. Shoppers can order 24 hours a day and return merchandise for any reason for a full refund. Other successful mail-order catalogs—including Talbots, Frontgate, and Lillian Vernon—target hardworking, home-oriented baby boomers who don't have time to visit, or would rather not visit, a retail store. To remain competitive and save time for customers, catalog companies maintain databases of customer information so they do not have to ask customers for their addresses and credit-card numbers. The companies also work with overnight shippers such as UPS and FedEx to speed up deliveries. Indeed, some products can be ordered as late as 12:30 A.M. and still arrive the same day by 10:30 A.M.

Telemarketing

Telemarketing is the use of the telephone to sell directly to consumers. It consists of outbound sales calls, usually unsolicited, and inbound calls—that is, orders through toll-free 800 numbers or fee-based 900 numbers.

Rising postage rates and decreasing long-distance phone rates have made *outbound* telemarketing an attractive direct-marketing technique. Skyrocketing field sales costs have also led marketing managers to use outbound telemarketing. Searching for ways to keep costs under control, marketing managers have learned how to pinpoint prospects quickly, zero in on serious buyers, and keep in close touch with regular customers. Meanwhile, they are reserving expensive, time-consuming, in-person calls for closing sales. So many consumers complained about outbound telemarketing calls, however, that Congress passed legislation establishing a national "do not call" list of consumers who do not want to receive unsolicited telephone calls. In addition, Congress passed laws requiring e-mail marketers to allow recipients to opt out of mass e-mails (spam). The laws also prohibit marketers from camouflaging their identity through false return addresses and misleading subject lines. A problem with the telemarketing law, however, is that it exempts nonprofits, so some companies have set up nonprofit subsidiaries to continue their calling activities. Some industry experts say the lists help them by eliminating nonbuyers, but others believe this legislation could have a long-term negative effect on telemarketing sales.[18]

Inbound telemarketing programs, which use 800 and 900 numbers, are mainly used to take orders, generate leads, and provide customer service. Inbound 800 telemarketing has successfully supplemented direct-response TV, radio, and print advertising for more than 25 years. The more recently introduced 900 numbers, which customers pay to call, are gaining popularity as a cost-effective way for companies to target customers. One of the major benefits of 900 numbers is that they allow marketers to generate qualified responses. Although the charge may reduce the total volume of calls, the calls that do come are from customers who have a true interest in the product.

telemarketing
The use of the telephone to sell directly to consumers.

ELECTRONIC RETAILING

Electronic retailing includes the 24-hour, shop-at-home television networks and online retailing.

Shop-at-Home Networks

The shop-at-home television networks are specialized forms of direct-response marketing. Shows display merchandise, with the retail price, to home viewers. Viewers can phone in their orders directly on a toll-free line and shop with a credit card. The shop-at-home industry has quickly grown into a multibillion-dollar business with a loyal customer following. Shop-at-home networks have the capability of reaching nearly every home that has a television set.

The best-known shop-at-home networks are the Home Shopping Network and the QVC (Quality, Value, Convenience) Network. Home shopping networks attract a broad audience through diverse programming and product offerings and are now adding new products to appeal to more affluent audiences. For instance, on QVC, cooking programs attract both men and women, fashion programs attract mostly women, and the NFL Team Shop attracts primarily men. Since it began broadcasting, the channel has sold everything from Sony electronics to Bugs Bunny to Gucci. With annual sales of almost $6 billion, QVC ships more than 150 million packages worldwide to about 10 million customers every year. The company owes its success in part to its customer files of more than 20 million people in 40 countries and to the fact that it introduces as many as 250 new products each week.[19]

Online Retailing

For years, shopping at home meant looking through catalogs and then placing an order over the telephone. For many people today, however, it now means turning on a computer, surfing retail Web sites, and selecting and ordering products online with the click of a mouse. **Online retailing,** or *e-tailing*, is a type of shopping available to consumers with access to the Internet. Over 70 percent of Americans have Internet access either at home or at work.

Online retailing has exploded in the last several years as consumers have found this type of shopping convenient and, in many instances, less costly. Consumers can shop without leaving home, choose from a wide selection of merchants, use shopping comparison services to search the Web for the best price, and then have the items delivered to their doorsteps. As a result, online shopping continues to grow at a rapid pace, with online sales accounting for roughly 8 percent of total retail sales. In fact, online sales surpassed $140 billion in 2005 and are expected to more than double by 2010 to over $325 billion annually.[20] Online retailing is also increasing in popularity outside the United States. Read more about e-tailing worldwide in the "Global Perspectives" box.

Broadcast and cable television networks are cultivating a new source of income by selling products online that are featured in their TV shows. Delivery Agent, a San Francisco company that calls itself the leader in shopping enabled entertainment, manages e-commerce for NBC, Bravo, and Martha Stewart Omnimedia, among others. The producers of Bravo's *Project Runway* contracted with Delivery Agent to sell the cloth-

online retailing
A type of shopping available to consumers with access to the Internet.

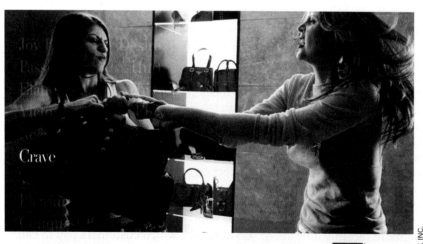
© BLUEFLY, INC.

Consumers appreciate the immediacy and convenience of online retailing. This advertisement for bluefly.com, an online retailer, emphasizes its current fashions and reduced prices.

Online Retailing Grows Worldwide

Consumers and marketers around the world are embracing the Internet and online retailing (both e-commerce and m-commerce). Millions of people from the United States, United Kingdom, Canada, continental Europe, India, and South Africa are choosing to shop over the Internet. More than 200 million individual subscribers already have Internet access, with the United States, China, Japan, South Korea, and the United Kingdom having the largest concentrations of subscribers. North America and western Europe account for almost half of all Internet access in the world, but the Middle East, Africa, eastern Europe, Australia, and New Zealand are the fastest-growing areas. Marketers definitely are vying for Internet consumers' attention. In recent years, online advertising has surpassed experts' estimates. In 2005, almost $14 billion was spent on online advertising in the United States, and $4 billion was spent in Europe, with the United Kingdom, France, and Germany leading the way.

Given the dramatic increases in the number of Web surfers and in spending on online advertising, online retailers have consistently enjoyed big payoffs during holiday shopping seasons. Online holiday sales surpassed $28 billion in the United States in 2005. The fastest-growing categories were apparel and accessories, computer software, home and garden, and toys and hobbies.

Online spending is increasing by about 30 percent annually worldwide, compared to 33 percent in the United States. The slightly higher U.S. rate probably occurs because more consumers in the United States have Internet access, particularly high-speed broadband. Unfortunately, the number of online fraud claims is keeping pace with the growth in spending. VeriSign estimates that more than 6 percent of online transactions are fraudulent and that 52 percent of the fraud takes place outside the United States.

Amazon.com is the best example of a successful global e-commerce business model. Amazon believes that it is very important to reach customers throughout the world. Therefore, it has five separate Web sites, each directed to a different nationality: a British site Amazon.co.uk, a French-language site Amazon.fr, a German-language site Amazon.de, a Japanese-language site Amazon.co.jp, and a Chinese-language site www.joyo.com. Each Web site is tailored to its country of origin and helps Amazon remain the leading online global retailer. In addition to online ads, such as pop-ups and banner ads, Amazon uses print media such as direct mail and newspaper inserts to encourage online purchasing.[21]

As Internet usage around the world increases, so will the number of online shoppers. How do you think that will affect traditional retailers? Do you think the Internet will create a truly global retail marketplace?

ing designed on the reality fashion competition show. After the challenge to create an outfit for My Scene Barbie, the Bravo.com site sold out of the 3,300 dolls wearing the winning design creation.[22]

Most traditional retailers have now jumped on the Internet bandwagon, allowing shoppers to purchase the same merchandise found in their stores from their Web site. Online retailing also fits well with traditional catalog companies, such as Lands' End and Eddie Bauer that already have established distribution networks. In a drastic turnabout in its retail strategy, computer software retailer Egghead closed all of its brick-and-mortar stores, moved its entire business onto the Web, and added ".com" to the end of its name. Software purchased at the company's site, **http://www.egghead.com**, which is now supported by Amazon.com, can be downloaded directly to the purchaser's computer.

As the popularity of online retailing grows, it is becoming critical that retailers be online and that their stores, Web sites, and catalogs be integrated. Customers expect to find the same brands, products, and prices whether they purchase online, on the phone, or in a store. Therefore, retailers are increasingly using in-store kiosks to help tie the channels together for greater customer service. Retailer and cataloger Williams-Sonoma, for example, has linked its store gift registry to its Web site, allowing brides to see who has bought what in real time. Banana Republic stores in New York and Santa Monica, California, have kiosks where customers can order items that aren't on the shelves. Kiosks are even more popular among retailers that target younger, more computer-oriented customers. For example, Van's (**http://www.vans.com**) sells alternative sportswear online as well as in 160 retail stores. Each of its eight skate parks is a combination retail store, entertainment venue, and alternative sports arena. In addition to the skating rink, each park has a lounge area where customers can hang out, watch customized videos, and

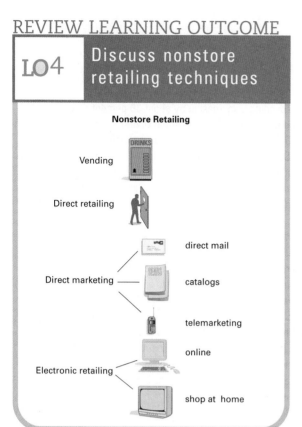

Nonstore Retailing

- Vending — DRINKS
- Direct retailing
- Direct marketing
  - direct mail
  - catalogs
  - telemarketing
- Electronic retailing
  - online
  - shop at home

surf Van's Web site at a bank of kiosks. Each kiosk not only offers a complete selection of Van's footwear, apparel, and accessories, but also includes a full-service pro shop that sells over 500 skateboards, bicycles, helmets, and other equipment and an information center with the latest tour, special event, and contest information.[23]

Online auctions run by Internet companies such as eBay and Amazon.com have enjoyed phenomenal success in recent years. With more than two million items for sale each day, ranging from antique clocks to car stereos, eBay is the leader in cyberspace auctions. Internet auction services like eBay run the Web service and collect a listing fee, plus a commission of 1 to 5 percent when a sale is completed. They also host auctions for other companies. For example, eBay and Sotheby's have a joint venture that offers fine art, rare coins, sports collectibles, jewelry, and antiques online. Each item carries a stamp of authenticity from Sotheby's or one of the 2,800 art and antiques dealers worldwide who have signed exclusive agreements with Sotheby's. The joint venture supports eBay's fine arts and antiques division and enables Sotheby's to offer online sales without the overhead expense of managing its own site.[24]

LO5 Franchising

A *franchise* is a continuing relationship in which a franchisor grants to a franchisee the business rights to operate or to sell a product. The **franchisor** originates the trade name, product, methods of operation, and so on. The **franchisee**, in return, pays the franchisor for the right to use its name, product, or business methods. A franchise agreement between the two parties usually lasts for 10 to 20 years, at which time it can be renewed if both parties are agreeable.

To be granted the rights to a franchise, a franchisee usually pays an initial, one-time franchise fee. The amount of this fee depends solely on the individual franchisor, but it generally ranges from $50,000 to $250,000 or higher. In addition to this initial franchise fee, the franchisee is expected to pay royalty fees, usually in the range of 3 to 7 percent of gross revenues. The franchisee may also be expected to pay advertising fees, which usually cover the cost of promotional materials and, if the franchise organization is large enough, regional or national advertising. A McDonald's franchise, for example, costs an initial $45,000 per store plus a monthly fee based on the restaurant's sales performance and base rent. In addition, a new McDonald's franchisee can expect start-up costs for equipment and pre-opening expenses to range from $511,000 to over $1 million. The size of the restaurant facility, area of the country, inventory, selection of kitchen equipment, signage, and style of decor and landscaping affect new restaurant costs.[25] Though the dollar amount will vary depending on the type of franchise, fees such as these are typical for all major franchisors, including Burger King, Jani-King, Athlete's Foot, Sonic, and Subway.

Franchising is not new. General Motors has used this approach since 1898, and Rexall drugstores, since 1901. Today, there are over half a million franchised establishments in the United States, with combined sales approaching $1 trillion, or about 40 percent of all retail trade. Although franchised restaurants attract most of those dollars, hundreds of retail and service franchises, such as Alphagraphics Printshops, Supercuts, and Sylvan Learning Systems, also are thriving. Indeed, there are over 320,000 franchises in 75 industries. Industries expected to see real growth in franchising include home repair, business support services, automotive repairs, hair salons, children's services, and telecommunications.[26] Exhibit 13.3 lists some facts about some of the largest and best-known U.S. franchisors. Exhibit 13.4 lists some Web sites that provide information about franchises.

franchisor
The originator of a trade name, product, methods of operation, and so on, that grants operating rights to another party to sell its product.

franchisee
An individual or business that is granted the right to sell another party's product.

Exhibit 13.3

Largest U.S. Franchisors

Franchisor	Type of Business	Total Units	Initial Investment
McDonald's	Fast food	Franchised units: 22,215 Company owned: 8,105	$511,000– $1,000,500
Southland (7-Eleven)	Convenience stores	Franchised units: 15,600 Company owned: 2,600	$83,000
Subway	Fast food	Franchised units: 21,000 Company owned: 2,600	$86,000– $250,000
Burger King	Fast food	Franchised units: 10,144 Company owned: 1,080	NA
KFC	Fast food	Franchised units: 5,000 Company owned: 1,252	NA
Pizza Hut	Pizza	Franchised units: 4,600 Company owned: 1,776	NA
Tandy (Radio Shack)	Consumer electronics	Franchised units: 1,921 Company owned: 5,121	NA
Taco Bell	Fast food	Franchised units: 5,743 Company owned: 1,284	NA
Dairy Queen	Ice cream, etc.	Franchised units: 6,000 Company owned: 70	$1 million– $2 million
Hooter's	Restaurant	Franchised units: 200 Company owned: 75	$500,000+
Jason's Deli	Fast food	Franchised units: 50 Company owned: 70	$700,000– $900,000
Marble Slab	Ice cream	Franchised units: 500 Company owned: 1	$180,000– $240,000
Quiznos Sub	Fast food	Franchised units: 1,950 Company owned: 15	$186,000– $265,000

SOURCE: http://www.franchise.org, January 2006.

Exhibit 13.4

Sources of Franchise Information

Some Web sites where people with francising-related questions can find answers:

- **Federal Trade Commission (http://www.ftc.gov)** Has a host of information consumers looking to buy a franchise might need. Click on the "for consumers" link and then on "Franchise & Business Opportunities." Contains information on FTC regulation as well as contact information for state regulators.

- **North American Securities Administrators Association (http://www.nasaa.org)** The umbrella group for state securities regulators offers links to find regulators and also has links to other governmental agencies.

- **International Franchise Association (http://www.franchise.org)** Contains information on such topics as buying a franchise and government relations. The site's FAQ section deals with some issues of franchise regulation.

- **American Franchisee Association (http://www.franchisee.org)** Represents franchisees and has information on legal resources, FTC regulations, and state law.

- **American Association of Franchisees & Dealers (http://www.aafd.org)** Offers legal and financial information.

Two basic forms of franchises are used today: product and trade name franchising and business format franchising. In *product and trade name franchising*, a dealer agrees to sell certain products provided by a manufacturer or a wholesaler. This approach has been used most widely in the auto and truck, soft drink bottling, tire, and gasoline service industries. For example, a local tire retailer may hold a franchise to sell Michelin tires. Likewise, the Coca-Cola bottler in a particular area is a product and trade name franchisee licensed to bottle and sell Coca-Cola's soft drinks.

Business format franchising is an ongoing business relationship between a franchisor and a franchisee. Typically, a franchisor "sells" a franchisee the rights to use the franchisor's format or approach to doing business. This form of franchising has rapidly expanded since the 1950s through retailing, restaurant, foodservice, hotel and motel, printing, and real estate franchises. Fast-food restaurants like McDonald's, Wendy's, and Burger King use this kind of franchising, as do other companies such as Hyatt Corporation, Unocal Corporation, and ExxonMobil Corporation. To be eligible to be a Domino's Pizza franchisee, you must have worked in a Domino's pizza store for at least one year. The company believes that after working in an existing location, you will have a better understanding of the company and its values and standards. Then potential franchisees must participate in a series of career development, franchise orientation, presentation skills, and franchise development programs.[27]

Like other retailers, franchisors are seeking new growth abroad. Hundreds of U.S. franchisors have begun international expansion and are actively looking for foreign franchisees to open new locations. KFC serves nearly 8 million customers daily at its more than 11,000 restaurants in over 80 countries and territories around the world, including Australia, China, Indonesia, Japan, and Saudi Arabia. KFC's parent company, Yum! Brands, Inc., the world's largest restaurant

LO5 Define franchising and describe its two basic forms

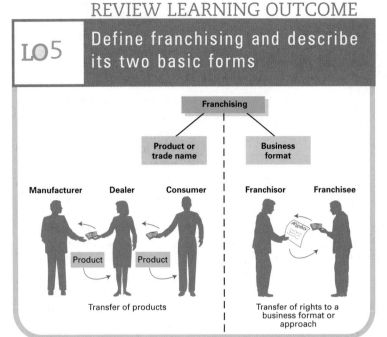

Franchising

Product or trade name — Business format

Manufacturer   Dealer   Consumer

Product   Product

Transfer of products

Franchisor   Franchisee

Transfer of rights to a business format or approach

system, attributes the franchise's success to its ability to adapt to local cultures and tastes without losing control of quality and brand image.[28] The International Franchise Association includes over 100 franchise organizations in countries from Argentina to Zimbabwe.

Franchisors usually allow franchisees to alter their business format slightly in foreign markets. For example, some McDonald's franchisees in Germany sell beer, and in Japan they offer food items that appeal to Japanese tastes, such as steamed dumplings, curry with rice, and roast pork cutlet burgers with melted cheese. McDonald's franchisees in India serve mutton instead of beef because most Indians are Hindu, a religion whose followers believe cows are a sacred symbol of the source of life. The menu also features rice-based Vegetable Burgers made with peas, carrots, red pepper, beans, and Indian spices as well as Vegetable McNuggets. But, in spite of menu differences, McDonald's foreign franchisees still maintain the company's standards of service and cleanliness.

LO6 Retail Marketing Strategy

Retailers must develop marketing strategies based on overall goals and strategic plans. Retailing goals might include more traffic, higher sales of a specific item, a more upscale image, or heightened public awareness of the retail operation. The strategies that retailers use to obtain their goals might include a sale, an updated decor, or a new advertisement. The key tasks in strategic retailing are defining and selecting a target market and developing the retailing mix to successfully meet the needs of the chosen target market.

DEFINING A TARGET MARKET

The first and foremost task in developing a retail strategy is to define the target market. This process begins with market segmentation, the topic of Chapter 7. Successful retailing has always been based on knowing the customer. Sometimes retailing chains flounder when management loses sight of the customers the stores should be serving. For example, Gap built a retail empire by offering updated, casual classics like white shirts and khaki pants that appealed to everyone from high school through middle age. But, as the chapter's opening example described, the company lost its focus—and its customers—when it shifted toward trendier fashions with a limited appeal.

Target markets in retailing are often defined by demographics, geographics, and psychographics. For instance, Bluefly.com, a discount fashion e-tailer, targets both men and women in their thirties, who have a higher-than-average income, read fashion magazines, and favor high-end designers. By understanding who its customers are, the company has been able to tailor its Web site to appeal specifically to its audience. The result is a higher sales rate than most e-tailers.[29]

When Beth McLaughlin launched a line of clothing stores, Torrid, aimed exclusively at teenaged girls sizes 12 to 26, she clearly identified her target. Her product offering was tailored to meet that target, as were her choices of location, pricing, and promotion. Torrid has expanded from 6 to 33 stores, with plans for another 19, as a result of McLaughlin's successful strategy.

© DOROTHY LOW PHOTOGRAPHY

Determining a target market is a prerequisite to creating the retailing mix. For example, Target's merchandising approach for sporting goods is to match its product assortment to the demographics of the local store and region. The amount of space devoted to sporting goods, as well as in-store promotions, also varies according to each store's target market. Similarly, American Eagle Outfitters offers fashionable, high-quality clothing at reasonable prices. AE is a lifestyle retailer that designs casual clothing such as jeans, pants, graphic T-shirts, outerwear, footwear, swimwear, and accessories that appeal to the 20-year-old with a hip, youthful, active attitude.[30]

CHOOSING THE RETAILING MIX

Retailers combine the elements of the retailing mix to come up with a single retailing method to attract the target market. The **retailing mix** consists of six Ps: the four Ps of the marketing mix (product, place, promotion, and price) plus presentation and personnel (see Exhibit 13.5).

The combination of the six Ps projects a store's image, which influences consumers' perceptions. Using these impressions of stores, shoppers position one store against another. A retail marketing manager must make sure that the store's positioning is compatible with the target customers' expectations. As discussed at the beginning of the chapter, retail stores can be positioned on three broad dimensions: service provided by store personnel, product assortment, and price. Management should use everything else—place, presentation, and promotion—to fine-tune the basic positioning of the store.

Exhibit 13.5
The Retailing Mix

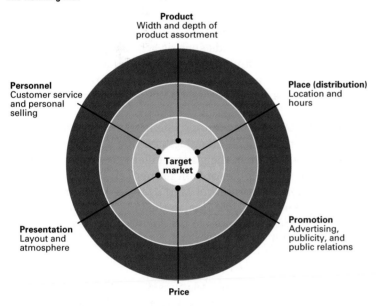

Product
Width and depth of product assortment

Place (distribution)
Location and hours

Personnel
Customer service and personal selling

Target market

Promotion
Advertising, publicity, and public relations

Presentation
Layout and atmosphere

Price

The Product Offering

The first element in the retailing mix is the **product offering,** also called the *product assortment* or *merchandise mix.* Retailers decide what to sell on the basis of what their target market wants to buy. They can base their decision on market research, past sales, fashion trends, customer requests, and other sources. A recent approach, called data mining, uses complex mathematical models to help retailers make better product mix decisions. Early users of the approach, such as Dillard's, Target, and Wal-Mart, use data mining to determine which products to stock at what price, how to manage markdowns, and how to advertise to draw target customers.

Developing a product offering is essentially a question of the width and depth of the product assortment. *Width* refers to the assortment of products offered; *depth* refers to the number of different brands offered within each assortment. Price, store design, displays, and service are important to consumers in determining where to shop, but the most critical factor is merchandise selection. This reasoning also holds true for online retailers. Amazon.com, for instance, is building the world's biggest online department store so that shoppers can get whatever they want with one click on their Web browsers. Like a traditional department store or mass merchandiser, Amazon offers considerable width in its product assortment with millions of different items, including books, music, toys, videos, tools and hardware, health and beauty aids, electronics, and software. Conversely, online specialty retailers, such as 1-800-Flowers.com, gloss.com makeup, and polo.com clothing, focus on a single category of merchandise, hoping to attract loyal customers with a larger depth of products at lower prices and better customer service. Many online retailers purposely focus on single product line niches that could never garner enough foot traffic to support a traditional brick-and-mortar store. For instance, The Mustard Place offers hundreds of different gourmet mustards, along with information on

retailing mix
A combination of the six Ps—product, place, promotion, price, presentation, and personnel—to sell goods and services to the ultimate consumer.

product offering
The mix of products offered to the consumer by the retailer; also called the *product assortment* or *merchandise mix.*

Publix

What brand name does Publix use for its private label? How extensive is the grocer's private-label product mix? Assess the growth potential for the private-label brand and propose other types of products that Publix could put under that label.

http://www.publix.com

Online

mustard and recipes.[31] Similarly, Fridgedoor.com claims to be the single largest stop for all things magnetic: novelty magnets, custom magnets, and magnetic supplies. It is the Web's largest refrigerator magnet retailer, with over 1,500 different types of magnets for sale.[32]

After determining what products will satisfy target customers' desires, retailers must find sources of supply and evaluate the products. When the right products are found, the retail buyer negotiates a purchase contract. The buying function can either be performed in-house or be delegated to an outside firm. The goods must then be moved from the seller to the retailer, which means shipping, storing, and stocking the inventory. The trick is to manage the inventory by cutting prices to move slow goods and by keeping adequate supplies of hot-selling items in stock. As in all good systems, the final step is to evaluate the entire process to seek more efficient methods and eliminate problems and bottlenecks.

As margins drop and competition intensifies, retailers are becoming ever more aware of the advantages of *private brands,* or those brands that are designed and developed using the retailer's name. Because the cost of goods typically makes up between 60 and 75 percent of a retailer's expenses, eliminating intermediaries can shave costs. As a result, prices of private-label goods are typically lower than for national brands, giving customers greater value. Private-label branding is not new. For decades, Sears has fashioned its Kenmore, Craftsman, and DieHard brands into household names. Wal-Mart has several successful private-label brands such as White Cloud paper products, Spring Valley nutritional supplements, Sam's American Choice laundry detergent, EverActive alkaline batteries, and EverStart auto batteries. Its Ol' Roy dog food and Sam's American Choice garden fertilizer are now the best-selling brands in their categories.

As the world's largest retailer, Wal-Mart's foray into private labels worries many brand marketers, such as Procter & Gamble, which manufactures Tide laundry detergent. Whereas Wal-Mart was once its biggest customer, the giant retailer is transforming itself into P&G's biggest competitor with the introduction of Sam's American Choice laundry soap that sells for 25 to 30 percent lower. And while Wal-Mart's private labels may not steal significant sales away from popular brands like Tide, in the long run smaller second- and third-tier brands that don't bring consumers to the shelves may have a difficult time surviving.

Promotion Strategy

Retail promotion strategy includes advertising, public relations and publicity, and sales promotion. The goal is to help position the store in consumers' minds. Retailers design intriguing ads, stage special events, and develop promotions aimed at their target markets. Today's grand openings are a carefully orchestrated blend of advertising, merchandising, goodwill, and glitter. All the elements of an opening—press coverage, special events, media advertising, and store displays—are carefully planned. For example, when Victoria's Secret opened its megastore in Dallas, the opening featured a $150 gift with a $50 purchase, free makeovers from a Victoria's Secret Fashion Show makeup artist, $10 gift cards that could be redeemed in the store, and an appearance by supermodel Heidi Klum.

Retailers' advertising is carried out mostly at the local level. Local advertising by retailers usually provides specific information about their stores, such as location, merchandise, hours, prices, and special sales. In contrast, national retail advertising generally focuses on image. For example, Target has used its "sign of the times" advertising campaign to effectively position itself as the "chic place to buy cheap."

Target's advertising campaign also takes advantage of cooperative advertising, another popular retail advertising practice. Traditionally, marketers would pay retailers to feature their products in store mailers, or a marketer would develop a TV campaign for the product and simply tack on several retailers' names at the end. But Target's advertising makes use of a more collaborative trend by integrating products such as Tide laundry detergent, Tums antacids, or Coca-Cola into the actual campaign. Another common form of cooperative advertising involves promotion of exclusive products. For example, Target hires famous designers to develop reasonably priced product lines available exclusively at Target stores.

Many retailers are forgoing media advertising these days in favor of direct-mail or frequent shopper programs. Direct-mail and catalog programs are luring many retailers, which hope they will prove to be a cost-effective means of increasing brand loyalty and spending by core customers. Nordstrom, for example, mails catalogs featuring brand-name and private-brand clothing, shoes, and accessories to target the shop-at-home crowd. Home repair outlets such as Lowe's and Home Depot also use direct mail, often around holidays when people have time off to complete needed repairs. Restaurants and small retailers have successfully used frequent diner or frequent shopper programs for years. Now many retail chains, like Gap, DSW, and Eddie Bauer, are offering frequent shopper programs with perks ranging from gift certificates to special "members only" sale prices. For example, customers with a Victoria's Secret Angel credit card are offered monthly specials on store merchandise, including items that generally are not put on sale to the public.

The Proper Location

The retailing axiom "location, location, location" has long emphasized the importance of place to the retail mix. The location decision is important first because the retailer is making a large, semipermanent commitment of resources that can reduce its future flexibility. Second, the location will affect the store's future growth and profitability.

Site location begins by choosing a community. Important factors to consider are the area's economic growth potential, the amount of competition, and geography. For instance, retailers like T. J. Maxx, Wal-Mart, and Target build stores in areas where the population is growing. Often these large retailers will build stores in new communities that are still under development. On the other hand, while population growth is an important consideration for fast-food restaurants, most also look for an area with other fast-food restaurants because being located in clusters helps to draw customers for each restaurant. Finally, for many retailers geography remains the most important factor in choosing a community. For example, Starbucks coffee looks for densely populated urban communities for its stores, Talbots looks for locations near upper-class neighborhoods, and Buckle stores look for locations in small, underserved cities.

After settling on a geographic region or community, retailers must choose a specific site. In addition to growth potential, the important factors are neighborhood socioeconomic characteristics, traffic flows, land costs, zoning regulations, and public transportation. A particular site's visibility, parking, entrance and exit locations, accessibility, and safety and security are also considered. Additionally, a retailer should consider how its store would fit into the surrounding environment. Retail decision makers probably would not locate a Dollar General store next door to a Neiman Marcus department store.

Retailers face one final decision about location: whether to have a freestanding unit or to become a tenant in a shopping center or mall.

Freestanding Stores   An isolated, freestanding location can be used by large retailers like Wal-Mart or Target and sellers of shopping goods like furniture and cars because they are "destination" stores. **Destination stores** are stores consumers seek out and purposely plan to visit. An isolated store location may have the advantages of low site cost or rent and no nearby competitors. On the other hand, it may be hard to attract customers to a freestanding location, and no other retailers are around to share costs.

Freestanding units are increasing in popularity as retailers strive to make their stores more convenient to access, more enticing to shop, and more profitable. Freestanding sites now account for more than half of all retail construction in the United States as more and more retailers are deciding not to locate in pedestrian malls. Perhaps the greatest reason for developing a freestanding site is greater visibility. Retailers often feel they get lost in huge centers and malls, but freestanding units can help stores develop an identity with shoppers. The ability to grow at faster rates through freestanding buildings has also

destination stores
Stores that consumers purposely plan to visit.

propelled the surge toward stand-alone units. Retailers like The Sports Authority, Linens N Things, Best Buy, and Bed Bath & Beyond choose to be freestanding to achieve their expansion objectives. An aggressive expansion plan may not allow time to wait for shopping centers to be built. Similarly, drugstore chains like Walgreens and Rite-Aid have been aggressively relocating their existing mall and shopping center stores to freestanding sites, especially street corner sites for drive-through accessibility.

Shopping Centers Shopping centers began in the 1950s when the U.S. population started migrating to the suburbs. The first shopping centers were *strip centers,* typically located along busy streets. They usually included a supermarket, a variety store, and perhaps a few specialty stores. Then *community shopping centers* emerged, with one or two small department stores, more specialty stores, a couple of restaurants, and several apparel stores. These community shopping centers provided off-street parking and a broader variety of merchandise.

Regional malls offering a much wider variety of merchandise started appearing in the mid-1970s. Regional malls are either entirely enclosed or roofed to allow shopping in any weather. Most are landscaped with trees, fountains, sculptures, and the like to enhance the shopping environment. They have acres of free parking. The *anchor stores* or *generator stores* (JCPenney, Sears, or major department stores) are usually located at opposite ends of the mall to create heavy foot traffic. Las Vegas's Fashion Show Mall takes the concept to the extreme. The mall has 2 million square feet of retail space and boasts over 250 stores, eight of which are anchor stores, including Neiman Marcus, Saks Fifth Avenue, Macy's, Bloomingdale Home, and Nordstrom.

According to shopping center developers, the newest generation of shopping centers are *lifestyle centers.* These new open-air shopping centers are targeted to upper-income shoppers with an aversion for "the mall" and seek to create an atmosphere that is part neighborhood park and part urban shopping center. Lifestyle centers typically combine outdoor shopping areas comprised of upscale retailers and restaurants, with plazas, fountains, and pedestrian streets. Newer centers like the Easton Town Center in Columbus, Ohio and the Legacy Town Center in Plano, Texas, also include luxury apartments and condominiums. Lifestyle centers are appealing to retail developers looking for an alternative to the traditional shopping mall, a concept rapidly losing favor among shoppers. According to the International Council of Shopping Centers, a New York City-based trade group, over 60 lifestyle centers were planned to open in 2006 and 2007. By stark contrast, only one new mall opened in 2006.[33]

Locating in a community shopping center or regional mall offers several advantages. First, the facilities are designed to attract shoppers. Second, the shopping environment, anchor stores, and "village square" activities draw customers. Third, ample parking is available. Fourth, the center or mall projects a unified image. Fifth, tenants also share the expenses of the mall's common area and promotions for the whole mall. Finally, malls can target different demographic groups. Some malls are considered upscale; others are aimed at people shopping for bargains.

Locating in a shopping center or mall does have disadvantages. These include expensive leases, the chance that common promotion efforts will not attract customers to a particular store, lease restrictions on merchandise carried and hours of operation, the anchor stores' domination of the tenants' association, and the possibility of having direct competitors within the same facility. Consumers have also become more pressed for time in recent years and are choosing more convenient stand-alone stores and neighborhood centers instead of malls. Faced with this trend, mall developers have improved the layout of many malls to make it

PHOTO COURTESY OF MALL OF AMERICA

In addition to being commercial centers, shopping malls were once a hub of community social activity. Lately, however, malls have struggled to compete against newer lifestyle centers and freestanding stores. Even with 520 stores, Mall of America regularly adds rides to its entertainment section to attract shoppers.

more convenient for customers to shop. For instance, the RiverTown Crossings center in Grandville, Michigan, clusters competing stores, like Abercrombie Kids, GapKids, Gymboree, and other kids' clothing stores in one section of the mall to accommodate time-strapped parents.[34]

Retail Prices

Another important element in the retailing mix is price. Retailing's ultimate goal is to sell products to consumers, and the right price is critical in ensuring sales. Because retail prices are usually based on the cost of the merchandise, an essential part of pricing is efficient and timely buying.

Price is also a key element in a retail store's positioning strategy. Higher prices often indicate a level of quality and help reinforce the prestigious image of retailers, such as Tiffany, Saks Fifth Avenue, Gucci, Cartier, and Neiman Marcus. On the other hand, discounters and off-price retailers, such as Target and T. J. Maxx, offer good value for the money. There are even stores, such as Dollar Tree, where everything costs one dollar. Dollar Tree's single-price-point strategy is aimed at getting customers to make impulse purchases through what analysts call the "wow factor"—the excitement of discovering that an item costs only a dollar.

A pricing trend among American retailers that seems to be here to stay is *everyday low pricing,* or EDLP. Introduced to the retail industry by Wal-Mart, EDLP offers consumers a low price all the time rather than holding periodic sales on merchandise. Even large retail giants, like Federated Department Stores, parent of Macy's and Bloomingdale's, have phased out deep discounts and sales in favor of lower prices every day. Similarly, Gap reduced prices on denim jeans, denim shirts, socks, and other items to protect and broaden the company's share of the casual clothes market. Supermarkets such as Albertson's and Winn-Dixie have also found success in EDLP.

Presentation of the Retail Store

The presentation of a retail store helps determine the store's image and positions the retail store in consumers' minds. For instance, a retailer that wants to position itself as an upscale store would use a lavish or sophisticated presentation.

The main element of a store's presentation is its **atmosphere,** the overall impression conveyed by a store's physical layout, decor, and surroundings. The atmosphere might create a relaxed or busy feeling, a sense of luxury or of efficiency, a friendly or cold attitude, a sense of organization or of clutter, or a fun or serious mood. For example, Wolfgang Puck restaurants feature tiles in the shape of a pizza on the floors, walls, and countertops. Urban Outfitters stores, targeted to Generation Y consumers, use raw concrete, original brick, rusted steel, and unfinished wood to convey an urban feel. Likewise, REI sporting-goods stores feature indoor rock-climbing walls, bike test trails, and rain rooms for testing outdoor gear.

The layout of retail stores is a key factor in their success. The goal is to use all space in the store effectively, including aisles, fixtures, merchandise displays, and nonselling areas. In addition to making shopping easy and convenient for the customer, an effective layout has a powerful influence on customer traffic patterns and purchasing behavior. For instance, Kohl's unique circular layout encourages customers to pass all of a store's departments to reach the checkout lanes. The stores are smaller than most department stores but have a wide aisle with plenty of room for customers and shopping carts. Each department is limited to five display racks on the main aisle. Displays are spaced widely and are set at varying heights so that customers can see everything in the department, including wall displays, from the main aisle. To further enhance the store's clean crisp presentation, merchandise is displayed from light to dark, which research suggests is most pleasing to the eye. Finally, to encourage last-minute, impulse purchases, Kohl's displays low-cost items at the checkout register. Together with other merchandising strategies, the store layout generates an average of over $300 in sales per square foot (this is a standard industry measure) in Kohl's almost 750 stores in 41 states and contributed to a sales increase of almost 15 percent in 2005.[35]

atmosphere
The overall impression conveyed by a store's physical layout, decor, and surroundings.

Layout also includes where products are placed in the store. Many technologically advanced retailers are using a technique called *market-basket analysis* to analyze the huge amounts of data collected through their point-of-purchase scanning equipment. The analysis looks for products that are commonly purchased together to help retailers place products in the right places. Wal-Mart uses market-basket analysis to determine where in the store to stock products for customer convenience. Bananas are placed not only in the produce section but also in the cereal aisle. Kleenex tissues are in the paper-goods aisle and also mixed in with the cold medicines. Measuring spoons are in the housewares and also hanging next to Crisco shortening. During October, flashlights are with the Halloween costumes as well as in the hardware aisle.

These are the most influential factors in creating a store's atmosphere:

- *Employee type and density:* Employee type refers to an employee's general characteristics—for instance, neat, friendly, knowledgeable, or service oriented. Density is the number of employees per thousand square feet of selling space. A discounter like Kmart has a low employee density that creates a "do-it-yourself," casual atmosphere. In contrast, Neiman Marcus's density is much higher, denoting readiness to serve the customer's every whim. Too many employees and not enough customers, however, can convey an air of desperation and intimidate customers.

- *Merchandise type and density:* The type of merchandise carried and how it is displayed add to the atmosphere the retailer is trying to create. A prestigious retailer like Saks or Bloomingdale's carries the best brand names and displays them in a neat, uncluttered arrangement. Discounters and off-price retailers, such as Marshall's and T. J. Maxx, may sell some well-known brands. But many carry seconds or out-of-season goods. Their merchandise is crowded into small spaces and hung on long racks by category—tops, pants, skirts, etc.—to create the impression that "We've got so much stuff, we're practically giving it away."

- *Fixture type and density:* Fixtures can be elegant (rich woods), trendy (chrome and smoked glass), or consist of old, beat-up tables, as in an antiques store. The fixtures should be consistent with the general atmosphere the store is trying to create. Apple has let its focus on design inform the look of its retail stores. Many Apple stores contain a signature glass staircase designed in part by CEO Steve Jobs, and all use large open tables to display company products. Because products are not cluttered on store shelves, it is easier for store visitors to play with them.[36]

- *Sound:* Sound can be pleasant or unpleasant for a customer. Classical music at a nice Italian restaurant helps create ambience, just as country-and-western music does at a truck stop. Music can also entice customers to stay in the store longer and buy more or eat quickly and leave a table for others. For instance, rapid music tends to make people eat more, chew less, and take bigger bites whereas slow music prompts people to dine more leisurely and eat less. Retailers can tailor their musical atmosphere to their shoppers' demographics and the merchandise they're selling. Music can control the pace of the store traffic, create an image, and attract or direct the shopper's attention. Starbucks has parlayed its unique in-store music selections

© APPLE COMPUTER, INC./PRNEWSFOTO

Apple reinvented how technology companies interact with customers by creating sleek company-owned stores that showcase entire product lines. The stores have been a critical factor in building and reinforcing Apple's brand with consumers.

into a new business with its Hear Music Channel on XM Satellite Radio, its Hear Music Cafés, and kiosks selling featured Hear Music artists in most Starbucks locations.

- *Odors:* Smell can either stimulate or detract from sales. The wonderful smell of pastries and breads entices bakery customers. Conversely, customers can be repulsed by bad odors such as cigarette smoke, musty smells, antiseptic odors, and overly powerful room deodorizers. If a grocery store pumps in the smell of baked goods, sales in that department increase threefold. Department stores have pumped in fragrances that are pleasing to their target market, and the response has been favorable. Not surprisingly, retailers are increasingly using fragrance as a key design element, as important as layout, lighting, and background music. Research suggests that people evaluate merchandise more positively, spend more time shopping, and are generally in a better mood when an agreeable odor is present. Retailers use fragrances as an extension of their retail strategy. The Rainforest Cafe, for instance, pumps fresh-flower extracts into its retail sections. Similarly, the Christmas Store at Disney World, which is open year-round, is infused with the scents of evergreen and spiced apple cider. Jordan's Furniture in Massachusetts and New Hampshire uses the scent of pine in its country-style sections to make the environment more interesting and encourage customers to linger longer.

- *Visual factors:* Colors can create a mood or focus attention and therefore are an important factor in atmosphere. Red, yellow, and orange are considered warm colors and are used when a feeling of warmth and closeness is desired. Cool colors like blue, green, and violet are used to open up closed-in places and create an air of elegance and cleanliness. For example, Starbucks Coffee uses an eggplant, golden yellow, and dark olive color combination so that customers will feel comfortable yet sophisticated. Some colors are better for display. For instance, diamonds appear most striking against black or dark blue velvet. Lighting can also have an important effect on store atmosphere. Jewelry is best displayed under high-intensity spotlights and cosmetics under more natural lighting. Many retailers have found that natural lighting, either from windows or skylights, can lead to increased sales. Outdoor lighting can also affect consumer patronage. Consumers often are afraid to shop after dark in many areas and prefer strong lighting for safety. The outdoor facade of the store also adds to its ambience and helps create favorable first impressions. For example, during a renovation in 2005, the façade of the Louis Vuitton store on the Champs Elysées in Paris was covered such that it looked like a giant signature suitcase. Without that exaggerated storefront, shoppers would have been unable to identify the store beneath the scaffolding.

Personnel and Customer Service

People are a unique aspect of retailing. Most retail sales involve a customer–salesperson relationship, if only briefly. When customers shop at a grocery store, the cashiers check and bag their groceries. When customers shop at a prestigious clothier, the salesclerks may help select the styles, sizes, and colors. They may also assist in the fitting process, offer alteration services, wrap purchases, and even offer a glass of champagne. Sales personnel provide their customers with the amount of service prescribed in the retail strategy of the store.

Retail salespeople serve another important selling function: They persuade shoppers to buy. They must therefore be able to persuade customers that what they are selling is what the customer needs. Salespeople are trained in two common selling techniques: trading up and suggestion selling. Trading up means persuading customers to buy a higher-priced item than they originally intended to buy. To avoid selling customers something they do not need or want, however, salespeople should take care when practicing trading-up techniques. Suggestion selling, a common practice among most retailers, seeks to broaden customers' original purchases with related items. For example, if you buy a new printer at Office Depot, the sales representative will ask if you would like to purchase paper, a USB cable, and/or extra ink cartridges. Similarly, McDonald's cashiers are trained to ask customers if they would like a hot apple pie with their hamburger and fries. Suggestion selling and trading up should always help shoppers recognize true needs rather than sell them unwanted merchandise.

LO6

List the major tasks involved in developing a retail marketing strategy

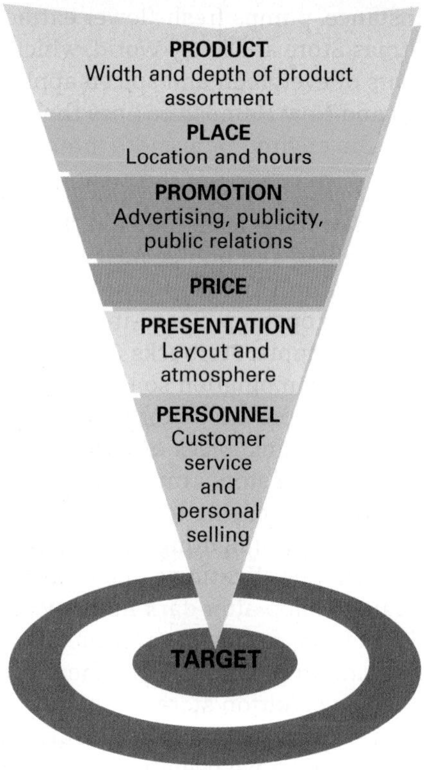

PRODUCT
Width and depth of product assortment

PLACE
Location and hours

PROMOTION
Advertising, publicity, public relations

PRICE

PRESENTATION
Layout and atmosphere

PERSONNEL
Customer service and personal selling

TARGET

Providing great customer service is one of the most challenging elements in the retail mix because customer expectations for service are so varied. What customers expect in a department store is very different from their expectations for a discount store. Customer expectations also change. Ten years ago, shoppers wanted personal one-on-one attention. Today, most customers are happy to help themselves as long as they can easily find what they need. For example, Home Depot has always had a reputation for great customer service. Shoppers enjoy talking to the store's knowledge-able staff in the busy, do-it-yourself, warehouse atmosphere. But as store sales increased, the company began receiving customer feedback that the salespeople seemed too busy to help and the stores were too cluttered. To meet customers' new expectations, the company changed its store policy to free up staff time to help customers and eliminated merchandise displays from the aisles.

Customer service is also critical for online retailers. Online shoppers expect a retailer's Web site to be easy to use, products to be available, and returns to be simple. Therefore, customer-friendly retailers like Bluefly.com design their sites to give their customers the information they need such as what's new and what's on sale. Other companies like Amazon.com and LandsEnd.com offer product recommendations and personal shoppers. Some retailers that have online, catalog, and traditional brick-and-mortar stores, such as Lands' End, Gap, and Williams-Sonoma, now allow customers to return goods bought through the catalog or online to their traditional store to make returns easier.

LO7

New Developments in Retailing

In an effort to better serve their customers and attract new ones, retailers are constantly adopting new strategies. Two recent developments are interactivity and m-commerce.

INTERACTIVITY

Adding interactivity to the retail environment is one of the most popular strategies in retailing in the past few years. Small retailers as well as national chains are using interactivity in stores to differentiate themselves from the competition. For some time, retailers have used "entertainment" retailing in the form of playing music, showing videos, hosting

Build-A-Bear is a 100 percent interactive retailing concept. Children choose an empty fabric shell and take it to a special station where they place a plush heart into their animal before a sales associate adds the stuffing. Children move to the next station to simulate washing and fluffing their animal. Finally they select an outfit to dress their animal before proceeding to the checkout.

special events, and sponsoring guest appearances, but the new interactive trend gets customers involved rather than just catching their eye. For example, at the American Girl store in Chicago, customers can purchase a doll made to look like them, take their dolls to the in-store American Girl café, go to the American Girl Theater, and even have their birthday parties. Similarly, Build-A-Bear enables customers to make their own stuffed animal by choosing which animal to stuff and then dressing and naming it. You can hold birthday parties there, too. Involvement isn't just for children, either. For Your Entertainment, one of the country's leading specialty retailers of movies, music, and games, regularly invites artists to perform in its stores. Performers may be local favorites or national superstars like Ziggy Marley and Michael Bolton. FYE even dedicates part of its Web site to a state-by-state touring schedule and allows local performers to sign up to play at its stores. Fans can request to see a local group perform at an FYE store or ask the stores to stock recordings by their local favorites. Visit FYE's Web site and check out a show near you![37]

M-COMMERCE

M-commerce (mobile e-commerce) enables consumers using wireless mobile devices to connect to the Internet and shop. M-commerce enjoyed early success overseas, but has been gaining acceptance and popularity in the United States. Essentially, m-commerce goes beyond text message advertisements to allow consumers to purchase goods and services using wireless mobile devices, such as mobile telephones, pagers, personal digital assistants (PDAs), and handheld computers. For example, Coca-Cola drinkers in Europe just dial a phone number on their mobile device, and the machine will signal them to select a drink; the transaction appears on the next phone bill. A new vehicle for m-commerce is the XM-enabled portable MP3 player. Devices like the Helix from Samsung and Inno from Pioneer allow users to bookmark songs they like when they hear them on XM Satellite Radio. Later, when the player is docked to an Internet-connected port, the marked songs will be bought and automatically downloaded from Napster, thanks to a relationship it has with XM.[38]

M-commerce users adopt the new technology because it saves time and offers more convenience in a greater number of locations. One study of m-commerce users who use Web-enabled devices to conduct transactions found that they consider relevant content, easy site navigation, and mobile device compatibility to be very important.[39]

REVIEW LEARNING OUTCOME

LO7 **Describe new developments in retailing**

Interactivity gets consumers involved in retail experience.

M-commerce is purchasing goods through mobile devices.

Quick Check

Now that you've read the chapter, do you get it? Take a moment for a quick check using this scale:

1 Not at all; 2 Not very well; 3 Ok; 4 Well; 5 Very Well

Can you . . .

____ construct a table that shows how the types of retailers differ according to service, assortment, price, and margin?

____ identify and describe the major types of retail operations?

____ explain the options available in nonstore retailing?

____ write a paragraph describing the two different types of franchising?

____ identify the elements in a retailing mix?

____ describe the components of a store's atmosphere?

____ list the numerous types of discount stores?

____ explain to a friend the difference between direct marketing, direct retailing, and direct mail?

____ explain the correlation between margin and price?

____ TOTAL

Score: 37–45, you're ready to move on to the applications; 28–36, skim the chapter one more time before moving on to the applications; 19–27, reread the sections giving you the most trouble and go to Thomson NOW for guided tutorials; 18 and under, you better reread the chapter to get a grasp of the fundamentals. If you've reread the chapter and still have a low score, visit your professor or TA during office hours.

Review and Applications

LO 1 Discuss the importance of retailing in the U.S. economy. Retailing plays a vital role in the U.S. economy for two main reasons. First, retail businesses contribute to our high standard of living by providing a vast number and diversity of goods and services. Second, retailing employs a large part of the U.S. working population—over 15 million people.

1.1 To fully appreciate the role retailing plays in the U.S. economy, it may be helpful to review a selection of press articles related to the retailing industry. Search for articles pertaining to retailing. Read a selection of articles, and report your findings to the class.

LO 2 Explain the dimensions by which retailers can be classified. Many different kinds of retailers exist. A retail establishment can be classified according to its ownership, level of service, product assortment, and price. On the basis of ownership, retailers can be broadly differentiated as independent retailers, chain stores, or franchise outlets. The level of service retailers provide can be classified along a continuum of high to low. Retailers also classify themselves by the breadth and depth of their product assortments; some retailers have concentrated product assortments, whereas others have extensive product assortments. Last, general price levels also classify a store, from discounters offering low prices to exclusive specialty stores where high prices are the norm. Retailers use these latter three variables to position themselves in the marketplace.

2.1 Form a team of three classmates to identify different retail stores in your city where pet supplies are sold. Include nonstore forms of retailing, such as catalogs, the Internet, or the local veterinarian. Team members should divide up and visit all the different retailing outlets for pet supplies. Prepare a report describing the differences in brands and products sold at each of the retailing formats and the differences in store characteristics and service levels. For example, which brands are sold via mass merchandiser, independent specialty store, or other venue? Suggest why different products and brands are distributed through different types of stores.

LO 3 Describe the major types of retail operations. The major types of retail stores are department stores, specialty retailers, supermarkets, drugstores, convenience stores, discount stores, and restaurants. Department stores carry a wide assortment of shopping and specialty goods, are organized into relatively independent departments, and offset higher prices by emphasizing customer service and decor. Specialty retailers typically carry a narrower but deeper assortment of merchandise, emphasizing distinctive products and a high level of customer service. Supermarkets are large self-service retailers that offer a wide variety of food products and some nonfood items. Drugstores are retail formats that sell mostly prescription and over-the-counter medications, health and beauty aids, cosmetics, and specialty items. Convenience stores carry a limited line of high-turnover convenience goods. Discount stores offer low-priced general merchandise and consist of four types: full-line discounters, specialty discount retailers, warehouse clubs, and off-price retailers. Finally, restaurants straddle the line between the retailing and services industries; although restaurants sell a product, food and drink, to final consumers, they can also be considered service marketers because they provide consumers with the service of preparing food and providing table service.

3.1 Discuss the possible marketing implications of the recent trend toward supercenters, which combine a supermarket and a full-line discount store.

3.2 Explain the function of warehouse clubs. Why are they classified as both wholesalers and retailers?

LO4 Discuss nonstore retailing techniques. Nonstore retailing, which is shopping outside a store setting, has three major categories. Automatic vending uses machines to offer products for sale. In direct retailing, the sales transaction occurs in a home setting, typically through door-to-door sales or party plan selling. Direct marketing refers to the techniques used to get consumers to buy from their homes or place of business. Those techniques include direct mail, catalogs and mail order, telemarketing, and electronic retailing, such as home shopping channels and online retailing.

4.1 Go to the Gift Center at online wine retailer Wine.com's Web site at **http://www.wine.com/**. How does this site help shoppers select gifts?

4.2 How much does the most powerful computer with the fastest modem, most memory, largest monitor, biggest hard drive, and all the available peripherals cost at **http://www.dell.com**? Then visit a store like Best Buy or Circuit City and price a comparable computer. How can you explain any price differences between the two retail operations? Explain any differences in features that you encountered. What conclusions can you draw from your research?

4.3 Most catalog companies also offer online shopping. Visit the Web site of one of your favorite catalogs to see if you can buy online. If so, surf the online catalog for a few minutes. Then compare the two retailing methods (paper and Internet) for prices, products, and so forth. Which do you prefer—the paper catalog or online shopping? Why?

4.4 Do you think it's harder for a retailer that sells primarily through its catalog (like Delia's) or one that sells primarily through its retail outlets (like Gap) to make the transition to successful e-tailing? Check out the two Web sites and compare how they present their products, their site functionality, and the integration of all their retail venues.
http://www.gap.com
http://www.delias.com

LO5 Define franchising and describe its two basic forms. Franchising is a continuing relationship in which a franchisor grants to a franchisee the business rights to operate or to sell a product. Modern franchising takes two basic forms. In product and trade name franchising, a dealer agrees to buy or sell certain products or product lines from a particular manufacturer or wholesaler. Business format franchising is an ongoing business relationship in which a franchisee uses a franchisor's name, format, or method of business in return for several types of fees.

5.1 What advantages does franchising provide to franchisors as well as franchisees?

5.2 Curves is the world's largest fitness franchise and the fastest-growing franchise of any kind. What do you need to do to become a Curves franchisee? Visit the Web page (**http://www.curves.com**) to find out. Does anything surprise you?

LO6 List the major tasks involved in developing a retail marketing strategy. Retail management begins with defining the target market, typically on the basis of demographic, geographic, or psychographic characteristics. After determining the target market, retail managers must develop the six variables of the retailing mix: product, promotion, place, price, presentation, and personnel.

6.1 Identify a successful retail business in your community. What marketing strategies have led to its success?

6.2 How can a company create an atmosphere on its Web site? Visit the pages of some of your favorite retailers to see if they have been able to re-create the store atmosphere on the Internet.

LO7 Describe new developments in retailing. Two major trends are evident in retailing today. First, adding interactivity to the retail environment is one of the most popular strategies in retailing in recent years. Small retailers as well as national chains are using interactivity to involve customers and set themselves apart from the competition. Second, m-commerce (mobile e-commerce) is gaining in popularity. M-commerce enables consumers to purchase goods and services using wireless mobile devices, such as mobile telephones, pagers, PDAs, and handheld computers.

7.1 Make a list of stores that actively incorporate some kind of interactivity or entertainment into their retailing strategy. Now, make a list of stores that do not, such as office supply stores. Compare your two lists. Select a company from your second list and draft a strategy to help it become more interactive.

Key Terms

Exercises

APPLICATION EXERCISE

After reading the chapter, you can see that differences in retailing are the result of strategy. To better understand the relationship between strategic retailing factors and consumer perceptions, you can conduct a simple observation exercise. First, pick a product to shop for, and then identify two stores where you have *never* shopped as places to look for your product. The two stores must be different types of retailers. For example, you can shop for a new HDTV at Best Buy (category killer) and at Hollywood Video (specialty retailer). Once you have identified what you are looking for and where you're going to look, visit each store and record your observations of specific strategic retailing factors.[40]

Activities

1. Go through each store and make careful observations on the following:
   - *Location:* Where is each store? How congested is the area of town where each store is located? What influence does the neighborhood have on your impression

of the store? Would you travel to this store under normal circumstances? Write a detailed paragraph on the location of each store.

- *Exterior atmosphere:* How convenient is parking (is there even parking?)? Is parking adequate? Other issues about parking (cleanliness and size of the lot, size of spaces, well-lit, etc.)? What kinds of stores are around the store you are visiting? Do you think being located next to them increases traffic at your store? Are direct competitors nearby? Is the building modern, historic, attractive, clean, and appealing? Is the entrance inviting to shoppers?

- *Interior atmosphere:* Compare the following attributes at each store: aisle width; lighting; number of customers; noise (background music, loudspeakers, etc.); store layout; signage; accessibility of the cashier; number of products available (depth and width of assortment); ability to inspect the product before purchase; quality of the fixtures (shelves, lights, etc.); availability of salespeople and their knowledge about the product; willingness of salespeople to help.

- *Product:* Is your product available? If not, is there a satisfactory substitute? What is your perception of the quality of goods offered? Why do you think as you do?

- *Price:* What is the price of the product/brand at this store? Is the price prominently marked? How do the prices at the two stores compare? How does the price compare to your expectations?

2. What are the three most important differences you observed between the stores?

3. From which of these two stores would you actually purchase the item? Why, specifically? List the factors that played a role in your decision. Which factor is most important to you? If you would not purchase the item at either store, why not?

4. Using the results of your research, write a short paper that outlines your observations. Conclude your paper with your answers to questions 2 and 3.

Entrepreneurship Case

BEST BUY GIVES A WHOLE NEW MEANING TO "THOUSANDS OF POSSIBILITIES. GET YOURS."

The promise of the long-awaited digital revolution has finally been fulfilled. Flat-panel televisions, MP3 players, wireless laptops, cell phones with Internet browsing capability, wirelessly networked computing devices for the home, digitally controlled home appliances, and more are no longer the toys of a future generation. They are here today, and Best Buy wants to sell them—all of them—to anyone with the money to burn on such luxury items. In addition to all the gee-whiz electronic merchandise, the company still sells coffee makers, vacuum cleaners, and washing machines, albeit slightly more expensive ones than before.

The new digital gadgets, however, are fast crossing the threshold from expensive luxury items to affordable common electronics. The upside is that more customers are able to buy such products; the downside is the negative pressure put on prices and revenues. If any retailer can find a way to survive and turn a profit in the fiercely competitive electronics and home appliance industry, it's Best Buy. Twenty years ago, when it operated under the name Sound of Music, a tornado ripped through its flagship store, and the company held a "best buy" sale to liquidate its merchandise and cover the costs of repairs. The success of the sale was the impetus for the name change to Best Buy, and the opening of its first superstore in 1984 marked the beginning of "big box" retailing as it is known today. Nine years later, the new-look national chain surpassed Circuit City as the number one retailer in the segment.

Best Buy's stores offer a dizzying array of products (its stores have nearly 25,000 separate items) at affordable prices. Usually located in small- or medium-sized outdoor shopping centers with other "big box" retailers, an average 40,000-square-foot Best Buy store is large enough to hold ample stock of all available items while still comfortably accommodating customers. Bright lights, concrete floors, wide and easily navigated aisles, oversize shopping carts, and a helpful but unobtrusive staff dressed in blue shirts and khaki pants have put Best Buy at the head of the retail class when it comes to customer satisfaction surveys. Best Buy's television commercials, which feature the tagline, "Thousands of Possibilities. Get Yours," communicate an accurate picture of the customer experience. Inside every Best Buy store, a canned deejay plays the latest popular music over the public address system; recently released DVDs play on big-screen TVs; and personal computers, video game modules, home stereo systems, and more are turned on and available for customers to tinker with.

The ability to connect with its customers has brought Best Buy a 16 percent share of the $130 billion North American market for electronics and related devices. It now operates 600 stores in the United States and plans to open 60 or so new stores each year for the near future. Competition, however, is stiffening. Best Buy's main threat now comes from discount superstore Wal-Mart, whose share of the market has climbed rapidly to just 5 percentage points behind Best Buy's. That development, combined with a downward pressure on prices for electronic devices similar to the pressures in the PC industry, has forced Best Buy to explore new and more profitable ways of meeting the needs of the market.

The firm's latest initiatives include selling more upscale and higher-margin merchandise, hiring highly trained sales "consultants" to assist with more complex and expensive purchases, staying open for longer hours on weekends, outsourcing lower-end items to China, and selling installation and connection services for its products. Those who prefer to shop in their pajamas can check out the possibilities online at BestBuy.com. Best Buy is also selling home entertainment packages direct to upscale homebuilders in cities such as Minneapolis, Dallas, and Las Vegas. For a nominal surcharge as low as $1,000, Best Buy will install, connect, and integrate the system while the house is being constructed, leaving the home's new owner to sit back and enjoy the show.[41]

Questions

1. What type of retailer is Best Buy?

2. Describe the six components of Best Buy's retailing mix. Is there anything you would change? Explain.

3. Do you agree with the strategy Best Buy has adopted to respond to its competition? Why or why not?

© NKP MEDIA, INC./THOMSON

COMPANY CLIPS

Sephora—Retailing for Success

From the beginning, Sephora has carried quality skincare products. Excellent retailing techniques, however, are the real driving force behinds Sephora's success. The company's open-sale environment allows consumers to try any product, or even take home a free sample, before they buy. A great location in the heart of the New York City retail district makes it easy for Sephora to attract potential buyers. Sephora also invests a lot of time and money into training their sales staff so that when customers enter the store, they gain a total shopping experience in which their every need is met. The salespeople are not paid on commission so they are free to give honest recommendations of products that would be best for their customers. As you watch the video, notice what other retailing methods Sephora uses to promote sales.

Questions

1. Visit www.Sephora.com and browse the online store. How does Sephora use the online environment to promote its products without the advantage of letting customers try before they buy?

2. Sephora is working out the details of a new loyalty program and they have asked you to give your input and advice. What do you tell them? How should they integrate this new program with the retailing mix they have already adopted?

BIZ FLIX

MAN'S FAVORITE SPORT/CORBIS

Man's Favorite Sport

Now that you understand retailing, you can appreciate the changes that retailing has experienced over the years. As an encore to your study, watch the film clip from *Man's Favorite Sport,* starring Rock Hudson as a salesman (Roger Willoughby) at Abercrombie & Fitch. In this scene, Roger enters his department and greets Major Phipps (Roscoe Karns), who is looking for a new fly rod to use in a local fishing competition. The scene shows an Abercrombie & Fitch of the 1960s, when the store was an upscale outdoor sporting-goods retailer, much like Orvis, Cabelas, and Galyan's. Now, however, the retailing mix for Abercrombie & Fitch is quite different. If you are unfamiliar with today's Abercrombie & Fitch, visit the company's Web site at **http://www.abercrombie.com**. How has the company changed its target market and its retailing mix? Even though the market and strategy have changed, is Abercrombie & Fitch the same type of retailer today as it was in the 1960s? Explain.

Marketing & You Results

If your score was on the low side, it means you don't find shopping in stores to be enjoyable. The higher your score, the more likely you are to think shopping is a fun activity. But beware: a high score can also indicate a tendency toward being a compulsive buyer!

Marketing Miscue

Retail Embargo of Harry Potter Book Violated

The sixth title in the magical tales of Harry Potter, *Harry Potter and the Half-Blood Prince*, was released on July 16, 2005, and quickly sold 10.8 million copies. This was a world record for the first printing of a book, but the records it broke were set by earlier books in the Harry Potter series. The fourth title, *Harry Potter and the Goblet of Fire*, was hailed as the "fastest-selling book in history" when it sold 3 million copies in the first 48 hours after its release in July 2000. Three years later, *Harry Potter and the Order of the Phoenix* took over the record. Only eight years after the publication of the first book in the series, *Harry Potter and the Sorcerer's Stone*, the Harry Potter series has sold over a quarter of a billion copies; the books have been translated into 61 languages and are distributed in more than 200 countries.

Like the other books in the series, the sixth title was introduced with much fanfare and secrecy. Author J. K. Rowling says she wants readers to be the first to know a book's contents. Therefore, there are no published previews of new Harry Potter books, so the media cannot leak any secrets and steal the thunder. Naturally, such secrecy increases the hype about the book. Harry Potter followers gather to wait in long lines for the 12:01 A.M. opening of bookstores on the release date. On Thursday, July 7, 2005, however, an employee at the Real Canadian Superstore in Coquitlam, British Columbia, inadvertently sold 14 copies of the new book nine days before the scheduled release. The employee, apparently not a Harry Potter fan, did not know about the sales embargo and sold the books by mistake.

Scholastic, a global publishing and media giant, is the American publisher of the Harry Potter book series. With revenues of over $2 billion, this publisher of children's material reaches a market of over 35 million children and 40 million parents. Though the company publishes over 750

new books annually, the release of a new Harry Potter book has a significant impact on both the company's image and its bottom line. Scholastic says that it ships the books in steel container trucks that require retailers to use bolt cutters to open containers just before midnight at the time of the planned release.

The Real Canadian Superstore, which sold the early copies, received its books from Raincoast Books, Ltd., the distributor of the Harry Potter books in Canada. Raincoast learned of the illegal early sales when a customer, in the spirit of preserving Harry mania, informed Raincoast that he had purchased a copy of the book from the superstore. Raincoast acted quickly and obtained an injunction from the British Columbia Supreme Court that forbade the purchasers from copying or disclosing any part of the book prior to 12:01 A.M. on July 16. In addition, Raincoast attempted to entice the purchasers of the 14 books to temporarily return their books by offering them Harry Potter memorabilia, including a J. K. Rowling autographed book plate. This was not the first time Harry Potter's publishers had gone to court to preserve the mystique surrounding the books. A similar situation occurred with the fifth book, when a bookstore clerk who claimed he was unaware of the restriction, sold copies that led one newspaper to plan an early review of the book. Thus, the 2005 injunction in British Columbia included a provision prohibiting the media from publishing advance reviews or articles discussing specific aspects of the book's plot or characters.

Although the early sales of the 14 books were clearly just a mistake by the superstore, some wondered whether the injunction actually created even more hype about the upcoming book release. The distribution mistake ultimately led to increased publicity for *Harry Potter and the Half-Blood Prince*.[1]

Questions

1. What is the distributor's role in creating and maintaining Harry mania?

2. Identify the major players in the distribution of Harry Potter books.

Critical Thinking Case

Whole Foods Thrives in a Declining Marketplace

In a marketplace where businesses are experiencing flat to declining growth, Whole Foods Market is gaining in share of wallet. Not only is the food chain profiting in grocery retailing, one of the toughest businesses in the world, but the company's goal is to more than double its sales to $10 billion by 2010. Whole Foods is challenging both the way supermarkets do business and the way consumers shop for food. Americans spend $430 billion a year on food at approximately 34,000 supermarkets. Yet the typical grocery retailer makes only one cent on every dollar spent in the store. This low margin is the impetus behind vendor allowances and slotting fees (fees paid by food producers to have a supermarket carry their products), which netted grocery stores close to $100 billion in 2003. Whole Foods refuses to take slotting fees, however, and accepted only about $1 million in other inducements in 2004. The company's niche is in organic foods that carry a price premium of 40 to 175 percent over regular goods—a niche market that provides Whole Foods with a profit margin that is triple the industry standard and sales per square foot of $800, double the industry standard.

In the mid-1950s, consumers were spending 17 percent of their total income on groceries. By 2005, however, consumers were spending only 6 percent of their total income on groceries. Major supermarket chains were experiencing shrinking profits or losses. Considering that 2004 profits fell nearly 30 percent at Safeway and 6 percent at Albertson's while A&P, Pathmark, and Winn-Dixie experienced almost $200 million in losses, can Whole Foods attain its sales goal by 2010? Just as important, how has this grocery retailer managed to increase its net income by 32 percent when other supermarket chains are experiencing shrinking profits or losses?

Whole Foods Market started in 1987 as a health food store in Austin, Texas. The company went public in 1992, and by the beginning of 2005 it had 166 stores (157 in the United States, 7 in Britain, and 2 in Canada) and 60 more stores under development in the three countries. Though the company ranks only twenty-first in grocery retailing

sales, it ranks fourth in both profits and in total stock market value among publicly held grocery store chains. Whole Foods was ranked 479 in *Fortune* magazine's list of the 500 largest publicly traded U.S. companies.

Its quality standards are what sets Whole Foods apart from traditional grocery retailers. With just over 12,000 organic farms in the United States, the farmers have few opportunities to use economies of scale to reduce costs. Additionally, organic farming is much more labor-intensive than conventional farming. Whole Foods passes these higher costs on to the consumer and does not attempt to compete on price. Thus, Whole Foods customers are ensured a high-quality offering and are willing to pay a higher price for that quality.

To reach its sales objective for 2010, Whole Foods is making food shopping an entertainment experience. The company intends to expand its customer base by making the shopping experience fun— one Whole Foods executive refers to its stores as food amusement parks. The company has already begun implementing its food entertainment strategy. Early in 2005, an 80,000-square-foot store opened in the company's hometown of Austin, Texas. Consumers can stroll the aisles with a glass of wine and watch the store's seafood team lob salmon back and forth, its pastry chefs roll dough, and its chefs prepare food for immediate (or later) consumption. Consumers can even become part of the ensemble by grinding their own flour or partaking in exchanges about the culinary arts. If the entertainment experience becomes too exhausting, the customer can take a break and get a massage (in the store, of course). Whole Foods stores in Atlanta, Georgia, already have or are planning a chocolate fountain (with free samples), wine-tasting stations, a wine and cheese island, a caviar and champagne station, and a grilling station with open flame to appeal to the southern love for brisket and ribs. For impatient New Yorkers, a Whole Foods store in New York City installed 26 cash registers and a line director to speed the checkout process.

The company has decided that the grocery consumers of the future will want either the cheapest groceries in town or the best groceries in town. Whole Foods wants to provide the best.[2]

Questions

1. Describe niche marketing as it pertains to Whole Foods and grocery retailing.

2. Compare the characteristics of Whole Foods with those of traditional grocery retailers.

PART 5

Promotion
Decisions

CROSS-FUNCTIONAL
CONNECTIONS

The marketing communications program is a critical element of the customer acquisition and retention process. When purchasing a product or service, however, customers do not think in terms of advertising, sales promotion, public relations, and personal selling; nor do they think in terms of marketing, manufacturing, accounting, finance, research and development, and human resources. Rather, the product or service received by the customer is the sum of all of the internal and external processes. It is the company's responsibility to make certain that the product/ service received by the customer is consistent with the message that the customer has received via the firm's integrated marketing communications.

Unfortunately, advertising and other promotional efforts tend to be a source of friction between marketing and financial managers. Such expenditures are generally viewed as cost elements rather than investments in the product or brand. Marketers, however, view these expenditures as investments in building the business. Customer satisfaction and repeat business depend on constant maintenance by the marketing department. In contrast, accountants view advertising and promotional expenses as variable costs. Unfortunately, viewed as variable costs, advertising expenses are tied directly to sales increases and decreases, so marketing budgets are often cut when they are needed most.

When a company's communications strategy

focuses on promoting the product's quality features, pressure is placed on R&D, manufacturing, and human resources to deliver quality. Unfortunately, a scientist or engineer's perception of quality may not be the same as the customer's. If a firm's communications program entices the consumer to try a product, the product must then be consistent with the consumer's expectations of quality. The initial perception of quality comes when the customer tries the product. For many products, this means usage at a basic level. For some products, however, especially those with a technological orientation, trying the product means that the customer has to first read the instruction book. In this situation, the instruction booklet serves as a form of marketing communication.

Another form of quality occurs in the employee–customer encounter. This encounter becomes the factory

. . . the sum of the external messages and internal operations produces a satisfied customer.

floor for both the salesperson and the customer. Even though the salesperson at the Apple Store may explain in detail how to download music to an Apple iPod, it is only when the customer tries the download at home alone that he or she learns to produce the recorded music. If unsuccessful, the customer is likely to call Apple for help. An employee at the call center will then attempt to help the customer navigate the download process again. The interaction with the call center becomes a long-lasting form of marketing communication between the customer and Apple Computer.

With so many products requiring technical support for installation and use, it is no longer sufficient for R&D engineers or manufacturing specialists to work only in their limited domains. Many firms now expect R&D and manufacturing to communicate directly with customers. Intuit understands the importance of these marketing communication interactions and sends its employees on "follow-me-home" calls. These visits enable salespeople to show the company's products and interact one-on-one with the company's customers. Interestingly, the follow-me-home program has led to long-term relationships, as product experts have continued their associations with customers. These relationships have become a critical form of marketing communications for Intuit. Companies should also include salespeople on cross-functional new-product development teams. Salespeople are the ones out in the field who see how customers use the com-

pany's products on a daily basis and hear what customers are saying about their preferences. Thus, salespeople can bring the voice of the customer into the firm. Personal selling is a component of integrated marketing communications where considerable interaction among functions occurs. The sales area must work closely with finance, accounting, and human resources with regard to compensation systems. While finance and accounting will generally focus on the profit aspect of the salesperson's objectives, human resources will have to work closely with the salesperson to develop the most appropriate compensation system for the types of accounts in the salesperson's territory. In today's business environment of teamwork and cross-selling, the human resources department may also be called on to help interview and train potential sales personnel.

A successful integrated marketing communications program requires marketing to work closely with R&D, manufacturing, finance, accounting, and human resources to establish appropriate goals and objectives for its marketing communications programs. It is the sum of the external messages and internal operations that produces a satisfied customer.

Questions

1. Why is marketing communications of particular concern to R&D and manufacturing?

2. How is personal selling functionally integrated?

Integrated Marketing
Communications

CHAPTER
14

Learning Outcomes

LO¹   Discuss the role of promotion in the marketing mix

LO²   Discuss the elements of the promotional mix

LO³   Describe the communication process

LO⁴   Explain the goals and tasks of promotion

LO⁵   Discuss the AIDA concept and its relationship to the promotional mix

LO⁶   Describe the factors that affect the promotional mix

LO⁷   Discuss the concept of integrated marketing communications

Subway—*eat fresh*

Hungry for a great sandwich? Go to your nearby Subway— it's probably closer than you think! Subway is the world's largest submarine sandwich restaurant chain in the world. In fact, it operates more units in the United States, Canada, and Australia than McDonald's does. One reason for Subway's success is high-quality food delivered consistently. Whenever and wherever you visit one of its 25,000+ restaurants in 83 countries, you will get the same choice of high-quality meats, vegetables, and condiments served on bread baked right in the restaurant.

Subway has achieved awareness and brand loyalty to a large degree by communicating very effectively with its target audience.

Becoming larger than McDonald's requires more than having an excellent product in a convenient location, however. Potential customers must be aware of you and believe in your brand. Subway has achieved awareness and brand loyalty to a large degree by communicating very effectively with its target audience. To create awareness, its promotional campaigns use traditional tools, such as TV advertising, radio, and billboards, and then supplement them with emerging media tools to create a preference for the Subway brand. For example, the company's Web site, **http://www.subway.com/**, features streaming video of the ads from the "Great Taste/Good for You" and "SUBWAY Eat Fresh!" campaigns. For several years,

Subway has sponsored Little League Baseball and Softball, NASCAR auto races, the American Heart Association's annual Heart Walk, and similar activities. Each event attracts many participants matching Subway's target demographic.

Subway has also tailored its promotional message to capitalize on the emerging social trends of nutrition, health, and wellness. The story of voluntary spokesman Jared Fogle, who lost 245 pounds in a year by eating only at Subway, became a centerpiece of Subway's marketing messages. Subway sent Jared on a world tour to talk about the importance of proper diet and exercise. The tour included the "Jared & Friends School Tour" designed to teach children the benefits of healthy living. The theme was so successful that Jared was invited to appear on *Oprah, Larry King Live,* and *48 Hours,* and his story was featured in national newspapers. Publicity from these events and Jared's appearances at other wellness venues such as California Governor Arnold Schwarzenegger's "Summit on Health, Nutrition, and Obesity" have done much to extend the impact of Subway's paid media programs. They also helped Subway to be named the number one franchise opportunity by *Entrepreneur* magazine in 2005—the thirteenth time in 17 years![1]

As you can see, Subway places considerable emphasis on promotion in its marketing mix. What types of promotional tools are available to companies, and what factors influence the choice of a particular promotion tool? Why is consistent integrated marketing important to the promotional plan? These questions and others will be answered as you read this chapter.

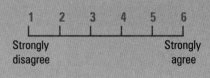

Marketing & You

Using the following scale, enter your opinions on the lines provided.

```
  1    2    3    4    5    6
  |____|____|____|____|____|
Strongly                Strongly
disagree                   agree
```

____ People frequently tell me about themselves.

____ I've been told that I'm a good listener.

____ I'm very accepting of others.

____ People trust me with their secrets.

____ I easily get people to "open up."

____ People feel relaxed around me.

____ I enjoy listening to people.

____ I'm sympathetic to people's problems.

____ I encourage people to tell me how they are feeling.

____ I can keep people talking about themselves.

Total your score, and see what it means after you read the chapter.

LO¹
The Role of Promotion in the Marketing Mix

Few goods or services, no matter how well developed, priced, or distributed, can survive in the marketplace without effective **promotion**—communication by marketers that informs, persuades, and reminds potential buyers of a product in order to influence their opinion or elicit a response.

Promotional strategy is a plan for the optimal use of the elements of promotion: advertising, public relations, personal selling, and sales promotion. As Exhibit 14.1 shows, the marketing manager determines the goals of the company's promotional strategy in light of the firm's overall goals for the marketing mix—product, place (distribution), promotion, and price. Using these overall goals, marketers combine the elements of the promotional strategy (the promotional mix) into a coordinated plan. The promotion plan then becomes an integral part of the marketing strategy for reaching the target market.

The main function of a marketer's promotional strategy is to convince target customers that the goods and services offered provide a competitive advantage over the competition. A **competitive advantage** is the set of unique features of a company and its products that are perceived by the target market as significant and superior to the competition. Such features can include high product quality, rapid delivery, low prices, excellent service, or a feature not offered by the competition. For example, as you read in the opening example, fast-food restaurant Subway promises fresh sandwiches that are better for you than a hamburger or pizza. Subway effectively communicates its competitive advantage through advertising featuring longtime "spokes-eater" Jared Fogle, who lost weight by eating at Subway every day.[2] Thus, promotion is a vital part of the marketing mix, informing consumers of a product's benefits and thereby positioning the product in the marketplace.

Exhibit 14.1
Role of Promotion in the Marketing Mix

REVIEW LEARNING OUTCOME

LO¹ Discuss the role of promotion in the marketing mix

The Promotional Mix

Most promotional strategies use several ingredients—which may include advertising, public relations, sales promotion, and personal selling—to reach a target market. That combination is called the **promotional mix.** The proper promotional mix is the one that management believes will meet the needs of the target market and fulfill the organization's overall goals. The more funds allocated to each promotional ingredient and the more managerial emphasis placed on each technique, the more important that element is thought to be in the overall mix.

ADVERTISING

Almost all companies selling a good or a service use some advertising, whether in the form of a multimillion-dollar campaign or a simple classified ad in a newspaper. **Advertising** is any form of impersonal paid communication in which the sponsor or company is identified. Traditional media—such as television, radio, newspapers, magazines, books, direct mail, billboards, and transit cards (advertisements on buses and taxis and at bus stops)—are most commonly used to transmit advertisements to consumers. With the increasing fragmentation of traditional media choices, marketers are using new methods to send their advertisements to consumers, such as Internet Web sites, e-mail, and interactive video technology located in department stores and supermarkets.

One of the primary benefits of advertising is its ability to communicate to a large number of people at one time. Cost per contact, therefore, is typically very low. Advertising has the advantage of being able to reach the masses (for instance, through national television networks), but it can also be microtargeted to small groups of potential customers, such as television ads on a targeted cable network or through print advertising in a trade magazine.

Although the cost per contact in advertising is very low, the total cost to advertise is typically very high. This hurdle tends to restrict advertising on a national basis to only those companies that are financially able to do so. For instance, Unilever spends between $20 million and $25 million annually advertising its Degree line of antiperspirants targeted at men. Moreover, in recent years Unilever has been spending about $2.5 million per ad to advertise Degree during the Super Bowl.[3] Smaller companies cannot match this level of spending for a national campaign. Chapter 15 examines advertising in greater detail.

Companies increasingly are using Internet advertising as a vital component in their marketing mix. Banner ads, viral marketing, and interactive promotions are all ways that marketers utilize the Internet to try and reach their target audience. But some consumers and lawmakers feel that consumers' privacy is being violated. Read about this issue in the "Ethics in Marketing" box.

PUBLIC RELATIONS

Concerned about how they are perceived by their target markets, organizations often spend large sums to build a positive public image. **Public relations** is the marketing function that evaluates public attitudes, identifies areas within the organization the public may be interested in, and executes a program of action to earn public understanding and acceptance. Public relations helps an organization communicate with its customers, suppliers, stockholders, government officials, employees, and the community in which it operates. Marketers use public relations not only to maintain a positive image but also to educate the public about the company's goals and objectives, introduce new products, and help support the sales effort.

In recent years, fast-food companies like McDonald's and soft drink companies like Coca-Cola have been criticized for contributing to childhood obesity, particularly in the United States. In response, the companies have undertaken public relations campaigns

promotional mix
The combination of promotional tools—including advertising, public relations, personal selling, and sales promotion—used to reach the target market and fulfill the organization's overall goals.

advertising
Impersonal, one-way mass communication about a product or organization that is paid for by a marketer.

public relations
The marketing function that evaluates public attitudes, identifies areas within the organization the public may be interested in, and executes a program of action to earn public understanding and acceptance.

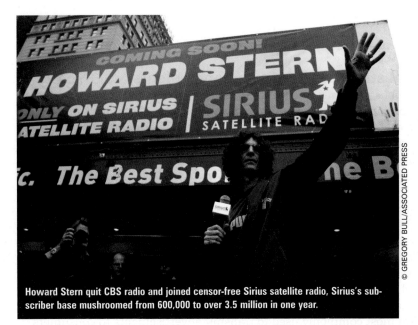

Howard Stern quit CBS radio and joined censor-free Sirius satellite radio, Sirius's subscriber base mushroomed from 600,000 to over 3.5 million in one year.

to try to minimize the impact on their reputations and ultimately sales. For example, Coca-Cola created the Beverage Institute for Health and Wellness to support nutrition research, education, and outreach. The company also spent $4 million to develop the "Live It" children's fitness campaign in schools across the country. Coke's nutrition communication manager says the campaign will not address childhood obesity or encourage students to drink Coke and that the company's logo will not appear on "Live It" materials. In addition to promoting the campaign, Coke is paying for campaign posters, pedometers, and nutrition education materials and offering prizes to children who meet the program's exercise goal of walking 10,000 steps in a week. Such efforts are designed to offset a push by the Center for Science in the Public Interest to persuade the Food and Drug Administration to require labels on sodas warning about obesity, tooth decay, and diabetes.[4]

A public relations program can generate favorable **publicity**—public information about a company, product, service, or issue appearing in the mass media as a new item. Organizations generally do not pay for the publicity and are not identified as the source of the information, but they can benefit tremendously from it. For example, the rapid growth of the satellite radio industry is partly due to publicity. Subscribers topped 12 million in 2005 and were expected to reach 15 million in 2006. Satellite radio's profile received a huge boost from the storm of publicity surrounding the decision by the country's most notorious and popular radio host, "shock jock" Howard Stern, to quit CBS radio and join censor-free Sirius satellite radio. Stern's first satellite broadcast was a major event, with the national media breathlessly reporting on the number of times he swore and looking for acceptable ways to report the more graphic—usually sexual—content of the show. After signing Stern, Sirius's subscriber base mushroomed from 600,000 to over 3.5 million in one year—the majority of new listeners were Stern fans who signed up to follow their hero. Although Sirius added Stern, XM Satellite Radio still has more subscribers at around 9 million. XM also benefited from the publicity Stern generated for the whole satellite broadcast medium and generated publicity of its own by signing up both Oprah Winfrey and reclusive music legend Bob Dylan to host their own shows.[5]

Although organizations do not directly pay for publicity, it should not be viewed as free. Preparing news releases, staging special events, and persuading media personnel to broadcast or print publicity messages cost money. Public relations and publicity are examined further in Chapter 15.

SALES PROMOTION

Sales promotion consists of all marketing activities—other than personal selling, advertising, and public relations—that stimulate consumer purchasing and dealer effectiveness. Sales promotion is generally a short-run tool used to stimulate immediate increases in demand. Sales promotion can be aimed at end consumers, trade customers, or a company's employees. Sales promotions include free samples, contests, premiums, trade shows, vacation giveaways, and coupons. A major promotional campaign might use several of these sales promotion tools. For example, Motorola, a sponsor of a mountain bike event called "24 Hours of Adrenalin," teamed up with Canadian Future Shop to debut the Motorola Gear Grab. This promotion gave ten people 24 seconds to grab as much Motorola gear as they could in a Future Shop store. Contestants worked in pairs

publicity
Public information about a company, product, service, or issue appearing in the mass media as a news item.

sales promotion
Marketing activities—other than personal selling, advertising, and public relations—that stimulate consumer buying and dealer effectiveness.

ETHICS in Marketing

Can E-mail Marketing Survive Anti-Spam Legislation?

ETHICS

Any American who logs onto the Internet is familiar with the ever-present spam filling our in-boxes in the form of e-mails offering herbal supplements, prescription drugs, low-interest loans, investment opportunities, free money, and other products. The term *spam* as the name for unwanted e-mails comes from a Monty Python skit in which a customer is urged to order Spam (the canned meat product) repeatedly until she screams "I don't want any Spam!"—which is how most of us feel today about the useless products and "phishing" scams we get in our e-mail. Spam raises serious moral issues, especially when it exposes children to pornography and vulnerable people to scams.

In an effort to curtail the flood of unsolicited commercial e-mails, Congress passed legislation that made it illegal for marketers to send unsolicited commercial e-mails using a false return address or subject line that conceals their identity and to harvest addresses from Web sites. In addition, e-mails are required to have a functioning opt-out mechanism that recipients can use to prevent future e-mails. Marketers who fail to comply can be sentenced to prison for up to five years.

The law curtailed some spamming, but 70 percent of the world's e-mail messages continue to be spam because so much spam originates outside the United States. Also, it is impossible to monitor the effectiveness of the required "opt-out" mechanisms. Although many companies include this option, it often does not work, even when the sender is a supposedly reputable firm. Officials at the Federal Trade Commission claim that the number of spam e-mails is leveling off and say that is evidence the law is working. In addition, the feds are hoping the guilty plea of the defendant in the first case prosecuted under the new anti-spam legislation will further discourage spam.

Spam is a serious problem for e-mail marketers. Consumers consider anything that doesn't interest them to be spam. But legally e-mail isn't spam if a consumer has opted-in to receive messages, and many consumers often forget they opted-in with a particular company. The problem is that if enough consumers claim a message is spam, Internet service providers will classify the marketer as a spammer and start blocking its message.

In spite of these problems, the news isn't all bad for e-mail marketers. About half of consumers take advantage of offers that arrive via e-mail. The number is up significantly in recent years. Discounts, markdowns, and free shipping offers persuade consumers to open messages, and the more messages opened, the more sales are made.[6]

Do you think spam or unsolicited commercial e-mail is an effective marketing tool? When does e-mail become spamming? Can spam be prevented?

---

and used Motorola two-way radios so that one partner could provide the other with the name, description, and location of a Motorola product—including cell phones and messaging devices—within the store. Contestants were also eligible for a grand prize of various Motorola and mountain biking gear.[7]

Often marketers use sales promotion to improve the effectiveness of other ingredients in the promotional mix, especially advertising and personal selling. Research shows that sales promotion complements advertising by yielding faster sales responses. Jose Cuervo International, a Mexican tequila manufacturer, launched the online marketing campaign "Endless Summer." The campaign asked tequila drinkers to register online to sign a petition asking Congress to change Labor Day from the first Monday in September to the last day of summer. As incentives for registration, Jose Cuervo offered a party pack, including margarita mix, a blender, a portable grill, a portable stereo, and a $250 party supplies gift certificate. Registered users were asked to forward e-mails and information about the petition to their friends.[8] Sales promotion is discussed in more detail in Chapter 16.

PERSONAL SELLING

Personal selling is a purchase situation involving a personal, paid-for communication between two people in an attempt to influence each other. In this dyad, both the buyer and the seller have specific objectives they wish to accomplish. The buyer may need to minimize cost or assure a

personal selling
A purchase situation involving a personal, paid-for communication between two people in an attempt to influence each other.

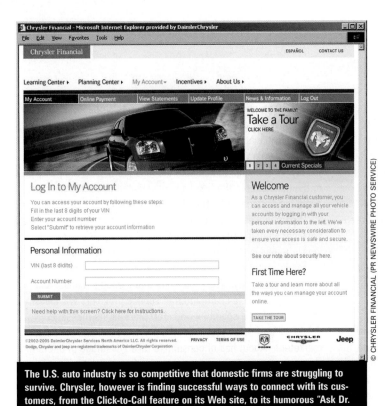

The U.S. auto industry is so competitive that domestic firms are struggling to survive. Chrysler, however is finding successful ways to connect with its customers, from the Click-to-Call feature on its Web site, to its humorous "Ask Dr. Z" advertising campaign featuring CEO Dieter Zetsche.

quality product, for instance, while the salesperson may need to maximize revenue and profits.

Traditional methods of personal selling include a planned presentation to one or more prospective buyers for the purpose of making a sale. Whether it takes place face-to-face or over the phone, personal selling attempts to persuade the buyer to accept a point of view or take some action. For example, a car salesperson may try to persuade a car buyer that a particular model is superior to a competing model in certain features, such as gas mileage, roominess, and interior styling. Once the buyer is somewhat convinced, then the salesperson may attempt to elicit some action from the buyer, such as a test-drive or a purchase. Frequently, in this traditional view of personal selling, the objectives of the salesperson are at the expense of the buyer, creating a win-lose outcome.

More current notions on personal selling emphasize the relationship that develops between a salesperson and a buyer. Initially, this concept was more typical in business-to-business selling situations, involving the sale of products like heavy machinery or computer systems. More recently, both business-to-business and business-to-consumer selling focus on building long-term relationships rather than on making a onetime sale. Relationship selling emphasizes a win-win outcome and the accomplishment of mutual objectives that benefit both buyer and salesperson in the long term. Rather than focusing on a quick sale, relationship selling attempts to create a long-term, committed relationship based on trust, increased customer loyalty, and a continuation of the relationship between the salesperson and the customer. Personal selling, like other promotional mix elements, is increasingly dependent on the Internet. Most companies use their Web sites to attract potential buyers seeking information on products and services. While some companies sell products direct to consumers online, many do not. Instead, they rely on the Web site to drive customers to their physical locations where personal selling can close the sale. Chrysler, a unit of DaimlerChrysler, added a "click-to-call" feature to its Web site that automatically calls a Chrysler representative who either answers questions or refers the call to a local dealer. About 80 percent of the calls are transferred to dealers, and 15 percent close the sale through personal selling. The new feature also collects customer feedback that can be used to improve customer service. For example, information on vehicle incentives and financing options was recently improved as a result of this new feature.[9] Personal selling is discussed further in Chapter 16.

REVIEW LEARNING OUTCOME

LO 2 Discuss the elements of the promotional mix

Maintain image and educate consumers

Reach the masses

Stimulate purchase

Advertising

Public Relations

Sales Promotion

Personal Selling

Build relationships

LO3
Marketing Communication

Promotional strategy is closely related to the process of communication. As humans, we assign meaning to feelings, ideas, facts, attitudes, and emotions. **Communication** is the process by which we exchange or share meanings through a common set of symbols. When a company develops a new product, changes an old one, or simply tries to increase sales of an existing good or service, it must communicate its selling message to potential customers. Marketers communicate information about the firm and its products to the target market and various publics through its promotion programs. Neiman Marcus, for example, set out to capture as many e-mail addresses as possible for a recent holiday promotions campaign. The focus of the campaign was "There is something for everyone at Neiman's." To build the database that launched the holiday campaign, Neiman's mailed print catalogs, sent over 750,000 e-mails, bought online ads, and hosted a "fantasy gift" press event. As an incentive for registration, Neiman's automatically entered all registered subscribers in its holiday sweepstakes, which awarded two Hummer 24-speed mountain bikes valued at $745. The press event and catalog featured everything from fantasy gifts—a Learjet valued at up to $12.7 million and a $27,000 luxury ice fishing house—to gifts under $100. Although official numbers were not released, Neiman's e-mails typically have an "extremely high" response rate.[10]

Communication can be divided into two major categories: interpersonal communication and mass communication. **Interpersonal communication** is direct, face-to-face communication between two or more people. When communicating face-to-face, people see the other person's reaction and can respond almost immediately. A salesperson speaking directly with a client is an example of an interpersonal marketing communication.

Mass communication involves communicating a concept or message to large audiences. A great deal of marketing communication is directed to consumers as a whole, usually through a mass medium such as television or newspapers. When a company advertises, it generally does not personally know the people with whom it is trying to communicate. Furthermore, the company is unable to respond immediately to consumers' reactions to its message. Instead, the marketing manager must wait to see whether people are reacting positively or negatively to the mass-communicated promotion. Any clutter from competitors' messages or other distractions in the environment can reduce the effectiveness of the mass-communication effort.

THE COMMUNICATION PROCESS

Marketers are both senders and receivers of messages. As *senders*, marketers attempt to inform, persuade, and remind the target market to adopt courses of action compatible with the need to promote the purchase of goods and services. As *receivers*, marketers attune themselves to the target market in order to develop the appropriate messages, adapt existing messages, and spot new communication opportunities. In this way, marketing communication is a two-way, rather than one-way, process. The two-way nature of the communication process is shown in Exhibit 14.2.

The Sender and Encoding

The **sender** is the originator of the message in the communication process. In an interpersonal conversation, the sender may be a parent, a friend, or a salesperson. For an advertisement or press release, the sender is the company or organization itself. For example, McDonald's fast-food restaurants launched a marketing campaign using the theme "I'm lovin' it." At the outset the objective of the campaign was to increase purchases of

communication
The process by which we exchange or share meanings through a common set of symbols.

interpersonal communication
Direct, face-to-face communication between two or more people.

mass communication
The communication of a concept or message to large audiences.

sender
The originator of the message in the communication process.

Exhibit 14.2
Communication Process

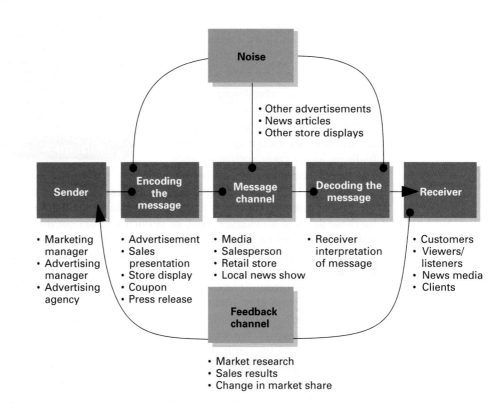

traditional menu items by children, teenagers, and young adults. To appeal to this market, McDonald's signed Justin Timberlake to sing a "hip-pop" jingle and do a voice-over in the commercial.

Encoding is the conversion of the sender's ideas and thoughts into a message, usually in the form of words or signs. Thus, to promote the message that a meal at McDonald's "is one of the simplest pleasures of daily life," the ad featured a mohawked dad with his mohawked child singing the jingle "I'm lovin' it." Marketers encoded the message by using the dad and child "lovin' it" at McDonald's.

A basic principle of encoding is that what matters is not what the source says but what the receiver hears. One way of conveying a message that the receiver will hear properly is to use concrete words and pictures. For example, in addition to visual images, the McDonald's "I'm lovin' it" jingle sung by Justin Timberlake explicitly conveyed the message:

> I'm lovin' it. Is this the place to eat? Since I don't cook, I'll just rock to the beat. I'm lovin' it. At the end of the day, to relieve the stress, we add a little play. I'm lovin' it. Sometimes we have mishaps. You just overcome it, adapt to setback. I'm lovin' it. I'm lovin' it.[11]

Message Transmission

Transmission of a message requires a **channel**—a voice, radio, newspaper, or other communication medium. A facial expression or gesture can also serve as a channel.

Reception occurs when the message is detected by the receiver and enters his or her frame of reference. In a two-way conversation such as a sales pitch given by a sales representative to a potential client, reception is normally high. In contrast, the desired receivers may or may not detect the message when it is mass communicated because most media are cluttered by **noise**—anything that interferes with, distorts, or slows down the transmission of information. In some media overcrowded with advertisers, such as newspapers and television, the noise level is high and the reception level is low. For example, competing network advertisements, other entertainment option advertisements, or other programming on the network itself might hamper reception of the McDonald's "I'm lovin' it" advertising campaign message. Transmission can also be hindered by situational factors such as physical surroundings like light, sound, location, and

encoding
The conversion of a sender's ideas and thoughts into a message, usually in the form of words or signs.

channel
A medium of communication—such as a voice, radio, or newspaper—for transmitting a message.

noise
Anything that interferes with, distorts, or slows down the transmission of information.

weather; the presence of other people; or the temporary moods consumers might bring to the situation. Mass communication may not even reach all the right consumers. Some members of the target audience were likely watching television when McDonald's advertisements were shown, but others probably were not.

The Receiver and Decoding

Marketers communicate their message through a channel to customers, or **receivers,** who will decode the message. **Decoding** is the interpretation of the language and symbols sent by the source through a channel. Common understanding between two communicators, or a common frame of reference, is required for effective communication. Therefore, marketing managers must ensure a proper match between the message to be conveyed and the target market's attitudes and ideas.

Even though a message has been received, it will not necessarily be properly decoded—or even seen, viewed, or heard—because of selective exposure, distortion, and retention (refer to Chapter 5). Even when people receive a message, they tend to manipulate, alter, and modify it to reflect their own biases, needs, knowledge, and culture. Differences in age, social class, education, culture, and ethnicity can lead to miscommunication, for example. Further, because people don't always listen or read carefully, they can easily misinterpret what is said or written. In fact, researchers have found that consumers misunderstand a large proportion of both printed and televised communications. Bright colors and bold graphics have been shown to increase consumers' comprehension of marketing communication. Even these techniques are not foolproof, however. A classic example of miscommunication occurred when Lever Brothers mailed out samples of its then new dishwashing liquid, Sunlight, which contains real lemon juice. The package clearly stated that Sunlight was a household cleaning product. Nevertheless, many people saw the word *sunlight,* the large picture of lemons, and the phrase "with real lemon juice" and thought the product was lemon juice.

McDonald's new food packaging supports the company's "I'm lovin' it" promotional message. The company has also ensured that the campaign has global reach by translating the phrase into numerous languages. The packaging depicts people enjoying the simple pleasures of life and furthers McDonald's creative intent to connect with customers worldwide in fresh and relevant ways.

Marketers targeting consumers in foreign countries must also worry about the translation and possible miscommunication of their promotional messages by other cultures. An important issue for global marketers is whether to standardize or customize the message for each global market in which they sell. For instance, McDonald's used the same "I'm lovin' it" advertising theme in other countries as part of its Worldwide Balance, Active Lifestyles Public Awareness Campaign. To do so, it extended the initial message to "It's what I eat and what I do . . . I'm lovin' it" and incorporated the message in TV commercials, print, outdoor, packaging, and Internet communications rolled out around the world.[12]

Feedback

In interpersonal communication, the receiver's response to a message is direct **feedback** to the source. Feedback may be verbal, as in saying "I agree," or nonverbal, as in nodding, smiling, frowning, or gesturing.

Because mass communicators like McDonald's are often cut off from direct feedback, they must rely on market research or analysis of viewer responses for indirect feedback. McDonald's might use such measurements as the percentage of television viewers who recognized, recalled, or stated that they were exposed to McDonald's messages. Indirect feedback enables mass communicators to decide whether to continue, modify, or drop a message. For example, the success of the "I'm lovin' it" campaign led McDonald's to use the theme in its 100-Days-Out Countdown to the 2006 Olympic Games, as one element of being the Top Sponsor and Official Restaurant of the Games.[13]

receiver
The person who decodes a message.

decoding
Interpretation of the language and symbols sent by the source through a channel.

feedback
The receiver's response to a message.

THE COMMUNICATION PROCESS AND THE PROMOTIONAL MIX

The four elements of the promotional mix differ in their ability to affect the target audience. For instance, promotional mix elements may communicate with the consumer directly or indirectly. The message may flow one way or two ways. Feedback may be fast or slow, a little or a lot. Likewise, the communicator may have varying degrees of control over message delivery, content, and flexibility. Exhibit 14.3 outlines differences among the promotional mix elements with respect to mode of communication, marketer's control over the communication process, amount and speed of feedback, direction of message flow, marketer's control over the message, identification of the sender, speed in reaching large audiences, and message flexibility.

From Exhibit 14.3, you can see that most elements of the promotional mix are indirect and impersonal when used to communicate with a target market, providing only one direction of message flow. For example, advertising, public relations, and sales promotion are generally impersonal, one-way means of mass communication. Because they provide no opportunity for direct feedback, it is more difficult to adapt these promotional elements to changing consumer preferences, individual differences, and personal goals.

Personal selling, on the other hand, is personal, two-way communication. The salesperson receives immediate feedback from the consumer and can adjust the message in response. Personal selling, however, is very slow in dispersing the marketer's message to large audiences. Because a salesperson can only communicate to one person or a small group of persons at one time, it is a poor choice if the marketer wants to send a message to many potential buyers.

THE IMPACT OF BLOGGING ON MARKETING COMMUNICATION

The Internet and related technologies are having a profound impact on marketing communication including the promotional mix. The rise of blogging, for example, has created a completely new way for marketers to manage their image, connect with consumers, and generate interest in and desire for their companies' products.

Despite what could be considered a national obsession with blogs, measuring blogging activity remains challenging. According to Technorati, the first blog search engine, there were 28.4 million blogs online in 2006, and that number was doubling every 5.5 months. In spite of the widespread popularity of blogging, a blog's life expectancy is short. Fewer than half of all blogs are receiving posts three months after their creation, and less than 10 percent are updated as often as weekly.[14] Moreover, a Gallup poll found

Exhibit 14.3

Characteristics of the Elements in the Promotional Mix

	Advertising	Public Relations	Sales Promotion	Personal Selling
Mode of Communication	Indirect and impersonal	Usually indirect and impersonal	Usually indirect and impersonal	Direct and face-to-face
Communicator Control over Situation	Low	Moderate to low	Moderate to low	High
Amount of Feedback	Little	Little	Little to moderate	Much
Speed of Feedback	Delayed	Delayed	Varies	Immediate
Direction of Message Flow	One-way	One-way	Mostly one-way	Two-way
Control over Message Content	Yes	No	Yes	Yes
Identification of Sponsor	Yes	No	Yes	Yes
Speed in Reaching Large Audience	Fast	Usually fast	Fast	Slow
Message Flexibility	Same message to all audiences	Usually no direct control over message	Same message to varied target audiences	Tailored to prospective buyer

that only 9 percent of Internet users read blogs frequently, 24 percent read them occasionally or less, and nearly 66 percent are not involved in blogging at all.[15]

The question then is whether blogging is a passing fad, representing at best an unreliable means of communicating, or an emerging trend. If it is a fad, why are marketers so interested in blogging as a promotional tool? The answer in part is that blogging alters the marketing communication process for the promotional elements that rely on mass communication—advertising, public relations, and sales promotion—by moving them away from impersonal, indirect communication toward a personalized, direct communication model.

Blogs can be divided into two broad categories: corporate blogs and noncorporate blogs. **Corporate blogs** are sponsored by a company or one of its brands and maintained by one or more of the company's employees. Corporate blogs disseminate marketing-controlled information. (Recall from Chapter 5 that marketing-controlled information is a source of product information that originates with marketers promoting the product.) Because blogs are designed to change daily, corporate blogs are dynamic and highly flexible, giving marketers the opportunity to adapt their messages more frequently than with any other communication channel. Initially, blogs were maintained by only the most technology-savvy companies. But today companies as diverse as Coca-Cola, Starwood Hotels, Honda, Nokia, Benetton, Ducati, Guinness, and HSBC have all launched corporate blogs. Undoubtedly, many more will appear in the near future.

In contrast, **noncorporate blogs** are independent and not associated with the marketing efforts of any particular company or brand. As such, noncorporate blogs function much like nonmarketing-controlled information: they provide a source of information and opinion perceived to be independent and more authentic than a corporate blog. Michael Marx loves Barq's root beer. He wears Barq's T-shirts, brings the beverage to parties, and calls it his "beer." He maintains a blog dedicated to Barq's, **http://www.thebarqsman.com,** where he collects news about the brand, Barq's commercials he likes, and musings on why Barq's is superior to other root beers. Thebarqsman.com is not affiliated with Coca-Cola, the owner of the Barq's brand, which had no idea of the blog's existence until a *New York Times* reporter writing a story on brand blogs mentioned it. Even though thebarqsman.com is dedicated to a single brand, Marx's blog is an example of a noncorporate blog.[16]

Both corporate and noncorporate blogs have had an impact on the communication model depicted in Exhibit 14.2. That model shows the feedback channel as primarily impersonal and numbers-driven. In the traditional communication process, marketers can see the results of consumer behavior (e.g., a drop in sales), but are only able to explain them using their judgment. Even the information generated by market research is not as natural as that gleaned from bloggers. Corporate blogs allow marketers to personalize the feedback channel by opening the door for direct conversation with consumers.

When marketers launch a corporate blog, they create an unfiltered feedback channel. In 2006 Enrico Minoli, CEO of Ducati, the Italian motorcycle brand, launched a

corporate blogs
Blogs that are sponsored by a company or one of its brands and maintained by one or more of the company's employees.

noncorporate blogs
Independent blogs that are not associated with the marketing efforts of any particular company or brand.

REVIEW LEARNING OUTCOME

LO 3   Describe the communication process

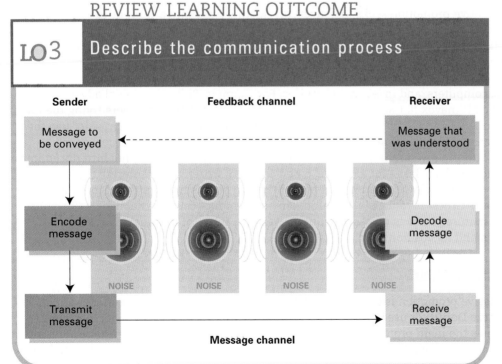

blog at **http://blog.ducati.com.** He vowed to write "openly about what's going on at Ducati." Within three days, his postings had generated 99 responses from motorcycle enthusiasts from Greece to Daytona Beach, who all seemed most pleased that the CEO himself was a motorbike enthusiast. They began peppering him with questions about when new models would hit production and chatted with each other about their own bikes and biking experiences. Minoli's blog put a face on the impersonal nature of a large corporation.[17]

Noncorporate blogs have also personalized the feedback channel. But while corporate blogs create a *direct*, personalized feedback channel for masses of consumers, noncorporate blogs represent an *indirect*, personalized feedback channel. Because noncorporate blogs are independent, they are often perceived as more authentic. Blogging experts offer marketers some solid advice for giving their blogs the honest quality many bloggers associate with noncorporate blogs: open the feedback channel. Todd Copilevitz, a consultant specializing in digital marketing, says, "Blogs are not an environment where you just hold forth opinion and don't accept feedback. You have to have your wits about you to understand it's not the same old PR machine."[18]

LO 4
The Goals and Tasks of Promotion

People communicate with one another for many reasons. They seek amusement, ask for help, give assistance or instructions, provide information, and express ideas and thoughts. Promotion, on the other hand, seeks to modify behavior and thoughts in some way. For example, promoters may try to persuade consumers to drink Pepsi rather than Coke, or to eat at Burger King instead of McDonald's. Promotion also strives to reinforce existing behavior—for instance, getting consumers to continue dining at Burger King once they have switched. The source (the seller) hopes to project a favorable image or to motivate purchase of the company's goods and services.

Promotion can perform one or more of three tasks: *inform* the target audience, *persuade* the target audience, or *remind* the target audience. Often a marketer will try to accomplish two or more of these tasks at the same time.

INFORMING

Informative promotion seeks to convert an existing need into a want or to stimulate interest in a new product. It is generally more prevalent during the early stages of the product life cycle. People typically will not buy a product or service or support a nonprofit organization until they know its purpose and its benefits to them. Informative messages are important for promoting complex and technical products such as automobiles, computers, and investment services. For example, Philips's original advertisement for the Magnavox flat-screen television showed young, urban consumers trying the flat-screen TV all over the house, including the ceiling. The ad focused on "how to" use the flat-screen TV rather than the Philips Magnavox brand or the technological capabilities.[19] Informative promotion is also important for a "new" brand being introduced into an "old" product class—for example, a new brand of frozen pizza entering the frozen pizza industry, which is dominated by well-known brands like Kraft's DiGiorno and Schwan's Grocery Products' Red Baron. The new product cannot establish itself against more mature products unless potential buyers are aware of it, value its benefits, and understand its positioning in the marketplace.

PERSUADING

Persuasive promotion is designed to stimulate a purchase or an action—for example, to eat more Doritos or use Verizon wireless mobile phone service. Persuasion normally becomes the main promotion goal when the product enters the growth stage of its life cycle. By this time, the target market should have general product awareness and some knowledge of how the product can fulfill their wants. Therefore, the promotional task switches from informing consumers about the product category to persuading them to buy the company's brand rather than the competitor's. At this time, the promotional message emphasizes the product's real and perceived competitive advantages, often appealing to emotional needs such as love, belonging, self-esteem, and ego satisfaction. For example, the latest advertisement for the Philips Magnavox flat-screen television still features young, urban consumers. But the ad focuses on the product's benefits such as lifestyle enhancements, technological features like HDTV and Dolby digital surround sound, and the superiority of the brand.[20]

Persuasion can also be an important goal for very competitive mature product categories such as many household items, soft drinks, beer, and banking services. In a marketplace characterized by many competitors, the promotional message often encourages brand switching and aims to convert some buyers into loyal users. For example, to persuade new customers to switch their checking accounts, a bank's marketing manager may offer a year's worth of free checks with no fees.

Critics believe that some promotional messages and techniques can be too persuasive, causing consumers to buy products and services they really don't need.

Tide
Consider Tide detergent's Web site as a promotional tool. Visit the site and decide whether you think the main goal of the site is informing, persuading, or reminding. Explain your choice.
http://www.tide.com

Online

REVIEW LEARNING OUTCOME

LO4 Explain the goals and tasks of promotion

- **Informative promotion**

  Increasing the awareness of a new brand, product class, or product attribute

  Explaining how the product works

  Suggesting new uses for a product

  Building a company image

- **Persuasive promotion**

  Encouraging brand switching

  Changing customers' perceptions of product attributes

  Influencing customers to buy now

  Persuading customers to call

- **Reminder promotion**

  Reminding consumers that the product may be needed in the near future

  Reminding consumers where to buy the product

  Maintaining consumer awareness

REMINDING

Reminder promotion is used to keep the product and brand name in the public's mind. This type of promotion prevails during the maturity stage of the life cycle. It assumes that the target market has already been persuaded of the good's or service's merits. Its purpose is simply to trigger a memory. Crest toothpaste, Tide laundry detergent, Miller beer, and many other consumer products often use reminder promotion. Similarly, Philips Magnavox could advertise just the brand rather than the benefits of the product.

LO5
Promotional Goals and the AIDA Concept

The ultimate goal of any promotion is to get someone to buy a good or service or, in the case of nonprofit organizations, to take some action (for instance, donate blood). A classic model for reaching promotional goals is called the **AIDA concept.**[21] The acronym stands for *attention, interest, desire,* and *action*—the stages of consumer involvement with a promotional message.

This model proposes that consumers respond to marketing messages in a cognitive (thinking), affective (feeling), and conative (doing) sequence. First, a promotion manager may focus on attracting a person's *attention* by training a salesperson to use a friendly greeting and approach, or by using loud volume, unusual color contrasts, bold headlines, movement, bright colors, and the like in an advertisement. Next, a good sales presentation, demonstration, or advertisement creates *interest* in the product and then, by illustrating how the product's features will satisfy the consumer's needs, arouses *desire*. Finally, a special offer or a strong closing sales pitch may be used to obtain purchase *action*.

AIDA concept
A model that outlines the process for achieving promotional goals in terms of stages of consumer involvement with the message; the acronym stands for *attention, interest, desire,* and *action.*

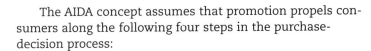
The AIDA concept assumes that promotion propels consumers along the following four steps in the purchase-decision process:

1. *Attention:* The advertiser must first gain the attention of the target market. A firm cannot sell something if the market does not know that the good or service exists. When Apple introduced the iPod, it was a new product for the company. To create awareness and gain attention for the new product, Apple had to advertise and promote it extensively through ads on TV, in magazines, and on the Internet. Because the iPod was a brand extension of the Apple computer, it required less effort than if it had been an entirely new brand. At the same time, because the iPod was an innovative new product line, the promotion had to get customers' attention and create awareness of a new idea from an established company.

2. *Interest:* Simple awareness of a brand seldom leads to a sale. The next step is to create interest in the product. A print ad or TV commercial cannot tell potential customers all the features and benefits of the iPod. Thus, Apple had to arrange iPod demonstrations and target messages to innovators and early adopters to create interest in the new portable music players.

3. *Desire:* Potential customers for the Apple iPod may like the concept of a portable music player, but they may not feel it is necessarily better than a Sony Walkman portable radio or a portable music player with fewer features. Therefore, Apple had to create brand preference with its iTunes Music Store, extended-life battery, clock and alarm, calendar and to-do list, photo storage, and other features. Specifically, Apple had to convince potential customers that the iPod was the best solution to meet their desire for a portable digital music player.

4. *Action:* Some potential target market customers may have been convinced to buy an iPod but had not yet made the actual purchase. To motivate them to take action, Apple continued advertising to more effectively communicate the features and benefits and also used promotions and price discounts.

© APPLE COMPUTER, INC.

Following the initial success of the iPod, to continue its market dominance of the portable digital music player market, Apple introduced new models such as the Nano and Shuffle that were smaller and lighter and yet had longer battery life and more storage. Then podcasting and video were added with access to thousands of network and cable shows and interfaces with auto, boat and home equipment—and the iPod became a "portable media player."

With each product innovation, the cycle of attention, interest, desire, and action began again. But with the familiarity and success of earlier models, the time frame became shorter. In fact, during the Christmas season in 2005, Apple was selling more than 100 iPods per minute, and by early 2006 it had sold over 42 million iPods. Moreover, according to Nielsen NetRatings, almost 21 million people, or about 14 percent of the Internet's active population, regularly visit the iTunes store.[22]

Most buyers involved in high-involvement purchase situations pass through the four stages of the AIDA model on the way to making a purchase. The promoter's task is to determine where on the purchase ladder most of the target consumers are located and design a promotion plan to meet their needs. For instance, if Apple learned from its market research that many potential customers were in the desire stage but had not bought an iPod for some reason, then Apple could place advertising on Yahoo or Google, and perhaps in video games as well, to target younger individuals who are the primary target market with specific messages to motivate them to take immediate action and buy an iPod.

The AIDA concept does not explain how all promotions influence purchase decisions. The model suggests that promotional effectiveness can be measured in terms of consumers progressing from one stage to the next. However, the order of stages in the model, as well as whether consumers go through all steps, has been much debated. For example, a purchase can occur without interest or desire, perhaps when a low-involvement product is bought on impulse. Regardless of the order of the stages or consumers' progression through these stages, the AIDA concept helps marketers by suggesting which promotional strategy will be most effective.[23]

AIDA AND THE PROMOTIONAL MIX

Exhibit 14.4 depicts the relationship between the promotional mix and the AIDA model. It shows that, although advertising does have an impact in the later stages, it is most useful in gaining attention for goods or services. In contrast, personal selling reaches fewer people at first, but salespeople are more effective at creating customer interest for merchandise or a service and at creating desire. For example, advertising may help a potential computer purchaser gain knowledge and information about competing brands, but the salesperson in an electronics store may be the one who actually encourages the buyer to decide that a particular brand is the best choice. The salesperson also has the advantage of having the computer physically there to demonstrate its capabilities to the buyer.

Public relations has its greatest impact in gaining attention for a company, good, or service. Many companies can attract attention and build goodwill by sponsoring community events that benefit a worthy cause such as antidrug and antigang programs. Such sponsorships project a positive image of the firm and its products into the minds of consumers and potential consumers. Good publicity can also help develop consumer desire for a product. Washington Mutual Financial Services invited 50,000 people to "Teacherpalooza: The World's Biggest Barbeque for the World's Greatest Teachers" in Chicago. The goal was to honor teachers and set a Guinness world record for the "World's Largest Barbeque." The barbeque featured performances by local teachers who competed for $15,000 prizes for the

Washington Mutual's Teacherpalooza in Chicago was successful in drawing attention to the company as a member of the Chicagoland community. With over 50,000 people attending, the public relations event also doubled as an attempt at entering the *Guinness Book of World Records*.

Exhibit 14.4
When the Elements of Promotion Are Most Useful

	Attention	Interest	Desire	Action
Advertising	●	●	○	●
Public Relations	●	●	●	●
Sales Promotion	○	○	●	○
Personal Selling	○	●	●	●

● Very effective   ○ Somewhat effective   ● Not effective

school they represented and live entertainment by Tim McGraw and Michelle Branch. A "Teacher Pavilion" described teacher-oriented financial services provided by Washington Mutual. Local news media cosponsored the event and were on hand to provide media coverage. The event exceeded all expectations, with broadcast television news stories and print coverage generating more than 4.7 million impressions and a total reach of more than 1.5 million households.[24]

Book publishers and movie studios often use public relations. For example, book publishers use public relations to get reviews of their new titles in major publications, such as *Publishers Weekly,* the *New York Times,* or the *Wall Street Journal.* Book authors also make appearances on talk shows and at bookstores to personally sign books and speak to fans. Similarly, movie marketers use prerelease publicity to raise the profile of their movies and to increase initial box-office sales. For example, most major motion picture studios have their own Web sites with multimedia clips and publicity photos of their current movies to attract viewers. Movie promoters include publicity gained from reviewers' quotes and Academy Award nominations in their advertising.

Sales promotion's greatest strength is in creating strong desire and purchase intent. Coupons and other price-off promotions are techniques used to persuade customers to buy new products. Frequent buyer sales promotion programs, popular among retailers, allow consumers to accumulate points or dollars that can later be redeemed for goods. Frequent buyer programs tend to increase purchase intent and loyalty and encourage repeat purchases. Many supermarket chains have developed loyalty programs patterned after the airlines' frequent flyer programs. Kroger's Plus Card members can go online and choose the coupons they want. The coupons are then downloaded to the member's Plus Card, and the savings can be redeemed when the member goes shopping with the card.

© R. ALCORN/THOMSON

REVIEW LEARNING OUTCOME

LO5 Discuss the AIDA concept and its relationship to the promotional mix

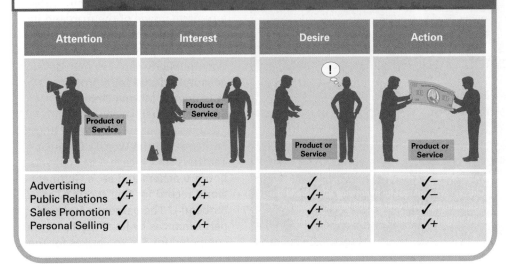

	Attention	Interest	Desire	Action
Advertising	✓+	✓+	✓	✓−
Public Relations	✓+	✓+	✓+	✓−
Sales Promotion	✓	✓	✓+	✓
Personal Selling	✓	✓+	✓+	✓+

LO6
Factors Affecting the Promotional Mix

Promotional mixes vary a great deal from one product and one industry to the next. Normally, advertising and personal selling are used to promote goods and services, and are supported and supplemented by sales promotion. Public relations helps develop a positive image for the organization and the product line. However, a firm may choose not to use all four promotional elements in its promotional mix, or it may choose to use them in varying degrees. The particular promotional mix chosen by a firm for a product or service depends on several factors: the nature of the product, the stage in the product life cycle, target market characteristics, the type of buying decision, funds available for promotion, and whether a push or a pull strategy will be used.

NATURE OF THE PRODUCT

Characteristics of the product itself can influence the promotional mix. For instance, a product can be classified as either a business product or a consumer product (refer to Chapters 6 and 9). As business products are often custom-tailored to the buyer's exact specifications, they are often not well suited to mass promotion. Therefore, producers of most business goods, such as computer systems or industrial machinery, rely more heavily on personal selling than on advertising. Informative personal selling is common for industrial installations, accessories, and component parts and materials. Advertising, however, still serves a purpose in promoting business goods. Advertisements in trade media may be used to create general buyer awareness and interest. Moreover, advertising can help locate potential customers for the sales force. For example, print media advertising often includes coupons soliciting the potential customer to "fill this out for more detailed information."

In contrast, because consumer products generally are not custom-made, they do not require the selling efforts of a company representative who can tailor them to the user's needs. Thus, consumer goods are promoted mainly through advertising to create brand familiarity. Television and radio advertising, consumer-oriented magazines, and increasingly the Internet and other highly targeted media are used extensively to promote consumer goods, especially nondurables. Sales promotion, the brand name, and the product's packaging are about twice as important for consumer goods as for business products. Persuasive personal selling is important at the retail level for shopping goods such as automobiles and appliances.

The costs and risks associated with a product also influence the promotional mix. As a general rule, when the costs or risks of using a product increase, personal selling becomes more important. Items that are a small part of a firm's budget (supply items) or of a consumer's budget (convenience products) do not require a salesperson to close the sale. In fact, inexpensive items cannot support the cost of a salesperson's time and effort unless the potential volume is high. On the other hand, expensive and complex machinery, new buildings, cars, and new homes represent a considerable investment. A salesperson must assure buyers that they are spending their money wisely and not taking an undue financial risk.

Social risk is an issue as well. Many consumer goods are not products of great social importance because they do not reflect social position. People do not experience much social risk in buying a loaf of bread or a candy bar. However, buying some shopping products and many specialty products such as jewelry and clothing does involve a social risk. Many consumers depend on sales personnel for guidance and advice in making the "proper" choice.

STAGE IN THE PRODUCT LIFE CYCLE

The product's stage in its life cycle is a big factor in designing a promotional mix (see Exhibit 14.5). During the *introduction stage,* the basic goal of promotion is to inform the target audience that the product is available. Initially, the emphasis is on the general product class—for example, mobile phones. The emphasis gradually changes to gaining attention for a particular brand,

Kellogg has launched a new public relations campaign featuring the Tonymobile, which is touring the United States (re)introducing families to Kellogg's family of characters: Toucan Sam, Dig 'Em, Snap! Crackle! and Pop! Competition in the breakfast food market is fierce, and Kellogg is using the Tonymobile to remind consumers about its cereals and cereal products.

Exhibit 14.5

Product Life Cycle and the Promotional Mix

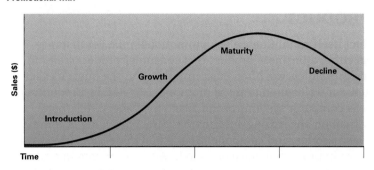

	Sales ($)			
	Introduction	Growth	Maturity	Decline

Time

| Preintroduction publicity; small amounts of advertising near introduction | Heavy advertising and public relations to build awareness; sales promotion to induce trial; personal selling to obtain distribution | Heavy advertising and public relations to build brand loyalty; decreasing use of sales promotion; personal selling to maintain distribution | Advertising slightly decreased — more persuasive and reminder in nature; increased use of sales promotion to build market share; personal selling to maintain distribution | Advertising and public relations drastically decreased; sales promotion and personal selling maintained at low levels |

such as Nokia, Samsung, Sony Ericsson, or Motorola. Typically, both extensive advertising and public relations inform the target audience of the product class or brand and heighten awareness levels. Sales promotion encourages early trial of the product, and personal selling gets retailers to carry the product.

When the product reaches the *growth stage* of the life cycle, the promotion blend may shift. Often a change is necessary because different types of potential buyers are targeted. Although advertising and public relations continue to be major elements of the promotional mix, sales promotion can be reduced because consumers need fewer incentives to purchase. The promotional strategy is to emphasize the product's differential advantage over the competition. Persuasive promotion is used to build and maintain brand loyalty to support the product during the growth stage. By this stage, personal selling has usually succeeded in getting adequate distribution for the product.

As the product reaches the *maturity stage* of its life cycle, competition becomes fiercer, and thus persuasive and reminder advertising are more strongly emphasized. Sales promotion comes back into focus as product sellers try to increase their market share.

All promotion, especially advertising, is reduced as the product enters the *decline stage*. Nevertheless, personal selling and sales promotion efforts may be maintained, particularly at the retail level.

TARGET MARKET CHARACTERISTICS

A target market characterized by widely scattered potential customers, highly informed buyers, and brand-loyal repeat purchasers generally requires a promotional mix with more advertising and sales promotion and less personal selling. Sometimes, however, personal selling is required even when buyers are well informed and geographically dispersed. Although industrial installations and component parts may be sold to extremely competent people with extensive education and work experience, salespeople must still be present to explain the product and work out the details of the purchase agreement.

Often firms sell goods and services in markets where potential customers are hard to locate. Print advertising can be used to find them. The reader is invited to call for more information or to mail in a reply card for a detailed brochure. As the calls or cards are received, salespeople are sent to visit the potential customers.

TYPE OF BUYING DECISION

The promotional mix also depends on the type of buying decision (routine or complex). For example, the most effective promotion for routine consumer decisions, like buying toothpaste or soft drinks, calls attention to the brand or reminds the consumer about the brand. Advertising and, especially, sales promotion are the most productive promotion tools to use for routine decisions.

If the decision is neither routine nor complex, advertising and public relations help establish awareness for the good or service. Suppose a man is looking for a bottle of wine to serve to his dinner guests. As a beer drinker, he is not familiar with wines, yet he has seen advertising for Robert Mondavi wine and has also read an article in a popular magazine about the Robert Mondavi winery. He may be more likely to buy this brand because he is already aware of it.

In contrast, consumers making complex buying decisions are more extensively involved. They rely on large amounts of information to help them reach a purchase decision. Personal selling is most effective in helping these consumers decide. For example, consumers thinking about buying a car usually depend on a salesperson to provide the information they need to reach a decision. Print advertising may also be used for high-involvement purchase decisions because it can often provide a large amount of information to the consumer.

AVAILABLE FUNDS

Money, or the lack of it, may easily be the most important factor in determining the promotional mix. A small, undercapitalized manufacturer may rely heavily on free publicity if its product is unique. If the situation warrants a sales force, a financially strained firm may turn to manufacturers' agents, who work on a commission basis with no advances or expense accounts. Even well-capitalized organizations may not be able to afford the advertising rates of publications like *Better Homes and Gardens, Reader's Digest,* and the *Wall Street Journal,* or the cost of running television commercials on *CSI* or the Super Bowl. The price of a high-profile advertisement in these media could support several salespeople for an entire year.

When funds are available to permit a mix of promotional elements, a firm will generally try to optimize its return on promotion dollars while minimizing the *cost per contact,* or the cost of reaching one member of the target market. In general, the cost per contact is very high for personal selling, public relations, and sales promotions like sampling and demonstrations. On the other hand, given the number of people national advertising reaches, it has a very low cost per contact.

Usually, there is a trade-off among the funds available, the number of people in the target market, the quality of communication needed, and the relative costs of the promotional elements. A company may have to forgo a full-page, color advertisement in *People* magazine in order to pay for a personal selling effort. Although the magazine ad will reach more people than personal selling, the high cost of the magazine space is a problem.

PUSH AND PULL STRATEGIES

The last factor that affects the promotional mix is whether to use a push or a pull promotional strategy. Manufacturers may use aggressive personal selling and trade advertising to convince a wholesaler or a retailer to carry and sell their merchandise. This approach is known as a **push strategy** (see Exhibit 14.6). The wholesaler, in turn, must often push the merchandise forward by persuading the retailer to handle the goods. The retailer then uses advertising, displays, and other forms of promotion to convince the consumer to buy the "pushed" products. This concept also applies to services. For example, the Jamaican Tourism Board targets promotions to travel agencies, which, in turn, tell their customers about the benefits of vacationing in Jamaica.

At the other extreme is a **pull strategy,** which stimulates consumer demand to obtain product distribution. Rather than trying to sell to the wholesaler, the manufacturer using a pull strategy focuses its promotional efforts on end consumers or opinion leaders. For example, BriteSmile Professional Teeth Whitening Centers sent office merchandising displays to dentists across the country to create a buzz and generate demand for its after-care whitening maintenance products, such as the

push strategy
A marketing strategy that uses aggressive personal selling and trade advertising to convince a wholesaler or a retailer to carry and sell particular merchandise.

pull strategy
A marketing strategy that stimulates consumer demand to obtain product distribution.

Exhibit 14.6

Push Strategy versus Pull Strategy

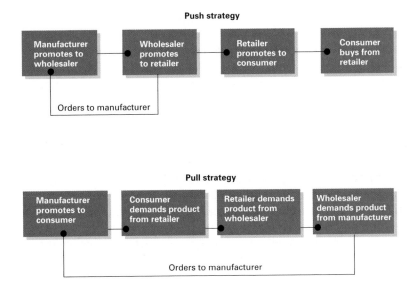

INTEGRATED MARKETING COMMUNICATIONS

CHAPTER 14

Sonicare sonic toothbrush, toothpaste, mouthwash, and mint gum.[25] As consumers begin demanding the product, the retailer orders the merchandise from the wholesaler. The wholesaler, confronted with rising demand, then places an order for the "pulled" merchandise from the manufacturer. Consumer demand pulls the product through the channel of distribution (see Exhibit 14.6). Heavy sampling, introductory consumer advertising, cents-off campaigns, and couponing are part of a pull strategy. For example, Smirnoff Ice sold almost 11 million cases in its first six months of national distribution. Contributing to those unprecedented numbers were extensive sampling, on-premise promotions, and $25 million in advertising.[26] Similarly, Splenda No Calorie Sweetner offered free samples, recipes, and a coupon to potential consumers who tried the product.[27]

Rarely does a company use a pull or a push strategy exclusively. Instead, the mix will emphasize one of these strategies. For example, pharmaceutical companies generally use a push strategy, through personal selling and trade advertising, to promote their drugs and therapies to physicians. Sales presentations and advertisements in medical journals give physicians the detailed information they need to prescribe medication to their patients. Most pharmaceutical companies supplement their push promotional strategy with a pull strategy targeted directly to potential patients through advertisements in consumer magazines and on television.

R. ALCORN/THOMSON

REVIEW LEARNING OUTCOME

LO6 Describe the factors that affect the promotional mix

- Nature of the product
- Product life cycle
- Target market characteristics
- Type of buying decision
- Funds available
- Push or pull strategy

Promotional Mix
% Advertising
% Public Relations
% Sales Promotion
% Personal Selling

LO7 Integrated Marketing Communications

Ideally, marketing communications from each promotional mix element (personal selling, advertising, sales promotion, and public relations) should be integrated— that is, the message reaching the consumer should be the same regardless of whether it is from an advertisement, a salesperson in the field, a magazine article, or a coupon in a newspaper insert.

From the consumer's standpoint, a company's communications are already integrated. Consumers do not think in terms of the four elements of promotion: advertising, sales promotion, public relations, and personal selling. Instead, everything is an "ad. In general, the only people who recognize the distinctions among these communications elements are the marketers themselves. Unfortunately, many marketers neglect this fact when planning promotional messages and fail to integrate their communication efforts from one element to the next. The most common rift typically occurs between personal selling and the other elements of the promotional mix.

This unintegrated, disjointed approach to promotion has propelled many companies to adopt the concept of **integrated marketing communications (IMC)**. IMC is the careful coordination of all promotional messages—traditional advertising, direct marketing, interactive, public relations, sales promotion, personal selling, event marketing, and other communications—for a product or service to assure the consistency of messages at every contact point where a company meets the consumer. Following the concept of IMC, marketing managers carefully work out the roles that various promotional ele-

integrated marketing communications (IMC)
The careful coordination of all promotional messages for a product or a service to assure the consistency of messages at every contact point where a company meets the consumer.

Moviemakers frequently use integrated marketing techniques to promote their films. Internet contests on Google, guide books from key cities in the story, and controversy over the movie's religious themes all contributed to the box-office success of the Da Vinci Code.

ments will play in the marketing mix. Timing of promotional activities is coordinated, and the results of each campaign are carefully monitored to improve future use of the promotional mix tools. Typically, a marketing communications director is appointed who has overall responsibility for integrating the company's marketing communications.

Movie marketing campaigns benefit greatly from an IMC approach. Those campaigns that are most integrated generally have more impact and make a deeper impression on potential moviegoers, leading to higher box-office sales. An integrated marketing approach was used to introduce the Da Vinci Code. Excitement about the release of the film gathered momentum months in advance as the trailer was shown on the Internet and television. Along with the release of the trailer, the movie was supported by numerous merchandising efforts. Bookstores and gift shops stocked hardback, paperback, and special illustrated editions, as well as *Da Vinci Code* walking tours of key cities in the story, playing cards, calligraphy sets, music CDs, video games, podcasts and more. Google and Sony launched a game called "The Sony Ericsson Da Vinci Code Trail" in 22 languages. Players competed against each other online and then in a real life challenge in Paris. The winner was awarded a two week trip to Rome, Paris, London, and New York. The game did more than promote the movie, however. "Da Vinci Code Trail" familiarized people with Google's services beyond search and drove traffic to Sony's Web site, which rose 30 percent as a result of the promotion. Finally, before the movie's release, there were over 500,000 English language posts on blogs like Technorati, Google, IceRocket, and BlogPulse. The integrated marketing campaign (plus the religious controversy surrounding the story) helped the film generate over $77 million at the box office on opening weekend.[28]

The IMC concept has been growing in popularity for several reasons. First, the proliferation of thousands of media choices beyond traditional television has made promotion a more complicated task. Instead of promoting a product just through mass-media options, like television and magazines, promotional messages today can appear in many varied sources. Furthermore, the mass market has also fragmented—more selectively segmented markets and an increase in niche marketing have replaced the traditional broad market groups that marketers promoted to in years past. For instance, many popular magazines now have Spanish-language editions targeted toward America's growing Hispanic population. Finally, marketers have slashed their advertising spending in favor of promotional techniques that generate immediate sales responses and those whose effects are more easily measured, such as direct marketing. Thus, the interest in IMC is largely a reaction to the scrutiny that marketing communications has come under and, particularly, to suggestions that uncoordinated promotional activity leads to a strategy that is wasteful and inefficient.

REVIEW LEARNING OUTCOME

LO7 Discuss the concept of integrated marketing communications

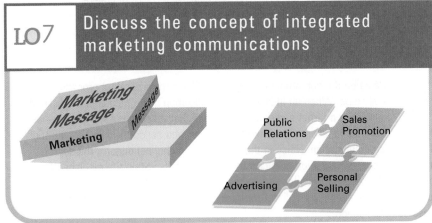

Quick Check ✔

Now that you've read the chapter, do you get it? Take a moment for a quick check using this scale:

1 Not at all; 2 Not very well; 3 Ok; 4 Well; 5 Very Well

Can you . . .

___ explain the role of promotion in the marketing mix?

___ identify the elements of the promotional mix?

___ explain the marketing communication process?

___ write a paragraph explaining the goals and tasks of promotion?

___ define the AIDA concept?

___ draw a diagram depicting how effective each element of the promotional mix is at each stage in the AIDA concept?

___ list the factors affecting the promotional mix?

___ compare a push strategy and a pull strategy?

___ explain the correlation between the promotional mix and IMC?

___ TOTAL

Score: 37–45, you're ready to move on to the applications; 28–36, skim the chapter one more time before moving on to the applications; 19–27, reread the sections giving you the most trouble and go to Thomson NOW for guided tutorials; 18 and under, you better reread the chapter to get a grasp of the fundamentals. If you've reread the chapter and still have a low score, visit your professor or TA during office hours.

Review and Applications

LO 1 Discuss the role of promotion in the marketing mix. Promotion is communication by marketers that informs, persuades, and reminds potential buyers of a product in order to influence an opinion or elicit a response. Promotional strategy is the plan for using the elements of promotion—advertising, public relations, sales promotion, and personal selling—to meet the firm's overall objectives and marketing goals. Based on these objectives, the elements of the promotional strategy become a coordinated promotion plan. The promotion plan then becomes an integral part of the total marketing strategy for reaching the target market along with product, distribution, and price.

1.1 What is a promotional strategy? Explain the concept of a competitive advantage in relation to promotional strategy.

LO 2 Discuss the elements of the promotional mix. The elements of the promotional mix include advertising, public relations, sales promotion, and personal selling. Advertising is a form of impersonal, one-way mass communication paid for by the source. Public relations is the function of promotion concerned with a firm's public image. Firms can't buy good publicity, but they can take steps to create a positive company image. Sales promotion is typically used to back up other components of the promotional mix by stimulating immediate demand. Finally, personal selling typically involves direct communication, in person or by telephone; the seller tries to initiate a purchase by informing and persuading one or more potential buyers.

2.1 As the promotional manager for a new line of cosmetics targeted to preteen girls, you have been assigned the task of deciding which promotional mix elements—advertising, public relations, sales promotion, and personal selling—should be used in promoting it. Your budget for promoting the preteen cosmetics line is limited. Write a promotional plan explaining your choice of promotional mix elements given the nature of the product, the stage in the product life cycle, the target market characteristics, the type of buying decision, available funds, and the use of a pull or push strategy.

LO 3 Describe the communication process. The communication process has several steps. When an individual or organization has a message it wishes to convey to a target audience, it encodes that message using language and symbols familiar to the intended receiver and sends the message through a channel of communication. Noise in the transmission channel distorts the source's intended message. Reception occurs if the message falls within the receiver's frame of reference. The receiver decodes the message and usually provides feedback to the source. Normally, feedback is direct for interpersonal communication and indirect for mass communication.

3.1 Why is understanding the target market a crucial aspect of the communication process?

LO4 Explain the goals and tasks of promotion. The fundamental goals of promotion are to induce, modify, or reinforce behavior by informing, persuading, and reminding. Informative promotion explains a good's or service's purpose and benefits. Promotion that informs the consumer is typically used to increase demand for a general product category or to introduce a new good or service. Persuasive promotion is designed to stimulate a purchase or an action. Promotion that persuades the consumer to buy is essential during the growth stage of the product life cycle, when competition becomes fierce. Reminder promotion is used to keep the product and brand name in the public's mind. Promotions that remind are generally used during the maturity stage of the product life cycle.

4.1 Why might a marketing manager choose to promote his or her product using persuasion? Give some current examples of persuasive promotion.

4.2 Choose a partner from class and go together to interview the owners or managers of several small businesses in your city. Ask them what their promotional objectives are and why. Are they trying to inform, persuade, or remind customers to do business with them? Also determine whether they believe they have an awareness problem or whether they need to persuade customers to come to them instead of to competitors. Ask them to list the characteristics of their primary market, the strengths and weaknesses of their direct competitors, and how they are positioning their store to compete. Prepare a report to present in class summarizing your findings.

LO5 Discuss the AIDA concept and its relationship to the promotional mix. The AIDA model outlines the four basic stages in the purchase decision-making process, which are initiated and propelled by promotional activities: (1) attention, (2) interest, (3) desire, and (4) action. The components of the promotional mix have varying levels of influence at each stage of the AIDA model. Advertising is a good tool for increasing awareness and knowledge of a good or service. Sales promotion is effective when consumers are at the purchase stage of the decision-making process. Personal selling is most effective in developing customer interest and desire.

5.1 Discuss the AIDA concept. How do these different stages of consumer involvement affect the promotional mix?

5.2 How does a Web site's ease of use affect its ability to create attention, interest, desire, and action? Visit the kitchen and bath pages of Kohler's Web site (**http://www.kohler.com**) and determine how successful the company is at moving consumers through the AIDA process.

LO6 Describe the factors that affect the promotional mix. Promotion managers consider many factors when creating promotional mixes. These factors include the nature of the product, product life-cycle stage, target market characteristics, the type of buying decision involved, availability of funds, and feasibility of push or pull strategies. Because most business products tend to be custom-tailored to the buyer's exact specifications, the marketing manager may choose a promotional mix that relies more heavily on personal selling. On the other hand, consumer products are generally mass produced and lend themselves more to mass promotional efforts such as advertising and sales promotion. As products move through different stages of the product life cycle, marketers will choose to use different promotional elements. For example, advertising is emphasized more in the introductory stage of the product life cycle than in the decline stage. Characteristics of the target market, such as geographic location of potential buyers and brand loyalty, influence the promotional mix as does whether the buying decision is complex or routine. The amount of funds a firm has to allocate to promotion may also help determine the promotional mix. Small firms with limited funds may rely more heavily on public relations, whereas larger firms may be able to afford broadcast or print advertising. Last, if a firm uses a push strategy to promote the product or service, the marketing manager may choose to use aggressive advertising and personal selling to wholesalers and retailers. If a pull strategy is chosen, then the manager often relies on aggressive mass promotion, such as advertising and sales promotion, to stimulate consumer demand.

6.1 Explain the difference between a "pull" and a "push" promotional strategy. Under what conditions should each strategy be used?

6.2 Use Radioguide.com (**http://www.radioguide.com**) to find a listing of radio Web sites in your area. View several of the stations' sites and compare the promotions featured. What conclusions can you draw about the target market of each station based on the types of promotions they are currently running? Would any of the promotions entice you to tune to a station that you normally don't listen to?

6.3 Visit **http://www.teenresearch.com**. What research can this company offer about the size and growth of the teen market, the buying power of teenagers, and their buying habits? Why might these statistics be important to a company targeting teenagers in terms of marketing communications and promotion strategy?

LO7 Discuss the concept of integrated marketing communications. Integrated marketing communications is the careful coordination of all promotional messages for a product or service to assure the consistency of messages at every contact point where a company meets the consumer—advertising, sales promotion, personal selling, public relations, as well as direct marketing, packaging, and other forms of communication. Marketing managers carefully coordinate all promotional activities to ensure that consumers see and hear one message. Integrated marketing communications has received more attention in recent years due to the proliferation of media choices, the fragmentation of mass markets into more segmented niches, and the decrease in advertising spending in favor of promotional techniques that generate an immediate sales response.

7.1 Discuss the importance of integrated marketing communications. Give some current examples of companies that are and are not practicing IMC.

7.2 What do you think is the role of Hallmark's Web site (**http://www.hallmark.com**) in the company's integrated marketing communications plan? What seems to be the marketing function of the site? Do you think the site is effective?

Key Terms

Exercises

APPLICATION EXERCISE 1

An important concept in promotion is semiotics, or the study of meaning and meaning-producing events. An understanding of semiotics can help you not only to identify objects (denotation) but also to grasp the utility of images and associations (connotation). By manipulating connotations of objects in advertising, you can create, change, or reinforce images for products. Thus, semiotics is a powerful tool for brand management and promotion.[30]

Activities

1. Make a list of ten images and associations that come to mind for each of the following items: baseball, vinyl record album, spoon, rubber band.

2. Look through magazines and see if you can find print advertisements that include each of the items (baseball, vinyl record album, spoon, rubber band) in a supporting role. What seems to be the message of each ad? How does the item help create or reinforce an image for the product being sold in the ad?

3. Think of an everyday object of your own. What are its likely connotations? For example, a dog in a car might signal a family vehicle, but a dog also connotes loyalty, "man's best friend," and dependability. What images and associations are likely with your item? Make a list of as many as you can.

4. Now use your object and list of associations to create an image for another product. Think of the likely connotations your object will have for a certain target market and how such connotations can support a brand image. For example, if your everyday object is a candle, you might choose lingerie for your product, based on a candle's romantic connotations.

APPLICATION EXERCISE 2

Many people are not aware of the rationale behind certain advertising messages. "Why do Infiniti ads show rocks and trees instead of automobiles?" "If car safety is so important, why do automobile ads often show cars skidding on wet, shiny surfaces?" "Target's ads are funky, with all the bright colors and product packaging, but what's the message?"

One way to understand the vagaries of the encoding process is to think of the popular board game *Taboo* by Hasbro. In this game, each team tries to get its members to guess a word without using obvious word clues. For example, to get the team to guess "apple," you may not say such words as *red, fruit, pie, cider,* or *core.* Sometimes advertising is like *Taboo* in that advertisers are not allowed to use certain words or descriptions. For example, pharmaceutical companies are not permitted to make certain claims or to say what a drug treats unless the ad also mentions the potential side effects. Language choices are also limited in advertising. To appreciate this, you can apply the *Taboo* game rules in an advertising format.[29]

Activities

1. Select a product from the list below, and then create a print advertisement or a television storyboard for that product. As part of the exercise, give your product a brand name. Taboo words, visuals, and concepts are given for each product type. Taboo items cannot be present in your work.

Product	Taboo Words, Visuals, and Concepts
Deodorant	Odor, underarm, perspiration, smell, sweat
Pain reliever	Pain, aches, fever, child-proof cap, gel
Soft drinks	Sugar-free, refreshing, thirst, swimwear, any celebrity

2. Now create a second ad or storyboard for your product. This time, however, you must use all the words, visuals, and concepts that are listed in the right column.

Product	Must-Use Words, Visuals, and Concepts
Deodorant	A romantic couple, monster trucks
Pain reliever	A mother and child, oatmeal, homework
Soft drinks	A cup of coffee, cookies, birthday cake, wine

Entrepreneurship Case

WICKED AWESOME! MUSICAL ENCHANTS RECORD CROWDS AFTER ROCKY START

When the curtains first lifted on the Broadway musical *Wicked,* it appeared that audiences had been scared away from the box office. The Gershwin Theater was rarely full, and a production that had cost over $14 million posted advance ticket sales of only $9 million. Crippled by cost overruns, cast changes, song rewrites, and a 2003 start date that was much later than projected, excitement and enthusiasm waned for what was once a much-anticipated show.

Based on Gregory Maguire's best-selling 1995 novel of the same name, the story is a prequel to Frank Baum's 1939 classic, *The Wizard of Oz.* The musical examines the lives of two teenage witches, Glinda and Elphaba, and wonders which one is truly evil. Glinda, a beautiful, ambitious, and popular blond, grows up to become the Good Witch; Elphaba, a green-skinned, intelligent, free-spirited rebel, develops into the nefarious Wicked Witch of the West. Elaborate sets, lighting, and costumes and a score by Academy Award–winning songwriter Stephen Schwartz did not impress the *New York Times,* however. Its scathing review claimed, "There's trouble in Emerald City . . . [it's] a sermon of a musical."

Unfazed, *Wicked* producer Marc Platt, a former Universal Pictures executive, never lost faith in his production. He remained convinced that if he could just get people in the door, they would leave completely captivated by what he considered a truly exceptional experience. So he cut ticket prices by 30 percent and watched as patrons began to make repeat ticket purchases during intermission. After the shows, swarms of enthralled teenage girls began to gather outside the stage door in hopes of meeting the cast.

As the target market emerged before his eyes, Platt leveraged his Hollywood experience to turn *Wicked* into a musical marketing machine. The hot ticket sales during show intermissions indicated that the show's success would hinge on word-of-mouth referrals from the show's core audience—teenage girls. To get more of them talking, Platt and the marketing team published feature articles on the show's Web site and seeded Internet chat rooms with *Wicked*-related topics. An all-out promotions blitz ensued.

Wicked lined up character endorsement deals with makeup manufacturer, Stila, and sent hot new stars Kristin Chenoweth and Idina Menzel to Sephora stores to give makeovers to teen fans with Glinda facial glitter and Elphaba lipstick. In an interesting twist on *American Idol, Wicked* karaoke contests at malls served as fake auditions that awarded real tickets to the most passionate fans. Radio promos in New York and Chicago were supported by advertising at Macy's and in *Elle Girl* magazine for a Halloween campaign that lasted a month.

As the show became profitable, two U.S. tours were launched. The shows routinely sell out, and yearly revenues are now close to $200 million. Tickets to the show on Broadway now command a record-tying $110, and the show's take is about $1.3 million a week in New York alone. Mike Isaacson, vice president of the Fox Theatre in St. Louis, sold an amazing $1.5 million worth of tickets a mere 48 hours after they went on sale. "This show is a rocket because it's attracting people from teenagers to grandparents," he mused.

Day-of-show raffles for tickets at sold-out venues give a few lucky patrons a chance to buy $25 tickets. Those raffles generally appeal to younger theatergoers, but those witch-wannabes bring mom and dad out for the night of mischief too. And their dollars help fund purchases of merchandise at the traveling OzDust Boutiques. Items like *Wicked*-branded golf balls, T-shirts, necklaces, and CDs of the show's musical numbers sell at the stands and at **http://www.wickedthemusical.com**. Sales generate weekly merchandise receipts of more than $300,000. But that doesn't surprise Marc Platt. Reflecting on the show's universal premise, he quips, "There's a little green girl inside all of us."[31]

Questions

1. Identify and describe the elements of *Wicked*'s promotional mix.

2. Did *Wicked* use a push or a pull promotional strategy? Explain.

3. As *Wicked* progresses through its life cycle, what changes would you recommend making to the current promotional mix? Why?

4. Describe how the AIDA process worked for various *Wicked* promotions. Which one do you think was most effective?

COMPANY CLIPS

Vans – Off the Wall and On Target

You have undoubtedly heard of Vans. The company has sold footwear, apparel, and extreme sports equipment for over 40 years using the distinct tagline, "Off the Wall." The company's founder wanted to control his own retail channel, so he transformed his manufacturing company into a marketing company. Always carefully protecting its unique brand image, Vans has crafted successful marketing messages and promotions that resonate with the youth culture that represents the company's target market. This video examines the carefully planned strategy that Vans developed to create loyalty in a fickle niche market.

Questions

1. Does Vans use a push or pull strategy to market its apparel? How does Steve feel about the two strategies?

2. What does Steve mean when he refers to tours and events as "planting seeds?"

3. Describe Vans' pyramid strategy. How does it protect the brand?

4. How does Steve's hands-on approach to events and promotion benefit the company?

BIZ FLIX

About a Boy

Now that you have a better grasp of marketing communications, you understand how messages can be designed to produce desired results. As an encore to your study, watch the film clip from *About a Boy*, starring Hugh Grant as happy, self-absorbed bachelor Will Lightman, who joins a support group for single parents as a way to meet women. Although Will has no children of his own, he finds himself inventing a son named Ned at his first Single Parents Alone Together (SPAT) meeting. Watching the clip, think about the communication process. How is Will's monologue like a promotional message? How is the AIDA concept at work in this scene? Explain. What other chapter concepts can you see in the clip if you think of it as a metaphor for marketing promotion?

Higher scores on this scale indicate that others perceive you to be responsive, warm, and a good listener. A high score also corresponds to a willingness to mentor others. If your score is low, it indicates that you don't actively encourage other people to share information about themselves with you. That doesn't mean you are a poor listener, however. Rather, you prefer not to take the initiative in the interaction.

Advertising and

CHAPTER

15

Public Relations

Learning Outcomes

LO ¹ Discuss the effects of advertising on market share and consumers

LO ² Identify the major types of advertising

LO ³ Discuss the creative decisions in developing an advertising campaign

LO ⁴ Describe media evaluation and selection techniques

LO ⁵ Discuss the role of public relations in the promotional mix

a new medium for advertising— **Bluetooth** enabled cell phones

Advertisers are constantly searching for a competitive edge, and cell phones may offer one. Ad agencies are testing the use of cell phones as a medium for delivering ads. The initial ads were mostly text messages, but as cell phone technology improves, video clips will become more popular. Two methods are being used for

The big appeal of cell phone advertising is that it is a good way to communicate with the youth market

cell phone advertising—opt-in lists and location-based advertising. Opt-in lists are targeted audiences who agree to receive messages. For instance, in the United States TV networks have used opt-in lists to announce new shows. A recent study suggests that 20 percent of wireless phone users would be receptive to targeted wireless phone advertising, particularly if advertisers agree to pay for premium services such as directory assistance, ring tones, and messaging. Procter & Gamble has used this approach with several of its products.

Location-based advertising gets the messages out by installing special transmitters on billboards and in prime locations for particular market segments, such as airports, train stations, and shopping malls. The transmitters are designed to identify individuals carrying cell phones with Bluetooth technology—a short-range wireless system that enables text, sound,

and video to be sent to the phone. When individuals pass within 100 yards of the transmitter, the transmitter sends a message asking if the individual wants to receive the message. In several tests, the response rate has been as high as 15 percent. Nike installed a huge Bluetooth-powered outdoor ad featuring tennis player Rafael Nadal in Plaza Cataluña, in Barcelona, Spain. By using their Bluetooth cell phone connection, users could download the new Nike Pro TV spot and an exclusive Nadal screensaver.

The big appeal of cell phone advertising is that it is a good way to communicate with the youth market, which buys a lot of products like music and movies but spends little time with traditional media like TV, newspapers, and magazines. For example, Maiden Group, PLC, an advertising agency based in the United Kingdom, promoted a new album by rock band Coldplay using 30-second spots featuring interviews with the musicians and clips from their music videos. The clips were used in six London train stations where large video advertising screens told cell phone users to switch on their Bluetooth phones to receive a message. The album became a number one hit in the United Kingdom, and the agency plans to use the approach with other promotions for this segment.[1]

How do you feel about cell phone advertising? Do you consider cell phone advertising to be like spam on your computer? Would subsidization of premium services motivate you to receive ads on your cell phone?

The Effects of Advertising

Advertising is defined in Chapter 14 as any form of impersonal, paid communication in which the sponsor or company is identified. It is a popular form of promotion, especially for consumer packaged goods and services. Advertising expenditures increase annually and were almost $300 billion in 2006. In 2005, 32 companies spent over $1 billion each; together, they accounted for about 22 percent of total ad spending. Among the top brands advertised by these companies were Verizon Communications, Olay, Crest, and Tylenol.[2]

Although total advertising expenditures seem large, the industry itself is fairly small. Only about 155,000 individuals are employed by the 12,000 or so advertising agencies. Another 240,000 people work in related services such as media buying, display advertising, and direct-mail advertising.[3]

The amount of money budgeted for advertising by some firms is staggering (see Exhibit 15.1). General Motors, Procter & Gamble and Time Warner each spend almost $4 billion annually in the United States on national advertising alone. That's about $10 million a day on national advertising. If local advertising, sales promotion, and public relations are included, this figure rises much higher. Over 100 companies spend more than $300 million each on advertising every year.[4]

Spending on advertising varies by industry. For example, the game and toy industry has one of the highest ratios of advertising dollars to sales. For every dollar of merchandise sold in the toy industry, about 12 to 15 cents is spent on advertising the toy to consumers. Book publishers spend roughly 27 cents on advertising for every dollar of book revenue. Other consumer goods manufacturers that spend heavily on advertising in relation to total sales include sugar and confectionery products manufacturers, leather manufacturers, watchmakers, perfume and cosmetic manufacturers, detergent makers, and wine and liquor companies.[5]

Exhibit 15.1

Top Ten Leaders by U.S. Advertising Spending

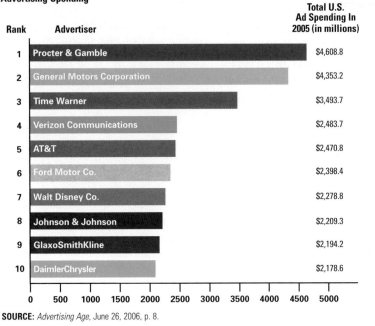

Rank	Advertiser	Total U.S. Ad Spending In 2005 (in millions)
1	Procter & Gamble	$4,608.8
2	General Motors Corporation	$4,353.2
3	Time Warner	$3,493.7
4	Verizon Communications	$2,483.7
5	AT&T	$2,470.8
6	Ford Motor Co.	$2,398.4
7	Walt Disney Co.	$2,278.8
8	Johnson & Johnson	$2,209.3
9	GlaxoSmithKline	$2,194.2
10	DaimlerChrysler	$2,178.6

SOURCE: *Advertising Age*, June 26, 2006, p. 8.

ADVERTISING AND MARKET SHARE

Today's most successful brands of consumer goods, like Ivory soap and Coca-Cola, were built by heavy advertising and marketing investments long ago. Today's advertising dollars are spent on maintaining brand awareness and market share.

New brands with a small market share tend to spend proportionately more for advertising and sales promotion than those with a large market share, typically for two reasons. First, beyond a certain level of spending for advertising and sales promotion, diminishing returns set in. That is, sales or market share begins to decrease no matter how much is spent on advertising and sales promotion. This phenomenon is called the **advertising response function.** Understanding the advertising response function helps marketers use budgets wisely. A market leader like Johnson & Johnson's Neutrogena typically spends proportionately less on advertising than a newcomer like Jergens' Natural Glow Daily Moisturizer brand. Jergens spends more on its brand to gain attention and increase market share. Neutrogena, on the other hand, spends only as much as is needed to maintain market share; anything more would produce diminishing benefits. Neutrogena has already captured the attention of the majority of its target market. It only needs to remind customers of its product.

advertising response function

A phenomenon in which spending for advertising and sales promotion increases sales or market share up to a certain level but then produces diminishing returns.

The second reason that new brands tend to require higher spending for advertising and sales promotion is that a certain minimum level of exposure is needed to measurably affect purchase habits. If Jergens advertised Natural Glow Daily Moisturizer in only one or two publications and bought only one or two television spots, it certainly would not achieve the exposure needed to penetrate consumers' perceptual defenses, gain attention, and ultimately affect purchase intentions. Instead, Natural Glow Daily Moisturizer was advertised in many different media for a sustained time.

THE EFFECTS OF ADVERTISING ON CONSUMERS

Advertising affects consumers' daily lives, informing them about products and services and influencing their attitudes, beliefs, and ultimately their purchases. The average U.S. citizen is exposed to hundreds of advertisements a day from all types of advertising media. In the television medium alone, researchers estimate that the average viewer watches at least six hours of commercial television messages a week. In addition, that person is exposed to countless print ads and promotional messages seen in other places. Advertising affects the TV programs people watch, the content of the newspapers they read, the politicians they elect, the medicines they take, and the toys their children play with. Consequently, the influence of advertising on the U.S. socioeconomic system has been the subject of extensive debate among economists, marketers, sociologists, psychologists, politicians, consumerists, and many others.

Though advertising cannot change consumers' deeply rooted values and attitudes, it may succeed in transforming a person's negative attitude toward a product into a positive one. For instance, serious or dramatic advertisements are more effective at changing consumers' negative attitudes. Humorous ads, on the other hand, have been shown to be more effective at shaping attitudes when consumers already have a positive image of the advertised brand.[6] For this reason, beer marketers often use humorous ads, such as Budweiser's musical tributes to "Real Men of Genius" (like Mr. Hot–Dog–Eating–Contest–Contestant), to communicate with their core market of young adults.

Advertising also reinforces positive attitudes toward brands. When consumers have a neutral or favorable frame of reference toward a product or brand, advertising often positively influences them. When consumers are already highly loyal to a brand, they may buy more of it when advertising and promotion for that brand increase.[7] This is why market leaders like General Motors and Procter & Gamble spend billions of dollars annually to reinforce and remind their loyal customers about the benefits of their cars and household products.

Advertising can also affect the way consumers rank a brand's attributes, such as color, taste, smell, and texture. For example, in years past car ads emphasized such brand attributes as roominess, speed, and low maintenance. Today, however, car marketers have added safety, versatility, and customization to the list. Safety features like antilock brakes, power door locks, and front and side air bags are now a standard part of the message in many carmakers' ads. Toyota Scion appeals to consumers' sense of individuality by allowing purchasers to custom-design their cars by selecting features such as the steering wheel color, multi-shade illuminated cup holders, and "sport" pedals.[8]

REVIEW LEARNING OUTCOME

LO I Discuss the effects of advertising on market share and consumers

Return on advertising expense (in sales or market share)

Building sales/share

Maintaining sales/share

Advertising response function

Money spent

Advertising can: ✓ change negative attitude to positive
✓ reinforce positive attitude
✓ affect how consumers rank brand attributes

Major Types of Advertising

The firm's promotional objectives determine the type of advertising it uses. If the goal of the promotion plan is to build up the image of the company or the industry, **institutional advertising** may be used. In contrast, if the advertiser wants to enhance the sales of a specific good or service, **product advertising** is used.

INSTITUTIONAL ADVERTISING

Historically, advertising in the United States has been product oriented. Today, however, companies market multiple products and need a different type of advertising. Institutional advertising, or corporate advertising, promotes the corporation as a whole and is designed to establish, change, or maintain the corporation's identity. It usually does not ask the audience to do anything but maintain a favorable attitude toward the advertiser and its goods and services. For example, when Time Warner dropped AOL from the company's corporate brand name, it hired a branding agency to develop institutional advertising to reposition the brand without the Internet unit and refocus the image on Time Warner as a media giant. In designing the "rebranding," executives did not want a radical change. Rather they wanted to "freshen" the previous image and maintain its favorable status. The logo itself changed in texture, color, and typeface. In addition to changing the logo on buildings, business cards, and stationery, the company changed its stock ticker symbol to reflect the new image.[9]

A form of institutional advertising called **advocacy advertising** is typically used to safeguard against negative consumer attitudes and to enhance the company's credibility among consumers who already favor its position. Often corporations use advocacy advertising to express their views on controversial issues. At other times, firms' advocacy campaigns react to criticism or blame, some in direct response to criticism by the media. Other advocacy campaigns may try to ward off increased regulation, damaging legislation, or an unfavorable outcome in a lawsuit. The tobacco companies have utilized "good citizen campaigns" in the United States and around the world in an effort to create a positive public image for themselves after losing several class-action suits and being accused of targeting children with their marketing campaigns. In an effort to improve its corporate image, Philip Morris has been spending more than $120 million a year promoting its environmental and community development programs, such as building homes for Habitat for Humanity, making donations to food banks, and supporting meal programs for seniors and shelters for battered women.[10]

PRODUCT ADVERTISING

Unlike institutional advertising, product advertising promotes the benefits of a specific good or service. The product's stage in its life cycle often determines which type of product advertising is used: pioneering advertising, competitive advertising, or comparative advertising.

Pioneering Advertising

Pioneering advertising is intended to stimulate primary demand for a new product or product category. Heavily used during the introductory stage of the product life cycle, pioneering advertising offers consumers in-depth information about the benefits of the product class. Pioneering advertising also seeks to create interest. Microsoft used pioneering advertising to introduce its new Windows and Office software products. To reposition its flagship products as more "user-friendly," the software giant added "XP"—short for "Experience"—to the Windows and Office upgrades.[11] Microsoft's $200 million four-month launch phase kicked off with two 15-second TV teaser spots, plus one 60-second and two 30-second TV spots that featured the Madonna song "Ray of Light." The print, outdoor, TV, and online campaign carried the tagline "Yes, you

institutional advertising
A form of advertising designed to enhance a company's image rather than promote a particular product.

product advertising
A form of advertising that touts the benefits of a specific good or service.

advocacy advertising
A form of advertising in which an organization expresses its views on controversial issues or responds to media attacks

pioneering advertising
A form of advertising designed to stimulate primary demand for a new product or product category.

can" and featured XP's signature look—blue skies with white clouds over a green field. The goal of Microsoft's pioneering campaign was to convince PC users to buy the upgrade because of the more intuitive interfaces and the ability to work seamlessly and easily with digital photographs, music files, and video.[12]

Pizza Hut
Papa John's

Can you find evidence of comparative advertising on either Pizza Hut's or Papa John's Web site?

http://www.pizzahut.com
http://www.papajohns.com

Online

Competitive Advertising

Firms use competitive or brand advertising when a product enters the growth phase of the product life cycle and other companies begin to enter the marketplace. Instead of building demand for the product category, the goal of **competitive advertising** is to influence demand for a specific brand. Often promotion becomes less informative and appeals more to emotions during this phase. Advertisements may begin to stress subtle differences between brands, with heavy emphasis on building recall of a brand name and creating a favorable attitude toward the brand. Automobile advertising has long used very competitive messages, drawing distinctions based on such factors as quality, performance, and image. Similarly, in an effort to obtain market share from competitors and build brand awareness in the wireless industry, Nextel Communications signed a ten-year title sponsorship agreement with NASCAR. NASCAR executives, interested in building a younger fan base, consider the telecom industry one of the best ways to reach younger consumers because they always have a cell phone "stuck" to their ear.[13]

Comparative Advertising

Comparative advertising directly or indirectly compares two or more competing brands on one or more specific attributes. Some advertisers even use comparative advertising against their own brands. Products experiencing sluggish growth or those entering the marketplace against strong competitors are more likely to employ comparative claims in their advertising. For instance, Miller Lite implemented a comparative advertising campaign in an attempt to regain market share from Bud Light. The focus of the campaign was that Miller Lite has the fewest simple carbohydrates of the leading light beers. The ads ended by stating that "Miller Lite has half the carbs of Bud Light."[14]

Before the 1970s, comparative advertising was allowed only if the competing brand was veiled and unidentified. In 1971, however, the Federal Trade Commission (FTC) fostered the growth of comparative advertising by saying that it provided information to the customer and that advertisers were more skillful than the government in communicating this information. Federal rulings prohibit advertisers from falsely describing competitors' products and allow competitors to sue if ads show their products or mention their brand names in an incorrect or false manner.

FTC rules also apply to advertisers making false claims about their own products. For example, a physicians' group filed false advertising complaints against the popular and long-lasting "milk mustache" ad campaign. The physicians said the ads, featuring sports figures, falsely claimed to enhance sports performances. In response to the physicians' petition, a federal panel was formed to determine whether there was a scientific consensus regarding the range of benefits attributed to milk. The panel's report supported most of the physicians' complaints and was turned over to the FTC for investigation.[15] In another case, the FTC required computer maker Gateway to reimburse customers after it charged them for an Internet access plan that was supposed to be free. Gateway offered one year of free Internet access as an incentive to buy Gateway Essential PCs, but customers found themselves paying $3.95 per hour for Net access.[16]

Companies must be careful with comparative advertising approaches in other countries as well. Germany, Italy, Belgium, and France, for example, do not permit advertisers to claim that their products are the best or better than competitors' products, both of which are common claims in the United States. In the Netherlands, car manufacturers cannot make claims in their advertising about the fuel consumption or environmental

competitive advertising
A form of advertising designed to influence demand for a specific brand.

comparative advertising
A form of advertising that compares two or more specifically named or shown competing brands on one or more specific attributes.

aspects of the car. Similarly, Lands' End ran afoul of a German law prohibiting lifetime guarantee claims, which happen to be one of Lands' End's guiding principles. The law has made it difficult for the direct retailer to sell its products and advertise its lifetime guarantee through the Internet and direct mail. In Italy, Absolut ran an ad claiming that it was the only vodka made from grain, which is perceived to produce a higher-quality vodka than potatoes do. Rival distributor Aosta Company, noting that two of its products were made from grain, filed a complaint against Absolut's Italian distributor, Seagram Italia.[17] Although comparative advertising has been legal in Italy since 1999, ads cannot make unsubstantiated claims. So authorities ordered the campaign stopped and Seagram Italia had to pull all ads. In South Korea, where comparative advertising is banned, ads for the domestic search engine Empas proclaim, "Empas Is No. 1, Yahoo! Is No. 6," and "If you can't find it with Yahoo!, try Empas." Yahoo! filed a complaint with Korea's Fair Trade Commission requesting that the ads be stopped.[18]

In other countries, hard-hitting comparative advertising will not be effective because it offends cultural values. For example, Arabic culture generally encourages people not to compete with one another, and the sharing of wealth is common practice. Therefore, comparative advertising is not consistent with social values in Arabic countries. Japanese advertisers have also been reluctant to use comparative advertising because it is considered confrontational and doesn't promote the respectful treatment of consumers or portray a company in a respectful light. Nevertheless, although the Japanese have traditionally favored soft-sell advertising approaches, consumers are witnessing a trend toward comparative ads.

REVIEW LEARNING OUTCOME

LO2 Identify the major types of advertising

LO3
Creative Decisions in Advertising

Advertising strategies typically are organized around an advertising campaign. An **advertising campaign** is a series of related advertisements focusing on a common theme, slogan, and set of advertising appeals. It is a specific advertising effort for a particular product that extends for a defined period of time. For example, XM Satellite Radio, the first subscription-based, digital-quality, satellite-transmitted radio service, developed an introductory advertising campaign around the theme "Radio to the Power of X." The company was attempting to persuade consumers to pay a monthly fee for what had always been free. Launched in movie theaters and then on TV, the $100 million ad campaign featured musicians and objects crashing to earth, each highlighting a different genre of satellite programming. B. B. King, Snoop Dogg, and David Bowie made appearances as they tumbled toward the ground. Other spots showed records raining on kids in a parking lot and a truck driver caught in a storm of cellos, trombones, and pianos. At the end of each spot, an XM tuner cycled through the channels until it rested on the appropriate genre. The idea was to convey the endless variety of programming offered on XM Satellite Radio and to set XM apart from its competitor, Sirius.[19]

advertising campaign
A series of related advertisements focusing on a common theme, slogan, and set of advertising appeals.

Before any creative work can begin on an advertising campaign, it is important to determine what goals or objectives the advertising should achieve. An **advertising objective** identifies the specific communication task that a campaign should accomplish for a specified target audience during a specified period. The objectives of a specific advertising campaign often depend on the overall corporate objectives and the product being advertised. For example, McIlhenny Company's Tabasco Hot Sauce launched a print advertising campaign with the objective of educating consumers about how to use the product and the variety of flavors offered. The ads featured product information embedded in the label, which was blown up to cover the entire page. The ad copy for the Garlic Pepper Sauce read: "The only one potent enough to ward off both hypothermia and vampires at once." The original Tabasco Pepper Sauce ad copy read: "It's like love, you always want more no matter how badly you got burned last time." The ad campaign increased sales by over 11 percent in the first four weeks. The print medium was also supported by participation in special events, such as the National Collegiate Tailgate Tour.[20]

The DAGMAR approach (Defining Advertising Goals for Measured Advertising Results) is one method of setting objectives. According to this method, all advertising objectives should precisely define the target audience, the desired percentage change in some specified measure of effectiveness, and the time frame in which that change is to occur. For example, the objectives for an advertising campaign for Coca-Cola's revamped POWERade brand might be to achieve a 15 percent increase in its share of the sports-drink market within eight months.

Once objectives are defined, creative work can begin on the advertising campaign. Advertising campaigns often follow the AIDA model, which was discussed in Chapter 14. Depending on where consumers are in the AIDA process, the creative development of an advertising campaign might focus on creating attention, arousing interest, stimulating desire, or ultimately leading to the action of buying the product. Specifically, creative decisions include identifying product benefits, developing and evaluating advertising appeals, executing the message, and evaluating the effectiveness of the campaign.

IDENTIFYING PRODUCT BENEFITS

A well-known rule of thumb in the advertising industry is "Sell the sizzle, not the steak"—that is, in advertising the goal is to sell the benefits of the product, not its attributes. An attribute is simply a feature of the product such as its easy-open package or special formulation. A benefit is what consumers will receive or achieve by using the product. A benefit should answer the consumer's question "What's in it for me?" Benefits might be such things as convenience, pleasure, savings, or relief. A quick test to determine whether you are offering attributes or benefits in your advertising is to ask "So?" Consider this example:

- *Attribute:* "POWERade's new line has been reformulated to combine the scientific benefits of sports drinks with B vitamins and to speed up energy metabolism." "So . . . ?"

- *Benefit:* "So, you'll satisfy your thirst with a great-tasting drink that will power you throughout the day."

Marketing research and intuition are usually used to unearth the perceived benefits of a product and to rank consumers' preferences for these benefits. Coke's rival, PepsiCo, has its own sports drink, Gatorade. Already positioned

Verizon has created a strong advertising appeal with its "Do you hear me now?" campaign. The company's unique selling proposition of nationwide wireless phone service has become its slogan: "We never stop working for you."

as *the* thirst-quencher, Gatorade's advertising touts its refueling benefits to serious athletes of mainstream sports. When Hollywood chewing gum lost its market leader status in France, the company conducted extensive research and identified several functional benefits for the "flavor" positioned gum such as fresh breath, white teeth, an energy boost, and decongestant. After repositioning the gum's functional benefits, sales increased by 28 percent.[21]

DEVELOPING AND EVALUATING ADVERTISING APPEALS

An **advertising appeal** identifies a reason for a person to buy a product. Developing advertising appeals, a challenging task, is typically the responsibility of the creative people in the advertising agency. Advertising appeals typically play off of consumers' emotions, such as fear or love, or address some need or want the consumer has, such as a need for convenience or the desire to save money.

Advertising campaigns can focus on one or more advertising appeals. Often the appeals are quite general, thus allowing the firm to develop a number of subthemes or minicampaigns using both advertising and sales promotion. Several possible advertising appeals are listed in Exhibit 15.2.

Exhibit 15.2
Common Advertising Appeals

Profit	Lets consumers know whether the product will save them money, make them money, or keep them from losing money
Health	Appeals to those who are body-conscious or who want to be healthy
Love or Romance	Is used often in selling cosmetics and perfumes
Fear	Can center around social embarrassment, growing old, or losing one's health; because of its power, requires advertiser to exercise care in execution
Admiration	Is the reason that celebrity spokespeople are used so often in advertising
Convenience	Is often used for fast-food restaurants and microwave foods
Fun and Pleasure	Are the key to advertising vacations, beer, amusement parks, and more
Vanity and Egotism	Are used most often for expensive or conspicuous items such as cars and clothing
Environmental Consciousness	Centers around protecting the environment and being considerate of others in the community

Choosing the best appeal from those developed normally requires market research. Criteria for evaluation include desirability, exclusiveness, and believability. The appeal first must make a positive impression on and be desirable to the target market. It must also be exclusive or unique; consumers must be able to distinguish the advertiser's message from competitors' messages. Most important, the appeal should be believable. An appeal that makes extravagant claims not only wastes promotional dollars but also creates ill will for the advertiser.

The advertising appeal selected for the campaign becomes what advertisers call its **unique selling proposition.** The unique selling proposition usually becomes the campaign's slogan. For example, Unilever's Degree antiperspirant, targeted at males aged 18 to 25, attempted to convey the brand's "never say die" personality by partnering with Ironman and NBC to create a TV special "Degree Road to the Ironman." The TV special was to correspond with the ad campaign carrying the slogan "Kicks in the Clutch," which was also Degree's unique selling proposition.[22] Similarly, POWERade's advertising campaign aimed at the sports enthusiast carries the slogan "Sport Is What You Make It." This is POWERade's unique selling proposition, implying that your can push yourself to the limit if you are motivated and use POWERade.[23]

Effective slogans often become so ingrained that consumers hearing the slogan immediately conjure up images of the product. For example, many consumers can easily name the companies and products behind these memorable slogans or even hum the jingle that goes along with them: "Have it your way," "Tastes great, less filling," "Ring around the collar," and "Tum te Tum Tum." Advertisers often revive old slogans or jingles

advertising appeal
A reason for a person to buy a product.

unique selling proposition
A desirable, exclusive, and believable advertising appeal selected as the theme for a campaign.

in the hope that the nostalgia will create good feelings with consumers. Maytag refreshed its campaign featuring its appliance pitchman by changing the actor who plays him and giving him a helper—the third change since the ads originated in 1967. And Hershey's Kit Kat bar's jingle "Gimme a Break" is so etched in consumers' minds that recently the agency hired a film crew to ask people on the street to sing the jingle for use on the Internet, in future ad campaigns, and in its Kit Kat "Gimme a Break" Café.[24]

EXECUTING THE MESSAGE

Message execution is the way an advertisement portrays its information. In general, the AIDA plan (see Chapter 14) is a good blueprint for executing an advertising message. Any ad should immediately draw the reader's, viewer's, or listener's attention. The advertiser must then use the message to hold interest, create desire for the good or service, and ultimately motivate action—a purchase.

The style in which the message is executed is one of the most creative elements of an advertisement. Exhibit 15.3 lists some examples of executional styles used by advertisers. Executional styles often dictate what type of media is to be employed to convey the message. Scientific executional styles lend themselves well to print advertising where more information can be conveyed. On the other hand, demonstration and musical styles are more likely found in broadcast advertising.

Testimonials by athletes are one of the more popular executional styles. Tiger Woods and Shaquille O'Neal are two of the most successful athlete spokespersons. Read Shaq's own words about the power of marketing and advertising in Exhibit 15.4.

Injecting humor into an advertisement is a popular and effective executional style. Selection of a humorous approach is based on the communications goal. Humorous executional styles are more often used in radio and television advertising than in print or

Exhibit 15.3

Ten Common Executional Styles for Advertising

Slice-of-Life	Depicts people in normal settings, such as at the dinner table or in their car. McDonald's often uses slice-of-life styles showing youngsters munching french fries and Happy Meals on family outings.
Lifestyle	Shows how well the product will fit in with the consumer's lifestyle. As their Volkswagen Jetta moves through the streets of the French Quarter, the Gen X drivers plug in a techno music CD and marvel at how the rhythms of the world mimic the ambient vibe inside their vehicle.
Spokesperson/ Testimonial	Can feature a celebrity, company official, or typical consumer making a testimonial or endorsing a product. Sarah Michelle Gellar, star of *Buffy the Vampire Slayer*, endorses Maybelline cosmetics while country singer Shania Twain introduced Revlon's ColorStay Liquid Lip. Dell, Inc. founder Michael Dell touts his vision of the customer experience via Dell in television ads.
Fantasy	Creates a fantasy for the viewer built around use of the product. Carmakers often use this style to let viewers fantasize about how they would feel speeding around tight corners or down long country roads in their cars.
Humorous	Advertisers often use humor in their ads, such as Snickers' "Not Going Anywhere for a While" campaign featuring hundreds of souls waiting, sometimes impatiently, to get into heaven.
Real/Animated Product Symbols	Creates a character that represents the product in advertisements, such as the Energizer bunny, Starkist's Charlie the Tuna, or General Mills' longtime icon, Betty Crocker, redesigned for the new millennium.
Mood or Image	Builds a mood or image around the product, such as peace, love, or beauty. De Beers ads depicting shadowy silhouettes wearing diamond engagement rings and diamond necklaces portrayed passion and intimacy while extolling that a "diamond is forever."
Demonstration	Shows consumers the expected benefit. Many consumer products use this technique. Laundry-detergent spots are famous for demonstrating how their product will clean clothes whiter and brighter. Fort James Corporation demonstrated in television commercials how its Dixie Rinse & ReUse disposable stoneware product line can stand up to the heat of a blowtorch and survive a cycle in a clothes washer.
Musical	Conveys the message of the advertisement through song. For example, Nike's ads depicting a marathoner's tortured feet, skier Picabo Street's surgery-scarred knee, and a surfer's thigh scarred by a shark attack while strains of Joe Cocker's "You Are So Beautiful" are heard in the background.
Scientific	Uses research or scientific evidence to give a brand superiority over competitors. Pain relievers like Advil, Bayer, and Excedrin use scientific evidence in their ads.

Exhibit 15.4

Dreamful Attraction: Shaquille O'Neal's Thoughts on Marketing and Advertising

While on the outside looking in, I did not realize that marketing was so complicated. I never knew that a person, such as an athlete, could have such a powerful effect on people's thought processes and purchasing behavior. The use of a well-known athlete in marketing a product or service can have a great impact on the sales of that product or service. Look at Michael Jordan. Almost overnight most every kid either was wearing or wanted to wear Air Jordan shoes.

Why does this happen? Is it the appeal of a great athlete or is it great marketing? The answer is "none of the above." It's both. In my years as a professional basketball player, I have seen firsthand the dramatic appeal that athletes have for the fans and public in general. Top-name athletes are like E. F. Hutton—when they talk, people listen. But why do they listen? I believe they listen to us, the athletes, because we have credibility. The effectiveness of celebrity endorsements depends largely on how credible and attractive the spokesperson is and how familiar people are with him or her. Companies sometimes use sports figures and other celebrities to promote products hoping they are appropriate opinion leaders.

Because of an athlete's fame and fortune, or attraction, the athlete can often have the right credibility to be a successful spokesperson. The best definition of credibility that I could find was by James Gordon in his book, *Rhetoric of Western Thought.* He said that attraction "can come from a person's observable talents, achievements, occupational position or status, personality and appearance, and style."* That may be why a famous athlete's personality and position can help him or her communicate more effectively than a not-so-famous athlete.

Credibility is a positive force in the persuasive promotion used predominantly by cola marketers like Pepsi because of what I like to call "dreamful attraction." For example, when I was young, I dreamed that I was like Dr. J., the famous basketball player for the Philadelphia 76ers. I would take his head off a poster and put my head on it. I wanted to be Dr. J. That is dreamful attraction. The youth of today are no different. Just the other day a kid stopped me and told me that he wanted to be like me. He had a dreamful attraction. This dreamful attraction can help sell products. In my case, Pepsi, Spalding, Kenner, and Reebok are hoping that they are able to package properly and market whatever dreamful attraction I might have for their target audience—kids.

There are many ways to communicate to my target audience. I find that the most effective way for me is through television commercials. This avenue gives me a chance to express myself and show my real feelings about a message we are trying to communicate—either visually or vocally. I feel that I have what Clint Eastwood has—"Sudden Impaq." My impact is revealed through my sense of humor and my nonverbal communication.

Why does Shaq sell? Communication. Although the verbal communication in many of my commercials is slim, the impact is still there. This makes me believe even more in the quote that who you are can almost be as important as what you say. But if you can blend the two together—who you are and what you have to say—then imagine how much more successful the communication message can be in the marketing process. Andre Agassi's favorite quote from his Canon commercial is "Image is everything." If it is not everything, it is almost everything. If you have the right image, match it with the right product, and market it properly, then success should follow.

I have been involved in commercials and the marketing of products for only a short time, but I have learned a great deal. If there is one formula for success in selling products, it would be this: Marketing plus credibility and image plus effective communications equals increase in sales—hopefully.

Now, you can call me Dr. Shaq, M.E. (Marketing Expert).

*James Gordon, *Rhetoric of Western Thought* (Dubuque, Iowa: Kendall-Hunt Publishing Co., 1976), 207.

The popular chimpanzee stars of CareerBuilder .com's Super Bowl ads are a perennial favorite. The company's campaigns showcase the hilarious tales of a human employee working in an office populated entirely by chimps.

magazine advertising where humor is less easily communicated. Humorous ads are typically used for lower-risk, low-involvement, routine purchases such as candy, cigarettes, soft drinks, and casual jeans, than for higher-risk purchases or those that are expensive, durable, or flamboyant.[25] Anheuser-Busch's consistent humorous approach to its Budweiser and Bud Light advertising campaigns has been credited with giving Bud a competitive edge in an image-conscious category that traditionally prefers upscale imports. Frogs, lizards, a ferret, and, of course, the "Whassup?" guys resonate with the core 21- to 27-year-old target market and have also secured a place in American pop culture.[26] Well-targeted humor can be effective in attracting and holding audience attention, particularly for women. For example, Altoids used humor to create and reinforce its quirky yet strong persona. With a significantly lower budget than key competitors, the Altoids campaign helped the product grow from a sleepy brand to the number one mint in America based on flavor.[27] But humorous advertising may not be effective in some situations, as for example, after the September 11 terrorist attacks on the Pentagon and the World Trade Center.

Executional styles for foreign advertising are often quite different from those we are accustomed to in the United States. Sometimes they are sexually oriented or aesthetically imaginative. For example, the *Financial Times* created the world's biggest newspaper by covering Hong Kong's tallest skyscraper in fabric that showed the front page. The skyscraper is also home to the newspaper's Asian headquarters. The outdoor advertising space is worth about $6 million.[28] European advertising avoids the direct-sell approaches common in U.S. ads and instead is more indirect, more symbolic, and, above all, more visual. Nike, known in the United States for "in-your-face" advertising and irreverent slogans such as "Just Do It," discovered that its brash advertising did not appeal to Europeans.

Sometimes a company will modify its executional styles to make its advertising more effective. For decades, Procter & Gamble has advertised shampoo in China using a demonstrational executional style. Television ads demonstrated how the science of shampoo worked and then showed a woman with nice, shiny hair. Because today's urban Chinese customers are more financially secure, they no longer make solely utilitarian purchases. To reflect that shift, Procter & Gamble has begun incorporating more of an emotional appeal into its advertisements. A new set of TV ads shows a woman emerging from an animated cocoon as a sophisticated butterfly. A voice over says, "Head & Shoulders metamorphosis—new life for hair."[29] See the "Global Perspectives" box in this chapter for some other examples of advertising around the world.

POSTCAMPAIGN EVALUATION

Evaluating an advertising campaign can be the most demanding task facing advertisers. How do advertisers know whether the campaign led to an increase in sales or market share or elevated awareness of the product? Most advertising campaigns aim to create an image for the good or service instead of asking for action, so their real effect is unknown. So many variables shape the

Determining how consumers will react to advertising can be a difficult proposition. During the 2004 Super Bowl, ad agency McKee Wallwork Henderson launched AdBowl IV. Viewers judged the commercials aired during the game and rated them on a scale of 1 (fumble) to 5 (touchdown).

GLOBAL Perspectives

Advertising Strategies Vary by Country

Global advertising positioning strategies use different tactics depending on the country. For example, China's ParkNshop, a discount retailer and supermarket, used animated shopping bags in a commercial. The commercial turns a typical shopping bag into an interactive shopping tool. To reinforce ParkNshop's image as a low-priced retailer, the bags in the commercial check the prices of the products before allowing them in the bag.

A Nokia advertising campaign for Australia, the Philippines, Vietnam, India, and China was designed to show consumers how a mobile phone can improve their lifestyles. The campaign, titled "We Never Stop Challenging the Future," was supported through TV, print, outdoor, and online advertising. One print ad showed a person stranded on a dirt road with the possibility of going in four different directions. The caption read "You could call for directions. Or use your phone to download maps. What if it could actually guide you home?" Another ad emphasized the phone's technological capabilities by showing a phone embedded in a man's hand.

The copy read "First we took away the antenna. Then we made it smaller. What if we made it disappear?" Both ads focused on how mobility could enhance a consumer's lifestyle.

To build its image internationally, Volkswagen launched an emotion-based campaign. Aware that consumers already associate the brand with quality and reliability, Volkswagen wanted to capitalize on the feelings underlying those product attributes. In Germany, Volkswagen launched a multifaceted campaign using a 20-page magazine and newspaper insert and a TV commercial. Subsequent 2-page print ads featured a picture of a VW car and a poem about the feelings associated with a VW automobile. The intent was that consumers viewing these ads would identify with the emotions that support their beliefs about the company.[30]

These examples illustrate how companies are using advertising to reach consumers in markets outside the United States. How do the domestic advertising campaigns by the same companies differ? Compare the advertisements and consider the similarities and differences.

effectiveness of an ad that, in many cases, advertisers must guess whether their money has been well spent. Despite this gray area, marketers spend a considerable amount of time studying advertising effectiveness and its probable impact on sales, market share, or awareness.

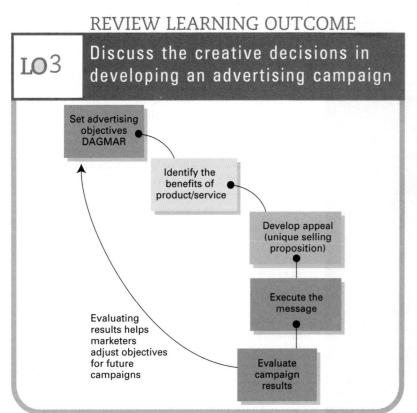
Testing ad effectiveness can be done either before or after the campaign. Before a campaign is released, marketing managers use pretests to determine the best advertising appeal, layout, and media vehicle. After advertisers implement a campaign, they often conduct tests to measure its effectiveness. Several monitoring techniques can be used to determine whether the campaign has met its original goals. Even if a campaign has been highly successful, advertisers still typically do a post-campaign analysis. They assess how the campaign might have been more efficient and what factors contributed to its success. For example, Hallmark's market researchers wanted to capitalize on aging baby boomers. Research indicated that baby boomers do not want to age, but since that is inevitable, boomers want to see the positive side of aging. Therefore, Hallmark created the "Time of Your Life" series that flattered their egos. The cards were not successful, however, because they were placed in the "over 50" section of the store and baby boomers do not want to shop in that section.[31]

LO4
Media Decisions in Advertising

A major decision for advertisers is the choice of **medium**—the channel used to convey a message to a target market. **Media planning**, therefore, is the series of decisions advertisers make regarding the selection and use of media, allowing the marketer to optimally and cost-effectively communicate the message to the target audience. Specifically, advertisers must determine which types of media will best communicate the benefits of their product or service to the target audience and when and for how long the advertisement will run.

Promotional objectives and the appeal and executional style of the advertising strongly affect the selection of media. It is important to understand that both creative and media decisions are made at the same time. Creative work cannot be completed without knowing which medium will be used to convey the message to the target market. For instance, creative planning will likely differ for an ad to be displayed on an outdoor billboard versus one placed in a print medium, such as a newspaper or magazine. In many cases, the advertising objectives dictate the medium and the creative approach to be used. For example, if the objective is to demonstrate how fast a product operates, a TV commercial that shows this action may be the best choice.

U.S. advertisers spend about $300 billion on media advertising annually. Almost one-half of that is spent on media monitored by national reporting services—newspapers, magazines, Yellow Pages, Internet, radio, television, and outdoor media. The remainder is spent on unmonitored media, such as direct mail, trade exhibits, cooperative advertising, brochures, coupons, catalogs, and special events. Exhibit 15.5 shows advertising spending by media type. As you can see, about 25 percent of every media dollar goes toward TV

medium
The channel used to convey a message to a target market.

media planning
The series of decisions advertisers make regarding the selection and use of media, allowing the marketer to optimally and cost-effectively communicate the message to the target audience.

ads, 20 percent toward
direct mail, and about 18
percent for newspaper ads.
But these traditional mass-
market media are declining
in usage and more targeted
media are growing.[32]

Exhibit 15.5

**Domestic Advertising
Spending by Media Type,
in billions**

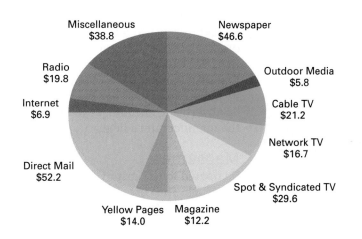

SOURCE: "Domestic Advertising Spending Totals," Special Report, June 27, 2005, *Advertising Age*,
http://www.adage.com, accessed January 2006.

MEDIA TYPES

Advertising media are
channels that advertisers
use in mass communica-
tion. The seven major
advertising media are
newspapers, magazines,
radio, television, outdoor
media, Yellow Pages, and the Internet. Exhibit 15.6 summarizes the advantages and disadvantages of these major channels. In recent years, however, alternative media vehicles
have emerged that give advertisers innovative ways to reach their target audience and
avoid advertising clutter.

Newspapers

The advantages of newspaper advertising include geographic flexibility and timeliness.
Because copywriters can usually prepare newspaper ads quickly and at a reasonable
cost, local merchants can reach their target market almost daily. Because newspapers
are generally a mass-market medium, however, they may not be the best vehicle for
marketers trying to reach a very narrow market. For example, local newspapers are not
the best media vehicles for reaching purchasers of specialty steel products or even tropi-
cal fish. These target consumers make up very small, specialized markets. Newspaper
advertising also encounters a lot of distractions from competing ads and news stories;
thus, one company's ad may not be particularly visible.

Exhibit 15.6

Advantages and Disadvantages of Major Advertising Media

Medium	Advantages	Disadvantages
Newspapers	Geographic selectivity and flexibility; short-term advertiser commitments; news value and immediacy; year-round readership; high individual market coverage; co-op and local tie-in availability; short lead time	Little demographic selectivity; limited color capabilities; low pass-along rate; may be expensive
Magazines	Good reproduction, especially for color; demographic selectivity; regional selectivity; local market selectivity; relatively long advertising life; high pass-along rate	Long-term advertiser commitments; slow audience buildup; limited demonstration capabilities; lack of urgency; long lead time
Radio	Low cost; immediacy of message; can be scheduled on short notice; relatively no seasonal change in audience; highly portable; short-term advertiser commitments; entertainment carryover	No visual treatment; short advertising life of message; high frequency required to generate comprehension and retention; distractions from background sound; commercial clutter
Television	Ability to reach a wide, diverse audience; low cost per thousand; creative opportunities for demonstration; immediacy of messages; entertainment carryover; demographic selectivity with cable stations	Short life of message; some consumer skepticism about claims; high campaign cost; little demographic selectivity with network stations; long-term advertiser commitments; long lead times required for production; commercial clutter
Outdoor Media	Repetition; moderate cost; flexibility; geographic selectivity	Short message; lack of demographic selectivity; high "noise" level distracting audience
Internet	Fastest-growing medium; ability to reach a narrow target audience; relatively short lead time required for creating Web-based advertising; moderate cost	Difficult to measure ad effectiveness and return on investment; ad exposure relies on "click-through" from banner ads; not all consumers have access to the Internet

Fox Network
ABC

What kind of advertising is done on the Fox Network's Web site? Compare this with the site for ABC. What differences do you notice? Why do you think a television network would choose not to sell ad space on its Web site?

http://www.fox.com
http://www.abc.com

Online

The main sources of newspaper ad revenue are local retailers, classified ads, and cooperative advertising. In **cooperative advertising,** the manufacturer and the retailer split the costs of advertising the manufacturer's brand. One reason manufacturers use cooperative advertising is the impracticality of listing all their dealers in national advertising. Also, coop advertising encourages retailers to devote more effort to the manufacturer's lines.

Magazines

Compared to the cost of other media, the cost per contact in magazine advertising is usually high. The cost per potential customer may be much lower, however, because magazines are often targeted to specialized audiences and thus reach more potential customers. The types of products most frequently advertised in magazines include automobiles, apparel, computers, and cigarettes.

One of the main advantages of magazine advertising is its market selectivity. Magazines are published for virtually every market segment. For instance, *Lucky* "The Magazine About Shopping" is a leading fashion magazine; *ESPN the Magazine* is a successful sports magazine; *Essence* is targeted toward African American women; *Marketing News* is a trade magazine for the marketing professional; and *The Source* is a niche publication geared to young urbanites with a passion for hip-hop music.

In 2006, Philips Electronics began an innovative advertising campaign in select magazines by sponsoring the magazines' contents page. Issues of four Time Warner magazines (*Time, Fortune, People,* and *Business 2.0*) featured the table of contents on the first page rather than several pages later. The inside front cover features a Philips ad with the following copy: "Philips Electronics is bringing the table of contents to the front of selected Time, Inc. magazines to make things easier for readers." In general, the placement of the contents page varies from magazine to magazine, but it is not uncommon for the contents to appear after numerous advertisements; as many as 24 pages of ads can appear before a magazine's contents page! Philips paid Time, Inc., $5 million to sponsor the contents pages in the four magazines for only one issue each.33

Radio

Radio has several strengths as an advertising medium: selectivity and audience segmentation, a large out-of-home audience, low unit and production costs, timeliness, and geographic flexibility. Local advertisers are the most frequent users of radio advertising, contributing over three-quarters of all radio ad revenues. Like newspapers, radio also lends itself well to cooperative advertising.

Radio advertising is enjoying a resurgence in popularity. As Americans become more mobile and pressed for time, media such as network television and newspapers have lost viewers and readers, particularly in the youth market. Radio listening, however, has grown in step with population increases mainly because its immediate, portable nature meshes so well with a fast-paced lifestyle. The ability to target specific demographic groups is a major selling point for radio stations, attracting advertisers pursuing narrowly defined audiences that are more likely to respond to certain kinds of ads and products. Radio listeners also tend to listen habitually and at predictable times, especially during "drive time," when commuters form a vast captive audience. Finally, satellite radio has attracted new audiences that are exposed to ads when allowed on that format.

Television

Because television is an audiovisual medium, it provides advertisers with many creative opportunities. Television broadcasters include network television, independent stations, cable television, and a relative newcomer, direct broadcast satellite television. ABC, CBS, NBC, and the Fox Network dominate network television, which reaches a wide and diverse market. Conversely, cable television and direct broadcast satellite systems, such as DirecTV and Dish Network, offer consumers a multitude of channels devoted exclusively to partic-

cooperative advertising
An arrangement in which the manufacturer and the retailer split the costs of advertising the manufacturer's brand.

Kanye Weset starred in this Pepsi commercial, which premiered during the MTV Video Music Awards. The ad promoted Pepsi, as well as one of West's albums.

ular audiences—for example, women, children, African Americans, nature lovers, senior citizens, Christians, Hispanics, sports fans, and fitness enthusiasts. Recent niche market entries include CSTV Network (college sports) and the NFL Network—focused exclusively on the sports enthusiast—and the casino and gambling channel. Because of its targeted channels, cable television is often characterized as "narrowcasting" by media buyers.

Advertising time on television can be very expensive, especially for network and popular cable channels. The top-ranked TV programs in recent years for "twenty-somethings" are aired on networks ABC, CBS, and Fox and on cable stations TNT and USA. The biggest draws are ABC's *Desperate Housewives, Lost,* and *Grey's Anatomy;* CBS's *CSI* and similar crime series; and Fox's *American Idol* and *24.* First-run prime-time shows and special events command the highest rates for a typical 30-second spot, with the least expensive ads costing about $300,000 and the more expensive ones $500,000. Super Bowl spots are the most expensive—a 30-second spot during the 2006 Super Bowl telecast cost advertisers an average of $2.5 million.[34]

One of the more successful recent television formats to emerge is the **infomercial,** a 30-minute or longer advertisement. Infomercials are an attractive advertising vehicle for many marketers because of the relatively inexpensive airtime and the lower production costs. Advertisers say the infomercial is an ideal way to present complicated information to potential customers, which other advertising vehicles typically don't allow time to do. Infomercials are being used by some mainstream marketers. In the last few years, companies such as Philips Electronics, Apple, Nissan, Mercedes, Nikon, and Microsoft have bought infomercial airtime. And a growing number of businesses are adding to the legitimacy of the medium by producing infomercials with a more polished look. Even Hollywood is cashing in on infomercials. Universal Pictures and other movie studios are using infomercials to introduce their latest movies.[35] To see some excerpts of infomercials, go to: **http://infomercial.tvheaven.com/.**

Probably the most significant trend to affect television advertising is the rise in popularity of digital video recorders (DVRs) like TiVo. For every hour of television programming, an average of 15 minutes is dedicated to nonprogram material (ads, public service announcements, and network promotions), so it's hardly surprising that viewers weary of ad breaks have embraced ad-skipping DVR technology as the solution to interruptions during their favorite shows. Marketers of the products featured in those advertisements are not the only ones trying to figure out ways to keep consumers from avoiding them; networks are also concerned about ad skipping. If consumers are not watching advertisements, then marketers will spend a greater proportion of their advertising budgets on alternative media, and a critical revenue stream for networks will disappear. While NBC ran a test in 2006 to measure the effectiveness of running shorter blocks of advertising, the company also said that it has no intention of changing its business model relative to advertising sales. The full impact of DVR technology on television as an advertising medium has yet to be determined.[36]

Outdoor Media

Outdoor or out-of-home advertising is a flexible, low-cost medium that may take a variety of forms. Examples include billboards, skywriting, giant inflatables, mini-billboards in malls and on bus stop shelters, signs in sports arenas, lighted moving signs in bus terminals and airports, and ads painted on cars, trucks, buses, water towers, manhole covers, drinking glass coasters, and even people, called "living advertising." Students in London "rented" their foreheads for temporary tattoos of brands and then walked around specified areas of the city.[37] The plywood scaffolding that rings downtown construction sites

infomercial
A 30-minute or longer advertisement that looks more like a TV talk show than a sales pitch.

can also carry ads. Manhattan's Times Square, with an estimated 1.5 million daily pedestrians, has been a popular area for outdoor advertising using scaffolding.

Outdoor advertising reaches a broad and diverse market and is, therefore, ideal for promoting convenience products and services as well as directing consumers to local businesses. One of outdoor's main advantages over other media is that its exposure frequency is very high, yet the amount of clutter from competing ads is very low. Outdoor advertising also has the ability to be customized to local marketing needs. For these reasons, local business establishments, such as local services and amusements, retailers, public transportation, and hotels and restaurants, are the leading outdoor advertisers. Outdoor advertising categories on the rise include telecommunications with a heavy emphasis on wireless services, financial services, and packaged goods.

Outdoor advertising is becoming more innovative. For instance, Absolut Vodka teamed up with IKEA furniture to produce a 19-by-49-foot billboard in Manhattan's SoHo district. The billboard shows a life-size studio apartment in the shape of an Absolut bottle that is filled with furniture from IKEA. The billboard is basically a fully furnished apartment with everything glued to the board and then turned on its side. New technology is enabling outdoor ads to become interactive and to be more like online ads. For example, Nike commissioned a 23-story interactive, digital billboard on New York's Times Square. People passing the display on the sidewalk could use their cell phones to temporarily control the billboard and design their own shoes.[38]

Unusual outdoor advertising campaigns are not limited to the United States. Snapple's launch in Mexico featured a giant street ad campaign with people going about their regular routines dressed as giant pieces of fruit, such as bananas and strawberries.[39] Adidas Japan created a "living billboard" in the form of a vertical soccer field on the side of a skyscraper. The billboard featured live players and a ball attached by ropes to the side of the building.[40] Virgin Atlantic Airlines painted an ad on the grass next to the runway at South Africa's Johannesburg International Airport to greet arriving and departing passengers. A world's first, the ad required 1,000 liters of paint and nine separate permits from different regulatory authorities due to the sensitive nature of the site.[41]

The Internet

The Internet has definitely changed the advertising industry. With ad revenues up dramatically in 2005 to almost $12 billion, the Internet has become a solid advertising medium. Online advertising is expected to double by 2010 and will represent about 10 percent of total U.S. ad dollars.[42] Internet advertising provides an interactive and versatile platform that offers rich data on consumer usage, enabling advertisers to improve their ad targetability and achieve measurable results.[43]

Popular Internet sites and search engines, such as Google and Yahoo!, as well as online service providers like America Online, generally sell advertising space to marketers to promote their goods and services. Internet surfers click on these ads to be linked to more information about the advertised product or service. Established brands such as General Motors, Anheuser-Busch, Procter & Gamble, and Verizon have been adjusting their budgets to include Internet advertising. And other firms are not far behind. For example, Vonage, Circuit City, Ameritrade Brokerage, Amazon.com, Overstock.com, Netflix.com, and Monster.com have been among the top 50 advertisers on the Internet in recent years.

The effectiveness of Internet advertising has been hotly debated, however. Early research on banner ads found response rates as high as 30 percent, but more recent studies indicate much lower response rates. With high-speed broadband spreading rapidly in the United States, advertisers increasingly are switching to other approaches. For example, marketers are using ads that float, sing, or dance; video commercials similar to traditional TV spots; and ads that pop up in another window, use larger, hard-to-miss shapes, and include both online and offline cross-promotions. The new formats include the *skyscraper,* a tall, skinny oblong at the side of a Web page, and the *rectangle,* a box much larger than a banner. These new formats are large enough for marketers to include their entire message so that users don't have to click through to another site.

One of the most popular approaches for Internet advertising is search engine ads. More than half of all U.S. Internet advertising in 2006 was on search engine portals, with Google getting the lion's share. In second place was Yahoo! followed by Microsoft's MSN. By 2010 search engine advertising is expected to exceed $11 billion in the United States and to be $33 billion worldwide.[44] Marketers' primary objective in using search engine ads is to enhance brand awareness. They do this through paid placement of ads tied to key words used in search engine searches—when someone clicks on the ad, the advertiser pays the search engine a fee.

Blockdot
Find out more about advergaming at Blockdot. Go to the company's web site and review its advergaming tools. Which ones do you think would be the most effective? Have you ever clicked through onto them? Why?
http://www.blockdot.com

Online

Another popular Internet advertising format is advergaming. In **advergaming**, companies put ad messages in Web-based or video games to advertise or promote a product, service, organization, or issue. Sometimes the entire game amounts to a virtual commercial, other times advertisers sponsor games or buy ad space for product placement in them. Organizations using advergaming include Disney, Viacom's Nickelodeon, and even the U.S. Army.[45] The format encourages users to register for sweepstakes and other promotions and play the game. For example, discount designer retailer Bluefly.com has run contests where shoppers register to win Jimmy Choo or Manolo Blahnik shoes (value approximately $600).

An increasingly popular Internet medium for advertising is the blog. Initially, blogs had no advertising. But the popularity of some blogs has made them an attractive medium for marketing messages. Budget Rent-A-Car recently bought ads on 177 blogs, Audi of America paid for advertising on 286 blogs, and MSNBC bought ads on more than 800 blogs.[46] Seed Media, which produces science publications in print and online, sells advertising on its network of more than 15 blogs just as it does in its magazine *Seed*. Seed Media contends that by advertising on its blog network, marketers will gain access to a group of bright, curious consumers who buy all kinds of products.[47]

advergaming
Placing advertising messages in Web-based or video games to advertise or promote a product, service, organization, or issue.

Alternative Media

To cut through the clutter of traditional advertising media, advertisers are creating new media vehicles to advertise their products, some ordinary and others quite innovative. Alternative media vehicles can include shopping carts in grocery stores, computer screen savers, DVDs, interactive kiosks in department stores, advertisements run before movies at the cinema, and "advertainments"—"mini movies" that promote a product and are shown via the Internet. For example, BMW shows films by recognized directors that run six to eight minutes and feature the cars in extreme situations.[48] Likewise, Coca-Cola sponsored a 25-minute advertainment program called "Sound Check" that was available only on TiVo. The program featured exclusive interviews, music videos, live shows, behind-the-scenes filming, and recordings by artists such as Ashanti, Sting, and Mary J. Blige.[49]

Indeed, almost anything can become a vehicle for displaying advertising. For instance, supermarkets have begun using "Flooranimation"—ads that are animated with graphics and sounds and installed on supermarket floors. Unanimated floor ads have been in use for some time, and research shows they increase sales 15 to 30 percent. Marketers are hoping that with animation and sound, sales will increase even more.[50] A company called Guerilla Video Projection Billboards places outdoor advertising and/or 30-second television commercials on buildings and

© MICRO TARGET MEDIA/PRNEWSFOTO (AP TOPIC GALLERY)

walls in busy restaurant and nightlife districts. The billboards, which can include motion graphics, sound, and additional advertising media, are an excellent way to communicate with consumers in the evenings in metro markets such as New York City, Chicago, Los Angeles, and San Francisco.[51] Marketers are also looking for more innovative ways to reach captive and often bored commuters. For instance, subway systems now show ads via lighted boxes installed along tunnel walls. As a train passes through the tunnel, the passengers view the illuminated boxes, which create the same kind of illusion as a child's flip book, in which the images appear to move as the pages are flipped rapidly.

When trying to reach males aged 18 to 34, video game advertising is emerging as an excellent medium, second only to prime-time *Monday Night Football*. The medium first attracted attention when Massive, Inc., (**http://www.massiveincorporated.com**) started a videogame advertising network and later established a partnership with Nielsen Entertainment, Inc., to provide ad ratings. Massive provides the capability to have ads with full motion and sound inserted into games played on Internet-connected computers. This is a big improvement over previous ads, which had to be inserted when the games were made and therefore quickly became obsolete. In 2006, Microsoft acquired Massive, a move that the company says will help it "deliver dynamic, relevant ads" across its online services including Xbox Live and MSN Games.[52]

As described in the chapter-opening vignette, cell phones are among the newest advertising media and are particularly useful for reaching the youth market. Today's data- and video-oriented phones can deliver advertisements and also have GPS capability, so they can receive "location-based" advertising; for example, a nearby restaurant can alert potential customers about specials. McDonald's enjoyed success doing this at locations in California where it gave away free McFlurry desserts. Marketers also are using text and video messages to notify customers of special deals, such as ring tone downloads. Cell phone advertising is less popular in the United States than in Europe and Asia, where cell phone owners use text messaging much more heavily. Although there is concern that cell phone spam will become as much of a problem as Internet spam, cell phone advertisers are targeting their ads to users who agree to receive the ads in exchange for premium services or who sign up on opt-in lists to learn about items that interest them, such as a particular band's next album or concert.[53]

MEDIA SELECTION CONSIDERATIONS

An important element in any advertising campaign is the **media mix,** the combination of media to be used. Media mix decisions are typically based on several factors: cost per contact, reach, frequency, target audience considerations, flexibility of the medium, noise level, and the life span of the medium.

Cost per contact is the cost of reaching one member of the target market. Naturally, as the size of the audience increases, so does the total cost. Cost per contact enables an advertiser to compare media vehicles, such as television versus radio or magazine versus newspaper, or more specifically *Newsweek* versus *Time*. An advertiser debating whether to spend local advertising dollars for TV spots or radio spots could consider the cost per contact of each. The advertiser might then pick the vehicle with the lowest cost per contact to maximize advertising punch for the money spent.

Reach is the number of different target consumers who are exposed to a commercial at least once during a specific period, usually four weeks. Media plans for product introductions and attempts at increasing brand awareness usually emphasize reach. For example, an advertiser might try to reach 70 percent of the target audience during the first three months of the campaign. Reach is related to a medium's ratings, generally referred to in the industry as *gross ratings points,* or GRP. A television program with a higher GRP means that more people are tuning in to the show and the reach is higher. Accordingly, as GRP increases for a particular medium, so does cost per contact.

Because the typical ad is short-lived and because often only a small portion of an ad may be perceived at one time, advertisers repeat their ads so that consumers will remember the message. **Frequency** is the number of times an individual is exposed to a message during a specific period. Advertisers use average frequency to measure the intensity of a specific medium's coverage. For example, Coca-Cola might want an aver-

media mix
The combination of media to be used for a promotional campaign.

cost per contact
The cost of reaching one member of the target market.

reach
The number of target consumers exposed to a commercial at least once during a specific period, usually four weeks.

frequency
The number of times an individual is exposed to a given message during a specific period.

age exposure frequency of five for its POWERade television ads. That means that each of the television viewers who saw the ad saw it an average of five times.

Media selection is also a matter of matching the advertising medium with the product's target market. If marketers are trying to reach teenage females, they might select *Seventeen* magazine. If they are trying to reach consumers over 50 years old, they may choose *Modern Maturity* magazine. A medium's ability to reach a precisely defined market is its **audience selectivity.** Some media vehicles, like general newspapers and network television, appeal to a wide cross section of the population. Others—such as *Brides, Popular Mechanics, Architectural Digest, Lucky,* MTV, ESPN, and Christian radio stations— appeal to very specific groups.

The *flexibility* of a medium can be extremely important to an advertiser. In the past, because of printing timetables, pasteup requirements, and so on, some magazines required final ad copy several months before publication. Therefore, magazine advertising traditionally could not adapt as rapidly to changing market conditions. While this is fast changing due to computer technology that creates electronic ad images and layouts, the lead time for magazine advertising is still considerably longer. Radio and Internet advertising, on the other hand, provide maximum flexibility. Usually, the advertiser can change a radio ad on the day it is aired, if necessary. Similarly, advertisements on the Internet can be changed in minutes with the click of a few buttons.

Noise level is the level of distraction associated with a medium. For example, to understand a televised promotional message, viewers must watch and listen carefully. But they often watch television with others, who may well provide distractions. Noise can also be created by competing ads, as when a street is lined with billboards or when a television program is cluttered with competing ads. About two-thirds of a newspaper's pages are now filled with advertising. A recent Sunday issue of the *Los Angeles Times* contained over one thousand ads, not counting the small classifieds. Even more space is dedicated to ads in magazines. For example, 85 percent of the space in the February/March issue of *Brides* magazine is typically devoted to advertisements. In contrast, direct mail is a private medium with a low noise level. Typically, no other advertising media or news stories compete for direct-mail readers' attention.

Media have either a short or a long life span. *Life span* means that messages can either quickly fade or persist as tangible copy to be carefully studied. For example, a radio commercial may last less than a minute. Listeners can't replay the commercial unless they have recorded the program. One way advertisers overcome this problem is by repeating radio ads often. In contrast, a magazine has a relatively long life span. A person may read several articles, put the magazine down, and pick it up a week later to continue reading. In addition, magazines often have a high pass-along rate. That is, one person will read the publication and then give it to someone else to read.

Media planners have traditionally relied on the above factors for selecting an effective media mix, with reach, frequency, and cost often the overriding criteria. Some experts, however, question the reliance media planners have traditionally placed on reach and frequency. For instance, well-established brands with familiar messages probably need fewer exposures to be effective, while newer brands or brands with unfamiliar messages likely need more exposures to become familiar.

Additionally, media planners have hundreds more media options today than they had 40 years ago when network television reigned. For instance, there are over 1,600 television stations across the country. In the Los Angeles market alone, there are now 79 radio stations, with 7 offering an "adult contemporary" format. The number of unique magazine titles has more than doubled over the last decade, with publications now targeting every possible market segment. Satellite television can now bring hundreds of channels into viewers' homes. The Internet provides media planners with even more targeted choices in which to send their messages. And alternative media choices are popping up in some very unlikely places. *Media fragmentation* is forcing media planners to pay as much attention to where they place their advertising, as to how often the advertisement is repeated. Indeed, experts recommend evaluating reach along with frequency in assessing the effectiveness of advertising. That is, in certain situations it may be important to reach potential consumers through as many media vehicles as possible. When this approach is considered, however, the budget must be large enough to achieve sufficient

audience selectivity
The ability of an advertising medium to reach a precisely defined market.

media schedule
Designation of the media, the specific publications or programs, and the insertion dates of advertising.

continuous media schedule
A media scheduling strategy in which advertising is run steadily throughout the advertising period; used for products in the latter stages of the product life cycle.

flighted media schedule
A media scheduling strategy in which ads are run heavily every other month or every two weeks, to achieve a greater impact with an increased frequency and reach at those times.

levels of frequency to have an impact. In evaluating reach versus frequency, therefore, the media planner ultimately must select an approach that is most likely to result in the ad being understood and remembered when a purchase decision is being made.

Advertisers also evaluate the qualitative factors involved in media selection. These qualitative factors include such things as attention to the commercial and the program, involvement, lack of distractions, how well the viewer likes the program, and other audience behaviors that affect the likelihood that a commercial message is being seen and, hopefully, absorbed. While advertisers can advertise their product in as many media as possible and repeat the ad as many times as they like, the ad still may not be effective if the audience is not paying attention. Research on audience attentiveness for television, for example, shows that the longer viewers stay tuned to a particular program, the more memorable they find the commercials. Holding power, therefore, can be more important than ratings (the number of people tuning in to any part of the program) when selecting media vehicles, challenging the long-held assumption that the higher the rating of a program, the more effective the advertising run during the program, even though it is more costly. For instance, *ER*, one of the top-rated shows among 25- to 54-year-olds, costs about $400,000 for a 30-second spot but ranks relatively low for holding power. In contrast, the low-rated *Candid Camera*, which ranks high in holding power, costs only about $55,000 for a 30-second spot.[54]

REVIEW LEARNING OUTCOME

LO4 Describe media evaluation and selection techniques

Media Choices

Type:
Magazine, Radio, Television, Newspaper, Outdoor, Alternative, Internet

Considerations:
Mix	(How much of each?)
Cost per contact	(How much per person?)
Reach	(How many people?)
Frequency	(How often?)
Audience selectivity	(How targeted is audience?)

flexibility
noise
life span
fragmentation

Scheduling:
continuous
flighted
pulsing
seasonal (e.g., back-to-school)

Winter Spring Summer Fall

MEDIA SCHEDULING

After choosing the media for the advertising campaign, advertisers must schedule the ads. A **media schedule** designates the medium or media to be used (such as magazines, television, or radio), the specific vehicles (such as *People* magazine, the show *Lost* on TV, or the American Top 40 national radio program), and the insertion dates of the advertising.

There are three basic types of media schedules:

- Products in the latter stages of the product life cycle, which are advertised on a reminder basis, use a **continuous media schedule.** A continuous schedule allows the advertising to run steadily throughout the advertising period. Examples include Ivory soap, Tide detergent, Bounty paper towels, and Charmin toilet tissue, which may have an ad in the newspaper every Sunday and a TV commercial on NBC every Wednesday at 7:30 P.M. over a three-month time period.

- With a **flighted media schedule,** the advertiser may schedule the ads heavily every other month or every two weeks to achieve a greater impact with an increased frequency and reach at those times. Movie studios might schedule television adver-

tising on Wednesday and Thursday nights, when moviegoers are deciding which films to see that weekend. A variation is the **pulsing media schedule,** which combines continuous scheduling with flighting. Continuous advertising is simply heavier during the best sale periods. A retail department store may advertise on a year-round basis but place more advertising during certain sale periods such as Thanksgiving, Christmas, and back-to-school.

- Certain times of the year call for a **seasonal media schedule.** Products like Contac cold tablets and Coppertone suntan lotion, which are used more during certain times of the year, tend to follow a seasonal strategy. Advertising for champagne is concentrated during the weeks of Christmas and New Year's, whereas health clubs concentrate their advertising in January to take advantage of New Year's resolutions.

New research comparing continuous media schedules and flighted ones finds that continuous schedules for television advertisements are more effective than flighting in driving sales. The research suggests that it may be more important to get exposure as close as possible to the time when someone is going to make a purchase. For example, if a consumer shops on a weekly basis, the best time to reach that person is right before he or she shops. Therefore, the advertiser should maintain a continuous schedule over as long a period of time as possible. Often called *recency planning,* this theory of scheduling is now commonly used for scheduling television advertising for frequently purchased products, such as Coca-Cola or Tide detergent. Recency planning's main premise is that advertising works by influencing the brand choice of people who are ready to buy.

LO⁵
Public Relations

Public relations is the element in the promotional mix that evaluates public attitudes, identifies issues that may elicit public concern, and executes programs to gain public understanding and acceptance. Like advertising and sales promotion, public relations is a vital link in a progressive company's marketing communication mix. Marketing managers plan solid public relations campaigns that fit into overall marketing plans and focus on targeted audiences. These campaigns strive to maintain a positive image of the corporation in the eyes of the public. Before launching public relations programs, managers evaluate public attitudes and company actions. Then they create programs to capitalize on the factors that enhance the firm's image and minimize the factors that could generate a negative image.

Many people associate public relations with publicity. *Publicity* is the effort to capture media attention—for example, through articles or editorials in publications or through human-interest stories on radio or television programs. Corporations usually initiate publicity through a press release that furthers their public relations plans. A company about to introduce a new product or open a new store may send press releases to the media in the hope that the story will be published or broadcast. Savvy publicity can often create overnight sensations.

SK Telecom developed a guerrilla marketing campaign to secure its position as the mobile communications leader in Korea. During the FIFA World Cup held in Korea, SK Telecom launched a campaign called "Be the Reds" named after Korean national soccer team, the Red Devils. The company invited sports fans to join the Red Devils' fan club and learn special team cheers. SK Telecom then distributed millions of free "Be the Reds" T-shirts. It sponsored TVs in commuter trains and massive television screens in highly populated public areas, all blazoned with the SK Telecom logo. Marketing activities were not permitted inside the stadium, but fans wearing their "Be the Reds" T-shirts blanketed the stands and screamed SK's team cheers. Recognition of the SK Telecom brand skyrocketed past that of the official sponsor. During the FIFA World Cup, SK Telecom signed up 96,000 new customers and increased its market share of Korean mobile communications service by 22 percent.[55]

pulsing media schedule
A media scheduling strategy that uses continuous scheduling throughout the year coupled with a flighted schedule during the best sales periods.

seasonal media schedule
A media scheduling strategy that runs advertising only during times of the year when the product is most likely to be used.

Corporate donations and sponsorships can also create favorable publicity. When two high school seniors wanted to go to college in California, but couldn't afford the tuition, they searched for corporate sponsors to pay for their education. The young entrepreneurs set up a Web site offering their services as "spokesguys" and posted photos of themselves wearing T-shirts and carrying surfboards inscribed with the message YOUR LOGO HERE. They got the attention of First USA, the country's largest Visa issuer, which decided to lend a hand. In exchange for the boys promoting fiscal responsibility to other college kids, First USA paid for their tuition and room and board. As a public relations investment, it's already paid off with the kind of publicity that money can't buy, including a story in the *New York Times*.[56]

Public relations departments may perform any or all of the following functions:

- *Press relations:* placing positive, newsworthy information in the news media to attract attention to a product, a service, or a person associated with the firm or institution

- *Product publicity:* publicizing specific products or services

- *Corporate communication:* creating internal and external messages to promote a positive image of the firm or institution

- *Public affairs:* building and maintaining national or local community relations

- *Lobbying:* influencing legislators and government officials to promote or defeat legislation and regulation

- *Employee and investor relations:* maintaining positive relationships with employees, shareholders, and others in the financial community

- *Crisis management:* responding to unfavorable publicity or a negative event

MAJOR PUBLIC RELATIONS TOOLS

Public relations professionals commonly use several tools, including new-product publicity, product placement, consumer education, sponsorship, and Web sites. Although many of these tools require an active role on the part of the public relations professional, such as writing press releases and engaging in proactive media relations, some techniques create their own publicity.

New-Product Publicity

Publicity is instrumental in introducing new products and services. Publicity can help advertisers explain what's different about their new product by prompting free news stories or positive word of mouth about it. During the introductory period, an especially innovative new product often needs more exposure than conventional, paid advertising affords. Public relations professionals write press releases or develop videos in an effort to generate news about their new product. They also jockey for exposure of their product or service at major events, on popular television and news shows, or in the hands of influential people. The chairman of Virgin Group, Richard Branson, helped promote a new line of consumer electronics, Virgin Pulse, distributed by Target. To get free publicity, Branson attended the release party wearing skin-colored leggings and a ripped T-shirt and holding a CD player over his private parts. Free publicity is one of the mainstays of the Virgin marketing approach. Branson also made guest appearances on *Friends* and *Baywatch* and rode down Fifth Avenue in a tank.[57]

Product Placement

Marketers are increasingly using product placement to reinforce brand awareness and create favorable attitudes. **Product placement** is a strategy that involves getting one's product, service, or name to appear in a movie, television show, radio program, magazine, newspaper, video game, video or audio clip, book, or commercial for another product; on the Internet; or at special events. Including an actual product such as a can of Pepsi adds a sense of realism to a movie, TV show, video game, book, or similar vehicle that a can simply marked "soda" cannot. Product placements are arranged through

product placement
A public relations strategy that involves getting a product, service, or company name to appear in a movie, television show, radio program, magazine, newspaper, video game, video or audio clip, book, or commercial for another product; on the Internet; or at special events.

barter (trade of product for placement), through paid placements, or at no charge when the product is viewed as enhancing the vehicle where it is placed.

Product placement expenditures amount to about $5 billion annually. Though this amount is small relative to other marketing expenditures, it is growing rapidly due to increasing audience fragmentation and the spread of ad-skipping technology, and it will likely double by 2010. More than two-thirds of product placements are in movies and TV shows, but placements in other alternatives are growing, particularly on the Internet and in video games. Most product placements are for transportation, clothing, food, beverages, home furnishings, travel, and leisure time activities. Companies like BMW, Lexus, Coca-Cola, Pepsi, Procter & Gamble, and Hershey have frequently used product placement as a public relations strategy. Indeed, Pepsi appeared in seven top-ranked films in one year. Digital technology now enables companies to "virtually" place their products in any audio or video production. Virtual placement not only reduces the cost of product placement for new productions but also enables companies to place products in previously produced programs, such as reruns of television shows and movies.

Companies obtain valuable product exposure, brand reinforcement, and increased sales through product placement, often at a much lower cost than in mass media like television ads. For example, Burger King products were woven into the *The Apprentice* when contestants wore Burger King uniforms and flipped burgers as part of a challenge; Ford sponsored the show *24*, with the main character, Jack Bauer, driving a Ford Expedition; and S.C. Johnson placed the ant killer RAID in an episode of the popular HBO series *The Sopranos*. When Red Stripe, a Jamaican-brewed beer, appeared in the movie *The Firm,* its U.S. sales increased more than 50 percent in the first month after the movie was released.[58]

Consumer Education

Some major firms believe that educated consumers are better, more loyal customers. BMW of North America, for example, sponsored an instructional driving school for teenagers in major cities across the United States. Teens received a special four-hour training session that included driving techniques, accident avoidance skills, and traction aid tricks from a professional driver. Financial planning firms often sponsor free educational seminars on money management, retirement planning, and investing in the hope that the seminar participants will choose the sponsoring organization for their future financial needs. Likewise, computer hardware and software firms, realizing that many consumers are intimidated by new technology and recognizing the strong relationship between learning and purchasing patterns, sponsor computer seminars and free in-store demonstrations.

Sponsorships

sponsorship
A public relations strategy in which a company spends money to support an issue, cause, or event that is consistent with corporate objectives, such as improving brand awareness or enhancing corporate image.

Sponsorships are increasing both in number and as a proportion of companies' marketing budgets, with worldwide sponsorship spending expected to exceed $30 billion in 2006. Probably the biggest reason for the increasing use of sponsorships is the difficulty of reaching audiences and differentiating a product from competing brands through the mass media. With a **sponsorship,** a company spends money to support an issue, cause, or event that is consistent with corporate objectives, such as improving brand awareness or enhancing corporate image. Most commonly, companies sponsor events such as festivals and fairs, conventions, expositions, sporting events, arts and entertainment spectaculars, and charity benefits. Typical examples of sponsorships include Jose Cuervo Tequila's sponsorship of the 2006 Pro Beach Volleyball Tour, Domino's Pizza's sponsorship of Michael Waltrip for the 2006 NASCAR season, Hilton Hotels' sponsorship of the Hilton Family Skating & Gymnastics Spectacular 2006 on NBC, Levi Strauss & Co.'s partnership with the San Francisco Giants to sponsor the right field section of the park to be named "Levi's Landing," and Anheuser-Busch's Bud Bowl 2006 that featured hip-hop star Snoop Dogg and rock band 3 Doors Down.[59]

Although companies have recently been turning to specialized events such as tie-ins with schools, charities, and other community service organizations, the most popular sponsorship events are still those involving sports, music, or the arts. For example, Vodafone, Coca-Cola, Saturn, Michelin, and Yamaha were among the sponsors of the 2005 Gravity Games extreme sporting event in Perth, Australia, which competes with ESPN's

© NIKE GOLF/PRNEWSFOTO (AP TOPIC GALLERY)

XGames. More than 55,000 people attended the games to watch 110 of the world's biggest names in action sports participate in freestyle motocross, skateboarding, wakeboarding, BMX, and aggressive in-line skating. Sponsors distributed free samples, hosted extreme athlete autograph sessions and sports demonstrations, and organized alternative music concerts.[60] Likewise, McDonald's expanded its "I'm lovin' it" campaign to include sponsorships of NASCAR, the Pro Beach Volleyball Tour, and the Big Mac Challenge—a 20-stop lifestyle-oriented car show including DJs and other youth-focused activities. Similarly, Yahoo! sponsored a video game tour to promote Yahoo! Music Unlimited, Napster forged a deal with the Dew Action Sports Tour, and MSN Music hosted Milwaukee's Summerfest and Manchester, Tennessee's Bonnaroo Music and Arts Festival.[61]

Marketers sometimes create their own events tied around their products. The state of Hawaii organized its own mall touring event, titled "Experience Aloha: Hawaii on Tour," to promote the islands as a tourist destination. The tour traveled to 22 U.S. cities for weekend mall visits that included hula dancers, chefs cooking Hawaiian cuisine, lei-making demonstrations, and a virtual reality film simulating a helicopter ride over Hawaii's islands. Many other states also sponsor events promoting tourism.

Corporations sponsor issues as well as events. Sponsorship issues are quite diverse, but the three most popular are education, health care, and social programs. Firms often donate a percentage of sales or profits to a worthy cause favored by their target market.

A special type of sponsorship, **cause-related marketing,** involves the association of a for-profit company with a nonprofit organization. Through the sponsorship, the company's product or service is promoted, and money is raised for the nonprofit. In a common type of cause-related sponsorship, a company agrees to donate a percentage of the purchase price of a particular item to a charity, but some arrangements are more complex. In the United Kingdom, for example, Blockbuster Entertainment Ltd. works with Starlight Children's Foundation to raise money, and Tesco supermarkets raise money for computers in schools. Similarly, in the United States Avon, Yoplait Yogurt, and BMW support the Susan G. Komen Breast Cancer Foundation, and J. P. Morgan Chase & Co. Bank works with St. Jude Children's Research Hospital. Findings from several studies suggest that some consumers consider a company's reputation when making purchasing decisions and that a company's community involvement boosts employee morale and loyalty.[62]

Internet Web Sites

Companies increasingly are using the Internet in their public relations strategies. Company Web sites are used to introduce new products, promote existing products, obtain consumer feedback, post news releases, communicate legislative and regulatory information, showcase upcoming events, provide links to related sites, release financial information, and perform many more marketing activities. Online reviews from opinion leaders and other consumers help marketers sway purchasing decisions in their favor. On its Web site for Playstation2 (http://www.playstation.com), Sony has online support, events and promotions, game trailers, and new and updated product releases such as Bode Miller Alpine Skiing 2006, King Kong, Madden NFL 06, Playboy Mansion and Jak X: Combat Racing. The site also includes message boards where the gaming community posts notes and chats, exchanges tips on games, votes on lifestyle issues like music and videos, and learns about promotional events.[63]

Web sites are also being incorporated into integrated marketing communications strategies. For example, CBS integrated broadcast advertising with product placement by placing a bonus scene from *CSI: Miami* on its Web site featuring a plot twist that was not revealed to television viewers until later in the season. The bonus scene page was sponsored by General Motors' Hummer brand, which also appeared in the bonus scene itself.[64]

More and more often, companies are also using blogs—both corporate and noncorporate—as a tool to manage their public images. Noncorporate blogs cannot be controlled, but marketers must monitor them to be aware of and respond to negative

cause-related marketing
A type of sponsorship involving the association of a for-profit company and a nonprofit organization; through the sponsorship, the company's product or service is promoted, and money is raised for the nonprofit.

information and encourage positive content. Wal-Mart has been especially active in cultivating bloggers to get the company's message out. Mona Williams, Wal-Mart's spokeswoman, says, "We reach out to bloggers in the same way we reach out to reporters. A lot of people are looking to bloggers for their news source, and this is a good way to get our message out."[65] The company has enlisted the services of a public relations firm to help it combat negative publicity. The publicist assigned to the Wal-Mart account, Marshall Manson, contacts bloggers who write pro-Wal-Mart content and asks if he can send them materials to use in their commentaries. Those who agree become champions for the giant retailer.[66]

In addition to "getting the message out," companies are using blogs to create communities of consumers who feel positively about the brand. The hope is that the positive attitude toward the brand will build into strong word-of-mouth marketing. Companies must exercise caution when diving into corporate blogging, however. Coca-Cola launched a blog authored by a fictional character that did little except parrot the company line. Consumers immediately saw the blog for what it was (a transparent public relations platform) and lambasted Coca-Cola for its insincerity.[67]

MANAGING UNFAVORABLE PUBLICITY

Although marketers try to avoid unpleasant situations, crises do happen. Coca-Cola had to issue an official apology to Chinese basketball star Yao Ming after Coke used his logo on its products in China without permission. The basketball star already had an agreement with Pepsi and Pepsi's brand Gatorade.[68] In our free-press environment, publicity is not easily controlled, especially in a crisis. **Crisis management** is the coordinated effort to handle the effects of unfavorable publicity, ensuring fast and accurate communication in times of emergency.

A good public relations staff is as important in bad times as in good. Companies must have a communication policy firmly in hand before a disaster occurs, because timing is uncontrollable. For example, in 2004, McDonald's was caught off-guard by the wave of negative publicity that followed the release of *Super Size Me*, a documentary film which chronicled the deterioration of filmmaker Morgan Spurlock's health while he experimented with an all-McDonald's diet. Two years later, in anticipation of a similar response to the movie version of Eric Schlosser's best seller *Fast Food Nation*, McDonald's contemplated dispatching a "truth squad" and a team of "ambassadors of the brand" to remind consumers that the restaurant offers a healthy menu and provides good jobs. The company has modified its menu to include more salads and apple dippers. McDonald's hopes new marketing communication focused on the importance of a balanced lifestyle will override any negative publicity resulting from the newer documentary.[69]

crisis management
A coordinated effort to handle all the effects of unfavorable publicity or of another unexpected unfavorable event.

When Wal-Mart became the target of negative publicity regarding its low wages and sparse benefits, publicist Marshall Manson sent a special missive to his network of bloggers. It revealed that various unions were hiring the homeless and day laborers to protest at nonunion businesses, including Wal-Mart. The unions paid the picketers minimum wage and gave them no benefits. Manson's release was used by numerous bloggers and represented a counterattack in the publicity war over Wal-Mart's employment practices.[70]

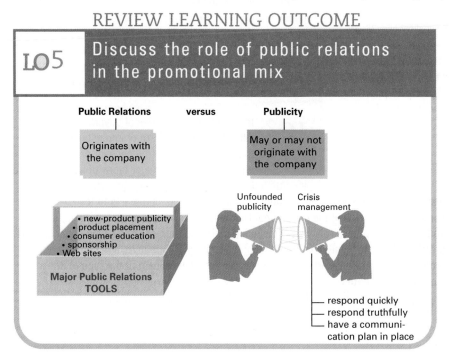

REVIEW LEARNING OUTCOME

LO5 Discuss the role of public relations in the promotional mix

Public Relations **versus** Publicity

Originates with the company

May or may not originate with the company

- new-product publicity
- product placement
- consumer education
- sponsorship
- Web sites

Major Public Relations TOOLS

Unfounded publicity   Crisis management

- respond quickly
- respond truthfully
- have a communication plan in place

Review and Applications

LO 1 Discuss the effects of advertising on market share and consumers. Advertising helps marketers increase or maintain brand awareness and, subsequently, market share. Typically, more is spent to advertise new brands with a small market share than to advertise older brands. Brands with a large market share use advertising mainly to maintain their share of the market. Advertising affects consumers' daily lives as well as their purchases. Although advertising can seldom change strongly held consumer attitudes and values, it may transform a consumer's negative attitude toward a product into a positive one. Additionally, when consumers are highly loyal to a brand, they may buy more of that brand when advertising is increased. Last, advertising can also change the importance of a brand's attributes to consumers. By emphasizing different brand attributes, advertisers can change their appeal in response to consumers' changing needs or try to achieve an advantage over competing brands.

1.1 Discuss the reasons why new brands with a smaller market share spend proportionately more on advertising than brands with a larger market share.

 1.2 Form a three-person team. Divide the responsibility for getting newspaper advertisements and menus for several local restaurants. While you are at the restaurants to obtain copies of their menus, observe the atmosphere and interview the manager to determine what he or she believes are the primary reasons people choose to dine there. Pool your information and develop a table comparing the restaurants in terms of convenience of location, value for the money, food variety and quality, atmosphere, and so on. Rank the restaurants in terms of their appeal to college students. Explain the basis of your rankings. What other market segment would be attracted to the restaurants and why? Do the newspaper advertisements emphasize the most effective appeal for a particular restaurant? Explain.

LO 2 Identify the major types of advertising. Advertising is any form of impersonal, paid communication in which the sponsor or company is identified. The two major types of advertising are institutional advertising and product advertising. Institutional advertising is not product oriented; rather, its purpose is to foster a positive company image among the general public, investment community, customers, and employees. Product advertising is designed mainly to promote goods and services, and it is classified into three main categories: pioneering, competitive, and comparative. A product's place in the product life cycle is a major determinant of the type of advertising used to promote it.

2.1 At what stage in a product's life cycle are pioneering, competitive, and comparative advertising most likely to occur? Give a current example of each type of advertising.

LO3 Discuss the creative decisions in developing an advertising campaign. Before any creative work can begin on an advertising campaign, it is important to determine what goals or objectives the advertising should achieve. The objectives of a specific advertising campaign often depend on the overall corporate objectives and the product being advertised. Once objectives have been defined, creative work can begin on the advertising campaign. Creative decisions include identifying the product's benefits, developing possible advertising appeals, evaluating and selecting the advertising appeals, executing the advertising message, and evaluating the effectiveness of the campaign.

3.1 What is an advertising appeal? Give some examples of advertising appeals you have observed recently in the media.

3.2 Design a full-page magazine advertisement for a new brand of soft drink. The name of the new drink and its package design are at your discretion. On a separate sheet, specify the benefits stressed or appeals made in the advertisement.

LO4 Describe media evaluation and selection techniques. Media evaluation and selection make up a crucial step in the advertising campaign process. Major types of advertising media include newspapers, magazines, radio, television, outdoor advertising such as billboards and bus panels, and the Internet. Recent trends in advertising media include video shopping carts, computer screen savers, cinema and DVD advertising, cell phones, and video games. Promotion managers choose the advertising campaign's media mix on the basis of the following variables: cost per contact, reach, frequency, characteristics of the target audience, flexibility of the medium, noise level, and the life span of the medium. After choosing the media mix, a media schedule designates when the advertisement will appear and the specific vehicles it will appear in.

4.1 What are the advantages of radio advertising? Why is radio expanding as an advertising medium?

4.2 You are the advertising manager of a sailing magazine, and one of your biggest potential advertisers has questioned your rates. Write the firm a letter explaining why you believe your audience selectivity is worth the extra expense for advertisers.

4.3 Identify an appropriate media mix for the following products:

   a. Chewing tobacco

   b. *People* magazine

   c. Weed-Eaters

   d. Foot odor killers

   e. "Drink responsibly" campaigns by beer brewers

4.4 How easy is it to find out about advertising options on the Internet? Go to Looksmart's and Yahoo's advertiser pages (**http://www.looksmart.com/aboutus/media** and **http://www.yahoo.com/info/advertising**). What kind of information do they require from you? Send an e-mail requesting information and compare what you recieve.

LO5 Discuss the role of public relations in the promotional mix. Public relations is a vital part of a firm's promotional mix. A company fosters good publicity to enhance its image and promote its products. Popular public relations tools include new-product publicity, product placements, consumer education, sponsorships, and Internet Web sites. An equally important aspect of public relations is managing unfavorable publicity to minimize damage to a firm's image.

5.1 How can advertising and publicity work together? Give an example.

5.2 As the new public relations director for a sportswear company, you have been asked to set public relations objectives for a new line of athletic shoes to be introduced to the teen market. Draft a memo outlining the objectives you propose for the shoe's introduction and your reasons for them.

5.3 Review the newspapers in your area for one week. Try to review several and varied newspapers (local, campus, cultural, countercultural, etc.) During this period, cut out all the event advertisements that list sponsors. Once you have your collection, spread them out so you can see them all at once. Identify any patterns or connections between the type of event and its sponsors. Identify companies that sponsor more than one event. What do sponsors tell you about target markets? After analyzing the ads, write a brief paragraph summarizing your discoveries.

Key Terms

Exercises

APPLICATION EXERCISE 1

You may think that creating advertising is easy. After all, you have a lot of experience with advertising, having been bombarded with advertisements since you were a child. But creating advertising presents real challenges. In this exercise, you will be challenged to create an ad for a new product for animal use that is based on a product used by humans. Some examples include bras for cows, claw polish for tigers, and "Minute Mice" for cats. You can pick any product and any animal, but the combination must make sense.[71]

Activities

1. You have been hired by the purveyor of your chosen product to create a print advertisement. Lay out your ad on a piece of paper that is no smaller than 8.5 by 11 inches and no larger than 11 by 14 inches. Include a headline, illustration, logo, and body copy. Your illustration may be either hand-drawn or clipped from a magazine.

2. Include the copy for your ad directly on the front of the ad unless your copy blocks are too large for you to be legible or neat. If that is the case, then label your copy blocks with letters, put them on the back of your ad, and write the corresponding letter in the appropriate place on the front of the ad.

3. Don't forget to pick your own brand name for the product or service (like "Minute Mice").

APPLICATION EXERCISE 2

In this age of 24-hour cable news channels, tabloid news shows, and aggressive local and national news reporters intent on exposing corporate wrongdoing, one of the most important skills for a manager to learn is how to deal effectively with the press. Test your ability to deal effectively with the press by putting yourself in the following situation. To make the situation more realistic read the scenario and then give yourself two minutes to write a response to each question.[72]

Activity

Today, in the nation's capital, a public-interest group held a press conference to release the results of a study that found that the food sold in most Chinese restaurants is high in fat. The group claims that the most popular Chinese dishes, including orange chicken, pork fried rice, and Hunan beef, contain nearly as much fat as the food you get from fast-food chains like McDonald's, Wendy's, and Burger King. (Much of it is fried or is covered with heavy sauces.) Furthermore, the group says that customers who hope to keep their cholesterol and blood pressure low by eating Chinese food are just fooling themselves.

A TV reporter from Channel 5 called you at Szechuan Palace, your Szechuan-style Chinese restaurant, to get your response to this study. When he and the camera crew arrived, he asked you the following questions:

1. "These new studies were based on lunches and dinners sampled from Chinese restaurants across the nation. A local company, Huntington Labs, has agreed to test foods from local restaurants so that we can provide accurate information to our viewers. Would you agree to let us sample the main dishes in your restaurant to test the level of calories, calories from fat, and cholesterol? Furthermore, can we take the cameras into your restaurant so that we can get your customers' reactions to these studies?"

2. "A new study released today claims that food sold in Chinese restaurants is on average nearly as fattening as that sold at fast-food restaurants. How healthy is the food that you serve at Szechuan?"

3. "Get the camera in close here [camera closes in to get the shot] because I want the audience at home to see that you don't provide any information on your menu about calories, calories from fat, or cholesterol. Without this information [camera pulls back to get a picture of you and the reporter], how can your customers know whether the food that you serve is healthy for them?"

Entrepreneurship Case

RACY PLACE MYSPACE MAKES BIG-TIME ADVERTISERS WARY

Suddenly, on the Internet, it's 1999. But instead of Hotmail, Yahoo! or ICQ, it's social networking site MySpace.com that is attracting Web surfers at a blistering pace. More than 180,000 visitors are registering every day at a Web site that attracted its first 60 million registered users in under 30 months. Already laying claim to about half the reach that monster players Yahoo! and Google enjoy, MySpace typically draws over 20 million unique visitors each month. And, by the time you read this, all of these statistics will probably have been surpassed, given the site's incomprehensible growth rate.

As Internet success stories go, the MySpace phenomenon is nothing short of spectacular. Rupert Murdoch's News, Inc., bought the site from parent company Intermix Media in 2005 for $580 million, but many observers think that was about one-fourth of what the site could have sold for had the board and the lead investors not rushed into the deal. What reminds industry observers of 1999, though, is that MySpace is a hot property, yet it has no visible business model beyond trading eyeballs for ad dollars.

So why aren't mega advertising dollars flooding the doors at corporate headquarters? A quick tour of MySpace.com would probably answer that question for anyone with a brain and a pulse. MySpace is an anything-goes, youth-oriented, social hub at the center of music, matchmaking, and social rendezvousing. Friends keep in touch with each other by posting their profiles, photos, music preferences, social events, and more to personalized Web pages. The pages they create can host automatically loaded music videos or tracks that start to play as soon as the Web page loads. Pictures are uncensored, as are avatars and messages posted to pages by friends or any registered visitor who happens to land there.

The only thing the site monitors is hate speech, but that may change in the wake of a 2005 controversy in which two sexual predators were convicted of luring minors into sex acts by trolling MySpace's public pages. Skin, lewd language, and descriptions of adult events and activities can be found whenever users care to share or search for them. Not all of the content on MySpace is mature or off-color, however. More than

350,000 music groups or individual performers are registered there, and mainstream acts post pages there so that fans can follow their activities. The Foo Fighters even allowed their album *In Your Honor* to air free for a week on MySpace before its official release.

The site also hosts hundreds of thousands, possibly millions, of unique video clips in 16 categories. There are blog listings, independent and user-generated film reviews, event listings, classifieds, discussion forums, and, of course, those personal pages and music samples. At least 45 percent of MySpace users are in advertisers' coveted under-25 age bracket. The minimum age requirement is 14, and therein lies the advertisers' rub. Advertising on MySpace raises ethical concerns and sparks fear of unwanted brand association, even though the user base is the most valued.

Though the site claims to generate tens of millions of dollars in ad revenue each month, that pales in comparison to what it could be making. David Cohen, the senior vice president of Interpublic Group's top ad agency, Universal McCann, considers the advertising opportunities on MySpace "a double-edged sword." He points out that user-generated content can be "risqué, in bad taste, et cetera." His *Fortune* 100 clients don't like the idea of placing advertisements for their products in an environment where they have little control over what appears beside them.

Still, MySpace has its supporters. As the fifth largest Web property on the Internet, it is always going to be attractive to somebody. HSBC, Cingular, Aquafina, and H&R Block have all bought ad space there; surely, many more deep-pocketed firms will follow. As Richard Doherty, research director of Envisioneering Group, asks, "If you pull away from MySpace, where do you go? Do you do due diligence on the next 10 [social networking sites]? Advertisers need this audience. This is a new double-digits-minutes eyeball magnet and advertisers have to be there."[73]

Questions

1. Do you think the MySpace environment will make it easier or more difficult for advertisers to induce ad viewers to follow the AIDA plan?

2. What kind of people or personalities might companies try to appeal to by advertising on MySpace?

3. Considering the effects of advertising on consumers, what are the risks that advertisers take in placing advertisements on MySpace?

4. Compose a list of the companies, products, and services that you think would benefit from advertising on MySpace.com. Are there any in particular that you think should stay away from MySpace, regardless of its popularity?

© NKP MEDIA, INC./THOMSON

COMPANY CLIPS

Vans – Off the Wall and On Message

Even though Vans generates $500 million a year in sales, the company uses only a small team to manage the company's advertising and public relations – Stacy and Chris. The Vans PR team (or duo) uses vertical advertising to cater to a core group of consumers. With only a small advertising budget, the team must develop partnerships with its advertisers and use tours and events to spread the Vans culture.

Questions

1. Who does Vans consider to be its core consumers? How does the company reach them with its marketing messages?
2. How does Vans choose causes for its cause-related marketing?
3. What does Vans do to ensure that its print ads fit the publications in which they appear?
4. Describe the role of the Internet in Vans's communication strategy.

ED TV/CORBIS

BIZ FLIX

Ed TV

After working through the advertising and public relations concepts in Chapter 15, you can see that promotional elements are often intertwined. As an encore to your study, watch the film clip from *Ed TV,* starring Rob Reiner (Whitaker), Ellen DeGeneres, and Matthew McConaughey as the star of a reality television series. The scene is taken from the film's opening sequence, in which Whitaker shows the advertising for "True TV" to an audience of press reporters. Watch the opening advertisement carefully. What kind of ad is it? Can you identify one (or more) executional styles or appeals? Could the advertisement be considered public relations? Why? What kind of public relations could it be? Can you envision other ways in which advertising and public relations could be intertwined?

High scores indicate that you like television advertising. Not only do you like it, but you think television ads have informational benefits. Low scores correspond to a more skeptical attitude toward television advertising. If you are skeptical about television ads, are you also skeptical about print ads and other forms of advertising? How much do you tune out (or tune in)?

Sales Promotion and
CHAPTER
16
Personal Selling

Learning Outcomes

LO 1   Define and state the objectives of sales promotion

LO 2   Discuss the most common forms of consumer sales promotion

LO 3   List the most common forms of trade sales promotion

LO 4   Describe personal selling

LO 5   Discuss the key differences between relationship selling and traditional selling

LO 6   List the steps in the selling process

LO 7   Describe the functions of sales management

XM Satellite *and* Sirius *compete for subscribers*

Satellite radio is no longer a fledgling medium. The two companies offering this service in the United States—XM Satellite Radio and Sirius—have over 10 million customers between them and are projected to surpass 40 million by 2010. Satellite radio offers over 150 stations ranging from commercial-free music to dozens of

Both companies have exclusive contracts with major automakers and are fighting for market share of American drivers.

sports, news, entertainment, and talk radio programs. The genres are as general as country or pop or as specific as big band/swing, reggae, and Broadway show tunes. Moreover, you can listen to the same radio station as you drive across the country and in different cities.

The two companies are competing fiercely. XM Satellite Radio, which had a one-year head start, has almost twice as many subscribers as Sirius. Both companies have exclusive contracts with major automakers and are fighting for market share of American drivers. XM and Sirius both provide coverage of Major League Baseball's All-Star Week and NFL preseason games. XM has a plug-and-play receiver that enables users to view scores for college games, pro football, baseball, basketball, hockey, tennis, and golf, as well as NASCAR results. Meanwhile, Sirius has an extensive package of college football games with live

play-by-play broadcasts and is launching a daily four-hour program "podcasting" self-published syndicated radio shows. In early 2006, Sirius signed notorious and often raunchy talk show host Howard Stern to a five-year $500 million contract in an effort to woo customers. Subscriptions to each company costs less than $13 per month.

XM Satellite is not sitting by idly. It now offers subscribers add-on devices that can tune in satellite radio and play MP3s. XM unveiled the new devices from partners Samsung and Pioneer at the Consumer Electronics Show in Las Vegas. Both products access satellite radio content while also playing MP3s or WMA (Windows Media Audio) files. This combination enables subscribers to buy a single portable music player. "This is a major milestone for both satellite radio and MP3, and it promises to fundamentally change the way people enjoy their music," says XM's CEO, Hugh Panero.

Unfortunately, the devices will not work with Apple's iTunes songs, so XM does not have access to the largest provider of legal online music. To help make up for this loss, XM has partnered with music rental service provider Napster. Customers can bookmark songs they hear on satellite radio, plug their device into a PC, and then purchase the tunes from a shared XM and Napster portal.[1]

Which market segments are likely to be most interested in satellite radio? Is the combination of podcasting, portable media players, and satellite broadcasting likely to attract many new subscribers? What is the better way to sell satellite radio—sales promotion or personal selling?

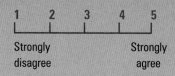

LO¹
Sales Promotion

In addition to using advertising, public relations, and personal selling, marketing managers can use sales promotion to increase the effectiveness of their promotional efforts. *Sales promotion* is marketing communication activities, other than advertising, personal selling, and public relations, in which a short-term incentive motivates consumers or members of the distribution channel to purchase a good or service immediately, either by lowering the price or by adding value.

Advertising offers the consumer a reason to buy; sales promotion offers an incentive to buy. Both are important, but sales promotion is usually cheaper than advertising and easier to measure. A major national TV advertising campaign often costs over $5 million to create, produce, and place. In contrast, promotional campaigns using the Internet or direct marketing methods can cost less than half that amount. It is also very difficult to determine how many people buy a product or service as a result of radio or TV ads. But with sales promotion, marketers know the precise number of coupons redeemed or the number of contest entries.

Sales promotion is usually targeted toward either of two distinctly different markets. **Consumer sales promotion** is targeted to the ultimate consumer market. **Trade sales promotion** is directed to members of the marketing channel, such as wholesalers and retailers. Sales promotion has become an important element in a marketer's integrated marketing communications program (see Chapter 14). Sales promotion expenditures have been steadily increasing over the last several years as a result of increased competition, the ever-expanding array of available media choices, consumers and retailers demanding more deals from manufacturers, and the continued reliance on accountable and measurable marketing strategies. In addition, product and service marketers that have traditionally ignored sales promotion activities, such as power companies and restaurants, have discovered the marketing power of sales promotion. In fact, annual expenditures on promotion marketing in the United States now exceed $300 billion.[2]

consumer sales promotion
Sales promotion activities targeting the ultimate consumer.

trade sales promotion
Sales promotion activities targeting a channel member, such as a wholesaler or retailer.

THE OBJECTIVES OF SALES PROMOTION

Sales promotion usually has more effect on behavior than on attitudes. Immediate purchase is the goal of sales promotion, regardless of the form it takes. Therefore, it seems to make more sense when planning a sales promotion campaign to target customers according to their general behavior. For instance, is the consumer loyal to your product or to your competitor's? Does the consumer switch brands readily in favor of the best deal? Does the consumer buy only the least expensive product, no matter what? Does the consumer buy any products in your category at all?

The objectives of a promotion depend on the general behavior of target consumers (see Exhibit 16.1). For example, marketers who are targeting loyal users of their product actually don't want to change behavior. Instead, they need to reinforce existing behavior or increase product usage. An effective tool for strengthening brand loyalty is the *frequent buyer program* that rewards consumers for repeat purchases. Other types of promotions are more effective with customers prone to brand switching or with those who are loyal to a competitor's product. A cents-off coupon, free sample, or eye-catching

REVIEW LEARNING OUTCOME

LO¹ Define and state the objectives of sales promotion

Sales Promotion

Consumer   Trade

Goal = Drive immediate purchase

= Influence <u>Behavior</u> not Attitude

Exhibit 16.1
Types of Consumers and Sales Promotion Goals

Type of Buyer	Desired Results	Sales Promotion Examples
Loyal customers People who buy your product most or all of the time	Reinforce behavior, increase consumption, change purchase timing	• Loyalty marketing programs, such as frequent buyer cards or frequent shopper clubs • Bonus packs that give loyal consumers an incentive to stock up or premiums offered in return for proofs of purchase
Competitor's customers People who buy a competitor's product most or all of the time	Break loyalty, persuade to switch to your brand	• Sampling to introduce your product's superior qualities compared to their brand • Sweepstakes, contests, or premiums that create interest in the product
Brand switchers People who buy a variety of products in the category	Persuade to buy your brand more often	• Any promotion that lowers the price of the product, such as coupons, price-off packages, and bonus packs • Trade deals that help make the product more readily available than competing products
Price buyers People who consistently buy the least expensive brand	Appeal with low prices or supply added value that makes price less important	• Coupons, price-off packages, refunds, or trade deals that reduce the price of the brand to match that of the brand that would have been purchased

SOURCE: From *Sales Promotion Essentials,* 2nd ed., by Don E. Schultz, William A. Robinson, and Lisa A. Petrison. Reprinted by permission of NTC Publishing Group, 4255 Touhy Ave., Lincolnwood, IL 60048.

display in a store will often entice shoppers to try a different brand. Consumers who do not use the product may be enticed to try it through the distribution of free samples.

Once marketers understand the dynamics occurring within their product category and have determined the particular consumers and consumer behaviors they want to influence, they can then go about selecting promotional tools to achieve these goals.

LO^2
Tools for Consumer Sales Promotion

Marketing managers must decide which consumer sales promotion devices to use in a specific campaign. The methods chosen must suit the objectives to ensure success of the overall promotion plan. Popular tools for consumer sales promotion are coupons and rebates, premiums, loyalty marketing programs, contests and sweepstakes, sampling, and point-of-purchase promotion. Consumer sales promotion tools have also been easily transferred to online versions to entice Internet users to visit sites, purchase products, or use services on the Web.

COUPONS AND REBATES

A **coupon** is a certificate that entitles consumers to an immediate price reduction when they buy the product. Coupons are a particularly good way to encourage product trial and repurchase. They are also likely to increase the amount of a product bought.

Coupon distribution has been growing in recent years. Almost 350 billion coupons are distributed to U.S. households annually, and this does not include the billions of coupons increasingly available over the Internet and in-store. Intense competition in the consumer packaged goods category and the annual introduction of over 1,200 new products have contributed to this trend. Though coupons are often criticized for reaching consumers who have no interest in the product or for encouraging repeat purchase by regular users, recent studies indicate that coupons promote new-product use and are likely to stimulate purchases. About 80 percent of all consumer packaged goods coupons are distributed via colorful FSIs (free standing inserts) that are delivered each week to over 60 million households in the Sunday newspaper. But recently marketers have been

coupon
A certificate that entitles consumers to an immediate price reduction when they buy the product.

expanding beyond FSIs to nontraditional channels, including the Internet where online coupon sites like coolsavings.com and valpak.com are emerging as major coupon distribution outlets.[3]

To overcome the low redemption rates for coupons, marketers are using new strategies. For example, by shortening the time in which coupons can be redeemed or reducing the requirement for multiple purchases, some marketers have increased the redemption rate by creating a greater sense of urgency to redeem the coupon. Some marketers are de-emphasizing their use of coupons in favor of everyday low pricing, while others are distributing single, all-purpose coupons that can be redeemed for several brands.

In-store coupons have become popular because they are more likely to influence customers' buying decisions. Instant coupons on product packages, coupons distributed from on-shelf coupon-dispensing machines, and electronic coupons issued at the checkout counter are achieving much higher redemption rates. Indeed, instant coupons are redeemed more than 15 times more frequently than traditional newspaper coupons, indicating that consumers are making more in-store purchase decisions.

Starbucks has taken in-store coupons to a new level by installing interactive units on grocery store shelves. Each unit provides consumers with product information related to brewing, coffee education, and a taste matcher. In one test the units resulted in a 200 percent increase in sales. Internet coupons are also gaining in popularity. For example, Kroger has launched "Coupons that you click. Not clip." on Kroger.com. Registered Kroger Plus Shoppers card members just log on to the Web site and click on the coupons they want. Coupons are automatically loaded on to the Kroger Plus card and redeemed at checkout when the shopper's Kroger Plus card is scanned.[4]

As marketing tactics grow more sophisticated, coupons are no longer viewed as a stand-alone tactic, but as an integral component of a larger promotional campaign. For example, Domino's Pizza teamed with eBay to launch a "Back to School" campaign focused on building the Domino's brand and driving consumers to **http://www.ebay.com**. The coupons arrived on pizza boxes. Customers then logged on to eBay for a chance to win one million eBay points (a cash value of $10,000) to be spent on eBay.com, textbook discounts, and Domino's gift certificates.[5]

Rebates are similar to coupons in that they offer the purchaser a price reduction; however, because the purchaser must mail in a rebate form and usually some proof of purchase, the reward is not as immediate. Traditionally used by food and cigarette manufacturers, rebates now appear on all types of products, from computers and software to film and cell phones. In the run-up to Super Bowl XL, Pepsi-Cola offered consumers a $10 dollar rebate as an incentive to stock up on the company's soda products and Frito-Lay brand chips in time for the big game.[6]

Manufacturers prefer rebates for several reasons. Rebates allow manufacturers to offer price cuts to consumers directly. Manufacturers have more control over rebate promotions because they can be rolled out and shut off quickly. Further, because buyers must fill out forms with their names, addresses, and other data, manufacturers use rebate programs to build customer databases. Perhaps the best reason of all to offer rebates is that although rebates are particularly good at enticing purchase, most consumers never bother to redeem them. The Federal Trade Commission estimates that only half of consumers eligible for rebates collect them.[7]

PREMIUMS

A **premium** is an extra item offered to the consumer, usually in exchange for some proof that the promoted product has been purchased. Premiums reinforce the consumer's purchase decision, increase consumption, and persuade nonusers to switch

rebate
A cash refund given for the purchase of a product during a specific period.

premium
An extra item offered to the consumer, usually in exchange for some proof of purchase of the promoted product.

brands. Premiums like telephones, tote bags, and umbrellas are given away when consumers buy cosmetics, magazines, bank services, rental cars, and so on. Probably the best example of the use of premiums is McDonald's Happy Meal, which rewards children with a small toy. Many companies have been built around furnishing clients with customized premiums. Because of the ubiquity of premiums, especially in trade relationships, it is getting harder to capture someone's attention with a premium. One British company, Novelty Gift Company, is hoping to change that. The company offers quirky gadgets like pink speakers shaped like pigs, a set of three iPod speakers shaped like a tripod, and a computer mouse that looks like a dragster.[8]

Premiums can also include more product for the regular price, such as two-for-the-price-of-one bonus packs or packages that include more of the product. Kellogg's, for instance, added two more pastries and waffles to its Pop Tarts and Eggo packages without increasing the price in an effort to boost market share lost to private-label brands and new competitors. The promotion was so successful the company decided to keep the additional product in its regular packaging. Another possibility is to attach a premium to the product's package. For example, when research showed that consumers who drink tequila are often trendsetters who entertain at home, 1800 Tequila launched a holiday promotion that included an instant camera and entertainment guide attached to the bottle.[9]

LOYALTY MARKETING PROGRAMS

Loyalty marketing programs, or **frequent buyer programs,** reward loyal consumers for making multiple purchases. Popularized by the airline industry through frequent flyer programs, loyalty marketing enables companies to strategically invest sales promotion dollars in activities designed to capture greater profits from customers already loyal to the product or company. This is critical, as studies show that consumer loyalty is on the decline. Forrester Research found that the percentage of consumers ranking price as more important than brand rose from 41 to 47 percent over three years. According to research conducted by Gartner, more than 75 percent of consumers have more than one loyalty card that rewards them with redeemable points. Furthermore, U.S. companies spend more than $1.2 billion annually on loyalty programs, and that amount is expected to rise in the future.[10]

The objective of loyalty marketing programs is to build long-term, mutually beneficial relationships between a company and its key customers. Frequent shopper card programs offered by many supermarkets and other retailers have exploded in popularity. Research from Forrester shows that 54 percent of primary grocery shoppers belong to two or more supermarket loyalty programs. Although this speaks to the popularity of loyalty cards, it also shows that customers are pledging "loyalty" to more than one store: 15 percent of primary grocery shoppers are cardholders in at least three programs, and 4 percent participate in four or five programs.[11] Combined with the statistics on the growing importance of price over brands, frequent shopper programs need to offer something more than just discounts to build customer loyalty. One of the more successful recent premium promotions is Starbucks' Duetto Card, which combines a Visa credit card with a reloadable Starbucks card. The card allows members to collect "Duetto Dollars" that can be redeemed for anything they want to purchase at a Starbucks location. Starbucks also sends members quarterly opportunities based on usage, such as product samples and previews. A year after its debut, fully 57 percent of Duetto cardholders said they were more likely to purchase Starbucks products as a result of the program.[12]

Cobranded credit cards are an increasingly popular loyalty marketing tool. Almost one billion direct marketing appeals for a cobranded credit card were sent to potential customers in the United States in 2005. Target, Gap, Sony and American Airlines are only a few examples of companies sponsoring cobranded Visa, MasterCard, or American Express cards. American Express has a program with Space Adventures, a company that offers simulated space flight experiences.[13]

loyalty marketing program
A promotional program designed to build long-term, mutually beneficial relationships between a company and its key customers.

frequent buyer program
A loyalty program in which loyal consumers are rewarded for making multiple purchases of a particular good or service.

Sweepstakes Online

How do online sweepstakes sites compare with the kind of sweepstakes entries you receive in the mail? Visit the popular sweepstakes site Sweepstakesonline.com. Do any of the contests interest you? Do you think the online pitches are ethical? Why or why not?

http://www.sweepstakesonline.com

Online

One unique frequent buyer program, called Stratus, is promoted as a gateway to a more glamorous lifestyle. The Stratus Visa card is underwritten by U.S. Bank and available only by invitation. Stratus cardholders pay an annual fee of $1,500 and are required to spend at least $100,000 per year on the card. Stratus partners include luxury catalog Vivre, luxury travel company Abercrombie and Kent, MarquisJet, Sony Cierge, and classic custom cigar company Zino Platinum, among others. Cardholders can redeem points for dinner at the Louvre, a private tour of the pyramids, a yoga class with Gwyneth Paltrow, or even trips in a private jet (furnished by MarquisJet, of course).[14]

Through loyalty programs, shoppers receive discounts, alerts on new products, and other enticing offers. In exchange, retailers are able to build customer databases that help them better understand customer preferences. Verizon Wireless builds loyalty with its "New Every Two" program. Consumers who have been Verizon customers for two years are eligible for a $100 credit toward a new digital phone.[15]

Companies increasingly are using the Internet to build customer loyalty through e-mail and blogs. Over 80 percent of supermarket chains are using e-mail to register customers for their loyalty programs and to entice them with coupons, flyers, and promotional campaigns.[16] Blogs are becoming a critical component of some companies' loyalty marketing programs. Blogging technology enables marketers to create a community of consumers who feel positively about the company's brand and to build deeper relationships with them. Starwood Hotels launched its corporate blog, TheLobby.com, in 2006. Although the blog is open to the public, the company is aiming the content specifically at members of the Starwood Preferred Guest loyalty program. Features include postings about special events at specific Starwood properties and how travelers can earn loyalty points through special promotions. The company's goal is to combine advertising with useful information to create a Web destination for its guests—and divert them away from other travel blogs that might contain negative postings about Starwood hotels.[17]

Companies like McDonald's and Cannondale are also using blogging technology to create communities around their brands. Robin Hopper, CEO of iUpload, the company that hosts the blogs for these two companies, says that companies publish blogs to build social networks around their brands. "It's a whole new way to market," he says. "People willingly provide all sorts of demographic information on blogs" that companies can use to target them more effectively.[18]

CONTESTS AND SWEEPSTAKES

Contests and sweepstakes are generally designed to create interest in a good or service, often to encourage brand switching. *Contests* are promotions in which participants use some skill or ability to compete for prizes. A consumer contest usually requires entrants to answer questions, complete sentences, or write a paragraph about the product and submit proof of purchase. Winning a *sweepstakes,* on the other hand, depends on chance or luck, and participation is free. Sweepstakes usually draw about ten times more entries than contests do.

While contests and sweepstakes may draw considerable interest and publicity, generally they are not effective tools for generating long-term sales. To increase their effectiveness, sales promotion managers must make certain the award will appeal to the target market. For example, Home & Garden Television Network's

Twenty brides-to-be, in wedding dresses and devil horns, run a difficult obstacle course in New York's Times Square for the chance to win $25,000 towards their dream wedding. The event was held to kick off the third season of BRIDEZILLAS, a show in cable network WE.

© WE TV/PRNEWSFOTO (AP TOPIC GALLERY)

annual "Dream Home Giveaway" sweepstakes awards a fully furnished, custom-built home to one lucky viewer. The promotion is cosponsored by General Motors, which fills the garage with a new sport-utility vehicle, and other home-related companies such as Sherwin-Williams paint, Lumber Liquidators flooring, California Closets, and Jeld-Wen windows and doors. The annual sweepstakes typically draws over four million entries.[19] Offering several smaller prizes to many winners instead of one huge prize to just one person often will increase the effectiveness of the promotion, but there's no denying the attractiveness of a jackpot-type prize.

Marketers have recently launched some of the biggest promotions ever. PepsiCo hosted a sweepstakes that featured a $1 billion giveaway. The winner was announced on a Warner Brothers television special hosted by Drew Carey. Pepsi also partnered with Apple Computer to give away 200 million free music downloads from iTunes.com. United Airlines launched a "Ticket to the World" that gives away free international travel tickets (previously only domestic tickets were given away), and Volkswagen launched a promotion that gave an Apple iPod to anyone who purchased a Beetle.[20]

SAMPLING

Consumers generally perceive a certain amount of risk in trying new products. Many are afraid of trying something they will not like (such as a new food item) or spending too much money and getting little reward. **Sampling** allows the customer to try a product risk-free. Sampling can increase retail sales by as much as 40 percent.[21] It is no surprise, therefore, that sampling has increased more than 20 percent annually in recent years.[22]

Sampling can be accomplished by directly mailing the sample to the customer, delivering the sample door-to-door, packaging the sample with another product, or demonstrating or sampling the product at a retail store or service outlet. Coca-Cola partnered with Domino's Pizza to sample its Coca-Cola Zero beverage. Every Domino's customer placing an order got a complimentary 20-ounce bottle of Coca-Cola Zero. To get the word out about a new flavor of ice cream, Ben & Jerry's Homemade deployed hot-air balloons to summer fairs and festivals in key markets and made guerrilla visits to office buildings in 13 cities.

© FREDERIC J. BROWN/AFP/GETTY IMAGES

Distributing samples can often mitigate the risks consumers perceive in trying a new product. As part of its global marketing strategy, Starbucks has aggressively expanded into Asia. A woman in Hong Kong samples a cup of coffee from "Mercury Man," a Starbucks employee who walks around with a pot of coffee on his back.

More than one million free scoops were served.[23] Similarly, when Masterfoods wanted to increase sales of its Dove "Promises" product line of dark and milk chocolates, it used both print media and sampling. To reach the upscale target market, samples were handed out at high-end hotels, spas, and gourmet cooking shows.[24]

Sampling at special events is a popular, effective, and high-profile distribution method that permits marketers to piggyback onto fun-based consumer activities—including sporting events, college fests, fairs and festivals, beach events, and chili cook-offs. For example, product sampling during tailgating at college and professional football stadiums allows marketers to reach anywhere from 10,000 to 50,000 consumers in a single afternoon. H.J. Heinz tests products such as new barbecue sauces and ketchups to get immediate feedback about what consumers like and dislike about the products.[25]

sampling
A promotional program that allows the consumer the opportunity to try a product or service for free.

Distributing samples to specific location types where consumers regularly meet for a common objective or interest, such as health clubs, churches, or doctors' offices, is one of the most efficient methods of sampling. What better way to get consumers to try a product than to offer a sample exactly when it is needed most? If someone visits a health club regularly, chances are he or she is a good prospect for a health-food product or vitamin supplement. Health club instructors are also handing out body wash, deodorant, and face cloths to sweating participants at the end of class, and, more surprisingly, hot drinks! Dunkin' Donuts used a sampling program in more than 200 health clubs to promote its new Latte Lite drink, a zero percent fat product that gives health-conscious consumers a lighter alternative.[26] Meanwhile, makers of stain removers and hand cleansers are giving away samples in mall food courts and petting zoos. Likewise, pharmaceutical companies offer free samples of new and expensive drugs as a tactic to entice doctors and consumers to become loyal to a product. This method of distributing samples is working. In fact, one recent study found that sampling events produced an average 36 percent increase in sales soon afterward.[27]

POINT-OF-PURCHASE PROMOTION

Point-of-purchase (P-O-P) promotion includes any promotional display set up at the retailer's location to build traffic, advertise the product, or induce impulse buying. Point-of-purchase promotions include shelf "talkers" (signs attached to store shelves), shelf extenders (attachments that extend shelves so products stand out), ads on grocery carts and bags, end-aisle and floor-stand displays, television monitors at supermarket check-out counters, in-store audio messages, and audiovisual displays. One big advantage of P-O-P promotion is that it offers manufacturers a captive audience in retail stores. Another advantage is that between 70 and 80 percent of all retail purchase decisions are made in-store, so P-O-P promotions can be very effective. P-O-P promotions can increase sales by as much as 65 percent. Strategies to increase sales include adding header or riser cards, changing messages on base or case wraps, adding inflatable or mobile displays, and using signs that advertise the brand's sports, movie, or charity tie-in.[28] When Hershey launched its new Swoops, a "chip" version of popular candy bars such as Almond Joy, Reese's, and Hershey Bars, it successfully used in-store displays to stimulate in-store, impulse purchases of the new candy.[29]

Corporations are cashing in on in-store purchasing decisions through more sophisticated P-O-P promotions. For example, MasterCard International sent 300,000 of its merchant and restaurant partners across the country P-O-P kits containing window clings, tent cards, employee buttons, register decals, coupons, and check presenter inserts customized by retail category. The promotion program, called Priceless P-O-P, awarded one cardholder five "prizes of a lifetime": an African safari, a visit from a celebrity chef, a behind-the-scenes tour of Space Center Houston, a trip to a racing school in England, and VIP passes to the My VH-1 Music Awards. MasterCard encouraged compliance among retailers with a mystery shopper program that sent teams into stores to award $50 gift cards to store employees whenever they encountered a Priceless P-O-P. Five random participants won $2,500 gift cards, and the staff at the store that produced the grand-prize winner earned a Major League Baseball prize package.[30]

ONLINE SALES PROMOTION

Online sales promotions have expanded dramatically in recent years. Marketers are now spending billions of dollars annually on such promotions. Sales promotions online have proved effective and cost-efficient, generating response rates three to five times higher than those of their off-line counterparts. The most effective types of online sales promotions are free merchandise, sweepstakes, free shipping with purchases, and coupons.

Eager to boost traffic, Internet retailers are busy giving away free services or equipment, such as personal computers and travel, to lure consumers not only to their own

point-of-purchase display
A promotional display set up at the retailer's location to build traffic, advertise the product, or induce impulse buying.

Web sites but to the Internet in general. Another goal is to add potential customers to their databases. For example, Heineken USA, Inc. launched the "Headline Hoax" online promotional campaign in which consumers (hoaxers) trick a friend (victim). The hoax is a fake headline with a photograph that looks as though it is on the front page of a major Web page such as Maximonline.com, FHM, or The Sporting News. The hoaxer can choose from a selection of pictures and headlines. One photo shows two football players attacking one another and the tackler has one hand inside the other's shirt and another hand pulling on his shorts; the headline reads "[Person's Name] is too touchy at touch football game." Once the victim opens this e-mail, other friends on the hoaxer's list are alerted to the joke. At the start of the campaign, Heineken had only 5,000 e-mail addresses in its database. Within six months, it had collected an additional 95,000 e-mail addresses. The program has been so successful that it has been updated and expanded to the "Heineken Holiday Headline Hoax" and similar programs.[31]

Marketers have discovered that online coupon distribution provides another vehicle for promoting their products. Online coupons have a redemption rate of around 15 percent, five to eight times the redemption rate for traditional coupons.[32] In fact, nearly 50 percent of consumers who purchase something online use a coupon or discount promotional code. According to CMS, a coupon-management company in Winston-Salem, North Carolina, over 7.9 million electronic coupons were redeemed in 2003.[33] In addition, e-coupons can help marketers lure new customers. For example, Staples.com jumped from 23rd to 14th among retail Web sites with the most buyers through an e-coupon promotion that offered $25 off on purchases of $75 or more.[34]

Online versions of loyalty programs are also popping up and although many types of companies have these programs, the most successful are those run by hotel and airline companies.

REVIEW LEARNING OUTCOME

LO 2 Discuss the most common forms of consumer sales promotion

CONSUMER SALES PROMOTION

- Coupons and rebates
- Premiums
- Loyalty marketing program
- Contests and sweepstakes
- Sampling
- P-O-P
- Online

LO 3
Tools for Trade Sales Promotion

Whereas consumer promotions *pull* a product through the channel by creating demand, trade promotions *push* a product through the distribution channel (see Chapter 12). When selling to members of the distribution channel, manufacturers use many of the same sales promotion tools used in consumer promotions—such as sales contests, premiums, and point-of-purchase displays. Several tools, however, are unique to manufacturers and intermediaries:

trade allowance
A price reduction offered by manufacturers to intermediaries, such as wholesalers and retailers.

- *Trade allowances:* A **trade allowance** is a price reduction offered by manufacturers to intermediaries such as wholesalers and retailers. The price reduction or rebate is given in exchange for doing something specific, such as allocating space for a new product or buying something during special periods. For example, a local Circuit City or Best Buy outlet could receive a special discount for running its own promotion on Sony Surround Sound Systems.

Trade shows and conventions, like the one advertised here, are an increasingly important part of sales promotion; they are an effective way to introduce new products to the marketplace.

- *Push money:* Intermediaries receive **push money** as a bonus for pushing the manufacturer's brand through the distribution channel. Often the push money is directed toward a retailer's salespeople. LinoColor, the leading high-end scanner company, produces a Picture Perfect Rewards catalog filled with merchandise retailers can purchase with points accrued for every LinoColor scanner they sell. The cover of the catalog features a wave runner that was brought to three industry trade shows and given away in a sweepstakes to one of the dealers who had visited all the product displays and passed a quiz. The program resulted in a 26 percent increase in LinoColor sales, and the manufacturer recruited 32 new dealers to carry the product line.[35]

- *Training:* Sometimes a manufacturer will train an intermediary's personnel if the product is rather complex—as frequently occurs in the computer and telecommunication industries. For example, representatives of a TV manufacturer like Toshiba may train salespeople in how to demonstrate the new features of the latest models of TVs to consumers. This is particularly helpful when salespeople must explain the features to older consumers who are less technology oriented.

- *Free merchandise:* Often a manufacturer offers retailers free merchandise in lieu of quantity discounts. For example, a breakfast cereal manufacturer may throw in one case of free cereal for every 20 cases ordered by the retailer. Occasionally, free merchandise is used as payment for trade allowances normally provided through other sales promotions. Instead of giving a retailer a price reduction for buying a certain quantity of merchandise, the manufacturer may throw in extra merchandise "free" (that is, at a cost that would equal the price reduction).

- *Store demonstrations:* Manufacturers can also arrange with retailers to perform an in-store demonstration. Food manufacturers often send representatives to grocery stores and supermarkets to let customers sample a product while shopping. Cosmetic companies also send their representatives to department stores to promote their beauty aids by performing facials and makeovers for customers.

- *Business meetings, conventions, and trade shows:* Trade association meetings, conferences, and conventions are an important aspect of sales promotion and a growing, multibillion-dollar market. At these shows, manufacturers, distributors, and other vendors have the chance to display their goods or describe their services to customers and potential customers. A recent study reported that, on average, the cost of closing a lead generated at an exhibition is 56 percent of the cost of closing a lead generated in the field—$625 versus $1,117.[36] Trade shows have been uniquely effective in introducing new products; they can establish products in the marketplace more quickly than advertising, direct marketing, or sales calls can. Companies participate in trade shows to attract and identify new prospects, serve current customers, introduce new products, enhance corporate image, test the market response to new products, enhance corporate morale, and gather competitive product information.

Trade promotions are popular among manufacturers for many reasons. Trade sales promotion tools help manufacturers gain new distributors for their products, obtain wholesaler and retailer support for consumer sales promotions, build or reduce dealer inventories, and improve trade relations. Car manufacturers annually

push money
Money offered to channel intermediaries to encourage them to "push" products—that is, to encourage other members of the channel to sell the products.

LO3 List the most common forms of trade sales promotion

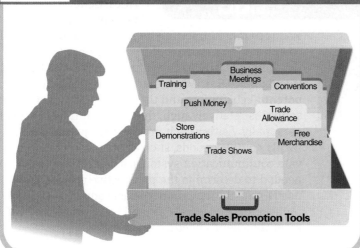

Trade Sales Promotion Tools

(Tools shown: Training, Business Meetings, Conventions, Push Money, Trade Allowance, Store Demonstrations, Free Merchandise, Trade Shows)

sponsor dozens of auto shows for consumers. Many of the displays feature interactive computer stations where consumers enter vehicle specifications and get a printout of prices and local dealer names. In return, the local car dealers get the names of good prospects. The shows attract millions of consumers, providing dealers with increased store traffic as well as good leads.

LO4 Personal Selling

As mentioned in Chapter 14, *personal selling* is direct communication between a sales representative and one or more prospective buyers in an attempt to influence each other in a purchase situation.

In a sense, all businesspeople are sales people. An individual may become a plant manager, a chemist, an engineer, or a member of any profession and yet still have to sell. During a job search, applicants must "sell" themselves to prospective employers in an interview. To reach the top in most organizations, individuals need to sell ideas to peers, superiors, and subordinates. Most important, people must sell themselves and their ideas to just about everyone with whom they have a continuing relationship and to many other people they see only once or twice. Chances are that students majoring in business or marketing will start their professional careers in sales. Even students in non-business majors may pursue a sales career.

Personal selling offers several advantages over other forms of promotion:

- Personal selling provides a detailed explanation or demonstration of the product. This capability is especially needed for complex or new goods and services.

- The sales message can be varied according to the motivations and interests of each prospective customer. Moreover, when the prospect has questions or raises objections, the salesperson is there to provide explanations. In contrast, advertising and sales promotion can only respond to the objections the copywriter thinks are important to customers.

- Personal selling can be directed only to qualified prospects. Other forms of promotion include some unavoidable waste because many people in the audience are not prospective customers.

- Personal selling costs can be controlled by adjusting the size of the sales force (and resulting expenses) in one-person increments. On the other hand, advertising and sales promotion must often be purchased in fairly large amounts.

- Perhaps the most important advantage is that personal selling is considerably more effective than other forms of promotion in obtaining a sale and gaining a satisfied customer.

Exhibit 16.2

Comparison of Personal Selling and Advertising/Sales Promotion

Personal selling is more important if . . .	Advertising and sales promotion are more important if . . .
The product has a high value.	The product has a low value.
It is a custom-made product.	It is a standardized product.
There are few customers.	There are many customers.
The product is technically complex.	The product is easy to understand.
Customers are concentrated.	Customers are geographically dispersed.
Examples: insurance policies, custom windows, airplane engines	**Examples:** soap, magazine subscriptions, cotton T-shirts

REVIEW LEARNING OUTCOME

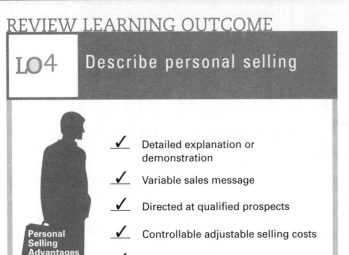

LO4 Describe personal selling

Personal Selling Advantages

✓ Detailed explanation or demonstration

✓ Variable sales message

✓ Directed at qualified prospects

✓ Controllable adjustable selling costs

✓ Effective at obtaining sale and gaining customer satisfaction

Personal selling may work better than other forms of promotion given certain customer and product characteristics. Generally speaking, personal selling becomes more important as the number of potential customers decreases, as the complexity of the product increases, and as the value of the product grows (see Exhibit 16.2). When there are relatively few potential customers and the value of the good or service is relatively high, the time and travel costs of personally visiting each prospect are justifiable. For highly complex goods, such as business jets or private communication systems, a salesperson is needed to determine the prospective customer's needs, explain the product's basic advantages, and propose the exact features and accessories that will meet the client's needs.

LO5 Relationship Selling

Until recently, marketing theory and practice concerning personal selling focused almost entirely on a planned presentation to prospective customers for the sole purpose of making the sale. Marketers were most concerned with making a one-time sale and then moving on to the next prospect. Whether the presentation took place face-to-face during a personal sales call or over the telephone (telemarketing), traditional personal selling methods attempted to persuade the buyer to accept a point of view or convince the buyer to take some action. Once the customer was somewhat convinced, then the salesperson used a variety of techniques in an attempt to elicit a purchase. Frequently, the objectives of the salesperson were at the expense of the buyer, creating a win-lose outcome. Although this type of sales approach has not disappeared entirely, it is being used less and less often by professional salespeople.

In contrast, modern views of personal selling emphasize the relationship that develops between a salesperson and a buyer. **Relationship selling**, or **consultative selling**, is a multistage process that emphasizes personalization and empathy as key ingredients in identifying prospects and developing them as long-term, satisfied customers. The old way was to sell a product, but with relationship selling, the objective is to build long-term branded relationships with consumers/buyers. Thus, the focus is on building mutual trust between the buyer and seller through the delivery of anticipated, long-term, value-added benefits to the buyer.

Relationship or consultative salespeople, therefore, become consultants, partners, and problem solvers for their customers. They strive to build long-term relationships with key accounts by developing trust over time. The emphasis shifts from a one-time sale to a long-term relationship in which the salesperson works with the customer to develop solutions for enhancing the customer's bottom line. Moreover, research has shown that positive customer-salesperson relationships contribute to trust, increased customer loyalty, and the intent to continue the relationship with the salesperson.[37] Thus, relationship selling promotes a win-win situation for both buyer and seller.

The end result of relationship selling tends to be loyal customers who purchase from the company time after time. A relationship selling strategy focused on retaining customers costs a company less than constantly prospecting and selling to new customers. Companies that focus on customer retention through high customer service gain 6 per-

relationship selling (consultative selling)
A sales practice that involves building, maintaining, and enhancing interactions with customers in order to develop long-term satisfaction through mutually beneficial partnerships.

cent market share per year, while companies that offer low customer service lose 2 percent market share per year.[38] In fact, it costs businesses six times more to gain a new customer than to retain a current one.[39]

Relationship selling is more typical with selling situations for industrial-type goods, such as heavy machinery or computer systems, and services, such as airlines and insurance, than for consumer goods. For example, Kinko's has built a long-term business relationship with PeopleSoft. The software maker now gives many of its training and educational materials printing jobs to Kinko's—a deal worth close to $5 million in revenues. Kinko's has forged such a close relationship with the company that Kinko's representatives are even invited to sit in on internal planning meetings in PeopleSoft's human resources department at the company's headquarters.

"Webinars" (online seminars lasting about an hour) are a popular way to support relationship selling tasks like lead generation, client support, sales training, and corporate meetings. For example, 3Com, a computer data networking system, held a webinar that was attended by 1,300 executives in 80 countries; the session generated 60 percent of 3Com's five-month lead generation goals. Similarly, SpectraLink, a provider of wireless phone and text messaging systems to Verizon and AT&T, uses webinars to give new-product demonstrations so that channel managers can focus on other tasks. DMReview, a web-based portal on technology, has found webinars to be so successful that it offers them continuously "on demand" on business intelligence and data mining topics. The webinars are cosponsored by major firms in insurance, banking, health care, and related fields. To maximize the opportunities provided by webcasting, marketers are using technology that effectively delivers content to other audiences using devices such as mobile phones, TiVo-type digital video recorders, and game consoles.[40]

Exhibit 16.3 lists the key differences between traditional personal selling and relationship or consultative selling. These differences will become more apparent as we explore the personal selling process later in the chapter.

REVIEW LEARNING OUTCOME

LO5

Discuss the key differences between relationship selling and traditional selling

Sales Increases Result from Creating Value

Initial Sale — Repeat Sale — Successive Sales

Traditional Sales

Relationship Selling

Exhibit 16.3

Key Differences between Traditional Selling and Relationship Selling

Traditional Personal Selling	Relationship or Consultative Selling
Sell products (goods and services)	Sell advice, assistance, and counsel
Focus on closing sales	Focus on improving the customer's bottom line
Limited sales planning	Consider sales planning as top priority
Spend most contact time telling customers about product	Spend most contact time attempting to build a problem-solving environment with the customer
Conduct "product-specific" needs assessment	Conduct discovery in the full scope of the customer's operations
"Lone wolf" approach to the account	Team approach to the account
Proposals and presentations based on pricing and product features	Proposals and presentations based on profit impact and strategic benefits to the customer
Sales follow-up is short term, focused on product delivery	Sales follow-up is long term, focused on long-term relationship enhancement

SOURCE: Robert M. Peterson, Patrick L. Schul, and George H. Lucas, Jr., "Consultative Selling: Walking the Walk in the New Selling Environment," National Conference on Sales Management, *Proceedings,* March 1996.

LO⁶
Steps in the Selling Process

Although personal selling may sound like a relatively simple task, completing a sale actually requires several steps. The **sales process**, or **sales cycle**, is simply the set of steps a salesperson goes through to sell a particular product or service. The sales process or cycle can be unique for each product or service, depending on the features of the product or service, characteristics of customer segments, and internal processes in place within the firm, such as how leads are gathered.

Some sales take only a few minutes, but others may take much longer to complete. Sales of technical products like a Boeing or Airbus airplane and customized goods and services typically take many months, perhaps even years, to complete. On the other end of the spectrum, sales of less technical products like copy machines or office supplies are generally more routine and may take only a few days. Whether a salesperson spends a few minutes or a few years on a sale, these are the seven basic steps in the personal selling process:

1. Generating leads
2. Qualifying leads
3. Approaching the customer and probing needs
4. Developing and proposing solutions
5. Handling objections
6. Closing the sale
7. Following up

Like other forms of promotion, these steps of selling follow the AIDA concept discussed in Chapter 14. Once a salesperson has located a prospect with the authority to buy, he or she tries to get the prospect's attention. A thorough needs assessment turned into an effective sales proposal and presentation should generate interest. After developing the customer's initial desire (preferably during the presentation of the sales proposal), the salesperson seeks action in the close by trying to get an agreement to buy. Follow-up after the sale, the final step in the selling process, not only lowers cognitive dissonance (refer to Chapter 5) but also may open up opportunities to discuss future sales. Effective follow-up will also lead to repeat business in which the process may start all over again at the needs assessment step.

sales process (sales cycle)
The set of steps a salesperson goes through in a particular organization to sell a particular product or service.

Traditional selling and relationship selling follow the same basic steps. They differ in the relative importance placed on key steps in the process (see Exhibit 16.4). Traditional selling efforts are transaction oriented, focusing on generating as many leads as possible, making as many presentations as possible, and closing as many sales as possible. Minimal effort is placed on asking questions to identify customer needs and wants or matching these needs and wants to the benefits of the product or service. In contrast, the salesperson practicing relationship selling emphasizes an up-front investment in the time and effort needed to uncover each customer's specific needs and wants and matches the product or service offering to them, as closely as possible. By doing the homework up front, the salesperson creates the conditions necessary for a relatively straightforward close. Let's look at each step of the selling process individually.

Exhibit 16.4

Relative Amount of Time Spent in Key Steps of the Selling Process

Key Selling Steps	Traditional Selling	Relationship/Consultative Selling
Generating leads	High	Low
Qualifying leads	Low	High
Approaching the customer and probing needs	Low	High
Developing and proposing solutions	Low	High
Handling objections	High	Low
Closing the sale	High	Low
Following up	Low	High

GENERATING LEADS

Initial groundwork must precede communication between the potential buyer and the salesperson. **Lead generation,** or **prospecting,** is the identification of those firms and people most likely to buy the seller's offerings. These firms or people become "sales leads" or "prospects."

Sales leads can be obtained in several different ways, most notably through advertising, trade shows and conventions, or direct-mail and telemarketing programs. One accounting firm used direct mail, telephone, sales visits, and seminars in a four-step process aimed at generating business-to-business leads. The initial step was a direct-mail piece, in the form of an introductory letter from a firm partner. The second piece, sent one month later, was a black and white direct-mail circular with company contact information. The third step was a follow-up call from a firm partner to arrange a meeting. In the last stage, partners contacted prospects who had initially declined appointments and invited them to attend a free tax seminar the following month. Of the 1,100 businesses targeted, 200 prospects set up meetings. Favorable publicity also helps to create leads. Company records of past client purchases are another excellent source of leads. Many sales professionals are also securing valuable leads from their firm's Internet Web site. For example, DaimlerChrysler's use of interactive media to create ongoing interaction with online consumers is paying off. The company recently sponsored 42 online video games featuring Chrysler, Jeep, and Dodge vehicles, generating more than 10,000 sales leads among the estimated 3.5 million consumers who downloaded the games. The company generates an estimated 40,000 sales leads monthly through its Web site and other online venues.[41]

Another way to gather a lead is through a **referral**—a recommendation from a customer or business associate. The advantages of referrals over other forms of prospecting include highly qualified leads, higher closing rates, larger initial transactions, and shorter sales cycles. Simply put, the salesperson and the company can earn more money in less time when prospecting using referrals. Referrals typically are as much as ten times more productive in generating sales than are cold calls. Unfortunately, although most clients are willing to give referrals, many salespeople do not ask for them. Effective sales training can help to overcome this reluctance to ask for referrals. To increase the number of referrals they receive, some companies even pay or send small gifts to customers or suppliers who provide referrals.

Networking is using friends, business contacts, coworkers, acquaintances, and fellow members in professional and civic organizations to identify potential clients. Indeed, a number of national networking clubs have been started for the sole purpose of generating leads and providing valuable business advice. The networking clubs usually have between 15 and 30 members in noncompeting business categories. During weekly breakfast or lunch meetings, each member is allowed to talk about the company he or she represents for an allotted period of time. Then members exchange lead cards. Research suggests that, on average, chapter members see an increase in business volume of between 16 and 25 percent after they've been with their group for three to six months. Increasingly, sales professionals are also using online networking sites such as Ryze, LinkedIn and Zero Degrees to connect with targeted leads and clients around the world, 24 hours a day. Some of LinkedIn's estimated 4.8 million users have reported

lead generation (prospecting)
Identification of those firms and people most likely to buy the seller's offerings.

referral
A recommendation to a salesperson from a customer or business associate.

networking
A process of finding out about potential clients from friends, business contacts, coworkers, acquaintances, and fellow members in professional and civic organizations.

LinkedIn
Ryze
Online networking groups are growing in popularity. Check out the sites for LinkedIn and Ryze to read more about how these groups work. Do they sound like something you would join? How could they benefit your career?

http://www.linkedin.com
http://www.ryze.com

Online

Networking is being transformed by the Internet. Sites like LinkedIn connect the contact lists of thousands of users, creating easily navigable networks comprised of millions of people working in nearly every industry.

response rates between 50 and 60 percent, versus 3 percent from direct marketing efforts.[42]

Before the advent of more sophisticated methods of lead generation, such as direct mail and telemarketing, most prospecting was done through **cold calling**—a form of lead generation in which the salesperson approaches potential buyers without any prior knowledge of the prospects' needs or financial status. Although this method is still used, many sales managers have realized the inefficiencies of having their top salespeople use their valuable selling time searching for the proverbial "needle in a haystack." Passing the job of cold calling to a lower-cost employee, typically an internal sales support person, allows salespeople to spend more time and use their relationship-building skills on prospects who have already been identified. Sales experts note that the days of cold calls and unannounced office visits have given way to referral-based and relationship selling.

QUALIFYING LEADS

When a prospect shows interest in learning more about a product, the salesperson has the opportunity to follow up, or qualify, the lead. Personally visiting unqualified prospects wastes valuable salesperson time and company resources. Often many leads go unanswered because salespeople are given no indication as to how qualified the leads are in terms of interest and ability to purchase. Unqualified prospects give vague or incomplete answers to a salesperson's specific questions, try to evade questions on budgets, and request changes in standard procedures like prices or terms of sale. In contrast, qualified leads who represent real prospects answer questions, value your time, and are realistic about money and when they are prepared to buy. Salespersons who are given accurate information on qualified leads are more than twice as likely to follow up.[43]

Lead qualification involves determining whether the prospect has three things:

- *A recognized need:* The most basic criterion for determining whether someone is a prospect for a product is a need that is not being satisfied. The salesperson should first consider prospects who are aware of a need but should not discount prospects who have not yet recognized that they have one. With a little more information about the product, they may decide they do have a need for it. Preliminary interviews and questioning can often provide the salesperson with enough information to determine whether there is a need.

- *Buying power:* Buying power involves both authority to make the purchase decision and access to funds to pay for it. To avoid wasting time and money, the salesperson needs to identify the purchasing authority and the ability to pay before making a presentation. Organizational charts and information about a firm's credit standing can provide valuable clues.

- *Receptivity and accessibility:* The prospect must be willing to see the salesperson and be accessible to the salesperson. Some prospects simply refuse to see salespeople. Others, because of their stature in their organization, will see only a salesperson or sales manager with similar stature.

Often the task of lead qualification is handled by a telemarketing group or a sales support person who *prequalifies* the lead for the salesperson. Prequalification systems free sales representatives from the time-consuming task of following up on leads to determine need, buying power, and receptiveness. Prequalification systems may even set up initial appointments with the prospect for the salesperson. The result is more time for the sales force to spend in front of interested customers. Software is increasingly being utilized in lead qualification. For example, one janitorial company initially considered anyone with a minimum of 75,000 square feet to be a prospect. But often properties are already under contract or have been contacted. Using software, the company was able to create a "smart" list that included only true prospects.[44]

Companies are increasingly using their Web sites to qualify leads. When qualifying leads online, companies want visitors to register, indicate the products and services they are interested in, and provide information on their time frame and resources. Leads from

cold calling
A form of lead generation in which the salesperson approaches potential buyers without any prior knowledge of the prospects' needs or financial status.

lead qualification
Determination of a sales prospect's (1) recognized need, (2) buying power, and (3) receptivity and accessibility.

the Internet can then be prioritized (those indicating a short time frame, for instance, given a higher priority) and then transferred to salespeople. Often Web site visitors can be enticed to answer questions with offers of free merchandise or information. Enticing visitors to register also enables companies to customize future electronic interactions—for example, by giving prospects who visit the Web site their choice from a menu of products tailored specifically to their needs.

APPROACHING THE CUSTOMER AND PROBING NEEDS

Before approaching the customer, the salesperson should learn as much as possible about the prospect's organization and its buyers. This process, called the **preapproach,** describes the "homework" that must be done by the salesperson before contacting the prospect. This may include consulting standard reference sources, such as Moody's, Standard & Poor's, or Dun & Bradstreet, or contacting acquaintances or others who may have information about the prospect. Another preapproach task is to determine whether the actual approach should be a personal visit, a phone call, a letter, or some other form of communication.

During the sales approach, the salesperson either talks to the prospect or secures an appointment for a future time in which to probe the prospect further as to his or her needs. Relationship selling theorists suggest that salespeople should begin developing mutual trust with their prospect during the approach. Salespeople should use the approach as a way of introducing themselves and their company and products. They must sell themselves before they can sell the product. Small talk that projects sincerity and some suggestion of friendship is encouraged because it builds rapport with the prospect, but remarks that could be construed as insincere should be avoided.

The salesperson's ultimate goal during the approach is to conduct a **needs assessment** to find out as much as possible about the prospect's situation. This involves interviewing the customer to determine his or her specific needs and wants and the range of options the customer has for satisfying them. The salesperson should be determining how to maximize the fit between what he or she can offer and what the prospective customer wants. As part of the needs assessment, the consultative salesperson must know everything there is to know about the following:

- *The product or service:* Product knowledge is the cornerstone for conducting a successful needs analysis. The consultative salesperson must be an expert on his or her product or service, including technical specifications, the product's features and benefits, pricing and billing procedures, warranty and service support, performance comparisons with the competition, other customers' experiences with the product, and current advertising and promotional campaign messages. For example, a salesperson who is attempting to sell a Xerox copier to a doctor's office should be very knowledgeable about Xerox's selection of copiers, their attributes, capabilities, technological specifications, and postpurchase servicing.

- *Customers and their needs:* The salesperson should know more about customers than they know about themselves. That's the secret to relationship and consultative selling, where the salesperson acts not only as a supplier of products and services but also as a trusted consultant and adviser. The professional salesperson doesn't just sell products. He or she brings to each client business-building ideas and solutions to problems. For the customer, consulting a professional salesperson is like having another vital person on the team at no cost. For example, if the Xerox salesperson is asking the "right" questions, then he or she should be able to identify copy-related areas where the doctor's office is losing or wasting money. By being familiar with the Xerox product lines and discovering the doctor's needs, in terms of copying capability, the Xerox salesperson can act as a "consultant" on how the doctor's office can save money and time, rather than just selling a copier.

preapproach
A process that describes the "homework" that must be done by a salesperson before he or she contacts a prospect.

needs assessment
A determination of the customer's specific needs and wants and the range of options the customer has for satisfying them.

- *The competition:* The salesperson must know as much about the competitor's company and products as he or she knows about his or her own company. *Competitive intelligence* includes many factors: who the competitors are and what is known about them; how their products and services compare; advantages and disadvantages; and strengths and weaknesses. In this case, the Xerox salesperson must be familiar with the products of competitors, such as Canon and Minolta. For example, if the Canon copy machine is less expensive than the Xerox copier, the doctor's office may be leaning toward purchasing the Canon. But if the Xerox salesperson can point out that the cost of long-term maintenance and toner cartridges is lower for the Xerox copier, offsetting its higher initial cost, the salesperson may be able to persuade the doctor's office to purchase the Xerox copier because of the long-term savings.

- *The industry:* Knowing the industry involves active research on the part of the salesperson. This means attending industry and trade association meetings, reading articles published in industry and trade journals, keeping track of legislation and regulation that affect the industry, awareness of product alternatives and innovations from domestic and foreign competition, and having a feel for economic and financial conditions that may affect the industry. Thus, the Xerox salesperson should stay on top of emerging technological innovations so that he or she can better serve customers looking for the latest and greatest technology. It is also important to be aware of economic downturns because businesses may be looking for less expensive financing options. In either case, the Xerox salesperson will be able to provide better service by knowing how industry trends may affect customers' office purchases.

Creating a *customer profile* during the approach helps salespeople optimize their time and resources. This profile is then used to help develop an intelligent analysis of the prospect's needs in preparation for the next step, developing and proposing solutions. Customer profile information is typically stored and manipulated using sales force automation software packages designed for use on laptop computers. Sales force automation software provides sales reps with a computerized and efficient method of collecting customer information for use during the entire sales process. Further, customer and sales data stored in a computer database can be easily shared among sales team members. The information can also be appended with industry statistics, sales or meeting notes, billing data, and other information that may be pertinent to the prospect or the prospect's company. The more salespeople know about their prospects, the better they can meet their needs.

Salespeople should wrap up their sales approach and need-probing mission by summarizing the prospect's need, problem, and interest. The salesperson should also get a commitment from the customer to some kind of action, whether it's reading promotional material or agreeing to a demonstration. This commitment helps qualify the prospect further and justify additional time invested by the salesperson. The salesperson should reiterate the action he or she promises to take, such as sending information or calling back to provide answers to questions. The date and time of the next call should be set at the conclusion of the sales approach as well as an agenda for the next call in terms of what the salesperson hopes to accomplish, such as providing a demonstration or presenting a solution.

DEVELOPING AND PROPOSING SOLUTIONS

Once the salesperson has gathered the appropriate information about the client's needs and wants, the next step is to determine whether his or her company's products or services match the needs of the prospective customer. The salesperson then develops a solution, or possibly several solutions, in which the salesperson's product or service solves the client's problems or meets a specific need.

These solutions are typically offered to the client in the form of a sales proposal delivered during a sales presentation. A **sales proposal** is a written document or professional presentation that outlines how the company's product or service will meet or

sales proposal
A formal written document or professional presentation that outlines how the salesperson's product or service will meet or exceed the prospect's needs.

sales presentation
A formal meeting in which the salesperson presents a sales proposal to a prospective buyer.

exceed the client's needs. The **sales presentation** is the formal meeting in which the salesperson has the opportunity to present the sales proposal. The presentation should be explicitly tied to the prospect's expressed needs. Further, the prospect should be involved in the presentation by being encouraged to participate in demonstrations or by exposure to computer exercises, slides, video or audio, flipcharts, photographs, and the like.

Technology has become an important part of presenting solutions for many salespeople. Pen manufacturer BIC uses the Internet to connect with its wholesale and convenience store customers. Before launching BIClink.com, BIC received 80 percent of its order volume by fax. Processing these orders was time-consuming, and the orders often were filled with errors. BIClink.com has eliminated the potential for errors and made it easier and faster to validate purchase order numbers, ship dates, case quantities, and pricing. When customers sign on (through a secure, password-protected system), the welcome screen is personalized with their company's name and the name of their BIC rep. On placing an order, customers receive both a hard copy and e-mail confirmation statement with the salesperson's name and contact information including e-mail, voice mail, phone, and fax numbers. Virtually all of BIC's customers now order online.[45]

Because the salesperson often has only one opportunity to present solutions, the quality of both the sales proposal and presentation can make or break the sale. Salespeople must be able to present the proposal and handle any customer objections confidently and professionally. For a powerful presentation, salespeople must be well prepared, use direct eye contact, ask open-ended questions, be poised, use hand gestures and voice inflection, focus on the customer's needs, incorporate visual elements that impart valuable information, know how to operate the audio/visual or computer equipment being used for the presentation, make sure the equipment works, and practice, practice, practice.[46] Nothing dies faster than a boring presentation. If the salesperson doesn't have a convincing and confident manner, then the prospect will very often forget the information. Prospects take in body language, voice patterns, dress, and body type. Often customers are more likely to remember how salespeople present themselves than what they say.

HANDLING OBJECTIONS

Rarely does a prospect say "I'll buy it" right after a presentation. Instead, the prospect often raises objections or asks questions about the proposal and the product. The potential buyer may insist that the price is too high, that he or she does not have enough information to make a decision, or that the good or service will not satisfy the present need. The buyer may also lack confidence in the seller's organization or product.

One of the first lessons that every salesperson learns is that objections to the product should not be taken personally as confrontations or insults. Rather, a salesperson should view objections as requests for information. A good salesperson considers objections a legitimate part of the purchase decision. To handle objections effectively, the salesperson should anticipate specific objections, such as concerns about price, fully investigate the objection with the customer, be aware of what the competition is offering, and, above all, stay calm. When Dell introduced its direct selling model, salespeople anticipated that customers would worry that they would not receive the same level of service and dedication as they would get from a reseller. As a result, the salespeople included assurances about service and support following the sale in their sales presentations.

Zig Ziglar, a renowned sales trainer, created a popular method for handling objections: "When an objection occurs, always use the fundamentals of FEEL, FELT, FOUND. It gives you an extra cushion of time and allows the prospect to identify with others." For example: "I see how you FEEL! Others have FELT the same way too until they FOUND . . . ." In the Xerox copier example, the doctor might say, "The copy machine seems to be very expensive." Using the Zig Ziglar method the salesperson would respond, "I see how you *feel*. Other doctors have *felt* the same way until they *found* out how much money they were saving after the first year."[47]

Often the salesperson can use the objection to close the sale. If the customer tries to pit suppliers against each other to drive down the price, the salesperson should be prepared to point out weaknesses in the competitor's offer and stand by the quality in his or her own proposal.

CLOSING THE SALE

At the end of the presentation, the salesperson should ask the customer how he or she would like to proceed. If the customer exhibits signs that he or she is ready to purchase and all questions have been answered and objections have been met, then the salesperson can try to close the sale. Customers often give signals during or after the presentation that they are ready to buy or are not interested. Examples include changes in facial expressions, gestures, and questions asked. The salesperson should look for these signals and respond appropriately.

Closing requires courage and skill. Naturally, the salesperson wants to avoid rejection, and asking for a sale carries with it the risk of a negative answer. A salesperson should keep an open mind when asking for the sale and be prepared for either a yes or a no. Rarely is a sale closed on the first call. In fact, the typical salesperson makes several hundred sales calls a year, many of which are repeat calls to the same client in an attempt to make a sale. Some salespeople may negotiate with large accounts for several years before closing a sale. As you can see, building a good relationship with the customer is very important. Often, if the salesperson has developed a strong relationship with the customer, only minimal efforts are needed to close a sale.

Negotiation often plays a key role in the closing of the sale. **Negotiation** is the process during which both the salesperson and the prospect offer special concessions in an attempt to arrive at a sales agreement. For example, the salesperson may offer a price cut, free installation, free service, or a trial order. Effective negotiators, however, avoid using price as a negotiation tool because cutting price directly affects a company's profitability. Because companies spend millions on advertising and product development to create value, when salespeople give in to price negotiations too quickly, it decreases the value of the product. Instead, effective salespeople should emphasize value to the customer, rendering price a nonissue. Salespeople should also be prepared to ask for trade-offs and try to avoid giving unilateral concessions. If you're making only a 50 percent margin on a product, and you need at least a 60 percent margin, raise your prices or drop the product. Moreover, if the customer asks for a 5 percent discount, the salesperson should ask for something in return, such as higher volume or more flexibility in delivery schedules.

More and more U.S. companies are expanding their marketing and selling efforts into global markets. Salespeople selling in foreign markets should tailor their presentation and closing styles to each market. Different personalities and skills will succeed in some countries and absolutely fail in others. For instance, if a salesperson is an excellent closer and always focuses on the next sale, doing business in Latin America might be difficult. The reason is that in Latin America people want to take a long time building a personal relationship with their suppliers.

FOLLOWING UP

Unfortunately, many salespeople have the attitude that making the sale is all that's important. Once the sale is made, they can forget about their customers. They are wrong. Salespeople's responsibilities do not end with making the sales and placing the orders. One of the most important aspects of their jobs is **follow-up**—the final step in the selling process, in which they must ensure that delivery schedules are met, that the goods or services perform as promised, and that the buyers' employees are properly trained to use the products.

In the traditional sales approach, follow-up with the customer is generally limited to successful product delivery and performance. A basic goal of relationship selling is to motivate customers to come back, again and again, by developing and nurturing long-term relationships. Most businesses depend on repeat sales, and repeat sales depend on thorough and continued follow-up by the salesperson. Finding a new customer is far more expensive than retaining an existing customer. When customers feel abandoned, cognitive dissonance arises and repeat sales decline. Today, this issue is more pertinent than ever because customers are far less loyal to brands and vendors. Buyers are more inclined to look for the best deal, especially in the case of poor after-the-sale follow-up.

negotiation
The process during which both the salesperson and the prospect offer special concessions in an attempt to arrive at a sales agreement.

follow-up
The final step of the selling process, in which the salesperson ensures that delivery schedules are met, that the goods or services perform as promised, and that the buyers' employees are properly trained to use the products.

More and more buyers favor building a relationship with sellers. One Farmers' Insurance agent suggests following up on insurance claims with a question to determine the customer's level of satisfaction. For example, he may ask "Were you happy with the way your claim was handled?" Depending on the response, the agent can either get a referral from the customer or try to fix any problems so that the customer does not choose another agency in the future. This agent also makes telephone and personal follow-up visits after a marriage, death, birth, or birthday in the customer's family. These visits are used as sales opportunities to cross-sell products such as life insurance.[48]

Automated e-mail follow-up marketing—a combination of sales automation and Internet technology—is enhancing customer satisfaction as well as bringing in more business for some marketers. Here's how it works: After the initial contact with a prospect, a software program automatically sends a series of personalized e-mail over a period of time. CollegeRecruiter.com is one company taking advantage of this technology. The company posts ads for businesses recruiting recent college graduates on its Web site and has seen phenomenal results from autoresponse marketing. Prospects start receiving a series of e-mails once they have visited the site and requested advertising rates. The first message goes out immediately. The next two go out in 4 to 11 days. From there, e-mails go out monthly. Using the automated follow-up e-mail system has helped CollegeRecruiter.com become the highest traffic career site used by job-hunting students and recent graduates. Its Web site regularly posts more than 100,000 job openings.[49]

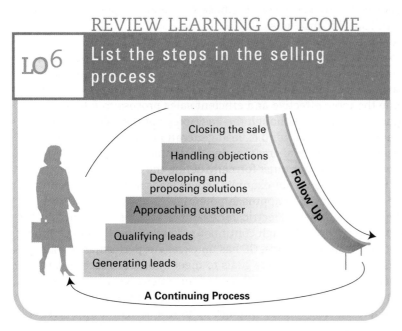

REVIEW LEARNING OUTCOME

LO6 List the steps in the selling process

Closing the sale

Handling objections

Developing and proposing solutions

Approaching customer

Qualifying leads

Generating leads

Follow Up

A Continuing Process

LO7
SALES MANAGEMENT

There is an old adage in business that nothing happens until a sale is made. Without sales there is no need for accountants, production workers, or even a company president. Sales provide the fuel that keeps the corporate engines humming. Companies like Cisco Systems, International Paper, and Johnson Controls, and several thousand other manufacturers would cease to exist without successful salespeople. Even companies like Procter & Gamble and Kraft Foods that mainly sell consumer goods and use extensive advertising campaigns still rely on salespeople to move products through the channel of distribution. Thus, sales management is one of marketing's most critical specialties. Effective sales management stems from a highly success-oriented sales force that accomplishes its mission economically and efficiently. Poor sales management can lead to unmet profit objectives or even to the downfall of the corporation.

Just as selling is a personal relationship, so is sales management. Although the sales manager's basic job is to maximize sales at a reasonable cost while also maximizing profits, he or she also has many other important responsibilities and decisions:

1. Defining sales goals and the sales process

2. Determining the sales force structure

3. Recruiting and training the sales force

4. Compensating and motivating the sales force

5. Evaluating the sales force

DEFINING SALES GOALS AND THE SALES PROCESS

Effective sales management begins with a determination of sales goals. Without goals to achieve, salesperson performance would be mediocre at best, and the company would likely fail. Like any marketing objective, sales goals should be stated in clear, precise, and measurable terms and should always specify a time frame for their fulfillment. Overall sales force goals are usually stated in terms of desired dollar sales volume, market share, or profit level. For example, a life insurance company may have a goal to sell $50 million in life insurance policies annually, to attain a 12 percent market share, or to achieve $1 million in profits. Individual salespeople are also assigned goals in the form of quotas. A **quota** is simply a statement of the salesperson's sales goals, usually based on sales volume alone but sometimes including key accounts (those with greatest potential), new accounts, repeat sales, and specific products.

Great sales managers focus not only on sales goals but also on the entire process that drives their sales organizations to reach those goals. Without a keen understanding of the sales process, a manager will never be successful—no matter how defined the sales goals or how great the sales reps. An important responsibility of the sales manager, therefore, is to determine the most effective and efficient sales process to follow in selling each different product and service. Although the basic steps of the sales process are the same as discussed earlier in the chapter (i.e., lead generation and qualification, approach and needs assessment, proposal creation and presentation, handling objections, closing, and follow-up), a manager must formally define the specific procedures salespeople go through to do their jobs—for example, where leads are generated, how they are qualified, what the best way is to approach potential clients, and what terms can be negotiated during closing. General Electric, for example, focuses on attracting, hiring, and keeping the right salespeople through continuous training and the development of an effective sales process for its sales force. GE has an excellent performance management program that gives an employee concrete goals to meet in order to receive a promotion. The company performs formal reviews three or four times a year and also provides an extensive product- and skills-training program that can last anywhere from one to two years. Salespeople are also rotated through up to five assignments before being placed in a permanent position to see what best suits the individual sales rep. When a GE rep finally makes a call, he or she is completely knowledgeable about the product being sold.[50]

DETERMINING THE SALES FORCE STRUCTURE

Because personal selling is so costly, no sales department can afford to be disorganized. Proper design helps the sales manager organize and delegate sales duties and provide direction for salespeople. Sales departments are most commonly organized by geographic regions, by product line, by marketing function performed (such as account development or account maintenance), by market or industry, or by individual client or account. The sales force for Hewlett-Packard could be organized into sales territories covering New England, the Midwest, the South, and the West Coast or into distinct groups selling different product lines. HP salespeople may also be assigned to a specific industry or market, for example, the telecommunications industry, or to key clients such as AT&T, Cingular, Virgin Mobile, and Verizon.

Market- or industry-based structures and key account structures are gaining popularity in today's competitive selling environment, especially with the emphasis on relationship selling. Being familiar with one industry or market allows sales reps to become experts in their fields and thereby offer better solutions and service. Further, by organizing the sales force around specific customers, many companies hope to improve customer service, encourage collaboration with other arms of the company, and unite salespeople in customer-focused sales teams. Internet advertising solutions company DoubleClick, for example, realigned its 175 salespeople into six vertical industry channels: automotive, business, entertainment and youth, technology, women and health, and travel. Previously, DoubleClick salespeople sold Internet ad space in a variety of different categories. Now salespeople can focus on one category, get a better understanding of the sites with related subject matter, and consult with advertisers about their competition.[51]

RECRUITING AND TRAINING THE SALES FORCE

Sales force recruitment should be based on an accurate, detailed description of the sales task as defined by the sales manager. For example, General Electric recruits over 1,000 students on 100 college campuses across the United States for entry-level, internship, and co-op positions. Its Web site provides prospective salespeople with explanations of different career entry paths and video accounts of what it is like to have a career at GE. Aside from the usual characteristics such as level of experience or education, what traits should sales managers look for in applicants? One of the most important traits of top performers is ego strength, or having a strong, healthy self-esteem and the ability to bounce back from rejection. Great salespeople also have a sense of urgency and competitiveness that pushes their sales to completion. Moreover, they have a desire to persuade people and close the sale. Effective salespeople are also assertive; they have the ability to be firm in one-to-one negotiations, to lead the sales process, and to get their point across confidently, without being overbearing or aggressive. They are sociable, willing to take risks, and capable of understanding complex concepts and ideas. Additionally, great salespeople are creative in developing client solutions, and they possess empathy—the ability to place oneself in someone else's shoes. Not surprisingly, virtually all successful salespeople say their sales style is relationship oriented rather than transaction oriented.[52]

After the sales recruit has been hired and given a brief orientation, training begins. A new salesperson generally receives instruction in company policies and practices, selling techniques, product knowledge, industry and customer characteristics, and nonselling duties such as filling out sales and market information reports or using a sales automation computer program. Firms that sell complex products generally offer the most extensive training programs. Once applicants are hired at General Electric, they enter one of the many "rotational" training programs depending on their interest and major. For example, the Sales and Marketing Commercial Leadership Program (CLP) is geared toward developing skills needed for a successful career at GE. The program ranges from one to two years, depending on which GE business area the employee selects, and includes several rotations between business headquarters and the field. On completing the program, the new employees are better prepared to sell GE products because of their high level of product knowledge and on-the-job experience interacting with customers.[53]

Most successful sales organizations have learned that training is not just for newly hired salespeople. Instead, training is offered to all salespeople in an ongoing effort to hone selling skills and relationship building. In pursuit of solid salesperson-client relationships, training programs now seek to improve salespeople's consultative selling and listening skills and to broaden their product and customer knowledge. In addition, training programs stress the interpersonal skills needed to become the contact person for customers. Because negotiation is increasingly important in closing a sale, salespeople are also trained to negotiate effectively without risking profits.

COMPENSATING AND MOTIVATING THE SALES FORCE

Compensation planning is one of the sales manager's toughest jobs. Only good planning will ensure that compensation attracts, motivates, and retains good salespeople. Generally, companies and industries with lower levels of compensation suffer higher turnover rates, which increase costs and decrease effectiveness. Therefore, compensation needs to be competitive enough to attract and motivate the best salespeople. Firms sometimes take profit into account when developing their compensation plans. Instead of paying salespeople on overall volume, they pay according to the profitability achieved from selling each product. Still other companies tie a part of the salesperson's total compensation to customer satisfaction assessed through periodic customer surveys.

The three basic compensation methods for salespeople are commission, salary, and combination plans. A typical commission plan gives salespeople a specified percentage of their sales revenue. A **straight commission** system compensates the salesperson only when a sale is made. On the other end of the spectrum, a **straight salary** system compensates a salesperson with a stated salary regardless of sales productivity. Most companies, however, offer a compromise between straight commission and straight salary plans. A *combination system* offers a base salary plus an incentive—usually a commission or a bonus. Combination systems have benefits for both the sales manager and the salesperson. The salary portion of the plan helps the manager control the sales force; the incentive provides motivation. For the salesperson, a combination plan offers an incentive to excel while minimizing the extremely wide swings in earnings that may occur when the economy surges or contracts too much. General Electric, Procter & Gamble, and Xerox are among the many large corporations that offer a base salary plus commission for sales representatives.

As the emphasis on relationship selling increases, many sales managers feel that tying a portion of a salesperson's compensation to a client's satisfaction with the salesperson and the company encourages relationship building. To determine this, sales managers can survey clients on a salesperson's ability to create realistic expectations and his or her responsiveness to customer needs. At PeopleSoft, the world's second largest applications software company, structure, culture, and strategies are built around customer satisfaction. Sales force compensation is tied to both sales quotas and a satisfaction metric that allows clients to voice their opinions on the service provided.[54]

Although the compensation plan motivates a salesperson to sell, sometimes it is not enough to produce the volume of sales or the profit margin required by sales management. Sales managers, therefore, often offer rewards or incentives, such as recognition at ceremonies, plaques, vacations, merchandise, and pay raises or cash bonuses. For example, Lorry I. Lokey, founder and chairman of the board of Business Wire, has invited employees from one of the company's 26 offices nationwide to join him on a free trip to a predetermined location, usually overseas. To qualify, employees must have celebrated their five-year anniversary with the company.[55] But, of course, cash awards are the most popular sales incentive and are used by virtually all companies. Another possibility is to reward salespeople with a Visa Gift Card, available from Visa in any amount between $25 and $600. The gift card, which functions like a credit card, can be personalized with a message about the salesperson's performance. It can then be reloaded at the employer's discretion. To recognize and further motivate employees, General Electric uses various rewards including stock options, recognition programs unique to each department, tuition assistance, and product discounts.[56] Rewards may help increase overall sales volume, add new accounts, improve morale and goodwill, move slow items, and bolster slow sales. They can also be used to achieve long-term or short-term objectives, such as unloading overstocked inventory and meeting a monthly or quarterly sales goal.

Motivation also takes the form of effective sales leadership on the part of the sales manager. An effective sales manager is inspirational to his or her salespeople, encouraging them to achieve their goals through clear and enthusiastic communications. He or she has a clear vision and commitment to the mission of the organization and the ability to instill pride and earn the respect of employees. Effective sales leaders continuously increase their knowledge and skill base while also encouraging others to do so. A recent study that assessed the attributes of sales leaders found that the best sales leaders share a number of key personality traits (see Exhibit 16.5), such as a sense of urgency, openness to new ideas, and a desire to take risks. These traits separate motivational sales leaders from mere sales managers. In motivating their sales force, sales managers must be careful not to encourage unethical behavior, as the "Ethics in Marketing" box explains.

EVALUATING THE SALES FORCE

The final task of sales managers is evaluating the effectiveness and performance of the sales force. To evaluate the sales force, the sales manager needs feedback—that is, regular information from salespeople. Typical performance measures include sales volume,

straight commission
A method of compensation in which the salesperson is paid some percentage when a sale is made.

straight salary
A method of compensation in which the salesperson receives a salary regardless of sales productivity.

Exhibit 16.5

Seven Key Leadership Traits of Effective Sales Leaders

Effective sales leaders . . .	
Are assertive	Assertive sales leaders know when and how to get tough and how to assert their authority.
Possess ego drive	Sales leaders with ego drive have the desire and ability to persuade their reps to take action.
Possess ego strength	Sales leaders with ego strength are able to make sure not only that they bounce back from rejection but also that their reps rebound, too.
Take risks	Risk-taking sales leaders are willing to go out on a limb in an effort to make a sale or enhance a relationship.
Are innovative	Innovative sales leaders stay open to new ideas and new ways of conducting business.
Have a sense of urgency	Urgent sales leaders understand that getting things done now is critical to winning and keeping business.
Are empathetic	Empathetic sales leaders help their reps grow by listening and understanding.

SOURCE: Table adapted from "The 7 Traits of Great Sales Leaders" by Geoffrey Brewer, *Sales & Marketing Management*, July 1997, 38–46. Reprinted with permission.

contribution to profit, calls per order, sales or profits per call, or percentage of calls achieving specific goals such as sales of products that the firm is heavily promoting.

Performance information helps the sales manager monitor a salesperson's progress through the sales cycle and pinpoint where breakdowns may be occurring. For example, by learning the number of prospects an individual salesperson has in each step of the sales cycle process and determining where prospects are falling out of the sales cycle, a manager can determine how effective a salesperson may be at lead generation, needs

ETHICS in Marketing

Promoting Ethical Behavior in Business

It is important for all companies to monitor their corporate cultures. This is especially true when salespeople are motivated by sales incentives. Salespeople's behavior often reflects the company's sales management program.

To develop a training program that will produce an ethical and successful sales force, sales managers should consider the company's mission statement, employee incentives, and compensation. When developing or modifying the mission statement, managers and employees should consider their customers' needs and wants. Salespeople who must try to sell unnecessary or unwanted products are more likely to cross ethical boundaries.

Sales managers should also consider what motivates employees to sell the company's product or service. Aside from compensation, many companies offer some type of incentive package, such as a trip, merchandise, or extra vacation time, that is based on the volume or dollars sold. Sales managers must also guard against unintended negative consequences of the incentives they offer.

Compensation policies are a major ethical issue for many sales-motivated organizations and must be designed to discourage unethical behavior.

Finally, sales managers should regularly evaluate and review the performance of their salespeople to make sure that they are not engaging in unethical behavior. In their book *The Psychology of Sales Call Reluctance,* George Dudley and Shannon Goodson

include a list labeled "How to Spot Unethical Self-Promoters." It provides a good guide to unethical salesperson behaviors. For example:

1. *Compulsive name-dropping:* Unethical salespeople know everybody you need them to know in order to impress you with their social network, contacts, and connections.
2. *Unshakable:* They are inappropriately calm and poised—even when you catch them in a lie.
3. *Dismissive:* When caught lying and confronted, they explain deception as a "harmless misunderstanding."
4. *Camouflage:* Their air of confidence and superiority conceals a history of legal problems and "misunderstandings."
5. *Fakes sincerity:* They tenaciously project phony sincerity because in their view, "everyone else is doing it."
6. *Mirror:* They repeatedly say whatever is necessary to make you think they acknowledge and closely identify with your values, interests, ambitions, and objectives.
7. *Aggressively advertise personal virtues:* They habitually package self-presentation with words like *integrity, openness, trust, principles,* and *honesty.*

Sales managers can use guidelines like these to identify individuals who may be using unethical approaches. By carefully reviewing performance and developing an incentive and compensation program that properly motivates employees, sales mangers can help to ensure that their company has an ethical sales force.[57]

Just as technology is affecting other areas of marketing, it is also a factor in personal selling. Although at first it was thought that technology would replace salespeople, it is now clear that sales support technology can enhance sales force productivity, as this ad for SanDisk makes apparent.

assessment, proposal generation, presenting, closing, and follow-up stages. This information can then tell a manager what sales skills may need to be reassessed or retrained. For example, if a sales manager notices that a sales rep seems to be letting too many prospects slip away after presenting proposals, it may mean he or she needs help with developing proposals, handling objections, or closing sales.

THE IMPACT OF TECHNOLOGY ON PERSONAL SELLING

Will the increasingly sophisticated technology now available at marketers' fingertips eliminate the need for salespeople? Experts agree that a relationship between the salesperson and customer will always be necessary. Technology, however, can certainly help to improve that relationship. Cell phones, laptops, pagers, e-mail, and electronic organizers allow salespeople to be more accessible to both clients and the company. Moreover, the Internet provides salespeople with vast resources of information on clients, competitors, and the industry. In fact, many companies are utilizing technology to stay more in touch with their own employees. For instance, IBM invited 320,000 employees to an electronic brainstorming session. A total of 52,600 employees logged on to the event to discuss issues of employee retention, work efficiency, quality, and teamwork. IBM has also added podcasting to its venues for internal communication, allowing global work teams to replace conference calls with podcasts that team members can download individually at convenient times.[58]

E-business, or buying, selling, marketing, collaborating with partners, and servicing customers electronically using the Internet, has had a significant impact on personal selling. Virtually all large companies and most medium and small companies are involved in e-commerce and consider it

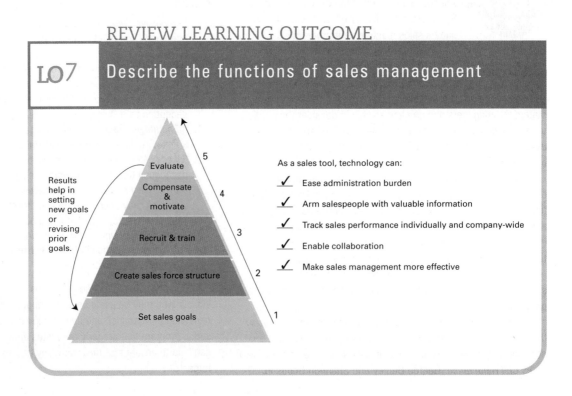

REVIEW LEARNING OUTCOME

LO 7 Describe the functions of sales management

Results help in setting new goals or revising prior goals.

5 Evaluate
4 Compensate & motivate
3 Recruit & train
2 Create sales force structure
1 Set sales goals

As a sales tool, technology can:

✓ Ease administration burden

✓ Arm salespeople with valuable information

✓ Track sales performance individually and company-wide

✓ Enable collaboration

✓ Make sales management more effective

to be necessary to compete in today's marketplace. For customers, the Web has become a powerful tool for finding accurate and up-to-date information on products, pricing, and order status. The Internet also cost-effectively processes orders and services requests. Although on the surface the Internet might look like a threat to the job security of salespeople, the Web is actually freeing sales reps from tedious administrative tasks, like shipping catalogs, placing routine orders, or tracking orders. This leaves them more time to focus on the needs of their clients.

Quick Check ✔

Now that you've read the chapter, do you get it? Take a moment for a quick check using this scale:

1 Not at all; 2 Not very well; 3 Ok; 4 Well; 5 Very Well

Can you . . .

___ explain what sales promotion is?

___ differentiate between forms of consumer and trade sales promotion?

___ explain the advantages of personal selling over other promotional tools?

___ outline the differences between traditional personal selling and relationship selling?

___ write a paragraph describing each step in the personal selling process?

___ explain the role sales managers play in the marketing organization?

___ describe the different ways sales reps can be compensated?

___ identify when personal selling is more appropriate than advertising and vice versa?

___ outline what criteria sales reps use to qualify a lead?

___ TOTAL

Score: 37–45, you're ready to move on to the applications; 28–36, skim the chapter one more time before moving on to the applications; 19–27, reread the sections giving you the most trouble and go to Thomson NOW for guided tutorials; 18 and under, you better reread the chapter to get a grasp of the fundamentals. If you've reread the chapter and still have a low score, visit your professor or TA during office hours.

Review and Applications

LO¹ Define and state the objectives of sales promotion. Sales promotion consists of those marketing communication activities, other than advertising, personal selling, and public relations, in which a short-term incentive motivates consumers or members of the distribution channel to purchase a good or service immediately, either by lowering the price or by adding value. The main objectives of sales promotion are to increase trial purchases, consumer inventories, and repeat purchases. Sales promotion is also used to encourage brand switching and to build brand loyalty. Sales promotion supports advertising activities.

1.1 What is the primary factor that determines sales promotion objectives? Name some different types of sales promotion techniques, and explain the type of customer they are intended to influence.

1.2 You have recently been assigned the task of developing promotional techniques to introduce your company's new product, a Cajun chicken sandwich. Advertising spending is limited, so the introduction will include only some low-budget sales promotion techniques. Write a sales promotion plan that will increase awareness of your new sandwich and allow your customer base to try it risk-free.

LO² Discuss the most common forms of consumer sales promotion. Consumer forms of sales promotion include coupons and rebates, premiums, loyalty marketing programs, contests and sweepstakes, sampling, and point-of-purchase displays. Coupons are certificates entitling consumers to an immediate price reduction when they purchase a product or service. Coupons are a particularly good way to encourage product trial and brand switching. Similar to coupons, rebates provide purchasers with a price reduction, although it is not immediate. To receive a rebate, consumers generally must mail in a rebate form with a proof of purchase. Premiums offer an extra item or incentive to the consumer for buying a product or service. Premiums reinforce the consumer's purchase decision, increase consumption, and persuade nonusers to switch brands. Rewarding loyal customers is the basis of loyalty marketing programs. Loyalty programs are extremely effective at building long-term, mutually beneficial relationships between a company and its key customers. Contests and sweepstakes are generally designed to create interest, often to encourage brand switching. Because consumers perceive risk in trying new products, sampling is an effective method for gaining new customers. Finally, point-of-purchase displays set up at the retailer's location build traffic, advertise the product, and induce impulse buying.

2.1 Discuss how different forms of sales promotion can erode or build brand loyalty. If a company's objective is to enhance customer loyalty to its products, what sales promotion techniques will be most appropriate?

2.2 What forms of consumer sales promotion might induce impulse purchases? What forms of sales promotion are more effective at persuading consumers to switch brands?

2.3 Consider the different consumer sales promotion tools. Give an example of how each type of tool has influenced you to purchase—or purchase more of—a product or service.

2.4 Not everyone thinks supermarket shopper cards are a bargain. Go to **http://www.nocards.org** and read several pages. Is the information on the site compelling? What do you think of shopper cards? You may want to use the Internet to research shopper cards in more detail before forming an opinion.

2.5 Contests and sweepstakes are very common in the entertainment industry. Radio stations have contests almost weekly (some daily); local television morning shows quiz viewers on trivia; even movies offer sweepstakes in conjunction with film previews and premiere nights. Think of a television or radio program unlikely to have contests or sweepstakes (things like *Cops, The View, Scooby Doo,* or your local classical music radio station, for example). Once you have chosen your program, design a contest or sweepstake to promote the show or the channel on which it airs. List the objectives and describe the rationale behind each part of your promotion.

2.6 How can uPromote.com (**http://www.upromote.com**) help you with your sales promotions efforts? What kind of marketing budget would you need to take advantage of its services? What kind of company would be best served by uPromote.com?

LO3 List the most common forms of trade sales promotion. Manufacturers use many of the same sales promotion tools used in consumer promotions, such as sales contests, premiums, and point-of-purchase displays. In addition, manufacturers and channel intermediaries use several unique promotional strategies: trade allowances, push money, training programs, free merchandise, store demonstrations, and meetings, conventions, and trade shows.

3.1 How does trade sales promotion differ from consumer sales promotion? How is it the same?

3.2 What are the main forms of trade sales promotion? Which type might be most enticing to a grocery store manager? To a buyer for a major electronics chain?

3.3 Form a team of three to five students. As marketing managers, you are in charge of selling Dixie cups. Design a consumer sales promotion plan and trade sales promotion plan for your product. Incorporate at least three different promotion tools into each plan. Share your results with the other teams in the class.

LO4 Describe personal selling. Personal selling is direct communication between a sales representative and one or more prospective buyers in an attempt to influence each other in a purchase situation. Broadly speaking, all businesspeople use personal selling to promote themselves and their ideas. Personal selling offers several advantages over other forms of promotion. Personal selling allows salespeople to thoroughly explain and demonstrate a product. Salespeople have the flexibility to tailor a sales proposal to the needs and preferences of individual customers. Personal selling is more efficient than other forms of promotion because salespeople target qualified prospects and avoid wasting efforts on unlikely buyers. Personal selling affords greater managerial control over promotion costs. Finally, personal selling is the most effective method of closing a sale and producing satisfied customers.

4.1 Discuss the role of personal selling in promoting products. What advantages does personal selling offer over other forms of promotion?

4.2 What are the major advantages of personal selling to the company selling a product? What are the advantages to the person or company buying the product?

LO5 Discuss the key differences between relationship selling and traditional selling. Relationship selling is the practice of building, maintaining, and enhancing interactions with customers in order to develop long-term satisfaction through mutually beneficial partnerships. Traditional selling, on the other hand, is transaction focused. That is, the salesperson is most concerned with making onetime sales and moving on to the next prospect. Salespeople practicing relationship selling spend more time understanding a prospect's needs and developing solutions to meet those needs.

5.1 What are the key differences between relationship selling and traditional methods of selling? What types of products or services do you think would be conducive to relationship selling?

5.2 Based on the key differences between traditional and relationship selling, which type of sales approach would you use as a salesperson? Do the different approaches require different personal strengths or attributes?

LO6 List the steps in the selling process. The selling process is composed of seven basic steps: (1) generating leads, (2) qualifying leads, (3) approaching the customer and probing needs, (4) developing and proposing solutions, (5) handling objections, (6) closing the sale, and (7) following up.

6.1 You are a new salesperson for a well-known medical software company, and one of your clients is a large group of physicians. You have just arranged an initial meeting with the office manager. Develop a list of questions you might ask at this meeting to uncover the group's specific needs.

6.2 What does sales follow-up entail? Why is it an essential step in the selling process, particularly from the perspective of relationship selling? How does it relate to cognitive dissonance?

6.3 How many ways can ZapData (**http://www.zapdata.com**) benefit salespeople? Which of its services would be most useful to marketing managers? Other businesspeople?

6.4 Consider each step in the selling process. Which steps could be conducted through technology (Internet, webinars, etc.)? Which are most important to handle "face-to-face"?

LO7 Describe the functions of sales management. Sales management is a critical area of marketing that performs several important functions. Sales managers set overall company sales goals and define the sales process most effective for achieving those goals. They determine sales force structure based on geographic, product, functional, or customer variables. Managers develop the sales force through recruiting and training. Sales management motivates the sales force through compensation planning, motivational tools, and effective sales leadership. Finally, sales managers evaluate the sales force through salesperson feedback and other methods of determining their performance.

7.1 What kinds of sales management opportunities are available at Amway and Quixtar? Use the companies' Web sites (**http://www.amway.com**; **http://www.quixtar .com**) to research one of these companies and determine its sales process, sales force structure, and how it recruits and trains its salespeople.

7.2 How does each of the sales management functions contribute to a successful, high-performing sales force?

Key Terms

Exercises

APPLICATION EXERCISE

Have you ever waited forever to get a fast-food hamburger? Have you even been left to languish in a dressing room by a salesperson who left for a coffee break? If so, you already know that sales and customer service are integral parts of marketing. While you are working on this chapter, keep a journal of your personal sales and/or customer service experiences with local merchants. Don't ignore the details. Even such things as how crowded a store or restaurant is when you visit may affect your perceptions of the service you received.[59]

Activities

1. Keep your journal for a week, recording all sales and service transactions, if possible, on the day they occur.

2. At the end of the week, examine your journal, and pick the most noteworthy entry. Provide the basic information about the transaction: company where it occurred, type of transaction (purchase, return, complaint, etc.), type of good or service involved, and so forth.

3. Once you have the outlined the situation, evaluate the experience. Use the information about selling in this chapter as support for your evaluation. For example, did the salesperson seem to treat the situation as an individual, discrete transaction, or did he or she seem interested in building a relationship?

4. Finally, make recommendations as to how the company can improve its sales and/or service. Suggestions should be logical and achievable (meaning you have to consider the cost of implementing your suggestion).

Entrepreneurship Case

RON POPEIL WHEELS, DEALS, HAS MASS APPEAL

At age 71, Ron Popeil is an avid inventor, tireless entrepreneur, clever marketer, and master salesman all in one. He just happens to be an American icon, too. The godfather of the infomercial, Popeil even has his famous Veg-O-Matic on display in the Smithsonian Institution as an American cultural artifact. His other famous products include the food dehydrator, the Ronco spray gun and the Popeil Pocket Fisherman.

As a teenager, Popeil helped his father sell his kitchen gadgets at local Woolworth's and later, in the 1950s, on the Chicago fair circuit. That is probably why his famous shtick, which included such memorable catch phrases as "But wait, there's more," "Price so low," and "Operators are standing by," always seemed like a blend between sincere eccentric inventor and excitable carnival barker. The combination suited him well and brought him enough financial success that he could afford to take his act to television. In the 1960s, he incorporated Ronco, and its name became synonymous with gadgets like the smokeless ashtray and Mr. Microphone.

Regardless of the product he is selling or the catchy pitch phrases he invents on the fly to sell them, Popeil is always sincere. "The easiest thing to do in the world is to sell a product I believe in," he has said. "If I spent two years creating a product, conceiving it, tinkering with it, I can get up and sell it. Who can sell it better than the guy who invented it?" Len Green, a professor in entrepreneurship at Babson University, says, "Ron is one of a kind. He is different from the rest because he not only invents, he sells. Most entrepreneurs come up with a concept and then give it to others to manufacture or sell. He's his own best salesman."

Though Popeil has suffered his fair share of flops, like spray-on hair and a brief bankruptcy in 1987, he has always managed to bounce back. Returning from bankruptcy, he relaunched the popular food dehydrator in 1990, and eight years later he designed and sold his most successful product ever, the Showtime rotisserie BBQ. Having sold over seven million units for four installments of $39.95 each, the rotisserie alone has grossed over $1 billion in sales. During the taping of the infomercial for that product, the live studio audience was treated to yet another of Popeil's catch phrases that has become part of the fabric of American speech. "Just set it and forget it!" is now used to sell all kinds of non-Popeil products from VCRs and digital video recorders to ovens and coffee makers.

Through the medium of television, Popeil was able to reach tens of millions of people. With an innate ability to invent or improve on everyday household products, his live product demonstrations captured the imaginations and dollars of generations of consumers. In 1976, he was even the subject of what was probably Dan Aykroyd's most famous bit on *Saturday Night Live.* Parodying Popeil, Aykroyd hawked "Rovco's Super Bass-O-Matic '76," which was capable of turning a bass or any other "small aquatic creature" into liquid without any "scaling, cutting or gutting."

Having recently sold Ronco to an investment group for over $55 million and accumulated a personal net worth of over $100 million, Popeil has had the last laugh. He will continue to serve as a product developer, pitchman, and consultant for the new company and already promises an even bigger hit than the Showtime rotisserie. Having identified a market of over 20 million Americans who fry turkeys every year, Popeil says he has a new fryer on the way that will make it possible to safely fry a 20-pound turkey in 70 minutes—indoors. Given that he has created over 150 products and invented personal selling via the mass marketing medium, there is little reason to doubt him.

As Barbara Gross, professor of marketing at California State University, Northridge, states, "His success speaks for itself; probably that has more to do with his personality. He's comfortable and sincere. He comes across like he really believes in it. When you hear him talk, you never feel like he's lying to you."[60]

1. What does Ron Popeil bring to personal selling that makes him so effective?

2. What trade sales promotion tools does he use? Why does he use sales promotion tools when he is selling direct to consumers?

3. Explain how Popeil's selling tactics allow him to achieve the desired objectives of sales promotions.

4. Do you think it is likely that America will ever see someone like Ron Popeil in the future? Why or why not?

COMPANY CLIPS

Vans—Off the Wall Promotions

Steve VanDorn, son of the founder, is the self-proclaimed "ambassador of fun" at Vans. Because Vans doesn't want to discount its products or lower prices, it has to find other ways to create value for consumers. So, to keep the brand energized, the company is constantly developing promotions that can only be described as fun, an important element for attracting trendsetting customers. The core of Vans's strategy revolves around unique and authentic contests and giveaways. The company relies on word-of-mouth advertising and credible personal selling. In this video segment, Vans marketers explain how they use Web sites, contests, giveaways, and athletic events to attract and keep customers.

Questions

1. How does Vans use giveaways and contests to market its products? Why do these strategies work so well for Vans?

2. How does Vans approach recruiting and training its sales force?

3. How have trade shows changed in recent years? What is Vans's main goal at trade shows today?

BIZ FLIX

Family Man (II)

Now that you have a better understanding of personal selling, you can see how selling techniques extend beyond the world of marketing. As an encore to your study, watch the second clip from *The Family Man,* starring Nicolas Cage as confirmed Wall Street bachelor Jack Campbell. After doing a good deed one Christmas, Jack wakes up to find himself married to his high school sweetheart and leading a very different life. Jack meets his former employer, Peter Lassiter, at his father-in-law's tire store where he now works. In this scene, Jack is trying to convince Lassiter to give him a job. Is Jack using a traditional or relationship selling approach? What makes you say so? Even though Jack is not selling a product, you can still see evidence of the personal selling process throughout the scene. Identify the steps of the selling process that you see in the clip. Does Jack execute them in order, or does he deviate from the process order?

High scores on this poll indicate a preference for using coupons, which may indicate that you are a comparison shopper. If your score was low, you probably don't see any economic benefits to using coupons, and you're likely not a comparison shopper. Instead, you probably prefer to buy what you want regardless of any coupon promotion.

Marketing Miscue

Burger King May Have Gone Too Far When It Sexualized Fast Food

The summer of 2005 was a rockin' time for Burger King, as the company launched its innovative new chicken strips. Introduced at various price points ($1.69 for six pieces, $2.69 for nine pieces, and $3.99 for a nine-piece Value Meal), BK Chicken Fries debuted with commercials featuring the company's Coq Roq (pronounced "cock rock") band and an interactive band Web site (http://www.coqroq.com).

BK Chicken Fries were designed to meet consumers' desire for great-tasting, high-quality chicken products that also offer value, portability, and fun. Burger King utilized all white meat chicken to meet the first two qualifications, with price set at a competitive level so that consumers would be getting good value for the money. The chicken fries were packaged in a container that had a built-in well for the dipping sauce and would fit into a car's cup holder. These were not the attributes that made the chicken fries famous, however. Rather, it was the way that Burger King portrayed the fun aspect of its new product.

Created by Miami-based Crispin Porter + Bogusky, the advertising campaign's television commercial featured a heavy metal band of masked chickens. The remarkable resemblance to the costumed heavy metal band Slipknot prompted a cease-and-desist letter from the band's attorney. According to the attorney's letter, Crispin Porter + Bogusky had approached the band's record label, Roadrunner, about Slipknot appearing in an unrelated Burger King ad—an offer that the band rejected because it did not want to be branded with burgers. The band claimed that Burger King's advertising, utilizing Slipknot's signature masks, was an effort to influence the Slipknot generation to purchase BK Chicken Fries.

The general public, however, was more upset about Coq Roq's interactive Web site. The site features videos showing the fictional chicken-headed band members, downloadable ring tones, and a photo gallery. While videos showing chickens with names such as "Fowl Mouth" and "The Talisman" trying to entice consumers to eat chicken are in questionable taste, the controversy centered on the photo gallery. When it debuted, the photo gallery hosted Polaroid-style photos of young women with handwritten captions such as "Groupies Love the Coq" and "Groupies Love Coq."

Within 24 hours, the captions had been erased, but Burger King refused to take any responsibility for the captions. Instead, the company blamed malfunctions in the Flash and XML programming for the captions appearing on the site and claimed it had no prelaunch knowledge of their presence. Burger King's spokesperson also said that the captions were removed as part of the tweaking involved in any new Web site and not because the company had received complaints.

The Coq Roq campaign was not Burger King's first advertising campaign to wander off the traditional family-oriented path. Ads for the restaurant's breakfast sandwiches depicted a masked BK mascot. In one spot, "Normal Joe" wakes up to find someone sharing his bed—the BK mascot who then offers him a breakfast sandwich. In another commercial, the BK mascot peeks in Normal Joe's window and offers him a breakfast sandwich. Promoting BK's Tendercrisp Bacon Cheddar Ranch sandwiches, Darius Rucker (Hootie of Hootie and the Blowfish) sings a revamped "have it your way" song with lyrics such as "there's a train of ladies coming with a nice caboose."

Historically, Burger King has presented itself as a family-oriented fast-food restaurant, with the slogan "Where Kids Are King." Parents were encouraged to bring their children to Burger King, and the restaurant would even give the kids a crown. This family image may have been tarnished by the chicken fries campaign and its Coq Roq band. At the same time, however, the company announced that BK Chicken Fries were one of its most successful product launches in recent years.[1]

Questions

1. Though controversial, the Coq Roq Web site created considerable buzz for Burger King. Given this, were the site's controversial aspects a mistake?

2. Some opponents of the campaign suggested that Burger King's sexualizing of its chicken fries could lead to even greater obesity in the youth demographic. What is Burger King's role in this social issue?

Critical Thinking Case

NASCAR Lifts Ban on Liquor Advertising

Stock car racing is one of the most popular professional sports in terms of television ratings. NASCAR is broadcast in over 150 countries and ranks behind only the National Football League in television sports viewing in the United States (and NASCAR has double the viewer base of the National Basketball Association). The three largest NASCAR-sanctioned racing series are the NEXTEL Cup Series, the Busch Series, and the Craftsman Truck Series, and there are over 1,500 additional races sanctioned in North America.

To reach the 75 million brand-loyal NASCAR fans (and possibly 75 million more "avid" fans) and an average of 125,000 spectators at each race, *Fortune* 500 companies sponsor NASCAR more than any other sport. It costs $15 million to $20 million a season to be a primary sponsor for one of the top racing teams. With a primary sponsorship, the sponsoring company gets to put company decals on the hood, the rear quarter panel, and the TV panel (above the rear bumper) of the race car. Sponsorship for a less successful racing team costs between $6 million and $10 million a season. With an associate sponsorship, which costs around $200,000 a season, the company gets to have one decal the size of an index card on the race car.

Though the cost of sponsorship might seem high, the television visibility and sales to the loyal fan base are the payoff. According to Performance Research, the average race-attending NASCAR fan is male, married, and 42 years old; he owns a home with around three cars per household and is employed full-time with an annual income between $35,000 and $50,000. These demographics are changing rapidly, though, as more and more women are being drawn to the sport. The television viewing fan base is even broader. Of particular interest to marketers and sponsors is the fact that 71 percent of NASCAR fans "almost always" or "frequently" select a product from a NASCAR sponsor simply because of the sponsorship (compared to 52 percent for tennis and 47 percent for PGA golf). In the same study, 57 percent indicated that they put more trust in products offered by NASCAR sponsors (compared to 16 percent for Olympic sponsors and 5 percent for World Cup Soccer sponsors).

From its beginning in 1949, NASCAR did not allow hard liquor sponsorship on its race cars. Though it accepted beer, cigarette, and chewing tobacco sponsors, there was concern that liquor sponsorships would be harmful to the sport's family-oriented image. In November 2004, however, citing the need for more corporate sponsors to keep race teams on the track, NASCAR lifted its ban on liquor advertising. Naturally, the decision was controversial.

Supporters of the long-standing ban on liquor advertising contended that liquor ads went against the association's family-oriented image. The American Medical Association suggested that the fastest-growing NASCAR audience was the 12- to 18-year-old segment and that advertising liquor on the race cars would send the wrong message to these teens. Additionally, the ban was consistent with network television's prohibition on liquor spots. On the flip side, however, was the fact that NASCAR allowed cars to be sponsored by beer companies (e.g., Dale Earnhardt Jr. was sponsored by Budweiser), even though one study had found that underage drinkers were nine times more likely to drink beer than other alcoholic beverages. Another study reported that less than 1 percent of teens consumed alcohol because of advertising. NASCAR felt that attitudes toward liquor companies had changed as the companies had developed reputations for responsible advertising and that this changing attitude was being reflected in television advertising. In 2004, more than 600 local and cable broadcast stations had begun running liquor spots to the tune of more than $100 million in advertising revenue.

NASCAR insisted that all advertising related to liquor sponsorship must have a strong responsible drinking component. For example, the race car and driver's attire sponsored by Jack Daniels said, "Pace Yourself, Drink Responsibly." Similarly, Crown Royal's sponsorship said, "Pacing is everything, especially when drinking." Additionally, merchandise bearing liquor sponsorship brands was not to be targeted to underage consumers. For example, miniature cars, which are popular among NASCAR fans, would only be marketed as collectors' items, and clothing items would not be available in child sizes. Purchasers would have to be of legal drinking age to buy merchandise carrying the liquor sponsor's brand name. On February 10, 2005, the first liquor logo crossed the finish line at a NASCAR race.[2]

Questions

1. Is NASCAR sending a mixed message to the public as it positions itself as a family-oriented sport sponsored by hard liquor companies?

2. Is liquor advertising a good fit with the NASCAR audience?

Pricing Decisions

CROSS-FUNCTIONAL CONNECTIONS

Pricing is the one element of the marketing mix that is "owned" by multiple groups within a company. Unfortunately, these owners of the pricing process do not always regard price as a strategic element of the business. Instead, they view it as a tactical component. Under this tactical viewpoint, price is considered to be on the cost side of the business rather than regarded as a strategic revenue generator. As both a strategic and a tactical capability, the pricing process engages numerous parties and organizational capital and invokes considerable cross-functional conflict.

There is usually little agreement across functions as to the best price for a particular product. Marketing is interested in pricing to provide value to the customer, while meeting competitors' prices. Because costs determine the floor on prices, the accounting group has traditionally identified with a cost-plus pricing approach. Naturally, finance has a keen interest in the pricing process in relation to its targets for return on investment. The relationship between price and demand has downstream effects on the manufacturing process, bringing production capabilities into the pricing decisions, particularly in relation to the company's ability to produce the number of units needed to break even. Research and development pays close attention to the introductory price of the product because this is considered to be the point at which development costs are recouped. With so many interested parties, it is hard to say if any one particular functional group is actually in charge of the final pricing decision!

The pricing decision must be viewed as an interactive process, with a strong need for cross-functional interaction. For example, if marketing identifies an initial price as too high to capture customer interest, R&D and manufacturing must be consulted to see if product features, product materials, or assembly processes can be modified to lower costs. Finance and accounting must be involved in reevaluating appropriate margins. With all of these parties interested in the outcome, it is not surprising that the pricing process is the source of immeasurable organizational friction.

A major breakthrough in the cross-functional ownership of the pricing process has been activity-based costing

It is safe to say that marketing has the broadest perspective on pricing because it is the function that looks at both internal cost issues and external demand pressures.

(ABC). Just as marketing and manufacturing have long focused on product customization, ABC provides the capability to customize price. The method requires input from marketing, accounting, and manufacturing. Essentially, ABC uses cost drivers to assign costs. The process requires a clear market segmentation approach based on customer needs. Activity-based costing allows the company to determine what will have to be done to satisfy customers' needs and to assign a cost to each of these activities. In this way, companies can distinguish between the truly profitable customers and those who may purchase in volume but require so much work (activities) that they are actually unprofitable.

Marketers have long acknowledged the importance of accounting information in the pricing process. The marketing group recognizes that accurate cost data are needed to make good pricing decisions, but criticizes traditional accounting methods for being too production oriented. Nonetheless, it is this cost information that points to the lowest possible price that can be charged for a product without losing money on a per item basis (considering traditional accounting methods). The activity-based system goes beyond the

cost of production and looks at how much it costs to maintain individual customer accounts. Ultimately, ABC allows marketers to price products or services to individual consumers based on the total cost to provide the product or service. From a marketer's perspective, for example, travel time to visit with a customer would be included as a cost and could be reflected in the price charged to that particular customer.

Technological changes have had a major impact on the pricing process. Think about the online search for airline tickets. The price of a trip between two cities can change by the hour. As the airline constantly updates its yield management report, the ticket price fluctuates to accommodate supply and demand. Such yield management systems would historically have fallen under the purview of the production function. With the advent of sophisticated technology, the yield management system now has direct, and immediate, input into the pricing process. With such sophisticated processes, one has to wonder what role marketing plays in the pricing of airline tickets.

Too many variables are at play in the pricing decision to say that the decision is the responsibility of any particular function. Rather, all functions have a need for functional-level input. Nevertheless, it is safe to say that marketing has the broadest perspective on pricing because it is the function that looks at both internal cost issues and external demand pressures.

Questions

1. Should marketing play the lead role in coordinating the pricing decision? Why or why not?

2. How is activity-based costing more market oriented than traditional accounting methods?

Pricing Concepts

© PORSCHE AG/PR NEWSWIRE PHOTO SERVICE (NEWSCOM)
© KK GAS/ISTOCKPHOTO INTERNATIONAL INC.

CHAPTER

17

Learning Outcomes

LO¹ Discuss the importance of pricing decisions to the economy and to the individual firm

LO² List and explain a variety of pricing objectives

LO³ Explain the role of demand in price determination

LO⁴ Understand the concept of yield management systems

LO⁵ Describe cost-oriented pricing strategies

LO⁶ Demonstrate how the product life cycle, competition, distribution and promotion strategies, customer demands, the Internet, and perceptions of quality can affect price

Porsche *goes off-road—and finds profits*

For over a decade, Americans had a love affair with their SUVs. Built on the chassis of successful pickup trucks, SUVs quickly became a rugged alternative to the equally popular mini-van. SUVs became a dominant force on the American road: in the early and mid-2000s, roughly 90 percent of the profits of General Motors and DaimlerChrysler

The sole reason this vehicle exists is that you might buy it—for $100,000.

were generated by sales of their SUVs, although these account for only one of every four vehicles sold.

During this same time period, the world's smallest truly independent car company took a look in its garage, realized that there were no SUVs in there, and decided to build one. Porsche Chief Executive Wendelin Wiedeking took a risky bet when he decided to steer the German sports-car icon into the market for big, bruising SUVs. Porsche aficionados cringed. Even the Porsche family shareholders balked, fearing the company's sports-car tradition and exclusive brand name didn't befit bulky off-roaders. But a determined Wiedeking prevailed, arguing that people would buy it. In fact, the sole reason this vehicle exists is that

you might buy it—for $100,000. Indeed, by early 2005, Porsche's SUV—the Cayenne—had sold over 100,000 units since its introduction in December 2002.

The Cayenne is a fearsome machine—one that can out-sports-car most sports cars and out-macho any other SUV. Step on the accelerator and the Cayenne's 5,600-pound bulk goes from idle to 60 in an extraordinary 5.6 seconds, and then keeps going until you hit 165 mph. It's by far the fastest SUV on the market.

Basically, Porsche sought to blunt criticism from the purists by smothering them with excess. Certainly, the Cayenne is faster than you need. It's also far heavier than you need. It's more stable in every turn than you need, and it's more comfortable than you need. And, of course, it can cross a roaring 22-inch-deep stream, too. All that excess comes at a hefty price, though. $100,000.[1]

What determines price in the marketplace? How are costs, revenues, and profits related? Can price influence perceived quality of a product? What causes buyers to be sensitive or insensitive to price changes?

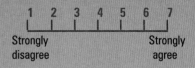

Price means one thing to the consumer and something else to the seller. To the consumer, it is the cost of something. To the seller, price is revenue, the primary source of profits. In the broadest sense, price allocates resources in a free-market economy. With so many ways of looking at price, it's no wonder that marketing managers find the task of setting prices a challenge.

WHAT IS PRICE?

Price is that which is given up in an exchange to acquire a good or service. Price is typically the money exchanged for the good or service. It may also be time lost while waiting to acquire the good or service. Standing in long lines at the airport first to check in and then to get through the security checkpoint procedures is a cost. In fact, these delays are one reason more people are selecting alternative modes of transportation for relatively short trips. Price might also include "lost dignity" for individuals who lose their jobs and must rely on charity to obtain food and clothing.

Consumers are interested in obtaining a "reasonable price." "Reasonable price" really means "perceived reasonable value" at the time of the transaction. One of the authors of this textbook bought a fancy European-designed toaster for about $45. The toaster's wide mouth made it possible to toast a bagel, warm a muffin, and, with a special $15 attachment, make a grilled sandwich. The author felt that a toaster with all these features surely must be worth the total price of $60. But after three months of using the device, toast burned around the edges and raw in the middle lost its appeal. The disappointed buyer put the toaster in the attic. Why didn't he return it to the retailer? Because the boutique had gone out of business, and no other local retailer carried the brand. Also, there was no U.S. service center. Remember, the price paid is based on the satisfaction consumers expect to receive from a product and not necessarily the satisfaction they actually receive.

Price can relate to anything with perceived value, not just money. When goods and services are exchanged, the trade is called barter. For example, if you exchange this book for a chemistry book at the end of the term, you have engaged in barter. The price you paid for the chemistry book was this textbook.

THE IMPORTANCE OF PRICE TO MARKETING MANAGERS

Prices are the key to revenues, which in turn are the key to profits for an organization. **Revenue** is the price charged to customers multiplied by the number of units sold. Revenue is what pays for every activity of the company: production, finance, sales, distribution, and so on. What's left over (if anything) is **profit.** Managers usually strive to charge a price that will earn a fair profit.

To earn a profit, managers must choose a price that is not too high or too low, a price that equals the perceived value to target consumers. If, in consumers' minds, a price is set too high, the perceived value will be less than the cost, and sales opportunities will be lost. Many mainstream purchasers of cars, sporting goods, CDs, tools, wedding gowns, and computers are buying "used or preowned" items to get a better deal. Pricing a new product too high may give some shoppers an incentive to go to a "preowned" or consignment retailer. Lost sales mean lost revenue. Conversely, if a price is too low, the consumer may perceive it as a great value, but the firm loses revenue it could have earned.

Trying to set the right price is one of the most stressful and pressure-filled tasks of the marketing manager, as trends in the consumer market attest:

- Confronting a flood of new products, potential buyers carefully evaluate the price of each one against the value of existing products.

- The increased availability of bargain-priced private and generic brands has put downward pressure on overall prices.

price
That which is given up in an exchange to acquire a good or service.

revenue
The price charged to customers multiplied by the number of units sold.

profit
Revenue minus expenses.

- Many firms are trying to maintain or regain their market share by cutting prices. For example, Dell has gained market share in the personal computer industry by aggressively cutting prices.

- The Internet has made comparison shopping easier.

REVIEW LEARNING OUTCOME

LO¹ Discuss the importance of pricing decisions to the economy and to the individual firm

Price × Sales Unit = Revenue

Revenue − Costs = Profit

Profit drives growth, salary increases, and corporate investment.

In the organizational market, where customers include both governments and businesses, buyers are also becoming more price sensitive and better informed. Computerized information systems enable the organizational buyer to compare price and performance with great ease and accuracy. Improved communication and the increased use of direct marketing and computer-aided selling have also opened up many markets to new competitors. Finally, competition in general is increasing, so some installations, accessories, and component parts are being marketed like indistinguishable commodities.

LO²
Pricing Objectives

To survive in today's highly competitive marketplace, companies need pricing objectives that are specific, attainable, and measurable. Realistic pricing goals then require periodic monitoring to determine the effectiveness of the company's strategy. For convenience, pricing objectives can be divided into three categories: profit oriented, sales oriented, and status quo.

PROFIT-ORIENTED PRICING OBJECTIVES

Profit-oriented objectives include profit maximization, satisfactory profits, and target return on investment. A brief discussion of each of these objectives follows.

Profit Maximization

Profit maximization means setting prices so that total revenue is as large as possible relative to total costs. (A more theoretically precise definition and explanation of profit maximization appear later in the chapter.) Profit maximization does not always signify unreasonably high prices, however. Both price and profits depend on the type of competitive environment a firm faces, such as whether it is in a monopoly position (being the only seller) or in a much more competitive situation. Also, remember that a firm cannot charge a price higher than the product's perceived value. Many firms do not have the accounting data they need for maximizing profits. It is easy to say that a company should keep producing and selling goods or services as long as revenues exceed costs. Yet it is often hard to set up an accounting system that can accurately determine the point of profit maximization.

Target
Wal-Mart
JCPenney
Shop for some kind of electronic device (DVD player, digital camera, MP3 player, etc.) on the Target, Wal-Mart, and JCPenney Web sites. How do the prices for the same product compare at the three retailers? Do they all even carry the same product? Compare the price on the Web with the price offered at the physical store and explain any discrepancies.

http://www.target.com
http://www.walmart.com
http://www.jcpenney.com

Online

Sometimes managers say that their company is trying to maximize profits—in other words, trying to make as much money as possible. Although this goal may sound impressive to stockholders, it is not good enough for planning. The statement "We want to make all the money we can" is vague and lacks focus. It gives management license to do just about anything it wants to do.

In attempting to maximize profits, managers can try to expand revenue by increasing customer satisfaction, or they can attempt to reduce costs by operating more efficiently. A third possibility is to attempt to do both. Recent research has shown that striving to enhance customer satisfaction leads to greater profitability (and customer satisfaction) than following a cost reduction strategy or attempting to do both.[2] This means that companies should consider allocating more resources to customer service initiatives, loyalty programs, and customer relationship management programs and allocating fewer resources to programs that are designed to improve efficiency and reduce costs. Both types of programs, of course, are critical to the success of the firm.

Satisfactory Profits

Satisfactory profits are a reasonable level of profits. Rather than maximizing profits, many organizations strive for profits that are satisfactory to the stockholders and management—in other words, a level of profits consistent with the level of risk an organization faces. In a risky industry, a satisfactory profit may be 35 percent. In a low-risk industry, it might be 7 percent. To maximize profits, a small-business owner might have to keep his or her store open seven days a week. However, the owner might not want to work that hard and might be satisfied with less profit.

Target Return on Investment

The most common profit objective is a target **return on investment (ROI)**, sometimes called the firm's return on total assets. ROI measures management's overall effectiveness in generating profits with the available assets. The higher the firm's ROI, the better off the firm is. Many companies—including DuPont, General Motors, Navistar, ExxonMobil, and Union Carbide—use a target ROI as their main pricing goal. In summary, ROI is a percentage that puts a firm's profits into perspective by showing profits relative to investment.

Return on investment is calculated as follows:

$$\text{Return on investment} = \frac{\text{Net profits after taxes}}{\text{Total assets}}$$

Assume that in 2007 Johnson Controls had assets of $4.5 million, net profits of $550,000, and a target ROI of 10 percent. This was the actual ROI:

$$\text{ROI} = \frac{\$550,000}{\$4,500,000}$$

$$= 12.2 \text{ percent}$$

As you can see, the ROI for Johnson Controls exceeded its target, which indicates that the company prospered in 2007.

Comparing the 12.2 percent ROI with the industry average provides a more meaningful picture, however. Any ROI needs to be evaluated in terms of the competitive environment, risks in the industry, and economic conditions. Generally speaking, firms seek ROIs in the 10 to 30 percent range. For example, General Electric seeks a 25 percent ROI, whereas Alcoa, Rubbermaid, and most major pharmaceutical companies strive for a 20 percent ROI. In some industries such as the grocery industry, however, a return of under 5 percent is common and acceptable.

A company with a target ROI can predetermine its desired level of profitability. The marketing manager can use the standard, such as 10 percent ROI, to determine whether a particular price and marketing mix are feasible. In addition, however, the manager must weigh the risk of a given strategy even if the return is in the acceptable range.

return on investment (ROI)
Net profit after taxes divided by total assets.

Exhibit 17.1

Two Ways to Measure Market Share (Units and Revenue)

Company	Units Sold	Unit Price	Total Revenue	Unit Market Share	Revenue Market Share
A	1,000	$1.00	$1,000,000	50%	25%
B	200	4.00	800,000	10	20
C	500	2.00	1,000,000	25	25
D	300	4.00	1,200,000	15	30
Total	2,000		$4,000,000		

SALES-ORIENTED PRICING OBJECTIVES

Sales-oriented pricing objectives are based either on market share or on dollar or unit sales. The effective marketing manager should be familiar with these pricing objectives.

Market Share

Market share is a company's product sales as a percentage of total sales for that industry. Sales can be reported in dollars or in units of product. It is very important to know whether market share is expressed in revenue or units because the results may be different. Consider four companies competing in an industry with 2,000 total unit sales and total industry revenue of $4 million (see Exhibit 17.1). Company A has the largest unit market share at 50 percent, but it has only 25 percent of the revenue market share. In contrast, company D has only a 15 percent unit share but the largest revenue share: 30 percent. Usually, market share is expressed in terms of revenue and not units.

Many companies believe that maintaining or increasing market share is an indicator of the effectiveness of their marketing mix. Larger market shares have indeed often meant higher profits, thanks to greater economies of scale, market power, and ability to compensate top-quality management. Conventional wisdom also says that market share and return on investment are strongly related. For the most part they are; however, many companies with low market share survive and even prosper. To succeed with a low market share, companies need to compete in industries with slow growth and few product changes—for instance, industrial component parts and supplies. Otherwise, they must vie in an industry that makes frequently bought items, such as consumer convenience goods.

market share
A company's product sales as a percentage of total sales for that industry.

The conventional wisdom about market share and profitability isn't always reliable, however. Because of extreme competition in some industries, many market share leaders either do not reach their target ROI or actually lose money. Freightliner, DaimlerChrysler's U.S. heavy-truck unit, aggressively fought for market share gains during the past decade. Though Freightliner grew to become the market leader with a 36 percent market share, its profits suffered. It lost hundreds of millions of dollars and slashed 8,000 jobs in an effort to cut costs.[3] The personal computer and food industries have also had this problem. Procter & Gamble switched from market share to ROI objectives after realizing that profits don't automatically follow from a large market share. PepsiCo says its new Pepsi challenge is to be number one in share of industry profit, not in share of sales volume.

Still, the struggle for market share can be all-consuming for some companies. For over a decade, Maxwell House and Folgers, the biggest U.S. coffee brands, have been locked in a struggle to dominate the market. Their weapons have been advertising, perpetual rounds of price cutting, and millions upon millions of cents-off coupons. At this point, Maxwell House, a unit of Kraft Foods, has regained a few drops of market share that it had lost to Folgers, a unit of Procter & Gamble, earlier in the war.

For over a decade, Folgers and Maxwell House have been locked in a struggle to dominate the coffee market. Numerous product extensions and modifications have been tried to persuade coffee drinkers to switch brands (or stay with their current brand). Now, however, both companies face a new and increasingly formidable competitor for market share: Starbucks.

© MICHAEL NEWMAN/PHOTOEDIT

PRICING CONCEPTS   CHAPTER 17

Maxwell House's strategy has been to advertise heavily (spending over $100 million a year) and to introduce new products that lure consumers with taste rather than price. Examples include ready-made coffee in refrigerator cartons and coffee syrup, both designed for consumers to pour and microwave as needed. Nevertheless, Folgers is still the nation's best-selling coffee, although the Kraft Foods brands, which include Yuban and Sanka, account for a 35 percent market share. P&G has 32 percent of the U.S. coffee market.

Research organizations like A. C. Nielsen and Information Resources, Inc., provide excellent market share reports for many different industries. These reports enable companies to track their performance in various product categories over time.

Sales Maximization

Rather than strive for market share, sometimes companies try to maximize sales. A firm with the objective of maximizing sales ignores profits, competition, and the marketing environment as long as sales are rising.

If a company is strapped for funds or faces an uncertain future, it may try to generate a maximum amount of cash in the short run. Management's task when using this objective is to calculate which price-quantity relationship generates the greatest cash revenue. Sales maximization can also be effectively used on a temporary basis to sell off excess inventory. It is not uncommon to find Christmas cards, ornaments, and other seasonal items discounted at 50 to 70 percent off retail prices after the holiday season. In addition, management can use sales maximization for year-end sales to clear out old models before introducing the new ones.

Maximization of cash should never be a long-run objective because cash maximization may mean little or no profitability. Without profits, a company cannot survive.

STATUS QUO PRICING OBJECTIVES

Status quo pricing seeks to maintain existing prices or to meet the competition's prices. This third category of pricing objectives has the major advantage of requiring little planning. It is essentially a passive policy.

Often firms competing in an industry with an established price leader simply meet the competition's prices. These industries typically have fewer price wars than those with direct price competition. In other cases, managers regularly shop competitors' stores to ensure that their prices are comparable. Target's middle managers visit competing Wal-Mart stores weekly to compare prices and then make adjustments.

status quo pricing
A pricing objective that maintains existing prices or meets the competition's prices.

demand
The quantity of a product that will be sold in the market at various prices for a specified period.

supply
The quantity of a product that will be offered to the market by a supplier at various prices for a specified period.

REVIEW LEARNING OUTCOME

LO2 List and explain a variety of pricing objectives

Profit-Oriented

- Profit maximization
  - Drive down costs
  - Increase revenue
- Satisfactory Profits
- Target ROI
  - Net profit after tax ÷ Total assets

Sales-Oriented

- Market Share
  - Unit
  - Revenue
- Sales Maximization
  - Generate cash

Status Quo

- Maintain Existing Price
  - Meet the competition
  - Passive policy

LO3
The Demand Determinant of Price

After marketing managers establish pricing goals, they must set specific prices to reach those goals. The price they set for each product depends mostly on two factors: the demand for the good or service and the cost to the seller for that good or service. When pricing goals are mainly sales oriented, demand considerations usually dominate. Other factors, such as distribution and promotion

Exhibit 17.2

Demand Curve and Demand Schedule for Gourmet Cookies

(a) Demand curve

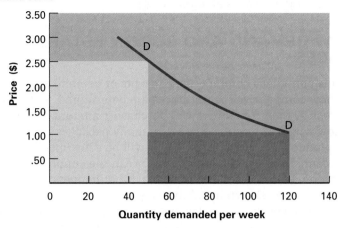

Quantity demanded per week

(b) Demand schedule

Price per package of gourmet cookies ($)	Packages of gourmet cookies demanded per week
3.00	35
2.50	50
2.00	65
1.50	85
1.00	120

Exhibit 17.3

Supply Curve and Supply Schedule for Gourmet Cookies

(a) Supply curve

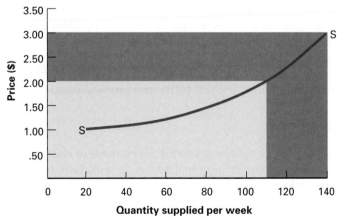

Quantity supplied per week

(b) Supply schedule

Price per package of gourmet cookies ($)	Packages of gourmet cookies supplied per week
3.00	140
2.50	130
2.00	110
1.50	85
1.00	25

strategies, perceived quality, demands of large customers, the Internet, and stage of the product life cycle, can also influence price.

THE NATURE OF DEMAND

Demand is the quantity of a product that will be sold in the market at various prices for a specified period. The quantity of a product that people will buy depends on its price. The higher the price, the fewer goods or services consumers will demand. Conversely, the lower the price, the more goods or services they will demand.

This trend is illustrated in Exhibit 17.2(a), which graphs the demand per week for gourmet cookies at a local retailer at various prices. This graph is called a demand curve. The vertical axis of the graph shows different prices of gourmet cookies, measured in dollars per package. The horizontal axis measures the quantity of gourmet cookies that will be demanded per week at each price. For example, at a price of $2.50, 50 packages will be sold per week; at $1.00, consumers will demand 120 packages—as the demand schedule in Exhibit 17.2(b) shows.

The demand curve in Exhibit 17.2 slopes downward and to the right, which indicates that more gourmet cookies are demanded as the price is lowered. In other words, if cookie manufacturers put a greater quantity on the market, then their hope of selling all of it will be realized only by selling it at a lower price.

One reason more is sold at lower prices than at higher prices is that lower prices bring in new buyers. This fact might not be so obvious with gourmet cookies, but consider the example of steak. As the price of steak drops lower and lower, some people who have not been eating steak will probably start buying it rather than hamburger. With each reduction in price, existing customers may also buy extra amounts. Similarly, if the price of gourmet cookies falls low enough, some people will buy more than they have bought in the past.

Supply is the quantity of a product that will be offered to the market by a supplier or suppliers at various prices for a specified period. Exhibit 17.3(a) illustrates the resulting supply curve for gourmet cookies. Unlike the falling demand curve, the supply curve for gourmet cookies slopes upward and to the right. At higher prices, gourmet cookie manufacturers will obtain more resources (flour, chocolate, eggs) and produce more gourmet cookies. If the price consumers are willing to pay for gourmet cookies increases, producers can afford to buy more ingredients.

Output tends to increase at higher prices because manufacturers can sell more packages of gourmet cookies and earn greater profits. The supply schedule in Exhibit 17.3(b) shows that at $2 suppliers are willing to place 110 packages of gourmet cookies on the market, but that they will offer 140 packages at a price of $3.

HOW DEMAND AND SUPPLY ESTABLISH PRICES

At this point, let's combine the concepts of demand and supply to see how competitive market prices are determined. So far, the premise is that if the price is X, then consumers will purchase Y amount of gourmet cookies. How high or low will prices actually go? How many packages of gourmet cookies will be produced? How many packages will be consumed? The demand curve cannot predict consumption, nor can the supply curve alone forecast production. Instead, we need to look at what happens when supply and demand interact—as shown in Exhibit 17.4.

At a price of $3, the public would demand only 35 packages of gourmet cookies. However, suppliers stand ready to place 140 packages on the market at this price (data from the demand and supply schedules). If they do, they would create a surplus of 105 packages of gourmet cookies. How does a merchant eliminate a surplus? It lowers the price.

At a price of $1, 120 packages would be demanded, but only 25 would be placed on the market. A shortage of 95 units would be created. If a product is in short supply and consumers want it, how do they entice the dealer to part with one unit? They offer more money—that is, pay a higher price.

Now let's examine a price of $1.50. At this price, 85 packages are demanded and 85 are supplied. When demand and supply are equal, a state called **price equilibrium** is achieved. A temporary price below equilibrium—say, $1.00—results in a shortage because at that price the demand for gourmet cookies is greater than the available supply. Shortages put upward pressure on price. As long as demand and supply remain the same, however, temporary price increases or decreases tend to return to equilibrium. At equilibrium, there is no inclination for prices to rise or fall.

An equilibrium price may not be reached all at once. Prices may fluctuate during a trial-and-error period as the market for a good or service moves toward equilibrium. Sooner or later, however, demand and supply will settle into proper balance.

Exhibit 17.4

Equilibrium Price for Gourmet Cookies

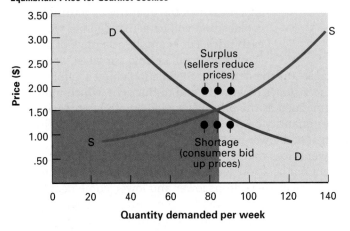

ELASTICITY OF DEMAND

price equilibrium
The price at which demand and supply are equal.

elasticity of demand
Consumers' responsiveness or sensitivity to changes in price.

elastic demand
A situation in which consumer demand is sensitive to changes in price.

inelastic demand
A situation in which an increase or a decrease in price will not significantly affect demand for the product.

To appreciate demand analysis, you should understand the concept of elasticity. **Elasticity of demand** refers to consumers' responsiveness or sensitivity to changes in price. **Elastic demand** occurs when consumers buy more or less of a product when the price changes. Conversely, **inelastic demand** means that an increase or a decrease in price will not significantly affect demand for the product.

Elasticity over the range of a demand curve can be measured by using this formula:

$$\text{Elasticity (E)} = \frac{\text{Percentage change in quantity demanded of good A}}{\text{Percentage change in price of good A}}$$

If *E* is greater than 1, demand is elastic.
If *E* is less than 1, demand is inelastic.
If *E* is equal to 1, demand is unitary.

Unitary elasticity means that an increase in sales exactly offsets a decrease in prices, so total revenue remains the same.

Elasticity can be measured by observing these changes in total revenue:

If price goes down and revenue goes up, demand is elastic.
If price goes down and revenue goes down, demand is inelastic.
If price goes up and revenue goes up, demand is inelastic.
If price goes up and revenue goes down, demand is elastic.
If price goes up or down and revenue stays the same, elasticity is unitary.

Columbia House
How can Columbia House offer so many DVDs for 49 cents? Go to the Web site to see what kind of deals Columbia House is offering right now. Compare the introductory offers to the pricing for subsequent purchases. What conclusions can you draw about Columbia House and about the elasticity of demand for DVDs based on the posted pricing for the initial sign-up and for subsequent purchases?

http://www.columbiahouse.com

Online

Exhibit 17.5(a) shows a very elastic demand curve. Decreasing the price of a Sony DVD player from $300 to $200 increases sales from 18,000 units to 59,000 units. Revenue increases from $5.4 million ($300 × 18,000) to $11.8 million ($200 × 59,000). The price decrease results in a large increase in sales and revenue.

Exhibit 17.5(b) shows a completely inelastic demand curve. The state of Nevada dropped its used-car vehicle inspection fee from $20 to $10. The state continued to inspect about 400,000 used cars annually. Decreasing the price (inspection fee) 50 percent did not cause people to buy more used cars. Demand is completely inelastic for inspection fees, which are required by law. Thus, it also follows that Nevada could double the original fee to $40 and double the state's inspection revenues. People won't stop buying used cars if the inspection fee increases—within a reasonable range.

Exhibit 17.6 presents the demand curve and demand schedule for three-ounce bottles of Spring Break suntan lotion. Let's follow the demand curve from the highest price to the lowest and examine what happens to elasticity as the price decreases.

Exhibit 17.5

Elasticity of Demand for Sony DVD Players and Auto Inspection Stickers

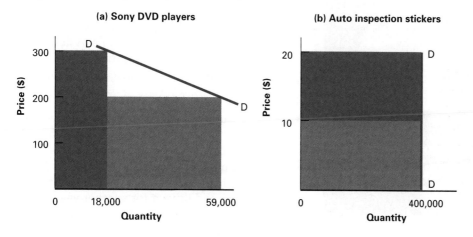

Inelastic Demand

The initial decrease in the price of Spring Break suntan lotion, from $5.00 to $2.25, results in a decrease in total revenue of $969 ($5,075 − $4,106). When price and total revenue fall, demand is inelastic. The decrease in price is much greater than the increase in suntan lotion sales (810 bottles). Demand is therefore not very flexible in the price range $5.00 to $2.25.

When demand is inelastic, sellers can raise prices and increase total revenue. Often items that are relatively inexpensive but convenient tend to have inelastic demand.

Elastic Demand

In the example of Spring Break suntan lotion, shown in Exhibit 17.6, when the price is dropped from $2.25 to $1.00, total revenue increases by $679 ($4,785 − $4,106). An increase in total revenue when price falls indicates that demand is elastic. Let's measure Spring Break's elasticity of demand when the price drops from $2.25 to $1.00 by applying the formula presented earlier:

unitary elasticity
A situation in which total revenue remains the same when prices change.

$$E = \frac{\text{Change in quantity/(Sum of quantities/2)}}{\text{Change in price/(sum of prices/2)}}$$

Exhibit 17.6

Demand for Three-Ounce Bottles of Spring Break Suntan Lotion

(a) Demand curve

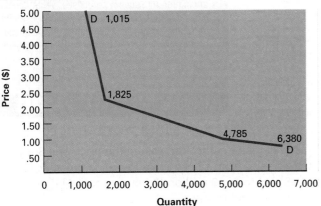

(b) Demand schedule

Price ($)	Quantity demanded	Total revenue (price × quantity)	Elasticity
5.00	1,015	$5,075 ●	⎤ Inelastic
2.25	1,825	4,106 ●	⎦
1.00	4,785	4,785 ●	⎤ Elastic
0.75	6,380	4,785 ●	⎦ Unitary

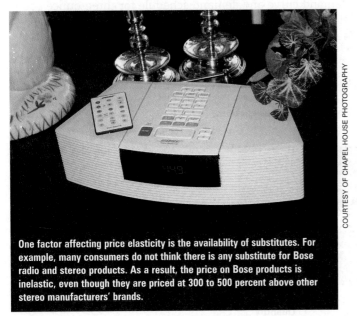

One factor affecting price elasticity is the availability of substitutes. For example, many consumers do not think there is any substitute for Bose radio and stereo products. As a result, the price on Bose products is inelastic, even though they are priced at 300 to 500 percent above other stereo manufacturers' brands.

$$= \frac{(4{,}785 - 1{,}825)/[(1{,}825 + 4{,}785)/2]}{(2.25 - 1.00)/[(2.25 + 1.00)/2]}$$

$$= \frac{2{,}960/3{,}305}{1.25/1.63}$$

$$= \frac{.896}{.767}$$

$$= 1.17$$

Because E is greater than 1, demand is elastic.

Factors That Affect Elasticity

Several factors affect elasticity of demand, including the following:

- Availability of substitutes: When many substitute products are available, the consumer can easily switch from one product to another, making demand elastic. The same is true in reverse: a person with complete renal failure will pay whatever is charged for a kidney transplant because there is no substitute. Interestingly, Bose stereo equipment is priced 300 to 500 percent higher than other stereo brands. Yet consumers are willing to pay the price because they perceive the equipment as being so superior to other brands that there is no acceptable substitute.

- Price relative to purchasing power: If a price is so low that it is an inconsequential part of an individual's budget, demand will be inelastic. For example, if the price of salt doubles, consumers will not stop putting salt and pepper on their eggs because salt is cheap anyway.

- Product durability: Consumers often have the option of repairing durable products rather than replacing them, thus prolonging their useful life. If a person plans to buy a new car and prices suddenly begin to rise, he or she may elect to fix the old car and drive it for another year. In other words, people are sensitive to the price increase, and demand is elastic.

- A product's other uses: The greater the number of different uses for a product, the more elastic demand tends to be. If a product has only one use, as may be true of a new medicine, the quantity purchased probably will not vary as price varies. A person will consume only the prescribed quantity, regardless of price. On the other hand, a product like steel has many possible applications. As its price falls, steel becomes more economically feasible in a wider variety of applications, thereby making demand relatively elastic.

- Rate of inflation: Recent research has found that when a country's inflation rate (the rate at which the price level is rising) is high, demand becomes more elastic. In other words, rising price levels make consumers more price sensitive. The research also found that during inflationary periods consumers base their timing (when to buy) and quantity decisions on price promotions. This suggests that a brand gains additional sales or market share if the product is effectively promoted or if the marketing manager keeps the brand's price increases low relative to the inflation rate.[4]

Examples of both elastic and inelastic demand abound in everyday life. In the summer of 2005, fans balked at high prices for concerts. Promoters lost money, and some shows including some by artists Christina Aguilera and Marc Anthony were canceled.

LO3 Explain the role of demand in price determination

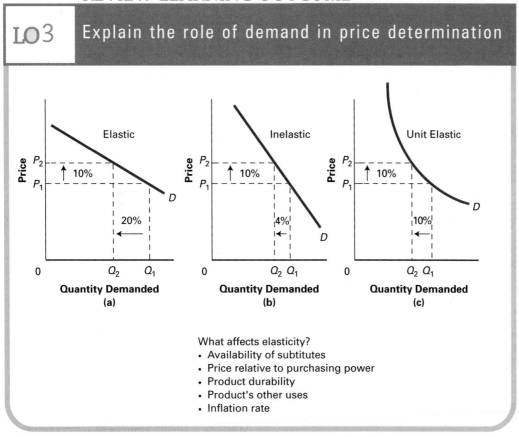

What affects elasticity?
- Availability of subtitutes
- Price relative to purchasing power
- Product durability
- Product's other uses
- Inflation rate

This is price elasticity in action. On the other hand, demand for some tickets was highly inelastic. The Rolling Stones are still selling out concerts with tickets priced at up to $400.[5]

When gasoline rose above $2 per gallon, the demand for big SUVs plummeted. Both Ford and General Motors cut SUV production plans as a result. Yet when GM initiated its employee discount program in May 2005, its sales rose 42 percent over the previous May and 47 percent over the previous June. When the employee discount program was discontinued, sales fell dramatically.[6]

LO4
The Power of Yield Management Systems

When competitive pressures are high, a company must know when it can raise prices to maximize its revenues. More and more companies are turning to yield management systems to help adjust prices. First developed in the airline industry, **yield management systems (YMS)** use complex mathematical software to profitably fill unused capacity. The software employs techniques such as discounting early purchases, limiting early sales at these discounted prices, and overbooking capacity. YMS now are appearing in other services such as lodging, other transportation forms, rental firms, retailers, and even hospitals.[7]

Yield management systems are spreading beyond service industries as their popularity increases. The lessons of airlines and hotels aren't entirely applicable to other industries, however, because plane seats and hotel beds are perishable—if they go empty, the revenue opportunity is lost forever. So it makes sense to slash prices to move toward capacity if it's possible to do so without reducing the prices that other customers pay. Cars and steel aren't so perishable. Still, the capacity to make these goods is perishable. An

yield management systems (YMS)
A technique for adjusting prices that uses complex mathematical software to profitably fill unused capacity by discounting early purchases, limiting early sales at these discounted prices, and overbooking capacity.

underused factory or mill is a lost revenue opportunity. So it makes sense to cut prices to use up capacity if it's possible to do so while getting other customers to pay full price.

By using a type of yield management system, Allstate has gotten smarter about what to charge which drivers. In the past customers were divided into three categories for car insurance. Now Allstate has more than 1,500 price levels. Agents used to simply refer to a manual to give customers a price; now they log on to a computer that uses complex algorithms to analyze 16 credit report variables, such as late payments and card balances, as well as data such as claims history for specific car models. Thus, safe drivers are rewarded, saving up to 20 percent over the old system, and high-risk drivers are penalized, paying up to 20 percent more. The system has worked so well that Allstate now applies it to other lines, such as homeowners' insurance.[8]

Yield management software is the reason that consumers now find prices at the 390 Longs Drug Stores in amounts like $2.07 or $5.84 instead of the traditional price-ending digits of .95 or .99. The company says the software has triggered a "category-by-category increase in sales and profit margins."[9] That's the main reason that DemandTec's YMS algorithms, and not manufacturers' suggested retail prices, now govern pricing in all Longs' stores in the continental United States.

With its lower cost structure and massive buying power, Wal-Mart has put pressure on everyone. Many retailers have fought back by slashing prices across the board—a foolhardy move, as many retailers have found out (think of Kmart). "You can't out-Wal-Mart Wal-Mart," said the CEO of Longs Drug Stores. "We'd lose that game."[10]

All the more reason, argues DemandTec's founder Michael Neal, to focus on better pricing. Neal explains that one DemandTec client, a retailer, began bargain pricing what it thought was a very price-sensitive product—diapers—to generate store traffic. But after running sales data through the pricing software, the client discovered that was not the case. Most price-conscious diaper shoppers had long since abandoned the store for bulk purchases at discounters such as Wal-Mart. As a result, the client raised prices on diapers, increasing margins without hurting sales or traffic.

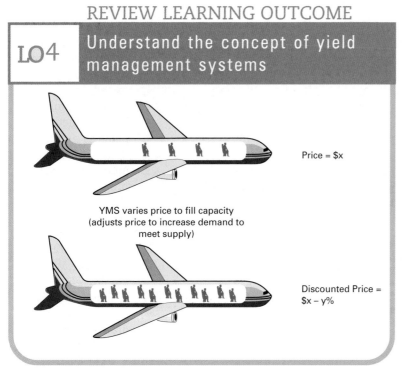
LO5
The Cost Determinant of Price

Sometimes companies minimize or ignore the importance of demand and decide to price their products largely or solely on the basis of costs. Prices determined strictly on the basis of costs may be too high for the target market, thereby reducing or eliminating sales. On the other hand, cost-based prices may be too low, causing the firm to earn a lower return than it should. Nevertheless, costs should generally be part of any price determination, if only as a floor below which a good or service must not be priced in the long run.

The idea of cost may seem simple, but it is actually a multifaceted concept, especially for producers of goods and services. A **variable cost** is a cost that varies with changes in the level of output; an example of a variable cost is the cost of materials. In contrast, a **fixed cost** does not change as output is increased or decreased. Examples include rent and executives' salaries.

variable cost
A cost that varies with changes in the level of output.

fixed cost
A cost that does not change as output is increased or decreased.

To compare the cost of production to the selling price of a product, it is helpful to calculate costs per unit, or average costs. **Average variable cost (AVC)** equals total variable costs divided by quantity of output. **Average total cost (ATC)** equals total costs divided by output. As the graph in Exhibit 17.7(a) shows, AVC and ATC are basically U-shaped curves. In contrast, average fixed cost (AFC) declines continually as output increases because total fixed costs are constant.

Marginal cost (MC) is the change in total costs associated with a one-unit change in output. Exhibit 17.7(b) shows that when output rises from seven to eight units, the change in total cost is from $640 to $750; therefore, marginal cost is $110.

All the curves illustrated in Exhibit 17.7(a) have definite relationships:

- AVC plus AFC equals ATC.

- MC falls for a while and then turns upward, in this case with the fourth unit. At that point diminishing returns set in, meaning that less output is produced for every additional dollar spent on variable input.

average variable cost (AVC)
Total variable costs divided by quantity of output.

average total cost (ATC)
Total costs divided by quantity of output.

marginal cost (MC)
The change in total costs associated with a one-unit change in output

Exhibit 17.7
Hypothetical Set of Cost Curves and a Cost Schedule

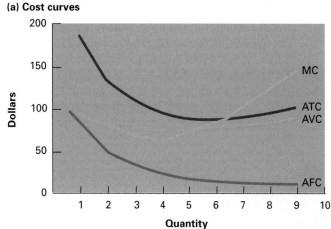

(a) Cost curves

(b) Cost schedule

	Total-cost data, per week				Average-cost data, per week			
(1) Total product (Q)	**(2)** Total fixed cost (TFC)	**(3)** Total variable cost (TVC)	**(4)** Total cost (TC)		**(5)** Average fixed cost (AFC)	**(6)** Average variable cost (AVC)	**(7)** Average total cost (ATC)	**(8)** Marginal cost (MC)
			TC = TFC + TVC		AFC = $\frac{TFC}{Q}$	AVC = $\frac{TVC}{Q}$	ATC = $\frac{TC}{Q}$	(MC) = $\frac{\text{change in TC}}{\text{change in Q}}$
0	$100	$ 0	$ 100		—	—	—	—
1	100	90	190		$100.00	$90.00	$190.00	$ 90
2	100	170	270		50.00	85.00	135.00	80
3	100	240	340		33.33	80.00	113.33	70
4	100	300	400		25.00	75.00	100.00	60
5	100	370	470		20.00	74.00	94.00	70
6	100	450	550		16.67	75.00	91.67	80
7	100	540	640		14.29	77.14	91.43	90
8	100	650	750		12.50	81.25	93.75	110
9	100	780	880		11.11	86.67	97.78	130
10	100	930	1,030		10.00	93.00	103.00	150

- MC intersects both AVC and ATC at their lowest possible points.

- When MC is less than AVC or ATC, the incremental cost will continue to pull the averages down. Conversely, when MC is greater than AVC or ATC, it pulls the averages up, and ATC and AVC begin to rise.

- The minimum point on the ATC curve is the least cost point for a fixed-capacity firm, although it is not necessarily the most profitable point.

Costs can be used to set prices in a variety of ways. For example, markup pricing is relatively simple. Profit maximization pricing and break-even pricing make use of the more complicated concepts of cost.

MARKUP PRICING

Markup pricing, the most popular method used by wholesalers and retailers to establish a selling price, does not directly analyze the costs of production. Instead, **markup pricing** uses the cost of buying the product from the producer, plus amounts for profit and for expenses not otherwise accounted for. The total determines the selling price.

A retailer, for example, adds a certain percentage to the cost of the merchandise received to arrive at the retail price. An item that costs the retailer $1.80 and is sold for $2.20 carries a markup of 40 cents, which is a markup of 22 percent of the cost ($.40 ÷ $1.80). Retailers tend to discuss markup in terms of its percentage of the retail price—in this example, 18 percent ($.40 ÷ $2.20). The difference between the retailer's cost and the selling price (40 cents) is the gross margin, as Chapter 13 explained.

The formula for calculating the retail price given a certain desired markup is as follows:

markup pricing
The cost of buying the product from the producer plus amounts for profit and for expenses not otherwise accounted for.

$$\text{Retail price} = \frac{\text{Cost}}{1 - \text{Desired return on sales}}$$
$$= \frac{\$1.80}{1.00 - .18}$$
$$= \$2.20$$

If the retailer wants a 30 percent return, then:

$$\text{Retail price} = \frac{\$1.80}{1.00 - .30}$$
$$= \$2.57$$

The reason that retailers and others speak of markups on selling price is that many important figures in financial reports, such as gross sales and revenues, are sales figures, not cost figures.

To use markup based on cost or selling price effectively, the marketing manager must calculate an adequate gross margin—the amount added to cost to determine price. The margin must ultimately provide adequate funds to cover selling expenses and profit. Once an appropriate margin has been determined, the markup technique has the major advantage of being easy to employ. Wal-Mart, for example, strives for a gross margin of around 16 percent.[11] Because supermarket chains, such as Safeway and Kroger, have typically had gross margins of 24 percent, they are now finding it extremely difficult to compete with Wal-Mart supermarkets. Wal-Mart is now the nation's largest grocery chain.

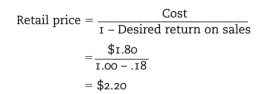

RETAIL PRICE $1055. ON YOUR WRIST $289. IN YOUR POCKET $766.

© COURTESY OF TIMEPIECES INTERNATIONAL

It is not uncommon for specialty retailers to mark up their merchandise by 100 percent, even more in industries like high fashion. This ad for Timepieces International touts the fact that by selling direct, it does not have "the usual mark-up to make" and so can offer this luxury watch at over 70 percent off the retail price.

Markups are often based on experience. For example, many small retailers mark up merchandise 100 percent over cost. (In other words, they double the cost.) This tactic is called **keystoning.** Some other factors that influence markups are the merchandise's appeal to customers, past response to the markup (an implicit demand consideration), the item's promotional value, the seasonality of the goods, their fashion appeal, the product's traditional selling price, and competition. Most retailers avoid any set markup because of such considerations as promotional value and seasonality.

PROFIT MAXIMIZATION PRICING

Producers tend to use more complicated methods of setting prices than distributors use. One is **profit maximization,** which occurs when marginal revenue equals marginal cost. You learned earlier that marginal cost is the change in total costs associated with a one-unit change in output. Similarly, **marginal revenue (MR)** is the extra revenue associated with selling an extra unit of output. As long as the revenue of the last unit produced and sold is greater than the cost of the last unit produced and sold, the firm should continue manufacturing and selling the product.

Exhibit 17.8 shows the marginal revenues and marginal costs for a hypothetical firm, using the cost data from Exhibit 17.7(b). The profit-maximizing quantity, where MR = MC, is six units. You might say, "If profit is zero, why produce the sixth unit? Why not stop at five?" In fact, you would be right. The firm, however, would not know that the fifth unit would produce zero profits until it determined that profits were no longer increasing. Economists suggest producing up to the point where MR = MC. If marginal revenue is just one penny greater than marginal costs, it will still increase total profits.

Exhibit 17.8
Point of Profit Maximization

Quantity	Marginal Revenue (MR)	Marginal Cost (MC)	Cumulative Total Profit
0	—	—	—
1	$140	$ 90	$ 50
2	130	80	100
3	105	70	135
4	95	60	170
5	85	70	185
*6	80	80	185
7	75	90	170
8	60	110	120
9	50	130	40
10	40	150	(70)

*Profit maximization.

keystoning
The practice of marking up prices by 100 percent, or doubling the cost.

profit maximization
A method of setting prices that occurs when marginal revenue equals marginal cost.

marginal revenue (MR)
The extra revenue associated with selling an extra unit of output or the change in total revenue with a one-unit change in output.

break-even analysis
A method of determining what sales volume must be reached before total revenue equals total costs.

BREAK-EVEN PRICING

Now let's take a closer look at the relationship between sales and cost. **Break-even analysis** determines what sales volume must be reached before the company breaks even (its total costs equal total revenue) and no profits are earned.

The typical break-even model assumes a given fixed cost and a constant average variable cost. Suppose that Universal Sportswear, a hypothetical firm, has fixed costs of $2,000 and that the cost of labor and materials for each unit produced is 50 cents. Assume that it can sell up to 6,000 units of its product at $1 without having to lower its price.

Exhibit 17.9(a) illustrates Universal Sportswear's break-even point. As Exhibit 17.9(b) indicates, Universal Sportswear's total variable costs increase by 50 cents every time a new unit is produced, and total fixed costs remain constant at $2,000 regardless of the level of output. Therefore, for 4,000 units of output, Universal Sportswear has $2,000 in fixed costs and $2,000 in total variable costs (4,000 units × $.50), or $4,000 in total costs.

Revenue is also $4,000 (4,000 units × $1), giving a net profit of zero dollars at the break-even point of 4,000 units. Notice that once the firm gets past the break-even point, the gap between total revenue and total costs gets wider and wider because both functions are assumed to be linear.

The formula for calculating break-even quantities is simple:

$$\text{Break-even quantity} = \frac{\text{Total fixed costs}}{\text{Fixed cost contribution}}$$

Exhibit 17.9

Costs, Revenues, and Break-Even Point for Universal Sportswear

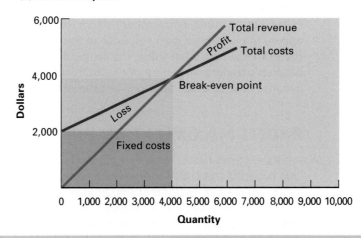

(a) Break-even point

(b) Costs and revenues

Output	Total fixed costs	Average variable costs	Total variable costs	Average total costs	Average revenue (price)	Total revenue	Total costs	Profit or loss
500	$2,000	$0.50	$ 250	$4.50	$1.00	$ 500	$2,250	($1,750)
1,000	2,000	0.50	500	2.50	1.00	1,000	2,500	(1,500)
1,500	2,000	0.50	750	1.83	1.00	1,500	2,750	(1,250)
2,000	2,000	0.50	1,000	1.50	1.00	2,000	3,000	(1,000)
2,500	2,000	0.50	1,250	1.30	1.00	2,500	3,250	(750)
3,000	2,000	0.50	1,500	1.17	1.00	3,000	3,500	(500)
3,500	2,000	0.50	1,750	1.07	1.00	3,500	3,750	(250)
*4,000	2,000	0.50	2,000	1.00	1.00	4,000	4,000	0
4,500	2,000	0.50	2,250	.94	1.00	4,500	4,250	250
5,000	2,000	0.50	2,500	.90	1.00	5,000	4,500	500
5,500	2,000	0.50	2,750	.86	1.00	5,500	4,750	750
6,000	2,000	0.50	3,000	.83	1.00	6,000	5,000	1,000

*Break-even point

Fixed cost contribution is the price minus the average variable cost. Therefore, for Universal Sportswear,

$$\text{Break-even quantity} = \frac{\$2,000}{(\$1.00 - \$.50)} = \frac{\$2,000}{\$.50}$$

$$= 4,000 \text{ units}$$

The advantage of break-even analysis is that it provides a quick estimate of how much the firm must sell to break even and how much profit can be earned if a higher sales volume is obtained. If a firm is operating close to the break-even point, it may want to see what can be done to reduce costs or increase sales. Moreover, in a simple break-even analysis, it is not necessary to compute marginal costs and marginal revenues because price and average cost per unit are assumed to be constant. Also, because accounting data for marginal cost and revenue are frequently unavailable, it is convenient not to have to depend on that information.

Break-even analysis is not without several important limitations. Sometimes it is hard to know whether a cost is fixed or variable. If labor wins a tough guaranteed-employment contract, are the resulting expenses a fixed cost? Are middle-level executives' salaries fixed costs? More important than cost determination is the fact that simple break-even analysis ignores demand. How does Universal Sportswear know it can sell 4,000 units at $1? Could it sell the same 4,000 units at $2 or even $5? Obviously, this information would profoundly affect the firm's pricing decisions.

LO5 Describe cost-oriented pricing strategies

Markup: Cost + x% = Price

Profit Maximization: Price set at point where MR = MC

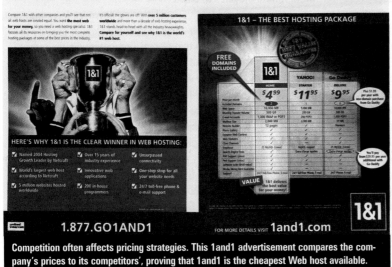

Break-even: Price set at point where total cost = total revenue

LO6 Other Determinants of Price

Other factors besides demand and costs can influence price. For example, the stages in the product life cycle, the competition, the product distribution strategy, the promotion strategy, and perceived quality can all affect pricing.

STAGES IN THE PRODUCT LIFE CYCLE

As a product moves through its life cycle (see Chapter 10), the demand for the product and the competitive conditions tend to change:

- Introductory stage: Management usually sets prices high during the introductory stage. One reason is that it hopes to recover its development costs quickly. In addition, demand originates in the core of the market (the customers whose needs ideally match the product's attributes) and thus is relatively inelastic. On the other hand, if the target market is highly price sensitive, management often finds it better to price the product at the market level or lower. For example, when Kraft Foods brought out Country Time lemonade, it was priced like similar products in the highly competitive beverage market because the market was price sensitive.

- Growth stage: As the product enters the growth stage, prices generally begin to stabilize for several reasons. First, competitors have entered the market, increasing the available supply. Second, the product has begun to appeal to a broader market, often lower-income groups. Finally, economies of scale are lowering costs, and the savings can be passed on to the consumer in the form of lower prices.

- Maturity stage: Maturity usually brings further price decreases as competition increases and inefficient, high-cost firms are eliminated. Distribution channels become a significant cost factor, however, because of the need to offer wide product lines for highly segmented markets, extensive service requirements, and the sheer number of dealers necessary to absorb high-volume production. The manufacturers that remain in the market toward the end of the maturity stage typically offer similar prices. Usually, only the most efficient remain, and they have comparable costs. At this stage, price increases are usually cost initiated, not demand initiated. Nor do price reductions in the late phase of maturity stimulate much demand. Because demand is limited and producers have similar cost structures, the remaining competitors will probably match price reductions.

- Decline stage: The final stage of the life cycle may see further price decreases as the few remaining competitors try

THE BIG HOSTING SHOWDOWN

Competition often affects pricing strategies. This 1and1 advertisement compares the company's prices to its competitors', proving that 1and1 is the cheapest Web host available.

to salvage the last vestiges of demand. When only one firm is left in the market, prices begin to stabilize. In fact, prices may eventually rise dramatically if the product survives and moves into the specialty goods category, as horse-drawn carriages and vinyl records have.

THE COMPETITION

Competition varies during the product life cycle, of course, and so at times it may strongly affect pricing decisions. Although a firm may not have any competition at first, the high prices it charges may eventually induce another firm to enter the market. Several Internet auto sellers, such as Autobytel.com, have sprung up in response to the perceived high profit margins earned by car dealers.

On the other hand, intense competition can sometimes lead to price wars. One company recently took action to avoid a calamitous price war by outsmarting its competition. A company (call it Acme) heard that its competitor was trying to steal some business by offering a low price to one of its best customers. Instead of immediately cutting prices, Acme reps visited three of its competitor's best clients and said they figured the client was paying x, the same price that the competitor had quoted to Acme's own customer. Within days, the competitor had retracted its low-price offer to Acme's client. Presumably, the competitor had received calls from three angry clients asking for the same special deal.

Competition in the global marketplace has often forced firms to lower prices. Carrefour, the world's second-largest retailer behind Wal-Mart, has cut prices in an attempt to gain market share. Carrefour's strategy is discussed in this chapter's "Global Perspectives" box.

GLOBAL Perspectives

Can Lowering Prices Help Carrefour Stay on Top?

In the Paris suburb of Villiers-en-Bière, at one of Carrefour's largest hypermarkets, big banners heralding price cuts hang from the ceiling. Small red tags touting the same are on the shelves. Three shopping carts filled with the same kinds of food are also on display, showing the difference in price between Carrefour's store brand goods and more expensive brands.

Flagging price cuts may seem like Retail 101, but it is a big gamble for Carrefour SA, the world's second-largest retailer behind Wal-Mart. Carrefour Chief Executive Daniel Bernard is telling store managers to cut their prices to build traffic and sales volume in an effort to win back the market share the company has lost in the aisles of relentless discounting chains.

Carrefour's strategy, in essence, has been to use its sheer size and market dominance as a tool to keep customers walking through its doors. But in the age of discounters, Carrefour has had to compete on price, too, and to leverage that size and market dominance to make its supply chain leaner. The gamble here is that Carrefour will make up for the price cuts an increase in sales volume.

Discounters all over the world, especially in Germany, the United Kingdom and the United States, have been baiting traditional retailers into price wars. Germany's biggest discounter, Aldi Group, has helped turn that country into the most price-conscious nation in Europe. Discounters make up fully 40 percent of the German retail market. In the United Kingdom, Tesco PLC and ASDA, a division of Wal-Mart, have forced grocers to cut prices

to stay competitive. In the United States, Wal-Mart has been stripping traditional grocers' profit margins as it continues to lure customers with low prices and vast selections.

Under Bernard's plan, executives at Carrefour's Paris headquarters have tightened their grip on individual store managers, who traditionally have had near-autonomy in managing their stores. The executives are pushing local store managers to have the lowest or next-lowest prices in their local markets on items from fruit to bicycles to DVDs.

In the supercompetitive retail market, however, lowering prices may not be enough when there are a slew of grocery marts and supercenter retailers that also are squeezing distributors, streamlining logistics, and relentlessly tracking customer preferences to cut costs. Even with its new measures, Carrefour is far less centralized than Wal-Mart or Tesco, the world's third-largest retailer, both of which use computers to extensively track customers and determine which items to stock. Wal-Mart and Tesco have developed lean supply chains to closely track and precisely price merchandise.[12]

Does Carrefour think that demand for its products is elastic or inelastic? What is the theoretical limit below which Carrefour should not lower prices? Carrefour is now the largest retailer in the rapidly growing Chinese market. Should it start lowering prices there as well? Many European villages deny building permits to retailers like Wal-Mart and Carrefour to protect small local merchants. Do you agree with this policy?

European Union Commissioner for Justice, Freedom and Security, Franco Frattini looks at counterfeit products displayed on a table at the EU Commission headquarters in Brussels. The European Commission has proposed minimum four-year jail terms as part of a new beefed up European Union law to fight counterfeiters and piracy.

DISTRIBUTION STRATEGY

An effective distribution network can often overcome other minor flaws in the marketing mix.[13] For example, although consumers may perceive a price as being slightly higher than normal, they may buy the product anyway if it is being sold at a convenient retail outlet.

Adequate distribution for a new product can often be attained by offering a larger-than-usual profit margin to distributors. A variation on this strategy is to give dealers a large trade allowance to help offset the costs of promotion and further stimulate demand at the retail level.

Manufacturers have gradually been losing control within the distribution channel to wholesalers and retailers, which often adopt pricing strategies that serve their own purposes. For instance, some distributors are **selling against the brand:** They place well-known brands on the shelves at high prices while offering other brands—typically, their private-label brands, such as Craftsman tools, Kroger canned pears, or Cost Cutter paper towels—at lower prices. Of course, sales of the higher-priced brands decline.

Wholesalers and retailers may also go outside traditional distribution channels to buy gray-market goods. As explained previously, distributors obtain the goods through unauthorized channels for less than they would normally pay, so they can sell the goods with a bigger-than-normal markup or at a reduced price. Imports seem to be particularly susceptible to gray marketing. Porsches, JVC stereos, and Seiko watches are among the brand-name products that have experienced this problem. Although consumers may pay less for gray-market goods, they often find that the manufacturer won't honor the warranty.

Manufacturers can regain some control over price by using an exclusive distribution system, by franchising, or by avoiding doing business with price-cutting discounters. Manufacturers can also package merchandise with the selling price marked on it or place goods on consignment. The best way for manufacturers to control prices, however, is to develop brand loyalty in consumers by delivering quality and value.

THE IMPACT OF THE INTERNET

The Internet, corporate networks, and wireless setups are linking people, machines, and companies around the globe—and connecting sellers and buyers as never before. This link is enabling buyers to quickly and easily compare products and prices, putting them in a better bargaining position. At the same time, the technology allows sellers to collect detailed data about customers' buying habits, preferences, and even spending limits so that the sellers can tailor their products and prices.

Picking a Product to Buy Online

The online shopping process begins with selecting a product. If you want a pet, camera, electronics product, or computer but don't know which brand, try http://www.activebuyersguide.com, which will help you narrow your choice. If you want help with outdoor gear, try http://outside.away.com. Once you select a brand, you can always get a second opinion at http://www.consumersearch.com. This is an expert site that aggregates reviews from many sources such as Consumer Digest, Consumer Reports, and PC World. For example, a quick click on sleeping bags led to reviews from Backpacker and Outside magazines. The problem with expert reviews is that each judgment reflects

selling against the brand
Stocking well-known branded items at high prices in order to sell store brands at discounted prices.

© YVES LOGGHE/ASSOCIATED PRESS

the views of a few people at most. Many shoppers find **http://www.consumerreview.com** or **http://www.epinions.com** helpful. These sites provide user opinions of hundreds of different products. Unfortunately, consumer reviews vary widely in quality. Some are quite terse whereas others tend to ramble on and on.

Using Shopping Bots

A shopping bot is a program that searches the Web for the best price for a particular item that you wish to purchase. Bot is short for robot. Shopping bots theoretically give pricing power to the consumer. The more information that the shopper has, the more efficient his or her purchase decision will be. When consumers use their money wisely, they can raise their standard of living by approximately one-third. This applies not only to purchasing but to the wise use of credit as well.

There are two general types of shopping bots. The first is the broad-based type that searches a wide range of product categories such as MySimon.com, dealtime.com, bizmate.com, pricegrabber.com, and PriceScan.com. These sites operate using a Yellow Pages type of model, in that they list every retailer they can find. The second is the niche-oriented type that searches for only one type of product such as computer equipment (CNET.com), books (Bookfinder.com), or CDs (CDPriceCompare.com).

Most shopping bots give preferential listings to those e-retailers that pay for the privilege. These so-called merchant partners receive about 60 percent of the click-throughs.[14] Typically, the bot lists its merchant partners first, not the retailer that offers the lowest price.

If a bot steers you to really low prices, be careful, as Internet fraud is huge. If you are considering buying from a site that you don't know, check out customer feedback at **http://www.resellerratings.com** or **http://ratingwonders.com.** Also, if a merchant's site doesn't answer questions about the product, call for details before giving out your credit-card information. Sometimes a really low price is for a reconditioned or refurbished item, or, in the case of clothing and similar items, it may be a "second." Also, ask about in-stock status, pricing breakdowns such as taxes and shipping, and return policies including restocking charges.

In summary, the Internet has shifted some shopping power to the consumer, but not all. Shopping bots help find lower prices, but the use of merchant partners means that the lowest prices may not be shown first. Also, bots tend to work better when the shopper has a specific item number as with electronics products. With other products, like wool sweaters, direct comparisons may be more difficult. There is no doubt, however, that the consumer has more pricing information than ever before.

Internet Auctions

The Internet auction business is huge. Part of the lure of buying online is that shoppers don't have to go to a flea market or use up a coveted weekend day or worry about the weather. Plus, bidding itself can be fun and exciting. Among the most popular consumer auction sites are the following:

- **http://www.auctions.amazon.com:** Links to Sotheby's for qualified sellers of high-end items.

- **http://www.ebay.com:** The most popular auction site.

- **http://www.auctions.yahoo.com:** Free listings and numerous selling categories including international auctions.

Even though consumers are spending billions on Internet auctions, business-to-business (B2B) auctions are likely to be the dominant form in the future. Recently, Whirlpool began holding online auctions. Participants bid on the price of the items that they would supply to Whirlpool, but with a twist: they had to include the date when Whirlpool would have to pay for the items. The company wanted to see which suppliers would offer the longest grace period before requiring payment. Five auctions held over five months helped Whirlpool uncover savings of close to $2 million and more than doubled the grace period.

Whirlpool's success is a sign that the B2B auction world is shifting from haggling over prices to niggling over parameters of the deal. Warranties, delivery dates, transportation methods, customer support, financing options, and quality have all become bargaining chips.

There is also a dark side to Internet auctions, however, especially those where most participants are consumers. Every day crooks lure hundreds of unsuspecting users with auctions that appear legitimate but are really a hollow shell. They hop from user ID to user ID, feeding the system with fake information and stolen credit cards so that the auction site can't tell who they are. In response to a dramatic increase in auction-fraud complaints, the Federal Trade Commission banded together with the National Association of Attorneys General to conduct Operation Bidder Beware, a nationwide crackdown and consumer-education campaign. In 2005, the FTC logged 50,000 auction-fraud complaints, more than six times as many as in 2001. "It's one of our top priorities," says Barbara Anthony, northeast regional director at the FTC. "It jeopardizes the e-commerce marketplace and the confidence consumers have in the Internet." These numbers include auctions on Yahoo.com and other sites, but the bulk of them are on eBay, which boasts 85 percent of the online auction market.[15]

Although the majority of transactions on eBay come off without a hitch, fraud may be more prevalent than the company lets on. The company reports that only 0.01 percent of all completed auctions are fraudulent, but the numbers don't include everyone who's been a victim of fraud.[16] They're based on the people who go through eBay's fraud-insurance claim process and thus don't include victims who for whatever reason fail to complete the process or don't start it in the first place because they don't see the point of applying for the maximum $175 reimbursement when they've lost, say, $3,000.

PROMOTION STRATEGY

Price is often used as a promotional tool to increase consumer interest. The weekly flyers sent out by grocery stores in the Sunday newspaper, for instance, advertise many products with special low prices. Crested Butte Ski Resort in Colorado tried a unique twist on price promotions. It made the unusual offer of free skiing between Thanksgiving and Christmas. Its only revenues were voluntary contributions from lodging and restaurant owners who benefited from the droves of skiers taking advantage of the promotion. Lodging during the slack period is now booked solid, and on the busiest days 9,000 skiers jam slopes designed for about 6,500. Crested Butte Resort no longer loses money during this time of the year.

Pricing can be a tool for trade promotions as well. For example, Levi's Dockers (casual men's pants) are very popular with white-collar men ages 25 to 45, a growing and lucrative market. Sensing an opportunity, rival pants-maker Bugle Boy began offering similar pants at cheaper wholesale prices, which gave retailers a bigger gross margin than they were getting with Dockers. Levi Strauss had to either lower prices or risk its $400 million annual Docker sales. Although Levi Strauss intended its cheapest Dockers to retail for $35, it started selling Dockers to retailers for $18 a pair. Retailers could then advertise Dockers at a very attractive retail price of $25.

DEMANDS OF LARGE CUSTOMERS

Manufacturers find that their large customers such as Wal-Mart, JCPenney, and other department stores often make specific pricing demands that the suppliers must agree to. Department stores are making greater-than-ever demands on their suppliers to cover the heavy discounts and markdowns on their own selling floors. They want suppliers to guarantee their stores' profit margins, and they insist on cash rebates if the guarantee isn't met. They are also exacting fines for violations of ticketing, packing, and shipping rules. Cumulatively, the demands are nearly wiping out profits for all but the very biggest suppliers, according to fashion designers and garment makers.

With annual sales of over $285 billion and 1.7 million "associates" (employees), Wal-Mart is the world's largest company. Wal-Mart is the largest customer of Disney brands, Procter & Gamble, Kraft, Gillette, Campbell Soups, and most of America's other leading branded manufacturers. Wal-Mart expects suppliers to offer their best price, period. There is no negotiation or raising prices later. When suppliers have raised prices, Wal-Mart has been known to keep sending the old amount.[17]

THE RELATIONSHIP OF PRICE TO QUALITY

When a purchase decision involves great uncertainty, consumers tend to rely on a high price as a predictor of good quality. Reliance on price as an indicator of quality seems to occur for all products, but it reveals itself more strongly for some items than for others.[18] Among the products that benefit from this phenomenon are coffee, stockings, aspirin, salt, floor wax, shampoo, clothing, furniture, perfume, whiskey, and many services. In the absence of other information, people typically assume that prices are higher because the products contain better materials, because they are made more carefully, or, in the case of professional services, because the provider has more expertise. In other words, consumers assume that "You get what you pay for."

Research has found that products that are perceived to be of high quality tend to benefit more from price promotions than products perceived to be of lower quality.[19] However, when perceived high- and lower-quality products are offered in settings where consumers have difficulty making comparisons, then price promotions have an equal effect on sales. Comparisons are more difficult in end-of-aisle displays, feature advertising, and the like.

Knowledgeable merchants take these consumer attitudes into account when devising their pricing strategies. **Prestige pricing** is charging a high price to help promote a high-quality image. A successful prestige pricing strategy requires a retail price that is reasonably consistent with consumers' expectations. No one goes shopping at a Gucci's shop in New York and expects to pay $9.95 for a pair of loafers. In fact, demand would fall drastically at such a low price. Bayer aspirin would probably lose market share over the long run if it lowered its prices. A new mustard packaged in a crockery jar was not successful until its price was doubled.

prestige pricing
Charging a high price to help promote a high-quality image.

REVIEW LEARNING OUTCOME

LO6 Demonstrate how the product life cycle, competition, distribution and promotion strategies, customer demands, the Internet, and perceptions of quality can affect price

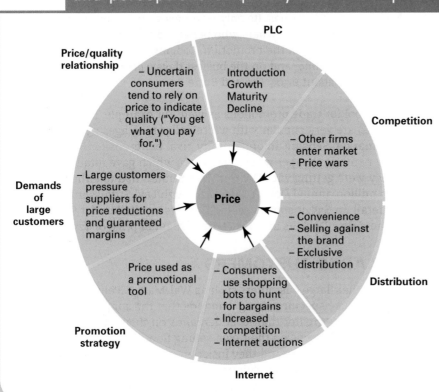

Some of the latest research on price-quality relationships has focused on consumer durable goods. The researchers first conducted a study to ascertain the dimensions of quality. These are (1) ease of use; (2) versatility (the ability of a product to perform more functions, e.g., special stitch types on sewing machines, or be more flexible, e.g., continuous temperature controls on microwave ovens); (3) durability; (4) serviceability (ease of obtaining quality repairs); (5) performance; and (6) prestige. The researchers found that when consumers focused on prestige and/or durability to assess quality, price was a strong indicator of perceived overall quality. Price was less important as an indicator of quality if the consumer was focusing on one of the other four dimensions of quality.[20]

Quick Check

Now that you've read the chapter, do you get it? Take a moment for a quick check using this scale:

1 Not at all; 2 Not very well; 3 Ok; 4 Well; 5 Very Well

Can you . . .

____ explain how price, revenue, and profit are related?

____ write the formula for target return on investment (ROI) and for the break-even quantity?

____ explain the three main categories of pricing objectives?

____ outline how supply and demand establish prices?

____ write a paragraph explaining elasticity of demand and what affects it?

____ explain how costs determine price?

____ explain to a friend what average variable cost, average total cost, marginal cost, and marginal revenue are?

____ describe how the stages of the PLC affect price?

____ articulate the relationship of price to quality?

____ discuss how promotion and distribution strategies affect price?

____ TOTAL

Score: 41–50, you're ready to move on to the applications; 31–40, skim the chapter one more time before moving on to the applications; 21–30, reread the sections giving you the most trouble and go to Thomson NOW for guided tutorials; 20 and under, you better reread the chapter to get a grasp of the fundamentals. If you've reread the chapter and still have a low score, visit your professor or TA during office hours.

Review and Applications

LO 1 Discuss the importance of pricing decisions to the economy and to the individual firm. Pricing plays an integral role in the U.S. economy by allocating goods and services among consumers, governments, and businesses. Pricing is essential in business because it creates revenue, which is the basis of all business activity. In setting prices, marketing managers strive to find a level high enough to produce a satisfactory profit.

1.1 Why is pricing so important to the marketing manager?

1.2 How does price allocate goods and services?

LO 2 List and explain a variety of pricing objectives. Establishing realistic and measurable pricing objectives is a critical part of any firm's marketing strategy. Pricing objectives are commonly classified into three categories: profit oriented, sales oriented, and status quo. Profit-oriented pricing is based on profit maximization, a satisfactory level of profit, or a target return on investment. The goal of profit maximization is to generate as much revenue as possible in relation to cost. Often, a more practical approach than profit maximization is setting prices to produce profits that will satisfy management and stockholders. The most common profit-oriented strategy is pricing for a specific return on investment relative to a firm's assets. The second type of pricing objective is sales oriented, and it focuses on either maintaining a percentage share of the market or maximizing dollar or unit sales. The third type of pricing objective aims to maintain the status quo by matching competitors' prices.

2.1 Give an example of each major type of pricing objective.

2.2 Why do many firms not maximize profits?

LO3 Explain the role of demand in price determination. Demand is a key determinant of price. When establishing prices, a firm must first determine demand for its product. A typical demand schedule shows an inverse relationship between quantity demanded and price: When price is lowered, sales increase; and when price is increased, the quantity demanded falls. For prestige products, however, there may be a direct relationship between demand and price: the quantity demanded will increase as price increases.

Marketing managers must also consider demand elasticity when setting prices. Elasticity of demand is the degree to which the quantity demanded fluctuates with changes in price. If consumers are sensitive to changes in price, demand is elastic; if they are insensitive to price changes, demand is inelastic. Thus, an increase in price will result in lower sales for an elastic product and little or no loss in sales for an inelastic product.

3.1 Explain the role of supply and demand in determining price.

3.2 If a firm can increase its total revenue by raising its price, shouldn't it do so?

3.3 Explain the concepts of elastic and inelastic demand. Why should managers understand these concepts?

LO4 Understand the concept of yield management systems. Yield management systems use complex mathematical software to profitably fill unused capacity. The software uses techniques such as discounting early purchases, limiting early sales at these discounted prices, and overbooking capacity. These systems are used in service and retail businesses and are substantially raising revenues.

4.1 Why are so many companies adopting yield management systems?

4.2 Explain the relationship between supply and demand and yield management systems.

LO5 Describe cost-oriented pricing strategies. The other major determinant of price is cost. Marketers use several cost-oriented pricing strategies. To cover their own expenses and obtain a profit, wholesalers and retailers commonly use markup pricing: They tack an extra amount onto the manufacturer's original price. Another pricing technique is to maximize profits by setting price where marginal revenue equals marginal cost. Still another pricing strategy determines how much a firm must sell to break even and uses this amount as a reference point for adjusting price.

5.1 Your firm has based its pricing strictly on cost in the past. As the newly hired marketing manager, you believe this policy should change. Write the president a memo explaining your reasons.

5.2 Why is it important for managers to understand the concept of break-even points? Are there any drawbacks?

LO6 Demonstrate how the product life cycle, competition, distribution and promotion strategies, customer demands, the Internet, and perceptions of quality can affect price. The price of a product normally changes as it moves through the life cycle and as demand for the product and competitive conditions change. Management often sets a high price at the introductory stage, and the high price tends to attract competition. The competition usually drives prices down because individual competitors lower prices to gain market share.

Adequate distribution for a new product can sometimes be obtained by offering a larger-than-usual profit margin to wholesalers and retailers. The Internet enables consumers to compare products and prices quickly and efficiently. Price is also used as a promotional tool to attract customers. Special low prices often attract new customers and entice existing customers to buy more. Large buyers can extract price concessions from vendors. Such demands can squeeze the profit margins of suppliers.

Perceptions of quality can also influence pricing strategies. A firm trying to project a prestigious image often charges a premium price for a product. Consumers tend to equate high prices with high quality.

6.1 Divide the class into teams of five. Each team will be assigned a different grocery store from a different chain. (An independent is fine.) Appoint a group leader. The group leaders should meet as a group and pick 15 nationally branded grocery items. Each item should be specifically described as to brand name and size of the package. Each team will then proceed to its assigned store and collect price data on the 15 items. The team should also gather price data on 15 similar store brands and 15 generics, if possible.

Each team should present its results to the class and discuss why there are price variations between stores, national brands, store brands, and generics.

As a next step, go back to your assigned store and share the overall results with the store manager. Bring back the manager's comments and share them with the class.

6.2 How does the stage of a product's life cycle affect price? Give some examples.

6.3 Go to Priceline.com. Can you research a ticket's price before purchasing it? What products and services are available for purchasing? How comfortable are you with naming your own price? Relate the supply and demand curves to customer-determined pricing.

Key Terms

Exercises

APPLICATION EXERCISE

Reliance on price as a predictor of quality seems to occur for all products. Does this mean that high-priced products are superior? Well, sometimes. Price can be a good predictor of quality for some products, but for others, price is not always the best way to determine the quality of a product or service before buying it. This exercise (and worksheet) will help you examine the price-quality relationship for a simple product: canned goods.[21]

Activities

1. Take a trip to a local supermarket where you are certain to find multiple brands of canned fruits and vegetables. Pick a single type of vegetable or fruit you like, such as cream corn or peach halves, and list five or six brands in the following worksheet:

(1) Brand	(2) Quality/ Rank (y)	Price			(6) d ($y - x$)	(7) d^2
		(3) Price/ Weight	(4) Price per Ounce	(5) Price Rank (x)		
TOTAL						

2. Before going any further, rank the brands according to which you think is the highest quality (1) to the lowest quality (5 or 6, depending on how many brands you find). This ranking will be y.

3. Record the price and the volume of each brand. For example, if a 14-ounce can costs $.89, you would list $.89/14 oz.

4. Translate the price per volume into price per ounce. Our 14-ounce can costs $.064 per ounce.

5. Now rank the price per ounce (we'll call it x) from the highest (1) to the lowest (5 or 6, again depending on how many brands you have).

6. We'll now begin calculating the coefficient of correlation between the price and quality rankings. The first step is to subtract x from y. Enter the result, d, in column 6.

7. Now calculate d^2 and enter the value in column 7. Write the sum of all the entries in column 7 in the final row.

8. The formula for calculating a price-quality coefficient r is as follows:

$$r_s = 1 - \frac{6\sum d^2}{(n^3 - n)}$$

In the formula, r_s is the coefficient of correlation, 6 is a constant, and n is the number of items ranked.

9. What does the result of your calculation tell you about the correlation between the price and the quality of the canned vegetable or fruit you selected? Now that you know this, will it change your buying habits?

Entrepreneurship Case
HDNET AIMS TO REDEFINE TELEVISION

If billionaire entrepreneur Mark Cuban had his way, the future would be today. The Web broadcasting pioneer earned nearly $2 billion when he and his partner sold their Broadcast.com business to Yahoo! for the princely sum of $5.7 billion at the height of the Internet frenzy in 2000. While looking to spend some of his newly found wealth on the latest and greatest in home entertainment systems, Cuban had his first experience with high-definition television. High-definition TV is a digital format that produces a picture resolution that can be up to ten times sharper than that of standard TVs (depending on screen pixel count), and it is typically presented in a wide-screen format along with digital surround sound. Cuban was so captivated by the amazing resolution on his new 100-inch projection set that he decided to start his own high-definition television network.

With a $100 million investment from Cuban, HDNet—the first-ever all-high-definition network—was off and running less than a year later. Three years later, HDNet boasts over 1,200 hours of original programming. In addition to the shows it produces, it has licensing contracts that double its programming inventory. HDNet also has broadcasting agreements that allow it to carry live sporting events from the National Hockey League, Major League soccer, and the NCAA. The company also operates HDNetMovies, which has scored deals with several major movie studios to convert their 35-millimeter films to a high-definition format.

Though HDNet's current subscriber base is estimated at around 1 million, industry statistics suggest that 60 million U.S. homes have television sets capable of delivering high-definition programming. With prices that started near $5,000 a couple of years ago, the prohibitive cost of the special television sets required to transmit high-definition programming was one of the company's major early hurdles. The other was the lack of available programming. High-definition shows must be produced on special equipment, and only a few major networks, such as NBC, CBS, ABC, HBO, Showtime, and the Discovery channel, have made the investment to do so.

Cuban has stayed the course, patiently waiting for prices of high-definition TV sets to drop to where they would have mass-market appeal. As with his Internet business, his timing appears to be perfect. Electronics retailer Best Buy now sells 27-inch high-definition TV sets for as low as $500. Of course, the discerning customer can spend as much as $9,000 in the same store for a top-of-the-line 60-inch model; but now that the television sets are affordable, adoption rates could be on the verge of exploding. Cuban, therefore, has turned his attention to securing distribution deals with major cable operators and satellite programmers.

His company has already locked in deals with all but three of the nation's largest cable television providers and with satellite broadcasters DirecTV and DISHNET. Both satellite programmers and the heavyweight cable-operating trio of Time Warner, Charter Communications, and Adelphia have begun to sell subscriptions to HDNet, which comes packaged with HDNetMovies. Those companies pay an as yet undisclosed amount of money back to Cuban for the rights to carry the channel and license HDNet's exclusive content. To reduce some of the technical confusion for customers, the satellite companies offer subscribers package deals. DirecTV's includes a dish, a high-definition receiver (required to transmit the signal to the high-definition TV), professional installation, and a year's worth of high-definition programming for $399. DISHNET offers a similar package, but throws in a TV for a total start-up cost of $1,000. Its subscriptions are priced separately and start at $110 per year. Cable operators charge a premium for HDNet and include it only with their high-end digital offerings, which generally cost around $100 per month. To entice skeptical consumers into signing up, some cable companies are offering 30-day free trials.

Mark Cuban truly believes that the story of high-definition television services will someday mirror that of FM radio or basic cable television. Of course, only time will tell if he is right, but one thing is for sure—with high-definition television, the future certainly *appears* brighter.[22]

Questions

1. How will demand and supply trends in the high-definition industry affect the price for HDNet's programming?

2. Based on how resellers are pricing HDNet for their subscribers, how would you characterize HDNet's pricing objectives?

3. From what you can discern about HDNet's stage in the product life cycle, competition, distribution, resellers' sales promotion strategies, customer demands, and perception of quality, submit a projection of what you think HDNet should charge carriers for access to its channels and original programming. Defend your answer.

COMPANY CLIPS

Acid+All = Serious Pricing

As long as people have stomach aches, companies will sell remedies. Acid+All is banking that America will continue its love affair with bad food and has made an interesting move into the antacid market. The tiny pills come packaged in a tin priced at $3.89, which clearly sets the product apart from competitors like Rolaids, Tums, and others. The gambit of staking out a position as a prestige product is high. Watch the video to see what issues helped forge the $3.89 unit price and if the company has been successful at this price point.

Questions

1. How do the product, place, and promotion elements of Acid+All's marketing mix influence the pricing strategy the company has chosen?

2. Would you expect demand for Acid+All to be elastic? Why or why not?

3. What role do the product life cycle, competition, and perceptions of quality play in Acid+All's suggested retail price?

4. Would you buy Acid+All for the $3.89 retail price? Why or why not?

BIZ FLIX

The Money Pit

Now that you have a basic understanding of the issues affecting price, you can see why pricing is the most flexible—and difficult—element of the marketing mix. As an encore to your study, watch the film clip from *The Money Pit,* starring Tom Hanks (Walter Fielding) and Shelley Long (Anna Crowley) as new homeowners. Problems with their dream home's plumbing, electricity, roof, and general structure force the owners to make a series of expensive repairs. Walter has tremendous difficulty finding contractors to make the needed repairs, however. In this scene, a plumber visits the house on the recommendation of his brother, a carpenter, who has put in a bid to do woodworking repairs. What chapter concepts can you identify in the scene? How do supply and demand determine the price the homeowners are willing to pay for the plumber's services? Based on what you see of the plumber, how elastic are his prices?

Marketing & You Results

High scores on this poll relate to a belief that you'll get more enjoyment and make better impressions if you buy high-priced brands. That is, you have a higher prestige sensitivity than someone with a lower score. If your score was low, compare it with your score for the Chapter 16 poll, which was probably high. That's because people with lower prestige sensitivities are more likely to use coupons!

Setting the Right Price

Learning Outcomes

LO¹ Describe the procedure for setting the right price

LO² Identify the legal and ethical constraints on pricing decisions

LO³ Explain how discounts, geographic pricing, and other pricing tactics can be used to fine-tune the base price

LO⁴ Discuss product line pricing

LO⁵ Describe the role of pricing during periods of inflation and recession

the ultimate discounter— **Ryanair**

Most airlines fight to trim costs. Ryanair struggles to find the few ounces of fat it hasn't already cut. The Irish no-frills carrier charges passengers for food, drinks, and newspapers. It uses tiny airports far from city centers and bargains for big discounts on landing fees. Employees pay for their own

The airline now carries more passengers in Europe than British Airways and is one of the world's most profitable airlines.

training and uniforms and are told to cut stationery costs by taking hotel notepads.

Ryanair won't consider ticket refunds, for any reason, even if the airline cancels a flight. "What part of 'no refund' don't you understand?" is Chief Executive Michael O'Leary's standard summary of his ticketing policy.

A former tax accountant, O'Leary is now squeezing the airline even tighter. Ryanair's new planes won't have window shades because they delay takeoff preparations as staff open them. Seatback magazine pockets are out, to cut cleaning time. New seats won't even recline, to shrink the repair bill.

And the airline—which has unusually stringent baggage limits—recently raised its excess baggage fee by 17 percent. "Stop bringing so much old rubbish with you," O'Leary says.

Ryanair has even converted some costs into revenues, or "reverse costs" in the company's lingo. Three Ryanair planes are flying billboards for Guinness stout and other products, each generating a onetime, six-figure net gain, according to O'Leary. Flight attendants are paid commissions for on-board food sales, including cups of airline coffee for about $3.50, allowing Ryanair to pay them less in salary.

Now Ryanair is pushing to increase nonticket revenues, such as in-flight sales, which already account for around 15 percent of revenue. It recently negotiated higher commissions on hotel and car reservations made through its Web site. The company doesn't have in-flight entertainment on planes now, but is considering adding it so that passengers could be charged for it.[1]

Ryanair is the ultimate discounter. Its pricing strategy, called penetration pricing, has been very successful. The airline now carries more passengers in Europe than British Airways and is one of the world's most profitable airlines. What are some of the pitfalls of penetration pricing? What is the complete opposite of penetration pricing, and what are the advantages of the opposing strategy? What are some price tactics that Ryanair could use to modify its base price?

LO¹
How to Set a Price on a Product or Service

Setting the right price on a product is a four-step process (see Exhibit 18.1):

1. Establish pricing goals.

2. Estimate demand, costs, and profits.

3. Choose a price strategy to help determine a base price.

4. Fine-tune the base price with pricing tactics.

The first three steps are discussed next; the fourth step is discussed later in the chapter.

Exhibit 18.1

Steps in Setting the Right Price on a Product

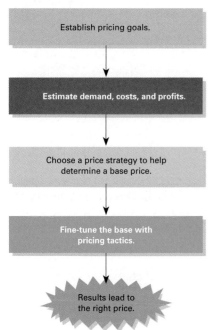

Establish pricing goals.

Estimate demand, costs, and profits.

Choose a price strategy to help determine a base price.

Fine-tune the base with pricing tactics.

Results lead to the right price.

ESTABLISH PRICING GOALS

The first step in setting the right price is to establish pricing goals. Recall from Chapter 17 that pricing objectives fall into three categories: profit oriented, sales oriented, and status quo. These goals are derived from the firm's overall objectives. If, for example, a company's objective is to be the dominant sales leader in an industry, then it will pursue a sales-oriented market share pricing goal. A conservative organization that is attempting to lower risks by being a follower, rather than attempting to be a market leader, may establish a status quo goal. This company is simply trying to preserve its position in the marketplace. Finally, a company committed to maximizing shareholder value will establish aggressive profit-oriented pricing goals.

A good understanding of the marketplace and of the consumer can sometimes tell a manager very quickly whether a goal is realistic. For example, if firm A's objective is a 20 percent target return on investment (ROI), and its product development and implementation costs are $5 million, the market must be rather large or must support the price required to earn a 20 percent ROI. Assume that company B has a pricing objective that all new products must reach at least 15 percent market share within three years after their introduction. A thorough study of the environment may convince the marketing manager that the competition is too strong and the market share goal can't be met.

All pricing objectives have trade-offs that managers must weigh. A profit maximization objective may require a bigger initial investment than the firm can commit or wants to commit. Reaching the desired market share often means sacrificing short-term profit because without careful management, long-term profit goals may not be met. Meeting the competition is the easiest pricing goal to implement. But can managers really afford to ignore demand and costs, the life-cycle stage, and other considerations? When creating pricing objectives, managers must consider these trade-offs in light of the target customer, the environment, and the company's overall objectives.

ESTIMATE DEMAND, COSTS, AND PROFITS

Chapter 17 explained that total revenue is a function of price and quantity demanded and that quantity demanded depends on elasticity. After establishing pricing goals, managers should estimate total revenue at a variety of prices. Next, they should determine corresponding costs for each price. They are then ready to estimate how much profit, if any, and how much market share can be earned at each possible price. These data become the heart of the developing price policy. Managers can study the options in light of revenues, costs, and profits. In turn, this information can help determine which price can best meet the firm's pricing goals.

CHOOSE A PRICE STRATEGY

The basic, long-term pricing framework for a good or service should be a logical extension of the pricing objectives. The marketing manager's chosen **price strategy** defines the initial price and gives direction for price movements over the product life cycle.

The price strategy sets a competitive price in a specific market segment, based on a well-defined positioning strategy. Changing a price level from premium to superpremium may require a change in the product itself, the target customers served, the promotional strategy, or the distribution channels. Thus, changing a price strategy can require dramatic alterations in the marketing mix. A carmaker cannot successfully compete in the superpremium category if the car looks and drives like an economy car.

A company's freedom in pricing a new product and devising a price strategy depends on the market conditions and the other elements of the marketing mix. If a firm launches a new item resembling several others already on the market, its pricing freedom will be restricted. To succeed, the company will probably have to charge a price close to the average market price. In contrast, a firm that introduces a totally new product with no close substitutes will have considerable pricing freedom.

Most companies do not do a good job of doing research to create a price strategy. A recent study found that only about 8 percent of the companies surveyed conducted serious pricing research to support the development of an effective pricing strategy. In fact, 88 percent of them did little or no serious pricing research. McKinsey & Co.'s Pricing Benchmark Survey estimated that only about 15 percent of companies do serious pricing research. A Coopers & Lybrand study found that 87 percent of the surveyed companies had changed prices in the previous year. Only 13 percent of the price changes, however, came after a scheduled review of pricing strategy.[2]

These numbers indicate that strategic pricing decisions tend to be made without an understanding of the likely buyer or the competitive response. Further, the research shows that managers often make tactical pricing decisions without reviewing how they may fit into the firm's overall pricing or marketing strategy. The data suggest that many companies make pricing decisions and changes without an existing process for managing the pricing activity. As a result, many of them do not have a serious pricing strategy and do not conduct pricing research to develop their strategy.[3]

Companies that do serious planning for creating a price strategy can select from three basic approaches: price skimming, penetration pricing, and status quo pricing. A discussion of each type follows.

price strategy
A basic, long-term pricing framework, which establishes the initial price for a product and the intended direction for price movements over the product life cycle.

price skimming
A pricing policy whereby a firm charges a high introductory price, often coupled with heavy promotion.

Price Skimming

Price skimming is sometimes called a "market-plus" approach to pricing because it denotes a high price relative to the prices of competing products. The term **price skimming** is derived from the phrase "skimming the cream off the top." Companies often use this strategy for new products when the product is perceived by the target market as having unique advantages. For example, Caterpillar sets premium prices on its construction equipment to support and capture its high perceived value. Genzyme Corporation introduced Ceredase as the first effective treatment for Gaucher's disease. The pill allows patients to avoid years of painful physical deterioration and lead normal lives. The cost of a year's supply for one patient can exceed $300,000.

Often companies will use skimming initially and then lower prices over time. This is called "sliding down the demand curve." Hardcover book publishers, such as HarperCollins and Random House, lower the price when the books are re-released in paperback. Calloway lowers the price of its old model golf clubs as new models hit the

© KATHY WILLENS/ASSOCIATED PRESS

Often companies will abandon a skimming strategy over time, but at Chanel that is not the case. Managers destroy unsold inventory as a way to maintain higher prices and avoid any suggestion of putting product on the market at a discount.

sales floor. Yet some manufacturers like Porsche and Cuisinart, the maker of kitchen appliances, maintain skimming prices throughout a product's life cycle. A manager of the factory that produces Chanel purses (retailing for over $2,000 each) told one of your authors that the company takes back unsold inventory and destroys it rather than selling it at a discount. Retailers such as Tiffany and Talbot's maintain skimming policies. Though both retailers occasionally have sales, their basic price strategy is price skimming.

Price skimming works best when the market is willing to buy the product even though it carries an above-average price. If, for example, some purchasing agents feel that Caterpillar equipment is far superior to competitors' products, then Caterpillar can charge premium prices successfully. Firms can also effectively use price skimming when a product is well protected legally, when it represents a technological breakthrough, or when it has in some other way blocked the entry of competitors. Managers may follow a skimming strategy when production cannot be expanded rapidly because of technological difficulties, shortages, or constraints imposed by the skill and time required to produce a product. As long as demand is greater than supply, skimming is an attainable strategy.

A successful skimming strategy enables management to recover its product development or "educational" costs quickly. (Often consumers must be "taught" the advantages of a radically new item, such as high-definition TV.) Even if the market perceives an introductory price as too high, managers can easily correct the problem by lowering the price. Firms often feel it is better to test the market at a high price and then lower the price if sales are too slow. They are tacitly saying, "If there are any premium-price buyers in the market, let's reach them first and maximize our revenue per unit." Successful skimming strategies are not limited to products. Well-known athletes, entertainers, lawyers, and hairstylists are experts at price skimming. Naturally, a skimming strategy will encourage competitors to enter the market.

Above all, if price skimming is to be successful, customers must perceive a high value for the product or service. Otherwise, failure can come at a high price. Iridium phones are an example of a technology-driven, feature-loaded, high-cost, high-price innovation. The phones were billed as a "use anywhere" mobile phone system. The original developers of the system poured $5 billion into a 66-satellite system. But phones and needed accessories took up so much space that they required a special briefcase. The purchase price for a phone system was $3,000, and airtime fees were $7 per minute. At the same time, cellular phones—with more limited coverage but adequate for many customers—were selling for less than $100 and were much more "user friendly." Though the Iridium system was technologically brilliant, it was clear from its inception that customers would neither pay the high purchase price nor accept the high user fees. Approximately 50,000 customers purchased phone systems, but this was well below the volume required to sustain the business. The original owners sold the system for $25 million.[4]

Penetration Pricing

Penetration pricing is at the opposite end of the spectrum from skimming. **Penetration pricing** means charging a relatively low price for a product in order to reach the mass market. The low price is designed to capture a large share of a substantial market, resulting in lower production costs. If a marketing manager has made obtaining a large market share the firm's pricing objective, penetration pricing is a logical choice.

Penetration pricing does mean lower profit per unit, however. Therefore, to reach the break-even point, it requires a higher volume of sales than would a skimming policy. If reaching a high volume of sales takes a long time, then the recovery of product development costs will also be slow. As you might expect, penetration pricing tends to discourage competition.

Procter & Gamble examined the electric toothbrush market and noted that most electric brushes cost over $50. The company brought out the Crest SpinBrush that works on batteries and sells for just $5. It is now the nation's best-selling toothbrush, manual or electric, and has helped the Crest brand of products become P&G's twelfth billion-dollar brand.[5]

A penetration strategy tends to be effective in a price-sensitive market. Price should decline more rapidly when demand is elastic because the market can be expanded through a lower price. Also, price sensitivity and greater competitive pressure should lead to a lower

penetration pricing
A pricing policy whereby a firm charges a relatively low price for a product initially as a way to reach the mass market.

initial price and a relatively slow decline in the price later or to a stable low price.

Although Wal-Mart is associated with penetration pricing, other chains have done an excellent job of following this strategy as well. Dollar stores, those bare-bones, strip-mall chains that sell staples at cut-rate prices, are now the fastest-growing retailers in America. They've become an alternative for a growing legion of shoppers who find Wal-Mart a bit too pricey or a bit too hard to get to. Led by Dollar General, Family Dollar, and Dollar Tree, the sector adds about 1,500 stores per year. Wal-Mart usually opens its huge stores on the edge of town. Dollar chains can put their much smaller stores right in downtown neighborhoods, closer to where people live. Parking is usually a snap, and shoppers can be in and out in less time than it takes to hike across a jumbo Wal-Mart lot. And as their name implies, the dollar stores offer low prices, sometimes even beating Wal-Mart. "Wal-Mart competes on price and assortment," says David A. Perdue, Dollar General's chief executive. "We compete on price and convenience."[6]

Dollar stores cut costs to the bone to be competitive with Wal-Mart. Family Dollar, for instance, prints one advertising circular a year. The stores approach labor the same way: Dollar General and Family Dollar employ about four people per store. And all the chains rely on closeout and stock-overrun merchandise for a portion of sales.

If a firm has a low fixed cost structure and each sale provides a large contribution to those fixed costs, penetration pricing can boost sales and provide large increases in profits—but only if the market size grows or if competitors choose not to respond. Low prices can attract additional buyers to the market. The increased sales can justify production expansion or the adoption of new technologies, both of which can reduce costs. And, if firms have excess capacity, even low-priced business can provide incremental dollars toward fixed costs.

Penetration pricing can also be effective if an experience curve will cause costs per unit to drop significantly. The experience curve proposes that per-unit costs will go down as a firm's production experience increases. On average, for each doubling of production, a firm can expect per-unit costs to decline by roughly 20 percent. Cost declines can be significant in the early stages of production. Manufacturers that fail to take advantage of these effects will find themselves at a competitive cost disadvantage relative to others that are further along the curve.

The big advantage of penetration pricing is that it typically discourages or blocks competition from entering a market. The disadvantage is that penetration means gearing up for mass production to sell a large volume at a low price. What if the volume fails to materialize? The company will face huge losses from building or converting a factory to produce the failed product. Skimming, in contrast, lets a firm "stick its toe in the water" and see if limited demand exists at the high price. If not, the firm can simply lower the price. Skimming lets a company start out with a small production facility and expand it gradually as price falls and demand increases.

Penetration pricing can also prove disastrous for a prestige brand that adopts the strategy in an effort to gain market share and fails. When Omega—once a more prestigious brand than Rolex—was trying to improve the market share of its watches, it adopted a penetration pricing strategy that succeeded in destroying the watches' brand image by flooding the market with lower-priced products. Omega never gained sufficient share on its lower-priced/lower-image competitors to justify destroying its brand image and high-priced position with upscale buyers. Lacoste clothing experienced a similar outcome from a penetration pricing strategy.

Status Quo Pricing

The third basic price strategy a firm may choose is status quo pricing, also called meeting the competition or going rate pricing (see also Chapter 17). It means charging a price identical to or very close to the competition's price. JCPenney, for example, makes sure it is charging comparable prices by sending representatives to shop at Sears stores.

LO 1 Describe the procedure for setting the right price

Establish price goals → Estimate demand costs, and profits → Choose a price strategy → Skimming (high) $ or Status quo (same) $ or Penetration (low) $

PRICE high / low

Choose a price strategy → Fine-tune base price → Set price $x.yy → Evaluate results → Fine-tune base price

Although status quo pricing has the advantage of simplicity, its disadvantage is that the strategy may ignore demand or cost or both. If the firm is comparatively small, however, meeting the competition may be the safest route to long-term survival.

LO 2 The Legality and Ethics of Price Strategy

As we mentioned in Chapter 3, some pricing decisions are subject to government regulation. Before marketing managers establish any price strategy, they should know the laws that limit their decision making. Among the issues that fall into this category are unfair trade practices, price fixing, price discrimination, and predatory pricing.

UNFAIR TRADE PRACTICES

In over half the states, **unfair trade practice acts** put a floor under wholesale and retail prices. Selling below cost in these states is illegal. Wholesalers and retailers must usually take a certain minimum percentage markup on their combined merchandise cost and transportation cost. The most common markup figures are 6 percent at the retail level and 2 percent at the wholesale level. If a specific wholesaler or retailer can provide "conclusive proof" that operating costs are lower than the minimum required figure, lower prices may be allowed.

The intent of unfair trade practice acts is to protect small local firms from giants like Wal-Mart and Target, which operate very efficiently on razor-thin profit margins. State enforcement of unfair trade practice laws has generally been lax, however, partly because low prices benefit local consumers.

PRICE FIXING

Price fixing is an agreement between two or more firms on the price they will charge for a product. For instance, two or more executives from competing firms might meet to decide how much to charge for a product or to decide which of them will submit the lowest bid on a certain contract. Such practices are illegal under the Sherman Act and the Federal Trade Commission Act. Offenders have received fines and sometimes prison terms. Price fixing is one area where the law is quite clear, and the Justice Department's enforcement is vigorous.

In the past several years, the Justice Department has vigorously pursued price-fixing cases. ISK Japan, a Japanese manufacturer of a coating for videotape, was fined $5 million for its role in a conspiracy to fix the prices of and allocate customers for video magnetic iron oxide (MIO) particles in the United States. Gemstar–TV Guide International paid $5.67 million in civil penalties and agreed to certain restrictions to resolve federal charges that the company had fixed prices. Hoechst AG, an international chemical conglomerate based in Germany, was fined $12 million for participating in a conspiracy to

unfair trade practice acts
Laws that prohibit wholesalers and retailers from selling below cost.

price fixing
An agreement between two or more firms on the price they will charge for a product.

suppress competition in the world markets for an industrial chemical used in the production of various products, including pharmaceuticals, herbicides, and plastic additives.[7] Uniroyal recently agreed to pay a $50 million fine for fixing prices on a synthetic rubber called neoprene.[8] The largest single fine to date is the $500 million fine paid by F. Hoffman–LaRoche for price fixing in the vitamin industry.[9]

The Justice Department also investigated five global paint manufacturers, including DuPont, Sherwin-Williams, and PPG Industries in the United States, for price fixing in the automotive refinishing industry. Supposedly, the paint firms met in Europe to fix wholesale prices in the United States. Concurrently, the Justice Department had at least 25 other price-fixing investigations under way in several industries.

Price-fixing prosecution is not limited to huge, global competitors. In San Diego, two groups of anesthesiologists recently settled federal charges that they conspired to set prices for Sharp Grossmont Hospital.[10]

Most price-fixing cases focus on high prices charged to customers. A reverse form of price fixing occurs when powerful buyers force their suppliers' prices down. Recently, Maine blueberry growers alleged that four big processors conspired to push down the price they would pay for fresh wild berries. A state court jury agreed and awarded millions in damages. In South Carolina, International Paper Company faces a lawsuit alleging that it conspired with its timber buyers to depress softwood prices in several states. In Alabama and Pennsylvania, federal antitrust enforcers targeted insurance companies that imposed contracts forcing down fees charged by doctors and hospitals. The insurers abandoned the practice.[11]

PRICE DISCRIMINATION

The Robinson-Patman Act of 1936 prohibits any firm from selling to two or more different buyers, within a reasonably short time, commodities (not services) of like grade and quality at different prices where the result would be to substantially lessen competition. The act also makes it illegal for a seller to offer two buyers different supplementary services and for buyers to use their purchasing power to force sellers into granting discriminatory prices or services.

Six elements are therefore needed for a violation of the Robinson-Patman Act to occur:

- There must be price discrimination; that is, the seller must charge different prices to different customers for the same product.

- The transaction must occur in interstate commerce.

- The seller must discriminate by price among two or more purchasers; that is, the seller must make two or more actual sales within a reasonably short time.

- The products sold must be commodities or other tangible goods.

- The products sold must be of like grade and quality, not necessarily identical. If the goods are truly interchangeable and substitutable, then they are of like grade and quality.

- There must be significant competitive injury.

The Robinson-Patman Act provides three defenses for the seller charged with price discrimination (in each case the burden is on the defendant to prove the defense):

- *Cost:* A firm can charge different prices to different customers if the prices represent manufacturing or quantity discount savings.

- *Market conditions:* Price variations are justified if designed to meet fluid product or market conditions. Examples include the deterioration of perishable goods, the obsolescence of seasonal products, a distress sale under court order, and a legitimate going-out-of-business sale.

- *Competition:* A reduction in price may be necessary to stay even with the competition. Specifically, if a competitor undercuts the price quoted by a seller to a buyer, the law authorizes the seller to lower the price charged to the buyer for the product in question.

PREDATORY PRICING

predatory pricing
The practice of charging a very low price for a product with the intent of driving competitors out of business or out of a market.

Predatory pricing is the practice of charging a very low price for a product with the intent of driving competitors out of business or out of a market. Once competitors have been driven out, the firm raises its prices. This practice is illegal under the Sherman Act and the Federal Trade Commission Act. Proving predatory pricing is difficult and expensive, however. The Justice Department must demonstrate that the predator, the destructive company, explicitly tried to ruin a competitor and that the predatory price was below the predator's average variable cost.

Prosecutions for predatory pricing suffered a major setback when a federal judge threw out a predatory pricing suit filed by the Justice Department against American

REVIEW LEARNING OUTCOME

LO 2   Identify the legal and ethical constraints on pricing decisions

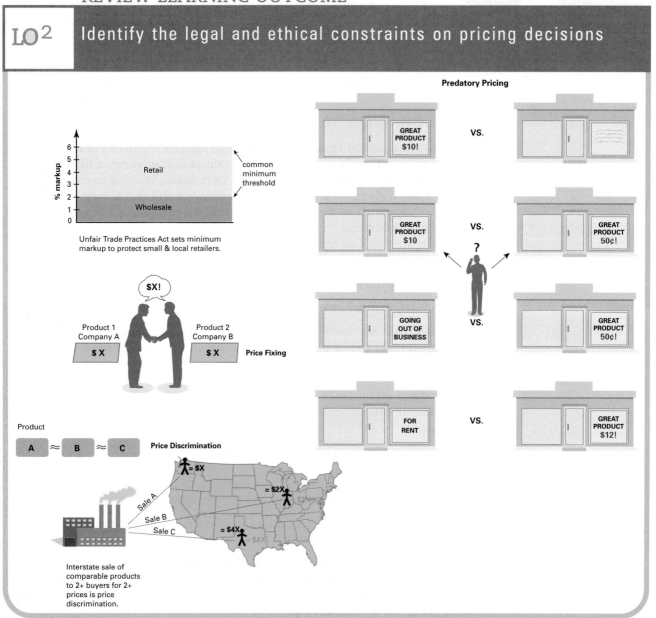

Unfair Trade Practices Act sets minimum markup to protect small & local retailers.

Price Fixing

Price Discrimination

Interstate sale of comparable products to 2+ buyers for 2+ prices is price discrimination.

Predatory Pricing

Airlines. Instead of using the traditional predatory pricing definition of pricing below average variable cost, the Justice Department had argued that the definition should be updated and that the test should be whether there was any business justification, other than driving away competitors, for American's aggressive pricing. Under that definition, the Justice Department attorneys thought they had a great case. Whenever a fledgling airline tried to get a toehold in the Dallas market, American would meet its fares and add flights. As soon as the rival retreated, American would jack its fares back up.

Under the average variable cost definition, however, the case would have been almost impossible to win. The reason is that like the high-tech industry, the airline industry has high fixed costs and low marginal costs. An airline's biggest expense is buying airplanes and labor. Once a flight is scheduled, the marginal cost of providing a seat for an additional passenger is almost zero. Thus, it is very difficult to prove that an airline is pricing below its average variable cost. The judge was not impressed by the Justice Department's argument, however, and stuck to the average variable cost definition of predatory pricing. The ruling has made proving predatory pricing very difficult.[12]

DHL, the package delivery company, has moved very aggressively into the U.S. market. It wants to increase its U.S. market share from less than 6 percent to 20 percent in five years. DHL is owned by Deutsche Post World Net, a $27 billion parent that has a postal monopoly in Germany and is the world's largest airfreight carrier. In the Americas alone, company revenue was over $7 billion in 2005. In Europe, DHL is ahead of FedEx and UPS.

"It's the German post office," said Dan McMackin, a UPS spokesman. "It has a government-sponsored monopoly on the delivery of letters. As it happens, the German Post Office has the second-highest stamp price in the world. The reason that's important to us and should be to consumers is it's like our post office, they cross-subsidize. In the private sector, it's illegal. They take some of the monies from the cost of stamps and then put them into . . . the rate they charge for you to ship a package. They can actually come into a market here and undercut a competitor by doing that."

FedEx and UPS asked the U.S. Department of Transportation to cancel DHL's registration, arguing that the post office profits amounted to predatory pricing in the United States. The department threw out the case, finding no evidence of "any unfair competition in the U.S. market by any of these DHL companies."[13]

LO3
Tactics for Fine-Tuning the Base Price

After managers understand both the legal and the marketing consequences of price strategies, they should set a base price, the general price level at which the company expects to sell the good or service. The general price level is correlated with the pricing policy: above the market (price skimming), at the market (status quo pricing), or below the market (penetration pricing). The final step, then, is to fine-tune the base price.

Fine-tuning techniques are short-run approaches that do not change the general price level. They do, however, result in changes within a general price level. These pricing tactics allow the firm to adjust for competition in certain markets, meet ever-changing government regulations, take advantage of unique demand situations, and meet promotional and positioning goals. Fine-tuning pricing tactics include various sorts of discounts, geographic pricing, and other pricing tactics.

DISCOUNTS, ALLOWANCES, REBATES, AND VALUE-BASED PRICING

base price
The general price level at which the company expects to sell the good or service.

A base price can be lowered using discounts and the related tactics of allowances, rebates, low or zero percent financing, and value-based pricing. Managers use the various forms of discounts to encourage customers to do what they would not ordinarily do, such as paying cash rather than using credit, taking delivery out of season, or performing

575

certain functions within a distribution channel.[14] The following are of the most common tactics:

- *Quantity discounts:* When buyers get a lower price for buying in multiple units or above a specified dollar amount, they are receiving a **quantity discount.** A **cumulative quantity discount** is a deduction from list price that applies to the buyer's total purchases made during a specific period; it is intended to encourage customer loyalty. In contrast, a **noncumulative quantity discount** is a deduction from list price that applies to a single order rather than to the total volume of orders placed during a certain period. It is intended to encourage orders in large quantities.

- *Cash discounts:* A **cash discount** is a price reduction offered to a consumer, an industrial user, or a marketing intermediary in return for prompt payment of a bill. Prompt payment saves the seller carrying charges and billing expenses and allows the seller to avoid bad debt.

- *Functional discounts:* When distribution channel intermediaries, such as wholesalers or retailers, perform a service or function for the manufacturer, they must be compensated. This compensation, typically a percentage discount from the base price, is called a **functional discount** (or **trade discount**). Functional discounts vary greatly from channel to channel, depending on the tasks performed by the intermediary.

- *Seasonal discounts:* A **seasonal discount** is a price reduction for buying merchandise out of season. It shifts the storage function to the purchaser. Seasonal discounts also enable manufacturers to maintain a steady production schedule year-round.

- *Promotional allowances:* A **promotional allowance** (also known as a **trade allowance**) is a payment to a dealer for promoting the manufacturer's products. It is both a pricing tool and a promotional device. As a pricing tool, a promotional allowance is like a functional discount. If, for example, a retailer runs an ad for a manufacturer's product, the manufacturer may pay half the cost. If a retailer sets up a special display, the manufacturer may include a certain quantity of free goods in the retailer's next order.[15]

- *Rebates:* A **rebate** is a cash refund given for the purchase of a product during a specific period. The advantage of a rebate over a simple price reduction for stimulating demand is that a rebate is a temporary inducement that can be taken away without altering the basic price structure. A manufacturer that uses a simple price reduction for a short time may meet resistance when trying to restore the price to its original, higher level.

- *Zero percent financing:* During the early and mid-2000s, new-car sales needed a boost. To get people back into automobile showrooms, manufacturers offered zero percent financing, which enabled purchasers to borrow money to pay for new cars without incurring an interest charge. The tactic created a huge increase in sales but not without cost to the manufacturers. A five-year interest-free car loan represented a cost of over $3,000 on a typical vehicle sold during the zero percent promotion. Automakers were still offering such incentives in 2006.

Value-Based Pricing

Value-based pricing, also called *value pricing,* is a pricing strategy that has grown out of the quality movement. Instead of figuring prices based on costs or competitors' prices, it starts with the customer, considers the competition, and then determines the appropriate price. The basic assumption is that the firm is customer driven, seeking to understand the attributes customers want in the goods and services they buy and the value of that bundle of attributes to customers. Because very few firms operate in a pure monopoly, however, a marketer using value-based pricing must also determine the value of

quantity discount
A price reduction offered to buyers buying in multiple units or above a specified dollar amount.

cumulative quantity discount
A deduction from list price that applies to the buyer's total purchases made during a specific period.

noncumulative quantity discount
A deduction from list price that applies to a single order rather than to the total volume of orders placed during a certain period.

cash discount
A price reduction offered to a consumer, an industrial user, or a marketing intermediary in return for prompt payment of a bill.

functional discount (trade discount)
A discount to wholesalers and retailers for performing channel functions.

seasonal discount
A price reduction for buying merchandise out of season.

promotional allowance (trade allowance)
A payment to a dealer for promoting the manufacturer's products.

rebate
A cash refund given for the purchase of a product during a specific period.

value-based pricing
Setting the price at a level that seems to the customer to be a good price compared to the prices of other options.

competitive offerings to customers. Customers determine the value of a product (not just its price) relative to the value of alternatives. In value-based pricing, therefore, the price of the product is set at a level that seems to the customer to be a good price compared with the prices of other options.

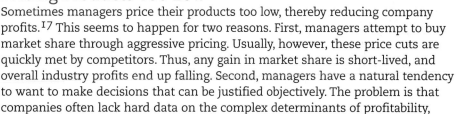

United Parcel Service
Go to UPS's Web site and do some quick cost comparison on sending the same package to a friend in town and to a friend out-of-state. Does the difference in cost surprise you? Do you think it is justified? Why or why not?

http://www.ups.com

Online

When two Wal-Mart supercenters and a rival regional grocery opened near a Kroger supermarket in Houston, the Kroger's sales dropped 10 percent. The store manager moved quickly to slash some prices and cut labor costs, for example, by buying ready-made cakes instead of baking them in-house and ordering precut salad-bar items from suppliers. Kroger employees used to stack displays by hand; now fruit and vegetables arrive stacked for display.

Such moves have helped Kroger cut worker-hours by 30 to 40 percent over the last four years and lower the prices of staples such as cereal, bread, milk, eggs, and disposable diapers. If Wal-Mart's supercenters continue to expand at their current pace, however, within this decade, more than three-quarters of the nation's Kroger's and Albertson's stores and more than half the Safeway outlets could be within ten miles of a Wal-Mart supercenter.

The fight for the minds of customers is already having an impact. Shoppers in competitive markets are seeing prices fall as Wal-Mart pushes rivals to match its value prices. Recently, a number of regional grocery chains have switched to value pricing. In the past, they offered weekly specials to attract shoppers and then made up the lost profit by keeping nonsale prices substantially higher. Now, stores like Costco and Wal-Mart have conditioned consumers to expect inexpensive goods every day.

California supermarket chain Raley's recently reduced the daily price on 7,000 items. Giant Eagle, Inc., of Pennsylvania has cut prices on 4,300 items, and Piggly Wiggly, operator of Fresh Brands, Inc., of Wisconsin, cut prices on 4,000 goods. Supermarkets generally carry about 30,000 items. Wegmans Food Markets, Inc., which serves parts of New York, New Jersey, and Virginia, has cut the prices of 10,000 items.[16]

Pricing Products Too Low

Sometimes managers price their products too low, thereby reducing company profits.[17] This seems to happen for two reasons. First, managers attempt to buy market share through aggressive pricing. Usually, however, these price cuts are quickly met by competitors. Thus, any gain in market share is short-lived, and overall industry profits end up falling. Second, managers have a natural tendency to want to make decisions that can be justified objectively. The problem is that companies often lack hard data on the complex determinants of profitability, such as the relationship between price changes and sales volumes, the link between demand levels and costs, and the likely responses of competitors to price changes. In contrast, companies usually have rich, unambiguous information on costs, sales, market share, and competitors' prices. As a result, managers tend to make pricing decisions based on current costs, projected short-term share gains, or current competitor prices rather than on long-term profitability.

The problem of "underpricing" can be solved by linking information about price, cost, and demand within the same decision support system. The demand data can be developed via marketing research. This will enable managers to get the hard data they need to calculate the effects of pricing decisions on profitability.

GEOGRAPHIC PRICING

Because many sellers ship their wares to a nationwide or even a worldwide market, the cost of freight can greatly affect the total cost of a product. Sellers may use several different geographic pricing tactics to moderate the impact of freight costs on distant customers. The following methods of geographic pricing are the most common:

FOB origin pricing
A price tactic that requires the buyer to absorb the freight costs from the shipping point ("free on board").

uniform delivered pricing
A price tactic in which the seller pays the actual freight charges and bills every purchaser an identical, flat freight charge.

zone pricing
A modification of uniform delivered pricing that divides the United States (or the total market) into segments or zones and charges a flat freight rate to all customers in a given zone.

freight absorption pricing
A price tactic in which the seller pays all or part of the actual freight charges and does not pass them on to the buyer.

- *FOB origin pricing:* **FOB origin pricing,** also called *FOB factory* or *FOB shipping point*, is a price tactic that requires the buyer to absorb the freight costs from the shipping point ("free on board"). The farther buyers are from sellers, the more they pay, because transportation costs generally increase with the distance merchandise is shipped.

- *Uniform delivered pricing:* If the marketing manager wants total costs, including freight, to be equal for all purchasers of identical products, the firm will adopt uniform delivered pricing, or "postage stamp" pricing. With **uniform delivered pricing,** the seller pays the actual freight charges and bills every purchaser an identical, flat freight charge. L.L. Bean uses uniform delivered pricing: if you purchase something from its catalog, you will be charged a flat freight rate.

- *Zone pricing:* A marketing manager who wants to equalize total costs among buyers within large geographic areas—but not necessarily all of the seller's market area—may modify the base price with a zone-pricing tactic. **Zone pricing** is a modification of uniform delivered pricing. Rather than using a uniform freight rate for the entire United States (or its total market), the firm divides it into segments or zones and charges a flat freight rate to all customers in a given zone. The U.S. Postal Service's parcel post rate structure is probably the best-known zone-pricing system in the country. Zone pricing can also have a darker side, as explained in this chapter's "Ethics in Marketing" box.

- *Freight absorption pricing:* In **freight absorption pricing,** the seller pays all or part of the actual freight charges and does not pass them on to the buyer. The man-

ETHICS in Marketing

Same Gasoline, Different Price

ETHICS

On a recent Wednesday, 72-year-old veterinarian Charles Hendricks filled up his Mercury Grand Marquis at a Chevron station in west Anaheim. On the other end of town, 22-year-old sandwich store manager Ryan Ketchum gassed up his Nissan Sentra at a Chevron station in Anaheim Hills. Both men bought regular gasoline. Both pumped the gas themselves. But there was one important difference: Hendricks paid $2.89 a gallon, whereas Ketchum paid $3.09—20 cents more a gallon for the same Chevron gas.

Such price variations may seem odd, but they are not unique to Anaheim. On any given day, in any major U.S. city, a single brand of gasoline will sell for a wide range of prices even when the cost to make and deliver the fuel is the same.

The primary culprit is zone pricing, a secret and pervasive oil company strategy to boost profits by charging dealers different amounts for fuel based on traffic volume, station amenities, nearby household incomes, the strength of competitors, and other factors. It's a controversial strategy, but the courts have thus far deemed it legal, and the Federal Trade Commission recently said the effect on consumers was ambiguous because some customers got hurt by higher prices while others benefited from lower ones.

To be sure, other industries vary prices by area too. Supermarkets, for instance, price the same brand of bread or cheese differently in different neighborhoods. But gasoline price patterns provoke a response that bread can't match, partly because other commodities don't fluctuate as wildly as gasoline does and their prices aren't posted by the side of the road.

Oil companies say the practice allows them to adapt to local market conditions by, for example, lowering prices to dealers who face stiff competition from high-volume sellers such as Costco Wholesale Corporation. Oil companies in California have that kind of control because they sell and deliver their fuel directly to most of the state's branded stations—those that sell gasoline under brand names such as Chevron, Arco, Shell, and 76. The refiners charge those dealers a wholesale price for the fuel, known as the dealer tank wagon price, based mostly on a carefully delineated map of price zones that have nothing to do with differences in costs.

The strategy is not unique to California, but it is especially powerful in that state because the five largest refiners, as sole suppliers to about 70 percent of the retail market, can readily influence pump prices by changing how much the dealers pay for fuel. Nationwide, refiners directly supply 35 percent of gasoline retailers, according to the Energy Department. In California, branded dealers are bound by long-term contracts that require them to buy fuel from the refiner at prices that are not negotiable. In other markets, refiners have less retail control because there are more unbranded competitors to challenge their pricing moves and because most branded stations can shop for fuel and buy through intermediaries instead of directly from the oil companies.[18]

A member of a consumer action group has said, "Zone pricing, on paper, sounds reasonable; in practice, its despicable!" What does this mean? Do you agree? The Western States Petroleum Association says, "It is a way for companies to price fairly in different areas." Do you agree? Do you think that the federal government should outlaw this type of zone pricing? Why?

ager may use this tactic in intensely competitive areas or as a way to break into new market areas.

- *Basing-point pricing:* With **basing-point pricing,** the seller designates a location as a basing point and charges all buyers the freight cost from that point, regardless of the city from which the goods are shipped. Thanks to several adverse court rulings, basing-point pricing has waned in popularity. Freight fees charged when none were actually incurred, called *phantom freight,* have been declared illegal.

OTHER PRICING TACTICS

Unlike geographic pricing, other pricing tactics are unique and defy neat categorization. Thus, we simply call this group "other." Managers use these tactics for various reasons—for example, to stimulate demand for specific products, to increase store patronage, and to offer a wider variety of merchandise at a specific price point. "Other" pricing tactics include a single-price tactic, flexible pricing, professional services pricing, price lining, leader pricing, bait pricing, odd–even pricing, price bundling, and two-part pricing. A brief overview of each of these tactics follows, along with a manager's reasons for using that tactic or a combination of tactics to change the base price.

Single-Price Tactic

A merchant using a **single-price tactic** offers all goods and services at the same price (or perhaps two or three prices). Retailers using this tactic include One Price Clothing Stores, Dre$$ to the Nine$, Your $10 Store, and Fashions $9.99. One Price Clothing Stores, for example, tend to be small, about 3,000 square feet. Their goal is to offer merchandise that would sell for at least $15 to $18 in other stores. The stores carry pants, shirts, blouses, sweaters, and shorts for juniors, misses, and large-sized women. The stores do not feature any seconds or irregular items, and everything is sold for $6.

Single-price selling removes price comparisons from the buyer's decision-making process. The consumer just looks for suitability and the highest perceived quality. The retailer enjoys the benefits of a simplified pricing system and minimal clerical errors. However, continually rising costs are a headache for retailers following this strategy. In times of inflation, they must frequently raise the selling price.

© AP/WIDE WORLD PHOTOS

KeepMedia is a Web site that offers consumers unlimited access to a database of magazine articles for a flat monthly rate of $4.95. In addition to using a single-price tactic, KeepMedia's pricing strategy represents penetration pricing in a market where online articles regularly cost around $3 per article. Pictured here is KeepMedia Chairman, Louis Borders.

basing-point pricing
A price tactic that charges freight from a given (basing) point, regardless of the city from which the goods are shipped

single-price tactic
A price tactic that offers all goods and services at the same price (or perhaps two or three prices).

flexible pricing (variable pricing)
A price tactic in which different customers pay different prices for essentially the same merchandise bought in equal quantities.

Flexible Pricing

Flexible pricing (or **variable pricing**) means that different customers pay different prices for essentially the same merchandise bought in equal quantities. This tactic is often found in the sale of shopping goods, specialty merchandise, and most industrial goods except supply items. Car dealers, many appliance retailers, and manufacturers of industrial installations, accessories, and component parts commonly follow the practice. It allows the seller to adjust for competition by meeting another seller's price. Thus, a marketing manager with a status quo pricing objective might readily adopt the tactic. Flexible pricing also enables the seller to close a sale with price-conscious consumers. If buyers show promise of becoming large-volume shoppers, flexible pricing can be used to lure their business.

The obvious disadvantages of flexible pricing are the lack of consistent profit margins, the potential ill will of high-paying purchasers, the tendency for salespeople to automatically lower the price to make a sale, and the possibility of a price war among sellers. The disadvantages of flexible pricing have led the automobile industry to experiment with one price for all buyers. General Motors has used a one-price tactic for some of its models, including the Saturn and the Buick Regal.

Professional Services Pricing

Professional services pricing is used by people with lengthy experience, training, and often certification by a licensing board—for example, lawyers, physicians, and family counselors. Professionals sometimes charge customers at an hourly rate, but sometimes fees are based on the solution of a problem or performance of an act (such as an eye examination) rather than on the actual time involved. A surgeon may perform a heart operation and charge a flat fee of $5,000. The operation itself may require only four hours, resulting in a hefty $1,250 hourly rate. The physician justifies the fee because of the lengthy education and internship required to learn the complex procedures of a heart operation. Lawyers also sometimes use flat-rate pricing, such as $500 for completing a divorce and $50 for handling a traffic ticket.

Those who use professional pricing have an ethical responsibility not to overcharge a customer. Because demand is sometimes highly inelastic, such as when a person requires heart surgery or a daily insulin shot to survive, there may be a temptation to charge "all the traffic will bear."[19]

Price Lining

When a seller establishes a series of prices for a type of merchandise, it creates a price line. **Price lining** is the practice of offering a product line with several items at specific price points. For example, Hon, an office furniture manufacturer, may offer its four-drawer file cabinets at $125, $250, and $400. The Limited may offer women's dresses at $40, $70, and $100, with no merchandise marked at prices between those figures. Instead of a normal demand curve running from $40 to $100, The Limited has three demand points (prices). Theoretically, the "curve" exists only because people would buy goods at the in-between prices if it were possible to do so. For example, a number of dresses could be sold at $60, but no sales will occur at that price because $60 is not part of the price line.

Price lining reduces confusion for both the salesperson and the consumer. The buyer may be offered a wider variety of merchandise at each established price. Price lines may also enable a seller to reach several market segments. For buyers, the question of price may be quite simple: all they have to do is find a suitable product at the predetermined price. Moreover, price lining is a valuable tactic for the marketing manager, because the firm may be able to carry a smaller total inventory than it could without price lines. The results may include fewer markdowns, simplified purchasing, and lower inventory carrying charges.

Price lines also present drawbacks, especially if costs are continually rising. Sellers can offset rising costs in three ways. First, they can begin stocking lower-quality merchandise at each price point. Second, sellers can change the prices, although frequent price line changes confuse buyers. Third, sellers can accept lower profit margins and hold quality and prices constant. This third alternative has short-run benefits, but its long-run handicaps may drive sellers out of business.

Leader Pricing

Leader pricing (or **loss-leader pricing**) is an attempt by the marketing manager to attract customers by selling a product near or even below cost in the hope that shoppers will buy other items once they are in the store. This type of pricing appears weekly in the newspaper advertising of supermarkets, specialty stores, and department stores. Leader pricing is normally used on well-known items that consumers can easily recognize as bargains at the special price. The goal is not necessarily to sell large quantities of leader items, but to try to appeal to customers who might shop elsewhere.[20]

Leader pricing is not limited to products. Health clubs offer a one-month free trial as a loss leader. Lawyers give a free initial consultation. And restaurants distribute two-for-one coupons and "welcome to the neighborhood" free meal coupons.

Bait Pricing

In contrast to leader pricing, which is a genuine attempt to give the consumer a reduced price, bait pricing is deceptive. **Bait pricing** tries to get the consumer into a store through false or misleading price advertising and then uses high-pressure selling to persuade the consumer to buy more expensive merchandise. You may have seen this ad or a similar one:

> REPOSSESSED . . . Singer slant-needle sewing machine . . . take over 8 payments of $5.10 per month . . . ABC Sewing Center.

This is bait. When a customer goes in to see the machine, a salesperson says that it has just been sold or else shows the prospective buyer a piece of junk no one would buy. Then the salesperson says, "But I've got a really good deal on this fine new model." This is the switch that may cause a susceptible consumer to walk out with a $400 machine. The Federal Trade Commission considers bait pricing a deceptive act and has banned its use in interstate commerce. Most states also ban bait pricing, but sometimes enforcement is lax.

Odd–Even Pricing

Odd–even pricing (or **psychological pricing**) means pricing at odd-numbered prices to connote a bargain and pricing at even-numbered prices to imply quality. For years, many retailers have priced their products in odd numbers—for example, $99.95 or $49.95—to make consumers feel they are paying a lower price for the product.

Contrary to popular belief that the ".99" part of a price such as $19.99 makes the difference in purchasing behavior, new research finds that it's the left digits—the numbers that come before the .99—that determine whether consumers perceive a penny reduction as a bargain. Research participants were shown product prices that ended either in nine (e.g., $19.99 and $23.59) or in zero (e.g., $20.00 and $23.60). In half the cases, when the price ending changed from zero to nine, the left digit changed and the price became lower (e.g., $20.00 changed to $19.99). For the other half, the left digit stayed the same (e.g., $23.60 changed to $23.59). When the left digit changed, participants thought the price with the nine ending (e.g., $19.99) was much cheaper than the price with the zero ending (e.g., $20.00). When the left digit did not change, however, participants perceived the nine- and the zero-ending prices (e.g., $23.60 versus $23.59) as essentially the same. These results demonstrate that the "left-digit effect," changing the left digits to a lower number (20 to 19) rather than the right digits (.60 to .59), is what affected the participants' perception of the price.[21]

Even-numbered pricing is sometimes used to denote quality. Examples include a fine perfume at $100 a bottle, a good watch at $500, or a mink coat at $3,000. The demand curve for such items would also be sawtoothed, except that the outside edges would represent even-numbered prices and, therefore, elastic demand.

Price Bundling

Price bundling is marketing two or more products in a single package for a special price. Examples include the sale of maintenance contracts with computer hardware and other office equipment, packages of stereo equipment, packages of options on cars, weekend hotel packages that include a room and several meals, and airline vacation packages. Microsoft offers "suites" of software that bundle spreadsheets, word processing, graphics, electronic mail, Internet access, and groupware for networks of microcomputers. Price bundling can stimulate demand for the bundled items if the target market perceives the price as a good value.

Services like hotels and airlines sell a perishable commodity (hotel rooms and airline seats) with relatively constant fixed costs. Bundling can be an important income stream for these businesses because the variable cost tends to be

Price bundling can encourage consumers to buy more than they may have originally planned to purchase. This Virgin Megastore advertisement offers deals on CDs purchased together, which customers may perceive as getting more for their money.

low—for instance, the cost of cleaning a hotel room or putting one more passenger on an airplane. Therefore, most of the revenue can help cover fixed costs and generate profits.

The automobile industry has a different motive for bundling. People buy cars only every three to five years. Thus, selling options is a somewhat rare opportunity for the car dealer. Price bundling can help the dealer sell a maximum number of options.

Bundling has also been used in the telecommunications industry. Companies offer local service, long distance, DSL Internet service, wireless, and even cable TV in various menus of bundling. Such bundling is not necessarily consumer focused. Telecom companies use bundling as a way to protect their market share and fight off competition by locking customers into a group of services. Comparison shopping may be difficult for consumers since they may not be able to determine how much they are really paying for each component of the bundle.

A related price tactic is **unbundling,** or reducing the bundle of services that comes with the basic product. Rather than raise the price of hotel rooms, some hotel chains have started charging registered guests for parking. To help hold the line on costs, some stores require customers to pay for gift wrapping.

Clearly, price bundling—for example, a theater series pass or a vacation package that combines airfare, lodging, and meals—can influence consumers' purchase behavior. But what about the decision to consume a particular bundled product or service, such as eating the daily lunch buffet or attending a particular theater performance? Some of the latest research has focused on how people consume certain bundled products or services. According to this research, the key to consumption behavior is how closely consumers can link the costs and benefits of the exchange.[22] In complex transactions like a holiday package, it may be unclear which costs are paying for which benefits. In such cases, consumers tend to mentally downplay their up-front costs for the bundled product, so they may be more likely to forgo a benefit that's part of the bundle, like a free dinner or a play.

Similarly, when people buy season tickets to a concert series, sporting event, or other activity, the sunk costs (price of the bundle) and the pending benefit (going to see an event) become decoupled. This reduces the likelihood of consumption of the event over time. For example, researchers found that theatergoers who purchased tickets to four plays were only 84 percent likely to use their first-play tickets and only 78 percent likely to use any given ticket across the four plays.[23] In contrast, theatergoers who purchased tickets to a single play were almost certain to use those tickets. This is consistent with the idea that in a one-to-one transaction (i.e., one payment, one benefit), the costs and benefits of that transaction are tightly coupled, resulting in strong sunk cost pressure to consume the pending benefit. In other words, "I bought this ticket, now I've got to use it."

In practice, these findings mean that a theater manager might expect a no-show rate of 20 percent when the percentage of season ticket holders is high, but a no-show rate of only 5 percent when the percentage of season ticket holders is low. With a high number of season ticket holders, a manager could oversell performances and maximize the revenue for the theater. Airlines routinely overbook in anticipation of a predictable percentage of no-shows.

The physical format of the transaction also figures in. A ski lift pass in the form of a booklet of tickets strengthens the cost-benefit link for consumers, whereas a single pass for multiple ski lifts weakens that link. Thus, the skier with a booklet of tickets is likely to use the ski lift more often than the skier who has just one pass, even though both paid the same amount at the outset.

Though price bundling of services can result in a lower rate of total consumption of that service, the same is not necessarily true for products. Consider the purchase of an expensive bottle of wine, which can be inventoried until needed. When the wine is purchased as a single unit, its cost and eventual benefit are tightly coupled. As a result, the cost of the wine will be quite important, and a person will likely reserve that wine for a special occasion. When purchased as part of a bundle (e.g., as part of a case of wine), however, the cost and benefit of that individual bottle of wine will likely become decoupled,

unbundling
Reducing the bundle of services that comes with the basic product.

reducing the impact of the cost on eventual consumption. As a result, a person will likely find the wine appropriate for many more (not-so-special) occasions. Thus, in contrast to the price bundling of services, the price bundling of physical goods could lead to an increase in product consumption.

Two-Part Pricing

Two-part pricing means establishing two separate charges to consume a single good or service. Tennis clubs and health clubs charge a membership fee and a flat fee each time a person uses certain equipment or facilities. In other cases they charge a base rate for a certain level of usage, such as ten racquetball games per month, and a surcharge for anything over that amount.

Consumers sometimes prefer two-part pricing because they are uncertain about the number and the types of activities they might use at places like an amusement park. Also, the people who use a service most often pay a higher total price. Two-part pricing can increase a seller's revenue by attracting consumers who would not pay a high fee even for unlimited use. For example, a health club might be able to sell only 100 memberships at $700 annually with unlimited use of facilities, for total revenue of $70,000. However, perhaps it could sell 900 memberships at $200 with a guarantee of using the racquetball courts ten times a month. Every use over ten would require the member to pay a $5 fee. Thus, membership revenue would provide a base of $180,000, with some additional usage fees throughout the year.

Princess Cruises
Carnival Cruises

How up-front are companies about their pricing penalties? Compare what you find out at Princess Cruises' Web page (type "penalties" into the search box) with what you find on Carnival Cruises' page. From a marketing standpoint, do you think it is better to hide penalties in the fine print or to clearly let the customer know in advance?

http://www.princesscruises.com
http://www.carnival.com

Online

two-part pricing
A price tactic that charges two separate amounts to consume a single good or service.

consumer penalty
An extra fee paid by the consumer for violating the terms of the purchase agreement.

CONSUMER PENALTIES

More and more businesses are adopting **consumer penalties**—extra fees paid by consumers for violating the terms of a purchase agreement (see Exhibit 18.2).

Businesses impose consumer penalties for two reasons: They will allegedly (1) suffer an irrevocable revenue loss and/or (2) incur significant additional transaction costs should customers be unable or unwilling to complete their purchase obligations. For the company, these customer payments are part of doing business in a highly competitive marketplace. With profit margins in many companies increasingly coming under pressure, organizations are looking to stem losses resulting from customers not meeting their obligations. However, the perceived unfairness of a penalty may affect some consumers' willingness to patronize a business in the future.

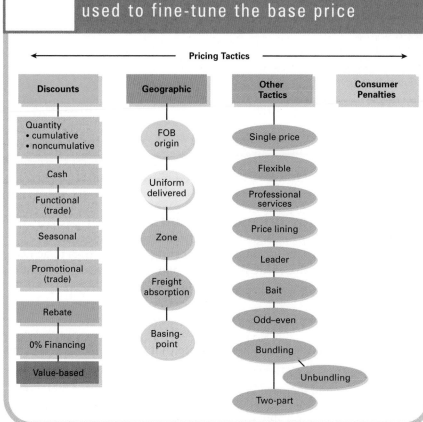

REVIEW LEARNING OUTCOME

LO3 Explain how discounts, geographic pricing, and other pricing tactics can be used to fine-tune the base price

Pricing Tactics

Discounts	Geographic	Other Tactics	Consumer Penalties
Quantity • cumulative • noncumulative	FOB origin	Single price	
Cash	Uniform delivered	Flexible	
Functional (trade)	Zone	Professional services	
Seasonal	Freight absorption	Price lining	
Promotional (trade)	Basing-point	Leader	
Rebate		Bait	
0% Financing		Odd–even	
Value-based		Bundling	
		Unbundling	
		Two-part	

Exhibit 18.2
Common Consumer Penalties

1. Airlines

- Some airlines charge a penalty of $100 for changing reservations on discount tickets.

2. Automobiles

- Penalties are imposed for early terminations of car leases. In some cases, deposits on canceled leases can be subject to penalties.
- Car owners in England pay penalties, administration fees, and commissions if they cancel an insurance policy early.

3. Banks

- Penalties are often associated with early withdrawal of certificates of deposit.
- Some banks charge penalties for too many withdrawals in a month.
- Some have monthly penalties of $5 to $10 if a client's balance falls below a minimum level.
- Banks can charge late fees, in addition to interest, for tardy payments.

4. Car Rentals

- Rental companies often have $25 to $100 penalties for no-shows for specialty vehicles. Budget, National, and Dollar/Thrifty are experimenting with no-show fees on all rentals.

5. Child Day Care

- Many day-care centers charge a penalty of up to $5 a minute when parents are late in picking up their children.

6. Cellular Phones

- Companies have cancellation penalties, often in the small print on the back of a contract, that can run as high as $525.

7. Credit and Debit Cards

- Some vendors now charge late fees (beyond normal interest). Lenders collect about $2 billion in late charges each year.
- GE Rewards MasterCard charges $25 a year for those who pay their bill each month, in full, on time. Advanta credit card company may charge $25 for six-month inactivity on an account and $25 to close an account.

8. Cruises

- If a cruise is sailing, even though there are hurricane warnings, some cruise lines will assess penalties if a passenger cancels.
- Even trip cancellation insurance will not ensure a refund if the traveler has embarked on the trip.
- Britain is trying to crack down on executive cancellation penalties on package holidays.
- The *Carnival Paradise* will disembark passengers found smoking.

9. Hotels

- Some hotels require 72 hours' cancellation notice, or the client must pay a penalty of one day's room cost.
- Most hotels have high charges for using in-room long-distance service.
- Hilton, Hyatt, and Westin have early departure fees ranging from $25 to $50.

10. Restaurants

- Some now charge up to $50 per person for no-show parties.

11. Retail Stores

- Circuit City and Best Buy are leading others in charging a 15 percent restocking fee on some items. A restocking fee is for putting a returned item back in inventory.

12. Trains

- Amtrak has a $20 penalty for a returned ticket and charges the same fee for changing a ticket.

13. Universities

- Universities will give only a partial tuition refund if a student becomes ill after a course begins.

SOURCE: Eugene Fram and Michael McCarthy, "The True Price of Penalties," *Marketing Management,* Fall 1999, 51.

LO⁴
Product Line Pricing

Product line pricing is setting prices for an entire line of products. Compared to setting the right price on a single product, product line pricing encompasses broader concerns. In product line pricing, the marketing manager tries to achieve maximum profits or other goals for the entire line rather than for a single component of the line.

RELATIONSHIPS AMONG PRODUCTS

The manager must first determine the type of relationship that exists among the various products in the line:

product line pricing
Setting prices for an entire line of products.

- If items are *complementary*, an increase in the sale of one good causes an increase in demand for the complementary product, and vice versa. For example, the sale of ski poles depends on the demand for skis, making these two items complementary.

- Two products in a line can also be *substitutes* for each other. If buyers buy one item in the line, they are less likely to buy a second item in the line. For example, if someone goes to an automotive supply store and buys paste Turtle Wax for a car, it is very unlikely that he or she will buy liquid Turtle Wax in the near future.

Beauty.com
Does Beauty.com use a product line pricing strategy? Choose a brand and view the product list and pricing sheet. What evidence do you see of product line pricing? Of other pricing strategies?

http://www.beauty.com

Online

- A *neutral* relationship can also exist between two products. In other words, demand for one of the products is unrelated to demand for the other. For instance, Ralston Purina sells chicken feed and Wheat Chex, but the sale of one of these products has no known impact on demand for the other.

JOINT COSTS

Joint costs are costs that are shared in the manufacturing and marketing of several products in a product line. These costs pose a unique problem in product pricing. In oil refining, for example, fuel oil, gasoline, kerosene, naphtha, paraffin, and lubricating oils are all derived from a common production process. Another example is the production of compact discs that combine photos and music.

Any assignment of joint costs must be somewhat subjective because costs are actually shared. Suppose a company produces two products, X and Y, in a common production process, with joint costs allocated on a weight basis. Product X weighs 1,000 pounds, and product Y weighs 500 pounds. Thus, costs are allocated on the basis of $2 for X for every $1 for Y. Gross margins (sales less the cost of goods sold) might then be as follows:

	Product X	Product Y	Total
Sales	$20,000	$6,000	$26,000
Less: cost of goods sold	15,000	7,500	22,500
Gross margin	$ 5,000	($1,500)	$ 3,500

This statement reveals a loss of $1,500 on product Y. Is that important? Yes, any loss is important. However, the firm must realize that overall it earned a $3,500 profit on the two items in the line. Also, weight may not be the right way to allocate the joint costs. Instead, the firm might use other bases, including market value or quantity sold.

REVIEW LEARNING OUTCOME

LO4 Discuss product line pricing

Products

A ● A   Complementary

A ● A   Substitute

A ● A   Neutral

Joint Costs

Raw Material   Production → Product A / Product B / Product C

Cost of processing divided among products A, B, & C = joint costs

joint costs
Costs that are shared in the manufacturing and marketing of several products in a product line.

Pricing during Difficult Economic Times

Pricing is always an important aspect of marketing, but it is especially crucial in times of inflation and recession. The firm that does not adjust to economic trends may lose ground that it can never make up.

INFLATION

When the economy is characterized by high inflation, special pricing tactics are often necessary. They can be subdivided into cost-oriented and demand-oriented tactics.

Cost-Oriented Tactics

One popular cost-oriented tactic is *culling products with a low profit margin* from the product line. However, this tactic may backfire for three reasons:

- A high volume of sales on an item with a low profit margin may still make the item highly profitable.

- Eliminating a product from a product line may reduce economies of scale, thereby lowering the margins on other items.

- Eliminating the product may affect the price-quality image of the entire line.

Another popular cost-oriented tactic is **delayed-quotation pricing,** which is used for industrial installations and many accessory items. Price is not set on the product until the item is either finished or delivered. Long production lead times force many firms to adopt this policy during periods of inflation. Builders of nuclear power plants, ships, airports, and office towers sometimes use delayed-quotation tactics.

Escalator pricing is similar to delayed-quotation pricing in that the final selling price reflects cost increases incurred between the time an order is placed and the time delivery is made. An escalator clause allows for price increases (usually across the board) based on the cost of living index or some other formula. As with any price increase, management's ability to implement such a policy is based on inelastic demand for the product.

About a third of all industrial product manufacturers now use escalator clauses. Many companies do not apply the clause in every sale, however. Often it is used only for extremely complex products that take a long time to produce or with new customers.

Another tactic growing in popularity is to hold prices constant but add new fees. Take the telecommunications industry, for instance. There are setup fees, change-of-service fees, service-termination fees, directory-assistance fees, regulatory assessment fees, number-portability fees, and cable hookup and equipment fees. Telecom and cable companies have been adding on numerous extra charges to boost revenues and cover expenses. All told, fees add 20 percent to the cost of wireless service, 15 percent to the cost of long distance, and at least 5 percent to cable and satellite service.[24] Financial services firms, airlines, and the travel industry are also notorious for adding on fees. American Airlines, for example, recently added a $250 fee (each way) to use your miles to upgrade to the next class of service on travel to Europe.

Any cost-oriented pricing policy that tries to maintain a fixed gross margin under all conditions can lead to a vicious cycle. For example, a price increase will result in decreased demand, which in turn increases production costs (because of lost economies of scale). Increased production costs require a further price increase, leading to further diminished demand, and so on.

Demand-Oriented Tactics

Demand-oriented pricing tactics use price to reflect changing patterns of demand caused by inflation or high interest rates. Cost changes are considered, of course, but mostly in the context of how increased prices will affect demand.

delayed-quotation pricing
A price tactic used for industrial installations and many accessory items, in which a firm price is not set until the item is either finished or delivered.

escalator pricing
A price tactic in which the final selling price reflects cost increases incurred between the time the order is placed and the time delivery is made.

© BONNIE JACOBS/ISTOCKPHOTO INTERNATIONAL INC.

Price shading is the use of discounts by salespeople to increase demand for one or more products in a line. Often shading becomes habitual and is done routinely without much forethought. Ducommun, a metals producer, is among the major companies that have succeeded in eliminating the practice. Ducommun has told its salespeople, "We want no deviation from book price" unless authorized by management.

To make the demand for a good or service more inelastic and to create buyer dependency, a company can use several strategies:

- *Cultivate selected demand:* Marketing managers can target prosperous customers who will pay extra for convenience or service. Neiman Marcus, for example, stresses quality. As a result, the luxury retailer is more lenient with suppliers and their price increases than is Dollar's Stores, a discounter. In cultivating close relationships with affluent organizational customers, marketing managers should avoid putting themselves at the mercy of a dominant firm. They can more easily raise prices when an account is readily replaceable. Finally, in companies where engineers exert more influence than purchasing departments do, performance is favored over price. Often a preferred vendor's pricing range expands if other suppliers prove technically unsatisfactory.

- *Create unique offerings:* Marketing managers should study buyers' needs. If the seller can design distinctive goods or services uniquely fitting buyers' activities, equipment, and procedures, a mutually beneficial relationship will evolve. Buyers would incur high changeover costs in switching to another supplier. By satisfying targeted buyers in a superior way, marketing managers can make them dependent. Cereal manufacturers have skirted around passing on costs by marketing unique value-added or multi-ingredient cereals, increasing the perceived quality of cereals and allowing companies to raise prices. These cereals include General Mills' Basic 4, Clusters, and Oatmeal Crisp; Post's Banana Nut Crunch and Blueberry Morning; and Kellogg's Mueslix, Nutri-Grain, and Temptations.

- *Change the package design:* Another way companies pass on higher costs is to shrink product sizes but keep prices the same. Scott Paper Company reduced the number of sheets in the smallest roll of Scott Clean paper towels from 96 to 60 and actually lowered the price by 10 cents a roll. The increases in costs for paper towels were tied to a 50 to 60 percent increase in the cost of pulp paper. The company also changed the names of the sizes to de-emphasize the magnitude of the rolls.

- *Heighten buyer dependence:* Owens-Corning Fiberglass supplies an integrated insulation service (from feasibility studies to installation) that includes commercial and scientific training for distributors and seminars for end users. This practice freezes out competition and supports higher prices.

Kellogg is no stranger to creating unique offerings to stimulate demand. It has extended many of its brands by creating cereal bars based on popular boxed cereals, and it has created new, boxed cereals designed to appeal to a variety of markets. One new cereal is Smorz. To create demand for Smorz, Kellogg hosted a summer kickoff event with one hundred third-graders, who participated in a Smores-making contest.

RECESSION

A recession is a period of reduced economic activity. Reduced demand for goods and services, along with higher rates of unemployment, is a common trait of a recession. Yet astute marketers can often find opportunity during recessions. A recession is an excellent time to build market share because competitors are struggling to make ends meet.

Two effective pricing tactics to hold or build market share during a recession are value-based pricing and bundling. *Value-based pricing,* discussed earlier in the chapter, stresses to customers that they are getting a good value for their money. Charles of the Ritz, usually known for its pricey products, introduced the Express Bar during a recession. A collection of affordable cosmetics and skin treatment products, the Express Bar sold alongside regular Ritz products in department stores. Although lower-priced products offer lower profit margins, Ritz found that increases in volume can offset slimmer margins. For example, the company found that consumers will buy two or three Express Bar lipsticks at a time.

Bundling or *unbundling* can also stimulate demand during a recession. If features are added to a bundle, consumers may perceive the offering as having greater value. For example, suppose that Hyatt offers a "great escape" weekend for $119. The package includes two nights' lodging and a continental breakfast. Hyatt could add a massage and a dinner for two to create more value for this price. Conversely, companies can unbundle offerings and lower base prices to stimulate demand. A furniture store, for example, could start charging separately for design consultation, delivery, credit, setup, and hauling away old furniture.

Recessions are a good time for marketing managers to study the demand for individual items in a product line and the revenue they produce. Pruning unprofitable items can save resources to be better used elsewhere. Borden's, for example, found that it made about 3,200 sizes, brands, types, and flavors of snacks—but got 95 percent of its revenues from just half of them.

Prices for fresh and frozen pork fell in the early 2000s, yet Hormel was able to increase both its sales and its profits. The company accomplished this by creating a whole new class of products. Hormel is increasingly turning its low-margin fresh pork— slabs that groceries and restaurants butcher themselves—into highly profitable heat-and-serve meals. These precut, value-added products, such as teriyaki-flavored loins, are easier for consumers to cook. Busy families were avoiding pork because they were not sure how to cook it properly. Grocers, eager to win business back from takeout restaurants, cleared refrigerator space eagerly.[25]

Prices often fall during a recession as competitors try desperately to maintain demand for their wares. Even if demand remains constant, falling prices mean lower profits or no profits. Falling prices, therefore, are a natural incentive to lower costs. During the past recession, companies implemented new technology to improve efficiency and then slashed payrolls. They also discovered that suppliers were an excellent source of cost savings; the cost of purchased materials accounts for slightly more than half of most U.S. manufacturers' expenses. General Electric's appliance division told 300 key suppliers that they had to reduce prices

REVIEW LEARNING OUTCOME

LO5 Describe the role of pricing during periods of inflation and recession

Inflation

$ → $$$

Cost-oriented tactics
- Contract product lines
- Delayed-quotation pricing
- Escalator pricing

Demand-oriented tactics
- Select demand
- Unique offering
- Change package design
- Increase buyer dependence

Recession

Price
- Value-based
- Bundling
- Unbundling

Product
- New products
- New product categories

Suppliers
- Renegotiate contracts
- Offer help
- Keep pressure on suppliers
- Reduce number of suppliers

10 percent or risk losing GE's business. Honeywell, Dow Chemical, General Motors, and DuPont made similar demands of their suppliers. Specific strategies that companies use with suppliers include the following:

- *Renegotiating contracts:* Sending suppliers letters demanding price cuts of 5 percent or more; putting out for rebid the contracts of those that refuse to cut costs.

- *Offering help:* Dispatching teams of experts to suppliers' plants to help reorganize and suggest other productivity-boosting changes; working with suppliers to make parts simpler and cheaper to produce.

- *Keeping the pressure on:* To make sure that improvements continue, setting annual, across-the-board cost reduction targets, often of 5 percent or more a year.

- *Paring down suppliers:* To improve economies of scale, slashing the overall number of suppliers, sometimes by up to 80 percent, and boosting purchases from those that remain.

Tough tactics like these help keep companies afloat during economic downturns.

Quick Check

Now that you've read the chapter, do you get it? Take a moment for a quick check using this scale:

1 Not at all; 2 Not very well; 3 Ok; 4 Well; 5 Very Well

Can you . . .

___ outline the procedure for setting the right price?

___ differentiate among penetration pricing, price skimming, and status quo pricing?

___ identify the legal constraints on pricing?

___ list the elements that need to be present for a violation of the Robinson-Patman Act?

___ list and define the different types of discounts marketers use?

___ explain the different types of geographic pricing?

___ compare the various pricing tactics marketers use?

___ explain how product line pricing works?

___ describe some of the common ways of allocating joint costs for a product line?

___ write a paragraph identifying pricing strategies marketers can use during inflation and recession?

___ TOTAL

Score: 41–50, you're ready to move on to the applications; 31–40, skim the chapter one more time before moving on to the applications; 21–30, reread the sections giving you the most trouble and go to Thomson NOW for guided tutorials; 20 and under, you better reread the chapter to get a grasp of the fundamentals. If you've reread the chapter and still have a low score, visit your professor or TA during office hours.

Review and Applications

LO 1 Describe the procedure for setting the right price. The process of setting the right price on a product involves four major steps: (1) establishing pricing goals; (2) estimating demand, costs, and profits; (3) choosing a price policy to help determine a base price; and (4) fine-tuning the base price with pricing tactics.

A price strategy establishes a long-term pricing framework for a good or service. The three main types of price policies are price skimming, penetration pricing, and status quo pricing. A price-skimming policy charges a high introductory price, often followed by a gradual reduction. Penetration pricing offers a low introductory price to capture a large market share and attain economies of scale. Finally, status quo pricing strives to match competitors' price.

1.1 A manufacturer of office furniture decides to produce antique-style rolltop desks reconfigured to accommodate personal computers. The desks will have built-in surge protectors, a platform for raising or lowering the monitor, and a number of other features. The high-quality, solid-oak desks will be priced far below comparable products. The marketing manager says, "We'll charge a low price and plan on a high volume to reduce our risks." Comment.

1.2 Janet Oliver, owner of a mid-priced dress shop, notes, "My pricing objectives are simple: I just charge what my competitors charge. I'm happy because I'm making money." React to Janet's statement.

1.3 What is the difference between a price policy and a price tactic? Give an example.

LO 2 Identify the legal and ethical constraints on pricing decisions. **Government regulation helps monitor four major areas of pricing: unfair trade practices, price fixing, predatory pricing, and price discrimination.** Many states have enacted unfair trade practice acts that protect small businesses from large firms that operate efficiently on extremely thin profit margins; the acts prohibit charging below-cost prices. The Sherman Act and the Federal Trade Commission Act prohibit both price fixing, which is an agreement between two or more firms on a particular price, and predatory pricing, in which a firm undercuts its competitors with extremely low prices to drive them out of business. Finally, the Robinson-Patman Act makes it illegal for firms to discriminate between two or more buyers in terms of price.

2.1 What are the three basic defenses that a seller can use if accused under the Robinson-Patman Act?

LO 3 Explain how discounts, geographic pricing, and other pricing tactics can be used to fine-tune the base price. **Several techniques enable marketing managers to adjust prices within a general range in response to changes in competition, government regulation, consumer demand, and promotional and positioning goals.** Techniques for fine-tuning a price can be divided into three main categories: discounts, allowances, rebates, and value-based pricing; geographic pricing; and other pricing tactics.

The first type of tactic gives lower prices to those that pay promptly, order a large quantity, or perform some function for the manufacturer. Value-based pricing starts with the customer, considers the competition and costs, and then determines a price. Additional tactics in this category include seasonal discounts, promotion allowances, and rebates (cash refunds).

Geographic pricing tactics—such as FOB origin pricing, uniform delivered pricing, zone pricing, freight absorption pricing, and basing-point pricing—are ways of moderating the impact of shipping costs on distant customers.

A variety of "other" pricing tactics stimulate demand for certain products, increase store patronage, and offer more merchandise at specific prices.

More and more customers are paying price penalties, which are extra fees for violating the terms of a purchase contract. The perceived fairness or unfairness of a penalty may affect some consumers' willingness to patronize a business in the future.

3.1 You are contemplating a price change for an established product sold by your firm. Write a memo analyzing the factors you need to consider in your decision.

3.2 Columnist Dave Barry jokes that federal law requires this message under the sticker price of new cars: "Warning to stupid people: Do not pay this amount." Discuss why the sticker price is generally higher than the actual selling price of a car. Tell how you think car dealers set the actual prices of the cars they sell.

3.3 Divide into teams of four persons. Each team should choose one of the following topics: skimming, penetration pricing, status quo pricing, price fixing, geographic pricing, adopting a single-price tactic, flexible pricing, or professional services pricing. Each team should then pick a retailer that it feels most closely follows the team's chosen pricing strategy. Go to the store and write down examples of the strategy. Interview the store manager and get his or her views on the advantages and disadvantages of the strategy. Each team should then make an oral report in class.

3.4 The U.S. Postal Service regularly raises the price of a first-class stamp but continues to operate in the red year after year. Is uniform delivered pricing the best choice for first-class mail? Explain your reasoning.

3.5 How is the "information age" changing the nature of pricing?

3.6 Have you ever paid a price penalty? How did it affect your attitude toward that company?

3.7 Imagine that you are a marketing manager for a mid-sized amusement park. You have attended an industry-wide meeting where a colleague gave a talk about new pricing strategies for amusement parks. You were very motivated by the seminar. On your return to work, write a memo to your boss outlining the pros and cons of the new pricing strategy. End your memo with a recommendation either for or against à la carte pricing of attractions (pricing each attraction separately rather than charging a single high entrance fee).

LO4 Discuss product line pricing. Product line pricing maximizes profits for an entire product line. When setting product line prices, marketing managers determine what type of relationship exists among the products in the line: complementary, substitute, or neutral. Managers also consider joint (shared) costs among products in the same line.

4.1 Develop a price line strategy for each of these firms:

   a. a college bookstore

   b. a restaurant

   c. a video rental firm

LO5 Describe the role of pricing during periods of inflation and recession. Marketing managers employ cost-oriented and demand-oriented tactics during periods of economic inflation. Cost-oriented tactics include dropping products with a low profit margin, using delayed-quotation pricing and escalator pricing, and adding fees. Demand-oriented pricing methods include price shading and increasing demand through cultivating selected customers, creating unique offerings, changing the package size, and heightening buyer dependence.

To stimulate demand during a recession, marketers use value-based pricing, bundling, and unbundling. Recessions are also a good time to prune unprofitable items from product lines. Managers strive to cut costs during recessions in order to maintain profits as revenues decline. Implementing new technology, cutting payrolls, and pressuring suppliers for reduced prices are common techniques used to cut costs. Companies also create new value-added products.

5.1 During a recession, what pricing strategies would you consider using to gain or maintain market share? Explain your answer.

5.2 After a decade of astounding growth and prosperity, Americans were challenged by the economic downturn of the early 2000s. As a result, pricing became an issue for many consumers looking to pinch pennies. This was also true in areas where penny-pinching isn't a common occurrence, like high-end retailers. Search the *Wall Street Journal* online archives (**http://www.wsj.com**) to find an article about pricing during a recession.

Key Terms

Exercises

APPLICATION EXERCISE

You read in the chapter about the dangers of pricing products too low. It seems so obviously wrong, but do companies really price their products so low that they won't make any money? After all, companies are in business to make money, and if they don't, they're probably not in business for very long. Let's take a deeper look at the effects of pricing products too low or creating too deep discounts during sale periods.[26]

Activity

1. The average markup for a produce department is 28 percent on selling price. When sold at 28 percent markup on selling price, bananas usually account for 25 percent of department sales and 25 percent of department markup. This week, because bananas were on special sale at the retailer's cost, the department sold twice as many pounds of bananas as usual. However, they were sold at zero markup. If all other things remain the same, what is the average markup on selling price for the entire produce department this week?

Entrepreneurship Case

DISCONNECTING CABLE CHANNELS FROM PRICING BUNDLES

When people go shopping, the grocery store doesn't make them buy broccoli if they are buying milk. Why then do cable and satellite TV companies make people pay for channels they don't watch, for example, highly targeted channels like Home and Garden Television (HGTV), Spike, and ESPN? Congressional lawmakers are interested in the cable industry's answer to this question. Several lawmakers are pushing for legislation that would prevent the cable industry from forcing consumers to buy a prix fixe menu of channels and would require the industry instead to offer à la carte service, or individual channels, in lieu of traditional packages. And the idea is gaining popularity.

This idea, and complaints about cable television service and rising rates, emerged at a Senate subcommittee hearing where legislators pilloried the cable industry for being unresponsive to consumers. One senator went so far as to say that cable subscribers "are being force-fed channels and features they don't want," and encouraged the industry to give consumers a choice. Another warned, "Do something about your rising rates or you're going to have trouble." The senators aren't alone in their frustration. Bipartisan members of the Federal Communications Commission have also signaled support for more personalized cable options. The industry, however, insists that such options will end up costing consumers more.

Fueling the debate is the spiraling price of cable TV service. According to a recent General Accounting Office study, cable programming rates jumped at least 34 percent during a recent three-year period, far outpacing the general rate of inflation (see Exhibit 18.3). The report attributed higher cable rates at least partially to billions of dollars of investments made by cable companies in original programming and upgraded technology. Cable companies are also paying more for sports programming; such fees rose 59 percent during the same period because of the higher prices being paid to sports teams and leagues to carry games.

Unbundling cable channels appeals to some consumers who hope it would lower monthly bills and give them more control over what their families are watching. Besides, the idea of paying for an individual channel isn't altogether new in the cable industry: plenty of consumers already pay extra for commercial-free channels such as

Exhibit 18.3

Cable Rates versus Inflation

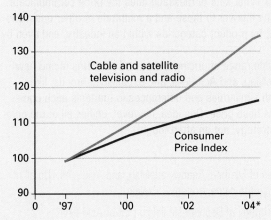

Cable TV in the United States continues to outpace the rate of inflation (1997–2004)

Cable and satellite television and radio

Consumer Price Index

* As of February.
Source: Bureau of Labor Statistics.

HBO and Showtime. Proponents of the à la carte plan say most cable subscribers watch the same channels all the time, so why should they pay for all the others? "The average household watches no more than a dozen to 17 channels," says Gene Kimmelman, head of Consumers Union, citing a report compiled by the FCC.

The movement to change how cable service is priced alarms the industry. Both programmers and operators say offering personalized selections to more then 70 million cable subscribers would shatter the economics of their business, forcing less popular channels out of business and potentially costing consumers more.

Cable operators say their entire business model is predicated on packaged offerings. That setup affords cable networks two revenue streams; advertising revenue and per-subscriber license fees from cable and satellite operators that distribute the programming. Any change in audience figures for a cable channel after it was removed from a package would severely hamper both revenue sources, they say. Furthermore, some industry members contend that an à la carte plan would severely limit individual networks' ability to generate original programming. This is a serious concern for companies like Scripps Networks, parent of the Food Network and HGTV, and Viacom, parent of Nickelodeon. For example, if Nickelodeon, which is available in 88 million homes including satellite customers, saw its distribution drop dramatically because of an à la carte system, the network would be making less money to put back into programming. Unbundling cable packages could have some serious unforeseen consequences.

"It could really destroy a business that is monumentally successful," adds Andy Heller, president of distribution for Time Warner's Turner Broadcasting, parent of TNT, the Cartoon Network, and CNN. He notes that the average monthly cable bill is less than the cost for a family of four to go to a baseball game nowadays.

Ironically, a cable operator in the New York City area tried to offer a channel on an à la carte basis but was not allowed to do so. An arbitration panel ruled against Cablevision Systems Corporation's effort to offer the New York sports channel YES individually to subscribers. YES challenged Cablevision's original decision not to bundle the channel with its basic service. The cable operator had said the YES channel, which carries Yankees games, was too costly.

Cable operators also say that selling channels separately presents technological problems. Only one-third of the country gets digital cable. The rest of the nation has older, analog systems in which it is more difficult to break down individual channel signals for each household. Given the technological costs of implementing an individualized system and the likelihood that fees would increase to make up for lost subscribers, subscribers could end up getting only a dozen or so channels for the same price they currently pay for a bundle.[27]

Questions

1. Is it legal for the government to intervene in industries whose prices outpace inflation? Is it appropriate?

2. What other pricing strategies could cable operators use that would maintain their revenue stream and check the escalating price of cable service?

3. Would you prefer an à la carte or a bundling pricing strategy for your cable service?

4. What would happen to the cable industry if it was deregulated in the same way as the telecommunications industry?

COMPANY CLIPS

Pricing Perspectives – Method, ReadyMadeMag, Sephora, Vans, and Acid+All

Setting the right price is one of the most challenging aspects of a marketer's job. How high a price will the market bear? What kind of message does the price communicate? How flexible can our price be? The answer to those and a multitude of other questions relating to price vary by industry, by product categories within an industry, and even by brand and store.

This video shows you a wide range of pricing issues and concerns facing new brands, like Method, ReadyMadeMag, and Acid+All, and established brands, like Sephora and Vans. There are both similarities and differences in the tools each company uses to set and fine-tune its base price. One idea, however, unifies all of the companies: pricing is a considered strategy, not an afterthought.

Questions

1. Compare the pricing strategies of Method, ReadyMadeMag, and Acid+All. Do all of these relatively new brands use the same strategy? Explain.

2. In what ways is the pricing strategy of Sephora similar to that of Acid+All?

3. Does it make sense for Method to use product line pricing? Why or why not?

4. What is Vans' primary strategy for setting prices on tickets to the Warped Tour it sponsors?

BIZ FLIX

Fast Times at Ridgemont High

Review this chapter's discussion of setting the right price and then watch the scene from *Fast Times at Ridgemont High.* This iconic teen film is set at a southern California high school. This scene comes from "The Dudes" sequence early in the film. Mike Damone (Robert Romanus) has some Van Halen concert tickets for sale. Does Mike follow the steps for setting a price described earlier in this chapter? For example, does he have a pricing goal or a price strategy? If *yes,* what are they? This chapter emphasizes the importance of legal and ethical issues in price strategy. Does either of these issues apply to the behavior shown in the scene? Review the section "Other Pricing Tactics" earlier in this chapter. Did Mike use any of the tactics?

High scores on this poll indicate that you are very sensitive to prices and that your price consciousness affects how you shop. Conversely, a lower score suggests that you are not very price conscious.

Marketing Miscue

A Pricing Execution Error at Dell

In a rare slip at Dell, Inc., a company known for its low-cost business model and close attention to operational detail, poor management of the average selling price resulted in a revenue shortfall in the second quarter of 2005. Basically, the company priced its computers too low. Though it shipped an industry-record 9.1 million computers during the quarter, the company failed to meet its quarterly revenue target.

According to Dell's Web site, the company's climb to market leadership has been the result of a persistent focus on delivering the best possible customer experience by the direct selling of computer products and services. The company was founded in 1984 by Michael Dell, and its corporate headquarters are in Round Rock, Texas. A worldwide supplier of computer systems, Dell manufactures computers in the United States, Brazil, Ireland, Malaysia, and China. The company holds the number one market position in the United States, the number three position in the Asia Pacific/Japan market, and the number two position in Europe. Worldwide, the company employs about 64,000 people.

Dell's products include servers, storage, printing and imaging systems, workstations, notebook computers, desktop computers, networking products, and software and peripheral products (e.g., plasma TVs, MP3 players, handhelds). Dell's service offerings include managed, professional, deployment, support, and training and certification services. Dell's pricing miscalculations occurred in its computer lines.

In 2005, personal computer makers were facing a mature market where continued growth was difficult. Worldwide PC sales were expected to grow 12.7 percent in 2005, but revenues were expected to grow only 0.5 percent. Such tepid growth prospects were squeezing PC makers from large (Dell) to small (Gateway). Desktop pricing was being forced down to new levels. Additionally, the notebook marketplace, which tends to generate higher margins, was experiencing price declines faster than anticipated. According to one industry expert, the quest for growth was forcing companies to test the limits of PC price elasticity.

During the second quarter, Dell's average selling price for its consumer computers dropped 13 percent, and the company experienced an average price decrease of 8 percent across all products and markets. Essentially, Dell was advertising its supercheap machines and offering revenue-draining promotions on the low-end machines (e.g., giving away printers with the purchase of cheap computers). Dell would have met expectations if it had simply priced the 9.1 million computers it sold in the second quarter just $10 to $15 higher. But the company was operating in a share-building model of growth and was not focusing on selling the more profitable machines. This was considered an unusual marketing strategy for the industry leader—a leader that did not need to slash prices to remain competitive with rival offerings. Thus, Dell's second quarter unit volume was high, but it undermined revenue growth.

Though Dell executives insisted that these were one-time, easily fixable pricing problems, industry analysts wondered whether Dell was losing its tactical edge. In their view, the company needed to return to selling higher-end, more profitable systems and be less aggressive in the battle for market share. In a marketplace where PC pricing had become more and more competitive, with low-end desktops priced as low as $299 and notebooks dipping below $500, there was concern that the company had not been able to quickly adjust its pricing model to drive revenue and meet expectations.

With competition heating up among notebook competitors (e.g., Hewlett-Packard, Gateway, Averatec), analysts expected that margins in the notebook market would be driven down. Though Dell had met industry expectations for profit margins on its notebooks, the analysts were concerned about its future profit margins in that sector. If they were to decline, Dell would be under additional pressure to get its pricing model back in line, while steering customers toward its more expensive computer products. Although the pricing error was a rare slipup for the company, it brought considerable attention to the operational detail required by a company as large as Dell.[1]

Questions

1. What type of marketing strategy was Dell pursuing? What was the role of pricing in this strategy?

2. How important are pricing decisions to the overall welfare of a company such as Dell?

Critical Thinking Case

Yahoo! Music Unlimited's Aggressive Pricing

In May 2005, Yahoo! Inc., introduced its Music Unlimited service for a low introductory price of $60 for a year's subscription or $7 for a month. For this low introductory fee, subscribers would receive unlimited listening access to a library of more than one million tracks. Subscribers who wanted to own a song, instead of just renting it, would pay 79 cents a song. A free seven-day trial of the service was included in the introductory offer.

At the time of the introduction, there were two product segments in the marketplace: the pay-per-download segment and the subscription services segment. Probably the best-known pay-per-download segment was Apple's iTunes, which charged 99 cents for a music download. Analysts believed that iTunes was the leading download service because of its relationship to the iPod. Although the average iPod owner purchased only around 25 songs, there were over 17 million iPod owners in 2005, and that number was expected to increase by another 5 million in 2006.

Yahoo! Music Unlimited's competitors in the subscription services market were RealNetworks' Rhapsody and Napster. They charged about $10 a month for a basic subscription and $15 a month for a portability subscription. One critical question for all three competitors was whether online music providers could change consumer behavior: Would music listeners readily switch from buying music to renting music? Would subscription services replace or even change the entire music purchasing experience? Another critical question was whether online music providers could actually make money on subscriptions: Could the online providers attract sufficient subscribers to survive, given that the providers had to pay the music label about $6 per person a month for a subscription that allowed users to listen to music only on their PC? For subscriptions that allowed downloads to portable players, label fees were around $8 per person per month. The music subscriber base was only 1.5 million in 2004, but that was twice as many as in 2003.

Competitively, Yahoo! Music Unlimited had its advantages and disadvantages. For one thing, Yahoo! was not relying solely on Music Unlimited for cash flow. Yahoo! was a widely diversified company, with a potential audience of 370 million visitors a month via its network of Web portals. Music Unlimited offered features that linked with many of Yahoo!'s other services. These features included Yahoo! Music Engine, Large Music Library, Yahoo! Messenger Integration, Personalization & Community, Music Portability, Instant Playlists, LAUNCHcast Integration, Access From Any PC, and Download Purchases. In contrast, the music service was the only business at Napster, and online subscriptions made up about 30 percent of RealNetworks' revenue. Yahoo! Music Unlimited could work on 10 different portable MP3 players. It was not compatible with Apple's iPod, however, and Apple had no incentive to make the iPod compatible with subscription service offerings.

With online music representing approximately 2 percent of total music sales, there was room for growth. According to data collected by Nielsen/NetRatings, almost 62 million people visited an online music site in April 2005. Male visitors slightly outnumbered female visitors, approximately 60 percent of the visitors were under the age of 45, and the majority had a household income of over $50,000.

Some projections even suggested that downloads and subscriptions would make the online music industry a $1 billion business in the United States by 2007.

Would Yahoo! be a major player in the subscription services marketplace? Would the fact that the costly infrastructure (e.g., servers, credit-card fees) was already in place at Yahoo! help the company move to the top of the online music industry? Or, was Yahoo! Music Unlimited's low introductory price essentially de-valuing music, and, if so, would this spark more battles with the music labels? Was the company also starting a price war with RealNetworks and Napster? If so, how long would this introductory price have to remain in place? Was this a sustainable business model for any company in the online music industry?[2]

Questions

1. What pricing objective is driving Yahoo! Music Unlimited?

2. What is the company's pricing strategy?

PART 7

Technology-Driven Marketing

CROSS-FUNCTIONAL CONNECTIONS

Technological advances have provided businesses with the ability to gather a vast amount of information about current and potential markets and to quickly and easily communicate company and product information to current and potential customers. To understand the marketplace and respond to marketplace demands, a company now requires internal technological linkages unheard of only a few decades ago. Today, information technology links marketing and its functional counterparts, making it possible for all functions to have access to the same valuable market information. Though connecting functional departments, customers, and suppliers in a single network offers enormous benefits, the process of bringing all of these groups together has not been without problems.

One of the major points of contention within organizations has been the necessary interaction between marketing and the information technology group. Information technologists, with backgrounds in computer science, mathematics, or engineering, have historically put little emphasis on interactions with customers. Nonetheless, these same information technologists are now charged with developing the company's Web site, which may be the customer's first and only contact with the company. What was once a brochure or print ad is now on the consumer's computer screen. Thus, the responsibility for the development and functional capabilities of a major element of the firm's marketing communications program—the company's Web site—is in the hands of information technology experts.

Companies often refer to marketers as the site/content *strategists* and information technologists as the site/content *implementers.* Unfortunately, this separation into strategy and implementation has tended to exacerbate the conflict between marketing and information technology.

business functions. For example, fulfilling customer requests for technical support electronically can dramatically improve customer satisfaction. Technicians are able to respond much more quickly to requests, bringing positive results to marketing in the form of satisfied customers and to engineering in that fewer engineers are needed for product support. Customers, however, now expect 24/7 service and want to receive responses to e-mail inquiries within a few hours, if not a few minutes.

Thus, technicians and support providers often suggest that marketers are creating unreasonable expectations among customers. At the same time, the ability to capture and interpret data coming into the customer support center has provided companies with a wealth of market and product intelligence.

Today, information technology links marketing and its functional counterparts, making it possible for all functions to have access to the same valuable market information.

The information technologists do not like "taking orders" from marketers about something that comes under their purview of computer expertise. Likewise, marketers fear that letting information technologists build the Web site will result in a site that is too technologically advanced to be easy to use and not visually appealing to the average customer.

Not only must technologists and marketers work together in developing the company's Web page, but the legal department must also be intimately involved in the process. Domain registration (similar to trademarks and trade names), intellectual property rights, hidden language (called metatext), taxation, and privacy policies are all areas in which legal assistance is of utmost importance. The marketing and information technology departments have to develop legally and ethically appropriate material that will also be interesting and easy to navigate. To its dismay, Rockstar Games learned about the financial ramifications of mistakes in this area with its release of *Grand Theft Auto: San Andreas* (see the Marketing Miscue after Part 7 for a discussion of this incident).

Once the marketers and information technologists have gotten past their functional biases and the lawyers have determined that a Web site is legally and ethically appropriate, doing business on the Internet requires interactions between marketing and other

Marketing direct to the consumer also provides manufacturing rewards. When a consumer places an order, advanced technological capabilities enable suppliers to receive electronic messages indicating the raw materials that will be needed to satisfy the customer's product demands. Raw materials can be shipped directly to the manufacturing facility. The manufacturing facility, having received the order transmission at the same time as its suppliers, can begin production immediately on receipt of the necessary supplies. Marketing on the Net also allows customers to receive their orders more quickly. No longer does the order have to work its way through various steps before finally reaching production (in a manufacturing company) or delivery (in retailing). Electronic order taking transmits the customer's order directly to the order fulfillment center, highlighting the need for close relations with the logistics and transportation people.

Without a doubt, today's marketers are expected to respond quickly to customer demands, and technology has enabled this rapid response. Through information technology, companies have been able to attract consumers. It is the successful interaction of all business functions, however, that keeps customers returning to these companies as loyal and repeat users.

Questions

1. How has today's technology altered the role of marketing both internally and externally?

2. What are some of the benefits of networking functional departments, customers, and suppliers?

Customer

Relationship Management (CRM)

Learning Outcomes

LO¹   Define customer relationship management

LO²   Explain how to identify customer relationships with the organization

LO³   Understand interactions with the current customer base

LO⁴   Outline the process of capturing customer data

LO⁵   Describe the use of technology to store and integrate customer data

LO⁶   Describe how to identify the best customers

LO⁷   Explain the process of leveraging customer information throughout the organization

Hilton Hotels *wows customers with CRM system*

In today's highly competitive lodging industry, a hotel needs a comprehensive customer relationship management (CRM) system. When successful, a CRM system enables an organization to acquire, retain, and grow customers in ways that would be impossible without it. What customers want most today, in addition to the product or service they are purchasing, is

What customers want most today is recognition, convenience, information, helpfulness, and excellent service every time they interact with a company.

recognition, convenience, information, helpfulness, and excellent service every time they interact with a company. With its CRM system, Hilton Hotels can examine occupancy, booking patterns, and specific customer information to meet these expectations. In addition to analyzing information about customers using its frequent guest program, Hilton Honors, the hotel chain can profile guests by name, zip code, phone number, or a combination of all three criteria. The system enables the chain to better serve customers, coordinate the loyalty programs, and develop unique marketing campaigns for individual hotels. This enables Hilton to be more cost-effective in managing its hotels and to deploy its marketing resources more effectively.

Perhaps most amazing is that the CRM system conducts these analyses in minutes, and sometime seconds, enabling customer service reps to respond almost instantaneously to both customer and manager requests. Users of the system can generate reports for any facility or for a specific location at a facility, determine rate plans for types of customers, identify seasonal booking patterns, and more. They can also drill down using data mining to track national accounts or individual guests; identify top meeting planners by name, location, and type of industry; and determine the purpose of travel such as business, pleasure, or both. According to Hilton's vice president for marketing, the system "can identify and profile market segments, the actual bookings, and then forecast advance booking patterns." For travelers, this means that a guest who has stayed with Hilton a hundred times will automatically get an upgrade and additional services, whereas a traveler staying with the chain only once or twice will get good service and additional help as needed, but not at the level of the more frequent customer.[1]

Hilton's CRM system is state of the art, but many companies are installing systems with similar capabilities. How do you think companies could use the information collected by CRM systems to better serve their customers? What additional information could marketers collect to help them develop more effective marketing campaigns?

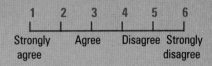

What Is Customer Relationship Management?

Customer relationship management (CRM) is the ultimate goal of a new trend in marketing that focuses on understanding customers as individuals instead of as part of a group. To do so, marketers are making their communications more customer-specific, like the personalized marketing efforts being used by Amazon.com. This movement initially was popularized as one-to-one marketing. But CRM is a much broader approach to understanding and serving customer needs than is one-to-one marketing.

Customer relationship management is a company-wide business strategy designed to optimize profitability, revenue, and customer satisfaction by focusing on highly defined and precise customer groups. This is accomplished by organizing the company around customer segments, establishing and tracking customer interactions with the company, fostering customer-satisfying behaviors, and linking all processes of the company from its customers through its suppliers. For example, Listen.com's Rhapsody player targets consumers who listen to streaming audio. Then, by requiring users to log in, Rhapsody tracks their musical preferences and usage. Listen.com can leverage this information to offer special promotions and make recommendations to specific target markets and individuals.

The difference between CRM and traditional mass marketing can be compared to shooting a rifle and a shotgun. If you have good aim, a rifle is the more efficient weapon to use. A shotgun, on the other hand, increases your odds of hitting the target when it is more difficult to focus. Instead of scattering messages far and wide across the spectrum of mass media (the shotgun approach), CRM marketers now are homing in on ways to effectively communicate with each individual customer (the rifle approach).

CRM is a strategy designed to optimize business performance by focusing on highly defined customer groups. This Surado ad for SCM SQL is a perfect example of what CRM systems seek to know: the real customer.

THE CUSTOMER RELATIONSHIP MANAGEMENT CYCLE

On the surface, CRM may appear to be a rather simplistic customer service strategy. But, though customer service is part of the CRM process, it is only a small part of a totally integrated approach to building customer relationships. CRM is often described as a closed-loop system that builds relationships with customers. Exhibit 19.1 illustrates this closed-loop system, one that is continuous and circular with no predefined starting or end point.[2]

To initiate the CRM cycle, a company must first *identify customer relationships with the organization.* This may simply entail learning who the customers are or where they are located, or it may require more detailed information on the products and services they are using. Bridgestone/Firestone, a tire manufacturer and tire service company, uses a CRM system called OnDemand5.[3] OnDemand5 initially gathers information from a point-of-sale interaction. The types of information gathered include basic demographic information, how frequently consumers purchase goods, how much they purchase, and how far they drive.

customer relationship management (CRM)
A company-wide business strategy designed to optimize profitability, revenue, and customer satisfaction by focusing on highly defined and precise customer groups.

Next, the company must *understand the interactions with current customers.* Companies accomplish this by collecting data on all types of communications a customer has with the company. Using its OnDemand5 system, Bridgestone/Firestone can add information based on additional interactions with the consumer such as multiple visits to a physical store location and purchasing history. In this phase, companies build on the initial information collected and develop a more useful database.

Using this knowledge of its customers and their interactions, the company then *captures relevant customer data on interactions.* As an example, Bridgestone/Firestone can collect such relevant information as the date of the last communication with a customer, how often the customer makes purchases, and whether the customer redeemed coupons sent through direct mail.

How can marketers realistically analyze and communicate with individual customers? How can huge corporations like FedEx and Williams-Sonoma manage relationships with each and every one of their millions of customers on a personal level? The answer lies in how information technology is used to implement the CRM system. Fundamentally, a CRM approach is no more than the relationship cultivated by a salesperson with the customer. A successful salesperson builds a relationship over time, constantly thinks about what the customer needs and wants, and is mindful of the trends and patterns in the customer's purchase history. A good salesperson often knows what the customer needs even before the customer knows. The salesperson may also inform, educate, and instruct the customer about new products, technology, or applications in anticipation of the customer's future needs or requirements.

This kind of thoughtful attention is the basis of successful CRM systems. Information technology is used not only to enhance the collection of customer data, but also to *store and integrate customer data* throughout the company and, ultimately, to "get to know" customers on a personal basis. Customer data are the firsthand responses that are obtained from customers through investigation or by asking direct questions. These initial data, which might include individual answers to questionnaires, responses on warranty cards, or lists of purchases recorded by electronic cash registers, have not yet been analyzed or interpreted.

The value of customer data depends on the system that stores the data and the consistency and accuracy of the data captured. Obtaining high-quality, actionable data from various sources is a key element in any CRM system. Bridgestone/Firestone accomplishes this by managing all information in a central database accessible by marketers. Different kinds of database management software are available, from extremely high-tech, expensive, custom-designed databases to standardized programs. NetERP, for example, offers users database technology in a standardized rather than a customized format and is available at a much lower cost.[4]

Every customer wants to be a company's main priority. Yet not all customers are equally important in the eyes of a business. Some customers are simply more profitable for the company than others. Consequently, the company must identify *its profitable and unprofitable customers.* Data mining is an analytical process that compiles actionable data about the purchase habits of a firm's current and potential customers. Essentially, data mining transforms customer data into customer information a company can use to make managerial decisions. The NetERP software allows managers to customize their "dashboard" to obtain real-time reports on top-selling items and gross sales over a given

Exhibit 19.1

A Simple Flow Model of the Customer Relationship Management System

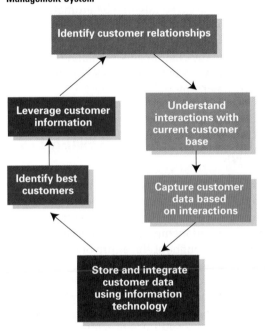

LO 1 Define customer relationship management

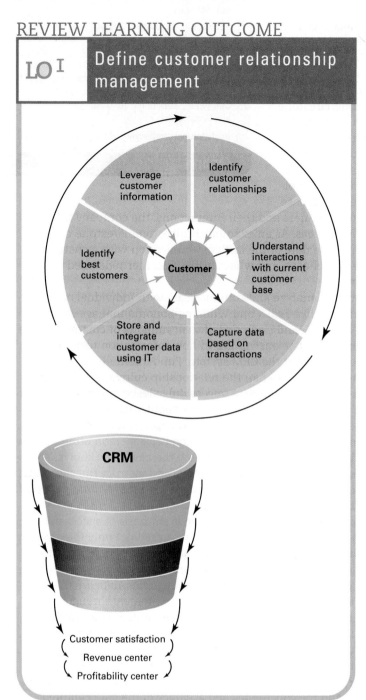

time period. Similarly, Bridgestone/Firestone uses OnDemand5 to analyze its data to determine which customers qualify for the MasterCare Select program. It also identifies customers who have not made a purchase in the past 8 to 12 months.

Once customer data are analyzed and transformed into usable information, the information must be *leveraged*. The CRM system sends the customer information to all areas of a business because the customer interacts with all aspects of the business (e.g., sales or marketing, operations, production, accounting). Essentially, the company is trying to enhance customer relationships by getting the right information to the right person in the right place at the right time.

Bridgestone/Firestone utilizes the information in its database to develop different marketing campaigns for each type of customer. For example, MasterCare Select customers receive free tire rotation, maps, roadside assistance, and lost-key service. Customers are also targeted by promotions aimed at increasing store visits, upgrades to higher-end tires, and purchases of additional services. Since the company customized its mailings to each type of customer, visits to stores have increased by more than 50 percent.[5]

IMPLEMENTING A CUSTOMER RELATIONSHIP MANAGEMENT SYSTEM

Our discussion of a CRM system has assumed two key points. First, customers take center stage in any organization. Second, the business must manage the customer relationship across all points of customer contact throughout the entire organization. The Seattle Mariners baseball team took proactive steps to increase customer attendance at games based on these two points. The team implemented a loyalty card program to help the Mariners "better understand the fans." By collecting information from every interaction a customer has with the Mariners, from visiting concession stands to purchasing online tickets and even frequenting retail

customer-centric
A philosophy under which the company customizes its product and service offering based on data generated through interactions between the customer and the company.

stores that sell Mariner merchandise, marketers were able to track the number of games consumers were attending. They sent reminder e-mails if a fan was close to achieving "season-ticket holder" status, and they also monitored complaints. For example, when the CRM system identified a complaint from a fan about the smell of garlic fries, the organization moved the fan to an area where there were no frequent consumers of garlic fries.[6]

In the next sections, we examine how a CRM system is implemented and follow the progression depicted in Exhibit 19.1 as we explain each step in greater detail.

LO 2
Identify Customer Relationships

Companies that have a CRM system follow a customer-centric focus or model. **Customer-centric** is an internal management philosophy similar to the marketing concept discussed in Chapter 1. Under this philosophy, the company customizes its product and service offering based on data generated through interactions between the customer and the company. This philosophy transcends all functional areas of the business (production, operations, accounting, etc.), producing an internal system where all of the company's decisions and actions are a direct result of customer information.

A customer-centric company builds long-lasting relationships by focusing on what satisfies and retains valuable customers. For example, Sony's Web site (**http://www.playstation.com**) focuses on learning, customer knowledge management, and empowerment to market its PlayStation gaming computer entertainment system. The PlayStation Web site is designed to create a community of users who can join PlayStation Underground where they will "feel like they belong to a subculture of intense gamers." To achieve this objective, the Web site offers online shopping, opportunities to try new games, customer support, and information on news, events, and promotions. The interactive features include online gaming and message boards.

The PlayStation is designed to support Sony's CRM system. When PlayStation users want to access amenities on the site, they are required to log in and supply information such as their name, e-mail address, and birth date. Users can opt to fill out a survey that asks questions about the types of computer entertainment systems they own, how many games are owned for each console, expected future game purchases, time spent playing games, types of games played, and level of Internet connectivity. Armed with this information, Sony marketers are then able to tailor the site, new games, and PlayStation hardware based on players' replies to the survey and use of the Web site.[7]

Customer-centric companies continually learn ways to enhance their product and service offerings. **Learning** in a CRM environment involves collecting customer information through comments and feedback on product and service performance. As just described, Sony uses its PlayStation Web site to gather information from surveys and message boards so that it can offer more customer-friendly products and services.

Each unit of a business typically has its own way of recording what it learns and perhaps even its own customer information system. The departments' different interests make it difficult to pull all of the customer information together in one place using a common format. To overcome this problem, companies using CRM rely on knowledge management. **Knowledge management** is a process by which customer information is centralized and shared in order to enhance the relationship between customers and the organization. Information collected includes experiential observations, comments, customer actions, and qualitative facts about the customer. For example, PlayStation marketers gather survey information and generate a computer file for each customer that is available to the call center as well as on the Web site. If a PlayStation user registers and purchases a yellow console but then wants to change to a silver console, he or she can call the customer service line, and the representative on the other end will change the order and indicate its availability, which brings us to the next concept—empowerment.[8]

As Chapter 1 explained, empowerment involves delegating authority to solve customers' problems. In other words, **empowerment** is the latitude organizations give their representatives to negotiate mutually satisfying commitments with customers. At Sony's PlayStation call center, a representative can change an order over the phone without having to wait for management's approval. Usually, organizational representatives are able to make such changes during interactions with customers through phone, fax, e-mail, Web communication, or face-to-face.

learning
An informal process of collecting customer data through customer comments and feedback on product or service performance.

knowledge management
The process by which learned information from customers is centralized and shared in order to enhance the relationship between customers and the organization.

empowerment
Delegation of authority to solve customers' problems quickly—usually by the first person that the customer notifies regarding the problem.

Sony's PlayStation system is one of the leaders in the video game market. To increase customer loyalty and ensure that the company's products meet the needs and wants of its target market, Sony designed a Web site that feels like an exclusive club for video gamers. And through player feedback, Sony can refine its site to match its customers' exact wants as they evolve.

LO2 Explain how to identify customer relationships with the organization

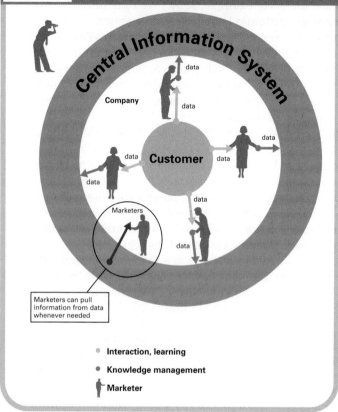

Central Information System

Company

data

data

data

Customer

data

data

data

Marketers

data

Marketers can pull information from data whenever needed

- Interaction, learning
- Knowledge management
- Marketer

An **interaction** is a touch point at which a customer and a company representative exchange information and develop learning relationships. With CRM the customer, and not the organization, defines the terms of the interaction, often by stating his or her preferences. The organization responds by designing products and services around customers' desired experiences. For example, students can purchase the Student Advantage Discount Card for a nominal fee and use it to obtain discounts from affiliated retailers, such as Dell, Foot Locker, Target, Timberland, and Barnes & Noble. Student Advantage tracks the cardholders' spending patterns and behaviors to gain a better understanding of what the college customer wants. Student Advantage then communicates this information to the affiliated retailers, who can tailor their discounts to meet college students' needs. Ultimately, everyone benefits from this program: cardholders get relevant discounts, and retailers enjoy increased sales.9

The success of CRM—building lasting and profitable relationships—can be directly measured by the effectiveness of the interaction between the customer and the organization. In fact, what further differentiates CRM from other strategic initiatives is the organization's ability to establish and manage interactions with its current customer base. The more latitude (empowerment) a company gives its representatives, the more likely the interaction will conclude in a way that satisfies the customer.

LO3
Understand Interactions of the Current Customer Base

The *interaction* between the customer and the organization is the foundation on which a CRM system is built. Only through effective interactions can organizations learn about the expectations of their customers, generate and manage knowledge about them, negotiate mutually satisfying commitments, and build long-term relationships.

Exhibit 19.2 illustrates the customer-centric approach for managing customer interactions. Following a customer-centric approach, an interaction can occur through a formal or direct communication channel, such as a phone, the Internet, or a salesperson. Interactions also occur through a previous relationship a customer has had with the organization, such as a past purchase or a survey response, or through some current transaction or request by the customer, such as an actual product purchase, a request for repair service, or a response to a coupon offer. In short, any activity or touch point a customer has with an organization, either directly or indirectly, constitutes an interaction.

Best Buy, an electronic retail superstore, offers a Performance Service Plan (PSP) on products bought in-store or online. The PSP guarantees products against damage and malfunctioning. If customers need assistance, they can contact the company by mail, phone, in-store, or online. All initial purchase contact information is kept in the customer database, along with copies of the PSP. If a customer calls the Customer Care 1-800 number, the representative will have access to all of this information and can either

interaction
The point at which a customer and a company representative exchange information and develop learning relationships.

help the customer or refer him or her to another representative. Thus, any form of communication with Best Buy whether initiated by the customer or by a company representative qualifies as an interaction or touch point.[10]

Companies that effectively manage customer interactions recognize that customers provide data to the organization that affect a wide variety of touch points. In a CRM system, **touch points** are all areas of a business where customers have contact with the company and data might be gathered. Touch points might include a customer registering for a particular service, a customer communicating with customer service for product information, a customer completing and returning the warranty information card for a product, or a customer talking with salespeople, delivery personnel, and product installers. In the Best Buy example, touch points include the initial customer-initiated purchase and the customer-initiated call to the Customer Care line. Data gathered at these touch points, once interpreted, provide information that affects touch points inside the company. For example, interpreted information may be redirected to marketing research, to develop profiles of extended warranty purchasers; to production, to analyze recurring problems and repair components; and to accounting, to establish cost-control models for repair service calls.

Exhibit 19.2

Customer-Centric Approach for Managing Customer Interactions

Current transaction

Channel ↔ Customer ↔ Past relationship

Requested service

Web-based interactions are an increasingly popular touch point for customers to communicate with companies on their own terms. Instead of wasting time with phone numbers and mail surveys, companies are publicizing their Web sites as the first touch point for customer interactions. Web users can evaluate and purchase products, make reservations, input preferential data, and provide customer feedback on services and products. Data from these Web-based interactions are then captured, compiled, and used to segment customers, refine marketing efforts, develop new products, and deliver a degree of individual customization to improve customer relationships.

When users log on to the Borders Books and Music Web site (teamed with Amazon), for example, as either members or guests, their queries and purchases are recorded and tracked. From that initial touch point, every time users enter the site, their preferences are shown first. If they have purchased any books or music in the past, the site will recommend new books or CDs from either the same or a similar author or artist. Similarly, if customers request a book by a particular author without making a purchase, they will be informed on a subsequent visit about new material that author has for sale.[11]

Another touch point is through **point-of-sale interactions** in stores or at information kiosks. Many point-of-sale software packages enable customers to easily provide information about themselves without feeling violated. The information is then used in two ways: for marketing and merchandising activities, and to accurately identify the store's best customers and the types of products they buy. Data collected at point-of-sale interactions is also used to increase customer satisfaction through the development of in-store services and customer recognition promotions. For example, Borders and Waldenbooks have joined together to offer a Platinum Visa Card that allows members to collect points for making purchases and redeem them for an in-store gift certificate. The companies can then track purchases and identify the best customers.

touch points
All possible areas of a business where customers communicate with that business

point-of-sale interactions
Communications between customers and organizations that occur at the point of sale, normally in a store.

LO3 Understand interactions with the current customer base

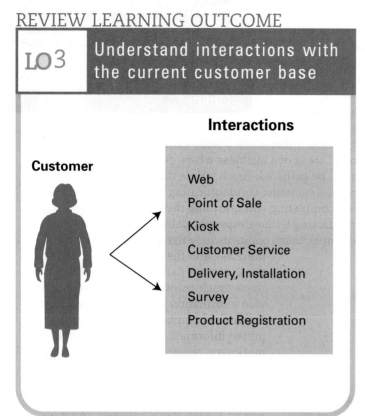

Interactions

Customer

Web

Point of Sale

Kiosk

Customer Service

Delivery, Installation

Survey

Product Registration

LO4 Capture Customer Data

Vast amounts of data can be obtained from the interactions between an organization and its customers. Therefore, in a CRM system, the issue is not how much data can be obtained, but rather what types of data should be acquired and how the data can effectively be used for relationship enhancement.

The traditional approach for acquiring data from customers is through channel interactions. Channel interactions include store visits, conversations with salespeople, interactions via the Web, traditional phone conversations, and wireless communications, such as cell phone conversations and satellite communications. In a CRM system, channel interactions are viewed as prime information sources based on the channel selected to initiate the interaction rather than on the data acquired. For example, if a consumer logs on to the Sony Web site to find out why a Sony device is not functioning properly and the answer is not available online, the consumer is then referred to a page where he or she can describe the problem. The Web site then e-mails the problem description to a company representative, who will research the problem and reply via e-mail. Furthermore, Sony will follow up with a brief satisfaction survey also sent via e-mail. Sony continues to use the e-mail mode of communication because the customer has established this as the preferred method of contact.[12]

Interactions between the company and the customer facilitate collection of large amounts of data. Companies can obtain not only simple contact information (name, address, phone number), but also data pertaining to the customer's current relationship with the organization—past purchase history, quantity and frequency of purchases, average amount spent on purchases, sensitivity to promotional activities, and so forth. GEICO Insurance Company, for example, at the time of policy renewal for its auto insurance customers, requests information pertaining to lifestyles (activities, interests, opinions, etc.), cultural factors (ethnicity, religion, etc.), and customer life stage (family composition, number and age of children, children living at home, etc.) for the purposes of pricing and customizing insurance packages for its customers. These data are also used for planning new product offerings such as vehicle maintenance insurance and gap insurance for lease customers along with cross-selling other GEICO services such as life insurance, home insurance, and marine insurance.[13]

In this manner, a lot of information can be captured from one individual customer across several touch points. Multiply this by the thousands of customers across all of the touch points with an organization, and the volume of data can rapidly become unmanageable for company personnel. The large volumes of data resulting from a CRM initiative can be managed effectively only through the use of technology. Furthermore, once customer data are collected, the question of who owns those data becomes extremely salient. In its privacy statement, Toysmart.com declared that it would never sell information registered at its Web site,

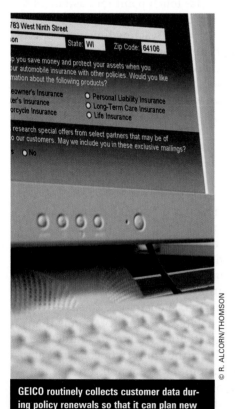

© R. ALCORN/THOMSON

GEICO routinely collects customer data during policy renewals so that it can plan new products and market new services towards its current customers. An important touch point for GEICO is its Web site.

LO4 Outline the process of capturing customer data

Collects customer information during every transaction, interaction.

Company

Information

Customer

→ Web
→ Point of sale
→ Kiosk
→ Customer service
→ Delivery, installation
→ Product use, consumption
→ Survey
→ Product registration

including children's names and birth dates, to a third party. When the company filed for bankruptcy protection, it said the information collected constituted a company asset that needed to be sold off to pay creditors. Despite the outrage at this announcement, many dot-com companies closing their doors found they had little in the way of assets and followed Toysmart's lead. The Maryland attorney general asked a U.S. Bankruptcy Court to reconsider its decision to allow garden-products seller MySeasons.com to sell its customer list despite its promise to keep customer information confidential.[14] In North Dakota, the issue was so alarming that voters overwhelmingly rejected a state law that would have allowed banks to sell customer information without written permission from the customers. Opponents of the law declared that customer information belongs to the customer, not the company.[15]

LO5
Store and Integrate Customer Data

Customer data are only as valuable as the system in which the data are stored and the consistency and accuracy of the data captured. Gathering data is further complicated by the fact that data needed by one unit of the organization, such as sales and marketing, often are generated by another area of the business or even a third-party supplier, such as an independent marketing research firm. Thus, companies must use information technology to capture, store, and integrate strategically important customer information. This process of centralizing data in a CRM system is referred to as data warehousing.

A **data warehouse** is a central repository (*database*) of customer data collected by an organization. Essentially, it is a large computerized file of all information collected in the previous phase of the CRM process, for example, information collected in channel, transaction, and product/service touch points. The core of the data warehouse is the **database**, "a collection of data, especially one that can be accessed and manipulated by computer software."[16] The CRM database focuses on collecting vital statistics on consumers, their purchasing habits, transaction methods, and product usage in a centralized repository that is accessible by all functional areas of a company. Traditionally, this information was stored in separate computer systems throughout the company. By utilizing a data warehouse, however, marketing managers can quickly access vast amounts of information required to make decisions. For example, Continental Airlines used to store data in a variety of operational systems that could not be integrated. As a result, managers did not have the depth and breadth of information to facilitate their decision-making capabilities. Now the Continental data warehouse centralizes data from 41 sources. The warehouse is accessible by 35 departments and 1,300 employees. The database content includes everything from flight schedules, seat inventory, and customer profiles to employee and crew payroll. Even aircraft parts and maintenance are being added to the system to aid in distribution decision making.[17]

data warehouse
A central repository for data from various functional areas of the organization that are stored and inventoried on a centralized computer system so that the information can be shared across all functional departments of the business.

database
A collection of data, especially one that can be accessed and manipulated by computer software.

When a company builds its database, the first step is to develop a list. Usually, this is in the form of a **response list,** based on customers who have indicated interest in a product or service, or a **compiled list,** created by an outside company that has collected names and contact information for potential consumers. Response lists tend to be especially valuable because past behavior is a strong predictor of future behavior and because consumers who have indicated interest in the product or service are more prone to purchase. Compiled lists usually are prepared by an outside company and are available for purchase. A compiled list generally includes names and addresses gleaned from telephone directories or membership rosters. Many lists are available, ranging from those owned by large list companies, such as Dun & Bradstreet for business-to-business data and Donnelley and R. L. Polk for consumer lists, to small groups or associations that are willing to sell their membership lists. Data compiled by large data-gathering companies usually are very accurate.

In this phase companies are usually collecting channel, transaction, and product/service information such as store, salesperson, communication channel, contact information, relationship, and brands. For example, when Philips wanted to determine how to best sell its CoolSkin Shaver accessories, it used existing information to expand its database. By sending an e-mail to registered users, Philips was able to collect information including whether consumers purchased online; if so, the "landing page" on the Web site; the number of "unsubscribes" when sent an e-mail; and the timeliness of response.[18]

A customer database becomes even more useful to marketing managers when it is enhanced to include more than simply a customer's or prospect's name, address, telephone number, and transaction history. Database enhancement involves purchasing information on customers or prospects to better describe their needs or determine how responsive they might be to marketing programs. Types of enhancement data typically include demographic, lifestyle, or behavioral information. Lands' End, for example, has enhanced its database to better understand purchasing patterns. The database not only pinpoints popular clothing items, but also attempts to explain why. In one instance, sales of raincoats increased sharply in the Northeast. Because the database is linked to regional weather information, analysts were able to explain the sudden boost in raincoat sales.[19]

Database enhancement can increase the effectiveness of marketing programs. By learning more about their best and most profitable customers, marketers can maximize the effectiveness of marketing communications and cross-selling. Database enhancement also helps a company find new prospects. Before opening a new store, H-E-B Grocery Company (http://www.heb.com) uses database enhancement and customer profiling to identify and learn as much as possible about potential customers. Each store is then designed to be unique and to offer the products those customers want. When the company opened one of its upscale Central Market stores in Fort Worth, Texas, customer profiles indicated that Fort Worth residents have a strong sense of Western heritage. The Fort Worth location, therefore, offers customers chipotle-smoked barbecue ribs, game birds, and briskets. The store has also adjusted the way it cuts and sells beef to meet local preferences, and it carries an expanded selection of peppers and fresh tortillas for its Hispanic customers. Once open, the stores continue to use databases to collect information about customer preferences and to tweak product offerings.

Multinational companies building worldwide databases often face difficult problems when pulling together internal data about their customers. Differences in language, computer systems, and data-collection methods can be huge obstacles to overcome. In spite of the challenges, many global companies are committed to building databases. Unilever is using the Internet not only to educate consumers about the brand but also to develop relationships with its customers by providing helpful information. Web site visitors can get information on removing stubborn stains and solving similar consumer problems. They also receive a discount on their next purchase in exchange for completing an online questionnaire. With diligent effort, Unilever has collected information on more than 30 million loyal customers from numerous countries.[20]

response list
A customer list that includes the names and addresses of individuals who have responded to an offer of some kind, such as by mail, telephone, direct-response television, product rebates, contests or sweepstakes, or billing inserts.

compiled list
A customer list that was developed by gathering names and addresses from telephone directories and membership rosters, usually enhanced with information from public records, such as census data, auto registrations, birth announcements, business start-ups, or bankruptcies.

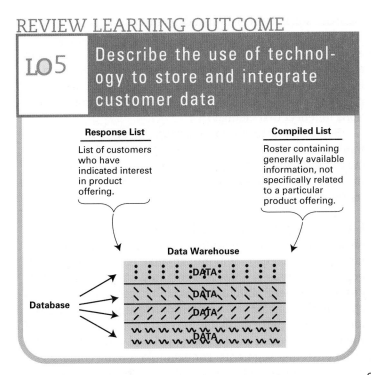

LO5 Describe the use of technology to store and integrate customer data

Response List

List of customers who have indicated interest in product offering.

Compiled List

Roster containing generally available information, not specifically related to a particular product offering.

Database

Data Warehouse

:::::: :DATA: : : : : :
\ \ \ \ \ \DATA\ \ \ \ \
/ / / / /DATA/ / / / /
∾∾∾∾∾∾DATA∾∾∾∾∾

LO⁶ Identifying the Best Customers

CRM manages interactions between a company and its customers. To be successful, companies must identify customers who yield high profits or potential profits. To do so, significant amounts of data must be gathered from customers, stored and integrated in the data warehouse, and then analyzed and interpreted for common patterns that can identify homogeneous customers who are different from other customer segments. Because not all customers are the same, organizations need to develop interactions that target *individual* customer needs and wants. Likewise, not all customers do generate the same revenue for a company. Recall, from Chapter 7, the 80/20 principle—80 percent of a company's revenue is generated by 20 percent of its customers. Therefore, the question becomes, how do we identify the 20 percent of our customer base that contributes 80 percent of our revenue? In a CRM system, the answer is data mining.

DATA MINING

Data mining is used to find hidden patterns and relationships in the customer data stored in the data warehouse. It is a data analysis approach that identifies patterns of characteristics that relate to particular customers or customer groups. Although businesses have been conducting such analyses for many years, the procedures typically were performed on small data sets containing as few as 300 to 400 customers. Today, with the development of sophisticated data warehouses, millions of customers' shopping patterns can be analyzed. Wal-Mart's data warehouse, believed to be second in size only to the Pentagon's, contains over 200 terabytes (trillions of characters) of customer transaction data. Wal-Mart uses its huge data warehouse to help each of its stores adapt its merchandising mix to local neighborhood preferences.

Using data mining, marketers can search the data warehouse, capture relevant data, categorize significant characteristics, and develop customer profiles. For example, in the Philips razor example, marketers were attempting to build a relationship with consumers through e-mail. By assessing response and nonresponse rates along with online purchases, they developed a profile of consumers likely to purchase CoolSkin accessories over the Internet. Moreover, once Philips was successful with CoolSkin accessories, it used this approach on other product lines.[21]

When using data mining, it is important to remember that the real value is in the company's ability to transform its data from operational bits and bytes into information marketers need for successful marketing strategies. Companies must go beyond merely creating a mailing list. They must analyze the data to identify and profile the best customers, calculate their lifetime value, and ultimately predict purchasing behavior through statistical modeling.

A wide range of companies have used data mining successfully. Albertson's Supermarkets use data mining to identify commonly purchased items that should be placed together on shelves and to learn what soft drinks sell best in different parts of the country. Using data mining, Camelot Music discovered that a large number of senior citizens were purchasing rap and alternative music. When managers investigated further, they discovered seniors were buying the music as gifts for their grandchildren. Finally, TheKnot.com, a Web site that helps plan weddings, asks users to register and provide basic information. Its

© DIGITAL VISION/GETTY IMAGES

database stores information and creates an initial profile of a customer. From the initial contact, the Web site gathers data as the customer uses the site. For example, when a user adds a product to the registry, the database is updated to reflect that change. Thus, if a consumer adds a different brand or product to the list, the site will tailor product recommendations to reflect that change.[22]

Before the information is leveraged, several types of analysis are often run on the data. These analyses include customer segmentation, recency-frequency-monetary analysis (RFM), lifetime value analysis (LTV), and predictive modeling.

Customer Segmentation

Recall that *customer segmentation* is the process of breaking large groups of customers into smaller, more homogeneous groups. This type of analysis generates a "profile" or picture of the customers' similar demographic, geographic, and psychographic traits as well as their previous purchase behavior; it focuses particularly on the best customers. Profiles of the best customers can be compared and contrasted with other customer segments. For example, a bank could segment consumers on frequency of usage, credit, age, and turnover. Once a profile of the best customer is developed using these criteria, it can be used to screen other potential consumers. Similarly, customer profiles can be used to introduce customers selectively to specific marketing actions. For example, young customers with an open mind can be introduced to home banking, and older, well-established customers to investment opportunities. See Chapter 7 for a detailed discussion of segmentation.

Recency-Frequency-Monetary Analysis (RFM)

Customers who have purchased recently and often and have spent considerable money are more likely to purchase again. Recency-frequency-monetary analysis (RFM) identifies those customers most likely to purchase again because they have bought recently, bought frequently, or spent a specified amount of money with the firm. Firms develop equations to identify the "best customers" (often the top 20 percent of the customer base) by assigning a score to customer records in the database on how often, how recently, and how much they have spent. Customers are then ranked to determine which ones move to the top of the list and which ones fall to the bottom. The ranking provides the basis for maximizing profits because it enables the firm to use the information in its customer database to select those persons who have proved to be good sources of revenue. Casino operator Harrah's Entertainment used data mining and RFM to identify 90 market segments that it can target with its marketing programs. Using direct feedback from the slots as to whether its strategies are working, Harrah's continuously tweaks its marketing tactics to focus on the most profitable segments.[23]

Lifetime Value Analysis (LTV)

Recency, frequency, and monetary data can also be used to create a lifetime value model on customers in the database. Whereas RFM looks at how valuable a customer currently is to a company, **lifetime value analysis (LTV)** projects the future value of the customer over a period of years. One of the basic assumptions in any lifetime value calculation is that marketing to repeat customers is more profitable than marketing to first-time buyers. That is, it costs more to find a new customer in terms of promotion and gaining trust than to sell more to a customer who is already loyal.

Customer lifetime value has a number of benefits. It shows marketers how much they can spend to *acquire* new customers, it tells them the level of spending to *retain* cus-

lifetime value analysis (LTV)
A data manipulation technique that projects the future value of the customer over a period of years using the assumption that marketing to repeat customers is more profitable than marketing to first-time buyers.

LO6 Describe how to identify the best customers

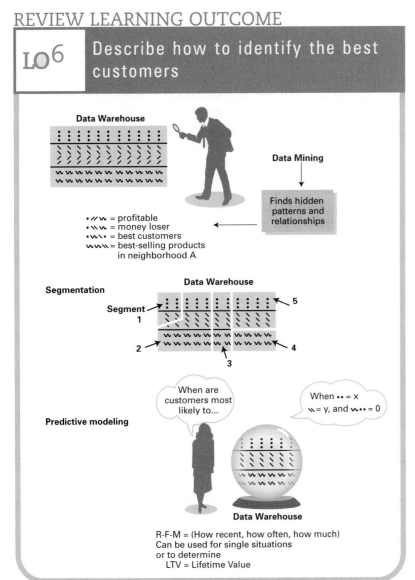

• //w = profitable
• \\w = money loser
• w\• = best customers
w\w\ = best-selling products
in neighborhood A

Segmentation

Segment 1

Predictive modeling

When are customers most likely to...

When •• = x
\\ = y, and w•• = 0

Data Warehouse

R-F-M = (How recent, how often, how much)
Can be used for single situations
or to determine
LTV = Lifetime Value

predictive modeling
A data manipulation technique in which marketers try to determine, based on some past set of occurrences, what the odds are that some other occurrence, such as a response or purchase, will take place in the future.

campaign management
Developing product or service offerings customized for the appropriate customer segment and then pricing and communicating these offerings for the purpose of enhancing customer relationships

tomers, and it facilitates targeting new customers who look as though they will be profitable customers. Cadillac has calculated the lifetime value of its top customers at $332,000. Similarly, Pizza Hut figures its best customers are worth $8,000 in bottom-line lifetime value.

Predictive Modeling

The ability to reasonably predict future customer behavior gives marketers a significant competitive advantage. Through **predictive modeling,** marketers try to determine, based on some past set of occurrences, what the odds are that some other occurrence, such as an Internet inquiry or purchase, will take place in the future. SPSS Predictive Marketing is one tool marketers can use to answer questions about their consumers. The software requires minimal knowledge of statistical analysis. Users operate from a prebuilt model, which generates profiles in three to four days. SPSS also has an online product that predicts Web site users' behavior. FT.com, the *Financial Times* Web site, uses the software to predict which subscribers may not renew their subscription and to convince users of free content to "subscribe" to FT.com.[24]

LO7 Leverage Customer Information

Data mining identifies the most profitable customers and prospects. Managers can then design tailored marketing strategies to best appeal to the identified segments. In CRM this is commonly referred to as leveraging customer information to facilitate enhanced relationships with customers. Exhibit 19.3 shows some common CRM marketing database applications.

CAMPAIGN MANAGEMENT

Through campaign management, all areas of the company participate in the development of programs targeted to customers. **Campaign management** involves monitoring and leveraging customer interactions to sell a company's products and to increase customer service. Campaigns are based directly on data obtained from customers through various interactions. Campaign management includes monitoring the success of the communications based on customer reactions through sales, orders, callbacks to the company, and the like. If a campaign appears unsuccessful, it is evaluated and changed to better achieve the company's desired objective. Stave Puzzles, the "Rolls-Royce" of puzzles, produces handcrafted wood puzzles. Each puzzle is unique and can be customized as the customer desires. Steve Richardson, the company's

Exhibit 19.3
**Common CRM Marketing
Database Applications**

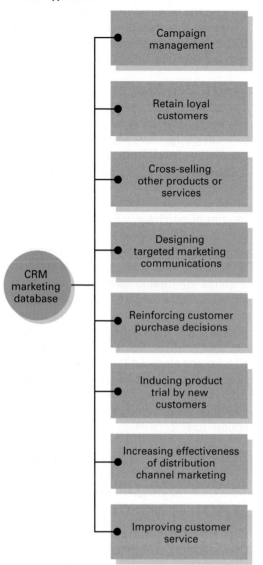

- Campaign management
- Retain loyal customers
- Cross-selling other products or services
- Designing targeted marketing communications
- Reinforcing customer purchase decisions
- Inducing product trial by new customers
- Increasing effectiveness of distribution channel marketing
- Improving customer service

CRM marketing database

cofounder, has narrowed his customer base to his "Hot Hundred" most valuable customers. To manage his customer base and ensure they are receiving optimal service, he tracks not only standard information, such as contact data and orders, but also birthdays, anniversaries, relationships between customers, phone conversations, inquiries, and workshop visits.[25]

Campaign management involves developing customized product and service offerings for the appropriate customer segment, pricing these offerings attractively, and communicating these offers in a manner that enhances customer relationships. Customizing product and service offerings requires managing multiple interactions with customers, as well as giving priority to those products and services that are viewed as most desirable for a specifically designated customer. Even within a highly defined market segment, individual customer differences will emerge. Therefore, interactions among customers must focus on individual experiences, expectations, and desires. Stave Puzzles customizes its marketing campaigns by tailoring mailouts to eight different segments. For example, the monthly buyers and top 10 percent of the customers receive individual reminder notes about special occasions and previous purchases.

RETAINING LOYAL CUSTOMERS

If a company has identified its best customers, then it should make every effort to maintain and increase their loyalty. When a company retains an additional 5 percent of its customers each year, profits will increase by as much as 25 percent. What's more, improving customer retention by a mere 2 percent can decrease costs by as much as 10 percent.[26] For example, The Palace of Auburn Hills, a sporting venue, is home to the NBA Detroit Pistons and the WNBA Detroit Shock. To increase game attendance, the arena developed its MyPal rewards card, which enables fans to receive e-mail updates. As a result, game attendance has increased for all types of consumers.[27]

Loyalty programs reward loyal customers for making multiple purchases. The objective is to build long-term mutually beneficial relationships between a company and its key customers. Marriot, Hilton, and Starwood Hotels, for instance, reward their best customers with special perks not available to customers who stay less frequently. Travelers who spend a specified number of nights per year receive reservation guarantees, upgrades to better rooms, welcome gifts like fruit baskets and wine in their rooms, free phone service, and access to concierge lounges. In addition to rewarding good customers, loyalty programs provide businesses with a wealth of information about their customers and shopping trends that can be used to make future business decisions. CVS, the U.S. drugstore chain with the most stores, has an ExtraCare program that allows customers to register for a card that is swiped prior to each purchase and gives discounts and offers special in-store promotions. The coupons and discounts are based on purchase history, which allows the company to sell more products. The ExtraCare program has also resulted in an increase in purchase frequency.[28]

CROSS-SELLING OTHER PRODUCTS AND SERVICES

CRM provides many opportunities to cross-sell related products. Marketers can use the database to match product profiles and consumer profiles so that they can cross-sell customers products that match their demographic, lifestyle, or behavioral characteristics. American Collegiate Marketing, a magazine subscription service targeted to students and educators (**http://www.magazineline.com**), uses past customer purchase information gleaned from its database of millions of magazine subscribers to feature new magazines that may interest the customer. Past purchase behavior may show that subscribers to *Sports Illustrated,* for instance, are also interested in general news magazines such as *Time* and *Newsweek.* Similarly, to increase purchasing across different departments and in different product lines, Wegmans Food Markets monitors sales using a frequent buyer card. Using data mining, it discovered that 80 percent of shoppers buying baby food also bought flowers. As a result, Wegmans was able to develop a more effective method for cross-selling products.[29]

Internet companies use product and customer profiling to reveal cross-selling opportunities while a customer is surfing their site. Past purchases on a particular Web site and the site a surfer comes from give online marketers clues about the surfer's interests and what items to cross-sell. Fry's Outpost electronics (**http://www.outpost.com**), a computer-goods e-tailer, adjusts the pages visitors see depending on what they click on at the site or what they purchased in the past. For instance, if a surfer always goes to computer game pages or has purchased games in the past, Outpost will automatically place offers for other game titles on part of the screen. Depending on what a shopper puts in a shopping cart, Outpost will flash promotions for related items—a leather case for someone who is buying a PDA, for example.

DESIGNING TARGETED MARKETING COMMUNICATIONS

Using transaction and purchase data, a database allows marketers to track customers' relationships to the company's products and services and modify the marketing message accordingly. For example, Kraft Foods teamed with Wegmans Food Markets to determine which advertising campaigns were most effective for frequent buyers of Kraft Macaroni & Cheese. Kraft used the results to better reach its frequent buyers in future campaigns.[30]

Customers can also be segmented into infrequent users, moderate users, and heavy users. A segmented communications strategy can then be developed based on which group the customer falls into. Communications to infrequent users might encourage repeat purchases through a direct incentive such as a limited-time price discount for ordering again. Communications to moderate users may use fewer incentives and more reinforcement of past purchase decisions. Communications to heavy users would be designed around loyalty and reinforcement of the purchase rather than price promotions. For example, Nike Store Toronto offers the Air Max Club (AMC), a loyalty club for customers. Club members can collect points and redeem them for gift certificates, movies, and books. Customers considered "most valuable" are identified when they swipe their card to collect points, thereby alerting the salesperson. A message on the salesperson's screen indicates that the customer should receive a special thank-you and possibly a prize. The system also generates customized coupons based on purchase history. The company has found that club members spend about 50 percent more than the average customer.[31]

REINFORCING CUSTOMER PURCHASE DECISIONS

As you learned in the consumer behavior chapter, cognitive dissonance is the feeling consumers experience when they recognize an inconsistency between their values and opinions and their purchase behavior. In other words, they doubt the soundness of their purchase decision and often feel anxious. CRM offers marketers an excellent opportunity to reach out to customers to reinforce the purchase decision. By thanking customers for their purchases and telling them they are important, marketers can help cement a long-term, profitable relationship. Guests staying at the quaint Village Country Inn nestled in the Green Mountains of Vermont receive a

Olay, a brand of Procter & Gamble, invites customers to join Club Olay, which offers special discounts, free samples, and the opportunity to purchase products before they're available in stores. But members are also able to communicate with the company by sharing their beauty secrets and entering various sweepstakes.

handwritten thank-you note from the inn's proprietors within a week of their stay. The note thanks the guests for visiting and encourages them to return in the future.

Updating customers periodically about the status of their order reinforces purchase decisions. Postsale e-mails also afford the chance to provide more customer service or cross-sell other products. Minutes after customers order merchandise from Amazon.com's Web site, for example, they receive an e-mail acknowledging their order. Every few days thereafter, customers receive updates that allow them to track the shipment of the order, from ship date to receipt. Similarly, Sumerset Houseboats builds customized, luxury houseboats priced at about $250,000 each. The company uses its Web site to monitor customer profiles, post company information, and communicate with customers. For example, it posts daily pictures of progress on houseboats being built. By reinforcing customers' decisions, Sumerset is able to offset the feeling of cognitive dissonance.[32]

INDUCING PRODUCT TRIAL BY NEW CUSTOMERS

Although significant time and money are expended on encouraging repeat purchases by the best customers, a marketing database is also used to identify new customers. Because a firm using a marketing database already has a profile of its best customers, it can easily use the results of modeling to profile potential customers. EATEL, a regional telecommunications firm, uses modeling to identify prospective residential and commercial telephone customers and successfully attract their business.

Marketing managers generally use demographic and behavioral data overlaid on existing customer data to develop a detailed customer profile that is a powerful tool for evaluating lists of prospects. For instance, if a firm's best customers are 35 to 50 years of age, live in suburban areas, own luxury cars, like to eat at Thai restaurants, and enjoy mountain climbing, then the company can find prospects already in its database or customers who currently are identified as using a competitor's product that match this profile. Procter & Gamble uses its Web site to test customer interest in new products. Customers who visit the Web site are encouraged to sign up for free trial samples and then provide feedback. P&G also uses the demographic data and customer feedback to make product and promotion decisions.

American ExpressPay keys contain a radio-frequency identification chip that enables cardholders to make instant purchases at places like Carl's Jr. restaurants. The ExpressPay keys are contactless versions of American Express credit cards, requiring the user to simply tap the card on a special reader to make a purchase.

INCREASING EFFECTIVENESS OF DISTRIBUTION CHANNEL MARKETING

In Chapter 12 you learned that a marketing channel is a business structure of interdependent organizations, such as wholesalers and retailers, which move a product from the producer to the ultimate consumer. Most marketers rely on indirect channels to move their products to the end user. Thus, marketers often lose touch with the customer as an individual since the relationship is really between the retailer and the consumer. Marketers in this predicament often view their customers as aggregate statistics because specific customer information is difficult to gather.

With CRM databases, manufacturers now have a tool to gain insight into who is buying their products. Instead of simply unloading products into the distribution channel and leaving marketing and relationship building to dealers, auto manufacturers today are using Web sites to keep in touch with customers and prospects, learn about their lifestyles and hobbies, understand their vehicle needs, and develop relationships in hopes these consumers will reward them with brand loyalty in the future. BMW and Mercedes-

Benz USA, as well as other vehicle manufacturers, have databases with names of millions of consumers who have expressed an interest.

With many brick-and-mortar stores setting up shop online, companies are now challenged to monitor purchases of customers who shop both in-store and online. This concept is referred to as multichannel marketing. After Lands' End determined that multichannel customers are the most valuable, the company targeted marketing campaigns toward retaining these customers and increased sales significantly. Talbot's and Victoria's Secret have also developed successful campaigns to serve multichannel customers.

Companies are also using radio-frequency identification (RFID) technology to improve distribution. The technology uses a microchip with an antenna that tracks anything from a soda can to a car. A computer can locate the product anywhere. The main implication of this technology is that companies will enjoy a reduction in theft and loss of merchandise shipments and will always know where merchandise is in the distribution channel. Moreover, as this technology is further developed, marketers will be able to gather essential information related to product usage and consumption.[33]

IMPROVING CUSTOMER SERVICE

CRM marketing techniques increasingly are being used to improve customer service. Boise Cascade Office Products uses CRM to compete against competitors like Staples and Office Depot. The company recently changed its culture to become more customer-centric. Sales reps are sent out to meet one-to-one with customers, and when customers place orders, either by phone or the Internet, information technology software automatically accesses their transaction history and customizes the response. In another competitive move, Boise Cascade acquired office products retailer OfficeMax. When the merger was announced, the company's chairman stated, "The combined office products business will be strategically stronger and better able to deliver compelling value to its customers through all channels and across all segments of the market."[34]

PRIVACY CONCERNS AND CRM

Before rushing out to invest in a CRM system and build a database, marketers should consider consumers' reactions to the growing use of databases. Many Americans and customers abroad are concerned about databases because of the potential for invasion of privacy. The sheer volume of information that is aggregated in databases makes this information vulnerable to unauthorized access and use. A fundamental aspect of marketing using CRM databases is providing valuable services to customers based on knowledge of what customers really value. It is critical, however, that marketers remember that these relationships should be built on trust. Although database technology enables marketers to compile ever-richer information about their customers that can be used to build and manage relationships, if these customers feel their privacy is being violated, then the relationship becomes a liability.

The popularity of the Internet for e-commerce and customer data collection and as a repository for sensitive customer data has alarmed privacy-minded customers. Online users complain loudly about being "spammed," and Web surfers, including

REVIEW LEARNING OUTCOME

LO7 Explain the process of leveraging customer information throughout the organization

Marketing Information

CRM Database

Applications

✓ Campaign management

✓ Retaining loyal customers

✓ Cross-selling other products and services

✓ Designing targeted marketing communications

✓ Reinforcing customer purchase decisions

✓ Inducing product trial by new customers

✓ Increasing effectiveness of distribution channel marketing

✓ Improving customer service

children, are routinely asked to divulge personal information to access certain screens or purchase goods or services. Internet users are disturbed by the amount of information businesses collect on them as they visit various sites in cyberspace. Indeed, many users are unaware of how personal information is collected, used, and distributed. The government actively sells huge amounts of personal information to list companies. State motor vehicle bureaus sell names and addresses of individuals who get driver's licenses. Hospitals sell the names of women who just gave birth on their premises. Consumer credit databases are often used by credit card marketers to prescreen targets for solicitations. Online and off-line privacy concerns are growing and ultimately will have to be dealt with by businesses and regulators.

Privacy policies for companies in the United States are largely voluntary, and regulations on how personal data are collected and used are being developed. But collecting data on consumers outside the United States is a different matter. For database marketers venturing beyond U.S. borders, success requires careful navigation of foreign privacy laws. For example, under the European Union's European Data Protection Directive, any business that trades with a European organization must comply with the EU's rules for handling information about individuals or risk prosecution. More than 50 nations have, or are developing, privacy legislation. Europe has the strictest legislation regarding the collection and use of customer data, and other countries are looking to that legislation when formulating their policies. The "Ethics in Marketing" box provides more perspectives on resolving CRM privacy issues.

ETHICS in Marketing

Privacy Issues Must Be Resolved for CRM's Success

CRM is a hot marketing topic and a popular business tool. But it also sparks hot debates regarding consumers' privacy. American businesses have collected consumer data for years. Policies and laws govern what businesses can do with that information once it is collected. Current laws cover several industries including finance, health care, retail, automotive and transportation, technology, and direct marketing. The Gramm-Leach-Bliley Act enforces privacy guidelines for financial information, the Health Insurance Portability and Accountability Act (HIPAA) regulates medical records, and the National Do-Not-Call list governs telemarketing. Most recently, the CAN-SPAM Act provided guidelines for e-mail.

Companies have taken initiatives, too. Many have developed independent privacy policies designed to govern how they collect, use, share, and protect the personal information of consumers and employees. According to the 2003 Benchmark Study of Corporate Privacy Practices Report, 98 percent of U.S. companies have a privacy policy in effect. Nevertheless, more than half of those companies feel their policy may be difficult to understand. One problem is that only 53 percent require mandatory training for policy enforcement. Consequently, consumer information is still vulnerable to unethical corporate practices.

Despite consumers' concerns, company executives realize that consumer information is very profitable. Companies can profit by sharing the information with a third party or by purchasing third-party information to build a more comprehensive database. As a result, companies are struggling to balance consumer trust and profitability. For example, the Walt Disney Company had a strict policy that did not allow it to share information collected on its Web site with third parties. Once executives realized the value of the information, however, they amended the privacy policy to enable third-party companies to send promotions to consumers. To ensure continued consumer trust, Disney allows consumers to opt in or opt out of third-party promotions. Additionally, Disney offers consumers updated privacy information on its Web site and sends e-mails to registered users explaining any privacy policy changes.[35]

How does a firm's privacy policy affect your purchasing decisions? Do you think it is ethical for a company to post a privacy policy but not have mandatory enforcement? What are the most important issues in establishing a privacy policy for a business?

Quick Check

Now that you've read the chapter, do you get it?
Take a moment for a quick check using this scale:

1 Not at all; 2 Not very well; 3 Ok; 4 Well; 5 Very Well

Can you . . .

___ diagram the customer relationship management cycle?

___ differentiate between learning and knowledge management?

___ identify the various interactions companies have with their customers?

___ explain to a friend what a data warehouse, database, response list, and compiled list are?

___ list and define the different types of data mining tools marketers use to identify the best customers?

___ describe the various ways marketers can use customer information?

___ compare the various pricing tactics marketers use?

___ explain why privacy concerns are an issue for companies implementing CRM?

___ TOTAL

Score: 33–40, you're ready to move on to the applications; 25–32, skim the chapter one more time before moving on to the applications; 17–24, reread the sections giving you the most trouble and go to Thomson NOW for guided tutorials; 16 and under, you better reread the chapter to get a grasp of the fundamentals. If you've reread the chapter and still have a low score, visit your professor or TA during office hours.

LO 1 Define customer relationship management. Customer relationship management (CRM) is a company-wide business strategy designed to optimize profitability, revenue, and customer satisfaction by focusing on highly defined and precise customer groups. This is accomplished by organizing the company around customer segments, encouraging and tracking customer interaction with the company, fostering customer-satisfying behaviors, and linking all processes of a company from its customers through its suppliers.

1.1 Identify the six components of the CRM process.

1.2 Form a team and identify several local businesses that would benefit from a CRM strategy. Select one business and outline a plan for implementing a CRM strategy for that business. You may want to visit the company and interview managers about their current initiatives. When you have completed your CRM plan, share it with the class—and the company.

1.3 General Motors installs the "OnStar" system in many of its vehicles. OnStar is a location, information, and communication system available to drivers who wish to subscribe to the service. Go to the OnStar Web site, **http://www.onstar.com**, and read about some of the services that are offered to consumers. Based on what you learn, write a short report describing the various ways that OnStar can be used as a CRM tool, specifically in the context of creating interactions, gathering customer data, and customizing service offerings to customers.

LO 2 Explain how to identify customer relationships with the organization. Companies that implement a CRM system adhere to a customer-centric focus or model. A customer-centric company focuses on learning the factors that build long-lasting relationships with valuable customers and then builds its system on what satisfies and retains those customers. Building relationships through CRM is a strategic process that focuses on learning, managing customer knowledge, and empowerment.

2.1 Briefly explain the concept of a customer-centric focus. Why is this so important in a CRM process?

2.2 What is meant by knowledge management? Why is it so important in a CRM system?

LO 3 Understand interactions with the current customer base. The interaction between the customer and the organization is considered to be the foundation on which a CRM system is built. Only through effective interactions can organizations learn about the expectations of their customers, generate and manage knowledge about them, negotiate mutually satisfying commitments, and build long-term relationships. Effective management of customer interactions recognizes that customers provide information to organizations across a wide variety of touch points. Consumer-centric organizations are implementing new and unique approaches for establishing interactions specifically for this purpose. They include Web-based interactions, point-of-sale interactions, and transaction-based interactions.

3.1 Develop a plan for establishing and managing interactions with a business's customers. In this plan, identify the key touch points for customers, explain how the data warehouse would be designed, and indicate the main interaction methods that would be promoted to the customer.

LO4 Outline the process of capturing customer data. Based on the interaction between the organization and its customers, vast amounts of information can be obtained. In a CRM system, the issue is not how much data can be obtained, but rather what type of data should be acquired and how those data can be used effectively for relationship enhancement. The channel, transaction, and product or service consumed all constitute touch points between a customer and the organization. These touch points represent possible areas within a business where customer interactions can take place and, hence, the opportunity for acquiring data from the customer.

4.1 Assume you are the manager for a Hard Rock Café. Your boss has asked you to evaluate how the company is using its Web site to gather customer data. Go to the Web site for the Hard Rock (**http://www.hardrock.com**) and provide a detailed critique on how the site is used for capturing customer data. Comment on the types of customer data the Web site is designed to capture, and explain how those data would benefit your local Hard Rock operation.

LO5 Describe the use of technology to store and integrate customer data. Customer data gathering is complicated because information needed by one unit of the organization (e.g., sales and marketing) is often generated by another area of the business or even a third-party supplier (e.g., an independent marketing research firm). Because of the lack of standard structure and interface, organizations rely on technology to capture, store, and integrate strategically important customer information. The process of centralizing data in a CRM system is referred to as data warehousing. A data warehouse is a central repository of customer information collected by an organization.

5.1 Briefly explain the concept of a data warehouse. In the context of a CRM framework, why is a data warehouse such an important tool?

5.2 What is being written about customer data in today's periodicals? Search your favorite database of articles using keywords like "customer data" and "data warehousing." Are certain industries better represented in the citation list generated by your search? Are certain issues more prevalent? Read a selection of at least three to four articles, and write a brief analysis of what is being discussed in the press regarding these CRM topics.

LO6 Describe how to identify the best customers. Customer relationship management, as a process strategy, attempts to manage the interactions between a company and its customers. To be successful, organizations must identify customers who yield high profitability or high potential profitability. To accomplish this task, significant amounts of information must be gathered from customers, stored and integrated in the data warehouse, and then analyzed for commonalities that can produce segments that are highly similar, yet different from other customer segments. A useful approach to identifying the best customers is recency-frequency-monetary (RFM) analysis. Data mining uses RFM, predictive modeling, and other approaches to identify significant relationships among several customer dimensions within vast data warehouses. These significant relationships enable marketers to better define the most profitable customers and prospects.

6.1 Explain the concept of data mining. Provide five examples of companies that are currently using data mining, and explain why each is using it.

LO7 Explain the process of leveraging customer information throughout the organization. One of the benefits of a CRM system is the capacity to share information throughout the organization. This allows an organization to interact with all functional areas to develop programs targeted to its customers. This process is commonly referred to as campaign management. Campaign management involves developing customized product/service offerings for the appropriate customer segment and pricing and communicating these offerings for the purpose of enhancing customer relationships.

7.1 Campaign management is a benefit derived by an organization's ability to leverage and disseminate information throughout the company. Briefly define campaign management and explain how a business may apply it to its daily operations. In your answer, select a particular business as an example of effective campaign management.

7.2 What kind of product testing is currently going on at the Procter & Gamble Web site (**http://www.pg.com**)? Sign up to participate and find out how the company implements its one-to-one marketing plan through its Web site.

Key Terms

campaign management	613	database	609	point-of-sale interactions	607
compiled list	610	empowerment	605	predictive modeling	613
customer relationship management (CRM)	602	interaction	606	response list	610
customer-centric	604	knowledge management	605	touch points	607
		learning	605		
data warehouse	609	lifetime value analysis (LTV)	612		

Exercises

APPLICATION EXERCISE

Understanding how companies use consumer information can be difficult if you have never had a job or internship that required you to use databases or customer profiles.[36]

Activity

1. Save all the direct-mail advertising that comes to your mailbox for at least a week. You may ask your parents or friends to collect direct mail that they receive as well.

2. Once you have your stack of mail, organize it according to the household that received it. For example, if friends and family helped you collect mail, then keep mail sent to each address together. Make a list of all material in each group.

3. To what kind of customer is each piece of mail targeted? What makes you think as you do?

4. Write out an aggregate profile for each address. If you were a direct marketer, what kind of products and services would you market to each? What kind of offers would you create?

5. Based on the content of the mail pieces, determine what kind of information the various companies have about you, your friends, or your family in their databases. Are there indications on the mailers about what kind of interactions the recipient has had with the sender of the marketing piece?

Entrepreneurship Case

THEY SHOULD HAVE 'DUNN' THIS MUCH SOONER! U.K. FIRM LEADS KROGER TURNAROUND

Supermarkets have long engaged in an intense struggle to interpret the mountains of data they compile from customer loyalty and frequent buyer cards. Though many are good at collecting information, few are actually effective at targeting appealing promotions based on what they learn from those cards. Falling behind on this important aspect of such a marketing-driven business almost cost Kroger its business life. Thankfully, little-known, London-based, relationship marketing specialist Dunnhumby was willing to come to the rescue.

Founded in 1989 by husband-and-wife team Edwina Dunn and Clive Humby, the firm gained acclaim for the work it did with cutting-edge U.K. grocer Tesco. The key to their success was the Tesco Club Card program that Dunnhumby created. The program boasts a reach of 10 million U.K. households and drives 85 percent of weekly store sales. Amazingly, the coupons Tesco sends to customers through the card program redeem at rates in the 20 to 40 percent range, compared to 1 to 2 percent for mass-marketed coupons.

Inspired by the Dunnhumby/Tesco success story, Kroger, the second largest U.S. retailer, convinced Dunnhumby to enter a joint venture based in the United States. In 2003, the two launched DunnhumbyUSA in an office down the street from Kroger's world headquarters in Cincinnati, Ohio, and immediately began the monumental task of trying to analyze the data from every transaction made on a Kroger Plus card.

Kroger claims that of the 42 million households that shop at its stores, more than 40 million have Kroger Plus cards. However, just 6.5 million of those provide over 50 percent of the company's sales. About 100 DunnhumbyUSA marketing strategists and mathematicians crunch Kroger's data on a daily basis, examining 27 sample products and developing categories by which to segment the top 15 percent of Kroger's customer base. Considering when and how they buy products from that special group, Dunnhumby develops what it calls a shopper's "DNA."

Cardholders are then placed in one of seven segments. The Traditional Homes group is so named for its members' affinity for scratch cooking and conventional fare; Budgeters are value-conscious shoppers; and the Finest category includes customers who frequently purchase gourmet, fresh, and imported foods. Adding yet another level of sophistication, Dunnhumby cross-references the original seven groups by another seven interest groups with names such as Family Care, Home Living, and Specialty Tastes shoppers.

Organizing shopper data into much more focused and detailed categories allows Kroger to send its core customers more relevant product offers. Instead of blasting them with weekly mailers, Kroger now issues just four two-piece mailers a year. The first piece is a letter to the shopper with several targeted coupons aimed at increasing spending in the store. The second is a brochure designed especially for the interest group that the household belongs to. It contains a vendor-sponsored page and a few more branded coupons based on the customer's second set of segmentation characteristics.

DunnhumbyUSA provides Kroger with more than analytics, however. Its U.S. office houses graphic designers and packaged goods specialists who work together with the technical staff to convert data tables into targeting strategies, in-store promotions, and carefully chosen product selections. DunnhumbyUSA assists Kroger in working better with its suppliers, too. The grocery giant has introduced its strategic partners to critical vendors such as Coca-Cola, Hershey, and General Mills.

The close interaction between Kroger and its largest vendors allows all parties involved to review more data and react quicker to developments in the marketplace so that they can create more value for the customer. Dunnhumby doesn't stop there, either. The firm's specialists coach Kroger's upper management to develop a strong customer focus, offer guidance in enhancing the effectiveness of Kroger employees, and supervise Kroger's development of its employee rewards program.

Dunnhumby's work is clearly paying off. After a miserable 2004, when Kroger lost over $100 million, the struggling supermarket experienced a dramatic reversal of fortune. Its 2005 net income tally was an astounding $958 million, and the company paid out is first dividend since 1988.[37]

Questions

1. What type of lists does DunnhumbyUSA interpret to improve Kroger's Plus Card program?

2. Describe the CRM system, including each of its components, that DunnhumbyUSA has implemented with Kroger.

3. Describe DunnhumbyUSA's approach to data mining.

4. How does DunnhumbyUSA leverage customer information? What other opportunities do you think it might explore in the future?

COMPANY CLIPS

Method – Spreading the News about Green Cleaning

It is not uncommon for companies to be a bit protective of their brands. As you read in Chapter 9, brand equity and perception are indicators of marketing success. But in today's fast-paced markets, much can be gained by turning ownership of the brand over to consumers. Method is a company that understands the benefits to this risky proposition. Founders Eric Ryan and Adam Lowry created a brand that its customers can take ownership of and have actually built a customer feedback channel that most businesses dream of achieving. Brand advocates, or Method's most enthusiastic customers, are the company's most vocal proponents and take an almost evangelical approach to sharing the benefits of green cleaning with the market.

Questions

1. How has Method identified customer relationships with the organization? What does the company do to nurture those relationships?

2. Identify the touch points mentioned in the video and list the types of information Method could gather at each one.

3. What is the role of technology in Method's CRM system?

BIZ FLIX

Casino (II)

Now that you have a basic understanding of customer relationship management, you can see how companies can use it to their advantage. As an encore to your study, watch the second film clip from Martin Scorsese's *Casino*, starring Robert De Niro (Sam Rothstein), Joe Pesci, and Sharon Stone. The scene for this chapter shows how the casino handles high rollers, or "whales," to attract their business. Even though this scene is not a literal depiction of a customer relationship management system, you can still see how the clip illustrates chapter concepts. For instance, in what way does the narration describe the customer relationship management cycle in Exhibit 19.1? And think about what Sam Rothstein seems to know about his customer. Does this mean he has a customer-centric focus? Why or why not?

Marketing & You Results

A low score on this poll suggests that you think it is acceptable to complain, whereas a high score suggests you think it is inappropriate to complain, even when you receive a bad product or service. People who perceive complaining to be most acceptable also tend to be aggressive, and those who regard complaining as inappropriate tend to be unassertive and generally passive.

Marketing Miscue

Game Code Violates Industry Rating

According to the Entertainment Software Association (ESA), the five top-selling video games by units sold in 2004 were *Grand Theft Auto: San Andreas, Halo 2, Madden NFL 2005, ESPN NFL 2K5,* and *Need for Speed: Underground 2.* Total video game sales in the United States in 2004 amounted to $6.2 billion or an estimated 203 million units. Demographically, 75 percent of heads of households play computer or video games. Approximately 35 percent of gamers are under 18 years old, 45 percent are 18 to 49 years old, and 20 percent are 50 or older. The average age of a gamer is 30.

The ESA was formed in 1994 to serve the business and public affairs needs of video and computer game companies. It has 25 game company members, including such well-known names as Activision, Electronic Arts, Konami, Microsoft, Nintendo, SEGA, Sony, Take-Two, Vivendi, and Warner Brothers. The ESA established the Entertainment Software Rating Board (ESRB) in 1994. The board's purpose is to apply and enforce ratings, advertising guidelines, and online privacy principles adopted by the computer and video game industry. In essence, the ESRB serves as a self-regulatory body for the interactive entertainment software industry. Unfortunately, in the summer of 2005, the ESRB had to slap the potentially crippling Adults Only (AO) rating on a member's game—the game that was the hottest-selling video game in 2004, *Grand Theft Auto: San Andreas.*

The ESRB has a two-part rating system. Appearing on a game's front cover is a rating symbol that indicates ages for which the game is appropriate: EC (Early Childhood, ages 3+), E (Everyone, ages 6+), E10+ (Everyone 10 and older), T (Teen, ages 13+), M (Mature, ages 17+), AO (Adults Only, ages 18+), and RP (Rating Pending). On a game's back cover is the content descriptor rating, which indicates content-specific elements of the game that led to a particular rating (e.g., alcohol, blood, crude humor, drugs, language, nudity, sexual violence, sexual content, violence). The ESRB rates more than 1,000 games a year. Approximately 54 percent of the games receive one of the Everyone ratings, 33 percent the Teen rating, and 12 percent the Mature rating. In 2004, less than 1 percent of reviewed games

received the Adults Only rating, which is reserved for titles with prolonged scenes of intense violence or graphic sexual content or nudity.

Ratings are issued before a game enters the market, but the ESRB took the unprecedented step of changing the rating of *Grand Theft Auto: San Andreas* from M to AO after the game had been on store shelves for nine months. The problem was the game's sexual content. The board's reviewers had not made an error in rating the game. In fact, the reviewers did not know that the sex scenes were in the game. Apparently, a gamer was able to crack the game's code and unlock information hidden in the program. This hidden code, referred to as the "hot coffee mod" (modification), allowed players to access sexually explicit mini-games via an Internet download. Initially, Take-Two Interactive Software, the parent company of the game's publisher Rockstar Games, denied that the explicit material existed on the game discs prior to modification, insisting that the material was the work of hackers. Eventually, the company took responsibility for the sex scenes, acknowledging that the scenes were created by internal developers and included on final copies distributed to retail outlets. Supposedly, the scenes were the result of dead code that did not make the final cut for the game but were too labor-intensive to delete completely. Instead, the code was programmed to be inaccessible to gamers.

Take-Two Interactive Software develops and publishes games through its wholly owned labels, Rockstar Games and Global Star Software. The *Grand Theft Auto* game series is one of its most popular brand franchises. The rating change cost the company an estimated $40 million to $50 million in sales because it drastically reduced the number of outlets that would carry the game. Wal-Mart, which controls around half of the video game market in the United States, refuses to sell AO-rated games, as does Best Buy. Other video game retail outlets including Target, Blockbuster, and Hollywood Video pulled the game from their shelves and were uncertain as to the game's future in their stores.

Not only did Take-Two suffer financially, but the U.S. House of Representatives passed a resolution to launch an investigation into whether Rockstar Games knew about the sex scenes prior to release of the game.[1]

Questions

1. Describe the marketing relationships that may have been damaged by technology's role in product development at Take-Two.

2. What (if anything) might the rating fiasco do to the ESRB's image?

Critical Thinking Case

Scripps Provides E-Offering with HGTVPro.com

By 2005, more than 10 million households in the United States had selected television programs by using video-on-demand services, and this number was expected to quadruple by 2010. Nevertheless, programmers and cable operators have had difficulty finding a business model that satisfies all parties in the video-on-demand relationship, including networks, distributors, advertisers, and viewers. Now, however, E. W. Scripps Company may have found the solution—video-on-demand online.

Headquartered in Cincinnati, Ohio, E. W. Scripps was founded in 1878 with a newspaper called *The Penny Press.* The newspaper's target audience was the emerging mass market of urban workers. The company grew to become a diverse media corporation with expertise in newspaper publishing, national lifestyle television networks, broadcast television, interactive media, and licensing/syndication. Today, Scripps operates daily and community newspapers in 18 markets and has ten broadcast television stations and five cable/satellite programming networks. Additionally, the company owns the Shop at Home Network, a television retailing offering, and Shopzilla, an online comparison shopping service.

In early 2005, E. W. Scripps set out to create a new television network using broadband, which allows viewers to access information via personal computers and cell phones. With an estimated 55 percent of homes having access to the Internet and 85 percent of offices having high-speed broadband, Scripps launched Scripps Network, a lifestyle network subsidiary, which is available in 95 countries on six continents. Already one of the biggest producers of cable content, Scripps Networks was the first major programmer to move into broadband with original content, taking content from its popular television brands into broadband channels. Because it was already producing 3,000 hours of content annually and thousands of Web-based video projects (with an average of 12 million visits a month), Scripps Networks could move into broadband channels at a relatively low cost.

Initially, Scripps's move into broadband focused on the Home & Garden Television network (HGTV) with HGTVPro. Scripps planned to follow this with Fine Living and the Food and DIY (do-it-yourself) networks. The company owns a library of 25,000 hours of television programming, which it reformatted for broadband viewing. Unlike half-hour programs on cable television, however, for broadband viewing the informative content has to be condensed into three to five minutes of streaming video. The broadband capability

also gives viewers access to content beyond the video in case they need more help for a particular project. For example, video viewers can access the "Best Practices" section of the Web site to supplement the streaming video. Viewers can also subscribe to HGTVProFile, the company's construction-related newsletter.

In its new venture, Scripps has had to deal with several issues related to advertising. The introduction of HGTVPro.com was supported by advertising, and users were not charged a fee for access. Although Scripps Networks does not allow product placement in its shows, it does permit online advertising on the Web site. GMC Truck, Lending Tree.com, and Whirlpool were three of the initial advertisers on the broadband Web site. Scripps recognizes that it needs to develop links for advertisers to reach viewers in a more efficient, relationship-oriented manner. Thus, it is considering a subscription model for its broadband channels. Subscribers would pay a fee to join an affinity group or club. Members would then be entitled to more extensive Web site access on the channel as well as to discounts from the advertisers. Another issue is that advertisers are demanding far greater broadband inventory than is available. Knowing this, Scripps does not want to lose potential advertising clients to its competitors. By the end of 2004, three other companies had made potentially threatening moves into the Internet mass communications marketplace: Dow Jones & Co. had acquired online financial publisher MarketWatch, Inc.; the Washington Post Company had purchased the online magazine *Slate;* and the New York Times Company had purchased About.com, which offers a diverse network of Web sites from food to sports.

Although not all of these issues have been resolved, Scripps's initiative appears to be successful. In its first 19 days of existence, there were 380,000 unique visits to HGTVPro.com. Within three months, more than 110,000 contractors and over one million consumers had registered for the free electronic newsletter. Thus, HGTVPro.com has allowed Scripps Networks to build on its recognized strength with the enormous success of its HGTV brand and maintain a competitive lead in the new video-on-demand online marketplace.[2]

Questions

1. Should HGTVPro.com allow product placement in its streaming videos? Why or why not?

2. What risks would be posed by moving to a fee-based subscription service?

A

accessory equipment Goods, such as portable tools and office equipment, that are less expensive and shorter-lived than major equipment.

adopter A consumer who was happy enough with his or her trial experience with a product to use it again.

advergaming Placing advertising messages in Web-based or video games to advertise or promote a product, service, organization, or issue.

advertising Impersonal, one-way mass communication about a product or organization that is paid for by a marketer.

advertising appeal A reason for a person to buy a product.

advertising campaign A series of related advertisements focusing on a common theme, slogan, and set of advertising appeals.

advertising objective A specific communication task that a campaign should accomplish for a specified target audience during a specified period.

advertising response function A phenomenon in which spending for advertising and sales promotion increases sales or market share up to a certain level but then produces diminishing returns.

advocacy advertising A form of advertising in which an organization expresses its views on controversial issues or responds to media attacks.

agents and brokers Wholesaling intermediaries who do not take title to a product but facilitate its sale from producer to end user by representing retailers, wholesalers, or manufacturers.

AIDA concept A model that outlines the process for achieving promotional goals in terms of stages of consumer involvement with the message; the acronym stands for *attention, interest, desire,* and *action.*

applied research An attempt to develop new or improved products.

aspirational reference group A group that someone would like to join.

assurance The knowledge and courtesy of employees and their ability to convey trust.

ATC. *See* average total cost.

atmosphere The overall impression conveyed by a store's physical layout, decor, and surroundings.

attitude A learned tendency to respond consistently toward a given object.

audience selectivity The ability of an advertising medium to reach a precisely defined market.

automatic vending The use of machines to offer goods for sale.

AVC. *See* average variable cost.

average total cost (ATC) Total costs divided by quantity of output.

average variable cost (AVC) Total variable costs divided by quantity of output.

B

baby boomers People born between 1946 and 1964.

bait pricing A price tactic that tries to get consumers into a store through false or misleading price advertising and then uses high-pressure selling to persuade consumers to buy more expensive merchandise.

base price The general price level at which the company expects to sell the good or service.

basic research Pure research that aims to confirm an existing theory or to learn more about a concept or phenomenon.

basing-point pricing A price tactic that charges freight from a given (basing) point, regardless of the city from which the goods are shipped.

BehaviorScan A scanner-based research program that tracks the purchases of 3,000 households through store scanners in each research market.

belief An organized pattern of knowledge that an individual holds as true about his or her world.

benefit segmentation The process of grouping customers into market segments according to the benefits they seek from the product.

brainstorming The process of getting a group to think of unlimited ways to vary a product or solve a problem.

brand A name, term, symbol, design, or combination thereof that identifies a seller's products and differentiates them from competitors' products.

brand equity The value of company and brand names.

brand loyalty A consistent preference for one brand over all others.

brand mark The elements of a brand that cannot be spoken.

brand name That part of a brand that can be spoken, including letters, words, and numbers.

break-even analysis A method of determining what sales volume must be reached before total revenue equals total costs.

business analysis The second stage of the screening process where preliminary figures for demand, cost, sales, and profitability are calculated.

business marketing The marketing of goods and services to individuals and organizations for purposes other than personal consumption.

business product (industrial product) A product used to manufacture other goods or services, to facilitate an organization's operations, or to resell to other customers.

business services Expense items that do not become part of a final product.

business-to-business electronic commerce The use of the Internet to facilitate the exchange of goods, services, and information between organizations.

business-to-business online exchange An electronic trading floor that provides companies with integrated links to their customers and suppliers.

buyer A department head who selects the merchandise for his or her department and may also be responsible for promotion and personnel.

buyer for export An intermediary in the global market that assumes all ownership risks and sells globally for its own account.

buying center All those persons in an organization who become involved in the purchase decision.

C

campaign management Developing product or service offerings customized for the appropriate customer segment and then pricing and communicating these offerings for the purpose of enhancing customer relationships.

cannibalization A situation that occurs when sales of a new product cut into sales of a firm's existing products.

capital-intensive Using more capital than labor in the production process.

cash cow In the portfolio matrix, a business unit that usually generates more cash than it needs to maintain its market share.

cash discount A price reduction offered to a consumer, an industrial user, or a marketing intermediary in return for prompt payment of a bill.

category killers Specialty discount stores that heavily dominate their narrow merchandise segment.

cause-related marketing A type of sponsorship involving the association of a for-profit company and a nonprofit organization; through the sponsorship, the company's product or service is promoted, and money is raised for the nonprofit.

Central America Free Trade Agreement (CAFTA) A trade agreement, instituted in 2005, that includes Costa Rica, the Dominican Republic, El Salvador, Guatemala, Honduras, Nicaragua, and the United States.

central-location telephone (CLT) facility A specially designed phone room used to conduct telephone interviewing.

chain stores Stores owned and operated as a group by a single organization.

channel A medium of communication—such as a voice, radio, or newspaper—for transmitting a message.

channel conflict A clash of goals and methods between distribution channel members.

channel control A situation that occurs when one marketing channel member intentionally affects another member's behavior.

channel leader (channel captain) A member of a marketing channel that exercises authority and power over the activities of other channel members.

channel members All parties in the marketing channel that negotiate with one another, buy and sell products, and facilitate the change of ownership between buyer and seller in the course of moving the product from the manufacturer into the hands of the final consumer.

channel partnering (channel cooperation) The joint effort of all channel members to create a supply chain that serves customers and creates a competitive advantage.

channel power The capacity of a particular marketing channel member to control or influence the behavior of other channel members.

CLT. *See* central-location telephone facility.

closed-ended question An interview question that asks the respondent to make a selection from a limited list of responses.

cobranding Placing two or more brand names on a product or its package.

code of ethics A guideline to help marketing managers and other employees make better decisions.

cognitive dissonance Inner tension that a consumer experiences after recognizing an inconsistency between behavior and values or opinions.

cold calling A form of lead generation in which the salesperson approaches potential buyers without prior knowledge of the prospects' needs or financial status.

commercialization The decision to market a product.

communication The process by which we exchange or share meanings through a common set of symbols.

comparative advertising A form of advertising that compares two or more specifically named or shown competing brands on one or more specific attributes.

competitive advantage The set of unique features of a company and its products that are perceived by the target market as significant and superior to the competition.

competitive advertising A form of advertising designed to influence demand for a specific brand.

competitive intelligence An intelligence system that helps managers assess their competition and vendors in order to become more efficient and effective competitors.

compiled list A customer list that was developed by gathering names and addresses from telephone directories and membership rosters, usually enhanced with information from public records, such as census data, auto registrations, birth announcements, business start-ups, or bankruptcies.

component lifestyles The practice of choosing goods and services that meet one's diverse needs and interests rather than conforming to a single, traditional lifestyle.

component parts Either finished items ready for assembly or products that need very little processing before becoming part of some other product.

computer-assisted personal interviewing An interviewing method in which the interviewer reads the questions from a computer screen and enters the respondent's data directly into the computer.

computer-assisted self-interviewing An interviewing method in which a mall interviewer intercepts and directs willing respondents to nearby computers where the respondent reads questions off a computer screen and directly keys his or her answers into a computer.

concentrated targeting strategy A strategy used to select one segment of a market for targeting marketing efforts.

concept test A test to evaluate a new-product idea, usually before any prototype has been created.

consumer behavior Processes a consumer uses to make purchase decisions, as well as to use and dispose of purchased goods or services; also includes factors that influence purchase decisions and product use.

consumer decision-making process A five-step process used by consumers when buying goods or services.

consumer penalty An extra fee paid by the consumer for violating the terms of the purchase agreement.

consumer product A product bought to satisfy an individual's personal wants.

Consumer Product Safety Commission (CPSC) A federal agency established to protect the health and safety of consumers in and around their homes.

consumer sales promotion Sales promotion activities targeting the ultimate consumer.

continuous media schedule A media scheduling strategy in which advertising is run steadily throughout the advertising period; used for products in the latter stages of the product life cycle.

contract manufacturing Private-label manufacturing by a foreign company.

control Provides the mechanisms for evaluating marketing results in light of the plan's objectives and for correcting actions that do not help the organization reach those objectives within budget guidelines.

convenience product A relatively inexpensive item that merits little shopping effort.

convenience sample A form of non-probability sample using respondents who are convenient or readily accessible to the researcher—for example, employees, friends, or relatives.

convenience store A miniature supermarket, carrying only a limited line of high-turnover convenience goods.

cooperative advertising An arrangement in which the manufacturer and the retailer split the costs of advertising the manufacturer's brand.

core service The most basic benefit the consumer is buying.

corporate blogs Blogs that are sponsored by a company or one of its brands and maintained by one or more of the company's employees.

corporate social responsibility A business's concern for society's welfare.

cost competitive advantage Being the low-cost competitor in an industry while maintaining satisfactory profit margins.

cost per contact The cost of reaching one member of the target market.

countertrade A form of trade in which all or part of the payment for goods or services is in the form of other goods or services.

coupon A certificate that entitles consumers to an immediate price reduction when they buy the product.

credence quality A characteristic that consumers may have difficulty assessing even after pur-

chase because they do not have the necessary knowledge or experience.

crisis management A coordinated effort to handle all the effects of unfavorable publicity or of another unexpected, unfavorable event.

cross-tabulation A method of analyzing data that lets the analyst look at the responses to one question in relation to the responses to one or more other questions.

culture The set of values, norms, attitudes, and other meaningful symbols that shape human behavior and the artifacts, or products, of that behavior as they are transmitted from one generation to the next.

cumulative quantity discount A deduction from list price that applies to the buyer's total purchases made during a specific period.

customer relationship management (CRM) A company-wide business strategy designed to optimize profitability, revenue, and customer satisfaction by focusing on highly defined and precise customer groups.

customer-centric A philosophy under which the company customizes its product and service offering based on data generated through interactions between the customer and the company.

customer satisfaction Customers' evaluation of a good or service in terms of whether it has met their needs and expectations.

customer value The relationship between benefits and the sacrifice necessary to obtain those benefits.

D

data warehouse A central repository for data from various functional areas of the organization that are stored and inventoried on a centralized computer system so that the information can be shared across all functional departments of the business.

database A collection of data, especially one that can be accessed and manipulated by computer software.

database marketing The creation of a large computerized file of customers' and potential customers' profiles and purchase patterns.

decision support system (DSS) An interactive, flexible computerized information system that enables managers to obtain and manipulate information as they are making decisions.

decline stage The fourth stage of the product life cycle, characterized by a long-run drop in sales.

decoding Interpretation of the language and symbols sent by the source through a channel.

delayed-quotation pricing A price tactic used for industrial installations and many accessory items, in which a firm price is not set until the item is either finished or delivered.

demand The quantity of a product that will be sold in the market at various prices for a specified period.

demographic segmentation Segmenting markets by age, gender, income, ethnic background, and family life cycle.

demography The study of people's vital statistics, such as their age, race and ethnicity, and location.

department store A store housing several departments under one roof.

derived demand The demand for business products.

destination stores Stores that consumers purposely plan to visit.

development The stage in the product development process in which a prototype is developed and a marketing strategy is outlined.

diffusion The process by which the adoption of an innovation spreads.

direct channel A distribution channel in which producers sell directly to consumers.

direct foreign investment Active ownership of a foreign company or of overseas manufacturing or marketing facilities.

direct marketing (direct-response marketing) Techniques used to get consumers to make a purchase from their home, office, or another nonretail setting.

direct retailing The selling of products by representatives who work door-to-door, office-to-office, or at home parties.

discount store A retailer that competes on the basis of low prices, high turnover, and high volume.

discrepancy of assortment The lack of all the items a customer needs to receive full satisfaction from a product or products.

discrepancy of quantity The difference between the amount of product produced and the amount an end user wants to buy.

disintermediation The elimination of intermediaries such as wholesalers or distributors from a marketing channel.

distribution resource planning (DRP) An inventory control system that manages the replenishment of goods from the manufacturer to the final consumer.

diversification A strategy of increasing sales by introducing new products into new markets.

dog In the portfolio matrix, a business unit that has low growth potential and a small market share.

DRP. *See* distribution resource planning.

drugstore A retail store that stocks pharmacy-related products and services as its main draw.

DSS. *See* decision support system.

dual distribution (multiple distribution) The use of two or more channels to distribute the same product to target markets.

dumping The sale of an exported product at a price lower than that charged for the same or a like product in the "home" market of the exporter.

E

EDI. *See* electronic data interchange.

80/20 principle A principle holding that 20 percent of all customers generate 80 percent of the demand.

elastic demand A situation in which consumer demand is sensitive to changes in price.

elasticity of demand Consumers' responsiveness or sensitivity to changes in price.

electronic data interchange (EDI) Information technology that replaces the paper documents that usually accompany business transactions, such as purchase orders and invoices, with electronic transmission of the needed information to reduce inventory levels, improve cash flow, streamline operations, and increase the speed and accuracy of information transmission.

electronic distribution A distribution technique that includes any kind of product or service that can be distributed electronically, whether over traditional forms such as fiber-optic cable or through satellite transmission of electronic signals.

empathy Caring, individualized attention to customers.

empowerment Delegation of authority to solve customers' problems quickly—usually by the first person that the customer notifies regarding a problem.

encoding The conversion of a sender's ideas and thoughts into a message, usually in the form of words or signs.

environmental management When a company implements strategies that attempt to shape the external environment within which it operates.

environmental scanning Collection and interpretation of information about forces, events, and relationships in the external environment that may affect the future of the organization or the implementation of the marketing plan.

escalator pricing A price tactic in which the final selling price reflects cost increases incurred between the time the order is placed and the time delivery is made.

ethics The moral principles or values that generally govern the conduct of an individual.

ethnographic research The study of human behavior in its natural context; involves observation of behavior and physical setting.

European Union A free trade zone encompassing 25 European countries.

evaluation Gauging the extent to which the marketing objectives have been achieved during the specified time period.

evoked set (consideration set) A group of brands, resulting from an information search, from which a buyer can choose.

exchange People giving up something to receive something they would rather have.

exclusive distribution A form of distribution that establishes one or a few dealers within a given area.

executive interviews A type of survey that involves interviewing businesspeople at their offices concerning industrial products or services.

experience curves Curves that show costs declining at a predictable rate as experience with a product increases.

experience quality A characteristic that can be assessed only after use.

experiment A method a researcher uses to gather primary data.

export agent An intermediary who acts like a manufacturer's agent for the exporter. The export agent lives in the foreign market.

export broker An intermediary who plays the traditional broker's role by bringing buyer and seller together.

exporting Selling domestically produced products to buyers in another country.

express warranty A written guarantee.

extensive decision making The most complex type of consumer decision making, used when buying an unfamiliar, expensive product or an infrequently bought item; requires use of several criteria for evaluating options and much time for seeking information.

external information search The process of seeking information in the outside environment.

F

factory outlet An off-price retailer that is owned and operated by a manufacturer.

family brand Marketing several different products under the same brand name.

family life cycle (FLC) A series of stages determined by a combination of age, marital status, and the presence or absence of children.

Federal Trade Commission (FTC) A federal agency empowered to prevent persons or corporations from using unfair methods of competition in commerce.

feedback The receiver's response to a message.

field service firm A firm that specializes in interviewing respondents on a subcontracted basis.

fixed cost A cost that does not change as output is increased or decreased.

FLC. *See* family life cycle.

flexible pricing (variable pricing) A price tactic in which different customers pay different prices for essentially the same merchandise bought in equal quantities.

flighted media schedule A media scheduling strategy in which ads are run heavily every other month or every two weeks, to achieve a greater impact with an increased frequency and reach at those times.

floating exchange rates Prices of different currencies move up and down based on the demand for and the supply of each currency.

FOB origin pricing A price tactic that requires the buyer to absorb the freight costs from the shipping point ("free on board").

focus group Seven to ten people who participate in a group discussion led by a moderator.

follow-up The final step of the selling process, in which the salesperson ensures that delivery schedules are met, that the goods or services perform as promised, and that the buyers' employees are properly trained to use the products.

Food and Drug Administration (FDA) A federal agency charged with enforcing regulations against selling and distributing adulterated, misbranded, or hazardous food and drug products.

four Ps Product, place, promotion, and price, which together make up the marketing mix.

frame error An error that occurs when a sample drawn from a population differs from the target population.

franchise The right to operate a business or to sell a product.

franchisee An individual or business that is granted the right to sell another party's product.

franchisor The originator of a trade name, product, methods of operation, and so on, that grants operating rights to another party to sell its product.

freight absorption pricing A price tactic in which the seller pays all or part of the actual freight charges and does not pass them on to the buyer.

frequency The number of times an individual is exposed to a given message during a specific period.

frequent buyer program A loyalty program in which loyal consumers are rewarded for making multiple purchases of a particular good or service.

full-line discount store A retailer that offers consumers very limited service and carries a broad assortment of well-known, nationally branded "hard goods."

functional discount (trade discount) A discount to wholesalers and retailers for performing channel functions.

G

gap model A model identifying five gaps that can cause problems in service delivery and influence customer evaluations of service quality.

General Agreement on Tariffs and Trade (GATT) A trade agreement that contained loopholes that enabled countries to avoid trade-barrier reduction agreements.

Generation X People born between 1965 and 1978.

Generation Y People born between 1979 and 1994.

generic product A no-frills, no-brand-name, low-cost product that is simply identified by its product category.

generic product name Identifies a product by class or type and cannot be trademarked.

geodemographic segmentation Segmenting potential customers into neighborhood lifestyle categories.

geographic segmentation Segmenting markets by region of the country or the world, market size, market density, or climate.

global brand A brand where at least 20 percent of the product is sold outside its home country or region.

global marketing Marketing that targets markets throughout the world.

global marketing standardization Production of uniform products that can be sold the same way all over the world.

global vision Recognizing and reacting to international marketing opportunities, using effective global marketing strategies, and being aware of threats from foreign competitors in all markets.

gross margin The amount of money the retailer makes as a percentage of sales after the cost of goods sold is subtracted.

group dynamics Group interaction essential to the success of focus-group research.

growth stage The second stage of the product life cycle when sales typically grow at an increasing rate, many competitors enter the market, large companies may start acquiring small pioneering firms, and profits are healthy.

H

heterogenity The variability of the inputs and outputs of services, which cause services to tend to be less standardized and uniform than goods.

horizontal conflict A channel conflict that occurs among channel members on the same level.

I

ideal self-image The way an individual would like to be.

IMC. *See* integrated marketing communications.

implementation The process that turns a marketing plan into action assignments and ensures that these assignments are executed in a way that accomplishes the plan's objectives.

implied warranty An unwritten guarantee that the good or service is fit for the purpose for which it was sold.

independent retailers Retailers owned by a single person or partnership and not operated as part of a larger retail institution.

individual branding Using different brand names for different products.

inelastic demand A situation in which an increase or a decrease in price will not significantly affect demand for the product.

inflation A measure of the decrease in the value of money, expressed as the percentage reduction in value since the previous year.

infomercial A 30-minute or longer advertisement that looks more like a TV talk show than a sales pitch.

informational labeling A type of package labeling designed to help consumers make proper product selections and lower their cognitive dissonance after the purchase.

InfoScan A scanner-based sales-tracking service for the consumer packaged-goods industry.

innovation A product perceived as new by a potential adopter.

inseparability The inability of the production and consumption of a service to be separated. Consumers must be present during the production.

institutional advertising A form of advertising designed to enhance a company's image rather than promote a particular product.

intangibility The inability of services to be touched, seen, tasted, heard, or felt in the same manner that goods can be sensed.

integrated marketing communications (IMC) The careful coordination of all promotional messages for a product or a service to assure the consistency of messages at every contact point where a company meets the consumer.

intensive distribution A form of distribution aimed at having a product available in every outlet where target customers might want to buy it.

interaction The point at which a customer and a company representative exchange information and develop learning relationships.

internal information search The process of recalling past information stored in the memory.

internal marketing Treating employees as customers and developing systems and benefits that satisfy their needs.

International Monetary Fund (IMF) An international organization that acts as a lender of last resort, providing loans to troubled nations, and also works to promote trade through financial cooperation.

interpersonal communication Direct, face-to-face communication between two or more people.

introductory stage The first stage of the product life cycle in which the full-scale launch of a new product into the marketplace occurs.

inventory control system A method of developing and maintaining an adequate assortment of materials or products to meet a manufacturer's or a customer's demand.

involvement The amount of time and effort a buyer invests in the search, evaluation, and decision processes of consumer behavior.

J

JIT. *See* just-in-time production.

joint costs Costs that are shared in the manufacturing and marketing of several products in a product line.

joint demand The demand for two or more items used together in a final product.

joint venture A venture in which a domestic firm buys part of a foreign company or joins with a foreign company to create a new entity.

just-in-time production (JIT) A process that redefines and simplifies manufacturing by reducing inventory levels and delivering raw materials just when they are needed on the production line.

K

keiretsu A network of interlocking corporate affiliates.

keystoning The practice of marking up prices by 100 percent, or doubling the cost.

knowledge management The process by which learned information from customers is centralized and shared in order to enhance the relationship between customers and the organization.

L

lead generation (prospecting) Identification of those firms and people most likely to buy the seller's offerings.

lead qualification Determination of a sales prospect's (1) recognized need, (2) buying power, and (3) receptivity and accessibility.

leader pricing (loss-leader pricing) A price tactic in which a product is sold near or even below cost in the hope that shoppers will buy other items once they are in the store.

learning A process that creates changes in behavior, immediate or expected, through experience and practice.

learning (Ch. 19, CRM) An informal process of collecting customer data through customer comments and feedback on product or service performance.

licensing The legal process whereby a licensor agrees to let another firm use its manufacturing process, trademarks, patents, trade secrets, or other proprietary knowledge.

lifestyle A mode of living as identified by a person's activities, interests, and opinions.

lifetime value analysis (LTV) A data manipulation technique that projects the future value of the customer over a period of years using the assumption that marketing to repeat customers is more profitable than marketing to first-time buyers.

limited decision making The type of decision making that requires a moderate amount of time for gathering information and deliberating about an unfamiliar brand in a familiar product category.

logistics The process of strategically managing the efficient flow and storage of raw materials, in-process inventory, and finished goods from point of origin to point of consumption.

logistics information system The link that connects all of the logistics components of the supply chain.

loyalty marketing program A promotional program designed to build long-term, mutually beneficial relationships between a company and its key customers.

LTV. *See* lifetime value analysis.

M

major equipment (installations) Capital goods such as large or expensive machines, mainframe computers, blast furnaces, generators, airplanes, and buildings.

mall intercept interview A survey research method that involves interviewing people in the common areas of shopping malls.

management decision problem A broad-based problem that uses marketing research in order for managers to take proper actions.

manufacturers' brand The brand name of a manufacturer.

marginal cost (MC) The change in total costs associated with a one-unit change in output.

marginal revenue (MR) The extra revenue associated with selling an extra unit of output or the change in total revenue with a one-unit change in output.

market People or organizations with needs or wants and the ability and willingness to buy.

market development A marketing strategy that entails attracting new customers to existing products.

market opportunity analysis (MOA) The description and estimation of the size and sales potential of market segments that are of interest to the firm and the assessment of key competitors in these market segments.

market orientation A philosophy that assumes that a sale does not depend on an aggressive sales force but rather on a customer's decision to purchase a product. It is synonymous with the marketing concept.

market penetration A marketing strategy that tries to increase market share among existing customers.

market segment A subgroup of people or organizations sharing one or more characteristics that cause them to have similar product needs.

market segmentation The process of dividing a market into meaningful, relatively similar, and identifiable segments or groups.

market share A company's product sales as a percentage of total sales for that industry.

marketing An organizational function and a set of processes for creating, communicating, and delivering value to customers and for managing customer relationships in ways that benefit the organization and its stakeholders.

marketing audit A thorough, systematic, periodic evaluation of the objectives, strategies, structure, and performance of the marketing organization.

marketing channel (channel of distribution) A set of interdependent organizations that ease the transfer of ownership as products move from producer to business user or consumer.

marketing concept The idea that the social and economic justification for an organization's existence is the satisfaction of customer wants and needs while meeting organizational objectives.

marketing-controlled information source A product information source that originates with marketers promoting the product.

marketing information Everyday information about developments in the marketing environment that managers use to prepare and adjust marketing plans.

marketing mix A unique blend of product, place, promotion, and pricing strategies designed to produce mutually satisfying exchanges with a target market.

marketing myopia Defining a business in terms of goods and services rather than in terms of the benefits that customers seek.

marketing objective A statement of what is to be accomplished through marketing activities.

marketing plan A written document that acts as a guidebook of marketing activities for the marketing manager.

marketing planning Designing activities relating to marketing objectives and the changing marketing environment.

marketing research The process of planning, collecting, and analyzing data relevant to a marketing decision.

marketing research aggregator A company that acquires, catalogs, reformats, segments, and resells reports already published by marketing research firms.

marketing research objective The specific information needed to solve a marketing research problem; the objective should be to provide insightful decision-making information.

marketing research problem Determining what information is needed and how that information can be obtained efficiently and effectively.

marketing strategy The activities of selecting and describing one or more target markets and developing and maintaining a marketing mix that will produce mutually satisfying exchanges with target markets.

markup pricing The cost of buying the product from the producer plus amounts for profit and for expenses not otherwise accounted for.

Maslow's hierarchy of needs A method of classifying human needs and motivations into five categories in ascending order of importance: physiological, safety, social, esteem, and self-actualization.

mass communication The communication of a concept or message to large audiences.

mass customization (build-to-order) A production method whereby products are not made until an order is placed by the customer; also a strategy that uses technology to deliver customized services on a mass basis.

mass merchandising A retailing strategy using moderate to low prices on large quantities of merchandise and lower service to stimulate high turnover of products.

materials-handling system A method of moving inventory into, within, and out of the warehouse.

materials requirement planning (MRP) (materials management) An inventory control system that manages the replenishment of raw materials, supplies, and components from the supplier to the manufacturer.

maturity stage The third stage of the product life cycle during which sales increase at a decreasing rate.

MC. *See* marginal cost.

measurement error An error that occurs when there is a difference between the information desired by the researcher and the information provided by the measurement process.

media mix The combination of media to be used for a promotional campaign.

media planning The series of decisions advertisers make regarding the selection and use of media, allowing the marketer to optimally and cost-effectively communicate the message to the target audience.

media schedule Designation of the media, the specific publications or programs, and the insertion dates of advertising.

medium The channel used to convey a message to a target market.

merchant wholesaler An institution that buys goods from manufacturers and resells them to businesses, government agencies, and other wholesalers or retailers and that receives and takes title to goods, stores them in its own warehouses, and later ships them.

Mercosur The largest Latin American trade agreement; includes Argentina, Bolivia, Brazil, Chile, Colombia, Ecuador, Paraguay, Peru, and Uruguay.

mission statement A statement of the firm's business based on a careful analysis of benefits sought by present and potential customers and an analysis of existing and anticipated environmental conditions.

modified rebuy A situation where the purchaser wants some change in the original good or service.

morals The rules people develop as a result of cultural values and norms.

motive A driving force that causes a person to take action to satisfy specific needs.

MR. *See* marginal revenue.

MRP. *See* materials requirement planning.

multiculturalism When all major ethnic groups in an area—such as a city, county, or census tract—are roughly equally represented.

multinational corporation A company that is heavily engaged in international trade, beyond exporting and importing.

multiplier effect (accelerator principle) Phenomenon in which a small increase or decrease in consumer demand can produce a much larger change in demand for the facilities and equipment needed to make the consumer product.

multisegment targeting strategy A strategy that chooses two or more well-defined market segments and develops a distinct marketing mix for each.

mystery shoppers Researchers posing as customers who gather observational data about a store.

N

NAICS. *See* North American Industry Classification System.

need recognition Result of an imbalance between actual and desired states.

needs assessment A determination of the customer's specific needs and wants and the range of options the customer has for satisfying them.

negotiation The process during which both the salesperson and the prospect offer special concessions in an attempt to arrive at a sales agreement.

networking A process of finding out about potential clients from friends, business contacts, coworkers, acquaintances, and fellow members in professional and civic organizations.

new buy A situation requiring the purchase of a product for the first time.

new product A product new to the world, the market, the producer, the seller, or some combination of these.

new-product strategy A plan that links the new-product development process with the objectives of the marketing department, the business unit, and the corporation.

niche One segment of a market.

niche competitive advantage The advantage achieved when a firm seeks to target and effectively serve a small segment of the market.

noise Anything that interferes with, distorts, or slows down the transmission of information.

nonaspirational reference group A group with which an individual does not want to associate.

noncorporate blogs Independent blogs that are not associated with the marketing efforts of any particular company or brand.

noncumulative quantity discount A deduction from list price that applies to a single order rather than to the total volume of orders placed during a certain period.

nonmarketing-controlled information source A product information source that is not associated with advertising or promotion.

nonprobability sample Any sample in which little or no attempt is made to get a representative cross section of the population.

nonprofit organization An organization that exists to achieve some goal other than the usual business goals of profit, market share, or return on investment.

nonprofit organization marketing The effort by nonprofit organizations to bring about mutually satisfying exchanges with target markets.

nonstore retailing Shopping without visiting a store.

norm A value or attitude deemed acceptable by a group.

North American Free Trade Agreement (NAFTA) An agreement between Canada, the United States, and Mexico that created the world's largest free trade zone.

North American Industry Classification System (NAICS) A detailed numbering system developed by the United States, Canada, and Mexico to classify North American business establishments by their main production processes.

O

observation research A research method that relies on four types of observation: people watching people, people watching an activity, machines watching people, and machines watching an activity.

odd–even pricing (psychological pricing) A price tactic that uses odd-numbered prices to connote bargains and even-numbered prices to imply quality.

off-price retailer A retailer that sells at prices 25 percent or more below traditional department store prices because it pays cash for its stock and usually doesn't ask for return privileges.

online retailing A type of shopping available to consumers with personal computers and access to the Internet.

one-to-one marketing An individualized marketing method that utilizes customer information to build long-term, personalized, and profitable relationships with each customer.

open-ended question An interview question that encourages an answer phrased in the respondent's own words.

opinion leader An individual who influences the opinions of others.

optimizers Business customers who consider numerous suppliers, both familiar and unfamiliar, solicit bids, and study all proposals carefully before selecting one.

order processing system A system whereby orders are entered into the supply chain and filled.

original equipment manufacturers (OEMs) Individuals and organizations that buy business goods and incorporate them into the products that they produce for eventual sale to other producers or to consumers.

outsourcing (contract logistics) A manufacturer's or supplier's use of an independent third party to manage an entire function of the logistics system, such as transportation, warehousing, or order processing.

P

penetration pricing A pricing policy whereby a firm charges a relatively low price for a product initially as a way to reach the mass market.

perception The process by which people select, organize, and interpret stimuli into a meaningful and coherent picture.

perceptual mapping A means of displaying or graphing, in two or more dimensions, the location of products, brands, or groups of products in customers' minds.

perishability The inability of services to be stored, warehoused, or inventoried.

personality A way of organizing and grouping the consistencies of an individual's reactions to situations.

personal selling A purchase situation involving a personal paid-for communication between two people in an attempt to influence each other.

persuasive labeling A type of package labeling that focuses on a promotional theme or logo with consumer information being secondary.

pioneering advertising A form of advertising designed to stimulate primary demand for a new product or product category.

planned obsolescence The practice of modifying products so those that have already been sold become obsolete before they actually need replacement.

planning The process of anticipating future events and determining strategies to achieve organizational objectives in the future.

PLC. *See* product life cycle.

point-of-purchase display A promotional display set up at the retailer's location to build traffic, advertise the product, or induce impulse buying.

point-of-sale interactions Communications between customers and organizations that occur at the point of sale, normally in a store.

portfolio matrix A tool for allocating resources among products or strategic business units on the basis of relative market share and market growth rate.

position The place a product, brand, or group of products occupies in consumers' minds relative to competing offerings.

positioning Developing a specific marketing mix to influence potential customers' overall perception of a brand, product line, or organization in general.

preapproach A process that describes the "homework" that must be done by a salesperson before he or she contacts a prospect.

predatory pricing The practice of charging a very low price for a product with the intent of driving competitors out of business or out of a market.

predictive modeling A data manipulation technique in which marketers try to determine, based on some past set of occurrences, what the odds are that some other occurrence, such as a response or purchase, will take place in the future.

premium An extra item offered to the consumer, usually in exchange for some proof of purchase of the promoted product.

prestige pricing Charging a high price to help promote a high-quality image.

price That which is given up in an exchange to acquire a good or service.

price bundling Marketing two or more products in a single package for a special price.

price equilibrium The price at which demand and supply are equal.

price fixing An agreement between two or more firms on the price they will charge for a product.

price lining The practice of offering a product line with several items at specific price points.

price shading The use of discounts by salespeople to increase demand for one or more products in a line.

price skimming A pricing policy whereby a firm charges a high introductory price, often coupled with heavy promotion.

price strategy A basic, long-term pricing framework, which establishes the initial price for a product and the intended direction for price movements over the product life cycle.

primary data Information that is collected for the first time; used for solving the particular problem under investigation.

primary membership group A reference group with which people interact regularly in an informal, face-to-face manner, such as family, friends, or fellow employees.

private brand A brand name owned by a wholesaler or a retailer.

probability sample A sample in which every element in the population has a known statistical likelihood of being selected.

problem child (question mark) In the portfolio matrix, a business unit that shows rapid growth but poor profit margins.

processed materials Products used directly in manufacturing other products.

product Everything, both favorable and unfavorable, that a person receives in an exchange.

product advertising A form of advertising that touts the benefits of a specific good or service.

product category All brands that satisfy a particular type of need.

product development A marketing strategy that entails the creation of new products for current customers; the process of converting applications for new technologies into marketable products.

product differentiation A positioning strategy that some firms use to distinguish their products from those of competitors.

product item A specific version of a product that can be designated as a distinct offering among an organization's products.

product life cycle (PLC) A biological metaphor that traces the stages of a product's acceptance, from its introduction (birth) to its decline (death).

product line A group of closely related product items.

product line depth The number of product items in a product line.

product line extension Adding additional products to an existing product line in order to compete more broadly in the industry.

product line pricing Setting prices for an entire line of products.

product mix All products that an organization sells.

product mix width The number of product lines an organization offers.

product modification Changing one or more of a product's characteristics.

product offering The mix of products offered to the consumer by the retailer; also called the *product assortment* or *merchandise mix*.

product placement A public relations strategy that involves getting a product, service, or company name to appear in a movie, television show, radio program, magazine, newspaper, video game, video or audio clip, book, or commercial for another product; on the Internet; or at special events.

production orientation A philosophy that focuses on the internal capabilities of the firm rather than on the desires and needs of the marketplace.

product/service differentiation competitive advantage The provision of something that is unique and valuable to buyers beyond simply offering a lower price than the competition's.

profit Revenue minus expenses.

profit maximization A method of setting prices that occurs when marginal revenue equals marginal cost.

promotion Communication by marketers that informs, persuades, and reminds potential buyers of a product in order to influence an opinion or elicit a response.

promotional allowance (trade allowance) A payment to a dealer for promoting the manufacturer's products.

promotional mix The combination of promotion tools—including advertising, public relations, personal selling, and sales promotion—used to reach the target market and fulfill the organization's overall goals.

promotional strategy A plan for the optimal use of the elements of promotion: advertising, public relations, personal selling, and sales promotion.

PSA. *See* public service advertisement.

psychographic segmentation Market segmentation on the basis of personality, motives, lifestyles, and geodemographics.

publicity Public information about a company, product, service, or issue appearing in the mass media as a news item.

public relations The marketing function that evaluates public attitudes, identifies areas within the organization the public may be interested in, and executes a program of action to earn public understanding and acceptance.

public service advertisement (PSA) Announcement that promotes a program of a federal, state, or local government or of a nonprofit organization.

pull strategy A marketing strategy that stimulates consumer demand to obtain product distribution.

pulsing media schedule A media scheduling strategy that uses continuous scheduling throughout the year coupled with a flighted schedule during the best sales periods.

purchasing power A comparison of income versus the relative cost of a set standard of goods and services in different geographic areas.

push money Money offered to channel intermediaries to encourage them to "push" products—that is, to encourage other members of the channel to sell the products.

push strategy A marketing strategy that uses aggressive personal selling and trade advertising to convince a wholesaler or a retailer to carry and sell particular merchandise.

pyramid of corporate social responsibility A model that suggests corporate social responsibility is composed of economic, legal, ethical, and philanthropic responsibilities and that the firm's economic performance supports the entire structure.

Q

quantity discount A price reduction offered to buyers buying in multiple units or above a specified dollar amount.

quota A statement of the individual salesperson's sales objectives, usually based on sales volume alone but sometimes including key accounts (those with greatest potential), new accounts, repeat sales, and specific products.

R

random error An error that occurs when the selected sample is an imperfect representation of the overall population.

random sample A sample arranged in such a way that every element of the population has an equal chance of being selected as part of the sample.

raw materials Unprocessed extractive or agricultural products, such as mineral ore, lumber, wheat, corn, fruits, vegetables, and fish.

reach The number of target consumers exposed to a commercial at least once during a specific period, usually four weeks.

real self-image The way an individual actually perceives himself or herself.

rebate A cash refund given for the purchase of a product during a specific period.

receiver The person who decodes a message.

recession A period of economic activity characterized by negative growth, which reduces demand for goods and services.

reciprocity The practice of business purchasers choosing to buy from their own customers.

recruited Internet sample A sample in which respondents are prerecruited and must qualify to participate. They are then e-mailed a questionnaire or directed to a secure Web site.

reference group A group in society that influences an individual's purchasing behavior.

referral A recommendation to a salesperson from a customer or business associate.

relationship commitment A firm's belief that an ongoing relationship with another firm is so important that the relationship warrants maximum efforts at maintaining it indefinitely.

relationship marketing A strategy that focuses on keeping and improving relationships with current customers.

relationship selling (consultative selling) A sales practice that involves building, maintaining, and enhancing interactions with customers in order to develop long-term satisfaction through mutually beneficial partnerships.

reliability The ability to perform a service dependably, accurately, and consistently.

repositioning Changing consumers' perceptions of a brand in relation to competing brands.

research design Specifies which research questions must be answered, how and when the data will be gathered, and how the data will be analyzed.

response list A customer list that includes the names and addresses of individuals who have responded to an offer of some kind, such as by mail, telephone, direct-response television, product rebates, contests or sweepstakes, or billing inserts.

responsiveness The ability to provide prompt service.

retailer A channel intermediary that sells mainly to consumers.

retailing All the activities directly related to the sale of goods and services to the ultimate consumer for personal, nonbusiness use.

retailing mix A combination of the six Ps—product, place, promotion, price, presentation, and personnel—to sell goods and services to the ultimate consumer.

return on investment (ROI) Net profit after taxes divided by total assets.

revenue The price charged to customers multiplied by the number of units sold.

ROI. *See* return on investment.

routine response behavior The type of decision making exhibited by consumers buying frequently purchased, low-cost goods and services; requires little search and decision time.

S

sales orientation The idea that people will buy more goods and services if aggressive sales techniques are used and that high sales result in high profits.

sales presentation A formal meeting in which the salesperson presents a sales proposal to a prospective buyer.

sales process (sales cycle) The set of steps a salesperson goes through in a particular organization to sell a particular product or service.

sales promotion Marketing activities—other than personal selling, advertising, and public relations—that stimulate consumer buying and dealer effectiveness.

sales proposal A formal written document or professional presentation that outlines how the salesperson's product or service will meet or exceed the prospect's needs.

sample A subset from a larger population.

sampling A promotional program that allows the consumer the opportunity to try the product or service for free.

sampling error An error that occurs when a sample somehow does not represent the target population.

satisficers Business customers who place an order with the first familiar supplier to satisfy product and delivery requirements.

scaled-response question A closed-ended question designed to measure the intensity of a respondent's answer.

scanner-based research A system for gathering information from a single group of respondents by continuously monitoring the advertising, promotion, and pricing they are exposed to and the things they buy.

scrambled merchandising The tendency to offer a wide variety of nontraditional goods and services under one roof.

screened Internet sample An Internet sample with quotas based on desired sample characteristics.

screening The first filter in the product development process, which eliminates ideas that are inconsistent with the organization's new-product strategy or are obviously inappropriate for some other reason.

search quality A characteristic that can be easily assessed before purchase.

seasonal discount A price reduction for buying merchandise out of season.

seasonal media schedule A media scheduling strategy that runs advertising only during times of the year when the product is most likely to be used.

secondary data Data previously collected for any purpose other than the one at hand.

secondary membership group A reference group with which people associate less consistently and more formally than a primary membership group, such as a club, professional group, or religious group.

segmentation bases (variables) Characteristics of individuals, groups, or organizations.

selective distortion A process whereby a consumer changes or distorts information that conflicts with his or her feelings or beliefs.

selective distribution A form of distribution achieved by screening dealers to eliminate all but a few in any single area.

selective exposure The process whereby a consumer notices certain stimuli and ignores others.

selective retention A process whereby a consumer remembers only that information that supports his or her personal beliefs.

self-concept How consumers perceive themselves in terms of attitudes, perceptions, beliefs, and self-evaluations.

selling against the brand Stocking well-known branded items at high prices in order to sell store brands at discounted prices.

sender The originator of the message in the communication process.

service The result of applying human or mechanical efforts to people or objects.

service mark A trademark for a service.

shopping product A product that requires comparison shopping because it is usually more expensive than a convenience product and is found in fewer stores.

simulated (laboratory) market testing The presentation of advertising and other promotion materials for several products, including a test product, to members of the product's target market.

simultaneous product development A team-oriented approach to new-product development.

single-price tactic A price tactic that offers all goods and services at the same price (or perhaps two or three prices).

social class A group of people in a society who are considered nearly equal in status or community esteem, who regularly socialize among themselves both formally and informally, and who share behavioral norms.

socialization process How cultural values and norms are passed down to children.

societal marketing orientation The idea that an organization exists not only to satisfy customer wants and needs and to meet organizational objectives but also to preserve or enhance individuals' and society's long-term best interests.

spatial discrepancy The difference between the location of a producer and the location of widely scattered markets.

specialty discount store A retail store that offers a nearly complete selection of single-line merchandise and uses self-service, discount prices, high volume, and high turnover.

specialty product A particular item that consumers search extensively for and are very reluctant to accept substitutes.

specialty store A retail store specializing in a given type of merchandise.

sponsorship A public relations strategy in which a company spends money to support an issue, cause, or event that is consistent with corporate objectives, such as improving brand awareness or enhancing corporate image.

star In the portfolio matrix, a business unit that is a fast-growing market leader.

status quo pricing A pricing objective that maintains existing prices or meets the competition's prices.

stickiness A measure of a Web site's effectiveness; calculated by multiplying the frequency of visits times the duration of a visit times the number of pages viewed during teach visit (site reach).

stimulus Any unit of input affecting one or more of the five senses: sight, smell, taste, touch, hearing.

stimulus discrimination A learned ability to differentiate among similar products.

stimulus generalization A form of learning that occurs when one response is extended to a second stimulus similar to the first.

straight commission A method of compensation in which the salesperson is paid some percentage when a sale is made.

straight rebuy A situation in which the purchaser reorders the same goods or services without looking for new information or investigating other suppliers.

straight salary A method of compensation in which the salesperson receives a salary regardless of sales productivity.

strategic alliance (strategic partnership) A cooperative agreement between business firms.

strategic business unit (SBU) A subgroup of a single business or a collection of related businesses within the larger organization.

strategic channel alliance A cooperative agreement between business firms to use the other's already established distribution channel.

strategic planning The managerial process of creating and maintaining a fit between the organization's objectives and resources and evolving market opportunities.

subculture A homogeneous group of people who share elements of the overall culture as well as unique elements of their own group.

supercenter A retail store that combines groceries and general merchandise goods with a wide range of services.

supermarket A large, departmentalized, self-service retailer that specializes in food and some nonfood items.

supplementary services A group of services that support or enhance the core service.

supplies Consumable items that do not become part of the final product.

supply The quantity of a product that will be offered to the market by a supplier at various prices for a specified period.

supply chain The connected chain of all of the business entities, both internal and external to the company, that perform or support the logistics function.

supply chain management A management system that coordinates and integrates all of the activities performed by supply chain members into a seamless process, from the source to the point of consumption, resulting in enhanced customer and economic value.

supply chain team An entire group of individuals who orchestrate the movement of goods, services, and information from the source to the consumer.

survey research The most popular technique for gathering primary data, in which a researcher interacts with people to obtain facts, opinions, and attitudes.

sustainability The idea that socially responsible companies will outperform their peers by focusing on the world's social problems and viewing them as opportunities to build profits and help the world at the same time.

sustainable competitive advantage An advantage that cannot be copied by the competition.

SWOT analysis Identifying internal strengths (S) and weaknesses (W) and also examining external opportunities (O) and threats (T).

T

tangibles The physical evidence of a service, including the physical facilities, tools, and equipment used to provide the service.

target market A defined group most likely to buy a firm's product; a group of people or organizations for which an organization designs, implements, and maintains a marketing mix intended to meet the needs of that group, resulting in mutually satisfying exchanges.

teamwork Collaborative efforts of people to accomplish common objectives.

telemarketing The use of the telephone to sell directly to consumers.

temporal discrepancy A situation that occurs when a product is produced but a customer is not ready to buy it.

test marketing The limited introduction of a product and a marketing program to determine the reactions of potential customers in a market situation.

touch points All possible areas of a business where customers communicate with that business.

trade allowance A price reduction offered by manufacturers to intermediaries, such as wholesalers and retailers.

trademark The exclusive right to use a brand or part of a brand.

trade sales promotion Sales promotion activities targeting a channel member, such as a wholesaler or retailer.

trust The condition that exists when one party has confidence in an exchange partner's reliability and integrity.

two-part pricing A price tactic that charges two separate amounts to consume a single good or service.

U

unbundling Reducing the bundle of services that comes with the basic product.

undifferentiated targeting strategy A marketing approach that views the market as one big market with no individual segments and thus uses a single marketing mix.

unfair trade practice acts Laws that prohibit wholesalers and retailers from selling below cost.

uniform delivered pricing A price tactic in which the seller pays the actual freight charges and bills every purchaser an identical, flat freight charge.

unique selling proposition A desirable, exclusive, and believable advertising appeal selected as the theme for a campaign.

unitary elasticity A situation in which total revenue remains the same when prices change.

universal product codes (UPCs) A series of thick and thin vertical lines (bar codes), readable by computerized optical scanners, that represent numbers used to track products.

universe The population from which a sample will be drawn.

unrestricted Internet sample A survey in which anyone with a computer and Internet access can fill out the questionnaire.

unsought product A product unknown to the potential buyer or a known product that the buyer does not actively seek.

UPCs. *See* universal product codes.

Uruguay Round An agreement to dramatically lower trade barriers worldwide; created the World Trade Organization.

usage-rate segmentation Dividing a market by the amount of product bought or consumed.

V

value The enduring belief that a specific mode of conduct is personally or socially preferable to another mode of conduct.

value-based pricing Setting the price at a level that seems to the customer to be a good price compared to the prices of other options.

variable cost A cost that varies with changes in the level of output.

vertical conflict A channel conflict that occurs between different levels in a marketing channel, most typically between the manufacturer and wholesaler or between the manufacturer and retailer.

W

want Recognition of an unfulfilled need and a product that will satisfy it.

warehouse membership clubs Limited-service merchant wholesalers that sell a limited selection of brand-name appliances, household items, and groceries on a cash-and-carry basis to members, usually small businesses and groups.

warranty A confirmation of the quality or performance of a good or service.

World Bank An international bank that offers low-interest loans, advice, and information to developing nations.

World Trade Organization (WTO) A trade organization that replaced the old General Agreement on Tariffs and Trade (GATT).

WTO. *See* World Trade Organization.

Y

yield management systems (YMS) A technique for adjusting prices that uses complex mathematical software to profitably fill unused capacity by discounting early purchases, limiting early sales at these discounted prices, and overbooking capacity.

Z

zone pricing A modification of uniform delivered pricing that divides the United States (or the total market) into segments or zones and charges a flat freight rate to all customers in a given zone.

CHAPTER 1

1. "The Art of Service," *Fast Company*, October 2005, 55. Used by permission.
2. "About Us," American Marketing Association (online). Available at **http://www.marketingpower.com**
3. Philip Kotler, *Marketing Management*, 11th ed. (Upper Saddle River, NJ: Prentice Hall, 2003), 66.
4. Robert Levering and Milton Moskowitz, "The 100 Best Companies to Work For," *Fortune*, January 24, 2005, 73.
5. Kotler, *Marketing Management*, 12.
6. Nora Isaacs, "Crash and Burn," upsideto-day.com, 186–192.
7. Flavia Ellen, Susan Kaufman, and Joan Levinstein, "Six Lessons from the Fast Lane," *Fortune*, October 6, 2004, online.
8. Ibid.
9. Isaacs, "Crash and Burn," 190.
10. Chris Penttila, "Setting Sale," *Entrepreneur*, August 2004, 58.
11. Valerie A. Zeithaml, Mary Jo Bitner, and Dwayne D. Gremler, *Services Marketing*, 4th ed. (New York: McGraw-Hill Irwin, 2006), 110.
12. "Building Business Around Customers: Know Thy Customer," *BusinessWeek*, September 12, 2005, 8.
13. Alexandra DeFelice, "A Century of Customer Love," *Customer Relationship Management*, June 2005, 43.
14. Zeithaml, Bitner, and Gremler, *Services Marketing*.
15. Ibid.
16. Vicki Powers, "CRM Claims the Corner Office," *Customer Relationship Management*, November 2004, 28–34.
17. Vicki Powers, "CRM Starts in the Executive Suite," *Customer Relationship Management*, March 2004, 13–14.
18. Robert Levering and Milton Moskowitz, "The 100 Best Companies to Work For," *Fortune*, January 2003, 127–152.
19. Levering and Moskowitz, "The 100 Best Companies to Work For," 2005.
20. O. M. Malik, "The New Land of Opportunity," *Business 2.0*, July 2004, 77. Used by permission.
21. **https://www.cia.gov/cia/publications/factbook/index.html**
22. The application exercises throughout the book are based on the winning entries in the "Best of the Great Ideas in Teaching Marketing" contest held in conjunction with the publication of the Eighth Edition of *Marketing*. Ideas came from marketing professors all across the country, who teach many different sizes and types of marketing courses. Information on ways to implement these great ideas in the classroom can be found in the Instructor Manual that accompanies this text.
23. Jena McGregor, "At Netflix, the Secret Sauce is Software," *Fast Company*, December 2005, 48–51; Jennifer Netherby, "Netflix Delivers Big Earnings Increase: Sets 5.9 Million Subs as Modest 2006 Goal," *Video Business*, January 30, 2006, 1; Steven Zeitchnik, "Download Dreams: Netflix Eager to Expand Online Efforts," *Daily Variety*, January 25, 2006, 5; Jennifer Moeller, "You've Got (Movies in the) Mail," *The Christian Science Monitor*, December 2, 2005, 15; Ben Fritz, "Freaky Disc Biz: Netflix Grows at Blockbuster's Expense," *Daily Variety*, October 20, 2005, 1; "All Queued Up: How the Netflix Distribution Network Supports the Company's Business Model," *Material Handling Management*, November 2005, 9.

CHAPTER 2

1. Nadine Heintz, "Hands On Case Study," *Inc.*, March 2005, 44–46; U.S. Newswire Medialink Worldwide, **http://releases.usnewswire.com**, December 5, 2005; **http://www.beaconstreetgirls.com**, December 5, 2005.
2. Greg Lindsay, "The Rebirth of Cool," *Business 2.0*, September 2004, 109–114.
3. Melanie Warner, "McDonald's Push a Boon for Produce," *The Star Telegram*, February 26, 2005, C1.
4. **http://www.benjerry.com**, December 1, 2005.
5. **http://www.nike.com**, December 5, 2005.
6. Ray A. Smith, "Buying a Suit That's Not Hot," *Wall Street Journal Online*, July 7, 2005.
7. Sarah Ellison, "Why Kraft Decided to Ban Some Food Ads to Children," *The Wall Street Journal*, October 31, 2005, A1; Hall Dickler Kent Goldstein and Wood LLC, "Kraft Foods to Junk Snack Ads for Kids," **www.marketingpower.com**, December 5, 2005; **www.kraft.com**, December 5, 2005.
8. This application exercise is based on the contribution of Robert O'Keefe, Philip R. Kemp, and J. Steven Kelly, all of DePaul University, to *Great Ideas in Teaching Marketing*, a teaching supplement that accompanies Lamb, Hair, and McDaniel's *Marketing*. Their entry titled "Using Environmental Scan Reports as a Means of Assessing Student Learning" received a first place award in the strategy category of the "Best of the Great Ideas in Teaching Marketing" contest held in conjunction with the publication of the Eighth Edition of *Marketing*.

9. Geoff Keighly, "The Phantasmagoria Factory," *Business 2.0*, January/February 2004, 103; Christopher J. Chipello, "Cirque du Soleil Seeks Partnerships to Create Entertainment Centers," *WSJ.com*, July 18, 2001; Steve Friess, "Cirque Dreams Big," *Newsweek*, July 14, 2003, 42; "Bravo Announces Programming Alliance with Cirque du Soleil; Original Series, Specials, and Documentaries to Air on Bravo, 'The Official U.S. Network of Cirque du Soleil,'" *Business Wire*, June 19, 2000; "Inhibitions Take the Night Off for International Gala Premiere of ZUMAN-ITY™; Another Side of Cirque du Soleil™ at New York–New York Hotel and Casino," *PR Newswire*, September 21, 2003; Laura Del Rosso, "'O' Dazzles with Air, Underground Acrobatics," *Travel Weekly*, August 5, 2002; Gigi Berardi, "Circus + Dance = Cirque du Soleil," *Dance Magazine*, September 2002.

MARKETING PLAN APPENDIX

The authors would like to thank e-motion software for allowing us to include its marketing plan in the Ninth Edition of *Marketing*. We greatly appreciate Mr. Keohane's contribution of a real plan used by his growing company, which demonstrates to students the level of detail and the elements required to build an effective plan.

CHAPTER 3

1. Marc Gunther, "Money and Morals at GE," *Fortune*, November 15, 2004, 176–182.
2. Marc Gunther, "Tree Huggers, Soy Lovers, and Profits," *Fortune*, June 23, 2003, 98–104.
3. Gunther, "Money and Morals at GE," 182. See also Donald Lichenstein, Minette Drumwright, and Bridgette Braig, "The Effect of Corporate Social Responsibility on Customer Donations to Corporate-Supported Nonprofits," *Journal of Marketing*, October 2004, 16–32.
4. This discussion is adapted from Archie B. Carroll, "The Pyramid of Corporate Social Responsibility: Toward the Moral Management of Organizational Stake-holders," *Business Horizons*, July/ August 1991, 39–48. See also Kirk Davidson, "Marketers Must Accept Greater Responsibilities," *Marketing News*, February 2, 1998, 6.
5. "America's Most Admired Companies," *Fortune*, March 7, 2003, 67.
6. Sankar Sen and C. B. Bhattacharya, "Does Doing Good Always Lead to Doing Better? Consumer Reactions to Corporate Responsibility," *Journal of Marketing Research*, May 2001, 225–243.

7. Gunther, "Tree Huggers, Soy Lovers, and Profits."

8. Marc Gunther, "Will Social Responsibility Harm Business?" *Wall Street Journal*, May 18, 2005, A2.

9. Based on Edward Stevens, *Business Ethics* (New York: Paulist Press, 1979). Reprinted with permission. Used with permission of Paulist Press.

10. Anusorn Singhapakdi, Skott Vitell, and Kenneth Kraft, "Moral Intensity and Ethical Decisionmaking of Marketing Professionals," *Journal of Business Research* 36, March 1996, 245–255; Ishmael Akaah and Edward Riordan, "Judgments of Marketing Professionals about Ethical Issues in Marketing Research: A Replication and Extension," *Journal of Marketing Research*, February 1989, 112–120. See also Shelby Hunt, Lawrence Chonko, and James Wilcox, "Ethical Problems of Marketing Researchers," *Journal of Marketing Research*, August 1984, 309–324; Kenneth Andrews, "Ethics in Practice," *Harvard Business Review*, September/October 1989, 99–104; Thomas Dunfee, Craig Smith, and William T. Ross, Jr., "Social Contracts and Marketing Ethics," *Journal of Marketing*, July 1999, 14–32; Jan Handleman and Stephen Arnold, "The Role of Marketing Actions with a Social Dimension: Appeals to the Institutional Environment," *Journal of Marketing*, July 1999, 33–48; David Turnipseed, "Are Good Soldiers Good? Exploring the Link between Organizational Citizenship Behavior and Personal Ethics," *Journal of Business Research*, January 2002, 1–16; Tim Barnett and Sean Valentine, "Issue Contingencies and Marketers' Recognition of Ethical Issues, Ethical Judgments and Behavioral Intentions," *Journal of Business Research*, April 2004, 338–346.

11. O. C. Ferrell, Debbie Thorne, and Linda Ferrell, "Legal Pressure for Ethical Compliance in Marketing," *Proceedings of the American Marketing Association*, Summer 1995, 412–413.

12. "Women-Owned Businesses Booming, but So Are Obstacles," *Associated Press Newswires*, April 11, 2000.

13. "Tech Companies Try Wooing Women with Girlie Marketing," *Wall Street Journal*, August 26, 2003, B1, B4.

14. "Female Persuasion," *Marketing Management*, July/August 2004, 6.

15. Ibid.

16. Ibid.

17. J. Walker Smith, "A Single-Minded Marketplace," *Marketing Management*, July/August 2004, 52.

18. Ibid.

19. Ibid.

20. J. Walker Smith, "Make Time Worth It," *Marketing Management*, July/August 2005, 56.

21. Michael Mandel, "The Real Reasons You're Working So Hard," *BusinessWeek*, October 3, 2005, 60.

22. Smith, "Make Time Worth It."

23. "Coming of Age in Consumerdom," *American Demographics*, April 2004, 14.

24. Ibid.

25. Martin Lindstrom, "Seen by Tweens," *Quirk's Marketing Research Review*, February 2004, 48–50.

26. Karen Akers, "Generation Y: Marketing to the Young and the Restless," *Successful Promotions*, January/February 2005, 33–38.

27. Ibid.

28. "The Echo Boomers," *CBSNews.com*, October 3, 2004.

29. Ibid.

30. "The Gen X Budget," *American Demographics*, July/August 2002, S5.

31. "Gen X Wants No-Debt," *American Demographics*, April 2004, 43.

32. "At Holiday Inn Select, Gen X Marks the Spot," *Brandweek*, September 19, 2005, 12.

33. Louise Lee, "Love Those Boomers," *BusinessWeek*, October 24, 2005, 94–101.

34. Ibid.

35. Dick Chay, "New Segments of Boomers Reveal New Marketing Implications," *Marketing News*, March 15, 2005, 24.

36. "America's Gray Area Dilemma," *American Demographics*, July/August 2004, 40.

37. "Manifest Destiny 3.0," *American Demographics*, September 2004, 29–34.

38. "U.S. Buying Power by Race," *Marketing News*, July 15, 2004, 11.

39. "Diversity in America," *American Demographics*, November 2002, S1–S15.

40. "Pepsi, Vowing Diversity Isn't Just Image Polish, Seeks Inclusive Culture," *Wall Street Journal*, April 19, 2005, B1.

41. "A Multicultural Mecca," *American Demographics*, May 2003, S4–S7.

42. "Give Me Your Tired, Your Poor, Your Beloved Products," *Business 2.0*, October 2005, 29–30.

43. "Wal-Mart's Hispanic Outreach," *Wall Street Journal*, May 31, 2005, B9.

44. "Net Serves As Best Tool to Connect with Hispanics," *Marketing News*, September 1, 2005, 29.

45. "Has This Group Been Left Behind?" *Brandweek*, March 14, 2005, 35.

46. Lafayette Jones, "A Sign of the Times," *Promo*, February 2, 2002.

47. "Marketing Intelligence," *Women's Wear Daily*, December 3, 2003, 20.

48. Joan Raymond, "The Multicultural Report," *American Demographics*, November 2001, S1–S4.

49. Ibid., S6.

50. Jerry Goodbody, "Taking the Pulse of Asian Americans," *Adweek's Marketing Week*, August 12, 2001, 32.

51. U.S. Census Bureau data with projections by the authors.

52. "The Rich Get Richer and That's OK," *BusinessWeek*, August 26, 2002, 90.

53. "The State," *BusinessWeek*, July 18, 2005, 16.

54. "Lagging behind the Wealthy, Many Use Debt to Catch Up," *Wall Street Journal*, May 17, 2005, A1.

55. Martha Barletta, "Capture the Power of the Purse," *Quirk's Marketing Research Review*, February 2005, 52–55; on the amount of private wealth, the Federal Reserve, as cited in PBS online, "To the Contrary, Hot Topics, Women and Philanthropy."

56. Ibid.

57. Diane Brady, "Reaping the Wind," *BusinessWeek*, October 11, 2004, 201.

58. "Safety Agency Takes Action on Baby Gear," *Wall Street Journal*, March 22, 2005, D1–D4.

59. http://www.privacy.org, March 24, 2005.

60. "The Great Data Heist," *Fortune*, May 16, 2005, 66–75.

61. "ChoicePoint to Exit Non-FCRA, Consumer-Sensitive Data Markets," http://www.choicepoint.com, March 4, 2005.

62. "Citi Notifies 3.9 Million Customers of Lost Data," MSNBC.com, June 7, 2005.

63. "These Wings Have a Name," *Brandweek*, February 7, 2005, 16–17.

64. "In Switch, Pepsi Makes Diet Cola Its New Flagship," *Wall Street Journal*, March 16, 2005, B1, B2.

65. "Home Economics," *BusinessWeek*, March 14, 2005, 12.

66. This application exercise is based on the contribution of Mark Andrew Mitchell (University of South Carolina-Spartanburg) to *Great Ideas in Teaching Marketing*, a teaching supplement that accompanies Lamb, Hair, and McDaniel's *Marketing*. Professor Mitchell's entry titled "The Guide to Ethnic Dining" was part of the "Best of the Great Ideas in Teaching Marketing" contest held in conjunction with the publication of the eighth edition of *Marketing*.

67. http://www.rockstargames.com; http://www.take2games.com; Logan Hill, "Why Rockstar Games Rock," *Wired.com*, July 2002; Michael Serazio, "Vice City Confidential: The 'Atari' Generation Grows Up," *Columbia.edu*, March 7, 2003; "The Games Kids Play: Are Mature Video Games Too Violent for Teens?" *Current Events*, February 7, 2003; "Deadly Inspiration? Teens Say Video Game Inspired Them in Deadly Highway Shooting," *ABCnews.com*, September 5, 2003; "Florida Officials Take Aim at Violent Games," *Reuters*, February 6, 2004; Andrew Bushell, "Popular Video Game Instructs Players to 'Shoot the Haitians'—New York AG Takes on Grand Theft Auto," *VillageVoice.com*, January 30, 2004; Christopher Byron, "Give Back Take-Two," *New York Post*, December 29, 2003.

CHAPTER 4

1. Robyn Meredith, "Split Personality," *Forbes*, October 17, 2005, 114–116.

2. http://www.trade.businessroundtable.org, November 22, 2005.

3. "Fortune Global 500," *Fortune*, July 25, 2005, 97–98.

4. "Borders Are So 20th Century," *BusinessWeek*, September 22, 2003, 68.

5. Marc Gunther, "Cops of the Global Village," *Fortune*, June 27, 2005, 158–164.

6. Theodore Levitt, "The Globalization of Markets," *Harvard Business Review*, May/June 1983, 92–102.

7. "Culture Course," *Wall Street Journal*, May 25, 2004, B1, B12. See also Richard Michon and Jean-Charles Chebat, "Cross-Cultural Mall Shopping Values and Habits: A Comparison between English- and French-Speaking Canadians," *Journal of Business Research*, August 2004, 883–892; Mitch

Griffin, Barry Babin, and Finn Christensen, "A Cross-Cultural Evaluation of the Materialism Construct: Assessing the Richins and Dawson's Materialism Scale in Denmark, France, and Russia," *Journal of Business Research*, August 2004, 893–900; Linda Ueltschy, Michel Laroche, Robert Tamila, and Peter Yannopoulos, "Cross-Cultural Invariance of Measures of Satisfaction and Service Quality," *Journal of Business Research*, August 2004, 901–912.

8. "It's August, Guess Where Everybody Is," *International Herald Tribune*, August 10, 2005, 11.

9. http://www.finfacts.com, November 22, 2005.

10. "To Put It in Perspective," *American Demographics*, June 2003, 9.

11. "World Bank Faults Tight Regulation," *Wall Street Journal*, October 7, 2003, A2, A10.

12. "Chávez Oil-Fueled Revolution," *BusinessWeek*, October 10, 2005, 57.

13. Remarks by Ambassador Garza at the "Hemisphere 2005" Conference in San Pedro, Mexico, May 13, 2005.

14. "Expanded EU Will Be an Uneven One," *Wall Street Journal*, September 22, 2003, A16.

15. "Corn Flakes Clash Shows the Glitches in European Union," *Wall Street Journal*, November 1, 2005, A1, A9.

16. "Intel Raided in EU Antitrust Investigation," *The Globe and Mail*, July 13, 2005, B8.

17. "EU Limits Coke's Sales Tactics in Settlement of Antitrust Case," *Wall Street Journal*, June 23, 2005, B6.

18. http://www.sba.gov, December 5, 2005.

19. "Entertainment/Character Licenses Generated Largest Share of Worldwide Sales," *Licensing Letter*, June 6, 2005.

20. http://www.franchise.org, December 5, 2005.

21. "Coke Bottler in Mexico Threatens to Cut Marketing," *Wall Street Journal*, November 1, 2005, B5.

22. "A Sneaker Maker Says China Partner Became Its Rival," *Wall Street Journal*, December 14, 2002, A1, A8.

23. Zeynep Emden, Attila Yaprak, and S. Tamer Causugil, "Learning from Experience in International Alliances: Antecedents and Firm Performance Implications," *Journal of Business Research*, July 2005, 883–901; Jane Lu and Louis Hébert, "Equity Control and the Survival of International Joint Ventures: A Contingency Approach," *Journal of Business Research*, June 2005, 736–745.

24. "Joint Problems," *Forbes*, October 17, 2005, 118.

25. "China: Joint Venture Construction Plans for Proposed 350,000 Automobile Engine Plant," *WWP-Report*, May 1, 2005.

26. "Visions of Sugar Plums South of the Border," *Wall Street Journal*, February 13, 2002, A15.

27. "Wal-Mart Opens 10 Brazil Stores in 2005, Eyes More Growth," *Dow Jones International News*, May 12, 2005.

28. "Wal-Mart: Struggling in Germany," *BusinessWeek Online*, April 11, 2005.

29. "Let a Thousand Brands Bloom," *BusinessWeek*, October 17, 2005, 58–60.

30. "Capturing a Piece of the Global Market," *BrandWeek*, June 20, 2005, 20.

31. "Machines for the Masses," *Wall Street Journal*, December 9, 2005, A4.

32. "Small Is Profitable," *BusinessWeek*, August 26, 2002, 112–114.

33. "Lattes Lure Brits to Coffee," *Wall Street Journal*, October 20, 2005, B1, B6.

34. "If Only 'Krispy Kreme' Meant 'Makes You Smarter,'" *Business 2.0*, August 2005, 108.

35. "China's Cultural Fabric Is a Challenge to Marketers," *Wall Street Journal*, January 21, 2004, B7.

36. "Solving China's Logistics Riddle," *Wall Street Journal*", October 15, 2003, A18, A19.

37. "India's Bumpy Ride," *Fortune*, October 31, 2005, 149–153.

38. "Dell May Have to Reboot in China," *BusinessWeek*, November 7, 2005, 46.

39. Matthew Myers, "Implications of Pricing Strategy—Venture Strategy Experience: An Application Using Optimal Models in an International Context," *Journal of Business Research*, June 2004, 591–600.

40. "U.S. Cuts Punitive Tariffs," *Quick Frozen Foods International*, January 1, 2005).

41. This application exercise is based on the contributions of Gregory J. Baleja (Alma College) and William C. Moncrief (Texas Christian University) to *Great Ideas in Teaching Marketing*, a teaching supplement that accompanies Lamb, Hair, and McDaniel's *Marketing*. Their entries titled "International Marketing: A Map Quiz" and "Using Geography in the International Marketing Class," respectively, were winners in the "Best of the Great Ideas in Teaching Marketing" contest held in conjunction with the publication of the Eighth Edition of *Marketing*.

42. Martin Lindstrom, "One Voice?" *Clickz.com*, February 26, 2002; Steve McClure, "New MTV Post in OZ, Japan: MTV Asia President to Assume Responsibility," *Billboard*, March 8, 2003, 59; "MTV Announces International Expansion Plans for Europe, Asia, and Latin America: Company to Add New Services in Regional Growth Markets Worldwide," *Business Wire*, March 9, 1996; Kerry Cappel, Catherine Belton, Tom Lowry, Manjeet Kripalani, Brian Bremner, and Dexter Roberts, "MTV's World," *BusinessWeek.com*, February 18, 2002.

PART 1

1. http://vtbear.stores.yahoo.net/; American Floral Endowment's Consumer Tracking Study, "Valentine's Day Statistics," http://www.growerflowers.com/SEholidaystats.asp, 2003; Associated Press, "Company Won't Pull Straitjacketed Bear," *ABC News*, 2005, http://abcnews.go.com/; Pam Belluck, "Toy's Message of Affection Draws Anger and Publicity," *New York Times*, January 22, 2005, http://www.nytimes.com; DHL Press Office, "DHL Survey Uncovers Valentine's Day Gift-Giving Habits," http://www.dhl-usa.com/, February 9, 2005; David Gram, "Crazy for You Bear Raises Ethics Questions," *Associated Press*, February 14, 2005, http://www.namiscc.org/News/2005/Winter/CrazyTeddy.htm; National Stigma Clearinghouse, "Vermont Teddy Bear Controversy," http://community-2.webtv.net/stigmanet/

2. "Doctors Not Influenced by Pharmaceutical Marketing Tactics," *Medical News Today*, December 8, 2004, http://www.medicalnewstoday.com/; Linda A. Johnson, "Web Sites New Twist in Celebrity Drug Ads," *AP News*, July 17, 2005, http://www.apdigitalnews.com/; Merrill Matthews, "Who's Afraid of Pharmaceutical Advertising?" *IPI Policy Report* no. 155, May 17, 2001; Ray Moynihan, "Who Pays for the Pizza? Redefining the Relationships between Doctors and Drug Companies," *BMJ (British Medical Journal)*, May 31, 2003, 1189–1192; Julie Schmit, "FDA Races to Keep Up with Drug Ads That Go Too Far," *USA Today*, May 30, 2005, http://www.usatoday.com; Shankar Vedantam and Marc Kaufman, "Doctors Influenced by Mention of Drug Ads," *Washington Post*, April 27, 2005, A01.

CHAPTER 5

1. Matthew Maier, "Hooking up with Gen Y," *Business 2.0*, October 2003, 49; http://www.virginmobileusa.com: "Company Exceeds Customer Expectations and Drives Active Use of Data Services and Mobile Content Favored by Youth Market," September 2005; "With New Offer, Just 35 Cents Per Day Buys 10 Cent Minutes All Day Long," May 2005; "Virgin Mobile USA and EMI Music's Virgin Records Offer Exclusive Content from Gorillaz Sophomore Disc, Demon Days," August 2005.

2. Michael Totty, "Information, Please," *Wall Street Journal*, October 29, 2001, R6; http://www.pg.com, accessed February 2006.

3. Emily Nelson, "P&G Checks Out Real Life," *Wall Street Journal*, May 17, 2001, B1.

4. "What's Hot in the Living Spaces of Young Adults?" *American Demographics*, September 2003, 14.

5. Jefferson Graham, "Portable Video Expected to Take Center Stage," *USA Today*, January 3, 2006, B1; http://www.apple.com/ipod/ipod.html; http://www.webopedia.com/TERM/M/MP3.html; http://www.mp3newswire.net/, accessed February 2006.

6. http://www.persil.com/persil_products/pfam_home/, February 2006; http://www.eu.pg.com/ourbrands/ariel.html, February 2006.

7. Ronald Alsop, "Survey Rates Companies' Reputations, and Many Are Found Wanting," *Wall Street Journal*, February 7, 2001, B1. See also Gordon Fairclough, "Philip Morris Seeks to Mold Its Image into an Altria State," *Wall Street Journal*, November 16, 2001, A3.

8. Ernest Beck, "Boosting Diageo's Spirits," *Wall Street Journal*, February 23, 2001, B1.

9. David P. Hamilton, "Not an Easy Sell: TiVo, ReplayTV and Other 'PVRs' Don't Take Off," *Wall Street Journal*, February 7, 2001, B1.

10. Ronald Alsop, "The Best Corporate Reputations in America: Johnson & Johnson (Think Babies!) Turns Up Tops," *Wall Street Journal*, September 23, 1999, B1. See also Alsop, "Survey Rates Companies' Reputations, and Many Are Found Wanting."

11. Princeton Research Survey Associates, "Consumer Behavior, Experiences and Attitudes: A Comparison by Age Groups," *AARP*, March 1999.

12. Amy Goldwasser, "What Is the Good Life? An A–Z Guide to Living Large," *Inc.*, October 2003, 71.

13. http://www.mystictan.com, accessed February 2006.

14. Philips Magnavox ad, *Business 2.0*, October 2003, 81.

15. Michael Totty, "Making the Sale," *Wall Street Journal*, September 24, 2001, R6.

16. Stephanie Thompson, "Marketers Embrace Latest Health Claims," *Advertising Age*, February 28, 2000, 20–22. See also John Urquhart, "A Health Food Hits Big Time," *Wall Street Journal*, August 3, 1999, B1, B4.

17. Sandra Yin, "Color Bind," *American Demographics*, September 2003, 24, 26.

18. Stephanie Thompson, "Fashion Week Gets TV Channel," *Advertising Age*, September 1, 2003, 3.

19. Cathleen Egan, "Kellogg, General Mills Battle over Bars," *Wall Street Journal*, March 26, 2001, B10.

20. Bill Stoneman, "Beyond Rocking the Ages: An Interview with J. Walker Smith," *American Demographics*, May 1998, 44–49.

21. Michael Weiss, "To Be about to Be," *American Demographics*, September 2003, 30–36.

22. Miriam Jordon, "Global Craze for Diet Drugs," *Wall Street Journal*, August 24, 2001, B1. See also Leslie Chang, "Bring Science to Weight Loss in China," *Wall Street Journal*, August 24, 2001, B1.

23. Bill Spindle, "Cowboys and Samurai: The Japanizing of Universal," *Wall Street Journal*, Mary 22, 2001, B1.

24. Joshua Harris Prager, "People with Disabilities Are Next Consumer Niche," *Wall Street Journal*, December 15, 1999, B1, B6.

25. Devon Spurgeon, "Hold the Oatmeal! Restaurants Now Court the Breakfast Burger Eater," *Wall Street Journal*, September 4, 2001, B1.

26. Eduardo Porter, "For Hispanic Marketers, Census Says It All," *Wall Street Journal*, April 24, 2001, B8. See also Dean Bonham, "Hispanic Fans Make It to Big Leagues," *Rocky Mountain News*, June 23, 2001, 5C.

27. Heidi J. Shrager, "Closed-Circle Commerce," *Wall Street Journal*, November 19, 2001, B1.

28. Ned Potter, "The World's Most Luxurious Car? Mercedes-Benz' Maybach Costs $350,000," *ABC Nightly News*, August 19, 2003; http://www.daimlerchrysler.com, accessed January 2006; Bruno J. Navarro, "Not for Housework," *Associated Press*, December 28, 2004.

29. Michael J. Weiss, "A Tale of Two Cheeses," *American Demographics*, February 1998, 16–17.

30. Rich Thomaselli, "James' Coke Deal Sets New Endorser Standard," *Advertising Age*, August 25, 2003, 3; http://quickstart.clari.net/qs_se/webnews/wed/dr/Ubkpjames.Rh90_DaL.html, accessed February 2006.

31. Jacek Slotala and Michal Sosnowski, "Poland's Marketing Paradox," *Brand Strategy*, February 2004, 56.

32. Barbara Cooke, "Radar Fine-Tuned to 'Cool' Sets Some Teens Apart," *Chicago Tribune*, March 5, 2000, 1.

33. Erin White, "Abercrombie Seeks to Send Teeny-Boppers Packing," *Wall Street Journal*, August 30, 2001, B1.

34. Norihiko Shirouzu, "Japan's High-School Girls Excel in Art of Setting Trends," *Wall Street Journal*, April 24, 1998, B1, B6.

35. Thompson, "Fashion Week Gets TV Channel."

36. http://www.alloyonline.com, accessed January 2006.

37. The material in this section comes from Rebecca Weeks, "Teens: Making or Breaking Brands?" http://www.imediaconnection.com, October 28 2004; http://www.nielsenbuzzmetrics.com/; and Troy Dreier, "AOL Launches Blog Service for Teens," *PC Magazine Online*, March 29, 2005.

38. Jonathan Eig, "Edible Entertainment," *Wall Street Journal*, October 24, 2001, B1.

39. *Advertising Age*, December 10, 2003, back cover.

40. Matthew Klein, "He Shops, She Shops," *American Demographics*, March 1998, 34–35.

41. Khanh T. L. Tran, "Women Assert Computer Games Aren't Male Preserve," *Wall Street Journal*, February 26, 2001, B1. See also Meeyoung Song, "Credit-Card Companies Cater to Korean Women," *Wall Street Journal*, June 6, 2001, B4.

42. Martha Barletta, "Capture the Power of the Purse," *Quirk's Marketing Research Review*, February 2005, 52–55.

43. Rebecca Gardyn, "Almost Adults," *American Demographics*, September 2003, 11; http://primetimetv.about.com and http://www.wchstv.com/newsroom/nielsen.shtml, accessed January 2006.

44. Vanessa O'Connell and Jon E. Hilsenrath, "Advertisers Are Cautious as Household Makeup Shifts," *Wall Street Journal*, May 15, 2001, B1.

45. Jean Halliday, "$45 Mil Campaign: Nissan Attempts to Sex Up Quest," *Advertising Age*, August 4, 2003, 7.

46. Nora J. Rifon and Molly Catherine Ziske, "Using Weight Loss Products: The Roles of Involvement, Self-Efficacy and Body Image," in 1995 *AMA Educators' Proceedings*, ed. Barbara B. Stern and George M. Zinkhan (Chicago: American Marketing Association, 1995), 90–98.

47. Lisa Vickery, Kelly Greene, Shelly Branch, and Emily Nelson, "Marketers Tweak Strategies as Age Groups Realign," *Wall Street Journal*, May 15, 2001, B1.

48. "FYI," *Advertising Age*, July 30, 2003, 2; http://www.adage.com; "Madonna to Star in Gap's Fall Ad Campaign," *USA Today*, July 15, 2003, 1C; http://www.usatoday.com/money/industries/retail/2003-07-15-madonna-gap_x.htm.

49. Sarah Hall, "What Color Is Your Cart?" *Self*, September 1999, 150; http://www.godiva.com, accessed January 2006.

50. Jane L. Levere, "New Campaign for Ivory Soap," *New York Times* online, October 25, 2001.

51. Joshua Rosenbaum, "Guitar Maker Looks for a New Key," *Wall Street Journal*, February 11, 1998, B1, B5.

52. Elizabeth J. Wilson, "Using the Dollarmetric Scale to Establish the Just Meaningful Difference in Price," in 1987 *AMA Educators' Proceedings*, ed. Susan Douglas et al. (Chicago: American Marketing Association, 1987), 107.

53. Sunil Gupta and Lee G. Cooper, "The Discounting of Discounts and Promotion Thresholds," *Journal of Consumer Research*, December 1992, 401–411.

54. Mark Stiving and Russell S. Winer, "An Empirical Analysis of Price Endings with Scanner Data," *Journal of Consumer Research*, June 1997, 57–67. See also Robert M. Schindler and Patrick N. Kirby, "Patterns of Rightmost Digits Used in Advertised Price: Implications for Nine-Ending Effects," *Journal of Consumer Research*, September 1997, 192–201.

55. Sheila Muto, "What's in an Address? Sometimes, a Better Image," *Wall Street Journal*, September 5, 2001, B14.

56. Stuart Elliot, "Growing Number of Airlines Resume Image Advertising," *New York Times* online, November 6, 2001.

57. Kevin Helliker, "How Hardy Are Upscale Gyms?" *Wall Street Journal*, February 9, 2001, B1.

58. Jim Carlton, "Recycling Redefined," *Wall Street Journal*, March 6, 2001, B1.

59. Stephanie Thompson, "Cole Haan Fashions an Effort for Women," *Advertising Age*, August 25, 2003, 6.

60. Miriam Jordan, "Debut of Rival Diet Colas in India Leaves a Bitter Taste," *Wall Street Journal*, July 21, 1999, B1, B4.

61. This application exercise is based on the contribution of P.J. Forrest (Mississippi College) to *Great Ideas in Teaching Marketing*, a teaching supplement that accompanies Lamb, Hair, and McDaniel's *Marketing*. Professor Forrest's entry titled "Print Ad Projects for Consumer Behavior" was a winner in the "Best of the Great Ideas in Teaching Marketing" contest held in conjunction with the publication of the eighth edition of *Marketing*.

62. Amy Chozick and Timothy Martin, "A Place for Cocoa Nuts?" *Wall Street Journal*, July 15, 2005, B1, B3; http://www.ethelschocolate.com; "Ethel's Launches First-Ever Approachable, Everyday Gourmet Chocolate and Chocolate Lounges; Opens First Two Stores in Chicago, Expected to Expand to Six by End of Summer," *PR Newswire*, June 6, 2005; Karen Hawkins, "Chocolate Lounges' Present Themselves as Sweet Alternatives to Coffee Shops, Bars," *Associated Press*, February 13, 2006; Melinda Murphy, "Trend Report: Chocolate Is Hot," *CBS News Online*, http://www.cbsnews.com/stories/2006/02/07/earlyshow/contributors/melindamurphy/main1289922.shtml.

CHAPTER 6

1. Based on Kevin Kelleher, "Giving Dealers a Raw Deal," *Business 2.0*, December 2004, 82, 84. Used by permission of *Business 2.0*.

2. Michael D. Hutt and Thomas W. Speh, *Business Marketing Management* (Cincinnati: South-Western, 2004), 4.

3. *Marketing News*, July 15, 2005, 29.

4. http://www.clickz.com/showPage.html?page=stats/sectors/b2b

5. NetGenesis, *E-Metrics: Business Metrics for the New Economy*, http://www.spss.com.

6. "B2B Ain't What It Used to Be," *eMarketer*, June 24, 2005, online.

7. *Wikipedia, the Free Encyclopedia*, July 26, 2005, online.

8. James Bandler, "As Kodak Eyes Digital Future, a Big Partner Starts to Fade," *Wall Street Journal Online*, January 23, 2004.

9. Janet Adamy, "Retail Exchanges Plan Merger to Vie with Wal-Mart," *Wall Street Journal*, April 26, 2005, B7.

10. David Bank, "Microsoft, SAP Plan a Joint Product," *Wall Street Journal*, April 26, 2005, B3.

11. Andy Pasztor, Jonathan Karp, and J. Lynn Lunsford, "Boeing, Lockheed Agree to Form Rocket Joint Venture, Ending Feud," *Wall Street Journal*, May 3, 2005, A3.

12. Erin White, "A Cheaper Alternative to Outsourcing: Choice Hotels and 1-800-Flowers Swap Call-Center Employees," *Wall Street Journal*, April 10, 2006, B3.

13. Robert M. Morgan and Shelby D. Hunt, "The Commitment-Trust Theory of Relationship Marketing" *Journal of Marketing* 58, no. 3 (1994): 23.

14. Ibid.

15. Leila Abboud, "How Eli Lilly's Monster Deal Faced Extinction—but Survived," *Wall Street Journal Online*, April 27, 2005.

16. Zang Dahong, "Shanghai Auto Wants to Be the World's Next Great Car Company," *Fortune*, October 4, 2004, 103–108.

17. U.S. Census Bureau, "North American Industry Classification System (NAICS)—United States," **http://www.census.gov/epcd/www/naics.html**.

18. Steve Butler, "B2B Exhanges' Transaction Activity," *eMarketer*, February 18, 2003, online.

19. **http://www.lockheedmartin.com**

20. "Right Channeling: Making Sure Your Best Customers Get Your Best Service," Right Now Technologies, online.

21. This application exercise is based on the contribution of Gregory B. Turner (College of Charleston) to *Great Ideas in Teaching Marketing*, a teaching supplement that accompanies Lamb, Hair, and McDaniel's *Marketing*. Professor Turner's entry titled "Student Ethics versus Practitioner Ethics" received an Honorable Mention in the "Best of the Great Ideas in Teaching Marketing" contest held in conjunction with the publication of the eighth edition of *Marketing*.

22. Jonathan Karp, "How Bikers' Water Backpack Became Soldiers' Essential," *Wall Street Journal*, July 19, 2005, B1, B2; "CamelBak Introduces New Line of Strength/Stealth Technology Responding to Law Enforcement and Military Needs; R&D Innovations Protect against Infrared Detection, Provide Strongest Hydration Reservoir Available," *PR Newswire*, January 27, 2005; Mark Riedy, "The Birth of CamelBak," *Mountain Bike*, Summer 2004, 104; "CamelBak Announces Chem-Bio Hydration Reservoir for Military, Law Enforcement and First Responders; New Reservoir Is World's Only Hands-Free Hydration System That Withstands Exposure to Chemical and Biological Agents to Provide Safe Drinking Water in All Combat Environments 24/7/365." *PR Newswire*, August 26, 2004.

CHAPTER 7

1. Ann Zimmerman and Kris Hudson, "Looking Upscale, Wal-Mart Begins a Big Makeover," *Wall Street Journal Online*, September 17, 2005. Used by permission.

2. Heather Landy, "Kiddie Cash," *Fort Worth Star-Telegram*, October 13, 2003, 8C.

3. "Marketing to Online Teens," *eMarketer*, May 11, 2004.

4. "Which Form of Media Influences Teens?" *eMarketer*, June 23, 2004, online.

5. Stephen J. Hasker and Andrew Somosi, "Marketing to Teens Online," *McKinsey Quarterly*, No. 4, 2004, online.

6. Aimee Deeken, "Teenage Tasteland," *Spring Magazine*, March 1, 2004, 22–24.

7. Ibid.

8. "Senior Power," *RetailWire*, September 14, 2005, online; Ylan Q. Mui, "Retailers Redesign as Boomers Hit 60," *Washington Post.com*, January 17, 2006, D01.

9. Kelly Greene, "When We're All 64," *Wall Street Journal*, September 26, 2005, R1.

10. Louise Lee, "Love Those Boomers," *BusinessWeek*, October 24, 2005, 94–102.

11. Ibid.

12. Jathon Sapsford, "Japan's Auto Makers Ply the Aged with 'Elder Car' Options," *Wall Street Journal*, November 5, 2004, B1.

13. Mui, "Retailers Redesign as Boomers Hit 60."

14. Jathon Sapsford, "As Japan's Elderly Ranks Swell, Toyota Sees New Path to Growth," *Wall Street Journal*, December 21, 2005, A1, A12. Reprinted with permission.

15. Deborah Ball and Christopher Lawton, "Wine Gets Wild and Crazy," *Wall Street Journal*, April 24, 2003, B1, B3.

16. Emily Fromm, "Marketing to Women," *Brandweek*, October 4, 2004, 21–28.

17. William Bulkeley, "Kodak Sharpens Digital Focus on Its Best Customers: Women," *Wall Street Journal*, July 6, 2005, A1.

18. Todd Wasserman, "Ameritrade Invests in Women Investors," *Brandweek*, February 14, 2005, 9.

19. "Hardware Store Chains Target Women Customers," *www.bizjournals.com*, October 24, 2005, 9.

20. Stephanie Kang, "Nike Targets Women with New Hip-Hop Line," *Wall Street Journal*, February 15, 2006, B4.

21. Jeremy Caplan, "Metrosexual Matrimony," *Time*, October 3, 2005, 67.

22. Rupa Rangananathan, "Resort Spa Uncovers Cultural Anthropology to Cultivate Male Clients," *RetailWire*, June 30, 2005, online.

23. "The New Mainstream: How the Buying Habits of Ethnic Groups Are Creating a New American Identity," *Knowledge@Wharton*, August 18, 2005, online.

24. Deborah L. Vence, "You Talking to Me?" *Marketing News*, March 1, 2004, 1, 9–11.

25. "Walgreens Launches an Exclusive Skin Care Line Targeted to Women of Color," *Yahoo.com*, September 13, 2005, online.

26. Vence, "You Talking to Me?" 9.

27. Juan Garcia and Roberto Gerdes, "To Win Latino Market, Know Pitfalls, Learn Rewards," *Marketing News*, March 1, 2004, 14, 19.

28. Deborah L. Vence, "Diversity Efforts More Segmented, Focused in 2004," *Marketing News*, January 10, 2004, 17, 19.

29. Michelle Conlin, "Unmarried America," *BusinessWeek*, October 20, 2003, 106–116.

30. Sarah Ellison and Carlos Tejada, "Mr., Mrs., Meet Mr. Clean," *Wall Street Journal*, January 30, 2003, B1, B3.

31. Dianne Hales, "What Your Car Says about You," *Parade*, May 15, 2005, 8.

32. "Work That's Never Done," *Brandweek*, March 2, 2003, 30–36.

33. Susan Warren, "Texas Grocer Thrives by Catering to Locals," *Wall Street Journal*, December 1, 2004, B1–B2.

34. **http://www.claritas.com**, April 30, 2006.

35. Carolyn Poirot, "If It Fuels Good, Eat It," *Fort Worth Star-Telegram*, August 11, 2003, E1.

36. Peter Grant and Jesse Drucker, "Phone, Cable Firms Rein in Consumers' Internet Use," *Wall Street Journal*, October 21, 2005, A1.

37. Don E. Shultz, "Behavior Changes: Do Your Segments?" *Marketing News*, July 22, 2002, 5.

38. Paula Andruss, "The Golden Age," *Marketing News*, April 1, 2005, 21, 26.

39. "The Sultan of Stitch," *Business 2.0*, September 2004, 56.

40. Sarah Bahari, "Plastic for Kids," *Fort Worth Star-Telegram*, May 22, 2005, F1, F7.

41. David Koenig, "Wal-Mart Targets Upscale Shoppers," *Forbes*, March 22, 2006, online.

42. Nisha Ramachandran, "Best Buy Shapes Up the Big Box," *USNews.com*, October 17, 2005, online.

43. Joshua Freed, "Best Buy to Tailor Store to Different Types of Shoppers," *Fort Worth Star-Telegram*, May 23, 2004, 12F.

44. Amy Merrick, "Gap's Greatest Generation?" *Wall Street Journal*, September 14, 2004, B1, B3.

45. Amy Merrick, "Gap Plans Five Forth & Towne Stores for Fall," *Wall Street Journal*, April 22, 2005, B1, B2.

46. Gerry Khermouch, "Call It the Pepsi Blue Generation," *BusinessWeek*, February 3, 2003, 96.

47. Don Peppers and Martha Rogers, "Customers Don't Grow on Trees," *Fast Company*, July 2005, 26.

48. Lior Arussy, "Be a Bag," *Customer Relationship Management*, March 2005, 24.

49. Julie Schlosser, "Cashing In on the New World of Me," *Fortune*, December 13, 2004, 244–250.

50. "Growth through Innovation," *RetailWire*, December 8, 2005, online.

51. Kenneth Hein, "ProFlowers to Grow Sales with Fresh Plan," *Brandweek*, November 1, 2004, 6.

52. Vijay Mahajan and Yoram Wind, "Get Emotional Product Positioning," *Marketing Management*, May/June 2002, 36–41.

53. Louise Lee, "Yes, We Have a New Banana," *BusinessWeek*, May 31, 2004, 70, 72.

54. Jenny McTaggart, "Taking a Bite Out of Baggers," *Brandweek*, June 27, 2005, 42–45.

55. Ibid.

56. Ibid.

57. This application exercise is based on the contribution of Kim McKeage (University of Maine) to *Great Ideas in Teaching Marketing*, a teaching supplement that accompanies Lamb, Hair, and McDaniel's *Marketing*. Professor McKeage's entry, titled "Students Practice Making Market/Product Grids on Themselves," received an Honorable Mention in the "Best of the Great Ideas in Teaching Marketing" contest held in conjunction with the publication of the eighth edition of *Marketing*.

58. "Las Vegas Tourism Agency Announces 1.3 Percent Rise in Visitor Totals for 2003," *Las Vegas Review-Journal*, February 14, 2004; Jennifer Bjorhus, "Las Vegas Tourism Authorities Campaign in Portland, Ore," *Knight Ridder/Tribune Business News*, June 4, 1999; Chris Jones, "Las Vegas Tourism Agency Executive Says Research, Marketing Are Key to Success," *Las Vegas Review-Journal*, April 6, 2003; Chris Jones, "Las Vegas Tourism Chief Opposes Ads; Board Members Object to 'Sin City' Phrase," *Las Vegas Review-Journal*, December 16, 2003; Chris Jones, "Las Vegas Tourism Officials Plan Marketing Blitz to Attract Canadian Tourists," *Travel Weekly*, March 3, 2003; Chris Jones, "New Las Vegas Tourism Ads Target Hispanics with Tradition-Focused Messages," *Las Vegas Review-Journal*, July 17, 2003; Chris Jones, "Las Vegas Tourism Authority Unveils Culturally Diverse Television Ads," *Las Vegas Review-Journal*, February 11, 2004.

CHAPTER 8

1. "College Communications 101," *Brandweek*, August 22, 2005, 16–18.

2. Evan Perez and Rick Brooks, "For Big Vendor of Personal Data, a Theft Lays Bare the Downside," *Wall Street Journal*, May 3, 2005, A1, A8.

3. Joseph Rydholm, "A Natural Extension," *Quirk's Marketing Research Review*, May 2002, 22–23, 69–70.

4. "Why Some Customers Are More Equal Than Others," *Fortune*, September 19, 1994, 215–224.

5. Sunil Gupta, Donald Lehmann, and Jennifer Ames Stuart, "Valuing Customers," *Journal of Marketing Research*, February 2004, 7–18.

6. "Couriers Deliver Customer Service," *Information Week*, June 3, 2002, 60.

7. "Cast Your Net," *Marketing News*, November 24, 2003, 15–19.

8. Ann Breese and Donald Bruzzone, "A Definite Impact," *Quirk's Marketing Research Review*, April 2004, 22–31.

9. "Recommended Search Strategy: Analyze Your Topic & Search with Peripheral Vision," **http://www.lib.berkeley.edu/TeachingLib/Enidez/Internet/Strategies.html** (May 9, 2005).

10. Alison Stein Wellner, "Watch Me Now," *American Demographics*, October 2002, S1–S8.

11. "How Cool Is That?" *Smart Money*, June 2005, 13.

12. Kurt Knapton and Steve Myers, "Demographics and Online Survey

Response Rates," *Quirk's Marketing Research Review*, January 2005, 58–68.

13. Chris Yalonis, "The Revolution in e-Research," *CASRO Marketing Research Journal*, 1999, 131 133; "The Power of On-line Research," *Quirk's Marketing Research Review*, April 2000, 46–48; Bil MacElroy, "The Need for Speed," *Quirk's Marketing Research Review*, July–August 2002, 22–27; Cristina Mititelu, "Internet Surveys: Limits and Beyond Limits," *Quirk's Marketing Research Review*, January 2003, 30–33; Nina Ray, "Cybersurveys Come of Age," *Marketing Research*, Spring 2003, 32–37; "Online Market Research Booming, According to Survey," *Quirk's Marketing Research Review*, January 2005; Roger Gates, "Internet Data Collection So Far," speech given to Kaiser Permanente, May 2005.

14. For information on building a panel, see Brian Wansink and Seymour Sudman, "Building a Successful Convenience Panel," *Marketing Research*, Fall 2002, 23–27.

15. Based on the author's conversation with Jerry Thomas, CEO Decision Analyst, Inc., September 20, 2005. This firm has one of the largest Internet panels in the world.

16. **http://www.ChannelM2.com**, November 2005.

17. This information on blogging comes from Pallavi Gogoi, "Smells Like Teen Marketing; 3iYing Teams Up with Design-Conscious Teen Girls in a Radical Approach to Pushing Everything from Tampons to Cell Phones," *BusinessWeek Online*, November 11, 2005; "Intelliseek to Provide AOL with Daily Blog Trend Analysis, *PR Newswire*, October 17, 2005; **http://www.nielsenbuzzmetrics.com/**; Justin Martin, "Blogging for Dollars: How Would You Like to Survey 20 Million Consumers in Two Minutes?" *Fortune*, December 12, 2005, 178; "Intelliseek's Enhanced BlogPulse Offers Data-Rich Blog Profiles," *PR Newswire*, July 21, 2005.

18. Carl McDaniel and Roger Gates, *Marketing Research*, 7th ed. (Hoboken: John Wiley & Sons, 2007)

19. "Snooping on a Shoestring," *Business 2.0*, May 2003, 64–66.

20. Becky Ebenkamp, "The Market Is the Message," "What If Teenagers Ruled the R&D Roost?" *Brandweek*, July 11, 2005, 16 and 17.

21. Gina Piccalo, "Fads Are So Yesterday," *Los Angeles Times*, October 9, 2005; Stephanie Kang, "Trying to Connect with a Hip Crowd," *Wall Street Journal*, October 13, 2005, B1.

PART 2

1. Michael Bazeley, "EBay Nation put to the Test," *San Jose Mercury News*, June 20, 2005, K0182; Rachel Konrad, "EBay Losing Allure for Some Entrepreneurs," *Associated Press Financial Wire*, June 26, 2005; Verne Kopytoff, "EBay Bids for Harmony," *San Francisco Chronicle*, June 23, 2005, C1; Paul J. Lim, "Bidding Adieu to EBay," *U.S. News & World Report*, February 28, 2005, 46.

2. This case is based on communications with Walter Roettger, President of Lyon College, and approved for publication on December 1, 2005.

CHAPTER 9

1. Kurt Badenhausen, "Brands Branching Out," *Forbes.com*, June 16, 2005.

2. Todd Wasserman, "P&G Tries to Absorb More Low-End Sales," *Brandweek*, September 26, 2005, 4.

3. Todd Wasserman, "P&G Seeks Right Ingredient to Wash Out Laundry Woes," *Brandweek*, August 8, 2005, 5.

4. Sandra O'Loughlin, "Sparkler on the Other Hand" *Brandweek*, April 19, 2005, 18.

5. Sonia Reyes, "Spam Sends $10M Message about Joys of Being Single," *Brandweek*, March 14, 2005, 10.

6. Kenneth Hein, "Parade of Drinks May Clog Channel," *Brandweek*, February 7, 2005, 4.

7. "Kraft Foods: Extending the Brand," *Fortune*, December 13, 2004, S20.

8. Christine Bittar, "J&J Prepares to Activate Viactiv Multivitamins Tack," *Brandweek*, October 25, 2004, 8.

9. Janet Adamy, "Heinz Sets Overhaul Plans in Motion," *Wall Street Journal*, September 20, 2005, A4.

10. Deborah Ball, "Italian Challenge: Water Everywhere, but Not on the Go," *Wall Street Journal*, May 28, 2005, A1, A8; **http://www.nestle.com.my/Media**, December 7, 2005; **http://www.nestle.com/Our_Brands/Bottled_Water/Overview/Bottled+Water.htm**, December 7, 2005.

11. Laurie Sullivan, "Retailers Ply Their Own Brands," *InternetWeek.com*, April 18, 2005.

12. "Private Label Widely Seen as 'Good Alternative' to Other Brands, According to A. C. Nielsen Global Survey," **http://biz.yahoo.com**, August 14, 2005.

13. Laurie Sullivan, "Brand This: Department Stores Capitalize on Their Names," **http://www.informationweek.com**, April 20, 2005.

14. Sullivan, "Retailers Ply Their Own Brands."

15. Matthew Boyle, "Brand Killers," *Fortune*, August 11, 2003, 89–100.

16. Jeremy Grant, "P&G Hits Back at Private Labels," *Financial Times*, May 3, 2006, 15.

17. Deborah L. Vence, "Product Enhancement," *Marketing News*, May 1, 2005, 19.

18. Julie Bennett, "Co-Branding Lets You Get a Pizza, Then Have Your Cake and Eat It, Too," *Wall Street Journal*, September 29, 2005, D8.

19. Vence, "Product Enhancement."

20. Brenda Cotter, "Maximize the Legal Value of Your Brands," *Brandweek*, August 22, 2005, 27.

21. Erin White, "Burberry Wants the Knockoffs to Knock It Off," *Fort Worth Star-Telegram*, May 28, 2003, 6F.

22. Mike Beirne, "Sweet Treats: Limited Editions, Energy Packs," *Brandweek*, June 20, 2005, 9.

23. Deborah Ball, "The Perils of Packaging: Nestlé Aims for Easier Openings," *Wall Street Journal*, November 17, 2005, B1.

24. Ibid.

25. Cynthia Arnold, "Way Outside the Box," *Marketing News*, January 29, 2003, 13.

26. Jonathan Asher, "Capturing a Piece of the Global Market," *Brandweek*, June 20, 2005, 20.

27. Ibid.

28. This application exercise is based on the contribution of Alice Griswold to *Great Ideas in Teaching Marketing*, a teaching supplement that accompanies Lamb, Hair, and McDaniel's *Marketing*. Professor Griswold's entry titled "The Oreo Debate" received an Honorable Mention in the "Best of the Great Ideas in Teaching Marketing" contest held in conjunction with the publication of the eighth edition of *Marketing*.

29. http://www.apple.com; Riva Richmond, "Apple's New GarageBand Makes Making Music Easy," *Dow Jones Newswires*, January 27, 2004; Walter Mossberg, "How to Become a Rock Star: Apple's Latest Music Offering Lets Closet Crooners Record and Mix Their Own Tunes," *WSJ.com*, February 4, 2004; Bob Massey, "Music-Making Made Slick," *Washington Post*, January 25, 2004, F07; Jonathan Seff, "Center of Attention—iPod Mini, iLife '04 Expand Apple's Digital Hub," http://www.macworld.com, March 2004.

CHAPTER 10

1. Sarah Ellison, "Studying Messy Habits to Sweep Up a Market," *Wall Street Journal*, July 14, 2005, B1. Used with permission.

2. Pete Engardio, "Scouring the Planet for Brainiacs," *BusinessWeek*, October 11, 2004, 102.

3. Patricia Sellers, "P&G: Teaching an Old Dog New Tricks," *Fortune*, May 31, 2004, 168.

4. "A Creative Corporation Toolbox," *BusinessWeek Online*, August 2005.

5. Bruce Nussbaum, "Get Creative," *BusinessWeek*, August 1, 2005, 64.

6. Renee Hopkins Callahan, Gwen Ishmael, and Leyla Namiranian, "The Case for In-the-Box Innovation," *Innovation Brochure* (Arlington, TX: Decision Analyst, 2005).

7. Matthew Boyle, "Reinventing Your Company," *Fortune*, September 6, 2004, 226.

8. "Changing the World," *Entrepreneur*, October 2003, 30.

9. Sellers, "P&G: Teaching an Old Dog New Tricks," 168.

10. David Welch, "The Second Coming of Cadillac," *BusinessWeek*, November 24, 2003, 79–80.

11. Ibid.

12. Callahan, Ishmael, and Namiranian, "The Case for In-the-Box Innovation."

13. Chris Penttila, "Keeping It Fresh," *Entrepreneur*, April 2005, 88.

14. Gary Fraser and Bryan Mattimore, "Slow Down, Speed Up New Product Growth," *Brandweek*, January 10, 2005, 18.

15. Bridget Finn, "Mining Blogs for Marketing Insight," *Business 2.0*, September 2005, 35.

16. Sellers, "P&G: Teaching an Old Dog New Tricks," 174.

17. Ibid.

18. David Kirkpatrick, "Innovation Do's and Don't's," *Fortune*, September 6, 2004, 240.

19. Sellers, "P&G: Teaching an Old Dog New Tricks," 174.

20. Paul Kaihla, "What Works," *Business 2.0*, August 2002, 65–70.

21. Louis Lavelle, "Inventing to Order," *BusinessWeek*, July 5, 2004, 84.

22. Penttila, "Keeping It Fresh," 86.

23. Sellers, "P&G: Teaching an Old Dog New Tricks," 174.

24. David Welch, "Detroit Tries It the Japanese Way," *BusinessWeek*, January 26, 2004, 76.

25. Joseph Weber, Stanley Holmes, and Christopher Palmeri, "'Mosh Pits' of Creativity," *BusinessWeek*, November 7, 2005, 98–100.

26. Ibid.

27. John Battelle, "The CTO in a GTO," *Business 2.0*, July 2004, 91.

28. Sarah Ellison and Charles Forelle, "Gillette's Smooth Bet: Men Will Pay More for Five-Blade Razor," *Wall Street Journal*, September 15, 2005, B1, B5.

29. Paul Lukas, "How Many Blades is Enough?" *Fortune*, October 31, 2005, 40.

30. Engardio, "Scouring the Planet for Brainiacs," 106.

31. Ibid., 106.

32. Robert D. Hof, "The Power of Us," *BusinessWeek*, June 20, 2005, 78–80.

33. Ibid., 76.

34. "Phytol Products Take Market Test," *Food Ingredients News*, August 2001, online.

35. Phillip Brasher, "Teens Sample Milk from Vending Machines," *Fort Worth Star-Telegram*, April 5, 2001, 10A.

36. Reed Tucker, "Air Purifiers Cause a Stink," *Fortune*, June 10, 2002, 40.

37. Timothy Aeppel, "Brothers of Invention," *Wall Street Journal*, April 19, 2004, B1. Reprinted with permission of *The Wall Street Journal*.

38. John Gaffney, "How Do You Feel about a $44 Tooth-Bleaching Kit?" *Business 2.0*, October 2001, 125–127.

39. Ibid.

40. Sellers, "P&G: Teaching an Old Dog New Tricks," 168.

41. Ibid., 178.

42. Joseph B. White and Norihiko Shirouzu, "Visionary Vehicles to Bring Chinese Cars to U.S. Market," *Wall Street Journal*, January 3, 2005, A4.

43. Sellers, "P&G: Teaching an Old Dog New Tricks," 178.

44. Kevin J. Clancy and Peter C. Krieg, "Product Life Cycle: A Dangerous Idea," *Brandweek*, March 1, 2004, 26.

45. Gerard J. Tellis, Stefan Stremersch, and Eden Yin, "When Will It Fly?" *The Economist*, August 9, 2003, 332.

46. James Bandler, "Ending Era, Kodak Will Stop Selling Most Film Cameras," *Wall Street Journal*, January 14, 2004, B1.

47. James Daly, "Restart, Redo, Recharge," *Business 2.0*, May 1, 2001, 11.

48. This application exercise is based on the contribution of Karen Stewart (Richard Stockton College of New Jersey) to *Great Ideas in Teaching Marketing*, a teaching supplement that accompanies Lamb, Hair, and McDaniel's *Marketing*. Professor Stewart's entry titled "New-Product Development" was a winner in the "Best of the Great Ideas in Teaching Marketing" contest held in conjunction with the publication of the eighth edition of *Marketing*.

49. Neil Parmar, "Idled Toy Inventors Find a Sweet Niche: 'Novelty' Candy," *Wall Street Journal*, July 21, 2005, B1, B3; "Novelties Engender Avid Fans," *MMR*, June 13, 2005, 64; "Timing Is Everything with Licensed Novelty Candy," *Confectioner*, March 2005, 32; "Securing Play Value: Novelty/Interactive Candy Isn't Just Playing Around; It's Aiming for a More Stable Shelf Spot," *Confectioner*, February 2005, 38.

CHAPTER 11

1. Elizabeth Weinstein, "Animal Shelters Upgrade Creature Comforts," *Wall Street Journal*, April 19, 2005, B1.

2. Valarie A. Zeithaml, Mary Jo Bitner, and Dwayne Gremler, *Services Marketing* (New York: McGraw-Hill, 2006).

3. Alex Frangos, "Border Patrol's New Look," *Wall Street Journal*, September 1, 2004, B1.

4. Bridget Finn, "Luring 'Em In," *Business 2.0*, March 2005, 44–46.

5. Zeithaml, Bitner, and Gremler, *Services Marketing*.

6. Kimberly Weisul, "A Shine on Their Shoes," *BusinessWeek*, December 5, 2005, 84.

7. Duff McDonald, "Roll Out the Blue Carpet," *Business 2.0*, May 2004, 53.

8. Montoko Rich, "Healthy Hospital Designs," *Wall Street Journal*, November 27, 2002, B1.

9. Zeithaml, Bitner, and Gremler, *Services Marketing*.

10. McDonald, "Roll Out the Blue Carpet."

11. Ibid.

12. Ibid.

13. Much of the material in this section is based on Christopher H. Lovelock and Jochen Wirtz, *Services Marketing*, 5th ed. (Upper Saddle River, NJ: Prentice Hall, 2004).

14. Michael Krauss, "Starbucks Adds Value by Taking on Wireless," *Marketing News*, February 3, 2003, 9.

15. Christopher Lawton, "Virgin Atlantic Brands Posh Flights," *Wall Street Journal*, April 7, 2005, B3.

16. Howard Shapiro, "A Hilton Is a Hilton Is a Hilton, Depending on What You Can Pay," *Fort Worth Star-Telegram*, June 27, 2004, 5H.

17. Mike Tierny, "The Nurse Will See You Now: Drugstore Mini-Clinics Tout Speed," *Atlanta Journal-Constitution*, December 6, 2005," http://www.ajc.com.

18. Lovelock and Wirtz, *Services Marketing*.

19. Amy Chozick, "Discount Airlines Hit Latin America," *Wall Street Journal*, June 8, 2005, D1.

20. Lovelock and Wirtz, *Services Marketing*.

21. Much of the material in this section is based on Leonard L. Berry and A. Parasuraman, *Marketing Services* (New York: Free Press, 1991), 132–150.

22. Weisul, "A Shine on Their Shoes."

23. Jennifer Alsever, "English to Go," *Business 2.0*, March 2005, 56.

24. Vicki Powers, "Finding Workers Who Fit," *Business 2.0*, November 2004, 74.

25. This exercise is based on the contribution of Stacia Wert-Gray (University of Central Oklahoma) and Gordon T. Gray (Oklahoma city University) to *Great Ideas in Teaching Marketing*, a teaching supplement that accompanies Lamb, Hair, and McDaniel's *Marketing*.

26. Claudia Peschiutta, "Theatres Scramble to Find New Program Publisher before Fall," *Los Angeles Business Journal*, July 29, 2002; Randy Gener, "Get with the (New) Program: There's Been a Big Shakeup in a Business That Audiences Take for Granted," *American Theatre* 20 (January 2003): 20; "Venerable Theater Guide Takes Its Enduring Show on the Road," *PR Week*, October 14, 2002, 14; Laura Weinert, "End Program: Will Acquisition of Performing Arts by National Playbill Damage West Coast Arts Coverage?" *Back Stage West*, July1, 2002, 1; Leonard Jacobs, "Theatre Mag Shake-up: Playbill Buys Stagebill; Show People to Debut," *Back Stage*, June 14, 2002, 2.

PART 3

1. http://www.apple.com/ipodnano/; Christopher Breen, "Review: iPod Nano," Playlist *Magazine*, September 9, 2005, http://www.playlistmag.com; Amanda Cantrell, "Mac Sales May Juice Apple's Earnings," *CNN/Money*, October 10, 2005, http://money.cnn.com/; Michael Bazeley, "EBay Nation Put to the Test," *San Jose Mercury News*, June 20, 2005, K0182; Michelle Meyers, "Problems Surfacing with iPod Nano Screen," *CNET News*, http://www.news.com, September 24, 2005; Greg Sandoval, "Apple: Small Number of iPod Nanos Flawed," *Associated Press*, September 28, 2005, http://www.apdigitalnews.com/.

2. Much of this case was prepared by Matt Miller in his case study, "Marketing the Dallas Mavericks to the Fort Worth Community," Texas Christian University, 2005. See also, "Mark Cuban," Billboard 2004 Digital Entertainment Conference & Awards, http://www.digitalentertainmentawards.com; Mark Cuban, "How to Win Fans and Influence People," *Special to SportsNation*, January 21, 2003, http://espn.go.com/.

CHAPTER 12

1. http://www.starbucks.com; Starbucks Annual Report, 2006; Steven Gray and Ethan Smith, "At Starbucks, a Blend of Coffee and Music Creates a Potent Mix," *Wall Street Journal*, July 19, 2005, A1, A11; "Starbucks Announces Record December Revenues," and "Starbucks to Open Next Evolution of Hear Music Coffeehouse in San Antonio and Miami," press releases January 2006, http://www.starbucks.com/aboutus; Scott Donaton, "Starbucks Must Not Forget What Made Success Possible," http://www.adage.com, January 13, 2003.

2. Steve Lohr, "Just Googling It Is Striking Fear into Companies," *New York Times*, November 6, 2005.

3. http://www.pumpbiz.com, January 2006.

4. Nicole Harris, "'Private Exchanges' May Allow B-to-B Commerce to Thrive After All," *Wall Street Journal*, March 16, 2001, B1; Michael Totty, "The Next Phase," *Wall Street Journal*, May 21, 2001, R8.

5. http://global.l-textile.com.

6. http://www.sears.com/sr/splash/landsend_splash.jsp?vertical-SEARS&adCell-P8&BV_UseBVCookie=Yes; http://www.avoncompany.com/about/gettingavon/.

7. http://www.meridiankiosks.com; http://www.meridiankiosks.com/Press.asp; http://www.meridiankiosks.com/Press_KioskMagazine_EA.asp; http://www.meridiankiosks.com/Press _Cheyney.asp.

8. "Pepsi, Starbucks Teaming Up," *Supermarket News*, October 31, 1994, 31; Starbucks Annual Report, 2006.

9. http://www.cisco.com/web/partners/pr67/pr303/partners_strategic_alliance_.html, January 2006.

10. Matthew Schifrin, "Partner or Perish," *Forbes Best of the Web*, May 21, 2001, 26; Jonathan Eig, "H.J. Heinz, Japan's Kagome Agree to Investments as Part of Alliance," *Wall Street Journal*, July 26, 2001, B11; http://www.kagome.com; http://www.heinz.com/jsp/index.jsp, January 2006.

11. http://www.edmunds.com/new/2006/ford/mustang/100613439/optionsresults.html?action=2&tid=edmunds.n.options.ntmv.1.1.Ford*, January 2006.

12. http://www.dod.mil/comptroller/icenter/learn/learnintro.htm and http://www.cmcusa.org/ManufacturingCounts, accessed February 2006.

13. Rob Wherry, "Ice Cream Wars: Dreyer's Conquered Supermarket Freezers. Now It's Going After the Corner Store," *Forbes*, May 28, 2001, 160; http://www.dreyersinc.com/newsroom/index.asp, January 2006.

14. Karen Lundegaard, "Bumpy Ride," *Wall Street Journal*, May 21, 2001, R21.

15. http://www.toyotaforklift.com; http://www.toyotaforklift.com/about_us/company_profile/toyotaphilosophy.aspx; Elena Eptako Murphy, "Buying on Price Alone Can Lead to High Operating Costs," *Purchasing.com*, September 4, 2003; http://www.manufacturing.net/pur/index.asp?layout-article&articleid=CA319650&industry=Industrial+Markets&industryid-21951.

16. http://www.dollartree.com/ReleaseDetail.cfm?ReleaseID=137166, January 2006.

17. http://www.sysco.com/aboutus/aboutus_story.html, January 2006.

18. Leigh Muzslay, "Shoes That Morph from Sneakers to Skates Are Flying Out of Stores," *Wall Street Journal*, July 26, 2001, B1; http://www.heelys.com, January 2006.

19. Shelly Branch, "P&G Buys Iams: Will Pet-Food Fight Follow?" *Wall Street Journal*, August 12, 1999, B1, B4; http://www.pg.com, and http://www.iams.com, January 2006.

20. http://www.target.com; http://www.finance.yahoo.com; http://finance.yahoo.com/q/pr?s-MOSS; Robert Berner, "Target's Aim: The Designer's Edge," *BusinessWeek Online*, February 27, 2002; http://www.businessweek.com/bwdaily/dnflash/feb2002/nf20020227_0567.htm.

21. Nick Wingfield, "How Apple's Store Strategy Beat the Odds," *Wall Street Journal*, May 17, 2006, B1.

22. J. Bandler, "Losing Focus: As Kodak Eyes Digital Future, a Big Partner Starts to Fade," *Wall Street Journal*, January 23, 2004, A1.

23. Tim Craig, "AMZN v. TRU: Cyber Heaven Turned Cyber Hell," *DSN Retailing Today*, July 19, 2004, 8; Mylene Mangalindan, "Game Over: How Amazon's Dream Alliance with Toys 'R' Us Went So Sour," *Wall Street Journal*, January 23, 2006, A1; Mylene Mangalindan, "Court Rules against Amazon in Toys Dispute," *Wall Street Journal*, March 3, 2006, B1.

24. http://www.kraft.com; http://kraft.com/corpresp.html.

25. Julie Schlosser, "Just Do It," *Fortune*, December 13, 2004, http://money.cnn.com/magazines/fortune/.

26. "Knowing What Customers Want," *Inc.*, August 2005, 22–24; http://www.zara.com, February 2006.

27. http://www.dell.com; Stacy Perman, "Automate or Die," *Business 2.0 Online*, July 2003.

28. http://www.amazon.com, February 2006.

29. "Item-Level RFID Takes a Step Forward," http://www.newsfactor.com/news, January 2006; "Walgreen to Use Tagged Displays," http://www.rfidjournal.com; http://www.ncr.com, February 2006.

30. http://www.roadway.com; http://www.inboundlogistics.com, February 2006.

31. Caitlin Kelly, "Rolling Onward," *Supply Chain Management*, September 30, 2001, online.

32. "Leveraged Procurement," http://www.outsourcing-supply-chain-management.com/leveraged.html, http://www.avendra.com and http://www.ford.com, February 2006.

33. Michael Selz, "Outsourcing Firms Venture Beyond Primary Functions," *Wall Street Journal*, June 26, 2001, B2.

34. http://www.appleinsider.com, February 2006.

35. Walter Mossberg, "ESPN Cellphone Has Great Sports Content but Many Trade-Offs," *Wall Street Journal*, February 16, 2006, B1.

36. Mei Fong, "IKEA Hits Home in China," *Wall Street Journal*, March 3, 2006, B1.

37. Ken Bensinger, "Can You Spot the Fake?" *Wall Street Journal*, February 16, 2001, W1; Todd Zaun and Karby Leggett, "Motorcycle Makers from Japan Discover Piracy Made in China," *Wall Street Journal*, July 25, 2001, A1.

38. Jon E. Hilsenrath, "Globalization Persists in Precarious New Age," *Wall Street Journal*, December 31, 2001, A1.

39. Kevin Hogan, "Borderline Savings," *Business 2.0*, May 17, 2001, 34.

40. Chuck Martin, "Oprah Fans Scoop Up Graeter's," *Cincinnati Enquirer*, June 4, 2002, online.

41. This application exercise is based on the contribution of John Beisel (University of Pittsburgh) to *Great Ideas in Teaching Marketing*, a teaching supplement that accompanies Lamb, Hair, and McDaniel's *Marketing*. The entry by Professor Beisel titled "Identifying Channels of Distribution" was a runner-up in the "Best of the Great Ideas in Teaching Marketing" contest held in conjunction with the publication of the eighth edition of *Marketing*.

42. Christopher Lawton, "Made-by-Viewers TV," *Wall Street Journal*, December 13, 2005, B1, B2; Steve Tomich, "Current TV: Think Outside, Get Inside the Box—Taking the Leap with a 'New TV' Network," *Digital Video Magazine*, January 1, 2006, 38; James Hibberd, "Progress Report: The New Nets; Three Rookies, All with Major Backers, Devise Strategies That Help Them Overcome the Odds and Find Their Place." *Television Week*, November 14, 2005, 26; Paul Gogh, "Gore: Current TV Aims for the Masses." *Hollywood Reporter*, October 10, 2005, 6.

CHAPTER 13

1. Lorrie Grant, "Not-So-Happy Holidays: Gap December Sales Fall Sharply," *USA Today*, January 6, 2006, B-1, and http://www.gapinc.com/public/About/about.shtml, http://www.msnbc.msn.com/id/9054063/, and http://www.businessweek.com/innovate/content/sep2005/id20050920_185520.htm, accessed February 2006.

2. Bureau of Labor Statistics, "Industry at a Glance: NAICS 42–45, Wholesale and Retail Trade," online at http://www.bls.gov, February 2006.

3. U.S. Census Bureau, Monthly Retail Trade Report, 2004; Betty W. Su, "The U.S. Economy to 2012: Signs of Growth," *Monthly Labor Review*, February 2006, vol. 127, no. 2, online at http://www.bls.gov.

4. Johnathan Thaw, "Why Sharper Image Is Playing the Hits Again," *Business 2.0 Online*, November 2003.

5. http://www.goya.com.

6. http://www.pigglywiggly.com; Matt Nannery, "Pigging Out," *Chain Store Age*, July 1999, 77.

7. http://www.exxonmobil.com.

8. http://www. walmart.com.

9. http://www.target.com.

10. http://www.familydollar.com, and http://www.dollargeneral.com.

11. J. Verdon, "$6.6B Deal Expected to Revive Chain, " *Hackensack Review*, March 19, 2005.

12. http://www.restaurant.org/trendmapper/, February 2006.

13. http://www.usatech.com.

14. http://www.meetmark.com.

15. Amy Lo, "Selling Dreams the Mary Kay Way," *AsiaWeek*, June 29, 2001.

16. Mickey Khan, "Pulling People to Test Drive Raised Range Rover Sales," *DM News Online*, November 14, 2003.

17. http://www.dell.com/us/en/gen/corporate, February 2006.

18. "New Anti-spam Measure Compels Consumers to Hit 'Reply' to E-mails," http://www.webfin.com, December 9, 2003; http://www.webfin.com/en/news/news.html/?id=43947.

19. http://www.qvc.com, February 2006.

20. http://doubleclick.com, http://www.shop.org, February 2006.

21. http://www.shop.org; http://www.comScore.com; http://www.amazon.com; http://www.emarketer.com; "Holiday Shopping: Online, Offline or Multichannel?" *eMarketer.com*, December 9, 2003; http://www.clickz.com, http://www.tns-mi.com, http://www.doubleclick.com, February 2006.

22. Abbey Klaassen, "Buy It from Radio Ads at the Push of a Button," *Advertising Age*, February 21, 2006, online.

23. http://www.vans.com, January 2006.

24. Alexander Peers and Nick Wingfield, "Sotheby's, eBay Team Up to Sell Fine Art Online," *Wall Street Journal*, January 31, 2002, B8; http://:search.sothebys.com, http://www.ebay.com, January 2006.

25. McDonald's Corporation, Inside the U.S. Franchising Fact Sheet, http://www.mcdonalds.com/corp/franchise/faqs2.html, January 2006.

26. International Franchise Association Web site, http://www.franchise.org, January 2006.

27. Domino's Pizza Web site, http://www.dominos.com/Franchise, January 2006.

28. http://www.kfc.com/about, January 2006.

29. http://www.bluefly.com.

30. www.ae.com and 2002 Annual Report.

31. http://www.mustard-place.com, February 2006.

32. http://www.thebestofchicago.com; http://www.Fridgedoor.com.

33. Thaddeus Herrick, "Fake Towns Rise, Offering Urban Life without the Grit: Mix of Office, Home and Play Threatens the Real Thing; But Where's the Grocery?" *Wall Street Journal*, May 31, 2006, A1.

34. http://www.rivertowncrossings.com/html/index4.asp, February 2006.

35. Calmetta Y. Coleman, "Kohl's Retail Racetrack," *Wall Street Journal*, March 13, 2001, B1; http://www.kohls.com.

36. Nick Wingfield, "How Apple's Store Strategy Beat the Odds," *Wall Street Journal*, May 17, 2006, B1;.

37. "Two Time Grammy Winner Michael Bolton Exclusively Touring FYE: For Your Entertainment Stores Nationwide," *PR Newswire*, December 4, 2003; http://www.fye.com.

38. Abbey Klaassen, "Buy It from Radio Ads."

39. Viswanath Venkatesh, V. Ramesh, and Anne P. Massey, "m-Commerce: Breaking Through the Adoption Barriers," Research at Smith, Fall 2003 vol. 4, no. 1; http://www.bearingpoint.com; http://www.bearingpoint.com/solutions/wireless_internet_solutions/mcommerce.html; "The Swipe and Sip Soda: Pepsi Taste-Tests New Wireless Credit Card System for Vending Machines," *mpulse: A Cooltown Magazine*, November 23, 2003; http://www.hpl.hp.com/techreports/2001/HPL-2001-22.pdf

40. This application exercise is based on the contribution of Amy Hubbert (University of Nebraska at Omaha) to *Great Ideas in Teaching Marketing*, a teaching supplement that accompanies Lamb, Hair, and McDaniel's *Marketing*. Professor Hubbert's entry titled "Discovery of Strategic Retailing Factors" was a winner in the "Best of the Great Ideas in Teaching Marketing" contest conducted in conjunction with the publication of the eighth edition of *Marketing*.

41. http://www.bestbuy.com; Mark Tatge, "Fun and Games," *Forbes*, January 12, 2004, 138; Scott Carlson, "Best Buy Extends Weekend Store Hours," *Saint Paul Pioneer Press*, February 17, 2004; Scott Carlson, "Best Buy, Target Stores Score High in Consumer-Approval Survey," *Saint Paul Pioneer Press*, January 30, 2004; Laura Heller, "Connected Life Blooms in the Desert," *DSN Retailing News*, February 9, 2004, 188.

PART 4

1. http://www.raincoast.com; http://www.scholastic.com; http://www.wikipedia.com; Nicholas Reed, "Harry Potter and the Vanishing Volumes," *Vancouver Sun*, July 12, 2005, A1; Tabassum Siddiqui, "Potter Purchases Bound to Secrecy," *Toronto Star*, July 12, 2005, A01.

2. Amy Culbertson, "The Aisles Have It!" *Fort Worth Star-Telegram*, March 19, 2005, K4065; Natalie Gott, "Whole Foods Offers New Ingredient to Grocery Shopping—Fun," *Miami Herald*, May 22, 2005, http://www.herald.com; Seth Lubove, "Food Porn," *Forbes*, February 14, 2005, 102; Chris Price, "Prices Don't Stop Whole Foods Shoppers in New Orleans," *New Orleans City Business*, February 14, 2005, http://www.neworleanscitybusiness.com; Christine VanDusen, "A Whole New Kind of Grocery Store," *Atlanta Journal-Constitution*, April 17, 2005, 1F.

CHAPTER 14

1. http://www.subway.com/subwayroot/AboutSubway/index.aspx, http://www.subway.com/subwayroot/AboutSubway/nascar/nascar.aspx, http://walking.about.com/cs/diet/a/subwaydiet2.htm, http://www.subway.com/subwayroot/MenuNutrition/Jared/index.aspx, and http://www.wjox690.com/goout.asp?u=http://www.subway.com, accessed February 2006.

2. Stuart Elliot, "Subway's New Campaign," *New York Times*, Febraury 22, 2003, online.

3. Theresa Howard, "Coca-Cola Ads to Kick Off Super Bowl with Pregame Show," *USA Today*, January 19, 2006, 3B; http://www.newyorkbusiness.com/news.cms?id=8349, accessed January 2006.

4. http://prweek.com/news/news_story.cfm?ID=239635&site=3, and http://prweek.com/news/news_story.cfm?ID=239635&site=3, accessed January 2006.

5. "Satellite Cured Radio Star," http://news.yahoo.com/, and "Oprah Signs Three-Year Deal with XM Satellite Radio," http://www.philly.com/mld/belleville/business/13837515.htm?source=rss&channel=belleville_business, accessed February 2006.

6. Wendy Davis, "E-Mail Marketers Face Holiday Backlash," http://publications.mediapost.com/, January 20, 2006, "1 in 3 Report Marketing Emails as Spam," http://www.mediabuyerplanner.com, Greg Sandoval, "Defendant in Spam Case Pleads Guilty," and Anne Broache, "FTC Says Federal Spam Law Has Worked," http://www.news.zdnet.com, accessed January 2006.

7. http://www.24hoursofadrenalin.com/twenty4/index.cfm?fuseaction=dsp_sponsors&showCountry=USA, accessed January 2006.

8. Mickey Khan, "Cuervo Works to Change Labor Day," *DMNews.com*, August 25, 2003.

9. Marji McClure, "Click to Call Helps Chrysler Drive Traffic to Dealers," *DMNews.com*.

10. Mickey Khan, "Neiman Marcus Eyes Fatter Database for Holidays," *DMNews.com*, October 23, 2003.

11. Rance Crain, "We're Not Lovin' McDonald's New Strategy Either," *AdAge.com*, September 22, 2003 online; Stuart Elliott, "Big New Campaign for McDonald's," *New York Times*, September 3, 2003 online; Bob Garfield, "Why We're Not Lovin' It," *AdAge.com*, September 8, 2003.

12. McDonald's press releases, http://www.mcdonald's.com, accessed January 2006.

13. http://www.mcdonalds.com/corp/news.html, accessed January 2006.

14. Jason Fry, "Blog Epitaphs? Get Me Rewrite!" *Wall Street Journal*, February 27, 2006, online; http://www.technorati.com/weblog/2006/02/81.html.

15. Fry, "Blog Epitaphs? Get Me Rewrite!"; http://poll.gallup.com.

16. Tania Ralli, "Brand Blogs Capture the Attention of Some Companies," *New York Times*, October 24, 2005, C6.

17. "Blogs Can Offer a Big Advantage to Brands—If They're Honest," *New Age Media*, March 23, 2006, 15.

18. Peter Sanders, "Starwood's Web Log Caters to Loyalty," *Wall Street Journal*, April 12, 2006, B3.

19. http://www.philips.com.

20. Ibid.

21. The AIDA concept is based on the classic research of E. K. Strong, Jr., as theorized in *The Psychology of Selling and Advertising* (New York: McGraw-Hill, 1925) and "Theories of Selling," *Journal of Applied Psychology* 9 (1925): 75–86.

22. Bob Keefe, "During the Holiday Quarter, Apple Sold 14 Million iPods, Which Equates to More Than 100 a Minute," *Atlanta Journal Constitution*, January 11 2006, p. C-1, and http://www.appleinsider.com, accessed January 2006.

23. Thomas E. Barry and Daniel J. Howard, A Review and Critique of the Hierarchy of Effects in Advertising," *International Journal of Advertising* 9 (1990), 121–135.

24. Washington Mutual Press Release, "Teacher Talent Competition, Free BBQ and Performances by Tim McGraw and Michelle Branch Highlight Festivities," *PR Newswire*, October 18, 2003; http://www.wamu.com; http://www.optsevents.com/ourclients_teacherpalooza.php, accessed January 2006.

25. Sandra Dolbow, "BriteSmile Sinks Its Teeth into $20M Push," *Brandweek*, December 17, 2001, 6.

26. Hilary Chura "Marketing 1000: Smirnoff Ice," *Advertising Age*, October 8, 2001, S10–S30.

27. http://www.freestuffonline.com.

28. http://www.prnewstoday.com/release.htm?cat=advertising&dat=20060510&rl=3159647en-3; http://www.bloggersblog.com/cgi-bin/bloggers-blog.pl?bblog=519061.

29. This application exercise is based on the contribution of Lyn R. Godwin (University of St. Thomas) to *Great Ideas in Teaching Marketing*, a teaching supplement that accompanies Lamb, Hair, and McDaniel's *Marketing*. Professor Godwin's entry titled "Taboo or Not Taboo: That Is the Question" was a runner-up in the "Best of the Great Ideas in Teaching Marketing" contest held in conjunction with the publication of the eighth edition of *Marketing*.

30. This application exercise is based on the contribution of David M. Blanchette (Rhode Island College) to *Great Ideas in Teaching Marketing*, a teaching supplement that accompanies Lamb, Hair, and McDaniel's *Marketing*. Professor Blanchette's entry titled "Applying Semiotics in Promotion" was a runner-up in the "Best of the Great Ideas in Teaching Marketing" contest held in conjunction with the publication of the eighth edition of *Marketing*.

31. Brooks Barnes, "How 'Wicked' Cast Its Spell," *Wall Street Journal*, October 22, 2005, A1, A4; http://www.wickedthemusical.com; http://broadwayworld.com.

CHAPTER 15

1. "Wireless Phone Advertising Has Promise," *Mobile Advertising, Brands and Affinity Marketing*, Reed Business, http://www.instat.com; Keith Shaw; "What's Scarier? Wireless Phone Advertising or a Donald Trump Ring Tone?" http://www.networkworld.com; Paul Korzeniowski, "Cell Phones Emerge as New Advertising Medium," http://www.technewsworld.com; http://www.marketingdirecto.com/noticias/noticia.php?idnoticia=16532, accessed January 2006; Aaron Patrick, "Commercials by Cellphone," *Wall Street Journal*, August 22, 2005, B1, B3.

2. "Leading National Advertisers," Special Report, June 27, 2005, http://www.adage.com, accessed January 2006.

3. http://www.census.gov, Industry Series Reports, Professional, Scientific, and Technical Services, Advertising & Related Services, NAICS code 5184, accessed January 2006.

4. "Leading National Advertisers."

5. http://www.adage.com.

6. Michael R. Solomon, *Consumer Behavior*, 6th ed. (Upper Saddle River, NJ: Prentice Hall, 2004), 275.

7. Tom Duncan, *Integrated Marketing Communications* (Burr Ridge, IL: McGraw-Hill, 2002), 257.

8. http://www.scion.com.

9. Tobi Elkin, "Time Warner Taps Branding Agency," *Advertising Age*, September 22, 2003, 1.

10. http://www.philipmorrisusa.com and http://www.altria.com, accessed January 2006.

11. Tobi Elkin, "Microsoft to Focus on Experience," *Advertising Age*, February 26, 2001, 26.

12 Tobi Elkin, "Window XP's $200 Million Launch Kicks Off," *AdAge.com*, October 11, 2001.

13. Sean Callahan, "Nextel Wins the Race to Sponsor NASCAR," *BtoB online*, July 14, 2003; Rich Thomaselli, "Nextel Link Takes Nascar to New Level," *Advertising Age*, October 27, 2003, S-7.

14. Bob Garfield, "This Time Miller Lite Gets It Right by Forgoing 'Creativity,'" *Advertising Age*, September 22, 2003, 45.

15. Maryann Napoli, *Health Facts*, October 2001, 2.

16. Sebastian Rupley, "No False Ads," *PC Magazine*, July 3, 2001, 64.

17. "Absolut Vodka Must Pull Campaign in Italy," http://www.adageglobal.com, February 2, 2001.

18. "Yahoo! Korea Complains about Comparative Ads," www.adage.com, September 21, 2001.

19. "Rainmakers," *Advertising Age's Creativity*, October 2001, 14.

20. Tabasco advertisement, *Advertising Age*, October 13, 2003, 8.

21. Emma Hall, "Case Study," *Advertising Age*, September 22, 2003, 18.

22. Hank Kim, "Unilever, Ironman Link for NBC Reality Special," *Advertising Age*, September 8, 2003, 6.

23. http://www.us.powerade.com/.

24. Laura Q. Hughes and Wendy Davis, "Revival of the Fittest," *Advertising Age*, March 12, 2001, 18–19; http://www.hersheys.com/chocolateworld/, accessed January 2006.

25. Solomon, *Consumer Behavior*.

26. Mike Beirne, "Can Your Beer Do This?" *Brandweek*, October 15, 2001, M50.

27. http://www.adweek.com/aw/national/article_display.jsp?vnu_content_id=1000475212 and http://www.leoburnett.com/ideas/altoids.asp, accessed January 2006.

28. "'FT' Creates World's Biggest Newspaper," *Advertising Age*, October 20, 2003.

29. Geoffrey A. Fowler, "For P&G in China, It's Wash, Rinse, Don't Repeat," *Wall Street Journal*, April 7, 2006.

30. "China Retailer Bags Spokesman," *Advertising Age*, November 24, 2003, 12; "Spotlight," *Advertising Age*, December 1, 2003, 18; Bill Britt, "Volkswagen Waxes Poetic to Stir Up Emotions and Sales," *Advertising Age*, September 29, 2003.

31. Pamela Paul, "Sell It to the Psyche," *Time*, September 15, 2003, 47; http://www.marketingpower.com.

32. http://www.adage.com.

33. Brian Steinberg, "Philips and Time Agree to Keep It Simple," *Wall Street Journal*, April 21, 2006, B3.

34. Steven Levingston, "Spots on Traditional TV Still the Biggest Show on Super Bowl Sunday," *Washington Post*, Saturday, January 14, 2006; http://www.usatoday.com/life/television/nielsen.htm, http://www.top5s.com/tvcable.htm, http://www.nielsenmedia.com, and http://money.cnn.com/2005/01/20/news/fortune500/superbowl_ads/, accessed January 2006.

35. Jim Edwards, "The Art of the Infomercial," *Brandweek*, September 3, 2001, 14.

36. Suzanne Vranica, "TV-Ad Test to Show If Less Is More; NBC Universal's Trial Run Will Measure Effectiveness of Fewer Commercials," *Wall Street Journal*, April 5, 2006, B3.

37. Erin White, "In-Your-Face Marketing: Ad Agency Rents Foreheads," *Wall Street Journal*, February 11, 2003, B2; http://www.commercialalert.org.

38. Mike Esterl, "Going Outside, Beyond the Billboard," *Wall Street Journal*, July 21, 2005, B3.

39. "Cadbury Rolls Snapple in Mexico," *Advertising Age*, October 13, 2003, 18.

40. Ryan Woo, "Adidas Wows Japan with Vertical Soccer Field," *Wall Street Journal*, September 22, 2003, B1.

41. http://www.theloerieawards.co.za/winners/search/?show=1 , accessed January 2006.

42. http://www.iab.net/; Razil Suarez, "The Value of Online Advertising," *E-Commerce Times*, http://www.ecommercetimes.com/story/47474, and "Internet Advertising to Double in Five Years," http://www.clickz.com, accessed January 2006.

43. David Ho, "Advertisers Ditch Pop-Ups for New Tricks," *Atlanta Journal-Constitution*, December 4, 2005, C-3.

44. John Mello, "Search Engine Ads Garner $5.75 Billion in 2005," January 10, 2006, http://www.ecommercetimes.com.

45. Michael McCarthy, "Disney Plans to Mix Ads, Video Games to Target Kids, Teens," *USA Today*, January 15, 2005, B-1.

46. Stuart Elliott, "Science Blogs as a Vehicle for Upscale Ads," *New York Times*, January 20, 2006, C2.

47. Ibid.

48. http://www.bmwfilms.com.

49. Tobi Elkin, "Coca-Cola's First TiVo Advertainment Airs Today," *AdAge.com*, October 9, 2003.

50. Jack Neff, "Floors in Stores Start Moving," *Advertising Age*, August 20, 2001, 15.

51. http://www.altterrain.com/light_projection_advertising.htm.

52. Christopher Lawton, "Videogame Ads Attempt Next Level," *Wall Street Journal*, Monday, July 25, 2005, B6; "Video Game Advertising Gets a Boost," *USA Today*, December 16, 2004, B-1; Derek Sooman, "World's First Video Game Advertising Network," October 20, 2004, http://www.techspot.com; http://www.massiveincorporated.com, accessed January 2006; http://www.microsoft.com/presspass/press/2006/may06/05-04MassiveIncPR.mspx, accessed May 20, 2006.

53. http://www.technewsworld.com/story/46630.html; Korzeniowski, "Cell Phones Emerge as New Advertising Medium"; http://www.marketingdirecto.com/noticias/noticia.php?idnoticia=16532.

54. Sally Beatty, "Ogilvy's TV-Ad Study Stresses 'Holding Power' Instead of Ratings," *Wall Street Journal*, June 4, 1999, B2; http://www.ogilvy.com/viewpoint, accessed January 2006.

55. Marketing Agencies Association (MAA) Worldwide Press Releases, October 27, 2003, http://www.maaw.org; Annie Smith Hughes, "SK Telecom Steals World Cup—and PMAA Grand Prix," *PROMO Magazine*, August 1, 2003, online.

56. Jean Sherman Chatzky, "Whose Name Here? It Seems No Event Is Too Personal to Have a Corporate Sponsor," *Money*, October 1, 2001, 196.

57. Alice Z. Cuneo, "Virgin Mobile Gets Naked," *Advertising Age*, October 27, 2003, 4; Claire Atkinson, "There's a Method to Branson's Madness," *Advertising Age*, October 20, 2003, 3, 54.

58. http://www.sourcewatch.org/index.php?title=Product_placement; Kris Oser, "How a Product Placement Strategy Worked for Yahoo," *AdAge.com*, January 31, 2005, http://adage.com/latestnews; http:// money.howstuffworks.com/product-placement.htm and Product Placement Spending in Media 2005, http://www.pqmedia.com, accessed January 2006.

59. http://www.sponsorship.com, http://www.dominos.com, http://www.hiltonworldwide.com, and http://www.anheuser-busch.com, accessed January 2006.

60. http://www.olntv.com/nw/article/view/681/?tf=nwArticle.tpl; http://www.espneventmedia.com/.

61. *IEG Sponsorship Report*, July 4, 2005, vol. 24, no. 12, http://www.iegsr.com.

62. http://www.stjude.org/corporate/0,2516,410_2034_16782,00.html, http://www.thinkbeforeyoupink.org/Pages/InfoMktgCampaigns.html, and http://www.bitc.org.uk/resources/research/research_publications/corp_survey_3.html, accessed January 2006.

63. http://www.playstation.com, accessed January 2006.

64. Gavin O'Malley, "CBS Puts *CSI Miami* Twist Online," November 16, 2005, http://publications.mediapost.com, and http://www.adverblog.com/archives/cat_integrated_marketing.htm, accessed January 2006.

65. Ann Zimmerman, "Wal-Mart Enlists Bloggers to Combat Negative News," *Wall Street Journal*, March 7, 2006, D7.

66. Ibid.

67. "Blogs Can Offer a Big Advantage to Brands—If They're Honest," *New Age Media*, March 23, 2006, 15.

68. "Coca-Cola Says Sorry to Yao Ming," *PromoXtra Newsletter*, October 23, 2003.

69. Janet Adamy and Richard Gibson, "McDonald's Isn't Slow to React to 'Fast-Food Nation' This Time," *Wall Street Journal*, April 12, 2006, B3.

70. Zimmerman, "Wal-Mart Enlists Bloggers to Combat Negative News."

71. This application exercise is based on the contribution of S. J. Garner (Eastern Kentucky University) to *Great Ideas in Teaching Marketing*, a teaching supplement that accompanies Lamb, Hair, and McDaniel's *Marketing*. Professor Garner's entry titled "Creating Advertising for Illegal Products/Services" was a runner-up in the "Best of the Great Ideas in Teaching Marketing" contest conducted in conjunction with the publication of the eighth edition of *Marketing*.

72. This application exercise is taken from Chuck Williams, *Management*, 3d ed. (Cincinnati: South-Western, 2005). The idea to include a crisis management exercise in this chapter came from a contribution by Jack K. Mandel (Nassau Community College) to *Great Ideas in Teaching Marketing*, a teaching supplement that accompanies Lamb, Hair, and McDaniel's *Marketing*. Professor Mandel's entry titled "Putting Students in the Line of Fire to Learn Crisis Management Techniques" received an honorable mention in the "Best of the Great Ideas in Teaching Marketing" contest held in conjunction with the publication of the eighth edition of *Marketing*.

73. Ethan Smith, "Can MySpace Work as Ad Space?" *Wall Street Journal*, July 22, 2005, B2; Kris Oser, "MySpace: Big Audience, Big Risks; News of Sexual Predators on Social-Networking Sites Gives Buyers Jitters," *Advertising Age*, February 20, 2006, 3; "News Corp. Subsidiary Sued by Founder of Company That Created MySpace.com," *PR Newswire*, February 23, 2006; "Social Networks: More Bubble than Profit?" *BusinessWeek Online*, February 28, 2006; http://www.myspace.com.

CHAPTER 16

1. Rodney Ho, "Shock Jock Boosts Stock of Burgeoning Satellite Radio," *Atlanta Journal–Constitution*, January 9, 2006, A-1, 10; Rodney Ho, "Unleashed: Howard Stern Moves His Shtick to Satellite," *Atlanta Journal–Constitution*, January 9, 2006, D-1, 3; http://www.xmradio.com; http://radio.about.com, accessed January 2006; Press release, August 11, 2003, http://www.xmradio.com; Undated AP release, "A Free Offer for Satellite Radio," http://www.sirius.com; Barry Willis, "Satellite Radio News," http://www.stereophile.com, August 11, 2003; Elizabeth Boston, "Satellite Radio Signs Up Another Automaker," *Ad Age Online*, April 16, 2003; Tom Jacobs, "XM and Sirius Get Busy," *The Motley Fool*, http://www.fool.com, August 12, 2003; Mike Langberg, "Satellite Radio Is Ready to Go Mainstream," *STLtoday.com*, July 23, 2003; Joseph B. White, "Car Makers Hope to Lure Buyers with Fancy New Audio Options," *Wall Street Journal*, July 21, 2003.

2. Annual Report: Industry Report *PROMO Magazine*; http://promomagazine.com, accessed January 2006.

3. http://www.cms.inmar.com/newsandevents; Find/SVP, "Cut It Out: Coupons Are On an Upswing," http://www.forbes.com, accessed January 2006.

4. http://www.kroger.com; Internet Coupons link at http://gs2.coolsavings.com/kroger/index.aspx

5. Mickey Kahn, "eBay Offers Will Ride on Domino's Pizza Boxes," *DM News Online*, August 22, 2003; http://www.dominos.com; Joint press release of eBay and Domino's, August 21, 2003.

6. Suzanne Vita Palazzo, "Countdown to Kickoff," *Grocery Headquarters*, December 2005, 43.

7. Bruce Mohl, "Retailers Simplify the Rebate Process," *Boston Globe*, November 7, 2004.

8. http://www.noveltygiftco.co.uk.

9. "Vodka," *PROMO Xtra Newsletter*, October 16, 2003.

10. http://www.ecommercetimes.com, accessed January 2006.

11. Matthew Haeberle, "Loyalty Is Dead: Great Experiences, Not Price, Will Create Loyal Customers," *Chain Store Age*, January 2004, 17.

12. "REPEAT/Starbucks," October 13, 2003; "Duetto Turns One," *Cardline*, October 22, 2004, 1.

13. Barbara Kiviat, "Plastic That Pays You Back: Rewards Can Help You Spend More at Your Favorite Stores. Should You Bite?" *Time*, March 14, 2004, 94.

14. "US Bank Will Issue Luxury Card," *Cardline*, April 16, 2004, 1; Stratus launch brochure, Stratus Rewards, Santa Monica, California, http://www.stratusrewards.com.

15. http://www.verizonwireless.com.

16. "Grocers' Use of E-Mail Growing," *Promo P&I*, August 2005, http://www.promomagazine.com, accessed January 2006.

17. Peter Sanders, "Starwood's Web Log Caters to Loyalty," *Wall Street Journal*, April 12, 2006, B3.

18. "The Inside Story on Company Blogs: Corporate America May Fear Critical Comments in Public Blogs, but It Isn't Ignoring the Medium's Potential for Improving Internal Communications," *BusinessWeek Online*, February 15, 2006.

19. http://www.hgtv.com/hgtv/pac_ctnt_988/text/0,,HGTV_22056_38648,00.html, accessed January 2006.
20. Jim Kirk, "Marketers Pull Out the Stops: PepsiCo Tries $1B Giveaway," *Chicago Tribune*, October 5, 2003; http://www.rep-am.com/business; "Pepsi Brings Music and Star Power to Super Bowl Advertising Game Plan; P. Diddy Starts a Trend and Cindy Crawford Switches Roles for Diet Pepsi; Pepsi and Apple Highlight Second iTunes Giveaway with 200 Million Songs," *PR Newswire*, February 2, 2005, http://www.pepsi.com.
21. Lafayette Jones, "Ethnic Product Sampling: The Hidden Opportunity," *Retail Merchandiser*, August 2001, 45.
22. Tim Parry, "Sampling—Teaching Tools," *PROMO Magazine*, http://www.promomagazine.com, accessed January 2006.
23. "Domino's Customers Get Free Coca-Cola Zero," *PROMO Xtra*, December 22, 2005, http://promomagazine.com, accessed January 2006; Stephanie Thompson, "Ben & Jerry's Goes Alternative with New Effort: Marketer Sticks to Its Grassroots Via Print, Radio," *Advertising Age*, May 8, 2000, 111.
24. Stephanie Thompson, "Dove Targets the Chocoholic," *Advertising Age*, September 15, 2003, 45.
25. Andy Cohen, "A Marketing Touchdown," *Sales & Marketing Management*, October 2001, 16.
26. "Dunkin' Donuts Targets Health Clubs with Sampling Program," *PROMO Xtra*, December 28, 2005, http://promomagazine.com, accessed January 2006.
27. Geoffrey A. Fowler, "When Free Samples Become Saviors," *Wall Street Journal*, August 14, 2001, B1, B4.
28. "Point-of-Purchase: $17 Billion," *PROMO Magazine*, October 29, 2001, 3; "In Praise of Promotion," *PROMO Xtra*, http://promomagazine.com, accessed January 2006.
29. Stephanie Thompason, "Hershey Sets $30M Push," *Advertising Age*, September 15, 2003, 3, 45.
30. "MasterCard Unwraps Priceless Holiday Prizes," *PROMO Xtra*, November 5, 2001, 22.
31. Mickey Khan, "Heinekin Hoaxes Are Real Deal for Building E-mail Names," *DM News Online*, October 7, 2003; http://www.heineken.com, accessed January 2006.
32. Deena M. Amato-McCoy, "Print & Save," *Grocery Headquarters*, October 2005, 89; Jeanette Best, "Online Coupons: An Engaging Idea," *Brandweek*, May 2, 2005, 20.
33. Catherine Seda, "What a Deal! Attract Customers with Online Coupons," *Entrepreneur*, December 2003, 104.
34. Roger O. Crocket, "Penny-Pinchers' Paradise," *BusinessWeek*, January 22, 2001, EB12.
35. Libby Estell, "Economic Incentives," *Sales & Marketing Management*, October 2001, S2-S4.
36. Ben Chapman, "The Trade Show Must Go On," *Sales & Marketing Management*, June 2001, 22.
37. Michael Beverland, "Contextual Influences and the Adoption and Practice of Relationship Selling in a Business-to-Business Setting: An Exploratory Study," *Journal of Personal Selling & Sales Management*, Summer 2001, 207.
38. Richard Morrison, "The Business Process of Customer Retention and Loyalty," *Customer Interaction Solutions*, October 2001, 4.
39. "The Right Questions and Attitudes Can Beef Up Your Sales, Improve Customer Retention," *Selling*, June 2001, 3.
40. Larry Rigs, "Hit 'Em Where They Work," *Direct*, October 15, 2003; http://www.directmag.com; http://www.dmreview.com, accessed January 2006; Webcast Essentials, supplement to *CRM Magazine*, 2005.
41. Jean Halliday, "Chrysler Web Offerings Draw Sales Leads," *Automotive News*, December 5, 2005, 22.
42. Alf Nucifora, "Need Leads? Try a Networking Group," *Business News New Jersey*, November 14, 2000, 22; Catherine Seda, "The Meet Market," *Entrepreneur*, August 2004, 68; Jim Dickie, "Is Social Networking an Overhyped Fad or a Useful Tool?," *Destination CRM*, January 21, 2005; Kristina Dell, "What Are Friends For?," *Time*, September 21, 2004.
43. B. Weitz, S. Castleberry, and J. Tanner, *Selling* (Burr Ridge, IL: McGraw-Hill/Irwin, 2004), 198–201.
44. Tracie Chancellor, "Create a 'Smart List' of Sales Leads by Using Latest Software Database," *Houston Business Journal Online*, September 8, 2003; http://www.bizjournals.com/Houston/stories/2003/09/08ocus4.html.
45. http://www.bicworld.com; http://www.BICLink.com.
46. http://www.presentations.com.
47. http://www.chanimal.com; "chatrooms" link at the "Overcoming Objections" Web page (link to http://www.chanimal.com/html/objections.html).
48. Troy Korsgaden, "Fine-tuning Your Agency's Office Systems," http://www.roughnotes.com/rnmagazine/2000/june00/06p116.htm
49. http://www.collegerecruiter.com, accessed January 2006.
50. http://www.ge.com.
51. http://www.doubleclick.com.
52. Weitz, Castleberry, and Tanner, *Selling*, 18–20.
53. http://www.ge.com.
54. http://www.oracle.com/index.html
55. http://home.businesswire.com/portal/site/home/index.jsp?epi-content=GENERIC&newsId=20051216005415&ndmHsc=v2*A1104584400000*B1135297768000*C1136120399000*DgroupByDate*J2*N1001680&newsLang=en&beanID=1234257777&viewID=news_view, accessed January 2006.
56. Kathleen Joyce, "In the Cards," *PROMO Magazine* September 1, 2003, http://www.promomagazine.com.
57. G. Dudley and S. Goodson, *The Psychology of Sales Call Reluctance* (Dallas: Behavioral Sciences Research Press, 1999); http://www.bsrpinc.com/research/unethical_survey_02.htm?Sex=F&Age=27&Country=usa&Education=5&Profession=Academic&Title=Instructor&submit=Continue; "How to Do the Right Thing: The 90-Day Plan," *Optimize*, February 2002, http://www.optimizemag.com; Dwight Ueda, "Sales Compensation," *Salary.com*, http://www.salary.com/advice/layouthtmls/advl_display_Cat14_Ser6_Par23.html.
58. Kathleen Cholewka, "E-Market Stats," *Sales & Marketing Management*, September 2001, 21; Jamie Smith Hopkins, "Corporations Podcast Their Marketing Nets," *Baltimore Sun*, December 11, 2005.
59. This application exercise is based on the contribution of John Ronchetto (University of San Diego) to *Great Ideas in Teaching Marketing*, a teaching supplement that accompanies Lamb, Hair, and McDaniel's *Marketing*. Professor Ronchetto's entry titled "Sales and Customer Service Experiential Journal and Paper" was a winner in the "Best of the Great Ideas in Teaching Marketing" contest held in conjunction with the publication of the eighth edition of *Marketing*.
60. "Ron Popeil, He of the Pocket Fisherman and Spray-On Hair, Has Perfected His Formula for Success: Invent, Market, and Sell with a Passion," *BusinessWeek Online*, October 3, 2005; Brent Hopkins, "How Ron Popeil Invented Himself," *Knight-Ridder/Tribune Business News*, August 31, 2005; Matt Myerhoff, "Infomercial King Sells Company, Ronco Goes Public for Expansion," *Los Angeles Business Journal*, July 29, 2005, 1; http://snltranscripts.jt.org/75/75qbassamatic.phtml.

PART 5

1. "Burger King Introduces Chicken Fries," *QSR Online*, July 26, 2005, http://www.qsrmagazine.com; "Slipknot's Burger King Beef," http://www.thesmokinggun.com, August 17, 2005; Mark Hinson, "Put on the Commercial Brake, BK," http://www.tallahassee.com, September 11, 2005; Joe Kovacs, "Fowl-Mouthed Slogans Too Hot for Burger King," *WorldNetDaily*, July 28, 2005, http://www.worldnetdaily.com; Michael Paoletta and Susan Butler, "For Burger King and Slipknot, a Game of Chicken," *Reuters Wired News*, August 29, 2005, http://www.wireservice.wired.com; Bruce George Wingate, "'Foq' Burger King: Does Burger King's Coq Roq Ad Campaign Truly Shake Up the Establishment's Old-Fashioned Chicken Mentality, or Are They Just Poultry Poseurs?" *Lifestyles, Fairfield County Weekly*, August 25, 2005, http://www.fairfieldweekly.com.
2. Rebecca Gladden, "When the Spirits Move Them," *Insider Racing News*, November 14, 2004, http://www.performanceresearch.com/; David Kiley, "A Green Flag for Booze," *BusinessWeek*, March 7, 2005, 95; Al Levine, "NASCAR Gets in the Spirit," *Atlanta Journal-Constitution*, February 20, 2005, 1A; Performance Research, "Loyal NASCAR Fans Please Stand Up," 2005, http://www.performanceresearch.com; Ben VanHouten, "The Need for Speed," *Restaurant Business*, March 15, 2005, 34+.

CHAPTER 17

1. "Cayenne Cash-In," *The Courier-Mail*, June 18, 2005, C33; "This SUV Can Tow an Entire Carmaker," *BusinessWeek*, January 19, 2004, 40; John Tagmos, "The Profit Machine," *Business 2.0*, September 2004, 172–173.
2. Roland Rust, Christine Moorman, and Peter R. Dickson, "Getting Return on Quality: Revenue Expansion, Cost Reduction, or Both?" *Journal of Marketing*, October 2002, 7–24.

3. "DaimlerChrysler's Freightliner Puts New Chief at the Wheel," *Wall Street Journal*, May 29, 2001, B4.

4. Tammo H. A. Bijmolt, Harald J. vanHeerde, and Rik G. M. Pieters, "New Empirical Generalizations on the Determinants of Price Elasticity," *Journal of Marketing Research*, May 2005, 141–156; Christian Homburg, Wayne Hoyer, and Nicole Koschate, "Customers' Reactions to Price Increases: Do Customer Satisfaction and Perceived Motive Fairness Matter?" *Journal of the Academy of Marketing Science*, Winter 2005, 36–49; Gadi Fibich, Arieh Gavious, and Oded Lowengart, "The Dynamics of Price Elasticity of Demand in the Presence of Reference Price Effects," *Journal of the Academy of Marketing Science*, Winter 2005, 66–78.

5. "Summer Concerts Try New Tactics to Fill Seats," *Wall Street Journal*, May 19, 2005, D1.

6. "After Discount Sales Binge, GM May Have Headache," *Chicago Tribune*, July 7, 2005.

7. "The Price Is Really Right," *BusinessWeek*, March 31, 2003, 62–66.

8. Michael Mendano, "Priced to Perfection," *Business2.com*, March 6, 2001, 40–41.

9. "The Power of Optimal Pricing," *Business 2.0*, September 2002, 68–70.

10. Ibid.

11. "Meet Your New Neighborhood Grocer," *Fortune*, May 13, 2002, 93–96.

12. Robert Guy Matthews, "Carrefour Rings Up Discounts," *Wall Street Journal*, September 17, 2004, B6.

13. See Joseph Cannon and Christian Homburg, "Buyer-Supplier Relationships and Customer Firm Costs," *Journal of Marketing*, January 2001, 29–43.

14. "How Shopping Bots Really Work," *MSN-MONEY*, July 11, 2005, **http://moneycentral.msn.com**.

15. "U.S., 29 States Crack Down on Illicit Internet Auctions," *Milwaukee Journal Sentinel*, May 1, 2003, 3A.

16. "eBay's Worst Nightmare," *Fortune*, May 26, 2003, 89–92.

17. "One Nation under Wal-Mart," *Fortune*, March 3, 2003, 65–78.

18. R. Chandrashekaran, "The Implications of Individual Differences in Reference to Price Utilization for Designing Effective Price Communications," *Journal of Business Research*, August 2001, 85–92.

19. Katherine Lemon and Stephen Nowlis, "Developing Synergies between Promotions and Brands in Different Price-Quality Tiers," *Journal of Marketing Research*, May 2002, 171–185. Also see Valerie Taylor and William Bearden, "The Effects of Price on Brand Extension Evaluations: The Moderating Role of Extension Similarity," *Journal of the Academy of Marketing Science*, Spring 2002, 131–140; and Raj Sethuraman and V. Srinivasan, "The Asymmetric Share Effect: An Empirical Generalization on Cross-Price Effects," *Journal of Marketing Research*, August 2002, 379–386.

20. Merrie Brucks, Valarie Zeithaml, and Gillian Naylor, "Price and Brand Name as Indictors of Quality Dimensions for Consumer Durables," *Journal of the Academy of Marketing Science*, Summer 2000, 359–374; and

Wilfred Amaldoss and Sanjay Jain, "Pricing of Conspicuous Goods: A Competitive Analysis of Social Effects," *Journal of Marketing Research*, February 2005, 30–42.

21. This application exercise is based on the contribution of Vaughn C. Judd (Auburn University, Montgomery) to *Great Ideas in Teaching Marketing*, a teaching supplement and accompanies Lamb, Hair, and McDaniel's *Marketing*. Professor Judd's entry titled "Analyzing the Price-Quality Relationship" was a winner in the "Best of the Great Ideas in Teaching Marketing" contest held in conjunction with the publication of the eighth edition of *Marketing*.

22. http://www.hd.net/; http://www.DirectTV.com; http://www.Adelphia.com; http://www.timewarner.com; Leigh Gallagher, "The Big Picture," *Forbes*, March 1, 2004, 78; Allison Roman, "All HD All the time: Mark Cuban's HDNet Is Typically Offered on Operators' Premium Tier," *Broadcasting & Cable*, January 26, 2004, 20; Meredith Amdur, "New Definition at TW; Cuban's HDNet Lands Carriage with Cabler," *Daily Variety*, December 18, 2003, 6.

CHAPTER 18

1. Keith Johnson and Daniel Michaels, "Big Worry for No-Frills Ryanair: Has It Gone as Low as It Can Go?" *Wall Street Journal*, July 1, 2004, A1, A10.

2. Kent Monroe and Jennifer Cox, "Pricing Practices That Endanger Profits," *Marketing Management*, September/October 2001, 42–46.

3. Thomas T. Nagle and George Cressman, "Don't Just Set Prices, Manage Them," *Marketing Management*, November/December 2002, 29–33; Jay Klompmaker, William H. Rogers, and Anthony Nygren, "Value, Not Volume," *Marketing Management*, June 2003, 45–48; Alison Wellner, "Boost Your Bottom Line by Taking the Guesswork Out of Pricing," *Inc.*, June 2005, 72–82.

4. George Cressman, "Reaping What You Sow," *Marketing Management*, March/April 2004, 34–40.

5. "Why P&G's Smile Is So Bright," *BusinessWeek*, August 12, 2002, 58–60.

6. "Out-Discounting the Discounter," *BusinessWeek*, May 10, 2004, 78–79. An interesting article on shoppers who use penetration pricing to their advantage is Edward J. Fox and Stephen J. Hoch, "Cherry-Picking," *Journal of Marketing*, January 2005, 46–62.

7. "The Price Fixing Series," *Multinational Monitor* 24, issue 3 (2003): 30.

8. "Price Fixing Investigations Sweep Chemical Industry," *Wall Street Journal*, June 22, 2004, A1, A6.

9. "Five Paint Firms Are Scrutinized for Price Fixing," *Wall Street Journal*, June 4, 2001, A3–A4.

10. "Doctor Group Settle Charges," *San Diego Union-Tribune*, May 31, 2003, C-3.

11. "How Driving Prices Lower Can Violate Antitrust Statutes," *Wall Street Journal*, January 24, 2004, A1, A11.

12. Dan Carney, "Predatory Pricing: Cleared for Takeoff," *BusinessWeek*, May 14, 2001, 50.

13. "DHL Goes On Offensive," *East Valley Tribune.com*, September 26, 2004.

14. Bruce Alford and Abhijit Biswas, "The Effects of Discount Level, Price Consciousness, and Sale Proneness on Consumers' Price Perception and Behavioral Intention," *Journal of Business Research*, September 2002, 775–783. Also see V. Kumar, Vibhas Madan, and Srini Srinivasan, "Price Discounts or Coupon Promotions: Does It Matter?" *Journal of Business Research*, September 2004, 933–941.

15. Pradeep Chintagunta, "Investigating Category Pricing Behavior at a Retail Chain," *Journal of Marketing Research*, May 2002, 141–154.

16. "Price War in Aisle 3," *Wall Street Journal*, May 27, 2003, B1, B16. Also see Kathleen Seiders and Glenn Voss, "From Price to Purchase," *Marketing Management*, December 2004, 38–43.

17. Joel Urbany, "Are Your Prices Too Low?" *Harvard Business Review*, October 2001, 26–27.

18. Elizabeth Douglass and Gary Cohen, "Zones of Contention in Gasoline Pricing," *LATIMES.com*, June 19, 2005.

19. To learn more about "pricing fairness," see Lan Xia, Kent Monroe, and Jennifer Cox, "The Price Is Unfair! A Conceptual Framework of Price Fairness Perceptions," *Journal of Marketing*, October 2004, 1–15.

20. David Bell, Ganesh Iyer, and V. Padmanabhar, "Price Competition under Stockpiling and Flexible Consumption," *Journal of Marketing Research*, August 2002, 292–303.

21. Thomas Manoj and Vicki Morwitz, "Penny Wise and Pound Foolish: The Left Digit Effect in Price Cognition," *Journal of Consumer Research*, June 2005, 54–64.

22. Dilip Soman and John Gourville, "Transaction Decoupling: The Effects of Price Bundling on the Decision to Consume," *MSI Report*, No. 98–131 (2002); Stefan Stremersch and Gerard J. Tellis, "Strategic Bundling of Products and Prices: A New Synthesis for Marketing," *Journal of Marketing*, January 2002, 55–71; "Forget Prices and Get People to Use the Stuff," *Wall Street Journal*, June 3, 2004, p. A2.

23. Dilip Soman and John Gourville, "Transaction Decoupling: How Price Bundling Affects the Decision to Consume," *Journal of Marketing Research*, February 2001, 30–44.

24. "Fees! Fees! Fees!" *BusinessWeek*, September 29, 2003, 99–104.

25. "How to Thrive When Prices Fall," *Fortune*, May 12, 2003, 131–134.

26. This application exercise is based on the contribution of William H. Brannen (Creighton University) to *Great Ideas in Teaching Marketing*, a teaching supplement that accompanies Lamb, Hair, and McDaniel's *Marketing*. Professor Brannen's entry titled "Can Your Marketing Students Solve the Banana Problem? Can You?" was a runner-up in the "Best of the Great Ideas in Teaching Marketing" contest held in conjunction with the publication of the eighth edition of *Marketing*.

27. Anne Maria Squeo and Joe Flint, "Should Cable Be à la Carte, Not Flat Rate?" *Wall Street Journal*, March 6, 2004, B1. Used with permission.

PART 6

1. http://www.dell.com; Louise Lee, "Dell's Shortfall, Dell's Challenge," *BusinessWeek Online*, August 16, 2005; Scott Morrison, "Pricing Pressures Squeeze Profits on PCs, Computers," *Financial Times, London Edition*, August 23, 2005, 21; Richard Waters, "PC Pricing Mistake Hits Dell Revenues," *Financial Times, London Edition*, August 12, 2005, 28; Dan Zehr, "Dell's Profit Rises, but Sales Fall Short," *Austin American Statesman*, August 12, 2005, D1.

2. Peter Burrows, Ben Elgin, Ronald Grover, Jay Greene, Heather Green, and Tom Lowry, "Online Music: Rewriting the Score," *BusinessWeek*, May 30, 2005, 34+; eMarketer, "New eMarketer Report Finds Digital Music Advances Substantially Changing Music Industry Landscape," *Market Wire*, July 14, 2005, http://www.marketwire.com; Gale Group, Inc., "Yahoo Shakes Up Music Subscription Market," *Business and Industry Online Reporter*, May 14, 2005, 1; Scott Kessler (interview), "Yahoo's Music Rivals Sing the Blues," *BusinessWeek Online*, May 12, 2005.

CHAPTER 19

1. http://www.destinationcrm.com/articles/?ArticleID=1273, http://archives.cnn.com/2001/TECH/industry/10/11/hilton.crm.idg/, http://www.computerworld.com/softwaretopics/crm/story/0,10801,64606,00.html, http://www.commweb.com/trends/trends_archive/52200283, and http://www.clickz.com/news/print.php/3590196, accessed April 2006.

2. Joseph Hair, Robert Bush, and David Ortinau, *Marketing Research: Within a Changing Information Environment*, 3d ed. (Burr Ridge, IL: McGraw-Hill/Irwin, 2006), 114.

3. http://www.ondemand5.com.

4. Robert Westervelt, "NetLedger Goes Beyond Hosted CRM," *Yahoo! News!*, July 30, 2003; http://www.netsuite.com/portal/products/neterp/main.shtml, accessed April, 2006.

5. Jeff Sweat, "Keep 'Em Happy," *Internet Week.com*, January 28, 2002.

6. http://seattle.mariners.mlb.com/NASApp/mlb/index.jsp?c_id=sea; Sweat, "Keep 'Em Happy."

7. http://www.playstation.com; SAP Customer Success Story, "Playstation.com Chooses mySAP CRM," http://www.hp.com.

8. Ibid.

9. http://www.studentadvantage.com/discountcard/

10. http://www.bestbuy.com.

11. "Heading to the Border: Borders Books and Music Celebrates Three Decades of Prosperity Thanks to Its Successful Retailing Recipe," *Shopping Center World*, December 1, 2001, http://retailtrafficmag.com/; http://www.amazon.com; http://www.cardmemberservices.com/ (follow link from amazon.com).

12. http://www.sony.com.

13. "Group 1 and iWay Software Partner to Enhance Enterprise Wide Data Quality and Customer Data Integration," Press Release: iWay Software, January 15, 2002.

14. http://www.oag.state.md.us/Press/2001/1217b01.htm, accessed April 2006.

15. "North Dakota Voters Reject Referendum to Allow Banks to Sell Customer Information without Written Permission," *Monday Business Briefing*, June 27, 2002.

16. *Random House Webster's Dictionary.*

17. Rick Whiting, "The Data-Warehouse Advantage," *Information Week.com*, July 28, 2003; John Courtmanche, "Continental Is Merging Databases, Testing Operational CRM," *1to1 Magazine*, May/June 2001.

18. "The Key to Effective CRM: Building an Interactive Dialog," http://www.marketing3.nl, presentation in Utrecht, The Netherlands, December 4, 2003.

19. Whiting, "The Data-Warehouse Advantage."

20. http://www.unilever.com.

21. "The Key to Effective CRM: Building an Interactive Dialog."

22. http://www.theknot.com; "TheKnot Ties in Consumers with Personalization," *Consumer-Centric Benchmarks for 2001 & Beyond*, http://www.risnews.com.

23. Jack Schofield, "Casino Rewards Total Loyalty," http://technology.guardian.co.uk/online/story/0,3605,1122850,00.html, accessed April 2006; Christina Binkley, "Lucky Numbers: A Casino Chain Finds a Lucrative Niche: The Small Spenders," *Wall Street Journal*, May 4, 2000, A1, A10; "Personal Touch for VIPs: Client-Tracking System Helps Harrah's Tailor Sales Efforts for Frequent Visitors," *Information Week*, November 4, 2003.

24. Rick Whiting, "Know Thy Customer," *Information Week.com*, March 3, 2003, and "Get a Jump on the Future," *Information Week.com*, May 19, 2003.

25. Jaimie Seaton, "Stave Solves the Relationship Puzzle," *1to1 Magazine*, August 4, 2003, http://www.1to1.com.

26. B. Weitz, S. Castleberry, and J. Tanner, *Selling* (Burr Ridge, IL: McGraw-Hill/Irwin, 2004), 184–185.

27. "The MyPal Rewards Program Scores Big with Fans," *1to1 Magazine*, April 2003; http://www.nba.com/pistons/roster; http://www.palacenet.com/.

28. Kim Steffen, "CVS Gives Customers ExtraCare," *1to1 Magazine*, April 2, 2001.

29. Lauren Paul, "Wegman's Proves to Kraft That Customer Differentiation Works," *1to1 Magazine*, November/December 2002.

30. Karen Schwartz, "Kraft Data Mining Transforms Marketing and Margins," *Consumer Goods Magazine*, September 2000, http://www.consumergoods.com.

31. Jane Zarem, "Nike's 'Smart' Loyalty Program," *1to1 Magazine*, March 2002.

32. Christopher Caggiano, "Building Customer Loyalty," *Inc. Magazine Online*, November 2003.

33. Kit Davis, "Track Star, RFID Is Racing to Market," *Consumer Goods Magazine*, June 2003, http://www.consumergoods.com.

34. "Boise Completes OfficeMax Merger," December 9, 2003, http://www.bc.com/; Jim Kirk, "Boise Taking Its Business Personally," *Chicago Tribune*, January 6, 2002, C1.

35. Janis Mara, "Companies Alter Privacy Policies," *Internetnews.com*, January 2, 2004, http://www.internetnews.com/; "Ponemon Institute, International Association of Privacy Professionals Release Results of Benchmark Privacy Practices Survey," June 4, 2003, http://www.privacyassociation.org/docs/BenchmarkSurvJTH.pdf.

36. This application exercise is based on the contribution of Kenneth J. Radig (Medaille College) to *Great Ideas in Teaching Marketing*, a teaching supplement that accompanies Lamb, Hair, and McDaniel's *Marketing*. Professor Radig's entry titled "Direct Mail Assignment" was a runner-up in the "Best of the Great Ideas in Teaching Marketing" contest held in conjunction with the publication of the Eighth Edition of *Marketing*.

37. Laura Baverman, "Kroger's Card Sharks," *Cincinnati Business Courier*, November 4, 2005, 1, 46; Lucia Moses, "Diving for Data; With Dunnhumby's Loyalty Marketing Know-How, Kroger Hopes to Unlock Valuable Secrets of Its Loyalty Card Data," *Supermarket News*, September 26, 2005, 72; "Kroger Ups 2005 Earnings; Will Pay Dividend," *Columbus Business First*, March 6, 2006, 11; Steven Gray, "Kroger Fights Goliath, and Investors Freeze," *Wall Street Journal*, June 14, 2006, C1.

PART 7

1. "Sex Scenes? Now, That's Going Too Far . . . ," *The News Tribune*, July 22, 2005, B06; Entertainment Software Association, http://www.theesa.com; Entertainment Software Rating Board, http://www.esrb.org; Victor Godinez, "Hidden Sex Scenes Bump Up New Grand Theft Auto Game to Adults Only," *Dallas Morning News*, July 21, 2005; Rachel Sa, "Grand Theft Auto Slapped with Severe AO Rating: Future Shop and Best Buy Will Pull Sexually Explicit Game from Shelves," *National Post (Canada)*, July 21, 2005, A6; Anna Zaijka, "Explicit Video Game Vanishes from Shelves," *Vallejo Times-Herald*, July 28, 2005.

2. http://www.hgtvpro.com; http://www.scripps.com; Bill Brewer, "Scripps Is Going Broadband," *Knoxville News-Sentinel*, May 16, 2005, C1; Allison Fass, "Advertising on Demand," *Forbes*, July 25, 2005, 72; Jon Lafayette, "Broadband on Scripps' Menu," *Television Week*, May 16, 2005, 1+; Duncan Mansfield, "Scripps Takes Latest Channel Direct to Web," *BusinessWeek Online*, March 21, 2005; Linda Moss, "Raging Debate on VOD Still Hasn't Delivered the Hits," *Multichannel News*, April 11, 2005, 1.

MARKETING & YOU (BY CHAPTER)

1. "Loyalty (Organization) - #228," *Marketing Scales Handbook: A Compilation of Multi-Item Measures*, eds. Gordon C. Bruner, Karen E. James, and Paul J. Hensel (Chicago: American Marketing Association, 2001), vol. 3, 369.

2. "Planning for the Sale - #784," *Marketing Scales Handbook: A Compilation of Multi-Item Measures*, eds. Gordon C. Bruner, Karen E. James, and Paul J. Hensel (Chicago: American Marketing Association, 2001), vol. 3, 1345

3. "Good Ethics Is Good Business - #635," *Marketing Scales Handbook: A Compilation of*

Multi-Item Measures, eds. Gordon C. Bruner II, Karen E. James, and Paul J. Hensel (American Marketing Association: Chicago, 2001), vol. 3, 1064.

4. "Cultural Openness - #116," Marketing Scales Handbook: A Compilation of Multi-Item Measures, eds. Gordon C. Bruner II, Karen E. James, and Paul J. Hensel (American Marketing Association: Chicago, 2001), vol. 3, 190.

5. "Compulsive Buying - #98," Marketing Scales Handbook: A Compilation of Multi-Item Measures, eds. Gordon C. Bruner II, Karen E. James, and Paul J. Hensel (American Marketing Association: Chicago, 2001), vol. 3, 157.

6. "Trust in Salesperson - #920," Marketing Scales Handbook: A Compilation of Multi-Item Measures, eds. Gordon C. Bruner II, Karen E. James, and Paul J. Hensel (American Marketing Association: Chicago, 2001), vol. 3, 1,600.

7. "Budget Constraints - #78," Marketing Scales Handbook: A Compilation of Multi-Item Measures, eds. Gordon C. Bruner II, Karen E. James, and Paul J. Hensel (American Marketing Association: Chicago, 2001), vol. 3, 128.

8. "Information Acquisition Process - #646," Marketing Scales Handbook: A Compilation of Multi-Item Measures, eds. Gordon C. Bruner II, Karen E. James, and Paul J. Hensel (American Marketing Association: Chicago, 2001), vol. 3, 1084.

9. "Brand Consciousness - #65, #66," Marketing Scales Handbook: A Compilation of Multi-Item Measures, eds. Gordon C. Bruner II, Karen E. James, and Paul J. Hensel (American Marketing Association: Chicago, 2001), vol. 3, 114-115.

10. "Market Maven - #230," Marketing Scales Handbook: A Compilation of Multi-Item Measures, eds. Gordon C. Bruner II, Karen E. James, and Paul J. Hensel (American Marketing Association: Chicago, 2001), vol. 3, 372.

11. "Attitude toward Charitable Organizations - #18," Marketing Scales Handbook: A Compilation of Multi-Item Measures, eds. Gordon C. Bruner II, Karen E. James, and Paul J. Hensel (American Marketing Association: Chicago, 2001), vol. 3, 28.

12. "Authority - #58," Marketing Scales Handbook: A Compilation of Multi-Item Measures, eds. Gordon C. Bruner II, Karen E. James, and Paul J. Hensel (American Marketing Association: Chicago, 2001), vol. 3, 101-102.

13. "Shopping Enjoyment - #363" and "Shopping Orientation - #368," Marketing Scales Handbook: A Compilation of Multi-Item Measures, eds. Gordon C. Bruner II, Karen E. James, and Paul J. Hensel (American Marketing Association: Chicago, 2001), vol. 3, 602-607.

14. "Openers - #715," Marketing Scales Handbook: A Compilation of Multi-Item Measures, eds. Gordon C. Bruner II, Karen E. James, and Paul J. Hensel (American Marketing Association: Chicago, 2001), vol. 3, 1217.

15. "Attitude toward Television Advertising - #455," Marketing Scales Handbook: A Compilation of Multi-Item Measures, eds. Gordon C. Bruner II, Karen E. James, and Paul J. Hensel (American Marketing Association: Chicago, 2001), vol. 3, 746.

16. "Coupon Use (Economic Benefits) - #115," Marketing Scales Handbook: A Compilation of Multi-Item Measures, eds. Gordon C. Bruner II, Karen E. James, and Paul J. Hensel (American Marketing Association: Chicago, 2001), vol. 3, 185.

17. "Price-Prestige Relationship - #265," Marketing Scales Handbook: A Compilation of Multi-Item Measures, eds. Gordon C. Bruner II, Karen E. James, and Paul J. Hensel (American Marketing Association: Chicago, 2001), vol. 3, 435.

18. "Price Consciousness - #264," Marketing Scales Handbook: A Compilation of Multi-Item Measures, eds. Gordon C. Bruner II, Karen E. James, and Paul J. Hensel (American Marketing Association: Chicago, 2001), vol. 3, 433.

19. "Attitude toward Complaining (Personal Norms) - #29," Marketing Scales Handbook: A Compilation of Multi-Item Measures, eds. Gordon C. Bruner II, Karen E. James, and Paul J. Hensel (American Marketing Association: Chicago, 2001), vol. 3, 49.

INTRODUCTION TO Marketing 9e

Business mission, 38–39, 58–59
Business mission statement, 37, 38–39
Business product distributors, 191
Business products, 186, 191, 197–199, 284, 285, 368–369. *See also* Industrial products
Business services, 199
Business-to-business electronic commerce (B2B e-commerce), 186–187
Business-to-business online exchange, 196
Buyer behavior, 47
Buyer considerations, 365
Buyer for export, 121
Buyers, 196, 364, 365, 367, 379, 380, 384, 404, 501
Buying, 196
Buying centers, 200–201, 204
Buying decisions
    consumer (*See* Consumer decision making)
    integrated marketing communications and, 456–457, 458
Buying processes, 224

C
CAD. *See* Computer-aided design (CAD)
CAFTA. *See* Central American Free Trade Agreement (CAFTA)
Cajuns, 160
California's Notice of Security Breach Law, 95
CAM. *See* Computer-aided manufacturing (CAM)
Campaign management, 613–614
CAN-SPAM Act of 2003, 92, 93–94
Cannibalization, 229
Capitalism, 113, 158
Careers/jobs, 16, 22–33
Cash cow, 45–46
Cash discounts, 576
Catalogs, 413, 416, 421
Category killers, 408–409, 410
Cause-related marketing, 490
CCOs. *See* Chief customer officers (CCOs)
Cease-and-Desist Order, 93
Celler-Kefauver Antimerger Act of 1950, 91
Central American Free Trade Agreement (CAFTA), 116
Central-location telephone (CLT) facility, 253
CEO, 11, 23
Certified Purchasing Manager (CPM), 196
Chain stores, 403
Channel, 446, 449
Channel alliances, 379
Channel captain, 377
Channel conflict, 377–379
Channel control, 377
Channel cooperation, 379
Channel leader, 377
Channel members, 362, 377, 379
Channel of distribution, 362. *See also* Marketing channels
Channel partnering, 379
Channel power, 377
Chief customer officers (CCOs), 11
Child labor laws, 156
Child Protection Act of 1990, 92
Child Protection and Toy Safety Act of 1969, 92
Children's Online Privacy Protection Act of 1998, 92
Chinese, as subculture, 160
CI. *See* Competitive intelligence (CI)
Citizenship, 67, 117, 203
City government, 192
Class brands, 243
Clayton Act of 1914, 91
Climate, 214
Closed-ended question, 255
Closing, in selling process, 518, 519
CLT facility. *See* Central-location telephone (CLT) facility
Cluster sample, 259
Cobranding, 96, 293–294

Cognitive dissonance, 151, 155, 615
Cold calling, 514
Commerce, FTC and, 93
Commercialization, 317
Commission, 522
Communication. *See also* Personal selling
    consumers and, 151–152, 157, 166
    corporate, 488
    customer-relationship management and, 615
    defined, 445
    integrated marketing (*See* Integrated marketing communications)
    interpersonal, 445
    marketing, 445–450
    marketing channels and, 368, 376
    marketing plan and, 50
    mass, 445, 447, 448
    postpurchase, 342
    products and, 321–322, 324
    service quality and, 338
    supply chain management and, 382
Communication process, 445–448
Community shopping centers, 422
Comparative advertising, 471–472
Compatibility, new products and, 321
Compensation, 521–522, 524
Competition, 7, 12, 74, 329, 354, 357, 401, 432, 499
    buying behavior and, 202
    capitalism and, 158
    competitive intelligence and, 269–270
    consumer buying decisions and, 175
    dumping and, 132
    foreign, 106, 108
    FTC and, 93
    geographic segmentation and, 215
    global, 96–97
    globalization and, 108
    integrated marketing communications and, 456
    in international services, 346
    marketing channels and, 370, 378
    positioning and, 233, 234
    pricing and, 542, 554–555, 558, 571, 572–573, 596
    products and, 318, 324
    relationship marketing and, 189
    repositioning and, 234
    undifferentiated targeting strategy and, 227
Competitive advantage, 9, 34–64
    business mission and, 38–39
    cost, 41–42
    defined, 440
    global issues in services marketing and, 346
    global marketing mix and, 130
    integrated marketing communications and, 451
    marketing channels and, 379
    marketing mix and, 48–49
    marketing plan and, 36–40, 49–51
    new products and, 310
    niche, 43
    product/service differentiation, 42–43
    relationship marketing and, 189
    services and, 339
    situation analysis and, 40–41
    strategic alternatives in, 44–47
    supply chain management and, 371
    sustainable, 43
    target market and, 47–48
Competitive advertising, 471, 472
Competitive arena, 8
Competitive capitalism, 113
Competitive environment, regulation of, 91, 95
Competitive factors, affecting marketing, 95–97
Competitive intelligence (CI), 269–270
Compiled list, 610, 611
Complementary branding, 293
Complexity, new products and, 320, 321
Component lifestyles, 75
Component parts, 198–199

Components, standardized, 286, 383
Computer-aided design (CAD), 42
Computer-aided manufacturing (CAM), 42
Computer-assisted personal interviewing, 253
Computer-assisted self-interviewing, 253
Concentrated targeting, 227–228, 229
Concentrated targeting strategy, 226, 227
Concept test, 312–313
Conceptual learning, 175
Conflict, 3, 377–379
Consent Decree, 93
Consideration set, 150
Consolidation, 368
Conspiracy, 572–573
Consultants, 312
Consultative selling, 510
Consumer behavior, 146, 175
Consumer buying decisions. *See* Consumer decision making
Consumer Credit Protection Act of 1968, 92
Consumer decision making, 144–183
    influences on, 155–178
    process for, 146–152
Consumer penalties, 583–584
Consumer Product Safety Act of 1972, 92, 314
Consumer Product Safety Commission (CPSC), 92
Consumers, 73, 75, 81. *See also* Customers
    advertising and, 469
    African American, 84
    Asian American, 85
    business marketing and (*See* Business markets/marketing)
    buying decisions for, 166
    in China, 125
    competition and, 96
    decision making for (*See* Consumer decision making)
    demographic makeup of, 119
    global marketing mix and, 127, 130
    globalization and, 110
    income of, 86–87
    integrated marketing communications and (*See* Integrated marketing communications)
    intermediaries and, 364
    in Japan, 129–130
    laws protecting, 92
    marketing channels and, 362, 363, 364, 367–369
    one-to-one marketing and, 230
    pricing and, 555–556
    privacy of, 93–95
    products and, 280, 284–286
    sales promotion and, 500, 501–507, 502–503
    Uruguay Round and, 115
Contests, 501, 504–505, 507
Continuous media schedule, 486
Contract logistics, 387–388
Contract manufacturing, 120, 123, 125
Control, in marketing plan, 50–51, 63–64
Convenience, 340–341
Convenience products, 284–285
Convenience sample, 259
Convenience stores, 403, 407, 410
Conventional morality, 70, 72
Cooperation, 12
Cooperative advertising, 480
Cooperative branding, 293
Copyrights, 115
Core service, 339, 342
Corporate blogs, 449
Corporate citizenship, at General Electric, 67
Corporate communication, 488
Corporate social responsibility, 68–69. *See also* Social responsibility
Corrective Advertising, 93
Cost
    average total, 549–550
    average variable, 549–550
    consumer involvement and, 152
    distribution decisions and, 358–359
    fixed, 548–550